FIRST CANADIAN EDITION

**ROBERT J. BRYM**
University of Toronto

**JOHN LIE**
University of Michigan

**ADIE NELSON**
University of Waterloo

**NEIL GUPPY**
University of British Columbia

**CHRIS McCORMICK**
St. Thomas University

Australia Canada Mexico Singapore Spain United Kingdom United States

**Sociology:**
**Your Compass for a New World**
**First Canadian Edition**
by Robert J. Brym, John Lie,
Adie Nelson, Neil Guppy, and
Chris McCormick

**Editorial Director and Publisher:**
Evelyn Veitch

**Executive Editor:**
Joanna Cotton

**Acquisitions Editor:**
Brad Lambertus

**Marketing Manager:**
Lenore Taylor

**Developmental Editor:**
Klaus Unger

**Production Editor:**
Julie van Veen

**Production Coordinator:**
Helen Jager Locsin

**Creative Director:**
Angela Cluer

**Cover and Interior Design:**
Van Mua

**Cover Design Modifications:**
Peter Papayanakis

**Copy Editor:**
Susan Broadhurst

**Proofreader:**
Dawn Hunter

**Compositor:**
Alicja Jamorski

**Printer:**
Transcontinental



Printed and bound in Canada
1 2 3 4 06 05 04 03

For more information contact Nelson, 1120 Birchmount Road, Scarborough, Ontario, M1K 5G4. Or you can visit our Internet site at http://www.nelson.com



**National Library of Canada Cataloguing in Publication**

Sociology: your compass for a new world/Robert J. Brym... [et al.].

ISBN 0-7747-3702-6

1. Sociology. I. Brym, Robert J., 1951–

HM586.S65 2003 301 C2002-904458-8

# DEDICATION

For our students

# About the Authors

**Robert J. Brym** is an internationally known scholar. He studied in Israel and Canada and received his Ph.D. from the University of Toronto, where he is now on faculty and especially enjoys teaching Introductory Sociology to 1500 students every year. He has won numerous awards for his teaching and scholarly work, including four Dean's Excellence Awards, the Oswald Hall Award for Undergraduate Teaching Excellence, and the Outstanding Contribution Award and the Distinguished Service Award of the Canadian Sociology and Anthropology Association. His main areas of research are political sociology, race and ethnic relations, and sociology of culture. His major works include *Intellectuals and Politics* (London and Boston: Allen & Unwin, 1980), *From Culture to Power: The Sociology of English Canada* (Toronto: Oxford University Press, 1989) with Bonnie Fox, *The Jews of Moscow, Kiev, and Minsk* (New York: New York University Press, 1994) with Rozalina Ryvkina, and *Sociology: Your Compass for a New World* (Belmont, CA: Wadsworth, 2003) with John Lie. In 2001, he was co-investigator for the world's first large-scale survey of Internet dating, sponsored by MSN.CA. His works have been translated into several languages. From 1986–89 Robert served as editor of the *Canadian Review of Sociology and Anthropology*, the journal of the Canadian Sociology and Anthropology Association. From 1992–97 he was editor of *Current Sociology*, the journal of the International Sociological Association. He is now editor of *East European Jewish Affairs*, published in London. He is currently involved in two research projects. With sociologists at the Institute of Sociology, Russian Academy of Sciences, Moscow, he is conducting a study of recruitment and mobility in the Russian civil service. As part of an international team of more than 100 sociologists and political scientists centred at the University of Michigan, he is analyzing the results of the 2000 World Values Survey of 86 countries, including Canada.

**John Lie** (pronounced "lee") was born in South Korea, grew up in Japan and Hawaii, and attended Harvard University. Currently professor of sociology at the University of Michigan, he has taught at the University of Hawaii at Manoa, the University of California at Berkeley, the University of Illinois at Urbana–Champaign, and Harvard University in the United States, as well as universities in Japan, South Korea, Taiwan, and New Zealand. He served as chair of the Department of Sociology at the University of Illinois at Urbana–Champaign. His main research interests are comparative macrosociology and comparative race and ethnic relations. John's major publications include *Blue Dreams: Korean Americans and the Los Angeles Riots* (Cambridge, MA: Harvard University Press, 1998), and *Multiethnic Japan* (Cambridge, MA: Harvard University Press, 2001). He has taught introductory sociology classes ranging in size from 3 to more than 700 students in several countries and hopes this book will stimulate your sociological imagination.

**Adie Nelson** obtained her Ph.D. at age 24 from the London School of Economics and Political Science. Her doctoral dissertation, *Kept Women* (London: Orbis, 1983), was later abridged and published in English, German, Italian, and Dutch. From 1985–88, she was a MacTaggart Postdoctoral Fellow at the University of Alberta. Since 1991, she has been on faculty at the University of Waterloo, where she regularly teaches courses in introductory sociology. A prolific writer, she is the author, co-author, and co-editor of more than a dozen books. Her work has also appeared in such journals as *The British Journal of Sociology*, *The Journal of Contemporary Ethnography*, *Qualitative Sociology*, and *Psychology of Women Quarterly*. Her areas of specialization are criminology, victimology, gender, and sexuality. Her current writing projects include textbooks on the sociology of law and on criminology, as well as a monograph on the commercialization of crime.

**Neil Guppy** was born in North Bay, Ontario. He attended university in Ontario, at both Queen's University (in physical and health education) and the University of Waterloo, receiving his Ph.D. in sociology in 1981. His first academic job was at the University of British Columbia, where he started in the Department of Anthropology and Sociology in 1979. He has served as an associate dean (students) in the Faculty of Arts, and since 1999 has been the associate vice-president (academic programs) at UBC. His research interests are in the areas of social inequality, education, research methodology, and the environment/resources. His most recent books include *Education in Canada: Recent Trends and Future Challenges* (1998, with Scott Davies), a third edition of *Successful Surveys: Research Methods and Practice* (2003, with George Gray), and a fourth edition of *Social Inequality in Canada: Patterns, Problems, and Policies* (2003, edited with Jim Curtis and Ed Grabb). In 1988–89 he won a University Killam Research Award at UBC and in 1992–93 he was awarded a University Killam Teaching Prize. He is the past editor of the Sage Series in International Sociology (London, England) and was a member of the publication board of the International Sociological Association from 1994–99.

**Chris McCormick** is a professor of criminology and acting chair of the Department of Criminology and Criminal Justice at St. Thomas University in Fredericton, New Brunswick. He has taught at Acadia, Dalhousie, Saint Mary's, and Mount Saint Vincent universities. He has published widely, including *Constructing Danger: The Mis/representation of Crime in the News* (1995) and *The Westray Chronicles: A Case Study in Corporate Crime* (1999). His current research is on early Canadian criminal justice history.

# BRIEF CONTENTS

# Contents

## PART II

**References, 569**
**Index, 607**

# PREFACE

## A Compass for a New World

> It was the best of times, it was the worst of times, it was the age of wisdom, it was the age of foolishness, it was the epoch of belief, it was the epoch of incredulity, it was the season of Light, it was the season of Darkness, it was the spring of hope, it was the winter of despair, we had everything before us, we had nothing before us, we were all going direct to Heaven, we were all going direct the other way—in short, the period was so far like the present period, that some of its noisiest authorities insisted on its being received, for good or for evil, in the superlative degree of comparison only.
>
> – Charles Dickens, *A Tale of Two Cities* (2002 [1859])

Dickens refers to the end of the eighteenth century, yet he offers a prophetic description of the times in which we live. We, too, set sail at the dawn of a new millennium, an age of superlatives, an age of uncertainty.

The Soviet Union was formally dissolved on December 21, 1991. On that day we learned that even a seemingly vast superpower can collapse and splinter almost overnight. One of the world's leading historians wrote that the twentieth century ended with the fall of the USSR, ushering in a new century of mounting indeterminacy (Hobsbawm, 1994). As if to prove the point, scientists announced on June 26, 2000, that they had finished sequencing the human genome, beginning a new era of scientific breakthroughs. Yet shortly after, the United Nations forecast that 85 million people will die of AIDS by 2020, convincing us (if we had not already been convinced) that, despite remarkable medical advances, the plague is still with us. Then, on September 11, 2001, terrorists attacked the World Trade Center in New York and the Pentagon in Washington, D.C., killing about 3000 people. We saw the world's mood and its political and economic outlook buoyant one day, uncertain the next.

The world is an unpredictable place. It is especially disorienting for students just entering adulthood. We wrote this book to show undergraduates that sociology can help them make sense of their lives, however uncertain they may appear to be. We hope it will serve as their sociological compass in the unpredictable new world of the twenty-first century. Moreover, we show that sociology can be a liberating practical activity, not just an abstract intellectual exercise. By revealing the opportunities and constraints we face, sociology can help us navigate our lives, teaching us who we are and what we can become in this particular social and historical context. We cannot know what the future will bring, but we can at least know the choices we confront and the likely consequences of our actions. From this point of view, sociology can help us create the best possible future. That has always been sociology's principal justification, and so it should be today.

## Unique Features

We have tried to keep sociology's main purpose and relevance front and centre in this book. As a result, *Sociology: Your Compass for a New World* differs from other major introductory sociology textbooks in six ways:

1. ***Drawing connections between one's self and the social world.*** To varying degrees, all introductory sociology textbooks try to show students how their personal experiences are connected to the larger social world. However, we employ two devices to make these connections clearer than in other textbooks. First, we illustrate key sociological ideas by using fresh examples that resonate deeply with student interests and experiences. For example, to show how radical subcultures often become commercialized, we analyze punk and rap music. To demonstrate how functionalists study religion, we discuss the Stanley Cup finals. To illustrate the use of two- and three-variable tables, we study data on the number of sex partners people had in the past year. To characterize contemporary processes of urbanization, we consider the growth of theme parks. To demonstrate the reach of globalization processes, we trace the use of English slang among Japanese teenagers. To portray various aspects of the mass media, we investigate the growth of the World Wide Web and its convergence with television and telephony. We think these examples speak directly to today's students about important sociological ideas in terms they understand, thus making the connection between self and society clear.

   We also developed several pedagogical features to draw the connection between students' experiences and the larger social world. "Where Do You Fit In?" is a question we ask in every chapter. In this feature, we repeatedly challenge students to consider how and why their own lives conform to, or deviate from, various patterns of social relations and actions. "It's Your Choice" is a feature of each chapter that sets out public policy alternatives on a range of pressing social issues. It teaches students that sociology can be a matter of the most urgent practical importance. Students also learn they can have a say in the development of public policy. "Sociology at the Movies" takes a universal and popular element of contemporary culture and renders it sociologically relevant. We provide brief reviews of movies, most of them recent releases, and highlight the sociological insights they contain.
2. ***What to think versus how to think.*** All textbooks teach students both *what* to think about a subject and *how* to think about it from a particular disciplinary perspective. In our judgment, however, introductory sociology textbooks usually place too much stress on the "what" and not enough on the "how." The result: They sometimes read more like encyclopedias than enticements to look at the world in a new way. We have tipped the balance in the other direction. To be sure, *Sociology: Your Compass for a New World* contains definitions and literature reviews. It features standard pedagogical aids such as a list of chapter aims at the beginning of each chapter and a "Summary," a "Glossary," a set of "Questions to Consider," a list of "Web Resources," and a list of "Suggested Readings" at the end of each chapter. However, we devote more space than other authors to showing how sociologists think. We typically relate an anecdote to highlight an issue's importance, present contending interpretations of the issue, and then adduce data to judge the merits of the various interpretations. We do not just refer to tables and graphs, but analyze them. When evidence warrants, we reject theories and endorse others. Thus, many sections of the book read more like a simplified journal article than an encyclopedia. If all this sounds just like what sociologists do professionally, then we have achieved our aim:

to present a less antiseptic, more realistic, and therefore intrinsically exciting account of how sociologists practise their craft. Said differently, one of the strengths of this book is that it does not present sociology as a set of immutable truths carved in stone tablets. Instead, it shows how sociologists actually go about the business of solving sociological puzzles.

3. ***Objectivity versus subjectivity.*** Sociologists since Max Weber have understood that sociologists—indeed, all scientists—are members of society whose thinking and research are influenced by the social and historical context in which they work. Yet a recent article in the *American Sociological Review* shows that introductory sociology textbooks present a stylized and not very sociological view of the research process. Textbooks tend to emphasize sociology's objectivity and the hypothetico-deductive method of reasoning, for the most part ignoring the more subjective factors that go into the research mix (Lynch and Bogen, 1997). We think this emphasis is a pedagogical error. In our own teaching, we have found that drawing the connection between objectivity and subjectivity in sociological research makes the discipline more appealing to students. It shows how research issues are connected to the lives of real flesh-and-blood women and men, and how sociology is related to students' existential concerns. Therefore, in each chapter of *Sociology: Your Compass for a New World*, we feature a "Personal Anecdote" that explains how certain sociological issues first arose in our own minds. We also place the ideas of important sociological figures in social and historical context. We show how sociological methodologies serve as a reality check, but we also make it clear that socially grounded personal concerns often lead sociologists to decide which aspects of reality are worth checking on in the first place. We believe *Sociology: Your Compass for a New World* is unique in presenting a realistic and balanced account of the role of objectivity and subjectivity in the research process.
4. ***Diversity and a global perspective.*** It is gratifying to see how much less parochial introductory sociology textbooks are today than they were just 20 years ago. Contemporary textbooks highlight gender and race issues. They broaden the student's understanding of the world by comparing Canada with other societies. They show how global processes affect local issues and how local issues affect global processes. *Sociology: Your Compass for a New World* is no different in this regard. We have made diversity and globalization prominent themes of this book. We incorporate a "Global Perspective" feature in each chapter. We make frequent and effective use of cross-national comparisons between Canada and countries as diverse as India and Sweden. And we remain sensitive to gender and race issues throughout. This has been easy for us because several of us are members of racial and ethnic minority groups. We are multilingual. We have lived in other countries for extended periods. And we have published widely on countries other than Canada. As you will see in the following pages, our backgrounds have enabled us to bring greater depth to issues of diversity and globalization than other textbooks.
5. ***Currency.*** Every book bears the imprint of its time. It is significant, therefore, that the first editions of most major North American introductory sociology textbooks were published about 15 years ago. Circa 1988, about 10 percent of Canadians owned personal computers. The World Wide Web did not exist. Genetic engineering was in its infancy. The USSR was a major world power. Nobody could imagine teenage boys committing mass murder at school with semi-automatic weapons. *Sociology: Your Compass for a New World* is one of the first North American introductory sociology textbooks of the twenty-first century, and it is the most up to date. This is reflected in the currency of our illustrations and references. For instance, we do not just recommend a few Web sites at the end of each chapter, as is typical in other introductory sociology textbooks. Instead, Web resources form an integral part of this book; fully one-sixth of our citations are Web sites. The currency of this book is also reflected in our "Technology Bytes" feature, which emphasizes the benefits and disadvantages of science and technology as they apply to each of sociology's

major sub-fields. It is reflected in the fact that we devote entire chapters to "The Mass Media" and "Technology and the Global Environment." And it is reflected in the book's theoretical structure.

It made sense in the 1980s to simplify the sociological universe for introductory students by claiming that three main theoretical perspectives (functionalism, symbolic interactionism, and conflict theory) pervade all areas of the discipline. By now, however, that approach is no longer adequate. Functionalism is less influential than it once was. Feminism is an important theoretical perspective in its own right. Conflict theory and symbolic interactionism have become internally differentiated. For example, there is no longer a single conflict theory of politics but at least three important variants. Highly influential new theoretical perspectives, such as postmodernism and social constructionism, have emerged, and not all of them fit neatly into the old categories. *Sociology: Your Compass for a New World* incorporates not just the latest research findings in sociology but also recent theoretical innovations that are given insufficient attention in other major textbooks.

6. ***Organization.*** Traditionally, introductory sociology textbooks come in two sizes. There is the 21- to 24-chapter volume, roughly 750 pages in length, and the 14- or 15-chapter "essentials" version, about 500 pages long. We used both types of books in our classrooms and discussed the question of textbook length with other instructors. We concluded that the 750-page tome is more than many instructors and students can handle in a semester, while the stripped-down 500-page version covers the field too superficially. We decided, therefore, to write *Sociology: Your Compass for a New World* in a concise style, combining some topics and eliminating some nonessential elements one finds in other textbooks. We believe that many instructors will find the 656 pages of *Sociology: Your Compass for a New World* crisp and to the point, without sacrificing any essential elements of the full-length introductory sociology textbook. We believe that *Sociology: Your Compass for a New World* overcomes frequently voiced problems associated with both longer and shorter works of its type.

## Ancillaries

A full range of high-quality ancillaries has been prepared to help instructors and students get the most out of *Sociology: Your Compass for a New World.*

### Supplements for Instructors

- ***Instructor's Manual.*** The Instructor's Manual has been prepared by Adie Nelson, University of Waterloo. It contains lecture outlines, supplemental lecture material, suggested activities for students, and Internet and InfoTrac® College Edition exercises.
- ***Test Bank.*** The Test Bank has been prepared by Paul Lamy, University of Ottawa. It consists of 75–100 multiple-choice questions and 15–20 true/false questions per chapter, all with rejoinders and page references. This supplement also includes 10–20 short answer and 5–10 extended essay questions per chapter.
- ***ExamView Computerized Test Bank.*** Create, deliver, and customize tests and study guides (both print and online) in minutes with this easy-to-use assessment and tutorial system. *ExamView* offers both a *Quick Test Wizard* and an *Online Test Wizard* that guide you step-by-step through the process of creating tests. The test appears on screen exactly as it will print or display online. Using *ExamView's* complete word processing capabilities, you can enter an unlimited number of new questions or edit existing questions.
- ***InfoTrac® College Edition.*** Ignite discussions or augment your lectures with the latest developments in sociology and societal change. Create your own course reader by selecting articles or by using the search keywords provided at the end of each chapter. *InfoTrac® College Edition* (available as a free option with this text) gives

you and your students four months of free access to an easy-to-use online database of reliable, full-length articles (not abstracts) from hundreds of top academic journals and popular sources. Among the journals available twenty-four hours a day, seven days a week are the *Canadian Review of Sociology and Anthropology*, the *Canadian Journal of Sociology*, *Canadian Ethnic Studies*, *Public Policy*, the *American Journal of Sociology*, *Social Forces*, *Social Research*, and *Sociology*. Contact your Nelson representative for more information. *InfoTrac® College Edition* is available only to North American college and university students. Journals are subject to change.

## Classroom Presentation Tools for the Instructor

- ***Microsoft®PowerPoint® series.*** Robert Brym wrote the PowerPoint® series that accompanies the book. Occasionally using animation to add variety and enhance visual appeal, the PowerPoint® series avoids cartoons and other graphical elements that distract students and trivialize the subject matter. Instead, it clearly outlines each chapter of the text and reproduces all of the textbook's figures. Instructors can access supplementary graphics that allow them to develop themes introduced in the text. The PowerPoint® series is also available as a set of acetates.
- ***The Nelson Sociology Video Collection.*** This seven-hour set of 31 video segments, each 5 to 23 minutes in length, was created to stimulate discussion of topics raised in sociology. Produced in conjunction with Face to Face Media (Vancouver), the Jesuit Communication Project (Toronto), and the National Film Board of Canada, the selections have been edited to optimize their impact in the classroom. Many of the selections are taken from films that have won national and international awards. Six of the selections are from the celebrated work of Gwynne Dyer, one of Canada's leading media intellectuals.
- ***Multimedia Manager for Sociology: A Microsoft® PowerPoint® Link Tool.*** The easy way to great multimedia lectures! This one-stop digital library and presentation tool helps you assemble, edit, and present custom lectures. The CD-ROM brings together art (figures, tables, photos) from the text itself, pre-assembled PowerPoint® lecture slides, and video. You can use the materials as they are or add your own materials for a truly customized lecture presentation.
- ***CNN Today Sociology Video Series, Volumes I–V.*** The *CNN Today* Sociology Video Series is an exclusive series jointly created by Wadsworth and *CNN* for the introduction to sociology course. Each video in the series consists of approximately 45 minutes of footage originally broadcast on *CNN* within the last several years and selected specifically to illustrate important sociological concepts. The videos are broken into short, two- to seven-minute segments that are perfect for classroom use as lecture launchers or to illustrate key sociological concepts. An annotated table of contents accompanies each video, with descriptions of the segments and suggestions for their possible use within the course.
- ***Demonstrating Sociology: ShowCase Presentation Software.*** This software package for instructors allows them to analyze data live in front of a classroom. It is a powerful yet easy-to-use statistical analysis package that lets professors show students how sociologists ask and answer questions using sociological theory. An accompanying resource book provides detailed "scripts" for using ShowCase in class. (This software is for Windows users with CD-ROM capability.)

## Supplements for Students

- ***Study Guide.*** The Study Guide was prepared by Geraint Osborne, John McTaggert, and Kierstin Hatt of Augustana University College in Camrose, Alberta. Each chapter of the guide includes learning objectives, chapter outlines, key terms, Internet resources, and multiple-choice and true/false questions with rejoinders and page references, as well as short answer and essay questions to enhance student understanding.

- ✦ ***Society in Question,*** Third Edition, by Robert J. Brym, is the only introductory sociology reader that combines Canadian and international readings. This reader provides balanced coverage of the approaches and methods in current sociology as well as unique and surprising perspectives on many major sociological topics. All readings have been chosen for their ability to speak directly to contemporary Canadian students about how sociology can enable them to make sense of their lives in a rapidly changing world.
- ✦ ***Sociological Footprints: Introductory Readings in Sociology,*** Ninth Edition, by Leonard Cargan and Jeanne Ballantine, Wright State University, is a collection of classical, contemporary, popular, and multicultural readings. The primary objective of this anthology is to provide a link between theoretical sociology and everyday life. The readings deal with such relevant topics as youth violence, globalization, terrorism, and technology.

## Web Site to Accompany *Sociology: Your Compass for a New World*

www.brymsociologycompass.nelson.com

- ✦ ***Companion Web Site.*** In terms of substance, visual appeal, and interactivity, the book's Web site contains an unusually rich collection of materials. Alone among introductory sociology Web sites, this one was written by one of the textbook authors, Robert Brym. All of the materials on the site are closely tied to themes introduced in the text. For each chapter of the book, the site features three online tests, one online research project, one interactive exercise, and four carefully chosen Web links. A separate set of online tests is provided for each of the interactive exercises. In addition, the site contains more than 100 lectures and interviews on a wide variety of sociological topics, many of them featuring leading sociologists. Students hear the lectures and interviews using the free RealPlayer™ plug-in. A "Research Centre" offers students easy access to a full range of official statistics. Instructors can download the Instructor's Manual and the Microsoft® PowerPoint® series directly from the site.

## Acknowledgements

Anyone who has gone sailing knows that when you embark on a long voyage you need more than a compass. Among other things, you need a helm operator blessed with a strong sense of direction and an intimate knowledge of likely dangers. You need at least one crew member who knows all the ropes and can use them to keep things intact and in their proper place. And you need sturdy hands to raise and lower the sails. On the voyage to complete the Canadian edition of this book, the crew demonstrated all these skills. Brad Lambertus, our acquisitions editor, saw this book's promise from the outset, understood clearly the direction we had to take to develop its potential, and on several occasions steered us clear of threatening shoals. We still marvel at how our developmental editor, Klaus Unger, was able to keep the many parts of this project in their proper order and prevent the whole thing from flying apart at the seams even in stormy weather. Copy editor Susan Broadhurst and proofreader Dawn Hunter certainly assisted in this regard. But above all we are indebted to our co-author Adie Nelson, the catalyst who came to the rescue in perilous seas. She knew just when to trim the jib, when to hoist the mainsail, and when to dump ballast. We are deeply indebted to her and to all surviving members of our crew for a successful voyage. Robin Hawkshaw of the University of British Columbia has been invaluable to the team in helping to complete this book.

This book would have been of far inferior quality if the following people had not generously shared their knowledge with us, offered painstaking criticisms of chapter drafts, and given us emotional support:

**Dean Behrens,** University of Toronto
**Nachman Ben-Yehuda,** Hebrew University of Jerusalem

**Steve Berkowitz,** University of Vermont
**Monica Boyd,** University of Toronto
**Clem Brooks,** University of Indiana
**Harvey Choldin,** University of Illinois, Urbana–Champaign
**Dan Clawson,** University of Massachusetts, Amherst
**Weizhen Dong,** University of Toronto
**John Fox,** McMaster University
**Rosemary Gartner,** University of Toronto
**Michael Goldman,** University of Illinois, Urbana–Champaign
**John Hannigan,** University of Toronto
**Randy Hodson,** Ohio State University
**David Hopping,** University of Illinois, Urbana–Champaign
**Elizabeth Jenner,** University of Illinois, Urbana–Champaign
**Baruch Kimmerling,** Hebrew University of Jerusalem
**Larisa Kosova,** Russian Center for Public Opinion Research, Moscow
**Rhonda Lenton,** York University
**Vladimir Magun,** Institute of Sociology, Russian Academy of Science, Moscow
**Jeff Manza,** Northwestern University
**John Myles,** University of Toronto
**Gregg Olsen,** University of Manitoba
**William Outhwaite,** University of Sussex, UK
**Jim Richardson,** University of New Brunswick
**Michael Shalev,** Hebrew University of Jerusalem
**Hira Singh,** York University
**Murray Straus,** University of New Hampshire
**Shelley Ungar,** University of Toronto
**Jack Veugelers,** University of Toronto

We are also grateful to the following colleagues who reviewed the manuscript and provided a wealth of helpful suggestions:

**Penny Biles,** Sheridan College
**Rudy Chernecki,** Durham College
**Art Clarke,** retired from Sir Sandford Fleming College
**Jim Jackson,** M.A., Humber College
**Graham Johnson,** University of British Columbia
**Patricia Kachuk,** University of British Columbia
**Heather A. Kitchin,** Acadia University
**Lisa Kowalchuk,** St. Mary's University
**Kim Luton,** University of Western Ontario
**Geraint Osborne,** Augustana University College
**Vincent Sacco,** Queen's University
**Bill Stuebing,** Red Deer College
**Pam Sugiman,** McMaster University

**Robert J. Brym**
**John Lie**
**Adie Nelson**
**Neil Guppy**
**Chris McCormick**

PART

I

# FOUNDATIONS

## IN THIS CHAPTER, YOU WILL LEARN THAT

- The causes of human behaviour lie partly in the patterns of social relations that surround and permeate us.
- Sociologists examine the connection between social relations and personal troubles.
- Sociologists are often motivated to do research by the desire to improve people's lives. At the same time, sociologists adopt scientific methods to test their ideas.
- Sociology originated at the time of the Industrial Revolution. The founders of sociology diagnosed the massive social transformations of their day. They also suggested ways of overcoming social problems created by the Industrial Revolution.
- Today's Postindustrial Revolution similarly challenges us. Sociology clarifies the scope, direction, and significance of social change. It also suggests ways of dealing with the social problems created by the Postindustrial Revolution.
- At the personal level, sociology can help clarify the opportunities and constraints you face. It suggests what you can become in today's social and historical context.

CHAPTER

1

# A Sociological Compass

## INTRODUCTION

### Why You Need a Compass for a New World

"When I was a child, a cleaning lady came to our house twice a month," Robert Brym recalls. "Her name was Lena White, and she was what we then called an 'Indian.' I was fond of Lena because she possessed two apparently magical powers. First, she could let the ash at the end of her cigarette grow five centimetres before it fell off. I sometimes used to play where Lena was working just to see how long she could scrub, vacuum, climb the stepladder, and chatter before the ash made its inevitable descent to the floor. Second, Lena could tell stories. My mother would serve us lunch at the kitchen table. During dessert, as we sipped tea with milk, Lena would spin tales about Gluskap, the Creator of the world.

"I liked Gluskap because he was mischievous and enormously powerful. He fought giants, drove away monsters, taught people how to hunt and farm, and named the stars. But he also got into trouble and learned from his mistakes. For example, one day the wind was blowing so hard Gluskap couldn't paddle his canoe into the bay to hunt ducks. So he found the source of the wind: the flapping wings of the Wind Eagle. He then tricked the Wind Eagle into getting stuck in a crevice where he could flap no more. Now Gluskap could go hunting. However, the air soon grew so hot he found it difficult to breathe. The water became dirty and began to smell bad, and there was so much foam on it he found it hard to paddle. When he complained to his grandmother, she explained that the wind was needed to cool the air, wash the earth, and move the waters to keep them clean. And so Gluskap freed the Wind Eagle and the winds returned to the earth. Gluskap decided it was better to wait for good weather and *then* go duck hunting rather than conquer the winds.

"Like the tale of the Wind Eagle, many of the Gluskap stories Lena told me were about the need for harmony among humans and between humans and nature. You can imagine my surprise, therefore, when I got to school and learned about the European exploration of what was called the New World. My teachers taught me all about the glories of the *conquest* of nature—and of other people. I learned that in the New World a Native population perhaps a hundredth as large as Europe's occupied a territory more than four times larger. I was taught that the New World was unimaginably rich in resources. European rulers saw that by controlling it they could increase their power and importance. Christians recognized new possibilities for spreading their religion. Explorers discerned fresh opportunities for rewarding adventures. A wave of excitement swelled as word spread of the New World's vast potential and challenges. I, too, became excited as I heard stories of conquest quite unlike the tales of Gluskap. Of course, I learned little about the violence required to conquer the New World.

"Forty years ago I was caught between thrilling stories of conquest and reflective stories that questioned the wisdom of conquest. Today, I think many people are in a similar position. On the one hand, we feel like the European explorers because we, too, have reached the frontiers of a New World. Like them, we are full of anticipation. Our New World is one of virtually instant long-distance communication, global economies and cultures, weakening nation-states, and technological advances that often make the daily news seem like reports from a distant planet. In a fundamental way, the world is not the same place it was just 50 years ago. Orbiting telescopes that peer to the fringes of the universe, human genetic code laid bare like a road map, fibre optic cable that carries trillions of bits of information per second, and spacecraft that transport robots to Mars help make this a New World.

"On the other hand, we understand that not all is hope and bright horizons. Our anticipation is mixed with dread. Gluskap stories make more sense than ever. Scientific breakthroughs are announced almost daily, but the global environment has never been in worse shape and AIDS is now the leading cause of death in Africa. Marriages and nations unexpectedly break up and then reconstitute themselves in new and unanticipated forms. We celebrate the advances made by women and racial minorities only to find that some people oppose their progress, sometimes violently. Waves of people migrate between continents, establishing cooperation but also conflict between previously separated groups. New technologies make work more interesting and creative for some, offering unprecedented opportunities to become rich and famous. They also make jobs more onerous and routine for others. The standard of living goes up for many people but stagnates for many more.

"Amid all this contradictory news, good and bad, uncertainty about the future prevails. That is why my colleagues and I wrote this book. We set out to show undergraduates that sociology can help them make sense of their lives, however uncertain they may appear to be. Five hundred years ago, the early European explorers of North and South America set themselves the preliminary task of mapping the contours of the New World. We set ourselves a similar task here. Their frontiers were physical; ours are social. Their maps were geographical; ours are sociological. But in terms of functionality, our maps are much like theirs. All maps allow us to find our place in the world and see ourselves in the context of larger forces. *Sociological* maps, as the famous American sociologist C. Wright Mills wrote, allow us to "grasp the interplay of [people] and society, of biography and history" (Mills, 1959: 4). This book, then, shows you how to draw sociological maps so you can see your place in the world, figure out how to navigate through it, and perhaps discover how to improve it. It is your sociological compass.

"We emphasize that sociology can be a liberating practical activity, not just an abstract intellectual exercise. By revealing the opportunities and constraints you face, sociology can help teach you who you are and what you can become in this particular social and historical context. We cannot know what the future will bring, but we can at least know the choices we confront and the likely consequences of our actions. From this point of view, sociology can help us create the best possible future. That has always been sociology's principal justification, and so it should be today."

## The Goals of This Chapter

In this chapter we aim to achieve three goals:

1. We first illustrate the power of sociology to dispel foggy assumptions and help us see the operation of the social world more clearly. To that end, we examine a phenomenon that at first glance appears to be solely the outcome of breakdowns in *individual* functioning: suicide. We show that, in fact, *social* relations powerfully influence suicide rates. This exercise introduces you to what is unique about the sociological perspective.
2. We show that, from its origins, sociological research has been motivated by a desire to improve the social world. Thus, sociology is not just a dry, academic exercise but a means of charting a better course for society. At the same time, however, sociologists adopt scientific methods to test their ideas, thus increasing their validity. We illustrate these points by briefly analyzing the work of the founders of the discipline.
3. We suggest that sociology can help you come to grips with your century, just as it helped the founders of sociology deal with theirs. Today we are witnessing massive and disorienting social changes. As was the case a hundred years ago, sociologists today try to understand social phenomena and suggest credible ways of improving their societies. By promising to make sociology relevant to you, this chapter should be viewed as an open invitation to participate in sociology's challenge.

But first things first. Before showing how sociology can help you understand and improve your world, we briefly examine the problem of suicide. That examination will help illustrate how the sociological perspective can clarify and sometimes overturn common-sense beliefs.

## THE SOCIOLOGICAL PERSPECTIVE

By analyzing suicide sociologically, you can put to a tough test the claim that sociology takes a unique, surprising, and enlightening perspective on social events. After all, suicide appears to be the supremely anti-social and nonsocial act. It is, in the first place, condemned by nearly everyone in society. Moreover, it is typically committed in private, far from the public's intrusive glare.

It is comparatively rare: In recent years, there have been about 13 suicides annually for every 100 000 people in Canada. (Canada's suicide rate places us 26th among the 82 countries that publish suicide statistics; see Figure 1.1.) And, finally, when you think about

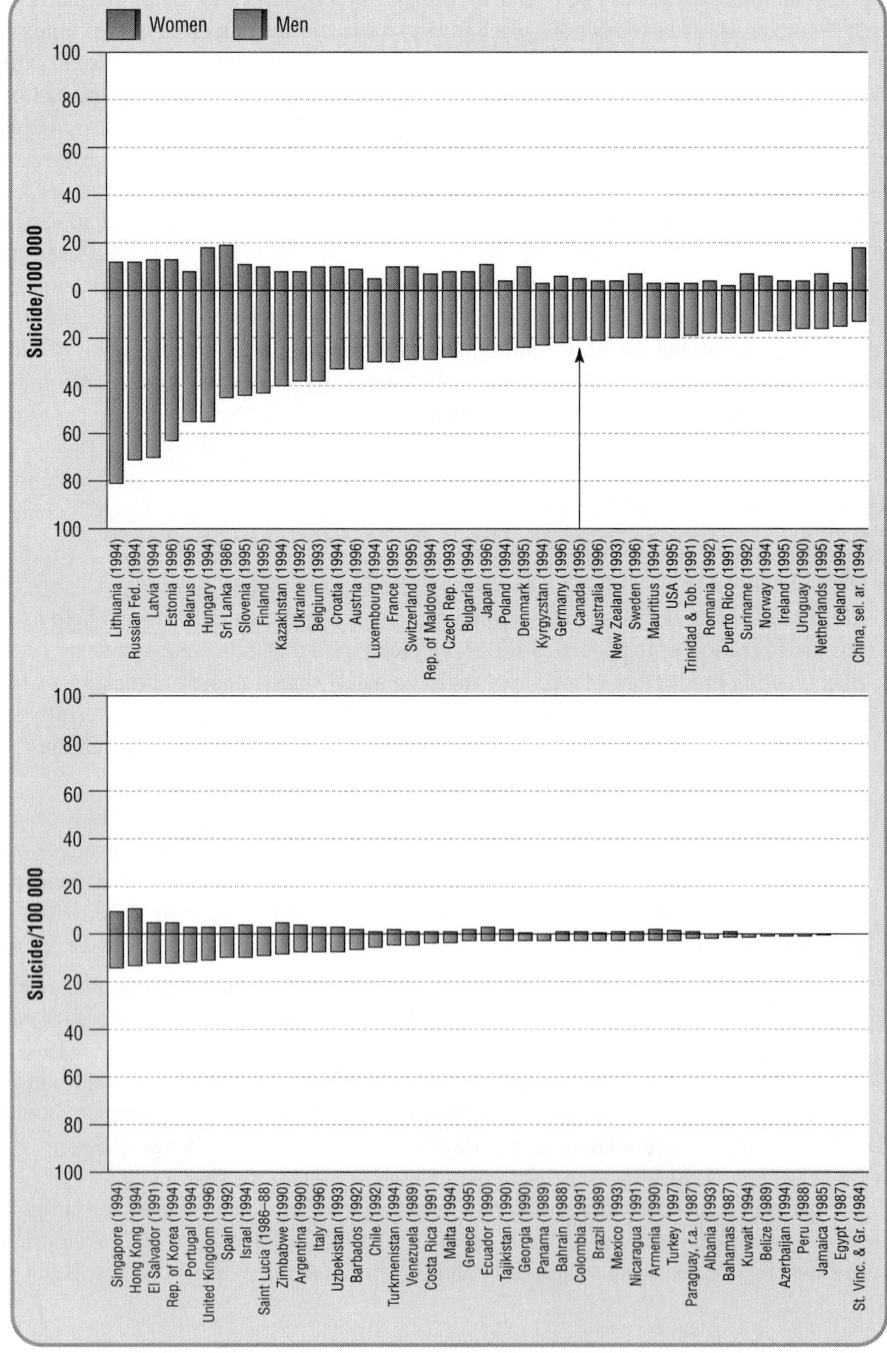


✦ **FIGURE 1.1** ✦
**Suicide Rates by Country and Sex, c. 1995**

Source: Schmidtke et al. (1998).

why people commit such acts, you are likely to focus on their individual states of mind rather than on the state of society. In other words, we are usually interested in the aspects of specific individuals' lives that caused them to become depressed or angry enough to do something as awful as killing themselves. We do not usually think about the patterns of social relations that might encourage or inhibit such actions in general. If sociology can reveal the hidden social causes of such an apparently nonsocial and anti-social phenomenon, there must be something to it!

## The Sociological Explanation of Suicide

At the end of the nineteenth century, Émile Durkheim (1951 [1897]) demonstrated that suicide is more than just an individual act of desperation that results from psychological disorder, as was commonly believed at the time. Suicide rates, Durkheim showed, are strongly influenced by social forces.

Durkheim made his case by examining the association between rates of suicide and rates of psychological disorder for different groups. The idea that psychological disorder causes suicide is supported, he reasoned, only if suicide rates tend to be high where rates of psychological disorder are high, and low where rates of psychological disorder are low. But his analysis of European government statistics, hospital records, and other sources revealed nothing of the kind. He discovered, for example, that there were slightly more women than men in insane asylums, but there were four male suicides for every female suicide. Jews had the highest rate of psychological disorder among the major religious groups in France, but they also had the lowest suicide rate. Psychological disorders occurred most frequently when a person reached maturity, but suicide rates increased steadily with age.

Clearly, suicide rates and rates of psychological disorder did not vary directly. In fact, they often appeared to vary inversely. Why? Durkheim argued that suicide rates vary as a result of differences in the degree of **social solidarity** in different categories of the population. According to Durkheim, the more a group's members share beliefs and values, and the more frequently and intensely they interact, the more social solidarity there is in the group. In turn, the more social solidarity there is in a group, the more firmly anchored individuals are to the social world, and the less likely they are to take their own life if adversity strikes. In other words, Durkheim expected high-solidarity groups to have lower suicide rates than low-solidarity groups—at least up to a certain point (see Figure 1.2).

To support his argument, Durkheim showed that married adults are half as likely as unmarried adults to commit suicide. That is because marriage creates social ties and a sort of moral cement that bind the individual to society. Similarly, he argued that women are less likely to commit suicide than men because women are more involved in the intimate

"Pacific." Alex Colville. 1967.

✦ **FIGURE 1.2** ✦

**Durkheim's Theory of Suicide**

Durkheim argued that, as the level of social solidarity increases, the suicide rate declines. Then, beyond a certain point, it starts to rise. Hence the U-shaped curve in this graph. Durkheim called suicides that occur in very high solidarity settings **altruistic**. They occur when norms very tightly govern behaviour. For example, when soldiers knowingly give up their lives to protect members of their unit, they commit altruistic suicide out of a deep sense of patriotism and comradeship. In contrast, suicide that occurs in very low solidarity settings is **anomic**, said Durkheim. That is, it results from vaguely defined norms governing behaviour.

Suicide rate
High
Low
Anomic suicide
Altruistic suicide
Low
High
Social solidarity

social relations of family life. Jews, Durkheim wrote, are less likely to commit suicide than Christians because centuries of persecution have turned them into a group that is more defensive and tightly knit. And the elderly are more prone than the young and the middle-aged to take their own lives in the face of misfortune, because they are most likely to live alone, to have lost a spouse, and to lack a job and a wide network of friends. In general, Durkheim wrote, "suicide varies with the degree of integration of the social groups of which the individual forms a part" (Durkheim, 1951 [1897]: 209). Of course, his generalization tells us nothing about why any particular individual may take his or her life. That issue is the province of psychology. But it does tell us that a person's likelihood of committing suicide decreases with the degree to which he or she is anchored in society. And it says something surprising and uniquely sociological about how and why the suicide rate varies from group to group.

## Suicide in Canada Today

Durkheim's theory is not just an historical curiosity. It sheds light on the factors that account for variations in suicide rates here and now. Consider Figure 1.3, which shows suicide rates by age and sex in Canada. Comparing rates for men and women, we immedi-

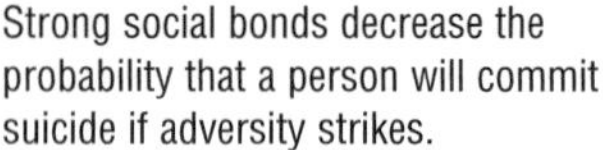

Strong social bonds decrease the probability that a person will commit suicide if adversity strikes.

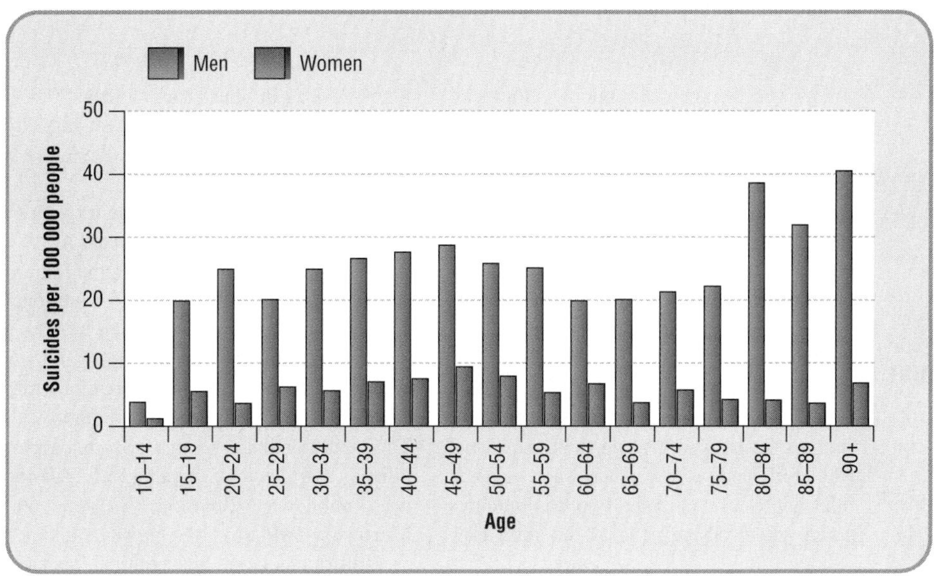


✦ **FIGURE 1.3** ✦
**Suicide by Age and Sex, Canada, 1997**

Source: Calculated from Statistics Canada (1999b: 126–9).

ately see that, as in Durkheim's France, men are about four times more likely than women to commit suicide (see also Figure 1.1, which shows that the relationship between sex and suicide is similar in nearly all countries). However, looking at differences between age groups, we see a striking difference between Durkheim's France and contemporary Canada. When Durkheim wrote, youth suicide was extremely rare. In Canada today, it is much more common, having increased substantially since the 1960s. That is why suicide rates do *not* increase steadily with age in Canada today, although they do rise substantially for men over the age of 79.

Although the rate of youth suicide was low in Durkheim's France, his theory of social solidarity helps us understand why it has risen so quickly in Canada. In brief, shared moral principles and strong social ties have eroded since the early 1960s, especially for Canada's youth. Consider the following facts:

- Church, synagogue, mosque, and temple attendance is down, particularly among young people. Well over half of Canadians attended religious services weekly in the 1960s. Today the figure is below one-third and is only 15 percent for people born after 1960.
- Unemployment is up, again especially for youth. Thus, the unemployment rate was in the 3-percent range for most of the 1960s. It rose steadily to the 10-percent range for most of the 1990s. As of March 2002, the most recent date for which unemployment figures are available as of this writing, the unemployment rate was 7.7 percent. Moreover, the unemployment rate is more than twice as high for Canadians under the age of 24 as it is for older Canadians.
- The rate of divorce has increased sixfold since the early 1960s. Births outside marriage are also much more common than they used to be. As a result, children are more often brought up in single-parent families than in the past. This suggests that they enjoy less frequent and intimate social interaction with parents and less adult supervision.

In sum, the figures cited above suggest that the level of social solidarity is now lower than it was just a few decades ago, especially for young people. Less firmly rooted in society, and less likely to share moral standards, young people in Canada today are more likely than they were four decades ago to take their own lives if they happen to find themselves in the midst of a deep personal crisis (see also Box 1.1).

BOX 1.1
IT'S YOUR CHOICE

### SUICIDE AND THE INNU OF LABRADOR

The Canadians with the highest suicide rate are Aboriginal peoples. For instance, the suicide rate among registered Indians is four times higher than for the Canadian population as a whole (Health Canada, 1994: 56). Among Canada's Aboriginal peoples, the 2000 Innu of Labrador have the highest suicide rate. They are in fact the most suicide-prone people on earth. Among the Innu, the suicide rate is nearly 13 times higher than for all Canadians (Rogan, 2001; Samson, Wilson, and Mazower, 1999).

Durkheim's theory of suicide helps explain the Innu people's tragic propensity to commit suicide. Over the past half-century, the Innu's traditional norms and values have been destroyed. Moreover, the Innu have been prevented from participating in stable and meaningful patterns of social interaction. In other words, social solidarity among the Innu has been cut to an abysmally low level.

How did this state of affairs come about? Historically, the Innu were a nomadic people who relied on hunting and trapping for their livelihood. In the mid-1950s, however, shortly after Newfoundland and Labrador became part of Canada, the provincial and federal governments were eager to gain control of traditional Innu land so as to encourage economic development. Government officials felt that if new roads, mines, lumbering operations, hydroelectric projects, and low-level flight training facilities for NATO air forces were to be built, the Innu would have to be concentrated in stable settlements. Furthermore, government officials believed that, to function in these new settlements, the Innu would have to learn practical and cultural skills associated with a modern industrial society. As a result, governments put tremendous pressure on the Innu to give up their traditional way of life and settle in places such as Davis Inlet and Sheshatsui, the two communities where about 85 percent of the Innu now reside.[1]

In the new communities, Canadian laws, schools, and churches strongly discouraged the Innu from hunting, practising their religion, and raising their children in the traditional way. For example, Canadian hunting regulations limited Innu access to their age-old livelihood. Priests are known to have beaten children who missed church or school to go hunting, thus introducing interpersonal violence into a culture that formerly knew none. Teachers transmitted North American and European skills and culture, often denigrating Innu practices. In effect, Canadian authorities staged an assault on Innu culture as a whole. At the same time, there were few alternative jobs in the new communities. Most Innu wound up living in despair and on welfare. In the absence of work, and lacking the stabilizing influence of their traditional culture, a people long known for their nonviolence and cooperative spirit became victims of widespread family breakdown, sexual abuse, drunkenness, and alcohol-related illness. Today in Sheshatsui, at least 20 percent of the children regularly get high by sniffing gasoline. In Davis Inlet, the figure is nearly 60 percent.

What is to be done about the tragedy of the Innu people? A study conducted in 1984 showed that a movement among the Innu to return to the land and their traditional hunting practices for up to seven months a year led to a dramatic improvement in their health. They lived a vigorous outdoor life. Alcohol abuse stopped. Diet improved. Their emotional and social environment stabilized and became meaningful. Suicide was unknown (Samson, Wilson, and Mazower, 1999: 25).

Unfortunately, a big political obstacle stands in the way of the Innu returning to their traditional lifestyle on a wide scale. Simply put, the governments of Canada and Newfoundland and Labrador will not allow it. A widespread Innu return to the land conflicts with government and private economic development plans. For instance, the Lower Churchill Falls hydroelectric project (the second-biggest hydroelectric project in the world) and the Voisey's Bay nickel mine (the world's biggest deposit of nickel) are located in the middle of traditional Innu hunting and burial grounds. The Innu are vigorously attempting to regain control of their land and what happens to it. They also want to be able to decide *on their own* when and how to use Canadian health services, training facilities, and the like. Whether some compromise can be worked out between government and private plans for economic development and the continuity of the Innu people is unclear. What is clear is that, as a Canadian citizen, the outcome is partly your choice.

## From Personal Troubles to Social Structures

You have known for a long time that you live in a society. But until now, you may not have fully appreciated that society also lives in you. That is, patterns of social relations affect your innermost thoughts and feelings, influence your actions, and thus help shape who you are. As we have seen, one such pattern of social relations is the level of social solidarity characteristic of the various groups to which you belong.

Sociologists call relatively stable patterns of social relations **social structures.** One of the sociologist's main tasks is to identify and explain the connection between people's personal troubles and the social structures in which people are embedded. This is harder work than it may seem at first. In everyday life, we usually see things mainly from our own point of view. Our experiences appear unique to each of us. If we think about them at all, social structures may appear remote and impersonal. To see how social structures operate inside us, we require sociological training.

An important step in broadening our sociological awareness involves recognizing that three levels of social structure surround and permeate us. Think of these structures as concentric circles radiating out from you:

1. **Microstructures** are patterns of intimate social relations. They are formed during face-to-face interaction. Families, friendship circles, and work associations are all examples of microstructures.

   Understanding the operation of microstructures can be useful. Let us say you are looking for a job. You might think you would do best to ask as many close friends and relatives as possible for leads and contacts. However, sociological research shows that people you know well are likely to know many of the same people. After asking a couple of close connections for help landing a job, you would therefore do best to ask more remote acquaintances for leads and contacts. People to whom you are *weakly* connected (and who are weakly connected among themselves) are more likely to know *different* groups of people. Therefore, they will give you more information about job possibilities and ensure that word about your job search spreads farther. You are more likely to find a job faster if you understand "the strength of weak ties" in microstructural settings (Granovetter, 1973).

2. **Macrostructures** are patterns of social relations that lie outside and above your circle of intimates and acquaintances.[2] Macrostructures include class relations, bureaucracies, and **patriarchy,** the traditional system of economic and political inequality between women and men in most societies (for some exceptions, see Chapter 9, Sexuality and Gender).

   Understanding the operation of macrostructures can also be useful. Consider, for example, one aspect of patriarchy. In our society, most married women who work full-time in the paid labour force are responsible for more housework, child care, and care for the elderly than their husbands. Governments and businesses support this arrangement insofar as they provide little assistance to families in the form of nurseries, after-school programs for children, seniors homes, and so forth. Yet an aspect of patriarchy—the unequal division of work in the household—is a major source of dissatisfaction with marriage, especially in families that cannot afford to buy these services privately. Thus, sociological research shows that where spouses share domestic responsibilities equally, they are happier with their marriages and less likely to divorce (Hochschild with Machung, 1989). When a marriage is in danger of dissolving, it is common for partners to blame themselves and each other for their troubles. However, it should now be clear that forces other than incompatible personalities often put stress on families. Understanding how the macrostructure of patriarchy crops up in everyday life, and doing something to change that structure, can thus help people lead happier lives.

3. The third level of society that surrounds and permeates us is composed of **global structures.** International organizations, patterns of worldwide travel and communication, and the economic relations between countries are examples of global structures. Global structures are increasingly important as inexpensive travel and communication allow all parts of the world to become interconnected culturally, economically, and politically.

   Understanding the operation of global structures can be useful, too. For instance, many people are concerned about the world's poor. They donate money to charities to help with famine relief. Some people also approve of the Canadian government giving foreign aid to poor countries. However, many of these same people do not appreciate that charity and foreign aid alone do not seem able to end world poverty. That is because charity and foreign aid have been unable to overcome the structure of social relations among countries that have created and now sustain global inequality.

Let us linger on this point for a moment. As we will see in Chapter 16 (Population, Urbanization, and Development), Britain, France, and other imperial powers locked some countries into poverty when they colonized them between the seventeenth and nineteenth centuries. In the twentieth century, the poor (or "developing") countries borrowed money from these same rich countries and Western banks to pay for airports, roads, harbours, sanitation systems, basic health care, and so forth. Today, poor countries pay far more to rich countries and Western banks in interest on those loans than they receive in aid and charity (see Figure 1.4). Thus, it seems that relying exclusively on foreign aid and charity can do little to help solve the problem of world poverty. Understanding how the global structure of international relations created and helps maintain global inequality suggests new policy priorities for helping the world's poor. One such priority might involve campaigning for the cancellation of foreign debt in compensation for past injustices. Some elements in the Canadian government have been promoting this policy for the past few years.

As these examples illustrate, personal problems are connected to social structures at the micro, macro, and global levels. Whether the personal problem involves finding a job, keeping a marriage intact, or figuring out a way to act justly to end world poverty, social-structural considerations broaden our understanding of the problem and suggest appropriate courses of action (see Box 1.2).

## The Sociological Imagination

Half a century ago, C. Wright Mills (1959) called the ability to see the connection between personal troubles and social structures the **sociological imagination.** He emphasized the difficulty of developing this quality of mind:

> When a society becomes industrialized, a peasant becomes a worker; a feudal lord is liquidated or becomes a businessman. When classes rise or fall, a [woman] is employed or unemployed; when the rate of investment goes up or down, a [woman] takes new heart or goes broke. When war happens, an insurance sales[person] becomes a rocket launcher; a store clerk, a radar [operator]; a wife lives alone; a child grows up without a father. Neither the life of an individual nor the history of a society can be understood without understanding both.
>
> Yet [people] do not usually define the troubles they endure in terms of historical change.... The well-being they enjoy, they do not usually impute to the big ups and downs of the society in which they live. Seldom aware of the intricate connection between the patterns of their own lives and the course of world history, ordinary [people] do not usually know what this connection means for the kind of [people] they are becoming and for the

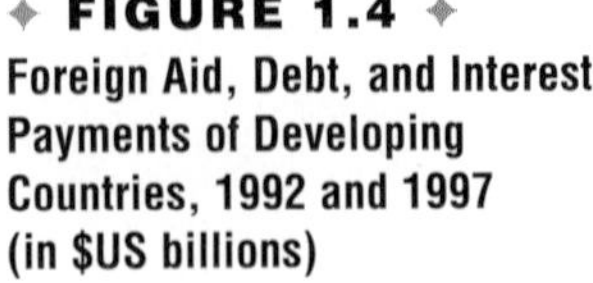

✦ **FIGURE 1.4** ✦
**Foreign Aid, Debt, and Interest Payments of Developing Countries, 1992 and 1997 (in $US billions)**

Source: World Bank (1999a; 1999b).

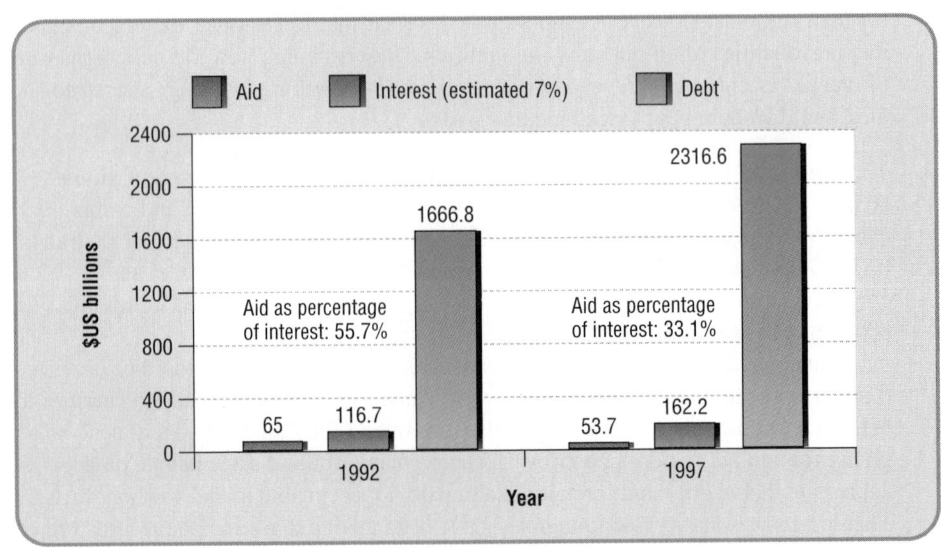

## BOX 1.2
## SOCIOLOGY AT THE MOVIES

Forrest Gump let life happen to him without ever understanding the larger social and historical forces impinging on him. His was a life entirely devoid of the sociological imagination.

### *FORREST GUMP* (1994)

*Forrest Gump* is a widely acclaimed cinematic tour of the United States from the 1950s to the 1980s. The movie stars Tom Hanks as Forrest Gump, a man with an IQ of 75. Although Forrest has limited intelligence and little education, he leads a remarkable life. He is a football hero in high school, wins the Congressional Medal of Honor during the Vietnam War, and manages to become a millionaire by buying stock in a start-up company called Apple Computers. In between, he teaches Elvis to swivel his hips, sits next to John Lennon in a television talk show, becomes a Ping-Pong champion, and meets several U.S. presidents. In short, Forrest leads a charmed life.

In contrast, the girl Forrest Gump falls in love with in elementary school—and whom he remains in love with for the rest of his life—becomes a hippie. She preaches flower power and peace while Forrest is fighting in Vietnam. Eventually, she becomes a drug addict, a stripper, and HIV-positive.

Between these two lives, one lucky, the other damaged, *Forrest Gump* manages to capture many important moments in U.S. and world history over a 40-year period. However, because Forrest is so limited intellectually, he cannot make much sense of his life or the world around him. He is naively optimistic. Remarkable things happen to him, but he never fully appreciates their significance. He never questions whether the social and historical events that swirl around and through him have negative consequences for some people, so he never tries to change them or even senses that they might need to be changed.

In contrast to Forrest's approach to life, the sociological imagination urges us to connect our biography with history and social structure—to make sense of our lives against a larger historical and social background and to act in light of our understanding. The message of the sociological imagination is similar to that of the classical Greek philosopher Socrates: "The unexamined life is not worth living."

What do you think about these two conflicting views? Would you like things to happen to you without really understanding what is going on? Or is it better to live an examined life? Had Forrest been equipped with the sociological imagination, would he have gotten more out of life? Have you ever tried to put events in your own life in the context of history and social structure? Did the exercise help you make sense of your life? Did it in any way lead to a life more worth living? Is the sociological imagination a worthy goal?

Although movies are just entertainment to many people, they often achieve by different means what the sociological imagination aims for. Therefore, in each chapter of this book, we review a movie to shed light on topics of sociological importance.

> kind of history-making in which they might take part. They do not possess the quality of mind essential to grasp the interplay of [people] and society, of biography and history, of self and world. They cannot cope with their personal troubles in such a way as to control the structural transformations that usually lie behind them.
>
> What they need...is a quality of mind that will help them to [see]...what is going on in the world and...what may be happening within themselves. It is this quality...that...may be called the sociological imagination. (Mills, 1959: 3–4)

The founders of sociology first developed the sociological imagination. It will therefore prove useful to sketch out the broad contours of their work.[3]

# THEORETICAL TRADITIONS IN SOCIOLOGY

## The Origins of Sociology

The term "sociology" was coined by the French social thinker Auguste Comte in 1838 (Comte, 1975). Comte tried to place the study of society on scientific foundations. He wanted to understand the social world as it is, not as he or anyone else imagined it should be. This was a highly original approach to the study of society. In ancient and medieval times, philosophers from diverse civilizations had sketched blueprints for the ideal society (see Figure 1.5). We see evidence of this in the work of Confucius in China, Ibn Khaldun in Tunisia, and Plato and Aristotle in Greece, to name only a few of the best-known figures. But Comte was swept up in the scientific revolution of his time. He was inspired by the astronomers and physicists of the modern era—Copernicus in Poland, Galileo in Italy, Newton in England. He wanted to test the validity of his ideas through careful observation of the real world rather than by assuming that "God" or "human nature" determined the shape of society.

Yet, despite Comte's breakthrough, there was a tension in his work. For although he was eager to adopt the scientific method in his study of society, he was a conservative thinker, motivated by strong opposition to rapid change in French society. His was a time not only of scientific but also of political and social revolution. Comte witnessed the democratic forces unleashed by the French Revolution, the early industrialization of society, and the rapid growth of cities. And what he saw shocked and angered him, because rapid social change was destroying many of the things he valued, especially unquestioning respect for authority. He therefore urged slow change and the preservation of much that was traditional in social life. Thus, at its very origin, sociological research was motivated by adherence to scientific methods of research *and* a vision of the ideal society.

The same sort of tension is evident in the work of the most important early figures in the history of sociology, Karl Marx, Émile Durkheim, and Max Weber. These three men lived in the period 1820–1920. They witnessed various phases of Europe's wrenching tran-

The Scientific Revolution began in Europe around 1550. Scientists proposed new theories about the structure of the universe and developed new methods to collect evidence so they could test those theories. Shown here is an astrolabe used by Copernicus to solve problems relating to the position of the sun, the planets, and the stars.

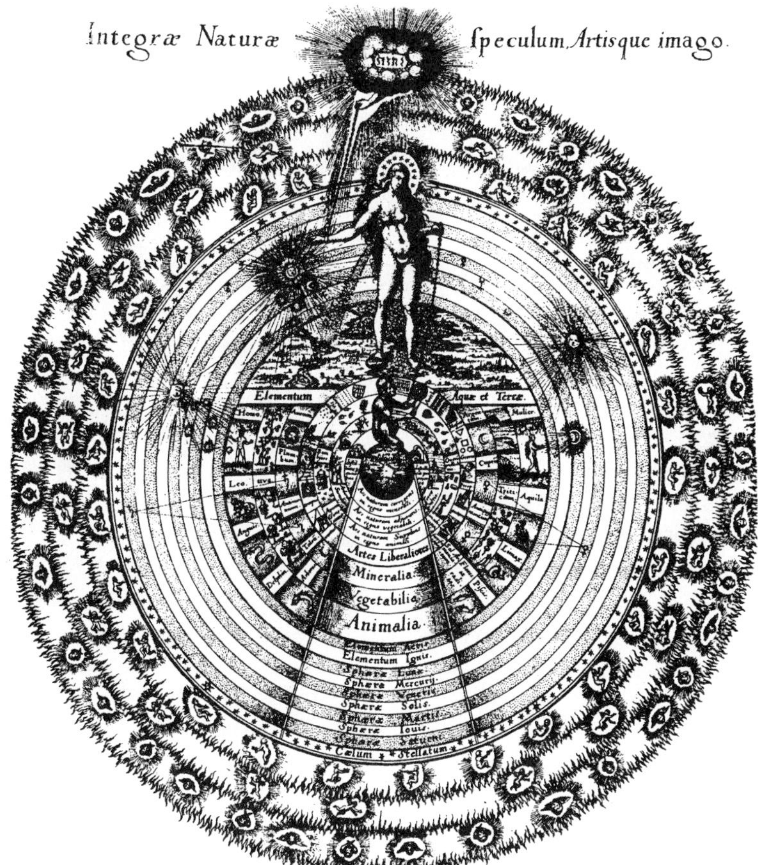


**✦ FIGURE 1.5 ✦**

**The European View of the World, about 1600**

In Shakespeare's time, most educated Europeans pictured a universe in which God ultimately determines everything. Thus, in this early seventeenth-century engraving, a chain extends from God's hand to the hand of a woman representing Nature; she in turn holds a chain extending to the "ape of Nature," representing humankind. This suggests that God and his intermediary, Nature, shape all human actions. Notice also that the engraving places humans at the centre of the universe, suggesting that God created the universe chiefly for human benefit. Finally, note that the engraving arranges all the elements of the universe—angels, heavenly objects, humans, animals, vegetables, minerals—in a hierarchy. It suggests that higher elements, such as the stars and the planets, influence lower elements, such as the fate of humans.

Source: Robert Fludd. *Ultriusque Cosmi Maioris Scilicet et Minoris Metaphysica, Physica Atqve Technica Historia.* 1617–19. (Oppenheim, Germany. Johan-Thedori de Bry.)

Eugene Delacroix. *Liberty Leading the People, July 28, 1830.* The democratic forces unleashed by the French Revolution suggested that people are responsible for organizing society and that human intervention can therefore solve social problems. As such, democracy was a foundation stone of sociology.

sition to industrial capitalism. They wanted to understand why people were moving from countryside to city, working agonizingly long hours in crowded and dangerous factories, losing faith in their religions, confronting faceless bureaucracies, and reacting to the conditions of their existence with strikes, crime, revolution, and war. Like Comte, these early sociologists were all committed to the scientific method of research. However, they also wanted to chart a better course for their societies. The ideas they developed are therefore not just diagnostic tools from which we can still learn much, but also, like many sociological ideas, prescriptions for combating social ills.

Diego Rivera. *Detroit Industry,* North Wall. 1932–33. Fresco (detail). Copyright 1997. The Detroit Institute of Arts. The so-called Second Industrial Revolution began in the early twentieth century. Wealthy entrepreneurs formed large companies. Steel became a basic industrial material. Oil and electricity fuelled much industrial production. At the same time, Henry Ford's assembly lines and other mass-production technologies transformed the workplace.

## Theory, Research, and Values

To clarify the tension in sociology between analysis and ideal, diagnosis and prescription, we can usefully distinguish three terms: theory, research, and values.

- Sociological ideas are generally stated in the form of theories. A **theory** is a tentative explanation of some aspect of social life that states how and why certain facts are related. For example, in his theory of suicide, Durkheim showed how facts about suicide rates are related to facts about social solidarity. This enabled him to explain suicide as a function of social solidarity.
- *After* theories are formulated, the sociologist can conduct research. **Research** is the process of carefully observing social reality to assess the validity of a theory. It is because research can call the validity of a theory into question that theories are said to be only "tentative" explanations. We discuss the research process in detail in Chapter 2, Research Methods.
- *Before* sociologists can formulate a theory, however, they must make certain judgments. For example, they must decide which problems are worth studying. They must make certain assumptions about how the parts of society fit together. If they are going to recommend ways of improving the operation of some aspect of society, they must have an opinion about what the ideal society ought to look like. As we will soon see, these issues are shaped in large measure by sociologists' values. **Values** are ideas about what is right and wrong. Inevitably, values help sociologists formulate and favour certain theories over others (Edel, 1965; Kuhn, 1970 [1962]). So sociological theories may be modified and even rejected because of research, but they are often motivated by sociologists' values.

Durkheim, Marx, and Weber initiated three of the major theoretical traditions in sociology—functionalism, conflict theory, and symbolic interactionism. A fourth perspective, feminism, has become popular in recent decades as a means of correcting some deficiencies of the three long-established traditions. It will become clear as you read this book that there are many more theories than just these four. However, because these four traditions have been especially influential in the development of sociology, we present a thumbnail sketch of each one here.

## Functionalism

Durkheim's theory of suicide is an early example of what sociologists now call **functionalism.** Functionalist theories incorporate these four features:

1. They stress that human behaviour is governed by relatively stable patterns of social relations or social structures. For example, Durkheim emphasized how suicide rates are influenced by patterns of social solidarity. Usually the social structures analyzed by functionalists are macrostructures.
2. Functionalist theories show how social structures maintain or undermine social stability. Typically, Durkheim analyzed how the growth of industries and cities in nineteenth-century Europe lowered the level of social solidarity and contributed to social instability, one aspect of which was a higher suicide rate.
3. Functionalist theories emphasize that social structures are based mainly on shared values or preferences. Thus, when Durkheim wrote about social solidarity, he sometimes meant the frequency and intensity of social interaction, but more often he thought of social solidarity as a kind of moral cement that binds people together.
4. Functionalism suggests that re-establishing equilibrium can best solve most social problems. Thus, Durkheim said social stability could be restored in late nineteenth-century Europe by creating new associations of employers and workers that would lower workers' expectations about what they could get out of life. If, said Durkheim, more people could agree on wanting less, social solidarity would rise and there would be fewer strikes, less suicide, and so on. Functionalism, then, was a conservative response to widespread social unrest in late nineteenth-century France. A more liberal or radical response would have been to argue that if people are expressing discontent because they are getting less out of life than they expect, discontent can be lowered by figuring out ways for them to get more out of life.

Although functionalist thinking influenced North American sociology at the end of the nineteenth century, it was only during the continent's greatest economic crisis ever, the Great Depression of 1929–39, that functionalism took deep root here (Russett, 1966). With 30 percent of the labour force unemployed and labour unrest rising, it is not entirely surprising that sociologists with a conservative frame of mind were attracted to a theory that focused on how social equilibrium could be restored. Functionalist theory remained popular for about 30 years. It experienced a minor revival in the early 1990s but never regained the dominance it enjoyed from the 1930s to the early 1960s.

Harvard sociologist Talcott Parsons was the foremost North American proponent of functionalism. Parsons is best known for identifying how various institutions must work to ensure the smooth operation of society as a whole. He argued that society is well integrated and in equilibrium when the family successfully raises new generations, the military successfully defends society against external threats, schools are able to teach students the skills and values they need to function as productive adults, and religions create a shared moral code among the people (Parsons, 1951).

Parsons was criticized for exaggerating the degree to which members of society share common values and social institutions contribute to social harmony. This led North America's other leading functionalist, Robert Merton, to propose that social structures may have different consequences for different groups of people. Merton noted that some of those consequences may be disruptive or **dysfunctional** (Merton, 1968 [1949]). Moreover, said Merton, although some functions are **manifest** (visible and intended), others are **latent** (unintended and less obvious). For instance, a manifest function of schools is to transmit skills from one generation to the next. A latent function of schools is to encourage

S. D. Clark (1910– ) received his Ph.D. from the University of Toronto. He became the first chair of the Department of Sociology at that institution. Born in Lloydminster, Alberta, he is especially well known for his studies of Canadian social development as a process of disorganization and reorganization on a series of economic frontiers (Clark, 1968 [1962]). The influence of functionalism on his work is apparent in his emphasis on the way society re-establishes equilibrium after experiencing disruptions caused by economic change.

John Porter (1921–79) was Canada's premier sociologist in the 1960s and 1970s. Born in Vancouver, he received his Ph.D. from the London School of Economics. He spent his academic career at Carleton University in Ottawa. There he served as chair of the Department of Sociology and Anthropology, dean of Arts and Science, and vice-president. His major work, *The Vertical Mosaic* (1965), is a study of class and power in Canada. Firmly rooted in conflict theory, it influenced a generation of Canadian sociologists in their studies on social inequality, elite groups, French–English relations, and Canadian–American relations.

the development of a separate youth culture that often conflicts with parents' values (Coleman, 1961; Hersch, 1998).

## Conflict Theory

The second major theoretical tradition in sociology emphasizes the centrality of conflict in social life. **Conflict theory** incorporates these features:

- It generally focuses on large, macrolevel structures, such as the relations among classes.
- It shows how major patterns of inequality in society produce social stability in some circumstances and social change in others.
- It stresses how members of privileged groups try to maintain their advantages while subordinate groups struggle to increase theirs. From this point of view, social conditions at a given time are the expression of an ongoing power struggle between privileged and subordinate groups.
- It typically leads to the suggestion that eliminating privilege will lower the level of conflict and increase the sum total of human welfare.

Conflict theory originated in the work of German social thinker Karl Marx. A generation before Durkheim, Marx observed the destitution and discontent produced by the Industrial Revolution and proposed a sweeping argument about the ways societies develop (Marx, 1904 [1859]; Marx and Engels, 1972 [1848]). Marx's theory was radically different from Durkheim's. Class conflict lies at the centre of his ideas.

Marx argued that owners of industry are eager to improve the way work is organized and to adopt new tools, machines, and production methods. These innovations allow them to produce more efficiently, earn higher profits, and drive inefficient competitors out of business. However, according to Marx, the drive for profits also causes capitalists to concentrate workers in larger and larger establishments, keep wages as low as possible, and invest as little as possible in improving working conditions. Thus, said Marx, in factory and in mine, a large and growing class of poor workers come to oppose a small and shrinking class of wealthy owners.

Marx felt that workers would ultimately become aware of belonging to the same exploited class. Their sense of "class consciousness," he wrote, would encourage the growth of working-class organizations, such as trade unions and labour parties. These organizations would eventually seek to put an end to private ownership of property and replace it with a system in which everyone shared property and wealth. This was the "communist" society envisaged by Marx.

Marx's specific predictions about the inevitable demise of capitalism are now largely discredited. Max Weber, a German sociologist who wrote his major works a generation after Marx, was among the first to point out some of the flaws in Marx's argument (Weber, 1946). Weber noted the rapid growth of the so-called "service" sector of the economy, with its many nonmanual (or "white-collar") workers and professionals. He argued that many members of these occupational groups would stabilize society because they enjoy higher status and income than manual (or "blue-collar") workers in the manufacturing sector. In addition, Weber showed that class conflict is not the only driving force of history. In his view, politics and religion are also important sources of historical change. Other writers pointed out that Marx did not appreciate how investment in technology would make it possible for workers to toil fewer hours under less oppressive conditions. Nor did he foresee that higher wages, better working conditions, and welfare state benefits would pacify manual workers. We see, then, that many of the particulars of Marx's theory were called into question by Weber and other sociologists.

Nevertheless, Marx's insights about the fundamental importance of conflict in social life are still highly influential in modern sociology. Conflict theory became especially popular in North America in the 1960s and 1970s, decades that were rocked by major labour unrest, peace demonstrations on university campuses, the rise of the black power movement, and the emergence of contemporary feminism. Strikes, demonstrations, and riots were almost daily occurrences in the 1960s and 1970s, and it seemed self-evident to many sociologists of that generation that conflict between classes, nations, races, and generations was the very essence of social life. Many of today's leading sociologists attended graduate school in this period. They were strongly influenced by the spirit of the times. As you will see throughout this book, they have made important contributions to conflict theory during their professional careers.

Erving Goffman (1922–82) was born in Toronto. He studied sociology and anthropology as an undergraduate at the University of Toronto. He completed his Ph.D. at the University of Chicago and pursued his academic career at the University of California, Berkeley, and the University of Pennsylvania. Goffman developed an international reputation for his "dramaturgical" approach to symbolic interactionism. This approach highlights the way people present themselves to others, managing their identities in order to create desired impressions on their "audience," in much the same way actors do on stage (Goffman, 1959 [1956]).

## Symbolic Interactionism

Above, we noted that Weber criticized Marx's interpretation of the development of capitalism. Among other things, Weber argued that early capitalist development was caused not just by favourable *economic* circumstances. In addition, he said, certain *religious* beliefs facilitated robust capitalist growth. In particular, sixteenth- and seventeenth-century Protestants believed that their religious doubts could be reduced, and a state of grace assured, if they worked diligently and lived modestly. Weber called this belief the **Protestant ethic.** He believed it had an unintended effect: People who adhered to the Protestant ethic saved and invested more than others. Thus, according to Weber, capitalism developed most robustly where the Protestant ethic took hold. He concluded that capitalism did not develop because of the operation of economic forces alone, as Marx argued. Instead, it depended partly on the religious meaning individuals attached to their work (Weber, 1958 [1904–5]).

The idea that subjective meanings must be analyzed in any complete sociological analysis found rich soil in North America in the late nineteenth and early twentieth centuries. Here was an idea that resonated deeply with the individualism of North American culture. A century ago, it was widely believed that individual talent and initiative could achieve just about anything on this continent of opportunity. Small wonder, then, that much of early North American sociology focused on the individual or, more precisely, on the connection between the individual and the larger society. For example, George Herbert Mead at the University of Chicago was the driving force behind the study of how individual identity is formed in the course of interaction with other people. We discuss his contribution in Chapter 4, Socialization. Here we note only that the work of Mead and his colleagues gave birth to symbolic interactionism, a distinctively North American theoretical tradition that continues to be a major force in sociology today.

Functionalist and conflict theories assume that people's group memberships—whether they are rich or poor, male or female, black or white—determine their behaviour. This can sometimes make people seem like balls on a pool table: They get knocked around and cannot choose their own destinations. We know from our everyday experience, however, that people are not like that. You often make choices, sometimes difficult ones. You sometimes change your mind. Moreover, two people with similar group memberships may react differently to similar social circumstances. That is because they interpret those circumstances differently.

Recognizing these issues, some sociologists focus on the subjective side of social life. They work in the symbolic interactionist tradition. **Symbolic interactionism** incorporates these features:

- ✦ It focuses on face-to-face communication in microlevel social settings. This distinguishes it from both the functionalist and the conflict approaches.
- ✦ It emphasizes that an adequate explanation of social behaviour requires understanding the subjective meanings people attach to their social circumstances.
- ✦ It stresses that people help to create their social circumstances and do not merely react to them.[4]
- ✦ By focusing on the subjective meanings people create in small social settings, symbolic interactionists validate unpopular and unofficial viewpoints. This increases our understanding and tolerance of people who may be different from us.

To understand symbolic interactionism better, let us return briefly to the problem of suicide. If a police officer discovers a dead person at the wheel of a car that has run into a tree, it may be difficult to establish with certainty whether the death was accidental or suicidal. Interviewing friends and relatives to discover the driver's state of mind just before the crash may help rule out the possibility of suicide. As this example illustrates, understanding the intention or motive of the actor is critical to understanding the meaning of a social action and explaining it. A state of mind must be interpreted, usually by a coroner, before the dead body becomes a suicide statistic (Douglas, 1967).

For surviving family and friends, suicide is almost always painful and embarrassing. Insurance policies often deny payments to beneficiaries in the case of suicide. As a result, coroners are inclined to classify deaths as accidental whenever such an interpretation is plausible. Being human, they want to minimize a family's pain after such a horrible event. Sociologists believe that, for this reason, official suicide rates are about one-third lower than actual suicide rates.

The study of the subjective side of social life reveals many such inconsistencies. It helps us go beyond the official picture, deepening our understanding of how society works and supplementing the insights gained from macrolevel analysis. Moreover, by stressing the importance and validity of subjective meanings, symbolic interactionists also increase respect for and tolerance of minority and deviant viewpoints.

## Feminism

Few women figured prominently in the early history of sociology. The strict demands placed on them by the nineteenth-century family and the lack of opportunity for women in the larger society prevented most of them from attaining a higher education and making major contributions to the discipline. The women who did make their mark on the discipline in its early years tended to have unusual biographies. These exceptional people introduced gender issues that were largely ignored by Marx, Durkheim, Weber, Mead, and other early sociologists. Appreciation for the sociological contribution of these pioneer women has grown in recent years as concern with gender issues has come to form a substantial part of the modern sociological enterprise.

Margrit Eichler (1942– ) was born in Berlin, Germany. She took her Ph.D. at Duke University in the United States before beginning her academic career in Canada. She served as chair of the Department of Sociology at the Ontario Institute for Studies in Education and is now head of the Women's Studies Program at the University of Toronto. She is internationally known for her work on feminist methodology (Eichler, 1987). Her work on family policy in Canada has influenced students, professional sociologists, and policymakers for nearly two decades (Eichler, 1988 [1983]).

For example, Harriet Martineau is often called the first female sociologist (Martineau, 1985). Born in England to a prosperous family in 1802, she never married. She was able to support herself comfortably from her journalistic writings. Martineau translated Comte into English. She wrote one of the first books on sociological research methods. She undertook critical studies of slavery, factory laws, and gender inequality. She was a leading advocate of voting rights and higher education for women, as well as gender equality in the family. As such, Martineau was one of the first feminists (Martineau, 1985).

Despite its encouraging beginnings, feminist thinking had little impact on sociology until the mid-1960s. It was then that the rise of the modern women's movement drew attention to the many remaining inequalities between women and men. Since then, feminist theory has had such a big influence on sociology it may now fairly be regarded as sociology's fourth major theoretical tradition. There are several variants of modern feminism (see Chapter 9, Sexuality and Gender). However, the various strands of **feminist theory** share the following features:

- ✦ It focuses on various aspects of patriarchy, the system of male domination in society. Patriarchy, feminists contend, is at least as important as class inequality in determining a person's opportunities in life, and perhaps more so.
- ✦ It holds that male domination and female subordination are determined not by biological necessity but by structures of power and social convention. From their point of view, women are subordinate to men only because men enjoy more legal, economic, political, and cultural rights.
- ✦ It examines the operation of patriarchy in both micro and macro settings.

- ✦ It contends that existing patterns of gender inequality can and should be changed for the benefit of all members of society. The main sources of gender inequality include differences in the way boys and girls are raised; barriers to equal opportunity in education, paid work, and politics; and the unequal division of domestic responsibilities between women and men.

In Table 1.1 we summarize the theoretical traditions outlined above. As you will see in the following pages, sociologists in Canada and elsewhere have elaborated and refined each of them. They have applied them to all of the discipline's branches. Some sociologists work exclusively within one tradition. Others conduct research that borrows from more than one tradition. But all sociologists are deeply indebted to the founders of the discipline. Standing on the shoulders of giants, we are able to see farther.

✦ **TABLE 1.1** ✦
**The Main Theoretical Traditions in Sociology**

| Theoretical Tradition | Main Level of Analysis | Main Focus | Main Question | Image of Ideal Society |
|---|---|---|---|---|
| Functionalism | Macro | Values | How do the institutions of society contribute to social stability? | A state of equilibrium |
| Symbolic interactionism | Micro | Meaning | How do individuals communicate so as to make their social settings meaningful? | Respect for the validity of minority views |
| Conflict theory | Macro | Class inequality | How do privileged groups seek to maintain their advantages and subordinate groups seek to increase theirs, often causing social change in the process? | The elimination of privilege, especially class privilege |
| Feminism | Micro and macro | Patriarchy | What social structures and interaction processes maintain male dominance and female subordination? | The elimination of gender inequality |

# THEIR REVOLUTION AND OURS

## The Industrial and Postindustrial Revolutions

As we have seen, the founders of the discipline devoted their lives to solving the great sociological puzzle of their time: the causes and consequences of the **Industrial Revolution.** The Industrial Revolution refers to the rapid economic transformation that began in Britain in the 1780s. It involved the application of science and technology to industrial processes, the creation of factories, and the formation of a large class of manual or "blue-collar" workers. Within about a century, the Industrial Revolution had taken firm root throughout Western Europe, North America, and Japan. A century after that, industry had begun implanting itself in most of the rest of the world.

As noted in our discussion of Marx, the industrial working class protested long workdays, low pay, and dangerous working conditions. Workers went on strike, formed unions, and joined political parties. Their protests forced governments to tax citizens in order to provide at least minimal protection against ill health, unemployment, and poverty. Working-class protest also forced employers to limit the length of the workday, improve working conditions, and raise wages. Employers were still able to increase their profits by making the organization of work more efficient and introducing new technologies.

Collecting taxes, administering social services, and investing heavily in technological change required the growth of government and business offices, hospitals, schools, universities, and research laboratories. Thus, the new "service" sector was born. Its employees came to be known as "white-collar" workers. Highly trained professionals were at the peak of the service sector. Secretaries and clerks were near its base. By 1980, more than half of all people working in Canada's paid labour force were in nonmanual occupations (Ornstein, 1983: 252).

Sociologists call this most recent transformation of human society the **Postindustrial Revolution.** Specifically, the Postindustrial Revolution refers to the technology-driven shift from manufacturing to service industries and the consequences of that shift for nearly all human activities (Bell, 1976; Toffler, 1990). The dimensions and consequences of postindustrialism form the great sociological puzzle of our time. In concluding this chapter, a review of some of the sociological issues raised by the Postindustrial Revolution is therefore in order. Since much of this book analyzes postindustrialism and its effects, the review will also prove useful as a brief guided tour to *Sociology: Your Compass for a New World.*

## Postindustrialism: A Sociological Compass

Ray Kurzweil is the inventor of reading machines for the blind, speech recognition technology, and music synthesizers. He also has an impressive track record forecasting technological change. In 1999, Kurzweil predicted that by 2030 computers will equal human intelligence and claim to have attained self-consciousness. Thanks to computer-assisted technological advances, such as genetic engineering, life expectancy will be greatly extended. Routine physical labour will be a thing of the past because hardly any humans will be needed in manufacturing, agriculture, or transportation. Inexpensive, routine production will be aided by "nanobots," microscopic machines that, among other things, assemble products molecule by molecule. Basic necessities will be available for the vast majority of people. By the end of the twenty-first century, Kurzweil continued, computers will fuse with humans. At that point, death will have been conquered because it will be

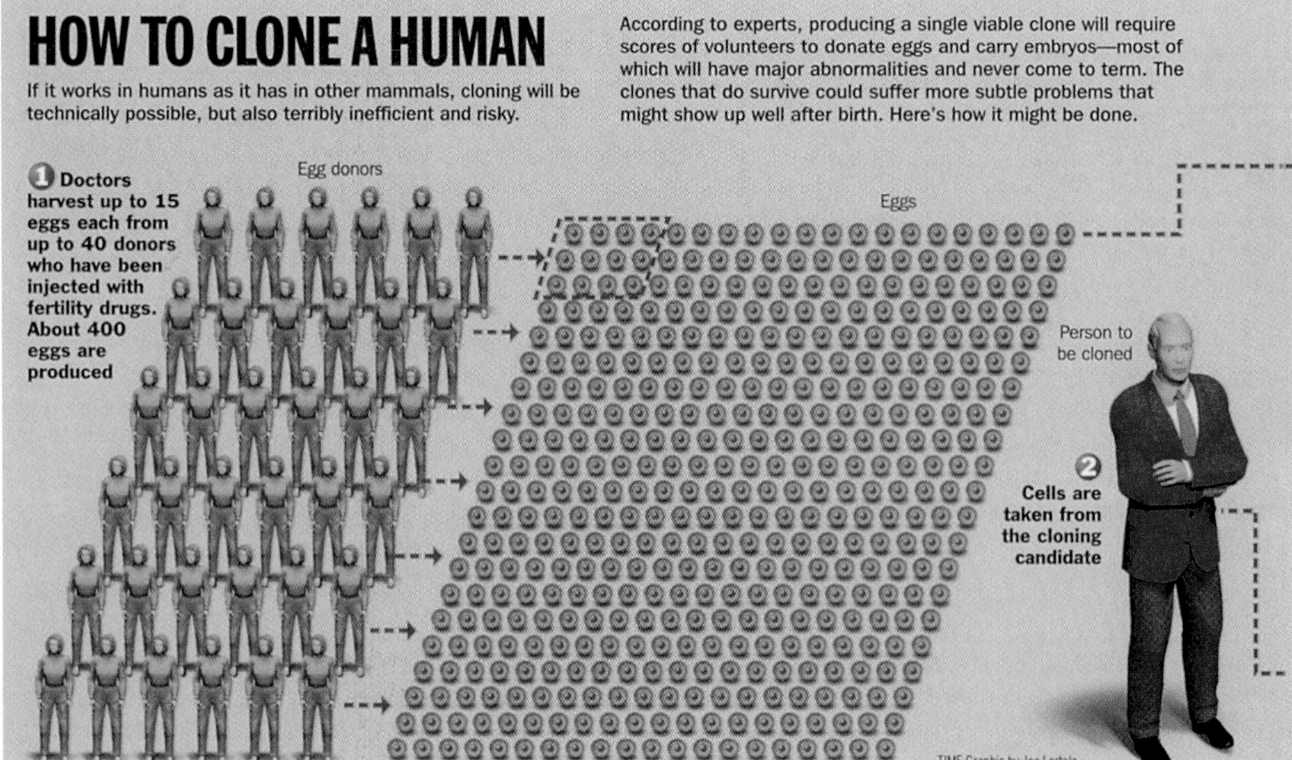

possible to scan and upload human consciousness to self-conscious computers, which will take a variety of physical forms (Kurzweil, 1999).[5]

Kurzweil's forecast of immortality by 2100 may seem far-fetched. However, many people strongly believe that postindustrialism is already increasing our freedom and creating many new opportunities, even for disadvantaged groups. Today, says a technology writer for the *New York Times*,

> [i]ndividuals are acquiring more control over their lives, their minds and their bodies, even their genes, thanks to the transformations in medicine, communications, transportation and industry. At the same time, these technologies are providing social benefits and undoing some of the damage of the past. Technology helps to conserve natural resources and diminish pollution.... The Information Revolution, besides enabling us to visit Mars at will, is fostering peaceful cooperation on Earth by decentralizing power. Political tyrants and demagogic warmongers are losing control now that their subjects have tools to communicate directly with one another. People are using the tools to do their jobs without leaving their families. They're forming new communities in cyberspace and forming new bonds with their neighbors in real space. Technology has the potential to increase individual freedom and strengthen community.... (Tierney, 1997: 46–7)

Most sociologists readily agree that postindustrialism promises more freedom and opportunity. However, sociologists also see many social-structural barriers to the realization of these promises. For most sociologists, the Postindustrial Revolution is so far only half a revolution. And it is uncertain how the second half will turn out.

The main unresolved issues confronting the postindustrial era may be sketched in the form of a compass—a sociological compass (see Figure 1.6). Each axis of the compass contrasts a postindustrial ideal (equality of opportunity, freedom) with its opposite (inequality of opportunity, constraint):

1. *Equality vs. inequality of opportunity*. Optimists forecast that postindustrialism will provide not just more opportunity to find creative, interesting, challenging, and

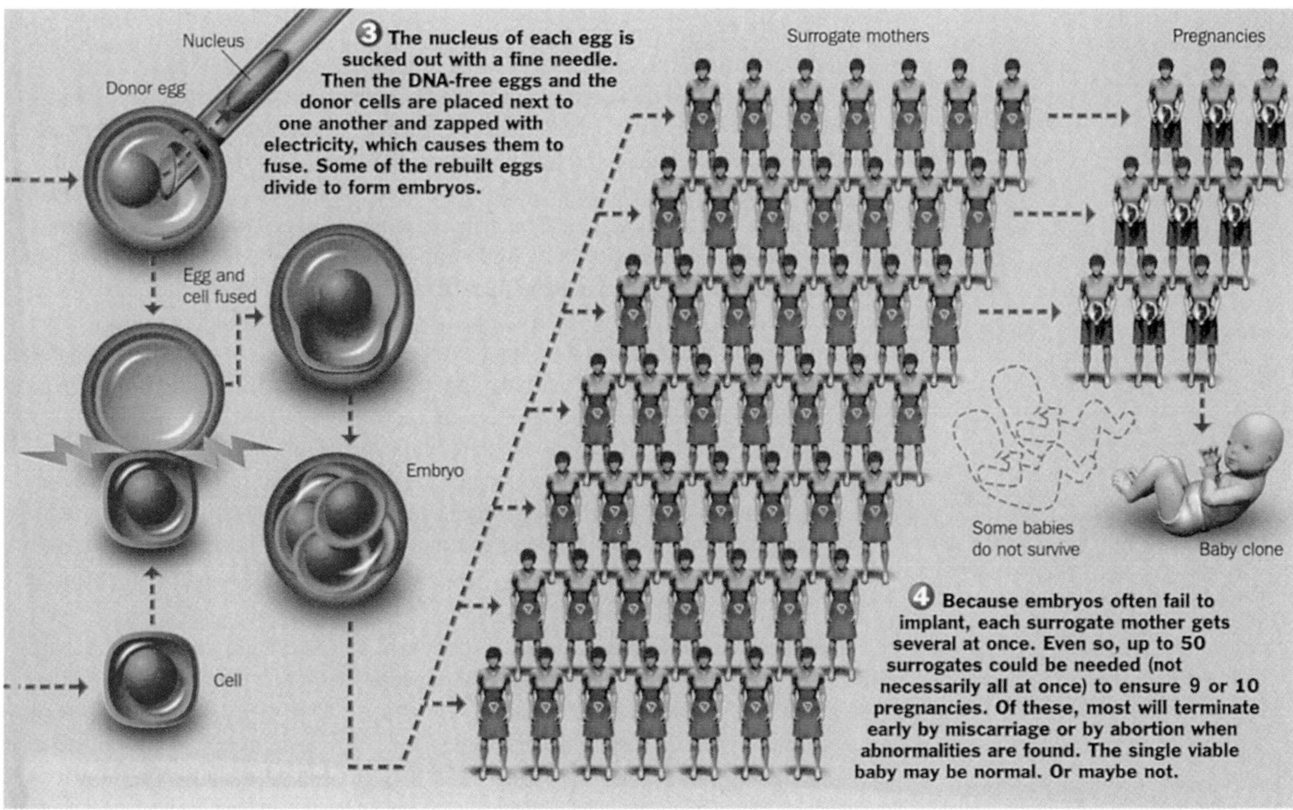

✦ **FIGURE 1.6** ✦
**A Sociological Compass**

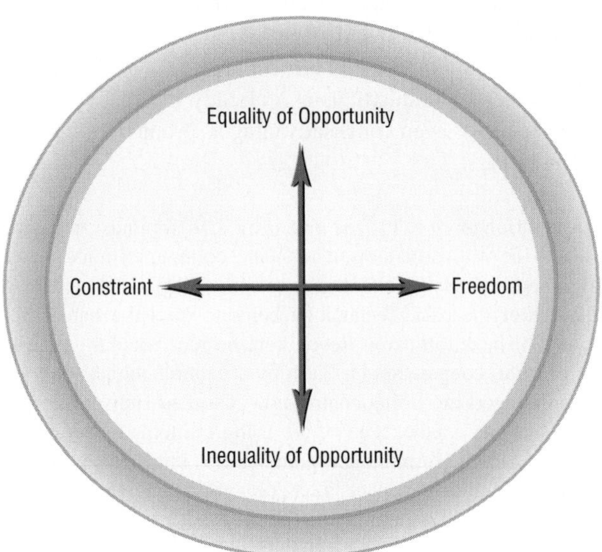


rewarding work. In addition, they say, the new era will generate more "equality of opportunity," that is, a better chance for *all* people to get a good education, influence government policy, and find good jobs.

You will certainly find evidence to support these optimistic claims in the following pages. For example, Chapters 7 (Social Stratification: Canadian and Global Perspectives) and 10 (Work and the Economy) show that the average standard of living and the number of good jobs are increasing in postindustrial societies such as Canada. In Chapters 9 (Sexuality and Gender) and 13 (Religion and Education) you will learn about the rapid strides women in particular are making in the economy, the education system, and other institutions. Chapter 8 (Race and Ethnicity) shows that postindustrial societies such as Canada are characterized by a decline in discrimination against members of ethnic and racial minorities. Chapter 11 (Politics) demonstrates that democracy is spreading quickly throughout the world.

Yet, as you read this book, it will also become clear that all of these seemingly happy stories have a dark underside. For example, it turns out that the number of routine jobs with low pay and few benefits is growing faster than the number of creative, high-paying jobs. Inequality between the wealthiest and poorest Canadians has grown in recent decades, as has inequality between the wealthiest and poorest nations. An enormous opportunity gulf still separates women and men. Racism and discrimination are still very much a part of the world in which we live. The quality of our health care system is declining just as our population is aging rapidly and most in need of health care (see Chapter 15, Health, Medicine, and Aging). Many of the world's new democracies are only superficially democratic, while Canadians and citizens of other postindustrial societies are increasingly cynical about the ability of their political systems to respond to their demands and are looking for alternative forms of political expression (see Chapter 17, Collective Action and Social Movements). In short, equality of opportunity is an undeniably attractive ideal, but it is far from clear that it is the inevitable outcome of the growth of postindustrial society.

2. *Individual freedom vs. individual constraint*. The same may be said of the ideal of freedom. In an earlier era, most people retained their religious, ethnic, racial, and sexual identities for a lifetime, even if they were not particularly comfortable with them. They often remained in social relationships that made them unhappy. One of the major themes of *Sociology: Your Compass for a New World* is that today many people are freer to construct their identities and form social relationships in ways that suit them. To a greater degree than ever before, it is possible to *choose* who you

want to be, who you want to associate with, and how you want to associate with them. The postindustrial era frees people from traditional constraints by encouraging virtually instant global communication, international migration, greater acceptance of sexual diversity and a variety of family forms, the growth of ethnically and racially diverse cities, and so forth. For instance, in the past, people often remained in marriages even if they were unhappy. Families often involved a father working in the paid labour force and a mother keeping house and raising children without pay. Today, people are freer to end unhappy marriages and create family forms that are better suited to their individual needs (see Chapter 12, Families). We take up the theme of increasing individual freedom in Chapters 3 (Culture), 4 (Socialization), 8 (Race and Ethnicity), 9 (Sexuality and Gender), 13 (Religion and Education), 14 (The Mass Media), and 16 (Population, Urbanization, and Development).

Again, however, we must face the less rosy aspects of postindustrialism. In many of the following chapters, we point out how increased freedom is experienced only within certain limits and how social diversity is limited by a strong push to conformity in some spheres of life. For example, we can choose a far wider variety of consumer products than ever before, but consumerism itself increasingly seems a compulsory way of life (see Chapter 3, Culture). Moreover, it is a way of life that threatens the natural environment (see Chapter 18, Technology and the Global Environment). Meanwhile, some new technologies, such as surveillance cameras, cause us to modify our behaviour and act in more conformist ways (see Chapter 6, Deviance and Crime). Large, impersonal bureaucracies and standardized products and services dehumanize both staff and customers (see Chapter 5, Interaction and Organization). The tastes and the profit motive of vast media conglomerates, most of them American-owned, govern most of our diverse cultural consumption and arguably threaten the survival of distinctive national cultures (see Chapter 14, The Mass Media). Powerful interests are trying to shore up the traditional nuclear family even though it does not suit some people (see Chapter 12, Families). As these examples show, the push to uniformity counters the trend toward growing social diversity. Moreover, postindustrialism may make us freer in some ways, but it also places new constraints on us.

## WHY SOCIOLOGY?

Sociology is more than just an intellectual exercise. It is also an applied science with practical, everyday uses. Students often ask: "Can I get a good job with a sociology degree?" "Exactly what kind of work could I do with a major in sociology?" "Aren't all the good jobs these days in technical areas and the natural sciences?" To answer these questions—and to help you decide whether a sociology or other social science major makes sense for you—consider the following data on the employment of Canadians with degrees in sociology and related fields.

A study based on 1988 data found that a higher percentage of sociology graduates were employed full-time than were graduates in the other social sciences (Guppy and Hedley, 1993). A study based mainly on 1996 data showed that

- the unemployment rate among social science graduates was lower than among graduates in math, physics, engineering, agriculture, and biology.
- between 1991 and 1996, there were more new jobs for people with social science degrees than for people with degrees in other fields.
- although women earned less than men in all fields in 1996, the discrepancy between men's and women's income was smallest among social science graduates (Allen, 1999).

On the basis of these figures it seems that sociology degrees promise more employment security for both men and women, and less income discrimination against women, than other degrees. It also seems that the postindustrial economy requires more new employees with a social science background than new employees with a background in some technical and scientific fields.

The immediate past president of Brazil, Fernando Henrique Cardoso, has a Ph.D. in sociology. So does the former president of the Liberal Party of Canada and current president of York University in Toronto, Lorna Marsden. Anthony Giddens, director of the London School of Economics and adviser to British Prime Minister Tony Blair, also holds a doctorate in sociology, as do Martin Goldfarb, president of Goldfarb Consultants International, and Donna Dasko, senior vice-president of Environics, two of Canada's leading public opinion firms with offices and affiliates around the world. Alex Himelfarb, Canada's highest-ranking civil servant (clerk of the Privy Council and secretary to the Cabinet in Ottawa) holds a sociology Ph.D., too. In all, there are more than 3000 people with sociology Ph.D.s in Canada. In addition, many thousands of Canadians have M.A.s and B.A.s in sociology. People with sociological training teach at various levels from high school to graduate school. They conduct research and give advice in a wide variety of settings. These include local, provincial, and federal governments, universities, corporations, the criminal justice system, public opinion firms, trade unions, social service agencies, international nongovernmental organizations, and private research and testing firms (Stephens, 1999; see Table 1.2). In addition, a sociology degree is excellent preparation for post-B.A. studies in a variety of fields including industrial relations, social work, and law. A major in sociology is not for everyone, but as these data make clear, it is associated with relatively good job prospects.

**✦ TABLE 1.2 ✦**
**Jobs Commonly Held by Canadian Sociology Graduates**

Source: Guppy and Hedley (1993).

**Government**
- community affairs officer
- urban/regional planner
- legislative aide
- affirmative action/employment equity worker
- foreign service officer
- human rights officer
- personnel coordinator

**Research**
- social research specialist
- consumer researcher
- data analyst
- market researcher
- survey researcher
- census officer/analyst
- demographer/population analyst
- system analyst

**Community Affairs**
- occupational/career counsellor
- homeless/housing worker
- public health/hospital administrator
- child development technician
- public administration assistant
- social assistance advocate
- resident planning aide
- group home worker
- rehabilitation program worker
- rural health outreach worker
- housing coordinator
- fundraising director/assistant
- caseworker/aide
- community organizer
- youth outreach worker

**Corrections**
- corrections officer
- criminology assistant
- police officer
- rehabilitation counsellor
- criminal investigator
- juvenile court worker
- parole officer

**Teaching**
- college/university placement worker
- public health educator
- teacher
- admissions counsellor

**Business**
- market analyst
- project manager
- sales representative
- real estate agent
- journalist
- public relations officer
- actuary
- insurance agent
- human resources manager
- production manager
- labour relations officer
- administrative assistant
- quality control manager
- merchandiser/purchaser
- computer analyst
- data entry manager
- publishing officer
- advertising officer
- sales manager

Sociology has benefits even for people who do not work as sociologists. For, although it offers no easy solutions as to how the goal of improving society may be accomplished, it does promise a useful way of understanding our current predicament and seeing possible ways of dealing with it.

The renowned English sociologist Anthony Giddens wrote that we live in an era "suspended between extraordinary opportunity...and global catastrophe" (Giddens, 1982: 166). A whole range of environmental issues, profound inequalities in the wealth of nations and of classes, racial and ethnic violence, and unsolved problems in the relations between women and men continue to stare us in the face and profoundly affect the quality of our everyday lives.

Despair and apathy is one possible response to these complex issues. But it is not a response that humans have often favoured. If it were our nature to give up hope, we would still be sitting around half-naked in the mud outside a cave.

People are more inclined to look for ways to improve their lives, and this period of human history is full of opportunities to do so. We have, for example, advanced to the point where for the first time we have the means to feed and educate everyone in the world. Similarly, it now seems possible to erode some of the inequalities that have always been with us and have always been the major source of human conflict. You sampled sociology's ability to tie personal troubles to public issues in our discussion of suicide. You reviewed the major perspectives or paradigms that enable sociologists to connect the personal with the social-structural. You saw sociology's ability to provide a historical and critical understanding of where we are and where we might head when we outlined the half-fulfilled promises of postindustrialism.

The questions raised in this book are tough to answer. Sharp controversy surrounds them all. However, if you try to grapple with them, you will enhance your understanding of your society's, and your own, possibilities. That, ultimately, is the purpose of sociology.

## SUMMARY

1. Durkheim showed that even apparently nonsocial and antisocial actions are influenced by social structures. Specifically, he showed how levels of social solidarity affect suicide rates.
2. Due to the rise in youth suicide, the pattern of suicide rates in Canada today is not exactly the same as in Durkheim's France. Nevertheless, Durkheim's theory explains the contemporary Canadian pattern well.
3. Sociologists analyze the connection between personal troubles and social structures.
4. Sociologists analyze the influence of three levels of social structure on human action: microstructures, macrostructures, and global structures.
5. Values suggest which sociological research questions are worth asking and how the parts of society fit together. A theory is a tentative explanation of some aspect of social life. It states how and why specific facts are connected. Research is the process of carefully observing social reality to assess the validity of a theory.
6. There are four major theoretical traditions in sociology. Functionalism analyzes how social order is supported by macrostructures. Conflict theory analyzes how social inequality is maintained and challenged. Symbolic interactionism analyzes how meaning is created when people communicate in microlevel settings. Feminism focuses on the social sources of patriarchy in both macro and micro settings.
7. The rise of sociology was stimulated by the scientific, industrial, and democratic revolutions of the nineteenth century.
8. The Postindustrial Revolution is the technology-driven shift from manufacturing to service industries and the consequences of that shift for virtually all human activities.
9. The causes and consequences of postindustrialism form the great sociological puzzle of our time. The tension between (a) equality of opportunity and inequality of opportunity, and (b) freedom and constraint are among the chief interests of sociology today.

## GLOSSARY

**Altruistic suicide** occurs in settings that exhibit very high levels of social solidarity, according to Durkheim. In other words, altruistic suicide results from norms very tightly governing behaviour.

**Anomic suicide** occurs in settings that exhibit low levels of social solidarity, according to Durkheim. In other words, anomic suicide results from vaguely defined norms governing behaviour.

**Conflict theory** generally focuses on large, macrolevel structures, such as the relations among classes. It shows how major patterns of inequality in society produce social stability in some circumstances and social change in others. It stresses how members of privileged groups try to maintain their advantages while subordinate groups struggle to increase theirs. And it typically leads to the suggestion that eliminating privilege will lower the level of conflict and increase the sum total of human welfare.

**Dysfunctions** are effects of social structures that create social instability.

**Ethnomethodology** is the study of how people make sense of what others do and say in terms of norms that exist independently of social actors. (See Note 4, page 29.)

**Feminist theory** claims that patriarchy is at least as important as class inequality in determining a person's opportunities in life. It holds that male domination and female subordination are determined not by biological necessity but by structures of power and social convention. It examines the operation of patriarchy in both micro and macro settings. And it contends that existing patterns of gender inequality can and should be changed for the benefit of all members of society.

**Functionalism** stresses that human behaviour is governed by relatively stable social structures. It underlines how social structures maintain or undermine social stability. It emphasizes that social structures are based mainly on shared values or preferences. And it suggests that re-establishing equilibrium can best solve most social problems.

**Global structures** are patterns of social relations that lie outside and above the national level. They include international organizations, patterns of worldwide travel and communication, and the economic relations between countries.

The **Industrial Revolution,** often regarded as the most important event in world history since the development of agriculture and cities, refers to the rapid economic transformation that began in Britain in the 1780s. It involved the large-scale application of science and technology to industrial processes, the creation of factories, and the formation of a working class.

**Latent functions** are invisible and unintended effects of social structures.

**Macrostructures** are overarching patterns of social relations that lie outside and above your circle of intimates and acquaintances. Macrostructures include classes, bureaucracies, and power systems such as patriarchy.

**Manifest functions** are visible and intended effects of social structures.

**Microstructures** are the patterns of relatively intimate social relations formed during face-to-face interaction. Families, friendship circles, and work associations are all examples of microstructures.

**Patriarchy** is the traditional system of economic and political inequality between women and men.

The **Postindustrial Revolution** refers to the technology-driven shift from manufacturing to service industries and the consequences of that shift for virtually all human activities.

The **Protestant ethic** is the sixteenth- and seventeenth-century Protestant belief that religious doubts can be reduced, and a state of grace assured, if people work diligently and live ascetically. According to Weber, the Protestant work ethic had the unintended effect of increasing savings and investment and thus stimulating capitalist growth.

**Research** is the process of carefully observing reality to assess the validity of a theory.

**Social solidarity** refers to (1) the degree to which group members share beliefs and values, and (2) the intensity and frequency of their interaction.

**Social structures** are relatively stable patterns of social relations.

The **sociological imagination** is the quality of mind that enables one to see the connection between personal troubles and social structures.

**Symbolic interactionism** focuses on face-to-face communication, or interaction in microlevel social settings. It emphasizes that an adequate explanation of social behaviour requires understanding the subjective meanings people attach to their social circumstances. It stresses that people help to create their social circumstances and do not merely react to them. And, by underscoring the subjective meanings people create in small social settings, it validates unpopular and unofficial viewpoints. This increases our understanding and tolerance of people who may be different from us.

A **theory** is a tentative explanation of some aspect of social life that states how and why certain facts are related.

**Values** are ideas about what is right and wrong.

## QUESTIONS TO CONSIDER

1. What is the difference between objectivity and subjectivity? What role do objectivity and subjectivity play in sociology?
2. What does Durkheim mean by "social solidarity"? How does he apply the term to the study of suicide? Comparing Canada 100 years ago with Canada today, how and why do you think the level of social solidarity has changed? What accounts for the change? What are some consequences of the change? Has the level of social solidarity changed more for some groups than for others? If so, why and with what consequences?
3. Do you think Canadians have more or less freedom and equality of opportunity now than they did 100 years ago? Do you think we will have more or less freedom and equality of opportunity in 100 years than we do today? Justify your argument.

## WEB RESOURCES

### Companion Web Site for This Book

http://www.brymsociologycompass.nelson.com

Begin by clicking on the Student Resources section of the Web site. Next, select the chapter you are currently studying from the pull-down menu. From the Student Resources page you will have easy access to InfoTrac College Edition®, MicroCase online exercises, and additional Web links. The Web site also has many useful tips to aid you in your study of sociology, including practice tests for each chapter.

### InfoTrac Search Terms

These search terms are provided to assist you in beginning to conduct research on this topic by visiting http://www.infotrac-college.com

**Conflict theory**
**Feminism**
**Functionalism**
**Social structure**
**Suicide**
**Symbolic interactionism**

### Recommended Web Sites

For an inspiring essay on the practice of the sociological craft by one of North America's leading sociologists, see Gary T. Marx, "Of Methods and Manners for Aspiring Sociologists: 36 Moral Imperatives," on the World Wide Web at http://web.mit.edu/gtmarx/www/37moral.html.

SocioWeb is a comprehensive guide to sociological resources on the World Wide Web at http://www.socioweb.com/~markbl/socioweb.

For descriptions of Departments of Sociology at universities throughout the world, visit http://www.socioweb.com/~markbl/socioweb/univ.

The Canadian Sociology and Anthropology Association (CSAA) is the professional organization of Canadian sociologists. Visit the CSAA Web site at http://alcor.concordia.ca/~csaa1.

## SUGGESTED READINGS

On the development of Canadian sociology, including theoretical debates and empirical findings, see:

Robert J. Brym. "Canadian Sociology: An Introduction to the Upper Thirteen," *The American Sociologist* (33: 2002), pp. 5–11.

Robert J. Brym with Bonnie J. Fox. *From Culture to Power: The Sociology of English Canada* (Toronto: Oxford University Press, 1989).

Robert J. Brym and Céline Saint-Pierre. "Canadian Sociology," *Contemporary Sociology* (26: 1997), pp. 543–6.

Harry Hiller, ed. "Legacy for a New Millennium," special issue of *The Canadian Journal of Sociology* (26, 3: 2001).

For an international perspective, in which leading sociologists from around the world assess the state of the discipline and its future, see Immanuel Wallerstein, ed. "The Heritage of Sociology and the Future of the Social Sciences in the 21st Century," *Current Sociology* (46, 2: 1998).

## NOTES

1. As this book went to press in the last weeks of 2002, 680 Innu were being relocated at government expense to 133 new homes in Natuashish, a modern village carved out of the wilderness 15 km west of Davis Inlet. It is unclear, however, how new homes will solve the complex social problems of the Innu.
2. Some sociologists also distinguish "mesostructures," social relations that link micro- and macrostructures.
3. More detailed discussion of these theories will be found throughout the book. For example, on functionalism, see Chapters 7, 12, and 14. On conflict theory, see Chapters 6, 7, 11, and 17. On symbolic interactionism, see Chapters 4, 5, 14, and 17. On feminism, see Chapters 4, 9, and 17.
4. By emphasizing how social reality is constructed in the course of interaction, symbolic interactionists downplay the importance of norms and understandings that precede any given interaction. **Ethnomethodology** tries to correct this shortcoming. Ethnomethodologists study how people make sense of what others do and say, but they stress that norms exist independently of social actors. Indeed, in the ethnomethodological view, everyday interactions could not take place without pre-existing shared norms. Say you pass an acquaintance, who offers a friendly "How are you?" If you proceed to outline in detail your financial situation, your love life, interesting developments at work, and so on, the acquaintance will quickly become annoyed. Most people expect "How are you?" to be answered with an equally brief reply. Violate the norm and communication quickly breaks down (Garfinkel, 1967).
5. Kurzweil's main detractor is Bill Joy, chief scientist at Sun Microsystems and a co-developer of the Java programming language. (Ironically, Joy is a pessimist while Kurzweil, who predicts immortality, has a name formed by a compound German word that means, roughly, "a short time.") Joy argues that new genetic entities and nanobots will be routinely programmed to make copies of themselves. For example, a

nanobot set up to make water from hydrogen and oxygen, or a virus genetically engineered to kill crop-damaging insects, will be programmed to self-replicate so the job can be accomplished faster. However, a programming error or a genetic mutation could result in the copying process getting out of control. An out-of-control virus mutation could kill crops rather than harmful insects. An out-of-control water-manufacturing nanobot could flood the world and leave it without land. Another danger, Joy asserts, is bound up with the fact that the new technologies democratize the ability of people to do evil. For example, unlike the construction of a nuclear bomb, the creation of a deadly virus will require relatively inexpensive, commercially available equipment. Therefore, a single crazed or politically motivated scientist will soon be able to do much damage to the world, claims Joy (2000). Joy's remarks have gained credibility since the terrorist attacks of September 11, 2001, and the subsequent anthrax attacks in the United States.

## IN THIS CHAPTER, YOU WILL LEARN THAT

- The practice of science is a social activity governed by rules defined and enforced by the scientific community.
- Scientific ideas differ from common sense and other forms of knowledge. Scientific ideas are assessed in the clear light of systematically collected evidence and public scrutiny.
- Sociological research depends not just on the rigorous testing of ideas but also on creative insight. Thus, the objective and subjective phases of inquiry are both important in good research.
- The main methods of collecting sociological data include systematic observations of natural social settings, experiments, surveys, and the analysis of existing documents and official statistics.
- Each data collection method has characteristic strengths and weaknesses. Each method is appropriate for different kinds of research problems.

CHAPTER

2

# RESEARCH METHODS

## SCIENCE AND EXPERIENCE

### OTTFFSSENT

"Okay, Mr. Smarty Pants, see if you can figure this one out." That's how Robert Brym's 11-year-old daughter, Talia, greeted him one day when she came home from school. "I wrote some letters of the alphabet on this sheet of paper. They form a pattern. Take a look at the letters and tell me the pattern."

Robert took the sheet of paper from Talia and smiled confidently. "Like most North Americans, I'd had a lot of experience with this sort of puzzle," says Robert. "For example, most IQ and SAT tests ask you to find patterns in sequences of letters, and you learn certain ways of solving these problems. One of the most common methods is to see if the 'distance' between adjoining letters stays the same or varies predictably. For example, in the sequence ADGJ, there are two missing letters between each adjoining pair. Insert the missing letters and you get the first 10 letters of the alphabet: A(BC)D(EF)G(HI)J.

"This time, however, I was stumped. On the sheet of paper Talia had written the letters OTTFFSSENT. I tried to use the distance method to solve the problem. Nothing worked. After 10 minutes of head scratching, I gave up."

"The answer's easy," Talia said, clearly pleased at her father's failure. "Spell out the numbers 1 to 10. The first letter of each word—one, two, three, and so forth—spells OTTFFSSENT. Looks like you're not as smart as you thought. See ya." And with that she bounced off to her room.

Robert comments: "Later that day, it dawned on me that Talia had taught me more than just a puzzle. She had shown me that experience sometimes prevents people from seeing things. My experience with solving letter puzzles by using certain set methods obviously kept me from solving the unusual problem of OTTFFSSENT." Said differently, reality (in this case, a pattern of letters) is not just a thing "out there" we can learn to perceive "objectively." As social scientists have appreciated for more than a century, *experience* helps determine how we perceive reality, including what patterns we see and whether we are able to see patterns at all (Hughes, 1967: 16).

The fact that experience filters perceptions of reality is the single biggest problem for sociological research. In sociological research, the filtering occurs in four stages (see Figure 2.1). First, as noted in Chapter 1, the real-life experiences and passions of sociologists motivate much research. That is, our *values* often help us decide which problems are worth investigating. These values may reflect the typical outlook of our class, race, gender, region, historical period, and so on. Second, our values lead us to formulate and adopt favoured *theories* for interpreting and explaining those problems. Third, sociologists' interpretations are influenced by *previous research*, which we consult to find out what we already know about a subject. And fourth, the *methods* we use to gather data mould our perceptions. The shape of our tools often helps determine which bits of reality we dig up.

Given that values, theories, previous research, and research methods filter our perceptions, you are right to conclude that we can never perceive society in a pure or objective form.[1] What we can do is use techniques of data collection that minimize bias. We can also clearly and publicly describe the filters that influence our perceptions. Doing so enables us to eliminate obvious sources of bias. It also helps others see biases we miss and try to correct for them. The end result is a more accurate perception of reality than is possible by relying exclusively on blind prejudice or common sense.

It is thus clear that a healthy tension pervades all sociological scholarship. On the one hand, researchers generally try to be objective in order to perceive reality as clearly as possible. They follow the rules of the scientific method and design data collection techniques to minimize bias. On the other hand, the values and passions that grow out of personal experience are important sources of creativity. As Max Weber said, we choose to study "only those segments of reality which have become significant to us because of their value-relevance" (Weber, 1964 [1949]: 76). So objectivity and subjectivity each play an important role in science, including sociology. Oversimplifying a little, we can say that although

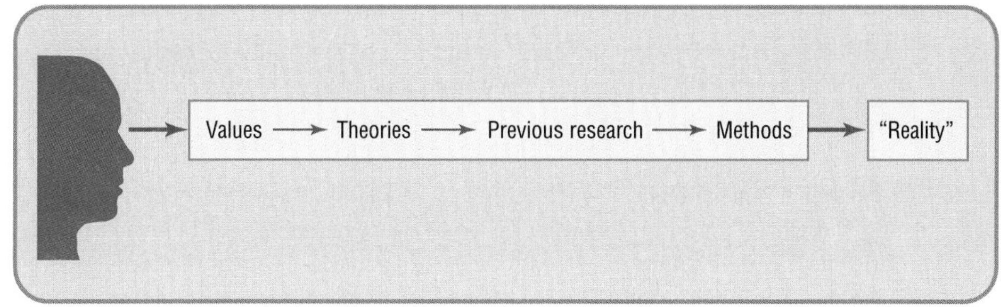


✦ **FIGURE 2.1** ✦
**How Research Filters Perception**

objectivity is a reality check, subjectivity leads us to define which aspects of reality are worth checking on in the first place.

Most of this chapter is about the reality check. It explores how sociologists try to adhere to the rules of the scientific method. We first contrast scientific and nonscientific thinking. We next discuss the steps involved in the sociological research process. We then describe the main methods of gathering sociological data and the decisions that have to be made during the research process. Finally, we return to the role of subjectivity in research.

## Scientific versus Nonscientific Thinking

In science, seeing is believing. In everyday life, believing is seeing. In other words, in everyday life our biases easily influence our observations. This often leads us to draw incorrect conclusions about what we see. In contrast, scientists, including sociologists, develop ways of collecting, observing, and thinking about evidence that minimize their chance of drawing biased conclusions.

On what basis do you decide statements are true in everyday life? Below we describe 10 types of nonscientific thinking (Babbie, 2000 [1973]). As you read about each one, ask yourself how frequently you think unscientifically. If you often think unscientifically, this chapter is for you.

1. "Chicken soup helps get rid of a cold. *It worked for my grandparents, and it works for me*." This statement represents knowledge based on *tradition*. Although some traditional knowledge is valid (sugar will rot your teeth), some is not (masturbation will not blind you). Science is required to separate valid from invalid knowledge.
2. "Weak magnets can be used to heal many illnesses. *I read all about it in the newspaper*." This statement represents knowledge based on *authority*. We often think something is true because we read it in an authoritative source or hear it from an expert. But authoritative sources and experts can be wrong. For example, nineteenth-century Western physicians commonly "bled" their patients with leeches to draw "poisons" from their bodies. This often did more harm than good. As this example suggests, scientists should always question authority to arrive at more valid knowledge.
3. "The car that hit the cyclist was dark brown. I was going for a walk last night when *I saw the accident*." This statement represents knowledge based on *casual observation*. Unfortunately, we are usually pretty careless observers. That is why good lawyers can often trip up eyewitnesses in courtrooms. Eyewitnesses are rarely certain about what they saw. In general, uncertainty can be reduced by observing in a conscious and deliberate manner and by recording observations. That is just what scientists do.
4. "If you work hard, you can get ahead. *I know because several of my parents' friends started off poor but are now comfortably middle class*." This statement represents knowledge based on *overgeneralization*. For instance, if you know a few people who started off poor, worked hard, and became rich you may think any poor person can become rich if he or she works hard enough. You may not know about the more numerous poor people who work hard and remain poor. Scientists, however, sample

Perhaps the first major advance in modern medicine took place when doctors stopped using unproven interventions in their treatment of patients. One such intervention involved using leeches to bleed patients, shown here in a medieval drawing.

cases that are representative of entire populations. This enables them to avoid overgeneralization. They also avoid overgeneralization by repeating research. This ensures that they do not draw conclusions from an unusual set of research findings.

5. "I'm right because *I can't think of any contrary cases*." This statement represents knowledge based on *selective observation*. Sometimes we unconsciously ignore evidence that challenges our firmly held beliefs. Thus, you may actually know some people who work hard but remain poor. However, to maintain your belief that hard work results in wealth, you may keep them out of mind. The scientific requirement that evidence be drawn from representative samples of the population minimizes bias arising from selective observation.
6. "Mr. Smith is poor even though he works hard, but that's because he has a disability. People with disabilities are the only *exception to the rule* that if you work hard you can get ahead." This statement represents knowledge based on *qualification*. Qualifications or "exceptions to the rule" are often made in everyday life, and they are in science, too. The difference is that in everyday life qualifications are easily accepted as valid, while in scientific inquiry they are treated as statements that must be carefully examined in the light of evidence.
7. "The Toronto Blue Jays won 50 percent of their baseball games over the last three months but 65 percent of the games they played on Thursdays. *Because it happened so often before*, I bet they'll win next Thursday." This statement represents knowledge based on *illogical reasoning*. In everyday life, we may expect the recurrence of events without reasonable cause, ignoring the fact that rare sequences of events occur just by chance. For example, it is possible for you to flip a coin 10 times and have it come up heads each time. On average, this will happen once every 1024 times you flip a coin 10 times. In the absence of any apparent reason for this happening, it is merely coincidental. It is illogical to believe otherwise. Scientists refrain from illogical reasoning. They also use statistical techniques to distinguish between events that are probably due to chance and those that are not.
8. "*I just can't be wrong*." This statement represents knowledge based on *ego-defence*. Even scientists may be passionately committed to the conclusions they reach in their research because they have invested much time, energy, and money in them. It is other scientists—more accurately, the whole institution of science, with its commitment to publishing research results and critically scrutinizing findings—that puts strict limits on ego-defence in scientific understanding.
9. "*The matter is settled once and for all*." This statement represents knowledge based on the *premature closure of inquiry*. This involves deciding that all the relevant evidence has been gathered on a particular subject. Science, however, is committed to the idea that all theories are only temporarily true. Matters are never settled.
10. "*There must be supernatural forces at work here*." This statement represents knowledge based on *mystification*. When we can find no rational explanation for a phenomenon, we may attribute it to forces that cannot be observed or fully understood. Although such forces may exist, scientists remain skeptical. They are committed to discovering observable causes of observable effects.

Even Albert Einstein, often hailed as the most intelligent person of the twentieth century, sometimes ignored evidence in favour of pet theories. However, the social institution of science, which makes ideas public and subjects them to careful scrutiny, often overcomes such bias.

## THE RESEARCH CYCLE

Sociological research seeks to overcome the kind of unscientific thinking described above. It is a cyclical process that involves six steps (see Figure 2.2).

First, the sociologist must *formulate a research question*. A research question must be stated so it can be answered by systematically collecting and analyzing sociological data. Sociological research cannot determine whether God exists or what is the best political system. Answers to such questions require faith more than evidence. Sociological research

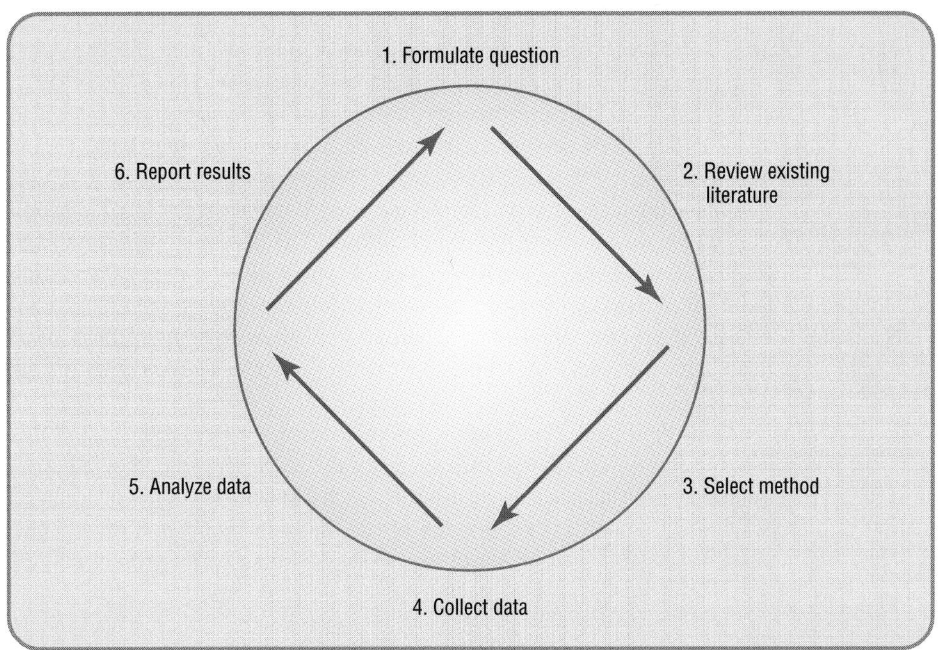


✦ **FIGURE 2.2** ✦
**The Research Cycle**

can determine why some people are more religious than others and which political systems create more opportunities for higher education. Answers to such questions require evidence more than faith.

Second, the *existing research literature must be reviewed.* Researchers must elaborate their research questions in the clear light of what other sociologists have already debated and discovered. Why? Because reading the relevant sociological literature stimulates researchers' sociological imaginations, allows them to refine their initial questions, and prevents duplication of effort.

*Selecting a research method* is the third step in the research cycle. As we will see in detail below, each data collection method has strengths and weaknesses. Each method is therefore best suited to studying a different kind of problem. When choosing a method, one must keep these strengths and weaknesses in mind. (In the ideal but, unfortunately, infrequent case, several methods are used simultaneously to study the same problem. This can overcome the drawbacks of any single method and increase confidence in one's findings.)

The fourth stage of the research cycle involves *collecting the data* by observing subjects, interviewing them, reading documents produced by or about them, and so forth. Many researchers think this is the most exciting stage of the research cycle, because it brings them face to face with the puzzling sociological reality that so fascinates them.

Other researchers find the fifth step of the research cycle, *analyzing the data,* the most challenging. During data analysis you can learn things that nobody ever knew before. This is when data confirm some of your expectations and confound others, requiring you to think creatively about familiar issues, reconsider the relevant theoretical and research literature, and abandon pet ideas.

Of course, research is not much use to the sociological community, the subjects of the research, or the wider society if researchers do not *publish the results* in a report, a scientific journal, or a book. That is the research cycle's sixth step. Publication serves another important function, too. It allows other sociologists to scrutinize and criticize the research. On that basis, errors can be corrected and new and more sophisticated research questions can be formulated for the next round of research. In this sense, the practice of science is a social activity governed by rules defined and enforced by the scientific community.

Throughout the research cycle, researchers must be mindful of the need to *respect their subjects' rights.* This means, in the first instance, that researchers must do their subjects no harm. This is the right to safety. People must have the right to decide whether they can be studied and, if so, in what way. Second, research subjects must have the right to decide whether their attitudes and behaviours may be revealed to the public and, if so, in what way. This is the right to privacy. Third, researchers cannot use data in a way that allows them to be traced to a particular subject. This is the subject's right to confidentiality. Fourth, subjects must be told how the information they supply will be used. They must also be allowed to judge the degree of personal risk involved in answering questions. This is the right to informed consent.

It would be wrong to think that the research cycle always begins at the first stage and then proceeds to stage two, then to stage three, and so forth. The research cycle is a useful way of thinking about the stages of research—an ideal, if you will—but the exact starting point and progression of research varies from one project to the next. For example, sometimes research begins with a personal puzzle, sometimes with alternative interpretations of observations collected in a project, and sometimes with a skeptical perspective on the research literature.

Bearing in mind this thumbnail sketch of the research cycle, we devote the rest of this chapter mainly to exploring the fourth and fifth stages of the research cycle, the gathering and analyzing of evidence. In this context we describe each of sociology's major research methods. These methods include the examination of existing documents and official statistics, experiments, surveys, and participant observation. We begin by describing participant observation research.

## Participant Observation

In **participant observation** research, the immediate social environment of the people being investigated becomes the sociological "laboratory." The participant-observer goes wherever people meet, from the ethnic slum (Whyte, 1981 [1943]) to the intensive care unit of a major hospital (Chambliss, 1996), from the white teenage heavy-metal gang (Gaines, 1990) to the audience of a daytime TV talk show (Grindstaff, 1997), from the gay community (Humphreys, 1975) to the Yukon International Storytelling Festival (Cruikshank, 1997).

Sociologists engage in participant observation when they attempt to observe a social milieu objectively *and* take part in the activities of the people they are studying (Lofland and Lofland, 1995 [1971]). By participating in the lives of their subjects, researchers are able to see the world from their subjects' point of view. This allows them to achieve a deep and sympathetic understanding of people's beliefs, values, and motives. In addition, participant observation requires that sociologists step back and observe their subjects' milieu from an outsider's point of view. This helps them see their subjects more objectively. In participant observation research, then, there is a tension between the goals of subjectivity and objectivity. As you will see, however, this is a healthy tension that enhances our understanding of many social settings.

A well-known example of participation observation research is Carl B. Klockars' analysis of the professional "fence," a person who buys and sells stolen goods (Klockars, 1974). Among other things, Klockars wanted to understand how criminals can knowingly hurt people and live with the guilt. Are criminals capable of this because they are "sick" or unfeeling? Klockars came to a different conclusion by examining the case of Vincent Swaggi (a pseudonym).

Swaggi buys cheap stolen goods from thieves and then sells them in his store for a handsome profit. His buying is private and patently criminal. His selling is public and, to his customers, it appears to be legal. Consequently, Swaggi faces the moral dilemma shared by all criminals to varying degrees. He has to reconcile the very different moral codes of the two worlds he straddles, cancelling out any feelings of guilt he derives from conventional morality.

"The way I look at it, I'm a businessman," says Swaggi. "Sure I buy hot stuff, but I never stole nothing in my life. Some driver brings me a couple of cartons, though, I ain't gonna turn him away. If I don't buy it, somebody else will. So what's the difference? I might as well make money with him instead of somebody else." Swaggi thus denies responsibility for his actions. He also claims his actions never hurt anyone:

> Did you see the paper yesterday? You figure it out. Last year I musta had $25,000 wortha merchandise from Sears. In this city last year they could'a called it Sears, Roebuck, and Swaggi. Just yesterday I read where Sears just had the biggest year in history, made more money than ever before. Now if I had that much of Sears's stuff can you imagine how much they musta lost all told? Millions, must be millions. And they still had their biggest year ever....You think they end up losing when they get clipped? Don't you believe it. They're no different from anybody else. If they don't get it back by takin' it off their taxes, they get it back from insurance. Who knows, maybe they do both.

And if he has done a few bad things in his life, then, says Swaggi, so has everyone else. Besides, he's also done a lot of good. In fact, he believes his virtuous acts more than compensate for the skeletons in his closet. Consider, for example, how he managed to protect one of his suppliers and get him a promotion at the same time:

> I had this guy bringin' me radios. Nice little clock radios, sold for $34.95. He worked in the warehouse. Two a day he'd bring me, an' I'd give him fifteen for the both of 'em. Well, after a while he told me his boss was gettin' suspicious 'cause inventory showed a big shortage.... So I ask him if anybody else is takin' much stuff. He says a couple of guys do. I tell him to lay off for a while an' the next time he sees one of the other guys take somethin' to tip off the boss. They'll fire the guy an' clear up the shortage. Well he did an' you know what happened? They made my man assistant shipper. Now once a month I get a carton delivered right to my store with my name on it. Clock radios, percolators, waffle irons, anything I want fifty off wholesale. (quoted in Klockars, 1974: 135–61)

Without Klockars' research, we might think that all criminals are able to live with their guilt only because they are pathological or lack empathy for their fellow human beings. But thanks partly to Klockars' research, we know better. We understand that criminals are able to avoid feeling guilty about their actions and get on with their work because they weave a blanket of rationalizations over their criminal activities. These justifications make their illegal activities appear morally acceptable and normal, at least to the criminals themselves. We understand this aspect of criminal activity better because Klockars spent 15 months befriending Swaggi and closely observing him on the job. He interviewed Swaggi for a total of about 400 hours, taking detailed "field notes" most of the time. He then wrote up his descriptions, quotations, and insights in a book that is now considered a minor classic in the sociology of crime and deviance (Klockars, 1974).

Why is observation *and* participation necessary in participant observation research? Because sociological insight is sharpest when researchers stand both inside and outside the lives of their subjects. Said differently, we see more clearly when we move back and forth between inside and outside. By immersing themselves in their subjects' world, by learning their language and their culture in depth, insiders are able to experience the world just as their subjects do.

Subjectivity can, however, go too far. After all, "natives" are rarely able to see their cultures with much objectivity and inmates of prisons and mental institutions do not have access to official information about themselves. It is only by regularly standing apart and observing their subjects from the point of view of outsiders that researchers can raise analytical issues and see things their subjects are blind to, or are forbidden from seeing.

Objectivity can also go too far. Observers who try to attain complete objectivity will often not be able to make correct inferences about their subjects' behaviour. That is because they cannot fully understand the way their subjects experience the world and cannot ask them about their experiences. Instead, observers who seek complete objectivity must rely only on their own experiences to impute meaning to a social setting. Yet the meaning a situation holds for observers may differ from the meaning it holds for their subjects.

In short, opting for pure observation or pure participation compromises the researcher's ability to see the world sociologically. Instead, participant observation requires the researcher to keep walking a tightrope between the two extremes of objectivity and subjectivity.

It is often difficult for participant-observers to gain access to the groups they wish to study. They must first win the confidence of their subjects, who must feel at ease in the presence of the researcher before they behave naturally. *Reactivity* occurs when the researcher's presence influences the subjects' behaviour (Webb et al., 1966). Reaching a state of nonreactivity requires patience and delicacy on the researcher's part. It took Klockars several months to meet and interview about 60 imprisoned thieves before one of them felt comfortable enough to recommend that he contact Swaggi. Klockars had to demonstrate genuine interest in the thieves' activities and convince them he was no threat to them before they opened up to him. Often, sociologists can minimize reactivity by gaining access to a group in stages. At first, researchers may simply attend a group meeting. After a time, they may start to attend more regularly. Then, when their faces are more familiar, they may strike up a conversation with some of the friendlier group members. Only later will they begin to explain their true motivation for attending.

Klockars and Swaggi are both white men. Their similarity made communication between them easier. In contrast, race, gender, class, and age differences sometimes make it difficult, and occasionally even impossible, for some researchers to study some groups. There are many participant-observation studies in which big social differences between sociologists and their subjects were overcome and resulted in excellent research (e.g., Liebow, 1967; Stack, 1974). On the other hand, one can scarcely imagine a sociologist nearing retirement conducting participant-observation research on youth gangs or an African-Canadian sociologist using this research method to study skinheads.

Most participant-observation studies begin as **exploratory research.** This means researchers at first have only a vague sense of what they are looking for, and perhaps no sense at all of what they will discover in the course of their study. They are equipped only with some hunches based on their own experience and their reading of the relevant research literature. They try, however, to treat these hunches as hypotheses. **Hypotheses** are unverified but testable statements about the phenomena that interest researchers. As they immerse themselves in the life of their subjects, their observations constitute sociological data that allow them to reject, accept, or modify their initial hypotheses. Indeed, researchers often purposely seek out observations that enable them to determine the validity and scope of their hypotheses. ("From previous research I know elderly people are generally more religious than young people, and that seems to be true in this community, too. But does religiosity vary among people of the same age who are rich, middle class, working class, and poor? If so, why? If not, why not?") Purposively choosing observations results in the creation of a grounded theory. A *grounded theory* is an explanation of a phenomenon based not on mere speculation but on the controlled scrutiny of one's subjects (Glaser and Straus, 1967).

## Methodological Issues

The great advantage of participant observation is that it lets researchers get "under the skin" of their subjects and discover their view of the world in its full complexity. It is an especially valuable technique when little is known about the group or phenomenon under investigation and the sociologist is interested in constructing a theory about it. But participant observation has drawbacks too. To understand them we must say a few words about measurement in sociology.

When researchers think about the social world, they use mental constructs or concepts such as "race," "class," "gender," and so forth. Concepts that can have more than one value are called **variables**. Height and wealth are variables. Perhaps less obviously, affection and perceived beauty are, too. Just as one can be 5'7" or 6'2", rich or poor, one can be passionately in love with, or indifferent to, the girl next door on the grounds that she is beautiful or plain. In each case, we know we are dealing with a variable because height, wealth, affection, and perceived beauty can take different values.

Once researchers identify the variables that interest them, they must decide which real-world observations correspond to each variable. Should "class," for example, be measured by determining people's annual income? Or should it be measured by determining their accumulated wealth, or years of formal education, or some combination of these or other indicators of rank? Deciding which observations to link to which variables is known as **operationalization**.

Sociological variables can sometimes be measured by casual observation. It is usually pretty easy to tell if someone is a man or a woman, and participant-observers can learn a great deal more about their subjects through extended discussion and careful observation. When researchers find out how much money their subjects earn, how satisfied they are with their marriages, whether they have ever been the victims of a criminal act, and so forth, they are measuring the values of the sociological variables embedded in their hypotheses.

Typically, researchers must establish criteria for assigning values to variables. At exactly what level of annual income can someone be considered "upper class"? What are the precise characteristics of settlements that allow them to be characterized as "urban"? What features of a person permit us to say she is a "leader"? Answers to such questions all involve measurement decisions.

And there's the rub. In any given research project, participant-observers usually work alone and usually investigate only one group or one type of group. Thus, when we read their research results we must be convinced of three things if we are to accept their findings. We must be confident the findings extend beyond the single case examined. We must be confident their interpretations are accurate. And we must be confident another researcher would interpret things in the same way. Let us examine each of these points in turn (see Figure 2.3):

1. *Would another researcher interpret or measure things in the same way?* This is the problem of **reliability**. If a measurement procedure repeatedly yields consistent results, we consider it reliable. However, in the case of participant-observation, there is usually only one person doing the measuring in only one setting. Therefore, there is really no way of knowing whether repeating the procedures would yield consistent results.
2. *Are the researcher's interpretations accurate?* This is the problem of **validity**, the problem of whether one can find confirmation of one's measures in the real world. If a measurement procedure measures what it is supposed to measure, then it is valid. Whether a measure is reliable has no bearing on its validity. Measuring a person's shoe with a ruler may give us a reliable indicator of that person's shoe size. That is because the ruler repeatedly yields the same results. However, regardless of consistency, shoe size as measured by a ruler is a totally invalid measure of a person's

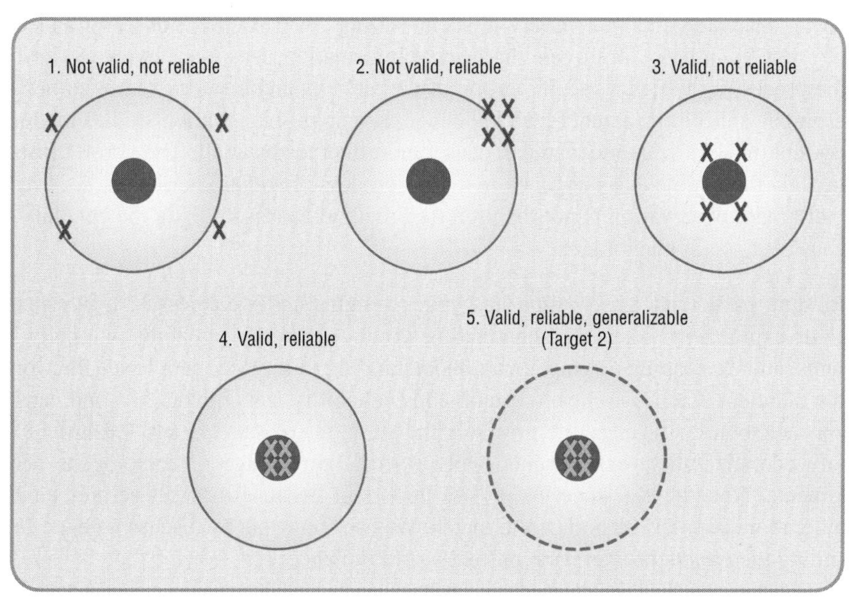


**✦ FIGURE 2.3 ✦**

**Measurement as Target Practice: Validity, Reliability, and Generalizability Compared**

Validity, reliability, and generalizability may be explained by drawing an analogy between measuring a variable and firing at a bull's eye. In case 1, shots (measures) are far apart (not reliable) and far from the bull's eye (not valid). In case 2, shots are close to one another (reliable) but far from the bull's eye (not valid). In case 3, shots are close to the bull's eye (valid) but far from one another (not reliable). In case 4, shots are close to the bull's eye (valid) and close to one another (reliable). In case 5, we use a second target. Our shots are again close to one another (reliable) and close to the bull's eye (valid). Because our measures were valid and reliable for both the first and second targets in cases 4 and 5, we conclude our results are generalizable.

annual income. Similarly, you may think you are measuring annual income by asking people how much they earn. Another interviewer at another time may get exactly the same result when posing the same question. But, despite this reliability, respondents may understate their true income. (A respondent is a person who answers the researcher's questions.) Our measure of annual income may therefore lack validity. Perfectly consistent measures may, in other words, have little truth-value.

In one sense, participant-observers have every right to feel they are on solid ground when it comes to the question of validity. If anyone can tell whether respondents are understating their true income, surely it is someone who has spent months or even years getting to know everything about their lifestyle. Still, doubts may creep in if the criteria used by the participant-observers to assess the validity of their measures are all *internal* to the settings they are investigating. Our confidence in the validity of researchers' measures increases if we are able to use *external* validation criteria. Consider age. Asking people their age is one way to determine how old they are. The problem with this measure is that people tend to exaggerate their age when they are young and minimize it when they are old. A more valid way to determine people's age is to ask them about their year of birth. Year of birth is generally reported more accurately than responses to the question "How old are you?" It is therefore a more valid measure of age. A still more valid measure of age can be found in the "year of birth" entry on people's birth certificates. The point is that validity increases if we have some external check on our measure of age.

3. *Do the research findings apply beyond the specific case examined?* This is the problem of **generalizability**, and it is one of the most serious problems faced by participant-observation studies. For example, Klockars studied just one professional fence in depth. Can we safely conclude his findings are relevant to all professional fences? Do we dare apply his insights to all criminals? Are we foolhardy if we generalize his conclusions to nearly all of us on the grounds that most of us commit deviant acts at one time or another and must deal with feelings of guilt? None of this is clear from Klockars' research. Nor are questions of generalizability clearly answered by many participant-observation studies, since they are usually studies of single cases.
4. Related to the issue of generalizability is that of **causality**, the analysis of causes and their effects. Information on how widely or narrowly a research finding applies can help us establish the causes of a social phenomenon. For instance, we might want to know how gender, race, class, parental supervision, police surveillance, and other factors shape the type and rate of juvenile delinquency. If so, we require information on types and rates of criminal activity among teenagers with a variety of social characteristics in a variety of social settings. A participant-observation study of crime is unlikely to provide that sort of information. It is more likely to clarify the process by which a specific group of people in a single setting learns to become criminal. Indeed, researchers who conduct participant-observation studies tend not to think in somewhat mechanical, cause-and-effect terms at all. They prefer instead to view their subjects as engaged in a fluid process of social interaction. As a result, participant-observation is not the preferred method for discovering the general causes of social phenomena.

In sum, participant-observation has both strengths and weaknesses. It is especially useful in exploratory research, constructing grounded theory, creating internally valid measures, and developing a sympathetic understanding of the way people see the world. It is often deficient when it comes to establishing reliability, generalizability, and causality. As you will soon learn, these are precisely the strengths of surveys and (with the exception of generalizability) experiments. Only a small percentage of sociologists conduct experiments. Nonetheless, experiments are important because they set certain standards that other more popular methods try to match. We can show this by discussing experiments concerning the effects of television on real-world violence.

## Experiments

In the mid-1960s, about 15 years after commercial TV was introduced in North America, rates of violent crime began to increase dramatically. Some people were not surprised. The first generation of North American children exposed to high levels of TV violence virtually from birth had reached their mid-teens. TV violence, some commentators said, legitimized violence in the real world, making it seem increasingly normal and acceptable. As a result, they concluded, North American teenagers in the 1960s and subsequent decades were more likely than pre-1960s teens to commit violent acts.

Social scientists soon started investigating the connection between TV and real-world violence using experimental methods. An **experiment** is a carefully controlled artificial situation that allows researchers to isolate hypothesized causes and measure their effects precisely (Campbell and Stanley, 1963). It uses a special procedure called **randomization** to create two similar groups. Randomization involves assigning individuals to the two groups by chance processes. It then introduces the hypothesized cause to only one of the groups. By comparing the state of the two groups before and after only one of the groups has been exposed to the hypothesized cause, an experiment can determine whether the presumed cause has the predicted effect.

Here is how an experiment on the effects of TV violence on aggressive behaviour might work:

1. *Selection of subjects.* Researchers advertise in local newspapers for parents willing to allow their children to act as research subjects. Fifty children are selected for the experiment.
2. *Random assignment of subjects to experimental and control groups.* At random, each child draws a number from 1 to 50 from a box. The researchers assign children who draw odd numbers to the **experimental group**. This is the group that will be exposed to a violent TV program during the experiment. They assign children who draw even numbers to the **control group**. This is the group that will not be exposed to a violent TV program during the experiment.

   Note that randomization and repetition make the experimental and control groups similar. That is, by assigning subjects to the two groups using a chance process, and repeating the experiment many times, researchers ensure that the experimental and control groups are likely to have the same proportion of boys and girls, members of different races, children highly motivated to participate in the study, and so forth. Random assignment eliminates bias by allowing a chance process and only a chance process to decide which group each child is assigned to.
3. *Measurement of dependent variable in experimental and control groups.* The researchers put small groups of children in a room and give them toys to play with. They observe the children through a one-way mirror, rating each child in terms of the aggressiveness of his or her play. This is the child's pre-test score on the dependent variable, aggressive behaviour. The **dependent variable** is the effect in any cause-and-effect relationship.
4. *Introduction of independent variable to experimental group.* The researchers show children in the experimental group an hour-long TV show in which many violent and aggressive acts take place. They do not show the film to children in the control group. In this experiment, the violent TV show is the independent variable. The **independent variable** is the presumed cause in any cause-and-effect relationship.
5. *Remeasurement of dependent variable in experimental and control groups.* Immediately after the children see the TV show, the researchers again observe the children in both groups at play. Each child's play is given a second aggressiveness rating—the post-test score.
6. *Assessment of experimental effect.* Post-test minus pre-test scores are calculated for both the experimental and the control groups. If the post-test minus pre-test score

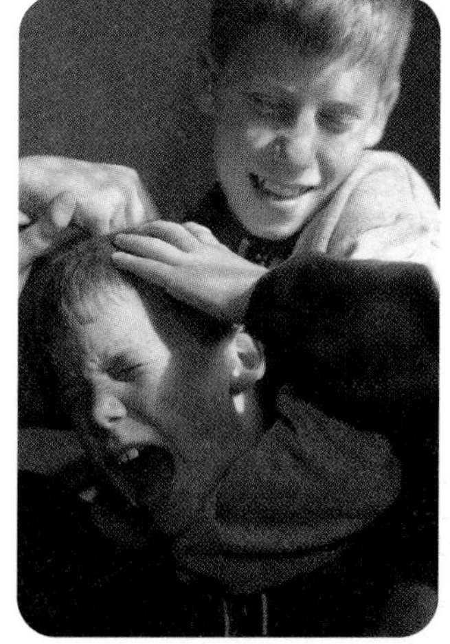

Aggressive behaviour among children is common, from siblings fighting to bullying in the schoolyard. Since the inception of home TV in the 1950s, social scientists have sought to find strong research designs capable of examining the causal effects, if any, of viewing violence on the "tube."

> for the experimental group is significantly greater than the post-test minus pre-test score for the control group, the researchers conclude the independent variable (watching violent TV) has a significant effect on the dependent variable (aggressive behaviour). This conclusion is warranted because the introduction of the independent variable is the only difference between the experimental and control groups.

As this example shows, an experiment is a precision instrument for isolating the single cause of theoretical interest and measuring its effect in an exact and repeatable way. But high reliability and the ability to establish causality come at a steep price. Cynics sometimes say experimental sociology allows researchers to know more and more about less and less. Many sociologists argue that experiments are highly artificial situations. They believe that removing people from their natural social settings usually lowers the validity of one's findings.

These misgivings are evident in experimental studies of the effects of TV violence (Felson, 1996). Experiments show that watching violent TV usually increases violent behaviour in the short term. However, in the real world, violent behaviour usually means attempting to harm another person physically. Shouting, hitting a doll, or kicking a toy is just not the same thing. In fact, such acts may enable children to relieve frustrations in a fantasy world, thus lowering their chance of acting violently in the real world. Moreover, in a laboratory situation, aggressive behaviour may be encouraged because it is legitimized. Simply showing a violent TV program may suggest to subjects how the experimenter expects them to behave during the experiment. Subjects who are influenced by the prestige of the researcher and the scientific nature of the experiment compound this problem. They will try to do what is expected of them in order not to appear poorly adjusted. (Changing people's behaviour by making them aware they are being studied is known as the *Hawthorne effect*. It is so named because researchers at the Western Electric Company's Hawthorne factory in the 1930s claimed to find that workers' productivity increased no matter how they changed their work environment. Productivity increased, they said, just because the researchers were paying attention to the workers.[2]) Finally, aggressive behaviour is not punished or controlled in the laboratory setting as it is in the real world. If a boy watching a martial arts movie stands up and delivers a karate blow to his younger brother, a parent is likely to take action to prevent a recurrence. This teaches the boy not to engage in such aggressive behaviour. This does not happen in the lab, where the lack of disciplinary control may facilitate unrealistically high levels of aggression.

In an effort to overcome the validity problem and still retain many of the benefits of experimental design, some sociologists have conducted experiments in natural settings. In such experiments, researchers forgo strict randomization of subjects. Instead, they compare groups that are already quite similar. They either introduce the independent variable themselves (this is called a *field experiment*) or observe what happens when the independent variable is introduced to one of the groups in the normal course of social life (this is called a *natural experiment*).

Some field experiments on media effects compare boys in institutionalized settings such as boarding schools. The researchers expose half the boys to violent TV programming. Measures of aggressiveness taken before and after the introduction of violent programming allow researchers to calculate its effect on behaviour. One reanalysis of 28 such studies yielded mixed results. Although 16 of the field experiments (57 percent) suggested that subjects engage in more aggression following exposure to violent films, 12 (43 percent) did not (Wood, Wong, and Chachere, 1991).

Natural experiments have compared rates of aggressive behaviour in Canadian and other towns with and without TV service, but their results are inconclusive. They are also muddied by the fact that there are substantial differences among the towns apart from the presence or absence of TV service. It is therefore unclear whether differences in child aggressiveness are due to media effects.

Because of the validity problems noted above, it has not been convincingly demonstrated that TV violence generally encourages violent behaviour. The sociological consensus is that TV violence probably does have an effect on a small percentage of viewers, but the effect is not large (Felson, 1996: 123). The extent of the effect is unclear partly because the experimental method makes it difficult to generalize from the specific groups studied to the entire population. The subjects of an experiment on media effects may be white, middle-class people from a city on the Prairies who read newspaper ads and are in a position to take a day off to participate in the experiment. This is hardly a representative group of Canadians. But experimentalists are rarely concerned that their subjects are representative of an entire population. As we will now see, one of the strong points of surveys is that they allow us to make safer generalizations.

## Surveys

### Sampling

Surveys are part of the fabric of everyday life in North America. You see surveys in action when the CBC conducts a poll to discover the percentage of Canadians who approve of the prime minister's performance, when someone phones to ask about your taste in breakfast cereal, and when the late advice columnist Ann Landers asked her readers, "If you had to do it over again, would you have children?" In every **survey**, people are asked questions about their knowledge, attitudes, or behaviour, either in a face-to-face or telephone interview or in a paper-and-pencil format.

Remarkably, Ann Landers found that fully 70 percent of parents would not have children if they could make the choice again. She then ran a shocking headline saying so. Should we have confidence in her finding? Hardly. As the letters from her readers indicated, many of the people who answered her question were angry with their children. All 10 000 respondents felt at least strongly enough about the issue to take the trouble to mail in their replies at their own expense. Like all survey researchers, Ann Landers aimed to study part of a group—**a sample**—in order to learn about the whole group—the **population** (in this case, all North American parents). The trouble is, she got replies from a *voluntary response sample*, a group of people who chose *themselves* in response to a general appeal. People who choose themselves are unlikely to be representative of the population of interest. In contrast, a *representative sample* is a group of people chosen so their characteristics closely match those of the population of interest. The difference in the quality of knowledge we can derive from the two types of samples cannot be overstated. Thus, a few months after Ann Landers conducted her poll, a scientific survey based on a

Researchers collect information using surveys by asking people in a representative sample a set of identical questions. People interviewed on a downtown street corner do *not* constitute a representative sample of Canadian adults. That is because the sample does not include people who live outside the urban core, underestimates the number of elderly people and people with disabilities, does not take into account regional diversity, and so forth.

representative sample found that 91 percent of North American parents *would* have children again (Moore, 1995: 178).

How can survey researchers draw a representative sample? You might think that setting yourself up in a public place such as a shopping mall and asking willing passersby to answer some questions would work. However, this sort of *convenience sample*, which chooses the people who are easiest to reach, is also highly unlikely to be representative. People who go to malls are richer than average. Moreover, a larger proportion of homemakers, retired people, and teenagers visit malls than can be found in the Canadian population as a whole. Convenience samples are almost always unrepresentative.

To draw a representative sample, respondents cannot select themselves, as in the Ann Landers case. Nor can the researcher choose respondents, as in the mall example. Instead, respondents must be chosen at random, and an individual's chance of being chosen must be known and greater than zero. A sample with these characteristics is known as a **probability sample** (see Box 2.1)

To draw a probability sample you first need a *sampling frame*. This is a list of all the people in the population of interest. You also need a randomizing method. This is a way of ensuring every person in the sampling frame has a known and non-zero chance of being selected.

Up-to-date membership lists of organizations are useful sampling frames if you want to survey members of organizations. But if you want to investigate, say, the religious beliefs of Canadians, then the membership lists of places of worship are inadequate. That is because many Canadians do not belong to such institutions. In a nationwide Canadian survey conducted in 1998, just 34 percent of Canadians said they attended religious services regularly (Clark, 1998). In such cases, you might turn to another frequently used sampling frame, the telephone directory. The telephone directory is now available for the entire country on CD-ROM. However, even the telephone directory lacks the names and addresses of some poor and homeless people (who do not have phones) and some rich people (who have unlisted phone numbers). Computer programs are available that dial residential phone numbers at random, including unlisted numbers. However, that still excludes about 1.3 percent of Canadian households from any survey relying on the telephone directory as a sampling frame.

As the example of the telephone directory shows, few sampling frames are perfect. Even the largest and most expensive survey in Canada, the census, missed an estimated 2 percent of the population in 2001. Researchers believe that much of the undercounted population is composed of specific and identifiable groups, thus introducing sampling bias (see "Analysis of Existing Documents and Official Statistics" on page 55). Nevertheless, researchers maximize the accuracy of their generalizations by using the least biased sampling frames available and adjusting their analyses and conclusions to take account of known sampling bias.

Once a sampling frame has been chosen or created, individuals must be selected by a chance process. One way to do this is by picking, say, the tenth person on your list and then every twentieth (or thirtieth, or hundredth) person after that, depending on how many people you need in your sample. A second method is to assign the number 1 to the first person in the sampling frame, the number 2 to the next person, and so on. Then you create a separate list of random numbers by using a computer or consulting a table of random numbers, which you can find at the back of almost any elementary statistics book. Your list of random numbers should have as many entries as the number of people you want in your sample. The individuals whose assigned numbers correspond to the list of random numbers are the people in your sample.

How many respondents do you need in a sample? That depends on how much inaccuracy you are willing to tolerate. Large samples give more precise results than small samples. For most sociological purposes, however, a random sample of 1500 people will give acceptably accurate results, even if the population of interest is the entire adult population of Canada. More precisely, if you draw 20 random samples of 1500 individuals each, 19 of them will provide estimates that will be accurate within 2.5 percent of actual population

## BOX 2.1
## SOCIOLOGY AT THE MOVIES

*The Blair Witch Project* is frightening partly because it lacks a sociological perspective.

### *THE BLAIR WITCH PROJECT* (1999)

In sociology, some big surveys cost a few million dollars. They employ hundreds of people as interviewers, data analysts, project managers, and so forth. They use computers and sophisticated software to analyze data. The typical Hollywood movie costs 10 times more than even big sociology research projects. It employs many more people and uses much more sophisticated technology for special effects.

You might think there is little room for small-scale work in either sociological research or movie making, but that isn't so. *The Blair Witch Project*, directed by Daniel Myrick and Eduardo Sanchez, cost just over $50 000 to make. It was a surprise hit in the summer of 1999, earning $75 million in its first week of national release. Besides raising hopes for all low-budget projects everywhere, the movie can also teach us something about research methods.

*The Blair Witch Project* begins as a research project. Three people trek to a small town to find out about the local witch legend. Like good researchers, they interview local people. Some respondents dismiss the legend. Others provide tantalizing hints that the witch really exists. The results of this research are inconclusive, so the three investigators decide to hike into the woods, hoping to discover for themselves whether the witch exists.

Unfortunately, they overestimate their skills as hikers and campers. They lose their map, soon get lost, and proceed to get on each other's nerves. Eventually, one of them disappears after an argument with the other two. (We don't know why he disappears—either because the Blair witch got him or because he was angry with his co-investigators.) The two remaining people then stumble upon an old, vacant house. Exploring the house, they hear odd noises. In the end, the two cameras fall to the floor. The video footage ends. Whether the two characters were attacked by the Blair witch or by their angry co-investigator is unclear.

The power of the movie—the reason it was so frightening to so many people—derives from the fact that it *lacks* a sociological viewpoint. After the three investigators conduct their interviews, anything resembling sociological research stops. Subsequently, our only sources of knowledge are the video cameras held by each of the three investigators. We are rarely given a panoramic view or a sense of context to improve our understanding of what is happening. The narrow perspectives of the three cameras certainly provide a sense of being there. Members of the audience feel they are seeing things just as the three investigators do, facing the unknown terror of the Blair witch, who is nowhere to be seen. But if the audience members were able to draw on other sources of information about the Blair witch or the angry co-investigator who left in a huff, if they were able to see things from a broader perspective than is afforded by the individual viewpoints of the three investigators, if they were able to make sense of the larger context of events, some of the terror might subside. For example, if the two remaining people had better evidence that the Blair witch was real, they might not have entered the house. If they had known their travelling companion was a deeply disturbed young man with violent tendencies, they might have taken steps to protect themselves rather than leave themselves open to assault. As the old saying goes, it's better to face the devil you know than the devil you don't know.

Sociologically speaking, *The Blair Witch Project* is unsatisfying because it doesn't escape the narrow, individual points of view provided by the three video cameras. In contrast, sociological research tries to get beyond individual points of view. For instance, by taking random samples rather than convenience samples in opinion surveys, researchers ensure that their data accurately reflect opinion in the population from which the samples are drawn. Similarly, by comparing experimental and control groups, researchers eliminate the possibility that variables other than the independent variable of interest are responsible for observed differences between the two groups. By using these and other research methods, sociologists avoid getting lost in the woods.

Homelessness is an increasing focus of public policy. But public support may not be adequate if the homeless are not counted properly in the census. Statistics Canada included a count of the homeless in the 2001 Census. However, because the count is based on information about the use of shelters and soup kitchens, combined with an attempt at street counts, these numbers are estimates.

values. Accordingly, we say that the estimate has a 2.5 percent "margin of error." Imagine, for example, that 50 percent of a random sample of 1500 respondents says it supports the Liberal party. This means that in 19 out of 20 samples of this size, support for the Liberals would be between 47.5 and 52.5 percent. If the survey showed that 52 percent of the respondents support the Liberals and 48 percent support the Canadian Alliance, the appropriate conclusion is *not* that the Liberals are in the lead. Instead, you should conclude that there is no detectable difference in support for the two parties given the 2.5 percent margin of error in the survey (see Figure 2.4).

In sum, probability sampling enables us to conduct surveys that permit us to generalize from a part (the sample) to the whole (the population) within known margins of error. Now let us consider the validity of survey data.

**✦ FIGURE 2.4 ✦**

**The Margin of Error in a Sample**

In a sample of 1500 people, 48 percent of the respondents support the Canadian Alliance and 50 percent support the Liberals. However, because the 2.5 percent margins of error overlap, we cannot be sure whether support for the two parties differs in the population. To conclude that support for the two parties differs in the population, the margins of error must not overlap.

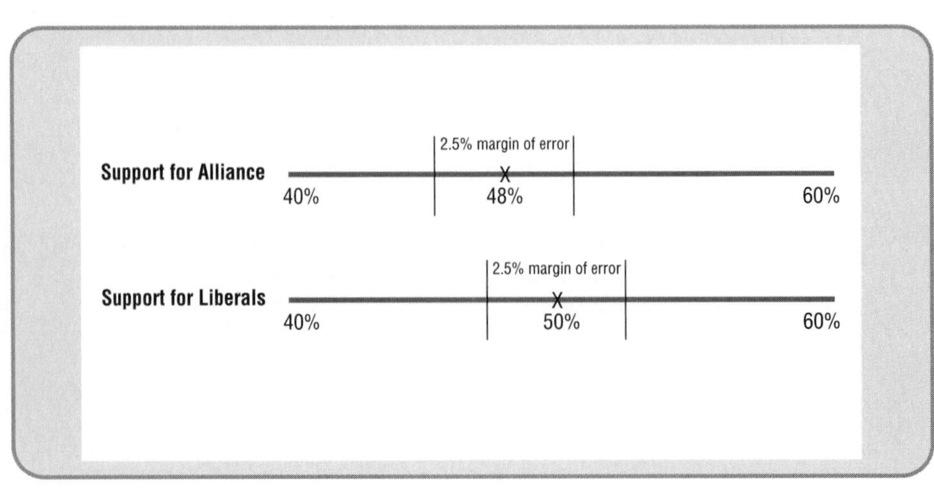

## Survey Questions and Validity

There are three main ways to conduct a survey. Sometimes, a *self-administered questionnaire* is used. For example, a form containing questions and permitted responses may be mailed to the respondent and returned to the researcher through the mail system. The main advantage of this method is that it is relatively inexpensive. It also has drawbacks. For one thing, it sometimes results in unacceptably low *response rates*. The response rate is the number of people who answer the questionnaire divided by the number of people asked to do so, expressed as a percentage. Moreover, if you use mail questionnaires, an interviewer is not present to explain problematic questions and response options to the respondent. *Face-to-face interviews* are therefore generally preferred over mail questionnaires. In this type of survey, questions and allowable responses are presented to the respondent by the interviewer during a meeting. However, training interviewers and sending them around to conduct interviews is very expensive. That is why *telephone interviews* have become increasingly popular over the past two or three decades. They can elicit relatively high response rates and are relatively inexpensive to administer.

Questionnaires can contain two types of questions. A *closed-ended question* provides the respondent with a list of permitted answers. Each answer is given a numerical code so the data can later be easily input into a computer for statistical analysis. *Open-ended questions* allow respondents to answer questions in their own words. They are particularly useful in exploratory research, where the researcher does not have enough knowledge to create a meaningful and complete list of possible answers. Open-ended questions are more time-consuming to analyze than closed-ended questions, although recent computer programs for analyzing text make the task much easier.

Researchers want the answers elicited by surveys to be valid, to actually measure what they are supposed to. To maximize validity, researchers must guard against several dangers. We have already considered one threat to validity in survey research: *undercounting* some categories of the population because of an imperfect sampling frame.

Survey researchers who put their questionnaires on the World Wide Web confront a recent variant of the problem of undercounting. Below each question they list allowable responses. Beside each allowable response they place a clickable box. They ask people who visit the Web site containing the questionnaire to read the questions and click the appropriate boxes indicating their responses. Respondents' answers are automatically stored in a computerized database as soon as they click. For non-Web surveys, people must be hired as "data entry clerks" to enter questionnaire responses into a computer. This expensive step is eliminated with Web surveys. Web surveys also save the cost of postage and interviewers. However, the people who respond to Web surveys select themselves in much the same fashion as the respondents to Ann Landers' parenthood question. Moreover, to answer a Web survey you have to have access to a computer connected to the Internet. A sample drawn from Internet users would not be representative of the Canadian population as a whole, let alone the population of a less-developed country, where Internet access is rare. In 2000, 42 percent of Canadians had never used the Internet and another 10 percent used it rarely. This 52 percent of Canadians tends to be elderly, have low incomes, and have no post-secondary education (Crompton, Ellison, and Stevenson, 2002). So although a Web survey of Internet users might have validity, a Web survey of the general population would likely give invalid results because of the unrepresentative nature of the sample on which it is based.

There are other threats to validity in survey research aside from undercounting. Even if an individual is contacted about a survey, he or she may refuse to participate in the survey. This threat to validity is known as *nonresponse*. If nonrespondents differ from respondents in ways that are relevant to the research topic, the conclusions one draws from the survey may be in jeopardy. For instance, some alcoholics may not want to participate in a survey on alcohol consumption because they regard the topic as sensitive. If so, a measure of the rate of alcohol consumption taken from the sample would not be an accurate reflection of the rate of alcohol consumption in the population. Actual alcohol consumption in the population would be higher than the rate in the sample.

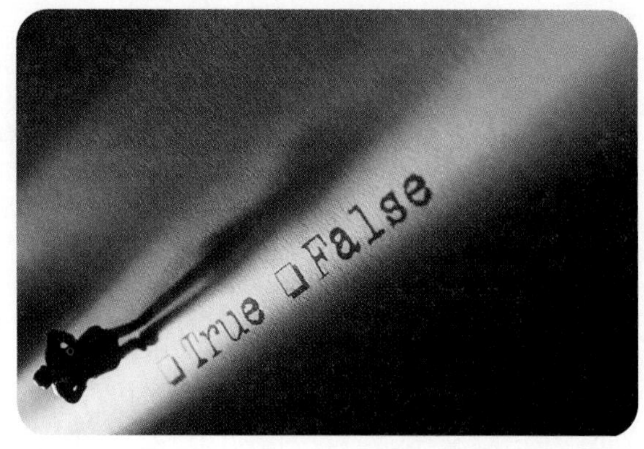


Survey researchers pay careful attention to nonresponse. They try to discover whether nonrespondents differ systematically from respondents so they can take this into account before drawing conclusions from their sample. They must also take special measures to ensure that the response rate remains acceptably high—generally, around 70 percent or more of people contacted. Proven tactics ensure a high response rate. Researchers can notify potential respondents about the survey in advance. They can remind them to complete and mail in survey forms. They can have universities and other prestigious institutions sponsor the survey. They can stress the practical and scientific value of the research. And they can give people small rewards, such as a dollar or two, for participating.

If respondents do not answer questions accurately, a third threat to validity is present: *response bias*. The survey may focus on sensitive, unpopular, or illegal behaviour. As a result, some respondents may not be willing to answer questions frankly. The interviewer's attitude, gender, or race may suggest that some responses are preferred. This can elicit biased responses. Some of these problems can be overcome by carefully selecting and training interviewers and closely supervising their work. Response bias on questions about sensitive, unpopular, or illegal behaviour can be minimized by having such questions answered in private (Smith, 1992).

Fourth, validity may be compromised because of *wording effects*. That is, the way questions are phrased or ordered can influence and invalidate responses. Experienced survey researchers have turned questionnaire construction into a respected craft. Increasingly, they refine the lessons learned from experience with evidence from field experiments. These experiments divide samples into two or more randomly chosen subsamples. Different question wording or ordering is then administered to the people in each subsample so that wording effects can be measured. Detected problems can then be resolved in future research.

Both experience and field experiments suggest that survey questions must be specific and simple. They should be expressed in plain, everyday language. They should be phrased neutrally, never leading the respondent to a particular answer and never using inflammatory terms. Because people's memories are often faulty, questions are more likely to elicit valid responses if they focus on important, singular, current events rather than less salient, multiple, past events. Breaking these rules lowers the validity of survey findings (Converse and Presser, 1986; Ornstein, 1998).

## Causality

In 1991, Erin Brockovich was down and out. She was a twice-divorced mother of three small children, and she had no university education. She had recently been seriously injured in a traffic accident, and she was unable to find work. She hired a law firm to argue her case but the $25 000 settlement covered only a fraction of her debts.[3]

Then came a turning point in Brockovich's life. She convinced the law firm that had settled her car accident case to hire her as a filing clerk at $1800 a month. Soon after she began working for the firm, Brockovich came across some medical records that piqued her curiosity. Her boss let her look into the matter. Brockovich's dogged investigation eventually established that a giant power utility had allowed a toxic chemical to leak into the groundwater of a nearby town, ruining the health of more than 600 residents. Although she was not a lawyer and had no formal education even as a law clerk or a paralegal, Brockovich spearheaded a court case that resulted in the largest legal settlement in North American history. In 1996, the power utility was ordered to pay $500 million to the victims. Brockovich herself received $3 million for her efforts. In 2000, these events were dramatized in the hit movie *Erin Brockovich*, starring Julia Roberts in the title role. The movie was nominated for five Academy Awards® and Roberts won the best actress award for her portrayal of Brockovich (Ellis, 2002).

Erin Brockovich's story is unusual for two reasons. First, crimes committed by big corporations are rarely prosecuted successfully, and even successful prosecutions typically result in modest settlements (see Chapter 6, Deviance and Crime). Second, unemployed divorced women with small children and no university education rarely compete successfully against big-time lawyers, regardless of how bright and energetic they may be. Due to lack of education and the demands of family, the cards are stacked too heavily against them (see Chapter 9, Sexuality and Gender). But what if we even out the playing field? What if we compare men and women who are more alike? What if we compare, say, male and female lawyers? Are male lawyers generally more successful? And if so, why? These are the questions sociologists Fiona Kay and John Hagan (1998) set out to answer in a survey of Ontario lawyers.[4]

Kay and Hagan analyzed self-administered questionnaires completed by a representative group of 905 lawyers. The respondents had all been called to the Ontario bar between 1975 and 1990, remained in practice in 1990, and had begun practice on a partnership track. Partnership is a measure of success in legal practice. Achieving the rank of partner means that a lawyer is one of the owners of his or her firm. Partnership enhances the lawyer's earnings and opens additional opportunities for career advancement. Kay and Hagan found that 46 percent of the men in their sample were partners, compared with just 25 percent of the women. That is, they found an **association** between gender and promotion. In general, an association exists between two variables if the value of one variable (in this case, partner vs. nonpartner) changes with the value of the other (in this case, male vs. female).

Why were men substantially more likely to become partners than women? One explanation for why some people have more successful careers focuses on their "human capital," that is, the investments they make in their occupation. In this view, success comes from improving one's education, work experience, and work skills. If women devote more attention than men to domestic labour and raising children, while men devote more attention to upgrading their education, work experience, and work skills, men will be more successful in their careers than women (Becker, 1991).

We can test human capital theory by comparing male and female lawyers who have invested *equally* in human capital. Our confidence in human capital theory would *increase* if female lawyers who have invested as much in human capital as male lawyers were as likely as male lawyers to become partners. Our confidence in human capital would *decrease* if male lawyers were more successful than female lawyers even when women and men make identical investments in their careers.

The hit film *Erin Brockovich* (2000) is based on a true story. In the film, Brockovich (played by Julia Roberts), a single mother of three children and a legal assistant, discovers that a power utility is illegally dumping cancer-causing chemicals into an unlined pond, causing high rates of cancer and other diseases in the area. Against all odds, Brockovich helps her boss win a case against the company. The film raises the question of why successful prosecutions of corporate crime are so rare. It also raises the question of why bright, energetic men often earn more than equally bright, energetic women.

How can we measure investment in human capital? The number of years since graduation from law school is one measure, because it indicates years of job experience. A second measure is the number of years spent in law practice. If one takes time off work to have children and raise them, one will have less work experience. Significantly, when Kay and Hagan compared male and female lawyers with equal years of job experience and time since graduation, they found that men were still more likely to become partners than women. Their findings thus decrease our confidence in human capital theory. That is because gender differences in success persist even when investment in human capital is the same for women and men.

Kay and Hagan (1998: 729) propose an alternative explanation for the greater career success of men: "[W]omen must display *greater* career commitment than men to receive the same, or even smaller, rewards [*our emphasis*]." Their data support this argument. For example, Kay and Hagan's survey data show that women's career prospects improve if they are eager to engage in various "extracurricular" activities that enhance the reputation of their firms and attract clients. Such activities include being honoured by a professional organization, receiving public recognition for their work, and serving as a member of the bench in the Law Society of Upper Canada. Men's career prospects are unaffected by these activities. This illustrates that, to advance to the level of partner, women must display greater career commitment than men.

In the course of developing an explanation for the association between gender and promotion, Kay and Hagan performed a causal analysis. They had to satisfy four conditions to establish causality. Since these four conditions must be satisfied in *any* causal analysis, they are worth considering at length.

Kay and Hagan had to be confident that the independent variable occurred before the dependent variable. This is the *time order* criterion. Time order is straightforward in the relationship between gender and promotion. Chronologically, gender precedes promotion.

Kay and Hagan had to establish the existence of a correlation between the independent and dependent variables. This is the *association* criterion. We saw that 46 percent of men and 25 percent of women received promotions to partners. The association is not perfect. A perfect association would involve 100 percent of men versus zero percent of women receiving promotion. But clearly the partnership experience of women and men differs substantially. If the difference between the percentages were 3 percent rather than 21 percent (46 – 25 = 21), we might be tempted to say the difference is very small and probably due to chance fluctua-

Men are usually more successful in the legal profession than women. By comparing male and female lawyers with similar levels of job experience, sociologists Fiona Kay and John Hagan (1998) found that female lawyers have to be more committed to their jobs than male lawyers are in order to be as successful.

tion, that is, the individuals who happened to be included in the sample. However, a 21 percent difference establishes a sizable association between gender and partnership.

Kay and Hagan had to show that the effect resulted from the cause and not from some other factor. This is the *spuriousness* criterion. It may be that an association between independent and dependent variables is erroneous since the association may be due to the effect of a third variable. For instance, in Scandinavia there is an association between storks and babies. The more storks in a region, the higher the birth rate. Does this mean that storks bring babies? Of course not. There are more storks *and* more babies in rural regions than in urban regions. If you look at rural regions only, there is no association at all between storks and the birth rate. The same holds true if you look at urban regions only. "Region" accounts for the association between storks and babies. It is a control variable. Statistical control removes the effect of a third variable (in this case, "region") from an association (in this case, between storks and babies). Statistical **control** shows how the third variable influences the original association. Because in this case controlling for region makes the original association disappear, we say that the association between storks and babies is spurious. In general, spuriousness exists between an independent and a dependent variable when the introduction of a causally prior control variable makes the initial association disappear.

Similarly, Kay and Hagan wanted to see whether the association between gender and promotion was spurious. To find out, they examined the effect of human capital on the association. They found that human capital had no effect on the association. That is, men were still more likely to be promoted than women even when comparing women and men who had made equal investments in human capital. Unlike the association between storks and babies after controlling for region, the association between gender and promotion after controlling for human capital remained strong. This suggests that in Kay and Hagan's research, the control variable (human capital) is *not* responsible for the original association (between gender and promotion).

Kay and Hagan had to show a mechanism or process linking the cause and the effect. This is the *rationale* criterion. Their rationale for the link between gender and promotion was the variable "work commitment." When Kay and Hagan controlled for work commitment, the association between gender and promotion disappeared. They found that if women displayed more work commitment than men, they were as likely as men to be promoted. This is similar to the storks and babies example with region controlled. Just as region accounted for the association between storks and babies, work commitment accounted for the association between gender and promotion. Kay and Hagan's causal reasoning is illustrated in Figure 2.5.

Analysis of survey data involves more than just testing for **spurious associations**. Many interesting and unexpected things can happen when a two-variable association is elaborated by controlling for a third variable (Hirschi and Selvin, 1972). The original association may remain unchanged. It may strengthen. It may weaken. It may disappear or

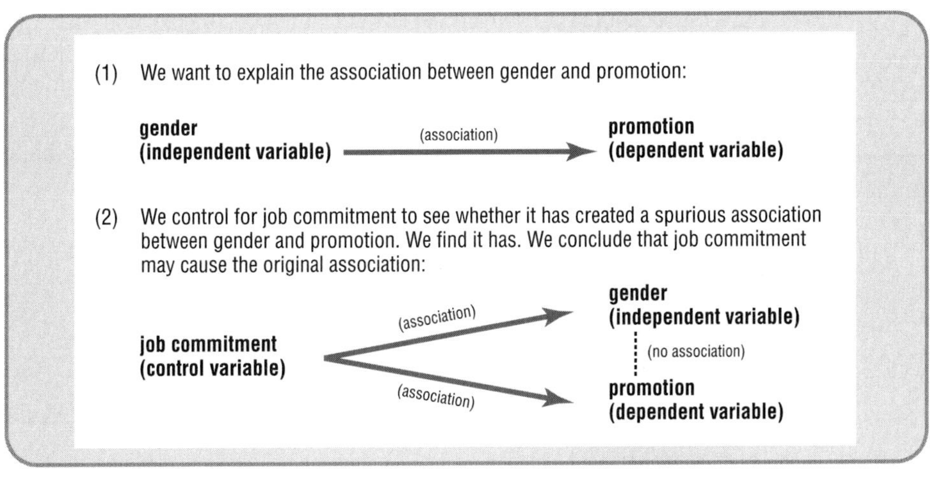


**✦ FIGURE 2.5 ✦**
**Establishing Causality by Testing an Association for Spuriousness**

weaken in only some categories of the control variable. It may even change direction entirely. Data analysis is therefore full of surprises, and accounting for the outcomes of statistical control requires a lot of creative theoretical thinking.

## Contingency Tables

A survey is not an ideal instrument for conducting exploratory research. It cannot provide the kind of deep and sympathetic understanding one gains from participant observation. On the other hand, surveys do produce results from which we can confidently generalize. If properly crafted, they provide valid measures of many sociologically important variables. Because they allow the same questions to be asked repeatedly, surveys enable researchers to establish the reliability of measures with relative ease. And finally, as we have just seen, survey data are useful for discovering relationships among variables, including cause-and-effect relationships.

One of the most useful tools for analyzing survey data is the contingency table. A **contingency table** is a cross-classification of cases by at least two variables that allows you to see how, if at all, the variables are associated. To understand this definition better, consider Table 2.1, taken from a nationwide Canadian poll conducted in 1999. One survey question was worded as follows: "As you may know, we have a number of genetically engineered or genetically modified foods in our food system. Do you strongly approve, somewhat approve, somewhat disapprove, or strongly disapprove of 'genetically engineered' or 'genetically modified' food?" Table 2.1 shows the results on this question for women and men. To simplify our analysis we combined the two categories of approval to form one category. We did the same for the two categories of disapproval. The table shows the number and percentage of Canadian women and men who approve and disapprove of genetically modified food. It allows us to see whether gender affects attitudes toward genetically modified food.

Note that gender, the independent variable (the presumed cause) is arrayed across the top of the table. Attitude toward genetically modified food (the presumed effect) is arrayed along the side of the table. The table consists of four cells, one defined by the cross-classification of approval and men, another by the cross-classification of approval and women, a third by the cross-classification of disapproval and men, and the fourth by the cross-classification of disapproval and women.

Although 2049 people were interviewed in the survey, 196 did not answer the question. All 1853 who responded can be assigned to cells of the table based on their characteristics. For example, men who approved of genetically modified food are assigned to the top left cell. Women who disapproved are placed in the lower right cell.

Do women and men differ in their attitude toward genetically modified food? Does the difference between the values of the independent variable produce a difference between the values of the dependent variable? Table 2.1 shows that 468 men and 295 women approved of genetically modified food. However, the absolute number of men and women in these cells tells us little because more men than women may have been interviewed. An easy way to take this into account is to convert the absolute numbers to percentages. Effectively, this asks: For every one hundred men, how many approved of genetically modified food? For every one hundred women, how many approved of genetically modified food?

✦ **TABLE 2.1** ✦

**Attitude toward Genetically Modified Food by Sex, Canada, 1999**

Source: Environics Research Group (1999).

| | Sex of Respondent | | |
|---|---|---|---|
| **Attitude to GM Food** | **Male** | **Female** | **Row Totals** |
| Approve | 468 (49.5%) | 295 (32.5%) | 763 (41.2%) |
| Disapprove | 478 (50.5%) | 612 (67.5%) | 1090 (58.8%) |
| Column totals | 946 (100.0%) | 907 (100.0%) | 1853 (100.0%) |

The percentages are in parentheses in the table: 49.5 percent of men approved of genetically modified food (468/946 × 100 = 49.5). The comparable figure for women is 32.5 percent. The independent variable (men versus women) produces a 17 percent difference in the approval of genetically modified food (49.5 – 32.5 = 17).

One reason for this difference might be that men are more politically conservative or right wing than women (Everitt, 1998; Howell and Day, 2000). A simple way to measure political preferences is to ask people which federal political party they would vote for "if an election were held today." In our analysis we have combined the Conservative Party with the Alliance/Reform Party on the political right, kept the Liberal Party as a centrist party on its own, and combined the NDP and the Bloc Québécois on the political left.

The analysis becomes more complex with three variables in the analysis. In Table 2.2 you will quickly notice that we effectively have a sub-table for men (on the left side) and another sub-table for women (on the right side). As well, since some respondents did not state a party preference, we have only 1503 people in this table.

Are there differences in levels of approval of genetically modified food among people who have different political party preferences? Yes and no. For men, those who support parties on the right or in the centre tend to approve of genetically engineered food by a small margin (52.7 and 54.8 percent, respectively). However, men who favour parties on the left are not as approving (36.1 percent). So, yes, for men party preference does make a difference in approval levels. For women, there are virtually no differences by party preference. Only about a third of women approve of genetically modified foods, and approval does not differ by party preference.

So we see that contingency tables are effective tools for causal analysis. They enable us to see whether there is an association between two variables and to examine the effects of control variables on the original association.

## Analysis of Existing Documents and Official Statistics

Apart from participant observation, experiments, and surveys, there is a fourth important sociological research method: the *analysis of existing documents and official statistics*. What do existing documents and official statistics have in common? They are created by people other than the researcher for purposes other than sociological research.

The three types of existing documents that sociologists have mined most widely and deeply are diaries, newspapers, and published historical works. For example, one of the early classics of American sociology, a study of Polish immigrants, is based on a close reading of immigrants' diaries and letters (Thomas and Znaniecki, 1958 [1918–20]). In recent decades, sociologists have made outstanding contributions to the study of political protest by systematically classifying nineteenth- and early twentieth-century French,

| Sex of Respondent | | Male | | | Female | | |
|---|---|---|---|---|---|---|---|
| | Political Preference | Right | Centre | Left | Right | Centre | Left |
| Attitude to GM Food | | | | | | | |
| Approve | | 149 (52.7%) | 207 (54.8%) | 48 (36.1%) | 57 (31.7%) | 123 (34.1%) | 55 (32.7%) |
| Disapprove | | 134 (47.3%) | 171 (45.2%) | 85 (63.9%) | 123 (68.3%) | 238 (65.9%) | 113 (67.3%) |
| Column totals | | 283 (100.0%) | 378 (100.0%) | 133 (100.0%) | 180 (100.0%) | 361 (100.0%) | 168 (100.0%) |

✦ **TABLE 2.2** ✦
**Attitude toward Genetically Modified Food by Sex, Controlling for Political Preference, Canada, 1999**

Source: Environics Research Group (1999).

Italian, and British newspaper accounts of strikes and demonstrations (Tilly, Tilly, and Tilly, 1975).

In recent decades, sociologists have tried to discover the conditions that led some countries to dictatorship and others to democracy, some to economic development and others to underdevelopment, some to become thoroughly globalized and others to remain less tied to global social processes. In trying to answer such broad questions, they have had to rely on published histories as their main source of data. No other method would allow the breadth of coverage and depth of analysis required for such comparative and historical work. For example, Barrington Moore spent a decade reading the histories of Britain, France, Russia, Germany, China, India, and other countries to figure out the social origins of dictatorship and democracy in the modern world (Moore, 1967). Immanuel Wallerstein canvassed the history of virtually the entire world to make sense of why some countries became industrialized while others remain undeveloped (Wallerstein, 1974–89). What distinguishes this type of research from purely historical work is the kind of questions posed by the researchers. Moore and Wallerstein asked the same kind of big, theoretical questions (and used the same kinds of research methods) as Marx and Weber. They have inspired a generation of younger sociologists to adopt a similar approach. Comparative-historical research is therefore one of the growth areas of the discipline.

Census data, police crime reports, and records of key life events are perhaps the most frequently used sources of official statistics. Canadian censuses have been conducted regularly since 1871. The modern census tallies the number of Canadian residents and classifies them by place of residence, race, ethnic origin, occupation, age, and hundreds of other variables (see Box 2.2). Statistics Canada publishes an annual Uniform Crime Reporting Survey that reports the number of crimes in Canada and classifies them by location and type of crime, the age and sex of offenders and victims, and other variables. Statistics Canada regularly publishes an *Annual Compendium of Vital Statistics* that reports births, deaths, marriages, and divorces by sex, age, and so forth.

Existing documents and official statistics have four main advantages over other types of data. First, they can save the researcher time and money. That is because they are usually available at no cost in libraries or on the World Wide Web. (See the Web Resources at the end of the chapter for useful Web sites containing official statistics.) Second, official statistics usually cover entire populations and are collected using rigorous and uniform methods, thus yielding high-quality data. Third, existing documents and official statistics are especially useful for historical analysis. The analysis of data from these sources is the only sociological method that does not require live subjects. Fourth, since the method does not require live subjects, reactivity is not a problem; the researcher's presence does not influence the subjects' behaviour.[5]

However, existing documents and official statistics share one big disadvantage. These data sources are not created with the researchers' needs in mind. They often contain biases that reflect the interests of the individuals and organizations that created them. Therefore, they may be less than ideal for research purposes and must always be treated cautiously.

To illustrate the potential bias of official statistics, consider how researchers compare the well-being of Canadians and people living in other countries. They sometimes use a measure called gross domestic product per capita (GDPpc). GDPpc is the total dollar value of goods and services produced in a country in a year divided by the number of people in the country. It is a convenient measure because all governments regularly publish GDPpc figures.

Most researchers are aware of a flaw in GDPpc, however. The cost of living varies from one country to the next. A dollar can buy you a cup of coffee in many Canadian restaurants but that same cup of coffee will cost you $6 in a Japanese restaurant. GDPpc looks at how many dollars you have, not at what the dollars can buy. Therefore, governments started publishing an official statistic called purchasing power parity (PPP). It takes the cost of goods and services in each country into account.

Significantly, however, both PPP and GDPpc ignore two serious problems. First, it is possible for GDPpc and PPP to go up while most people in a society become worse off. The richest people may earn all of the newly created wealth while the incomes of most

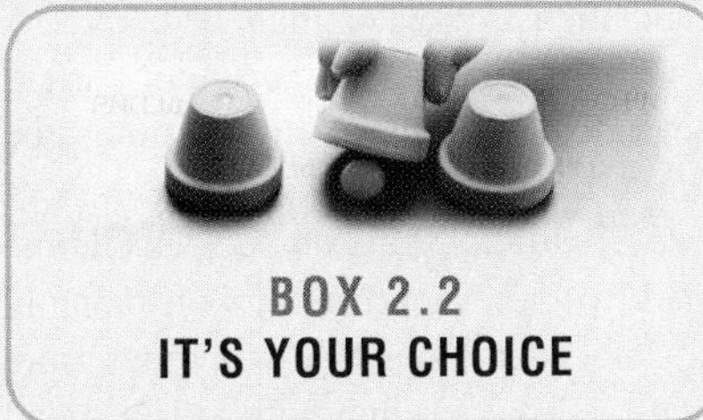

BOX 2.2
IT'S YOUR CHOICE

## WHO SHOULD BE COUNTED IN THE CANADIAN CENSUS?

It may seem odd to say so, but the census is a political document. Often seen as little more than a dry, scientific compilation of numbers, of interest mainly to bureaucrats and bean-counters, the census is actually a record of the political interests and power struggles that have shaped Canadian history (Brym, 1999; Curtis, 2001). In particular, the census has always counted certain kinds of people and excluded other. By rendering some people and groups "invisible" it profoundly influences social policy.

The census excluded some people right from the beginning. Jean Talon completed New France's first census in 1666. The count: 3215 French settlers. Talon did not count the much larger population of Aboriginal peoples, did not even try to estimate their number and socio-economic characteristics. That is because the first "Canadian" census was not a neutral tally of all residents of New France but a means of providing information that could be used to help wrest control of the territory from the Aboriginal peoples and establish a stable and prosperous French colony. Talon needed the numbers to rationalize the taxation of the French colonists, to further their economic development, to organize new colonization efforts, and, by implication, to interfere with, and even destroy, the livelihoods and lives of the Native population. The fact that Aboriginal peoples were not counted only added to the sense that they did not count. In this sense, the first census added to the mythology that New France was empty, virgin territory, just waiting for European colonists to exploit its riches. Could there be a more political purpose?

That was the seventeenth century. You might think that the tendency of the census to exclude some kinds of people is ancient history. If so, you would be wrong. The census still undercounts Aboriginal peoples. Members of dozens of reserves and settlements refuse to participate in the census as an act of political protest. They simply do not recognize the authority of the federal government. In addition, the census undercounts homeless people, who by definition have no fixed address. Still other Canadians refuse to participate in the census because they regard it as an invasion of their privacy.

The census has always counted certain kinds of people and excluded others. By rendering some people and groups "invisible" it profoundly influences social policy.
"Above the Street." Tom Campbell. 1995.

Apart from undercounting certain types of individuals, the census renders certain *characteristics* of individuals invisible and denies the existence of certain *groups*. For example:

- Until 1981, the census required every Canadian to specify one and only one ethnic or cultural origin. A person born to a Ukrainian-Canadian mother and an Italian-Canadian father may have felt attached to Ukrainian, Italian, *and* Canadian cultures. But such multiple ethnic attachments were not recognized by the census. People who felt they were of mixed heritage were counted as individuals in the census, but their multiple ethnic attachments were rendered invisible.
- Remarkably, it was only in 1996 that the census listed "Canadian" as a possible response to the ethnic question. Suddenly, "Canadian" became the most frequently chosen ethnic origin in the country. At midnight between May 13 and 14, 1996, Canada "lost" millions of citizens who had formerly specified European, Asian, African, and other ancestries. Before the 1990s, the census made the Canadian ethnic group invisible.
- Until recently the census let people say they were from Jamaica or China but it did not allow them to identify themselves as members of a "visible minority." The recognition of the diverse *racial* origins of Canadians is something quite new.
- Some people lived common law before 1981. However, the 1981 Census was the first to ask people if they were living common law.
- Women did most of the country's domestic labour before 1996 (as they do today), but only in 1996 did the census recognize unpaid domestic labour by asking questions about it.

So, we see that people who perform domestic labour, people living common law, members of visible minorities, members of the Canadian ethnic group, and people who identify with more than one ethnic group have been slighted by the Canadian census until recently. Homeless people and Aboriginal peoples are still slighted. This matters because government programs and government funding are based on census counts. If some types of people are undercounted, what negative implications might this have for them? Can you think of types of people other than those listed above who are rendered invisible by the Canadian census? Should they be counted, too? As a Canadian citizen, it's your choice.

people fall. Any measure of well-being that ignores the *distribution* of well-being in society is biased toward measuring the well-being of the well-to-do. Second, in some countries the gap in well-being between women and men is greater than in others. A country like Kuwait ranks quite high on GDPpc and PPP. However, women benefit far less than men do from that country's prosperity. A measure of well-being that ignores the gender gap is biased toward measuring the well-being of men.

This story has a happy ending. Realizing the biases in official statistics such as GDPpc and PPP, social scientists at the United Nations created two new measures of well-being in the mid-1990s. First, the human development index (HDI) combines PPP with a measure of average life expectancy and average level of education. The reasoning of the UN social scientists is that people living in countries that distribute well-being more equitably will live longer and be better educated. Second, the gender empowerment measure (GEM) combines the percentage of parliamentary seats, good jobs, and earned income controlled by women.

Table 2.3 lists the countries ranked first through fifth on all four measures of well-being we have mentioned. As you can see, the list of the top five countries differs for each measure. There is no "best" measure. Each measure has its own bias, and researchers have to be sensitive to these biases, as they must whenever they use official statistics.

## THE IMPORTANCE OF BEING SUBJECTIVE

In the following chapters, we show how participant observation, experiments, surveys, and the analysis of existing documents and official statistics are used in sociological research. You are well equipped for the journey. By now you should have a pretty good idea of the basic methodological issues that confront any sociological research project. You should also understand the strengths and weaknesses of some of the most widely used data collection techniques.

Our synopsis of sociology's "reality check" should not obscure the fact that sociological research questions often spring from real-life experiences and the pressing concerns of the day. But prior to sociological analysis, we rarely see things as they are. We see them as *we* are. Then, a sort of waltz begins. Subjectivity leads; objectivity follows. When the dance is finished, we see things more accurately.

Feminism provides a prime example of this process. Here is a *political* movement of people and ideas that, over the past 35 years, has helped shape the sociological *research* agenda. The division of labour in the household, violence against women, the effects of child-rearing responsibilities on women's careers, the social barriers to women's participation in politics and the armed forces, and many other related concerns were sociological "non-issues" before the rise of the modern feminist movement. Sociologists did not study these problems. Effectively, they did not exist for the sociological community (although they did, of course, exist for women). But subjectivity led. Feminism as a political movement brought these and many other concerns to the attention of the Canadian public.

✦ **TABLE 2.3** ✦
**Rank of Countries by Four Measures of Well-Being**

Source: Adapted from United Nations (1999a; 1999b; 1999c).

| Countries Ranked . . . | 1st | 2nd | 3rd | 4th | 5th |
|---|---|---|---|---|---|
| **Measure of Well-Being** | | | | | |
| Gross Domestic Product per Capita (1997) | Luxembourg | Bermuda | Switzerland, Liechtenstein | Norway | Japan |
| Purchasing Power Parity (1995) | Luxembourg | Brunei | United States | Switzerland | Hong Kong |
| Human Development Index (1995) | Canada | France | Norway | United States | Iceland |
| Gender Empowerment Measure (1998) | Norway | Sweden | Denmark | Finland | New Zealand |

Objectivity followed. Large parts of the sociological community began doing rigorous research on feminist-inspired issues and greatly refined our knowledge about them.

The entire sociological perspective began to shift as a growing number of scholars abandoned gender-biased research (Eichler, 1988; Tavris, 1992). Thus, approaching sociological problems from an exclusively male perspective is now less common than it used to be. For instance, it is less likely in 2003 than in 1973 that a sociologist would study work but ignore unpaid housework as one type of labour. Similarly, using data on one sex to draw conclusions about all people is now generally frowned upon. As these advances in sociological thinking show, and as has often been the case in the history of the discipline, objective sociological knowledge has been enhanced as a result of subjective experiences. And so the waltz continues. As in *Alice in Wonderland,* the question now is, "Will you, won't you, will you, won't you, join the dance?"

APPENDIX

# FOUR STATISTICS YOU SHOULD KNOW

In this book we sometimes report the results of sociological research in statistical form. You need to know four basic statistics to understand this material:

1. The *mean* (or arithmetic average). Imagine we know the height and annual income of the first nine people who entered your sociology classroom today. The height and income data are arranged in Table 2.4. From Table 2.4 you can calculate the mean by summing the values for each student or *case* and dividing by the number of cases. For example, the nine students are a total of 609 inches tall. Dividing 609 by 9, we get the mean height—67.7 inches.
2. The *median*. The mean can be deceiving when some cases have exceptionally high or low values. For example, in Table 2.4, the mean income is \$37 667, but because one lucky fellow has an income of \$200 000, the mean is higher than the income of seven of the nine students. It is therefore a poor measure of the centre of the income distribution. The median is a better measure. If you order the data from the lowest to the highest income, the median is the value of the case at the midpoint. The median income in our example is \$15 000. Four students earn more than that; four earn less. (Note: If there is an even number of cases, the midpoint is the average of the middle two values.)
3. *Correlation*. We have seen how valuable contingency tables are for analyzing relationships among variables. However, for variables that can assume many values, such as height and income, contingency tables become impracticably large. In such cases, sociologists prefer to analyze relationships among variables using *scatterplots*. Markers in the body of the graph indicate the score of each case on both the independent and dependent variables. The pattern formed by the markers is inspected visually and through the use of statistics. The strength of the association between the two variables is measured by a statistic called the *correlation coefficient* (signified as $r$). The value of $r$ can vary from –1.0 to 1.0. If the markers are scattered

**✦ TABLE 2.4 ✦**
**The Height and Annual Income of Nine Students**

| Student | Height (in inches) | Income ($000) |
|---|---|---|
| 1 | 67 | 5 |
| 2 | 65 | 8 |
| 3 | 60 | 9 |
| 4 | 64 | 12 |
| 5 | 72 | 40 |
| 6 | 68 | 15 |
| 7 | 70 | 20 |
| 8 | 69 | 30 |
| 9 | 74 | 200 |

around a straight, upward-sloping trend line, *r* takes a positive value. A positive *r* suggests that, as the value of one variable increases, so does the value of the other (see Figure 2.6, scatterplot 1). If the markers are scattered around a straight, downward-sloping trend line, *r* takes a negative value. A negative *r* suggests that, as the value of one variable increases, the value of the other decreases (see Figure 2.6, scatterplot 2). Whether positive or negative, the magnitude (or absolute value) of *r* decreases the more widely scattered the markers are from the line. If the degree of scatter is very high, $r = 0$. That is, there is no association between the variables (see Figure 2.6, scatterplot 3). However, a low *r* or an *r* of zero may derive from a relationship between the two variables that does not look like a straight line. It may look like a curve. As a result, it is always necessary to inspect scatterplots visually and not just rely on statistics like *r* to interpret the data.

**4.** A *rate* lets you compare the values of a variable among groups of different size. For example, let's say 1000 women got married last year in a city of 100 000 people and 2000 women got married in a city of 300 000 people. If you want to compare the likelihood of women getting married in the two cities, you have to divide the number of women who got married in each city by the total number of women in each city. Since 1000/100 000 = 0.01, or 1 percent, and 2000/300 000 = 0.00666 or 0.67 percent, we can say that the *rate* of women marrying is higher in the first city even though fewer women got married there last year. Note that rates are often expressed in percentage terms. In general, dividing the number of times an event occurs (e.g., a woman getting married) by the total number of people to whom the event could occur in principle (e.g., the number of women in a city) will give you the rate at which an event occurs.

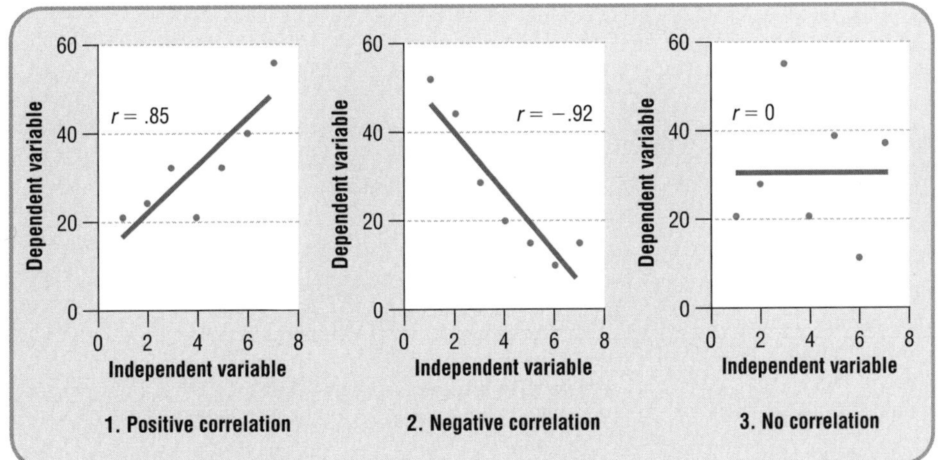


**FIGURE 2.6**
Correlation

## SUMMARY

1. The aim of science is to arrive at knowledge that is less subjective than other ways of knowing. A degree of objectivity is achieved by testing ideas against systematically collected data and leaving research open to public scrutiny.
2. The subjective side of the research enterprise is no less important than the objective side. Creativity and the motivation to study new problems from new perspectives arise from individual passions and interests.
3. Certain methodological issues have to be addressed in any research project to maximize its scientific value. These issues include reliability (consistency in measurement), validity (precision in measurement), generalizability (assessing the applicability of findings beyond the case studied), and causality (assessing cause-and-effect relations among variables).
4. One of the main sociological methods is participant observation, which involves carefully observing people's face-to-face interactions and actually participating in their lives over a long period of time. Participant observation is particularly useful for exploratory research, constructing grounded theory, and validating measures on the basis of internal criteria. Issues of external validity, reliability, generalizability, and causality make participant observation less useful for other research purposes.
5. An experiment is a carefully controlled artificial situation that allows researchers to isolate hypothesized causes and measure their effects by randomizing the allocation of subjects to experimental and control groups and exposing only the experimental group to an independent variable. Experiments get high marks for reliability and their analysis of causality, but issues of validity and generalizability make them less than ideal for many research purposes.
6. In a survey, people are asked questions about their knowledge, attitudes, or behaviour, either in a face-to-face or telephone interview or in a paper-and-pencil format. Surveys rank high on reliability and validity as long as researchers train interviewers well, phrase questions carefully, and take special measures to ensure high response rates. Generalizability is achieved through probability sampling, statistical control, and the analysis of causality by means of data manipulation.
7. Existing documents and official statistics are inexpensive and convenient sources of high-quality data. However, they must be used cautiously since they often reflect the biases of the individuals and organizations that create them rather than the interests of the researcher.

## GLOSSARY

An **association** exists between two variables if the value of one variable changes with the value of the other.

**Causality** means that a change in the independent variable ($x$) produces a change in the dependent variable ($y$). In analyzing survey data, we establish causality by demonstrating that (a) there is an association between $x$ and $y$, (b) $x$ precedes $y$, and (c) the introduction of a causally prior control variable does not result in the original association disappearing.

A **contingency table** is a cross-classification of cases by at least two variables that allows you to see how, if at all, the variables are associated.

**Control** in statistics refers to removing the influence of one or more variables on the association between an independent and a dependent variable.

A **control group** in an experiment is the group that is not exposed to the independent variable.

A **dependent variable** is the presumed effect in a cause-and-effect relationship.

An **experiment** is a carefully controlled artificial situation that allows researchers to isolate hypothesized causes and measure their effects precisely.

An **experimental group** in an experiment is the group that is exposed to the independent variable.

**Exploratory research** is an attempt to describe, understand, and develop a theory about a social phenomenon in the absence of much previous research on the subject.

**Generalizability** exists when research findings apply beyond the specific case examined.

A **hypothesis** is an unverified but testable statement about the relationship between two or more variables.

An **independent variable** is the presumed cause in a cause-and-effect relationship.

**Operationalization** is the procedure by which researchers establish criteria for assigning values to variables.

**Participant observation** involves carefully observing people's face-to-face interactions and actually participating in their lives over a long period of time, thus achieving a deep and sympathetic understanding of what motivates them to act in the way they do.

A **population** is the entire group about which the researcher wishes to generalize.

In a **probability sample**, the units have a known and non-zero chance of being selected.

Random means "by chance"—for example, having an equal and non-zero probability of being sampled. **Randomization** involves assigning individuals to groups by chance processes.

**Reliability** is the degree to which a measurement procedure yields consistent results.

A **sample** is the part of the population of research interest that is selected for analysis.

A **spurious association** exists between an independent variable and a dependent variable when the introduction of a causally prior control variable makes the initial association disappear.

In a **survey**, people are asked questions about their knowledge, attitudes, or behaviour, either in a face-to-face or telephone interview or in a paper-and-pencil format.

**Validity** is the degree to which a measure actually measures what it is intended to measure.

A **variable** is a concept that can take on more than one value.

## QUESTIONS TO CONSIDER

1. What is the connection between objectivity and subjectivity in sociological research?
2. What criteria do sociologists apply to select one method of data collection over another?
3. What are the methodological strengths and weaknesses of various methods of data collection?

## WEB RESOURCES

### Companion Web Site for This Book

http://www.brymsociologycompass.nelson.com

Begin by clicking on the Student Resources section of the Web site. Next, select the chapter you are currently studying from the pull-down menu. From the Student Resources page you will have easy access to InfoTrac College Edition®, MicroCase online exercises, and additional Web links. The Web site also has many useful tips to aid you in your study of sociology, including practice tests for each chapter.

### InfoTrac Search Terms

These search terms are provided to assist you in beginning to conduct research on this topic by visiting http://www.infotrac-college.com

**Census**
**Historical sociology**
**Participant observation**
**Sociology experiment**
**Sociological survey**

### Recommended Web Sites

Bill Trochim at Cornell University has put together a comprehensive and impressive sociological research methods course at http://trochim.human.cornell.edu/.

For a comprehensive listing of Web sites devoted to qualitative research, go to http://www.nova.edu/ssss/QR/web.html.

"Statistics Every Writer Should Know" is an exceptionally clear presentation of basic statistics on the World Wide Web at http://www.robertniles.com/stats/.

The World Wide Web contains many rich sources of official statistics. In preparing this book we relied heavily on data from the Web sites of Statistics Canada, http://www.statcan.ca/start.html, and the United Nations http://www.un.org.

## SUGGESTED READINGS

Earl Babbie. *The Practice of Social Research*, 9th ed. (Belmont, CA: Wadsworth, 2000 [1973]). This book is generally considered to be the best single-volume introduction to sociological research methods. Babbie is a real craftsman, and he explains in detail how to use all the tools in the sociologist's kit.

Margrit Eichler. *Nonsexist Research Methods: A Practical Guide* (Boston: Unwin Hyman, 1988). Shows how social science research has systematically produced biased findings by considering men the normal standard against which everyone should be judged and measured, and it provides remedies.

William Foote Whyte. *Street Corner Society: The Social Structure of an Italian Slum*, 3rd ed. (Chicago: University of Chicago Press, 1981 [1943]). This is perhaps the most famous and frequently cited participant observation study of all time. A must read for all aspiring sociologists.

## NOTES

1. Some scholars think it is possible to examine data without any preconceived notions and then formulate theories on the basis of this examination. However, they seem to form a small minority (Medawar, 1996: 12–32).
2. Subsequent analysis questioned the existence of a productivity effect in the Hawthorne study (Franke and Kaul, 1978). However, the general principle derived from the Hawthorne study—that social science researchers can influence their subjects—is now widely accepted (Webb et al., 1966).
3. Throughout, we convert U.S. dollars to Canadian dollars.
4. For clarity, we simplify Kay and Hagan's analysis.
5. When researchers finish analyzing survey data, they typically deposit computer-readable files of the data in an archive. This allows other researchers to conduct secondary analyses of survey data years later. Such data are widely used. They are not collected by government departments, but they have all the advantages of official statistics listed above, although they are based on samples rather than populations. The largest social science data archive includes Canadian data and is housed at the University of Michigan's Inter-University Consortium for Political and Social Research (ICPSR). The ICPSR Web site, at http://www.icpsr.umich.edu/, allows visitors to conduct elementary data analyses online.

PART

II

# Basic Social Processes

CHAPTER 3
Culture

CHAPTER 4
Socialization

CHAPTER 5
Interacton and Organization

CHAPTER 6
Deviance and Crime

## IN THIS CHAPTER, YOU WILL LEARN THAT

- Culture is the sum of shared ideas, practices, and material objects that people create to adapt to, and thrive in, their environments.
- Humans have thrived in their environments because of their unique ability to think abstractly, cooperate with one another, and make tools.
- Although sociologists recognize that biology sets broad human limits and potentials, most sociologists do not believe that specific human behaviours and social arrangements are biologically determined.
- In some respects, the development of culture makes people freer. For example, culture has become more diversified and consensus has declined in many areas of life, allowing people more choice in how they live.
- In other respects, the development of culture puts limits on who we can become. For example, the culture of buying consumer goods has become a virtually compulsory national pastime. Increasingly, therefore, people define themselves by the goods they purchase.

CHAPTER

3

# CULTURE

## CULTURE AS PROBLEM SOLVING

If you follow or participate in sports, you probably know that many athletes perform little rituals before each game. Consider Canadian hockey legend Wayne Gretzky. He never got his hair cut while playing on the road because the last time he did, his team lost. He always put his equipment on in the same order: left shin pad, left stocking, right shin pad, right stocking, pants, left skate, right skate, shoulder pads, left elbow pad, right elbow pad, and finally, jersey—with the right side tucked into his pants. During warm-up, he would always shoot his first puck far to the right of the goal. When he went back to the dressing room, he would drink a Diet Coke, a glass of ice water, a Gatorade, and another Diet Coke—in that order. Goalie Patrick Roy juggles a puck between periods and bounces it on the ground. "Then I put it in a special place where no one will find it and make off with it, otherwise...so the legend goes, bad luck could befall the culprit and he would suddenly turn into an alligator" ("Mad about Hockey: Superstitions," 2002). Meanwhile, forward Bruce Gardiner dips his hockey stick in a toilet before taking to the ice (Arace, 2000).

Wayne Gretzky. Culture can solve practical problems: Although some sports rituals are undoubtedly stranger than others, athletes often create a little culture to help them manage stress.

In baseball, Nomar Garciaparra, the star shortstop of the Boston Red Sox, can take 10 seconds to pull on his batting gloves repeatedly and kick the dirt with the toes of his cleats before he swings the bat. He believes this routine brings him luck. Garciaparra has other superstitious practices as well. For example, he never changes his cap. And although his name is really Anthony, he adopted Nomar, his father's name spelled backwards, for good luck.

Garciaparra's nervous pre-batting dance, as well as the superstitious practices of other athletes, makes some people chuckle. But these rituals put athletes at ease. Garciaparra's ritual certainly didn't hurt his league-leading .372 batting average in 2000. As Garciaparra says: "I have some superstitions, definitely, and they're always going to be there. I think a lot of people have them...[It] definitely helps because it gets you in the mind set" ("Garciaparra Explains His Superstitions," 2000).

Like soldiers going off to battle, undergraduate students about to write final exams, and other people in high-stress situations, athletes invent practices to help them stop worrying and focus on the job at hand. Some wear a lucky piece of jewellery or item of clothing. Others say special words or a quick prayer. Still others cross themselves. And then there are those who engage in more elaborate rituals. For example, two sociologists interviewed 300 university students about their superstitious practices before final exams. One student felt she would do well only if she ate a sausage and two eggs sunny-side up on the morning of each exam. She had to place the sausage vertically on the left side of her plate and the eggs to the right of the sausage so they formed the "100" percent she was aiming for (Albas and Albas, 1989). Of course, the ritual had a more direct influence on her cholesterol level than on her grades. Yet indirectly it may have had the desired effect. To the degree it helped relieve her anxiety and relax her, she may have done better on her exams.

When some people say *culture*, they refer to opera, ballet, art, and fine literature. For sociologists, however, this definition is too narrow.[1] Sociologists define **culture** broadly as all the ideas, practices, and material objects that people create to deal with real-life problems. For example, when the university student invented the ritual of preparing for exams by eating sausage and eggs arranged just so, she was creating culture in the sociological sense. This practice helped the student deal with the real-life problem of high anxiety.

Similarly, tools help people solve the problem of how to plant crops and build houses. Religion helps people face the problem of death and how to give meaning to life. Tools and religion are also elements of culture because they, too, help people solve real-life problems. Note, however, that religion, technology, and many other elements of culture differ from the superstitious practices of athletes and undergraduates in one important respect. Superstitions are often unique to the individuals who create them. In contrast, religion and technology are widely shared. They are even passed on from one generation to the next. How does cultural sharing take place? By means of communication and learning. Thus, shared culture is *socially* transmitted. We conclude that culture is composed of the socially transmitted ideas, practices, and material objects that enable people to adapt to, and thrive in, their environments.

## The Origins of Culture

You can appreciate the importance of culture for human survival by considering the predicament of early humans about 100 000 years ago. They lived in harsh natural environments. They had poor physical endowments, being slower runners and weaker fighters than many other animals. Yet, despite these disadvantages, they survived. More than that, they prospered and came to dominate nature. This was possible largely because they were the smartest creatures around. Their sophisticated brains enabled them to create cultural survival kits of enormous complexity and flexibility. These cultural survival kits contained three main tools. Each tool was a uniquely human talent. Each gave rise to a different element of culture.

The first tool in the human cultural survival kit was **abstraction,** the capacity to create general ideas or ways of thinking that are not linked to particular instances. **Symbols,** for example, are one important type of idea. They are things that carry particular meanings. Languages, mathematical notations, and signs are all sets of symbols. Symbols allow us to classify experience and generalize from it. For example, we recognize that we can sit on many objects but that only some of those objects have four legs, a back, and space for one person. We distinguish the latter from other objects by giving them a name: chairs. By the time a baby reaches the end of her first year, she has heard that word repeatedly and understands that it refers to a certain class of objects. True, a few chimpanzees have been taught how to make some signs with their hands. In this way, they have learned a few dozen words and how to string together some simple phrases. Yet even these extraordinarily intelligent animals cannot learn any rules of grammar, teach other chimps what they know, or advance much beyond the vocabulary of a two-year-old human (Pinker, 1994). Abstraction beyond the most rudimentary level is a uniquely human capacity. The ability to abstract enables humans to learn and transmit knowledge in a way no other animal can.

**Cooperation** is the second main tool in the human cultural survival kit. It is the capacity to create a complex social life. This is accomplished by establishing **norms,** or generally accepted ways of doing things. When we raise children and build schools, we are cooperating to reproduce and advance the human race. When we create communities and industries, we are cooperating by pooling resources and encouraging people to acquire specialized skills. This enables them to accomplish things that no person could possibly do on his or her own. An enormous variety of social arrangements and institutions, ranging from health care systems through forms of religious worship to political parties, demonstrates the advanced human capacity to cooperate and follow norms. Of course, there is also plenty of war, crime, and revolution in the world. However, even when people engage in conflict they must cooperate and respect norms or fail to achieve their survival aims. The armed robber who is left stranded by his getaway driver will be caught; the navy captain whose sailors mutiny will lose the battle.

By acquiring specialized skills, people are able to accomplish things that no person could possibly do on his or her own.

**Production** is the third main tool in the human cultural survival kit. It involves making and using tools and techniques that improve our ability to take what we want from nature. Such tools and techniques are known as **material culture.** Of course, all animals take from nature in order to subsist, and an ape may sometimes use a rock to break another object. But only humans are sufficiently intelligent and dexterous to *make* tools and use them to produce everything from food to computers. Understood in this sense, production is a uniquely human activity.

Table 3.1 illustrates each of the basic human capacities and their cultural offshoots with respect to three types of human activity: medicine, law, and religion. It shows, for all three types of activity, how abstraction, cooperation, and production give rise to specific kinds of ideas, norms, and elements of material culture. In medicine, theoretical ideas about the way our bodies work are evaluated using norms about how to test theories experimentally. Experimentation, in turn, results in the production of new medicines and therapies. These are part of material culture. In law, values, or shared ideas about what is right and wrong, are embodied in a legal code, or norms defining illegal behaviour and punishments for breaking the law. The application of the law requires the creation of courts and jails, which are also part of material culture. Religious folklore—traditional ideas about

✦ **TABLE 3.1** ✦
**The Building Blocks of Culture**

Source: Adapted from Bierstedt (1963).

| Human Capacities | | | |
|---|---|---|---|
| | **Abstraction** | **Cooperation** | **Production** |
| | ↓ | ↓ | ↓ |
| | **Ideas** | **Norms** | **Material Culture** |
| **Elements of Culture** | | | |
| | | **Cultural Activities** | |
| Medicine | Theories | Experiments | Treatments |
| Law | Values | Laws | Courts, jails |
| Religion | Religious folklore | Religious customs | Church art, architecture |

how the universe was created, the meaning of life, and so forth—is expressed in religious customs regarding how to worship and how to treat fellow human beings. Religious folklore and customs can give rise to material culture that includes churches, their associated art and architecture, and so forth. As these examples suggest, then, the capacity for abstraction, cooperation, and production are evident in all spheres of culture.

In concluding this discussion of the origins of culture, we must note that people are usually rewarded when they follow cultural guidelines and punished when they do not. These rewards and punishments aimed at ensuring conformity are known as **sanctions.** Taken together they are called the system of **social control.** Rewards (or positive sanctions) include everything from praise and encouragement to money and power. Punishments (or negative sanctions) range from avoidance and contempt to physical violence and arrest. Punishment is more severe for the violation of core norms. These are norms that people feel are essential for the survival of their group or their society. Sociologist William Graham Sumner (1940 [1907]) called such core norms *mores* (the Latin word for customs, pronounced MORE-ays). Punishment is less severe for the violation of less important norms (which Sumner called *folkways*).

Despite efforts to control them, people often reject elements of existing culture and create new elements of culture. Reasons for this are discussed below and in Chapters 6 (Deviance and Crime), 14 (The Mass Media), and 17 (Collective Action and Social Movements). Here it is enough to say that just as social control is needed to ensure stable patterns of interaction, so resistance to social control is needed to ensure cultural innovation and social renewal. Stable but vibrant societies are able to find a balance between social control and cultural innovation.

## CULTURE AND BIOLOGY

We have seen how the human capacity for abstraction, cooperation, and production enables us to create culture and makes us distinctively human. This capacity is built on a solid biological foundation. For example, without supple vocal chords we could not speak. Without the ability to grasp small objects we could not make tools. Without complex brains we could not even conceive of sophisticated social institutions such as universities and armies. Biology, as every sociologist recognizes, sets broad human limits and potentials, including the potential to create culture.

However, some students of human behaviour who are trained as biologists go a step farther. Practitioners of what originated as sociobiology and is now commonly known as evolutionary psychology claim that genes—chemical units that carry traits from parents to children—account not just for physical characteristics but also for specific behaviours and social practices (Wilson, 1975). From their point of view, genes determine not just whether our eyes are blue or brown, but also whether we are law abiding, whether we are sexually faithful to our partners, and just about every other aspect of our social behaviour. This kind of argument has become increasingly popular since the early 1970s. The overwhelming majority of sociologists disagrees with it, however. It is therefore worth devoting a few paragraphs to the misconceptions of evolutionary psychology (see also Chapter 9, Sexuality and Gender).

Evolutionary psychology's starting point is Charles Darwin's theory of evolution. Darwin (1859) observed wide variations in the physical characteristics of members of each species. For example, some deer can run quickly. Others run slower. The colouring of some frogs lets them blend perfectly into their surroundings. The colouring of other frogs does not camouflage them as well. Some tigers are more ferocious than others. Because of such variations, some members of each species—the quicker deer, the better-camouflaged frog, the more ferocious tiger—are more likely to survive. In general, the species members who are best adapted to their environments (or "fittest") are most likely to live long enough to have offspring. Therefore, concluded Darwin, the species characteristics that endure are those that increase the survival chances of the species.

Contemporary evolutionary psychologists make similar arguments about human behaviour and social arrangements. Typically, *they first identify a supposedly universal human behavioural trait.* For example, they claim that men are more likely than women to want many sexual partners.

*They next offer an explanation as to why this behaviour increases survival chances.* Thus, to continue with our example, they account for supposedly universal male promiscuity and female fidelity as follows: Every time a man ejaculates, he produces hundreds of millions of sperm, and he can achieve this feat from puberty until old age. In contrast, a woman typically releases fewer than 400 mature eggs from her ovaries over her entire lifetime—one egg per month between puberty and menopause in periods when she is not pregnant. From these observed sex differences, evolutionary psychologists jump to the assertion that men and women develop different "reproductive strategies" to increase the chance they will reproduce their genes. Specifically, because a woman produces few eggs, she improves her chance of reproducing her genes if she has a mate who stays around to help and protect her during those few occasions when she is pregnant, gives birth, and nurses a small infant. Because a man's sperm is so plentiful, he improves his chance of reproducing his genes if he tries to impregnate as many women as possible. In short, women's desire for a single mate and men's desire for many sexual partners is simply the way men and women play out the game of survival of the fittest. Even male rapists, writes one evolutionary psychologist, may just be "doing the best they can to maximize their [reproductive] fitness" (Barash, 1981: 55).

*The final part of the evolutionary psychologists' argument is that the behaviour in question cannot be changed.* Once metal pathways are stamped into a computer's circuit boards they determine how electrical current can flow. In much the same way, the characteristics that maximize the survival chances of a species supposedly become encoded or "hardwired" in our genes. It follows that what exists is necessary.

Most sociologists and many biologists and psychologists are critical of the reasoning of evolutionary psychologists. In the first place, *many behaviours discussed by evolutionary psychologists are not universal and some are not even that common.* Consider male promiscuity. Is it true that men are promiscuous and that women are not? Canadian research shows a trend toward convergence in the sexual behaviour of women and men (Hobart, 1996: 151; Nelson and Robinson, 2002: 313). In the United States in 1996, only a small minority of adult American men (20 percent) claimed they had more than one sex partner in the previous year (see Table 3.2). The figure for adult American women is lower, but not dramatically so (11 percent). Moreover, if we consider married adults only, the figures fall to 4 percent for men and 2 percent for women, a small and statistically insignificant difference (see Table 3.3). True, some groups of men are more promiscuous than others. For example, 41 percent of unmarried American men claim to have had more than one sex partner in the previous year. The proportion is higher still for unmarried young men. You can exercise your sociological imagination to explain why certain social arrangements such as the institution of marriage and male youth culture account for variations in promiscuity. For present purposes, however, the important point is that the evolutionary

**✦ TABLE 3.2 ✦**
**Number of Sex Partners by Respondent's Sex, United States, 1996 (in percent)**

Source: National Opinion Research Center (1999).

| | Respondent's Sex | |
|---|---|---|
| **Number of Sex Partners** | **Male** | **Female** |
| 0 or 1 | 80 | 89 |
| More than 1 | 20 | 11 |
| Total | 100 | 100 |
| *n* | 870 | 1 008 |

**✦ TABLE 3.3 ✦**
**Number of Sex Partners by Respondent's Sex, United States, 1996, Married Respondents Only (in percent)**

Source: National Opinion Research Center (1999).

| | Respondent's Sex | |
|---|---|---|
| **Number of Sex Partners** | **Male** | **Female** |
| 0 or 1 | 96 | 98 |
| More than 1 | 4 | 2 |
| Total | 100 | 100 |
| *n* | 487 | 605 |

psychologists' claim that men *in general* are highly promiscuous, and much more promiscuous than women, is false. So are many of their other claims about so-called behavioural constants or universals.

The second big problem with evolutionary psychology is that one of its key arguments—that specific behaviours and social arrangements are associated with specific genes—has never been verified. Researchers *have* identified gene mutations associated with many diseases, including more than 20 types of hereditary cancer (Fearon, 1997). Most people are optimistic that these discoveries will lead to new medical treatments. But what is true for diseases is not true for behaviours and social arrangements. No convincing evidence supports the view that specific behaviours and social arrangements are associated with specific genes. Therefore, when it comes to supporting their key argument, evolutionary psychologists have little to stand on apart from a fragile string of maybes and possibilities: "[W]e *may* have to open our minds and admit the *possibility* that our need to maximize our [reproductive] fitness *may* be whispering somewhere deep within us and that, *know it or not,* most of the time we are heeding these whisperings [*our emphasis*]" (Barash, 1981: 31). Maybe. Then again, maybe not.

Finally, even if researchers eventually discover an association between particular genes and particular behaviours, it would be wrong to conclude that variations among people are due just to their genes. Why? Because, in the words of R. C. Lewontin, one of the world's leading geneticists, "variations among individuals within species are a unique consequence of both genes *and environment* in a constant interaction . . . [and] random variation in growth and division of cells during development [*our emphasis*]" (Lewontin, 1991: 26–7). Genes *never* develop without environmental influence. The genes of a human embryo, for example, are profoundly affected by whether the mother consumes the recommended daily dosage of calcium or nearly overdoses daily on crack cocaine. And what the mother consumes is, in turn, determined by many social factors. Even if one inherits a mutant cancer gene, the chance of developing cancer is strongly influenced by diet, exercise, tobacco consumption, and factors associated with occupational and environmental pollution. Some cancers are more heritable than others, but even the most heritable cancers seem to be much more strongly influenced by environmental than genetic factors (Fearon, 1997; Hoover, 2000; Kevles, 1999; Lichtenstein et al., 2000; Remennick, 1998). It follows that the pattern of your life is not entirely hardwired by your genes (see Figure 3.1). Changes in social environment do produce physical and, to an even greater degree, behavioural change. However, to determine the effects of the social environment on human behaviour, we have to abandon the premises of evolutionary psychology and develop sociological skills for analyzing the effects of social structure and culture. We begin that task by first considering how it is possible to observe culture in an unbiased fashion.

**FIGURE 3.1**

**A Genetic Misconception**

When scientists announced they had finished sequencing the human genome on June 26, 2000, some people thought all human characteristics could be read from the human genetic "map." They cannot. The functions of most genes are still unknown. Moreover, because genes mutate randomly and interact with environmental (including social) conditions, the correspondence between genetic function and behavioural outcome is highly uncertain.

Source: "Human Genome..." (2000).

## CULTURE FROM THE INSIDE AND THE OUTSIDE

"I was once introduced to an interesting woman at a party and began a conversation with her that started agreeably," recalls Robert Brym. "Within 10 minutes, however, I found myself on the other side of the room, my back pressed hard against the wall, trying to figure out how I could politely end our interaction. I wasn't immediately aware of the reason for my discomfort. Only after I told the woman I had to make an important phone call and had left the room did I realize the source of the problem: She had invaded my culturally defined comfort zone. Research shows that the average North American prefers to stand 75 to 90 centimetres away from strangers or acquaintances when they are engaged in face-to-face interaction (Hall, 1959: 158–80). But this woman had recently arrived from her home in a part of the Middle East where the culturally defined comfort zone is generally smaller. She stood only about 60 centimetres away from me as we spoke. Without thinking about it, I retreated half a step. Without thinking about it, she advanced half a step. And soon we had waltzed across the faculty club lounge, completely unaware of what we were doing, until I had no more room to retreat and had to concoct a means of escape."

As this example shows, culture, despite its central importance in human life, is often invisible. That is, people tend to take their own culture for granted; it usually seems so sensible and natural they rarely think about it. In contrast, people are often startled when confronted by cultures other than their own. That is, the ideas, norms, and techniques of other cultures frequently seem odd, irrational, and even inferior.

Judging another culture exclusively by the standards of one's own is known as **ethnocentrism.** Ethnocentrism impairs sociological analysis (see Box 3.1). This can be illustrated by a practice that seems bizarre to many Westerners: cow worship among Hindu peasants in India.

Hindu peasants refuse to slaughter cattle and eat beef because, for them, the cow is a religious symbol of life. Pin-up calendars throughout rural India portray beautiful women with the bodies of fat, white cows, milk jetting out of each teat. Cows are permitted to wander the streets, defecate on the sidewalks, and stop to chew their cud in busy intersections or on railroad tracks, causing traffic to come to a complete halt. In Madras, police

## BOX 3.1 SOCIOLOGY AT THE MOVIES

*Austin Powers: The Spy Who Shagged Me* (1999)

### *AUSTIN POWERS: THE SPY WHO SHAGGED ME* (1999)

All Austin Powers movies are about super-spy Austin Powers battling his arch-enemy Dr. Evil, who plans to destroy the world. In *The Spy Who Shagged Me* (1999), Austin Powers and Dr. Evil—both played by Toronto's Mike Myers—happen to have been frozen in the 1960s and thawed in the 1990s. Dr. Evil figures he can defeat Austin Powers if he returns to 1969 in a time machine and steals the legendary sexual energy or "mojo" from Powers' still-frozen body. However, the mojo-less Powers remains steadfast in his determination to save the world and, along the way, recapture the mojo that makes him "deadly to his enemies" and, despite his bad teeth, "irresistible to women." He is assisted in his efforts by beautiful and cheerfully randy CIA agent Felicity Shagwell (played by Heather Graham). The film, like its predecessor, is half-satire and half-tribute to the hugely popular spy movies and TV series of the 1960s and 1970s (*Our Man Flint, The Thomas Crown Affair, The Avengers, The Man from U.N.C.L.E., Get Smart*) and, especially, the Sean Connery–era James Bond films.

*The Spy Who Shagged Me* is funny because the audience is well aware of the enormous cultural changes that have taken place over the past three or four decades, while Austin Powers is not. We laugh at his assumption that it is still fashionable—if not the height of sophistication—to don a velvet jumpsuit, frilly shirt, heavy necklace, and big, dark-framed glasses. We roar at his presumption that using the slang of the 1960s ("Yeah, baby!") will make him a "groovy" guy. And what of his efforts to prove himself an expert at "shagging"? We might consider his attempts at seduction to be blatant sexual harassment. If he could read our minds, Austin Powers would no doubt look bemused—or simply call us "uptight."

Apart from being a funny movie, *The Spy Who Shagged Me* also has sociological significance. For one thing, it forcefully reminds us that no culture is static. Cultural changes that occur within even a few short decades can be profound. Many of the fashions, expressions, and behaviours we take for granted and think of as "cool" today will likely seem ridiculous to us tomorrow. You might even consider putting together a scrapbook of today's fads and fashions, to be opened in just a few years. Inevitably, when the time comes to open your "time capsule," you will experience a mixture of nostalgia and amusement.

The sociological significance of *The Spy Who Shagged Me* lies also in the way it gently mocks certain aspects of our culture today. Rather than assuming that our current culture is superior to the culture of the past, it pokes fun at New Age thinking, the many support groups for chemical addictions and other problems that dot the social scene (the so-called recovery movement), concerns over political correctness, and, of course, our seemingly endless fascination with determining which fashionable coffee chain churns out the best cup of java. By making the contemporary world a foreign world to Austin Powers, the movie invites us to turn a critical eye on our own culture. This, to be sure, is no easy task. As the anthropologist Ralph Linton (1936) observed many years ago, "[t]he last thing a fish would ever notice would be water." Much of the sociological value of *The Spy Who Shagged Me* is that it makes us notice the water.

stations maintain fields where stray cows that have fallen ill can graze and be nursed back to health. The government even runs old-age homes for cows where dry and decrepit cattle are kept free of charge. All this seems utterly inscrutable to most Westerners, for it takes place amid poverty and hunger that could presumably be alleviated if only the peasants would slaughter their "useless" cattle for food instead of squandering scarce resources feeding and protecting them.

Many Westerners find the Indian practice of cow worship bizarre. However, cow worship performs a number of useful economic functions and is in that sense entirely rational. By viewing cow worship exclusively as an outsider (or, for that matter, exclusively as an insider), we fail to see its rational core.

According to anthropologist Marvin Harris, however, ethnocentrism misleads many Western observers (Harris, 1974: 3–32). Cow worship, it turns out, is an economically rational practice in rural India. For one thing, Indian peasants cannot afford tractors, so cows are needed to give birth to oxen, which are in high demand for plowing. For another, the cows produce hundreds of millions of pounds of recoverable manure, about half of which is used as fertilizer and half as a cooking fuel. With oil, coal, and wood in short supply, and with the peasants unable to afford chemical fertilizers, cow dung is, well, a godsend. What is more, cows in India don't cost much to maintain since they eat mostly food that is not fit for human consumption. And they represent an important source of protein and a livelihood for members of low-ranking castes, who have the right to dispose of the bodies of dead cattle. These "untouchables" eat beef and form the workforce of India's large leather craft industry. The protection of cows by means of cow worship is thus a perfectly sensible and highly efficient economic practice. It only seems irrational when judged by the standards of Western agribusiness.

We can draw much the same lesson from Robert Brym's hurried exit from the faculty club lounge. Culture is most clearly visible from the margins, as it were. We see its contours most sharply if we are neither too deeply immersed in it (as Robert was during his conversation) nor too much removed from it (as many Western observers are when they analyze cow worship in India). Said differently, if you refrain from taking your own culture for granted and judging other cultures by the standards of your own, you will have taken important first steps toward developing a sociological understanding of culture.

## THE TWO FACES OF CULTURE

Culture has two faces. First, culture provides us with an opportunity to exercise our *freedom*. We create elements of culture in our everyday life to solve practical problems and express our needs, hopes, joys, and fears.

However, creating culture is just like any other act of construction in that we need raw materials to get the job done. The raw materials for the culture we create consist of cultural elements that either existed before we were born or other people created since our birth. We may put these elements together in ways that produce something genuinely new. But there is no other well to drink from, so existing culture puts limits on what we can think and do. In that sense, culture *constrains* us. This is culture's second face.

Because culture can be seen both as an opportunity for freedom and as a source of constraint, we examine both faces of culture below. We begin with the view that culture is an opportunity for freedom. We first establish that people are not just passive recipients but active producers and interpreters of culture. Next, we show that the range of cultural choices available to us has never been greater because we live in a society characterized by unparalleled cultural diversity. We then show how globalization processes contribute to the diversification of culture and broaden the range of cultural choices open to us. We argue that this has led to the emergence of a new, "postmodern" era of culture. After developing the idea that culture is a source of freedom, we turn to culture's flip side as a source of social constraint.

## Culture as Freedom

### Cultural Production

Until the 1960s, many sociologists argued that culture is simply a "reflection" of society. Using the language of Chapter 2, Research Methods, we can say they regarded culture as a dependent variable. Television, for example, became a household necessity after the Second World War. Sociologists noted that its spread depended on the existence of an affluent and technologically advanced society. Moreover, they said, the programming content of television revealed much about the concerns and aspirations of people in post–Second World War society. As a part of both material and symbolic culture, then, television was said to reflect the society from which it emerged.

More recently, sociologists have emphasized culture as an *independent* variable. Increasingly, they stress that people do not just accept culture passively. That is, we are hardly inert and empty vessels into which society pours a defined assortment of beliefs, symbols, and values. Instead, we actively produce and interpret culture, creatively fashioning it to suit our own needs.

British literary critic Richard Hoggart (1958) and social historian E. P. Thompson (1968) wrote pioneering works emphasizing how people produce and interpret culture. Hoggart and Thompson showed how working-class people shape the cultural milieux in which they live. For instance, religious ideas and secular reading materials may be created for members of the working class by people in higher-class positions—"from the outside," as it were. What then happens, according to Hoggart and Thompson, is that members of the working class make sense of these elements of culture on their own terms. In general, audiences always change ideas to make them meaningful to themselves. This line of thought was developed by sociologist Stuart Hall (1980) and his colleagues, who showed how people mould culture to fit their sense of self. It gave rise to the field of cultural studies, which overlaps the sociology of culture (Griswold, 1992; Long, 1997; Wolff, 1999). Later in this chapter and again in Chapter 14, The Mass Media, we take up some of the themes introduced by Hoggart, Thompson, and Hall.

### Cultural Diversity

The fact that people actively produce and interpret culture means that, to a degree, we are at liberty to choose how culture influences us. We are increasingly able to exercise that ability because there is more to choose from. Like many societies in the world, Canadian society is undergoing rapid cultural diversification, partly due to changes in the countries of origin of immigrants to Canada. Although for decades immigrants have made up about 16 percent of Canada's population (and, in 1996, accounted for 17.4 percent), they are now arriving from places such as Asia and the Caribbean rather than traditional sources of immigrants in Europe. Ethnically and racially, Canada is a more heterogeneous society now than it has ever been during its history. According to the 1996 Census, about 3.2 million Canadians (about 11 percent of the population) are members of visible minority groups. Based on recent projections, the visible minority groups population will increase to around 7 million by 2016, just under a fifth of Canada's projected total population (Statistics Canada, 1998a: 75).

The cultural diversification of Canadian society is evident in all aspects of life, from the growing popularity of Latino and Brazilian music, through the increasing influence of Asian design in clothing and architecture, to the ever-broadening international assortment of foods consumed by most Canadians. Marriage between people of different ethnic groups is widespread, and interracial marriage is increasingly accepted (See Chapter 12, Families).

At the political level, however, cultural diversity has become a source of conflict. This is nowhere more evident than in the debates that have surfaced in recent years concerning curricula in the Canadian educational system.

Although each province and territory in Canada holds jurisdiction over education, it was common until recent decades for schools across Canada to stress the common elements of our culture, history, and society. Students learned the historical importance of the "charter groups"—the English and the French—in Canada's history. School curricula typically neglected the contributions of non-whites and non-French/non-English to Canada's historical, literary, artistic, and scientific development. Moreover, students learned little about the less savoury aspects of Canadian history, including Canada's racist immigration policies that actively sought to preserve Canada's "English stock" by restricting or denying entry to certain groups (see Chapter 8, Race and Ethnicity). In general, history books were written from the perspective of the victors, not the vanquished.

For the past few decades, some educators have argued that the experiences of women as well as Aboriginal peoples, visible minorities, and other disadvantaged groups must be incorporated into Canada's classrooms. In the words of one group of experts, "The purpose of schooling must be to 'empower'...[minority groups], to give them the ability to participate fully in struggles, large and small, to gain respect, dignity and power" (Gaskell, McLaren, and Novogrodsky, 1995: 105). Such advocates of multiculturalism in education suggest we must bring our educational system in line with Canada's status as the first officially multicultural society in the world. They point out that, unlike the United States, which has been described by some as a unicultural "melting pot," Canada has attempted to preserve and promote multiculturalism as an ideal. For example, in launching its multiculturalism policy in 1971, the Canadian government declared that Canada, while officially bilingual, had no "official" culture—that is, none of the distinguishable cultures in Canada took precedence over the others. Moreover, with the passage of the Canadian Multicultural Act in 1988, the federal government confirmed its commitment to the recognition of all Canadians "as full and equal participants in Canadian society." In short, multiculturalists argue that, to the extent that existing curricula are biased, both in what is included and in what is excluded, our schools are failing to provide students with the type of education a country truly devoted to multiculturalism must demand.

Canada continues to diversify culturally.

Most critics of multiculturalism in education do not argue against teaching cultural diversity. What they fear is that multicultural education is being taken too far (Fekete, 1994; Glazer, 1997; Schlesinger, 1991; Stotsky, 1999; see Box 3.2). Specifically, they say multiculturalism has three negative consequences:

1. Critics believe that multicultural education hurts minority students by forcing them to spend too much time on noncore subjects. To get ahead in the world, they say, one needs to be skilled in English and math. By taking time away from these subjects, multicultural education impedes the success of minority group members in the work world. (Multiculturalists counter that minority students develop pride and self-esteem from a curriculum that stresses cultural diversity. They argue that this helps minority students get ahead in the work world.)
2. Critics also believe that multicultural education causes political disunity and results in more interethnic and interracial conflict. Therefore, they want school and post-secondary curricula to stress the common elements of the national experience and highlight Europe's contribution to our culture. (Multiculturalists reply that political unity and interethnic and interracial harmony simply maintain inequality in Canadian society. Conflict, they say, while unfortunate, is often necessary to achieve equality between majority and minority groups.)
3. Finally, critics of multiculturalism complain that it encourages the growth of **cultural relativism.** Cultural relativism is the opposite of ethnocentrism. It is the belief that all cultures and all cultural practices have equal value. The trouble with this view is that some cultures oppose the most deeply held values of most Canadians. Other cultures promote practices that most Canadians consider inhumane. Should we respect racist and anti-democratic cultures, such as the apartheid regime that existed in South Africa from 1948 until 1992? What about female circumcision, which is still widely practised in Somalia, Sudan, and Egypt (see Box 3.2)? Or the Australian Aboriginal practice of driving spears through the limbs of criminals (Garkawe, 1995)? Critics argue that to the degree it promotes cultural relativism, a truly multicultural system of education might encourage respect for practices that are abhorrent to most Canadians. (Multiculturalists reply that cultural relativism need not be taken to such an extreme. *Moderate* cultural relativism encourages tolerance, and it should be promoted.)

Clearly, multiculturalism in education is a complex and emotional issue that requires much additional research and debate. It is worth pondering here, however, because it says something important about the state of Canadian culture today and, more generally, about how world culture has developed since our remote ancestors lived in tribes. In general, as we will now see, cultures tend to become more heterogeneous over time, with important consequences for everyday life.

## From Diversity to Globalization

In preliterate or tribal societies, cultural beliefs and practices are virtually the same for all group members. For example, many tribal societies organize **rites of passage.** These are cultural ceremonies that mark the transition from one stage of life to another (e.g., baptisms, confirmations, weddings) or from life to death (e.g., funerals). These religious rituals involve elaborate body painting, carefully orchestrated chants and movements, and so forth. They are conducted in public. No variation from prescribed practice is allowed. Culture is homogeneous (Durkheim, 1976 [1915]).

In contrast, preindustrial Western Europe and North America were rocked by artistic, religious, scientific, and political forces that fragmented culture. The Renaissance, the Protestant Reformation, the Scientific Revolution, the French and American revolutions—between the fourteenth and eighteenth centuries, all of these movements involved people questioning old ways of seeing and doing things. Science placed skepticism about established authority at the very heart of its method. Political revolution proved there was nothing ordained about who should rule and how they should do so. Religious dissent

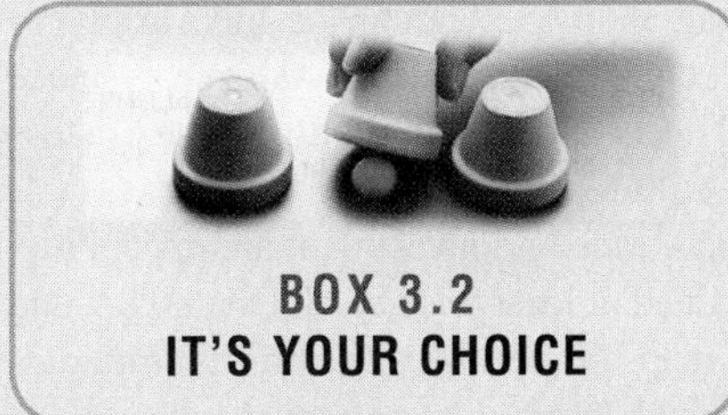

## BOX 3.2 IT'S YOUR CHOICE

### FEMALE GENITAL MUTILATION

In the early 1990s, a Somali woman, Khadra Hassan Farah, sought refugee status in Canada. Khadra had fled her country with her 10-year-old daughter, Hodan, fearing that if she remained, her daughter would be forced to undergo female genital mutilation. In 1993, Khadra and her daughter were granted refugee status after immigration officials ruled that Hodan's "right to personal security would be greatly infringed" if she were forced to return to Somalia (Amnesty International, 1998).

Female genital mutilation is defined by the World Health Organization as "all procedures involving partial or total removal of the external female genitalia or other injury to the female genital organs whether for cultural or other non-therapeutic reasons" (World Health Organization, 1998a). These procedures are usually performed without anesthesia by elderly women who lack medical training. Female genital mutilation results in pain, humiliation, psychological trauma, and loss of sexual pleasure. It is also associated with infection, shock, injury to neighbouring organs, and severe bleeding in the short term. In the long term, it is associated with infertility, chronic infections in the urinary tract and reproductive system, increased susceptibility to hepatitis B and HIV/AIDS, and so on.

Although frequently associated with Islam, female genital mutilation is a social custom, not a religious practice (Ontario Consultants on Religious Tolerance, 2000a). According to data compiled by the World Health Organization, it is nearly universal in Somalia, Djibouti, and Egypt, and very common in other parts of Africa (see Table 3.4). More than 132 million women and girls worldwide have undergone female genital mutilation. About 2 million girls are at risk of undergoing it every year (World Health Organization, 1998a).

Female genital mutilation is typically performed as a rite of passage on girls between the ages of 4 and 14. In some cultures, it is believed to enhance female fertility. However, it is most commonly based on the assumption that women are naturally "unclean" and "masculine" inasmuch as they possess a vestige of a "male" sex organ, the clitoris. From this point of view, women who have not experienced genital mutilation are thought to be more likely to demonstrate "masculine" levels of sexual interest and activity. They are thought to be less likely to remain virgins before marriage and remain faithful within marriage.

**TABLE 3.4**
**Estimates of the Prevalence of Female Genital Mutilation in Africa**

| Country | Prevalence (%) |
|---|---|
| Benin | 50 |
| Burkina Faso | 70 |
| Cameroon | 20 |
| Central African Republic | 43 |
| Chad | 60 |
| Côte d'Ivoire | 43 |
| Democratic Republic of the Congo | 5 |
| Djibouti | 98 |
| Egypt | 97 |
| Eritrea | 90 |
| Ethiopia | 85 |
| Gambia | 80 |
| Ghana | 30 |
| Guinea | 60 |
| Guinea-Bissau | 50 |
| Kenya | 50 |
| Liberia | 60 |
| Mali | 94 |
| Mauritania | 25 |
| Niger | 20 |
| Nigeria | 40 |
| Senegal | 20 |
| Sierra Leone | 90 |
| Somalia | 98 |
| Togo | 50 |
| Uganda | 5 |
| United Republic of Tanzania | 10 |

Source: Adapted from World Health Organization (1998a).

Accordingly, female genital mutilation is designed to lessen or totally eradicate feelings of sexual arousal in women.

Reactions to female genital mutilation can be grouped into two broad categories. The first is a "human rights perspective," according to which female genital mutilation is simply a manifestation of gender-based oppression and the violence that women experience in societies worldwide. Adopting this perspective, female genital mutilation was first identified as a form of violence against women by the United Nations in 1993. This perspective is also reflected in a growing number of international, regional, and national agreements that commit governments to preventing female genital mutilation, assisting women at risk of undergoing it, and punishing people who commit it. For example, female genital mutilation is illegal in Canada (Hussein, 1995; Scott, 2000). Moreover, section 273.3 of the Criminal Code prohibits anyone from removing children who are ordinarily resident in Canada and subjecting them to female genital mutilation.

Proponents of the second perspective on female genital mutilation are commonly known as "cultural relativists." They view interventions that interfere with the practice as little more than ethnocentric and neo-imperialist attacks on African cultures. From their point of view, all talk of "universal human rights" denies cultural sovereignty to less powerful peoples. Moreover, opposition to female genital mutilation is thought to undermine tolerance and multiculturalism while reinforcing racist attitudes. Accordingly, cultural relativists argue that we should affirm the right of other cultures to practise female genital mutilation even if we regard it as destructive, senseless, oppressive, and abhorrent. The fact that other cultures regard female genital mutilation as meaningful and as serving useful functions should be respected.

Which of these perspectives do you find more compelling? Do you believe that certain principles of human decency transcend the particulars of any particular culture? If so, what are those principles? If you do not believe in the existence of any universal principles of human decency, then does anything go? Would you agree that, say, genocide is acceptable if the great majority of people in a particular society favour it? Or are there limits to your cultural relativism? In a world where supposedly universal principles often clash with the principles of particular cultures, where do you draw the line? It's your choice.

ensured that the Catholic Church would no longer be the supreme interpreter of God's will in the eyes of all Christians. Authority and truth became divided as never before.

Cultural fragmentation picked up steam during industrialization, as the variety of occupational roles grew and new political and intellectual movements crystallized. Its pace is quickening again today in the postindustrial era. This is due to **globalization,** the process by which formerly separate economies, states, and cultures are being tied together.

The roots of globalization are many. International trade and investment are expanding. Even the most patriotic of Canadians has probably dined at least once at McDonald's—and even a business as "American" as McDonald's now reaps 60 percent of its profits from outside the United States. Indeed, McDonald's international operations are expected to grow at four times the rate of its U.S. outlets (Commins, 1997). At the same time, members of different ethnic and racial groups are migrating and coming into sustained contact with one another. A growing number of people date, court, and marry across religious, ethnic, and racial lines. Influential "transnational" organizations such as the International Monetary Fund, the World Bank, the European Union, Greenpeace, and Amnesty International are multiplying. Relatively inexpensive international travel and communication make contacts among people from diverse cultures routine. The mass media make Tom Cruise and *Survivor* nearly as well known in Warsaw as in Winnipeg. MTV brings rock music to the world via MTV Canada, MTV Latino, MTV Brazil, MTV Europe, MTV Asia, MTV Japan, MTV Mandarin, and MTV India (Hanke, 1998). Globalization, in short, destroys political, economic, and cultural isolation, bringing people together in what Canadian media analyst Marshall McLuhan (1964) called a "global village." As a result of globalization, people are less obliged to accept the culture into which they are born and freer to combine elements of culture from a wide variety of historical periods and geographical settings. Globalization is a schoolboy in Bombay, India, listening to Bob Marley on his MP3 player as he rushes to slip into his Levis, wolf down a bowl of Kellogg's Basmati Flakes, and say goodbye to his parents in Hindi because he's late for his English-language school.

A good indicator of the influence and extent of globalization is the spread of English since 1600. In 1600, English was the mother tongue of between 4 million and 7 million people. Not even all people in England spoke it. Today, 750 million to 1 billion people speak English worldwide, more than half as a second language. With the exception of the many varieties of Chinese, English is the most widespread language on earth.[2] More than half the world's technical and scientific periodicals are written in English, as are three-quarters of the world's letters, telexes, and telegrams and 80 percent of the non-numerical

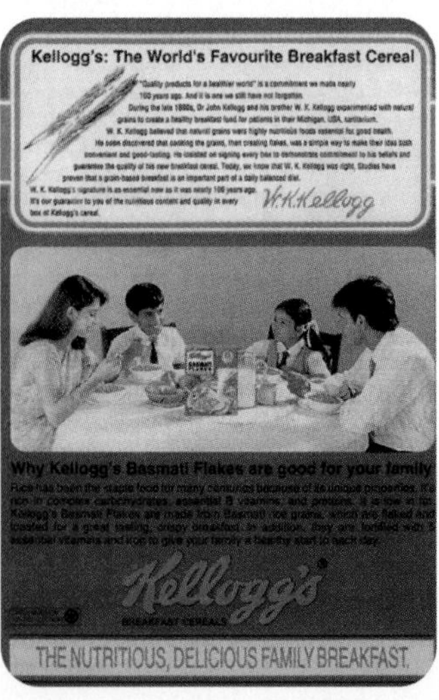


The idea of globalization first gained prominence in marketing strategies in the 1970s. In the 1980s, companies such as Coca-Cola and McDonald's expanded into non-Western countries to find new markets. Today, Kellogg's markets products in more than 160 countries. Basmati Flakes cereal was first produced by the Kellogg's plant in Tajola, India, in 1992.

data stored in the world's computers. English is the official language of the Olympics, of the Miss Universe contest, of navigation in the air and on the seas, and of the World Council of Churches.

English is dominant because Britain and the United States have been the world's most powerful and influential countries—economically, militarily, and culturally—for 200 years (someone once defined language as a dialect backed up by an army). In recent decades, the global spread of capitalism, the popularity of Hollywood movies and American TV shows, and widespread access to instant communication via telephone and the Internet have increased the reach of the English language (see Figure 3.2). There are now more speakers of excellent English in India than in Britain, and when a construction company jointly owned by German, French, and Italian interests undertakes a building project in Spain, the language of business is English (McCrum, Cran, and MacNeil, 1992).

Even in Japan, where relatively few people speak the language, English words are commonly used. For example, when you learn to open a computer file's *ai-kon* (icon) you are told to *daburu-kurikku* (double-click) the *mausu* (mouse). In view of the extensive use of English in Japan, *The Japanese Times,* one of Tokyo's four English-language daily newspapers, ran a story a few years ago noting the pressures of globalization and suggesting it might be time for Japan to switch to English. True, the Health and Welfare Ministry banned excessive use of English in its documents a couple of years ago, but, as one Japanese newspaper noted, given the popularity of English words, it's doubtful there will be much *foro-uppu* (follow-up).

For Japanese teenagers, English is certainly considered very cool. A 15-year-old girl, wearing her trademark *roozu sokusu* (loose socks), might greet a friend sporting new sunglasses with a spirited *chekaraccho* (Check it out, Joe). If she likes the shades, she might say they're *cho beri gu* (ultra-good) and invite her friend *deniru* (to go to a Denny's restaurant) or *hageru* (to go to a Häagen-Dazs ice cream outlet). Of course, the girl might also *disu* (diss, or show disrespect toward) her friend. She might come right out and inform him that the new shades look *cho beri ba* (ultra-bad) or *cho beri bu* (ultra-blue, depressing, or ultra-ugly). If so, the situation that develops could be a little *denjarasu* (dangerous). Terms of affection, such as *wonchu* (I want you), might not be exchanged. The budding relationship might go nowhere. Nonetheless, we can be pretty sure that Japanese teenagers' use of English slang will intensify under the pressures of globalization (Kristof, 1997).

## Postmodernism

Some sociologists think so much cultural fragmentation and reconfiguration has taken place in the last few decades that a new term is needed to characterize the culture of our

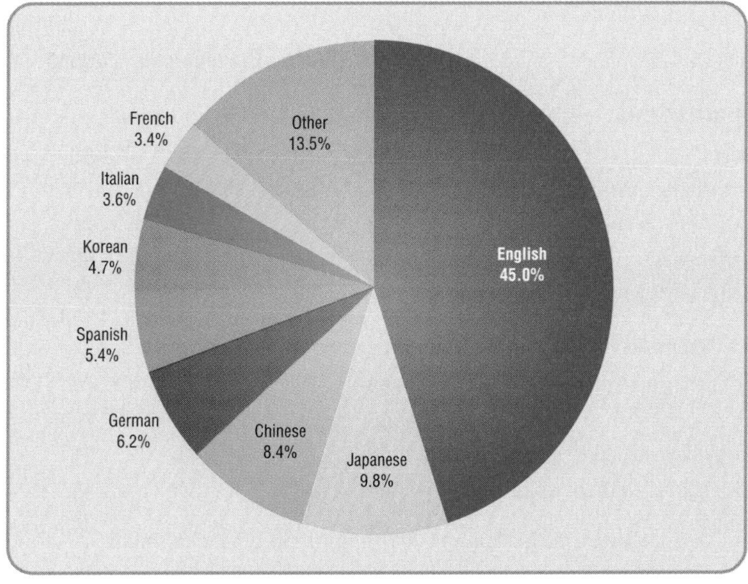


✦ **FIGURE 3.2** ✦
**Internet Usage by Language Group, June 2001**

Source: Global Reach (2001).

times: **postmodernism.** Scholars often characterize the last half of the nineteenth century and the first half of the twentieth century as the era of modernity. During this hundred-year period, belief in the inevitability of progress, respect for authority, and consensus around core values characterized much of Western culture. In contrast, postmodern culture involves an eclectic mix of elements from different times and places, the erosion of authority, and the decline of consensus around core values. Let us consider each of these aspects of postmodernism in turn.

*An eclectic mix of elements from different times and places.* In the postmodern era, it is easier to create individualized belief systems and practices by blending facets of different cultures and historical periods. Consider religion. Although the vast majority of Canadians say they believe in God and continue to identify themselves as Christians, increasing numbers now identify themselves as adherents of Eastern non-Christian religions or as having "no religion" (Clark, 1998; Vanier Institute of the Family, 2000: 14; see Chapter 13, Religion and Education). In addition, Canadians are increasingly showing a willingness to feast off of a religious "smorgasboard" that combines a conventional menu with a wide assortment of other supernatural beliefs and practices including astrology, tarot, New Age mysticism, psychic phenomena, and communication with the dead (Bibby, 1987: 233; Bibby, 2001: 195). This is clear from a series of questions that were asked of Canadians teenagers and adults in two national surveys carried out in 2000 (Bibby, 2001). It is evident that religious beliefs and practices are not always drawn from conventional sources (see Table 3.5). Simply put, there are many more ways of worshipping than there used to be. For example, one can easily construct a personalized religion involving, say, belief in the divinity of Jesus *and* yoga (Melton, 1996 [1978]). In the words of one journalist: "In an age when we trust ourselves to assemble our own investment portfolios and cancer therapies, why not our religious beliefs?" (Creedon, 1998). Individuals thus draw on religions much like consumers shop in a mall. They practise religion à la carte. Meanwhile, churches, synagogues, and other religious institutions have diversified their menus to appeal to the spiritual, leisure, and social needs of religious consumers and retain their loyalties in the competitive market for congregants and parishioners (Finke and Stark, 1992).

The mix-and-match approach we see when it comes to religion is evident in virtually all spheres of culture. Purists may scoff at this sort of cultural blending. However, it probably has an important positive social consequence. It seems likely that people who engage in cultural blending are usually more tolerant and appreciative of ethnic, racial, and religious groups other than their own.

*The erosion of authority.* Half a century ago, Canadians were more likely than they are today to defer to authority in the family, schools, politics, medicine, and so forth. As the

✦ **TABLE 3.5** ✦
**Beliefs across Generations, Canada, 2000**

Source: Bibby (2001: 252).

| "I believe..." | Adults | Teens | Grandparents | Parents | Younger Adults |
|---|---|---|---|---|---|
| **Conventional** | | | | | |
| God exists | 81% | 73 | 85 | 81 | 78 |
| God or a higher power cares about you | 73 | 68 | 77 | 72 | 71 |
| Jesus was the Divine Son of God | 72 | 65 | 77 | 71 | 68 |
| In life after death | 68 | 78 | 64 | 69 | 72 |
| Have felt the presence God/higher power | 47 | 36 | 51 | 47 | 42 |
| **Less Conventional** | | | | | |
| In near-death experiences | 68 | 76 | 57 | 71 | 76 |
| In ESP | 66 | 59 | 59 | 70 | 67 |
| Personally have experienced precognition | 58 | 63 | 46 | 61 | 68 |
| Can have contact with the spirit world | 45 | 43 | 30 | 48 | 57 |
| In astrology | 34 | 57 | 31 | 34 | 36 |

A hallmark of postmodernism is the combining of cultural elements from different times and places. Architect I. M. Pei unleased a storm of protest when his 22-metre glass pyramid became an entrance to the Louvre in Paris. It created a postmodern nightmare in the eyes of some critics.

social bases of authority and truth have multiplied, however, we are more likely to challenge authority. Authorities once widely respected, including parents, physicians, and politicians, have come to be held in lower regard by many people. In the 1950s, Robert Young played the firm, wise, and always-present father in the TV hit *Father Knows Best.* Fifty years later, Homer Simpson plays a fool in *The Simpsons.* Compared with Canadian teenagers in 2000, Canadian teenagers in the 1980s—merely two decades ago—were more likely to express confidence in our police, our politicians, our court systems, and the leadership of religious organizations (Bibby, 2001: 193). Today, both young and old Canadians are likely to be critical of social institutions, including those, such as religious organizations, that previously enjoyed special veneration (see Table 3.6). The rise of Homer Simpson and the decline of confidence in government both reflect the societywide erosion of traditional authority (Nevitte, 1996).

*The decline of consensus around core values.* Half a century ago, people's values remained quite stable over the course of their adult lives and many values were widely accepted. Today, value shifts are more rapid and consensus has broken down on many

**✦ TABLE 3.6 ✦**
**Confidence in Institutions across Generations, Canada, 2000**

Source: Adapted from Bibby (2001: 245).

**Percentage Indicating Have "A Great Deal" or "Quite a Bit" of Confidence, by Institution and Generation**

| | Adults | Teens |
|---|---|---|
| Police | 67% | 62 |
| Schools | 47 | 63 |
| Computer industry | 45 | 51 |
| Court system | 40 | 52 |
| Newspapers | 41 | 60 |
| Radio | 41 | 48 |
| Major business | 37 | 48 |
| Religious organizations | 33 | 40 |
| Television | 29 | 44 |
| Music industry | 27 | 54 |
| Provincial government | 26 | 41 |
| Federal government | 24 | 41 |
| Movie industry | 22 | 60 |

issues. For example, in the middle of the twentieth century, the great majority of adults remained loyal to one political party from one election to the next. However, specific issues and personalities have increasingly eclipsed party loyalty as the driving forces of Canadian politics (Clarke et al., 1996; Nie, Verba, and Petrocik, 1979 [1976]). Today, people are more likely to vote for different political parties in succeeding elections than they were in 1950.

The decline of consensus may also be illustrated by considering the fate of Big Historical Projects. For most of the past 200 years, consensus throughout the world was built around Big Historical Projects. Various political and social movements convinced people they could take history into their own hands and create a glorious future just by signing up. German Nazism was a Big Historical Project. Its followers expected the Reich to enjoy 1000 years of power. Communism was an even bigger Big Historical Project, mobilizing hundreds of millions of people for a future that promised to end inequality and injustice for all time. However, the biggest and most successful Big Historical Project was not so much a social movement as a powerful idea—the belief that progress is inevitable, that life will always improve, due mainly to the spread of democracy and scientific innovation.

The twentieth century was unkind to Big Historical Projects. Russian communism lasted 74 years. German Nazism endured a mere 12. And the idea of progress fell on hard times as 100 million soldiers and civilians died in wars; the forward march of democracy took wrong turns into fascism, communism, and regimes based on religious fanaticism; and pollution due to urbanization and industrialization threatened the planet. In the postmodern era, more and more people recognize that apparent progress, including scientific advances, often have negative consequences (Scott, 1998; see Figure 3.3). As the poet e e cummings once wrote, nothing recedes like progress.

Postmodernism has many parents, teachers, politicians, religious leaders, and not a few university professors worried. Given the eclectic mixing of cultural elements from different times and places, the erosion of authority, and the decline of consensus around core values, how can we make binding decisions? How can we govern? How can we teach children and adolescents the difference between right and wrong? How can we transmit accepted literary tastes and artistic standards from one generation to the next? These are the kinds of issues that plague people in positions of authority today.

Although their concerns are legitimate, many authorities seem not to have considered the other side of the coin. The postmodern condition, as we have described it above, empowers ordinary people and makes them more responsible for their own fate. It frees people to adopt religious, ethnic, and other identities they are comfortable with, as opposed to identities imposed on them by others. It makes them more tolerant of difference. That is no small matter in a world torn by group conflict. And the postmodern attitude encourages healthy skepticism about rosy and naive scientific and political promises.

Thus, the news about postmodern culture is not all bad. However, as you will now see, it's not all good either.

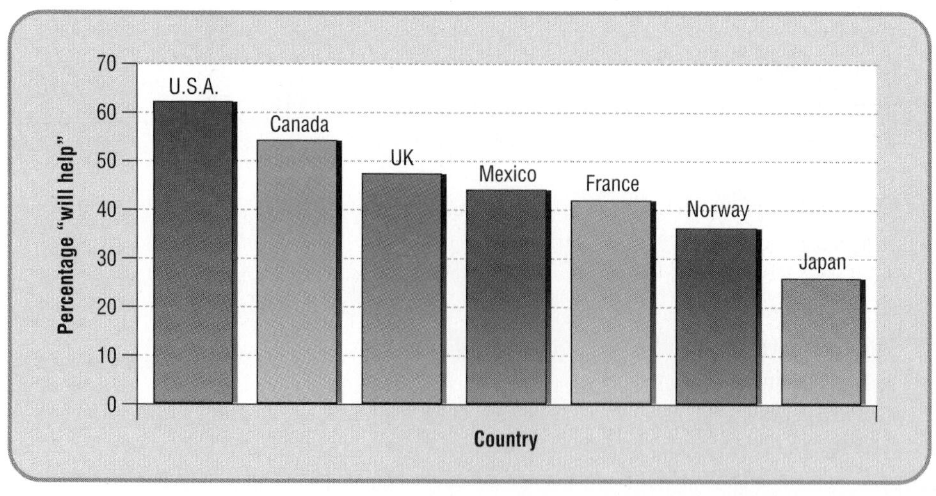


✦ **FIGURE 3.3** ✦

**Does Science Benefit Humanity? (in percent)**

"In the long run, do you think the scientific advances we are making will help or harm humankind?"

Source: *World Values Survey* (1994).

## Culture as Constraint

We noted above that culture has two faces. One we labelled *freedom*, the other *constraint*. Diversity, globalization, and postmodernism are all aspects of the new freedoms that culture allows us today. We now turn to an examination of two contemporary aspects of culture that act as constraining forces on our lives: rationalization and consumerism.

### Rationalization

In fourteenth-century Europe, an upsurge in demand for textiles caused loom owners to look for ways of increasing productivity. To that end, they imposed longer hours on loom workers. They also turned to a new technology for assistance: the mechanical clock. They installed public clocks in town squares. The clocks, known as *werkglocken* (work clocks) in German, signalled the beginning of the workday, the timing of meals, and quitting time.

Workers were accustomed to enjoying many holidays and a fairly flexible and vague work schedule regulated only approximately by the seasons and the rising and setting of the sun. The regimentation imposed by the work clocks made life more difficult. So the workers staged uprisings to silence the clocks. But to no avail. City officials sided with the employers and imposed fines for ignoring the *werkglocken.* Harsher penalties, including death, were imposed on anyone trying to use the clocks' bells to signal a revolt (Thompson, 1967).

Now, more than 600 years later, many people are, in effect, slaves of the *werkglock.* This is especially true of big-city North American couples who are employed full-time in the paid labour force and have preteen children. For them, life often seems an endless round of waking up at 6:30 a.m., getting everyone washed and dressed, preparing the kids' lunches, getting them out the door in time for the school bus or the car pool, driving to work through rush-hour traffic, facing the speedup at work that resulted from the recent downsizing, driving back home through rush-hour traffic, preparing dinner, taking the kids to their soccer game, returning home to clean up the dishes and help with homework, getting the kids washed, brushed, and into bed, and (if you haven't brought some office work home) grabbing an hour of TV before collapsing, exhausted, for 6.5 hours before the story repeats itself. Life is less hectic for residents of small towns, unmarried people, couples without small children, retirees, and the unemployed. But the lives of most people are so packed with activities that time must be carefully regulated, each moment precisely parcelled out so that we may tick off item after item from an ever-growing list of tasks that need to be completed on schedule (Schor, 1992).

After more than 600 years of conditioning, it is unusual for people to rebel against the clock in the town square any more. In fact, we now wear a watch on our wrist without giving it a second thought, as it were. This signifies that we have accepted and internalized the regime of the *werkglock.* Allowing clocks to precisely regulate our activities seems the most natural thing in the world—which is a pretty good sign that the internalized *werkglock* is, in fact, a product of culture.

Have we come to depend too heavily on the *werkglock*? Harold Lloyd in *Safety Last* (1923).

Is the precise regulation of time rational? It certainly is rational as a means of ensuring the goal of efficiency. Minding the clock maximizes how much work you get done in a day. The regulation of time makes it possible for trains to run on schedule and university classes to begin punctually. But is minding the clock rational as an end in itself? For many people, it is not. They complain that the precise regulation of time has gotten out of hand. Life has simply become too hectic for many people to enjoy. In this sense, a *rational means* (the *werkglock*) has been applied to a *given goal* (maximizing work) but has led to an *irrational end* (a hectic life).

This, in a nutshell, is Max Weber's thesis about the rationalization process. **Rationalization,** in Weber's usage, means (a) the application of the most efficient means to achieve given goals, and (b) the unintended, negative consequences of doing so. Weber claimed that rationality of means has crept into all spheres of life, leading to unintended consequences that dehumanize and constrain us (see Figure 3.4).

Weber believed that the rationalization process is exemplified by bureaucracies—large, impersonal organizations composed of many clearly defined positions arranged in a hierarchy (see Chapter 5, Interaction and Organization). Modern bureaucracies, Weber said, are increasingly influential organizations. The factory, the government office, the military, the system of higher education, and the institutions of science are all bureaucratically organized. Yet bureaucracies are composed of nonelected officials. Consequently, they concentrate power and threaten democracy. Moreover, bureaucracies discourage officeholders from considering what the goals of their organization ought to be. Bureaucrats are asked only to determine the best way of achieving the goals defined by their superiors. Officeholders thus lose their spontaneity, their inventiveness, and all opportunity to act heroically. It is "horrible to think," wrote Weber, "that the world could one day be filled with nothing but those little cogs, little men clinging to little jobs and striving towards bigger ones . . ." (quoted in Mayer, 1944: 127).

Sociologist George Ritzer argues that, just as the modern bureaucracy epitomized the rationalization process for Weber at the turn of the twentieth century, the McDonald's restaurant is the epitome of rationalization today (Ritzer, 1993; 1996). Instead of adapting institutions to the needs of people, says Ritzer, people must increasingly adapt to the needs of "McDonaldization." We are dehumanized in the process (Leidner, 1993; Reiter, 1991).

As Ritzer shows, McDonald's has lunch down to a science. The meat and vegetables used to prepare your meal must meet minimum standards of quality and freshness. Each food item contains identical ingredients. Each portion is carefully weighed and cooked according to a uniform and precisely timed process. McDonald's executives have carefully thought through every aspect of your lunch. They have turned its preparation into a model of rationality. With the goal of making profits, they have optimized food preparation to make it as fast and as cheap as possible.

Unfortunately, however, the rationalization of lunch dehumanizes both staff and customers. For instance, meals are prepared by nonunionized, uniformed workers who receive minimum wage. They must execute their tasks quickly and within specific time limits. To boost sales, they must smile as they recite fixed scripts ("Would you like some fries with

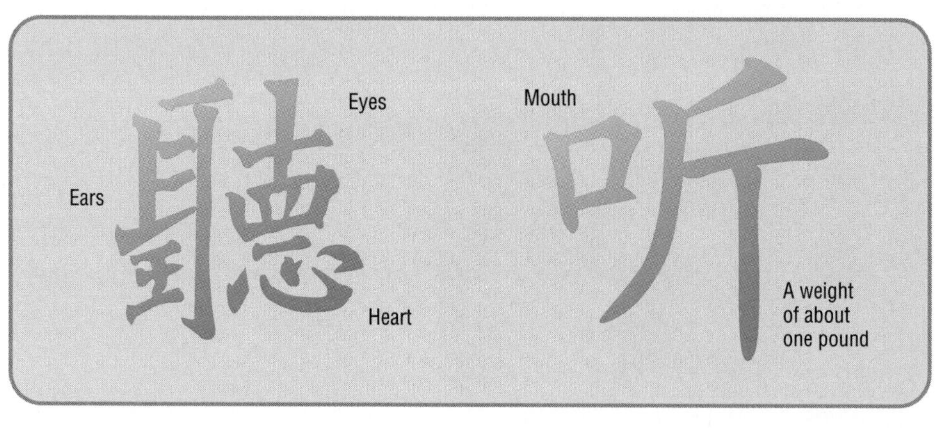


✦ **FIGURE 3.4** ✦

**The Rationalization of Chinese Script**

Reprinted here are the Chinese characters for "listening" *(t'ing)* in traditional Chinese script (left) and simplified, modern script (right). Each character is composed of several word-symbols. In classical script, listening is depicted as a process involving the eyes, the ears, and the heart. It implies that listening demands the utmost empathy and involves the whole person. In contrast, modern script depicts listening as something that merely involves one person speaking and the other "weighing" speech. Modern Chinese script has been rationalized. Has empathy been lost in the process?

your burger?"). Nearly half of all McDonald's employees are so dissatisfied with their work they quit after a year or less. To deal with this problem, McDonald's is now field testing vending machines that will be used to replace staff and boost sales. Anyone for an e-burger ("McDonald's Testing E-burgers," 1999)?

Meanwhile, customers are expected to spend as little time as possible eating the food—hence the drive-through window, chairs designed to be comfortable for only about 20 minutes, and small express outlets in subways and department stores where customers eat standing up or on the run. Customers are also expected to eat unhealthy food. A Big Mac, small fries, medium Coke, and apple Danish can provide up to 67 percent of your recommended daily calorie intake and 88 percent of your recommended daily fat intake (calculated from McDonald's Corporation, 1999). This is why physicians and nutritionists regularly decry the popularity of fast food.

Nonetheless, powerful forces make the Big Mac popular. On the demand side, fast food fits the rushed lifestyle of many individuals and families in the more affluent countries of the world and the growing middle class in the developing countries (more than half of McDonald's sales are now outside North America). On the supply side, one can make big profits by turning meal preparation into a mass production industry. Motivated by these forces, rationality of means (turning lunch into a science) results in irrationality of ends (dehumanizing staff and customers).

As the examples of the *werkglock,* bureaucracy, and McDonald's show, rationalization enables us to do just about everything more efficiently, but at a steep cost. Because it is so widespread, rationalization is one of the most constraining aspects of culture today. In Weber's view, it makes life in the modern world akin to living inside an "iron cage."

The second constraining aspect of culture to examine is consumerism. **Consumerism** is the tendency to define ourselves in terms of the goods and services we purchase.

## Consumerism

In 1998, apparel sales in North America were lagging. As a result, the Gap launched a new ad campaign to help revitalize sales. The company hired Hollywood talent to create a slick and highly effective series of TV spots for khaki pants. According to the promotional material for the ad campaign, the purpose of the ads was to "reinvent khakis," that is, to stimulate demand for the pants. In *Khakis rock,* "skateboarders and in-line skaters dance, glide, and fly to music by the Crystal Method." In *Khakis groove,* "hip-hop dancers throw radical moves to the funky beat of Bill Mason." In *Khakis swing,* "two couples break away from a crowd to demonstrate swing techniques to the vintage sounds of Louis Prima" (Gap.com, 1999).

About 55 seconds of each ad featured the dancers. During the last five seconds, the words "Gap khakis" appeared on the screen. The Gap followed a similar approach in its 2000 ad campaign, inspired by the 1957 musical *West Side Story.* The 30-second spots

"McDonaldization" is a global phenomenon, as this busy McDonald's restaurant in Beijing, China, suggests.

replaced the play's warring street gangs, the Jets and the Sharks, with fashion factions of their own, the Khakis and the Jeans. Again, most of the ad was devoted to the riveting dance number. The pants were mentioned for only a few seconds at the end.

As the imbalance between stylish come-on and mere information suggests, the people who created the ads understood well that it was really the appeal of the dancers that would sell the pants. They knew that to stimulate demand for their product, they had to associate the khakis with desirable properties such as youth, good health, coolness, popularity, beauty, and sex. As an advertising executive said in the 1940s: "It's not the steak we sell. It's the sizzle."

Because advertising stimulates sales, there is a tendency for business to spend more on advertising over time. Because advertising is widespread, most people unquestioningly accept it as part of their lives. In fact, many people have *become* ads. When your father was a child and quickly threw on a shirt, allowing a label to hang out, your grandmother might have admonished him to "tuck in that label." In contrast, many people today proudly display consumer labels as marks of status and identity. Advertisers teach us to associate the words *Gucci* and *Nike* with different kinds of people, and when people display these labels on their clothes they are telling us something about the kind of people they are. Advertising becomes us.

Where do you fit in? If you don't display labels on your clothes, what does your reluctance to do so tell people about who you are? If you do display labels on your clothes, which ones are they? What do the labels tell others about who you are? Do your friends display clothing labels similar to yours? What about people you dislike? Do you think it is reasonable to conclude that clothing labels are cultural artifacts that increase the solidarity of social groups and segregate them from other groups?

The rationalization process, when applied to the production of goods and services, enables us to produce more efficiently, to have more of just about everything than our parents did. But it is consumerism, the tendency to define ourselves in terms of the goods we purchase, that ensures all the goods we produce will be bought. Of course, we have a lot of choice. We can select from dozens of styles of running shoes, cars, toothpaste, and all the rest. We can also choose to buy items that help define us as members of a particular **subculture,** adherents of a set of distinctive values, norms, and practices within a larger culture. But, regardless of individual tastes and inclinations, nearly all of us have one thing in common: we tend to be good consumers. We are motivated by advertising, which is based on the accurate insight that people will likely be considered cultural outcasts if they fail to conform to stylish trends. By creating those trends, advertisers push us to buy even if we must incur large debts to do so (Schor, 1999). That is why North Americans' "shop-till-you-drop" lifestyle prompted French sociologist Jean Baudrillard to remark pointedly that even what is best is compulsory (Baudrillard, 1988 [1986]).

What is being sold here? The pants or the attitude?

As is the case for rationalization, consumerism has unintended, negative consequences. For example, our culture of excessive consumption causes environmental degradation. We discuss this problem in detail in Chapter 18, Technology and the Global Environment. In addition, consumerism is remarkably effective in taming expressions of freedom and individualism, including acts of dissent and rebellion. That is, deviations from mainstream culture often lose their power to drive change and are turned simply into means of making money. Some examples from the world of popular music will help illustrate the point:

✦ Ozzy Osbourne is the godfather of heavy metal. Beginning in the late 1960s, he and his band, Black Sabbath, inspired Metallica, KISS, Judas Priest, Marilyn Manson, and others to play loud, nihilistic music, reject conventional morality, embrace death and violence, and foment youthful rebellion and parental panic. In 1982, he bit the head off a bat during a performance and urinated on the Alamo. He was given rabies shots for the former and arrested for the latter. Around the same time, Tipper Gore, wife of the future presidential candidate, formed the Parental Music Resources Committee (PMRC) to fight against violence and sex in the lyrics of popular music. Osbourne was one of the PMRC's principal targets. The Prince of Darkness, as he was often called, was about as rebellious a figure as one could imagine in 1982. Flash forward 20 years. Osbourne, now 53, has the sixth most popular show on American television among 18- to 34 year-olds, just behind *Survivor* in the ratings. MTV placed a dozen cameras throughout his Beverly Hills mansion, and every Tuesday night viewers get to see everything that goes on in the Osbourne household for half an hour. According to *USA Today*, it turns out that Osbourne is "a lot like anyone's adorable dad. Shuffles a bit. Forgets things. Worries about the garbage. Snores on the couch while the TV blares. Walks the dog" (Gundersen, Keveney, and Oldenburg, 2002: 1A).

  The Osbourne family does a lot of swearing. Ozzy's 17-year-old daughter sometimes sports pink hair and his 16-year-old son wears dark nail polish. But CNN's Greta Van Susteren says she finds the Osbournes "charming," while Rosie O'Donnell told Ozzy's wife, Sharon: "What I love most about [your show] is not only the relationship you have with Ozzy—and you obviously adore each other—but the honesty with which you relate to your children. The love is so evident between all of you. It's heartwarming" (Gundersen, Keveney, and Oldenburg, 2002: 2A). *The Osbournes*, it turns out, is a comfort to many people. It proves that the frightening rejection of mainstream culture in the 1970s and 1980s was just a passing phase and that things of eternal value—especially the nuclear family and commercialism—remain intact. Ozzy Osbourne has thus been transformed from the

Ozzy Osbourne (holding plaque) *en famille.*

epitome of rebellion against society to a family man, a small industry, and a media icon. In April 2002 alone, he appeared on the covers of *Time*, *Entertainment Weekly*, and *Rolling Stone* and on *The Rosie O'Donnell Show* and *Live! With Regis & Kelly*.

- Punk rock is another genre of musical rebellion from the 1970s. In the UK, the most important early punk rockers were the Sex Pistols and the Clash. Punk rockers tore their clothes, wore dog collars around their necks, cut their hair in Mohawks, tattooed bar codes on their necks, and shoved safety pins through their ears—all to illustrate how society devalued and degraded people. In 1977, when Queen Elizabeth II celebrated her Silver Jubilee, the Sex Pistols released "God Save the Queen," an attack on the monarchy. Because the song was banned from the airwaves and most record stores, they hired a boat to follow the queen's flotilla down the Thames. According to one account, "[t]heir raggedy fans crowded onto London's bridges and swung from the lampposts, screaming and ecstatically chucking debris onto the boat as it blasted out the vicious lyrics: 'God save the Queen / she ain't no human being / she made you a moron / a potential H-bomb / God save the Queen / we mean it maaan!'" (McLaren, 2002). Flash forward 15 years. The queen is now celebrating her fiftieth year on the throne. Punk rocker Vic Garbage, who blasted "God Save the Queen" for eight hours straight from his public housing complex in 1977 and wore a "Stuff the Wedding" T-shirt when Prince Charles and Lady Diana married, is proud of his red, white, and blue haircut and is playing a gig in the conservative northern town of Bolton in honour of the queen. Punk has been tamed. Remastered classics from the punk "revolution" are available in lovely boxed sets at HMV. A display of desecrated queen's heads is featured at an East End London art gallery. The Sex Pistols' Johnny Rotten is upset he wasn't asked to play at the official Buckingham Palace concert celebrating the queen's 50 years on the throne. "I've come to the point of view," says Rotten, "that, bad as it all is, it's my kind of bad, and I have paid for it, and I want to celebrate it somehow" (McLaren, 2002). As is the case with heavy metal, punk has for the most part been commercialized and declawed.
- And then there is hip-hop (Brym, 2001a). Originating in the 1970s in the squalor of inner-city American ghettoes, hip-hop was at first a highly politicized rebellion. Early hip-hop artists glorified the mean streets of the inner city and held the police, the mass media, and other pillars of white society in utter contempt, blaming them for arbitrary arrests, the political suppression of black activists, and the malicious spreading of lies about African-Americans. However, by the time Public Enemy became a hit in the late 1980s, MTV had aired its first regular program devoted to the genre and much of hip-hop's audience was composed of white middle-class youth. Hip-hop artists were quick to see the potential of commercialization. Some members of Wu-Tang Clan had their own lines of clothes, Versace was marketing clothing influenced by ghetto styles, and Puff Daddy (who later was made over as P. Diddy) was reminding his audience: "Nigga get money, that's simply the plan" (from his 1999 CD, *Forever*). No less than with heavy metal and punk, hip-hop's radicalism gave way to the lures of commercialism.

In sum, the stories of heavy metal, punk, and hip-hop are testimony to the capacity of postmodern culture to constrain expressions of freedom, individualism, dissent, and rebellion (Frank and Weiland, 1997). They are compelling illustrations of postmodern culture's second face.

## SUMMARY

1. Humans have been able to adapt to their environments because they can create culture. In particular, the ability to create symbols, make tools, and cooperate has enabled humans to thrive.
2. No hard evidence supports the view that specific human behaviours and social arrangements are biologically determined, although biology does set human limits and potentials.

3. We can see the contours of culture most sharply if we are neither too deeply immersed in it nor too much removed from it. Understanding culture requires refraining from taking your own culture for granted and judging other cultures by the standards of your own.
4. Culture has two faces. In some respects, culture provides us with increasing opportunities to exercise our freedom. The growth of multiculturalism, globalization, and postmodernism reflects this tendency. In other respects, culture constrains us, putting limits on what we can become. The growth of rationalization and consumerism reflects this tendency.
5. Advocates of multiculturalism in education want school and post-secondary curricula to reflect the country's growing ethnic and racial diversity. They also want school and post-secondary curricula to stress that all cultures have equal value. They believe that multicultural education will promote self-esteem and economic success among members of racial and ethnic minorities and promote our government's policy of multiculturalism. Critics fear that multiculturalism results in declining educational standards. They believe that multicultural education causes political disunity and interethnic and interracial conflict. And they argue that it promotes an extreme form of cultural relativism.
6. The globalization of culture has resulted from the growth of international trade and investment, ethnic and racial migration, influential "transnational" organizations, and inexpensive travel and communication.
7. Postmodernism involves an eclectic mixing of elements from different times and places, the decline of authority, and the erosion of consensus around core values.
8. Rationalization involves the application of the most efficient means to achieve given goals and the unintended, negative consequences of doing so. Rationalization is evident in the growth and operation of bureaucracies, in the increasingly regulated use of time, and in many other areas of social life.
9. Consumerism is the tendency to define ourselves in terms of the goods we purchase. Excessive consumption puts limits on who we can become, constrains our capacity to dissent from mainstream culture, and degrades the natural environment.

## GLOSSARY

**Abstraction** is the human capacity to create general ideas or ways of thinking that are not linked to particular instances. For example, languages, mathematical notations, and signs allow us to classify experience and generalize from it.

**Consumerism** is the tendency to define ourselves in terms of the goods we purchase.

**Cooperation** is the human capacity to create a complex social life.

**Cultural relativism** is the belief that all cultures have equal value.

**Culture** is the sum of practices, languages, symbols, beliefs, values, ideologies, and material objects that people create to deal with real-life problems. Cultures enable people to adapt to, and thrive in, their environments.

**Ethnocentrism** is the tendency to judge other cultures exclusively by the standards of one's own.

**Globalization** is the process by which formerly separate economies, states, and cultures are being tied together.

**High culture** is culture consumed mainly by upper classes.

**Mass culture** (see Popular culture).

**Material culture** is composed of the tools and techniques that enable people to get tasks accomplished.

**Norms** are generally accepted ways of doing things.

**Popular culture** (or **mass culture**) is culture consumed by all classes.

**Postmodernism** is characterized by an eclectic mix of cultural elements and the erosion of consensus.

**Production** is the human capacity to make and use tools. It improves our ability to take what we want from nature.

**Rationalization** is the application of the most efficient means to achieve given goals and the unintended, negative consequences of doing so.

**Rites of passage** are cultural ceremonies that mark the transition from one stage of life to another (e.g., baptisms, confirmations, weddings) or from life to death (e.g., funerals).

**Sanctions** are rewards and punishments intended to ensure conformity to cultural guidelines.

The system of **social control** is the sum of sanctions in society by means of which conformity to cultural guidelines is ensured.

A **subculture** is a set of distinctive values, norms, and practices within a larger culture.

A **symbol** is anything that carries a particular meaning, including the components of language, mathematical notations, and signs. Symbols allow us to classify experience and generalize from it.

## QUESTIONS TO CONSIDER

1. We imbibe culture but we also create it. What elements of culture have you created? Under what conditions were you prompted to do so? Was your cultural contribution strictly personal or was it shared with others? Why?
2. Select a subcultural practice that seems odd, inexplicable, or irrational to you. By interviewing members of the subcultural group and reading about them, explain how the subcultural practice you chose makes sense to members of the subcultural group.
3. Do you think the freedoms afforded by postmodern culture outweigh the constraints it places on us? Why or why not?

# WEB RESOURCES

## Companion Web Site for This Book

http://www.brymsociologycompass.nelson.com

Begin by clicking on the Student Resources section of the Web site. Next, select the chapter you are currently studying from the pull-down menu. From the Student Resources page you will have easy access to InfoTrac College Edition®, MicroCase online exercises, and additional Web links. The Web site also has many useful tips to aid you in your study of sociology, including practice tests for each chapter.

## InfoTrac Search Terms

These search terms are provided to assist you in beginning to conduct research on this topic by visiting http://www.infotrac-college.com

**Consumerism**
**Culture**
**Globalization**
**Multiculturalism**
**Postmodernism**
**Rationalization**

## Recommended Web Sites

Bernard Barber, "Jihad vs. McWorld," on the World Wide Web at http://www.theatlantic.com/politics/foreign/barberf.htm is a brief, masterful analysis of the forces that are simultaneously making world culture more homogeneous and more heterogeneous. The article was originally published in *The Atlantic Monthly* (March 1992). For the full story, see Bernard Barber, *Jihad vs. McWorld: How Globalism and Tribalism Are Reshaping the World* (New York: Ballantine Books, 1996).

Adbusters is an organization devoted to analyzing and criticizing consumer culture. Its provocative Web site is at http://adbusters.org.

Sarah Zupko's Cultural Studies Center is our favourite site on the sociology of popular culture. Visit it at http://www.popcultures.com/.

The Resource Center for Cyberculture Studies is an organization devoted to studying emerging cultures on the World Wide Web. Its Web site is at http://www.com.washington.edu/rccs/.

# SUGGESTED READINGS

Wendy Griswold. "The Sociology of Culture: Four Good Arguments (and One Bad One)," *Acta Sociologica* 35 (1992): 322–8. Concisely analyzes major issues in the subfield.

R. C. Lewontin. *Biology as Ideology: The Doctrine of DNA* (New York: HarperCollins, 1991). A brilliant short critique of sociobiology, evolutionary psychology, and related ideologies by one of the world's leading scientists.

Mark Anthony Neal. *What the Music Said: Black Popular Music and Black Public Culture* (New York: Routledge, 1999). A fine case study in the sociology of culture. Shows how post–Second World War black popular music emerged from the struggle to maintain community in the face of poverty and brutality.

# NOTES

1. Sociologists call opera and so forth **high culture** to distinguish it from **popular** or **mass culture**. Although high culture is consumed mainly by the upper classes, popular or mass culture is consumed by all classes.

2. Concern over the possible erosion of the French language led, in part, to the 1969 passage of Canada's Official Languages Act and the 1977 passage of the French Language Charter (Bill 101) in Quebec, which established French as the only official language of education, work, and the public sector in the province.

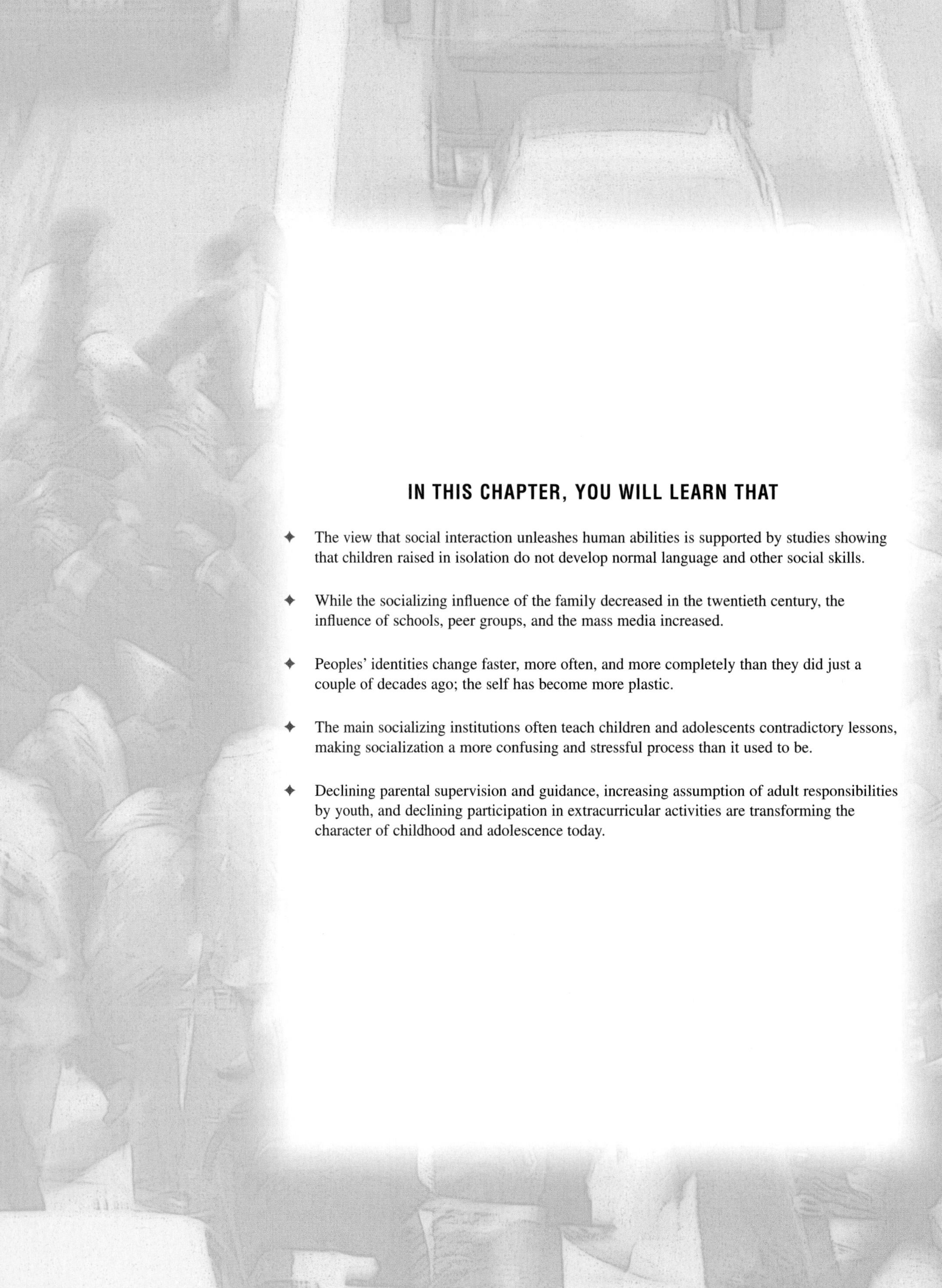

## IN THIS CHAPTER, YOU WILL LEARN THAT

- The view that social interaction unleashes human abilities is supported by studies showing that children raised in isolation do not develop normal language and other social skills.
- While the socializing influence of the family decreased in the twentieth century, the influence of schools, peer groups, and the mass media increased.
- Peoples' identities change faster, more often, and more completely than they did just a couple of decades ago; the self has become more plastic.
- The main socializing institutions often teach children and adolescents contradictory lessons, making socialization a more confusing and stressful process than it used to be.
- Declining parental supervision and guidance, increasing assumption of adult responsibilities by youth, and declining participation in extracurricular activities are transforming the character of childhood and adolescence today.

CHAPTER

4

# SOCIALIZATION

## SOCIAL ISOLATION AND THE CRYSTALLIZATION OF SELF-IDENTITY

One day in the year 1800, a 10- or 11-year-old boy walked out of the woods in southern France. He was filthy, naked, unable to speak, and had not been toilet trained. After being taken by the police to a local orphanage, he repeatedly tried to escape and refused to wear clothes. No parent ever claimed him. He became known as "the wild boy of Aveyron." A thorough medical examination found no major abnormalities of either a physical or a mental nature. Why, then, did the boy seem more animal than human? Apparently because, until he walked out of the woods, he had been raised in isolation from other human beings (Shattuck, 1980).

Similar horrifying reports lead to the same conclusion. Occasionally a child is found locked in an attic or a cellar, where he or she saw another person for only short periods each day to receive food. Like the wild boy of Aveyron, such children rarely develop normally. Typically, they remain disinterested in games. They cannot form intimate social relationships with other people. They develop only the most basic language skills.

Some of these children may suffer from congenitally subnormal intelligence. It is uncertain how much and what type of social contact they had before they were discovered. Some may have been abused. Therefore, their condition may not be due only to social isolation. However, these examples do at least suggest that the ability to learn culture and become human is only a potential. To be actualized, **socialization** must unleash this human potential. Socialization is the process by which people learn their culture—including norms, values, and roles—and become aware of themselves as they interact with others.

More convincing evidence of the importance of socialization in unleashing human potential comes from a study conducted by René Spitz (Spitz, 1945; 1962). Spitz compared children who were being raised in an orphanage with children who, for medical reasons, were being raised in a nursing home. Both institutions were hygienic and provided good food and medical care. However, while their mothers cared for the babies in the nursing home, just 6 nurses cared for the 45 orphans. The orphans, therefore, had much less contact with other people. Moreover, from their cribs, the nursing home infants could taste a slice of society. They saw other babies playing and receiving care. They saw mothers, doctors, and nurses talking, cleaning, serving food, and providing medical treatment. In contrast, it was established practice in the orphanage to hang sheets from the cribs to prevent the infants from seeing the activities of the institution. Depriving the infants of social stimuli for most of the day apparently made them less demanding.

In the 1960s, researchers Harry and Margaret Harlow placed baby rhesus monkeys in various conditions of isolation to witness and study the animals' reactions. Among other things, they discovered that baby monkeys raised with an artifical mother made of wire mesh, a wooden head, and the nipple of a feeding tube for a breast were later unable to interact normally with other monkeys. However, when the artifical mother was covered with a soft terry cloth, the infant monkeys clung to it in comfort and later revealed less emotional distress. Infant monkeys preferred the cloth mother even when it had less milk than the wire mother. The Harlows concluded that emotional development requires affectionate cradling.

Social deprivation had other effects, too. Because of the different patterns of child care described above, by the age of 9 to 12 months the orphans were more susceptible to infections and had a higher death rate than the babies in the nursing home. By the time they were two to three years old, all the children from the nursing home were walking and talking, compared with fewer than 8 percent of the orphans. Normal children begin to play with their own genitals by the end of their first year. Spitz found that the orphans began this sort of play only in their fourth year. He took this as a sign that they might have an impaired sexual life when they reached maturity. This had happened to rhesus monkeys raised in isolation. Spitz's natural experiment thus amounts to quite compelling evidence for the importance of childhood socialization in making us fully human. Without childhood socialization, most of our human potential remains unlocked.

The formation of a sense of self continues in adolescence, a particularly turbulent period of rapid self-development. Consequently, many people can remember experiences from their youth that helped crystallize their self-identity. Do you? Robert Brym clearly recalls one such defining moment.

"I can date precisely the pivot of my adolescence," says Robert. "I was in grade 10. It was December 16. At 4 p.m. I was a nobody, and knew it. Half an hour later, I was walking home from school, delighting in the slight sting of snowflakes melting on my upturned face, knowing I had been swept up in a sea change.

"About 200 students sat impatiently in the auditorium that last day of school before the winter vacation. We were waiting for Mr. Garrod, the English teacher who headed the school's drama program, to announce the cast of *West Side Story.* I was hoping for a small speaking part and was not surprised when Mr. Garrod failed to read my name as a chorus member. However, as the list of remaining characters grew shorter, I became despondent. Soon only the leads remained. I knew that an unknown kid in grade 10 couldn't possibly be asked to play Tony, the male lead. Leads were almost always reserved for more experienced grade 12 students.

"Then came the thunderclap. 'Tony,' said Mr. Garrod, 'will be played by Robert Brym.'

"'Who's Robert Brym?' whispered a girl two rows ahead of me. Her friend merely shrugged in reply. If she had asked *me* that question, I might have responded similarly. Like nearly all 15-year-olds, I was deeply involved in the process of figuring out exactly who I was. I had little idea of what I was good at. I was insecure about my social status. I wasn't sure what I believed in. In short, I was a typical teenager. I had only a vaguely defined sense of self.

"A sociologist once wrote that 'the central growth process in adolescence is to define the self through the clarification of experience and to establish self-esteem' (Friedenberg, 1959: 190). From this point of view, playing Tony in *West Side Story* turned out to be the first section of a bridge that led me from adolescence to adulthood. Playing Tony raised my social status in the eyes of my classmates, made me more self-confident, taught me I could be good at something, helped me to begin discovering parts of myself I hadn't known before, and showed me that I could act rather than merely be acted upon. In short, it was through my involvement in the play (and, subsequently, in many other plays throughout high school) that I began to develop a clear sense of who I am."

The crystallization of self-identity during adolescence is just one episode in a lifelong process of socialization. To paint a picture of the socialization process in its entirety, we must first review the main theories of how one's sense of self develops during early childhood. We then discuss the operation and relative influence of society's main socializing institutions or "agents of socialization": families, schools, peer groups, and the mass media. In these settings, we learn, among other things, how to control our impulses, think of ourselves as members of different groups, value certain ideals, and perform various roles. (A **role** is the behaviour expected of a person occupying a particular position in society.) You will see that these institutions do not always work hand in hand to produce happy, well-adjusted adults. They often give mixed messages and are often at odds with each other. That is, they teach children and adolescents different and even contradictory lessons. You will also see that although recent developments give us more freedom to decide who we are, they can make socialization more disorienting than ever before. Finally, in the concluding section of this chapter, we examine how decreasing supervision and guidance by adult family members, increasing assumption of adult responsibilities by youth, and declining participation in extracurricular activities are changing the nature of childhood and adolescence today. Some analysts even say that childhood and adolescence are vanishing before our eyes. Thus, the main theme of this chapter is that the development of one's self-identity is often a difficult and stressful process—and it is becoming more so.

It is during childhood that the contours of one's self are first formed. We therefore begin by discussing the most important social-scientific theories of how the self originates in the first years of life.

## THEORIES OF CHILDHOOD SOCIALIZATION

### Freud

Socialization begins soon after birth. Infants cry out, driven by elemental needs, and are gratified by food, comfort, or affection. Because their needs are usually satisfied immediately, they do not at first seem able to distinguish themselves from their main caregivers, usually their mothers. However, social interaction soon enables infants to begin developing a self-image or sense of **self**—a set of ideas and attitudes about who they are as independent beings.

Sigmund Freud proposed the first social-scientific interpretation of the process by which the self emerges (Freud, 1962 [1930]; 1973 [1915–17]). Freud was the Austrian founder of psychoanalysis. He referred to the part of the self that demands immediate gratification as the **id.** According to Freud, a self-image begins to emerge as soon as the id's demands are denied. For example, at a certain point, parents usually decide not to feed and comfort a baby every time it wakes up in the middle of the night. The parents' refusal at first incites howls of protest. Eventually, however, the baby learns certain practical lessons from the experience—to eat more before going to bed, sleep for longer periods, and put itself back to sleep if it wakes up. Equally important, the baby begins to sense that its needs differ from those of its parents, that it has an existence independent of others, and that it must somehow balance its needs with the realities of life.

Because of many such lessons in self-control, including toilet training, the child eventually develops a sense of what constitutes appropriate behaviour and a moral sense of right and wrong. Soon a personal conscience or, to use Freud's term, a **superego,** crystallizes. The superego is a repository of cultural standards. In addition, the child develops a third component of the self, the **ego.** According to Freud, the ego is a psychological mechanism that, in well-adjusted individuals, balances the conflicting needs of the pleasure-seeking id and the restraining superego.

Sigmund Freud (1856–1939) was the founder of psychoanalysis. Many issues have been raised about the specifics of his theories. Nevertheless, his main sociological contribution was his insistence that the self emerges during early social interaction and that early childhood experience exerts a lasting impact on personality development.

In Freud's view, the emergence of the superego is a painful and frustrating process. In fact, said Freud, to get on with our daily lives we have to repress memories of denying the id immediate gratification. Repression involves storing traumatic memories in a part of the self that we are not normally aware of: the **unconscious.** Repressed memories influence emotions and actions even after they are stored away. Particularly painful instances of childhood repression may cause psychological problems of various sorts later in life, requiring therapy to correct. However, some repression is the cost of civilization. As Freud said, we cannot live in an orderly society unless we deny the id (Freud, 1962 [1930]).

Researchers have called into question many of the specifics of Freud's argument. Three criticisms stand out:

1. *The connections between early childhood development and adult personality are more complex than Freud assumed.* Freud wrote that when the ego fails to balance the needs of the id and the superego, individuals develop personality disorders. Typically, he said, this occurs if a young child is raised in an overly repressive atmosphere. To avoid later psychiatric problems, Freud and his followers recommended raising young children in a relaxed and permissive environment. Such an environ-

ment is characterized by prolonged breastfeeding, nursing on demand, gradual weaning, lenient and late bladder and bowel training, frequent mothering, freedom from restraint and punishment, and so forth. However, sociological research reveals no connection between these aspects of early childhood training and the development of well-adjusted adults (Sewell, 1958). One group of researchers who were influenced by Freud's theories tracked people from infancy to age 32 and made *incorrect* predictions about personality development in two-thirds of the cases. They "had failed to anticipate that depth, complexity, problem-solving abilities, and maturity might derive from painful [childhood] experiences" (Coontz, 1992: 228).

2. *Many sociologists criticize Freud for gender bias in his analysis of male and female sexuality.* Freud argued that psychologically normal women are immature and dependent on men because they envy the male sexual organ. Women who are mature and independent he classified as abnormal. We discuss this fallacy in detail in Chapter 9, Sexuality and Gender.
3. *Sociologists often criticize Freud for neglecting socialization after childhood.* Freud believed that the human personality is fixed by about the age of five. However, sociologists have shown that socialization continues throughout the life course (see Box 4.1). We devote much of this chapter to exploring socialization after early childhood.

**BOX 4.1**
**SOCIOLOGY AT THE MOVIES**

### *AFFLICTION* (1997)

Nick Nolte and James Coburn in *Affliction*

Nearly everyone accepts the importance of socialization in shaping people's personalities. In casual conversation, we talk about the influence of family and friends, neighbourhood and school, and other agents of socialization in making us who we are. *Affliction,* starring Nick Nolte, Sissy Spacek, and James Coburn, is a powerful movie about socialization and its legacy. Based on a novel by Russell Banks, it shows that some individuals cannot overcome the impact of early socialization, while others can.

James Coburn plays an alcoholic and abusive father. He thinks nothing of beating his wife and two children. Nick Nolte plays the elder son who is afflicted by his father's curse. When he was a child, he was afraid of his father. As an adult, he tries to overcome his father's influence, yet he cannot resist the lure of alcohol and violence. He is an unsuccessful police officer, and he has trouble maintaining the love and respect of the women around him: his ex-wife, his daughter, and his new girlfriend. Although he tries to be caring and responsible, his dependence on alcohol, his quick temper, and his inclination to violence ultimately doom his good intentions. In the end, tragedy befalls him.

The movie is not, however, fatalistic. It does not suggest that childhood socialization casts the adult personality in stone. The movie's narrator, the younger brother, managed to break away from the affliction. The younger brother does not tell the audience how this came about. However, he does give us a clue. He left his family and community to pursue higher education in the city. That is, he found another life, another set of social influences. Adult socialization in a new social context set him free.

As *Affliction* shows, then, socialization has a big impact on all of us. Childhood socialization is not, however, one's destiny. In making us think about the different paths taken by the two brothers, *Affliction* offers a good case study in the power—and limitations—of childhood socialization.

Despite the shortcomings listed above, the sociological implications of Freud's theory are profound. His main sociological contribution was his insistence that the self emerges during early social interaction and that early childhood experience exerts a lasting impact on personality development. As we will now see, the great North American social psychologist George Herbert Mead took these ideas in a still more sociological direction.

## Mead

A century ago, sociologist Charles Horton Cooley introduced the idea of the "looking glass self." Cooley wrote that, when we interact with others, they gesture and react to us. Just as we see our physical body reflected in a mirror, so we see our social selves reflected in people's gestures and reactions. In other words, our feelings about who we are depend largely on how we see ourselves judged by others (Cooley, 1902).

George Herbert Mead (1934) took up and developed the idea of the looking glass self. Like Freud, Mead noted that a subjective and impulsive aspect of the self is present from birth. Mead called it simply the **I.** Again like Freud, Mead argued that a repository of culturally approved standards emerges as part of the self during social interaction. Mead called this objective, social component of the self the **me.** However, while Freud focused on the denial of the id's impulses as the mechanism that generates the self's objective side, Mead drew attention to the unique human capacity to "take the role of the other" as the source of the me.

Mead understood that human communication involves seeing yourself from the point of view of other people. How, for example, do you interpret your mother's smile? Does it mean "I love you," "I find you humorous," or something else entirely? According to Mead, you can know the answer only if you use your imagination to take your mother's point of view for a moment and see yourself as she sees you. In other words, you must see yourself objectively, as a "me," to understand your mother's communicative act. All human communication depends on being able to take the role of the other, wrote Mead. The self thus emerges from people using symbols such as words and gestures to communicate. It follows that the "me" is not present from birth. It emerges only gradually during social interaction.

Much socialization takes place informally, with the participants unaware they are being socialized. These girls are learning gender roles as they go to the mall dressed like Britney Spears.

Unlike Freud, Mead did not think that the emergence of the self was traumatic. On the contrary, he thought it was fun. Mead saw the self as developing in four stages of role-taking. At first, children learn to use language and other symbols by *imitating* important people in their lives, such as their mother and father. Mead called such people **significant others.** Second, children pretend to *be* other people. That is, they use their imaginations to role-play in games such as "house," "school," and "doctor." Third, by the time they reach the age of about seven, children learn to play complex games requiring that they simultaneously take the role of *several* other people. In baseball, for example, the infielders have to be aware of the expectations of everyone in the infield. A shortstop may catch a line drive. If she wants to make a double play, she must be aware almost instantly that a runner is trying to reach second base and that the person playing second expects her to throw there. If she hesitates, she probably cannot execute the double play. Once a child can think in this complex way, she can begin the fourth stage in the development of the self. This involves taking the role of what Mead called the **generalized other.** Years of experience may teach an individual that other people, employing the cultural standards of their society, usually regard her as funny or temperamental or intelligent. A person's image of these cultural standards and how they are applied to her is what Mead meant by the generalized other.

## Recent Developments

Since Mead, psychologists have continued to study childhood socialization. For example, they have identified the stages in which thinking and moral skills develop from infancy to the late teenage years. Let us briefly consider some of their most important contributions.

The Swiss psychologist Jean Piaget divided the development of thinking (or cognitive) skills during childhood into four stages (Piaget and Inhelder, 1969). In the first two years of life, he wrote, children explore the world only through their five senses. Piaget called this the *sensorimotor* stage of cognitive development. At this point in their lives, children's knowledge of the world is limited to what their senses tell them. They cannot think using symbols.

According to Piaget, children begin to think symbolically between the ages of two and seven. He called this the *preoperational* stage of cognitive development. Language and imagination blossom during these years. However, children are still unable to think abstractly. Piaget illustrated this by asking five- and six-year-olds to inspect two identical glasses of coloured water. He then asked them whether the glasses contained the same amount of water. All the children agreed that they did. Next, the children watched Piaget pour the water from one glass into a wide, low beaker and the water from the second glass into a narrow, tall beaker. Obviously, the water level was higher in the second beaker although the volume of water was the same in both containers. Piaget then asked each child whether the two beakers contained the same amount of water. Nearly all the children said that the narrow, tall beaker contained more water. Clearly, the abstract concept of volume had no meaning for them.

In contrast, most seven- or eight-year-old children understood that the volume of water is the same in both beakers, despite the different water levels. This suggests that abstract thinking begins at about the age of seven. Moreover, between the ages of 7 and 11, children are able to see the connections between causes and effects in their environment. Piaget called this the *concrete operational* stage of cognitive development. Finally, by about the age of 12, children develop the ability to think more abstractly and critically. This is the beginning of what Piaget called the *formal operational* stage of cognitive development.

Social psychologist Lawrence Kohlberg took Piaget's ideas in a somewhat different direction. He showed how children's *moral* reasoning—their ability to judge right from wrong—also passes through developmental stages (Kohlberg, 1981). Kohlberg argued that young children distinguish right from wrong only on the basis of whether something gratifies their immediate needs. At this stage of moral growth, which Kohlberg labelled the *preconventional* stage, what is "right" is simply what satisfies the young child. For example, from the point of view of a two-year-old, it is entirely appropriate to grab a cookie from a playmate and eat it. An abstract moral concept like theft has no meaning for the very young child.

Teenagers, in contrast, begin to think about right and wrong in terms of whether specific actions please their parents and teachers and are consistent with cultural norms. This is the *conventional* stage of moral growth in Kohlberg's terminology. At this stage, a child understands that theft is a proscribed act and that getting caught stealing will result in punishment.

Some people never advance beyond conventional morality. Others, however, develop the capacity to think abstractly and critically about moral principles. This is Kohlberg's *postconventional* stage of moral development. At this stage, one may ponder the meaning of such abstract terms as freedom, justice, and equality. One may question whether the laws of one's society or the actions of one's parents, teachers, or other authorities conform to lofty moral principles. For instance, a 19-year-old who believes that the settlement of Europeans in North America involved the theft of land from Aboriginal peoples is thinking in postconventional moral terms. Such an adolescent is applying abstract moral principles independently and is not merely accepting their interpretation by authorities.

Modern psychology has done much to reveal the cognitive and moral dimensions of childhood development. However, from a sociological point of view, the main problem with this body of research is that it minimizes the extent to which society shapes the way we think. Thus, most psychologists assume that people pass through the same stages of mental development and think in similar ways, regardless of the structure of their society and their position in it. Many sociologists disagree with these assumptions.

A few psychologists do, too. The Belarussian psychologist Lev Vygotsky and the American educational psychologist Carol Gilligan offer the most sociological approaches to thinking about cognitive and moral development, respectively. For Vygotsky, ways of thinking are determined not so much by innate factors as they are by the nature of the social institutions in which individuals grow up. Consider, for example, the contrast between ancient China and Greece. The rice agriculture of ancient southern China required substantial cooperation among neighbours. It was centrally organized in a complex hierarchy within a large state. Harmony and social order were therefore central to ancient Chinese life. Ancient Chinese thinking, in turn, tended to stress the importance of mutual social obligation and consensus rather than debate. Ancient Chinese philosophies focused on the way in which wholes, not analytical categories, caused processes and events. In contrast, the hills and seashores of ancient Greece were suited more to small-scale herding and fishing than large-scale, centrally organized agriculture. Ancient Greek society was less socially complex than that of ancient China, it was politically decentralized, and it gave its citizens more personal freedom. As a result, ancient Greek thinking stressed personal agency. Debate was an integral part of politics. Philosophies tended to be analytical, which means, among other things, that processes and events were viewed as the result of discrete categories rather than whole systems. Markedly different civilizations grew up on these different cognitive foundations; ways of thinking depended less on innate characteristics than on the structure of society (Cole, 1995; Nisbett et al., 2001; Vygotsky, 1987).

In a like manner, Gilligan emphasized the sociological foundations of moral development in her studies of boys and girls. She attributed differences in the moral development of boys and girls to the different cultural standards parents and teachers pass on to them (Brown and Gilligan, 1992; Gilligan, 1982; Gilligan, Lyons, and Hanmer, 1990). For example, Gilligan found that, unlike boys, girls suffer a decline in self-esteem between the ages of 5 and 18.[1] She attributed this to their learning our society's cultural standards over time. Specficially, our society tends to define the ideal woman as eager to please and therefore nonassertive. Most girls learn this lesson as they mature, and their self-esteem suffers as a result. The fact that girls encounter more male and fewer female teachers and other authority figures as they age reinforces this lesson, according to Gilligan.

Influenced more by the approaches of Vygotsky and Gilligan than Piaget and Kohlberg, we now assess the contribution of various agents of socialization to the development of the self. These agents of socialization include families, schools, peer groups, and the mass media. We emphasize differences in socialization between societies, social groups, and historical periods. Our approach to socialization, therefore, is rigorously sociological.

In her research, Carol Gilligan attributes differences in the moral development of boys and girls to the different cultural standards parents and teachers pass on to them. By emphasizing that moral development is socially differentiated and does not follow universal rules, Gilligan has made a major sociological contribution to our understanding of childhood development.

## AGENTS OF SOCIALIZATION

### The Family

Freud and Mead understood well that the family is the most important agent of **primary socialization,** the process of mastering the basic skills required to function in society during childhood. They argued that, for most babies, the family is the world. This is as true today as it was a hundred years ago. The family is well suited to providing the kind of careful, intimate attention required for primary socialization. The family is a small group. Its members are in frequent face-to-face contact. Child abuse and neglect exist, but most parents love their children and are therefore highly motivated to care for them. These characteristics make most families ideal, even today, for teaching small children everything from language to their place in the world.

The family into which one is born also exerts an *enduring* influence over the course of one's entire life. Consider the long-term effect of the family's religious atmosphere, for instance. Social scientists who have sought to understand who becomes involved in religious organizations have come to the basic conclusion that the principal way in which religious groups grow is through the recruitment and retention of children whose parents already belong to the group. In addition, a few outsiders are brought into the religious groups through relational ties they have forged with group members through friendship and marriage (Bibby, 2001: 115). Parents, then, remain the key source of their children's religious identification throughout life. Even among those Canadians who may claim, at some point, to have abandoned the religious faith of their parents—or claim to have no religious identification whatsoever—many will still readopt the religious identities of their parents "when they want to secure 'rites of passage' such as marriage and the baptism of children" (Bibby, 2001: 200). Clearly, the religious atmosphere of the family into which one is born exerts a strong influence on one's religious practice as an adult.

Despite the continuing importance of the family in socialization, things have changed since Freud and Mead wrote their important works in the early 1900s. They did not foresee how the relative influence of various socialization agents would alter during the next century. The influence of some socialization agents increased, while the influence of others—especially the family—declined.

The family is still an important agent of socialization, although its importance has declined since the nineteenth century.

The socialization function of the family was more pronounced a century ago, partly because adult family members were more readily available for child care than they are today. As industry grew, families left farming for city work in factories and offices. Especially after the 1950s, many women had to work outside the home for a wage to maintain an adequate standard of living for their families. Fathers, for the most part, did not compensate by spending more time with their children. In fact, because divorce rates have increased, and many fathers have less contact with their children after divorce, children probably see less of their fathers on average now than they did a century ago. As a result of these developments, child care—and therefore child socialization—became a big social problem in the twentieth century. The question of "who's minding the kids?" now results in a variety of answers (see Figure 4.1). By century's end, "about 40 percent of Canada's 2.3 million children under the age of six received some form of non-parental childcare while one or both parents worked for pay or studied" (Vanier Institute of the Family, 2000: 160). On average, our country's youngest children now receive 27 hours a week of non-parental care. Among children aged 6 to 11, about 1 in 4 also receives regular care from someone other than his or her own parents (see Figure 4.2).

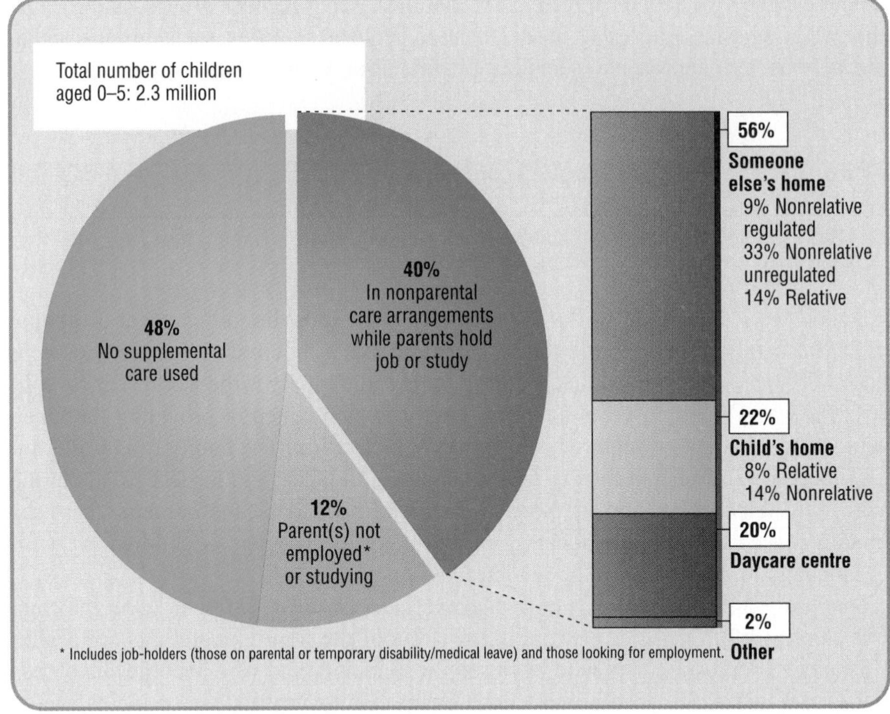


✦ **FIGURE 4.1** ✦

**Percentage of Children Age 0–5 in Nonparental Child Care While Parent(s) Work or Study (1994–1995)**

Source: Adapted from Statistics Canada, "National Longitudinal Survey of Children and Youth," Documentation and Data files, 1994–1995, Catalogue 89M0015, November 30, 1997.

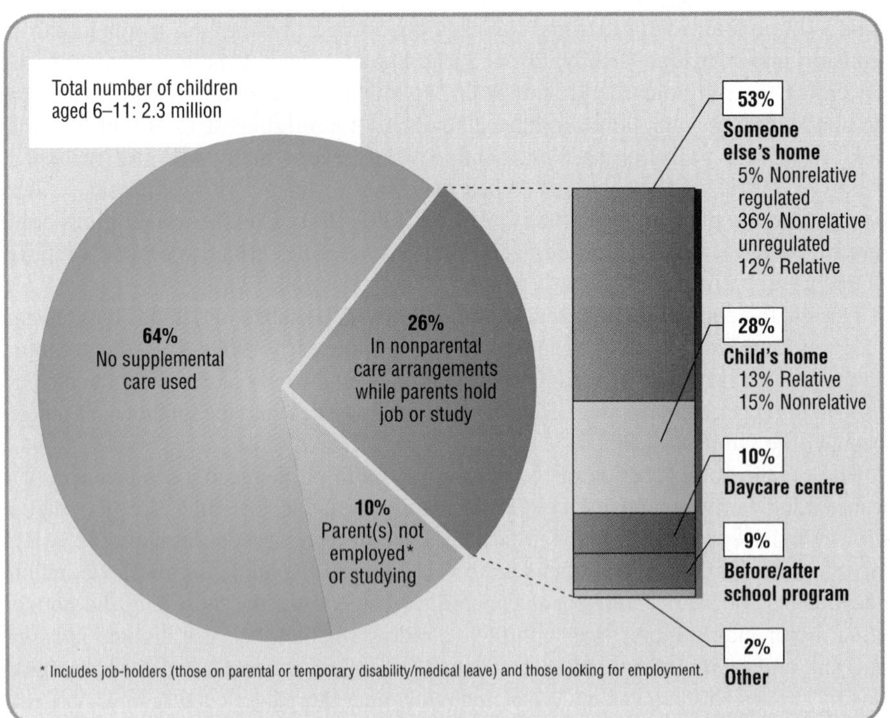


✦ **FIGURE 4.2** ✦

**Percentage of Children Age 6–11 in Nonparental Child Care (Outside of School Hours) While Parent(s) Work or Study (1994–1995)**

Source: Adapted from Statistics Canada, "National Longitudinal Survey of Children and Youth," Documentation and Data files, 1994–1995, Catalogue 89M0015, November 30, 1997.

Note: percentages may not total 100% because of rounding.

## Schools

For children over the age of five, the child-care problem was partly resolved by the growth of the public school system, which was increasingly responsible for **secondary socialization,** or socialization outside the family after childhood. Industry needed better trained and educated employees. Therefore, by the early 1900s, every province had established a "compulsory education" rule, which prescribed the minimum and maximum ages between which a child had to attend school. The precise cut-offs they established varied. Nevertheless, by the end of the twentieth century, more than 14 million Canadians aged 15 and older (two-thirds) had completed at least high school. Indeed, the 1996 Census was the first census in Canada to record a higher number of university graduates than of people reporting less than a grade nine education (Health Canada, 1999a). In 1999, 14.8 percent of Canadians had a university degree, while 11.0 percent had less than a grade nine education (*Canadian Global Almanac 2002*, 2001: 80). This makes Canadians among the most highly educated people in the world.

Although schools help prepare students for the job market, they do not necessarily give students an accurate picture of what the job market requires. In 1992, for example, a nationwide U.S. survey highlighted the mismatch between the ambitions of American high-school students and the projected needs of the American economy in 2005 (Schneider and Stevenson, 1999: 77–8; see Figure 4.3). The number of high-school students wanting to become lawyers and judges was five times the projected number needed. The number who wanted to become writers, artists, entertainers, and athletes was 14 times higher than expected openings in 2005. At the other extreme, in 2005 there will be five times more administrative and clerical jobs than students interested in such work. And there will be seven times more service jobs than teenagers wanting them. High-school students, it seems safe to say, often have unrealistically high expectations about the kinds of jobs they are likely to get when they finish their education.

In 2000, a national survey of Canadians teenagers also found that the vast majority has very high expectations when it comes to their future careers. Whether or not they expected to graduate from university, teens believed that they would be able to pursue careers, obtain the jobs they desired upon graduation, and stay with the same career for life (Bibby, 2001: 139). Optimism abounds, it seems, among most young Canadian and American students. Few, it seems, realistically anticipate the current "education–jobs" gap (Livingstone, 1999) and the widespread unemployment and underemployment that exist for even highly educated people in Canada as well as the United States, France, Germany, the United Kingdom, and other economically powerful countries (see Chapter 13, Religion and Education).

Instructing students in academic and vocational subjects, however, is just one part of the school's job. In addition, a **hidden curriculum** teaches students what will be expected

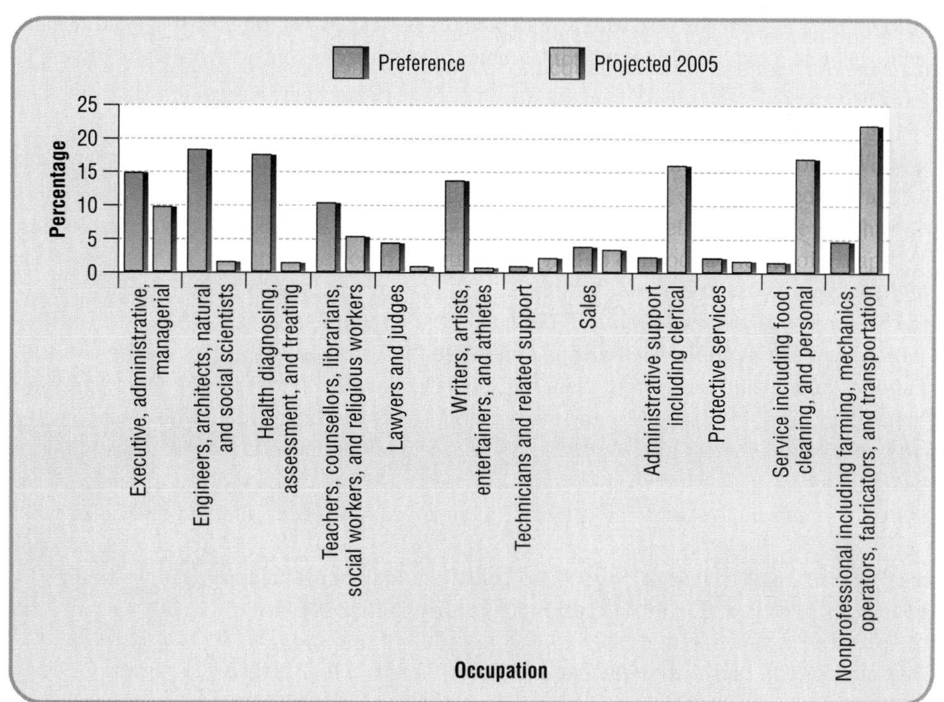


✦ **FIGURE 4.3** ✦
**Adolescent Job Preferences and Projected Jobs in Paid Labour Force, United States, 2005 (in percent)**

Source: Schneider and Stevenson (1999: 77).

of them in the larger society once they graduate. The hidden curriculum teaches them how to be conventionally "good citizens." Most parents approve of this instruction. According to one survey conducted in several highly industrialized countries in 1998, the capacity of schools to socialize students is more important to the public than all academic subjects except mathematics (Galper, 1998).

What is the content of the hidden curriculum? In the family, children tend to be evaluated on the basis of personal and emotional criteria. As students, however, they are led to believe that they are evaluated solely on the basis of their performance on impersonal, standardized tests. They are told that similar criteria will be used to evaluate them in the work world. The lesson is, of course, only partly true. As you will see in Chapters 8 (Race and Ethnicity), 9 (Sexuality and Gender), and 13 (Religion and Education), it is not just performance, but also class, gender, sexual orientation, and racial criteria that help determine success in school and in the work world. But the accuracy of the lesson is not the issue here. The important point is that the hidden curriculum has done its job if it convinces students that they are judged on the basis of performance alone. Similarly, a successful hidden curriculum teaches students punctuality, respect for authority, the importance of competition in leading to excellent performance, and other conformist behaviours and beliefs that are expected of "good citizens."

Many students from poor and racial minority families reject the hidden curriculum in whole or in part. Their experience, and the experience of their friends, peers, and family members, may make them skeptical about the ability of school to open job opportunities for them. As a result, they rebel against the authority of the school. Expected to be polite and studious, they openly violate rules and neglect their work.

Believing that school does not lead to economic success can act as a **self-fulfilling prophecy,** an expectation that helps cause what it predicts. W. I. Thomas and Dorothy Swaine Thomas had a similar idea in stating what became known as the **Thomas theorem:** "Situations we define as real become real in their consequences" (Thomas, 1966 [1931]: 301). For example, believing that school won't help you get ahead may cause you to do poorly in school, and performing poorly makes it more likely you will wind up near the bottom of the class structure (Willis, 1984 [1977]).

Teachers, for their part, can also develop expectations that turn into self-fulfilling prophecies. In one famous study, two researchers informed the teachers in a primary school that they were going to administer a special test to the pupils to predict intellectual "blooming." In fact, the test was just a standard IQ test. After the test, they told teachers which students they could expect to become high achievers and which they could expect

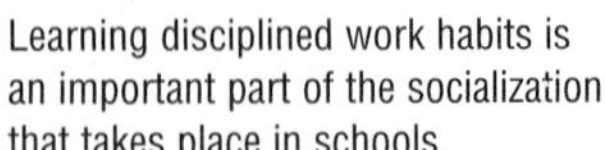
Learning disciplined work habits is an important part of the socialization that takes place in schools.

to become low achievers. In fact, the researchers assigned pupils to the two groups at random. At the end of the year, the researchers repeated the IQ test. They found that the students singled out as high achievers scored significantly higher than those singled out as low achievers. Since the only difference between the two groups of students was that teachers expected one group to do well and the other to do poorly, the researchers concluded that teachers' expectations alone influenced students' performance (Rosenthal and Jacobson, 1968). The clear implication of this research is that if a teacher believes that poor or minority children are likely to do poorly in school, chances are they will.

## Peer Groups

A second socialization agent whose importance increased in the twentieth century is the **peer group.** Peer groups consist of individuals who are not necessarily friends but are about the same age and of similar status. (**Status** refers to a recognized social position an individual can occupy.) Peer groups help children and adolescents separate from their families and develop independent sources of identity. They are especially influential over such lifestyle issues as appearance, social activities, and dating. In fact, from middle childhood through adolescence, the peer group is often the dominant socializing agent.

As you probably learned from your own life experience, there is often conflict between the values promoted by the family and those promoted by the adolescent peer group. Adolescent peer groups are controlled by youth, and through them young people begin to develop their own identities. They do this by rejecting some parental values, experimenting with new elements of culture, and engaging in various forms of rebellious behaviour, including the consumption of alcohol, cigarettes, and drugs (see Figure 4.4). In contrast, families are controlled by parents. They represent the values of childhood. Under these circumstances, such issues as hair and dress styles; music; curfews; tobacco, drug, and alcohol use; and political views are likely to become points of conflict between the generations.

We should not, however, overstate the significance of adolescent–parent conflict. For one thing, the conflict is usually temporary. Once adolescents mature, the family exerts a more enduring influence on many important issues. Research shows that families have more influence than peer groups over the educational aspirations and the political, social, and religious preferences of adolescents and university students (Davies and Kandel, 1981; Milem, 1998). Without minimizing the importance of the peer group in the lives of adolescents, the impact of families remains significant. A survey of 3500 Canadian high-school students found that 91 percent said that how they live their lives has been *influenced*

Gender segregation during schoolyard play.

✦ **FIGURE 4.4** ✦

**Percentage of Americans Age 12–17 Who Used Cigarettes, Alcohol, Marijuana, or Cocaine in Month prior to Survey, 1990–1997**

Source: U.S. Department of Health and Human Services (1999: 22).

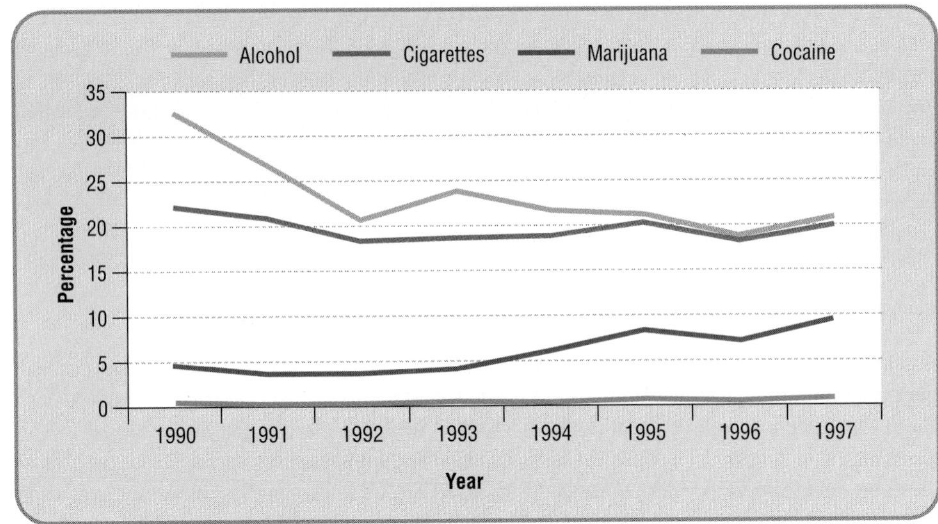


by the way they were brought up, and a clear majority feel that their parents, and especially their mothers, continue to have an impact on how they live their daily lives (Bibby, 2001: 55). Admittedly, not all the teens in this survey said their parents' influence was positive. However, approximately 7 in 10 teens reported high levels of enjoyment from their mothers and 6 in 10 teens said the same about their fathers. In addition, even though Canadian teens report that they are more likely to turn to their friends than to family members when they face a serious problem (approximately 4 in 10 versus 2 in 10, respectively), another 2 in 10 said they look equally to both.

A second reason why we should not exaggerate the extent of adolescent–parent discord is that peer groups are not just sources of conflict. They also help *integrate* young people into the larger society. A recent study of preadolescent children in a small North American city illustrates the point. Over a period of eight years, sociologists Patricia and Peter Adler conducted in-depth interviews with school children between the ages of 8 and 11. They lived in a well-to-do community comprising about 80 000 whites and 10 000 racial minority group members (Adler and Adler, 1998). In each school they visited, they found a system of cliques arranged in a strict hierarchy, much like the arrangement of classes and racial groups in adult society. In schools with a substantial number of visible minorities, cliques were divided by race. Visible minority cliques were usually less popular than white cliques. In all schools, the most popular boys were highly successful in competitive and aggressive achievement-oriented activities, especially athletics. The most popular girls came from well-to-do and permissive families. One of the main bases of their popularity was that they had the means and the opportunity to participate in the most interesting social activities, ranging from skiing to late-night parties. Physical attractiveness was also an important basis of girls' popularity. Thus, elementary-school peer groups prepared these youngsters for the class and racial inequalities of the adult world and the gender-specific criteria that would often be used to evaluate them as adults, such as competitiveness in the case of boys and attractiveness in the case of girls. (For more on gender socialization, see the discussion of the mass media below and Chapter 9, Sexuality and Gender.) What we learn from this research is that peer groups function not only to help adolescents form an independent identity by separating them from their families, but also to teach them how to adapt to the ways of the larger society.

## The Mass Media

Like the school and the peer group, the mass media have also become increasingly important socializing agents in the twenty-first century. The mass media include television, radio, movies, videos, CDs, audiotapes, the Internet, newspapers, magazines, and books.

The fastest-growing mass medium is the Internet. Worldwide, the number of Internet users jumped from 40 million in 1995 to 280 million in 2000 to an estimated 760 million in 2003 ("Global Internet Statistics (by Language)," 2002; see Figure 4.5).

However, TV viewing consumes more of the average Canadian's free time than any other mass medium (see Table 4.1). In 1999, almost all Canadians (99 percent) owned at least one colour television set (Statistics Canada, 2001c). Statistics Canada Time-Use Survey collected national survey data showing that watching TV is the most time-consuming activity in which Canadian men and women occupy their "free time." Although about 9 out of 10 Canadians read newspapers on a regular basis, 8 out of 10 read magazines, and 7 out of 10 have read at least one book in the previous year (Vanier Institute of the Family, 2000: 168), free time typically becomes prime time. On average, in 1998, Canadian men and women spent more time each day watching television than socializing in homes or other settings, playing sports, or enjoying a meal at a restaurant (*Canadian Global Almanac 2000*, 1999: 75). In 1999, Canadians spent an average of 21.6 hours per week watching television (down from a record high of 23.5 hours in 1988) (Statistics

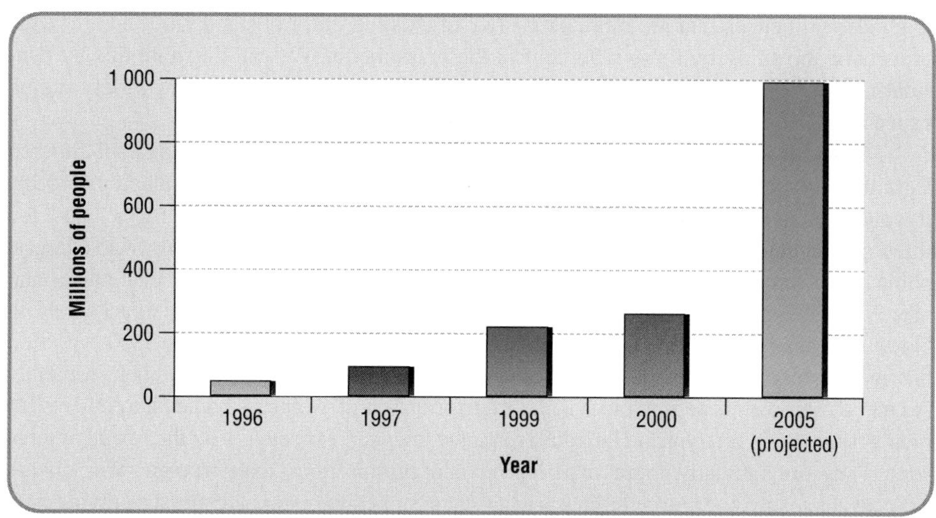


**✦ FIGURE 4.5 ✦**

**Number of Internet Users, 1996–2005 (predicted)**

Source: "Face of the Web Study Pegs Global Internet Population at More Than 300 Million" (1999).

**✦ TABLE 4.1 ✦**

**How Canadians Spend Their "Free Time," by Gender,[1] 1998**

Source: Adapted from *Canadian Global Almanac 2000* (1999).

[1] Average over a seven-day week by Canadians over the age of 15.

| | Average Hours Spent per Day by Participants in that Activity | | Percentage Participating | |
|---|---|---|---|---|
| **Activity** | **Men** | **Women** | **Men** | **Women** |
| Socializing | 3.0 | 2.8 | 62 | 70 |
| Restaurant meals | 1.6 | 1.5 | 20 | 18 |
| Socializing (in homes) | 2.5 | 2.3 | 49 | 61 |
| Other socializing | 2.7 | 2.6 | 12 | 12 |
| Television, reading, and other passive leisure | 3.3 | 3.1 | 87 | 84 |
| Watching television | 3.0 | 2.7 | 80 | 75 |
| Reading books, magazines, newspapers | 1.3 | 1.4 | 30 | 34 |
| Other passive leisure | 1.1 | 1.1 | 9 | 9 |
| Sports, movies, and other entertainment events | 2.6 | 2.8 | 6 | 6 |
| Active leisure | 2.6 | 2.2 | 41 | 39 |
| Active sports | 2.3 | 1.7 | 26 | 22 |
| Other active leisure | 2.4 | 2.1 | 21 | 22 |

Canada, 2001c). Heavy users of TV are concentrated among socially disadvantaged groups, and that trend is intensifying over time (Hao, 1994; Robinson and Bianchi, 1997).

Children and adolescents use the mass media for entertainment and stimulation. The mass media also help young people cope with anger, anxiety, and unhappiness. Finally, the cultural materials provided by the mass media help young people construct their identities—for example, by emulating the appearance and behaviour of appealing movie stars, rock idols, and sports heroes. In performing these functions, the mass media offer youth much choice. Many Canadians have access to scores of radio stations and TV channels, hundreds of magazines, thousands of CD titles, hundreds of thousands of books, and millions of Web sites. Most of us can gain access to hip-hop, heavy metal, or Haydn with equal ease. Thus, although adolescents have little choice over how they are socialized by their family and their school, the very proliferation of the mass media gives them more say over which media messages will influence them. To a degree, the mass media allow adolescents to engage in what sociologist Jeffrey Jensen Arnett (1995) calls **self-socialization,** or choosing socialization influences from the wide variety of mass media offerings.

Although people are to some extent free to choose socialization influences from the mass media, they choose some influences more often than others. Specifically, they tend to choose influences that are more pervasive, fit existing cultural standards, and are made especially appealing by those who control the mass media. We can illustrate this by considering how we learn gender roles from the mass media. **Gender roles** are widely shared expectations about how males and females are supposed to act.

The social construction of gender roles by the mass media begins when small children learn that only a kiss from Snow White's Prince Charming will save her from eternal sleep. It continues in magazines, romance novels, television, advertisements, music, and the Internet. It is big business. For example, Toronto's Harlequin Enterprises, the world's largest publisher of romance fiction, sells more than 200 million books a year in 23 languages and more than 100 national markets. About one in every six mass-market paperbacks sold in North America is a Harlequin romance. The average romance reader spends $800 a year on the genre. Most readers of Harlequin romances consume between 3 and 20 books a month. A central theme in these romances is the transformation of women's bodies into objects for men's pleasure. In the typical Harlequin romance, men are expected to be the sexual aggressors. They are typically more experienced and promiscuous than women. Women are expected to desire love before intimacy. They are assumed to be sexually passive, giving only subtle cues to indicate their interest in male overtures. Supposedly lacking the urgent sex drive that preoccupies men, women are often held accountable for moral standards and contraception (e.Harlequin.com, 2002; Grescoe, 1996; Jensen, 1984; see Figure 4.6).

Boys and girls do not passively accept such messages about appropriate gender roles. They often interpret them in unique ways and sometimes resist them. For the most part, however, they try to develop skills that will help them perform gender roles in a conventional way (Eagley and Wood, 1999: 412–3). Of course, conventions change. It is important to note in this regard that what children learn about femininity and masculinity today is less sexist than what they learned just a few generations ago. For example, comparing *Cinderella* and *Snow White* with *Mulan,* we see immediately that children going to Disney movies today are sometimes presented with more assertive and heroic female role models than the passive heroines of the 1930s and 1940s. On the other hand, the amount of change in gender socialization should not be exaggerated. *Cinderella* and *Snow White* are still popular movies. Moreover, for every *Mulan* there is a *Little Mermaid,* a movie that simply modernizes old themes about female passivity and male conquest. In the end, the Little Mermaid's salvation comes through her marriage. The vast majority of heroic, gutsy, smart, and enterprising leads in nearly all children's movies are still boys (Douglas, 1994: 296–7).

As the learning of gender roles through the mass media suggests, then, not all media influences are created equal. We may be free to choose which media messages influence us, but most people are inclined to choose the messages that are most widespread, most closely aligned with existing cultural standards, and made most enticing by the mass media. In the case of gender roles, these messages are those that support conventional expectations about how males and females are supposed to act.

Frantically she got up, her eyes flooding with tears, knocking over her chair in her desperate attempt to avoid crying in front of Alex and completely humiliating herself. But as she tried to run to the sanctuary of the bathroom the length of her bathrobe hampered her, and she had only taken a few steps before Alex caught up with her, bodily grabbed hold of her and swung her around to face him, his own face taut with emotion . . .

'Men aren't worth loving . . .'

'No?' Alex asked her huskily.

'No,' Beth repeated firmly, but somehow or other her denial had lost a good deal of its potency. Was that perhaps because of the way Alex was cupping her face, his mouth gently caressing hers, his lips teasing the stubbornly tight line of hers, coaxing it to soften and part. . .?

As Alex continued to kiss her the most dizzying sweet sensation filled Beth.

She had the most overpowering urge to cling blissfully to Alex and melt into his arms like an old-fashioned Victorian maiden. Behind her closed eyelids she could have sworn there danced sunlit images of tulle and confetti scented with the lilies of a bridal bouquet, and the sound of a triumphant 'Wedding March' swelled and boomed and gold sunbeams formed a circle around her.

Dreamily Beth sighed, and then smiled beneath Alex's kiss, her own lips parting in happy acquiescence to the explorative thrust of his tongue.

Alex was dressed casually, in jeans and a soft shirt. Beneath her fingertips Beth could feel the fabric of that shirt, soft and warm, but the body that lay beneath it felt deliciously firm . . . hard, masculine, an unfamiliar and even forbidden territory that her fingers were suddenly dangerously eager to explore.

✦ **FIGURE 4.6** ✦
**A Harlequin Romance**

Source: Jordan (1999: 97–8).

## Resocialization and Total Institutions

In concluding our discussion of socialization agents, we must underline the importance of **resocialization** in contributing to the lifelong process of social learning. Resocialization takes place when powerful socializing agents deliberately cause rapid change in people's values, roles, and self-conception, sometimes against their will.

You can see resocialization at work in the ceremonies that are staged when someone joins a fraternity, a sorority, the Canadian Armed Forces, or a religious order. Such a ceremony, or **initiation rite,** signifies the transition of the individual from one group to another and ensures his or her loyalty to the new group. Initiation rites require new recruits to abandon old self-perceptions and assume new identities. Often they are composed of a three-stage ceremony involving (a) separation from one's old status and identity (ritual rejection), (b) degradation, disorientation, and stress (ritual death), and (c) acceptance of the new group culture and status (ritual rebirth).

Much resocialization takes place in what sociologist Erving Goffman (1961) called **total institutions.** Total institutions are settings where people are isolated from the larger society and under the strict control and constant supervision of a specialized staff. Asylums and prisons are examples of total institutions. Because of the "pressure cooker" atmosphere in such institutions, resocialization in total institutions is often rapid and thorough, even in the absence of initiation rites.

A famous failed experiment illustrates the immense resocializing capacity of total institutions (Haney, Banks, and Zimbardo, 1973; Zimbardo, 1972). In the early 1970s, a group of researchers created their own mock prison. They paid about two dozen male volunteers to act as guards and inmates. The volunteers were mature, emotionally stable, intelligent university students from middle-class homes in the United States and Canada. None had a criminal record. By the flip of a coin, half the volunteers were designated prisoners, the other half guards. The guards made up their own rules for maintaining law and order in the mock prison. The prisoners were picked up by city police officers in a squad car, searched, handcuffed, fingerprinted, booked at the police station, and taken blindfolded to the mock prison. At the mock prison, each prisoner was stripped, deloused, put into a uniform, given a number, and placed in a cell with two other inmates.

Not all initiation rites or "rites of passage" involve resocialization, in which powerful socializing agents deliberately cause rapid change in people's values, roles, and self-conception, sometimes against their will. Some rites of passage are a normal part of primary and secondary socialization and merely signify the transition from one status to another. Here, an Italian family celebrates the first communion of a young boy.

To better understand what it means to be a prisoner or a prison guard, the researchers wanted to observe and record social interaction in the mock prison for two weeks. However, they were forced to end the experiment abruptly after only six days because what they witnessed frightened them. In less than a week, the prisoners and prison guards could no longer tell the difference between the roles they were playing and their "real" selves. Much of the socialization these young men had undergone over a period of about 20 years was quickly suspended.

About a third of the guards began to treat the prisoners like despicable animals, taking pleasure in cruelty. Even the guards who were regarded by the prisoners as tough but fair stopped short of interfering in the tyrannical and arbitrary use of power by the most sadistic guards.

All the prisoners became servile and dehumanized, thinking only about survival, escape, and their growing hatred of the guards. Had they been thinking as university students, they could have walked out of the experiment at any time. Some of the prisoners did, in fact, beg for parole. However, by the fifth day of the experiment they were so programmed to think of themselves as prisoners that they returned docilely to their cells when their request for parole was denied.

This experiment suggests that your sense of self and the roles you play are not as fixed as you may think. Radically alter your social setting and, like the university students in the experiment, your self-conception and patterned behaviour are also likely to change. Such change is most evident among people undergoing resocialization in total institutions. However, the sociological eye is able to observe the flexibility of the self in all social settings—a task made easier by the fact that the self has become more flexible over time. We now turn to an examination of the growing flexibility of the self.

## THE FLEXIBLE SELF

Older sociology textbooks acknowledge that the development of the self is a lifelong process. They note that when young adults enter a profession and get married, they must learn new occupational and family roles. If they marry someone from an ethnic, racial, or religious group other than their own, they are likely to adopt new cultural values or at least modify old ones. Retirement and old age present an entirely new set of challenges. Giving up a job, seeing children leave home and start their own families, losing a spouse and close friends—all these changes later in life require people to think of themselves in new ways, to redefine who they are.

In our judgment, however, older treatments of adult socialization underestimate the plasticity or flexibility of the self (Mortimer and Simmons, 1978). We believe that, today, people's identities change faster, more often, and more completely than they did just a couple of decades ago.

One important factor contributing to the growing flexibility of the self is globalization. As we saw in Chapter 3, Culture, people are now less obliged to accept the culture into which they are born. Because of globalization, they are freer to combine elements of culture from a wide variety of historical periods and geographical settings.

A second factor that increases our freedom to design our selves is our growing ability to fashion new bodies from old. People have always defined themselves partly in terms of their bodies; your self-conception is influenced by whether you're a man or a woman, tall or short, healthy or ill, conventionally good looking or plain. But our bodies used to be fixed by nature. People could do nothing to change the fact that they were born with certain features and grew older at a certain rate.

Now, however, you can change your body, and therefore your self-conception, radically and virtually at will—if, that is, you can afford it. Bodybuilding, aerobic exercise, and weight reduction regimes are more popular than ever. In 1999, Canada spent US$130 million on weight management programs. Only six rich countries—all of them with much larger populations than Canada's—spent more (Ash, 2001: 51). For those who want to see quicker results, plastic surgery allows people to buy new breasts, noses, lips, eyelids, and hair—and to remove unwanted fat, skin, and hair from various parts of their bodies. More than 7.4 million North Americans had cosmetic surgery in 2000. The top five cosmetic surgical procedures (which accounted for 76 percent of total surgeries performed) were nose reshaping (rhinoplasty—$4000), liposuction ($2000 per area), eyelid surgery ($5000), breast augmentation ($6000), and facelifts ($8000) (CBC, 2001). Although the vast majority of cosmetic surgery consumers in Canada are women, the number of Canadian men opting for cosmetic surgery has doubled in the past two decades. Men account for between one-quarter and one-third of Canadians seeking to redesign their appearance (Chisholm, 1996). Although teenaged females are reportedly seeking plastic surgery in record numbers, with nose alterations, ear pinnings, and breast implants the three most commonly performed cosmetic surgeries among this age group, 44 percent of the total cosmetic surgeries performed in Canada are on those between the ages of 35 and 50. One in three Canadians undergoing cosmetic surgery each year is a repeat customer (CBC, 2001; Nelson and Robinson, 2002: 144–5).

Some forms of surgery obviously result in far more drastic changes than others. Sex-change operations, while infrequent, are no longer a rarity. Organ transplants are routine. At any given time, about 3000 Canadians are waiting for a replacement organ (Health Canada, 1999a). There is a brisk illegal international trade in human hearts, lungs, kidneys, livers, and eyes that enables well-to-do people to enhance and extend their lives (Rothman, 1998).

As if all this were not enough to change how people think of themselves, Dr. Robert J. White of Case Western Reserve University School of Medicine in Cleveland has started to perform whole-body transplants. In 1998, he removed the head of a rhesus monkey and connected it by tubes and sutures to the trunk of another monkey. The new entity lived and gained consciousness, although it was paralyzed below the neck because there is no way yet to connect the millions of neurons bridging the brain and the spinal column. Could the same operation be done on a human? No problem, says White. Because the human body is larger and we know more about human anatomy than monkey anatomy, the operation would in fact be simpler than it is on monkeys. And, notes White, because research on spinal regeneration is advancing rapidly, it is only a matter of time before it will be possible to create a fully functional human out of one person's head and another's body (ABC Evening News, 30 April 1998; Browne, 1998). We used to think of our selves as congruent with our bodies but the two have now become disjointed. As a result, the formerly simple question, "Who are you?" has grown complex.

Further complicating the process of identity formation today is the growth of the Internet and its audiovisual component, the World Wide Web. In the 1980s and early 1990s, most observers believed that social interaction by means of computer would involve only the exchange of information between individuals (Wellman et al., 1996). It turns out they were wrong. Computer-assisted social interaction profoundly affects how people think of themselves.

Internet users interact socially by exchanging text, images, and sound via e-mail, Internet phone, video conferencing, computer-assisted work groups, and participation in **virtual communities.** Virtual communities have the most radical implications for the way we see ourselves. Virtual communities are associations of people, scattered across the country or the planet, who communicate via computer and modem about subjects of common interest. Some virtual communities cater to people's interest in specialized subjects, such as reggae music, BMWs, or white-water canoeing. Others are multiple user dimensions (MUDs), computer programs that allow thousands of people to role-play and engage in a sort of collective fantasy. These programs define the aims and rules of the virtual community and the objects and spaces it contains. Users log on to the MUD from their PCs around the world and define their character (their "identity") any way they wish. They interact with other users either by exchanging text messages or by having their avatars (graphical representations) act and speak for them.

The first MUD was created in 1979 at the University of Essex in England. In June 2002, there were nearly 1800 MUDs worldwide and probably more than a million MUD users ("The MUD Connector," 2002). MUD users form social relationships. They exchange confidences, give advice, share resources, get emotionally involved, and talk about sex. Although their true identities are usually concealed, they sometimes decide to meet and interact in real life.

Some people may dismiss all this as yet another computer game played mainly by bored university students, a sort of high-tech version of Dungeons and Dragons. The fact is, however, that a large and growing number of people are finding that virtual communities affect their identities in profound ways (Dibbell, 1993). Specifically, because virtual communities allow people to interact using concealed identities, MUD users are free to assume new identities and are encouraged to discover parts of themselves they were formerly unaware of. In virtual communities, shy people can become bold, normally assertive people can become voyeurs, old people can become young, straight people can become gay, women can become men.

Take Doug, a university student interviewed by sociologist Sherry Turkle. Doug plays four characters distributed across three different MUDs: a seductive woman, a macho cowboy type, a rabbit who wanders through its MUD introducing people to each other, and a fourth character Doug would "rather not even talk about because my anonymity there is very important to me. Let's just say that I feel like a sexual tourist." Doug often divides his computer screen into separate windows, devoting a couple of windows to MUDs and a couple to other applications. This allows him, in his own words, to

> split my mind . . . I can see myself as being two or three or more. And I just turn on one part of my mind and then another when I go from window to window. I'm in some kind of argument in one window and trying to come on to a girl in a MUD in another, and another window might be running a spreadsheet program or some other technical thing for school . . . And then I'll get a real-time message . . . that's RL [real life] . . . RL is just one more window . . . and it's not usually my best one. (quoted in Turkle, 1995: 13)

Turkle (1995: 14) comments:

> [I]n the daily practice of many computer users, windows have become a powerful metaphor for thinking about the self as a multiple, distributed system. The self is no longer simply playing different roles in different settings at different times, something that a person experiences when, for example, she wakes up as a lover, makes breakfast as a mother, and drives to work as a lawyer. The life practice of windows is that of a decentred self that exists in many worlds and plays many roles at the same time . . . MUDs . . . offer parallel identities, parallel lives.

Since Turkle did her research in the first half of the 1990s, other forms of Internet community building have surpassed the importance of MUDs. The most widely used are ICQ and MSN Messenger Service. These are instant messaging programs that allow users to interact in real time either in an unstructured way or focused on certain themes of their own choosing. ICQ and MSN "chat groups" have role-playing capabilities, but they are usually less formally organized than MUDs. Millions of people use ICQ and MSN Messenger Service daily (ICQ.com, 2002). Regardless of the forum, however, experience on the Internet reinforces our main point. In recent decades, the self has become increasingly flexible and people are freer than ever to shape their selves as they choose (Brym and Lenton, 2001).

However, this freedom comes at a cost, particularly for young people. In concluding this chapter, we consider some of the socialization challenges Canadian youths face today. To set the stage for this discussion, we first examine the emergence of *childhood* and *adolescence* as categories of social thought and experience some 400 years ago.

# DILEMMAS OF CHILDHOOD AND ADOLESCENT SOCIALIZATION

## The Emergence of Childhood and Adolescence

In preindustrial societies, children are thought of as small adults. From a young age, they are expected to conform as much as possible to the norms of the adult world. That is largely because children are put to work as soon as they can contribute to the welfare of their families. Often, this means doing chores by the age of 5 and working full-time by the age of 10 or 12. Marriage, and thus the achievement of full adulthood, is common by the age of 15 or 16.

Until the late 1600s, children in Europe and North America fit this pattern. It was only in the late 1600s that the idea of childhood as a distinct stage of life emerged. At that time, the feeling grew among well-to-do Europeans and North Americans that boys should be permitted to play games and receive an education that would allow them to develop the emotional, physical, and intellectual skills they would need as adults. Girls continued to be treated as "little women" (the title of Louisa May Alcott's 1869 novel) until the nineteenth century. Most working-class boys did not enjoy much of a childhood until the twentieth century. Thus, it is only in the last century that the idea of childhood as a distinct and prolonged period of life became universal in the West (Ariès, 1962 [1960]).

The idea of childhood emerged when and where it did because of social necessity and social possibility. Prolonged childhood was *necessary* in societies that required better-educated adults to do increasingly complex work. That is because childhood gave young people a chance to prepare for adult life. Prolonged childhood was *possible* in societies where improved hygiene and nutrition allowed most people to live more than 35 years, the average life span in Europe in the early 1600s. In other words, before the late 1600s, most people did not live long enough to permit the luxury of childhood. Moreover, there was no social need for a period of extended training and development before the comparatively simple demands of adulthood were thrust upon young people.

In general, wealthier and more complex societies whose populations enjoy a long average life expectancy stretch out the pre-adult period of life. For example, we saw that in Europe in 1600, most people reached mature adulthood by the age of about 16. In contrast, in countries such as Canada today, most people are considered to reach mature adulthood only around the age of 30, by which time they have completed their formal education, married, and "settled down." Once teenagers were relieved of adult responsibilities, a new term had to be coined to describe the teenage years: *adolescence*. Subsequently, the term *young adulthood* entered popular usage as an increasingly large number of people in their late teens and twenties delayed marriage to attend university (see Table 4.2).

Although these new terms describing the stages of life were firmly entrenched in North America by the middle of the twentieth century, some of the categories of the population they were meant to describe soon began to change dramatically. Somewhat excitedly, a number of analysts began to write about the "disappearance" of childhood and adolescence altogether (Friedenberg, 1959; Postman, 1982). Although undoubtedly overstating their case, these social scientists identified some of the social forces responsible for the changing character of childhood and adolescence in recent decades. Let us examine these social forces in the concluding section of this chapter.

## Problems of Childhood and Adolescent Socialization Today

When you were between the ages of 10 and 17, how often were you at home or with friends but without adult supervision? How often did you have to prepare your own meals or take care of a younger sibling while your parent or parents were at work? How many hours a week did you spend cleaning house? How many hours a week did you have to work at a part-time job to earn spending money and save for university? How many hours

✦ **TABLE 4.2** ✦

**The Stages of Life in Canada and Russia**

Source: Adapted from Markowitz (2000); United Nations (2000a).

*Note:* Among industrialized countries, those that are wealthiest and enjoy the longest life expectancy seem to distinguish more *stages* of life, each with distinct needs and features. For example, Russia is among the poorest of industrialized countries and its average life expectancy is only about 65 years. There, only two age groups are distinguished between birth and the age of 29: children and youth. In contrast, Canada is among the richest of the industrialized countries and its average life expectancy is longer. Here, six age groups are commonly distinguished between birth and age 29: infants, toddlers, children, preteens, teenagers (or adolescents), and young adults. Some people in Canada also distinguish different groups among the elderly: the young old (aged 65–74), the old (75–84), and the old old (85+). See Chapter 15, Health, Medicine, and Aging. As this example suggests, long life and material well-being allow people to invent new terms for more age groups and focus on the special needs of each one.

| **Canada** | | **Russia** | |
|---|---|---|---|
| GDP per capita, 2000: $32 274 | | GDP per capita, 1999 est.: $1948 | |
| Average life expectancy, 1997: | | Average life expectancy, 1995 est.: | |
| 76.2 years (men); | | 60.0 years (men); | |
| 81.8 years (women) | | 72.5 years (women) | |
| Infants | 0–2 | Children *(deti)* | 0–16 |
| Toddlers | 3–5 | | |
| Children | 6–10 | | |
| Preteens | 11–12 | | |
| Teenagers (or adolescents) | 13–17 (or 20) | Youth *(molodezh)* | 17–29 |
| Young adults | 18 (or 21)–25 (or 30) | | |
| Adults | 26 (or 31)–40 (or 45) | Adults *(vzroslie)* | 30–44 |
| Middle-aged | 41 (or 46)–64 | Older adults *(pozhilie)* | 45–54 (women), 59 (men) |
| Elderly | 65+ | Elderly/pensioners *(starie/pensioneri)* | 55 (women), 60 (men) |

a week did you spend on extracurricular activities associated with your school? on TV viewing and other mass media use? If you were like most Canadian preteens and teenagers, many of your waking hours outside of school were spent without adult supervision and/or assuming substantial adult responsibilities such as those listed above. You are unlikely to have spent much time on extracurricular activities associated with your school but quite a lot of time viewing TV and using other mass media.

Declining adult supervision and guidance, increasing mass media and peer group influence, and the increasing assumption of substantial adult responsibilities to the neglect of extracurricular activities have done much to change the socialization patterns of Canadian youth over the past 40 years or so. Let us consider each of these developments in turn.

- *Declining adult supervision and guidance.* In her recent six-year, in-depth study of adolescence, Patricia Hersch wrote that "in all societies since the beginning of time, adolescents have learned to become adults by observing, imitating and interacting with grown-ups around them" (Hersch, 1998: 20). However, in contemporary North America, notes Hersch, adults are increasingly absent from the lives of adolescents. Why? According to Hersch, "society has left its children behind as the cost of progress in the workplace" (Hersch, 1998: 19). What she means is that more adults are working longer hours than ever before. Consequently, they have less time to spend with their children than they used to. We examine some reasons for the increasing demands of paid work in Chapters 5 (Interaction and Organization) and 10 (Work and the Economy). Here, we stress a major consequence for youth: Young people are increasingly left alone to socialize themselves and build their own community. This community sometimes revolves around high-risk behaviour. To be sure, more is involved in high-risk behaviour than socialization patterns (see Box 4.2). However, it is not coincidental in this connection that girls are less likely to engage in juvenile crime than boys. That is partly because parents tend to supervise and socialize their sons and daughters differently (Hagan, Simpson, and Gillis, 1987). Parents typically exert more control over girls, supervising them more closely and socializing them to avoid risk. These research findings suggest that many of the teenage behaviours commonly regarded as problematic result from declining adult guidance and supervision.
- *Increasing media influence.* Declining adult supervision and guidance also leaves North American youth more susceptible to the influence of the mass media and peer

groups. As one parent put it, "When they hit the teen years it is as if they can't be children anymore. The outside world has invaded the school environment" (quoted in Hersch, 1998: 111). In an earlier era, family, school, church, and community usually taught young people more or less consistent beliefs and values. Now, however, the mass media offer a wide variety of cultural messages, many of which differ from each other and from those taught in school and at home. The result for many adolescents is confusion (Arnett, 1995). Should the 10-year-old girl dress modestly or in a sexually provocative fashion? Should the 14-year-old boy devote more time to

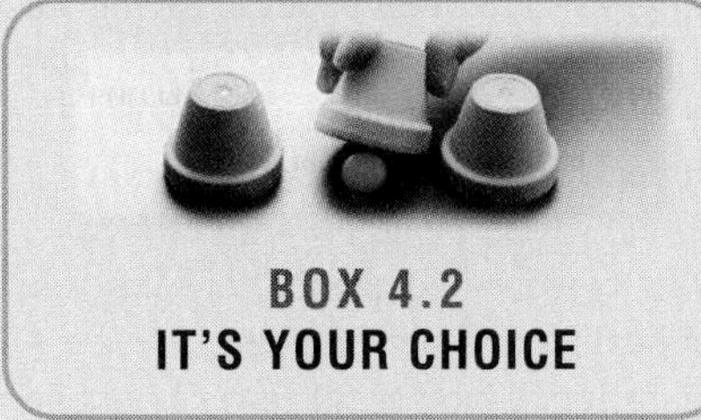

BOX 4.2
IT'S YOUR CHOICE

## SOCIALIZATION VERSUS GUN CONTROL

Students from W.R. Myers High School in Taber, Alberta, console each other following a memorial service for slain student Jason Lang. Are acts of violence committed by teenagers best understood as the result of faulty socialization, inadequate controls on firearms, or some combination of both?

On April 29, 1999, Columbine High School in Littleton, Colorado, was the scene of a mass shooting by two students. The students murdered 13 people (12 fellow students and 1 teacher) and then turned their guns on themselves.

After the massacre at Columbine High School, newspapers, magazines, Internet chat rooms, and radio and television talk shows were abuzz with the problem of teenage violence. "What is to be done?" people asked. One solution that seems obvious to many Canadians is to limit the availability of firearms. Their reasoning is simple: All advanced industrial societies except the United States restrict gun ownership, and only the United States has a serious problem with teenagers shooting one another. Other countries do have problems with teenage violence, however. For example, just eight days after the shooting rampage at Columbine, a 15-year-old boy in Taber, Alberta, gunned down one teen and wounded another in a school hallway. Exactly one year after the Columbine massacre, a teenager in an Ottawa-area high school stabbed four students and one staff member before his principal convinced him to surrender (*Maclean's,* 2000: 20). However, in countries where guns are less readily available, such as Canada, Australia, Britain, or Japan, teenage violence does not generally lead to mass killings. According to a 1995 Canadian government report, the rate of homicide using firearms per 100 000 people is 2.2 in Canada, 1.8 in Australia, 1.2 in Japan, 1.3 in Britain, and 9.3 in the United States (Department of Justice, Canada, 1995).

In the United States, however, most political discussions about teenage violence focus on the problem of socialization, not on gun control. Soon after the Littleton tragedy, for example, the U.S. House of Representatives passed a "juvenile crime bill." It cast blame on the entertainment industry, especially Hollywood movies, and the decline of "family values." Henry Hyde, an Illinois Republican, complained: "People were misled and disinclined to oppose the powerful entertainment industry" (quoted in Lazare, 1999: 57). Tom DeLay, a Republican congressman from Texas, worried: "We place our children in daycare centres where they learn their socialization skills . . . under the law of the jungle . . ." (quoted in Lazare, 1999: 58). In other words, according to these American politicians, teenage massacres result from poor childhood socialization: the corrupting influence of Hollywood movies and declining family values.

Some politicians want to reintroduce Christianity to public schools to help overcome this presumed decay. DeLay thus reported an e-mail message he received. It read: "'Dear God, why didn't you stop the shootings at Columbine?' And God writes, 'Dear student, I would have, but I wasn't allowed in school'" (quoted in Lazare, 1999: 57–8). One consequence of the Littleton massacre was not a gun control bill, but a bill to display the Ten Commandments in public schools.

What do you think? Is the problem of students shooting each other a problem of socialization, lack of gun control, or a combination of both? In answering this question, think about the situation in Canada as well as other countries and refer back to the discussion of media influence in Chapter 2, Research Methods.

attending church, synagogue, temple, or mosque—or to playing electric guitar in the garage? Should you "just say no" to drugs? The mass media and peer groups often pull young people in different directions from the school and the family, leaving them uncertain about what constitutes appropriate behaviour and making the job of growing up more stressful than it used to be.

- *Declining extracurricular activities and increasing adult responsibilities.* As the opening anecdote about Robert Brym's involvement in high-school drama illustrates, extracurricular activities are important for adolescent personality development. That is because they provide opportunities for students to develop concrete skills and thereby make sense of the world and their place in it. In schools today, academic subjects are too often presented as disconnected bits of knowledge that lack relevance to the student's life. Drama, music, and athletics programs are often better at giving students a framework within which they can develop a strong sense of self, for they are concrete activities with clearly defined rules. By training and playing hard on a hockey team, mastering a string or a band instrument, or acting in plays, you can learn something about your physical, emotional, and social capabilities and limitations, about what you are made of, and about what you can and cannot do. These are just the sorts of activities adolescents require for healthy self-development.

  However, if you're like most young Canadians today, you spent fewer hours per week on extracurricular activities associated with school than your parents did when they went to school. Educators estimate that only about a quarter of today's high-school students take part in sports, drama, music, and so forth (Hersch, 1998). Many of them are simply too busy with homework, household chores, child-care responsibilities, and part-time jobs to enjoy the benefits of school activities outside the classroom. The survey of 3500 Canadian teenagers referred to earlier in this chapter found that half of them said they were working at jobs averaging 15 hours a week (Bibby, 2001: 35).

Some analysts wonder whether the assumption of so many adult responsibilities, the lack of extracurricular activities, declining adult supervision and guidance, and increasing mass media and peer group influence are causing childhood and adolescence to disappear. As early as 1959, one sociologist spoke of "the vanishing adolescent" in North American society (Friedenberg, 1959). More recently, another commentator remarked: "I think that we who were small in the early sixties were perhaps the last generation...who actually had a childhood, in the . . . sense of . . . a space distinct in roles and customs from the world of adults, oriented around children's own needs and culture rather than around the needs and culture of adults" (Wolf, 1997: 13; see also Postman, 1982). Childhood and adolescence became universal categories of social thought and experience in the twentieth century. Under the impact of the social forces discussed above, however, the experience and meaning of childhood and adolescence now seem to be changing radically.

## SUMMARY

1. Studies show that children raised in isolation do not develop normally. This corroborates the view that social interaction unleashes human potential.
2. Freud developed the first social-scientific theory of how the self develops. He called the part of the self that demands immediate gratification the id. He argued that a self-image begins to emerge when the id's demands are denied. Because of many lessons in self-control, a child eventually develops a sense of what constitutes appropriate behaviour, a moral sense of right and wrong, and a personal conscience or superego. The superego is a repository of cultural standards. A third component of the self, the ego, then develops. In psychologically healthy individuals, the ego balances the demands of the id and superego.
3. Like Freud, Mead noted that a subjective and impulsive aspect of the self is present from birth. He called it the "I." Mead also argued that a repository of culturally approved standards emerges as part of the self during social interaction. Mead called it the "me." However, Mead drew attention to the unique human capacity to "take the role of the other" as the source of the me. At first the child imitates and then pretends to be his or her significant others. Next, the child learns to play complex games in which he or she must understand several roles simultaneously. Finally, a person's image of cultural standards and how they are applied to him or her stimulates the growth of what Mead called "the generalized other."
4. In the twentieth century, the increasing socializing influence of schools, peer groups, and the mass media was matched by the decreasing socializing influence of the family.
5. People's self-conceptions are subject to more flux now than they were even a few decades ago. Cultural globalization, medical advances, and computer-assisted communication are among the factors that have made the self more plastic.
6. Decreasing parental supervision and guidance, the increasing assumption of substantial adult responsibilities by children and adolescents, declining participation in extracurricular activities, and increased mass media and peer group influence are causing changes in the character and experience of childhood and adolescence. According to some analysts, childhood and adolescence as they were known in the first half of the twentieth century are disappearing.

## GLOSSARY

The **ego,** according to Freud, is a psychological mechanism that balances the conflicting needs of the pleasure-seeking id and the restraining superego.

**Gender roles** are widely shared expectations about how males and females are supposed to act.

The **generalized other,** according to Mead, is a person's image of cultural standards and how they apply to him or her.

A **hidden curriculum** teaches students what will be expected of them as conventionally good citizens once they leave school.

The **I,** according to Mead, is the subjective and impulsive aspect of the self that is present from birth.

The **id,** according to Freud, is the part of the self that demands immediate gratification.

An **initiation rite** is a ritual ordeal that signifies the transition of the individual from one group to another and ensures his or her loyalty to the new group.

The **me,** according to Mead, is the objective component of the self that emerges as people communicate symbolically and learn to take the role of the other.

One's **peer group** is composed of people who are about the same age and of similar status as the individual. The peer group acts as an agent of socialization.

**Primary socialization** is the process of acquiring the basic skills needed to function in society during childhood. Primary socialization usually takes place in a family.

**Resocialization** occurs when powerful socializing agents deliberately cause rapid change in one's values, roles, and self-conception, sometimes against one's will.

A **role** is the behaviour expected of a person occupying a particular position in society.

**Secondary socialization** is socialization outside the family after childhood.

The **self** consists of your ideas and attitudes about who you are.

A **self-fulfilling prophecy** is an expectation that helps bring about what it predicts.

**Self-socialization** involves choosing socialization influences from the wide variety of mass media offerings.

**Significant others** are people who play important roles in the early socialization experiences of children.

**Socialization** is the process by which people learn their culture—including norms, values, and roles—and become aware of themselves as they interact with others.

**Status** refers to a recognized social position an individual can occupy.

The **superego,** according to Freud, is a part of the self that acts as a repository of cultural standards.

The **Thomas theorem** states: "Situations we define as real become real in their consequences."

**Total institutions** are settings in which people are isolated from the larger society and under the strict control and constant supervision of a specialized staff.

The **unconscious,** according to Freud, is the part of the self that contains repressed memories we are not normally aware of.

A **virtual community** is an association of people, scattered across the country, continent, or planet, who communicate via computer and modem about a subject of common interest.

## QUESTIONS TO CONSIDER

1. Do you think of yourself in a fundamentally different way from the way your parents (or other close relatives or friends at least 20 years older than you) thought of themselves when they were your age? Interview your parents, relatives, or friends to find out. Pay particular attention to the way in which the forces of globalization may have altered self-conceptions over time.
2. Have you ever participated in an initiation rite in university, in the military, or in a religious organization? If so, describe the ritual rejection, ritual death, and ritual rebirth that made up the rite. Do you think the rite increased your identification with the group you were joining? Did it increase the sense of solidarity—the "we-feeling"—of group members?
3. List the contradictory lessons that different agents of socialization taught you as an adolescent. How have you resolved these contradictory lessons? If you have not resolved them, how do you intend to do so?

## WEB RESOURCES

### Companion Web Site for This Book

http://www.brymsociologycompass.nelson.com

Begin by clicking on the Student Resources section of the Web site. Next, select the chapter you are currently studying from the pull-down menu. From the Student Resources page you will have easy access to InfoTrac College Edition®, MicroCase online exercises, and additional Web links. The Web site also has many useful tips to aid you in your study of sociology, including practice tests for each chapter.

### InfoTrac Search Terms

These search terms are provided to assist you in beginning to conduct research on this topic by visiting http://www.infotrac-college.com

**Hidden curriculum**
**Initiation rite**
**Peer group**
**Primary socialization**
**Secondary socialization**

### Recommended Web Sites

A useful summary of major ideas in the sociological study of socialization can be found at http://www.nwmissouri.edu/nwcourses/martin/general/socialization/168108.thml.

For the socialization experiences that characterize different generations, go to a major search engine on the Web, such as Yahoo at http://www.yahoo.com/, and search for "teenagers," "generation X," "baby boomers," "the elderly," and so on.

Initiation rites (or rites of passage) are conveniently summarized in the online version of the *Encarta* encyclopedia. Go to the Encarta search engine at http://encarta.msn.com/ and search for "rites of passage."

## SUGGESTED READINGS

Patricia A. Adler and Peter Adler. *Peer Power: Preadolescent Culture and Identity* (New Brunswick, NJ: Rutgers University Press, 1998). The best sociological study of the role of peer groups in preadolescent socialization.

Reginald W. Bibby. *Canada's Teens: Today, Yesterday, and Tomorrow* (Toronto: Stoddart, 2001). A highly readable analysis that draws on nationwide surveys of Canadian teens and adults.

Sigmund Freud. *Civilization and Its Discontents.* James Strachey, trans. (New York: W. W. Norton, 1962 [1930]). Freud's classic explanation of how there can be no civilization without repression.

Patricia Hersch. *A Tribe Apart: A Journey into the Heart of American Adolescence* (New York: Ballantine Books, 1998). An insightful portrait of adolescents today.

## NOTE

1. Although subsequent research found that boys tend to score somewhat higher than girls on self-esteem, it failed to find a decline in the self-esteem of teenage girls. See Kling et al. (1999).

## IN THIS CHAPTER, YOU WILL LEARN THAT

- People interact for a variety of reasons. One important motivation is to gain valued resources. However, if one party competes too eagerly for valued resources, preventing others from benefiting, interaction breaks down.
- Competition is only one basis for interaction. Other bases include domination, which depends on fear, and cooperation, which depends on trust.
- For people to interact, they must understand the basic values and norms held by others. They also must accept their own and others' roles and statuses. To a degree, people work out these elements of interaction during interaction itself.
- Bureaucracies are large, impersonal organizations that operate with varying degrees of efficiency.
- Efficient bureaucracies are those that keep hierarchy to a minimum, distribute decision making to all levels of the bureaucracy, and keep lines of communication open among different units of the bureaucracy.

# CHAPTER 5

# INTERACTION AND ORGANIZATION

## THE STRUCTURE OF SOCIAL INTERACTION

In 1941, the large stone and glass train station was one of the proudest structures in Smolensk, a provincial capital of about 100 000 people on Russia's western border. Always bustling, it was especially busy on the morning of June 28. Besides the usual passengers and well-wishers, hundreds of Soviet Red Army soldiers were nervously talking, smoking, writing hurried letters to their loved ones, and sleeping fitfully on the station floor waiting for their train. Nazi troops had invaded the nearby city of Minsk in Belarus a couple of days before. The Soviet soldiers were being positioned to defend Russia against the inevitable German onslaught.

Robert Brym's father, then in his twenties, had been standing in line for nearly two hours to buy food when he noticed flares arching over the station. Within seconds, Stuka bombers, the pride of the German air force, swept down, releasing their bombs just before pulling out of their dive. Inside the station, shards of glass, blocks of stone, and mounds of earth fell indiscriminately on sleeping soldiers and nursing mothers alike. Everyone panicked. People trampled over one another to get out. In minutes, the train station was rubble.

Nearly two years earlier, Robert's father had managed to escape Poland when the Nazis invaded his hometown near Warsaw. Now, he was on the run again. By the time the Nazis occupied Smolensk a few weeks after their dive bombers destroyed its train station, Robert's father was deep in the Russian interior serving in a workers' battalion attached to the Soviet Red Army.

"My father was one of 300 000 Polish Jews who fled eastward into Russia before the Nazi genocide machine could reach them," says Robert. "The remaining 3 million Polish Jews were killed in various ways. Some died in battle. Many more, like my father's mother and younger siblings, were rounded up like diseased cattle and shot. However, most of Poland's Jews wound up in the concentration camps. Those deemed unfit were shipped to the gas chambers. Those declared able to work were turned into slaves until they could work no more. Then they, too, met their fate. A mere 9 percent of Poland's 3.3 million Jews survived the Second World War.

"Two questions always perplexed my father about the war. How was it possible for many thousands of ordinary Germans—products of what he regarded as the most advanced civilization on earth—to murder millions of defenceless and innocent Jews, Gypsies, homosexuals, and people with mental disabilities systematically in the death camps? And why did the innocents often march to the gas chambers without protest rather than make it as difficult as possible for the Nazis to carry out their vile plans?"

To answer these questions adequately, we must borrow ideas from the sociological study of interaction and organization. Consider first the question of how ordinary German citizens could commit the crime of the century. The conventional, nonsociological answer is that many Nazis were evil, sadistic, or deluded enough to think that Jews and other undesirables threatened the existence of the German people. Therefore, in the Nazi mind, the innocents had to be killed. This is the answer of the 1993 movie *Schindler's List* and other accounts (Goldhagen, 1996).

Yet it is far from the whole story. Sociologists emphasize two other factors:

1. Structures of authority tend to render people obedient. Most people find it difficult to disobey authorities because they fear ridicule, ostracism, and punishment. This was strikingly demonstrated in an experiment conducted by social psychologist Stanley Milgram (1974). Milgram informed his experimental subjects they were taking part in a study on punishment and learning. He brought each subject to a room where a man was strapped to a chair. An electrode was attached to the man's wrist. The experimental subject sat in front of a console that contained 30 switches with labels ranging from "15 volts" to "450 volts" in 15-volt increments. Labels ranging from "SLIGHT SHOCK" to "DANGER: SEVERE SHOCK" were pasted below the switches. The experimental subjects were told to administer a 15-volt shock for the man's first wrong answer and then to increase the voltage each time he made an

German industrialist Oskar Schindler (Liam Neeson, centre) searches for his plant manager Itzhak Stern among a trainload of Polish Jews about to be deported to Auschwitz-Birkenau in *Schindler's List*. The movie turns the history of Nazism into a morality play, a struggle between good and evil forces. It does not probe into the sociological roots of good and evil.

error. The man strapped in the chair was in fact an actor and did not actually receive a shock. However, as the experimental subject increased the current, the actor began to writhe in apparent pain, shouting for mercy and begging to be released. If the experimental subjects grew reluctant to administer more current, Milgram assured them that the man strapped in the chair would be just fine and insisted that the success of the experiment depended on the subject's obedience. The subjects were, however, free to abort the experiment at any time. Remarkably, 71 percent of experimental subjects were prepared to administer shocks of 285 volts or more even though the switches at that level were labelled "INTENSE SHOCK," "EXTREME INTENSITY SHOCK," and "DANGER: SEVERE SHOCK" and despite the fact that the actor appeared to be in great distress at this level of current.

Milgram's experiment teaches us that as soon as we are introduced to a structure of authority, we are inclined to obey those in power. This is the case even if the authority structure is brand new and highly artificial, even if we are free to walk away from it with little penalty, even if we think that by remaining in its grip we are inflicting terrible pain on another human being. In this context, the actions and inactions of German citizens in the Second World War become more understandable if no more forgivable.[1]

2. Bureaucracies are highly effective structures of authority. The Nazi genocide machine was bureaucratically organized, and that made it more effective. As Max Weber (1978a [1968]) defined the term, a **bureaucracy** is a large, impersonal organization composed of many clearly defined positions arranged in a hierarchy. A bureaucracy has a permanent, salaried staff of qualified experts and written goals, rules, and procedures. Staff members always try to find ways to run their organization more efficiently. "Efficiency" means achieving the bureaucracy's goals at the least cost. The goal of the Nazi genocide machine was to kill Jews and other undesirables. To achieve that goal with maximum efficiency, the job was broken into many small tasks. Most officials performed only one function: checking train schedules, organizing entertainment for camp guards, maintaining supplies of Zyklon B gas, removing ashes from the crematoria, and so forth. The full horror of what was happening eluded many officials, or at least it could be conveniently ignored as they concentrated on their jobs, most of them far removed from the gas chambers and death camps in occupied Poland (see Figure 5.1). Many factors account for variations in Jewish victimization rates across Europe during the Second World War (Fein, 1979; Marrus, 1987). One was bureaucratic organization. Not coincidentally, the proportion of Jews killed was highest not in the Nazi-controlled countries where

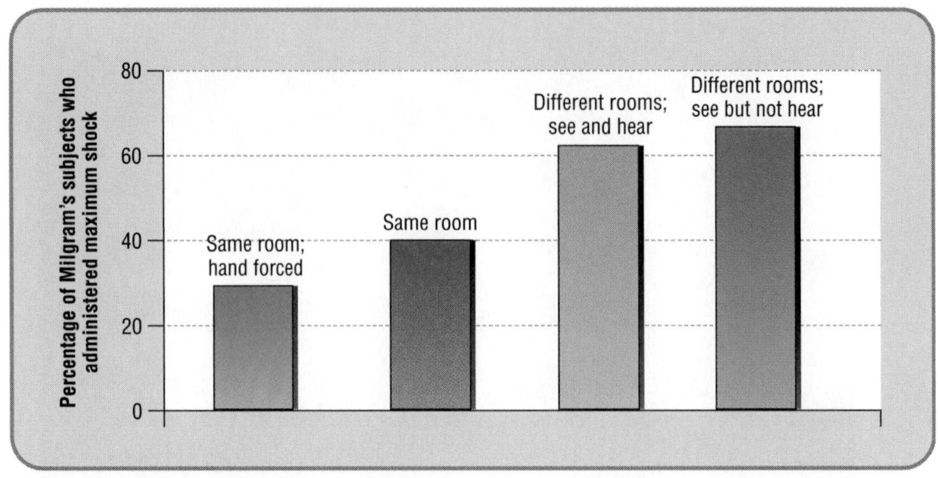


✦ **FIGURE 5.1** ✦
**Obedience to Authority Increases with Separation from the Negative Effects of One's Actions**

Milgram's experiment supports the view that separating people from the negative effects of their actions increases the likelihood of compliance. When subject and actor were in the same room and the subject was told to force the actor's hand onto the electrode, 30% of subjects administered the maximum 450-volt shock. When subject and actor were merely in the same room, 40% of subjects administered the maximum shock. When subject and actor were in different rooms but the subject could see and hear the actor, 62.5% of subjects administered the maximum shock. When subject and actor were in different rooms and the actor could be seen but not heard, 65% of subjects administered the maximum shock.

Source: Milgram (1974).

the hatred of Jews was most intense (e.g., Romania), but in countries where the Nazi bureaucracy was best organized (e.g., Holland) (Arendt, 1977 [1963]; Bauman, 1991 [1989]; Hilberg, 1961; Sofsky, 1997 [1993]).

In short, the sociological reply to the first question posed by Robert's father is that it was not just blind hatred but the social organization of authority and, in particular, its bureaucratic structure, that made it possible for the Nazis to kill innocent people so ruthlessly.

And why did the innocents only sometimes resist their oppressors rather than always fight them tooth and nail? The short sociological answer is that they had few resources with which to fight. Not only did they lack the most rudimentary weapons, but they had also been systematically stripped of their strength, health, dignity, and courage when they were shaven, deloused, starved, intimidated, worked half to death, and beaten by the camp guards. Jews with resources did fight the Nazis. They were the second most highly decorated ethnic group in the Soviet Red Army (next to the Russians themselves). They fought heroically in the underground resistance movement. They organized uprisings against the Nazis in Warsaw and other places (Dawidowicz, 1975). Only in the camps, where Jews lacked nearly all means of resistance, did their interaction with the Nazis tend to take the form of fearful compliance.

The kinds of issues raised above lie at the heart of the sociological study of interaction and organization. How is social interaction maintained? What are the most efficient forms of social organization? In one form or another, these questions have concerned social thinkers for centuries. They are our chief focus here.

How is social interaction maintained? **Social interaction** involves people communicating face to face, acting and reacting in relation to other people. Social interaction is structured around three elements. First, each person engaged in social interaction tends to adhere to specific norms or generally accepted ways of doing things. Second, each person acts according to the demands of a particular role or set of expected behaviours. Third, each person assumes a certain status or recognized position in the interaction. But if norms, roles, and statuses are the building blocks of social interaction, what is the cement that holds them together? In other words, why do people maintain stable patterns of interaction in the first place? This is the most fundamental sociological question one can ask, for it is really a question about how society is at all possible. As we will see, there are three main ways of maintaining social interaction and thereby cementing society: by means of domination (as in the concentration camps), by means of competition, and by means of cooperation. In the first half of this chapter, we investigate each of these modes of interaction.

What are the most efficient forms of social organization? Much interaction takes place in **social groups,** clusters of people who identify with one another and adhere to defined norms, roles, and statuses. Social groups are usually distinguished from **social categories,** or people who share a similar status but do not identify with one another. There are many

In primary groups such as families, norms, roles, and statuses are agreed upon but are not set down in writing. Social interaction creates strong emotional ties. It extends over a long period. It involves a wide range of activities. It results in group members knowing one another well.

kinds of social groups. However, sociologists make a basic distinction between primary and secondary groups. In **primary groups,** norms, roles, and statuses are agreed upon but are not set down in writing. Social interaction leads to strong emotional ties. It extends over a long period. It involves a wide range of activities. It results in group members knowing one another well. The family is the most important primary group.

**Secondary groups** are larger and more impersonal than primary groups. Compared with primary groups, social interaction in secondary groups creates weaker emotional ties. It extends over a shorter period. It involves a narrow range of activities. It results in most group members having at most a passing acquaintance with one another. Your sociology class is an example of a secondary group.

Bureaucracy, which we defined above, is one type of secondary group. Bureaucracies are widespread because they are often more efficient than other kinds of secondary groups—that is, they achieve similar goals at a lower cost. But, despite its success, is bureaucracy always the most efficient type of secondary group? We devote much of the second half of this chapter to answering that question.

First, however, we examine the way social interaction is maintained in situations involving domination, competition, and cooperation. We begin by analyzing the competitive character of much everyday conversation.

## THREE MODES OF SOCIAL INTERACTION

### Interaction as Competition and Exchange

Have you ever been in a conversation where you can't get a word in edgewise? If you are like most people, this is bound to happen to you from time to time. The longer this kind of one-sided conversation persists, the more neglected you feel. You may make increasingly less subtle attempts to turn the conversation your way. But if you fail, you may decide to end the interaction altogether. If this experience repeats itself—if the person you are talking to monopolizes conversations repeatedly—you are likely to want to avoid getting into conversations with him or her in the future. Maintaining interaction (and maintaining a relationship) requires that the needs of both parties for attention is met.

Most people do not consistently try to monopolize conversations. If they did, there would not be much talk in the world. However, a remarkably large part of all conversations involves a subtle competition for attention. Consider the following snippet of dinner conversation:

> John: "I'm feeling really starved."
> Mary: "Oh, I just ate."
> John: "Well, I'm feeling really starved."
> Mary: "When was the last time you ate?"

Sociologist Charles Derber recorded this conversation (Derber, 1979: 24). John starts by saying how hungry he is. The attention is on him. Mary replies that she's not hungry. Attention shifts to her. John insists he's hungry, shifting attention back to him. Mary finally allows the conversation to focus on John by asking him when he last ate. John thus "wins" the competition for attention.

Derber recorded 1500 conversations in family homes, workplaces, restaurants, classrooms, dormitories, and therapy groups. He concluded that North Americans usually try to turn conversations toward themselves, and they usually do so in ways that go unnoticed. Nonetheless, says Derber, the typical conversation is a covert competition for attention. In Derber's words, there exists

> a set of extremely common conversational practices which show an unresponsiveness to other's topics and involve turning them into one's own. Because of norms prohibiting blatantly egocentric behavior, these practices are often exquisitely subtle . . . Although conversationalists are free to introduce topics about themselves, they are expected to maintain an appearance of genuine interest in those about others in a conversation. A delicate face-saving system requires that people refrain from openly disregarding others' concerns and keep expressions of disinterest from becoming visible. (Derber, 1979: 23)

You can observe the competition for attention yourself. Tape-record a couple of minutes of conversation in your dorm, home, or workplace. Then play back the tape. Evaluate each statement in the conversation. Does the statement try to change which person is the subject of the conversation? Or does it say something about the other conversationalist(s) or ask them about what they said? How does not responding, or merely saying "uh-huh" in response, operate to shift attention? Are other conversational techniques especially effective in shifting attention? Who "wins" the conversation? What is the winner's gender, race, and class position? Is the winner popular or unpopular? Do you think there is generally a connection between the person's status in the group and his or her ability to win? (Hint: Sociological research shows that men interrupt conversations more than women and more often become the focus of attention [Tannen, 1994a; 1994b].) You might even want to record yourself in conversation. Where do you fit in?

Derber is careful to point out that conversations are not winner-take-all competitions. Unless both people in a two-person conversation receive some attention, the interaction is likely to cease. It follows that conversation typically involves the exchange of attention. Furthermore, attention is only one valued resource that people trade during social interaction. Other media of exchange include pleasure, approval, prestige, information, and money.

The idea that social interaction involves trade in valued resources is the central insight of **exchange theory** (Blau, 1964; Homans, 1961). A variant of this approach is **rational choice theory** (Coleman, 1990; Hechter, 1987). Rational choice theory focuses less on the resources being exchanged than on the way interacting people weigh the benefits and costs of interaction. According to rational choice theory, interacting people always try to maximize benefits and minimize costs. Business people want to keep their expenses to a minimum so they can keep their profits as high as possible. Similarly, everyone wants to gain the most from their interactions—socially, emotionally, and economically—while paying the least.

Undoubtedly, one can explain many types of social interaction in terms of exchange and rational choice theories. However, some types of interaction cannot be explained in these terms. For example, people often act in ways they consider fair or just, even if this does not maximize their personal gain (Frank, 1988; Gamson, Fireman, and Rytina, 1982). Some people even engage in altruistic or heroic acts from which they gain nothing at all. They do so although altruism and heroism can sometimes place them at considerable risk.

Consider a woman who hears a drowning man cry "help" and decides to risk her life to save him (Lewontin, 1991: 73–4). Some analysts assert that such a hero is willing to save the drowning man because she thinks the favour may be returned in the future. This seems far-fetched to us. In the first place, there is close to a zero probability that today's rescuer will be drowning someday and that the man who is drowning today will be present to save her. Second, a man who cannot swim well enough to save himself is just about the last person on earth you would want to try to rescue you if the need arose. Third, heroes typically report they decide to act in an instant, before there is a chance to weigh any costs and benefits at all. Heroes respond to cries for help based on emotion (which, physiologists tell us, takes 1/125 of a second to register in the brain), not calculation (which takes seconds or even minutes to register).

When people behave fairly or altruistically, they are interacting with others based on norms they have learned—norms that say they should act justly and help people in need, even if substantial costs are attached. Such norms are ignored for the most part by exchange and rational choice theorists. Exchange and rational choice theorists assume that most of the norms relevant to social interaction are like the "norm of reciprocity," which states that you should try to do for others what they try to do for you, because if you do not, then others will stop doing things for you (Homans, 1950). But social life is richer than this narrow view suggests. Interaction is not all selfishness. Moreover, as you will now see, we cannot assume what people want. That is because norms (as well as roles and statuses) are not presented to us fully formed. Nor do we mechanically accept them when they are presented to us. Instead, we constantly negotiate and modify norms, roles, and statuses as we interact with others.

## Interaction as Impression Management

> The best way of impressing [advisers] with your competence is asking questions you know the answer to. Because if they ever put it back on you, "Well what do you think?" then you can tell them what you think and you'd give a very intelligent answer because you knew it. You didn't ask it to find out information. You ask it to impress people.
>
> —a third-year medical student

Pierre Trudeau in the midst of "Trudeau-mania," 1967. Impression management involves manipulating the way you present yourself so that others will view you in the best possible light. It is especially important for politicians to be adept at impression management since their success depends heavily on voters' opinions of them.

Soon after they enter medical school, students become adept at **impression management.** That is, they learn how to manipulate the way they present themselves so they can appear in the best possible light and be judged competent by their teachers and patients. As Jack Haas and William Shaffir (1987) show in their study of professional socialization at McMaster University medical school, students adopt a new, medical vocabulary and wear a white lab coat to set themselves off from patients. They try to model their behaviour after that of doctors who have authority over them. They may ask questions they know the answer to so they can impress their teachers. When dealing with patients, they may hide their ignorance under medical jargon to maintain their authority. By engaging in these and related practices, medical students reduce the distance between their premedical-school selves and the role of doctor. By the time they finish medical school, they have reduced the distance so much that they no longer see any difference at all between who they are and the role of doctor. They come to take for granted a fact they once had to socially construct—the fact that they are doctors (Haas and Shaffir, 1987: 53–83).

Haas and Shaffir's study is an application of symbolic interactionism, a theoretical approach introduced in Chapter 1. Symbolic interactionists regard people as active, creative, and self-reflective. Whereas exchange theorists assume what people want, symbolic interactionists argue that people create meanings and desires in the course of social interaction. According to Herbert Blumer (1969), symbolic interactionism is based on three principles. First, "human beings act toward things on the basis of the meaning which these things have for them." Second, "the meaning of a thing" emerges from the process of social interaction. Third, "the use of meanings by the actors occurs through a process of interpretation" (Blumer, 1969: 2; see also Berger and Luckmann, 1966; Strauss, 1993; Wiley, 1994).

Although there are several distinct approaches to symbolic interactionism (Denzin, 1992), probably the most widely applied approach is **dramaturgical analysis.** As first developed by Canadian-born sociologist Erving Goffman (1959 [1956]), dramaturgical analysis takes literally Shakespeare's line from *As You Like It:* "All the world's a stage and all the men and women merely players."

From Goffman's point of view, we are constantly engaged in role-playing. This is most clearly evident when we are "front stage," that is, in public settings that require the use of props, set gestures, and memorized lines. A server in a restaurant, for example, must dress in a uniform, smile, and recite fixed lines. ("How are you? My name is Sam and I'm your server today. May I get you something from the bar before you order your meal?") When the server goes "backstage," he or she can relax from the front stage performance and discuss it with fellow actors ("Those kids at table six are driving me nuts!"). Thus, we often distinguish between our public roles and our "true" selves. When we do so, we experience what Goffman calls **role distance.** Note, however, that even backstage we engage in role-playing and impression management. It's just that we are less likely to be aware of it. For instance, in the kitchen, a server may try to present herself in the best possible light in order to impress another server so she can eventually ask him out on a date. Thus, the implication of dramaturgical analysis is that there is no single self, just the ensemble of roles we play in various social contexts.

By emphasizing how social reality is constructed in the course of interaction, symbolic interactionists downplay the importance of norms and understandings that precede any given interaction. **Ethnomethodology** tries to correct this shortcoming. Ethnomethodology is the study of the methods ordinary people use, often unconsciously, to make sense of what others do and say. Ethnomethodologists stress that everyday interactions could not take place without pre-existing shared norms and understandings. To illustrate this point, Harold Garfinkel (1967: 44) got one of his students to interpret a casual greeting in an unexpected way:

| | |
|---|---|
| Acquaintance: | [waving cheerily] How are you? |
| Student: | How am I in regard to what? My health, my finances, my schoolwork, my peace of mind, my . . . ? |
| Acquaintance: | [red in the face and suddenly out of control] Look! I was just trying to be polite. Frankly, I don't give a damn how you are. |

As this example shows, social interaction requires tacit agreement between the actors about what is normal and expected. Without shared norms and understandings, there can be no sustained interaction; people are likely to get upset and end an interaction when the assumptions underlying the stability and meaning of daily life are violated.

Assuming the existence of shared norms and understandings, let us now inquire briefly into the way people communicate in face-to-face interaction. This may seem a trivial issue, but as you will soon see, having a simple conversation is actually a wonder of intricate complexity.

## Verbal and Nonverbal Communication

Fifty years ago, an article appeared in the British newspaper *News Chronicle*, trumpeting the invention of an electronic translating device at the University of London. According to the article, "[a]s fast as [a user] could type the words in, say, French, the equivalent in Hungarian or Russian would issue forth on the tape" (quoted in Silberman, 2000: 225). The report was an exaggeration, to put it mildly. It soon became a standing joke that if you ask a computer to translate "The spirit is willing, but the flesh is weak" into Russian, the output will read "The vodka is good, but the steak is lousy." Today, we are closer to high-quality machine translation than we were in the 1950s. However, a practical Universal Translator exists only on Star Trek.

The main problem with computerized translation systems is that computers find it difficult to make sense of the social and cultural context in which language is used. The same words may mean different things in different settings, so computers, lacking contextual cues, routinely botch translations. For this reason, metaphors are notoriously problematic for computers. The following machine translation, which contains both literal and metaphorical text, illustrates this point:

> English original:
> Babel Fish is a computerized translation system that is available on the World Wide Web (at http://babel.altavista.com/translate.dyn). You can type a passage in a window and receive a nearly instant translation in one of four languages. Simple, literal language is translated fairly accurately. But when understanding requires an appreciation of social context, as most of our everyday speech does, the computer can quickly get you into a pickle. What a drag!
>
> Machine translation from English to French:
> Le poisson de Babel est un système de traduction automatisé qui est disponible sur le World Wide Web (à http://babel.altavista.com/translate.dyn). Vous pouvez taper un passage dans un Window et recevoir une traduction presque instantanée dans un de quatre langages. Le langage simple et littéral est traduit assez exactement. Mais quand la compréhension exige une appréciation de contexte social, en tant que majeure partie de notre discours journalier, l'ordinateur peut rapidement vous entrer dans des conserves au vinaigre. Quelle drague!
>
> Machine translation from French back to English:
> The fish of Babel is an automated translation system which is available on the World Wide Web (with http://babel.altavista.com/translate.dyn). You can type a passage in Window and receive an almost instantaneous translation in one of four languages. The simple and literal language is translated rather exactly. But when comprehension requires an appreciation of social context, as a major part of our daily speech, the computer can quickly enter you preserves to the vinegar. What a dredger!

Despite the complexity involved in accurate translation, human beings are much better at it than computers. Why is this so? A hint comes from computers themselves. Machine translation works best when applications are restricted to a single social context—say, weather forecasting or oil exploration. In such cases, specialized vocabularies and meanings specific to the context of interest can be built into the program. Ambiguity is thus reduced and computers can "understand" the meaning of words well enough to translate them reasonably accurately. Similarly, humans must be able to reduce ambiguity and make sense of words to become good translators. They do so by learning the nuances of meaning in different cultural and social contexts over an extended period of time.

Mastery of one's own language happens the same way. People are able to understand one another not just because they are able to learn words—computers can do that well enough—but also because they can learn the social and cultural contexts that give words meaning. They are greatly assisted in that task by nonverbal cues.

Let us linger for a moment on the question of how nonverbal cues enhance meaning. Sociologists, anthropologists, and psychologists have identified numerous nonverbal means of communication that establish context and meaning. The most important types of nonverbal communication involve the use of facial expressions, gestures, body language, and status cues.

*Facial expressions, gestures, and body language.* The April 2000 issue of *Cosmopolitan* magazine featured an article advising female readers on "how to reduce otherwise evolved men to drooling, panting fools." Basing his analysis on the work of several psychologists, the author of the article first urges readers to "[d]elete the old-school seductress image (smoky eyes, red lips, brazen stare) from your consciousness." Then, he writes, you must "[u]pload a new inner temptress who's equal parts good girl and wild child." This involves seven steps: (1) Establish eye contact by playing sexual peekaboo. Gaze at him, look away, peek again, and so on. By interrupting the intensity of your gaze, you heighten his anticipation of the next glance. The trick is to hold his gaze long enough to rouse his interest yet briefly enough to make him want more. Three seconds of gazing followed by five seconds of looking away seems to be the ideal. (2) Sit down with your legs crossed to emphasize their shapeliness. Your toes should be pointed toward the man who interests you and should reach inside the one-metre "territorial bubble" that defines his personal space. (3) Touch your body in places where you would like him to touch you so he will get the subliminal message that you are imagining his caresses. (4) Speak quietly. The more softly you speak, the more intently he must listen. Speaking just above a whisper will grab his full attention and force him to remain fixed on you. (5) Invade his personal space and enter his "intimate zone" by finding an excuse to touch him. Picking a piece of lint off his jacket and then leaning in to tell him in a whisper what you have done ought to do the trick. Then you can tell him how much you like his cologne. (6) Raise your arm to flip your hair. This gesture subliminally beckons him forward. (7) Finally, smile—and when you do, tilt your head to reveal your neck because it is sexually arousing (Willardt, 2000). If things progress, another article in the same issue of *Cosmopolitan* explains how you can read his body language to tell whether he is lying (Dutton, 2000).

Whatever we may think of the soundness of *Cosmopolitan's* advice or the image of women and men it seeks to reinforce, this example drives home the point that social interaction typically involves a complex mix of verbal and nonverbal messages. The face alone is capable of more than 1000 distinct expressions reflecting the whole range of human emotion. Arm movements, hand gestures, posture, and other aspects of body language send many more messages to one's audience (Birdwhistell, 1970; Wood and Henry, 2002). See Figure 5.2.

Despite the wide variety of facial expressions in the human repertoire, most researchers believed until recently that the facial expressions of six emotions are similar across cultures. These six emotions are happiness, sadness, anger, disgust, fear, and surprise (Ekman, 1978). A smile, it was believed, looks and means the same to advertising executives in Manhattan and members of an isolated tribe in Papua New Guinea. Researchers concluded that the facial expressions that express these basic emotions are reflexes rather than learned responses.

Since the mid-1990s, however, some researchers have questioned whether a universally recognized set of facial expressions reflects basic human emotions. Among other things, critics have argued that "facial expressions are not the readout of emotions but displays that serve social motives and are mostly determined by the presence of an audience" (Fernandez-Dols, Sanchez, Carrera, and Ruiz-Belda, 1997: 163; Harrigan and Tiang, 1997). From this point of view, a smile will reflect pleasure if it serves a person's interest

✦ **FIGURE 5.2** ✦

**Among other things, body language communicates the degree to which people conform to gender roles, or widely shared expectations about how males or females are supposed to act. In these photos, which postures suggest power and aggressiveness? Which suggest pleasant compliance? Which are "appropriate" to the sex of the person?**

to present a smiling face to his or her audience. On the other hand, a person may be motivated to conceal anxiety by smiling or to conceal pleasure by suppressing a smile.

Some people are better at deception than others. Most people find it hard to deceive others because facial expressions are hard to control. If you have ever tried to stop yourself from blushing you will know exactly what we mean. Sensitive analysts of human affairs—not just sociologists trained in the fine points of symbolic interaction, but police detectives, lawyers, and other specialists in deception—can often see through phony performances. They know that a crooked smile, a smile that lasts too long, or a smile that fades too quickly may suggest that something fishy is going on beneath the superficial level of impression management. Still, smooth operators can fool experts. Moreover, experts can be mistaken. Crooked smiles and the like may be the result of innocent nervousness rather than deception.

No gestures or body postures mean the same thing in all societies and all cultures. In our society, people point with an outstretched hand and an extended finger. However, people raised in other cultures tip their head or use their chin or eyes to point out something. We nod our heads "yes" and shake them "no," but others nod "no" and shake "yes."

Finally, we must note that in all societies people communicate by manipulating the space that separates them from others (Hall, 1959; 1966). This is well illustrated in our *Cosmopolitan* example, where women are urged to invade a man's "personal space" and "intimate zone" to arouse his interest. Sociologists commonly distinguish four zones that surround us. The size of these zones varies from one society to the next. In North America, an intimate zone extends about 45 cm from the body. It is restricted to people with whom we want sustained, intimate physical contact. A personal zone extends from about 45 cm to 1.25 m away. It is reserved for friends and acquaintances. We tolerate only a little physical intimacy from such people. The social zone is situated in the area roughly 1.25 m to 3.5 m away from us. Apart from a handshake, no physical contact is permitted from people we restrict to this zone. The public zone starts around 3.5 m from our bodies. It is used to distinguish a performer or a speaker from an audience.

*Status cues.* Aside from facial expressions, gestures, and body language, a second type of nonverbal communication takes place by means of **status cues,** or visual indicators of other people's social position. Erving Goffman (1959 [1956]) observed that when individuals come into contact, they typically try to acquire information that will help them define the situation and make interaction easier. This is accomplished in part by attending to status cues. Elijah Anderson (1990) developed this idea by studying the way African-Americans and European-Americans interact on the street in two adjacent urban neighbourhoods. Members of both groups visually inspect strangers before concluding that they are not dangerous. They make assumptions about others on the basis of skin colour, age, sex, companions, clothing, jewellery, and the objects they carry with them. They evaluate the movements of strangers, the time of day, and other factors to establish how dangerous they might be. In general, children pass inspection easily. White women and men are treated with greater caution, but not as much caution as black women and black men. Urban dwellers are most suspicious of black male teenagers. People are most likely to interact verbally with individuals who are perceived as the safest.

Although status cues may be useful in helping people define the situation and thus greasing the wheels of social interaction, they also pose a social danger. This is because status cues can quickly degenerate into **stereotypes,** or rigid views of how members of various groups act, regardless of whether individual group members really behave that way. Stereotypes create social barriers that impair interaction or prevent it altogether. For instance, police officers routinely stop young black male drivers without cause to check for proper licensing, possession of illegal goods, and so on. In this case, a social cue has become a stereotype that guides police policy. Young black males, the great majority of whom never commit an illegal act, often view the police practice as harassment. Racial stereotyping therefore helps to worsen relations between the black community and law enforcement officials (see Figure 5.3).

As these examples show, then, face-to-face interaction may at first glance appear to be straightforward and unproblematic. Most of the time it is. However, underlying the taken-for-granted surface of human communication is a wide range of cultural assumptions, unconscious understandings, and nonverbal cues that make interaction possible.

## Interaction and Power

So far we have made four main points:

1. One of the most important forces that cement social interaction is the competitive exchange of valued resources. People communicate to the degree they get something valuable out of the interaction. Simultaneously, however, they must engage in a

✦ **FIGURE 5.3** ✦

**Probability of Being Stopped by the Police, Toronto, by Race, Sex, and Age, 1992–1994 (*n* = 1257)**

Black male drivers are more likely to be stopped by the police than any other race/sex group. White and Asian female drivers are least likely to be stopped. Black males with higher education are more likely to be stopped than black males with lower education. How does stereotyping influence the chance of being stopped by the police?

Source: Wortley, Brownfield, and Hagan (1996).

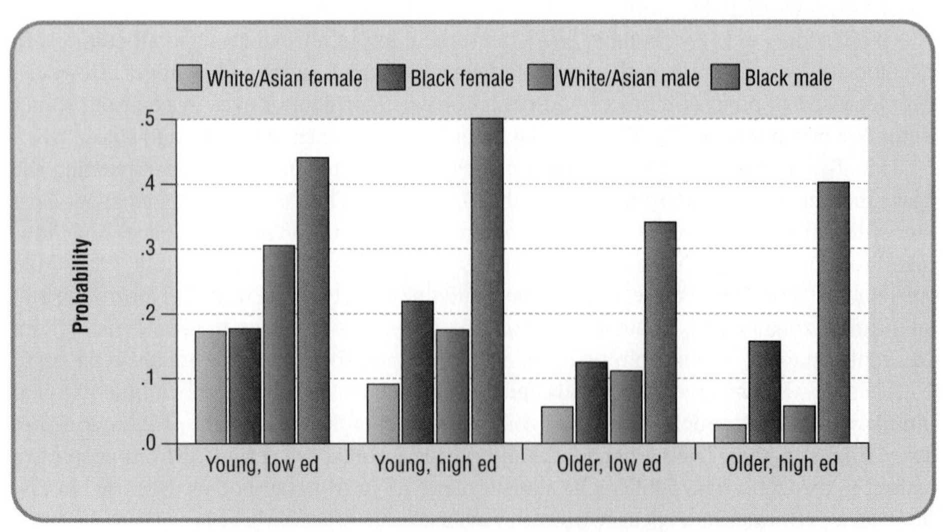

careful balancing act. If they compete too avidly and prevent others from getting much out of the social interaction, communication will break down. This is exchange and rational choice theory in a nutshell.

2. Nobody hands values, norms, roles, and statuses to us fully formed. Nor do we accept them mechanically. We mould them to suit us as we interact with others. For example, we constantly engage in impression management so others will see the roles we perform in the best possible light. This is a major argument of symbolic interactionism and its most popular variant, dramaturgical analysis.
3. Norms do not emerge entirely spontaneously during social interaction either. In general form, they exist before any given interaction takes place. Indeed, sustained interaction would be impossible without pre-existing shared understandings. This is the core argument of ethnomethodology.
4. Nonverbal mechanisms of communication greatly facilitate social interaction. These mechanisms include facial expressions, hand gestures, body language, and status cues.

We now want to highlight a fifth point that has so far been lurking in the background of our discussion. When people interact, their statuses are often arranged in a hierarchy. Those on top enjoy more power than those on the bottom. The degree of inequality strongly affects the character of social interaction between the interacting parties (Bourdieu, 1977 [1972]; Collins, 1975, 1982; Gamson, Fireman, and Rytina, 1982; Molm, 1997).

Max Weber (1947: 152) defined **power** as "the probability that one actor within a social relationship will be in a position to carry out his [or her] own will despite resistance." We can clearly see how the distribution of power affects interaction by examining male–female interaction. Women are typically socialized to assume subordinate positions in life, men to assume superordinate positions. As we saw in Chapter 4, Socialization, this is evident in the way men usually learn to be aggressive and competitive, women co-operative and supportive (see also Chapter 9, Sexuality and Gender). Because of this learning, men often dominate conversations. Thus, conversation analyses conducted by Deborah Tannen show that men are more likely than women to engage in long monologues and interrupt when others are talking. They are also less likely to ask for help or directions because doing so would imply a reduction in their authority. Much male–female conflict results from these differences. A stereotypical case is the lost male driver and the helpful female passenger. The female passenger, seeing that the male driver is lost, suggests that they stop and ask for directions. The male driver does not want to ask for directions because he thinks that would make him look incompetent. If both parties remain firm in their positions, an argument is bound to result (Tannen, 1994a, 1994b; see Box 5.1).

To get a better grasp on the role of power in social interaction, it is useful to consider two extreme cases and the case that lies at the midpoint between the extremes (see Figure 5.4 and Table 5.1).[2] **Domination** represents one extreme type of interaction. In social interaction based on domination, nearly all power is concentrated in the hands of people of similar status, while people of different status enjoy almost no power. Guards versus inmates in a concentration camp, and landowners versus slaves on plantations in the antebellum South, were engaged in social interaction based on domination. In extreme cases of domination, subordinates live in a state of near-constant fear.

The other extreme involves interaction based on **cooperation.** Here, power is more or less equally distributed between people of different status. Cooperative interaction is based on feelings of trust. For example, as we will see in Chapter 12, Families, marriages are happier when spouses share housework and child care equitably. Perceived inequity breeds resentment and dissatisfaction, harms intimacy, and increases the chance that people will have extramarital affairs and divorce. In contrast, high levels of trust between spouses are associated with marital stability and enduring love (Wood and Henry, 2002).

Between the two extremes of interaction based on domination and interaction based on trust is interaction based on **competition.** In this mode of interaction, power is

✦ **FIGURE 5.4** ✦
**Interpersonal Power by Mode of Interaction**

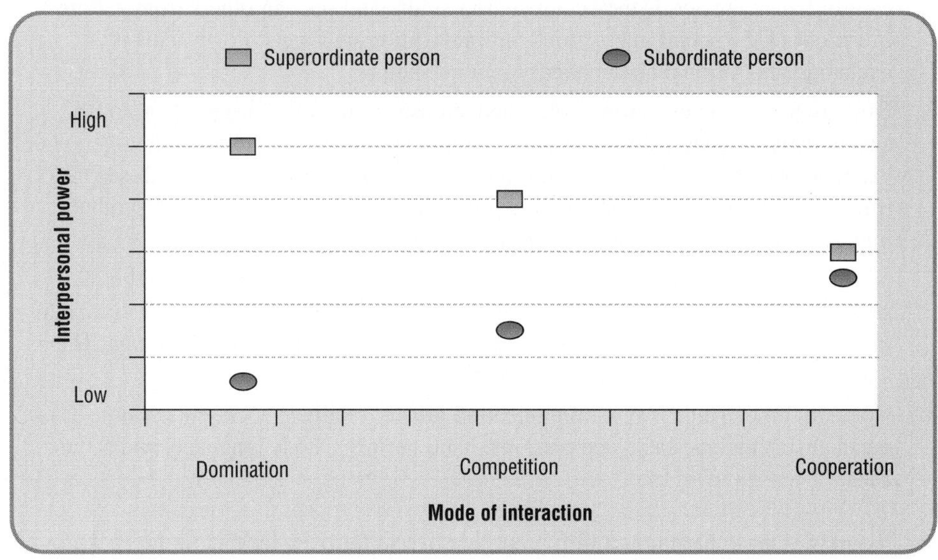


✦ **TABLE 5.1** ✦
**Main Modes of Interaction**

| **Mode of Interaction** | Domination | Competition | Cooperation |
|---|---|---|---|
| **Level of Inequality** | High | Medium | Low |
| **Characteristic Emotion** | Fear | Envy | Trust |
| **Efficiency** | Low | Medium | High |

unequally distributed but the degree of inequality is less than in systems of domination. Most of the social interactions analyzed by exchange and rational choice theorists are of this type. If trust is the prototypical emotion of relationships based on cooperation, and varying degrees of fear the characteristic emotion of subordinates involved in relationships based on domination, envy is an important emotion in competitive interactions.

Significantly, the mode of interaction in an organization strongly influences its efficiency or productivity, that is, its ability to achieve its goals at the least possible cost. Thus, African-American slaves on plantations in the antebellum South and Jews in Nazi concentration camps were usually regarded as slow and inept workers by their masters (Collins, 1982: 66–9). This characterization was not just a matter of prejudice. Slaves are inefficient workers. That is because, in the final analysis, it is only the fear of coercion that motivates them to work. Yet, as psychologists have known for half a century, punishment is a far less effective motivator than reward (Skinner, 1953). Slaves hate their tedious and often back-breaking labour, they get next to nothing in exchange for it, and therefore they typically do as little of it as they can get away with.

In a competitive mode of interaction, subordinates receive more benefits, including prestige and money. Prestige and money are stronger motivators than the threat of coercion. Thus, if bosses pay workers reasonably well, and treat them with respect, they will work more efficiently than slaves even if they do not particularly enjoy their work or identify with the goals of the company. Knowing that they can make more money by working harder, and that their efforts are appreciated, workers will often put in extra effort (Collins, 1982: 63–5).

The most efficient workers, however, are those who enjoy their work and identify with their employer. Keeping decision making as democratic as possible, giving workers some decision-making autonomy, and ensuring that salaries and perks are not too highly skewed

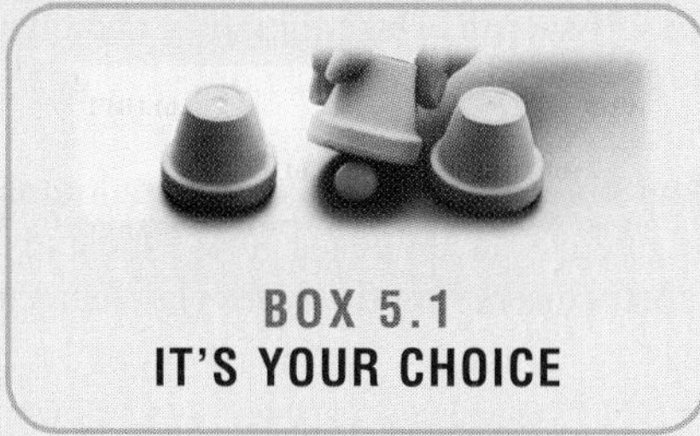

BOX 5.1
IT'S YOUR CHOICE

### ALLOCATING TIME FAIRLY IN CLASS DISCUSSIONS

Professors are accustomed to hearing student complaints. Sometimes these are reasonable; sometimes they are not. While serving as chair of his department, one of the authors of this book, John Lie, received a puzzling complaint from a self-proclaimed feminist taking a women's studies class. She said: "The professor lets the male students talk in class. They don't seem to have done much of the reading, but the professor insists on letting them say something even when they don't really have anything to say." John later talked to the professor, who claimed she was only trying to let different opinions come out in class.

Policy debates often deal with important issues at the provincial, national, and international levels. However, they may revolve around everyday social interaction. For instance, as this chapter's discussion of Deborah Tannen's work suggests, gender differences in conversational styles have a big impact on gender inequality. Thus, many professors use class participation to evaluate students. Your grade may depend in part on how often you speak up and whether you have something interesting to say. But Tannen's study suggests that men tend to speak up more often and more forcefully than women. Men are more likely to dominate classroom discussions. Therefore, does the evaluation of class participation in assigning grades unfairly penalize female students? If so, what policies can you recommend that might overcome the problem?

One possibility is to eliminate class participation as a criterion for student evaluation. However, most professors would object to this approach on the grounds that good discussions can demonstrate students' familiarity with course material, sharpen one's ability to reason logically, and enrich everyone's educational experience. A post-secondary school lacking energetic discussion and debate would not be much of an educational institution.

A second option is systematically to encourage women to participate in classroom discussion. A third option is to allot equal time for women and men or to give each student equal time. Criticisms of such an approach come readily to mind. Shouldn't time be allocated only to people who have done the reading and have something interesting to say? That is the point made by the student who complained to John Lie. Encouraging everyone to speak or forcing each student to speak for a certain number of minutes, even if they do not have something interesting to contribute, would probably be boring or frustrating for better-prepared students.

As you can see, there is no obvious solution to the question of how time should be allocated in class discussions. In general, the realm of interpersonal interaction and conversation is an extremely difficult area in which to impose rules and policies. So what, if anything, should your professor do to ensure that class discussion time is allocated fairly?

in favour of those on top all help to create high worker morale and foster a more cooperative work environment. For example, company picnics, baseball games, and, in Japan, the singing of company songs before the workday begins all help workers feel they are in harmony with their employer and are playing on the same team. Similarly, although sales meetings and other conferences have an instrumental purpose (the discussion of sales

Social interaction is not based entirely on selfishness. Love, for example, is based on trust. Gustav Klimt. "The Kiss." 1907–8.

strategies, new products, etc.), they also offer opportunities for friendly social interaction that increase workers' identification with their employer. When workers identify strongly with their employers, they will be willing to undergo self-sacrifice, take initiative, and give their best creative effort, even without the prospect of material reward. The old saying, "A job well done is reward enough," is a good motto for a cooperative work environment.

In the next section, we have more to say about competition versus cooperation as modes of interaction. As you will see, modes of interaction influence how efficiently bureaucracies operate. We introduce this theme by first considering the types and sources of bureaucratic inefficiency.

## BUREAUCRACIES AND NETWORKS

### Bureaucratic Inefficiency

At the beginning of this chapter we noted that Weber regarded bureaucracies as the most efficient type of secondary group. This runs against the grain of common knowledge. In everyday speech, when someone says "bureaucracy," people commonly think of bored clerks sitting in small cubicles spinning out endless trails of "red tape" that create needless waste and frustrate the goals of clients (see Box 5.2). The idea that bureaucracies are efficient may seem very odd indeed.

Real events often reinforce the common view. Consider, for instance, the case of the *Challenger* space shuttle, which exploded shortly after takeoff on January 28, 1986. All seven crew members were killed. The weather was cold, and the flexible O-rings that were supposed to seal the sections of the booster rockets had become rigid. This allowed burning gas to leak. The burning gas triggered the explosion. Some engineers at NASA and at the company that manufactured the O-rings knew they would not function properly in cold weather. However, this information did not reach NASA's top bureaucrats:

> [The] rigid hierarchy that had arisen at NASA . . . made communication between departments formal and not particularly effective. [In the huge bureaucracy,] most communication was done through memos and reports. Everything was meticulously documented, but critical details tended to get lost in the paperwork blizzard. The result was that the upper-level managers were kept informed about possible problems with the O-rings . . . but they never truly understood the seriousness of the issue. (Pool, 1997: 257)

As this event shows, then, bureaucratic inefficiencies can have tragic consequences.

How can we reconcile the reality of bureaucratic inefficiencies—even tragedies—with Weber's view that bureaucracies are the most efficient type of secondary group? The answer is twofold. First, we must recognize that when Weber wrote about the efficiency of bureaucracy, he was comparing it with older organizational forms. These operated on the basis of either traditional practice ("We do it this way because we've always done it this way") or the charisma of their leaders ("We do it this way because our chief inspires us to do it this way"). Compared with such "traditional" and "charismatic" organizations, bureaucracies are generally more efficient. Second, we must recognize that Weber thought bureaucracies could operate efficiently only in the ideal case. He wrote extensively about some of bureaucracy's less admirable aspects in the real world. In other words, he understood that reality is often messier than the ideal case. So should we. In reality, bureaucracies vary in efficiency. Therefore, rather than proclaiming bureaucracy efficient or inefficient, it makes sense to find out what makes bureaucracies work well or poorly. The knowledge can then be applied to improving the operation of bureaucracies.

Sociologists lodge four main criticisms against bureaucracies. First is the problem of **dehumanization.** Rather than treating clients and personnel as people with unique needs, bureaucracies sometimes treat clients as standard cases and personnel as cogs in a giant machine. This frustrates clients and lowers worker morale. Second is the problem of

## BOX 5.2 SOCIOLOGY AT THE MOVIES

In *Ikiru,* Kanji Watanabe, played by Takashi Shamura, finds solace from bureaucracy and the prospect of death by helping to create a small park for children in his neighbourhood.

### *IKIRU* (1952)

Mounds of paperwork, cluttered office desks, long lines of complaining citizens, and indifferent clerks who quietly shuffle papers—this image of bureaucracy can be found in all modern and postmodern societies. Few people are without a story or two of frustrating struggles against one bureaucracy or another. Most movies depict bureaucracy as perpetually mired in red tape and as an impersonal, soulless machine.

*Ikiru,* directed by the Japanese filmmaker Akira Kurosawa, is a profound portrait of the individual versus bureaucracy. Many film critics consider it one of the top 10 films of the twentieth century.

At the beginning of the film, the main character, Kanji Watanabe, seems little more than a living corpse. As a minor clerk in a large city bureaucracy, he spends much of the day plodding through documents. He is a true bureaucratic ritualist. He does not see and does not seem to care about the people whom he is supposed to be serving. He simply shuffles paper.

One day, however, Watanabe learns he is suffering from stomach cancer and has only a year left to live. Without a word, he leaves his job of 30 years. He decides to devote his remaining time to finding meaning in life. But he is alone in the world. His wife is dead; his son is indifferent; his co-workers are strangers. Watanabe decides to go to a bar for the first time in his life and drink himself into oblivion, but he finds the experience meaningless.

Then Watanabe spots a pretty young woman from his office. Perhaps she can divert his attention from his looming mortality? In the end, she does, though not in the way Watanabe expected. She inspires him to do something small that will make the world a better place. He hears about a struggle to create a small park for children in his neighbourhood. Soon after, he devotes all of his energy to turning the idea of the park into a reality. Ironically, he spends much of his time battling an uncooperative bureaucracy staffed by uncaring and indifferent officials.

In the end, Watanabe dies. Initially, those who had fought with him vow to go on, to realize the dead man's dream. Soon, however, the rhythm of bureaucratic life resumes. Nearly everyone returns to his or her role as a functionary. As a charismatic leader of a small social movement, the hero briefly made an impact on his society. In the end, however, the wheels of bureaucracy grind on.

Can you think of a situation in which you or someone you know attempted to challenge and reform a bureaucracy? Can change come from within the bureaucracy or does it need to come from outside? Can individuals overcome bureaucratic inertia or are they doomed to be rolled over by the wheels of bureaucracy?

**bureaucratic ritualism** (Merton, 1968 [1949]). Bureaucrats sometimes get so preoccupied with rules and regulations they make it difficult for the organization to fulfil its goals. Third is the problem of **oligarchy,** or "rule of the few" (Michels, 1949 [1911]). Some sociologists have argued there is a tendency in all bureaucracies for power to become increasingly concentrated in the hands of a few people at the top of the organizational pyramid. This is particularly problematic in political organizations because it hinders democracy and renders leaders unaccountable to the public. Fourth is the problem of **bureaucratic inertia.** Bureaucracies are sometimes so large and rigid they lose touch with reality and continue their policies even when their clients' needs change. Like the *Titanic*, they find it difficult to shift course and steer clear of dangerous obstacles.

Two main factors underlie bureaucratic inefficiency: size and social structure. Consider size first. There is something to be said for the view that bigger is almost inevitably more problematic. Some of the problems caused by size are evident even when you think about the difference between two-person and three-person relationships (known respectively as dyads and triads). When only two people are involved in a relationship, they may form a strong social bond. If they do, communication is direct and usually unproblematic. Once a third person is introduced, however, a secret may be kept, a coalition of two against one may crystallize, and jealousy may result. Thus, triads are usually more unstable and conflict-ridden than dyads (Simmel, 1950).

Problems can multiply in groups of more than three people. For example, as Figure 5.5 shows, although there can be only one relationship between two people, there can be three relationships among three people and six relationships among four people. The number of potential relationships increases exponentially with the number of people, so there are 325 possible relationships among 25 people and 1225 possible relationships among 50 people. The possibility of clique formation, rivalries, conflict, and miscommunication rise as quickly as the number of possible social relationships in an organization.

The second factor underlying bureaucratic inefficiency is social structure. Figure 5.6 shows a typical bureaucratic structure. Note that it is a hierarchy. The bureaucracy has a head. Below the head are three divisions. Below the divisions are six departments. As you move up the hierarchy, the power of the staff increases. Note also the lines of communication that join the various bureaucratic units. Staff members in the departments report only to their divisions. Staff members in the divisions report only to the head.

Usually, the more levels in a bureaucratic structure, the more difficult communication becomes. That is because people have to communicate indirectly, through division heads, rather than directly with each other. Information may be lost, blocked, reinterpreted, or distorted as it moves up the hierarchy; or there may simply be so much information that the top levels become engulfed in a "paperwork blizzard" that prevents them from clearly seeing the needs of the organization and its clients. Bureaucratic heads may have only a vague and imprecise idea of what is happening "on the ground" (Wilensky, 1967).

Consider also what happens when the lines of communication directly joining divisions or departments are weak or nonexistent. As the lines joining units in Figure 5.6 suggest, department A1 may have information that could help department A2 do its job better but may have to communicate that information indirectly, through the division level. There the information may be lost, blocked, reinterpreted, or distorted. Thus, just as people who have authority may lack information, people who have information may lack the authority to act on it directly (Crozier, 1964 [1963]).

Below we consider some ways of overcoming bureaucratic inefficiency. As you will see, these typically involve establishing patterns of social relations that flatten the bureaucratic hierarchy and cut across the sort of bureaucratic rigidities illustrated in Figure 5.6. As a useful prelude to this discussion, we first note some shortcomings of Weber's analysis of bureaucracy. Weber tended to ignore both bureaucracy's "informal" side and the role of

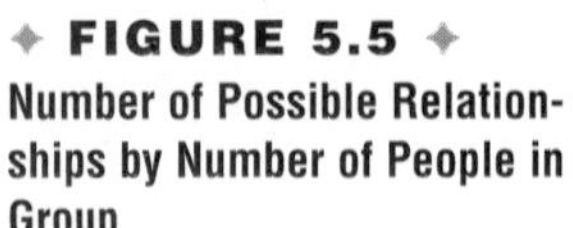
✦ **FIGURE 5.5** ✦
**Number of Possible Relationships by Number of People in Group**

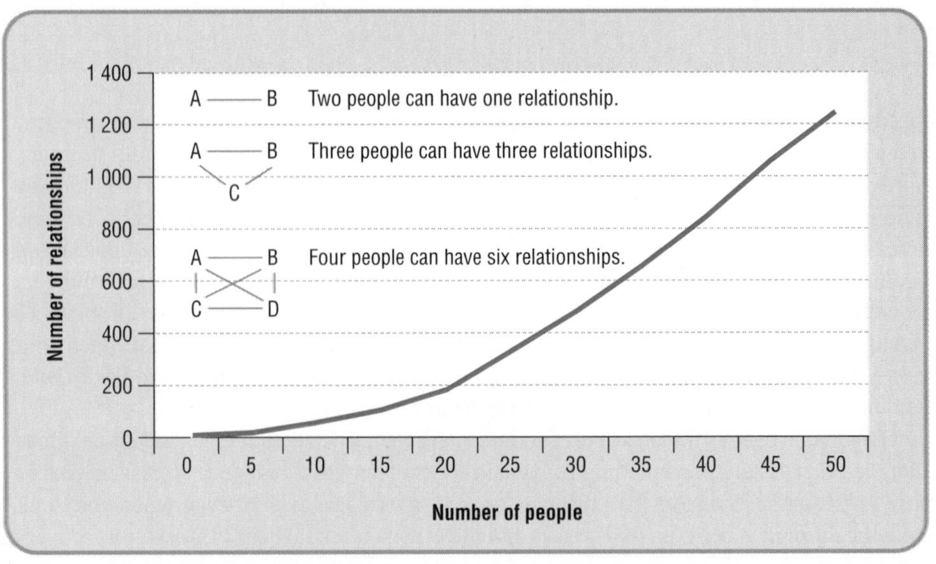

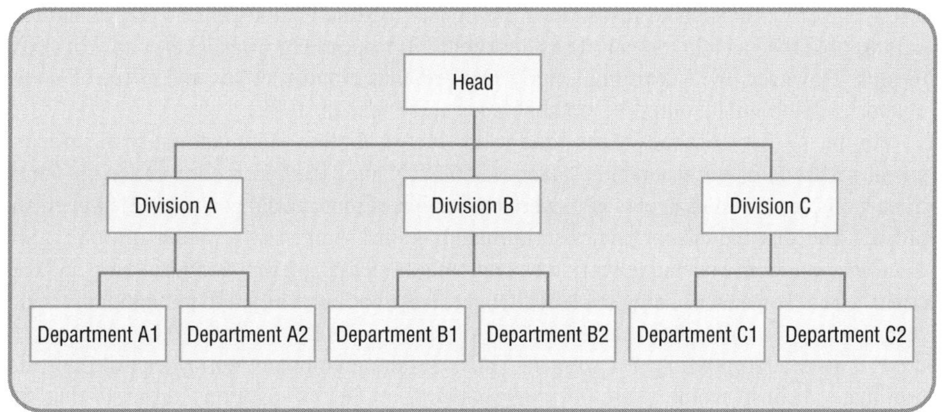


✦ **FIGURE 5.6** ✦
**Bureaucratic Structure**

leadership in influencing bureaucratic performance. Yet, as you will learn, it is precisely by paying attention to such issues that bureaucracies can be made more efficient.

## Bureaucracy's Informal Side

Weber was concerned mainly with the formal structure or "chain of command" in a bureaucracy. He paid little attention to the fact that intricate webs of social relations, known as social networks, underlie the chain of command. A **social network** is a bounded set of individuals who are linked by the exchange of material or emotional resources. The patterns of exchange determine the boundaries of the network. Members exchange resources more frequently with one another than with nonmembers. They also think of themselves as network members. Social networks may be formal (defined in writing) but they are often informal (defined only in practice) (Wellman and Berkowitz, 1997 [1988]).

Evidence for the existence of social networks and their importance in the operation of bureaucracies goes back to the 1930s. Officials at the Hawthorne plant of the Western Electric Company near Chicago wanted to see how various aspects of the work environment affected productivity. They sent social scientists in to investigate. Among other things, researchers found workers in one section of the plant had established a norm for daily output. Workers who failed to meet the norm were helped by co-workers until their output increased. Workers who exceeded the norm were chided by co-workers until their productivity

Parents can help their graduating children find jobs by getting them "plugged into" the right social networks. Here, in the 1968 movie *The Graduate*, a friend of the family advises Dustin Hoffman that the future lies in the plastics industry.

fell. Company officials and researchers previously regarded employees merely as individuals who worked as hard or as little as they could in response to wage levels and work conditions. However, the Hawthorne study showed that employees are members of social networks that regulate output (Roethlisberger and Dickson, 1939).

In the 1970s, Rosabeth Moss Kanter conducted another landmark study of informal social relations in bureaucracies (Kanter, 1977). Kanter studied a corporation in which most women were sales agents who were locked out of managerial positions. However, she did not find that the corporation discriminated against women as a matter of policy. She did find a male-only social network whose members shared gossip, went drinking, and told sexist jokes. The cost of being excluded from the network was high: To get good raises and promotions, one had to be accepted as "one of the boys" and be sponsored by a male executive. This was impossible for women. Thus, despite a company policy that did not discriminate against women, an informal network of social relations ensured that the company discriminated against women in practice.

Despite their overt commitment to impersonality and written rules, bureaucracies rely profoundly on informal interaction to get the job done (Barnard, 1938; Blau, 1963 [1955]). This is true even at the highest levels. For example, executives usually decide important matters in face-to-face meetings, not in writing or over the phone. That is because people feel more comfortable in intimate settings, where they can get to know "the whole person." Meeting face to face, people can use their verbal and nonverbal interaction skills to gauge other people's trustworthiness. Socializing—talking over dinner, for example—is an important part of any business because the establishment of trust lies at the heart of all social interactions that require cooperation (Gambetta, 1988).

## Leadership

Apart from overlooking the role of informal relations in the operation of bureaucracies, Weber also paid insufficient attention to the issue of leadership. Weber thought the operation of a bureaucracy is determined largely by its formal structure. However, sociologists now realize that leadership style also has a bearing on bureaucratic performance (Barnard, 1938; Ridgeway, 1983; Selznick, 1957).

Research shows that the least effective leader is the one who allows subordinates to work things out largely on their own, with almost no direction from above. This is known as **laissez-faire leadership,** from the French expression "let them do." At the other extreme is **authoritarian leadership.** Authoritarian leaders demand strict compliance from subordinates. They are most effective in a crisis, such as a war or in the emergency room of a hospital. They may earn grudging respect from subordinates for achieving the group's goals in the face of difficult circumstances, but they rarely win popularity contests. **Democratic leadership** offers more guidance than the laissez-faire variety but less control than the authoritarian type. Democratic leaders try to include all group members in the decision-making process, taking the best ideas from the group and moulding them into a strategy with which all can identify. Except for in crisis situations, democratic leadership is usually the most effective leadership style.

In sum, contemporary researchers have modified Weber's characterization of bureaucracy in two main ways. First, they have stressed the importance of informal social networks in shaping bureaucratic operations. Second, they have shown that democratic leaders are most effective in noncrisis situations because they tend to distribute decision-making authority and rewards widely. As you will now see, these are important lessons when it comes to thinking about how to make bureaucracies more efficient.

## Overcoming Bureaucratic Inefficiency

In the business world, large bureaucratic organizations sometimes find themselves unable to compete against smaller, innovative firms, particularly in industries that are changing quickly (Burns and Stalker, 1961). That is partly because innovative firms tend to have flatter and more democratic organizational structures, such as the network illustrated in Figure 5.7.

Compare the flat network structure in Figure 5.7 with the traditional bureaucratic structure in Figure 5.6 on page 141. Note that the network structure has fewer levels than the traditional bureaucratic structure. Moreover, in the network structure, lines of communication link all units. In the traditional bureaucratic structure, information flows only upward.

Much evidence suggests that flatter bureaucracies with decentralized decision making and multiple lines of communication produce more satisfied workers, happier clients, and bigger profits (Kanter, 1977, 1983, 1989). Some of this evidence comes from Sweden and Japan. There, beginning in the early 1970s, corporations such as Volvo and Toyota were at the forefront of bureaucratic innovation. They began eliminating middle-management positions. They allowed worker participation in a variety of tasks related to their main functions. They delegated authority to autonomous teams of a dozen or so workers that were allowed to make many decisions themselves. They formed "quality circles" of workers to monitor and correct defects in products and services. As a result, product quality, worker morale, and profitability improved. Today, these ideas have spread well beyond the Swedish and Japanese automobile industry and are evident in such North American corporate giants as General Motors, Ford, Boeing, and Caterpillar.

In the 1980s and 1990s, companies outside the manufacturing sector introduced similar bureaucratic reforms, again with positive effects. Consider the case of Bob R., who works as a field technician for a major telephone company. His company created small teams of field technicians who are each responsible for keeping a group of customers happy. The technicians set their own work schedule. They figure out when they need to do preventive maintenance, when they need to conduct repairs, and when it is time to try to sell customers new services. Bob describes his new job as follows:

> I've been at the company for twenty-three years, and I always thought we were overmanaged, overcontrolled, and oversupervised. They treated us like children. We're having a very good time under the new system. They've given us the freedom to work on our own. This is the most intelligent thing this company has done in years. It's fun. (quoted in Hammer, 1999: 87)

Managers and workers in many industries have offered similar testimonies to the benefits of more democratic, network-like structures.

## Why All Bureaucracies Are Not Flatter

If flatter, more democratic organizations are more efficient, why are all bureaucracies not flatter? Research on this subject is still sketchy. However, on the basis of available research, it appears there are forces outside organizations—in the "organizational environment"—that affect their willingness to undertake bureaucratic reform along the lines described above (Aldrich, 1979; Martin, 1992; McKelvey, 1982; Meyer and Scott, 1983).

For example, due to the nature of the organizational environment in which some companies find themselves, they can earn healthy profits without flat bureaucracies. Therefore, they have little incentive to experiment with bureaucratic reform. Other external circumstances enable or compel companies to develop flatter bureaucracies to gain an edge over competitors.

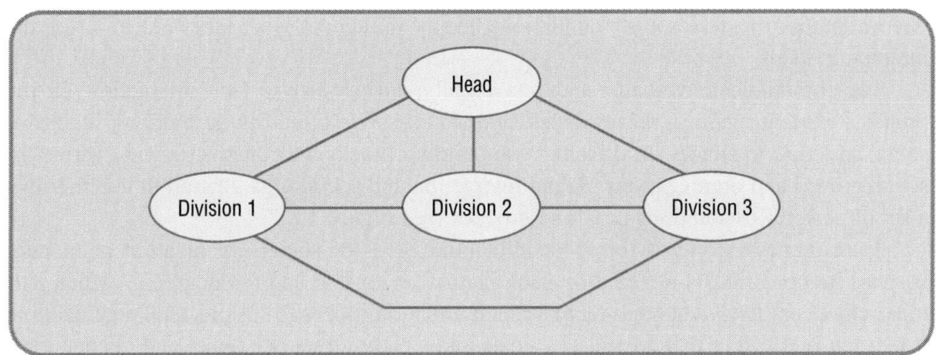


✦ **FIGURE 5.7** ✦
**Network Structure**

Consider large North American multinational corporations. Many of them became big in the first half of the twentieth century. They faced few international competitors at that time. In contrast, many big Japanese and German corporations matured or revived in the highly competitive post–Second World War international environment. Intense international competition gave them a bigger incentive to develop more efficient organizational structures than the North American firms. Thus, for 30 or 40 years after the Second World War, large Japanese and German corporations were ahead of their North American counterparts in developing flat organizational structures (Harrison, 1994).

Similarly, many large North American companies matured when external sources of supply were scarce. For instance, when IBM entered the computer market in the 1950s, it had to produce all components internally because nobody else was making them. This led IBM to develop a large, hierarchical bureaucracy. In contrast, in the 1970s, Japanese computer manufacturers could rely on many external suppliers. Therefore, they could develop flatter organizational structures (Podolny and Page, 1998).

Significantly, Silicon Valley, the centre of the North American computer industry today, is full of companies that fit the flatter "Japanese" organizational pattern (McCarthy, 1999). That is because these companies originated in the 1980s and 1990s, when external suppliers were abundant and international competition was intense. In general, intense international competition in the immediate post–Second World War era encouraged many big North American companies to adopt Japanese-style bureaucratic reforms by the 1980s and 1990s (Tsutsui, 1998). We thus see how the organizational environment that lies outside a company affects the kind of bureaucratic structure it creates.

A company's willingness to undertake bureaucratic reform also depends on the distribution of the costs and benefits of reform to company personnel. In turn, the distribution of costs and benefits depends partly on factors outside the company itself. For example, the threat of imminent plant closures and large-scale job loss has led some unions to support bureaucratic reform. In the 1990s, Quebec unions eagerly supported democratization and innovation in large corporations for just these reasons; they concluded that the benefits were huge compared with the alternative (Lowe, 2000: 147). On the other hand, where plant closures and large-scale job loss are not imminent, many workers and their unions suspect that the real aim of bureaucratic reform is not to give workers greater skill, a stronger voice, and more fulfilment. Instead, they believe that flatter bureaucracies intensify work and are really designed to achieve higher productivity and profits for the corporation at the expense of workers. In such circumstances, workers may resist bureaucratic reform (Lowe, 2000: 138–55; Russell, 1999). Again we see how the organization's environment influences a company's desire and ability to flatten its bureaucratic structure.

## CONCLUSION

Let us sum up the main lessons of this chapter.

Although face-to-face interaction may seem natural and spontaneous, this chapter shows just how socially structured interaction really is. Interaction can be based on social relations of domination, competition, or cooperation. Whether interaction is grounded in one or another of these social foundations deeply influences what takes place during the interaction itself.

We communicate verbally and nonverbally during face-to-face interaction. In the process, we learn values, norms, roles, and statuses. We mould these building blocks of social structure to suit us. And from these building blocks we construct a wide variety of social groups and organizations. Social interaction and social organization fit together like a set of nested Russian dolls or Chinese boxes (see Figure 5.8).

Bureaucracy is one of the most influential types of social organization in modern society. Its operation is affected by such factors as its size and the degree to which it is hierarchical or "flat." Although more efficient than traditional forms of social organization, it is often ineffective in achieving its goals and satisfying its personnel and clients. Flat-

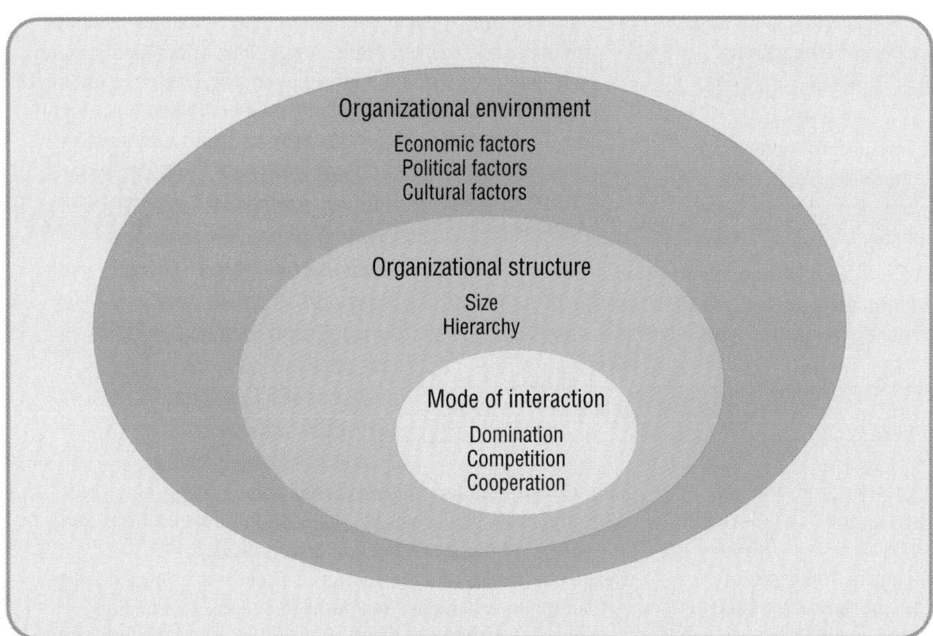


✦ **FIGURE 5.8** ✦
**The Structure of Interaction and Organization**

tening bureaucratic structures—making them more democratic and opening up lines of communication within them—often helps overcome these inefficiencies. However, people do not have a free hand to undertake such bureaucratic reform. They are constrained by social forces outside organizations. We conclude that organizations, like interactions, exist in a socially structured context. Analyzing that context sociologically helps us understand both the opportunities and the constraints we face as we interact with others outside and inside social groups.

## SUMMARY

1. According to exchange and rational choice theories, the competitive exchange of valued resources cements social interaction. People communicate to the degree they get something valuable out of the interaction. However, if they compete too avidly and prevent others from getting much out of the social interaction, communication will break down.
2. According to symbolic interactionism and its most popular variant, dramaturgical analysis, values, norms, roles, and statuses are not handed to us fully formed. Nor do we accept them mechanically. We mould them to suit us as we interact with others.
3. According to ethnomethodology, norms do not emerge entirely spontaneously during social interaction. In general form, they exist before any given interaction takes place. Interaction would be impossible without pre-existing shared understandings.
4. Nonverbal mechanisms of communication greatly facilitate social interaction. These mechanisms include facial expressions, hand gestures, body language, and status cues.
5. When people interact, their statuses are often arranged in a hierarchy. Those on top enjoy more power than those on the bottom. The degree of inequality strongly affects the character of social interaction between the interacting parties.
6. The three main modes of interaction are domination (in which inequality between superordinates and subordinates is high), cooperation (in which inequality is low), and competition (in which inequality is moderate). Although varying degrees of fear pervade interaction based on domination, envy is characteristic of competitive interaction and trust suffuses cooperative interaction. Efficiency is highest in cooperative interaction and lowest in interaction based on domination.
7. Bureaucratic inefficiency is evident in dehumanization (treating clients as standard cases and personnel as cogs in a giant machine), bureaucratic ritualism (a preoccupation with rules and regulations that makes it difficult for the organization to fulfil its goals), oligarchy (concentration of power in the hands of a few people), and bureaucratic inertia (rigidity that causes organizations to lose touch with reality and continue their policies even when clients' needs change).
8. In general, inefficiency increases with the size and degree of hierarchy in bureaucracies. By flattening bureaucratic structures, decentralizing decision-making authority, and opening lines of communication among bureaucratic units, efficiency can often be improved.
9. Social networks, or a bounded set of individuals who are linked by the exchange of material or emotional resources,

underlie the chain of command in all bureaucracies and affect their operation. Weber ignored this aspect of bureaucracy.

10. Weber also downplayed the importance of leadership in the functioning of bureaucracy. However, research shows that democratic leadership improves the efficiency of bureaucratic operations in noncrisis situations, authoritarian leadership works best in crises, and laissez-faire leadership is the least effective form of leadership in all situations.
11. Bureaucracies can often be made more efficient by flattening their structures, decentralizing decision-making authority, and opening lines of communication between bureaucratic units.
12. Social forces outside corporations may facilitate or hinder bureaucratic reform. For example, intense competition and the availability of external suppliers encourage the growth of flatter bureaucracies. Similarly, workers facing mass layoffs or the threat of plant closure may be inclined to support bureaucratic reform as a means of preventing job loss. Workers in less threatening circumstances may suspect bureaucratic reform is just a means of getting them to work more intensely. They may therefore oppose it.

## GLOSSARY

**Authoritarian leaders** demand strict compliance from subordinates. They are most effective in a crisis, such as a war or in the emergency room of a hospital.

**Bureaucracies** are large, impersonal organizations composed of many clearly defined positions arranged in a hierarchy. Bureaucracies have a permanent, salaried staff of qualified experts and written goals, rules, and procedures. Staff members always try to find ways to run the bureaucracy more efficiently.

**Bureaucratic inertia** refers to the tendency of large, rigid bureaucracies to continue their policies even when their clients' needs change.

**Bureaucratic ritualism** involves bureaucrats becoming so preoccupied with rules and regulations they make it difficult for the organization to fulfil its goals.

**Competition** is a mode of interaction in which power is unequally distributed but the degree of inequality is less than in systems of domination. Envy is an important emotion in competitive interactions.

**Cooperation** is a basis for social interaction in which power is more or less equally distributed between people of different status. The dominant emotion in cooperative interaction is trust.

**Dehumanization** occurs when bureaucracies treat clients as standard cases and personnel as cogs in a giant machine. This frustrates clients and lowers worker morale.

**Democratic leadership** offers more guidance than the laissez-faire variety but less control than the authoritarian type. Democratic leaders try to include all group members in the decision-making process, taking the best ideas from the group and moulding them into a strategy with which all can identify. Outside crisis situations, democratic leadership is usually the most effective leadership style.

**Domination** is a mode of interaction in which nearly all power is concentrated in the hands of people of similar status. Fear is the dominant emotion in systems of interaction based on domination.

**Dramaturgical analysis** views social interaction as a sort of play in which people present themselves in the best possible light.

**Ethnomethodology** is the study of how people make sense of what others do and say by adhering to pre-existing norms.

**Exchange theory** holds that social interaction involves trade in valued resources.

**Impression management** is the process by which people present themselves in the best possible light.

**Laissez-faire leaders** allow subordinates to work things out largely on their own, with almost no direction from above. They are the least effective type of leader.

**Oligarchy** means "rule of the few." There is a supposed tendency in all bureaucracies for power to become increasingly concentrated in the hands of a few people at the top of the organizational pyramid.

**Power** is the probability that one actor within a social relationship will be in a position to carry out his or her own will despite resistance.

In **primary groups,** norms, roles, and statuses are agreed upon but are not set down in writing. Social interaction leads to strong emotional ties, extends over a long period, and involves a wide range of activities. It results in group members knowing one another well.

**Rational choice theory** focuses on the way interacting people weigh the benefits and costs of interaction. According to rational choice theory, interacting people always try to maximize benefits and minimize costs.

**Role distance** is awareness of the difference between our public roles and our "true" selves.

**Secondary groups** are larger and more impersonal than primary groups. Compared with that in primary groups, social interaction in secondary groups creates weaker emotional ties, extends over a shorter period, and involves a narrow range of activities. It results in most group members having at most a passing acquaintance with one another.

A **social category** is composed of people who share a similar status but do not identify with one another.

A **social group** is a cluster of people who identify with one another and adhere to defined norms, roles, and statuses.

**Social interaction** involves people communicating face to face, acting and reacting in relation to other people.

A **social network** is a bounded set of individuals who are linked by the exchange of material or emotional resources. The patterns of exchange determine the boundaries of the network. Members exchange resources more frequently with one another than with nonmembers. They also think of themselves as network members. Social networks may be formal (defined in writing), but they are more often informal (defined only in practice).

**Status cues** are visual indicators of other people's social position.

**Stereotypes** are rigid views of how members of various groups act, regardless of whether individual group members really behave that way.

## QUESTIONS TO CONSIDER

1. Think about your everyday interactions with friends, professors, and parents. In each case, how do the exchange of valued resources, the dictates of power, and the influence of norms shape your interactions?
2. If you were starting your own business, how would you organize it? Why? Base your answer on theories and research discussed in this chapter.

## WEB RESOURCES

### Companion Web Site for This Book

http://www.brymsociologycompass.nelson.com

Begin by clicking on the Student Resources section of the Web site. Next, select the chapter you are currently studying from the pull-down menu. From the Student Resources page you will have easy access to InfoTrac College Edition®, MicroCase online exercises, and additional Web links. The Web site also has many useful tips to aid you in your study of sociology, including practice tests for each chapter.

### InfoTrac Search Terms

These search terms are provided to assist you in beginning to conduct research on this topic by visiting http://www.infotrac-college.com

**Bureaucracy**
**Dramaturgical analysis**
**Exchange theory**
**Rational choice theory**
**Social network**

### Recommended Web Sites

Erving Goffman's *The Presentation of Self in Everyday Life* (1959 [1956]) is a classic in the analysis of social interaction. A synopsis of the book can be found at http://www.cfmc.com/adamb/writings/goffman.htm and excerpts can be found at http://www2.pfeiffer.edu/~lridener/courses/impmgt.html and http://www2.pfeiffer.edu/~lridener/courses/goffself.html.

If you need convincing that social interaction on the Internet can have deep emotional and sociological implications, read Julian Dibbell's "A Rape in Cyberspace" (1993), on the World Wide Web at http://www.levity.com/julian/bungle.html. This compelling article is especially valuable in showing how social structure emerges in virtual communities.

For social interaction on the World Wide Web, visit "The MUD Connector" at http://www.mudconnect.com/. The Society for the Study of Social Interaction is a professional organization of sociologists who study social interaction. Visit their Web site at http://sun.soci.niu.edu/~sssi/.

## SUGGESTED READINGS

Erving Goffman. *The Presentation of Self in Everyday Life* (Garden City, NY: Anchor, 1959 [1956]). The classic dramaturgical analysis and the model for many later works.

Graham Lowe. *The Quality of Work: A People-Centred Agenda* (Toronto: Oxford University Press, 2000). A clear-headed analysis of the higher-quality work Canadians want and the social forces promoting and hindering that desire.

Rosabeth Moss Kanter. *Men and Women of the Corporation* (New York: Basic Books, 1977). A landmark study of gender in corporate America. Shows how social interaction shapes social organizations and how social organizations shape social interaction.

Julia Wood and Angela Henry. *Everyday Encounters: An Introduction to Interpersonal Communication*, 2nd Canadian ed. (Toronto: Nelson, 2002). A lucid and engaging primer with useful Canadian examples.

## NOTES

1. Significantly, a study of Christians who helped Jews in Second World War Europe found that their heroism was not related to their educational attainment, political orientation, religious background, or even their attitudes toward Jews. What the rescuers had in common was that they were not well integrated in society. That is, for one reason or another, they were poorly socialized and therefore less inclined than nonheroes to respect authority (Tec, 1986).
2. The following discussion of power and social interaction is based mainly on Amitai Etzioni's (1975) classic analysis and Collins' useful essay on power (Collins, 1982: 60–85).

## IN THIS CHAPTER, YOU WILL LEARN THAT

- Deviance and crime vary among cultures, across history, and from one social context to another.
- Rather than being inherent in the characteristics of individuals or actions, deviance and crime are socially defined and constructed. The distribution of power is especially important in the social construction of deviance and crime.
- Following dramatic increases in the 1960s and 1970s, Canadian crime rates peaked in the early 1990s and have been falling steadily since that time. The decline is due mainly to more effective policing, a declining number of young people in the population, and a booming economy.
- Statistics show that a disproportionately large number of Aboriginal peoples are arrested, convicted, and imprisoned. Explanations for this include the low social and economic standing of Aboriginal peoples, the commission of offences more likely to generate an official response from the criminal justice system, a decline in informal mechanisms of social control within Aboriginal communities, and racial discrimination in the criminal justice system.
- There are many theories of deviance and crime. Each theory illuminates a different aspect of the process by which people break rules and are defined as deviants and criminals.
- As in deviance and crime, conceptions of appropriate punishment vary culturally and historically.
- In some respects modern societies are characterized by less conformity than pre-modern societies, but in other respects they tolerate less deviance.
- Imprisonment is one of the main forms of punishment in industrial societies.
- Fear of crime may be subject to manipulation by commercial and political groups that benefit from it.
- There are cost-effective and workable alternatives to a regime of punishment.

CHAPTER

6

# DEVIANCE AND CRIME

## THE SOCIAL DEFINITION OF DEVIANCE AND CRIME

Canadians' television viewing habits are fairly consistent from one week to the next. If the week's programming does not include such major sporting events as the Stanley Cup finals, the Grey Cup, or the Olympics, nor such celebrity-laden programs as the Academy Awards® or the Emmy Awards, we likely opt for a crime show. Topping the list of the 10 most-watched television programs in Canada between August 28, 2000, and September 2, 2001, was *The Sopranos*; in third place was *Law and Order* (*Canadian Global Almanac 2002*, 2001: 627). Recognizing the potential allure of crime to Canadian television viewers, the CBC attempted as early as the 1950s to manufacture an appealing big-budget crime drama, *RCMP*. Now, of course, Canadians can join with millions of American viewers and dine on a long list of crime-related programs, including *The Practice, Crossing Jordan, CSI, 24, Judging Amy, Blue Murder, The District, COPS, Texas Justice,* and *Diagnosis Murder*. If one were to list all the crime shows on network cable and satellite, one might conclude that we are a society obsessed with crime.

For the last three decades, when asked to identify the top 10 social issues that concern them, Canadians have consistently placed crime among their top three social concerns (Bibby, 1995: 94–5). Since the 1970s, national surveys also find that Canadians believe that crime in general, and violent crime in particular, is on the rise (Fedorowycz, 1999). Over the same time period, the majority of Canadian adults have told survey researchers that they feel the courts are too lenient with offenders, particularly young offenders, and the death penalty should be used in at least some cases (Besserer, 2002). Teenage Canadians hold similar attitudes. In 2001, for example, about 7 in 10 expressed support for making the Young Offender's Act "tougher," while the same number supported the occasional use of the death penalty (Bibby, 1995, 2001: 45).

Why is there so much concern with crime in Canada and so much support for a "get-tough" approach? Since we commonly think of criminals as "the bad guys," we might be excused for thinking that Canada contains a disproportionately large number of bad people who have broken the law. For the sociologist, however, this is an oversimplification for two reasons. First, the term *crime* simply indicates a technical violation of the criminal law. Knowing that someone has broken the law tells us little about his or her moral character and whether he or she is "good" or "bad." Consider, for example, that in the 1970s a popular CBC game show called *This Is the Law* took a tongue-in-cheek approach to the topic of crime. Each week on the show, panellists watched sketches in which "crimes" were being enacted. After the police had arrested the "villain" in the sketch, the panellists were asked to guess exactly what crime had been committed. The show's writers, it seemed, had no problem finding "ample examples of loony laws worldwide to keep the program stocked with fresh material and the panellists guessing" (Statistics Canada, 1998a: 508). One Canadian "crime" featured on this program was the "fraudulent practice of witchcraft," or fortune-telling. Another was a B.C. law that prohibited hairdressers in the province from advertising the price of haircuts.

Nelson Mandela spent decades of his life imprisoned in South Africa for activities designed to end apartheid. Today Mandela is hailed as a hero. In 1993, he was awarded the Nobel Peace Prize and served as the first democratically elected state president of South Africa from 1994 until 1999.

Second, it would be useful to bear in mind that a list of famous people who have been labelled criminals would include Socrates, Jesus, Martin Luther, Louis Riel, Mahatma Gandhi, Martin Luther King, Jr., and Nelson Mandela. For most people today, these historical figures are heroes. In contrast, people who planned and participated in the extermination of Jews, Roma ("Gypsies"), and homosexuals in Nazi Germany were acting in a way that was defined in Germany as law-abiding behaviour.

Most of you would consider the actions taken by the Nazis in Germany, rather than the actions of Jesus or Martin Luther, to be deviant or criminal. That is because norms and laws have changed dramatically. Today, anyone who advocates or promotes genocide has committed a crime under Canadian law. Section 319 of the Criminal Code prohibits the wilful promotion of hatred against any identifiable group or "any section of the public distinguished by colour, race, sexual orientation, religion, or ethnic group." It also specifies that any one doing so may be punished with a term of imprisonment for up to two years.

It is evident, then, that definitions of deviance and crime change over time. For example, homosexuality used to be considered a crime and then a sickness, but an increasing proportion of Canadians now recognize homosexuality as a legitimate sexual orientation (Mooney et al., 2001). Similarly, acts that are right and heroic for some people are wrong and treacherous for others. If you ask any of the law enforcement officials and members of the Canadian Armed Forces who were brought in during the 1990 Oka crisis on the Kanehsatake reserve in Quebec, they will almost certainly tell you that the Mohawk Warriors Society was composed of common criminals whose actions led to the death of an officer of the Sûreté du Québec. If you ask a member of the Mohawk Warriors Society or others who supported the Mohawks in their efforts, they will tell you that the blockade represented a peaceful attempt to direct national attention to a land dispute between the reserve and the municipality. Sociologists, however, will not jump to hasty conclusions. Instead, they will try to understand how social definitions, social relationships, and social conditions led to both the events and the labelling of the Warriors as criminal by the police, the military, and, later, the courts.

That is the approach to deviance and crime we take in this chapter. We first discuss how deviance and crime are socially defined. We then analyze crime patterns in Canada: who commits crimes and what accounts for changing crime rates over time. Next we assess the major theories of deviance and crime. Finally, we examine the social determinants of different types of punishment. We turn first to the social definition of crime.

## Types of Deviance and Crime

**Deviance** involves breaking a norm. If you were the only man in a university classroom full of women, you probably would not be considered deviant. However, if a man were to use a woman's restroom, we would likely regard him as deviant. That is because deviance is not merely departure from the statistical average, but rather implies violating an accepted rule of behaviour.

Many deviant acts go unnoticed or are considered so trivial they warrant no punishment. However, people who are observed committing more serious acts of deviance are typically punished, either informally or formally. **Informal punishment** is mild. It may involve raised eyebrows, gossip, ostracism, "shaming," or **stigmatization** (Braithwaite, 1989). When people are stigmatized, they are negatively evaluated because of a marker that distinguishes them from others (Goffman, 1963). One of this book's authors, John Lie, was stigmatized as a young child and often bullied by elementary school classmates because he had a Korean name in a Japanese school. "I was normal in other ways," says John. "I played the same sports and games, watched the same television shows, and looked, dressed, and acted like other Japanese students. However, my one deviation was enough to stigmatize me. It gave licence to some of my classmates to beat me up from time to time. I wondered at the time why no rules banned bullying and why no law existed against what I now call racial discrimination. If such a law did exist, my classmates would have been subject to formal punishment, which is more severe than informal punishment." **Formal punishment** results from people breaking laws, which are norms stipulated and enforced by government bodies. For example, criminals may be formally punished by having to serve time in prison or perform community service.

Sociologist John Hagan (1994) usefully classifies various types of deviance and crime along three dimensions (see Figure 6.1). The first dimension is the *severity of the social response*. At one extreme, homicide and other very serious forms of deviance result in the most severe negative reactions, such as life imprisonment or capital punishment. At the other end of the spectrum, some people may do little more than express mild disapproval of slight deviations from a norm, such as wearing a nose ring.

The second dimension of deviance and crime is the *perceived harmfulness* of the deviant or criminal act. Although some deviant acts, such as sexual assault, are generally seen as very harmful, others, such as tattooing, are commonly regarded as being of little consequence. Note that actual harmfulness is not the only issue here. *Perceived* harmfulness is. Coca-Cola

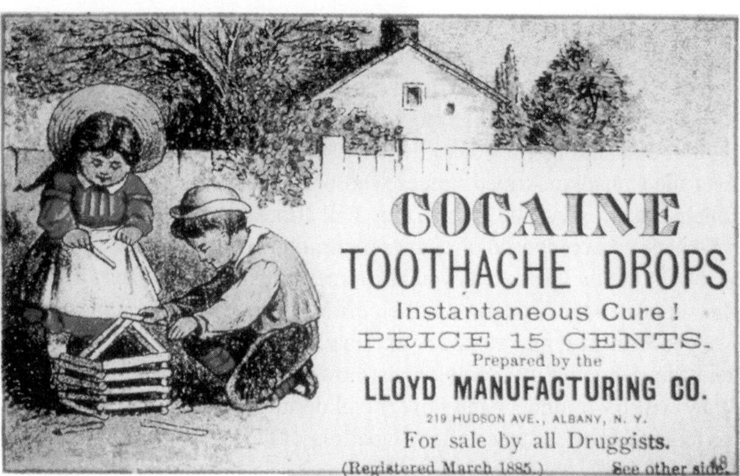


One of the determinants of the seriousness of a deviant act is its perceived harmfulness. Perceptions vary historically, however. For instance, until the early part of the twentieth century, cocaine was considered a medicine. It was an ingredient of Coca-Cola and toothache drops, and in these forms was commonly given to children.

got its name because, in the early part of this century, it contained a derivative of cocaine. Now cocaine is an illegal drug because people's perceptions of its harmfulness changed.

The third characteristic of deviance is the *degree of public agreement* about whether an act should be considered deviant. For example, people disagree about whether smoking marijuana should be considered a crime, especially since it may have therapeutic value in treating pain associated with cancer. In contrast, virtually everyone agrees that murder is seriously deviant. Note, however, that even the social definition of murder varies over time and across cultures and societies. Thus, at the beginning of the twentieth century, Inuit communities sometimes allowed newborns to freeze to death. Life in the far north was precarious. Killing newborns was not considered a punishable offence if community members agreed that investing scarce resources in keeping the newborn alive could endanger everyone's well-being. Similarly, whether we classify the death of a miner as an accident or murder depends on the kind of worker safety legislation in existence. Some societies have more stringent worker safety rules than others, and deaths considered accidental in some societies are classified as criminal offences in others (McCormick, 1999). So we see that, even when it comes to consensus crimes, social definitions are variable.

As Figure 6.1 shows, Hagan's analysis allows us to classify four types of deviance and crime:

**✦ FIGURE 6.1 ✦**
**Types of Deviance and Crime**

Source: Hagan (1994).

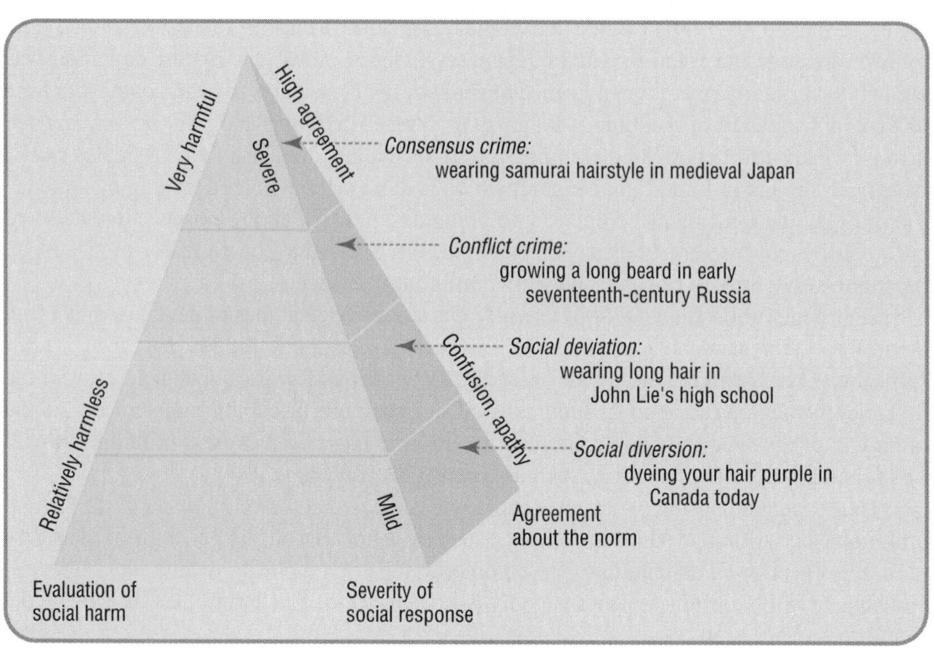

1. **Social diversions** are minor acts of deviance such as participating in fads and fashions like dyeing one's hair purple. People usually perceive such acts as harmless. They evoke, at most, a mild societal reaction such as amusement or disdain. That is because many people are apathetic or unclear about whether social diversions are in fact deviant.
2. **Social deviations** are more serious acts. Large proportions of people agree they are deviant and somewhat harmful, and they are usually subject to institutional sanction. For example, John Lie's high school in Hawaii had a rule making long hair on boys a fairly serious deviation punishable by a humiliating public haircut.
3. **Conflict crimes** are deviant acts that the state defines as illegal, but the definition is controversial in the wider society. For instance, Tsar Peter the Great of Russia wanted to Westernize and modernize his empire, and he viewed long beards as a sign of backwardness. On September 1, 1698, he imposed a fine on beards in the form of a tax. Many Russians disagreed with his policy. Others agreed that growing long beards harmed Russia because it symbolized Russia's past rather than future. Due to this disagreement in the wider society about the harmfulness of the practice, wearing a long beard in late seventeenth-century Russia may be classified as a conflict crime.
4. Finally, **consensus crimes** are widely recognized to be bad in themselves. There is little controversy over their seriousness. The great majority of people agree that such crimes should be met with severe punishment. For instance, in medieval Japan, hairstyle was an important expression of people's status. If you were a peasant and sported the hairstyle of the samurai (warrior caste), you could be arrested and even killed because you were seen to be calling the entire social order into question.

As these examples show, then, people's conceptions of deviance and crime vary substantially over time and between societies. Under some circumstances, an issue that seems quite trivial to us, such as hairstyle, can be a matter of life and death.

Transvestites dress in clothing generally considered appropriate to members of the opposite sex. Is transvestitism a social diversion, a social deviation, a conflict crime, or a consensus crime? Why?

BOX 6.1
IT'S YOUR CHOICE

### VIOLENCE AND HOCKEY: DEVIANT, CRIMINAL, OR NORMATIVE?

In February 2000, Marty McSorley, a defenceman for the Boston Bruins, was suspended indefinitely by the NHL after he hit the head of Donald Brashear of the Vancouver Canucks hard with his stick. Brashear was left unconscious with blood flowing from his nose. He was later diagnosed with a head injury and a serious concussion. At the time of the incident, McSorley had already accumulated more than 3300 career penalty minutes, the third-highest total in NHL history (Mickleburgh, 2000a).

A frequent fighter and hard-nosed player during 17 NHL seasons, McSorley is perhaps most familiar to Canadians as the unofficial on-ice bodyguard for Wayne Gretzky when both played for the Edmonton Oilers in the 1980s. Later, McSorley resumed this role when he was sent to the Los Angeles Kings as part of the Gretzky deal in 1988. Despite his reputation, when first queried by reporters about his attack on Brashear, McSorley emphasized that his actions had been wrong and that he had attempted to apologize to Brashear: "It was a very stupid play. It wasn't something that I thought about doing.... I embarrassed my hockey team. I apologize to Brashear and the fans that had to watch that.... I got way carried away" (in Maki, 2000).

Reactions to the incident were varied. Some players found McSorley's hit deplorable. Others, however, saw it as just part of the game and were shocked when Vancouver police charged McSorley with assault. This marked the first time an NHL player had faced criminal charges stemming from on-ice acts.

That October, McSorley arrived at a Vancouver provincial courthouse accompanied by Wayne Gretzky, who said he was there to support his friend (Mickleburgh, 2000b). During the trial, McSorley entered a plea of not guilty. While acknowledging that he had been sent onto the ice "on a specific mission to 'get Brashear,' who had irritated the Bruins throughout the game," McSorley maintained that the injuries Brashear sustained were not the result of a deliberate act but, rather, accidental (Mickleburgh, 2000a: A9).

In the end, McSorley was found guilty of assault. However, his penalty was light—an 18-month conditional discharge coupled with a ban from playing in any sporting event in which Brashear was on the opposing team. The judge did, however, express the opinion that violence in hockey should be curtailed. "Mr. McSorley must be used as an example," Judge William Kitchen said. "Everyone must understand this type of violence will not be tolerated, either on the street or in the hockey arenas." Gary Bettman, president of the NHL, quickly issued a statement asserting that "[c]learly, this incident was not representative of NHL hockey or NHL players" (Mickleburgh, 2000a).

Violence, of course, does not only erupt at the professional level of hockey. To date, there have been relatively few on-ice incidents in Canada or the United States that have resulted in criminal charges being laid. Moreover, those who have faced charges have generally been acquitted or given only light sanctions (Grange, 2000). Proving that someone deliberately set out to harm another may be difficult when outbursts of aggression are seen as inevitable by-products of intense competition or simply as part of the game.

Bill McMurty, a Toronto lawyer who wrote a report on amateur hockey, observed: "Hockey is the only sport in the history of sport anywhere in the world that not only tolerates fighting, but rewards it. You breed McSorleys from the age of 10 and up, and there may only be 30 or 40 in the NHL, but there might be 3000 or 4000 who are aspiring to get there. It breeds a culture of violence" (Grange, 2000).

Do you agree or disagree with the police's decision to charge Marty McSorley with assault for his attack on Brashear? Do you believe that the judge was right in finding him guilty? in imposing only a light penalty? Should athletes involved in contact sports be exempt from criminal laws prohibiting assault? If so, would you extend this exemption to cases that result in severe injury to—or the death of—another player? If not, do you think we should crack down on sports violence? Should we charge more athletes? impose harsher penalties? It's your choice.

## Power and the Social Construction of Crime and Deviance

To truly understand deviance and crime, you have to study how people socially construct norms and laws. The school of sociological thought known as **social constructionism** emphasizes that various social problems, including crime, are *not* inherent in certain actions themselves. Instead, some people are in a position to create norms and pass laws that stigmatize other people. Therefore, one must study how norms and laws are created (or "constructed") to understand why particular actions are defined as deviant or criminal in the first place.

Power is a crucial element in the social construction of deviance and crime. Power, you will recall from Chapter 5 (Interaction and Organization), is "the probability that one actor within a social relationship will be in a position to carry out his [or her] own will despite resistance" (Weber, 1947: 152). An "actor" may be an entire social group. Relatively powerful social groups are generally able to create norms and laws that suit their interests. Relatively powerless social groups are usually unable to do so.

The powerless, however, often struggle against stigmatization. If their power increases, they may succeed in their struggle. We can illustrate the importance of power in the social construction of crime and deviance by considering crimes against women and white-collar crime.

## Crimes against Women

We argued above that definitions of crime are usually constructed so as to bestow advantages on the more powerful members of society and disadvantages on the less powerful. As you will learn in detail in Chapter 9 (Sexuality and Gender), women are generally less powerful than men in all social institutions. Has the law therefore been biased against women? We believe it has.

Until recently, many types of crimes against women were largely ignored in Canada and most other parts of the world. This was true even when the crime involved nonconsensual sexual intercourse, an act that was defined under Canadian criminal law as "rape" before 1983 and is now considered a form of "sexual assault." Admittedly, rapes involving strangers were sometimes severely punished. But so-called "date rapes" or "acquaintance rapes" involving a friend or an acquaintance were rarely prosecuted. And, until 1983, Canadian law viewed marital rape as a contradiction in terms, as if it were logically impossible for a married woman to be raped by her spouse. In her research, Susan Estrich (1984) found that law professors, judges, police officers, rapists, and even victims did not think date rape was "real rape." Similarly, judges, lawyers, and social scientists rarely discussed physical violence against women and sexual harassment until the 1970s. Governments did not collect data on the topic, and few social scientists showed any interest in what has now become a large and important area of study.

Today, the situation has improved. To be sure, as Diana Scully's (1990) study of convicted rapists shows, sexual assault is still associated with a low rate of prosecution. Rapists often hold women in contempt and do not regard sexual assault as a real crime. Yet a series of changes to criminal law in Canada emphasizes that nonconsensual sexual acts are sexual assaults. These new laws have helped raise people's awareness of date, acquaintance, and marital rape. Sexual assault is more often prosecuted now than it used to be. The same is true for other violence against women and sexual harassment.

Why the change? In part, because women's position in the economy, the family, and other social institutions has improved over the past 30 years. Women now have more autonomy in the family, earn more, and enjoy more political influence. They also created a movement for women's rights that heightened concern about crimes disproportionately affecting them. For instance, until very recently, male sexual harassment of female workers was considered normal. Following Catharine MacKinnon's path-breaking work on the subject, however, feminists succeeded in having the social definition of sexual harassment transformed (MacKinnon, 1979). Sexual harassment is now considered a social deviation and, in some circumstances, a crime. Increased public awareness of the extent of sexual harassment has probably made it less common. We thus see how social definitions of crimes against women have changed with a shift in the distribution of power between women and men.

## White-Collar Crime

**White-collar crime** refers to illegal acts "committed by a person of respectability and high social status in the course of his [or her] occupation" (Sutherland, 1949: 9). Such crimes include embezzlement, false advertising, tax evasion, insider stock trading, fraud, unfair labour practices, copyright infringement, and conspiracy to fix prices and restrain trade. Sociologists often contrast white-collar crimes with **street crimes.** The latter include arson, breaking and entering, robbery, assault, and other illegal acts. While street crimes are committed disproportionately by people from lower classes, white-collar crime is committed disproportionately by people from middle and upper classes.

Many sociologists think white-collar crime is more costly to society than street crime. Tax evasion alone has been estimated to cost Canadians approximately $30 billion a year (Gabor, 1994). Bre-X, reputedly one of the world's largest stock frauds, cost investors $6 billion. In this case, the Calgary-based company's geologist had sought to make worthless mining property seem valuable by salting core samples with gold. After his actions became known, the market for Bre-X stock collapsed and the company's shares became worthless (Hagan, 2000). Yet white-collar criminals, including corporations, are infrequently prosecuted. They are convicted even less often. This is true even in extreme cases, when white-collar crimes result in environmental degradation or death due, for example, to the illegal relaxation of safety standards. Among the best-known cases in Canada is the failure of managers in the Johns-Manville Corporation to alert workers to the serious health hazards posed by asbestos, even though the risks had been known since the turn of the century. Similarly, the report of an official inquiry into the 1992 explosion at the Westray coal mine in Pictou County, Nova Scotia, which instantly killed 26 miners, was tellingly entitled *The Westray Story: A Predictable Path to Disaster*. It noted that the managers at Westray had displayed a "disdain for safety and appeared to regard safety-conscious workers as the wimps in the organization" (Hagan, 2000: 463; see Box 6.2).

White-collar crime results in few prosecutions and still fewer convictions for two main reasons. First, much white-collar crime takes place in private and is therefore difficult to detect. For example, corporations may illegally decide to fix prices and divide markets, but executives make these decisions in boardrooms and private clubs that are not generally subject to police surveillance. Second, corporations can afford legal experts, public relations firms, and advertising agencies that advise their clients on how to bend laws, build up their corporate image in the public mind, and influence lawmakers to pass laws "without teeth" (Blumberg, 1989; Clinard and Yeager, 1980; Hagan, 1989; Sherrill, 1997; Sutherland, 1949). Moreover, when prosecutions are successful, the punishment is usually light (Snider, 1999).

Governments, too, commit serious crimes. However, it is difficult to punish political leaders (Chambliss, 1989). Authoritarian governments often call their critics terrorists, and even torture people who are fighting for democracy, but such governments rarely have to account for their deeds (Herman and O'Sullivan, 1989). Even the United States government, with its democratic ideals, sometimes behaves criminally. In the late 1980s, for example, while the United States was engaged in a war on drugs, the CIA participated in the drug trade to help arm the right-wing Contra military forces in Nicaragua (Scott and Marshall, 1991). When called to account for behaviour such as this, a common claim made is that the end justifies the means. That is, good motives excuse bad behaviour. This claim is also commonly advanced in the case of so-called "blue-collar crimes" committed by police officers or agencies. For example, in the 1980s, the federal McDonald Commission of Inquiry into Certain Activities of the RCMP revealed that members of the RCMP had effectively put themselves above the law in their attempts to enforce the law. The end of law enforcement was seen to justify any means, including acts that, "if undertaken by any other citizen, would have resulted in substantial periods of incarceration" (Brannigan, 1984: 63). These acts were not minor wrongdoings but included such manifestly criminal conduct as arson, breaking and entering, theft, contravening the Post Office Act, kidnapping and forcible detention, and invasion of privacy. Nevertheless, when confronted with evidence of wide-scale and systemic wrongdoing by the RCMP, the Canadian government at the time showed a marked reluctance to treat these acts as crimes. As sociologist Augustine Brannigan (1984: 65) observed of the Canadian government's response to the findings of the McDonald Commission: "The opinion of the government seems to be that whatever the police need to do in order to do their job is *ipso facto* legal."

In sum, white-collar crime is underdetected, underprosecuted, and underconvicted because it is the crime of the powerful and the well-to-do. The social construction of crimes against women has changed over the past 30 years, partly because women have become more powerful. In contrast, the social construction of white-collar crime has changed very little since 1970 because upper classes are no less powerful now than they were then.

BOX 6.2
SOCIOLOGY AT THE MOVIES

John Travolta in *A Civil Action*

### *A CIVIL ACTION* (1998)

*A Civil Action* is based on a true story. John Travolta plays a personal-injury lawyer who hosts a radio show. In response to a call from a woman representing a group of parents in Woburn, Massachusetts, he comes face to face with a horrible case of industrial pollution. Many parents in the town have lost children to leukemia, and they believe that a local factory caused the disease by dumping waste chemicals into the city's water supply.

At first, Travolta doesn't want to get involved. He tells the families that a lawsuit makes sense only if the defendant has a lot of money or a large insurance policy. However, on his way home from meeting with the parents, he is caught speeding on a freeway. By chance, he notices trucks and railway cars streaming by bearing the logos of W. R. Grace and Beatrice Food. He suddenly realizes that the plant is associated with two large corporations and that he and the parents can make a great deal of money in this case.

White-collar crime doesn't get as much attention as other kinds of crime, but *A Civil Action* casts a spotlight on the problem. In addition, it shows some reasons why prosecuting large corporations is difficult. First, corporations can afford to hire brilliant legal minds, such as the lawyer played by Robert Duvall in *A Civil Action*. Second, because of the difficulty of finding evidence—the frequent absence of a "smoking gun"—proving a case of corporate crime is often difficult. Third, corporations are in a financial position to offer out-of-court settlements without admitting their guilt. This is what happens in *A Civil Action*. The lawyer played by Travolta finally finds a W. R. Grace worker who admits to dumping toxic chemicals. Although the corporation is willing to offer a modest out-of-court settlement, its executives refuse to admit responsibility or apologize for their negligence. Meanwhile, Travolta's firm spends all its resources prosecuting the case, and Travolta finds himself virtually penniless. The movie ends well, however. Travolta manages to get the federal government's Environmental Protection Agency (EPA) interested in the Woburn case, and the EPA lawyers succeed in their appeal.

As you think about white-collar crime, you should contrast it with street crime. You should also consider the way both types of crime are portrayed in the movies. For example, in *Pulp Fiction* (1994), also starring John Travolta, we get an inside view of the world of organized and street crime, including the drug trade, racketeering, and gambling. The filmmaker introduces the viewer to the character behind each criminal act. The characters are often made to seem likeable or at least interesting. Nonetheless, most viewers would insist on stiff penalties for drug trading or murder. In contrast, in *A Civil Action*, we never see the faces of the people responsible for the negligence that led to the deaths of the children. Many members of the public are indifferent to corporate crimes, although they may kill more people than street crimes. Why do you think white-collar and street crimes are portrayed so differently in the movies? Why do you think most members of the public think so differently about the two types of crime?

## Crime Rates

Some crimes are more common than others, and rates of crime vary over place and time and among different social groups. We will now describe some of these variations. Then we will review the main sociological explanations of crime and deviance.

First, a word about crime statistics: Information on crime collected by the police is our main source of information on crime in Canada. Since 1962, Canada has used a system called the Canadian Uniform Crime Reports (UCR) that was developed by Statistics

Canada and the Canadian Association of Chiefs of Police. Under this system, information is collected from more than 400 municipal police departments across Canada on 91 detailed categories of crime. The information is then compiled and published each year with counts and calculated rates per 100 000 population. Offences are grouped into major categories of crime. For example, "crimes of violence" group together such acts as homicide, attempted homicide, assault, abduction, sexual assault, and robbery. "Property offences" include breaking and entering, theft of motor vehicles, possession of stolen goods, fraud, and so on. UCRs also provide information on the number of persons charged with different types of offences, with separate counts for adults and youths, males and females.

These statistics have several shortcomings. First, much crime is not reported to the police. This is particularly true in relation to so-called **victimless crimes,** such as communicating for the purposes of prostitution, illegal gambling, and the use of illegal drugs. Although all of these acts involve violations of the law, there is no complaining party who steps forward and identifies himself or herself as a victim. In addition, many common or "level 1" assaults go unreported because the assailant is a friend or relative of the victim. Many victims of sexual assault are also reluctant to report the crime because they are afraid they will be humiliated, or not believed, and stigmatized by making it public. Moreover, authorities and the wider public decide which criminal acts to report and which to ignore. If, for instance, the authorities decide to crack down on drugs, more drug-related crimes will be counted, not because there are more drug-related crimes but because more drug criminals are apprehended. Changes in legislation, which either create new offences or amend existing offences, will also influence the number of recorded offences. Recognizing these difficulties, students of crime often supplement official crime statistics with other sources of information.

**Self-report surveys** are especially useful. In such surveys, respondents are asked to report their involvement in criminal activities, either as perpetrators or as victims. Self-report data compensate for many of the problems associated with official statistics but are still subject to concealment as well as exaggeration. In general, self-report surveys report approximately the same rate of serious crime as official statistics but find two or three times the rate of less serious crimes. In consequence, *indirect measures* of crime are sometimes used as well. For instance, sales of syringes are a good index of the use of illegal intravenous drugs. Indirect measures are unavailable for many types of crime, however.

Self-report surveys are also useful because they remind us that a majority of Canadians, young and old, has engaged in some type of "criminal" activity. As a result, they remind us that committing an act in violation of the law does not always or automatically result in being officially labelled a "criminal." The process of criminal labelling can be likened to a funnel that is broad at one end and narrow at the other (see Figure 6.2). To be officially identified as a "criminal," an individual's law-violating behaviour must first be observed and felt to justify action. The behaviour must be reported to the police who, in turn, must respond to the incident, decide that it warrants further investigation, file a report, and make an arrest. Next, the person accused must appear at a preliminary hearing, an arraignment, and a trial. If the person does not plead guilty, there is always the possibility that he or she will not be convicted because his or her guilt has not been proven "beyond a reasonable doubt." At every stage, then, a person who has, in fact, violated the law, may nevertheless avoid official labelling as a criminal. If we review Figure 6.2, it becomes evident why generalizations based on samples of incarcerated offenders may not apply beyond inmate populations.

In **victimization surveys,** people are asked whether they have been victims of crime. Here as well, however, responses are influenced by people's willingness and ability to discuss criminal experiences frankly. Although these types of surveys date back to the mid-1960s in the United States, no national victimization survey was done in Canada until 1988 (Fattah, 1991). For Statistics Canada's 1999 General Social Survey (GSS), 26 000 people aged 15 and older were interviewed by telephone and asked if they had been victimized by crime and, if so, where and when the crime had occurred and whether it been reported to the police. In addition, respondents were queried on their perceptions of the level of crime in their neighbourhood, their personal fear of crime, and their views on the criminal jus-

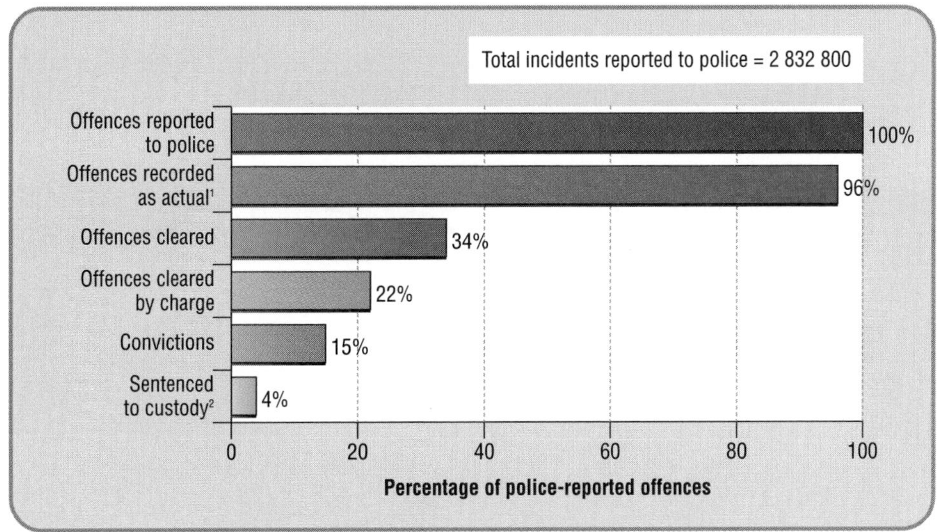


✦ **FIGURE 6.2** ✦

**Caseload within the Canadian Criminal Justice System, 1996**

Source: Adapted from *Juristat,* "Youth Court Statistics 1995–96 Highlights" "Adult Criminal Court Statistics, 1995–96" and "Canadian Crime Statistics, 1996," Catalogue 85-002, Vol. 17, No. 8, Vol. 17, No. 6 and Vol. 17, No. 10.

1 An offence is considered "actual" when, following an initial investigation, the police confirm that a criminal offence has occurred. An offence is "cleared" when police are satisfied that they have identified an offender. However, it may not be possible to lay a charge against an offender because he or she is dead, under age 12, has diplomatic immunity, is already in prison, and so on. If, in the view of the police, it is possible to lay a charge against an offender, the offence is cleared by charge.

2 Includes secure custody only for young offenders and any custodial sentence for adults.

tice system (Tufts, 2000). In addition, the International Crime Victim Survey (ICVS) collected victimization data using the same questionnaire in many countries, including Canada, in 1989, 1992, 1996–97, and 2000 (Besserer, 2002). It examines householders' experience with crime, policing, crime prevention, and feelings of being unsafe. This survey has found that, on average, 55 percent of victimization incidents are reported to police, with property crimes more likely to be reported than crimes against persons. In part, this reflects the general requirement by insurance companies that individuals seeking compensation for property stolen or damaged as the result of a criminal act file a police report. Although victimization surveys provide detailed information about crime victims, they provide less reliable data about offenders.

Bearing these caveats in mind, what does the official record show? Most Canadians would be understandably alarmed to hear that, in 2000, 2.4 million Criminal Code incidents (excluding traffic and drug incidents) were reported to Canadian police agencies. They might assume that these incidents were reflected in the dramatic crimes reported each day in newspaper headlines and on the nightly news. However, that is not the case. In 2000, 55 percent of Criminal Code incidents involved property crimes, 13 percent involved violent crimes, and 34 percent involved other Criminal Code offences, primarily mischief and disturbing the peace. Some Canadians may still find it alarming to note that in 2000 our police-reported crime rate was 7655 incidents per 100 000 population. The bad news is that the 2000 Canadian crime rate is 47 percent higher than it was in 1970 (Logan, 2001: 4). However, we can take some comfort from the fact that Canada's crime rate in 2000 was at its lowest rate since 1978. The long crime wave that began its upswing in the early 1960s peaked and then fell in the 1990s. For the past decade, the crime rate has been decreasing by about 3 percent annually (see Figure 6.3).

In addition, the rates of many of the most serious crimes decreased or remained stable. For example, the homicide rate, which has declined since the mid-1970s, remained at a low rate of 1.8 per 100 000. To put this in perspective, although in 2000 there were 542 homicides in Canada, this figure is actually less than the number of homicides reported in some individual American cities. In 2000, there were 15 517 homicides in the United States (Gannon, 2001; see Figure 6.4). Since 1991, the rate of robbery has also consistently declined. The rates of the two most serious forms of sexual assault—sexual assault with a weapon and aggravated sexual assault—also continued to decline, while the rate of the least serious form—"level 1" sexual assault—remained stable.

In addition, Canada's rate of property crime has declined since 1991. Although there were about 1.3 million property crimes reported to Canadian police agencies in 2000, this nevertheless resulted in Canada's lowest property crime rate since 1993. Moreover, although Canada saw a 9 percent increase in the rate of drug offences (an upward trend

✦ **FIGURE 6.3** ✦
**Crime Rate, Canada, 1962–2000**

Source: Statistics Canada (2000).

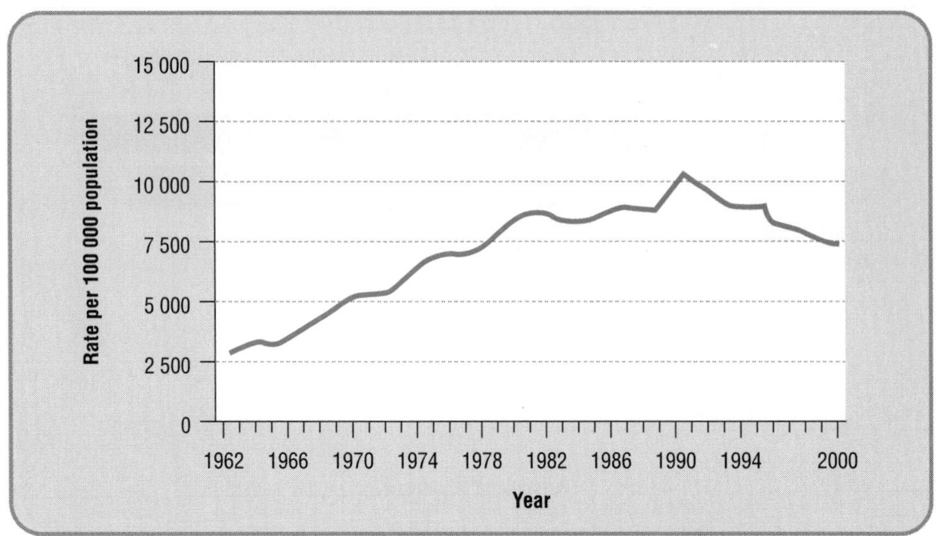


that started in the mid-1990s), cannabis offences accounted for three-quarters of all drug-related offences and more than one-third of these were for simple possession. The good news is evident. How do we explain it?

First, the "war against crime" is increasingly fought by large numbers of well-trained soldiers: "Veritable armies of law enforcement and correctional officers have grown phenomenally since the 1960s, not only in manpower but in programs and technical sophistication" (Mohr and Spencer, 1999: 588). It has been suggested that recent declines in Canada's crime rate may reflect the introduction of community policing initiatives, enforcement efforts that target specific types of crime and purposefully attempt to reduce their incidence, the refinement of case management methods, improvements within the field of forensics, and efforts directed toward crime prevention (Logan, 2001: 3).

Second, young men are most prone to street crime, but Canada is aging and the number of young people in the population has declined (see Figure 6.5). Although those between the ages 15 and 24 have a high risk of offending, this high-risk age group has decreased in size by 6 percent since 1991 (Logan, 2001: 3). Unlike the 1960s, when the baby boom generation (that is, those born between 1947 and 1966) came into their years of highest risk, the 1990s saw the products of the baby bust years (1967 to 1979). Simply put, "[t]here has been a smaller pool of people who are at the greatest risk with respect to criminal behaviour" (John Howard Society, 1999a: 2).

✦ **FIGURE 6.4** ✦
**Rates of Homicide, Canada and the United States, 1961–2000**

Source: Gannon (2001).

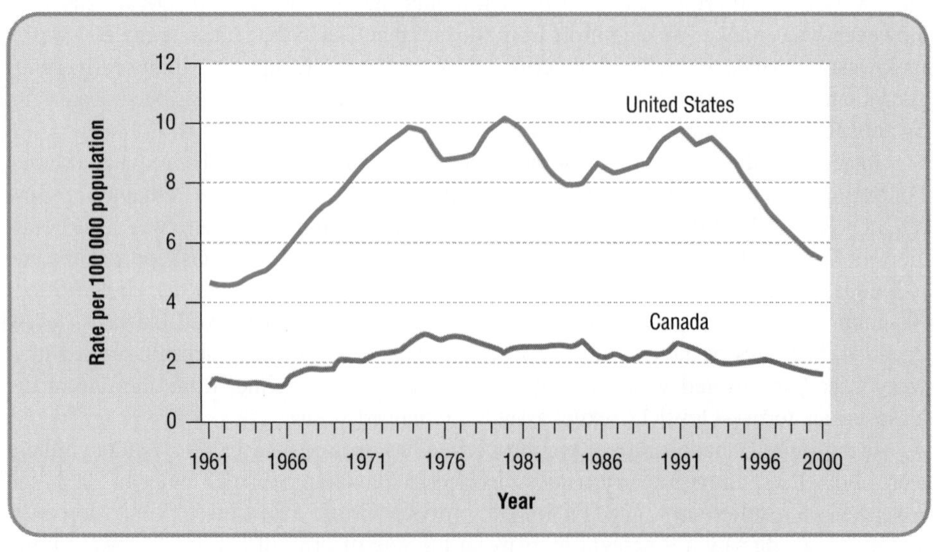

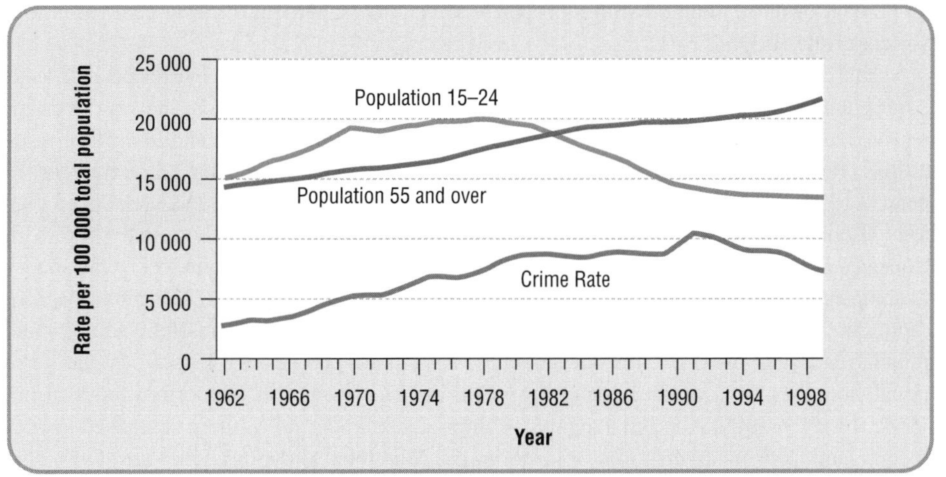


✦ **FIGURE 6.5** ✦
**Crime Rate and Selected Demographics, Canada, 1962–2000**

Source: Logan (2001).

Note: the Population 15–24 and Population 55 and over lines refer to changes in the population for those age groups and not changes in crime rates.

Third, following a steep recession in 1990–91, the economy boomed in the 1990s and has grown every year since 1993. Economic conditions, then, may have favoured a decrease in crime. It is notable here that a 1993 study conducted by Statistics Canada concluded that the variable most strongly correlated with the crime rate was the male unemployment rate (John Howard Society, 1999b: 3).

Finally, and more controversially, some American researchers argue that declining crime rates may be linked to the legalization of abortion (Donahue and Levitt, 2001). Specifically, they observe that, in the United States, the crime rate started to decline 19 years after abortion was legalized in that country. They suggest that this occurred because, beginning in 1972 with the legalization of abortion, there were proportionately fewer unwanted children in the population. They argue that unwanted children are more prone to criminal behaviour than wanted children because they tend to receive less parental supervision and guidance. In Canada, no comparable research has been conducted to date.

Please note that we have not claimed that putting more people in prison and imposing tougher penalties for crime help to account for lower crime rates. We will explain why these actions generally do not result in lower crime rates later in the chapter, when we discuss **social control** (methods of ensuring conformity) and punishment. We will also probe one of the most fascinating questions raised by official statistics: If crime rates fell in the 1990s, what accounts for our increased enthusiasm for get-tough policies, our expanding prison population, and our widespread and growing fear of crime?

## Criminal Profiles

Canadian adult criminal court statistics[1] for the fiscal year 2000–01 indicate that 83 percent of cases involved a male accused. Males accounted for 85 percent of crimes against a person, 78 percent of crimes against property, and 86 percent of Criminal Code traffic violations. Women accounted for a significant percentage of offenders in only a small number of crimes. Specifically, they accounted for 43 percent of those involved in morals-sexual offences (primarily soliciting prostitution), 44 percent of those charged with abduction (mainly child-related), 28 percent of those charged with fraud, and 27 percent of those charged with theft (including shoplifting) (Thomas, 2002: 4). This pattern reappears for cases processed in the youth courts of Canada. In 2000–01, males accounted for 8 in 10 youth court cases (deSouza, 2002: 5). However, with every passing year women compose a slightly bigger percentage of arrests (Hartnagel, 2000). This change is partly due to the fact that, in the course of socialization, traditional social controls and definitions of femininity are less often being imposed on women (see Chapter 9, Sexuality and Gender).

Most crime is committed by people who have not reached middle age. The 15- to 24-year-old age cohort is the most prone to criminal behaviour. Although this age cohort represented merely 14 percent of the total Canadian population in 2000, they accounted for

45 percent of those charged with a property crime and 31 percent of those charged with a violent crime (Logan, 2001: 3).

Analysis of official statistics also reveals that race is a factor in who is arrested. Although Aboriginal peoples represent 2 percent of the adult population in Canada, they are overrepresented as a proportion of those incarcerated in both federal and provincial/territorial institutions. For the past two decades, Aboriginal peoples have consistently accounted for 15 percent to 18 percent of admissions to both provincial/territorial and federal sentenced custody (Lonmo, 2001: 8; see Figure 6.6). The overrepresentation of Aboriginal peoples in Canada's prisons is particularly marked in the Prairie provinces (see Figure 6.7). One survey of inmates in Canada's adult correctional facilities found that although Aboriginal peoples represent 9 percent of Manitoba's population, they account for 61 percent of the adult inmate population in that province. In Alberta, where Aboriginal peoples make up 4 percent of the population, they account for 34 percent of adult inmates (Robinson, Porporino, and Millson, 1999). In 1999–2000, Aboriginal peoples comprised the majority of those sentenced to both federal and provincial/territorial institutions in Manitoba and Saskatchewan. They also accounted for the majority of those incarcerated in federal institutions in the Northwest Territories and Nunavut and territorial institutions in Yukon (Lonmo, 2001: 8).

In recent years, changes made by Parliament to the sentencing provisions of the Canadian Criminal Code have attempted to address the overrepresentation of Aboriginal peoples in Canada's inmate population. For example, section 718.2 specifies that "all available sanctions other than imprisonment that are reasonable in the circumstances should be considered for all offenders, *with particular attention to the circumstances of aboriginal offenders*" (emphasis added). Although being Aboriginal does not automatically result in a lesser sentence, the Supreme Court of Canada has urged judges, when sentencing an Aboriginal offender, to recognize the "broad systemic and background factors affecting Aboriginal people" (Lonmo, 2001: 8).

Nevertheless, Aboriginal peoples continue to be overrepresented in Canada's prison population. Compared with non-Aboriginal inmates, Aboriginal inmates are more likely to have had more extensive contact with both the criminal justice system and the correctional system, to have come from dysfunctional backgrounds, and to have served prison sentences for defaulting on court-ordered fines. Aboriginal women are particularly overrepresented in Canada's correctional institutions (La Prairie, 1996).

Several explanations for the overrepresentation of Aboriginal peoples in Canada's prisons may be found in the literature (Hartnagel, 2000). First, a disproportionately large number of Aboriginal peoples are poor. Although the great majority of poor people are law abiding, poverty and its disabilities are associated with elevated crime rates. Second is the

✦ **FIGURE 6.6** ✦

**Aboriginal Peoples as a Proportion of Total Admissions to Sentenced Custody, 1979–1980 to 1999–2000**

Source: Lonmo (2001).

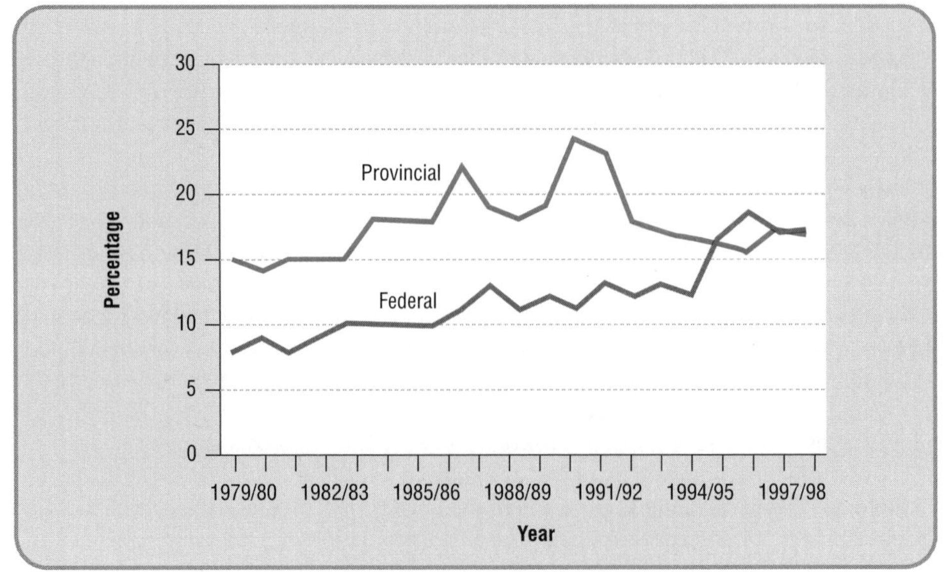

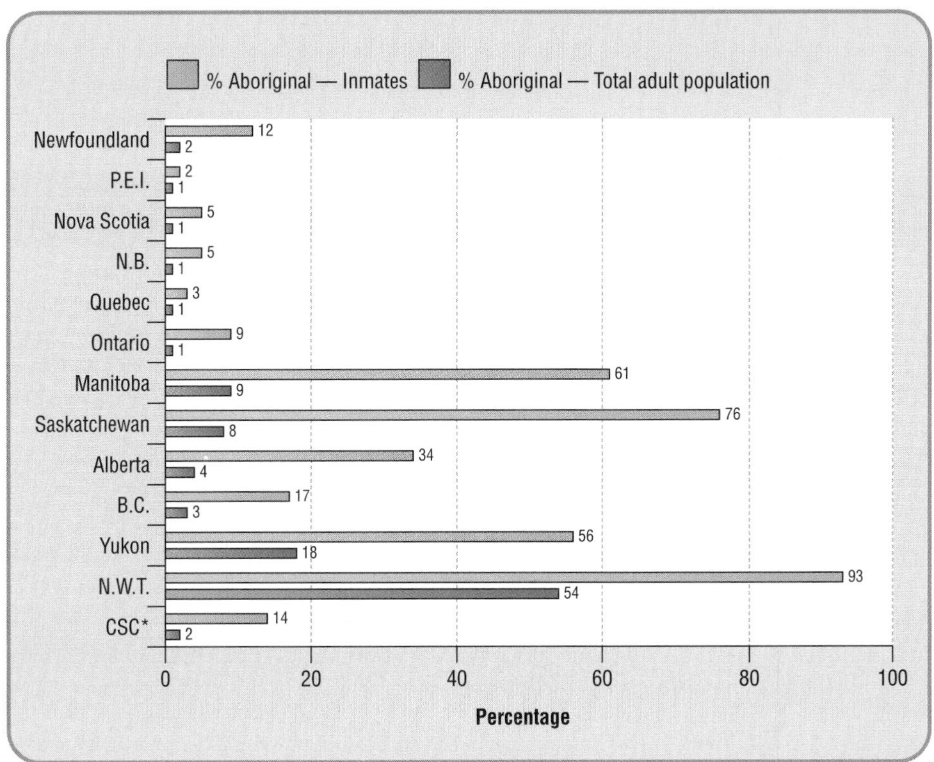


✦ **FIGURE 6.7** ✦

**Aboriginal Peoples—Proportion of Adult Population and Inmates by Jurisdiction**

Source: Robinson, Porporino, and Millson (1999).

*Federal population and population within federal Correctional Services Canada facilities.

closely related point that Aboriginal peoples may commit crimes that are more detectable than those committed by non-Aboriginal people. For example, as we have seen, "street crimes" are generally more detectable than "suite crimes," and they more often lead to prosecution and conviction. Third, the police, the courts, and other institutions may discriminate against Aboriginal peoples. As a result, Aboriginal peoples may be more likely to be apprehended, prosecuted, and convicted. Fourth, contact with Western culture has disrupted social life in many Aboriginal communities (see Chapter 8, Ethnicity and Race). This has led to a weakening of social control over community members. Some people think that certain "races" are *inherently* more law abiding than others, but they are able to hold such an opinion only by ignoring the powerful *social* forces that cause so many Aboriginal peoples to be incarcerated in Canada (Roberts and Gabor, 1990).

In the 1957 classic *12 Angry Men*, the character played by Henry Fonda convinces the members of a jury to overcome their prejudices, examine the facts dispassionately, and allow a disadvantaged minority youth accused of murdering his father to go free.

## Explaining Deviance and Crime

> Lep: "I remember your li'l ass used to ride dirt bikes and skateboards, actin' crazy an' shit. Now you want to be a gangster, huh? You wanna hang with real muthaf____and tear shit up, huh? Stand up, get your li'l ass up. How old is you now anyway?"
>
> Kody: "Eleven, but I'll be twelve in November."
>
> —Sanyika Shakur (1993: 8)

"Monster" Scott Kody eagerly joined the notorious gang the Crips in South Central Los Angeles in 1975 when he was in grade six. He was released from Folsom Prison on parole in 1988, at the age of 24. Until about three years before his release, he was one of the most ruthless gang leaders in Los Angeles and the California prison system. In 1985, however, he decided to reform. He adopted the name Sanyika Shakur, became a black nationalist, and began a crusade against gangs. Few people in his position have chosen that path. In Kody's heyday, about 30 000 gang members roamed Los Angeles County. Today there are an estimated 150 000.

What makes engaging in crime an attractive prospect? In general, why do deviance and crime occur at all? Sociologists have proposed dozens of explanations. However, we can group them into two basic types. **Motivational theories** identify the social factors that *drive* people to commit deviance and crime. **Constraint theories** identify the social factors that *impose* deviance and crime (or conventional behaviour) on people. Let us briefly examine three examples of each type of theory.

### Motivational Theories

#### Strain Theory

You will recall Durkheim's idea that the absence of clear norms—*anomie*—can result in elevated rates of suicide and other forms of deviant behaviour (see Chapter 1, A Sociological Compass). Robert Merton's **strain theory,** summarized in Table 6.1, extends Durkheim's insight (Merton, 1938). Merton argued that cultures often teach people to value material success. Just as often, however, societies do not provide enough legitimate opportunities for everyone to succeed. As a result, some people experience strain. Most of them will force themselves to adhere to social norms despite the strain (Merton called this *conformity*). The rest adapt in one of four ways. They may drop out of conventional society (*retreatism*). They may reject the goals of conventional society but continue to follow its rules (*ritualism*). They may protest against convention and support alternative values (*rebellion*). Or they may find alternative and illegitimate means of achieving their society's goals (*innovation*)—that is, they may become criminals. The "American Dream," as Merton referred to it, of material success starkly contradicts the lack of opportunity available to poor youths. As a result, poor youths sometimes engage in illegal means of attaining socially approved of goals.

#### Subcultural Theory

A second type of motivational theory, known as **subcultural theory,** emphasizes the importance of social groups. It suggests that deviant and criminal acts, including the formation of criminal gangs, are a *collective* adaptation to social conditions. Moreover, this collective adaptation involves the formation of a subculture with distinct norms and values.

✦ **TABLE 6.1** ✦
**Merton's Strain Theory of Deviance**

| | | Institutionalized Means | | |
|---|---|---|---|---|
| | | **Accept** | **Reject** | **Create New** |
| **Cultural Goals** | **Accept** | Conformity | Innovation | — |
| | **Reject** | Ritualism | Retreatism | — |
| | **Create New** | — | — | Rebellion |

Source: Adapted from Merton (1938).

Members of this subculture reject the legitimate world that, they feel, has rejected them (Cohen, 1955).

The literature emphasizes three features of criminal subcultures. First, depending on the availability of different subcultures in their neighbourhoods, delinquent youths may turn to different types of crime. In some areas, delinquent youths are recruited by organized crime, such as the Mafia. In areas that lack organized crime networks, delinquent youths are more likely to create violent gangs. Thus, the relative availability of different subcultures influences the type of criminal activity to which one turns (Cloward and Ohlin, 1960).

A second important feature of criminal subcultures is that their members typically spin out a whole series of rationalizations for their criminal activities. These justifications make their illegal activities appear morally acceptable and normal, at least to the members of the subculture. Typically, criminals deny personal responsibility for their actions ("What I did harmed nobody"). They condemn those who pass judgment on them ("I'm no worse than anyone else"). They claim their victims get what they deserve ("She had it coming to her"). And they appeal to higher loyalties, particularly to friends and family ("I had to do it because he dissed my gang"). The creation of such justifications and rationalizations enables criminals to clear their consciences and get on with the job. Sociologists call such rationalizations **techniques of neutralization** (Sykes and Matza, 1957; see also the case of the professional fence in Chapter 2, Research Methods).

Finally, although deviants may depart from mainstream culture in many ways, they are strict conformists when it comes to the norms of their own subculture. They tend to share the same beliefs, dress alike, eat similar food, and adopt the same mannerisms and speech patterns. Whether among professional thieves (Conwell, 1937) or young gang members (Short and Strodtbeck, 1965), deviance is strongly discouraged *within* the subculture. Paradoxically, deviant subcultures depend on internal conformity.

The main problem with strain and subcultural theories is that they exaggerate the connection between class and crime. Many self-report surveys find, at most, a weak tendency for criminals to come disproportionately from lower classes. Some self-report surveys report no such tendency at all, especially among young people and for less serious types of crime (Weis, 1987). A stronger correlation exists between *serious street crimes* and class. Armed robbery and assault, for instance, are more common among people from lower classes. A stronger correlation also exists between *white-collar* crime and class. Middle- and upper-class people are most likely to commit white-collar crimes. Thus, generalizations about the relationship between class and crime must be qualified by taking into account the severity and type of crime (Braithwaite, 1981). Note also that official statistics usually exaggerate class differences because they are more accurate barometers of street crime than suite crime. It is obvious that there is generally more police surveillance in lower-class neighbourhoods than upper-class boardrooms.

According to Edwin Sutherland's theory of differential association, people who are exposed to more deviant than nondeviant experiences as they grow up are likely to become deviants. As in *The Sopranos*, having family members and friends in the Mafia predisposes one to Mafia involvement.

## Learning Theory

Apart from exaggerating the association between class and crime, strain and subcultural theories are problematic because they tell us nothing about which adaptation someone experiencing strain will choose. Even when criminal subcultures beckon ambitious adolescents who lack opportunities to succeed in life, only a minority joins up. Most adolescents who experience strain and have the opportunity to join a gang reject the life of crime and become conformists and ritualists, to use Merton's terms. Why?

Edwin Sutherland (1939) addressed both the class problems and the choice problems more than 60 years ago by proposing a third motivational theory, which he called the theory of **differential association.** The theory of differential association is still one of the most influential ideas in the sociology of deviance and crime. In Sutherland's view, a person learns to favour one adaptation over another because of his or her life experiences or socialization. Specifically, everyone is exposed to both deviant and nondeviant values and behaviours as they grow up. If you happen to be exposed to more deviant than nondeviant experiences, chances are you will learn to become a deviant yourself. You will come to value a particular deviant lifestyle and consider it normal. Everything depends, then, on the exact mix of deviant and conformist influences a person faces. For example, a substantial body of participant-observation and survey research has failed to discover widespread cultural values prescribing crime and violence in the inner city (Sampson, 1997: 39). Most inner-city residents follow *conventional* norms, and that is one reason most inner-city adolescents do not learn to become gang members. Those who do become gang members tend to grow up in very specific situations and contexts that teach them the value of crime.

Significantly, the theory of differential association holds for people in all class positions. For instance, Sutherland applied the theory of differential association in his path-breaking research on white-collar crime. He noted that white-collar criminals, like their counterparts on the street, learn their skills from associates and share a culture that rewards rule breaking and expresses contempt for the law (Sutherland, 1949).

## Constraint Theories

Motivational theories ask how some people are driven to break norms and laws. Constraint theories, in contrast, pay less attention to people's motivations. How are deviant and criminal "labels" imposed on some people? How do various forms of social control fail to impose conformity on them? How does the distribution of power in society shape deviance and crime? These are the kinds of questions posed by constraint theorists.

### Labelling Theory

A few years ago in Saskatchewan, after a night of heavy drinking, two 20-year-old university students, Alex Ternowetsky and Steven Kummerfield, both white and middle class, picked up Pamela George, an Aboriginal single mother who occasionally worked as a prostitute, in downtown Regina. They drove the 28-year-old woman outside the city limits, demanded that she perform oral sex on them without pay, and then savagely beat her death. Although originally charged with first degree murder, a jury later found them guilty of the lesser charge of manslaughter. In a controversial move, Justice Ted Malone of the Saskatchewan Court of Queen's Bench instructed the jurors to consider that the two men had been drinking and that George was "indeed a prostitute." Members of the victim's family were appalled and Native leaders were outraged. Tone Cote of the Yorkton Tribal Council suggested the sentence was too lenient and would send the message that "[i]t's all right for little white boys to go out on the streets, get drunk and use that for an excuse to start hunting down our people."

In a variety of ways, this case, and the comments it raised, were eerily reminiscent of an earlier murder that had occurred in The Pas, Manitoba, in 1971. In that year, a 19-year-old Cree high-school student, Helen Betty Osborne, was abducted by four young white men from the main street in a practice known as "squaw hopping." Osborne was stabbed more than 50 times with a screwdriver when she resisted being raped and was left to bleed to death. For more than 16 years, no charges were laid against any of the youths, even though most people in the town probably knew about the youths' involvement in the murder (Griffiths and Yerbury, 1995: 394).

A chief insight of **labelling theory** is that deviance results not just from the actions of the deviant but also from the responses of others, who define some actions as deviant and other actions as normal. As the above examples suggest, the term *deviant* or *criminal* is not automatic when one engages in rule-violating behaviour. Some individuals escape being labelled as deviants despite having engaged in deviant behaviour. Others, however, who do not engage in deviant or criminal acts may find themselves wrongfully accused and labelled as either deviant or criminal.

For example, if an adolescent misbehaves in high school a few times, teachers and the principal may punish him. However, his troubles really begin if the school authorities and the police label him a delinquent or, more formally, as a young offender. Surveillance of his actions will increase. Actions that authorities would normally not notice or would define as of little consequence are more likely to be interpreted as proof that he, indeed, is a delinquent or criminal "type." He may be ostracized from nondeviant cliques in the school and eventually socialized into a deviant subculture. Over time, immersion in the deviant subculture may lead the adolescent to adopt "delinquent" as his **master status,** or overriding public identity. More easily than we may care to believe, what starts out as a few incidents of misbehaviour can amplify into a criminal career because of labelling (Matsueda, 1988, 1992).

That labelling plays an important part in who is caught and who is charged with crime was demonstrated more than 30 years ago by Aaron Cicourel (1968). Cicourel examined the tendency to label rule-breaking adolescents as juvenile delinquents if they came from families in which the parents were divorced. He found that police officers tended to use their discretionary powers to arrest adolescents from divorced families more often than adolescents from intact families who committed similar delinquent acts. Judges, in turn, tended to give more severe sentences to adolescents from divorced families than to adolescents from intact families who were charged with similar delinquent acts. Sociologists and criminologists then collected data on the social characteristics of adolescents who were charged as juvenile delinquents, "proving" that children from divorced families were more likely to become juvenile delinquents. Their finding reinforced the beliefs of police officers and judges. Thus, the labelling process acted as a self-fulfilling prophecy.

### Control Theory

All motivational theories assume that people are good and require special circumstances to make them bad. A popular type of constraint theory assumes that people are bad and require special circumstances to make them good. According to **control theory,** the rewards of deviance and crime are many. Proponents of this approach argue that nearly everyone wants fun, pleasure, excitement, and profit. Moreover, they say, if we could get away with it, most of us would commit deviant and criminal acts to acquire more of these valued things. For control theorists, the reason most of us don't engage in deviance and crime is that we are prevented from doing so. The reason deviants and criminals break norms and laws is that social controls are insufficient to ensure their conformity.

Travis Hirschi developed the control theory of crime (Hirschi, 1969; Gottfredson and Hirschi, 1990). He argued that adolescents are more prone to deviance and crime than adults because they are incompletely socialized and therefore lack self-control. Adults and adolescents may both experience the impulse to break norms and laws, but adolescents are less likely to control that impulse. Hirschi went on to show that the adolescents who are most prone to delinquency are likely to lack four types of social control. They tend to have few social *attachments* to parents, teachers, and other respectable role models, few legitimate *opportunities* for education and a good job, few *involvements* in conventional institutions, and weak *beliefs* in traditional values and morality. Because of the lack of control stemming from these sources, they are relatively free to act on their deviant impulses.

Other sociologists have applied control theory to gender differences in crime. They have shown that girls are less likely to engage in delinquency than boys because families typically exert more control over girls, supervising them more closely and socializing them to avoid risk (Hagan, Simpson, and Gillis, 1987; Peters, 1994). Sociologists have also applied control theory to different stages of life. Just as weak controls exercised by family and school are important in explaining why some adolescents engage in deviant or criminal acts, job and marital instability make it more likely that some adults will be unable to resist the temptations of deviance and crime (Sampson and Laub, 1993).

Labelling and control theories have little to say about why people regard certain kinds of activities as deviant or criminal in the first place. For the answer to that question, we must turn to conflict theory, a third type of constraint theory.

### Conflict Theory

The day after Christmas, 1996, JonBenet Ramsey was found strangled to death in the basement of her parents' US$800 000 home in Boulder, Colorado. The police found no footprints in the snow surrounding the house and no sign of forced entry. The investigators concluded that nobody had entered the house during the night when, according to the coroner, the murder took place. The police did find a ransom note saying that the child had been kidnapped. A linguistics expert from Vassar later compared the note with writing samples of the child's mother. In a 100-page report, the expert concluded that the child's mother was the author of the ransom note. It was also determined that all the materials used in the crime had been purchased by the mother. Finally, it was discovered that JonBenet had been sexually abused. Although by no means an open-and-shut case, enough evidence was available to cast a veil of suspicion over the parents. Yet, apparently due to the lofty position of the Ramsey family in their community, the police treated them in an extraordinary way. On the first day of the investigation, the commander of the Boulder police detective division designated the Ramseys an "influential family" and ordered that they be treated as victims, not suspects (Oates, 1999: 32). The father was allowed to participate in the search for the child. In the process, he may have contaminated crucial evidence. The police also let him leave the house unescorted for about an hour. This led to speculation that he might have disposed of incriminating evidence. Because the Ramseys are millionaires, they were able to hire accomplished lawyers who prevented the Boulder police from interviewing them for four months and a public relations team that reinforced the idea that the Ramseys were victims. A grand jury decided on October 13, 1999, that nobody would be charged with the murder of JonBenet Ramsey.

Regardless of the innocence or guilt of the Ramseys, the way their case was handled adds to the view that the law applies differently to rich and poor. That is the perspective of **conflict theory.** In brief, conflict theorists maintain that the rich and the powerful impose deviant and criminal labels on the less powerful members of society, particularly those who challenge the existing social order. Meanwhile, they are usually able to use their money and influence to escape punishment for their own misdeeds.

Steven Spitzer (1980) conveniently summarizes this school of thought. He notes that capitalist societies are based on private ownership of property. Moreover, their smooth functioning depends on the availability of productive labour and respect for authority. When thieves steal, they challenge private property. Theft is therefore a crime. When so-called "bag ladies" and drug addicts drop out of conventional society, they are defined as deviant because their refusal to engage in productive labour undermines a pillar of capitalism. When young, politically volatile students or militant trade unionists strike or otherwise protest against authority, they, too, represent a threat to the social order and are defined as deviant or criminal.

Of course, says Spitzer, the rich and the powerful engage in deviant and criminal acts too. But, he adds, they tend to be dealt with more leniently. Industries can grievously harm people by damaging the environment, yet serious charges are rarely brought against the owners of industry. White-collar crimes are less severely punished than street crimes, regardless of the relative harm they cause. Compare the crime of break and enter with fraud, for example. Fraud almost certainly costs society more than break and enters. But breaking and entering is a street crime committed mainly by lower-class people, while fraud is a white-collar crime committed mainly by middle- and upper-class people. Not surprisingly, therefore, in Canada in 2000–01, 61 percent of convicted break and enter cases but just 35 percent of convicted fraud cases resulted in a prison sentence (Thomas, 2002: 9). Laws and norms may change along with shifts in the distribution of power in society. However, according to conflict theorists, definitions of deviance and crime, and also punishments for misdeeds, are always influenced by who's on top.

And so we see that many theories contribute to our understanding of the social causes of deviance and crime. Some forms of deviance and crime are better explained by one theory than another. Different theories illuminate different aspects of the process by which people are motivated to break rules and be defined as rule breakers. Our overview should make it clear that no one theory is best. Instead, taking many theories into account allows us to develop a fully rounded appreciation of the complex processes surrounding the social construction of deviance and crime.

# SOCIAL CONTROL AND PUNISHMENT

## Trends in Social Control

No discussion of crime and deviance would be complete without considering in some depth the important issues of social control and punishment, for all societies seek to ensure that their members obey norms and laws. All societies impose sanctions on rule breakers. However, the *degree* of social control varies over time and from one society to the next. *Forms* of punishment also vary. Below we focus on how social control and punishment have changed historically.

Consider first the difference between preindustrial and industrial societies. Beginning in the late nineteenth century, many sociologists argued that preindustrial societies are characterized by strict social control and high conformity, while industrial societies are characterized by less stringent social control and low conformity (Tönnies, 1957 [1887]). Similar differences were said to characterize small communities versus cities. As the old German proverb says, "city air makes you free."

There is much truth in this point of view. Whether they are fans of opera or reggae, connoisseurs of fine wine or marijuana, city dwellers in industrial societies find it easier than people in small preindustrial communities to belong to a group or subculture of their choice. In general, the more complex a society, the less likely many norms will be widely shared. In fact, in a highly complex society such as Canada today, it is difficult to find an area of social life in which everyone is alike, or where one group can impose its norms on the rest of society without resistance.

Nonetheless, some sociologists believe that social control has intensified over time, at least in some ways. They recognize that individuality and deviance have increased but insist this has happened only within quite strict limits, beyond which it is now *more* difficult to move. In their view, many crucial aspects of life have become more regimented, not less.

Much of the regimentation of modern life is tied to the growth of capitalism and the state. Factories require strict labour regimes, with workers arriving and leaving at a fixed time and, in the interim, performing fixed tasks at a fixed pace. Workers initially rebelled against this regimentation since they were used to enjoying many holidays and a flexible and vague work schedule regulated only approximately by the seasons and the rising and setting of the sun. But they had little alternative as wage labour in industry overtook feudal arrangements in agriculture (Thompson, 1967). Meanwhile, institutions linked to the

In preindustrial societies, criminals who committed serious crimes were put to death, often in ways that seem cruel by today's standards. One method involved hanging the criminal with starving dogs.

growth of the modern state—or regulated by its armies, police forces, public schools, health care systems, and various other bureaucracies—also demanded strict work regimes, curricula, and procedures. These institutions existed on a much smaller scale in preindustrial times or did not exist at all. Today they penetrate our lives and sustain strong norms of belief and conduct (Foucault, 1977 [1975]).

Electronic technology makes it possible for authorities to exercise more effective social control than ever before. With millions of cameras mounted in public places and workplaces, some sociologists say we now live in a "surveillance society" (Lyon and Zureik, 1996). Spy cameras enable observers to see deviance and crime that would otherwise go undetected and take quick action to apprehend rule breakers. Moreover, when people are aware of the presence of spy cameras, they tend to alter their behaviour. For example, attentive shoplifters migrate to stores that lack electronic surveillance. On factory floors and in offices, workers display more conformity to management-imposed work norms. On campuses, students are inhibited from engaging in organized protests (Boal, 1998).

Thanks to computers and satellites, intelligence services in Canada, the United States, Britain, Australia, and New Zealand now monitor all international telecommunications traffic, always on the lookout for threats. As easily as you can find the word *anomie* in your sociology essay using the search function of your word processor, national security agencies can scan digitized telephone and e-mail traffic in many languages for key words and word patterns that suggest unfriendly activity (Omega Foundation, 1998). However, the system, known as Echelon, is also used to target sensitive business and economic secrets from Western Europe, and some people have expressed the fear that it could be used on ordinary citizens, robbing them of their privacy. Meanwhile, credit information on 95 percent of North American consumers is available for purchase, the better to tempt you with credit cards, marketing ploys, and junk mail. When you browse the Web, information about your browsing patterns is collected in the background by many of the sites you visit, again largely for marketing purposes. Most large companies monitor and record their employees' phone conversations and e-mail messages. These are all efforts to regulate behaviour, enforce conformity, and prevent deviance and crime more effectively using the latest technologies available (Garfinkel, 2000).

A major development in social control that accompanied industrialization was the rise of the prison. Today, prisons figure prominently in the control of criminals the world over. North Americans, however, have a particular affinity for the institution, as we will now see.

## The Prison

In October 2001, a 63-year-old man suffering from Parkinson's disease and addicted to cocaine was arrested in Ottawa. A passerby had noticed that the man had a 32-gauge shotgun in his gym bag and notified the police. The man, who was charged with possession of a weapon, did not resist arrest. This fact was not, perhaps, surprising, for the man's knowledge of the Canadian criminal justice system was vast. Roger Caron, dubbed Mad Dog Caron by the press, had first been sentenced to prison at the age of 16 for breaking and entering. He had spent most of his adult life as an inept robber, going in and out of eastern Canada's major prisons: Guelph, Kingston, Collins Bay, Millhaven, Stoney Mountain, St. Vincent De Paul, Dorchester, and an institution reserved for the criminally insane—Penetanguishene.

While incarcerated in the 1970s and after having already spent almost 20 years in prison, Caron wrote a chilling account of his lifetime behind bars. He was still in prison when his book, *Go-Boy!,* was published in 1978. The book describes, in harrowing detail, the harshness of the prison experience—the violence, the intense hatreds that fester, the hard labour, the horrors of solitary confinements, the twisted, manipulative friendships formed within a prison setting, and the brutal use of corporal punishment. He describes the use of the "paddle"—"three leather straps with wooden handles, so thick and coarse as to barely sag. Each one was perforated with hundreds of tiny holes designed to trap and rip the flesh from the buttocks." He writes that when this form of punishment was first administered to him in 1955, "[w]hite searing pain exploded throughout my being and blood

Roger Caron, who was 16 years old when he was first sentenced to prison for breaking and entering, has spent much of his life behind bars. His acclaimed book, *Go-Boy!* provides a chilling account of his life in almost all the major prisons in eastern Canada.

gushed from my lips as I struggled to stifle a scream. It was brutal and it was horrible" (Caron, 1979: 59; see also Farrell, n.d.).

*Go-Boy!* was honoured in 1978 with the Governor General's Award for literature and, in the years that followed, Caron wrote other books. However, he was unable to leave his past life totally. Following imprisonment for another botched robbery attempt, Caron was released from prison in 1998 and was still on parole at the time of his 2001 arrest. Regardless of the initial factors that caused Caron to turn to crime, it was his experiences within prison that turned him into a career criminal (CyberPress, 2001).

Caron's experience follows a pattern known to sociologists for a long time. Prisons are agents of socialization, and new inmates often become more serious offenders as they adapt to the culture of the most hardened, long-term prisoners (Wheeler, 1961).

Because prison often turns criminals into worse criminals, it is worth pondering the institution's origins, development, and current dilemmas. As societies industrialized, imprisonment became one of the most important forms of punishment for criminal behaviour (Garland, 1990; Morris and Rothman, 1995). In preindustrial societies, criminals were publicly humiliated, tortured, or put to death, depending on the severity of their transgressions. In the industrial era, depriving criminals of their freedom by putting them in prison seemed less harsh, more "civilized" (Durkheim, 1973 [1899–1900]).

Some people still take a benign view of prisons, even seeing them as opportunities for *rehabilitation.* They believe that prisoners, while serving time, can be taught how to be productive citizens upon release. In Canada, this rehabilitative ethos predominated in the 1950s and early 1970s, when many prisons sought to reform criminals by offering them psychological counselling, drug therapy, skills training, education, and other programs that would help at least the less violent offenders reintegrate into society (McMahon, 1992: xvii).

Today, however, many Canadians scoff at the idea that prisons can rehabilitate criminals. We have adopted a much tougher line and politicians routinely campaign on promises of a get-tough approach to crime and to criminals. Some people see prison as a means of *deterrence.* In this view, people will be less inclined to commit crimes if they know they are likely to get caught and serve long and unpleasant prison terms. Others think of prisons as institutions of *revenge.* They believe that depriving criminals of their freedom and forcing them to live in poor conditions is fair retribution for their illegal acts. Still others see prisons as institutions of *incapacitation.* From this viewpoint, the chief function of the prison is simply to keep criminals out of society as long as possible to ensure they can do no more harm (Feeley and Simon, 1992; Simon, 1993; Zimring and Hawkins, 1995).

No matter which of these views predominates, one thing is clear: The Canadian public has demanded that more criminals be arrested and imprisoned. And it has gotten what it wants. In 2000, Canada had 31 467 people in prison, for a rate of 118 per 100 000 population. In

1999–2000, Canada's prison population was composed of 12 816 inmates in federal institutions and 18 651 inmates in various forms of provincial/territorial custody. Although Canada's incarceration rate is higher than those of countries such as Scotland, Australia, or Germany, it is much lower than that of the United States (see Figure 6.8). In the United States, more than 2 million people are imprisoned, for a rate of 699 per 100 000. The United States currently has more people behind bars than any other country on earth. Only in Russia, now an impoverished country suffering from widespread corruption and social breakdown, is the incarceration rate close to that of the United States, at 675 per 100 000 (Sentencing Project, 2001).

## Moral Panic

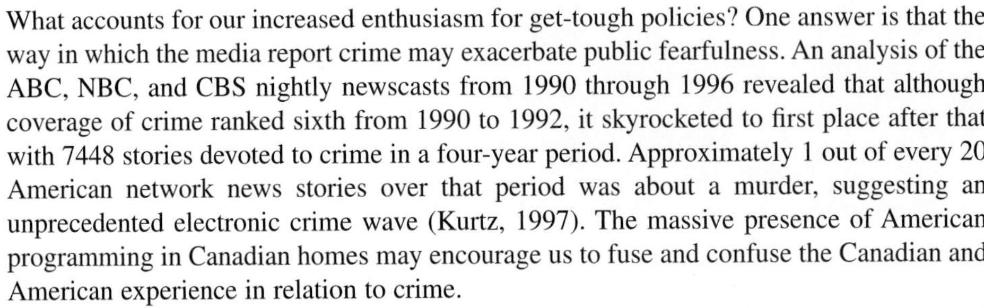

What accounts for our increased enthusiasm for get-tough policies? One answer is that the way in which the media report crime may exacerbate public fearfulness. An analysis of the ABC, NBC, and CBS nightly newscasts from 1990 through 1996 revealed that although coverage of crime ranked sixth from 1990 to 1992, it skyrocketed to first place after that with 7448 stories devoted to crime in a four-year period. Approximately 1 out of every 20 American network news stories over that period was about a murder, suggesting an unprecedented electronic crime wave (Kurtz, 1997). The massive presence of American programming in Canadian homes may encourage us to fuse and confuse the Canadian and American experience in relation to crime.

The National Media Archive examined 98 Canadian supper-hour TV newscasts that aired on three dates in 1997. *Chaos news*—news reports on crime, accidents, and natural disasters—accounted for 22 percent of local Canadian TV news items. Canadian newscasts were more likely than American newscasts to feature news about government and "soft news" (e.g., general human-interest stories and stories about entertainment, the arts, and culture). In general, American stations were also much more likely to lead or begin their newscasts with a report on crime, accidents, disasters, or other forms of chaos. Nevertheless, to the extent we believe that the crimes that draw headlines are "typical" of crime in Canada, we may believe that the battle to win the "war against crime" requires the most punitive measures.

✦ **FIGURE 6.8** ✦

**Number of Inmates per 100 000 Population (2000)**

Source: The Sentencing Project (2001).

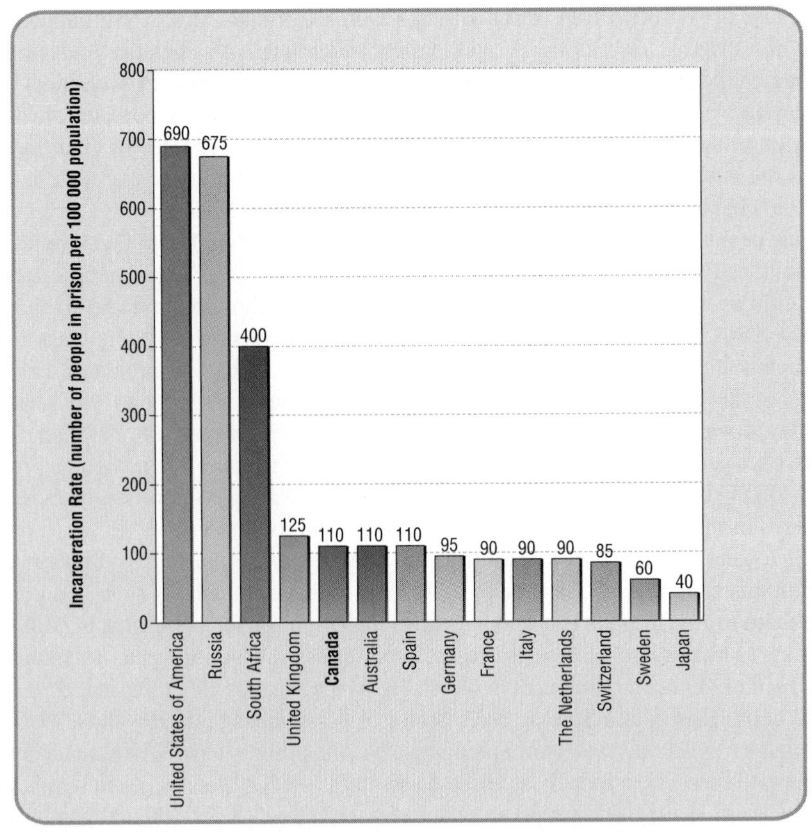

In short, media presentations of the crime problem may serve to promote a **moral panic.** That is, in response to lurid headlines that direct attention to the most notorious—and atypical—crimes and criminals, the public may prematurely conclude that all crime is violent and predatory, that all criminals are "dangerous," and that our current crime rate signals a grave threat to our society's well-being (Cohen, 1972; Goode and Ben-Yehuda, 1994). Are you part of the moral panic? Have you and your family taken special precautions to protect yourself from the "growing wave" of criminality? Even if you're not part of the moral panic, chances are you know someone who is. Therefore, to put things in perspective, you will need to recall an important fact from our discussion of recent trends in crime rates: According to official statistics, the moral panic is taking place during a period when major crime indexes are *falling*.

Why, then, the moral panic? Does anyone benefit from it? There may be several interested parties. First, the mass media benefit from moral panic because it allows them to rake in hefty profits. They publicize every major crime because crime draws big audiences, and big audiences mean more revenue from advertisers. After all, a front-page photograph of Karla Homolka or Paul Bernardo still generates newspaper sales a decade after their convictions—even if the story that accompanies it is abbreviated or banal. Fictional crime programs also draw tens of millions of viewers to their TVs. Second, the criminal justice system is a huge bureaucracy with thousands of employees. They benefit from moral panic because increased spending on crime prevention, control, and punishment secures their jobs and expands their turf. Third, the moral panic is useful politically. Since the early 1970s, many politicians have based entire careers on get-tough policies. At election time, many politicians make "combatting crime" a focal point of their campaign promises.

Intensive media coverage of the most notorious and violent crimes and criminals may lead to a heightened fear of crime and demands for tougher penalties. Here, Karla Homolka, who with her husband, Paul Bernardo, was responsible for the sexual assault and brutal murder of Tammy Homolka, Leslie Mahaffy, and Kristen French in the early 1990s.

## Alternative Forms of Punishment

The two most contentious issues concerning the punishment of criminals are these: (a) Should the death penalty be reintroduced to punish the most violent criminals? and (b) Should alternative strategies be used? In concluding this chapter, we briefly consider each of these issues.

### Capital Punishment

Although capital punishment has not been employed in Canada since 1962 and was formally abolished in this country in 1976, the state retains the right to bring it back. As well, evidence suggests that a majority of Canadians favour its reintroduction. Although support for the reinstatement of capital punishment is somewhat lower in Quebec and marginally higher in the Prairie provinces, on a national level, support for the death penalty has been remarkably consistent over time. Consider, for example, that in the fall of 1945, a Gallup poll reported that 80 percent of Canadians were in favour of capital punishment; in 1995, 82 percent were in favour of the death penalty in at least some instances (Bibby, 1995, 2001).

Although the death penalty ranks high as a form of revenge, it is questionable whether it is much of a deterrent. First, murder is often committed in a rage, when the perpetrator is not thinking entirely rationally. As such, the murderer is unlikely to coolly consider the costs and consequences of his or her actions. Second, critics point out that the United States has a much higher murder rate than Canada and Western European nations that do not practise capital punishment (Mooney et al., 2001: 131).

Moreover, one must remember that capital punishment, where it is actually practised, is hardly a matter of blind justice. This is particularly evident if we consider the racial distribution of people who are sentenced to death and executed in the United States. Murdering a white person in the United States is much more likely to result in a death sentence than murdering a black person. For example, in Florida in the 1970s, an African-American who killed a white person was 40 times more likely to receive the death penalty than an African-American who killed another African-American. Moreover, a white person who murders a black person very rarely is sentenced to death, but a black person who murders a white person is one of the most likely to get the death penalty. Thus, of the 80 white people who murdered African-Americans in Florida in the 1970s, not one was charged with a capital crime. In Texas, 1 was—out of 143 (Black, 1989; Haines, 1996; Tonry, 1995). Given this patent racial bias, we cannot view the death penalty as a justly administered punishment.

Sometimes people favour capital punishment because it saves money. They argue that killing someone outright costs less than keeping the person alive in prison for the rest of his or her life. However, after trials and appeals, a typical execution costs the taxpayer several times *more* than a 40-year stay in a maximum-security prison (Haines, 1996).

Finally, in assessing capital punishment, one must remember that mistakes are common. Nearly 40 percent of death sentences in the United States since 1977 have been overturned because of new evidence or mistrial (Haines, 1996). In Canada, the wrongful convictions of Donald Marshall, Guy Paul Morin, David Milgaard—and many others in recent times—for murders they did not commit should be sufficient to remind us that the wheels of justice do not always turn smoothly.

## Alternative Strategies

In recent years, analysts have suggested two main reforms to our current prison regime. First, some analysts have argued that we reconsider our stance on rehabilitation. Advocates of rehabilitation suggest that the rate of **recidivism,** or the extent to which convicted offenders commit another crime, can be reduced through programs such as educational and job training, individual and group therapy, substance abuse counselling, and behaviour modification. Second, they have argued that, whenever possible, we should attempt to *reduce* rather than increase our rate of incarcerated offenders. Drawing on labelling theory, they suggest we pursue a policy of *radical nonintervention*, diverting offenders away from formal processing in the criminal justice system. Proponents of this idea say that at least part of the increase in crime we have witnessed in the past four decades is attributable to the introduction of new and broadened definitions of criminal conduct. They believe that charging and imprisoning more and more Canadians, especially youth, is unlikely to help these individuals develop prosocial behaviour. Accordingly, they advise us to seek alternative methods that divert adults and juveniles from formal criminal justice system processing.

Although alternative procedures vary from province to province, their use generally arises after the police or Crown prosecutor recommends that an offender be considered suitable for "diversion." One example of an alternative measure is a victim–offender reconciliation program (VORP) in which victim and offender meet under controlled circumstances. The victim has an opportunity to describe the impact of the criminal event on himself or herself and the offender might, for example, be required to apologize and agree to compensate the victim financially. In 1998–99, 33 173 youth cases were dealt with through alternative measures programs (Tufts, 2000: 10). These cases were more likely to involve male than female offenders. Young offenders selected for inclusion in these programs were usually over 15 years of age and they generally completed the provisions of the agreements they made. Most cases referred for diversion involved theft under $5000 (e.g., shoplifting). This is not surprising, since to be recommended for diversion, the offence must be minor. As well, to be considered candidates for diversion, offenders must first acknowledge that they are guilty of the act they have been accused of committing.

In like fashion, proponents of *decarceration* recommend that options such as fines (the most commonly used penal sanction in Canada), probation, and community service become more widely used as alternatives to imprisonment. However, not everyone views this strategy as desirable. It has been argued that the increased use of community programs does not truly reduce the numbers of individuals subject to formal social control. Rather, such strategies may simply "widen the net" through the creation of more intensive, intrusive, and prolonged control mechanisms. These efforts might more accurately be labelled *transcarceration* rather than *decarceration* (Lowman, Menzies, and Palys, 1987). Noting such objections, some analysts suggest that we go farther still and lobby for legislative reform that would *decriminalize* certain categories of conduct currently prohibited under Canadian criminal law, such as marijuana possession. This last suggestion serves to remind us, yet again, that *crime* and *deviance* are social constructs.

## SUMMARY

1. Deviance involves breaking a norm. Crime involves breaking a law. Both crime and deviance evoke societal reactions that help define the seriousness of the rule-breaking incident.
2. The seriousness of deviant and criminal acts depends on the severity of the societal response to them, their perceived harmfulness, and the degree of public agreement about whether they should be considered deviant or criminal.
3. Acts that rank lowest on these three dimensions are called social diversions. Next come social deviations and then come conflict crimes. Consensus crimes rank highest.
4. Definitions of deviance and crime are historically and culturally variable. These definitions are socially defined and constructed. They are not inherent in actions or in the characteristics of individuals.
5. Power is a key element in defining deviance and crime. Powerful groups are generally able to create norms and laws that suit their interests. Less powerful groups are usually unable to do so.
6. The increasing power of women has led to greater recognition of crimes committed against them. However, no similar increase has occurred in the prosecution of white-collar criminals because the distribution of power between classes has not changed much in recent decades.
7. Crime statistics come from official sources, self-report surveys, and indirect measures. Each source has its strengths and weaknesses.
8. The long crime wave that began its upswing in the early 1960s peaked and fell in the 1990s and, for the last nine years, has decreased each year by an average of 3 percent. This stemmed, in part, from a smaller proportion of young men in the population and a booming economy.
9. Aboriginal peoples experience disproportionately high arrest, conviction, and incarceration rates. However, it would be inaccurate to conclude that race and crime are causally related. This finding may be a consequence of individual and institutional bias. Moreover, race and social class are closely related in that Aboriginal peoples are overrepresented in the lower classes.
10. Theories of deviance include motivational theories (strain theory, subcultural theory, and the theory of differential association) and constraint theories (labelling theory, control theory, and conflict theory). Different theories illuminate different aspects of the process by which people are motivated to break rules and be defined as rule breakers.
11. All societies seek to ensure that their members obey norms and laws by imposing sanctions on rule breakers. However, the degree and form of social control vary historically and culturally.
12. Although some sociologists say that social control is weaker and deviance is greater in industrial societies than in preindustrial societies, other sociologists note that in some respects social control is greater in industrial societies.
13. The prison has become an important form of punishment in modern industrial societies. Prisons now focus less on rehabilitation than on isolating and incapacitating inmates.
14. There is increasing enthusiasm for get-tough policies toward criminals. However, our response to crime may arise, in part, because of media presentations that focus attention on the most violent—and least representative—types of crime committed.
15. A variety of commercial and political groups benefit from the moral panic over crime and therefore encourage it.
16. Although the death penalty ranks high as a form of revenge, it is doubtful whether it acts as a serious deterrent. Moreover, where it exists, the death penalty is administered in a racially biased manner, does not save money, and sometimes results in tragic mistakes.
17. The question of how we should respond to crime results in many different strategies being suggested. These range from the reintroduction of capital punishment to the suggestion that we decriminalize various types of conduct that are currently prohibited under Canadian law.

## GLOSSARY

**Conflict crimes** are illegal acts that many people consider harmful to society. However, many people think they are not very harmful. They are punishable by the state.

**Conflict theory** holds that deviance and crime arise out of the conflict between the powerful and the powerless.

**Consensus crimes** are illegal acts that nearly all people agree are bad in themselves and harm society greatly. The state inflicts severe punishment for consensus crimes.

**Constraint theories** identify the social factors that impose deviance and crime (or conventional behaviour) on people.

**Control theory** holds that the rewards of deviance and crime are ample. Therefore, nearly everyone would engage in deviance and crime if they could get away with it. The degree to which people are prevented from violating norms and laws accounts for variations in the level of deviance and crime.

**Deviance** occurs when someone departs from a norm.

**Differential association** theory holds that people learn to value deviant or nondeviant lifestyles depending on whether their social environment leads them to associate more with deviants or nondeviants.

**Formal punishment** takes place when the judicial system penalizes someone for breaking a law.

**Informal punishment** involves a mild sanction that is imposed during face-to-face interaction, not by the judicial system.

**Labelling theory** holds that deviance results not so much from the actions of the deviant as from the response of others, who label the rule breaker a deviant.

One's **master status** is one's overriding public identity.

A **moral panic** occurs when many people fervently believe that some form of deviance or crime poses a profound threat to society's well-being.

**Motivational theories** identify the social factors that drive people to commit deviant and criminal acts.

**Recidivism rates** tell us what proportion of people are re-arrested after an initial arrest.

In **self-report surveys,** respondents are asked to report their involvement in criminal activities, either as perpetrators or victims.

**Social constructionism** is a school of sociological thought that emphasizes how some people are in a position to create norms and pass laws that define others as deviant or criminal.

**Social control** refers to methods of ensuring conformity.

**Social deviations** are noncriminal departures from norms that are nonetheless subject to official control. Some members of the public regard them as somewhat harmful while other members of the public do not.

A **social diversion** is a minor act of deviance that is generally perceived as relatively harmless and that evokes, at most, a mild societal reaction such as amusement or disdain.

People who are **stigmatized** are negatively evaluated because of a marker that distinguishes them from others.

**Strain theory** holds that people may turn to deviance when they experience strain. Strain results when a culture teaches people the value of material success and society fails to provide enough legitimate opportunities for everyone to succeed.

**Street crimes** include arson, break and enter, assault, and other illegal acts disproportionately committed by people from lower classes.

**Subcultural theory** argues that gangs are a collective adaptation to social conditions. Distinct norms and values that reject the legitimate world crystallize in gangs.

**Techniques of neutralization** are the rationalizations that deviants and criminals use to justify their activities. Techniques of neutralization make deviance and crime seem normal, at least to the deviants and criminals themselves.

**Victimization surveys** are surveys in which people are asked whether they have been victims of crime.

**Victimless crimes** involve violations of the law in which no victim has stepped forward and been identified.

**White-collar crime** refers to an illegal act committed by a respectable, high-status person in the course of work.

## QUESTIONS TO CONSIDER

1. Has this chapter changed your view of criminals and the criminal justice system? If so, how? If not, why not?
2. Do you think different theories are useful in explaining different types of deviance and crime? Or do you think that one or two theories explain all types of deviance and crime while other theories are not very illuminating? Justify your answer using logic and evidence.
3. Do TV crime shows and crime movies give a different picture of crime in Canada than this chapter provides? What are the major differences? Which picture do you think is more accurate? Why?

## WEB RESOURCES

### Companion Web Site for This Book

http://www.brymsociologycompass.nelson.com

Begin by clicking on the Student Resources section of the Web site. Next, select the chapter you are currently studying from the pull-down menu. From the Student Resources page you will have easy access to InfoTrac College Edition®, MicroCase online exercises, and additional Web links. The Web site also has many useful tips to aid you in your study of sociology, including practice tests for each chapter.

### InfoTrac Search Terms

These search terms are provided to assist you in beginning to conduct research on this topic by visiting http://www.infotrac-college.com

**Moral panic**
**Prison**
**Stigma**
**Street crime**
**White-collar crime**

### Recommended Web Sites

For a measure of how widespread corruption is in the governments of every country in the world, visit http://www.GWDG.DE/~uwww/icr.htm.

What makes crime news? For interesting material on this subject, visit http://www.fsu.edu/~crimdo/lecture2.html. See also http://www.fsu.edu/~crimdo/lecture4.html for material on the varieties of crime depicted by the mass media.

Cross-national data on rates of incarceration can be found at http://www.sentencingproject.org/pubs/tsppubs/9030data.html.

## SUGGESTED READINGS

Michel Foucault. *Discipline and Punish: The Birth of the Prison.* Alan Sheridan, trans. (New York: Pantheon, 1977 [1975]). One of the most influential and stimulating analyses of the development of the prison.

Rick Linden, ed. *Criminology: A Canadian Perspective*, 4th ed. (Toronto: Harcourt Canada, 2000). An introductory-level textbook on criminology with chapters written by many of Canada's top criminologists.

Mike Maguire, Rod Morgan, and Robert Reiner, eds. *The Oxford Handbook of Criminology* (Oxford, UK: Clarendon Press, 1994). Everything you always wanted to know about crime and criminology. Although the focus is on Britain, the book is full of interesting ideas and covers current controversies.

## NOTE

1. Data are drawn from an analysis of adult criminal courts in eight provinces and territories; at the time that the analysis was conducted, data were unavailable for New Brunswick, Manitoba, British Columbia, the Northwest Territories, and Nunavut.

PART

III

# INEQUALITY

## IN THIS CHAPTER, YOU WILL LEARN THAT

- Income is unequally distributed in Canada and government plays a small, but important, role in redistributing money to children and families who are poor.
- Income inequality in Canada is lower than in the United States but consistent with most other postindustrial societies.
- As societies develop, inequality at first increases. Then, after passing the early stage of industrialization, inequality in society declines. In the postindustrial stage of development, inequality begins to increase again.
- Most theories of social inequality focus on its economic roots.
- Prestige and power are important noneconomic sources of inequality.
- Although some sociologists used to think that talent and hard work alone determine one's position in the socio-economic hierarchy, it is now clear that being a member of certain groups limits one's opportunities for success. In this sense, social structure shapes the distribution of inequality.

CHAPTER

# 7

# Social Stratification: Canadian and Global Perspectives

# PATTERNS OF SOCIAL INEQUALITY

## Shipwrecks and Inequality

Writers and filmmakers sometimes use shipwreck stories to illustrate patterns of social inequality. The shipwreck is a literary device allowing writers to erase the social conventions of power and privilege. Marooned on a deserted island or floundering with a sinking ship, differences of wealth and power are unimportant. Society is effectively eradicated.

Daniel Defoe's *Robinson Crusoe*, first published in 1719, is a classic novel in this tradition. Defoe writes of an Englishman marooned on a deserted island. The man's strong will, hard work, and inventiveness turn the island into a thriving colony. Defoe was one of the first writers to portray the work ethic of capitalism favourably. He believed that people get rich if they possess the virtues of good businesspeople—and stay poor if they don't.

The 1974 Italian movie *Swept Away* tells almost exactly the opposite story.[1] In the movie a beautiful woman, one of the idle rich, cruises in the Mediterranean. She treats the hard-working deckhands in a condescending and abrupt way. The deckhands do their jobs but seethe with resentment. Then comes a storm. The beautiful woman and one handsome deckhand are swept onto a deserted island. The deckhand asserts his masculine prowess on an initially unwilling and reluctant woman. The two survivors soon have passionate sex and fall in love.

All is well until their rescue. Upon returning to the mainland, the woman resumes her haughty ways. She turns her back on the deckhand; he becomes a common labourer again. Thus, the movie sends the audience three harsh messages, each contrasting with themes in Defoe's *Robinson Crusoe*. First, you do not have to work hard to be rich, because you can inherit wealth. Second, hard work does not always make you rich. Third, something about the structure of society causes inequality, for it is only on the deserted island, without society as we know it, that class inequality disappears. *Swept Away* also focuses attention on unequal power between the sexes. The two survivors are not equals; male privilege exerts itself in a context in which class differences have been obliterated. Here, then, is a fourth harsh message. Inequality has many interrelated dimensions, including class, sex, and race, and different contexts highlight different conditions of power and exploitation.

And then there is *Titanic*, a characteristically American take on the shipwreck-and-inequality theme (see Box 7.1). At one level, the movie shows that class differences are important. For example, in first class living conditions are luxurious, while in third class they are cramped. Indeed, on the Titanic, class divisions spell the difference between life and death. After the *Titanic* strikes an iceberg off the coast of Newfoundland, the ship's crew prevents second- and third-class passengers from entering the few available lifeboats. Priority goes to first-class passengers.

As the tragedy of the *Titanic* unfolds, however, a different theme emerges. Under some circumstances, we learn, class differences can be erased. In the movie, the sinking of the *Titanic* is the backdrop to a fictional love story about a wealthy young woman in first class and a working-class youth from the decks below. The sinking of the *Titanic* and the collapse of its elaborate class structure give the young lovers an opportunity to cross class divisions and profess devotion to each other. At another level, then, *Titanic* is an optimistic tale that holds out hope for a society in which class differences no longer matter, a society much like that of the "American Dream."

*Robinson Crusoe*, *Swept Away*, and *Titanic* raise many of the issues we address in this chapter. What are the sources of social inequality? Do determination, industry, and ingenuity shape the distribution of advantages and disadvantages in society, as the tale of *Robinson Crusoe* portrays? Or is *Swept Away* more accurate? Do certain patterns of social relations underlie and shape that distribution? Is *Titanic*'s first message of social class differences still valid? Does social inequality still have big consequences for the way we live? What about *Titanic*'s second message? Can people overcome or reduce inequality in society? If so, how?

## BOX 7.1 SOCIOLOGY AT THE MOVIES

### *TITANIC* (1997)

When the character played by Leonardo DiCaprio goes to the first-class cabin for dinner in *Titanic,* it turns out that a first-class ticket is not the only thing he is missing. He also lacks appropriate dinner attire and the knowledge and tastes expected of someone who can afford to travel first class. He is able to borrow a dinner jacket. However, the conversation at the dinner table is foreign to him. Being a working-class youth, he has little knowledge of the arts or other matters that interest the rich and the highly educated. To make matters worse, his dinner companions look down on him as a member of a lower class. Only the character played by Kate Winslet sees something special in him. She is already falling in love.

The world of the luxury ship *Titanic* is highly stratified. Sumptuous ballrooms and suites are reserved for the rich. They are spacious, well appointed, and well served. Dingy and cramped living and sleeping quarters are reserved for the poor. Their cabins even lack windows. Still worse off are the workers in the boiler room. They must shovel coal for hours on end, suffering from heat, dust, and exhaustion.

In the movie, the characters played by Leonardo DiCaprio and Kate Winslet overcome class barriers and fall in love. However, their sentiments are clearly exceptional. Class differences matter even after the great ship strikes the iceberg. First-class passengers are given preference in access to the lifeboats. Lower-class ticket holders and workers on the ship are left to drown.

What does *Titanic* teach us about social stratification? Should we conclude that social stratification pervades all aspects of life? Or does love often overcome class differences? You can treat these questions empirically. Among the marriages and dating relationships in your circle of friends, families, and relatives, what proportion involve partners from different classes? A high proportion suggests that love often trumps class. A low proportion suggests that class usually overcomes love, or doesn't even allow it to blossom.

To answer these questions, we first sketch the pattern of social inequality both in Canada and globally. We pay special attention to change over time. We then critically review the major theories of social inequality. We assess explanations for differences in inequality in the light of logic and evidence. From time to time, we take a step back and identify issues needing resolution before we can achieve a fuller understanding of social inequality, one of the fundamentally important aspects of social life.

## Economic Inequality in Canada

The musical *Cabaret*, set in the 1930s, contains a song based on the popular saying "Money makes the world go round." More recently, Madonna reiterated the same premise with the lyrics in "Material Girl": "They can beg and they can plead / But they can't see the light (that's right) / 'Cause the boy with the cold hard cash / Is always Mister Right" (Brown and Rans, 1984).

Money is power. That was the message in *Cabaret* and again in "Material Girl." Decade by decade, the saying "everything has its price" becomes more and more accurate. We live in a "buyable" world. Ours is a material world. The market for body parts, or even bodies, is lucrative (see Technology Bytes). Buying babies from surrogate mothers or kidneys from strangers, once unheard of, is increasingly common.

The selling of blood, sperm, and ova is common in many countries. An international trade in the body parts of the living, and the dead, flourishes. These body parts are often used for education and research purposes. More controversial is the practice of purchasing human organs, in particular kidneys, for transplantation. In the typical supply and demand equation of modern commerce, as demand for available organs escalates, the supply of body parts expands. As the Bellagio Task Force Report on Transplantation, Bodily Integrity and the International Traffic in Organs states, the global organ shortage "has encouraged the sale of organs, nowhere more conspicuously than in India. It has also stimulated the use of organs from executed prisoners, nowhere more systematically than in China. Thus, residents of Gulf States and other Asian countries frequently travel to India to obtain a kidney" (Rothman et al., 1997).

People selling body parts are almost invariably poor. People buying body parts are invariably rich. Though not a common practice, an increasing number of wealthy people travel to foreign countries with their own surgeons in tow in an attempt to prolong life through the purchase and use of body parts.

In North America, and especially in the United States, poor people are more likely than rich people to suffer illnesses that could be alleviated by organ transplantation. However, they are less likely to be offered transplant opportunities (Wallich and Mukerjee, 1996). Especially in the United States, this is largely the result of the poor not having adequate private health insurance to cover transplantation expenses. However, it is also the case that the poor are more likely to be organ donors, even in Canada, because "the typical donor is still young and a victim of accidental or deliberate violence—which tends to strike the disadvantaged in disproportionate numbers" (Wallich and Mukerjee, 1996).

After weighing evidence and argument, the Bellagio Task Force "found no unarguable ethical principle that would justify a ban on the sale of organs" (Rothman et al., 1997). In particular, they note that "a prohibition on sale might well cost would-be recipients their lives and infringe in important ways on the autonomy of would-be sellers" (Rothman et al., 1997). This latter point is particularly germane because it touches on a key debate about social inequality. From what perspective or standpoint can we make judgments about inequality and human misery? Who should make the choice between grinding poverty on the one hand and the sale of a kidney on the other? An easy response is to claim this is a false dichotomy. No one should have to make such a choice! Too easy. Such a response ignores all of human history, in which social inequality, the context of such a horrible choice, has existed always and everywhere.

Materialism, the attempt to satisfy needs by buying products or experiences, is a defining characteristic of modern society. Never have so many people, at least in the Western industrial world, been able to share so widely in material comforts (such as central heating, ample food, appropriate clothing, and so forth). Economic prosperity has made Canada one of the best countries in the world in which to live.

The growth of prosperity in the post–Second World War Canadian economy is easy to illustrate. Figure 7.1 shows the growth in the average earnings of Canadian households. In the early 1950s, Canadian families had earnings of only about $3500. Today the typical Canadian family enjoys an income close to $60 000. In part, this increase is misleading since a soft drink that once cost a dime now costs a dollar. Such price inflation accounts for well over half the rise in incomes.

Nevertheless, the purchasing power of family incomes (what you can get for a dollar) also rose after the Second World War as a consequence of greater economic productivity. Therefore, the line in Figure 7.1 rises over time both because the cost of living increases and because people have become more productive. The productivity gains that spurred higher incomes occurred both because of the increased skill of workers and because of the increased use of sophisticated technology. Greater productivity generated substantial real increases in family income in the 1960s and 1970s, as Figure 7.1 shows.

Notice also from Figure 7.1 that the average earnings of Canadian families have increased at a slower rate recently. That is, the slope of the income line is flatter in the 1980s and 1990s than it was earlier. Recall, too, that the number of earners in a family increased over this recent interval as more women entered the paid labour force. Even so,

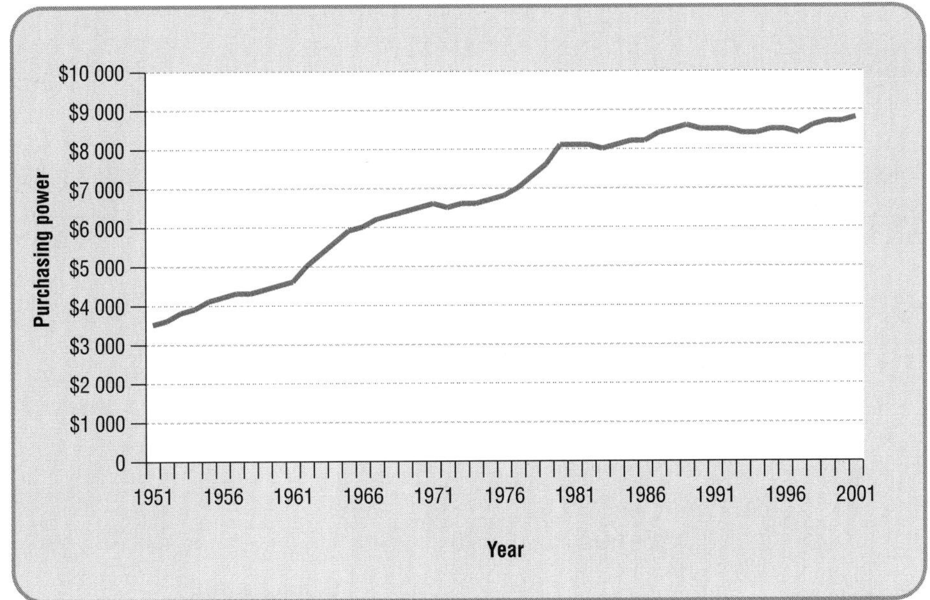


✦ **FIGURE 7.1** ✦

**Purchasing Power of Canadian Families, 1951 to 2001 (in 1951 dollars)**

Source: Adapted from various Statistics Canada documents.

the purchasing power of family earnings did not grow much. This has led to several recent public debates. Notably, the widespread demand for reduced taxes is in part a reaction to this relatively flat earnings trajectory. Despite working harder and longer, family incomes have not grown proportionately. Coupled with this is the common awareness that the days of the single-breadwinner family of the 1950s and 1960s are past. Most families now have at least two earners, but the prospect of buying a house, and owning more of it than the bank, is still a struggle.

Figure 7.1 simplifies reality because it is based on averages. Economic prosperity and the perks of materialism are not equally shared. In your own experience you will have witnessed inequality on a visit to "skid row" or the inner-city areas of many of our biggest communities. You may have seen the lineups for food banks or the poverty of some rural farmers. Here is a language and lifestyle of used clothes, of baloney and canned spam, of fleas and roaches, of despair and depression. There is also a language of booze, illicit sex, welfare cheats, laziness, and cunning deceit. We will return to these contrasting descriptions later.

At the other end of the money spectrum is the luxury of our richest neighbourhoods, places you may have lived in or visited. This is the world of million-dollar homes with indoor swimming pools and outdoor tennis courts, multi-car garages, and in-house security systems to deter those who might steal a piece of art. Here is a language and lifestyle of Gucci and Hugo Boss, of caviar and roast duckling, of coddled poodles and parakeets, of ambition and success. Here, too, is a different language, one of idle richness, of misbegotten inheritance, of greedy landlords, and of fraud and cunning deceit. This, too, is a contrast to which we will return.

The vast majority of us live between these two extremes. Many of us may have tasted both caviar and baloney, petted poodles and scratched fleas, but relatively few Canadians have continuing experience with either abject poverty or substantial wealth. How do we measure inequality that falls between these two extremes? Not all families earn $60 000 per year, even though that is close to the average. How do we understand fluctuations or variations around this average, and most important, how they have changed? Is economic inequality growing or receding?

Social scientists have come up with a simple yet powerful way to display patterns of inequality. Here is the method, by way of analogy. Among your classmates, think of how much money each person might have earned in the past few months. A few with well-paying, steady jobs may have earned more than $5000. Put those people at the front of a line, the highest earner first. Others will have struggled to find consistent work or may have

The Thomsons, Canada's wealthiest family, rank 13th on the *Forbes Magazine* list of the world's richest people. Ken Thomson, 78, has handed over the reins of the Thomson publishing empire to his son, David. This is an example of success due to both hard work and family connections (see Table 7.3).

opted not to work. Put them at the back of the line, with the lowest earner at the very end of the line.

Now, step two: Add up how much everyone in the line has earned. (Imagine you have 100 students in your lineup and in sum they earned $300 000). As step three, divide the line into five equal groups with 20 percent of your classmates in each group—technically, these groups are known as quintiles. As step four, add up how much the members of each of the five groups or quintiles earned. The group at the head of the line will have earned the most given how we constructed the line (imagine that together the members of this group earned $120 000). The group at the back of the line will have earned the least (imagine that they collectively earned $12 000). As the final step, we can calculate the percentage of money each group earned. The top quintile has 40 percent of the earnings ($120000/ $300 000 × 100) while the bottom quintile has only 4 percent. The remainder (56 percent) is shared by the other three quintiles.

A completely unequal distribution would result if the top quintile held 100 percent of the money. The opposite, a completely equal distribution, would result if each quintile held 20 percent of the money. This concept of the share of income held by each quintile is frequently used to investigate income inequality in Canada and elsewhere. It is an easy idea to visualize, and by looking at how the share of income changes over time, it allows researchers to determine whether inequality is growing or shrinking.

For the past several decades, Statistics Canada has used the Survey of Consumer Finances to gather income data for a sample of the Canadian population. This sample, recently including about 35 000 Canadian households, provides information useful in examining poverty, male–female wage differences, ethnic income inequality, and so forth. The share of income held by each quintile in the survey is also routinely reported by Statistics Canada (Statistics Canada, 2000d).

Figure 7.2 shows that for 1998, the most recent year for which data are available, the lowest quintile of income earners received 4.3 percent of all income, while the top quin-

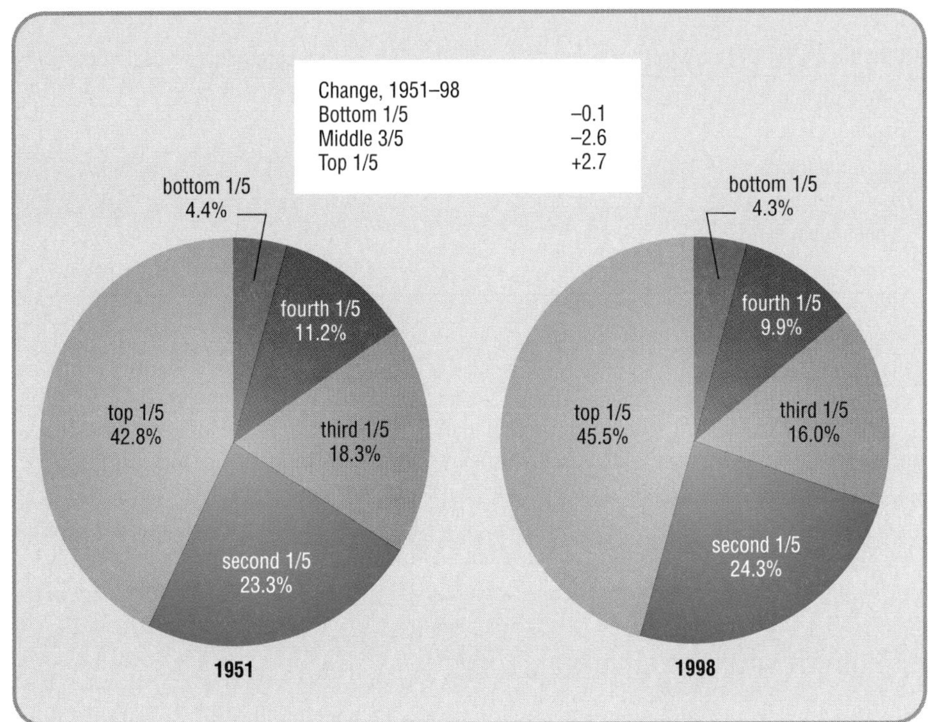


✦ **FIGURE 7.2** ✦

**The Distribution of Total Income among Families and Unattached Individuals, Canada, 1951 and 1998**

Source: Statistics Canada (2000d).

tile received 45.5 percent of all income. Almost half of all income was held by the richest 20 percent of individuals and families. In dollar terms, the average income of the lowest quintile was $10 688 as compared with the average for the top quintile of $113 374 (Statistics Canada, 2000d).

This level of inequality can be put into perspective in two ways. First, how does income inequality in Canada compare with income inequality among our neighbours in the United States? Income inequality is slightly less marked in Canada than in the United States. In the United States, the lowest quintile shares 3.6 percent of all income, compared with 4.3 percent in Canada. At the upper end, the richest Americans capture 49.2 percent of all income, compared with 45.5 percent in Canada.

A second perspective is gained by asking how income inequality has changed within Canada over the last 50 years. Figure 7.2 shows that the distribution has changed relatively little over the past five decades. For example, in 1998 the bottom quintile received 4.3 percent of income, while in 1951 the comparable figure was 4.4 percent. At the top end, the richest quintile has increased its share of income over the past 50 years from 42.8 percent of income to 45.5 percent. This growth occurred mainly at the expense of the middle class. More broadly, from the mid-1980s there is growing evidence of widening income inequality in Western industrial countries, including Canada (Förster and Pellizzari, 2000).

The incomes reported above and in Figure 7.2 are pre-tax incomes. This is the money Canadians receive prior to paying taxes. Given frequent media reference to Canada as a "welfare state," one might imagine that after-tax income is distributed differently. The concept of a welfare state implies the imagery of Robin Hood, taking from the rich and giving to the poor. To what degree does the Canadian state act like Robin Hood?

As Table 7.1 illustrates, in 1998 the government did redirect some income from the highest earners in Canada (the top quintile) to each of the other quintiles. Compared with their pre-tax share of total income, the richest quintile of earners saw their income share decline by 2.7 percent, from 45.5 to 42.8 percent. The after-tax incomes of all other quintiles rose modestly. A Robin Hood outcome would have seen the greatest rise in the lowest quintile, but that was not the case. This implies that in Canada the state is hardly as generous as Robin Hood.

✦ **TABLE 7.1** ✦
**Percentage Share of Pre-tax and After-tax Income by Quintile, 1998, for Families and Unattached Individuals**

Source: Statistics Canada (2000d).

| Quintile | Total Pre-tax Income Share | Total After-tax Income Share | Gain/Loss |
|---|---|---|---|
| Lowest quintile | 4.3 | 5.0 | +0.7 |
| Second quintile | 9.9 | 11.0 | +1.1 |
| Third quintile | 16.0 | 16.7 | +0.7 |
| Fourth quintile | 24.3 | 24.4 | +0.1 |
| Highest quintile | 45.5 | 42.8 | –2.7 |

Furthermore, over the course of the later part of the twentieth century, the redistributive effort of governments declined in Canada. The after-tax income share for the lowest quintile fell to 5.0 percent in 1998, down from 5.8 percent in 1989. In contrast, over that same decade, the after-tax income of the richest quintile grew from 40.6 to 42.8 percent. Using a variety of measures of income (e.g., market income, after-tax income), Statistics Canada (2000d: 74) concludes that, for Canada, "income inequality grew more rapidly in the latter half of the 1990s."

## Explanations of Income Inequality

Why do some people fall into the highest quintile and others into the lowest quintile? What explains the distribution of income? Obviously your job has a significant influence. Bank managers are paid more than bank tellers, schoolteachers more than daycare workers. As well, people who work more earn more. But these are rather obvious factors that predict earnings. Although these factors cannot be ignored, are there more general themes that might explain income inequality?

We know that some individuals earn sizable salaries because of their natural talent. Jarome Iginla (hockey), Victoria Bertram (ballet), Ben Heppner (opera), Laurie Kane (golf), Shania Twain (popular music), and Mike Weir (golf) are Canadians whose success on the world stage has provided them with substantial earnings. The principal reason for their excellence is a natural endowment in dance, music, or athletics. A genetic gift sets them apart. At the other end of the economic spectrum, some people have the genetic misfortune of bearing the hardship of Down's syndrome, schizophrenia, or autism. Exactly how genetics is involved in myriad conditions like these is unknown, but the consequence is that fewer people with Down's syndrome or schizophrenia are able to succeed economically. For the vast majority of people, however, genetic factors have relatively little explanatory power in determining economic success. Our genetic differences provide some insight into income inequality, but in comparison with other explanatory factors, genes play a relatively modest role.[2]

Even for those Canadians with a natural talent in the performing arts or athletics, the role of effort is essential. Talent alone is insufficient. All great performers speak emphatically about effort. Practice, the hours of dedication to the basics of one's profession, is common to all who enjoy significant success. Effort is also significant for many Canadians who spend long hours at work—whether amassing "billable" hours in a law practice, doing the "endless" chores in a small business, or working overtime at a construction site. Hard work usually pays off, although, as the film *Swept Away* signalled, and as many will know from personal experience, diligence and perseverance might be necessary conditions for rewards, but they are not sufficient. Effort alone does not result in high income (see Figure 7.3).

Raw talent needs to be honed. Education, tutelage, training, coaching, schooling—these are crucial ways in which skills are developed and nurtured. For the vast majority of income earners, it is their level of ability to communicate persuasively, think critically, reason logically, and work creatively that affects the occupations they hold and the incomes they receive. Our natural talent and our effort are important ingredients in this process, to be sure, but education matters. Indeed, the importance of education as a deter-

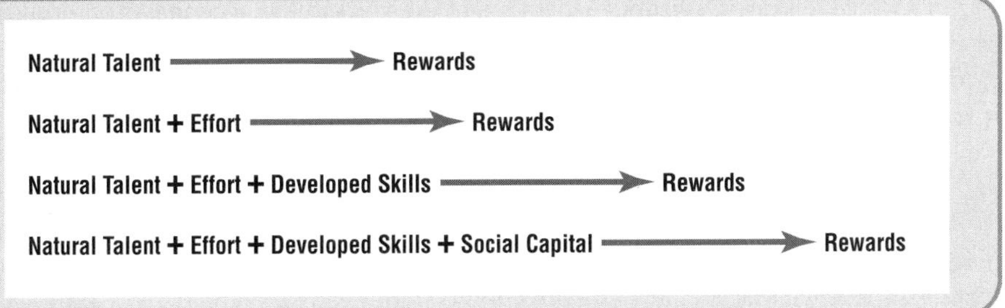


✦ **FIGURE 7.3** ✦
**A Simplified Schematic of Explanations for Income Inequality**

minant of occupation and income continues to increase (Baer, 1999). As the Canadian occupational structure moves further away from its traditional resource-based foundation to a more mature knowledge-driven economy, the importance of education will continue to grow (see Table 7.2).

Human capital theory stresses the increasing centrality of education as a factor affecting economic success. If physical capital is understood as investment in industrial plants and equipment, human capital is investment in education and training. In a manner analogous to the way productivity increases by upgrading manufacturing plants and introducing new technology, productivity gains can also result from investment in the skills and abilities of people. Knowledge-intensive jobs (that is, jobs requiring advanced skills) are increasing in Canada. Better-educated workers are more skilled and productive in these jobs because they have made investments in acquiring the research skills and knowledge base essential to the new economy (Betcherman and Lowe, 1997).

Much evidence supports a human capital interpretation of the link between schooling and incomes (Baer, 1999). However, this is not a complete explanation for why people earn what they earn. In Chapter 2 (Research Methods), we discussed the work of Kay and Hagan (1998). We saw that in the legal profession, almost everyone makes the same human capital investment. Everyone acquires a law degree, yet economic rewards vary even for people with the same experience and type of legal practice.

✦ **TABLE 7.2** ✦
**Median Annual Income, Full-Time Workers, Selected Occupations, Canada, 2001**

Source: Government of Canada (2001b).

| Occupation | Median Annual Income | Range of Incomes (bottom 20% – top 20%) |
|---|---|---|
| General and family physicians | $78 100 | $23 400 – $105 000 |
| Judges, lawyers, Quebec notaries | $62 400 | $20 100 – $94 700 |
| Police and firefighters | $52 481 | $33 185 – $63 022 |
| University professors and assistants | $52 300 | $17 900 – $63 200 |
| Engineers, professional | $51 200 | $30 000 – $69 200 |
| Airplane pilots, flight engineers, instructors | $50 800 | $16 400 – $72 300 |
| Computer programmers | $40 500 | $24 600 – $68 100 |
| Electricians | $38 400 | $18 500 – $40 500 |
| Average for all occupations | $37 400 | |
| Motor vehicle and transit drivers | $34 300 | $13 200 – $61 800 |
| Plumbers | $34 200 | $20 100 – $61 100 |
| Secretaries, recorders, transcriptionists | $29 100 | $17 800 – $36 900 |
| Bank tellers | $25 900 | $18 300 – $32 300 |
| Security guards | $25 394 | $14 306 – $39 469 |
| Cleaners | $25 100 | $12 400 – $41 100 |
| Cooks and chefs | $23 100 | $12 700 – $34 700 |
| Textile sewing machine operators and related Workers in fabric, fur, and leather | $22 700 | $15 900 – $39 800 |
| Technical occupations in personal service | $20 400 | $10 400 – $30 400 |

Part of the reason why people with the same amount of human capital may receive different economic rewards is that they possess different amounts of social capital. **Social capital** refers to people's networks or connections. Individuals are more likely to succeed if they have strong bonds of trust, cooperation, and mutual respect and obligation with well-positioned individuals or families. Knowing the right people, and having strong links to them, helps in attaining opportunities (Coleman, 1988).

A related version of this argument is captured in the notion of cultural capital as proposed by the French sociologist Pierre Bourdieu (Bourdieu and Passeron, 1990). Bourdieu focuses on taste and aesthetics—*savoir faire*. Cultural capital emphasizes a set of social skills people have, their ability to impress others, to use language and images effectively, and to influence and persuade people. While the notion of social capital stresses your networks and connections with others, the idea of cultural capital emphasizes your impression management skills, your ability to influence others. In different ways, both concepts emphasize being part of the right "social club."

What both concepts also have in common is the idea that families higher in the social hierarchy enjoy more capital of all types. Connections and culture help you find a good job. Hiring new recruits, then, depends on the talent, effort, and skills that people bring to the interview, but it also depends on the connections and culture that people have. Indeed, culture and connections often influence who gets an interview.

In summary, natural talent and effort are important, and for a few occupations very significant (e.g., opera singer, golfer). For most Canadians, level of education (or developed skill) is a critical factor in finding continuous, well-paying employment. In addition, social or cultural capital is consequential for many in finding economic success. Explaining an individual's position in the income hierarchy depends on several factors, but the four themes or perspectives outlined in Figure 7.3 are crucial.

## Income versus Wealth

Remember that the previous section has focused on explanations for differences among Canadians in the income they earn. Income differs from wealth. Your wealth is what you own. For most adults, this includes a house (minus the mortgage), a car (minus the car loan), and some appliances, furniture, and savings (minus the credit card balance). Your income, on the other hand, is what you earn over a given period of time. Typically, wealth is more unequally distributed than income.

Indeed, in 1999, 73.1 percent of all the wealth in the country was controlled by the richest 20 percent of the population. The richest 10 percent (decile) of Canadians control 55.7 percent of all wealth (Morissette, Zhang, and Drolet, 2002). From 1984 to 1999 the wealthiest decile saw its proportion of the country's total wealth increase by 3.9 percent, from 51.8 to 55.7 (see also Davies, 2003). Table 7.3 lists the wealthiest 10 Canadians or Canadian families, the richest of the rich. All of them are substantial billionaires.

Both the sizes and the sources of the fortunes listed in Table 7.3 are noteworthy. First, even if the average Canadian family saved every penny it earned, it would take 20 000 years to earn $1 billion. Second, even if you spent $1000 a day, you could not spend $1 billion in a lifetime. It would take nearly 2800 years (or about 35 lifetimes) to spend $1 billion at the rate of $1000 a day (assuming you did not invest the unspent portion to earn interest, dividends, or capital gains).

What are the sources for the fortunes listed in Table 7.3? For at least five of the names on the list (Thomson, Irving, Bombardier, Weston, and Bronfman), inheritance is a critical factor. These are family dynasties. Thomson, Irving, and Weston are families whom John Porter (1965) and Wallace Clement (1975) called members of the "Canadian corporate elite." These families are among a select group of Anglo-Canadians who have held inordinate influence in Canadian economic and political circles through several generations.

Skoll is an "instant" billionaire, having amassed his fortune through e-commerce. Several other "instant" billionaires have arrived and departed the top 10 in the past several years due to fluctuations in technical and research-driven sectors. On the whole, Table 7.3 suggests a mix of opportunism, business acumen, and family fortune as key determinants

**✦ TABLE 7.3 ✦**
**Wealthiest 10 Canadians, 2002**

Source: Brieger et al. (2002).

| Individual or Family | Estimated Wealth | Assets and Notes |
|---|---|---|
| Kenneth Thomson | $27.71 billion | Former Chairman, Thomson Corp., moving from a newspaper empire to an e-information and solutions company; chairman and director, Woodbridge Company Limited (the Thomson family holding company); http://www.thomson.com |
| Galen Weston | $10.24 billion | George Weston Ltd., founded 1882; Loblaws; President's Choice; Zehrs; Connors Seafood; owns more than 20 salmon farms; Holt Renfrew; http://www.weston.ca |
| Bombardier family | $4.65 billion | Bombardier Aerospace; Ski-doo snowmobiles; production sites in Canada, United States, Mexico, Austria, Germany, Switzerland, etc.; http://www.bombardier.com |
| James Pattison | $3.81 billion | Auto sales; food; media |
| Jeff Skoll | $3.43 billion | e-Bay |
| Eugene Melnyk | $3.3 billion | Pharmaceuticals (Biovail Corp.) |
| Irving family | $3.2 billion | Irving Oil; JD Irving Ltd; reputed to have revenues as large as the province of New Brunswick; http://www.irvingoil.com or http://www.jdirving.com |
| Paul Desmarais, Sr. | $2.79 billion | Financial services (Great West Lifeco, Investors Group); publishing (La Presse, Power Corp.) |
| Bernard Sherman | $2.73 billion | Pharmaceuticals (Apotex) |
| Charles Bronfman | $2.38 billion | Entertainment; telecommunications |

of wealth. Most of these family names are Anglo-Canadian, although Bombardier (French) and Bronfman (Jewish) hint at the growing diversity among elite families in Canada (see Ogmundson and McLaughlin, 1992).

For most Canadians, measures of net worth (that is, wealth minus debt) are more telling. For the majority of Canadians, investment in a family home is their chief asset. And although real estate values have risen sharply in many areas over the past few decades, home ownership typically involves mortgage support from a bank. A growing proportion of Canadians owns stocks or share investments. In 1989, fewer than one-quarter of Canadians had direct or indirect (that is, via pensions) stock ownership, but this rose to 37 percent in 1996 and to 49 percent in 2000 (Toronto Stock Exchange, 2000).

## Income and Poverty

At the other extreme of the income distribution are the homeless. In recent decades the number of people with "no fixed address" has increased considerably. We do not know how many Canadians are homeless. Yet, in cities across the country, people sleep under bridges, in back allies, behind dumpsters, and in thickets in public parks. They do so night after night, month after month.

Homelessness is one manifestation of poverty. Exactly how many Canadians are poor is a matter of intense debate. Poverty lacks an agreed-upon definition. A first disagreement occurs around whether poverty should be defined in absolute or relative terms. An absolute definition of poverty focuses on bare essentials, suggesting that poor families have resources inadequate to acquire the basic necessities of life (e.g., food, shelter, clothing). Agreement on "bare essentials" depends on values and judgments (see Sarlo, 2001). What is essential varies from time to time, place to place, and group to group. Many of our ancestors lived without indoor plumbing, and some Canadians still do, but most people would define indoor plumbing as essential. A family could survive on a steady diet of cod and potatoes, but most would define such a family as poor.

What constitutes "bare essentials" depends on social context. Again, most Canadians would agree that the poverty experienced in Angola or Haiti or Ethiopia is not what should be used to define poverty in Canada. That is because most people think of poverty in relation to the social and economic context in which people live. Central heating is a necessity in Canada's cold climate, but not in Ethiopia or Haiti.

A relative poverty line also has certain drawbacks. Two issues are central: relative to what, and how relative? Whether poverty ought to be defined narrowly in terms of economic measures (e.g., income) or more broadly with respect to community standards (e.g., safety of working conditions, environmental quality, housing stock) illustrates this second area of disagreement. Most definitions tend to be narrow, focusing primarily on income. But even if a relative poverty line is defined narrowly, how relative ought it to be? One-third of average income? one-half? some other fraction?

Yet another disagreement plagues any definition. Should poverty be defined on the basis of income or on the basis of consumption? Since "bare essentials" is a core idea in any definition of poverty, it makes good sense to ask about, and measure, poverty as the cost of purchasing "bare essentials." Deprivation occurs when a family cannot acquire the essentials, not necessarily when income is too low. Income and consumption are correlated, of course, but people with high net wealth can live off their savings even with low income.

In one sense, the definition of poverty means little to a homeless man sleeping on top of a hot air vent. The immediate experience of poverty by families in remote coastal communities, by single parents in the urban core, and by farmers on the Prairies is unaffected by whether poverty is defined absolutely or relatively, narrowly or broadly, by income or by consumption. However, the definition of poverty is consequential for these people because social policies are enacted, or not enacted, based on levels and trends in poverty. Definitions matter.

Social policy has a profound impact on the distribution of opportunities and rewards in Canada. Politics can reshape the distribution of income and the system of inequality by changing laws governing people's right to own property. Witness First Nations' land claims. Politicians can also alter patterns of inequality by entitling people to various welfare benefits and by redistributing income through tax policies. When politicians de-emphasize poverty, legislative efforts to maintain or expand welfare benefits and redistribute income are less likely. A definition of poverty showing fewer poor Canadians implies little need for government action. Conversely, for politicians and political parties supporting the poor, a definition of poverty showing a growing proportion of poor people is beneficial to their cause.

In addition to poverty definitions having political consequences, they are important research tools for the sociologist. A democratic society depends on the full participation of all citizens—everyone has the right to vote, anyone can run for political office, and the voice of everyone should influence political choices. As the National Council on Welfare (1999d: 4) argues, the proportion of Canadians who are poor is "one measure of how well our democracy is working." Can someone without a permanent home, someone in a family with bare cupboards, or someone with hand-me-down clothes participate fully in our national affairs?

Unlike some other countries, such as the United States, Canada does not have an official definition of poverty. Indeed, Statistics Canada argues that there is no internationally accepted definition of poverty and that any definition is arbitrary. Therefore, it does not attempt to estimate the number of Canadians who are poor (Fellegi, 2000: 124). Instead, Statistics Canada reports what it calls a "low income cut-off." This cut-off conveys "the income level at which a family may be in straitened circumstances because it has to spend a greater proportion of its income on necessities than the average family of similar size" (Statistics Canada, 2000d: 122). The threshold is reported for seven different family sizes and for five sizes of community since "straitened circumstances" depend on the number of people in your family and the place you live. Most advocates for the poor interpret these thresholds, shown for 2000 in Table 7.4, as poverty lines. For example, in Canada's largest

| | Community Size | | | | |
|---|---|---|---|---|---|
| Family Size | Cities of 500 000+ | 100 000 to 499 999 | 30 000 to 99 999 | Fewer than 30 000 | Rural areas |
| 1 | $17 060 | $14 985 | $14 638 | $13 345 | $11 613 |
| 2 | $23 123 | $20 312 | $19 842 | $18 086 | $15 744 |
| 3 | $29 393 | $25 819 | $25 221 | $22 990 | $20 010 |
| 4 | $33 844 | $29 722 | $29 038 | $26 472 | $23 039 |
| 5 | $36 975 | $32 476 | $31 726 | $28 921 | $25 173 |
| 6 | $40 137 | $35 249 | $34 437 | $31 391 | $27 325 |
| 7+ | $43 168 | $37 917 | $37 040 | $33 766 | $29 389 |

**✦ TABLE 7.4 ✦**
**National Council on Welfare Estimates of Statistics Canada's Low Income Cut-offs, 2000**

Source: National Council of Welfare (2000).

cities (e.g., Halifax, Montreal, Toronto, Vancouver), a family of four with an income of $33 844 after government transfer payments such as GST credits and Canada Child Tax Benefit would be considered poor.

Using the Statistics Canada low income cut-off as a measure of the poverty line, the National Council on Welfare (2000: 9) estimated that 16.4 percent of the Canadian population, or "over 4.9 million people in Canada, including 1.3 million children, lived in poverty in 1998." One of the difficulties of interpreting this figure is that it includes children, individuals not living in families, and families. Figure 7.4 avoids that complication by charting the percentage of Canadian children (under age 18) living in poverty. As the figure reveals, approximately one in five Canadian children live in poverty, a rate that increased through the 1990s. The poverty rate for families headed by single-parent mothers was 54.2 percent (representing 314 000 families).

Table 7.3 shows a poverty line. People with incomes at or below this line are considered poor. However, two different attributes of the poverty line need to be stressed. First, there is the risk of being poor, as measured by the poverty rate (16.4 percent in 1998). That is, what proportion of Canadians fall at or below this poverty line? Second, there is the severity of poverty—in essence, the gap between what a poor family receives in income and the poverty line. Often referred to the as "depth of poverty," this gap shows how close, or how far, families are from the poverty line. For example, poor single-parent mothers were typically $9230 below the poverty line, whereas poor couples over the age of 65 were $3488 below the poverty line on average (with the line adjusted for family size and

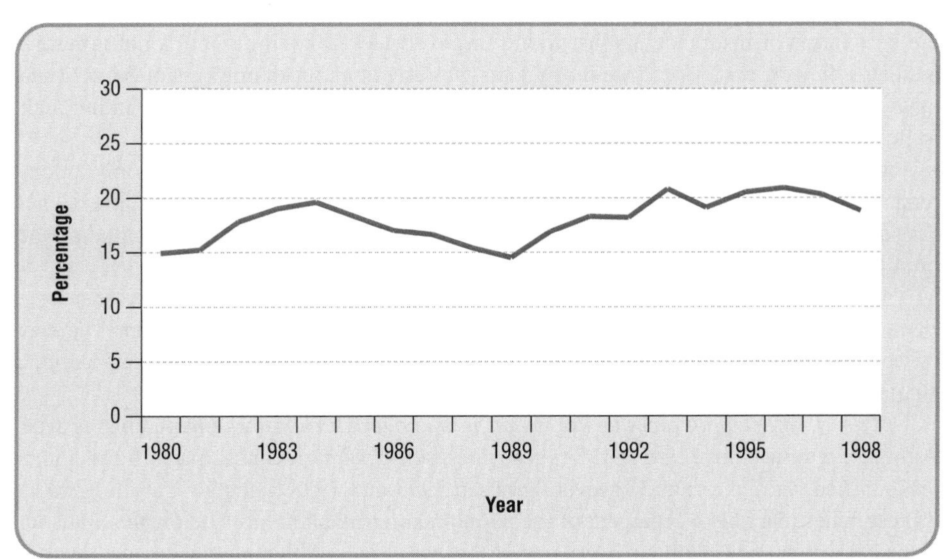


**✦ FIGURE 7.4 ✦**
**Poverty Rate for Children in Canada, 1980–1998**

Source: National Council of Welfare, Child Poverty Profile (1998).

community). Among the poorest of the poor in 1998 was an almost equal number of unattached Canadian women and men, more than 500 000 in total, with incomes of less than 50 percent of the poverty line, or $8243 in our biggest cities.

But behind these lines and numbers lurks the experience of being poor. "When I was about six," Neil Guppy remembers, "I was in a grocery store in Timmins, Ontario, with my father. At the cash register, I noticed that the man in front of us had several cans of dog food along with a few other things. Maybe because I had a wonderful dog of my own, I asked him what kind of dog he had, and he mumbled something in response. I didn't understand and so I asked him again. This time I thought he said, 'Cheap meat.' I didn't know what he meant, so I shut up. I asked my dad what the man had said as we left the store. He explained that maybe the man had bought the food for himself, and that he did so because it was the cheapest way to buy meat. I didn't want to believe my dad; surely the man had a dog.

"It just didn't seem right. Why should some families have to eat dog food? But then I remembered how the guy looked—very skinny, very worn clothes, very old boots, and very forlorn. I still didn't want to believe my dad, but that was when the reality of poverty first sunk in for me. I finally started to understand that when my parents told me some people were poor, that's what they meant.

"I grew up in rural northern Ontario, went to school with Cree kids from Coral Rapids, spent many hot summer days on my great-grandparents' farm outside Sturgeon Falls. I never experienced poverty myself, but I saw it first-hand. Homes with no running water were common. Outhouses were standard. Broken windows and furniture were widespread. Social scientists often think about poverty and wealth as two extremes on an income continuum. But the experience of poverty is not something even on the same scale as wealth. The experience of poverty is not just about a lack of money. To be poor in our material world is to lack hope, to feel despair, and to pray for your children."

We noted earlier the contrasting images sometimes constructed to portray the poor. Are people poor because they are lazy drunks or are they poor despite working hard? This imagery leads many people to differentiate between the "deserving" and the "undeserving" poor. Research conducted in the past few decades continues to show that many popular images about the poor are inaccurate.

*Myth 1: People are poor because they don't want to work.* In most poor families at least one family member works. In 1998, 65 percent of poor families with heads of household under age 65 had one family member working at least part of the year. The National Council of Welfare (2000: 44) estimates that "some 261,000 unattached persons—or 24 percent of all poor unattached persons under 65—were poor in 1998 even though they worked between 49 and 52 weeks. Some 94,000 families—or 10 percent of all poor families with heads under 65—were poor even when husbands and wives together worked for 103 or more weeks during the year." Although a good job is one of the best forms of insurance against living in poverty, even having a job is not a perfect insulator. In part, that is because individuals working at a minimum wage of $8 per hour have annual incomes of $16 640, which is below the poverty line for single individuals in big cities (Lee, 2000: 57–63).

*Myth 2: The overwhelming majority of poor people are immigrants.* It is only among recent immigrants, who arrived in the 1990s, that poverty rates are significantly higher than among people who are Canadian born (Lee, 2000). It seems that after an initial period of adjustment immigrants are less likely to be poor than are the native born.

*Myth 3: The welfare rolls are crammed with young people who ought to be earning a living.* In 1997 the National Council on Welfare (1998c) reported that only about 4 percent of welfare recipients were under the age of 20, and only 16 percent were under 25. Among single parents on welfare, only 3 percent were under the age of 20.

*Myth 4: Most poor people are trapped in poverty.* To some extent, this is true. Although families move into and out of poverty, some people, such as many of the homeless, do find it to be a trap. However, between 1993 and 1998 Statistics Canada (2000d: 89) estimates that only 3.3 percent of the population received incomes below the Statistics Canada low income cut-offs in every one of those six years. Although low income touched

1 in 5 Canadians over that 6-year interval, 1 in 30 Canadians were stuck with incomes below the poverty level in every year.

## Explaining Poverty

Why are some Canadians poor? Explanations vary. At one level, because poverty is a social construction—who is poor depends upon the definition—the explanations focus on definitions. This highlights the politics of poverty where levels and trends can be simply a consequence of definition. Accepting that some Canadians are poor, although granting that the number will vary depending upon definition, there is then a second level of explanation. Here the question is, "Why are some people/families poor and others not?" Answers to this question vary from individual-level explanations to structural explanations.

Individual level explanations focus on the attributes of people who are poor, asking how these people differ from people who are not poor. Put crudely, this type of explanation focuses on causes that lie "within the person." Someone is poor, on this logic, because of a personal attribute such as low intelligence or behaviour abnormality.

Some evidence suggests that individual attributes do explain a small amount of poverty. For example, we know that people with physical disabilities or schizophrenia have a higher risk of living in poverty than do others. Not all people with disabilities or with schizophrenia live in poverty, and the vast majority of people living in poverty have neither disabilities nor schizophrenia. On balance, this type of evidence teaches us that poverty is, for the most part, not a consequence of individual attributes even though these are important in some cases.

A related form of explanation focuses more on the attitudes of individuals—not on attributes that are inherited, but on attributes or stigmas that are acquired. A social-psychological type of explanation emphasizes low self-esteem, lack of achievement motivation, and an inability to delay gratification. Poverty is perpetuated, on this logic, because poor families employ inadequate child-rearing practices, practices that enhance bad attitudes. A related version of this argument stresses a "culture of poverty," a way of thinking and acting shared among poor families. This culture reinforces and perpetuates itself through poor upbringing and ill-formed personalities.

This type of reasoning is often dismissed by sociologists as "blaming the victim." You are poor, on this reasoning, because you have a poor work ethic, shoddy morals, no aspirations, no discipline, no fortitude, and so forth. Various objections undermine this type of explanation. First, there is a cause and effect, or chicken and egg, problem. People who are poor may develop "bad attitudes," but these may result from poverty and not be causes of poverty. The culture of poverty might provide an adequate description for some circumstances, but it is not an adequate explanation in general. Put slightly differently, descriptions of poverty stressing a culture of depression, lack of hope, and fatalism may be accurate, but these effects of poverty ought not to be confused with the causes of poverty. Second, many people who are poor do work, are religious, don't smoke or drink, and so on. Therefore, evidence that supports explanations founded on these personal deficits is often lacking.

Another form of explanation, one with greater currency in sociology, stresses the social organization of society, or sub-systems in society, as explanations of poverty. The organization of our economy, for example, affects poverty. Capitalist economies feature cyclical booms and busts, periods of low unemployment and high profits followed by high unemployment and low profits. Especially during recessions, some people are likely to be poor. Unemployment is an accepted part of our economic organization and some people who cannot find jobs will be poor. Low-wage jobs are also a part of the economy and some people in low-skill, nonunionized, part-year jobs will not earn enough to escape poverty. As Krahn and Lowe (1998: 405) summarize the situation: "a weak work ethic and a lack of effort" are seldom the explanation for individual poverty; "much more often the problem is one of not enough good jobs."

Other analysts stress social policy as a factor affecting poverty levels. For example, as noted above, if you received the minimum hourly wage while working full time, full year, you would still be poor, especially if you had children to support. In this sense we have in minimum wage legislation a social policy that creates a group of working poor. The social world is not quite so simple, of course, and if minimum wages were to rise, so too might the level of unemployment because some employers might not be able to afford higher wages. Debate over these issues continues, but the point is that our social policies affect the well-being of people, and understanding the consequences of policies is critical.

The system of tax collection and tax allocation illustrates another way that social policies affect poverty. A progressive taxation system is one in which a greater proportion of income is paid in tax as incomes rise. For example, those who earn $100 000 pay a larger percentage of their income as tax than do those who earn $50 000. In Canada, although our income tax system is progressive, the overall tax system is relatively neutral. Most Canadian families pay about the same percentage of their total income in tax. This occurs because two interrelated factors undermine the "Robin Hood" effect of progressive income taxes. First, other taxes, such as GST and fuel taxes, are flat or neutral. They are not based on the income of the taxpayer. Second, those who earn more are able to shelter much of their income from taxation (e.g., in registered education saving plans, in registered retirement savings plans, through capital gains tax exemptions, and so forth). The net effect, as we saw above, is a system that does little to actually redistribute income, and therefore relatively little to erode poverty.

Finally, other sociologists would stress ways of thinking, or ideological perspectives, as explanations for poverty. Negative images of various groups lead to an undervaluing of the ways of life of some people, such as First Nations and people with disabilities. Discrimination follows from this undervaluing, and discrimination seriously effects poverty. Undervaluing of talents and identities leads to less success in finding jobs. Even when employment is found, the work is more often unsteady and low paying.

Is poverty an inevitable feature of society? It may be, at least to the extent that inequality is known to exist in all societies. However, the extent of poverty in Canada could be reduced if we chose to follow the examples of Western European nations. Many countries in Western Europe have poverty rates well below Canada's. That is because many European governments have established job training and child-care programs that allow poor people to take jobs with livable wages and benefits. This is, however, clearly a political choice. Many Canadians argue that providing welfare benefits dampens the work ethic and actually perpetuates poverty (see Box 7.2). Although the Western European evidence does not support that view, the political will does not currently exist in Canada to change our social policies to alleviate poverty.

In sum, sociological explanations look not to the personal qualities of the poor but to the organization of society as ways of explaining why some people are poor and why poverty persists in Canada. Notice, too, that the solutions to poverty vary depending on the approach. One solution is to define the problem in a way that minimizes poverty. Still another solution looks to change poor people through job-training and job-search programs for adults and compensatory education programs for children so they are better able to find well-paying work. Another set of solutions looks at the organization of society and asks whether we could change the way we do things so as to benefit the poor. This would involve altering the tax system, encouraging the creation of good jobs, reducing discrimination, and the like.

## International Differences

### Global Inequality

Despite growing income inequality in recent years and a large low-income population, Canada is one of the richest countries in the world. Angola is a world apart. Angola is an African country of 11 million people. About 650 000 of its citizens have been killed in a civil war that has been raging since 1975, when the country gained independence from Portugal. Angola is one of the poorest nations on earth.

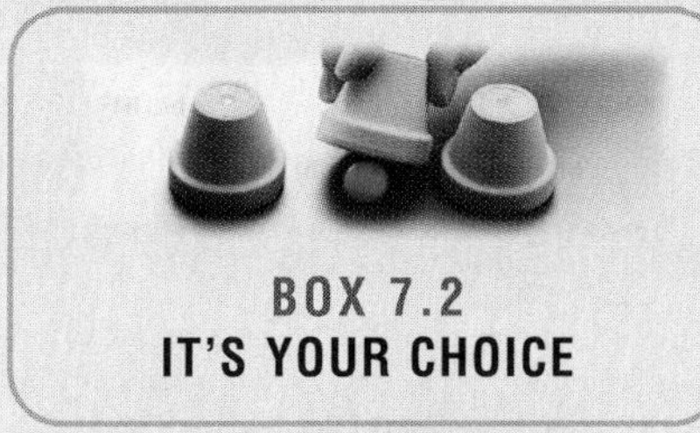

## BOX 7.2
## IT'S YOUR CHOICE

### INCOME REDISTRIBUTION AND TAXATION

The idea of rugged individualism implies that our personal fortunes ought to rest on our own shoulders. To each according to his or her abilities is often held up as a supreme principle. Those who work hard, who persevere, who make wise decisions—those individuals supposedly deserve rewards, like Robinson Crusoe. By implication, those who are lazy and unwise deserve less.

A contrasting idea, the idea of collective responsibility, implies that as members of a community we ought to look out for each other. In this view, "to each according to his or her need" ought to be a supreme principle. Those who have, ought to share. The interests of the many ought to come before the riches of a few.

Few Canadians support either of these extreme ideas, but examples of each principle are easy to find. The unequal distribution of income in Canada and the high salaries of the presidents of large corporations are consistent with the theme of rugged individualism. Government support for post-secondary education and health care illustrates the theme of collective responsibility. Both of these themes represent contrasting social policies, one focused on the supremacy of individual rights, the other emphasizing collective responsibility and the common good.

How much tax revenue should governments collect, and should they redistribute that revenue in ways that benefit lower income groups? Should governments act like Robin Hood and transfer some tax money to the poor? Should governments support hospitals and schools with tax dollars, or should individual families pay directly for medical care and education? These are questions of social policy.

Here are some of the arguments for and against income redistribution, arguments that are fundamental to some of the major political debates in many countries in recent years. What choices would you make if you and your colleagues could run government for a few years?

*Against Redistribution*

1. Taking from the rich and giving to the poor decreases the motivation for people in either group to work hard.
2. The cost of redistribution is high. Taking from one group and giving to another requires some agency first to collect money and then to allocate it.
3. Some individuals and families will cheat and deceive. Some will hide or misrepresent their earnings, either to pay less in tax or to receive more through welfare. Redistribution promotes both tax cheats and welfare frauds.

*For Redistribution*

1. A society with a reasonable degree of equality is a better place to live than a society with heightened levels of inequality.
2. An extra dollar to a poor family is more helpful than an extra dollar to a rich family.
3. Improving the material well-being of a poor family through benevolence enhances the social well-being of a rich family.
4. Aid to poorer families reduces the risk of crime and political conflict since poorer families are thereby less likely to seek illegal means of earning income or to unite in protest over living conditions.

Most Angolans live in houses made of cardboard, tin, and cement blocks. Most houses lack running water. Average income is about $1000 a year. On average, there is 1 telephone for every 140 people and 1 television for every 220 people. Inflation runs at about 90 percent per year. Adding to the misery of Angola's citizens are the millions of landmines that lie scattered throughout the countryside, regularly killing and maiming innocent passersby. Approximately 85 percent of the population survives on subsistence agriculture.

However, multinational companies such as Exxon and Chevron drill for oil in Angola. Oil exports account for nearly half the country's wealth. In the coastal capital of Luanda, an enclave of North Americans who work for Exxon and Chevron live in gated, heavily guarded communities that contain luxury homes, tennis courts, swimming pools, maids, and SUVs. Here, side by side in the city of Luanda, is a microcosm of the chasm separating rich from poor in the world.

Some countries, such as Canada, are rich. Others, such as Angola, are poor. When sociologists study such differences between countries, they are studying **global inequality.** However, it is possible for country A and country B to be equally rich while, inside country A, the gap between rich and poor is greater than inside country B. When sociologists compare such differences, they are studying **cross-national variations in internal stratification.**

The United States, Canada, Japan, Australia, and a dozen or so Western European countries, including Germany, France, and the UK, are the world's richest postindustrial societies. The world's poorest countries cover much of Africa, South America, and Asia. Inequality

Inequality on a global scale: Angola, 2000. *Left*: An amputated Angolan boy, victim of a landmine, hops home in Luanda. *Right*: Children relax at home in Luanda's North American enclave, built by Exxon for its supervisors and executives and their families.

between rich and poor countries is staggering. Nearly a fifth of the world's population lacks adequate shelter, and more than a fifth lacks safe water. About a third of the world's people are without electricity, and more than two-fifths lack adequate sanitation. In Canada, there are 635 phone lines for every 1000 people, but in Cambodia, Congo, and Afghanistan there is only 1 line per 1000 people. Although life expectancy is 79 years in Canada, it is 40 years or fewer in Uganda, Sierra Leone, and Zambia (see Table 7.5). Canada has one of the highest enrolment rates in the world for post-secondary education but, in countries such as Ethiopia, Mali, and Burkina Faso, fewer than 50 percent of children are enrolled in primary schools. People living in poor countries are also more likely than people in rich countries to experience extreme suffering on a mass scale. For example, because of political turmoil in many poor countries, an estimated 20 to 22 million people have been driven from their homes by force in recent years (Hampton, 1998). There are still about 27 million slaves in Mozambique, Sudan, and other African countries (Bales, 1999).

We devote much of Chapter 16 (Population, Urbanization, and Development) to analyzing the causes, dimensions, and consequences of global inequality. You will learn that much of the wealth of the rich countries has been gained at the expense of the poor countries. We also discuss possible ways of dealing with this most vexing of social issues. For the moment, having merely noted the existence of the problem, we focus on the second type of international difference: cross-national variations in internal stratification.

## Internal Stratification

Levels of global inequality aside, how does internal stratification differ from one country to the next? We can answer this question by first examining the **Gini index,** named after

✦ **TABLE 7.5** ✦

**United Nations Indicators of Human Development, 1995, Top Five and Bottom Five Countries**

Source: United Nations (1998a: 130–2).

*Note:* The United Nations publishes an annual index that combines three measures of "human development": life expectancy, adult literacy, and GDP per capital. This table lists the five countries that scored highest and lowest on the index in 1995 and gives the value of each measure for each of the 10 countries.

| Country and Overall Rank | Life Expectancy (years) | Adult Literacy (percent) | GDP per Capita ($US) |
|---|---|---|---|
| 1. Canada | 79.1 | 99.0 | 21 916 |
| 2. France | 78.7 | 99.0 | 21 176 |
| 3. Norway | 77.6 | 99.0 | 22 427 |
| 4. United States of America | 76.4 | 99.0 | 26 977 |
| 5. Iceland | 79.2 | 99.0 | 21 064 |
| 170. Burundi | 44.5 | 35.3 | 637 |
| 171. Mali | 47.0 | 31.0 | 565 |
| 172. Burkina Faso | 46.3 | 19.2 | 784 |
| 173. Niger | 47.5 | 13.6 | 765 |
| 174. Sierra Leone | 34.7 | 31.4 | 625 |
| Least Developed Countries | 51.2 | 49.2 | 1 008 |
| Industrial Countries | 74.2 | 98.6 | 16 337 |
| World | 63.6 | 77.6 | 5 990 |

the Italian economist who invented it. The Gini index is a measure of income inequality. Its value ranges from zero to one. A Gini index of zero indicates that every household (or every income recipient) in the country earns exactly the same amount of money (when each quintile earns 20 percent of the income). At the opposite pole, a Gini index of one indicates that a single household earns the entire national income. These are theoretical extremes. In the real world, nearly all societies have Gini indices between 0.2 and 0.5.

Figure 7.5 shows the Gini index for nine selected countries using the most recent international income data available. Of the nine countries, Sweden has the lowest Gini index (0.222) while Canada has the third lowest at (0.280). Figure 7.5 also shows the percentage of people in each country living below the low-income line (defined as 50 percent of median income). This definition of inequality confirms that among wealthy, postindustrial societies, income inequality is relatively modest in Canada.

## Development and Internal Stratification

What accounts for cross-national differences in internal stratification, such as those described above? Later, you will learn that political factors explain some of the differences. For the moment, however, we focus on how socio-economic development affects internal stratification.

Over the course of human history, as societies became richer and more complex, the level of social inequality first increased, then tapered off, then began to decline, and finally began to rise again (Lenski, 1966; Lenski, Nolan, and Lenski, 1995). Figure 7.6 illustrates the relationship between economic development and internal stratification. To account for this pattern, sociologists have analyzed how technology produces wealth and how that wealth is controlled in five types of societies.

*Foraging societies.* For the first 90 000 years of human existence, people lived in nomadic bands of fewer than 100 people. To survive, they hunted wild animals and foraged for wild edible plants. Life was precarious. Some foragers and hunters were undoubtedly more skilled than others, but they did not hoard food. Instead, they shared food to ensure the survival of all band members. They produced little or nothing above what they required for subsistence. There were no rich and poor, no economic inequality.

*Horticultural and pastoral societies.* About 12 000 years ago, people established the first agricultural settlements. They were based on horticulture (the use of small hand tools to cultivate plants) and pastoralism (the domestication of animals). These technological innovations enabled people to produce wealth, that is, a surplus above what they needed for subsistence. A small number of villagers controlled the surplus. Thus, significant economic inequality emerged.

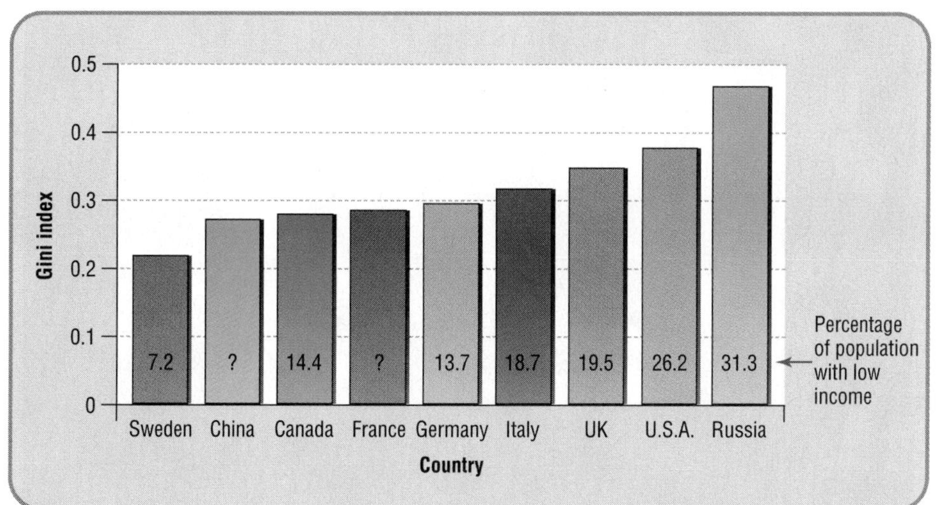


**✦ FIGURE 7.5 ✦**
**Household Income Inequality and Low Income, Selected Countries, 1992–1997**

Source: Luxemburg Income Study (1999a; 1999b).

*Note:* If the Gini index = 1, all income is earned by one household, If the Gini index = 0, all income is shared equally by all households. The low income line is 50% of median Income.

✦ **FIGURE 7.6** ✦
**Inequality and Development**

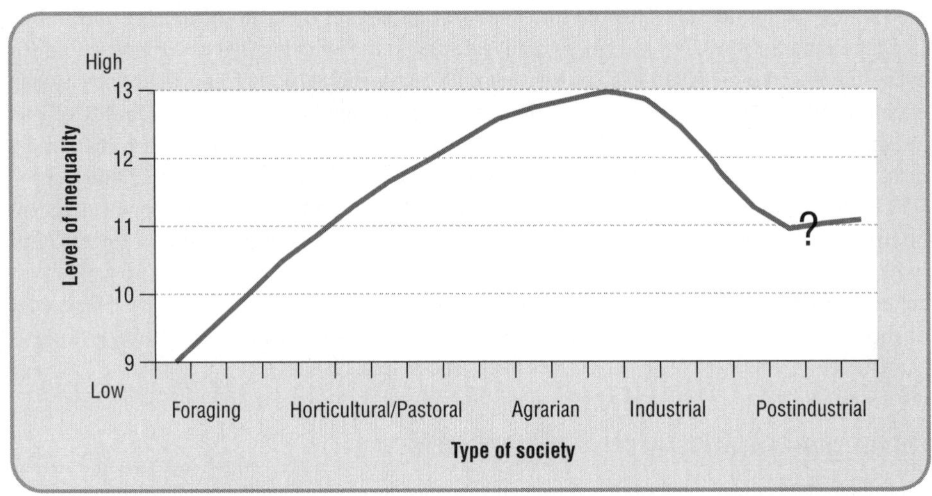


*Agrarian societies.* About 5000 years ago, people developed plow agriculture. By attaching oxen and other large animals to plows, farmers could increase the amount they produced. Again thanks to technological innovation, surpluses grew. With more wealth came still sharper levels of inequality.

Agrarian societies developed religious beliefs justifying steeper inequality. People came to believe that kings and queens ruled by "divine right." They viewed large landowners as "lords." Moreover, if you were born a peasant, you and your children were likely to remain peasants. If you were born a lord, you and your children were likely to remain lords. In the vocabulary of modern sociology, we say that stratification in agrarian societies was based more on **ascription** than **achievement.** That is, a person's position in the stratification system was determined more by the features he or she was born with (ascribed characteristics) than his or her accomplishments (achieved characteristics). Another way of saying this is that there was little **social mobility,** or movement up and down the stratification system.

A nearly purely ascriptive society existed in agrarian India. Society was divided into **castes,** four main groups and many subgroups arranged in a rigid hierarchy. Being born into a particular caste meant you had to work in the distinctive occupations reserved for that caste and marry someone from the same or an adjoining caste. The Hindu religion

Vincent Van Gogh. *The Potato Eaters* (1889). Most people in agrarian societies were desperately poor. In the early 1800s in Ireland, for example, potatoes supplied about 80 percent of the peasant's diet. On average, each peasant consumed about 10 potatoes a day. The economic surplus was much larger than in horticultural and pastoral societies, but much of the surplus wound up in the hands of royalty, the aristocracy, and religious authorities.

strictly reinforced the system (Srinivas, 1952). For example, Hinduism explained people's place in the caste system by their deeds in a previous life. If you were good, being born into a higher caste in your next life presumably rewarded you. If you were bad, being born into a lower caste presumably punished you. Belief in the sanctity of caste regulated even the most mundane aspects of life. Thus, someone from the lowest caste could dig a well for a member of the highest caste, but once the well was dug, the well digger could not do so much as cast his shadow on it. If he did, the well was considered polluted and upper-caste people were forbidden to drink from it.

Caste systems have existed in industrial times. For example, the system of **apartheid** existed in South Africa from 1948 to 1992. While the white minority enjoyed the best jobs and other privileges, apartheid consigned the large black majority to menial jobs. It also prevented marriage between blacks and whites and erected separate public facilities for members of the two races. Asians and people of "mixed race" enjoyed privileges between these two extremes. However, apartheid was an exception. For the most part, industrialism causes a decline in inequality.

*Industrial societies.* The Industrial Revolution began in Britain in the 1780s. A century later, it had spread to all of Western Europe, North America, Japan, and Russia.

The tendency of industrialism to lower the level of inequality was not apparent in the first stages of industrial growth. If you've ever read a Dickens novel such as *Oliver Twist,* you know that hellish working conditions and deep social inequalities characterized early industrialism.

However, improvements in the technology and social organization of manufacturing soon made it possible to produce more goods at a lower cost per unit. This raised living standards for the entire population. Moreover, in industrial societies, birth was no longer destiny. Businesses required a literate, numerate, and highly trained workforce. To raise profits, they were eager to identify and hire the most talented people. They encouraged everyone to develop their talents and rewarded them for doing so by paying higher salaries. Political pressure from below also played an important role in reducing inequality. Workers struggled for the right to form and join unions and expand the vote to all adult citizens. They used union power and their growing political influence to win improvements in the conditions of their existence.

Although, as you will see later, barriers remained, social mobility became more widespread than ever before. Even traditional inequality between women and men began to break down because of the demand for talent and women's struggles to enter the paid workforce on an equal footing with men. Why hire an incompetent man over a competent woman when you can profit more from the services of a capable employee? Put in this way, women's demands for equality made good business sense. For all these reasons, then, stratification declined as industrial societies developed.

*Postindustrial societies.* The microelectronics and biotechnology revolution of the past 50 years is ushering in a new type of society in which the engine of economic growth depends less on turning raw resources into finished products and more on an educated workforce using scientific ideas to produce more goods and services. It would be foolhardy to make definitive statements about long-term trends in social inequality in postindustrial societies, because the postindustrial era is only a few decades old. However, in Canada and some other postindustrial countries, social inequality has been increasing recently, and it is possible this trend will continue.

Again, technological factors seem to be partly responsible for this trend. Many high-technology jobs have been created at the top of the stratification system over the past few decades. These jobs pay well. At the same time, new technologies have made many jobs routine. Routine jobs require little training, and they pay poorly. Because the number of routine jobs is growing more quickly than the number of jobs at the top of the stratification system, the overall effect of technology today is to increase the level of inequality in society. We emphasize that this trend may be a function only of the early years of post-industrialism. However, when we examine these developments in detail in Chapter 10 (Work and the Economy), you will see that inequality seems likely to continue to grow at least until the end of the first decade of the twenty-first century.

Having described some basic patterns and trends in social stratification, we now examine how sociologists have explained it. We begin with Karl Marx, who formulated the first major sociological theory of stratification 150 years ago (Marx and Engels, 1972 [1848]; Marx, 1904 [1859]).

# THEORIES OF STRATIFICATION

## Conflict Perspectives

### Marx

In medieval Western Europe, peasants worked small plots of land owned by landlords. Peasants were legally obliged to give their landlords a set part of the harvest and to continue working for them under any circumstance. In turn, landlords were required to protect peasants from marauders. They were also obliged to open their storehouses and feed the peasants if crops failed. This arrangement was known as **feudalism.**

According to Marx, by the late 1400s, several forces were beginning to undermine feudalism. Most important was the growth of exploration and trade, which increased the demand for many goods and services in commerce, navigation, and industry. By the 1600s and 1700s, some urban craftsmen and merchants had opened small manufacturing enterprises and saved enough capital to expand production. However, they faced a big problem. To increase profits they needed more workers. Yet the biggest potential source of workers—the peasantry—was legally bound to the land. Thus, feudalism had to wither if agricultural peasants were to become industrial workers. In Scotland, for example, enterprising landowners recognized they could make more money raising sheep and selling wool than by having their peasants till the soil. So they turned their cropland into pastures, forcing peasants off the land and into the cities. The former peasants had no choice but to take jobs as urban workers.

In Marx's view, relations between workers and industrialists first encouraged rapid technological change and economic growth. After all, industrial owners wanted to adopt new tools, machines, and production methods so they could produce more efficiently and earn higher profits. But this had unforeseen consequences. In the first place, some owners, driven out of business by more efficient competitors, were forced to become members of the working class. Together with former peasants pouring into the cities from the countryside, this caused the working class to grow. Second, the drive for profits motivated owners to concentrate workers in larger and larger factories, keep wages as low as possible, and invest as little as possible in improving working conditions. Thus, as the ownership class grew richer and smaller, the working class grew larger and more impoverished.

Marx felt that workers would ultimately become aware of their exploitation. Their sense of **class consciousness** would, he wrote, encourage the growth of unions and workers' political parties. These organizations would eventually try to create a communist system in which there would be no private wealth. Instead, under communism, everyone would share wealth, said Marx.

We must note several points about Marx's theory. First, according to Marx, a person's **class** is determined by the source of his or her income, or, to use Marx's term, by one's "relationship to the means of production." For example, members of the capitalist class (or **bourgeoisie**) own means of production, including factories, tools, and land. However, they do not do any physical labour. They are thus in a position to earn profits. In contrast, members of the working class (or **proletariat**) do physical labour. However, they do not own means of production. They are thus in a position to earn wages. It is the source of income, not the amount, that distinguishes classes in Marx's view.

A second noteworthy point about Marx's theory is that it recognizes more than two classes in any society. For example, Marx discussed the **petty bourgeoisie.** This is a class of small-scale capitalists who own means of production but employ only a few workers or none at all. This situation forces them to do physical work themselves. In Marx's view, however, members of the petty bourgeoisie are bound to disappear as capitalism develops because they are economically inefficient. Just two great classes characterize every economic era, said Marx: landlords and serfs during feudalism, bourgeoisie and proletariat during capitalism.

Finally, it is important to note that some of Marx's predictions about the development of capitalism turned out to be wrong. Nevertheless, Marx's ideas about **social stratification** have stimulated thinking and research on social stratification until today, as you will see below.

## A Critique of Marx

Marx's ideas strongly influenced the development of sociological conflict theory (see Chapter 1, A Sociological Compass). Today, however, more than 120 years after Marx's death, it is generally agreed that Marx did not accurately foresee some specific aspects of capitalist development:

- Industrial societies did not polarize into two opposed classes engaged in bitter conflict. Instead, a large and heterogeneous middle class of "white-collar" workers emerged. Some of them are nonmanual employees. Others are professionals. Many of them enjoy higher income and status than manual workers. With a bigger stake in capitalism than propertyless manual workers, nonmanual employees and professionals have generally acted as a stabilizing force in society. To take account of these changes, some neo-Marxists recognize two main divisions in the social relations of work. Although owners control the assets of the business and determine its purpose, in today's large industrial organizations they cannot immediately supervise or direct the work of every employee. This is especially the case when a company is owned by a great many people, as it is in many major corporations today. Therefore, a class of supervisors has arisen. This class, sometimes called the "new middle class" to illustrate its recency and its intermediate position, is defined by relations of authority and supervision. New middle-class workers take direction from owners and are responsible for coordinating and directing the work of other employees. Sociologists Wallace Clement and John Myles (1994) provide an excellent application of this new way of thinking about class in their comparative analysis of the Canadian, American, and Scandinavian class structures.
- Marx correctly argued that investment in technology makes it possible for capitalists to earn high profits. However, he did not expect investment in technology also to make it possible for workers to earn higher wages and toil fewer hours under less oppressive conditions. Yet that is just what happened. Their improved living standard tended to pacify workers, as did the availability of various welfare state benefits, such as employment insurance.
- Communism took root not where industry was most highly developed, as Marx predicted, but in semi-industrialized countries such as Russia in 1917 and China in 1948. Moreover, instead of evolving into classless societies, new forms of privilege emerged under communism. For example, in communist Russia, money income was more equal than in the West. However, membership in the Communist Party, and particularly membership in the so-called *nomenklatura,* a select group of professional state managers, brought special privileges. These included exclusive access to stores where they could purchase scarce Western goods at nominal prices, luxurious country homes, free trips abroad, and so forth. According to a Russian quip from the 1970s, "under capitalism, one class exploits the other, but under communism it's the other way around."

## Weber

Writing in the early 1900s, Max Weber foretold most of these developments. For example, he did not think communism would create classlessness. He also understood the profound significance of the growth of the middle class. As a result, Weber developed an approach to social stratification much different from Marx's.

Weber, like Marx, saw classes as economic categories (Weber, 1946: 180–95). However, he did not think a single criterion—ownership versus non-ownership of property—determines class position. Class position, wrote Weber, is determined by one's "market situation," including the possession of goods, opportunities for income, level of education, and degree of technical skill. From this point of view, there are four main classes according to Weber: large property owners, small property owners, propertyless but relatively highly educated and well-paid employees, and propertyless manual workers. Thus, white-collar employees and professionals emerge as a large class in Weber's scheme.

If Weber broadened Marx's idea of class, he also recognized that two types of groups other than class have a bearing on the way a society is stratified: status groups and parties.

**Status groups** differ from one another in the prestige or social honour they enjoy and in their style of life. Consider members of a particular minority ethnic community who have recently immigrated. They may earn relatively high income but endure relatively low prestige. The longer-established members of the majority ethnic community may look down on them as vulgar "new rich." If their cultural practices differ from those of the majority ethnic group, their style of life may also become a subject of scorn. Thus, the position of the minority ethnic group in the social hierarchy does not derive just from its economic position but also from the esteem in which it is held.

In Weber's usage, **parties** are not just political groups but, more generally, organizations that seek to impose their will on others. Control over parties, especially large bureaucratic organizations, does not depend just on wealth or another class criterion. One can head a military, scientific, or other bureaucracy without being rich, just as one can be rich and still have to endure low prestige.

So we see why Weber argued that to draw an accurate picture of a society's stratification system, one must analyze classes, status groups, and parties as somewhat independent bases of social inequality. But to what degree are they independent of one another? Weber said that the importance of status groups as a basis of stratification is greatest in precapitalist societies. Under capitalism, classes and parties (especially bureaucracies) become the main bases of stratification.

## Functionalism

Marx and Weber were Germans who wrote their major works between the 1840s and the 1910s. Inevitably, their theories bear the stamp of the age in which they wrote. The next major developments in the field occurred in the United States in the mid-twentieth century. Just as inevitably, these innovations were coloured by the optimism, dynamism, and prejudices of that time and place.

Consider first in this connection the **functional theory of stratification,** proposed by Kingsley Davis and Wilbert Moore at the end of the Second World War (Davis and Moore, 1945). Davis and Moore observed that jobs differ in importance. A judge's work, for example, contributes more to society than the work of a janitor. This presents a problem: How can people be motivated to undergo the long training they need to serve as judges, physicians, engineers, and so forth? Higher education is expensive. You earn little money while training. Long and hard study rather than pleasure seeking is essential. Clearly, an incentive is needed to motivate the most talented people to train for the most important jobs. The incentives, said Davis and Moore, are money and prestige. More precisely, social stratification is necessary (or "functional") because the prospect of high rewards motivates people to undergo the sacrifices needed to get a higher education. Without substantial inequality, they conclude, the most talented people would have no incentive to become judges, physicians, and so forth.

Although the functional theory of stratification may at first seem plausible, we can conduct what Max Weber called a "thought experiment" to uncover one of its chief flaws. Imagine a society with just two classes of people—physicians and farmers. The farmers grow food. The physicians tend the ill. Then, one day, a rare and deadly virus strikes. The virus has the odd property of attacking only physicians. Within weeks, there are no more doctors in our imaginary society. As a result, the farmers are much worse off. Cures and

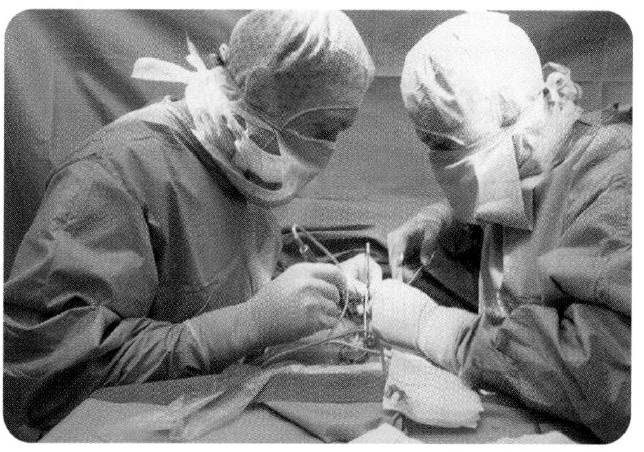

According to the functional theory of stratification, "important" jobs require more training than "less important" jobs. The promise of big salaries motivates people to undergo that training. Therefore, the functionalists conclude, social stratification is necessary. As the text makes clear, however, one of the problems with the functional theory of stratification is that it is difficult to establish which jobs are important, especially when one takes a historical perspective.

treatments for their ailments are no long available. Soon the average farmer lives fewer years than his or her predecessors. The society is less well off, though it survives.

Now imagine the reverse. Again we have a society composed of only physicians and farmers. Again a rare and lethal virus strikes. This time, however, the virus has the odd property of attacking only farmers. Within weeks, the physicians' stores of food are depleted. After a few more weeks, the physicians start dying of starvation. The physicians who try to become farmers catch the new virus and expire. Within months, there is no more society. Who, then, does the more important work, physicians or farmers? Our thought experiment suggests that farmers do, for without them society cannot exist.

From a historical point of view, we can say that *none* of the jobs regarded by Davis and Moore as "important" would exist without the physical labour done by people in "unimportant" jobs. To sustain the witch doctor in a tribal society, hunters and gatherers had to produce enough for their own subsistence plus a surplus to feed, clothe, and house the witch doctor. To sustain the royal court in an agrarian society, serfs had to produce enough for their own subsistence plus a surplus to support the royal family. By using taxes, tithes, and force, government and religious authorities have taken surpluses from ordinary working people for thousands of years. Among other things, these surpluses were used to establish the first institutions of higher learning in the thirteenth century. Out of these, modern universities developed.

The question of which occupations are most important is not clear-cut. To be sure, physicians earn a lot more money than farmers today and they also enjoy a lot more prestige. But that is not because their work is more important in any objective sense of the word. (On the question of why physicians and other professionals earn more than nonprofessionals, see Chapter 13, Religion and Education).

Other problems with the functional theory of stratification have been noted (Tumin, 1953). We mention two of the most important. First, the functional theory of stratification stresses how inequality helps society discover talent. However, it ignores the pool of talent lying undiscovered because of inequality. Bright and energetic adolescents may be forced to drop out of high school to help support themselves and their families. Capable and industrious high-school graduates may be forced to forgo a post-secondary education because they can't afford it. Inequality may encourage the discovery of talent, but only among those who can afford to take advantage of the opportunities available to them. For the rest, inequality prevents talent from being discovered.

Second, the functional theory of stratification fails to examine how advantages are passed from generation to generation. Like Robinson Crusoe, the functional theory correctly emphasizes that talent and hard work often result in high material rewards. However, it is also the case that inheritance allows parents to transfer wealth to children regardless of their talent. For example, glancing back at Table 7.3, we see that more than half of the largest personal fortunes in Canada were inherited. Other examples strengthen the point. The McCain brothers in New Brunswick are very rich Canadians not because of their talent (although they do have talent) but principally because their father gave them a food-processing empire.

Even rich people who do not inherit large fortunes often start near the top of the stratification system. Bill Gates, for example, is the richest person in the world. He did not inherit his fortune. However, his father was a partner in one of the most successful law firms in Seattle. Gates himself went to the most exclusive and expensive private schools in the city, followed by a stint at Harvard. In the late 1960s, his high school was one of the first in the world to boast a computer terminal connected to a nearby university mainframe. Gates' early fascination with computers dates from this period. Gates is without doubt a highly talented man, but surely the social advantages he was born with, and not just his talents, helped to elevate him to his present lofty status (Wallace and Erickson, 1992). An adequate theory of stratification must take inheritance into account, while recognizing how inequality prevents the discovery of talent.

Many of the ideas reviewed above emphasize the economic sources of inequality. However, as Weber correctly pointed out, inequality is not based on money alone. It is also based on prestige and power. We now turn to an examination of these noneconomic sources of inequality.

## NONECONOMIC DIMENSIONS OF INEQUALITY

### Power

In November 1997, seven teenagers in Victoria, B.C.—six girls and one boy—attacked their schoolmate, 14-year-old Reena Virk. They beat her unconscious and left her to drown. In March 2000, Hamed Nastoh, also 14, killed himself by jumping off the Pattullo Bridge between New Westminster and Surrey, B.C. Nine months later, 14-year-old Dawn-Marie Wesley of Mission, B.C., hanged herself in her bedroom with a dog leash. In April 2002, 14-year-old Emmet Fralick of Halifax shot and killed himself.

What do the cases of Virk, Nastoh, Wesley, and Fralick have in common? All four teenagers were bullied by their classmates. Three of them felt they had no recourse but to take their own lives. As Dawn-Marie Wesley wrote in her suicide note: "If I try to get help it will get worse. They are always looking for a new person to beat up and they are the toughest girls. If I ratted they would get suspended and there would be no stopping them. I love you all so much" (quoted in O'Malley and Ali, 2001).

Bullying was probably part of your upbringing, too. Recall your years in the schoolyard. Remember how some people had the power to "name," while others were forced to "wear" those names? "Four eyes," "fatty," and "darkie," were common names in many schools. If you had the misfortune of needing glasses, having a visible birthmark, or even having an unusual name, you might have been the victim of this verbal abuse.

It was a mocking, disdainful abuse. Many were put down, derided for petty reasons. They were publicly shamed and humiliated. Why? Because it made those with the power to name feel superior, it made them proud. In addition, the peer group was a vital place to earn points and win friends. To become one of the in-crowd, you were often required to disparage outsiders. If you were part of the out-crowd, you were often required to disparage members of the in-crowd as a sort of defence aimed at maintaining your self-esteem. Often it was groups or cliques who did the mocking. Social class, or ethnicity, or grade level, or neighbourhood often defined those groups.

Bullying is power in action. Max Weber defined power as the ability of individuals or groups to get their own way, even in the face of resistance from others (Weber, 1947: 152). As Weber would note, name-calling is a form of getting your way, even if others try to resist. "Sticks and stones will break my bones but names will never hurt me." What nonsense! The power of ideas can be devastating. Names can hurt. Naming can traumatize. Some kids commit suicide because they can no longer withstand the torment of the bully's cry. Naming is about power.

According to the Anti-Bullying Public Awareness Campaign, "Bullying is the assertion of power through aggression. Bullies acquire power over their victims physically, emotionally, and socially." As they grow up bullies may move on to other types of violence or abuse.

Source: Department of Justice Canada http://canada.justice.gc.ca/en/news/nr/2002/doc_30447.html. Retrieved October 2, 2002.

Weber's definition of power has several intriguing ramifications. For one thing, power is often misunderstood as binary—you either have it or you don't. In this version the holders of power attain what they want, and they are understood to do so by preventing others from attaining their desired ends. For example, urban transit is typically expanded in ways that disrupt less well-off communities, but minimize disruption in affluent neighbourhoods. Rezoning of permit increased urban density rarely occurs in prosperous neighbourhoods. Threats to the property values of wealthy homeowners are more frequently repelled than are threats of redevelopment in less wealthy areas of the community. This generalization, although not true in every instance, tends to be accurate because of the differential power possessed by the wealthy; they can influence local governments to avoid outcomes they see as undesirable. However, people in poorer neighbourhoods are not powerless, and although they are more likely to lose most political struggles, resistance is common.

Power, we conclude, is not all or nothing. It must be understood as relational even if one group, such as the wealthy, typically has more than another, such as the poor. Failure to realize this relational quality of power has led some analysts to underestimate the importance of resistance and conflict in the social world.

However, the use of power is often invisible. This is one of its most important attributes. Often, wealthy homeowners do not have to do anything to gain advantages in municipal affairs, because others implicitly understand that to take them on would be futile. The power to accomplish specific ends often relies on an ability to define or set the agenda. People with power win many battles without having to fight them. Indeed, those who most frequently use coercive force often have less power than those who win by defining the situation in a way that benefits their particular ends.

The power to set the rules, to influence or shape the parameters of debate, is where power is often exercised but unseen. The application of visible sanctions is not an adequate measure of power because sanctions often do not have to be applied—an outcome is won based on the sanctions one is capable of exercising.

Another complication arises in distinguishing between power and authority. I may comply with your requests not because you force me to do so but because I believe your requests are legitimate. However, legitimate authority is not a type of power. Rather, it is a basis for power. Compliance occurs not because of sanctions, sometimes not even because of sanctions that others could apply. Instead, compliance occurs because of agreement. We agree that bringing a gun to school is inappropriate or that stopping at stop signs is essential. Most people do both of these things not out fear of sanctions, but because they agree that these are sensible, legitimate practices.

Power also occurs in a more inclusive sense that can perhaps best be explained by way of illustration. Norbert Elias (1994 [1939]) has written about the processes underlying the development of modern table manners. Remember those early lessons in your own home—about sitting properly, about chewing properly, and about not playing with your food.

In the thirteenth century it was common, for example, to grab a joint of meat from a platter, take a few bites, and throw the joint back onto the platter for someone else to enjoy. Likewise, picking your nose while eating and spitting at your feet were common occurrences. Over the course of several centuries, a "civilizing process" occurred as people came increasingly to regulate their own action to avoid the shame and ridicule associated with such vulgar behaviour as spitting at the table (see our earlier discussion regarding norms). The instinctual or animalistic side of human life was gradually replaced by a social order brought about largely through self-control or self-restraint. Power at this microlevel of self-constraint is a form of internalized control.

This sense of moral regulation, as some have called it, is important in its consequences for various groups. The power of regulation, in Elias' examples, was something that was self-imposed. In the guise of sexuality, ethnicity/ancestry, or disability, this power to name and define actions as illegitimate or abnormal has had profound consequences for people's identity, opportunity, and well-being. For example, Valverde (1991) analyzes the cultural stereotypes Anglo-Canadians held about Chinese men in the early 1900s, including their supposedly widespread use of opium. These stereotypes undercut the masculine prowess of Chinese men while supporting the "naturalness" and potency of white male sexuality. More generally, the concept of moral regulation has been understood as a way of making the social organization of life, the ways in which we act and interact, appear natural and normal (Hunt, 1999; Valverde, 1994).

The ability to define what is appropriate or acceptable also lies behind the notions of social and cultural capital discussed earlier. The creation of exclusive social clubs, or social circles, captures a powerful idea in society. The process of social closure can be seen perhaps most clearly in the caste system of India. Membership in the elite caste is enforced by birthright, and its members enjoy a position of privilege maintained at the expense of others.

In modern Canada, the idea of birthright providing continuing guarantees of privilege runs against the grain of meritocratic ideals. In a meritocracy people are rewarded on the basis of merit or achievement rather than on the basis of birth or connections. Nevertheless, the ability of well-to-do families to pass their privileges to the next generation is a feature of Canadian society, as we will see below.

In part this ability to ensure intergenerational transmission of privilege is a question of power. In particular, membership in elite circles in Canada depends on owning property and credentials. Living in wealthy neighbourhoods, owning vacation homes in exclusive places, such as Muskoka in Ontario or Whistler in B.C., and owning substantial business interests all provide one with property that can be used to reinforce exclusive circles and that can be passed along from one generation to the next. Likewise, earning professional degrees from the best universities, especially in medicine, dentistry, law, and business, helps to entrench one's position in privileged social circles, and this process also acts to reproduce privilege.

It is an attractive life, the life of well-to-do families. It is a life in which one can take access to privilege for granted, where concern about money for next week's groceries is not all-consuming. It is a life in which exercise in the form of water sports in the summer and skiing in the winter is common, where vacations in foreign places are expected and assumed. It is a life in which books, music, live theatre, and the opera are routine. Most important, for purposes of this text, it is a life that one looks forward to living and that one can transmit to one's sons and daughters. There is, of course, some caricature in the above description. Life among well-to-do families is not always rosy, but the prospects of it being rosy are far greater for the well-to-do than for the impoverished.

The examples used in this discussion also show that power is manifest in different ways (Grabb, 1999). There is economic power, as witnessed by the power of large corporations to control the market place and influence consumer choice. There is political power in the sense of being able to establish laws and policies that benefit certain groups. The state also exercises power through its role in gathering information and in surveillance. Military might is also a form of political power.

Finally, there is ideological power—the power to shape ideas and frame discussions. For instance, in the course of human history, the idea of possessing "private property" is of recent vintage, historically speaking. The ability of the wealthy to evict tenants and enclose their land for their own personal interests was one of the most important struggles of recent centuries. Acceptance of the idea of private property was critical to this transformation. In fact, this example also illustrates that all three forms of power—economic, political, and ideological—often operate in concert.

The Canadian Charter of Rights and Freedoms, introduced in 1982, illustrates another form of ideological/political power. Section 15(1) of the Charter notes:

> 15. (1) Every individual is equal before and under the law and has the right to the equal protection and equal benefit of the law without discrimination and, in particular, without discrimination based on race, national or ethnic origin, colour, religion, sex, age or mental or physical disability.

Moreover, the Charter allows for affirmative action or employment equity measures that redress historical disadvantage. Specifically, section 15(2) reads:

> 15. (2) Subsection (1) does not preclude any law, program or activity that has as its object the amelioration of conditions of disadvantaged individuals or groups including those that are disadvantaged because of race, national or ethnic origin, colour, religion, sex, age or mental or physical disability.

Section 15(2) allows the federal government to have in place an equity policy that offers preferential hiring for women, Aboriginal peoples, members of visible minority groups, and people with disabilities. Historically these groups have been underrepresented in the civil service, especially in higher-level management positions. This equity policy is legal because it works to redress a historical imbalance. It is most often used to ensure more open competition. No systematically collected evidence shows that this policy has meant hiring less qualified people from underrepresented groups, but resistance to these types of policies occurs because some people, such as young white males, believe that these policies act to their detriment.

Certain forms of inequality are legal in Canada. For example, car rental companies have age restrictions on who can rent a car. The minimum wage is lower for young people than for adults. People can be forced to retire at age 65. Even though age is mentioned in section 15(1) of the Charter, restrictions based on age are legal if they comply with section 1 of the Charter, which "guarantees the rights and freedoms set out in [the Charter] subject only to such reasonable limits prescribed by law as can be demonstrably justified in a free and democratic society." The Supreme Court of Canada has ruled that mandatory retirement at age 65 is legal because it is a "reasonable limit" that is "demonstrably justifiable." The Charter clearly reflects political power, but in important ways it is "ideological power" that determines what constitutes "reasonable limits" and defines what is "demonstrably justifiable."

## Prestige and Taste

Let us now consider another noneconomic dimension of social stratification: prestige or honour.

Weber, you will recall, said status groups differ from one another in terms of their lifestyles and the honour in which they are held. Here we may add that members of status groups signal their rank by means of material and symbolic culture. That is, they seek to distinguish themselves from others by displays of "taste" in fashion, food, music, literature, manners, travel, and so forth.

The difference between "good taste," "common taste," and "bad taste" is not inherent in cultural objects themselves. Rather, cultural objects that are considered to be in the best taste are generally those that are least accessible.

To explain the connection between taste and accessibility, let us compare Bach's *The Well-Tempered Clavier* with Gershwin's *Rhapsody in Blue*. A survey by French sociologist

Pierre Bourdieu showed different social groups prefer these two musical works (Bourdieu, 1984 [1979]: 17). Well-educated professionals, high-school teachers, professors, and artists prefer *The Well-Tempered Clavier.* Less well-educated clerks, secretaries, and junior commercial and administrative executives favour *Rhapsody in Blue.* Why? The two works are certainly very different types of music. Gershwin evokes the jazzy dynamism of big-city America early in the twentieth century, Bach the almost mathematically ordered courtly life of early eighteenth-century Germany. But one would be hard-pressed to argue that *The Well-Tempered Clavier* is intrinsically superior music. Both are great art. Why then do more highly educated people prefer *The Well-Tempered Clavier* to *Rhapsody in Blue?* Because, according to Bourdieu, during their education they acquire specific cultural tastes associated with their social position. These tastes help to distinguish them from people in other social positions. Many of them come to regard lovers of Gershwin condescendingly, just as many lovers of Gershwin come to think of Bach enthusiasts as snobs. These distancing attitudes help the two status groups remain separate.

Bach is known for such musical innovations as counterpoint (playing two or more melodies simultaneously) and the fugue (in which instruments repeat the same melody with slight variations). His music is complex, and to really appreciate it one may require some formal instruction. Many other elements of "high culture," such as opera and abstract art, are similarly inaccessible to most people because fully understanding them requires special education.

However, it is not just education that makes some cultural objects less accessible than others. Purely financial considerations also enter the picture. A Mercedes costs four times more than a Ford, and a winter ski trip to Whistler can cost four times more than a week in a modest motel near the beach on Lake Erie or the Bay of Fundy. Of course, one can get from point A to point B quite comfortably in a Ford and have a perfectly enjoyable vacation in different places. Still, most people would prefer the Mercedes and Whistler, at least partly because they signal higher status. Access to tasteful cultural objects, then, is as much a matter of cost as education.

The differences among "good taste," "common taste," and "bad taste" are not inherent in cultural objects themselves. Rather, cultural objects that are considered to be in the best taste are generally those that are least accessible. *Below.* Don Cherry. *Right.* Karen Kain in the National Ballet of Canada's production of *Swan Lake.*

Often, rich people engage in conspicuous displays of consumption, waste, and leisure not because they are necessary, useful, or pleasurable but simply to impress their peers and inferiors (Veblen, 1899). This is evident if we consider how clothing acts as a sort of language that signals one's status to others (Lurie, 1981).

For thousands of years, certain clothing styles have indicated rank. In ancient Egypt, only people in high positions were allowed to wear sandals. The ancient Greeks and Romans passed laws controlling the type, number, and colour of garments one could wear and the type of embroidery with which they could be trimmed. In medieval Europe, too, various aspects of dress were regulated to ensure that certain styles were specific to certain groups.

European laws governing the dress styles of different groups fell into disuse after about 1700. That is because a new method of control emerged as Europe became wealthier. From the eighteenth century on, the cost of clothing came to designate a person's rank. Expensive materials, styles that were difficult to care for, heavy jewellery, and superfluous trimmings became all the rage. It was not for comfort or utility that rich people wore elaborate powdered wigs, heavy damasked satins, the furs of rare animals, diamond tiaras, and patterned brocades and velvets. Such raiment was often hot, stiff, heavy, and itchy. One could scarcely move in many of these getups. And that was just their point—to prove not only that the wearer could afford enormous sums for handmade finery but also that he or she did not have to work to pay for them.

Today, we have different ways of using clothes to signal status. For instance, designer labels loudly proclaim the dollar value of garments. Another example: A great variety and quantity of clothing are required to maintain appearances. Thus, the well-to-do athletic type may have many different and expensive outfits that are "required" for jogging, hiking, cycling, aerobics, golf, tennis, and so forth. In fact, many people who really can't afford to obey the rules of conspicuous consumption, waste, and leisure feel compelled to do so anyway. As a result, they go into debt to maintain their wardrobes. Doing so helps them maintain prestige in the eyes of associates and strangers alike, even if their economic standing secretly falters.

## SOCIAL MOBILITY

Mordecai Richler's *The Apprenticeship of Duddy Kravitz* is one of the true classics of modern Canadian literature (Richler, 1959). Made into a 1974 film starring Richard Dreyfuss as Duddy, it is the story of a poor 18-year-old Jewish Montrealer in the mid-1940s desperately seeking to establish himself in the world. To that end, he waits on tables, smuggles drugs, drives a taxi, produces wedding and bar mitzvah films, and rents out pinball machines. He is an obnoxious charmer with relentless drive, a young man so fixed on making it that he is even willing to sacrifice his girlfriend and his only co-worker to achieve his goals. One cannot help but admire Duddy for his ambition and his artfulness even while one is shocked by his guile and his single-mindedness.

Part of what makes *The Apprenticeship of Duddy Kravitz* universally appealing is that it could be a story about anyone on the make. It is not just some immigrants and their children who may start out as pushy little guys engaged in shady practices and unethical behaviour. As Richler reminds us in many places, some of the wealthiest establishment families in Canada and elsewhere started out in just this way. Duddy, then, is a universal symbol of "upward mobility"—and the compromises one must sometimes make to achieve it.

Much of our discussion to this point has focused on how we describe inequality and how we explain its persistence. Here we take up a different, although related, set of questions. Is our position within the system of inequality fixed? To what extent, if at all, are we trapped in a disadvantaged social position or assured of maintaining an advantaged position? Canada is not a caste system. But at birth, do all people have the same freedom to gain wealth and fame? Are the opportunities we enjoy, our "life chances," equally accessible to everyone?

Sociologists use the term social mobility to refer to the dynamics of the system of inequality and, in particular, to movement up and down the stratification system. If we think about inequality as either a hierarchy of more or less privileged positions or a set of higher and lower social classes, an important question is how much opportunity people have to change positions. Typically, change has been measured using one of two benchmarks: your first position in the hierarchy (e.g., your first full-time job) or the position of your parents in the hierarchy. Comparing your first job to your current job is an examination of occupational or **intragenerational mobility.** Comparing the occupation(s) of parents to their children's current occupation is an examination of the inheritance of social position or **intergenerational mobility.**

Whichever benchmark is used, social mobility analysts are interested in the openness or fluidity of society. In open or fluid societies, there is greater equality of access to all positions in the hierarchy of inequality, both the low and the high. Regardless of your social origins, in more open societies you are more likely to rise or fall to a position that reflects your capabilities. In contrast, in closed or rigid societies, your social origins have major consequences for where you are located in the hierarchy of inequality. In such societies, poverty begets poverty, and wealth begets wealth. In feudal Europe or in the Indian caste system, your birth determined your fate—you were a peasant or a lord based on the position of the family to which you were born.

More recently, societies have become more open in that your social origin does not completely determine your fate. Your chances in life are less dependent on the circumstances of your birth. Think about the changes in Canadian society over the last century. A mainly agrarian, resource-based economy has transformed into a modern, advanced postindustrial nation. We have experienced substantial growth in well-paying occupations in finance, marketing, management, and the professions. To what extent have people from all walks of life, from all economic backgrounds, been able to benefit from this transformation? This introduces a second, related theme to discussions of mobility—equality of opportunity.

As you can imagine from our earlier discussion, in the 1950s and 1960s proponents of the functional theory of stratification and human capital theory imagined that equality of opportunity would pervade society. They argued that as more and more skilled jobs are created in the new economy, the best and the brightest must rise to the top to take those jobs and perform them diligently. We would then move from a society based on ascription to one based on achievement. In a system of inequality based on ascription, your family's station in life determines your own fortunes. Conversely, in a system based on achievement, your own talents, your own merit, determines your lot in life. If you achieve good grades in school, your chance of acquiring a professional or managerial job rises.

Other sociologists, however, have cautioned that this scenario of high individual social mobility might not follow from the transformation of the economy. These theorists, focusing more on the reproduction of inequality, emphasized how advantaged families have long attempted to ensure that their offspring inherit their advantages (Collins, 1979).

On the world stage, Blossfeld and Shavit (1993) demonstrated that in 11 of 13 advanced industrial countries, little evidence supports the view that there is greater equality of opportunity in societies with expanding education systems (Sweden and the Netherlands are the two exceptions). In short, the openness or fluidity of the system of inequality did not increase over the last half of the twentieth century.

Richard Wanner (1999) has tested these ideas at the post-secondary level using Canadian data. He set himself the task of testing the idea that "Canada's investment in educational expansion reduced the amount of ascription in educational attainment" (Wanner, 1999: 409). What he was asking was this: Has the growth of education—more high schools, more colleges and universities—benefited people from all social backgrounds equally?

If ascription is weaker now than in previous decades, then parents' **socio-economic status (SES)** should now have less effect on a child's education. In simple terms, if in earlier decades the chances of children from poorer families going to university were small, these chances should have increased in more recent decades if ascription was weakening. As measures of socio-economic background, Wanner used mother's and father's education and father's occupation. He tested his central question using detailed information from a sample of 31 500 Canadians.

What did he find? That class-based ascription still operates strongly. Despite the fact that more Canadians are acquiring more years of schooling and more degrees than ever before, the long arm of family socio-economic background continues to exert a strong hold on educational attainment. The link between family advantage and children's educational achievement has not weakened.

Explanations for how and why this occurs remain a matter of controversy (Davies, 1999). The school system has become increasingly differentiated. Many routes through high-school vocational programs and college diploma programs are taken by students from lower socio-economic backgrounds. Students from higher socio-economic backgrounds typically continue on to university. Also, new high-school programs have proliferated. These include storefront schools for "at-risk" students in poorer neighbourhoods, language immersion streams, private schools, and enriched learning tracks. These types of schools tend to enrol students from different socio-economic backgrounds.

More recently, data from the National Longitudinal Survey of Children and Youth has demonstrated socio-economic differences in children's preparedness or readiness for school (Ross, Roberts, and Scott, 2000). Children from households with incomes below $20 000 are 4.5 times more likely to have delayed vocabulary development than are children from families with incomes at or above $50 000. Not only are they themselves less ready for school learning, but because family incomes are similar in the same neighbourhood, these students often find themselves in schools with others who are less well prepared (Hertzman, 2000). A recent international study has replicated these findings, showing that a family's socio-economic status affects a student's reading literacy, in this case among 15-year-olds. Importantly, however, the effect of socio-economic status was less pronounced in Canada than in other countries (OECD, 2001).

Sociologists have also distinguished "equality of opportunity" from "equality of condition" to emphasize this point. Although everyone might have the legal opportunity to go to school, not everyone is socially able to take advantage of these opportunities. Coming to kindergarten hungry or not having been in high-quality child care before age five has an effect on how well a child will begin his or her formal schooling career. Equality of opportunity focuses on chances of participation, while equality of condition focuses on chances of succeeding. By way of analogy, we may all be able to enter the race, but if you come with track shoes and good coaching and I come with boots and no coaching, your chances of winning are higher, assuming that we have equal athletic skills.

## POLITICS AND THE PERCEPTION OF CLASS INEQUALITY

We expect you have had some strong reactions to our review of sociological theories and research on social stratification. You may therefore find it worthwhile to reflect more systematically on your own attitudes to social inequality. To start with, do you consider the family in which you grew up to have been lower class, working class, middle class, or upper class? Do you think the gaps between classes in Canadian society are big, moderate, or small? How strongly do you agree or disagree with the view that big gaps between classes are needed to motivate people to work hard and maintain national prosperity? How strongly do you agree or disagree with the view that inequality persists because it benefits the rich and the powerful? How strongly do you agree or disagree with the view that inequality persists because ordinary people don't join together to get rid of it? Answering these questions will help you clarify the way you perceive and evaluate the Canadian class structure and your place in it. If you take note of your answers, you can compare them with the responses of representative samples of Canadians, which we review below.

Surveys show that few Canadians have trouble placing themselves in the class structure when asked to do so. Most Canadians consider themselves to be middle class or working class. They also think that the gaps between classes are relatively large. But do Canadians think that these big gaps between classes are needed to motivate people to work hard, thus increasing their own wealth and the wealth of the nation? Some Canadians think so, but most do not. A survey conducted in 18 countries, including Canada, asked more than 22 000 respondents if large differences in income are necessary for national prosperity. Canadians were among the most likely to disagree with that view (Pammett, 1997: 77).

So, Canadians know that they live in a class-divided society. They also tend to think that deep class divisions are not necessary for national prosperity. Why then do Canadians think inequality continues to exist? The 18-nation survey cited above sheds light on this issue. One of the survey questions asked respondents how strongly they agree or disagree with the view that "inequality continues because it benefits the rich and powerful." Most Canadians agreed with that statement. Only about a quarter of them disagreed with it in any way. Another question asked respondents how strongly they agree or disagree with the view that "inequality continues because ordinary people don't join together to get rid of it." Again, most Canadians agreed, with less than a third disagreeing in any way (Pammett, 1997: 77–8).

Despite widespread awareness of inequality and considerable dissatisfaction with it, most Canadians are opposed to the government playing an active role in reducing inequality. Most do not want government to provide citizens with a basic income. They tend to oppose government job-creation programs. They even resist the idea that government should reduce income differences through taxation (Pammett, 1997: 81). Most Canadians remain individualistic and self-reliant. On the whole, they persist in the belief that opportunities for mobility are abundant and that it is up to the individual to make something of those opportunities by means of talent and effort.

Significantly, however, all of the attitudes summarized above vary by class position. For example, discontent with the level of inequality in Canadian society is stronger at the bottom of the stratification system than at the top. The belief that Canadian society is full of opportunities for upward mobility is stronger at the top of the class hierarchy than at the bottom. One finds considerably less opposition to the idea that government should reduce inequality as one moves down the stratification system. This permits us to conclude that, if Canadians allow inequality to persist, it is because the balance of attitudes—and of power—favours continuity over change. We take up this important theme again in Chapter 11 (Politics), where we discuss the social roots of politics.

## SUMMARY

1. Income inequality has been a recurring feature of Canadian society, with a slight increase in inequality in the late 1990s.
2. The extent of income inequality in Canada is similar to that in most other highly industrialized countries, but less than in the United States.
3. Inequality increases as societies develop from the foraging to the early industrial stage. With increased industrialization, inequality declines. Inequality then increases in the early stages of postindustrialism.
4. Marx's theory of inequality distinguishes among classes on the basis of their role in the productive process. It predicts inevitable conflict between workers and owner, and the birth of a communist system.
5. Weber distinguished among classes on the basis of their "market relations." His model of stratification included four main classes. He argued that class consciousness may develop under some circumstances but is by no means inevitable. Weber also emphasized prestige and power as important sources of inequality.
6. Davis and Moore's functional theory of stratification argues that (1) some jobs are more important than others, (2) people must make sacrifices to train for important jobs, and (3) inequality is required to motivate people to undergo these sacrifices. In this sense, stratification "functions" as a system of motivation.
7. People often engage in conspicuous consumption, waste, and leisure to signal their position in the social hierarchy.
8. Explanations for inequality in Canada range from the individual to the structural. Sociologists stress structural arguments, arguments that focus on how the organization of society, or the social relations among Canadians, affects the position of individuals and groups in the social hierarchy.

## GLOSSARY

An **achievement**-based stratification system is one in which the allocation of rank depends on a person's accomplishments.

**Apartheid** was a caste system based on race that existed in South Africa from 1948 to 1992. It consigned the large black majority to menial jobs, prevented marriage between blacks and whites, and erected separate public facilities for members of the two races. Asians and people of "mixed race" enjoyed privileges between these two extremes.

An **ascription**-based stratification system is one in which the allocation of rank depends on the features with which a person is born.

The **bourgeoisie** are owners of the means of production, including factories, tools, and land. They do not do any physical labour. Their income derives from profits.

A **caste** system is an almost pure ascription-based stratification system in which occupation and marriage partners are assigned on the basis of caste membership.

**Class,** in Marx's sense of the term, is determined by one's relationship to the means of production. In Weber's usage, class is determined by one's "market situation."

**Class consciousness** refers to being aware of membership in a class.

**Cross-national variations in internal stratification** are differences among countries in their stratification systems.

**Feudalism** was a legal arrangement in pre-industrial Europe that bound peasants to the land and obliged them to give their landlords a set part of the harvest. In exchange, landlords were required to protect peasants from marauders and open their storehouses to feed the peasants if crops failed.

The **functional theory of stratification** argues that (1) some jobs are more important than others, (2) people must make sacrifices to train for important jobs, and (3) inequality is required to motivate people to undergo these sacrifices.

The **Gini index** is a measure of income inequality. Its value ranges from zero (which means that every household earns exactly the same amount of money) to one (which means that all income is earned by a single household).

**Global inequality** refers to differences in the economic ranking of countries.

**Intergenerational mobility** is social mobility that occurs between generations.

**Intragenerational mobility** is social mobility that occurs within a single generation.

**Parties,** in Weber's usage, are organizations that seek to impose their will on others.

The **petty bourgeoisie,** in Marx's usage, is the class of small-scale capitalists who own means of production but employ only a few workers or none at all, forcing them to do physical work themselves.

The **proletariat,** in Marx's usage, is the working class. Members of the proletariat do physical labour but do not own means of production. They are thus in a position to earn wages.

**Social capital** refers to the networks or connections that individuals possess.

**Social mobility** refers to movement up or down the stratification system.

**Social stratification** refers to the way in which society is organized in layers or strata.

**Socio-economic status (SES)** combines income, education, and occupational prestige data in a single index of one's position in the socio-economic hierarchy.

**Status groups** differ from one another in terms of the prestige or social honour they enjoy, and also in terms of their style of life.

## QUESTIONS TO CONSIDER

1. How do you think the Canadian and global stratification systems will change over the next 10 years? over the next 25 years? Why do you think these changes will occur?
2. Why do you think many Canadians oppose more government intervention to reduce the level of inequality in society? Before answering, think about the advantages that inequality brings to many people and the resources at their disposal for maintaining inequality.
3. Compare the number and quality of public facilities such as playgrounds, public schools, and libraries in various parts of your community. How is the distribution of public facilities related to the socio-economic status of neighbourhoods? Why does this relationship exist?
4. Scientific advances in both microelectronics and biotechnology are significant features of this decade. How might these influence, and in turn be influenced by, inequality in contemporary Canada?

# WEB RESOURCES

## Companion Web Site for This Book

http://www.brymsociologycompass.nelson.com

Begin by clicking on the Student Resources section of the Web site. Next, select the chapter you are currently studying from the pull-down menu. From the Student Resources page you will have easy access to InfoTrac College Edition®, MicroCase online exercises, and additional Web links. The Web site also has many useful tips to aid you in your study of sociology, including practice tests for each chapter.

## InfoTrac Search Terms

These search terms are provided to assist you in beginning to conduct research on this topic by visiting http://www.infotrac-college.com

**Class**
**Class consciousness**
**Global inequality**
**Poverty**
**Social mobility**

## Recommended Web Sites

For comprehensive statistics about Canada, go to Statistics Canada at http://www.statcan.ca.

For information about Canada's efforts at national and international poverty reduction, see the Poverty Reduction Web site at http://www.acdi-cida.gc.ca/poverty.

For financial information about Canada's publicly traded companies, go to the Toronto Stock Exchange at http://www.tse.com.

For research on social and economic security, visit the Canadian Council on Social Development at http://www.ccsd.ca/.

For publications and statistics on international economic and social issues, go to http://www.oecd.org.

To learn about the projects, services, and products of the World Bank Group, go to http://www.worldbank.org/.

For a good site about researching the issues of globalization, go to http://www.polity.co.uk/global/research.htm.

# SUGGESTED READINGS

James Curtis, Edward Grabb, and Neil Guppy, eds. *Social Inequality in Canada: Patterns, Problems and Policies,* 4th ed (Scarborough, ON: Prentice Hall Allyn and Bacon Canada Inc., 2003). A collection of readings on core aspects of inequality in Canada.

Wallace Clement and John Myles. *Relations of Ruling: Class and Gender in Postindustrial Societies* (Montreal: McGill-Queen's University Press, 1994). An outstanding study of patterns of Canadian inequality in comparative perspective.

David B. Grusky, ed. *Social Stratification: Class, Race, and Gender in Sociological Perspective* (Boulder, CO: Westview, 1994). An anthology of key articles in the field of social stratification.

# NOTES

1. In fall 2002 Madonna and her director husband, Guy Ritchie, released a remake of the movie.
2. This statement is contentious. Intelligence is hereditary in part, and how smart you are has some effect on economic success. But three issues are worth noting. What is intelligence? What causal role does genetics play in affecting measured intelligence? How strong a causal link is there between intelligence and economic success?

## IN THIS CHAPTER, YOU WILL LEARN THAT

- Race and ethnicity are socially constructed labels or categories. These labels, which have profound consequences for people's lives, distinguish people by perceived physical or cultural differences.
- Racial and ethnic labels and identities change over time and place. Relations among racial and ethnic groups help shape these labels and identities.
- In Canada, racial, ethnic, and ancestral groups are blending over time. However, this tendency is weaker among members of highly disadvantaged groups, especially First Nations peoples and very recent refugee immigrants.
- Identifying with a racial or ethnic group can be economically, politically, and emotionally advantageous or disadvantageous.
- Racial and ethnic inequality is likely to persist in Canada.

CHAPTER

8

# RACE AND ETHNICITY

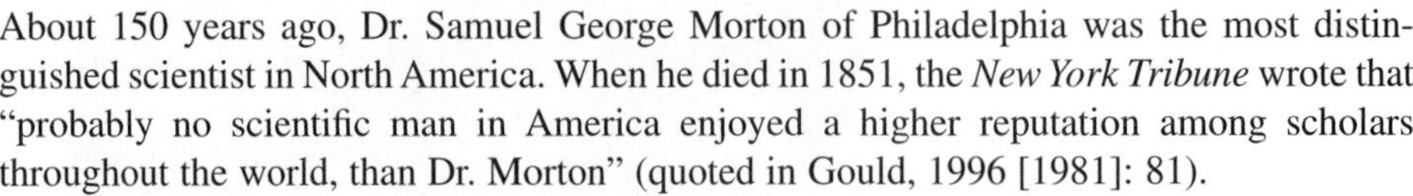

## DEFINING RACE AND ETHNICITY

### The Great Brain Robbery

About 150 years ago, Dr. Samuel George Morton of Philadelphia was the most distinguished scientist in North America. When he died in 1851, the *New York Tribune* wrote that "probably no scientific man in America enjoyed a higher reputation among scholars throughout the world, than Dr. Morton" (quoted in Gould, 1996 [1981]: 81).

Among other things, Morton collected and measured human skulls. The skulls came from various times and places. Their original occupants were members of different races. Morton believed he could show that the bigger your brain, the smarter you were. To prove his point he packed BB-sized shot into a skull until it was full. Next he poured the shot from the skull into a graduated cylinder. He then recorded the volume of shot in the cylinder. Finally, he noted the race of the person from whom each skull came. This, he thought, allowed him to draw conclusions about the average brain size of different races.

As he expected, Morton found that the races ranking highest in the social hierarchy had the biggest brains, while those ranking lowest had the smallest brains. He claimed that the people with the biggest brains were whites of European origin. Next were Asians. Then came Native North Americans. The people at the bottom of the social hierarchy—and those with the smallest brains—were blacks.

Morton's research had profound sociological implications, for he claimed to show that the system of social inequality in the United States and throughout the world had natural, biological roots. If, on average, members of some racial groups are rich and others poor, some highly educated and others illiterate, some powerful and others powerless, that was, said Morton, due to differences in brain size and mental capacity. Moreover, since he used science to show that Native North Americans and blacks *naturally* rest at the bottom of the social hierarchy, his ideas were used to justify two of the most oppressive forms of domination and injustice: colonization and slavery.

Despite claims of scientific objectivity, not a shred of evidence supported Morton's ideas. For example, in one of his three main studies, Morton measured the capacity of skulls robbed from Egyptian tombs. He found that the average volume of black people's skulls was 4 cubic inches (65.5 ml) smaller than the average volume of white people's skulls. This seemed to prove his case. Today, however, we know that three main issues compromise his findings:

1. Morton claimed to be able to distinguish the skulls of white and black people by the shapes of the skulls. However, even today archaeologists cannot precisely determine race by skull shape. As a result, it is unclear whether the skulls Morton identified as "Caucasian" belonged to white people and those identified as "Negroid" or "Negro" belonged to black people.
2. Morton's skulls formed a small, unrepresentative sample. Morton based his conclusions on only 72 specimens. This is a very small number on which to base any generalization. Moreover, those 72 skulls are not representative of the skulls of white and black people in ancient Egypt or any other time and place. They are just the 72 skulls that Morton happened to have access to. For all we know, they are highly unusual.
3. Even if we ignore these first two problems, 71 percent of the skulls Morton identified as "Negroid" or "Negro" were women's, compared with only 48 percent of the skulls he identified as "Caucasian." Yet women's bodies are on average smaller than men's bodies. To make a fair comparison, Morton would have had to ensure that the sex composition of the white and black skulls was identical. He did not. Instead, he biased his findings in favour of finding larger white skulls. When we compare Morton's black and white female skulls, the white skulls are only 2 cubic inches (32.8 ml) bigger. When we compare his black and white male skulls, the white skulls are 1 cubic inch (16.4 ml) *smaller* (Gould, 1996 [1981]: 84, 91, 92).

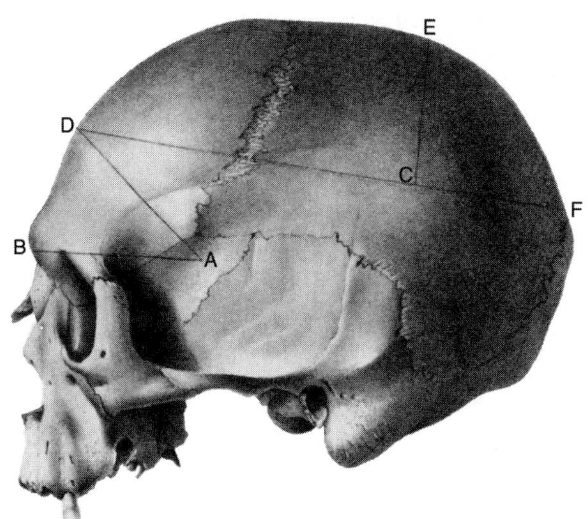


In the nineteenth century, brain size was falsely held to be one of the main indicators of intellectual capacity. Average brain size was incorrectly said to vary by race. Researchers who were eager to prove the existence of such correlations are now widely regarded as practitioners of a racist quasi-science.

Scientifically speaking, Morton's findings are meaningless. Yet they were influential for a long time. Some people still believe them. For example, about 40 years ago, the author of an article about race in the *Encyclopedia Britannica,* the world's most authoritative general reference source, wrote that blacks have "a rather small brain in relation to their size" (Buxton, 1963: 864A). That claim was repeated in a controversial book written by a Canadian psychologist in the mid-1990s (Rushton, 1995). Yet there is no more evidence today than there was in 1850 that whites have bigger brains than blacks.[1]

## Race, Biology, and Society

Biological arguments about racial differences have grown more sophisticated over time. However, the scientific basis of these arguments is just as shaky now as it always was.

In medieval Europe, some aristocrats saw blue veins underneath their pale skin but could not see blue veins underneath the peasants' suntanned skin. They concluded that the two groups must be racially distinct. The aristocrats called themselves "blue bloods." They ignored the fact that the colour of blood from an aristocrat's wound was just as red as the blood from a peasant's wound.

About 80 years ago, some scholars expressed the belief that racial differences in average IQ scores were genetically based. Typically, in 1927 a Canadian professor by the name of Peter Sandiford argued that Canada must institute selective immigration to ensure that only the best and the brightest arrive on our shores and that we kept out "misfits" and "defectives." He encouraged the recruitment of people of British, German, and Danish stock, and discouraged the recruitment of Poles, Italians, and Greeks. Sandiford provided IQ test results supporting his selective immigration policy. He felt that his data showed the mental superiority of Northern Europeans in comparison with Eastern and Southern Europeans. However, his testing results also provided what he regarded as "profoundly disturbing" evidence. People of Japanese and Chinese ancestry had the highest intelligence scores. This he had not predicted. He dismissed this finding by asserting that a few clever Asians had apparently entered Canada. They were exceptions, he wrote, and should not detract from the "need" to keep Asians out of Canada, too (McLaren, 1990).

Similarly, in the United States, Jews scored below non-Jews on IQ tests in the 1920s. This was used as an argument against Jewish immigration. More recently, African-Americans have on average scored below European-Americans on IQ tests. Some people say this justifies slashing budgets for schools in the inner city, where many African-Americans live. Why invest good money in inner-city schooling, such people ask, if low IQ scores are rooted in biology and therefore fixed (Herrnstein and Murray, 1994)? However, the people who argued against Jewish immigration and better education for inner-city African-Americans ignored two facts. First, Jewish IQ scores rose as Jews moved up the class hierarchy and could afford better education. Second, enriched educational facilities have routinely boosted the IQ scores of inner-city African-American children (Campbell and Ramey, 1994; Frank Porter Graham Child Development Center, 1999; Hancock, 1994; Steinberg, 1989 [1981]). Much evidence shows that the social setting in which one is raised and educated has a big impact on IQ. The claim that racial differences in IQ scores are biologically based is about as strong as evidence that aristocrats have blue blood (Cancio, Evans, and Maume, 1996; Fischer et al., 1996; see Chapter 13, Religion and Education).[2]

If one cannot reasonably maintain that racial differences in average IQ scores are based in biology, what about differences in singing ability or athletic prowess or crime rates? For example, some people insist that, for genetic reasons, people of African descent are better than whites at singing and sports, and more prone to crime. Is there any evidence to support this belief?

At first glance, the supporting evidence might seem strong. Consider sports. Aren't 87 percent of NBA players and 75 percent of NFL players black? Don't blacks of West African descent hold the 200 fastest 100-metre-dash times, all under 10 seconds? Don't North and East Africans regularly win 40 percent of the top international distance-running honours yet represent only a fraction of 1 percent of the world's population (Entine, 2000)? Although these facts are undeniable, the argument for the genetic basis of black athletic superiority begins to falter once we consider two additional points. First, no gene linked to general athletic superiority has yet been identified. Second, athletes of African descent do not perform unusually well in many sports, such as swimming, hockey, cycling, tennis, gymnastics, and soccer. The idea that people of African descent are in general superior athletes is simply untrue.

Sociologists have identified certain *social* conditions that lead to high levels of participation in sports (as well as entertainment and crime). These operate on all groups of people, whatever their race. Specifically, people who face widespread prejudice and discrimination often enter sports, entertainment, and crime in disproportionately large numbers for lack of other ways to improve their social and economic position. For such people, other avenues of upward mobility tend to be blocked. (**Prejudice** is an attitude that judges a person on his or her group's real or imagined characteristics. **Discrimination** is unfair treatment of people due to their group membership.) For example, it was not until the 1950s that prejudice and discrimination against North American Jews began to decline appreciably. Until then, Jews played a prominent role in some professional sports. For instance, when the New York Knicks played their first game on November 1, 1946, beating the Toronto Huskies 68–66, the starting lineup for New York consisted of Ossie Schechtman, Stan Stutz, Jake Weber, Ralph Kaplowitz, and Leo "Ace" Gottlieb—a nearly all-Jewish squad ("New York Knicks History," 2000). Similarly, Koreans in Japan today are subject to much prejudice and discrimination. They often pursue careers in sports and entertainment. In contrast, Koreans in Canada face less prejudice and discrimination. Few of them become athletes and entertainers. Instead, they are often said to excel in engineering and science. As these examples suggest, then, social circumstances have a big impact on athletic and other forms of behaviour.

The idea that people of African descent are genetically superior to whites in athletic ability is the complement of the idea that they are genetically inferior to whites in intellectual ability. Both ideas have the effect of reinforcing black–white inequality.[3] For although there are just a few thousand professional athletes in North America, there are millions of pharmacists, graphics designers, lawyers, systems analysts, police officers, nurses, and people in other interesting occupations that offer steady employment and good pay. By promoting only the Vince Carters and Shaquille O'Neals of the world as suitable role models for youth, the idea of "natural" black athletic superiority and intellectual inferiority in effect asks blacks to bet on a high-risk proposition—that they will make it in professional sports. At the same time, it deflects attention from a much safer bet—that they can achieve upward mobility through academic excellence (Doberman, 1997; Guppy and Davies, 1998).

An additional problem undermines the argument that genes determine the behaviour of racial groups. It is impossible to neatly distinguish races based on genetic differences. A high level of genetic mixing has taken place among people of various races throughout the world. In North America, for instance, it was not uncommon for white male slave owners to rape black female slaves, who then gave birth to children of mixed race. Many Europeans had children with Aboriginal peoples in the eighteenth and nineteenth centuries. We know from the census that ethnic and racial intermarriage has been increasing in Canada at least since 1871. In the 2001 Census, more than 35 percent of Canadians reported multiple ethnic or racial identities. Usually, people who report multiple ethnic or racial identities have parents of different ethnic or racial origins (Kalbach and Kalbach, 1998). A growing number of North Americans are similar to Tiger Woods. Woods claims he is of "Cablinasian" ancestry—part Caucasian, part black, part Native American Indian, and part Asian. As these examples illustrate, the difference among "black," "white," "Asian," and so forth is often anything but clear-cut.

Some respected scholars believe we all belong to one human race, which originated in Africa (Cavalli-Sforza, Menozzi, and Piazza, 1994). They argue that subsequent migration, geographical separation, and inbreeding led to the formation of more or less distinct races. However, particularly in modern times, humanity has experienced so much intermixing that race as a biological category has lost nearly all meaning. Some biologists and social scientists therefore suggest we drop the term *race* from the vocabulary of science.

Most sociologists, however, continue to use the term *race*. They do so because *perceptions* of race continue to affect the lives of most people profoundly. Everything from your wealth to your health is influenced by whether others see you as black, white, brown, or something else. Race as a *sociological* concept is thus an invaluable analytical tool. It is invaluable, however, only to the degree that people who use the term remember that it refers to *socially significant* physical differences (e.g., skin colour) rather than to biological differences that shape behaviour patterns.

Said differently, perceptions of racial difference are socially constructed and often arbitrary. The Irish and the Jews in North America were regarded as "blacks" by many people a hundred years ago, and today some northern Italians still think of southern Italians from Sicily and Calabria as "blacks" (Gilman, 1991; Ignatiev, 1995; Roediger, 1991). During the Second World War, some people made arbitrary physical distinctions between Chinese allies and Japanese enemies that helped justify the Canadian policy of placing Japanese-Canadians in internment camps (see Figure 8.1). These examples show that racial distinctions are social constructs, not biological givens.

Athletic heroes such as Donovan Bailey are often held up as role models for African-Canadian youth even though the chance of "making it" as an athlete is much less than the chance of getting a post-secondary education and succeeding as a professional. Racial stereotypes about black athletic prowess and intellectual inferiority are often reinforced through the idolization of sporting heroes.

**✦ FIGURE 8.1 ✦**
***Time* Magazine Explains How to Make Arbitrary Racial Distinctions, 1941**

Source: "How to Tell Your Friends from the Japs" (1941).

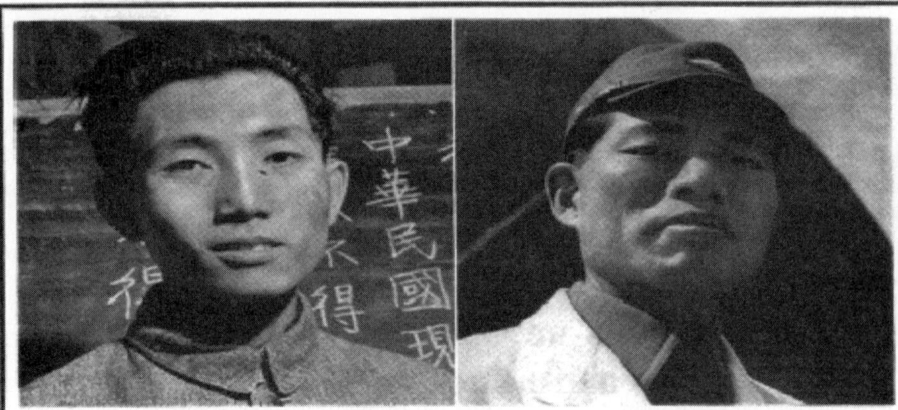


*Chinese* *Japanese*

HOW TO TELL YOUR FRIENDS FROM THE JAPS

Of these four faces of young men (*above*) and middle-aged men (*below*) the two on the left are Chinese, the two on the right Japanese. There is no infallible way of telling them apart, because the same racial strains are mixed in both. Even an anthropologist, with calipers and plenty of time to measure heads, noses, shoulders, hips, is sometimes stumped. A few rules of thumb—not always reliable:

▶ Some Chinese are tall (average: 5 ft. 5 in.). Virtually all Japanese are short (average: 5 ft. 2½ in.).

▶ Japanese are likely to be stockier and broader-hipped than short Chinese.

▶ Japanese—except for wrestlers—are seldom fat; they often dry up and grow lean as they age. The Chinese often put on weight, particularly if they are prosperous (in China, with its frequent famines, being fat is esteemed as a sign of being a solid citizen).

▶ Chinese, not as hairy as Japanese, seldom grow an impressive mustache.

▶ Most Chinese avoid horn-rimmed spectacles.

▶ Although both have the typical epicanthic fold of the upper eyelid (which makes them look almond-eyed), Japanese eyes are usually set closer together.

▶ Those who know them best often rely on facial expression to tell them apart: the Chinese expression is likely to be more placid, kindly, open; the Japanese more positive, dogmatic, arrogant.

In Washington, last week, Correspondent Joseph Chiang made things much easier by pinning on his lapel a large badge reading "Chinese Reporter—NOT *Japanese*—Please."

▶ Some aristocratic Japanese have thin, aquiline noses, narrow faces and, except for their eyes, look like Caucasians.

▶ Japanese are hesitant, nervous in conversation, laugh loudly at the wrong time.

▶ Japanese walk stiffly erect, hard-heeled. Chinese, more relaxed, have an easy gait, sometimes shuffle.

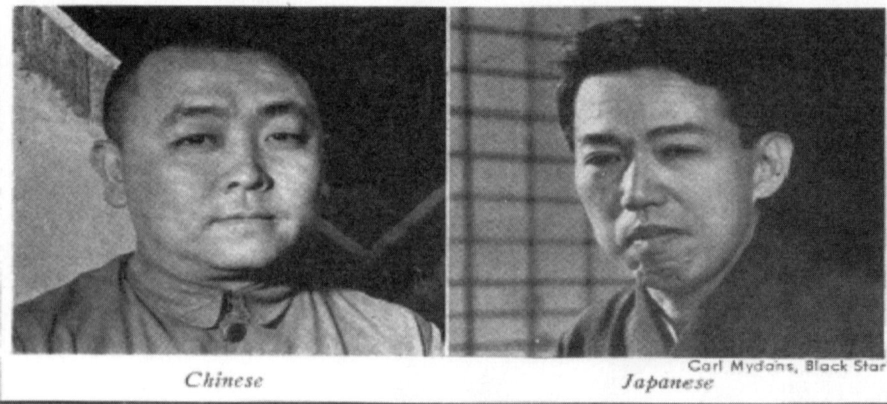

Carl Mydans, Black Star

*Chinese* *Japanese*

Finally, then, we can define **race** as a social construct used to distinguish people in terms of one or more physical markers. However, this definition raises an interesting question. If race is merely a social construct and not a useful biological term, why are perceptions of physical difference used to distinguish groups of people in the first place? Why, in other words, does race matter? Most sociologists believe that race matters because it allows social inequality to be created and perpetuated. The English who colonized Ireland, the Americans who went to Africa looking for slaves, and the Germans who used the Jews as a scapegoat to explain their deep economic and political troubles after the First World War, all created systems of racial domination. (A **scapegoat** is a disadvantaged person or category of people that others blame for their own problems.) Once colonialism, slavery, and concentration camps were established, behavioural differences developed between subordinates and superordinates. For example, North American slaves and Jewish concentration camp inmates, with little motivating them to work hard except the ultimate threat of the master's whip, tended to do only the minimum work necessary to survive. Their masters noticed this and characterized their subordinates as inherently slow and unreliable workers (Collins, 1982: 66–9). In this way, racial stereotypes are born. The stereotypes then embed themselves in literature, popular lore, journalism, and political debate. This reinforces racial inequalities (see Figure 8.2). We thus see that race matters to the degree that it helps create and maintain systems of social inequality.

## Ethnicity, Culture, and Social Structure

Race is to biology as ethnicity is to culture. A *race* is a socially defined category of people whose perceived *physical* markers are deemed significant. An **ethnic group** is composed of people whose perceived *cultural* markers are deemed significant. Ethnic groups differ from one another in terms of language, religion, customs, values, ancestors, and the like. However, just as physical distinctions don't *cause* differences in the behaviour of various races, so cultural distinctions are often not by themselves the major source of differences in the behaviour of various ethnic groups. In other words, ethnic values and other elements of ethnic culture have less of an effect on the way people behave than we commonly believe. That is because *social structural* differences frequently underlie cultural differences.

An example will help drive home the point. People often praise Jews, Koreans, and other economically successful groups for their cultural values, including an emphasis on education, family, and hard work. People less commonly notice, however, that Canadian immigration policy has been highly selective. For the most part, the Jews and Koreans who arrived in Canada were literate, urbanized, and skilled. Some even came with financial assets (Brym, Shaffir, and Weinfeld, 1993; Li, 1995; Wong and Ng, 1998). They certainly confronted prejudice and discrimination, but far less than that reserved for the descendants of slaves or members of Canada's Aboriginal peoples. These *social-structural* conditions facilitated Jewish and Korean success. They gave members of these groups a firm basis on which to build and maintain a culture emphasizing education, family, and other middle-class virtues. In contrast, descendants of slaves and members of Canada's Aboriginal

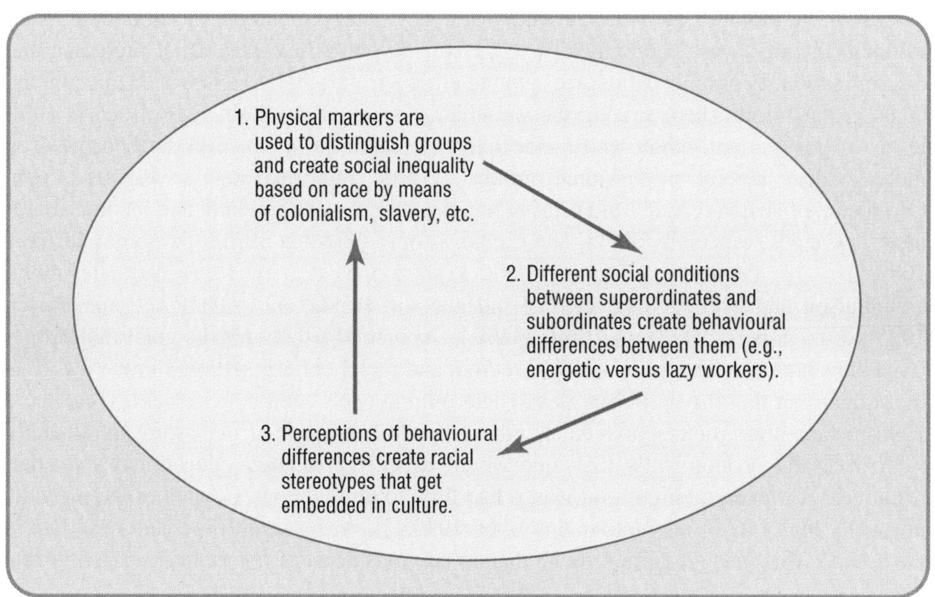


**FIGURE 8.2**
**The Vicious Circle of Racism**

peoples were typically illiterate and unskilled, and they experienced more prejudice and discrimination than other ethnic or racial groups in Canada. These social-structural disadvantages—not their culture—made them less economically successful than Jews and Koreans on average.

In general, much Canadian research supports the argument that culture in and of itself is unimportant in determining the economic success of racial or ethnic groups. There *are* substantial differences in average annual income between some racial groups. For example, the average annual income of Aboriginal peoples is substantially below that of white Canadians. So is the average annual income of non-white immigrants. The point, however, is that these differences are due largely to such factors as how many years of education the average Aboriginal Canadian has and how many years the non-white immigrant has been in the country. There are practically no income differences between white Canadians and the Canadian-born children of non-white immigrants. A professor of law who happens to be an Aboriginal Canadian earns as much as a white professor of law. The problem is that there are so few Aboriginal professors of law (see Box 8.1).

As we saw in our brief comparison of Koreans and Jews with Aboriginal peoples, what really matters in determining the economic success of an ethnic or racial group are the *resources* people possess, such as education, literacy, urbanity, and financial assets. We may now add that what also matters in determining economic success are the kinds of *economic opportunities* open to people. The latter point can be seen clearly if we compare Canada in the mid-twentieth century with Canada today.

Half a century ago, Canada was a society sharply stratified along ethnic and racial lines. The people with the most power and privilege were of British origin. WASPs (White Anglo-Saxon Protestants) in particular controlled almost all the big corporations in the country and dominated politics. Immigrants who arrived later enjoyed less power and privilege. Even among them, big economic differences were evident, with European immigrants enjoying higher status than immigrants of Asian ancestry, for example. Canada in the 1950s, then, was a racially and ethnically divided society. Ethnic and racial groups were culturally very different from one another and wide economic gaps separated them.

John Porter, one of the founders of modern Canadian sociology, called mid-twentieth-century Canada an ethnically and racially stratified "vertical mosaic." He thought the retention of ethnic and racial culture was a big problem in Canada because it hampered the upward mobility of immigrants. In his view, the "Canadian value system" encouraged the retention of ethnic culture, making Canada a low mobility society (Porter, 1965, 1979: 91).

By the 1970s, however, many Canadian sociologists, including Porter himself, had to reject or at least qualify their view that ethnic and racial culture determines economic success or failure. Events upset their earlier assumptions. The Canadian economy grew quickly in the decades after the Second World War. Many members of ethnic and racial **minority groups** were economically successful despite ethnic and racial prejudice and discrimination. Economic differences among ethnic groups and, to a lesser degree, among racial groups diminished. Among the wealthiest Canadians, and among politicians at all levels of government, ethnic and racial diversity increased. Such diversity became even more evident among professional groups. Visible minority status, whether Asian, Caribbean, or Hispanic, had little bearing on educational, occupational, and income attainment in Canada, especially among the Canadian-born (Boyd et al., 1985; Brym with Fox, 1989: 103–13; Guppy and Davies, 1998; Lian and Matthews, 1998; Nakhaie, 1997; Ogmundson and McLaughlin, 1992; Pendakur and Pendakur, 1998; Pineo and Porter, 1985; Reitz, in press; Reitz and Breton, 1994). Apparently, then, for the great majority of Canadians after the Second World War, ethnic and racial culture mattered much less than the structure of mobility opportunities in determining one's economic success. True, in the 1990s, recent immigrants who were members of visible minority groups were significantly less successful economically than one would expect given their educational and other resources. However, their cultural values had little to do with that. Canada experienced an unusually high rate of unemployment in the 1990s, hovering near 10 percent until late in the decade. This made it more difficult than in previous decades for recently arrived visible

BOX 8.1
## SOCIOLOGY AT THE MOVIES

*Atanarjuat: The Fast Runner* (2002)

### *ATANARJUAT: THE FAST RUNNER* (2002)

North of the Northwest Territories, beyond Hudson Bay, in the eastern Arctic wilderness of Nunavut, lies the town of Igloolik, population 1200. Archaeological evidence suggests that people have been living continuously in Igloolik for 4000 years. *Atanarjuat: The Fast Runner*, based on an ancient Inuit legend, shows us, without sentimentality or political correctness, what life must have been like in Igloolik before the arrival of Europeans. It also says something profound about the sources of an ethnic group's well-being and its destruction.

*Atanarjuat* was hailed as a "masterpiece" and an instant "classic" by *The New York Times*, and as an "astonishing epic" by Roger Ebert in the *Chicago Sun-Times*. It won a raft of prestigious international film awards, including prizes at the world's two most important film festivals: the Camera d'Or at Cannes for Best First Feature Film and the Best Film Award at the Toronto International Film Festival.

*Atanarjuat* is full of sex and violence, but it's no Hollywood blockbuster. It is a three-hour film. The first hour slowly uncovers the routines of Inuit life on its own terms. Relying on the memories of elders and sketches from the journal of Admiral William Parry's 1922 expedition, the film's director, Zacharias Kunuk, faithfully recreates a world composed of women cleaning animal skins, children chasing each other across the drifts, men racing dogsleds across the barrens, couples making love, families feasting on raw walrus meat, throat singing, rituals, startling Arctic light, and endless snow.

All is balance and cooperation until an evil shaman suddenly appears. He casts a spell that divides the community and results in the murder of the camp leader. The community's new leader ridicules and beats down his chief rival.

Twenty years pass. The sons of the camp leader and his rival continue the conflict into the next generation. Atanarjuat (played by Natar Ungalaaq), the son of the rival, wins the hand of the beautiful young woman promised to the leader's son. The leader's son vows revenge. He spears Atanarjuat's elder brother through a tent, killing him. In the most exciting and visually compelling sequence in the movie, Atanarjuat runs for his life across the ice, naked, his feet bleeding.

In time, however, harmony is restored. A kindly couple takes Atanarjuat in and nurses him back to physical and spiritual health. The "fast runner" eventually returns to his community. There he faces his foes, reclaims his family name, and restores order to the community.

At one level, *Atanarjuat* can be appreciated as a faithful reproduction of a lost way of life and a beautiful rendering of ancient folklore. At another level, it can be interpreted as a metaphor for the destruction of Aboriginal communities and the hope for their restoration on new foundations. Before European contact, Aboriginal communities everywhere were, of course, "primitive" by Western standards. Perhaps their most "primitive" features were their ideals of internal cooperation and harmony with nature. European contact hit these communities in much the same way the evil shaman disrupted Igloolik. We see evidence of the lingering effects of European contact throughout this book, in our discussions of crime (Chapter 6, Deviance and Crime), social stratification (Chapter 7, Social Stratification: Canadian and Global Perspectives), health (Chapter 15, Health, Medicine, and Aging), and environmental racism (Chapter 18, Technology and the Global Environment). Some people view the "backwardness" of Aboriginal cultures, their lack of fit with the requirements of modern living, as the chief reason Aboriginal communities experience so many troubles today. That, however, is like blaming a victim for his or her own suffering. Many Canadians take a different stance: They recognize the role of European contact in destroying the harmony of Aboriginal communities. Like Atanarjuat, they are seeking ways of re-establishing that lost harmony under new social conditions. Whether they can run fast enough is an open question.

minority immigrants to succeed economically. Their relative lack of success reinforces our point. In addition to the resources one possesses, it is the structure of opportunities for economic advancement, not ethnic or racial culture, that determines income, occupational, and educational attainment.

In sum, we see that racial and ethnic inequality is much more deeply rooted in social structure than in biology and culture. The biological and cultural aspects of race and ethnicity are secondary to their sociological character when it comes to explaining inequality. Moreover, the distinction between race and ethnicity is not as simple as the difference between biology and culture. As noted above for the Irish and the Jews, groups once socially defined as races may be later redefined as ethnicities, even though they do not change biologically. Social definitions, not biology and not culture, determine whether a group is viewed as a race or an ethnic group. The interesting question from a sociological point of view is why social definitions of race and ethnicity change. We now consider that issue.

## RACE AND ETHNIC RELATIONS

### Labels and Identity

John Lie moved with his family from South Korea to Japan when he was a baby. He moved from Japan to Hawaii when he was 10 years old, and again from Hawaii to the American mainland when he started university. The move to Hawaii and the move to the U.S. mainland changed the way John thought of himself in ethnic terms.

In Japan, Koreans form a minority group. Before 1945, when Korea was a colony of Japan, some Koreans were brought to Japan to work as miners and unskilled labourers. The Japanese thought the Koreans who lived there were beneath and outside Japanese society (Lie, 2001). Not surprisingly, then, Korean children in Japan, including John, were often teased and occasionally beaten by their Japanese schoolmates. "The beatings hurt," says John, "but the psychological trauma resulting from being socially excluded by my classmates hurt more. In fact, although I initially thought I was Japanese like my classmates, my Korean identity was literally beaten into me.

"When my family emigrated to Hawaii, I was sure things would get worse. I expected Americans to be even meaner than the Japanese. (By Americans, I thought only of white European-Americans.) Was I surprised when I discovered that most of my schoolmates were not white European-Americans, but people of Asian and mixed ancestry! Suddenly I was a member of a numerical majority. I was no longer teased or bullied. In fact, I found that students of Asian and non-European origin often singled out white European-Americans (called *haole* in Hawaiian) for abuse. We even had a 'beat up *haole* day' in school. Given my own experiences in Japan, I empathized somewhat with the white Americans. But I have to admit that I also felt a great sense of relief and an easing of the psychological trauma associated with being Korean in Japan.

"As the years passed, I finished public school in Hawaii. I then went to college in Massachusetts and got a job as a professor in Illinois and then in Michigan. I associated with, and befriended, people from various racial and ethnic groups. My Korean origin became a less and less important factor in the way people treated me. There was simply less prejudice and discrimination against Koreans during my adulthood in the United States than in my early years in Japan. I now think of myself less as Japanese or Korean than as American. Sometimes I even think of myself as a Midwesterner. My ethnic identity has changed over time in response to the significance others have attached to my Korean origin. I now understand what the French philosopher Jean-Paul Sartre meant when he wrote that 'the anti-Semite creates the Jew'" (Sartre, 1965 [1948]: 43).

The details of John Lie's life are unique. But experiencing a shift in racial or ethnic identity is common. Social contexts, and in particular the nature of one's relations with members of other racial and ethnic groups, shape and continuously reshape one's racial

According to the 2001 Census, the top 15 ethnic groups in Canada, other than British and French, include Canadians of German, Ukrainian, Aboriginal, Chinese, South Asian, Portuguese, and Filipino origins. This underscores that multiculturalism is, indeed, a fundamental characteristic of Canadian society and a growing reality in our daily lives.

and ethnic identity. Change your social context and your racial and ethnic self-conception eventually changes, too (Miles, 1989; Omi and Winant, 1986).

Consider Italian Canadians. Around 1900, Italian immigrants thought of themselves as people who came from a particular town or perhaps a particular province, such as Sicily or Calabria. They did not usually think of themselves as Italians. Italy became a unified country only in 1861. A mere 30 years later, many Italian citizens still did not identify with their new Italian nationality. In both Canada and the United States, however, government officials and other residents identified the newcomers as Italians. The designation at first seemed odd to many of the new immigrants. However, over time it stuck. Immigrants from Italy started thinking of themselves as Italian-Canadians because others defined them that way. A new ethnic identity was born (Yancey, Ericksen, and Leon, 1979).

As symbolic interactionists emphasize, the development of racial and ethnic labels, and ethnic and racial identities, is typically a process of negotiation. For example, members of a group may have a racial or ethnic identity, but outsiders may impose a new label on them. Group members then reject, accept, or modify the label. The negotiation between outsiders and insiders eventually results in the crystallization of a new, more or less stable ethnic identity. If the social context changes again, the negotiation process begins anew.

One such case involves the labelling of the indigenous peoples of North America by European settlers. When Christopher Columbus landed in North America in 1492, he assumed he had reached India. He called the indigenous peoples Indians and the misnomer stuck—not only among European settlers, but also among many indigenous peoples themselves. Indigenous peoples still identified themselves in tribal terms—as Mi'kmaq or Mohawk or Haida—but they typically thought of themselves collectively and *in opposition to European settlers* as Indians. A new identity was thus grafted onto tribal identities because indigenous peoples confronted a group that had the power to impose a name on them.

In time, however, an increasingly large number of indigenous people began to reject the term *Indian*. White settlers and their governments took land from the indigenous peoples, forced them onto reserves, and thus caused their resentment, anger, and solidarity to grow. Especially since the 1960s, indigenous North Americans have begun to fight back culturally and politically, asserting pride in their languages, art, and customs and making legal claims to the land that had been taken from them (see below). One aspect of their resistance involved questioning use of the term *Indian*. In Canada, many of them preferred instead to be called Native Canadians, indigenous peoples, Aboriginal Canadians, or First Nations. These new terms, especially the last one, were all assertions of new-found pride.

Today, many North Americans of European origin accept these new terms out of respect for indigenous North Americans and in recognition of their neglected rights. New, more or less stable ethnic identities have thus been negotiated as the power struggle between indigenous peoples and more recent settlers continues. As the social context changed, the negotiation of ethnic identities proceeded apace.

## Ethnic and Racial Labels: Imposition versus Choice

The idea that race and ethnicity are socially constructed does not mean that everyone can always choose their racial or ethnic identity freely. There are wide variations over time and from one society to the next in the degree to which people can exercise such freedom of choice. Moreover, in a given society at a given time, different categories of people are more or less free to choose. To illustrate these variations, we next discuss the way in which the government of the former Soviet Union imposed ethnicity on the citizens of that country. We then contrast imposed ethnicity in the former Soviet Union with the relative freedom of ethnic choice in Canada. In the Canadian case, we also underline the social forces that make it easier to choose one's ethnicity than one's race.

### State Imposition of Ethnicity in the Soviet Union

Until it formally dissolved in 1991, the Soviet Union was the biggest and one of the most powerful countries in the world (see Chapter 10, Work and the Economy, and Chapter 11, Politics). Stretching over 2 continents and 11 time zones, it was composed of 15 republics—Russia, Ukraine, Kazakhstan, and so forth—with a combined population larger than that of the United States. In each republic, the largest ethnic group was the so-called "titular" ethnic group of that republic: Russians in Russia, Ukrainians in Ukraine, Kazakhs in Kazakhstan, and so forth.[4] More than 100 minority ethnic groups also lived in the republics. As Figure 8.3 shows, in some republics the combined number of minority ethnic group members was greater than that of the titular ethnic group.

The vast size and ethnic heterogeneity of the Soviet Union required that its leaders develop strategies to prevent the country from falling apart at the seams. One such strategy involved weakening the boundaries between the republics so "a new historical community, the Soviet people" could come into existence (Bromley, 1982 [1977]: 270). The creation of a countrywide educational system and curriculum, the spread of the Russian language, and the establishment of propaganda campaigns trumpeting remarkable national achievements helped create a sense of unity among many Soviet citizens.

A second strategy promoting national unity involved the creation of a system that allowed power and privilege to be shared among ethnic groups. This was accomplished administratively through the "internal passport" system. Beginning in the 1930s, Soviet governments issued identity papers or internal passports to all citizens at the age of 16. The fifth entry in each passport noted the bearer's ethnicity. Adolescents were obliged to adopt the ethnicity of their parents. Only if the parents were of different ethnic backgrounds could a 16-year-old choose the ethnicity of the mother or the father.

The internal passport system enabled officials to apply strict ethnic quotas in recruiting people to institutions of higher education, professional and administrative positions, and political posts. Ethnic quotas were even used to determine where people could reside. Thus, ethnicity became critically important in determining some of the most fundamental aspects of one's life. To ensure the loyalty of the disparate and far-flung republics to the central government, officials granted advantages to members of titular ethnic groups living in their own republics. That is, you enjoyed the best opportunities for educational, occupational, and political advancement if you were a Russian living in Russia, a Ukrainian living in Ukraine, and so forth. If you happened to be a member of a titular ethnic group living outside your republic, you were at a disadvantage in this regard. And if you happened to be a member of a nontitular ethnic group, you were most disadvantaged (Brym with Ryvkina, 1994: 6–16; Karklins, 1986; Zaslavsky and Brym, 1983).

By thus organizing many basic social processes along ethnic lines, the government imposed ethnic labels on its citizens. Despite efforts to create a new "Soviet people," traditional

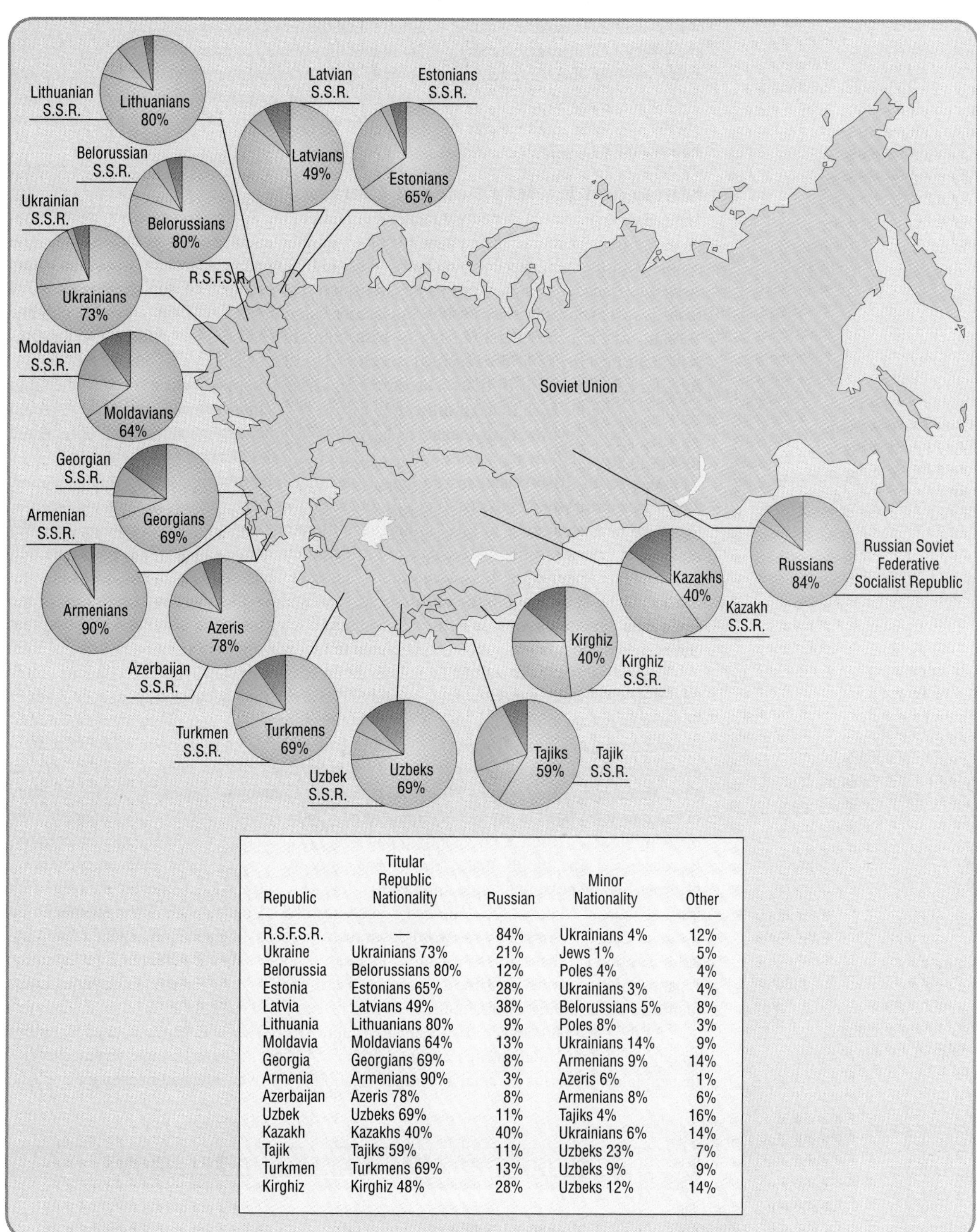


| Republic | Titular Republic Nationality | Russian | Minor Nationality | Other |
|---|---|---|---|---|
| R.S.F.S.R. | — | 84% | Ukrainians 4% | 12% |
| Ukraine | Ukrainians 73% | 21% | Jews 1% | 5% |
| Belorussia | Belorussians 80% | 12% | Poles 4% | 4% |
| Estonia | Estonians 65% | 28% | Ukrainians 3% | 4% |
| Latvia | Latvians 49% | 38% | Belorussians 5% | 8% |
| Lithuania | Lithuanians 80% | 9% | Poles 8% | 3% |
| Moldavia | Moldavians 64% | 13% | Ukrainians 14% | 9% |
| Georgia | Georgians 69% | 8% | Armenians 9% | 14% |
| Armenia | Armenians 90% | 3% | Azeris 6% | 1% |
| Azerbaijan | Azeris 78% | 8% | Armenians 8% | 6% |
| Uzbek | Uzbeks 69% | 11% | Tajiks 4% | 16% |
| Kazakh | Kazakhs 40% | 40% | Ukrainians 6% | 14% |
| Tajik | Tajiks 59% | 11% | Uzbeks 23% | 7% |
| Turkmen | Turkmens 69% | 13% | Uzbeks 9% | 9% |
| Kirghiz | Kirghiz 48% | 28% | Uzbeks 12% | 14% |

✦ **FIGURE 8.3** ✦

**Ethnic Groups in the Soviet Union by Republic, 1979**

Source: Perry-Castañeda Library Map Collection (2000).

ethnic identities remained strong. In 1991, when the Soviet Union ceased to exist, Russians knew they were Russians and Latvians knew they were Latvians partly because the ethnicity entry in their internal passports had circumscribed their opportunities in life for more than 60 years. Only in 1997 did the Russian government finally introduce new internal passports without the notorious fifth entry, thus bringing an end to the era of administratively imposed ethnicity in that country.

### Ethnic and Racial Choice in Canada

The situation in Canada is vastly different from that of the Soviet Union before 1991. Canadians are freer to choose their ethnic identity than citizens of the Soviet Union were. The people with the most freedom to choose are white European-Canadians whose ancestors arrived in Canada more than two generations ago. For example, identifying oneself as an Irish-Canadian no longer has negative implications, as it did in, say, 1900. Then, in a city like Toronto, where a substantial number of Irish immigrants were concentrated, the English-Protestant majority typically regarded working-class Irish Catholics as often drunk, inherently lazy, and born superstitious. This strong anti-Irish sentiment, which often erupted into conflict, meant the Irish found it difficult to escape their ethnic identity even if they wanted to. Since then, however, Irish-Canadians have followed the path taken by many other white European groups. They have achieved upward mobility and blended with the majority.

As a result, Irish-Canadians no longer find their identity imposed on them. Instead, they may *choose* whether to march in a St. Patrick's Day parade, enjoy the remarkable contributions of Irish authors to English-language literature and drama, and take pride in the athleticism and precision of Riverdance. For them, ethnicity is largely a *symbolic* matter, as it is for the other white European groups that have undergone similar social processes. Herbert Gans defines **symbolic ethnicity** as "a nostalgic allegiance to the culture of the immigrant generation, or that of the old country; a love for and a pride in a tradition that can be felt without having to be incorporated in everyday behaviour" (Gans, 1991: 436).

In contrast, most Afro-Canadians lack the freedom to enjoy symbolic ethnicity. They may well take pride in their cultural heritage. However, their identity as people of African descent is not an option because a considerable number of non-blacks are racists and impose it on them daily. **Racism** is the belief that a visible characteristic of a group, such as skin colour, indicates group inferiority and justifies discrimination. Recent surveys show that somewhere between 30 and 55 percent of Canadians (depending on the wording of the question) hold racist views (Henry et al., 2001: 147–51). In his autobiography, the black militant Malcolm X poignantly noted how racial identity can be imposed on people. He described one of his black Ph.D. professors as "one of these ultra-proper-talking Negroes" who spoke and acted snobbishly. "Do you know what white racists call black Ph.D.s?" asked Malcolm X. "He said something like, 'I believe that I happen not to be aware of that . . . ' And I laid the word down on him, loud: 'Nigger!'" (X, 1965: 284). Malcolm X's point is that it doesn't matter to a racist whether a black person is a professor or a panhandler, a genius or a fool, a saint or a criminal. Where racism is common, racial identities are compulsory and at the forefront of one's self-identity.

As the contrast between Irish-Canadians and Afro-Canadians suggests, then, relations among racial and ethnic groups can take different forms. We now discuss several theories that explain why forms of racial and ethnic relations vary over time and from place to place.

## THEORIES OF RACE AND ETHNIC RELATIONS

### Ecological Theory

Nearly a century ago, Robert Park proposed an influential theory of how race and ethnic relations change over time (Park, 1950 [1914]). His ecological theory focuses on the struggle for territory. He distinguished five stages in the process by which conflict among ethnic and racial groups emerges and is resolved:

As Malcolm X noted, it doesn't matter to a racist whether a black person is a professor or a panhandler, a genius or a fool, a saint or a criminal. Where racism is common, racial identities are compulsory and at the forefront of one's self-identity.

1. *Invasion*. One racial or ethnic group tries to move into the territory of another. The territory may be as large as a country or as small as a city neighbourhood.
2. *Resistance*. The established group tries to defend its territory and institutions against the intruding group. It may use legal means, violence, or both.
3. *Competition*. If the established group does not drive out the newcomers, the two groups begin to compete for scarce resources. These resources include housing, jobs, public park space, political positions, and so on.
4. *Accommodation and cooperation*. Over time, the two groups work out an understanding of what they should segregate, divide, and share. **Segregation** involves the spatial and institutional separation of racial or ethnic groups. For example, the two groups may segregate churches, heritage associations, and newspapers; divide political positions in proportion to the size of the groups; and share public parks equally.
5. *Assimilation*. **Assimilation** is the process by which a minority group blends into the majority population and eventually disappears as a distinct group. Park argued that assimilation is bound to occur as accommodation and cooperation allow trust and understanding to develop. Eventually, goodwill allows ethnic groups to fuse socially and culturally. Where there were formerly two or more groups, only one remains.

Park's theory stimulated important and insightful research (e.g., Suttles, 1968). However, it applies to some ethnic groups better than others. In North America, it applies best of all to whites of European origin. As Park predicted, many whites of European origin stopped thinking of themselves as Italian-Canadian or Irish-Canadian or German-Canadian after their families were in Canada for three or four generations. Today, they think of themselves just as Canadians (Boyd, 1999; Boyd and Norris, 2001). That is because, over time, they achieved rough equality with members of the majority group and, in the process, began to blend in with them. The story of the Irish is fairly typical. During the first half of the twentieth century, Irish-Canadians experienced upward mobility. By the middle of the century they earned about as much as others of British origin (the Scottish and the English). The tapering off of working-class Irish immigration prevented the average status of the group from falling. As their status rose, Irish-Canadians increasingly intermarried with members of other ethnic groups. Use of the Irish language, Gaelic, virtually disappeared. The Irish became less concentrated in particular cities and less segregated in certain neighbourhoods. Finally, conflict among most majority-group Canadians declined. With variations, a similar story may be told about Italian-Canadians, German-Canadians, and so forth.

However, the story does not apply to all Canadians. Park's theory resonates less well with the experiences of Aboriginal peoples, Québécois, Afro-Canadians, and Asian-Canadians in particular. For reasons we will now explore, some racial and ethnic groups seem stuck between Park's third and fourth stages (competition and accommodation/cooperation).

## The Theory of Internal Colonialism

The main weakness of Park's theory is that it pays insufficient attention to the *social-structural* conditions that prevent some groups from assimilating. Robert Blauner examined one such condition, which he called **internal colonialism** (Blauner, 1972; Hechter, 1974). Blauner's work is important because it stimulated the development of several theories that emphasize the social-structural (and especially class) roots of race and ethnicity.

*Colonialism* involves people from one country invading another. In the process, the invaders change or destroy the native culture. They gain virtually complete control over the native population. They develop the racist belief that the native inhabitants are inherently inferior. And they confine the natives to work considered demeaning. Internal colonialism involves much the same processes but within the boundaries of a single country. Internal colonialism prevents assimilation by segregating the colonized in terms of jobs, housing, and social contacts ranging from friendship to marriage. To varying degrees, Russia, China, France, Great Britain, Canada, Australia, the United States and other countries have engaged in internal colonialism. In Canada, the main victims of internal colonialism are Aboriginal peoples, the Québécois, and people of African descent.

## Canada's Aboriginal Peoples

The single word that best describes the treatment of Canada's Aboriginal peoples by European immigrants in the nineteenth century is *expulsion*. **Expulsion** is the forcible removal of a population from a territory claimed by another population. Expulsion is dramatically illustrated by the plight of the Beothuk, the Aboriginal inhabitants of what is today Newfoundland and Labrador. The Beothuk were Algonkian-speaking hunter-gatherers who probably numbered fewer than a thousand people at the time of European contact.

In the sixteenth century, European fishermen used Newfoundland and Labrador as a fishing port, returning to Europe each year after the fishing season. In the seventeenth century, year-round European settlement began. This caused a revolution in the life of the Beothuk because the Europeans viewed them as a nuisance. They offered incentives to Mi'kmaq Indians from Nova Scotia to kill off the Beothuk. The Beothuk population declined and gradually withdrew from European contact.

As European settlement grew in the eighteenth century, the Beothuk were squeezed into the interior. There they competed for scarce resources with fur traders. Eventually the Beothuk were reduced to a small refugee population along the Exploits River system living off the meagre resources of the Newfoundland and Labrador interior. The expulsion of the Beothuk from their traditional territories due to European colonization led to their eventual extinction. Today, about all that remains of the Beothuk aside from their tragic history and a few artifacts is a statue outside the Newfoundland and Labrador provincial legislature.

The story of the Beothuk is an extreme case. However, *all* First Nations tribes had broadly similar experiences. In the 1700s and 1800s, as the European settlers' fur trade gave way to the harvesting of timber, minerals, oil, and gas, Aboriginal peoples were shunted aside so the Canadian economy could grow. At the time, Europeans thought they were "assimilating" the Aboriginal peoples. The Indian Act spoke of the need to transform a hunting-gathering people into an agricultural labour force (Menzies, 1999). Sir John A. Macdonald, Canada's first prime minister, spoke of the need "to do away with the tribal system and assimilate the Indian people in all respects with the inhabitants of the Dominion, as speedily as they are fit to change" (quoted in Montgomery, 1965: 13). In contrast, many Aboriginal peoples understood the settlers' actions—the passage of the Indian Act, the establishment of the reserve system, the creation of residential schools, and so forth—less as an attempt to assimilate them than as an attempt to obliterate their heritage. It is in this sense that the government of Canada has been accused by some Aboriginal peoples of perpetuating cultural genocide (Cardinal, 1977). **Genocide** is the intentional extermination of an entire population defined as a "race" or a "people."

Adding insult to injury, early historical writing about Canada depicted the First Nations as either irrelevant or evil. Typically, in *The History of the Dominion of Canada*, a book widely used in Canadian schools at the turn of the twentieth century, only five pages

✦ **FIGURE 8.4** ✦
**The Canadian Policy of Assimilation**
In its annual report of 1904, the Department of Indian Affairs published the photographs of Thomas Moore of the Regina Industrial School, "before and after tuition." These images are "a cogent expression of what federal policy had been since Confederation and what it would remain for many decades. It was a policy of assimilation, a policy designed to move Aboriginal communities from their 'savage' state to that of 'civilization' and thus to make in Canada but one community—a non-Aboriginal one" (Milloy, 1999).

Source: Saskatchewan Archives Board, R-82239[1] and R-82239[2].

were devoted to Aboriginal peoples (Clement, 1897). They are described as "cruel," "rude," "false" and "crafty" "savages," and "ferocious villains" who plotted against the Europeans with "fiendish ingenuity" (see also Roberts, 1915; Richardson, 1832; and the overview by Francis, 1992). Canadian schoolbooks continued to portray Aboriginal peoples in pretty much this way until the mid-twentieth century (see Figure 8.4).

So we see that, throughout North America, the confrontation with European culture undermined the way of life of the Aboriginal peoples. Due to internal colonialism and, in particular, expulsion from their traditional lands, Canada's Aboriginal peoples were prevented from practising their traditional ways and from assimilating into the larger society. Most of them languished on reservations and, in more recent times, in urban slums. There they experienced high rates of unemployment, poverty, ill health, and violence. The history of Canada's Aboriginal peoples raises in the most distressing way possible the issue of whether and in what form white society should take responsibility for past injustices.

## The Québécois

A second form of internal colonialism involves not expulsion but **conquest,** the forcible capture of land and the economic and political domination of its inhabitants. For example, as part of their centuries-long struggle to control North America, the English conquered New France and its 60 000 *Canadien* settlers in 1759. They thereby created a system of ethnic stratification that remained in place for more than 200 years and that turned out to be a major source of political conflict (McRoberts, 1988 [1976]).

The British recognized that any attempt to impose their language, religion, laws, and institutions in the former French colony could result in unacceptably high levels of resistance and conflict. Therefore, they tried to accommodate farmers and the Catholic clergy by reinforcing their rights and privileges. The British believed this would win the allegiance of these two *Canadien* groups, who would in turn help build loyalty to Britain among the population as a whole. In contrast, the British undermined the rights and privileges of *Canadien* merchants engaged mainly in the fur trade. They took over virtually all large-scale commerce. In this manner, big business became a British domain. Agriculture, religion, and politics remained the province of the French. This pattern of ethnic stratification remained intact for two centuries. True, by 1950 most farmers had been transformed

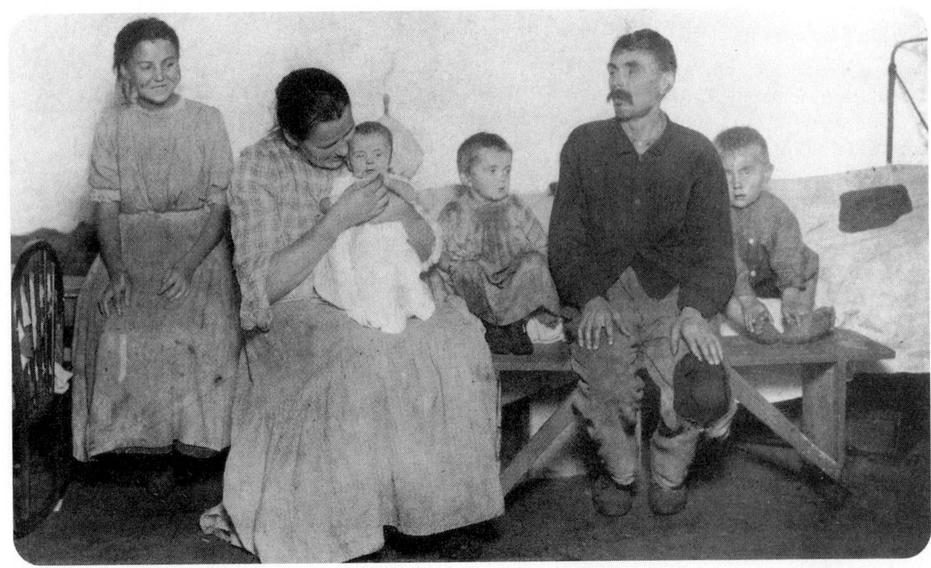

Many white Canadians lived in poor urban ghettos in the nineteenth and early twentieth centuries. However, a larger proportion of them experienced upward mobility than was the case for Afro-Canadians in the late twentieth century. This photo shows a Manitoba tenement in 1912.

into urban, industrial workers. A contingent of Québécois had become physicians, lawyers, and members of the "new middle class" of administrators, technicians, scientists, and intellectuals. However, the upper reaches of the stratification system remained overwhelmingly populated by people of British origin. Social separation reinforced economic segregation. The French and the British tended to speak different languages, live in different towns and neighbourhoods, interact occasionally, befriend one another infrequently, and intermarry rarely. Characteristically, the novel that became emblematic of the social relations between French and English in Quebec is entitled *Two Solitudes* (MacLennan, 1945).

Apart from its rigid system of ethnic stratification, Quebec in the middle of the twentieth century was remarkable because of its undeveloped government services. Health, education, and welfare were largely controlled by the Catholic Church. Intervention of the government in economic matters was almost unknown. Due to this political backwardness, members of Quebec's new middle class, together with blue-collar workers, began campaigning to modernize the provincial political system in the late 1940s. They pressed for more liberal labour laws that would recognize the right of all workers to form unions and strike. They wanted state control over education and a new curriculum that stressed the natural and social sciences rather than classical languages and catechism. They desired a government that would supply a wide range of social services to the population. They demanded that the state provide better infrastructure for economic development and assist francophone entrepreneurs expand their businesses. The partial realization of these aims in the 1960s came to be known as the Quiet Revolution.

However, the modernization of the Quebec state failed to resolve four issues:

1. *The potential demographic decline of the Québécois.* By 1981, Québécois women were giving birth to fewer children on average than women in any other province. In fact, they were having fewer than the 2.1 children women must bear on average to ensure that the size of the population does not decline (Romaniuc, 1984: 14–8). Noticing this trend in the 1970s, many Québécois felt they were becoming an endangered species.
2. *The assimilation of immigrants into English culture.* Fears of demographic decline were reinforced by the preference of most new immigrants to have their children educated in English-language schools. Together with the falling birth rate, this development threatened to diminish the size—and therefore, potentially, the power—of Quebec's francophone population.
3. *Persistent ethnic stratification.* The Quiet Revolution helped create many thousands of jobs for highly educated francophones—but almost exclusively in the government bureaucracy, the educational system, and in new Crown corporations such as Hydro-

Québec. It became apparent in the 1970s that management positions in the private sector remained the preserve of English-origin Canadians.

4. *The continued use of English as the language of private industry.* English remained the language of choice in the private sector because the largest and technologically most advanced businesses were controlled by English-Canadians and Americans. This situation was felt particularly keenly when the expansion of the state sector, and therefore the upward mobility of the francophone new middle class, slowed in the 1970s.

Because of the issues just listed, many Québécois felt that the survival and prosperity of their community required active state intervention in non-francophone institutions. For example, many Québécois came to believe that most shares of banks, trust companies, and insurance firms should be held in Quebec and that these financial institutions should be obliged to reinvest their profits in the province. They argued that the state should increase its role as economic planner and initiator of development and should forbid foreign ownership of cultural enterprises. Finally, the Québécois increasingly demanded compulsory French-language education for the children of most immigrants, obligatory use of French among private-sector managers, and French-only signs in public places. Most Québécois regarded these proposals as the only means by which their community could survive and attain equality with other groups. Moreover, since the Quebec state did not have the legal authority to enact some of the proposed changes, they felt that the province ought to negotiate broader constitutional powers with the federal government. A large minority of Québécois went a step further. They became convinced that Quebec ought to become a politically sovereign nation, albeit a nation economically associated with Canada.

The pro-independence Parti Québécois won the provincial election in 1976. In 1980, it held a referendum to see whether Quebecers favoured "sovereignty-association." Nearly 60 percent voted "no." A second referendum was held in 1995. This time, the forces opposed to sovereignty-association won by the narrowest of margins—about 1 percent. The Parti Québécois promises to hold additional referenda until it gets the result it wants. Thus, as Canada entered the twenty-first century, its future was still uncertain due to the economic, social, and cultural segregation of the Québécois from English Canada that is a legacy of the conquest.

## Afro-Canadians

We have seen that internal colonialism, whether it is accomplished by means of expulsion or conquest, creates big barriers to assimilation than can endure for centuries. A third form of internal colonialism—slavery—creates similar barriers. **Slavery** is the ownership and control of people.

By about 1800, 24 million Africans had been captured and placed on slave ships headed to North, Central, and South America. Due to violence, disease, and shipwreck, fewer than half survived the passage. Black slaves were bought and sold in Canada at least until the 1820s (see Figure 8.5). Only in 1833, when the British government banned slavery throughout the British Empire, did the practice become illegal in Canada. Slavery was abolished in the United States 30 years later.

It is true that the extent of slavery in Canada paled in comparison with its widespread use in the United States, where tobacco and cotton production depended entirely on the work of dirt-cheap black labour. It is also true that for decades Canada served as the terminus of the "underground railway," a network of assistance that smuggled escaped slaves out of the United States to freedom in Canada. As Martin Luther King, leader of the American civil rights movement in the 1960s, said in 1967:

> Deep in our history of struggle for freedom Canada was the North Star. The Negro slave...knew that far to the north a land existed where a fugitive slave, if he survived the horrors of the journey, could find freedom. The legendary underground railroad started in the south and ended in Canada.... Our spirituals, now so widely admired around the world, were often codes. We sang of "heaven" that awaited us, and the slave masters listened in innocence, not realizing that we were not speaking of the hereafter. Heaven was the word

Jacob Lawrence. *The Migration of the Negro, Panel No. 57.* 1940–1941. Jacob Lawrence's "The Great Migration" series of paintings illustrates the mass exodus of African-Americans from the South to the North in search of a better life. Many former plantation slaves came to Canada using the "underground railway," settling in southern Ontario in particular. It was neither a railway nor was it underground, but it was a powerful network of blacks and whites who opposed slavery. Ontario was a prime destination because in 1793 Lieutenant Governor John Graves Simcoe signed the Upper Canadian Act Against Slavery.

> for Canada and the Negro sang of the hope that his escape on the underground railroad would carry him there. One of our spirituals, "Follow the Drinking Gourd," in its disguised lyrics contained directions for escape. The gourd was the big dipper, and the North Star to which its handle pointed gave the celestial map that directed the flight to the Canadian border. (King, 1967: 1)

What King neglected to mention is that after the American Civil War (1861–65) the practice of encouraging black settlement in Canada was reversed. Government policy required the rejection of most immigration applications by black people. This policy reflected a deeply felt prejudice on the part of the Canadian population that persisted throughout the twentieth century (Goldstein, 1978; Sissing, 1996). Moreover, social relations between Canadians of African descent and the white European majority were anything but intimate and based on equality. Until the mid-twentieth century, Afro-Canadians tended to do unskilled labour and be residentially and socially segregated—for example, in the Halifax community of Africville, established around 1850 by runaway American slaves (Clairmont and Magill, 1999 [1974]).

**TO BE SOLD,**

A **BLACK WOMAN, named** PEGGY, aged about forty years ; and a Black boy her ſon, named JUPITER, aged about fifteen years, both of them the property of the Subſcriber.

The Woman is a tolerable Cook and waſher woman and perfectly underſtands making Soap and Candles.

The Boy is tall and ſtrong of his age, and has been employed in Country buſineſs, but brought up principally as a Houſe Servant—They are each of them Servants for life. The Price for the Wowan is one hundred and fifty Dollars—for the Boy two hundred Dollars, payable in three years with Intereſt from the day of Sale and to be properly ſecured by Bond &c.—But one fourth leſs will be taken in ready Money.

PETER RUSSELL.

York, Feb. 10th 1806.

**✦ FIGURE 8.5 ✦**

**Black Slave for Sale**

Many distinguished persons were slave owners, including Peter Russell, who held positions in the executive and legislative councils and became administrator of Upper Canada.

Source: Upper Canada Gazette, February 10, 1806.

Canadian immigration policy was liberalized in the 1960s. Racial and ethnic restrictions were removed. Immigrants were now admitted on the basis of their potential economic contribution to Canadian society (about 56 percent of all immigrants in 1996), their close family ties with Canadians (about 30 percent of the total), or their refugee status (about 13 percent of the total) (Citizenship and Immigration Canada, 1997). As a result, Canada became a much more racially and ethnically diverse society (see Table 8.1). For example, more than 271 000 people came to Canada from the Caribbean and more than 148 000 came from Africa between 1961 and 1996. Some of these new immigrants had completed post-secondary education. Others attended colleges and universities in Canada. The social standing of Canada's black community thus improved significantly. Nonetheless, Canadians of African descent still tend to interact little with white Canadians of European descent, especially in their intimate relations, and they still tend to live in different neighbourhoods. Like the aftermath of expulsion and conquest, the aftermath of slavery—prejudice, discrimination, disadvantage, and segregation—continues to act as a barrier to assimilation.

You can easily judge for yourself the strength of social barriers between Canadians of different ethnic and racial backgrounds. You can also determine how this barrier has changed over time. Draw up a list of your five closest friends and note the ethnic or racial background of each one. Now ask one of your parents to do the same for *their* five closest friends. Finally, ask one of your grandparents to draw up a similar list. How racially and ethnically diverse is your friendship network? How do you explain its racial and ethnic diversity or lack of diversity? How racially and ethnically diverse is your friendship network compared with the friendship network of your parent and grandparent? How do you explain differences between generations? Now, instead of focusing on friends, perform the same exercise for your cousins and the cousins of your parent and grandparent. How racially and ethnically diverse is your kinship network? How diverse it is compared with the kinship network of your parent and grandparent? How do you explain differences among generations? Finally, compare the racial and ethnic diversity of friendship and kinship networks. For each generation (yours, your parent's, and your grandparent's), is the kinship or the friendship network more racially and ethnically diverse? Why? Where do you and your family fit into the web of racial and ethnic diversity that composes Canadian society?

## The Theory of the Split Labour Market and the Case of Asian-Canadians

We have seen how the theory of internal colonialism explains the persistence of inequality and segregation between racial and ethnic groups. A second theory that focuses on the social-structural barriers to assimilation is the theory of the split labour market, first proposed by sociologist Edna Bonacich (1972). Bonacich's theory explains why racial identities are reinforced by certain labour market conditions. In brief, she argues that where low-wage workers of one race and high-wage workers of another race compete for the

**✦ TABLE 8.1 ✦**
**Immigrants by Place of Birth and Period of Immigration, Canada, 1996 (in percent)**

Source: Statistics Canada (2002c).

| Place of Birth | Immigrated before 1961 | Immigrated 1961–90 | Immigrated 1991–96 |
|---|---|---|---|
| United Kingdom | 25.2 | 12.7 | 2.4 |
| Northern and Western Europe (excluding UK) | 26.9 | 6.9 | 3.1 |
| Southern Europe | 21.6 | 15.1 | 5.0 |
| Eastern Europe | 16.6 | 6.4 | 8.5 |
| Asia | 3.1 | 32.6 | 57.0 |
| Caribbean, Bermuda, and Africa | 0.1 | 12.6 | 12.9 |
| Other | 6.5 | 13.7 | 11.1 |
| Total | 100.0 | 100.0 | 100.0 |

same jobs, high-wage workers are likely to resent the presence of low-wage competitors and conflict is bound to result. Consequently, racist attitudes develop or are reinforced.

This is certainly what happened during the early years of Asian immigration in Canada. Chinese, then Japanese, and later Sikhs were allowed into Canada from about the 1850s to the early 1920s for one reason: to provide scarce services and cheap labour in the booming West. Chinese-owned restaurants, grocery stores, laundries, and import businesses dotted the West and especially British Columbia by the early twentieth century (Li, 1998; Whitaker, 1987). Numerically more important, however, were the Asian labourers who worked in lumbering, mining, and railway construction. For example, 15 000 Chinese men were allowed into Canada to complete construction of the final and most difficult section of the Canadian Pacific Railway (CPR), which involved blasting tunnels and laying rail along dangerous Rocky Mountain passes. The Chinese were paid half the wages of white workers. It is said that they "worked like horses." It is also said that they "dropped like flies" due to exposure, disease, malnutrition, and explosions. Four Chinese workers died for every mile of track laid.

Asian immigration in general was widely viewed as a threat to cherished British values and institutions, an evil to be endured only as long as absolutely necessary. Therefore, once the CPR was completed in 1885, the Chinese were no longer welcome in British Columbia. A prohibitively expensive "head tax" equal to two months' wages was placed on each Chinese immigrant. The tax was increased tenfold in 1903 (see Figure 8.6). In 1923, Chinese immigration was banned altogether. During the Great Depression, more than 28 000 Chinese were deported because of high unemployment, and Asian immigration did not resume on a large scale until the 1960s, when racial criteria were finally removed from Canadian immigration regulations.

Underlying European-Canadian animosity against Asian immigration was a split labour market. The fact that Asian immigrants were willing to work for much lower wages than European-Canadians fuelled deep resentment among European-Canadians, especially when the labour market was flooded with far too many job seekers. European-Canadians formed "exclusion leagues" to pressure the government to restrict Asian immigration, and on occasion they even staged anti-Asian riots. Such actions solidified racial identities among both the throwers and the victims of the bricks and made assimilation impossible (on the 1907 anti-Asian riots in Vancouver, see Chapter 17, Collective Action and Social Movements).

In sum, the theory of split labour markets, like the theory of internal colonialism, emphasizes the social-structural roots of race and ethnicity and helps overcome the main weakness of Park's ecological theory. The groups that have had most trouble assimilating into the British values and institutions that dominate Canadian society are those that were subjected to expulsion from their native lands, conquest, slavery, and split labour markets. These circumstances left a legacy of racism that created social-structural impediments to assimila-

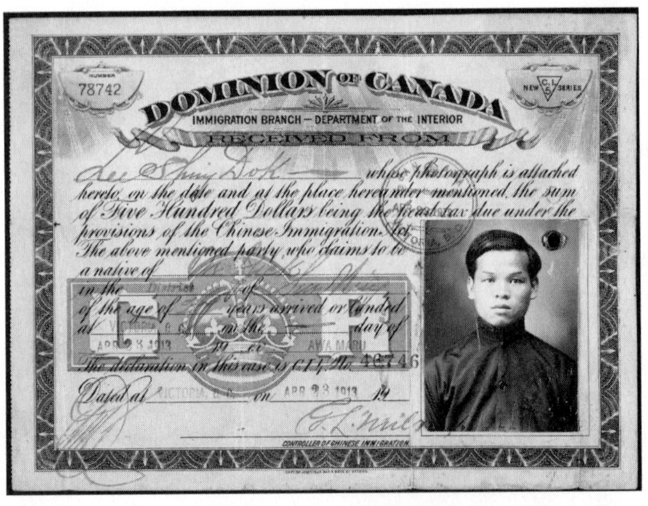
NUMBER 78742

NEW C.I. 5 SERIES

DOMINION OF CANADA

IMMIGRATION BRANCH — DEPARTMENT OF THE INTERIOR

RECEIVED FROM

Lee Shing Doh whose photograph is attached hereto, on the date and at the place hereunder mentioned, the sum of Five Hundred Dollars being the head tax due under the provisions of the Chinese Immigration Act. The above mentioned party who claims to be a native of ______ in the District of ______ of the age of ______ years arrived or landed at VICTORIA, B.C. on the ______ day of APR 23 1913 19__ AWA MARU

The declaration in this case is C.I. 4. No. 46746

Dated at VICTORIA, B.C. on APR 23 1913 19__

CONTROLLER OF CHINESE IMMIGRATION

**✦ FIGURE 8.6 ✦**
**Head Tax Certificate**
In another example of legislated racism, immigrants from China were required by law to pay a "head tax" to enter Canada between 1885 and 1923. The tax began as a fee of $50 and rose to as high as $500.

Source: National Archives of Canada/ C149236.

tion—impediments such as forced segregation in low-status jobs and low-income neighbourhoods. By focusing on factors like these, we arrive at a more realistic picture of the state of race and ethnic relations in the Canada than is afforded by ecological theory alone.

## Some Advantages of Ethnicity

The theories of internal colonialism and split labour markets emphasize how social forces outside a racial or ethnic group force its members together, preventing their assimilation into the dominant values and institutions of society. It focuses on the disadvantages of race and ethnicity. Moreover, it deals only with the most disadvantaged minorities. The theory has less to say about the internal conditions that promote group cohesion and in particular about the value of group membership. Nor does it help us to understand why some European Canadians such as those of Greek or Polish or German origin continue to participate in the life of their ethnic communities, even if their families have been in the country more than two or three generations.

A review of the sociological literature suggests that three main factors enhance the value of ethnic group membership for some white European-Canadians who have lived in the country for many generations:

1. *Ethnic group membership can have economic advantages.* The economic advantages of ethnicity are most apparent for immigrants, who comprised nearly 18 percent of the Canadian population in 2001 (see Figure 8.7). Immigrants often lack extensive social contacts and fluency in English or French. Therefore, they commonly rely on members of their ethnic group to help them find jobs and housing. In this way, immigrant communities become tightly knit. However, some economic advantages extend into the third generation and beyond. For example, community solidarity is an important resource for "ethnic entrepreneurs." These are businesspeople who operate largely within their ethnic community. They draw on their community for customers, suppliers, employees, and credit, and they may be linked economically to the homeland as importers and exporters. They often pass on their businesses to their children, who in turn can pass the businesses on to the next generation. In this way, strong economic incentives encourage some people to remain ethnic group members, even beyond the immigrant generation (Bonacich, 1973; Fong and Ooka, forthcoming; Light, 1991; Portes and Manning, 199).
2. *Ethnic group membership can be politically useful.* Consider, for instance, the way some Canadians reacted to the rise of separatism in Quebec in the 1960s. To bridge the growing divide between francophone Quebec and the rest of the country, the

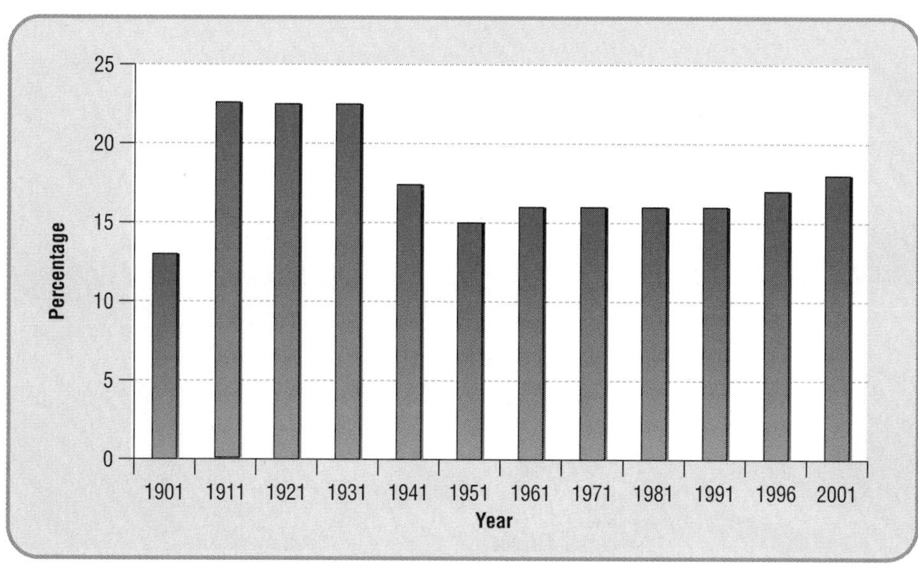


✦ **FIGURE 8.7** ✦
**Percent of Canada's Population Foreign-Born, 1901–2001**

Source: Adapted from Canada Census 1996.

federal government under Pierre Trudeau's Liberals promoted a policy of *bilingualism*. French and English were made official languages. This meant that federal government services would be made available in both languages and instruction in French, including total immersion instruction, would be encouraged in English schools. Members of some ethnic groups, such as people of Ukrainian origin in western Canada, felt neglected and alienated by this turn of events. They saw no reason why the French should be accorded special status and wanted a share of the resources available for promoting ethnic languages and cultures. As a result, the Trudeau government proclaimed a new policy of *multiculturalism* in 1971. Now federal funds became available for the promotion of Ukrainian and all other ethnic cultures in Canada. This entire episode of Canadian ethnic history bolstered western support for the Liberal Party and softened western opposition to bilingualism. Moreover, it helped stimulate ethnic culture and ethnic identification throughout the country. We thus see that ethnicity can be a political tool for achieving increased access to resources. This is part of the reason for the persistence of ethnic identification for some white European-Canadians whose families have lived in the country for many generations.

3. *Ethnic group membership tends to persist because of the emotional support it provides*. Like economic benefits, the emotional advantages of ethnicity are most apparent in immigrant communities. Speaking the ethnic language and sharing other elements of one's native culture are valuable sources of comfort in an alien environment. Even beyond the second generation, however, ethnic group membership can perform significant emotional functions. For example, some ethnic groups have experienced unusually high levels of prejudice and discrimination involving expulsion or attempted genocide. For people who belong to such groups, the resulting trauma is so severe it can be transmitted for several generations. In such cases, ethnic group membership offers security in a world still seen as hostile long after the threat of territorial loss or annihilation has disappeared (Bar-On, 1999). Another way in which ethnic group membership offers emotional support beyond the second generation is by providing a sense of rootedness. Especially in a highly mobile, urbanized, technological, and bureaucratic society such as ours, ties to an ethnic community can be an important source of stability and security (Isajiw, 1978).

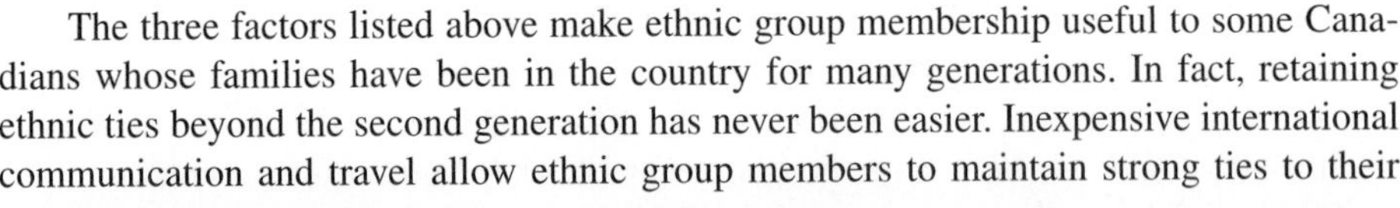
The three factors listed above make ethnic group membership useful to some Canadians whose families have been in the country for many generations. In fact, retaining ethnic ties beyond the second generation has never been easier. Inexpensive international communication and travel allow ethnic group members to maintain strong ties to their

Pier 21 is located at 1055 Marginal Road, Halifax, Nova Scotia. It played an important role in the lives of many immigrants to Canada. It opened its doors in 1928. As the era of ocean travel was coming to an end in March 1971, the Immigration Service left Pier 21.

With the introduction of the point system in 1967, nationality and race were removed as selection criteria from the Immigration Act. Of the more than 250 000 people who came to Canada last year, more than 50 percent came from 10 source countries: China, India, Pakistan, the Philippines, Korea, the United States, Iran, Romania, Sri Lanka, and Britain.

ancestral homeland in a way that was never possible in earlier times. Immigration used to involve cutting all or most ties to one's country of origin. Travel by sea and air was expensive, long-distance telephone rates were prohibitive, and the occasional letter was about the only communication most immigrants had with their relatives in the old country. This lack of communication encouraged assimilation in people's newly adopted countries. Today, however, ties to the ancestral communities are often maintained in ways that sustain ethnic culture. For example, about 50 000 Jews have immigrated from the former Soviet Union to Canada since the early 1970s, settling mainly in Toronto. They frequently visit relatives in the former Soviet Union and Israel, speak with them on the phone, and use the Internet to exchange e-mail with them. They also receive Russian-language radio and TV broadcasts, act as conduits for foreign investment, and send money to relatives abroad (Brym, 2001b; Brym with Ryvkina, 1994; Markowitz, 1993). This sort of intimate and ongoing connection with the motherland is typical of most recent immigrant communities in North America. Thanks to inexpensive international travel and communication, some ethnic groups have become **transnational communities** whose boundaries extend among countries. Characteristically, the Ticuani Potable Water Committee in Brooklyn has been raising money for the farming community of Ticuani in the Mixteca region of Mexico for 25 years. Its seal reads *"Por el Progreso de Ticuani: Los Ausentes Siempre Presentes. Ticuani y New York"* (translation: "For the Progress of Ticuani: The Absent Ones Always Present. Ticuani and New York"). The phrase "the absent ones always present" nicely captures the essence of transnational communities, whose growing number and vitality facilitate the retention of ethnic group membership beyond the second generation (Portes, 1996).

In sum, ethnicity remains a vibrant force in Canadian society for a variety of reasons. Even some white Canadians whose families settled in this country more than two generations ago have reason to identify with their ethnic group. Bearing this in mind, what is the likely future of race and ethnic relations in Canada? We conclude by offering some tentative answers to that question.

## THE FUTURE OF RACE AND ETHNICITY IN CANADA

The world is composed of more than 200 countries and more than 5000 ethnic and racial groups. As a result, no country is ethnically and racially homogeneous and in many countries, including Canada, the largest ethnic group forms less than half the population (see Figure 8.8). Canada's British roots remain important. Our parliamentary democracy is based on the British model; the queen's representative, the governor general, is our titular head of state; we still celebrate May 24, Queen Victoria's birthday; and English is the country's predominant language, with more than 60 percent of Canadians claiming it as their mother tongue. Nonetheless, Canada is one of the most racially and ethnically heterogeneous societies in the world.

As racial and ethnic diversity has increased, Canadian ethnic and race relations have changed radically. Two hundred years ago, Canada was a society based on expulsion, conquest, slavery, and segregation. Today, we are a society based on segregation, pluralism, and assimilation, **pluralism** being understood as the retention of racial and ethnic culture combined with equal access to basic social resources. Thus, on a scale of tolerance, Canada has come a long way in the past 200 years (see Figure 8.9).

✦ **FIGURE 8.8** ✦
**Estimates of Ethnic Origins of Canadian Population**

Source: Statistics Canada, Census of Canada (various years).

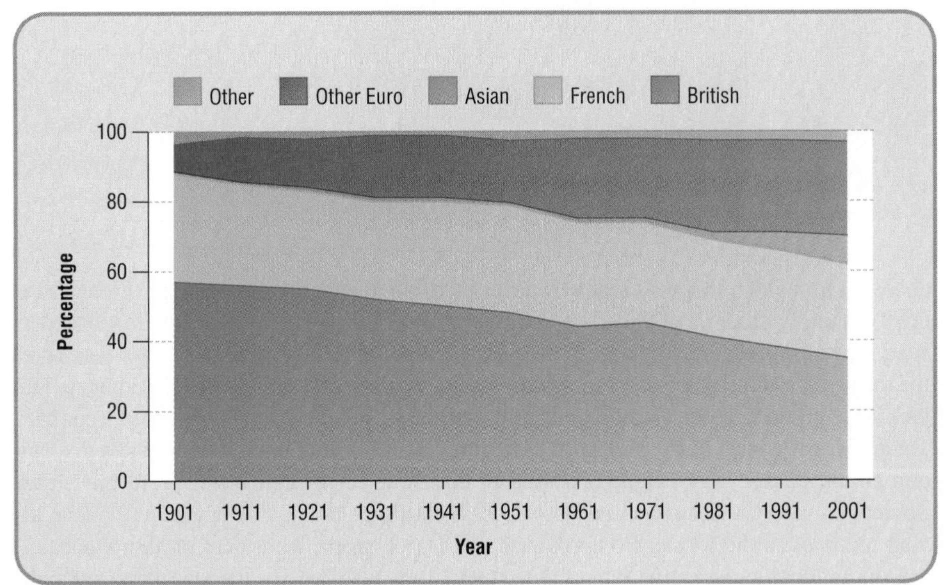


✦ **FIGURE 8.9** ✦
**Six Degrees of Separation: Types of Ethnic and Racial Group Relations**

Source: Adapted from Kornblum (1997 [1988]: 385).

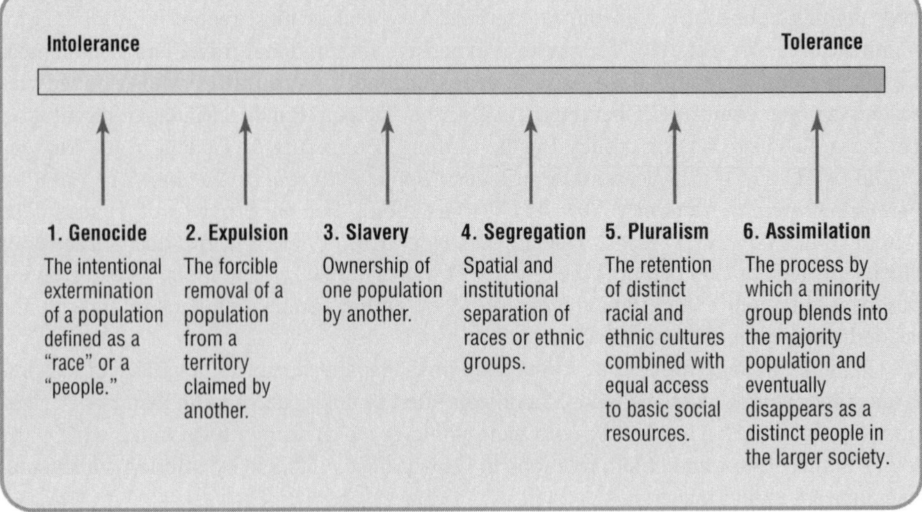

In comparison with most other countries, too, Canada is a relatively tolerant land. In the late twentieth and early twenty-first centuries, racial and ethnic tensions in some parts of the world erupted into wars of secession and attempted genocide. Conflict among Croats, Serbs, and other ethnic groups tore Yugoslavia apart. Russia fought a bloody war against its Chechen ethnic minority that, as of this writing, continues. In Rwanda, Hutu militia and soldiers massacred many thousands of Tutsi civilians. A few years later, Tutsi soldiers massacred many thousands of Hutu civilians. Comparing Canada with such poor countries may seem to stack the deck in favour of concluding that Canada is a relatively tolerant society. However, even when we compare Canada with other rich, stable, postindustrial countries, our society seems relatively tolerant by most measures (see Figure 8.10).

Due to such factors as intermarriage and immigration, the growth of tolerance in Canada is taking place in the context of increasing ethnic and racial diversity. Given continuing migration in the coming decades, Canada will become even more of a racial and ethnic mosaic than it is now (Pendakur, 2000). However, if present trends continue, the racial and ethnic mosaic will continue to be vertical. That is, some groups, especially Aboriginal peoples, will be disproportionately clustered at the bottom of the socio-economic hierarchy. Unless dramatic changes occur they will continue to enjoy less wealth, income, education, good housing, health care, and other social rewards than other Canadians.

Political initiatives could decrease the verticality of the Canadian mosaic, speeding up the movement from segregation to pluralism and assimilation for the country's most disadvantaged groups. Such political initiatives include compensation for historical injustices (see Box 8.2), **affirmative action** or employment equity programs that encourage the hiring of qualified members of disadvantaged minorities, government-subsidized job training and child care, improvements in public education, and the shoring up of Canada's faltering medicare system. All these initiatives would benefit disadvantaged Canadians the most. However, the country does not seem much in the mood for such expensive reforms at the moment. Canada is therefore likely to remain a vertical mosaic for some time to come.

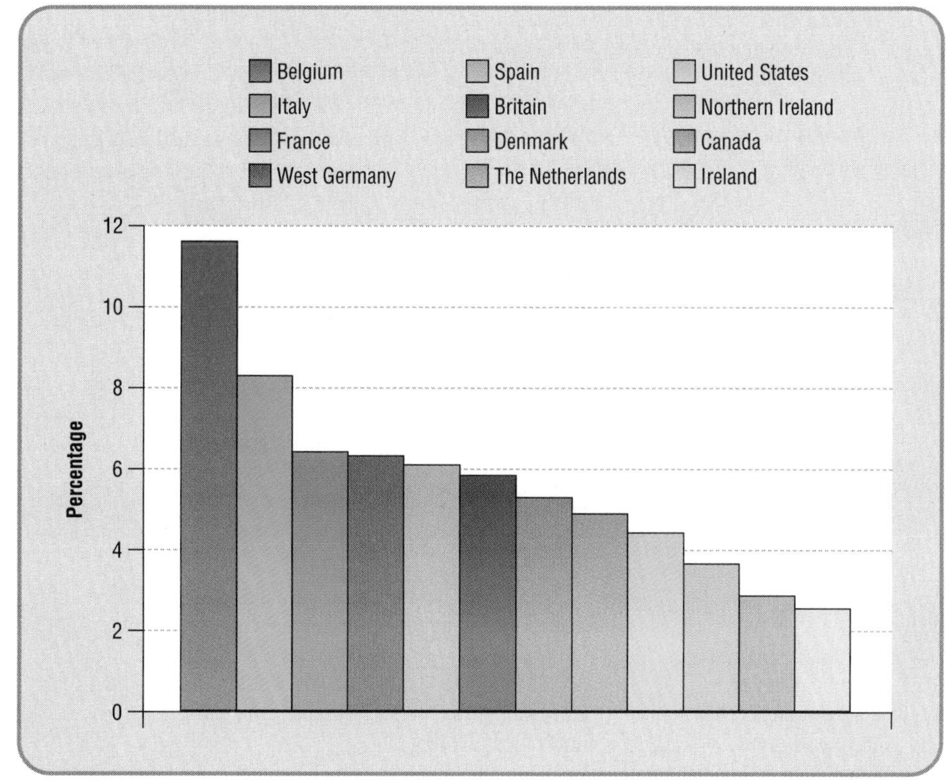


**✦ FIGURE 8.10 ✦**

**Percentage Opposed to Person of Another Race, Immigrants, or Foreign Workers Living Next Door, 12 Postindustrial Countries, 1990**

Source: Nevitte (1996: 231).

BOX 8.2
IT'S YOUR CHOICE

### SHOULD WE PAY THE PRICE OF PAST WRONGS?

July 28, 2001, was a hot, muggy day in Toronto and Randall Robinson added to the heat with his fiery oration to the African Canadian Legal Clinic (ACLC). "We're owed at least $11 trillion," he exhorted; "America must pay for slavery." The Harvard-educated Robinson was championing the cause of reparations for the descendants of American slaves—monetary compensation for past injustices. Americans of African descent, he argued, have been "bottom-stuck" since they were slaves. Their disadvantaged position today, he argued, is the legacy of slavery.

Although slavery was abolished in Canada 170 years ago, Robinson's arguments were endorsed by the ACLC and other Canadian groups that are not of African descent. Japanese-, Chinese-, Aboriginal, and Jewish-Canadians all had representatives and gave advice at the meeting of the ACLC in July 2001:

- *Japanese-Canadians*. In 1942, three months after Japan attacked Pearl Harbor, the Canadian government invoked the War Measures Act. All people of Japanese origin residing within 160 km of the Pacific Coast were removed from their homes. With about 24 hours' notice, almost 21 000 Japanese-Canadians, 75 percent of them Canadian citizens, were moved to prisoner of war camps, work camps, and internment camps. Japanese-Canadians have sought reparations for this historical injustice.
- *Chinese-Canadians*. As noted above, the descendants of many Chinese-Canadians were forced to pay a highly discriminatory head tax between 1885 and 1903. Chinese-Canadians have requested compensation for this mistreatment.
- *Aboriginal peoples*. Many Aboriginal children were taken from their parents and placed in residential schools in the twentieth century. Many of them were physically and sexually abused in these schools. Aboriginal peoples also claim that much land was illegally taken from them. They, too, have sought a redress of grievances.
- *Jewish-Canadians*. The Nazis enslaved and slaughtered European Jews by the million during the Second World War. Jews were the first group in recent decades to seek reparations (from the German government) for the historical injustices they suffered.

In the past, what was past was past. The vanquished were vanquished. The powerful wrote the history books and took no responsibility for what their ancestors had done. Today, things are different. Aggrieved groups in Canada and around the world are demanding reparations (Torpey, 2001). The recognition of fundamental human rights, signified first by the Human Rights Declaration of the United Nations in 1948, and the widespread delegitimization of racial and ethnic discrimination have provided fertile terrain for this historical turn. The mobilization of shame has triggered a revolutionary change in how some people and governments view past injustices.

What do you think about the reparations issue? Should *you* compensate Afro-Canadians for slavery, Chinese-Canadians for the head tax, Japanese-Canadians for the internment camps, and Aboriginal peoples for residential schools and land? How responsible should *you* be for events that took place 50 or 200 years ago? In 1988 the Canadian government condemned the internment of Japanese-Canadians during the Second World War, offered individual and community compensation to Japanese-Canadians, and provided a $24 million endowment for the Canadian Race Relations Foundation. Does this seem fair to you? What about the far larger demands of Aboriginal peoples for self-government and land rights given that they were pushed onto reserves to make way for exploration and resource development? Should Canada recognize its guilt and compensate those who have suffered? If not, why not? If so, should limits be placed on reparations? Why or why not? As a Canadian citizen, it's your choice.

## SUMMARY

1. Race is not a purely biological category. Ethnicity is not a purely cultural category. Both are socially constructed ideas that we use to distinguish people based on physical or cultural differences. These distinctions have profound consequences for people's lives.
2. Racial and ethnic labels and identities are variables. They change over time and place, and are affected by relations among racial and ethnic groups. Cordial group relations hasten the blending of labels and identities.
3. Racial and ethnic groups are blending over time, as members of society become more tolerant. However, this tendency is weak among members of highly disadvantaged groups. That is because such groups remain highly segregated in jobs, housing, and social contacts. To a considerable degree, this is a historical legacy of internal colonialism and split labour markets.
4. Identifying with a racial or ethnic group can have economic, political, and emotional rewards. This accounts for the persistence of ethnic identity among many white Canadians, even after their families have been in Canada for more than two generations.
5. Racial and ethnic inequalities are likely to persist. In addition to affirmative action or employment equity programs, more job training, improvements in public education, and subsidized health care and child care would promote equality. However, Canada does not seem to favour these expensive reforms at this time.

# GLOSSARY

**Affirmative action or employment equity** is a policy that gives preference to minority group members if equally qualified people are available for a position.

**Assimilation** is the process by which a minority group blends into the majority population and eventually disappears as a distinct group.

**Conquest** is the forcible capture of land and the economic and political domination of its inhabitants.

**Discrimination** is unfair treatment of people due to their group membership.

An **ethnic group** is composed of people whose perceived cultural markers are deemed socially significant. Ethnic groups differ from one another in terms of language, religion, customs, values, ancestors, and the like.

**Expulsion** is the forcible removal of a population from a territory claimed by another population.

**Genocide** is the intentional extermination of an entire population defined as a "race" or a "people."

**Internal colonialism** involves one race or ethnic group subjugating another in the same country. It prevents assimilation by segregating the subordinate group in terms of jobs, housing, and social contacts.

A **minority group** is a group of people who are socially disadvantaged although they may be in the numerical majority.

**Pluralism** is the retention of racial and ethnic culture combined with equal access to basic social resources.

**Prejudice** is an attitude that judges a person on his or her group's real or imagined characteristics.

**Race** is a social construct used to distinguish people in terms of one or more physical markers, usually with profound effects on their lives.

**Racism** is the belief that a visible characteristic of a group, such as skin colour, indicates group inferiority and justifies discrimination.

A **scapegoat** is a disadvantaged person or category of people that others blame for their own problems.

**Segregation** involves the spatial and institutional separation of racial or ethnic groups.

**Slavery** is the ownership and control of people.

**Symbolic ethnicity** is a nostalgic allegiance to the culture of the immigrant generation, or that of the old country, that is not usually incorporated in everyday behaviour.

**Transnational communities** are communities whose boundaries extend among countries.

# QUESTIONS TO CONSIDER

1. How do you identify yourself in terms of your race or ethnicity? Do conventional ethnic and racial categories, such as black, white, Hispanic, and Asian, "fit" your sense of who you are? If so, why? If not, why not?
2. Do you think racism is becoming a more serious problem in Canada and worldwide? Why or why not? How do trends in racism compare with trends in other forms of prejudice, such as sexism? What accounts for similarities and differences in these trends?
3. What are the costs and benefits of ethnic diversity in your university? Do you think it would be useful to adopt a policy of affirmative action or employment equity to make the student body and the faculty more ethically and racially diverse? Why or why not?

# WEB RESOURCES

## Companion Web Site for This Book

http://www.brymsociologycompass.nelson.com

Begin by clicking on the Student Resources section of the Web site. Next, select the chapter you are currently studying from the pull-down menu. From the Student Resources page you will have easy access to InfoTrac College Edition®, MicroCase online exercises, and additional Web links. The Web site also has many useful tips to aid you in your study of sociology, including practice tests for each chapter.

## InfoTrac Search Terms

These search terms are provided to assist you in beginning to conduct research on this topic by visiting http://www.infotrac-college.com

**Affirmative action**
**Assimilation**
**Discrimination**
**Racism**
**Transnational community**

## Recommended Web Sites

For information on the history and cultures of the people of Canada, visit Canadian Heritage at http://www.pch.gc.ca/english.htm.

For a site that promotes cooperation between Aboriginal peoples and other Canadians, go to the Assembly of First Nations Web site at http://www.afn.ca/.

To share the Japanese-Canadian experience, go to http://www.jcnm.ca.

For issues relevant to Chinese-Canadians, go to http://www.ccnc.ca.

For information about the United Nations human rights program, go to http://www.unhchr.ch/hchr_un.htm.

## SUGGESTED READINGS

Stephen Jay Gould. *The Mismeasure of Man*, rev. ed. (New York: Norton. 1996 [1981]). A Pulitzer Prize–winning study of the abuse of science in the study of racial differences, written by the late Harvard biologist who was arguably the most famous scientist of the late twentieth century.

Charles Taylor. *Multiculturalism: Examining the Politics of Recognition* (Princeton, NJ: Princeton University Press, 1994). This book by Canada's foremost philosopher argues for the recognition of the value of other cultures, claiming that recognition is central to the growth of dignity and meaningful participation in social life for all people.

Alan C. Cairns. *Citizens Plus: Aboriginal Peoples and the Canadian State* (Vancouver: UBC Press, 2000). A highly readable overview of the confrontation between Aboriginal peoples and European-Canadians, including a stimulating analysis and critique of possible solutions to Aboriginal issues.

## NOTES

1. Controversy surrounds the terminology used throughout this chapter. Some scholars prefer to emphasize common descent and culture by using terms such as "Afro-Canadian" and "Euro-Canadian" rather than "black" and "white." However, terms that emphasize descent and culture can be ethnocentric. For example, there are millions of black immigrants from former British and French colonies in Europe. Therefore, "Euro-Canadian" does not accurately signify the white majority in Canada. Because there is no perfect set of terms to denote racial or ethnic communities, we use "white" and "Euro-Canadian" as well as "black" and "Afro-Canadian."
2. Although sociologists commonly dispute a genetic basis of mean intelligence for races, evidence suggests that individual differences in intelligence are partly genetically transmitted (Bouchard et al., 1990; Lewontin, 1991: 19–37; Scarr and Weinberg, 1978; Schiff and Lewontin, 1986).
3. The genetic argument also belittles the athletic activity itself by denying the role of training in developing athletic skills.
4. In Soviet terminology, these groups were called "nationalities."

## IN THIS CHAPTER, YOU WILL LEARN THAT

- Although biology determines sex, social structure and culture largely determine gender, or the expression of culturally appropriate masculine and feminine roles.
- The social construction of gender is evident in the way parents treat babies, teachers treat pupils, and the mass media portray ideal body images.
- The social forces pushing people to assume conventionally masculine or feminine roles are compelling.
- The social forces pushing people toward heterosexuality operate with even greater force.
- The social distinction between men and women serves as an important basis of inequality in the family and the workplace.
- Male aggression against women is rooted in gender inequality.

CHAPTER

9

# SEXUALITY AND GENDER

## SEX VERSUS GENDER

### Is It a Boy or a Girl?

On April 27, 1967, what was supposed to be a routine circumcision of an eight-month-old male twin at the St. Boniface Hospital in Winnipeg, Manitoba, turned out to be anything but routine. Whether because of mechanical malfunction, physician error, or some combination of the two, the infant's penis was burned off by the heated needle on the electric cauterizing machine. A parade of specialists informed the boy's distraught parents that their son's prognosis was grim. Medical technology of the time did not permit the reconstruction of a penis that would resemble a normal organ in appearance or sexual function; at best, attempts at phallic reconstruction would result in a conduit for urine. A psychiatric report prepared on the boy's projected future concluded that "he will be unable to live a normal sexual life from the time of adolescence: that he will be unable to consummate marriage or have normal heterosexual relations, in that he will have to recognize that he is incomplete, physically defective and that he must live apart" (Colapinto, 2001: 16).

Approximately 10 months after the accident, the child's parents experienced a glimmering of hope when they saw John Money, a psychologist at the renowned John Hopkins Hospital in Baltimore, being interviewed on television. Money had been the driving force behind the creation of the world's first "sex change" clinic at John Hopkins (Bullough, 2000). Money was already well known at that time for his research on infant **hermaphrodites.** Hermaphrodites are persons who are born with ambiguous genitals because of a hormone imbalance in the womb. It was Money's opinion that infants with "unfinished genitals" should be *assigned* into whichever sex seemed most suitable, physically converted through surgery and hormone treatments, and reared in accordance with their newly assigned sex (Money and Ehrhardt, 1972). For example, he advised that a male infant born with a penis under one inch (2.5 cm) in length be assigned to the female sex. Clinical castration and other genital surgery would be followed by a program of hormonal, mental, and social conditioning. The child, while young, would *not* be informed of his ambiguous sexual status at birth. Rather, his parents would treat him as a girl and rear him accordingly. According to Money, these strategies would lead to the child's eventual possession of a self-identity that was consistent with the assigned sex.

In a surge of optimism, the Winnipeg couple wrote to Dr. Money and he promptly wrote back, urging them to bring their child to Baltimore without delay. After consultation with various physicians and with Money, the parents agreed to have their son's sex reassigned. In anticipation of what would follow, the boy's parents stopped cutting his hair, dressed him in feminine clothes, and changed his name from Bruce to Brenda. Surgical castration was performed when the twin was 22 months old.

Early reports of the child's progress (Money and Ehrhardt, 1972) seemed to indicate the primacy of nurture (i.e., environment) over nature (i.e., biology) in the making of boys and girls. In stark contrast to her biologically identical brother, Brenda was described as disdaining "cars and gas pumps and tools" and fascinated by "dolls, a doll house and a doll carriage." The mother of the reassigned twin reported that, at the age of four and a half, Brenda preferred and took pleasure in her feminine clothing, helped with household chores (while her brother did not), and was neat and tidy. "[S]he is so feminine. I've never seen a little girl so neat and tidy...and yet my son is quite different. I can't wash his face for anything.... She is very proud of herself, when she puts on a new dress, or I set her hair" (Money and Ehrhardt, 1972). These stereotypical preferences and activities were all taken as indicators of successful conformity to a feminine gender and of the power of gender to override biological sex (Money and Ehrhardt, 1972: 11).

The "twins case" generated worldwide attention and textbooks in both medicine and the social sciences were rewritten to incorporate Money's reports of the child's progress. For example, in his introductory text, *Sociology*, Ian Robertson (1977) confidently asserted that Money's work proved that "children can *easily* be raised as a member of the opposite sex" (*our emphasis*). Marlene Mackie's *Gender Relations in Canada: Further Explanations* (1991: 69) also reported that, "This oft-cited case...suggests that social assignment outweighs biology in determining gender identity and behaviour."

However, later reports on the reassigned twin cast doubt on the apparent success of the transformation (Diamond and Sigmundson, 1999). Although feminine in appearance, "by all accounts of family, teachers, guidance clinic workers and relatives, this illusion...disappeared the second Brenda moved, spoke, walked or gestured" (Colapinto, 2001: 57). Brenda insisted on urinating standing up, refused to undergo the further "feminizing" surgeries that had been planned for her, and, from age seven, daydreamed of her ideal future self "as a twenty-one-year-old male with a mustache, a sports car, and surrounded by admiring friends" (Colapinto, 2001: 93). She experienced various difficulties, including academic failure and rejection and ridicule from her classmates, who dubbed her "Cavewoman" (Diamond, 1982). At age 9, Brenda had a nervous breakdown; at age 14, in a state of acute despair, she attempted suicide (Colapinto, 2001: 96, 262).

In 1980, Brenda learned the details of her sex reassignment from her father. At age 16, she decided to be reassigned once more and to live as a man rather than a woman. Advancements in medical technology made it possible for the twin, who adopted the name David, to have an artificial penis constructed. At age 25, David married a woman and adopted her three children (Gorman, 1997). In 2000, he allowed a journalist to write his biography and reveal his true identity in an attempt to set the published record straight—"a published record which expressly denied the extraordinary torments he had undergone and which, to David's everlasting horror, had led to similar anguish for untold numbers of children" (Colapinto, 2001: 282). David observed, "I don't have the kind of education that these scientists and doctors and psychologists have, but to me it's very ignorant. If a woman lost her breasts, do you turn her into a guy? To make her feel 'whole and complete'?... [Y]ou can't be something that you're not. You have to be *you*" (Colapinto, 2001: 264–5, emphasis in original).

The story of Bruce/Brenda/David introduces the first big question of this chapter. What makes us male or female? Of course, part of the answer is biological. Your **sex** depends on whether you were born with distinct male or female genitals and a genetic program that released either male or female hormones to stimulate the development of your reproductive system.

However, the case of Bruce/Brenda/David also shows that more is involved in becoming male or female than biological sex differences.

Recalling his brother's conflicted childhood, David's identical twin remarked: "I recognized Brenda as my sister, but she never, ever acted the part. When I say there was nothing feminine about Brenda...I mean there was *nothing* feminine. She walked like a guy. Sat with her legs apart. She talked about guy things, didn't give a crap about cleaning house, getting married, wearing makeup. We both wanted to play with guys, build forts and have snowball fights and play army" (Colapinto, 2001: 57, emphasis in original). As this quotation suggests, being male or female involves not just biology but also certain

Definitions of "male" and "female" traits vary across societies. For example, the ceremonial dress of male Wodaabe nomads in Niger may appear "feminine" by conventional North American standards.

"masculine" and "feminine" feelings, attitudes, and behaviours. Accordingly, sociologists distinguish biological sex from sociological **gender.** Your gender is composed of the feelings, attitudes, and behaviours typically associated with being male or female. **Gender identity** is your identification with, or sense of belonging to, a particular sex—biologically, psychologically, and socially. When you behave according to widely shared expectations about how males or females are supposed to act, you adopt a **gender role.**

Contrary to first impressions, the case of Bruce/Brenda/David suggests that, unlike sex, gender is not solely determined by biology. Research suggests that babies first develop a vague sense of being a boy or a girl at about the age of one. They develop a full-blown sense of gender identity between the ages of two and three (Blum, 1997). It is likely that by the time the surgery was performed to transform Bruce into Brenda, the child had already developed a male gender identity. He had, after all, been raised as a boy by his parents and treated as a boy by his brother for the first 17 months of his life. He had presumably seen boys behaving differently from girls on TV and in storybooks. Despite his parents' efforts to reinforce his identity as a girl, these early childhood lessons and the continuing role model of masculinity provided by his twin brother may have been influential.

Although some analysts maintain that the now famous twin study was doomed to fail from the outset (Colapinto, 2001: xvii), others remain convinced that if gender reassignment occurs before the age of 18 months, it can be "successful" (Crieghton and Mihto, 2001; Lightfoot-Klein et al., 2000). However, what criteria should we use in proclaiming the success or failure of such attempts? Recall that early pronouncements of the "successful" reassignment of Bruce/Brenda directed attention to the child exhibiting stereotypical "feminine" behaviour and attitudes. Later reports on the "failure" of the reassignment emphasized the twin's "masculine" behaviour and attitudes. It seems that in both cases, we witness the power of stereotyped attitudes, behaviours, and physical appearances to affect our understanding of the connection between gender and sex.

## Chapter Plan

The first half of this chapter helps you better understand what makes us male or female. We first outline two competing theories of gender differences. The first theory argues that gender is inherent in our biological makeup and is merely reinforced by society. The second argues that gender is constructed mainly by social influences. For reasons outlined below, we side with the second viewpoint.

After establishing our theoretical approach, we examine how people learn gender roles during socialization in the family and at school. Then we show how everyday social interactions and advertising reinforce gender roles.

We next discuss how members of society enforce **heterosexuality**—the preference for members of the opposite sex as sexual partners. For reasons that are still poorly understood, some people resist and even reject the gender roles that are assigned to them because of their biological sex. When this occurs, negative sanctions are often applied to force them to conform or to punish them for their deviance. Members of society are often eager to use emotional and physical violence to enforce conventional gender roles.

The second half of the chapter examines one of the chief consequences of people learning conventional gender roles. Gender, as currently constructed, creates and maintains social inequality. We illustrate this in two ways. We first investigate why gender is associated with an earnings gap between women and men in the paid labour force. We then show how gender inequality encourages sexual harassment and sexual assault. In concluding our discussion of sexuality and gender, we discuss some social policies that sociologists have recommended to decrease gender inequality and improve women's safety.

# THEORIES OF GENDER

## Essentialism[1]

As just noted, most arguments about the origins of gender differences in human behaviour adopt one of two perspectives. Some analysts see gender differences as a reflection of naturally evolved dispositions. Sociologists call this perspective **essentialism** (Weeks, 2000). That is because it views gender as part of the nature or "essence" of one's biological makeup. Other analysts see gender differences as a reflection of the different social positions occupied by women and men. Sociologists call this perspective **social constructionism.** That is because it views gender as "constructed" by social structure and culture. We now summarize and criticize essentialism. We then turn to social constructionism.

### Freud

Sigmund Freud (1977 [1905]) offered an early and influential essentialist explanation of male–female differences. He believed that differences in male and female anatomy account for the development of distinct masculine and feminine gender roles.

According to Freud, children around the age of three begin to pay attention to their genitals. As a young boy becomes preoccupied with his penis, he unconsciously develops a fantasy of sexually possessing the most conspicuous female in his life: his mother. Soon, he begins to resent his father because only his father is allowed to possess the mother sexually. Because he has seen his mother or another girl naked, the boy also develops anxiety that his father will castrate him for desiring his mother.[2] To resolve this fear, the boy represses his feelings for his mother. That is, he stores them in the unconscious part of his personality. In due course, this repression allows him to begin identifying with his father. This leads to the development of a strong, independent masculine personality.

In contrast, the young girl begins to develop a feminine personality when she realizes she lacks a penis. According to Freud:

> [girls] who notice the penis of a brother or playmate, strikingly visible and of large proportions, at once recognize it as the superior counterpart of their own small and inconspicuous organ, and from that time forward fall a victim to envy for the penis . . . She has seen it and knows that she is without it and wants to have it. (quoted in Steinem, 1994: 50)

Due to her "penis envy," the young girl soon develops a sense of inferiority, according to Freud. She also grows angry with her mother, who, she naively thinks, is responsible for cutting off the penis she must have once had. She rejects her mother and develops an unconscious sexual desire for her father. Eventually, however, realizing she will never have a penis, the girl comes to identify with her mother. This is a way of vicariously acquiring her father's penis in Freud's view. In the "normal" development of a mature woman, the girl's wish to have a penis is transformed into a desire to have children. However, says Freud, since women are never able to resolve their penis envy completely, they are "naturally" immature and dependent on men. This dependence is evident from the "fact" that women can be fully sexually satisfied only by vaginally induced orgasm.[3] Thus, a host of gender differences in personality and behaviour follows from the anatomical sex differences that children observe around the age of three.

### Sociobiology and Evolutionary Psychology

For the past 25 years, sociobiologists and evolutionary psychologists have offered a second essentialist theory. We introduced this theory in Chapter 3, Culture. According to sociobiologists and evolutionary psychologists, all humans instinctively try to ensure that their genes are passed on to future generations. However, men and women develop different strategies to achieve this goal. A woman has a bigger investment than a man in ensuring the survival of their offspring, because she produces only a small number of eggs during her reproductive life and, at most, can give birth to about 20 children. It is therefore in a woman's best interest to maintain primary responsibility for her genetic children and to look around for the best mate with whom to intermix her precious eggs. He is the man who can best help support the children after birth. In contrast, most men can produce as many as a billion sperm in a single ejaculation and this number can be replicated within 24 to 48 hours (Saxton, 1990: 94–5). Thus, a man increases the chance his and only his genes will be passed on to future generations if he is promiscuous yet jealously possessive of his partners. Moreover, since men compete with other men for sexual access to women, men evolve competitive and aggressive dispositions that include physical violence (DeSteno and Salovey, 2001). Women, says one evolutionary psychologist, are greedy for money, while men want casual sex with women, treat women's bodies as their property, and react violently to women who incite male sexual jealousy. These are "universal features of our evolved selves" that contribute to the survival of the human species (Buss, 2000). Thus, from the point of view of sociobiology and evolutionary psychology, gender differences in behaviour are based in biological differences between women and men.

## A Critique of Essentialism

Sociologists have lodged four main criticisms against essentialist arguments such as those of Freud and the sociobiologists and evolutionary psychologists.

*First, essentialists ignore the historical and cultural variability of gender and sexuality.* There are wide variations from one society to the next in the level of gender inequality, the rate of male violence against women, the criteria used for mate selection, and all other gender differences that appear universal to the essentialists. This variability deflates the idea that biological constants account for innate behavioural differences between women and men. Three examples help illustrate this point:

1. Women's tendency to stress the good provider role in selecting male partners, and men's tendency to stress women's domestic skills, decrease in societies with low levels of gender inequality (Eagley and Wood, 1999). Thus, by changing the level of gender inequality in society, you can change male and female criteria for mate selection.
2. Social situations involving competition and threat stimulate production of the hormone testosterone in women, causing them to act more aggressively. This happens when women become, say, corporate lawyers or police officers (Blum, 1997: 158–88). Thus, by allowing women to take jobs that stress competition and threat, you can change their level of aggressiveness.[4]
3. Gender differences are declining rapidly. Literally hundreds of studies conducted mainly in the United States and Canada show that women are developing traits that were traditionally considered masculine. Women have become more assertive, competitive, independent, and analytical in the last three decades (Biegler, 1999; Twenge, 1997). They play more aggressive sports, choose more math and science courses, do better in standardized tests, take more nontraditional jobs, and earn more money than they used to. One recent study found that, if current trends continue, the difference between male and female math and science scores will disappear in 30 to 40 years (Duffy, Gunther, and Walters, 1997; Nowell and Hedges, 1998: 210). In what may be a first, standardized math tests administered in Ontario in 1998 and 1999 to all grade three and grade six students found that girls outscored boys by 3 percent in grade three and by 2 percent in grade six (Galt, 1999). It seems that by making school curricula and teaching methods less sexist, increasing opportunities for women to pursue higher education and obtain a wider variety of jobs, and so forth, a whole range of gender differences starts to disappear. As these examples show, then, gender differences are not inherent in men and women. They vary with social conditions.

*The second problem with essentialism is that it tends to generalize from the average, ignoring variations within gender groups.* On average, women and men do differ in some respects. For example, one of the best-documented gender differences is that men are on average more verbally and physically aggressive than women. However, when sociobiologists and evolutionary psychologists say that men are *inherently* more aggressive than women, they make it seem as if this is true of all men and all women. As Figure 9.1 shows, it is not. When trained researchers measure verbal or physical aggressiveness, scores vary widely within gender groups. Aggressiveness is distributed so that there is considerable overlap between women and men. Thus, many women are more aggressive than the average man and many men are less aggressive than the average woman.

*Third, no evidence directly supports the essentialists' major claims.* Sociobiologists and evolutionary psychologists have not identified any of the genes that, they claim, cause male jealousy, female nurturance, the unequal division of labour between men and women, and so forth. They are simply assumed to exist. Similarly, Freudians have not collected any experimental or survey data that show boys are more independent than girls because of their emotional reactions to the discovery of their sex organs.

*Finally, essentialists' explanations for gender differences ignore the role of power.* Sociobiologists and evolutionary psychologists assume that existing behaviour patterns help ensure the survival of the species. However, their assumption overlooks the fact that men are usually in a position of greater power and authority than women. Behavioural differences between women and men therefore may result not from any biological imperative but from men being in a position to establish their preferences over the interests of women (see Box 9.1). Indeed, from this point of view, sociobiology and evolutionary psychology may be seen as examples of the exercise of male power, that is, as a rationalization for male domination and sexual aggression. Much the same may be said of Freud's interpretation. *Must* young girls define themselves in relation to young boys by focusing on their lack of a penis? There is no reason why young girls' sexual self-definitions cannot focus positively on their own reproductive organs, including their unique ability to bear children. Freud simply assumes that men are superior to women and then invents a speculative theory that justifies gender differences.

## Social Constructionism

Social constructionism is the main alternative to essentialism. We illustrate social constructionism by first considering how boys and girls learn masculine and feminine roles in the family and at school. We then show how gender roles are maintained in the course of everyday social interaction and through advertising in the mass media. We begin our discussion of social constructionism by examining the effect of a North American icon—the Barbie doll—on girls' gender roles.

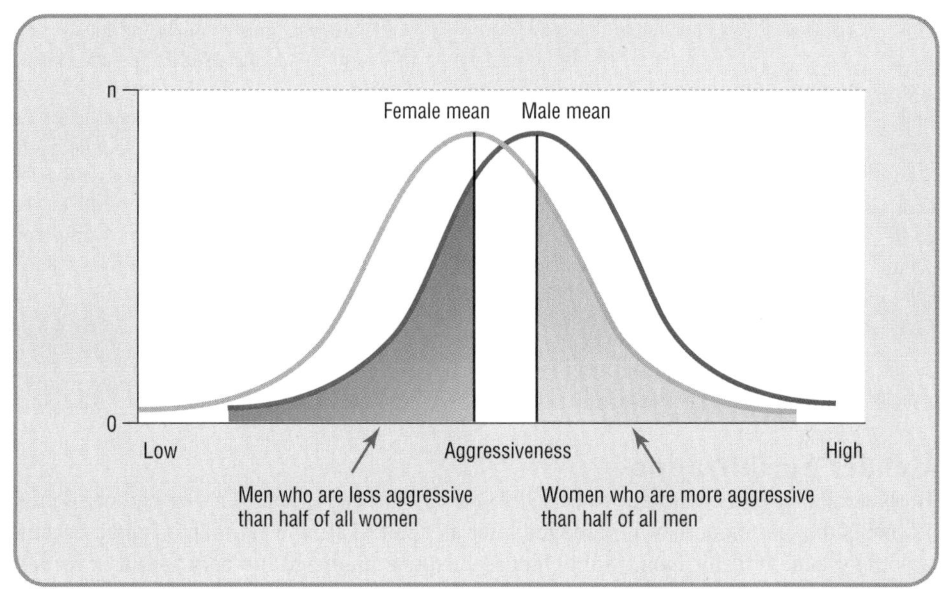


**✦ FIGURE 9.1 ✦**
**The Distribution of Aggressiveness among Men and Women**

BOX 9.1
SOCIOLOGY AT THE MOVIES

### *THE HANDMAID'S TALE* (1990)

Handmaid Offred (played by Natasha Richardson) receives instruction on the virtues of serving as a baby machine in *The Handmaid's Tale* (1990).

Based on Canadian novelist Margaret Atwood's book of the same name, *The Handmaid's Tale* is set in Gilead, a republic that has replaced what was once the United States. The women of Gilead are having fewer babies than are needed to maintain the country's population. In response to this national emergency, the government has decreed fertile women to be state property. They are forced to act as "handmaids" for couples who cannot have children because of the wife's infertility. Handmaids are valuable only because they have healthy ovaries and can be impregnated. They are subjected to monthly examinations to ensure that they remain fertile. Those who become pregnant are praised and applauded by other women in the streets of Gilead. Those who do not face torture, banishment, or death. All handmaids are called by the first name of the couple's husband preceded by "of." Therefore, if the husband's name is Fred, the handmaid's name is Offred, signifying that she is the property *of Fred*.

*A Handmaid's Tale* is the story of one Offred, played by Natasha Richardson. She is the handmaid to the Commander (played by Robert Duvall) and his wife, Serena Joy (played by Faye Dunaway). The movie begins with Offred's forcible abduction by Gilead's soldiers, who murder her husband. Offred is then taken to an institution where, along with other women, she is resocialized as a handmaid. What do the handmaids learn? That the low birth rate in Gilead is God's vengeance for the sexual excesses and "anarchy" that once ran rampant. That the civil war that turned the United States into Gilead was a holy war, fought to restore God's rule on earth. That women's quest for equal rights with men was contrary to God's will. That the most sacred and noble duty of all handmaids is to bear children.

Soon after Offred arrives at the home of the Commander she must be impregnated. The act of intercourse between Offred and the Commander is governed by elaborate rules specifying, among other things, that Serena Joy must be present. Months pass. Offred does not become pregnant. During her monthly examination, Offred's doctor tells her that, since none of the Commander's previous handmaids became pregnant, it is likely the Commander is sterile. Startled, she asks whether men in Gilead are not also subject to medical exams and is informed that they are not. The doctor reminds her of the grave consequences she will face if she does not become pregnant and volunteers his services. He tells her that he has performed this service for many other handmaids. Offred refuses his offer, pointing out that the penalty for such acts is death.

Later, however, Serena Joy makes a similar suggestion to Offred, telling her that the family's trusted chauffeur, Nick (played by Aidan Quinn), would make a suitable candidate. Offred agrees. Offred and Nick have sex and establish an intimate relationship. She becomes pregnant with his child.

Offred, however, soon rebels against her role as a handmaid. She remembers and values the freedoms she used to enjoy. She becomes aware that the puritanical moral code imposed on Gilead's citizens does not apply to prominent citizens such as the Commander. While living in the Commander's home, Offred forms an association with another handmaid who is a member of a resistance movement. Acting on the orders of this movement, Offred kills the Commander. She escapes with Nick's help since he, it turns out, is also a member of the resistance.

This provocative movie is a cautionary tale, a reminder of what has been and what could be. Some North American feminists have criticized new reproductive technologies, especially surrogate motherhood, as a means by which men gain control over women's bodies, women's bodies are turned into commodities, and poor women are exploited by those who are well off (French, 1992; Nelson and Robinson, 2002: 379). Some members of the religious right in North America would like to restrict women's role in society to that of wives and mothers. We also have the recent example of the Taliban in Afghanistan, which did not even allow women to attend school so they could better serve men's needs. Is *The Handmaid's Tale* just science fiction or is it a mirror to the present and a warning about the future?

## Gender Socialization

Barbie dolls have been around since 1959. Based on the creation of a German cartoonist, Barbie is the first modern doll modelled after an adult. (Lili, the German original, became a pornographic doll for men.) Some industry experts predicted mothers would never buy dolls with breasts for their little girls. Were *they* wrong! Mattel now sells about 10 million

Barbies and 20 million accompanying outfits annually. The Barbie trademark is worth US$1 billion.

What do girls learn when they play with Barbie? The author of a Web site devoted to Barbie undoubtedly speaks for millions when she writes: "Barbie was more than a doll to me. She was a way of living: the Ideal Woman. When I played with her, I could make her do and be ANYTHING I wanted. Never before or since have I found such an ideal method of living vicariously through anyone or anything. And I don't believe I am alone. I am certain that most people have, in fact, lived their dreams with Barbie as the role player" (Elliott, 1995; see also Nicolaiedis, 1998; Turkel, 1998).

One dream that Barbie stimulates among many girls concerns body image. After all, Barbie is a scale model of a woman with a 40-18-32 figure (Hamilton, 1996: 197). Researchers who compared Barbie's gravity-defying proportions with the actual proportions of several representative groups of adult women concluded that the probability of this body shape was less than 1 in 100 000 (Norton et al., 1996). Ken's body shape is far more realistic at 1 in 50.

Nevertheless, for more than 40 years, Barbie has served as an identifiable symbol of stereotypical female beauty (Magro, 1997). Her pre-set Barbie Workout Scale registers a lithe 110 pounds. The closets of her (pink) house are jammed with outfits. Bathrooms, gyms, and beauty parlours feature prominently among the Barbie sets available. Her quest for physical perfection seems largely geared to the benefit of Ken, her "anatomically challenged boyfriend" (Nelson and Robinson, 2002: 131). When girls play with Barbie, they learn to want to be slim, blonde, shapely, and, implicitly, pleasing to men.

A comparable story, with competition and aggression as its theme, could be told about how boys' toys, such as GI Joe, teach stereotypical male roles. True, a movement to market more gender-neutral toys arose in the 1960s and 1970s. However, it has now been overtaken by the resumption of a strong tendency to market toys based on gender. As *The Wall Street Journal* pointed out, "gender-neutral is out, as more kids' marketers push single-sex products" (Bannon, 2000: B1). For example, in 2000, Toys "Я" Us unveiled a new store design that included a store directory featuring Boy's World and Girl's World. The Boy's World section listed action figures, sports collectibles, remote-controlled cars, Tonka trucks, boys' role-playing games, and walkie-talkies. The Girl's World section listed Barbie dolls, baby dolls, collectible horses, play kitchens, housekeeping toys, girls' dress-up, jewellery, cosmetics, and bath and body products.

Yet toys are only part of the story of gender socialization and hardly its first or final chapter. Early research reported that, from birth, infant boys and girls who are matched in length, weight, and general health are treated differently by parents—and by fathers, in particular. Girls tend to be identified as delicate, weak, beautiful, and cute, boys as strong, alert, and well coordinated (Rubin, Provenzano, and Lurra, 1974). Recent attempts to update and extend this investigation found that although parents' gender-stereotyped perceptions of newborns have declined, especially among fathers, they have not disappeared entirely (Fagot, Rodgers, and Leinbach, 2000; Gauvain et al., 2002; Karraker, Vogel, and Lake, 1995). When viewing videotape of a nine-month-old infant, adult experimental subjects tend to label its startled reaction to a stimulus as "anger" if the child has earlier been

A movement to market more gender-neutral toys emerged in the 1960s and 1970s. However, it has now been overtaken by the resumption of a strong tendency to market toys based on gender.

identified by the experimenters as a boy and as "fear" if it has earlier been identified as a girl, *whatever the infant's actual sex* (Condry and Condry, 1976; see also Martin, 1999).

Parents, and especially fathers, are more likely to encourage their sons to engage in boisterous and competitive play and discourage their daughters from doing likewise. In general, parents tend to encourage girls to engage in cooperative, role-playing games (Fagot, Rodgers, and Leinbach, 2000; Gauvain et al., 2002; Parke, 2001, 2002). These different play patterns lead to the heightened development of verbal and emotional skills among girls, and to more concern with winning and the establishment of hierarchy among boys (Tannen, 1990). Boys are more likely than girls to be praised for assertiveness, and girls are more likely than boys to be rewarded for compliance (Kerig, Cowan, and Cowan, 1993). Given this early socialization, it seems perfectly "natural" that boys' toys stress aggression, competition, spatial manipulation, and outdoor activities, while girls' toys stress nurturing, physical attractiveness, and indoor activities (Hughes, 1995 [1991]). Still, what seems natural must be continuously socially reinforced. Presented with a choice between playing with a tool set and a dish set, preschool boys are about as likely to choose one as the other—unless the dish set is presented as a girl's toy and they think their fathers would view playing with it as "bad." Then, they tend to pick the tool set (Raag and Rackliff, 1998).

It would take someone who has spent very little time in the company of children to think they are passive objects of socialization. They are not. Parents, teachers, and other authority figures typically try to impose their ideas of appropriate gender behaviour on children, but children creatively interpret, negotiate, resist, and self-impose these ideas all the time. Gender, we might say, is something that is done, not just given (Messner, 2000; West and Zimmerman, 1987). This is nowhere more evident than in the way children play.

Consider the fourth- and fifth-grade classroom that sociologist Barrie Thorne (1993) observed. The teacher periodically asked the children to choose their own desks. With the exception of one girl, they always segregated *themselves* by gender. The teacher then drew upon this self-segregation in pitting the boys against the girls in spelling and math contests. These contests were marked by cross-gender antagonism and expression of within-gender solidarity. Similarly, when children played chasing games in the schoolyard, groups often *spontaneously* crystallized along gender lines. These games had special names, some of which, such as "chase and kiss," had clear sexual meanings. Provocation, physical contact, and avoidance were all sexually charged parts of the game.

Although Thorne found that contests, chasing games, and other activities often involved self-segregation of boys and girls, she observed many cases of boys and girls playing together. She also noticed quite a lot of "boundary crossing." Boundary crossing involves boys playing stereotypically girls' games and girls playing stereotypically boys' games. The most common form of boundary crossing involved girls who were skilled at specific sports that were central to the boys' world—sports such as soccer, baseball, and basketball. If girls demonstrated skill at these activities, boys often accepted them as participants. Finally, Thorne noticed occasions where boys and girls interacted without strain and without strong gender identities coming to the fore. For instance, activities requiring cooperation, such as a group radio show or art project, lessened attention to gender. Another situation that lessened strain between boys and girls, causing gender to recede in importance, occurred when adults organized mixed-gender encounters in the classroom and in physical education periods. On such occasions, adults legitimized cross-gender contact. Mixed-gender interaction was also more common in less public and crowded settings. Thus, boys and girls were more likely to play together and in a relaxed way in the relative privacy of their neighbourhoods. In contrast, in the schoolyard, where they were under the close scrutiny of their peers, gender segregation and antagonism were more evident.

In sum, Thorne's research makes two important contributions to our understanding of gender socialization. First, children are actively engaged in the process of constructing gender roles. They are not merely passive recipients of adult demands. Second, while schoolchildren tend to segregate themselves by gender, boundaries between boys and girls are sometimes fluid and sometimes rigid, depending on social circumstances. In other words, the content of children's gendered activities is by no means fixed.

In her research on schoolchildren, sociologist Barrie Thorne noticed quite a lot of "boundary crossing" between boys and girls. Most commonly, boys accepted girls as participants in soccer, baseball, and basketball games if girls demonstrated skill at these sports.

This is not to suggest that adults have no gender demands and expectations. They do, and their demands and expectations contribute importantly to gender socialization. For instance, schoolteachers and guidance counsellors may still expect boys to do better in the sciences and math and girls to achieve higher marks in English (Lips, 1999). Parents may also reinforce these stereotypes in their evaluation of different activities (Eccles, Jacobs, and Harold, 1990). Although not all studies comparing mixed- and single-sex schools suggest that girls do much better in the latter (Bornholt, 2001; Jackson and Smith, 2000), many do. Sharlene Hesse-Biber and Gregg Lee Carter (2000: 99–100) summarize this body of research and are worth quoting at length:

> [In girls-only schools], female cognitive development is greater; female occupational aspirations and their ultimate attainment are increased; female self-confidence and self-esteem are magnified. Moreover, . . . females receive better treatment in the classroom; they are more likely to be encouraged to explore—and to have access to—wider curriculum opportunities; and teachers have greater respect for their work. Finally, females attending single-sex schools have . . . more egalitarian attitudes towards the role of women in society than do their counterparts in mixed-sex schools.... Single-sex schools accrue these benefits for girls for a variety of reasons . . . : (1) a diminished emphasis on "youth culture," which centers on athletics, social life, physical attractiveness, heterosexual popularity, and negative attitudes toward academics; (2) the provision of more successful same-sex role models (the top students in all subjects and all extracurricular activities [are] girls); (3) a reduction in sex bias in teacher-student interaction (there are [no] boys around [who] can be "favoured"); and (4) elimination of sex stereotypes in peer interaction (generally, cross-sex peer interaction in school involves male dominance, male leadership, and, often, sexual harassment).

Adolescents must usually start choosing courses in school by the age of 14 or 15. By then, their **gender ideologies** are well formed. Gender ideologies are sets of interrelated ideas about what constitutes appropriate masculine and feminine roles and behaviour. One aspect of gender ideology becomes especially important around grades 9 and 10: adolescents' ideas about whether, as adults, they will focus mainly on the home, paid work, or a combination of the two. Adolescents usually make course choices with gender ideologies in mind. Boys are strongly inclined to consider only their careers in making course choices. Most girls are inclined to consider both home responsibilities and careers, although a minority considers only home responsibilities and another minority considers only careers. As a result, boys tend to choose career-oriented courses, particularly in math and sciences, more often than girls (Eccles et al., 1999). In college and university, the pattern is accentuated. In 1997–98, women accounted for 29 percent of all Canadian university students in mathematics and the physical sciences, and 22 percent of those in engineering and the applied sciences (Normand, 2000: 87).

Young women tend to choose courses that lead to lower-paying jobs because they expect to devote a large part of their lives to child rearing and housework (Eccles et al., 1999). When Canadian undergraduates (821 women and 535 men) were asked to identify their preference, 53 percent of the women but only 6 percent of the men selected "graduation, full-time work, marriage, children, stop working at least until youngest child is in school, then pursue a full-time job" as their preferred lifestyle sequence (Schroeder, Blood, and Maluso, 1993).

These choices sharply restrict women's career opportunities and earnings in science and business. In 1996, women accounted for three out of every five people working full-year, full-time in the 25 lowest-paying occupations in Canada. The average earnings of women in these occupations was $16 674 (Statistics Canada, 1998a). We examine the wage gap between women and men in depth in the second half of this chapter.

## The Mass Media and Body Image

The social construction of gender does not stop at the school steps. Outside school, children, adolescents, and adults continue to negotiate gender roles as they interact with the mass media. If you systematically observe the roles played by women and men in television, movies, magazines, music videos, TV commercials, and print media advertisements, you will probably discover a pattern noted by sociologists since the 1970s. Women will more frequently be seen cleaning house, taking care of children, modelling clothes, and acting as objects of male desire (Signorielli, 1998). Men will more frequently be seen in aggressive, action-oriented, and authoritative roles. The effect of these messages on viewers is much the same as that of the Disney movies and Harlequin romances we discussed in Chapter 4, Socialization. They reinforce the normality of traditional gender roles. As we will now see, many people even try to shape their bodies after the body images portrayed in the mass media.

The human body has always served as a sort of personal billboard that advertises gender. However, historian Joan Jacobs Brumberg (1997) makes a good case for the view that the importance of body image to our self-definition has grown over the past century. Just listen to the difference in emphasis on the body in the diary resolutions of two typical white, middle-class North American girls, separated by a mere 90 years. From 1892: "Resolved, not to talk about myself or feelings. To think before speaking. To work seriously. To be self restrained in conversation and actions. Not to let my thoughts wander. To be dignified. Interest myself more in others." From 1982: "I will try to make myself better in any way I possibly can with the help of my budget and baby-sitting money. I will lose weight, get new lenses, already got new haircut, good makeup, new clothes and accessories" (quoted in Brumberg, 1997: xxi).

As body image became more important for one's self-definition in the course of the twentieth century, the ideal body image became thinner, especially for women. For example, although Miss America beauty pageant winners became only somewhat taller between 1922 and 1999, they became much thinner (Curran, 2000). As one eating disorders expert observed, "Beauty pageants, like the rest of our media-driven culture, give young women in particular a message, over and over again, that it's exceedingly important to be thin to be considered successful and attractive" (Harry Brandt, as quoted in Curran, 2000).[5]

Why did body image become more important to people's self-definition during the twentieth century? Why was slimness stressed? Part of the answer to both questions is that more North Americans grew overweight as their lifestyles became more sedentary. As they became better educated, they also grew increasingly aware of the health problems associated with being overweight. The desire to slim down was, then, partly a reaction to bulking up. But that is not the whole story. The rake-thin models who populate modern ads are not promoting good health. They are promoting an extreme body shape that is virtually unattainable for most people. Supermodel Elle MacPherson ("The Body") not only has 44-inch legs, but also measurements of 36-24-35 (a hip to waist ratio of .69) (Tovee et al., 1997).

If models are "statistical rarities who can combine tall lean bodies with curves" (Etcoff, 1999: 193), dieting cannot bring about a model's shape. Nevertheless, Canadians spent $130 million on weight management products in 1999 (Ash, 2001: 51). Ads for industries that profit from our cultural obsession with weight bombard us daily with the message that only certain body types are appealing and acceptable.

Beauty pageant winners have become significantly thinner in recent decades.

Survey data show just how widespread dissatisfaction with our bodies is and how important a role the mass media play in generating our discomfort. For example, a 1997 survey of North American university graduates showed that 56 percent of women and 43 percent of men were dissatisfied with their overall appearance (Garner, 1997). Only 3 percent of the dissatisfied women, but 22 percent of the dissatisfied men, wanted to gain weight. This reflects the greater desire of men for muscular, stereotypically male physiques. Most of the dissatisfied men, and even more of the dissatisfied women (89 percent), wanted to lose weight. This reflects the general societal push toward slimness and its greater effect on women. According to the 1996–1997 National Population Health Survey, even though Canadian women are almost five times more likely than Canadian

The low-cal and diet food industry promotes an ideal of slimness that is often impossible to attain and that generates widespread body dissatisfaction.

men to be *underweight* (14 percent and 3 percent, respectively), they are more likely to report recent attempts to lose weight: "This desire to lose weight extended to many women who were already within the healthy weight range" (Health Canada, 1999b: 118).

Figure 9.2 reveals gender differences in body ideals in a different way. It compares North American women's and men's attitudes toward their stomachs. It also compares women's attitudes toward their breasts with men's attitudes toward their chests. It shows, first, that women are more concerned about their stomachs than men are. Second, it shows that men are more concerned about their chests than women are about their breasts. Clearly, then, people's body ideals are influenced by their gender. Note also that Figure 9.2 shows trends over time. North Americans' anxiety about their bodies increased substantially between 1972 and 1997.

Table 9.1 suggests that advertising is highly influential in creating anxiety and insecurity about appearance, and particularly about body weight. We see that in 1997 nearly 30 percent of North American women compared themselves with the fashion models they saw in advertisements, felt insecure about their own appearance, and wanted to lose weight as a result. Among women who were dissatisfied with their appearance, the percentages were much larger, with about 45 percent making comparisons with fashion models and two-thirds feeling insecure and wanting to lose weight. It seems safe to conclude that fashion models stimulate body dissatisfaction among many North American women.

Body dissatisfaction, in turn, motivates many women to diet. Because of anxiety about their weight, 84 percent of North American women said they had dieted in the 1997 survey. The comparable figure for men was 54 percent. Just how important is it for people to achieve their weight goals? According to the survey, it's a life or death issue: 24 percent of

✦ **FIGURE 9.2** ✦
**Body Dissatisfaction, North America, 1972–1997 (in percent, $n$ = 4000)**

Source: Garner (1997).

*Note:* The *n* of 4000 refers to the 1997 survey only. The number of respondents in the earlier surveys was not given.

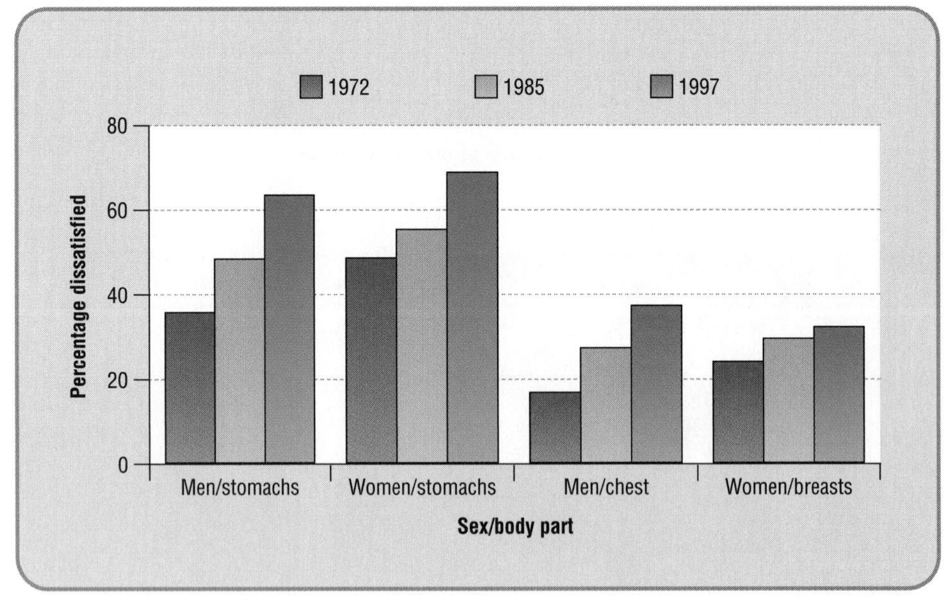


✦ **TABLE 9.1** ✦
**The Influence of Fashion Models on Feelings about Appearance, North America, 1997 (in percent; $n$ = 4000)**

Source: Adapted from Garner (1997).

| | Men | Women | Extremely Dissatisfied Women |
|---|---|---|---|
| *I always or often:* | | | |
| Compare myself with models in magazines | 12 | 27 | 43 |
| Carefully study the shape of models | 19 | 28 | 47 |
| *Very thin or muscular models make me:* | | | |
| Feel insecure about my weight | 15 | 29 | 67 |
| Want to lose weight | 18 | 30 | 67 |

women and 17 percent of men said they would willingly trade more than three years of their lives to achieve their weight goals.

Body dissatisfaction prompts some people to take dangerous and even life-threatening measures to reduce their size. In the 1997 survey, 50 percent of female smokers and 30 percent of male smokers said they smoke to control their weight. Other surveys suggest that between 1 percent and 5 percent of North American women suffer from anorexia nervosa (characterized by weight loss, excessive exercise, food aversion, distorted body image, and an intense and irrational fear of body fat and weight gain). About the same percentage of North American female university students suffer from bulimia, characterized by cycles of binge eating and purging (through self-induced vomiting and/or the use of laxatives, purgatives, or diuretics). For university men, the prevalence of bulimia is between 0.2 and 1.5 percent (Averett and Korenman, 1996: 305–6).

## Male–Female Interaction

The gender roles children learn in their families, at school, and through the mass media form the basis of their social interaction as adults. For instance, by playing team sports, boys tend to learn that social interaction is most often about competition, conflict, self-sufficiency, and hierarchical relationships (leaders versus the led). They understand the importance of taking centre stage and boasting about their talents (Messner, 1995 [1989]). Since many of the most popular video games for boys exclude female characters (*Game Boy* wasn't named *Game Boy* for nothing!), use women as sex objects, or involve violence against women, they reinforce some of the most unsavoury lessons of traditional gender socialization (Dietz, 1998). On the other hand, by playing with dolls and baking sets, girls tend to learn that social interaction is most often about maintaining cordial relationships, avoiding conflict, and resolving differences of opinion through negotiation (Subrahmanyam and Greenfield, 1998). They are informed of the importance of giving advice and not promoting themselves or being bossy.[6]

Because of these early socialization patterns, misunderstandings between men and women are common. A stereotypical example: Harold is driving around lost. However, he refuses to ask for directions because doing so would amount to an admission of inadequacy and therefore a loss of status. Meanwhile, it seems perfectly "natural" to Sybil to want to share information, so she urges Harold to ask for directions. The result: conflict between Harold and Sybil (Tannen, 1990: 62).

Gender-specific interaction styles also have serious implications for who gets heard and who gets credit at work. Here are some examples uncovered by Deborah Tannen's research (1994a: 132–59):

- A female office manager doesn't want to seem bossy or arrogant. She is eager to preserve consensus among her co-workers. So she spends a good deal of time soliciting their opinions before making an important decision. She asks questions, listens attentively, and offers suggestions. She then decides. But her boss perceives her approach as indecisive and incompetent. He wants to recruit leaders for upper-management positions, so he overlooks the woman and selects an assertive man for a senior job that just opened up.
- Male managers are inclined to say "I" in many situations where female managers are inclined to say "we"—as in "I'm hiring a new manager and I'm going to put him in charge of my marketing division" or "This is what I've come up with on the Lakehill deal." This sort of phrasing draws attention to one's personal accomplishments. In contrast, Tannen heard a female manager talking about what "we" had done, when in fact she had done all the work alone. This sort of phrasing camouflages women's accomplishments.

The contrasting interaction styles illustrated above can result in female managers not getting credit for competent performance. That may be why women sometimes complain about a **glass ceiling,** a social barrier that makes it difficult for them to rise to the top level of management. As we will soon see, factors other than interaction styles, such as outright discrimination and women's generally greater commitment to family responsibilities, also support the glass ceiling. Yet gender differences in interaction styles play an independent role in constraining women's career progress.

## Homosexuality

The preceding discussion outlines some powerful social forces that push us to define ourselves as conventionally masculine or feminine in behaviour and appearance. For most people, gender socialization by the family, the school, and the mass media is compelling, and sustained by daily interactions. A minority of people, however, resists conventional gender roles. For example, the term **transgendered** is used to refer to those who "transgress societal gender norms...defy rigid, bipolar gender constructions, and...present a breaking and/or blurring of cultural/stereotypical gender roles" ("Defining a Common Language," n.d.). The terms *transgender, transgendered,* and *transgenderist* are used interchangeably to convey "rising above" traditional gender roles (Cole et al., 2000: 151). About 1 in every 5000 to 10 000 people in North America is transgendered. Some transgendered people are **transsexuals.** Transsexuals are individuals who want to alter their gender by changing their appearance or resorting to medical intervention. Transsexuals believe they were born with the "wrong" body. They identify with, and want to live fully as, members of the "opposite" sex. They often take the lengthy and painful path to a sex change operation. About 1 in every 30 000 people in North America is a transsexual (Nolen, 1999). **Homosexuals** are people who prefer sexual partners of the same sex, and **bisexuals** are people who enjoy sexual partners of either sex. People usually call homosexual men *gay* and homosexual women *lesbians*. The most comprehensive survey of sexuality conducted in North America reports that 2.8 percent of American men and 1.4 percent of American women think of themselves as homosexual or bisexual. However, 10.1 percent of men and 8.6 percent of women think of themselves as homosexual or bisexual, *or* have had some same-sex experience or desire (see Table 9.2; Laumann et al., 1994: 299). In 2000, about 6 percent of Torontonians identified themselves as homosexual or bisexual ("Homosexuality and Bisexuality," 2000). Due to widespread animosity toward homosexuals, some people who have wanted or engaged in same-sex acts do not identify themselves as gay, lesbian, or bisexual (Flowers and Buston, 2001; Herdt, 2001).

Homosexuality has existed in every society. Some societies, such as ancient Greece, have encouraged it. More frequently, however, homosexual acts have been forbidden. In both the past and present, most laws prohibiting homosexual behaviour have targeted male rather than female homosexuality (Brown, 2000). For example, a survey designed to investigate laws and attitudes in relation to homosexuality in 210 countries throughout the world (excluding the United States) reported that female homosexuality was currently legal in 49 countries and illegal in 44 countries. In the laws of 98 countries, female homosexuality was not mentioned. Male homosexuality was legal in 58 countries and illegal in 84 countries. Only 49 countries excluded mention of male homosexuality (*ILGA Annual Report 1996–1997*). Homosexuals were not identified as a distinct "category" of people until the 1860s, when the term *homosexuality* was coined. The term *lesbian* is of even more recent vintage.

✦ **TABLE 9.2** ✦

**Homosexuality in the United States, 1992 (in percent; *n* = 3432)**

Source: Michael et al. (1994: 40).

| | Men | Women |
|---|---|---|
| Identified themselves as homosexual or bisexual | 2.8 | 1.4 |
| Had sex with person of same sex in past 12 months | 3.4 | 0.6 |
| Had sex with person of same sex at least once since puberty | 5.3 | 3.5 |
| Felt desire for sex with person of same sex | 7.7 | 7.5 |
| Had some same-sex desire or experience or identified themselves as homosexual or bisexual | 10.1 | 8.6 |

We do not yet understand well why some individuals develop homosexual orientations. Some scientists believe that the cause of homosexuality is mainly genetic (Hamer et al., 1993; Pillard and Bailey, 1998), others think it is chiefly hormonal, while still others point to life experiences during early childhood as the most important factor (Brannock and Chapman, 1990; Doell, 1995). According to the American Psychological Association, homosexuality "emerges for most people in early adolescence without any prior sexual experience...[it] is not changeable" (American Psychological Association, 1998). Similarly, many North Americans, as well as gay rights advocates, believe that sexual orientation is not a choice. A national U.S. study of homosexual men found that 90 percent believed they were born with their homosexual orientation and only 4 percent felt that environmental factors were the sole cause (Lever, 1994). Gallup poll findings also suggest that the general public increasingly supports the idea that homosexuality is not so much a "preference" as an innate orientation (13 percent in 1977 compared with 34 percent in 1999; Gallup Organization, 2000). Beliefs about the causes of homosexuality are also related to people's attitudes toward homosexuals. For example, one national poll reported that "those who believe homosexuals choose their sexual orientation are far less tolerant of gays and lesbians and more likely to conclude homosexuality should be illegal than those who think sexual orientation is not a matter of personal choice" (Rosin and Morin, 1999: 8).

In general, sociologists are less interested in the origins of homosexuality than in the way it is socially constructed, that is, in the wide variety of ways it is expressed and repressed (Plummer, 1995). It is important to note in this connection that homosexuality has become less of a stigma over the past century. Two factors are chiefly responsible for this, one scientific, the other political. In the twentieth century, sexologists—psychologists and physicians who study sexual practices scientifically—first recognized and stressed the wide diversity of existing sexual practices. Alfred Kinsey was among the pioneers in this field. He and his colleagues interviewed thousands of men and women. In the 1940s, they concluded that homosexual practices were so widespread that homosexuality could hardly be considered an illness affecting a tiny minority (Kinsey, Pomeroy, and Martin, 1948; Kinsey et al., 1953).

Sexologists, then, provided a scientific rationale for belief in the normality of sexual diversity. However, it was sexual minorities themselves who provided the social and political energy needed to legitimize sexual diversity among an increasingly large section of the public. Especially since the middle of the twentieth century, gays and lesbians have built large communities and subcultures, particularly in major urban areas such as Vancouver, Winnipeg, Toronto, and Montreal (Greenhill, 2001; Ingram, 2001). They have gone public

On April 1, 2001, the Netherlands recognized full and equal marriage rights for homosexual couples. Within hours, Dutch citizens were taking advantage of the new law. The Dutch law is part of a worldwide trend to legally recognize long-term same-sex unions.

with their lifestyles (Owen, 2001). They have organized demonstrations, parades, and political pressure groups to express their self-confidence and demand equal rights with the heterosexual majority (Goldie, 2001). This has done much to legitimize homosexuality and sexual diversity in general.

Yet opposition to people who don't conform to conventional gender roles remains strong at all stages of the life cycle. When you were a child, did you ever laugh at a girl who, say, liked to climb trees and play with toy trucks? Did you ever call such a girl a "tomboy"? When you were a child, did you ever tease a boy who, say, liked to bake with his sister's Easy Bake Oven? Did you ever call such a boy a "sissy"? If so, your behaviour was not unusual. Children are typically strict about enforcing conventional gender roles. They often apply sanctions against playmates who deviate from convention (Fineran, 2002; Tigert, 2001).

Among adults, such opposition is just as strong. What is your attitude today toward transgendered people, transsexuals, and homosexuals? Do you, for example, think relations between adults of the same sex are always, or almost always, wrong? If so, you are again not unusual. A national survey of Canadians conducted in 2000 found that almost one in three Canadians believed same-sex relations were "always wrong." Although discouraging to some, this figure represents an increase in Canada's acceptance of homosexuality over the past three decades; in 1975, for example, 63 percent of Canadians viewed homosexuality in this way (*Maclean's*, 2002: 12). Similarly, a survey conducted in 2000 found that "for the first time in the seven years it had been asking the question, less than half of Canadians [48 percent] opposed same-sex marriage" (Bricker and Greenspon, 2001: 267). A 2001 Gallup poll "found majority support for gay adoption, indicating another milestone" (Bricker and Greenspon, 2001: 267). Nevertheless, many Canadians still feel that homosexuals should not be entitled to the same rights and privileges as others in our society. For example, although the vast majority of Canadians now find it acceptable for gays to work as salespersons (93 percent), members of Parliament (86 percent), or physicians (82 percent), there is less support for their working as junior school teachers (67 percent) or members of the clergy (63 percent).

Antipathy to homosexuals is so strong among some people that they are prepared to back up their beliefs with force. A 1998 study of about 500 young adults in the San Francisco Bay area (probably the most sexually tolerant area in North America) found that 1 in 10 admitted physically attacking or threatening people they believed were homosexuals. Twenty-four percent reported engaging in anti-gay name-calling. Among male respondents, 18 percent reported acting in a violent or threatening way and 32 percent reported name-calling. In addition, a third of those who had *not* engaged in anti-gay aggression said they would do so if a homosexual flirted with, or propositioned, them (Franklin, 1998). Such actions appear to be widespread. A survey of more than 3000 high-school students found that students who reported having engaged in same-sex relations were more than three times as likely as others to report not going to school because they felt unsafe, more than twice as likely to report having been threatened or injured with a weapon at school, and significantly more likely to report that their property was deliberately damaged or stolen at school (Faulkner and Cranston, 1998; see also Bush and Sainz, 2001).

The consequences of homophobia can be devastating. For example, when 14-year-old Christian Hernandez told his best friend that he was gay, the consequences proved disastrous. "He told me he couldn't accept it," recalls Hernandez. "And he began to spread it around." For two years, the Niagara Falls student was teased and harassed almost daily. After school one day, a group of boys waited for him. Their leader told Hernandez that "he didn't accept faggots, that we brought AIDS into the world" and stabbed him in the neck with a knife. Hernandez required a week's hospitalization. When he told his parents what had happened, his father replied that he'd "rather have a dead son than a queer son" (Fisher, 1999).

However, it should be emphasized that not all victims of so-called "gay bashing" are homosexual or bisexual. Victims are targeted because the perpetrator *perceives* them as such. As a result, "no one is safe from hate crimes and...it is in everyone's interest to stop this epidemic of hate" (National Coalition of Anti-Violence Programs, 1998: 4).

Research suggests that some anti-gay crimes may result from repressed homosexual urges on the part of the aggressor (Adams, Wright, and Lohr, 1998). From this point of view, aggressors are "homophobic" or afraid of homosexuals because they cannot cope with their own, possibly subconscious, homosexual impulses. Their aggression is a way of acting out a denial of these impulses. However, although this psychological explanation may account for some anti-gay violence, it seems inadequate when set alongside the finding that fully half of all young male adults admitted to some form of anti-gay aggression in the San Francisco study cited above. An analysis of the motivations of these San Franciscans showed that some of them did commit assaults to prove their toughness and heterosexuality. Others committed assaults just to alleviate boredom and have fun. Still others believed they were defending themselves from aggressive sexual propositions. A fourth group acted violently because they wanted to punish homosexuals for what they perceived as moral transgressions (Franklin, 1998). It seems clear, then, that anti-gay violence is not just a question of abnormal psychology but a broad cultural problem with several sources.

On the other hand, anecdotal evidence suggests that opposition to anti-gay violence is also growing. The 2001 murder of Aaron Webster in Vancouver led to a public outcry. In the wake of his murder, NDP MP Svend Robinson introduced a Private Member's Bill that would include sexual orientation among the grounds protected by hate crimes legislation[7] (see Box 9.2). The 1999 movie *Boys Don't Cry* also raised awareness of the problem of violence directed against sexual minorities. The movie, for which Hilary Swank won the Best Actress Oscar®, tells the true story of Teena Brandon, a young woman with a sexual identity crisis. She wants a sex-change operation but can't afford one. So she decides to change her name to Brandon Teena and "pass" as a man. She soon develops an intimate relationship with a woman by the name of Lana Tisdel. Tisdel eventually learns that Teena is anatomically a female. However, when Lana's ex-boyfriend and his friend discover the truth about Teena, they beat, rape, and ultimately murder her. Teena's only transgression was that she wanted to be a man.

In sum, strong social and cultural forces lead us to distinguish men from women and heterosexuals from homosexuals. We learn these distinctions throughout the socialization process, and we continuously construct them anew in our daily interactions. Most people use positive and negative sanctions to ensure that others conform to conventional heterosexual gender roles. Some people resort to violence to enforce conformity and punish deviance.

Our presentation also suggests that the social construction of conventional gender roles helps create and maintain social inequality between women and men. In the remainder of this chapter, we examine the historical origins and some of the present-day consequences of gender inequality.

Especially since the middle of the twentieth century, gays and lesbians have gone public with their lifestyles. They have organized demonstrations, parades, and political pressure groups to express their self-confidence and demand equal rights with the heterosexual majority. This has done much to legitimize homosexuality and sexual diversity in general.

BOX 9.2
IT'S YOUR CHOICE

### HATE CRIME LAW AND HOMOPHOBIA

On November 17, 2001, Aaron Webster, a 42-year-old gay man, was beaten to death in a vicious attack in Vancouver. Tim Chisholm, Aaron's friend for 15 years, discovered Aaron's bloodied body, naked except for his hiking boots, in a parking lot in Stanley Park. Aaron had been bludgeoned with either a baseball bat or a pool cue by a group of three to four men. After phoning 911, Chisholm attempted CPR on his unconscious friend. It was no use. Aaron died in Chisholm's arms before help could arrive.

This brutal murder is believed to have been British Columbia's first fatal "gay bashing." At a memorial service for Webster that drew more than 1500 people, Vancouver Police Inspector Dave Jones identified Webster as the victim of "a hate crime, pure and simple" and pledged that the city's police department would "do everything in our power" to find the perpetrators and "bring them to justice" (Associated Press, 2001; Nagle, 2001).

One issue raised by Webster's death concerns the definition of hate crime (Wetzel, 2001). Hate crimes are criminal acts motivated by a victim's race, religion, or ethnicity. Under section 319 of the Canadian Criminal Code, the wilful promotion of hatred against any identifiable group (that is, "any section of the public distinguished by colour, race, religion, or ethnic group") and the advocating of genocide are crimes punishable by up to two years imprisonment. In 1999, following the gay bashing of a student in Fredericton, Justice Minister Anne McLellan announced that she would introduce amendments to protect lesbians and gays from hate crimes. She did not do so. Following Webster's murder, MP Svend Robinson introduced a Private Member's Bill that sought to include sexual orientation among the grounds protected by hate crimes legislation.

If hate motivates a crime, Canadian law requires that the perpetrator be punished more severely than otherwise. Under section 718.2 of the Canadian Criminal Code, "evidence that [an offence] was motivated by bias, prejudice or hate based on race, national or ethnic origin, colour, religion, sex, age, mental or physical disability, sexual orientation or any other similar factor" is to be considered an aggravating circumstance only in sentencing convicted offenders. For example, assaulting a person during an argument generally carries a lighter punishment than assaulting a person because he or she is gay or Jewish or black. However, despite this provision in law, "gay-bashers are often able to rely on the discredited 'homosexual panic' defence, claiming they were justified in committing murder because the victim 'came on' to them" (EGALE, 2001).

Do you think crimes motivated by the victim's sexual orientation are the same as crimes motivated by the victim's race, religion, or ethnicity? If so, why? If not, why not? Do you think crimes motivated by the perceived sexual orientation of the victim should be included in the legal definition of hate crime? If so, why? If not, why not?

## GENDER INEQUALITY

### The Origins of Gender Inequality

Contrary to what essentialists say, men have not always enjoyed much more power and authority than women. Substantial inequality between women and men has existed for only about 6000 years. It was socially constructed. Three major socio-historical processes account for the growth of gender inequality. Let us briefly consider each of them.

### Long-Distance Warfare and Conquest

The anthropological record suggests that women and men were about equal in status in nomadic hunting-and-gathering societies, the dominant form of society for 90 percent of human history. Rough gender equality was based on the fact that women produced a substantial amount of the band's food, up to 80 percent in some cases (see Chapter 12, Families). The archeological record from "Old Europe" tells a similar story. Old Europe is a region stretching roughly from Poland in the north to the Mediterranean island of Crete in the south, and from Switzerland in the west to Bulgaria in the east (see Figure 9.3). Between 7000 and 3500 BCE, men and women enjoyed approximately equal status throughout the region. In fact, the religions of the region gave primacy to fertility and creator goddesses. Kinship was traced through the mother's side of the family. Then, sometime between 4300 and 4200 BCE, all this began to change. Old Europe was invaded by successive waves of warring peoples from the Asiatic and European northeast (the Kur-

Women's domestic role was idealized in the nineteenth century.

gans) and the deserts to the south (the Semites). Both the Kurgan and Semitic civilizations were based on a steeply hierarchical social structure in which men were dominant. Their religions gave primacy to male warrior gods. They acquired property and slaves by conquering other peoples and imposed their religions on the vanquished. They eliminated, or at least downgraded, goddesses as divine powers. God became a male who willed that men

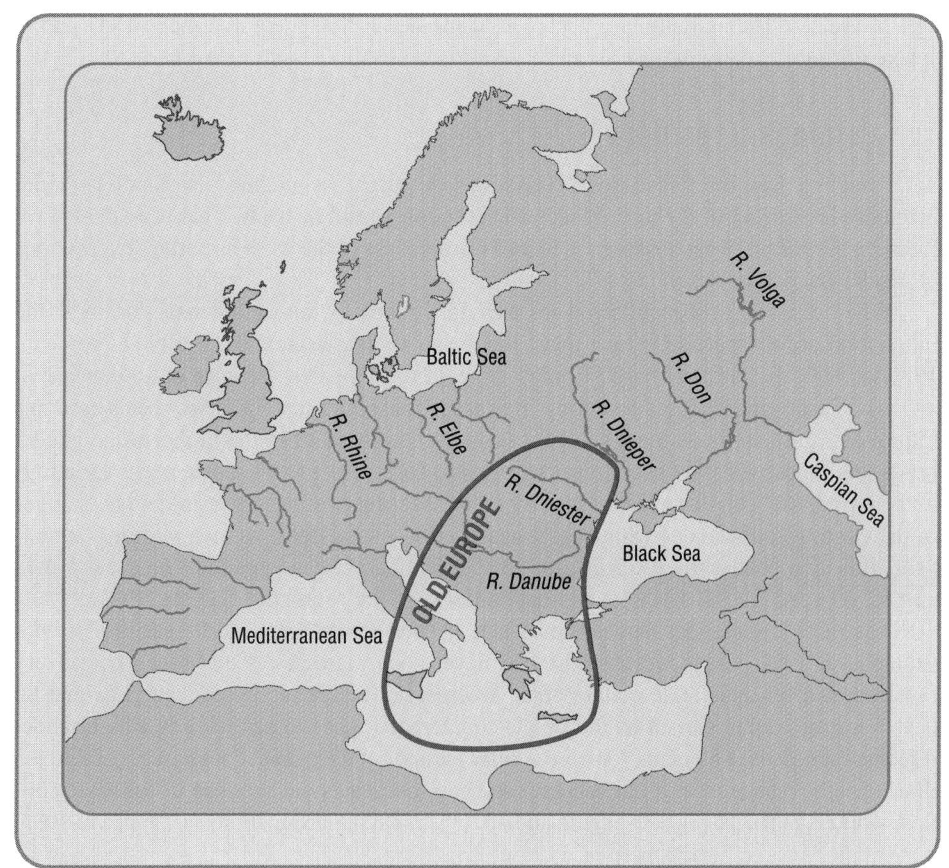


✦ **FIGURE 9.3** ✦
**Old Europe**

Source: Gimbutas (1982: 16).

should rule women. Laws reinforced women's sexual, economic, and political subjugation to men. Traditional Judaism, Christianity, and Islam all embody ideas of male dominance, and they all derive from the tribes that conquered Old Europe in the fifth millennium BCE (Eisler, 1995 [1987]; see also Lerner, 1986).

### Plow Agriculture

Long-distance warfare and conquest catered to men's strengths and so greatly enhanced male power and authority. Large-scale farming using plows harnessed to animals had much the same effect. Plow agriculture originated in the Middle East around 5000 years ago. It required that strong adults remain in the fields all day for much of the year. It also reinforced the principle of private ownership of land. Since men were on average stronger than women, and since women were restricted in their activities by pregnancy, nursing, and childbirth, plow agriculture made men more powerful socially. Thus, men owned land and ownership was passed from father to the eldest son (Coontz and Henderson, 1986).

### The Separation of Public and Private Spheres

In the agricultural era, economic production was organized around the household. Men may have worked apart from women in the fields, but the fields were still part of the *family* farm. In contrast, during the early phase of industrialization, men's work moved out of the household and into the factory and the office. Most men became wage or salary workers. Some men assumed decision-making roles in economic and political institutions. Yet while men went public, women who could afford to do so remained in the domestic or private sphere. The idea soon developed that this was a natural division of labour. This idea persisted until the second half of the twentieth century, when a variety of social circumstances, ranging from the introduction of the birth control pill to women's demands for entry into higher education, finally allowed women to enter the public sphere in large numbers.

So we see that, according to social constructionists, gender inequality derives not from any inherent biological features of men and women but from three main socio-historical circumstances: the arrival of long-distance warfare and conquest, the development of plow agriculture, and the assignment of women to the domestic sphere and men to the public sphere during the early industrial era.

## The Earnings Gap Today

After reading this brief historical overview, you might be inclined to dismiss gender inequality as a thing of the past. If so, your decision would be hasty. That is evident if we focus on the earnings gap between men and women, one of the most important expressions of gender inequality today.

When data were first collected in 1967 in Canada on female-to-male earnings, the ratio stood at 58.4 percent. Since that time, it has increased notably. For example, from 1989 to 1993, the ratio increased from 66 percent to 72 percent because of an increase in average female earnings and a stalling in average male earnings. In 1994, men's earnings improved significantly as the result of a surge in employment in the higher-wage goods-producing industries and the earnings ratio fell to 69.8 percent. "In short, recent variations in the ratio have been due more to improving or faltering earnings for men than to changes in the earning for women" (Statistics Canada, 1997a). In 1997, women working in full-year, full-time jobs earned an average of $30 717, while comparably employed men earned, on average, $41 848; the earnings ratio was 73.4 (Statistics Canada, 1999a).

The hourly wage gap between men and women varies among different groups. For example, in 1997, single women who had never been married earned 96 cents for every dollar earned by their male counterparts. Women with a university education earned 85 cents for every dollar earned by their male counterparts, and women without a high school diploma earned only 69 cents for every dollar earned by their male counterparts. Table 9.3 illustrates the persistence of the gender wage gap in the average earnings of full-year, full-time workers in the 10 highest-paying and 10 lowest-paying occupations in Canada in 1995.

**✦ TABLE 9.3 ✦**

**Number of Earners Who Worked Full Year, Full Time in 1995 in the 10 Highest-Paying and 10 Lowest-Paying Occupations and Their Average Earnings by Sex, for Canada, 1995 (20% Sample Data)**

| Average 1995 earnings $ | Both sexes | Men | Women |
|---|---|---|---|
| **All occupations** | **37 556** | **42 488** | **30 130** |
| **Total—10 highest-paying occupations** [1] | **80 206** | **86 139** | **58 943** |
| Judges | 126 246 | 128 791 | 117 707 |
| Specialist physicians | 123 976 | 137 019 | 86 086 |
| General practitioners and family physicians | 107 620 | 116 750 | 81 512 |
| Dentists | 102 433 | 109 187 | 71 587 |
| Senior managers—Goods production, utilities, transportation, and construction | 99 360 | 102 971 | 58 463 |
| Senior managers—Financial, communications carriers, and other business services | 99 117 | 104 715 | 71 270 |
| Lawyers and Quebec notaries | 81 617 | 89 353 | 60 930 |
| Senior managers—Trade, broadcasting, and other services n.e.c. | 79 200 | 84 237 | 48 651 |
| Primary production managers (except agriculture) | 76 701 | 78 421 | 48 479 |
| Securities agents, investment dealers, and traders | 75 911 | 90 391 | 47 323 |
| **Total—10 lowest-paying occupations** [1] | **17 729** | **20 238** | **16 564** |
| Sewing machine operators | 17 613 | 20 664 | 17 340 |
| Cashiers | 17 553 | 20 557 | 16 977 |
| Ironing, pressing, and finishing occupations | 17 322 | 19 297 | 16 499 |
| Artisans and craftspersons | 16 943 | 20 555 | 13 565 |
| Bartenders | 16 740 | 18 899 | 14 940 |
| Harvesting labourers | 16 426 | 18 683 | 14 465 |
| Service station attendants | 16 203 | 16 520 | 14 947 |
| Food service counter attendants and food preparers | 15 487 | 17 912 | 14 681 |
| Food and beverage servers | 14 891 | 18 192 | 13 861 |
| Babysitters, nannies, and parents' helpers | 12 713 | 15 106 | 12 662 |

Source: Adapted from Statistics Canada, Catalogue No. 93F0029XDB96005 in the Nation Series.

1 Although athletes were in the 25 highest-paying occupations and trappers and hunters were in the 25 lowest-paying occupations, their very small numbers rendered their income statistics unreliable. Hence, the individuals in these occupations were excluded from the highest- and lowest-paying groups.

Four main factors contribute to the gender gap in earnings. Let us consider each of them in turn (Bianchi and Spain, 1996; England, 1992).

*Gender discrimination.* In February 1985, when Microsoft, the software giant, employed about 1000 people, it hired its first two female executives. According to a well-placed source involved in the hiring, both women got their jobs because Microsoft was trying to win a U.S. Air Force contract. Under the government's guidelines, it didn't have enough women in top management positions to qualify. The source quotes then 29-year-old Bill Gates, president of Microsoft, as saying: "Well, let's hire two women because we can pay them half as much as we will have to pay a man, and we can give them all this other 'crap' work to do because they are women" (quoted in Wallace and Erickson, 1992: 291).

This incident is a clear illustration of **gender discrimination,** rewarding women and men differently for the same work. Discrimination on the basis of sex is against the law in Canada, and equity laws have helped increase the female–male earnings ratio. Yet progress is slow. The female–male earnings ratio for full-time, full-year workers increased 14 percent between 1967 and 1999. At that rate of improvement, women will be earning as much as men by 2060, around the time that most first-year university students taking this course will be in their seventies (Statistics Canada, 2000h).

*Women tend to be concentrated in low-wage occupations and industries.* The second factor leading to lower earnings for women is that the programs they select in high school and afterwards tend to limit them to jobs in low-wage occupations and industries. The concentration of women in certain occupations and men in others is referred to as

Although women have entered many traditionally "male" occupations since the 1970s, they are still concentrated in lower-paying clerical and service occupations and underrepresented in higher-paying manual occupations.

*occupational sex segregation.* Although women have made big strides since the 1970s, especially in managerial employment, they are still concentrated in lower-paying clerical and service occupations and underrepresented in higher-paying manual occupations (see Table 9.4). This is particularly true for women of colour, First Nations women, and women with disabilities. For example, "[a]mong those who were employed in 1995 or 1996, 44% of visible minority women aged 15–64 who held a bachelor's degree or higher were working in clerical, sales, or service jobs, compared with 25% of other women with a degree. In addition, 4% of university-educated visible minority women were employed as manual workers, compared with 1% of non-visible workers" (Chard, 2000: 229). In contrast to visible minority men, who are concentrated in professional occupations and service jobs in higher proportions than Canadians overall, visible minority women are more likely than Canadian women as a whole to be concentrated in manual labour. Similarly, working-aged women with disabilities are less likely than working-age men with disabilities to be employed (41 percent versus 56 percent; Shain, 1995).

*Heavy domestic responsibilities reduce women's earnings.* Raising children can be one of the most emotionally satisfying experiences in life. However, it is time-consuming *work* that decreases the time available for education, training, and paid work. Since women are disproportionately involved in child rearing, they suffer the brunt of this economic reality. Women also do more housework and elder care than men (Sauve, 2002; see also Chapter 12, Families). In most countries, including Canada, women do between two-thirds and three-quarters of all unpaid child care, housework, and care for the elderly (Boyd, 1997: 55). As a result, they devote fewer hours to paid work than men, experience more labour-force interruptions, and are more likely than men to take part-time jobs. Part-time jobs pay less per hour and offer fewer benefits than full-time work. Even when they work full-time in the paid labour force, women continue to shoulder a disproportionate share of domestic responsibilities, working, in effect, a "double shift" (see Chapter 12, Families).

✦ **TABLE 9.4** ✦

**Distribution of Employment, by Occupation, 1987, 1994, and 1999**

Source: Adapted from Statistics Canada, Catalogue No. 89-503-XPE.

1 Includes occupations that are not classified.

| | 1987 | 1994 | 1999 |
|---|---|---|---|
| | **Women as a % of total employed in occupation** | **Women as a % of total employed in occupation** | **Women as a % of total employed in occupation** |
| **Managerial** | | | |
| Senior management | 16.9 | 19.8 | 26.8 |
| Other management | 30.6 | 36.9 | 35.7 |
| Total management | 28.9 | 35.1 | 35.1 |
| **Professional** | | | |
| Business and finance | 40.7 | 44.6 | 49.4 |
| Natural sciences/engineering/mathematics | 16.7 | 17.0 | 19.6 |
| Social sciences/religion | 47.8 | 56.5 | 58.2 |
| Teaching | 57.3 | 59.4 | 62.1 |
| Doctors/dentists/other health | 44.1 | 48.7 | 47.1 |
| Nursing/therapy/other health-related | 87.3 | 87.1 | 86.5 |
| Artistic/literary/recreational | 50.4 | 53.6 | 54.8 |
| Total professional | 49.8 | 52.2 | 51.8 |
| Clerical and administrative | 74.4 | 74.9 | 75.3 |
| Sales and service | 55.7 | 56.4 | 58.7 |
| Primary | 20.0 | 21.3 | 21.6 |
| Trades, transport, and construction | 5.3 | 5.4 | 6.2 |
| Processing, manufacturing, and utilities | 30.2 | 29.2 | 29.8 |
| **Total[1]** | **43.0** | **45.3** | **45.9** |

This affects how much time they can devote to their jobs and careers, with negative consequences for their earnings (Waldfogel, 1997). In Canada, nearly one-fifth of the wage gap between women and men can be attributed to the fact that women have less work experience, and the situation in other highly developed countries is similar (Wright, Baxter, and Birkelund, 1995).

*Finally, work done by women is commonly considered less valuable than work done by men because it is viewed as involving fewer skills.* Women tend to earn less than men because the skills involved in their work are often undervalued (Figart and Lapidus, 1996; Sorenson, 1994). For example, kindergarten teachers (nearly all of whom are women) earn less than office machine repair technicians (nearly all of whom are men). It is, however, questionable whether it takes less training and skill to teach a young child the basics of counting and cooperation than it takes to get a photocopier to collate paper properly. As this example suggests, we apply somewhat arbitrary standards to reward different occupational roles. In our society, these standards systematically undervalue the kind of skills needed for jobs where women are concentrated.

We thus see that the gender gap in earnings is based on several *social* circumstances rather than any inherent difference between women and men. This means that people can reduce the gender gap if they want to. Below, we discuss social policies that could create more equality between women and men. But first, to stress the urgency of such policies, we explain how the persistence of gender inequality encourages sexual harassment and rape.

## Male Aggression against Women

Serious acts of aggression between men and women are common. The great majority are committed by men against women. For example, in 1997, more than 27 000 sexual assaults were reported to the police in Canada. More than 8 out of 10 victims (84 percent) were women, and nearly all (98 percent) of the accused perpetrators were men (Integration Analysis Program, 1999: 272). Among young singles, the rate of sexual assault is higher than in the population as a whole.

Even though "rapists" have typically been thought of as deranged individuals, research on *acquaintance rape*—sexual assaults committed by someone the victim knows—demonstrates that "normal" men are capable of acts of coercive sexuality (Meyer, 1984; Senn et al., 2000). One study (DeKeseredy and Kelly, 1993) found that 20.2 percent of female Canadian post-secondary students said they gave in to unwanted sexual intercourse because they were overwhelmed by a man's continued arguments and pressure, 6.6 percent reported they had unwanted sexual intercourse because a man threatened or used some degree of physical force, and 13.6 percent claimed that, while they were either intoxicated or under the influence of drugs, a man had attempted unwanted sexual intercourse.

Another study found that half of first- and second-year university women reported unwanted attempts at intercourse by males of their acquaintance. In 83 percent of cases, they knew the men at least moderately well. One-third of these attempts were accompanied by "strong" physical force and another third by "mild" physical force. The women seemed constrained by traditional roles in their responses, which were largely passive and accepting; 37 percent did nothing. Only a minority gave a strong verbal response (26 percent) or a physical response (14 percent). Half of the attacks succeeded; the stronger the victim's response, the less likely it was that the attempted rape was completed. None of the women reported the attack to the authorities and half talked to no one about it. The remainder told friends. Only 11 percent ended the relationship, whereas almost three-quarters either accepted or ignored the attack. Half continued to be friends (25 percent) or dating or sex partners (25 percent). Most blamed themselves at least partially (Murnen, Perot, and Byrne, 1989).

Over the past decade, college and university administrations as well as other groups have begun to deal with this serious hazard of dating. For example, the Canadian Federation of Students (CFS, 2001) has a long-standing "No Means No" campaign that includes a fact sheet on date rape and, more recently, on date rape drugs. The campaign's message is that, "when it comes to sex, 'no means no' and there is no excuse for not understanding 'no.'"

Why do men commit more frequent (and more harmful) acts of aggression against women than women commit against men? It is *not* because men on average are *physically* more powerful than women. Greater physical power is more likely to be used to commit acts of aggression when norms justify male domination and men have much more *social* power than women. When women and men are more equal socially, and norms justify gender equality, the rate of male aggression against women is lower. This is evident if we consider various types of aggressive interaction, including sexual assault and sexual harassment (see also the discussion of wife abuse in Chapter 12, Families).

## Sexual Assault

Some people think rapists are men who suffer a psychological disorder that compels them to achieve immediate sexual gratification even if violence is required. Others think rape occurs because of flawed communication. They believe some victims give mixed signals to their assailants by, for example, drinking too much and flirting with them.

Such explanations are not completely invalid. Interviews with victims and perpetrators show that some offenders do suffer from psychological disorders. Others misinterpret signals in what they regard as sexually ambiguous situations (Hannon et al., 1995). But such cases account for only a small proportion of the total. Men who commit sexual assault are rarely mentally disturbed, and it is abundantly clear to most assailants that they are doing something their victims strongly oppose.

What then accounts for sexual assault being as common as it is? A sociological answer is suggested by the fact that sexual assault is sometimes not about sexual gratification at all. Some offenders cannot ejaculate or even achieve an erection. Significantly, however, all forms of sexual assault involve domination and humiliation as principal motives. It is not surprising, therefore, that some offenders were physically or sexually abused in their youth. They develop

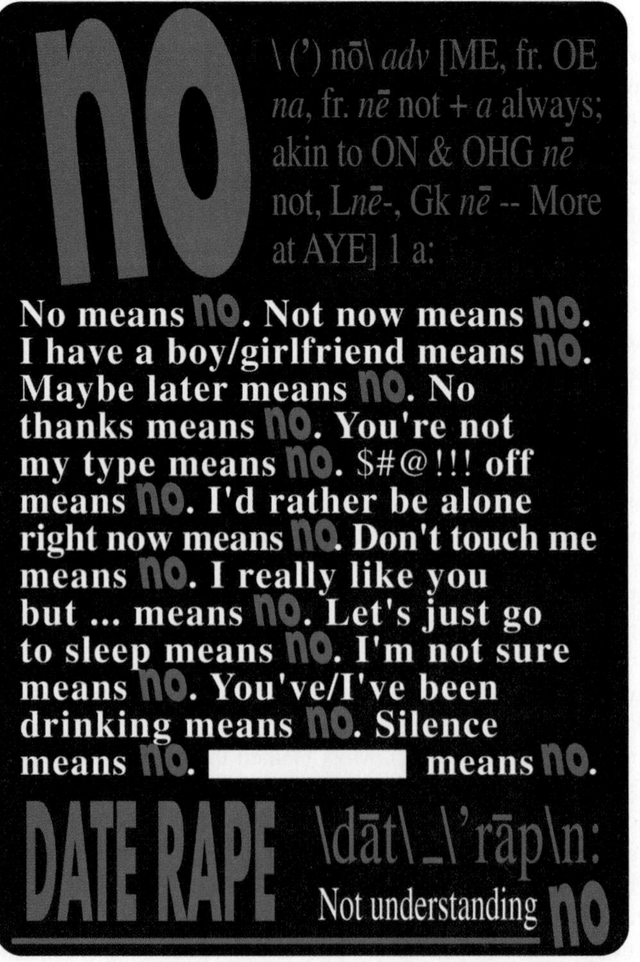


This poster suggests that men still need to be reminded that no means no.

a deep need to feel powerful as psychological compensation for their early powerlessness. Others are men who, as children, saw their mothers as potentially hostile figures who needed to be controlled, or as mere objects available for male gratification. They saw their fathers as emotionally cold and distant. Raised in such an atmosphere, rapists learn not to empathize with women. Instead, they learn to want to dominate them (Lisak, 1992).

Psychological factors aside, certain *social* situations also increase the rate of sexual aggression. One such situation is war. In war, conquering male soldiers often feel justified in wanting to humiliate the vanquished, who are powerless to stop them. Rape is often used for this purpose, as was especially well documented in the ethnic wars that accompanied the breakup of Yugoslavia in the 1990s (Human Rights Watch, 1995).

The relationship between male dominance and sexual aggression is evident in research on fraternities. Many college and university fraternities tend to emphasize male dominance and aggression as a central part of their culture. Sociologists who have interviewed fraternity members have shown that most fraternities try to recruit members who can reinforce a macho image and avoid any suggestion of effeminacy and homosexuality. Research also shows that fraternity houses that are especially prone to sexual assault tend to sponsor parties that treat women in a particularly degrading way. By emphasizing a very narrow and aggressive form of masculinity, some fraternities tend to facilitate sexual assault on campuses (Boswell and Spade, 1996).

Another social circumstance that increases the likelihood of sexual assault is participation in athletics. Of course, the overwhelming majority of athletes are not rapists. However, there are proportionately more rapists among men who participate in athletics than among nonathletes (Welch, 1997). That is because many sports embody a particular vision of masculinity in North American culture: competitive, aggressive, and domineering. By recruiting men who display these characteristics and by encouraging the development of these characteristics in athletes, sports can contribute to "off-field" aggression, including sexual aggression. Furthermore, among male athletes, there is a distinct hierarchy of sexual aggression. Male athletes who engage in contact sports are more prone to be rapists than other athletes. There are proportionately even more rapists among athletes involved in collision and combative sports, notably football (Welch, 1997).

Sexual assault, we conclude, involves using sex to establish dominance. Its incidence is highest in situations where early socialization experiences predispose men to want to control women, where norms justify the domination of women, and where a big power imbalance between men and women exists.

## Sexual Harassment

There are two types of sexual harassment. **Quid pro quo sexual harassment** takes place when sexual threats or bribery are made a condition of employment decisions. (The Latin phrase *quid pro quo* means "something for something.") **Hostile environment sexual harassment** involves sexual jokes, comments, and touching that interferes with work or creates a hostile work environment. Research suggests that relatively powerless women are the most likely to be sexually harassed. Specifically, women who are young, unmarried, and employed in nonprofessional jobs are most likely to become objects of sexual harassment, particularly if they are temporary workers, if the ratio of women to men in the workplace is low, and if the organizational culture of the workplace tolerates sexual harassment (Rogers and Henson, 1997; Welsh, 1999). However, female doctors (Schneider and Phillips, 1997) and lawyers (Rosenberg, Perlstadt, and Phillips, 1997) also report high rates of sexual harassment, in the first case by male patients and in the second by male colleagues.

Ultimately, male aggression against women, including sexual harassment and sexual assault, is encouraged by a lesson most of us still learn at home, in school, at work, through much of organized religion, and in the mass media—that it is natural and right for men to dominate women. To be sure, recent decades have witnessed important changes in the way women's and men's roles are defined. Nevertheless, in the world of paid work, in the household, in government, and in all other spheres of life, men still tend to command substantially more power and authority than women. Daily patterns of gender domination, viewed as legitimate by most people, are built into our courtship, sexual, family, and work norms. From this point of view, male aggression against women is simply an expression of male authority by other means.

This does not mean that all men endorse the principle of male dominance, much less that all men are inclined to engage in sexual assault or other acts of aggression against women. Indeed, scholars increasingly speak of *masculinities* in the plural, rather than the singular, to acknowledge differences among men and to emphasize that "masculinity" is neither innate nor a fixed entity (Messerschmidt, 1993). Many men favour gender equality, and most men never abuse a woman. Nevertheless, the fact remains that many aspects of our culture legitimize male dominance, making it seem valid or proper. For example, pornography, jokes about "dumb blondes," and leering might seem examples of merely harmless play. At a subtler, sociological level, however, they are assertions of the appropriateness of women's submission to men. Such frequent and routine reinforcements of male authority increase the likelihood that some men will consider it their right to assault women physically or sexually if the opportunity to do so exists or can be created. "Just kidding" has a cost. For instance, researchers have found that university men who enjoy sexist jokes are most likely to report engaging in acts of sexual aggression against women (Ryan and Kanjorski, 1998).

We thus see that male aggression against women and gender inequality are not separate issues. Gender inequality is the foundation of aggression against women. In concluding this chapter, we consider how gender inequality can be decreased in the coming decades. As we proceed, you should bear in mind that gender equality is not just a matter of justice. It is also a question of safety.

## Toward 2060

The twentieth century witnessed growing equality between women and men in many countries. In Canada, the decline of the family farm made children less economically useful and more costly to raise. As a result, women started having fewer children. The industrialization of Canada, and then the growth of the economy's service sector, increased demand for women in the paid labour force (see Figure 9.4). This gave them substantially more economic power and also encouraged them to have fewer children. The legalization and availability of contraception made it possible for women to exercise unprecedented control over their own bodies. The women's movement fought for, and won, increased rights for women on a number of economic, political, and legal fronts. All these forces brought about a massive cultural shift, a fundamental reorientation of thinking on the part of many Canadians about what women could and should do in society.

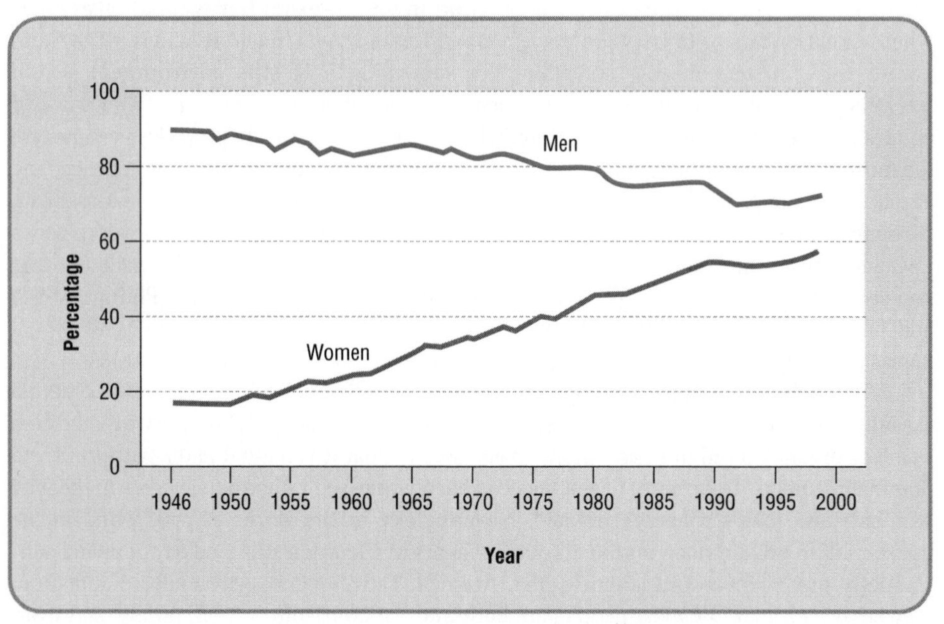


✦ **FIGURE 9.4** ✦
**Percentage of Employed Adults Ages 25 and Older, Canada: 1946–1999**

Source: Crompton and Vickers (2000: 8).

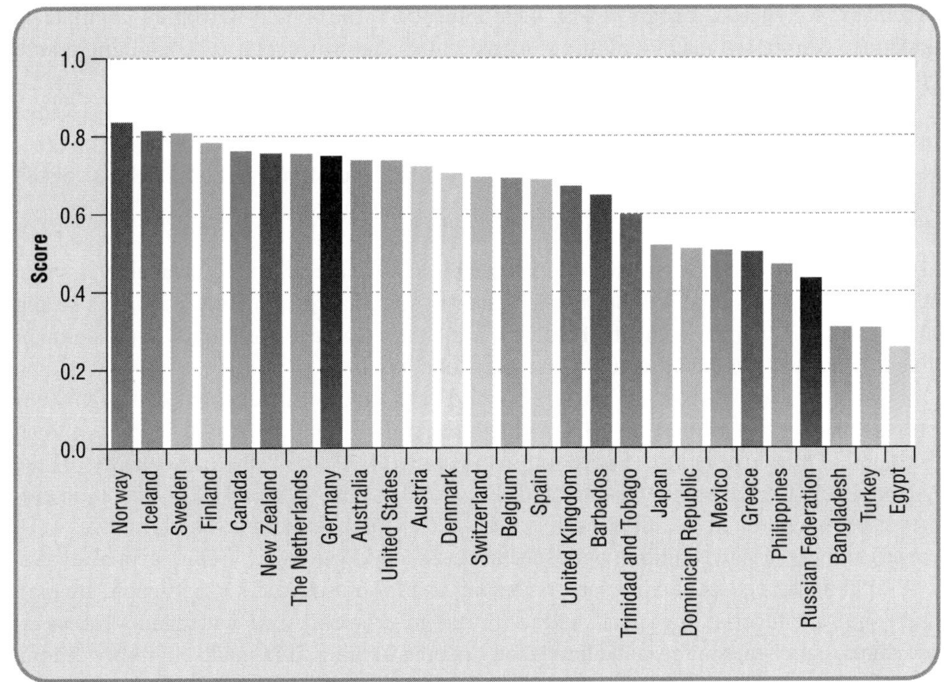


**FIGURE 9.5**
**Comparison of Selected Countries Ranked According to Gender Empowerment Measure, 2001**

Source: Adapted from United Nations Development Programme (2001).

One indicator of the progress of women is the Gender Empowerment Measure (GEM). The GEM is computed by the United Nations. It takes into account women's share of seats in Parliament; women's share of administrative, managerial, professional, and technical jobs; and women's earning power. A score of 1.0 indicates equality with men on these three dimensions.

As Figure 9.5 shows, Norway, Iceland, Sweden, and Finland were the most gender-egalitarian countries in the world in 2001. They had GEM scores ranging from 0.836 to 0.783. This means that women in these countries are about 80 percent of the way to equality with men on these three dimensions. Canada ranked fifth in the world with a GEM score of 0.763.

In general, there is more gender equality in rich than in poor countries. Thus, the top 11 countries, shown in Figure 9.5, are all rich. This suggests that gender equality is a function of economic development. However, our analysis of the GEM data suggests that there are some exceptions to the general pattern. They show that gender equality is also a function of government policy. Thus, in some of the former communist countries of Eastern Europe—such as the Czech Republic (ranked at 26), Slovakia (27), Latvia (28), and Poland (32)—gender equality is *higher* than one would expect given their level of economic development. Meanwhile, in some of the Islamic countries, gender inequality is *lower* than one would expect given their level of economic development (e.g., Kuwait, a rich country, has high gender inequality). These anomalies exist because the former communist countries made gender equality a matter of public policy while many Islamic countries do just the opposite. To cite just one extreme case, in 1996 authorities in the Islamic country of Afghanistan made it illegal for girls to attend school and women to work in the paid labour force. (The situation has improved since the overthrow of the Taliban regime in 2001.)

The GEM figures suggest that Canadian women still have a considerable way to go before they achieve equality with men. We have seen, for example, that the gender gap in earnings is shrinking but will disappear only in 2060—and then only if it continues to diminish at the same rate as during the last third of the twentieth century. That is a big "if," because progress is never automatic.

Socializing children at home and in school to understand that women and men are equally adept at all jobs is important in motivating them to excel in nontraditional fields. Hiring more women to compensate for past discrimination in hiring, firing, promotion, and training is also important. However, without in any way belittling the need for such initiatives, we should recognize that their impact will be muted if women continue to undertake disproportionate domestic responsibilities and if occupations containing a high concentration of women continue to be undervalued in monetary terms.

Two main policy initiatives will probably be required in the coming decades to bridge the gender gap in earnings. One is the development of a better childcare system. The other is the development of a policy of comparable worth. Let us consider both of these issues.

## Child Care

High-quality, government-subsidized, affordable child care is widely available in most Western European countries, but not in Canada (see Chapter 12, Families). As a result, many Canadian women with small children are either unable to work outside the home or able to work outside the home only on a part-time basis.

Child-care options and the quality of child care vary by social class. Although well-off parents may pay as much as $850 a month per child for high-quality care in downtown Toronto or Ottawa, others are forced to rely on unregulated care "where the quality of care is completely unpredictable" (National Council on Welfare, 1999c: 4). This situation creates risks for children's health and safety and anxiety for their parents. For those who work irregular hours or have children with special needs, child care may simply be unavailable.

Although the costs of child care in general, and for preschoolers in particular, are high and rising, the federal, provincial, and territorial governments have cut funding for social programs, cut or frozen fee subsidies to low-income families, and made eligibility criteria for subsidies more restrictive. It is therefore not surprising that informal care by relatives, neighbours, and paid caregivers is the most common form of child care in Canada for children whose parents work in the paid labour force (Baker and Lero, 1996). Currently, non-parental child care is provided to 40 percent of all Canadian children under the age of five. Of these children, 56 percent are cared for in someone else's home, 22 percent are cared for in their own home, 20 percent are cared for in a daycare centre, and 2 percent have other arrangements (Vanier Institute of the Family, 2001).

In 1997, Quebec introduced a comprehensive family policy that attempts to integrate family benefits, paid parental leave, child care, and kindergarten. Its child-care component heralded universally available, affordable child care in that province. The aim was to make every child in Quebec able to receive child care for $5 a day (and for as little as $2 a day for certain low-income families) by 2001. In March 2000, British Columbia became the second jurisdiction in North America to move toward publicly funded child care for all families "rich, poor, and the large majority in between" (Canadian Council on Social Development, 2001: 6). Elsewhere in Canada, however, the provision of child care continues to be "severely compromised on three fronts: the availability of spaces to meet the needs of children and their families, the affordability of care and the quality of services provided" (National Council on Welfare, 1999b: 44). A Canadian study that estimated the benefits of a high-quality, affordable universal system of child care and early child-care education costing $7.9 billion calculated that if such a system existed, the value of the increased employment of mothers would be worth $6.2 billion and the improvement in child development worth $4.3 billion (Cleveland and Krashinsky, 1998) Yet, until the child-care situation described above changes, women, particularly those in the middle and lower classes, will continue to suffer economically from the lack of accessible, affordable child care.

## Equal Pay for Work of Equal Value

On paper, Canadian women have had the right to equal pay for the same jobs done by men since the 1950s. Unfortunately, although early laws proclaimed lofty goals, they failed to result in fair wages. Because of occupational sex segregation, few men and women were doing the same jobs, and "women's" jobs paid less than "men's" jobs.

In the 1980s, researchers found women earn less than men partly because jobs in which women are concentrated are valued less than jobs in which men are concentrated. They therefore tried to establish gender-neutral standards by which they could judge the dollar value of work. These standards include such factors as the education and experience required to do a particular job and the level of responsibility, amount of stress, and working conditions associated with it. Researchers felt that, by using these criteria to compare jobs in which women and men are concentrated, they could identify pay inequities. The underpaid could then be compensated accordingly. In other words, women and men would receive **equal pay for work of equal value,** even if they did different jobs. During the mid-1980s, some governments amended the law to state that women should be paid equally for work of equal value. This amendment required employers to compare the rates of pay for women and men in dissimilar jobs that nevertheless involved the same skill, effort, responsibility, and working conditions. In 1985, Manitoba became the first Canadian province to demand that its public sector be proactive and implement plans for "equal pay for work of equal value"—or **pay equity,** as it came to be called. Pay equity is now official policy in 10 of 13 Canadian jurisdictions (Alberta, Saskatchewan, and the Northwest Territories are the exceptions). However, provisions vary widely. Enforcement mechanisms are meagre and employers have found various ways to argue that unequal wages do not signify discrimination based on sex. Thus, while pay equity is undoubtedly a significant step toward achieving gender equality, inequity remains, as evidenced by the persistence of the wage gap between working men and women.

## THE WOMEN'S MOVEMENT

Improvements in the social standing of women do not depend just on the sympathy of government and business leaders. Progress on this front has always depended in part on the strength of the organized women's movement. This is likely to be true in the future, too. In concluding this chapter, it is therefore fitting to consider the state of the women's movement and its prospects.

The "first wave" of the women's movement emerged during the late 1800s and lasted into the early 1920s. The most important public achievements of this movement in Canada were the right to vote and the right (granted in 1929) to be considered *persons*, and not chattels, under Canadian law (Nelson and Robinson, 2002). In 1916, women in Alberta, Manitoba, and Saskatchewan were granted the right to vote in provincial elections. The

The "first wave" of the women's movement achieved its main goal—the right of women to vote—as a result of much demonstrating, lobbying, organizing, and persistent educational work.

following year, women in British Columbia were granted this right. Women achieved this right in Nova Scotia in 1918, in New Brunswick in 1919, in Prince Edward Island in 1922, in Newfoundland in 1925, and in Quebec in 1940. These rights were first granted to white women. Women from certain ethnic and racial groups did not receive the franchise until later (Nelson and Robinson, 2002).

In the mid-1960s, the "second wave" of the women's movement started to grow. Second-wave feminists were inspired in part by the successes of the civil rights movement in the United States. They felt that women's concerns were largely ignored—despite persistent and pervasive gender inequality. Like their counterparts more than a century earlier, they held demonstrations, lobbied politicians, and formed women's organizations to further their cause. They demanded equal rights with men in education and employment, the elimination of sexual violence, and women's control over reproduction. However, the second wave of the women's movement did not always or consistently recognize, include, or champion the needs of all Canadian women equally. It is only recently that the second wave of the women's movement has begun to respond positively to the claim that white, middle-class feminists have "denied, dismissed, and denigrated" the experiences of women of different races, abilities, and classes (Cassidy, Lord, and Mandell, 1998: 26).

Currently, there is considerable intellectual diversity in the modern feminist movement concerning ultimate goals. Three main streams may be distinguished (Tong, 1989).

*Liberal feminism* is the most popular current in the women's movement today. Its advocates believe that the main sources of women's subordination are learned gender roles and the denial of opportunities to women. Liberal feminists advocate nonsexist methods of socialization and education, more sharing of domestic tasks between women and men, and extending to women all the educational, employment, and political rights and privileges men enjoy.

*Socialist feminists* regard women's relationship to the economy as the main source of women's disadvantages. They believe that the traditional nuclear family emerged along with inequalities of wealth. In their opinion, once men possessed wealth, they wanted to ensure that their property would be transmitted to their children, particularly their sons. They accomplished this in two ways. First, men exercised complete economic control over their property, thus ensuring it would not be squandered and would remain theirs and theirs alone. Second, they enforced female monogamy, thus ensuring that their property would be transmitted only to *their* offspring. Thus, according to socialist feminists, the economic and sexual oppression of women has its roots in capitalism. Socialist feminists also assert that the reforms proposed by liberal feminists are inadequate, because they can do little to help

The "second wave" of the women's movement started to grow in the mid-1960s. Members of the movement advocated equal rights with men in education and employment, the elimination of sexual violence, and women's control over reproduction.

working-class women, who are too poor to take advantage of equal educational and work opportunities. Socialist feminists conclude that only the elimination of private property and the creation of economic equality can bring about an end to the oppression of all women.

*Radical feminists,* in turn, find the reforms proposed by liberals and the revolution proposed by socialists inadequate. Patriarchy—male domination and norms justifying that domination—is more deeply rooted than capitalism, say the radical feminists. After all, patriarchy predates capitalism. Moreover, it is just as evident in self-proclaimed communist societies as it is in capitalist societies. Radical feminists conclude that the very idea of gender must be changed to bring an end to male domination. Some radical feminists argue that new reproductive technologies, such as in vitro fertilization, are bound to be helpful in this regard because they can break the link between women's bodies and child-bearing (see Chapter 12, Families). However, the revolution envisaged by radical feminists goes beyond the realm of reproduction to include all aspects of male sexual dominance. From their point of view, pornography, sexual harassment, restrictive contraception, sexual assault, incest, sterilization, and physical assault must be eliminated in order for women to reconstruct their sexuality on their own terms.

This thumbnail sketch by no means exhausts the variety of streams of contemporary feminist thought. For example, since the mid-1980s, *anti-racist* and *postmodernist* feminists have criticized liberal, socialist, and radical feminists for generalizing from the experience of white women and failing to understand how women's lives are rooted in particular historical and racial experiences (hooks, 1984). These new currents have done much to extend the relevance of feminism to previously marginalized groups.

Partly because of the political and intellectual vigour of the women's movement, some feminist ideas have gained widespread acceptance in Canadian society over the past three decades. For example, the 1995 General Social Survey data show that the majority of Canadians, men and women, agree or strongly agree that being able to have a paying job is either important or very important for their personal happiness. As well, approximately 7 out of 10 Canadian men and women agree or strongly agree that both spouses should contribute to household income. However, these values appear to conflict with other attitudes and beliefs. The same survey found that although 67 percent of women and 59 percent of men agree or strongly agree that employed mothers can maintain warm relationships with their children of any age, 59 percent of men and 51 percent of women agree or strongly agree that preschool-age children are likely to suffer if both parents are employed. Moreover, 46 percent of women and 44 percent of men agree or strongly agree with the statement that a "job is alright, but what most women really want is a home and children" (Ghalam, 1997: 16). It appears that the tapestry of our social lives features interwoven threads of the new and the old.

Many people, especially men, continue to oppose the women's movement. In fact, in recent years several anti-feminist men's groups have sprung up to defend traditional male privileges. It is apparently difficult for some men to accept feminism because they feel that the social changes advocated by feminists threaten their traditional way of life and perhaps even their sexual identity.

Our own experience suggests that those who breach traditional gender roles may expect to face at least some opposition. For example, Adie Nelson recalls that when she was expecting her first child, she received a stern lecture from another faculty member on the "catastrophic effect" that her continued employment would "undoubtedly" have on her child, particularly if the child was a male. "My colleague informed me that if I had a son and continued to work, I 'held the scalpel' to my son's 'psychic emasculation,'" Adie recalls. "Supposedly, my employment not only placed my child at risk, but my husband as well. According to my colleague, as the direct result of my being employed, my husband (a 6'2", 220-pound police officer) would become a 'prancing, flaming homosexual' and, before long, leave me for a man." Adie's reaction? She observes: "Well, it's obvious that not all dinosaurs are extinct."

## SUMMARY

1. The way that culturally appropriate masculine and feminine roles are expressed depends on a variety of social conditions, especially the level of gender inequality.
2. Males and females are channelled into gender-appropriate roles by parents, teachers, and the mass media.
3. While society pushes people to assume conventionally masculine or feminine roles, it demands heterosexuality with even greater force.
4. The social distinction between men and women serves as a major basis of inequality in the family and the workplace.
5. The gender gap in earnings derives from outright discrimination against women, women's disproportionate domestic responsibilities, women's concentration in low-wage occupations and industries, and the undervaluation of work typically done by women.
6. Male aggression against women is rooted in gender inequality.
7. Among the major reforms that can help eliminate the gender gap in earnings and reduce the overall level and expression of gender inequality are (a) the development of an affordable, accessible system of high-quality daycare, and (b) the remuneration of men and women on the basis of their work's actual worth.

## GLOSSARY

**Bisexuals** are people who enjoy sexual partners of either sex.

**Equal pay for work of equal value** refers to the equal dollar value of different jobs. It is established in gender-neutral terms by comparing jobs in terms of the education and experience need to do them and the stress, responsibility, and working conditions associated with them.

**Essentialism** is a school of thought that views gender differences as a reflection of biological differences between women and men.

Your **gender** is your sense of being male or female and your playing masculine and feminine roles in ways defined as appropriate by your culture and society.

**Gender discrimination** involves rewarding men and women differently for the same work.

**Gender identity** is one's identification with, or sense of belonging to, a particular sex—biologically, psychologically, and socially.

A **gender ideology** is a set of ideas about what constitutes appropriate masculine and feminine roles and behaviour.

A **gender role** is the set of behaviours associated with widely shared expectations about how males or females are supposed to act.

The **glass ceiling** is a social barrier that makes it difficult for women to rise to the top level of management.

**Hermaphrodites** are people born with ambiguous genitals because of a hormone imbalance in their mother's womb.

**Heterosexuals** are people who prefer members of the opposite sex as sexual partners.

**Homosexuals** are people who prefer sexual partners of the same sex. People usually call homosexual men *gay* and homosexual women *lesbians*.

**Hostile environment sexual harassment** involves sexual jokes, comments, and touching that interferes with work or creates an unfriendly work environment.

**Pay equity** is equal pay for work of equal value.

**Quid pro quo sexual harassment** takes place when sexual threats or bribery are made a condition of employment decisions.

Your **sex** depends on whether you were born with distinct male or female genitals and a genetic program that released either male or female hormones to stimulate the development of your reproductive system.

**Social constructionism** is a school of thought that views gender differences as a reflection of the different social positions occupied by women and men.

**Transgendered** is used to indicate a "rising above" traditional gender roles and refers to those who wittingly breach societal gender norms and present in ways that blur any distinction between male/female and masculine/feminine.

**Transsexuals** believe they were born with the "wrong" body. They identify with, and want to live fully as, members of the "opposite" sex.

## QUESTIONS TO CONSIDER

1. By interviewing your family members and using your own memory, compare the gender division of labour in (a) the households in which your parents grew up, and (b) the household(s) in which you grew up. Then, imagine the gender division of labour you would like to see in the household you hope to live in about 10 years from now. What accounts for change over time in the gender division of labour in these households? Do you think your hopes are realistic? Why or why not?
2. In your own case, rank the relative importance of your family, your schools, and the mass media in your gender socialization. What criteria do you use to judge the importance of each socialization agent?

3. Systematically note the roles played by women and men on TV programs and ads one evening. Is there a gender division of labour on TV? If so, describe it.
4. Are you a feminist? If so, which of the types of feminism discussed in this chapter do you find most appealing? Why? If not, what do you find objectionable about feminism? In either case, what is the ideal form of gender relations in your opinion? Why do you think this form is ideal?

## WEB RESOURCES

### Companion Web Site for This Book

http://www.brymsociologycompass.nelson.com

Begin by clicking on the Student Resources section of the Web site. Next, select the chapter you are currently studying from the pull-down menu. From the Student Resources page you will have easy access to InfoTrac College Edition®, MicroCase online exercises, and additional Web links. The Web site also has many useful tips to aid you in your study of sociology, including practice tests for each chapter.

### InfoTrac Search Terms

These search terms are provided to assist you in beginning to conduct research on this topic by visiting http://www.infotrac-college.com

**Gender**
**Gender discrimination**
**Gender role**
**Glass ceiling**
**Sexual harassment**

### Recommended Web Sites

For a useful discussion of women and work worldwide see the article "Women, Gender and Work: Part II" by Janneke Plantenga and Johan Hansen, available on the World Wide Web at http://www.ilo.org/public/english/support/publ/revue/sommaire/138-4.htm.

To learn about the history of women and gender in Canada, go to http://www.hartford-hwp.com/archives/44/index-eb.html.

For information on gender roles and stereotyping in children's literature, see http://www.indiana.edu/~eric_rec/ieo/bibs/childgen.html.

A variety of useful links can be found at Gender.org.uk: http://www.gender.org.uk.

Visit the Web site of Status of Women Canada (SWC) at http://www.swc-cfc.gc.ca/direct.html.

For more on the United Nations Gender Empowerment Measure (GEM), discussed in the text, see http://www.undp.org/index5.html.

## SUGGESTED READINGS

Deborah Blum. *Sex on the Brain: The Biological Differences Between Men and Women* (New York: Penguin, 1997). The subtitle is a misnomer. This Pulitzer Prize–winning science writer discusses not just the biological differences between men and women but the interaction between biology and environment.

Terry Goldie. *in a queer country: Gay & Lesbian Studies in the Canadian Context* (Vancouver: Arsenal Pulp Press, 2001). A fascinating collection featuring essays of enormous breadth, originality, and variety that celebrates both cultural and sexual difference.

Riane Eisler. *The Chalice and the Blade: Our History, Our Future* (New York: HarperCollins, 1995 [1987]). The big picture on gender inequality. Eisler's brilliant examination of the archaeological record uncovers the historical origins of gender inequality and suggests that now, for the first time in 7000 years, we are in a position to put an end to it.

## NOTES

1. We are grateful to Rhonda Lenton for her ideas on essentialism and its critique. See Lenton (2001).
2. Freud called this set of emotions the *Oedipus complex* after the ancient Greek legend of Oedipus. Oedipus was abandoned as a child. When he became an adult he accidentally killed his father and unwittingly married his mother. Discovering his true relationship to his mother, he blinded himself and died in exile.
3. Freud called this set of emotions the *Electra complex* after the ancient Greek legend of Electra. Electra persuaded her brother to kill their mother and their mother's lover to avenge their father's murder. Incidentally, some sexologists call into question the existence of vaginal orgasm and stress the importance of clitoral stimulation (Masters, Johnson, and Kolodny, 1992, 1994). This viewpoint emerged around the same time as the modern feminist movement and as more and more people came to view sexuality not just as a means of reproduction but also as a means of enjoyment.
4. Women born with higher testosterone levels may gravitate to more stereotypically male jobs in the first place. However, given what we know about how high-stress jobs increase testosterone levels, it also seems likely that these biological tendencies are accentuated or dampened by occupational demands. This argument is reinforced by research on girls born with unusually high testosterone levels. They prefer rough, aggressive play, but that preference is almost always ratcheted down when they start playing with other girls, who direct them toward standard girls' games. Nature provides, but society helps to decide (Blum, 1997: 158–88).
5. This message is borne out by research in the United States, Germany, and Britain that finds that upwardly mobile women "are much thinner than their counterparts who marry men of the same social class or lower" (Etcoff, 1999: 200–1).
6. Displaying direct aggression is more strongly associated with peer rejection for girls than for boys (Bukowski et al., 1993). Also, compared with boys, girls demonstrate higher levels of indirect or relational aggression—acts designed to damage another's peer relationships or reputation (e.g., gossiping, spreading malicious rumours, exclusionary acts)—than boys (Crick, 1997).
7. Although Justice Minister Anne McLellan said she would "consider" amending this section of the Code "if" there was "general agreement" by the provinces, no such change had occurred by the time this book went to press (EGALE, 2001).

PART

IV

# INSTITUTIONS

CHAPTER 10
WORK AND THE ECONOMY

CHAPTER 11
POLITICS

CHAPTER 12
FAMILIES

CHAPTER 13
RELIGION AND EDUCATION

CHAPTER 14
THE MASS MEDIA

CHAPTER 15
HEALTH, MEDICINE, AND AGING

## IN THIS CHAPTER, YOU WILL LEARN THAT

- Three work-related revolutions—one in agriculture, one in manufacturing, and one in the provision of services—have profoundly altered the ways in which people earn a living and how societies are organized.
- In the past few decades, the number of "good" jobs has grown, but so too has the number of "bad" jobs.
- With varying degrees of success, people seek to control work through unions, professional organizations, corporations, and markets.
- The growth of large corporations and global markets has shaped the transformation of work in recent decades and will shape the choices you face as a member of the labour force and a citizen.

CHAPTER

10

# WORK AND THE ECONOMY

## THE PROMISE AND HISTORY OF WORK

### Salvation or Curse?

The computerization of the office began in earnest about 20 years ago. Soon, the image of the new office was as familiar as a Dilbert cartoon. It was a checkerboard of 3-m × 3-m cubicles. Three padded walls, 2 m high, framed each cubicle. Inside, a computer terminal sat on a desk. A worker quietly tapped away at a keyboard, seemingly entranced by the glow of a video screen.

Sociologist Shoshana Zuboff visited many such offices soon after they were computerized. She sometimes asked the office workers to draw pictures capturing their job experience before and after computerization. The pictures were strikingly similar. Smiles changed to frowns, mobility became immobility, sociability was transformed into isolation, freedom turned to regimentation. Two of the workers' pictures are reprinted in Figure 10.1. Work automation and standardization emerge from these drawings as profoundly degrading and inhuman processes (Zuboff, 1988).

The image conveyed by these drawings is only one view of the transformation of work in the Information Age. There is another, and it is vastly different. Bill Gates argues that computers reduce our work hours. They make goods and services cheaper by removing many distribution costs of capitalism (think of Chapters.Indigo.ca reducing the need for bookstores). Computers also allow us to enjoy our leisure time more (Gates with Myhrvold and Rinearson, 1996). This vision is well captured by the arresting December 1999 cover of *Wired* magazine, reprinted as Figure 10.2. According to *Wired*, computers liberate us. They allow us to become more mobile and more creative. Computerized work allows our imaginations to leap and our spirits to soar.

✦ **FIGURE 10.1** ✦
**One View of the Effects of Computers on Work**
Shoshana Zuboff asked office workers to draw pictures representing how they felt about their jobs before and after a new computer sytem was introduced. Here are "before" and "after" pictures drawn by two office workers. Notice how even the flower on one worker's desk wilted after the new computer system was introduced.

Source: Zuboff (1988: 146–7).

Before

After

"Before I was able to get up and hand things to people without having someone say, what are you doing? Now, I feel like I am with my head down, doing my work."

Before

After

"My supervisor is frowning because we shouldn't be talking. I have on the stripes of a convict. It's all true. It feels like a prison in here."

✦ **FIGURE 10.2** ✦
**Another View of the Effect of Computers on Work**
*Wired* magazine is always on high about the benefits of computer technology.

Source: *Wired* (1999).

These strikingly different images form the core questions of the sociology of work, and they will be our focus in this chapter. Is work a salvation or a curse? Or is it perhaps both at once? Is it more accurate to say that work has become more of a salvation or a curse over time? Or is work a salvation for some and a curse for others?

To answer these questions, we first trace the evolution of work from pre-agrarian to postindustrial times. As you will see, we have experienced three work-related revolutions in the past 10 000 years. Each revolution has profoundly altered the way we sustain ourselves and the way we live. Next, we examine how job skills have changed over the past century. We also trace changes in the number and distribution of "good" and "bad" jobs over time. We then analyze how people have sought to control work through unions, professional organizations, corporations, and markets. Finally, we place our discussion in a broader context. The growth of large corporations and markets on a global scale has shaped the transformation of work over the past quarter-century. Understanding these transformations will help you understand the work-related choices you face both as a member of the labour force and as a citizen.

## Three Revolutions

The **economy** is the social institution that organizes the production and distribution of goods and services. Conventionally, analysts divide the economy into three sectors. The *primary* sector includes farming, fishing, logging, and mining. In the *secondary* sector, raw materials are turned into finished goods, for example the manufacture of furniture or cars. Finally, in the *tertiary* sector, services are bought and sold. These services include the work of nurses, teachers, lawyers, hairdressers, computer programmers, and so forth. Often, the three sectors are referred to as the *agricultural*, *manufacturing*, and *service* sectors.

Three truly revolutionary events have taken place in the history of human labour. In each revolution, a different economic sector rose to dominance. First came the agricultural revolution, then the revolution in manufacturing, and finally the revolution in services (Gellner, 1988; Lenski, 1966).

## The Development of Agriculture

Nearly all humans lived in nomadic tribes until about 10 000 years ago. Then, people in the fertile valleys of the Middle East, Southeast Asia, and South America began to herd cattle and cultivate crops using simple hand tools. Stable human settlements spread in these areas. About 5000 years ago, farmers invented the plow. By attaching plows to large animals, they substantially increased the amount of land under cultivation. **Productivity**—the amount produced for every hour worked—soared.

Although nowadays few people think of Canada as an agricultural nation, in the wheat boom of the late 1800s Canada was a world leader. In addition, the harvesting of fish, fur, and timber were important elements of Canada's primary sector. The Biblical phrase "hewers of wood and drawers of water" was sometimes applied to Canadians and it was apt. In 1900, more than 40 percent of the Canadian paid workforce was employed in agriculture, with a smaller percentage involved in resource extraction, such as cutting timber, mining, or fishing. These commodities are, in the lexicon of Canadian social science, *staples*. The harvesting and extracting of these staples, whether nickel from Sudbury, Ontario, oil from Leduc, Alberta, or cod from Petty Harbour, Newfoundland, propelled early economic development in Canada.

## The Development of Manufacturing

International exploration and commerce helped stimulate the growth of markets from the fifteenth century onward. **Markets** are social relations that regulate the exchange of goods and services. In a market, the prices of goods and services are established by their relative abundance (*supply*) and their relative appeal (*demand*). About 225 years ago, the steam engine, railroads, and other technological innovations greatly increased the ability of producers to supply markets. This was the era of the Industrial Revolution. Beginning in England, the Industrial Revolution spread to Western Europe, North America, Russia, and Japan within a century.

Although Canada began as a staples economy, a stronger manufacturing sector gradually developed. This is especially the case in southern Ontario and Quebec, where firms such as Bombardier, Magna, Nortel, and GM Canada compete on a world scale. In other regions, manufacturing is far more fragile and the historic roots of the staples economy remain strong. For example, if you were to visit Leduc, Petty Harbour, or Sudbury, you would see little of the manufacturing focus that characterizes Oshawa, Oakville, or Windsor. Canadian manufacturing strength varies significantly by region (Clement, 1997).

A Canadian engineering feat, the longest bridge over ice-covered waters in the world (at 12.9 km), was recently completed linking Borden-Carleton, Prince Edward Island, and Cape Tormentine, New Brunswick. This historic bridge opened June 1, 1997, bringing a new age of transportation to Atlantic Canada.

## The Development of the Service Sector

Even in pre-agrarian societies, a few individuals specialized in providing services rather than producing goods. For example, a person considered adept at tending to the ill, forecasting the weather, or predicting the movement of animals might be relieved of hunting responsibilities to focus on these services. However, such jobs were rare because productivity was low. Nearly everyone had to do physical work for the tribe to survive. Even in early agricultural societies, it took 80 to 100 farmers to support one nonfarmer (Hodson and Sullivan, 1995: 10).

Only at the beginning of the nineteenth century in Western Europe and North America did productivity increase to the point where a quarter of the labour force could be employed in services. By 1960 more than half the labour force of the highly industrialized countries was providing services. Forty years later, the figure was close to 75 percent (see Figure 10.3).

The rapid change in the composition of the labour force during the final decades of the twentieth century was made possible in large part by the computer. The computer automated many manufacturing and office procedures. It created jobs in the service sector as quickly as it eliminated them in manufacturing. Thus, the computer is to the service sector as the steam engine was to manufacturing and the plow was to agriculture. Especially in the areas of financial services and communications, the Canadian service sector has boomed.

Besides increasing productivity and causing shifts between sectors in employment, the agricultural, industrial, and service revolutions altered the way work was socially organized. For one thing, the **division of labour** increased. That is, work tasks became more specialized with each successive revolution. In pre-agrarian societies there were four main jobs: hunting wild animals, gathering wild edible plants, raising children, and tending to the tribe's spiritual needs. In contrast, a postindustrial society such as Canada boasts thousands of different kinds of jobs.

In some cases, increasing the division of labour involves creating new skills (e.g., Web site design, laser eye surgery). Some new jobs require long periods of study. Foremost among these are the professions, such as medicine, law, and engineering. In other cases, increasing the division of labour involves breaking a complex range of skills into a series of simple routines. For example, a hundred years ago, a butcher's job involved knowing how to dissect an entire cow. In today's meat-packing plant there are large stock scalpers, belly shavers, crotch busters, gut snatchers, gut sorters, snout pullers, ear cutters, eyelid removers, stomach washers (also known as belly bumpers), hind leg pullers, front leg toenail pullers, and oxtail washers. A different person performs each routine. None requires much skill.

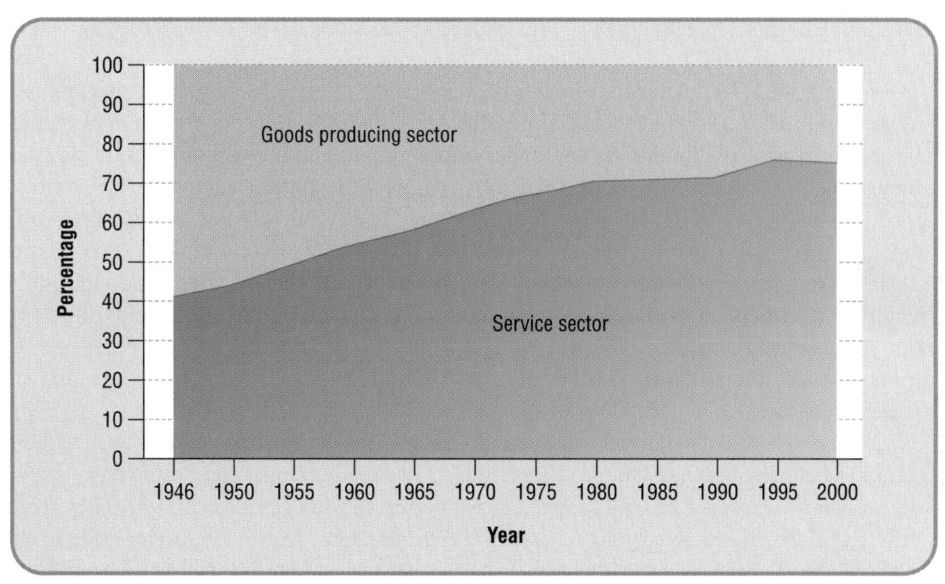


✦ **FIGURE 10.3** ✦
**Estimated Distribution of Canadian Labour Force in Goods Production and Services, 1946–2000**

Source: Adapted from Crompton and Vickers (2000).

If the division of labour increased as one work revolution gave way to the next, then social relations among workers also changed. In particular, work relations became more hierarchical. Although work used to be based on cooperation among equals, it now involves superordinates exercising authority and subordinates following commands. Owners oversee executives. Executives oversee middle managers. Middle managers oversee ordinary workers. Increasingly, work hierarchies are organized bureaucratically. That is, clearly defined positions and written goals, rules, and procedures govern the organization of work. Workplaces have grown enormously in size and many Canadians work in large organizations.

## "GOOD" VERSUS "BAD" JOBS

John Lie once got a job as a factory worker in Honolulu. "The summer after my second year in high school," John recalls, "I decided it was time to earn some money. I had expenses, after all, but only an occasionally successful means of earning money: begging my parents. Scouring the 'help wanted' ads in the local newspaper, I soon realized I wasn't really qualified to do anything in particular. Some friends at school suggested I apply for work at a pineapple-canning factory. So I did.

"At the factory, an elderly man asked me a few questions and hired me. I was elated—but only for a moment. A tour of the factory floor ruined my mood. Row upon row of conveyor belts carried pineapples in various states of disintegration. Supervisors hastened the employees to work faster yet make fewer mistakes. The smell, the noise, and the heat were unbearable. After the tour, the interviewer announced I would get the graveyard shift (11 p.m. to 7 a.m.) at minimum wage.

"The tour and the prospect of working all night finished me off. Now dreading the idea of working in the factory, I wandered over to a mall. I bumped into a friend there. He told me a bookstore was looking for an employee (9 to 5, no pineapple smell, and air conditioned, although still minimum wage). I jumped at the chance. Thus, my career as a factory worker ended before it ever began.

"A dozen years later, just after I got my Ph.D., I landed one of my best jobs ever. I taught for a year in South Korea. However, my salary hardly covered my rent. I needed more work desperately. Through a friend of a friend, I found a second job as a business consultant in a major corporation. I was given a big office with a panoramic view of Seoul and a personal secretary who was both charming and efficient. I wrote a handful of sociological reports that year on how bureaucracies work, how state policies affect workers, how the world economy had changed in the past two decades, and so on. I got to accompany the president of the company on trips to the United States. I spent most of my days reading books. I also went for long lunches with colleagues and took off several afternoons a week to teach."

What is the difference between a "good" job and a "bad" job, as these terms are usually understood? As John Lie's anecdote illustrates, bad jobs don't pay much and require the performance of routine tasks under close supervision. Working conditions are unpleasant, sometimes dangerous. Bad jobs require little formal education. In contrast, good jobs often require higher education. They pay well. They are not closely supervised and they encourage the worker to be creative in pleasant surroundings. Other distinguishing features of good and bad jobs are not apparent from the anecdote. Good jobs offer secure employment, opportunities for promotion, and other significant benefits. In a bad job, you can easily be fired, you receive few if any fringe benefits, and the prospects for promotion are few (Adams, Betcherman, and Bilson, 1995; Lowe, 2000). Bad jobs are often called "dead-end" jobs.

Notice that social scientists who discuss today's service revolution tend to have both good and bad jobs in mind. On the other hand, some social scientists prefer the term *knowledge revolution* to describe the current transformation of work (Drucker, 1993). They focus almost exclusively on good jobs, ignoring the tremendous growth of service jobs in the food and beverage industry or the transportation industry. Most jobs fall between the two extremes sketched above. They have some mix of good and bad features. But what can we say about the overall mix of jobs in Canada? Are there more good jobs than bad jobs? And what does the future hold? Are good jobs or bad jobs likely to become more plentiful? What are your job prospects? These are tough questions, not least because some conditions that influence the mix of good and bad jobs are unpredictable. Nonetheless, social research sheds some light on these issues (Krahn and Lowe, 1998; Beaudry and Green, 1998).

## The Deskilling Thesis

Harry Braverman (1974) proposed one view of the future of work about 30 years ago. Braverman argued that owners (capitalists) organize work to maximize profits. One way to increase profits is to break complex tasks into simple routines. This increased division of labour in the workforce has three important consequences. First, machinery can be used to replace workers. Second, given the simplification of work routines, less skilled, cheaper labour can be used. Third, employees can be controlled more directly since less worker discretion and skill is needed to complete each task. As a result, the future of work, as Braverman saw it, involves a **deskilling** trend.

Deskilling can be best understood as a separation between conception and execution in a job. In the 1910s, for example, Henry Ford introduced the assembly line with just this aim in mind. The assembly line enabled Ford to produce affordable cars for a mass market. Workers executed highly specialized, repetitive tasks requiring little skill at a pace set by their supervisors. Automotive designers and managers conceived of the end product and the machinery necessary to build it. The workers merely executed the instructions of their superiors. The term **fordism** is now often used to refer to this mass production assembly-line work.

Around the same time, Frederick W. Taylor developed the principles of **scientific management.** After analyzing the movements of workers as they did their jobs, Taylor trained them to eliminate unnecessary actions and greatly improve their efficiency. Workers became cogs in a giant machine known as the modern factory.

Many criticisms were lodged against Braverman's deskilling thesis in the 1970s and 1980s. Perhaps the most serious criticism was that he was not so much wrong as irrelevant. That is, even if his characterization of factory work was accurate (and we will see below that in some respects it was not), factory workers represent only a small proportion of the labour force. They represent a smaller proportion with every passing year. In 1974, the year Braverman's book was published, less than a quarter of the Canadian labour force was employed in manufacturing. By 2000, the figure had declined to approximately 15 percent.

Science fiction writer Isaac Asimov's claim that the factory of the future will employ only a man and a dog is clearly an exaggeration. (The man will be there to feed the dog, said Asimov. The dog will be there to keep the man away from the machinery.) However, it is clear that the manufacturing sector is shrinking and the service sector is expanding.

Charlie Chaplin's 1929 movie *Modern Times* was a humorous critique of the factory of his day. In the movie, Chaplin gets a tick and moves like a machine on the assembly line. He then gets stuck on a conveyor belt and run through a machine. Finally, he is used as a test dummy for a feeding machine. The film thus suggests that workers were being used for the benefit of the machines rather than the machines being used for the benefit of the workers.

The vital question, according to some of Braverman's critics, is not whether jobs are becoming worse in manufacturing but whether good jobs or bad jobs are growing in services, the sector that accounts for about three-quarters of Canadian jobs today. Put another way, does the Braverman deskilling thesis apply to both industrial labour and service work?

Shoshana Zuboff's analysis of office workers, mentioned at the beginning of this chapter, made it appear that Braverman's insights apply beyond the factory walls (Zuboff, 1988; see Lowe, 1987 on the evolution of office work in Canada). Zuboff argues that the computerization of the office in the 1980s involved increased supervision of deskilled work. And she is right, at least in part. The computer did eliminate many jobs and routinize others. It allowed supervisors to monitor every keystroke, thus taking worker control to a new level. Today, employees who consistently fall behind a prescribed work pace or use their computers for personal e-mail, surfing the Web, and other pastimes can easily be identified and then retrained, disciplined, or fired. In the 1980s and 1990s, some analysts feared that good jobs in manufacturing were being replaced by bad jobs in services. From this point of view, the entire labour force was experiencing a downward slide (Bluestone and Harrison, 1982; Rifkin, 1995).

## Part-Time Work

The growth of part-time work in Canada has added to concern about erosion of meaningful, dignified employment. The proportion of part-time workers in the Canadian labour force increased by more than 100 percent between 1976 and 2000. In 2000, just under one-fifth of all people in the Canadian labour force were part-timers, working fewer than 30 hours a week (Pold, 2001: 13).

For two reasons, the expansion of part-time work is not a serious problem in itself. First, some part-time jobs are good jobs in the sense we defined above. Second, some people want to work part time and can afford to do so (Marshall, 2001a). For example, some people who want a job also want to devote a large part of their time to family responsibilities. Part-time work affords them that flexibility. Similarly, many high-school and university students who work part time are happy to do so. Perhaps you have joined the ranks of part-time retail clerks and fast-food servers to help pay for tuition, a car, a vacation, or a wardrobe.

Although the growth of part-time jobs is not problematic for voluntary part-time workers or people who have good part-time jobs, an increasingly large number of people depend on part-time work for the necessities of full-time living. And the plain fact is that most part-time jobs are bad jobs. Thus, part-time workers make up about two-thirds of the people working at or below minimum wage. Moreover, the fastest-growing category of part-time workers is composed of *involuntary* part-timers. Today, according to official statistics, one-third of part-time workers want to be working more hours. And official statistics underestimate the scope of the problem. Surveys show that about one-third of women officially classified as voluntary part-time workers would work more hours if good child care or elder care was available (Duffy, Glenday, and Pupo, 1997).

The downside of part-time work is not only economic, however. Nor is it just a matter of coping with the dull routine illustrated in our discussion of "McDonaldization" in Chapter 5, Interaction and Organization. If you've ever had a bad part-time job, you know that one of its most difficult aspects involves maintaining your self-respect in the face of low pay, benefits, security, status, and creativity. In the words of Dennis, a McDonald's employee interviewed by sociologist Robin Leidner: "This isn't really a job . . . It's about as low as you can get. Everybody knows it" (quoted in Leidner, 1993: 182).

And, Dennis might have added, nearly everybody lets you know they know it. Ester Reiter (1991) studied fast-food workers in Toronto, many of whom are teenagers working part time. These workers are trained, Reiter noted, to keep smiling no matter how demanding or rude their customers may be. The trouble is you can only count backwards from 100 so many times before feeling utterly humiliated. Anger often boils over.

The difficulty of maintaining one's dignity as a fast-food worker is compounded by the high premium most young people place on independence, autonomy, and respect. The problem this creates for teenagers who take jobs in fast-food restaurants is that their constant deference to customers violates the norms of youth culture. Therefore, fast-food workers are typically stigmatized by their peers. They are frequently the brunt of insults and ridicule (Newman, 1999: 97).

Fast-food workers undoubtedly represent an extreme case of the indignity endured by part-timers. However, the problem exists in various guises in many part-time jobs. For instance, if you work as a "temp" in an office, you are more likely than other office workers to be the victim of sexual harassment (Welsh, 1999). You are especially vulnerable to unwanted advances because you lack power in the office and are considered "fair game." Thus, the form and depth of degradation may vary from one part-time job to another but, as your own work experience may show, degradation seems to be a universal feature of this type of deskilled work.

## A Critique of the Deskilling Thesis

The deskilling thesis undoubtedly captures one important tendency in the history of work, a trend toward the simplification of previously complex jobs. However, it paints an incomplete picture. Analyses such as Braverman's and Zuboff's are too narrowly focused. They analyze specific job categories near the bottom of the occupational hierarchy. Consequently, they do not provide evidence of what is occurring across the entire occupational structure. For instance, Zuboff analyzed lower-level service workers such as data entry personnel and routine claims processors in a health insurance company. Her research, while helping us understand the bottom range of the service sector, ignores the top.

Taking a broader perspective and examining the entire occupational structure, two lines of argument potentially undermine the deskilling thesis. First, not all jobs are being deskilled. Second, deskilling may be occurring primarily in jobs characteristic of the old economy (e.g., assembly-line manufacturing) but not in the new economy (e.g., biotechnology, infomatics). In fact, even on Ford's assembly line, not all jobs were deskilled. A new group of workers was required to design the assembly line and the new production machinery. New jobs higher up the skill hierarchy were therefore necessary.

In general, if deskilling has occurred for some jobs, has upskilling or reskilling of other jobs offset this trend or have new high-skilled jobs been introduced? This is not an easy question to answer. How do you measure changes in skill across all jobs in the labour force? For one thing, the meaning of skill is itself contentious. As we saw in Chapter 9, Sexuality and Gender, women's work has long been undervalued because the skills women bring to jobs have been devalued (Creese and Began, 1999). Jobs requiring more training and education might be thought of as requiring more skill, but many occupational groups work to inflate the credentials needed for job entry so that the prestige and remuneration of the occupation rises (Rinehart, 2001). More-skilled jobs might be thought of as those receiving more income, but here too unions and professional associations work to increase earnings in ways that may be unconnected to skill (see the discussion of unions and professional organizations below).

Although the definition of skill is contentious, this makes research on skills more difficult, not impossible. Research on work requires nuance and sophistication. It should be conducted using multiple methods (such as surveys of the workplace and of earnings, and comparative participant observation studies of jobs).

One reason social commentators have assumed that deskilling is occurring is because of the rise of the service sector. For example, many jobs in the fast-food business are dead-end jobs. However, although there are many low-paying jobs in services, there are also many high-paying jobs. Moreover, the distribution of income in services is practically the same as that in manufacturing. That is, there are just as many high-paid jobs as low-paid jobs in both sectors. On some measures of job quality, such as job security, service jobs are on average better than manufacturing jobs (Meisenheimer II, 1998). Thus, the decline of the manufacturing sector and the rise of the service sector do not imply a downward slide in the skills of the entire labour force. Indeed, based on evidence from a national survey of Canadians, Clement and Myles (1994: 72) note that "the net result of the shift to services has been to increase the requirements for people to think on the job." Generalizing about the entire labour force from case studies of just a few job categories is dangerous, but wide-ranging studies such as that of Clement and Myles (1994) across a wide array of jobs and skills are very rare.

Table 10.1 uses national survey evidence from five countries to examine the skill levels of workers in both the goods producing and the service sectors. Respondents on the survey were asked a series of questions about the requirements of their jobs, such as whether they designed and put into practice important aspects of their work. Skilled jobs were taken to be those requiring high levels of both conceptual autonomy and complexity. The results show that in all countries jobs in the service sector require higher levels of skill than do jobs in the goods producing sector. This international evidence is compelling. It undermines the idea of deskilling in the overall workforce since higher skill requirements are reported in the service economy, which is the fastest growing.

Even if we examine the least-skilled service workers—fast-food servers, video store clerks, parking lot attendants, and the like—we find reason to question one aspect of the deskilling thesis. For although these jobs are dull and pay poorly, they are not as "dead end" as they are frequently made out to be. The least-skilled service workers tend to be under the age of 25 and tend to hold their jobs only briefly. After working in these entry-level jobs for a short time, most men move on to blue-collar jobs and most women move on to clerical jobs. These are not great leaps up the socio-economic hierarchy, but the fact that they are common suggests that work is not all bleak and hopeless even at the bottom of the service sector (Jacobs, 1993; Myles and Turegun, 1994).

Braverman and Zuboff underestimated the continuing importance of skilled labour in the economy. Assembly lines and computers may deskill many factory and office jobs, but if deskilling is to take place, then some members of the labour force must invent, design, advertise, market, install, repair, and maintain complex machines, including computerized and robotic systems. Most of these people have better jobs than the factory and office workers analyzed by Braverman and Zuboff. Moreover, although technological innovations kill off entire job categories, they also create entire new industries with many good jobs.

Thus, 30 years ago, Santa Clara County in California was best known for its excellent prunes. Today, it has been transformed into Silicon Valley, home to many tens of thousands of electronic engineers, computer programmers, graphics designers, venture capitalists, and so forth. On a smaller scale, Kanata (on the outskirts of Ottawa), Waterloo, and Vancouver are similar success stories. The introduction of new production techniques may even increase a country's competitive position in the world market. This can lead to employment gains at both the low end and the high end of the job hierarchy as consumers abroad rush to purchase relatively low-cost goods.

Our analysis of good and bad jobs raises another question. To what extent, if at all, is the introduction of information technology influencing the nature and quality of work? At the start of the chapter we used the introduction of computers to illustrate the rise of the service sector. What consequence has the introduction of the computer had on the self-reported skills workers use and the income they derive from work? Hughes and Lowe (2000) examined both these questions by comparing workers who do and do not make use of computers at work. They found that people who use computers at work make use of very similar skills when compared with their colleagues who do not use computers. They

**✦ TABLE 10.1 ✦**

**Percentage of Employees in Skilled Jobs by Sector and Country**

Source: Clement and Myles (1994: 76).

| | Country | | | | |
|---|---|---|---|---|---|
| **Economic Sector** | **Canada** | **United States** | **Norway** | **Sweden** | **Finland** |
| Goods producing sector | 26 | 25 | 31 | 23 | 25 |
| Service sector | 42 | 38 | 47 | 43 | 46 |
| Difference between sectors | 16 | 13 | 16 | 20 | 21 |

Workers in the speaker assembly and packing area, Paradigm Loudspeakers, Mississauga, ON.

found that people using computers tend to earn more, but the effect of computer use on earnings was smaller than the effects of other factors. For example, the earnings difference between women and men was greater than the earnings difference between people who did and did not use computers at work.

The information technology revolution has transformed work, but there is little systematic evidence that it has degraded work or created a polarization in earnings between those who use this new technology and others who do not (Marshall, 2001b). Its transformative impact has been in plant and office automation, where many people's lives have been disrupted through job loss or reclassification. Overall, however, there is no systematic evidence that newer forms of workplace technology have caused the jobs in Canada to decline in number or become less skilled (Goyder, 1997).

## The Social Relations of Work

What have changed significantly with the rise of a more knowledge-intensive economy are the *social relations* of work. The industrial revolution ushered in an era of work that might best be described as requiring brute labour and obedience to authority. With the spinning jenny, the assembly line, and the increasing use of machinery in production, more and more work became industrialized, whether with printing presses, welding torches, or sewing machines. Workers were closely supervised in factory settings and an increasing division of labour meant that the skill content of certain jobs eroded.

It is misleading, however, to think that it takes less skill now to produce the goods and services we use than it did in previous centuries. One might reach this conclusion by focusing on the skills associated with specific jobs or job tasks, but not if one focuses on the skills associated with the entire process of providing goods and services. In short, rather than examining discrete parts of a specialized division of labour, it is important to attend to the entire process of producing goods and services. If anything, this process requires more skill because of the complexity of goods and services we now produce.

As Clement and Myles (1994) argue, the skill content of the entire labour process has risen, although much of that skill content now resides in managerial and administrative spheres. After the Industrial Revolution a managerial revolution evolved, a revolution involving the separation of conception and execution. More of the job of conception shifted to the managerial and administrative realm. Before the mass-produced sweater, individual artisans determined the patterns and colours they would use. Now, workers in most textile sweatshops have little discretion over what they produce. Managers decide on patterns and colours and they pass along orders to supervisors who direct shop floor production.

The rise of a managerial class that began with the advent of the manufacturing era has intensified in the postindustrial service revolution. Many service sector jobs are knowledge intensive and, as Clement and Myles (1994: 80) show, "postindustrial services employ more skilled managers than firms in goods and distribution." As well, these managers tend less often to have surveillance and supervision roles, and more often to have real decision-making power. The net result is the rise of a new middle class with greater power to make decisions about what is to be done and how it is to occur.

The newer social relations of work can be seen perhaps most starkly in Silicon Valley. Some top executives in Silicon Valley earn more than $100 million annually. Even at less lofty levels, there are many thousands of high-paying, creative jobs in the Valley, more than half of them dependent on the high-tech sector (Bjorhus, 2000). Amid all this wealth, however, the electronics assembly factories in Silicon Valley are little better than high-tech sweatshops. Most workers in the electronics factories earn less than 60 percent of the Valley's average wage. They work long hours and are frequently exposed to toxic solvents, acids, and gases. Semiconductor workers therefore suffer industrial illnesses at three times the average rate for other manufacturing jobs. Although the opulent lifestyles of Silicon Valley's millionaires are often featured in the mass media, one must remember that a more accurate picture of the Valley also incorporates those who execute the wishes of the knowledge workers and executives. It is not just single jobs that are changing, but the full spectrum of jobs that is being transformed.

Figure 10.4 illustrates the changing nature of the Canadian occupational structure. Based on projections by Industry Canada, the chart shows those areas of the economy, across a set of skill dimensions, that are expected to grow in the next decade. This pattern is consistent with the pattern of growing income inequality discussed in Chapter 7, Social Stratification: Canadian and Global Perspectives. There, you will recall, we noted growing inequality between the top 20 percent of income earners and the remaining 80 percent.

## Labour Market Segmentation

The processes sketched above are taking place in the last of the three stages of labour market development identified by David Gordon and his colleagues (Gordon, Edwards, and Reich, 1982). The period from about 1820 to 1890 was one of *initial proletarianization* in North America. During this period, a large industrial working class replaced craft workers in small workshops. Then, from the end of the nineteenth century until the start of the Second World War, the labour market entered the phase of *labour homogenization*. Extensive mechanization and deskilling took place during this stage. Finally, the third phase of labour market development is that of **labour market segmentation.** During this stage, which began after the Second World War and continues to the present, large business organizations emerged: GM Canada, Air Canada, Bombardier, Bell Canada Enterprises (BCE), and many others. Thousands of small businesses continue to exist at this stage. However, different kinds of jobs are associated with small businesses and large business organizations. Good jobs with security and relatively high wages tend to be concentrated in large firms while smaller businesses cannot afford the same wages and job

The electronics assembly factories in Silicon Valley and similar places are little better than high-tech sweatshops.

| Emerging (Growth) Sector | University | College/Technical | High School or Less Than High School |
|---|---|---|---|
| **Environment** | Biophysicist, agrologist, forest management, environmental engineer | Air quality specialist, environmental technologist, pollution prevention officer, regulations officer | Landfill equipment operator, sylviculture and forestry worker, aquaculture and marine harvest labourer |
| **Biotechnology** | Biologist, biophysics, engineering, food science and technology, pharmacy, bioethics | Chemical technician, biological technician, water supply manager, inspector in public and environmental health | Information clerk; reporting, scheduling, and distribution occupations; labourer |
| **Multimedia** | Lawyer specializing in protecting intellectual property rights, translator, network architect, information librarian | Animation designer, Web designer, production designer, ideas manager, videographer | Product tester, librarian and information clerk |
| **Aerospace** | Aeronautics specialist, aerospace engineer, software engineering, astrophysicist, sales and marketing specialist | Mechanic, aircraft inspector, machinist, tool and die maker, industrial design technologist | Assembler, machining, aircraft electronic assembler |

✦ **FIGURE 10.4** ✦
**Sample Occupations in Emerging Sectors**

Source: Adapted from Human Resources Development Canada (2000).

security provisions. The result is a *segmented* labour market. In these two different settings, workers, and the work they do, have different characteristics:

- The **primary labour market** is composed disproportionately of highly skilled, well-educated workers. They are employed in large corporations that enjoy high levels of capital investment. In the primary labour market, employment is relatively secure, earnings are high, fringe benefits are generous, and opportunities for advancement within the firm are good. Often the work is unionized because workers have the collective ability to exert pressure on their large employer.
- The **secondary labour market** contains a disproportionately large number of women and members of ethnic minorities, especially recent immigrants. Employees in the secondary labour market tend to be unskilled and lack higher education. They work in small firms with low levels of capital investment. Employment is insecure, earnings are low, fringe benefits are meagre, and mobility prospects are limited. These firms are often subcontracted by large corporations that minimize their risk by off-loading seasonal work (e.g., in logging and oil exploration) and work for which demand is volatile (e.g., in auto parts supply and house construction).

This characterization may seem to advance us only a little beyond our earlier distinction between good jobs and bad jobs. However, proponents of labour market segmentation theory offer fresh insights into two important issues. First, they argue that work is found in different ways in the two labour markets. Second, they point out that social barriers make it difficult for individuals to move from one labour market to the other. To appreciate the significance of these points, it is vital to note that workers do more than just work. They also seek to control their work and prevent outsiders from gaining access to it. Some workers are more successful in this regard than others. Understanding the social roots of their success or failure permits us to see why the primary and secondary labour markets remain distinct. Therefore, we now turn to a discussion of forms of worker control.

## Worker Resistance and Management Response

One of the criticisms lodged against Braverman's analysis of factory work is that he inaccurately portrays workers as passive victims of management control. In reality, workers often resist the imposition of task specialization and mechanization by managers. They go on strike, change jobs, fail to show up for work, sabotage production lines, and so forth (Burawoy, 1979; Clawson, 1980; Dunk, 1991).

Eventually, worker resistance causes management to modify its organizational plans. For example, Henry Ford was forced to double wages to induce his workers to accept the monotony, stress, and lack of autonomy associated with assembly line production. Even so, gaining the cooperation of workers proved difficult. Therefore, beginning in the 1920s, some employers started to treat their employees better and less like cogs in a giant machine. They hoped to improve the work environment and thus make their employees more loyal and productive.

In the 1930s, the **human relations school of management** emerged as a challenge to Frederick W. Taylor's scientific management approach. Originating in studies conducted at the Hawthorne plant of the Western Electric Company near Chicago, the human relations school of management advocated less authoritarian leadership on the shop floor. They encouraged careful selection and training of personnel and greater attention to human needs and employee job satisfaction (see Chapter 5, Interaction and Organization).

Over the next 70 years, owners and managers of big companies in all the rich industrialized countries realized they had to make more concessions to labour if they wanted a loyal and productive workforce. These concessions included not just higher wages but more decision-making authority about product quality, promotion policies, job design, product innovation, company investments, and so forth. The biggest concessions to labour were made in countries with the most powerful trade union movements, such as Sweden (see Chapter 11, Politics, and Chapter 17, Collective Action and Social Movements). In these countries, large proportions of eligible workers are members of unions (almost 90 percent in Sweden; see Olsen, 2002: 134). Moreover, unions are organized in nationwide umbrella organizations that negotiate directly with centralized business organizations and governments over wages and labour policy in general. At the other extreme is the United States, where less than 14 percent of the workforce is in a union (Olsen, 2002: 134).

Canada is located between these two extremes, although closer to the American than the Swedish model. In Canada, more than 3.5 million employees are union members (just over 30 percent of the workforce; see Akyeampong, 1999). Here, there is no centralized, nationwide bargaining among unions, businesses, and governments. Two indicators of the relative inability of Canadian workers to wrest concessions from their employers are given in Figures 10.5 and 10.6. In contrast to workers in Europe, Canadians work more hours per week than people in many other rich industrialized countries do. They also have fewer paid vacation days per year. However, Canadian workers are better off than their American counterparts on these two measures.

In the realm of industry-level decision making, too, Canadian workers lag behind workers in Western Europe and Japan. We can see this if we briefly consider the two main types of decision-making innovations that have been introduced in the factories of the rich industrialized countries since the early 1970s:

1. *Reforms that give workers more authority on the shop floor* include those advanced by the **quality of work life** movement. *Quality circles* originated in Sweden and Japan. They involve small groups of a dozen or so workers and managers collaborating to improve both the quality of goods produced and the communication between workers and managers. In some cases, this approach has evolved into a system that results in high productivity gains and worker satisfaction. For example, at Saab's main auto plant in Trolhattan, Sweden, the assembly line was eliminated (Krahn and Lowe, 1998: 239). Robots took over the arduous job of welding. In the welding area, groups of 12 workers program the computers, maintain the robots, ensure quality control, perform administrative tasks, and clean the area. Elsewhere

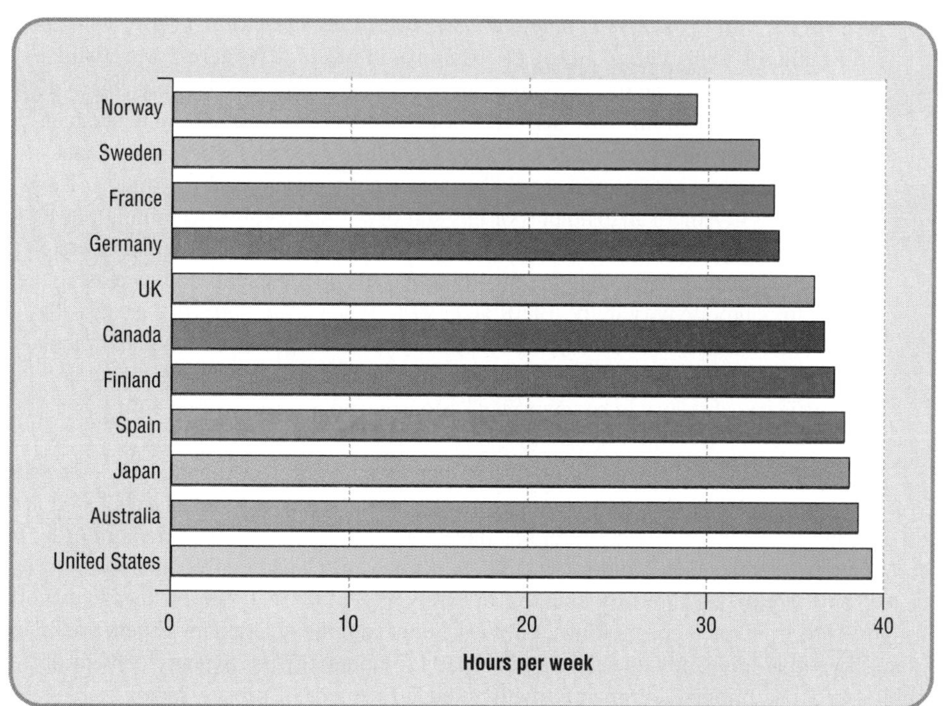


✦ **FIGURE 10.5** ✦
**Average Hours Worked per Week, Selected Countries, 1997–1998**

Source: "Mild Labor: The World at Work and Play" (1999).

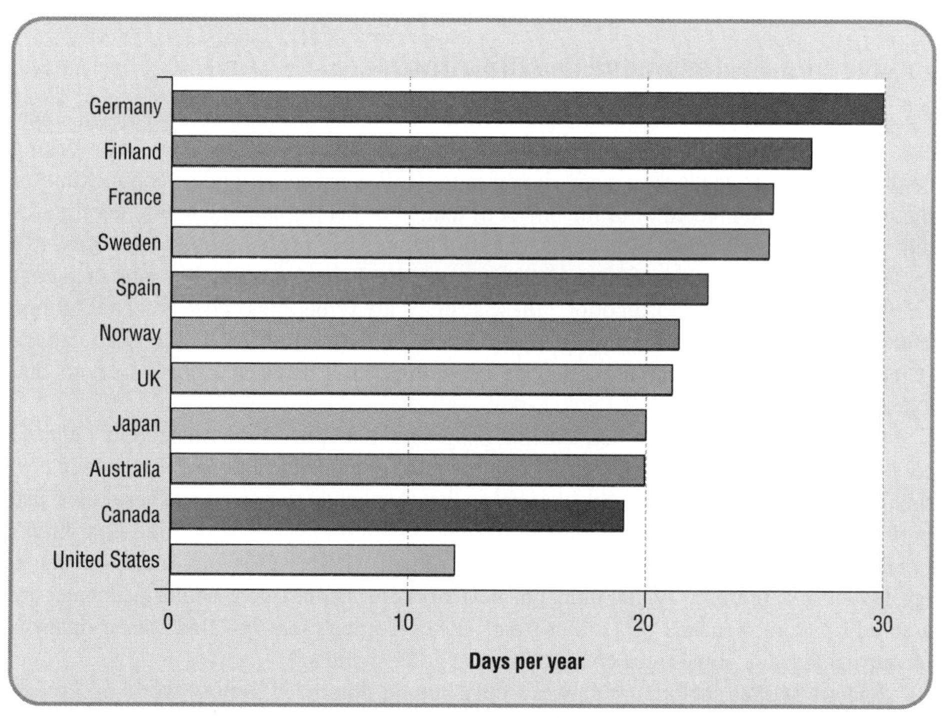


✦ **FIGURE 10.6** ✦
**Average Paid Vacation Days per Year, Selected Countries, 1997–1998**

Source: "Mild Labor: The World at Work and Play" (1999).

in the plant, autonomous teams build up inventory in "buffer zones" and decide themselves how to use it, thus introducing considerable flexibility into their schedule. All workers are encouraged to take advantage of many in-plant opportunities to upgrade their skills. Quality circles have been introduced in some Canadian industries, including automotive and aerospace. However, they are less widespread here than in Western Europe and Japan.

2. *Reforms that allow workers to help formulate overall business strategy* give workers more authority than quality circles. For example, in much of Western Europe workers are consulted not just on the shop floor but in the boardroom. In Germany, this system is known as **codetermination.** German workers' councils review and influence management policies on a wide range of issues, including when and where new plants should be built and how capital should be invested in technological innovation. There are a few North American examples of this sort of worker involvement in high-level decision making, mostly in the auto industry. Worker participation programs were widely credited with improving the quality of North American cars and increasing the auto sector's productivity in the 1980s and 1990s, making it competitive again with Japanese carmakers. However, "[w]orker participation programs have had a difficult birth in North America. No broad policy agenda guides their development, and no systematic social theory lights their way" (Hodson and Sullivan, 1995: 449).

Unions have clearly played a key role in increasing worker participation in industrial decision making since the 1920s and especially since the 1970s. To varying degrees, owners and managers of big corporations have conceded authority to workers in order to create a more stable, loyal, and productive workforce. In Canada, governments too have ceded some workplace authority to unionized workers. Public sector employees who work for government, Crown corporations, public schools, and the health care system are much more likely than their private sector counterparts to be unionized. Seventy percent of the public sector is unionized compared with about 20 percent of private sector employees. Understandably, workers who enjoy more authority in the workplace, whether unionized or not, have tried to protect the gains they have won. As we will now see, they have thereby contributed to the separation of primary and secondary labour markets.

## Unions and Professional Organizations

**Unions** are organizations of workers that seek to defend and promote their members' interests. By bargaining with employers, unions have succeeded in winning improved working conditions, higher wages, and more worker participation in industrial decision making for their members. One indicator of the power of unions is that the average hourly earnings of unionized workers is about $20, compared with about $16 for nonunionized workers.

In conjunction with employers, unions have also helped develop systems of labour recruitment, training, and promotion. These systems are sometimes called **internal labour markets** because they control pay rates, hiring, and promotions within corporations (Creese, 1999). At the same time, they reduce competition between a firm's workers and external labour supplies.

In an internal labour market, training programs that specify the credentials required for promotion govern advancement through the ranks. Seniority rules specify the length of time one must serve in a given position before being allowed to move up. These rules also protect senior personnel from layoffs according to the principle of "last hired, first fired." Finally, in internal labour markets, recruitment of new workers is usually limited to entry-level positions. In this way, the intake of new workers is controlled. Senior personnel are assured of promotion and protection from outside competition. For this reason, internal labour markets are sometimes called "labour market shelters."

Labour market shelters operate not only among unionized factory workers. Professionals, such as doctors, lawyers, and engineers, have also created highly effective labour market shelters. **Professionals** are people with specialized knowledge acquired through extensive higher education. They enjoy a high degree of work autonomy and usually regulate themselves and enforce standards through professional associations. The Canadian Medical Association is probably the best known and certainly one of the most powerful professional associations in the country. Professionals exercise authority over clients and subordinates. They operate according to a code of ethics that emphasizes the altruistic nature of their work. Finally, they specify the credentials needed to enter their professions and thus maintain a cap on the supply of new professionals. This reduces competition, ensures high demand for their services, and keeps their earnings high. In this way, the professions act as labour market shelters, much like unions. (For further discussion of professionalization, see Chapter 13, Religion and Education.)

## Barriers between the Primary and Secondary Labour Markets

We saw above that many workers in the secondary labour market do not enjoy the high pay, job security, and benefit packages shared by workers in the primary labour market, many of whom are members of unions and professional associations. We may now add that these workers find it difficult to exit the "job ghettos" of the secondary labour market. That is because three social barriers make the primary labour market difficult to penetrate:

1. *Often, there are few entry-level positions in the primary labour market.* One set of circumstances that contributes to the lack of entry-level positions in the primary labour market is corporate "downsizing" and plant shutdowns. These took place on a wide scale in Canada and the United States throughout the 1980s and early 1990s (see below and Box 10.1). The lack of entry-level positions is especially acute during periods of economic recession. A recession is usually defined as a period of six months or more during which the economy shrinks and unemployment rises. Canada was in the grip of recession just under 20 percent of the time between 1973 and the time of this writing (2002). Big economic forces such as plant shutdowns and recessions prevent upward mobility and often result in downward mobility.
2. *Workers often lack informal networks linking them to good job openings.* People often find out about job availability through informal networks of friends and acquaintances (Granovetter, 1995). These networks typically consist of people with the same ethnic and racial backgrounds. Recent immigrants, and especially refugees, who compose a disproportionately large share of workers in the secondary labour market and tend to be nonwhite, are less likely than others to find out about job openings in the primary labour market, where the labour force is disproportionately white. Even within ethnic groups, the difference between getting good work and having none is sometimes a question of having the right connections.
3. *Workers usually lack the required training and certification for jobs in the primary labour market.* What is more, due to their low wages and scarce leisure time, they usually cannot afford to upgrade either their skills or their credentials. Due to impersonal economic forces, a lack of network ties, and insufficient education, people often get stuck, usually permanently, in the secondary labour market.

## The Time Crunch and Its Effects

Although the quality of working life is much higher in the primary labour market than in the secondary labour market, one must be careful not to exaggerate the differences. Overwork and lack of leisure have become central features of our culture, and this is true in both labour markets. We are experiencing a growing time crunch. All the adults in most Canadian households work full time in the paid labour force and many adolescents work part time. Some people work two jobs to make ends meet. Many office workers, managers, and professionals work 10, 12, or more hours a day due to tight deadlines, demands for high productivity, and a trimmed-down workforce.

Over the past 50 years the average number of hours people spend working at their primary job has remained stable at between 35 and 40 per week. However, if

BOX 10.1
SOCIOLOGY AT THE MOVIES

Michael Moore directs *Roger and Me.*

### *ROGER AND ME* (1989)

Scene 1: An auto factory in Flint, Michigan. Scene 2: General Motors' chief executive officer, Roger Smith, announces he's closing the factory. Scene 3: Newspaper headlines proclaim that GM is opening plants in Mexico. Scene 4: Michael Moore, the director of the movie *Roger and Me*, tries to interview Roger Smith so he can get him to face up to the consequences of his corporate decisions for the ordinary citizens of Flint. Moore is repeatedly rebuffed. Scene 5: During a gala Christmas party, Smith talks about generosity and "the total Christmas experience." The scene is interlaced with shots of the families of fired auto workers being evicted from their homes. In one shot, a decorated Christmas tree is thrown on top of a family's belongings.

*Roger and Me* is an infuriating yet funny movie about deindustrialization and its impact on former GM workers in Flint. Over a decade, GM laid off more than 30 000 workers in the city and moved their jobs to Mexico. Flint, once prosperous, was soon dubbed by *Money* magazine as the worst place to live in the United States. In the movie, Michael Moore connects corporate decision making to everyday life in the United States and industrial policy abroad. We see how multinational corporations can close factories in one country, thereby exporting jobs to low-wage countries such as Mexico and overturning the lives of ordinary workers. Moore's attempts to interview Smith and discuss these issues are consistently irreverent and hilarious. When he tries to see Smith at his office, he offers the security guards his Chuck E. Cheese discount card for identification.

*Roger and Me* was released when many scholars and politicians were expressing fears that the North American labour force was on a downward slide because of deindustrialization. In cities such as Flint, some laid-off workers moved away. Others stayed but were unable to find work and so contributed to the rising poverty rate. The situation was similar in many communities in Canada in the 1980s due to the shutdown of factories, fish plants, pulp and paper mills, and sawmills. Like Flint, many Canadian communities—especially so-called single-industry towns such as Elliot Lake, Ontario; Sydney, Nova Scotia; and Tumbler Ridge, B.C.—never recovered. *Roger and Me* remains a testament to the suffering of laid-off employees when neither corporations nor governments assume any responsibility for compensating, retraining, and relocating them.

you reflect on the growth of part-time labour discussed earlier, something else must be happening to balance the fewer hours that these individuals spent at work. The offset comes from a growing number of Canadians working longer hours (Shields, 1999). For example, in 1995 almost one-quarter of all Canadian men and 9 percent of Canadian women in the paid labour force worked 41 or more hours per week. In 2000, 14 percent of Canadians in the paid labour force worked for pay 50 or more hours a week, up from 11 percent in 1976. In 1999, the figure was 38 percent among senior managers, the most overworked job category. Among transport and equipment operators, the second-most overworked job category, the figure was 27 percent. Among teachers and professors, the sixth-most overworked job category, the figure was 18 percent (Lowe, 2001: 8, 9). Add to this the heavy demands of family life, especially for women, and one can readily understand why stress, depression, aggression, and substance abuse are on the rise, in both the secondary and the primary labour markets. According to one human resources expert:

> People are on the edge, and acting it out in the workplace. They're yelling obscenities at each other, coming into work chronically late, throwing food in the cafeteria, and crying in the hallways. It's not just a matter of acting a little inappropriately any more. No, it's gotten far worse than that. Nice people are having trouble with alcohol, drugs, depression and acting aggressively at work.
>
> And these aren't isolated instances—instead, they're a composite picture from chronic work distress, as well as difficulties trying to deal with personal life overload from marital problems, single parenthood, financial worries and the like. The stress is so great that people are snapping. And no one has to tell you that it's getting worse. (Solomon, 1999: 48–49)

Stress is often defined as the feeling that one is unable to cope with life's demands given one's resources. Work is the leading source of stress throughout the world. In one study of office workers in 16 countries, including Canada, 54 percent of the respondents cited work as a current cause of stress in their lives and 29 percent cited money problems—which are also work-related since one's job is the main source of income for most people ("Work-related Stress: A Condition Felt 'Round the World,'" 1995). The rate of severe depression is also on the rise. In some countries, including Canada, people born after 1955 are three times more likely to experience serious depression than their grandparents (Weissman, 1992). According to a recent World Health Organization study, severe depression is the second-leading contributor to "disease burden" (years lived with a disability) in the rich postindustrial countries. It is predicted to rise to the number-one position by 2020 (Vernarec, 2000).

There are three main reasons why leisure is on the decline and the pace of work is becoming more frantic for those who are employed in the paid labour force (Schor, 1992). First, big corporations are in a position to invest increasingly enormous resources in advertising. As we saw in Chapter 3, Culture, advertising is pushing Canadians to consume goods and services at higher and higher levels all the time. Shopping has become an end in itself for many people, a form of entertainment and, in some cases, a deeply felt "need." Second, most corporate executives apparently think it is more profitable to push employees to work more hours rather than hire more workers and pay expensive benefits for new employees. Third, as we have just discussed, most Canadian workers in the private sector are not in a position to demand reduced working hours and more vacation time because few of them are unionized. They lack clout and suffer the consequences in terms of stress, depression, and other work-related ailments.

Bedtime at Yahoo! Inc. In high-tech industries, working on very little sleep is common. Here, David Filo, co-founder of Yahoo!, takes a nap under his desk.

## THE PROBLEM OF MARKETS

One conclusion we can draw from the preceding discussion is that the secondary labour market is a relatively **free market.** That is, the supply and demand for labour regulates wage levels and other benefits. If supply is high and demand is low, wages fall. If demand is high and supply is low, wages rise. People who work in the secondary labour market lack much power to interfere in the operation of the forces of supply and demand.

In contrast, the primary labour market is a more **regulated market.** Wage levels and other benefits are established not just by the forces of supply and demand but also by the power of workers and professionals. As we have seen, they are in a position to influence the operation of the primary labour market to their own advantage.

An unregulated market creates gross inequalities. Here, an account of a wife sold by her husband for nine-pence in Britain in 1823.

ACCOUNT OF THE

**SALE of a WIFE, by J. NASH,**

**IN THOMAS-STREET MARKET,**

On the 29th of May, 1823.

This day another of those disgraceful scenes which of late have so frequently annoyed the public markets in this country took place in St. Thomas's Market, in this city; a man (if he deserves the name) of the name of John Nash, a drover, residing in Rose-mary-street, appeared there leading his wife in a halter, followed by a great concourse of spectators; when arrived opposite the Bell-yard, he publicly announced his intention of disposing of his better half by Public Auction, and stated that the biddings were then open; it was a long while before any one ventured to speak, at length a young man who thought it a pity to let her remain in the hands of her present owner, generously bid 6d.! In vain did the anxious seller look around for another bidding, no one could be found to advance one penny, and after extolling her qualities, and warranting her sound, and free from vice, he was obliged, rather than keep her, to let her go at that price. The lady appeared quite satisfied, but not so the purchaser, he soon repented of his bargain, and again offered her to sale, when being bid nine-pence, he readily accepted it, and handed the lady to her new purchaser, who, not liking the transfer, made off with her mother, but was soon taken by her purchaser, and claimed as his property, to this she would not consent but by order of a magistrate, who dismissed the case. Nash, the husband, was obliged to make a precipitate retreat from the enraged populace.

Copy of Verses written on the Occasion:

COME all you kind husbands who have scolding wives,
Who thro' living together are tired of your lives,
If you cannot persuade her nor good natur'd make her
Place a rope round her neck & to market pray take her

Should any one bid, when she's offer'd for sale,
Let her go for a trifle lest she should get stale,
If six-pence be offer'd, & that's all can be had,
Let her go for the same rather than keep a lot bad.

Come all jolly neighbours, come dance sing & play,
Away to the wedding where we intend to drink tea;
All the world assembles, the young and the old,
For to see this fair beauty, as we have been told.

Here's success to this couple to keep up the fun,
May bumpers go round at the birth of a son;
Long life to them both, and in peace & content
May their days and their nights for ever be spent.

Shepherd, Printer, No. 6, on the Broad Weir, Bristol.

This suggests that the freer the market, the higher the resulting level of social inequality. In fact, in the freest markets, many of the least powerful people are unable to earn enough to subsist. A few of the most powerful people can amass unimaginably large fortunes. That is why the secondary labour market cannot be entirely free. Canadian governments have had to establish a legal minimum wage to prevent the price of unskilled labour from dropping below the point at which people are literally able to make a living (see Box 10.2). Similarly, in the historical period that most closely approximates a completely free market for labour—late eighteenth-century England—starvation became so widespread and the threat of social instability so great the government was forced to establish a system of state-run "poor houses" that provided minimal food and shelter for people without means (Polanyi, 1957 [1944]).

The question of whether free or regulated markets are better for society lies at the centre of much debate in economics and politics (Kuttner, 1997). For many economic sociologists, however, that question is too abstract. In the first place, regulation is not an either/or issue but a matter of degree. A market may be more or less regulated. No markets are completely unregulated. For example, various regulations and regulators monitor the Toronto Stock Exchange, the Ontario Securities Commission chief among them. Without some regulation, markets could not function. Second, markets may be regulated by different groups of people with varying degrees of power and different norms and values. Therefore, the costs and benefits of regulation may be socially distributed in many different ways. Sociological analysis can sort out the costs and benefits of different degrees of market regulation for various categories of the population. These, then, are the main insights of economic sociology as applied to the study of markets: (1) The structure of markets varies widely across cultures and historical periods. (2) The degree and type of regulation depends on how power, norms, and values are distributed among various social groups (Lie, 1992).

The economic sociologist's approach to the study of markets is different from that of the dominant trend in contemporary economics, known as the "neoclassical" school (Becker, 1976; Mankiw, 1998). Instead of focusing on how power, norms, and values shape markets, neoclassical economists argue that free markets maximize economic growth. We may use the minimum wage to illustrate their point. According to neoclassical

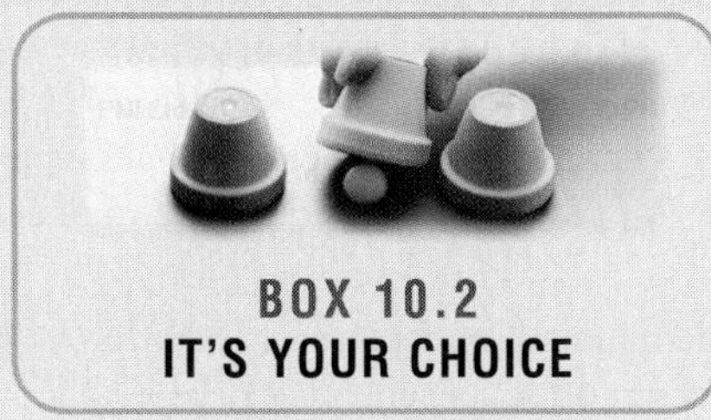

## BOX 10.2
## IT'S YOUR CHOICE

### THE MINIMUM WAGE

"Flipping burgers at Mickey D's is no way to make a living," a young man once told John Lie. Having tried his hand at several minimum-wage jobs as a teenager, John knew the young man was right.

In Canada, the provinces set the minimum wage. In 2001 it ranged from $5.50 in Newfoundland to $8.00 in B.C., with most provinces around the $7.00 range. At about $7 an hour a minimum-wage job may be fine for teenagers, many of whom are supported by their parents. However, it is difficult to live on one's own, much less to support a family, on a minimum-wage job, even if you work full time. This is the problem with the minimum wage. It does not amount to a living wage for many people.

In the 1990s about 60 percent of the 300 000 or so Canadians who received minimum wages for their work were adults over the age of 18. Most were women, many of them single mothers. Use $7 per hour as the base and calculate the annual income of someone working 52 weeks per year at 40 hours per week. The result: $14 560. This falls below the poverty line. Welcome to the "working poor." Could you live on $14 560 a year, especially if you had to support a child?

Given the thousands of Canadians who cannot lift themselves and their children out of poverty even if they work full time, many scholars and policymakers suggest raising the minimum wage (Goldberg and Green, 1999). Others disagree (Law, 1999). They fear that raising the minimum wage would decrease the number of available jobs. Others disagree in principle with government interference in the economy. Some scholars and policymakers even advocate the abolition of the minimum wage.

What do you think? Should the minimum wage be raised? Should someone working full time be entitled to live above the poverty level? Or should businesses be entitled to hire workers at whatever price the market will bear? It's your choice.

economists, if the minimum wage is eliminated entirely, everyone will be better off. For example, in a situation where labour is in low demand and high supply, wages will fall. This will increase profits. Higher profits will in turn allow employers to invest more in expanding their businesses. The new investment will create new jobs, and the rising demand for labour will drive wages up. Social inequality may increase but eventually *everyone* will be better off thanks to the operation of the free market.[1]

One difficulty with the neoclassical theory is that, in the real world, resistance to the operation of free markets increases as you move down the social hierarchy from the wealthiest and most powerful members of society to the poorest and least powerful. People at the low end of the social hierarchy usually fight against falling wages. The resulting social instability can disrupt production and investment. The riots in Argentina in late 2001 are a recent example. A social environment full of strikes, riots, and industrial sabotage is unfavourable to high productivity and new capital investment. That is why the economic system of a society at a given time is a more or less stable set of compromises between advocates and opponents of free markets. Markets are only as free as people are prepared to tolerate, and their degree of tolerance varies historically and among cultures (Berger and Dore, 1996; Doremus et al., 1998).

In the rest of this chapter, we offer several illustrations of how sociologists analyze markets. First, we compare capitalism and communism, the two main types of economic system in the twentieth century. Second, we examine the ability of big corporations to shape Canadian markets today. Finally, we extend our analysis of corporate and free market growth to the global level. We identify advocates and opponents of these developments and sketch the main work-related decisions that face us in the early twenty-first century.

## Capitalism and Communism

### Capitalism

The world's dominant economic system today is **capitalism.** Capitalist economies have two distinctive features:

1. *Private ownership of property.* In capitalist economies, individuals and corporations own almost all the means of producing goods and services. Individuals and corporations are therefore free to buy and sell land, natural resources, buildings, manufactured goods, medical services, and just about anything else. Like individuals, **corporations** are legal entities. They can enter contracts and own property. However, corporate ownership has two advantages over individual ownership. First, corporations are taxed at a lower rate than individuals. Second, the corporation's owners are not normally liable if the corporation harms consumers or goes bankrupt. Instead, the corporation itself is legally responsible for damage and debt. Incorporation ensures limited liability for owners.
2. *Competition in the pursuit of profit.* The second hallmark of capitalism is that producers, motivated by the lure of profits, compete to offer consumers desired goods and services at the lowest possible price. A purely capitalist economy is often called a laissez-faire system. *Laissez-faire* is French for "allow to do." In a laissez-faire system, the government does not interfere in the operation of the economy at all; it allows producers and consumers to do what they want. Adam Smith was an eighteenth-century Scottish economist who first outlined the operation of the ideal capitalist economy. According to Smith, everyone benefits from laissez-faire. The most efficient producers make profits while consumers can buy at low prices. If everyone pursues their narrow self-interest, unimpeded by government, the economy will achieve "the greatest good for the greatest number," said Smith (1776/1981).

In reality, no economy is purely laissez-faire. The state had to intervene heavily to create markets in the first place. For example, 500 years ago the idea that land is a commodity that can be bought, sold, and rented on the free market was utterly foreign to the Aboriginal peoples who lived in the territory that is now North America. To turn the land into a marketable commodity, European armies had to force Aboriginal peoples off the land and eventually onto reserves. Governments had to pass laws regulating the ownership, sale, and rent of land. Without the military and legal intervention of government, no market for land would exist.

Today, governments must also intervene in the economy to keep the market working effectively. For instance, governments create and maintain an economic infrastructure (roads, ports, etc.) to make commerce possible. They pass laws governing the minimum wage, occupational health and safety, child labour, and industrial pollution to protect workers and consumers from the excesses of corporations. If very large corporations get into financial trouble, they can expect the government to bail them out on the grounds that their bankruptcy would be devastating to the economy. For example, when Chrysler was facing financial ruin in the 1970s, the U.S. federal government stepped in with low-interest loans and other help to keep the corporation afloat. The Canadian government also plays an influential role in establishing, promoting, and supporting many leading industries, especially those that require large outlays on research and development, such as Bombardier and Monsanto. Agriculture Canada, for example, works closely with corporate interests in the cultivation and export of Canadian wheat. Industry Canada plays a leading role in promoting Canadian products abroad. The foundations of the Internet in the late 1960s and the subsequent development of the World Wide Web depended fundamentally on the support of the U.S. government. One of the most contentious issues of government intervention is the policy of both the Canadian and the United States governments to subsidize farmers, often paying them not to grow or harvest crops in order to keep prices up, despite widespread hunger in many regions of the world.

**✦ TABLE 10.2 ✦**

**The 10 Most Competitive and 10 Least Competitive Capitalist Economies in the World, 2002 (*n* = 49)**

| Country | Competitiveness Score |
|---|---|
| 1. United States | 100.0 |
| 2. Finland | 84.4 |
| 3. Luxembourg | 84.3 |
| 4. The Netherlands | 82.8 |
| 5. Singapore | 81.2 |
| 6. Denmark | 80.4 |
| 7. Switzerland | 79.5 |
| 8. Canada | 79.0 |
| 9. Hong Kong | 77.8 |
| 10. Ireland | 76.2 |
| . . . | |
| 40. Philippines | 41.5 |
| 41. Mexico | 41.4 |
| 42. India | 40.7 |
| 43. Russia | 39.0 |
| 44. Colombia | 38.1 |
| 45. Poland | 30.2 |
| 46. Turkey | 28.0 |
| 47. Indonesia | 26.9 |
| 48. Venezuela | 26.9 |
| 49. Argentina | 26.0 |

Source: International Institute for Management Development (2002).

*Note*: Many countries, especially poor ones, are not on this list because comprehensive economic data are unavailable for them.

As these examples of government intervention suggest, we should see Adam Smith's ideal of a laissez-faire economy as just that: an ideal. In the real world, markets are free to varying degrees, but none is or can be entirely free. Which capitalist economies are the freest and which are the least free? The International Institute for Management Development in Switzerland publishes a widely respected annual index of competitiveness for 49 capitalist countries. The index is based on the amount of state ownership of industry and many other indicators of market freedom. Table 10.2 (page 311) gives the overall scores for the 10 most competitive and 10 least competitive economies in 2002. The United States tops the list. It is the most competitive economy in the world with a score of 100. Canada is in eighth position, with Russia ranking forty-third and Argentina in forty-ninth place.

## Communism

Like laissez-faire capitalism, communism is an ideal. **Communism** is the name Karl Marx gave to the classless society that, he said, is bound to develop out of capitalism. Socialism is the name he gave to the transitional phase between capitalism and communism. No country in the world is communist in the pure sense of the term. About two dozen countries in Asia, South America, and Africa consider themselves socialist. These include China, North Korea, Vietnam, and Cuba. As an ideal, communism is an economic system with two distinct features:

1. *Public ownership of property*. Under communism, the state owns almost all the means of producing goods and services. Private corporations do not exist. Individuals are not free to buy and sell goods and services. The purported aim of public ownership is to ensure that all individuals have equal wealth and equal access to goods and services.
2. *Government planning*. Five-year state plans establish production quotas, prices, and most other aspects of economic activity. The political officials who design the state plans, and not the forces of supply and demand, determine what is produced, in what quantities, and at what prices. A high level of control of the population is required to implement these rigid state plans. As a result, democratic politics is not allowed to interfere with state activities. Only one political party exists—the Communist Party. Elections are held regularly, but only members of the Communist Party are allowed to run for office (Zaslavsky and Brym, 1978). In contrast to a capitalist "competitive" economy, communism is often thought of as a "command" economy.

Several highly industrialized countries, including Sweden, Denmark, Norway, and, to lesser degree, France and Germany, are "democratic socialist" societies. Like Canada, they are prosperous and enjoy multi-party elections. However, their governments intervene in the economy much more than we are used to in Canada. At their core, however, and despite their name, the democratic socialist countries are capitalist. The great bulk of property is privately owned and competition in the pursuit of profit is the main motive for business activity.

Until recently, the countries of Central and Eastern Europe were single-party, socialist societies. The most powerful of these countries was the Soviet Union, which was composed of Russia and 14 other socialist republics. In perhaps the most surprising and sudden change in modern history, the countries of the region began introducing capitalism and holding multi-party elections in the late 1980s and early 1990s.

The collapse of socialism in Central and Eastern Europe was due to several factors. For one thing, the citizens of the region enjoyed few civil rights. For another, their standard of living was only about half as high as that of people in the rich industrialized countries of the West. The gap between East and West grew as the arms race between the Soviet Union and the United States intensified in the 1980s. The standard of living fell as the Soviet Union mobilized its economic resources to try to match the quantity and quality of military goods produced by the United States. Dissatisfaction was widespread and expressed itself in many ways, including strikes and political demonstrations. It grew as television and radio signals beamed from the West made the gap between socialism and capitalism more apparent to the citizenry. Eventually, the communist parties of the region felt they could no longer govern effectively and so began to introduce reforms.

In the 1990s, some Central and East European countries were more successful than others in introducing elements of capitalism and raising their citizens' standard of living. The Czech Republic was among the most successful. Russia and most of the rest of the former Soviet Union were least successful. Many factors account for the different success rates, but perhaps the most important is the way in which different countries introduced reforms. The Czechs introduced both of the key elements of capitalism, private property and competition, in the pursuit of profit. The Russians, however, introduced private property without much competition. Specifically, the Russian government first allowed prices to rise to market levels. This made many basic goods too expensive for a large part of the population, which was quickly impoverished. Next, the government sold off state-owned property to individuals and corporations. However, the only people who could afford to buy the factories, mines, oil refineries, airlines, and other economic enterprises were organized criminals and former officials of the Communist Party. They alone had access to sufficient capital and insider information about how to make the purchases (Handelman, 1995). The effect was to make Russia's level of socio-economic inequality among the highest in the world.

A crucial element lacking in the Russian reform was competition. A few giant corporations control nearly every part of the Russian economy. They tend not to compete against each other. Competition would drive prices down and efficiency up. However, these corporations are so big they can agree among themselves to set prices at levels that are most profitable for them. They thus have little incentive to innovate. Moreover, they are so big and rich they have enormous influence over government. When a few corporations are so big they can behave in this way, they are called **oligopolies**.[2] Russia is full of them. The lack of competition in Russia has prevented the country from experiencing much economic growth since reforms began more than a decade ago (Brym, 1996a, 1996b, 1996c).

## The Corporation

Oligopolies can constrain innovation in all societies. They can force consumers to pay higher prices. They can exercise excessive influence on governments. However, in Canada and other Western countries, so-called "antitrust" laws limit their growth. In 1889, Canada first introduced legislation restricting businesses from combining or colluding to control markets. Replaced in 1923 by the Combines Investigation Act, the law allows government to review corporate mergers and acquisitions. Bank mergers have been a recent point of contention in Canada, with several of our largest banks wanting to merge in order to compete more successfully internationally. Resistance to such mergers is based on concern about job losses and restricted consumer banking choices.

However, the law has been only partly effective in stabilizing the growth of oligopolies. You need look no further than your local gas station to find an example that continues to suggest price competition is not as vigorous as the idea of "antitrust" implies. In the 1970s, Robert Bertrand, then director of the Investigations and Research Branch, Combines Investigation Act, wrote a 7-volume, 1700-page report implying that big oil companies engaged in monopoly practices. James Lorimer (1981) published extracts from the report under the provocative title, "Canada's Oil Monopoly: The Story of the $12 Billion Rip-off of Canadian Consumers."

Canadian banking provides an apt illustration of corporate concentration (although the beer industry, retail gas sales, or the movie theatre industry would provide equally compelling cases). First, there are only 11 domestic banks. Several of them are so small you have likely never heard of them. These include Citizens Bank of Canada and First Nations Bank of Canada. Second, the top four banks, as ranked by the value of their assets, control about 85 percent of all banking assets in the country. Even adding all the credit unions and trust companies in Canada, as well as all the foreign bank subsidiaries, the top four banks

In 1974, charges were laid against K. C. Irving Ltd. for monopoly ownership of all five daily newspapers in New Brunswick. The Crown failed to show that the Irving monopoly was detrimental to the public, so the monopoly remains in place. In general, Canadian laws preventing the growth of oligopolies and monopolies have been ineffectual. Today, in addition to newspapers, the Irving family enjoys dominant interests in New Brunswick's petroleum industry (including oil refining and gas stations), forest industry (including pulp and paper mills, lumber production, building supplies and equipment, and cardboard box and paper bag production), agriculture (including potato farming, fertilizer and chemical sales, farm machinery, and potato buying and processing), transportation (including shipbuilding, tugboats, fishing vessels, bus lines and parts, aircraft, trucking and truck building), and construction (including engineering consulting, industrial equipment and machinery, and plumbing and heating). Shown here in a 1979 photo is K.C. Irving, the founder of the Irving empire.

still control well over three-quarters of all assets. When Canada Trust was purchased by Toronto Dominion Bank in 2000, this asset concentration increased. Such concentration is a world apart from the early nineteenth century, when most businesses, including banks, were family owned and served only local markets (National Council on Welfare, 1998b; Whittington, 1999).

Recent mergers and acquisitions in the global automotive industry also illustrate corporate concentration. Chrysler and Daimler-Benz merged in a deal worth US$39 billion. Other new partnerships in recent years involved Volkswagen's takeover of Rolls Royce, Ford's takeover of Volvo's car division, and the alliance between Renault and Nissan. Such mergers create enormous organizations.

It is also important to note that a significant effect of Canadian competition law is to encourage big companies to diversify. That is, rather than increasing their share of control in their own industry, corporations often move into new industries, the better to avoid antitrust laws. Big companies that operate in several industries at the same time are called **conglomerates.** For example, Bell Canada Enterprises (BCE) is not just a telephone company. It owns CTV, *The Globe and Mail*, Sympatico, Teleglobe, and ExpressVu, among other companies. It is a giant conglomerate with more than 50 000 employees and assets of more than $22 billion. BCE is one example of the rapidly expanding conglomerates operating the world over. Big companies are swallowed up by still bigger ones in wave after wave of corporate mergers (Mizruchi, 1982, 1992).

Outright ownership of a company by a second company in another industry is only one way corporations may be linked. **Interlocking directorates** are another. Interlocking directorates are formed when an individual sits on the board of directors of two or more noncompeting companies. (Antitrust laws prevent an individual from sitting on the board of directors of a competitor.) For instance, in 2001 the board of directors of BCE included, among others, the president of George Weston Limited (who owns Loblaws), the chair of the board of Nova Chemicals, and the president and chief executive officer of Canadian National Railways. Such interlocks enable corporations to exchange valuable information and form alliances for their mutual benefit. They also create useful channels of communication to, and influence over, government since some board members of major corporations are likely to be former senior politicians. In 2002, for example, former prime minister Brian Mulroney became a member of the board of directors of Quebecor World, the largest commercial print media services company in the world (Carroll, 1986; Marchak, 1991).

Of course, small businesses continue to exist. In Canada, 78 percent of all businesses have fewer than five employees, and 97 percent have fewer than 50 employees (see Table 10.3). Small firms, which are a critical feature of the Canadian economy, are particularly important in the service sector. However, compared with large firms, profits in small firms are typically low, and bankruptcies are common. Small firms often use outdated production and marketing techniques. Jobs in small firms frequently have low wages and meagre benefits.

A sizable portion of the Canadian labour force works in large corporations. Specifically, about 4 in 10 workers are employed in firms with more than 500 employees, even though the percentage of such firms is very small (0.2 percent). Canada's largest private sector employer is the Loblaws food chain, owned by George Weston Ltd., with more than 100 000 employees. Onex Corporation, a conglomerate that many people have never heard of, employs more than 80 000 Canadians in diverse firms that include interests in airline catering, electronics manufacturing, sugar refining, and automotive parts.

## Globalization

As noted above, in the 1980s and early 1990s, Canada was hit by a wave of corporate "downsizing" (Grayson, 1985). Especially in the older manufacturing industries, thousands of blue-collar workers and middle managers were fired. In places such as Cape Breton, Nova Scotia; Ocean Falls, B.C.; and Ingersol, Ontario, the consequences were dev-

| Size of Firm | Percent of All Firms | Percent of All Employees |
|---|---|---|
| Fewer than 50 employees | 37.0 | 97.4 |
| Between 50 and 499 employees | 23.0 | 2.4 |
| 500 or more employees | 40.0 | 0.2 |

✦ **TABLE 10.3** ✦
**Number of Employees and Number of Firms by Size of Firm, 1996**

Source: Statistics Canada (2000i), 1997 Employment Dynamics [most recent data available].

astating. Unemployment soared. Social problems such as alcoholism and wife abuse became acute. Some people blamed government for the plant shutdowns. They said taxes were so high, big corporations could no longer make decent profits. Others blamed the unemployed themselves. They said powerful unions drove up the hourly wage to the point where companies were losing money.

In the 1980s, workers, governments, and corporations got involved as unequal players in the globalization of the world economy. Japan and Germany had fully recovered from the devastation of the Second World War. With these large and robust industrial economies now firing on all cylinders, American- and Canadian-based multinationals were forced to cut costs and become more efficient to remain competitive. On a scale far larger than ever before, they began to build branch plants in low-wage countries such as Mexico and China to take advantage of cheap labour and low taxes. Multinational corporations based in Japan and other highly industrialized countries did the same.

However, although multinational corporations could easily move investment capital from one country to the next, workers were rooted in their communities and governments were rooted in their nation-states. Multinationals thus had a big advantage over the other players in the globalization game. They could threaten to move plants unless governments and workers made concessions. They could play one government off another in the bidding war for new plants. And they could pick up and leave when it became clear that relocation would do wonders for their bottom line.

Today, more than 20 years after the globalization game began in earnest, it is easier to identify the winners than the losers. The clear winners are the stockholders of the multinational corporations, whose profits have soared. The losers, at least initially, were blue-collar workers. To cite just one example, in the past two decades General Motors has cut its workforce in Canada and the United States by about one-third in the face of stiff competition from automotive giants in Japan and Germany, in particular.

Even while these cuts were being made, however, some large manufacturers were hiring. For instance, employment at Bombardier grew dramatically, and this Canadian-owned vehicle and aerospace firm is now a world leader. In the service sector, employment soared, as we have seen. Corporations such as Loblaws, Molson Breweries, and the Hudson Bay Company employ tens of thousands of Canadians.

## Globalization in the Less Developed Countries

It is still too soon to tell whether the governments and citizens of the less developed countries will be losers or winners in the globalization game. On the one hand, it is hard to argue with the assessment of the rural Indonesian woman interviewed by Diane Wolf. She prefers the regime of the factory to the tedium of village life. In the village, the woman worked from dawn till dusk doing household chores, taking care of siblings, and feeding the family goat. In the factory, she earns less than $1 a day sewing pockets on men's shirts in a hot factory. Yet because work in the factory is less arduous, pays something, and holds out the hope of even better work for future generations, the woman views it as nothing less than liberating (Wolf, 1992). Many workers in other regions of the world where branch plants of multinationals have sprung up in recent decades feel much the same way. A wage of $3 an hour is excellent pay in Mexico, and workers rush to fill jobs along Mexico's northern border with the United States.

Yet the picture is not all bright. The governments of developing countries attract branch plants by imposing few if any pollution controls on their operations. This has dangerous effects on the environment. Typically, fewer jobs are available than the number of workers who are drawn from the countryside to find work in the branch plants. This results in the growth of urban slums that suffer from high unemployment and unsanitary conditions. High-value components are often imported. Therefore, the branch plants create few good jobs involving design and technical expertise. Finally, some branch plants—particularly clothing and shoe factories in Asia—exploit children and women, requiring them to work long workdays at paltry wages and in unsafe conditions.

Companies such as Nike and the Gap have been widely criticized for conditions in their overseas sweatshops. Nike is the market leader in sports footwear. It has been at the forefront of moving production jobs overseas to places such as Indonesia. There, Nike factory workers make about 10 cents an hour. That is why labour costs account for only about 4 percent of the price of a pair of Nike shoes. Workdays in the factories stretch as long as 16 hours. Substandard air quality and excessive exposure to toxic chemicals such as toluene are normal. An international campaign aimed at curbing Nike's labour practices has had only a modest impact. For example, in 1999, wages in the Indonesian factories were raised about a penny an hour ("The Nike Campaign," 2000).

Meanwhile, the Gap has invested heavily in the Northern Mariana Islands near Guam. Strictly speaking, the Marianas are not a poor foreign country since they form a U.S. commonwealth territory with a status similar to that of Puerto Rico. But they might as well be. Garment manufacturing is the biggest source of income on the islands and the Gap (which also owns Banana Republic and Old Navy) is the biggest employer. What attracts the Gap to the Marianas are below-minimum U.S. wage rates, duty-free access to U.S. markets, and the right to sew "Made in U.S.A." labels on clothes manufactured there (Bank of Hawaii, 1999). However, work conditions are horrific. Many workers live in guarded dormitories surrounded by barbed wire preventing their escape. And they work 12 to 18 hours a day without overtime. At the very least, cases like the Gap in the Marianas and Nike in Indonesia suggest that the benefits of foreign investment are unlikely to be uniformly beneficial for the residents of developing countries in the short term.

Some people in the rich, industrialized countries oppose the globalization of commerce. Shown here are demonstrators marching the streets of Calgary in June 2002 as part of a protest against the meeting of the G8 economic summit in Kananaskis, Alberta.

"As a movement we could be organizing regional actions that are based around community needs and desires, which are at odds with capitalist driven globalization. Regional organizers should build links with community struggles, to organize against oppression, both outside and within our movements. Organizers could use the Kananaskis G8 summit as a rallying point for the connection of local and international movements. We need to analyze the way that we organize, to make our actions and movements accessible and radical. We need to commit to do the hard work of helping to build an anti-racist, anti-imperialist, multiracial, feminist, queer liberationist, and anti-authoritarian movement against global capitalism" (http://g8.activist.ca/calltoaction/local.html).

## The Future of Work and the Economy

Although work and the economy have changed enormously over the years, one thing has remained constant for centuries. Businesses have always looked for ways to cut costs and boost profits. Two of the most effective means they have adopted for accomplishing these goals involve introducing new technologies and organizing the workplace in more efficient ways. Much is uncertain about the future of work and the economy. However, it is a pretty good bet that businesses will continue to follow these established practices.

Just how these practices will be implemented is less predictable. For example, it is possible to use technology and improved work organization to increase productivity by complementing the abilities of skilled workers. Worldwide, the automotive, aerospace, and computer industries have tended to adopt this approach. They have introduced automation and robots on a wide scale. They constantly upgrade the skills of their workers. And they have proven the benefits of small autonomous work groups for product quality, worker satisfaction, and therefore the bottom line. On the other hand, new technology and more efficient work organization can be used to replace workers, deskill jobs, and employ low-cost labour—mainly women and minority group members—on a large scale. Women are entering the labour force at a faster rate than men are. Competition from low-wage industries abroad remains intense. Therefore, the second option is especially tempting in some industries.

Our analysis suggests that each of the scenarios sketched above will tend to predominate in different industries. As a result, good jobs in the primary sector and bad jobs in the secondary sector are likely to continue. The pressure of competition will continue to prompt innovation and restructuring. However, we have also suggested that workplace struggles have no small bearing on how technologies are implemented and work is organized. To a degree, therefore, the future of work and the economy is up for grabs.

## SUMMARY

1. The first work-related revolution began about 10 000 years ago when people established permanent settlements and started herding and farming. The second work-related revolution began 220 years ago when various mechanical devices such as the steam engine greatly increased the ability of producers to supply markets. The third revolution in work is marked by growth in the provision of various services. It accelerated in the final decades of the twentieth century with the widespread use of the computer.
2. Each revolution in work increased productivity and the division of labour, caused a sectoral shift in employment, and made work relations more hierarchical. However, for the past 30 years the degree of hierarchy has been lowered in some industries, resulting in productivity gains and more worker satisfaction.
3. Deskilling and the growth of part-time jobs are two of the main trends in the workplace in the twentieth century. However, skilled labour has remained very important in the economy.
4. Good jobs have become more plentiful but the number of bad jobs is also growing rapidly. The result is a segmentation of the labour force into primary and secondary labour markets. Various social barriers limit mobility from the secondary to the primary labour market.
5. Workers have resisted attempts to deskill and control jobs. As a result, business has had to make concessions by giving workers more authority on the shop floor and in formulating overall business strategy. Such concessions have been biggest in countries where workers are more organized and powerful.
6. Unions and professional organizations have established internal labour markets to control pay rates, hiring, and promotions in organizations and reduce competition with external labour supplies.
7. Markets are free or regulated to varying degrees. No market that is purely free or completely regulated could function for long. A purely free market would create unbearable inequalities and a completely regulated market would stagnate.
8. Corporations are the dominant economic players in the world today. They exercise disproportionate economic and political influence by forming oligopolies, conglomerates, and interlocking directorates.
9. Growing competition among multinational corporations has led big corporations to cut costs by building more and more branch plants in low-wage, low-tax countries. Stockholders have profited from this strategy. However, the benefits for workers in both the industrialized and the less developed countries have been mixed.

## GLOSSARY

**Capitalism** is the dominant economic system in the world today. Private ownership of property and competition in the pursuit of profit characterize capitalist economies.

**Codetermination** is a German system of worker participation that allows workers to help formulate overall business strategy. German workers' councils review and influence management policies on a wide range of issues, including when and where new plants should be built and how capital should be invested in technological innovation.

**Communism** is a social and economic system in which property is owned by public bodies and government planning, not the market, determines production and distribution. Public ownership implies that workers share in the value of goods and services produced.

**Conglomerates** are large corporations that operate in several industries at the same time.

**Corporations** are legal entities that can enter into contracts and own property. They are taxed at a lower rate than individuals and their owners are normally not liable for the corporation's debt or any harm it may cause the public.

**Deskilling** refers to the process by which work tasks are broken into simple routines requiring little training to perform. Deskilling is usually accompanied by the use of machinery to replace labour wherever possible and increased management control over workers.

The **division of labour** refers to the specialization of work tasks. The more specialized the work tasks in a society, the greater the division of labour.

The **economy** is the institution that organizes the production, distribution, and exchange of goods and services.

**Fordism** is a method of industrial management based on assembly-line methods of production of cheap, uniform commodities in high volume that incorporates the principles of *scientific management.*

In a **free market,** prices are determined only by supply and demand.

The **human relations school of management** emerged as a challenge to Taylor's scientific management approach in the 1920s. It advocated less authoritarian leadership on the shop floor, careful selection and training of personnel, and greater attention to human needs and employee job satisfaction.

**Interlocking directorates** are formed when an individual sits on the board of directors of two or more noncompeting companies.

**Internal labour markets** are social mechanisms for controlling pay rates, hiring, and promotions within corporations while reducing competition between a firm's workers and external labour supplies.

**Labour market segmentation** is the division of the market for labour into distinct settings. In these settings, work is found in different ways and workers have different characteristics. There is also a slim chance of moving from one setting to another.

**Markets** are social relations that regulate the exchange of goods and services. In a market, the prices of goods and services are established by how plentiful they are (*supply*) and how much they are wanted (*demand*).

**Oligopolies** are giant corporations that control part of an economy. They are few in number and tend not to compete against one another. Instead, they can set prices at levels that are most profitable for them.

The **primary labour market** is composed mainly of highly skilled or well-educated white males. They are employed in large corporations that enjoy high levels of capital investment. In the primary labour market, employment is secure, earnings are high, and fringe benefits are generous.

**Productivity** refers to the amount of goods or services produced for every hour worked.

**Professionals** are people with specialized knowledge acquired through extensive higher education.

The **quality of work life** movement originated in Sweden and Japan. It involves small groups of a dozen or so workers and managers collaborating to improve both the quality of goods produced and the communication between workers and managers.

In a **regulated market,** various social forces limit the capacity of supply and demand to determine prices.

**Scientific management** is a system of improving productivity developed in the 1910s by Frederick W. Taylor. After analyzing the movements of workers as they did their jobs, Taylor trained them to eliminate unnecessary actions and greatly improve their efficiency. This has also been referred to as *taylorism.*

The **secondary labour market** contains a disproportionately large number of women and members of ethnic minorities, particularly recent immigrants. Employees in the secondary labour market tend to be unskilled and lack higher education. They work in small firms with low levels of capital investment. Employment is insecure, earnings are low, and fringe benefits are meagre.

**Unions** are organizations of workers that seek to defend and promote their members' interests.

## QUESTIONS TO CONSIDER

1. Women are entering the labour force at a faster rate than men are. Members of visible minority ethnic groups are entering the labour force at a much faster rate than whites. What policies must companies adopt if they hope to see women and members of ethnic and racial minorities achieve workplace equality with white men?
2. The computer is widely regarded as a labour-saving device and has been adopted on a wide scale. Yet, on average, Canadians work more hours per week now than they did 20 or 30 years ago. How do you explain this paradox?
3. Most of the less developed countries have been eager to see multinational corporations establish branch plants on their soil. What sorts of policies must less developed countries adopt to ensure maximum benefits for their populations from these branch plants? Would it be beneficial if the less developed countries worked out a common approach to this problem rather than competing against each other for branch plants?

## WEB RESOURCES

### Companion Web Site for This Book

http://www.brymsociologycompass.nelson.com

Begin by clicking on the Student Resources section of the Web site. Next, select the chapter you are currently studying from the pull-down menu. From the Student Resources page you will have easy access to InfoTrac College Edition®, MicroCase online exercises, and additional Web links. The Web site also has many useful tips to aid you in your study of sociology, including practice tests for each chapter.

### InfoTrac Search Terms

These search terms are provided to assist you in beginning to conduct research on this topic by visiting http://www.infotrac-college.com

**Capitalism**
**Corporation**
**Communism**
**Deskilling**
**Free market**

### Recommended Web Sites

For information on the Canadian economy, trade, and jobs go to Industry Canada at http://www.ic.gc.ca/.

For the unionized worker's perspective, see the Canadian Labour Congress at http://www.clc-ctc.ca.

For research on social and economic justice, see the Canadian Centre for Policy Alternatives at http://www.policyalternatives.ca/.

For information to help Canadians successfully participate in the workforce, go to Human Resources Development Canada at http://www.hrdc-drhc.gc.ca/.

For international information on social justice and human and labour rights, see the International Labour Organization at http://www.ilo.org.

## SUGGESTED READINGS

Randy Hodson and Teresa Sullivan. *The Social Organization of Work*, 2nd ed. (Belmont, CA: Wadsworth, 1995). The latest edition of an American undergraduate textbook in the sociology of work.

Harvey Krahn and Graham Lowe. *Work, Industry, and Canadian Society,* 3rd ed. (Toronto: Nelson, 1998). The most widely used undergraduate text on work and industry in Canadian universities and colleges.

Karl Polanyi. *The Great Transformation: The Political and Economic Origins of Our Time* (Boston: Beacon, 1957 [1944]). The classic account of the rise and decline of free market society.

James Rinehart. *The Tyranny of Work: Alienation and the Labour Force*, 4th ed. (Toronto: Harcourt, 2001). A good Canadian text with a focus specifically on issues of work alienation.

## NOTES

1. There is no necessary contradiction between one aspect of the sociologist's and the neoclassical economist's approaches to markets. As markets become less regulated, average wealth may grow and the gap between rich and poor may increase at the same time. As we saw in Chapter 7, Social Stratification: Canadian and Global Perspectives, this is exactly what has been happening in the United States, and to a lesser extent in Canada, for nearly 30 years. Note also that a less influential school of economic thought, known as "institutionalism," is much closer to the sociological perspective on markets than the neoclassical school.
2. A *monopoly* is a single producer that completely dominates a market.

## IN THIS CHAPTER, YOU WILL LEARN THAT

- Political sociologists analyze the distribution of power in society and its consequences for political behaviour and public policy.
- Sociological disputes about the distribution of power often focus on how social structures, and especially class structures, influence political life.
- Some political sociologists analyze how state institutions and laws affect political behaviour and public policy.
- Three waves of democratization have swept the world in the past 175 years.
- Societies become highly democratic only when their citizens win legal protections of their rights and freedoms. This typically occurs when their middle and working classes become large, organized, and prosperous.
- Enduring social inequalities limit democracy even in the richest countries.

# CHAPTER 11

# POLITICS

# INTRODUCTION

## Free Trade and Democracy

Just four days before the most important Canadian election of the twentieth century, the outcome seemed clear. A Gallup poll published November 17, 1988, showed the Liberals with a commanding 43 percent of the popular vote. The Progressive Conservatives (PCs) trailed far behind at 31 percent. The New Democratic Party (NDP) stood at 22 percent.

Then, a mere 100 hours before the first votes were cast, a little-known organization, the Canadian Alliance for Trade and Job Opportunities (CATJO), swung into high gear. With a campaign budget larger than that of the two opposition parties combined, CATJO funded a media blitz promoting the PCs and their free trade policies. A barrage of brochures, newspaper ads, and radio and television commercials supported the idea that Canadian prosperity depends on the removal of all taxes and impediments to trade between Canada and the United States. CATJO argued that if goods and services could be bought and sold across the border without hindrance, and capital invested without restraint, good jobs would proliferate and Canada's future would be assured.

Prior to the media blitz, an Angus Reid poll disclosed that most Canadians disagreed with CATJO's rosy assessment. They opposed free trade by a margin of 54 percent to 35 percent. A majority of Canadians sensed that free trade might open Canada to harmful competition with giant American companies, thus leading to job losses and deteriorating living standards. Yet the CATJO onslaught succeeded in overcoming some of these fears. Its media campaign hammered the pro–free trade message into the minds of the Canadian public and drew attention away from the opposition. Then, on election day, the unexpected happened. The PCs won with 43 percent of the popular vote. A mere six weeks later, on January 1, 1989, the Canada–U.S. Free Trade Agreement was implemented.

Who backed CATJO? Its sole sponsor was the Business Council on National Issues (BCNI), an organization composed of the chief executive officers of 150 of Canada's leading corporations. These were people with a clear stake in free trade. Their companies stood to benefit from increased business activity between Canada and the United States and unrestricted freedom to invest wherever profits promised to be higher (Richardson, 1996). Whether the Canadian people as a whole have benefited from free trade is a matter of ongoing debate.[1]

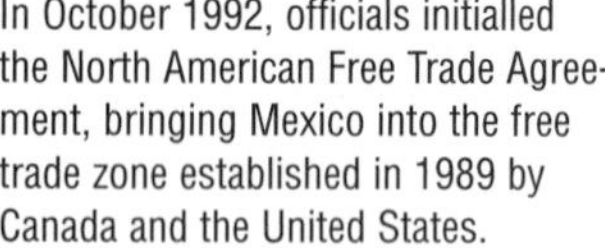

In October 1992, officials initialled the North American Free Trade Agreement, bringing Mexico into the free trade zone established in 1989 by Canada and the United States.

The free trade election raises important political questions. Does the victory of the PCs illustrate the operation of government "of the people, by the people, for the people," as Abraham Lincoln defined democracy in his famous speech at Gettysburg in 1863? The war certainly allowed a diverse range of Canadians to express conflicting views. In the end, the people did get the government they elected. This suggests that Lincoln's characterization of politics applied as well to Canada in 1988 as it did to the United States in 1863.

However, the access of big business to a bulging war chest might lead one to doubt that Lincoln's definition applies. Few groups can act like CATJO and put together $18 million for a media campaign aimed at swaying the hearts and minds of the Canadian people. Should we therefore conclude that (in the words of one wit) Canada is a case of government "of the people, by the lawyers, for the businessmen?"[2]

The free trade election of 1988 raises questions that lie at the heart of political sociology. What accounts for the degree to which a political system responds to the demands of all its citizens? As you will see, political sociologists have often answered this question by examining the effects of social structures, especially class structures, on politics. Although this approach contributes much to our understanding of political life, it is insufficient by itself. A fully adequate theory of democracy requires that we also examine how state institutions and laws affect political processes. We elaborate these points in the second section of this chapter.

From the mid-1970s until the early 1990s, a wave of competitive elections swept across many formerly nondemocratic countries. Most dramatically, elections were held in the former Soviet Union at the end of this period. Many Western analysts were ecstatic. By the mid-1990s, however, it became clear that their optimism was naive. Often, the new regimes turned out to be feeble and limited democracies. As a result, political sociologists began to reconsider the social preconditions of democracy. We review of some of their work in this chapter's third section. We conclude that genuine democracy is not based just on elections. In addition, large classes of people must win legal protection of their rights and freedoms for democracy to take root and grow. This has not yet happened in most of the world.

Some analysts believe that politics in the rich industrialized countries is less likely to be shaped by class inequality in the future. Others hold that the marriage of home computers and elections will allow citizens to get more involved in politics by voting often and directly on the Internet. Our reading of the evidence is different. In concluding this chapter, we argue that persistent class inequality is the major barrier to the progress of democracy in countries such as Canada.

Before developing these themes, however, we define some key terms.

## What Is Politics? Key Terms

Politics is a machine that determines "who gets what, when, and how" (Lasswell, 1936). **Power** fuels the machine. Power is the ability to control others, even against their will (Weber, 1947: 152). Having more power than others gives you the ability to get more valued things sooner. Having less power than others means you get fewer valued things later. Political sociology's chief task is figuring out how power drives different types of political machines.

The use of power sometimes involves force. For example, one way of operating a system for distributing jobs, money, education, and other valued things is by throwing people who do not agree with the system in jail. In this case, people obey political rules because they are afraid to disobey. More often, however, people agree with the distribution system or at least accept it grudgingly. For instance, most people pay their taxes without much pressure from the Canada Customs and Revenue Agency. They pay their parking tickets without serving jail time. They recognize the right of their rulers to control the political machine. When most people basically agree with how the political machine is run, raw power becomes **authority.** Authority is legitimate, institutionalized power. Power is *legitimate* when people regard its use as valid or justified. Power is *institutionalized* when the norms and statuses of social organizations govern its use. These norms and statuses define how authority should be used, how individuals can achieve authority, and how much authority is attached to each status in the organization.

Max Weber (1947) wrote that authority can have one of three bases:

1. **Traditional authority**. Particularly in tribal and feudal societies, rulers inherit authority through family or clan ties. The right of a family or clan to monopolize leadership is widely believed to derive from the will of a god.
2. **Legal-rational authority.** In modern societies, authority derives from respect for the law. Laws specify how one can achieve office. People generally believe these laws are rational. If someone achieves office by following these laws, his or her authority is respected.
3. **Charismatic authority.** Sometimes extraordinary, charismatic individuals challenge traditional or legal-rational authority. They claim to be inspired by a god or some higher principle that transcends other forms of authority. Most people believe this claim. One such principle is the idea that all people are created equal. Charismatic figures sometimes emerge during a **political revolution,** an attempt by many people to overthrow existing political institutions and establish new ones. Political revolutions take place when widespread and successful movements of opposition clash with crumbling traditional or legal-rational authority.

Politics takes place in all social settings. Such settings include intimate face-to-face relationships, families, and universities. However, political sociology is mainly concerned with institutions that *specialize* in the exercise of power and authority. Taken together, these institutions form the **state.** The state is composed of institutions that formulate and carry out a country's laws and public policies. In performing these functions, the state regulates citizens in **civil society.** Civil society is "made up of areas of social life—the domestic world, the economic sphere, cultural activities and political interaction—which are organized by private or voluntary arrangements between individuals and groups outside the direct control of the state" (Held, 1987: 281; see Figure 11.1).

In turn, citizens in civil society control the state to varying degrees. In an **authoritarian** state, citizen control is sharply restricted. In a **totalitarian** state it is virtually nonexistent. In a **democracy,** citizens exert a relatively high degree of control over the state. They do this partly by choosing representatives in regular, competitive elections.

**✦ FIGURE 11.1 ✦**
**The Institutions of State and Civil Society**

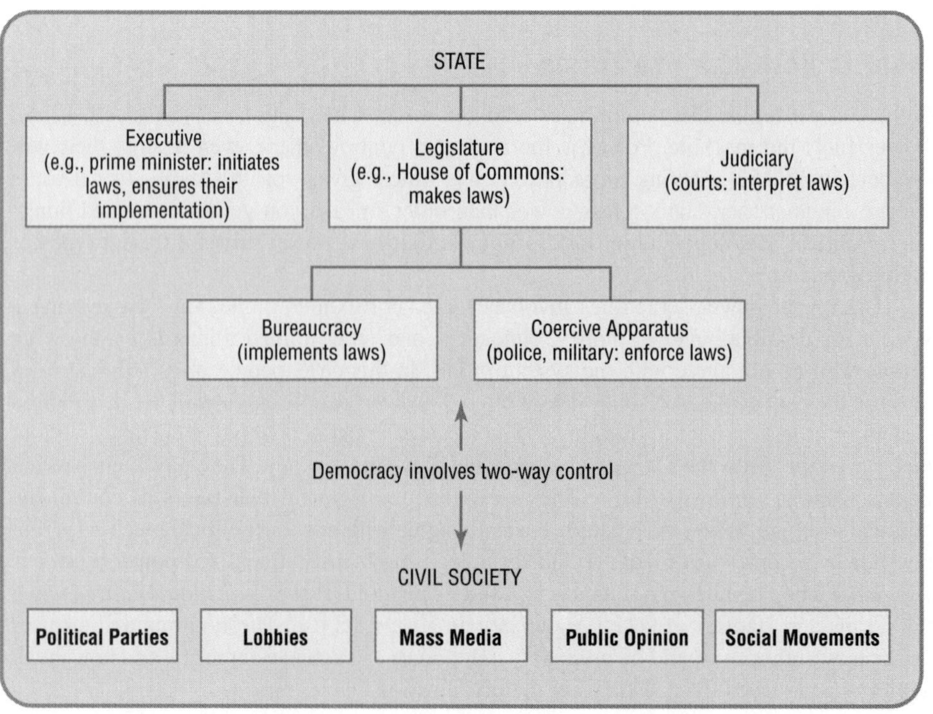

The three faces of authority according to Weber: traditional authority (King Louis XIV of France, circa 1670), charismatic authority (Vladimir Lenin, Bolshevik leader of the Russian Revolution of 1917), and legal-rational authority (Jean Chrétien campaigning in the 2000 Canadian federal election).

In modern democracies, citizens do not control the state directly. They do so through several organizations. **Political parties** compete for control of government in regular elections. They put forward policy alternatives and rally adult citizens to vote. Special interest groups such as trade unions and business associations form **lobbies.** They advise politicians about their members' desires. They also remind politicians how much their members' votes, organizing skills, and campaign contributions matter. The **mass media** keep a watchful and critical eye on the state. They keep the public informed about the quality of government. **Public opinion** refers to the values and attitudes of the adult population as a whole. It is expressed mainly in polls and letters to lawmakers, and gives politicians a reading of citizen preferences. Finally, when dissatisfaction with normal politics is widespread, protest sometimes takes the form of **social movements.** A social movement is a collective attempt to change all or part of the political or social order. Social movements help to keep governments responsive to the wishes of the citizenry (see Chapter 17, Collective Action and Social Movements).

Bearing these definitions in mind, we now consider the merits and limitations of four sociological theories of democracy.

## THEORIES OF DEMOCRACY

### Pluralist Theory

In the early 1950s, New Haven, Connecticut, was a city of about 150 000 people. It had seen better times. As in many other North American cities, post–Second World War prosperity and new roads had allowed much of the white middle class to resettle in the suburbs. This eroded the city's tax base. It also left much of the downtown to poor and minority-group residents. Some parts of New Haven became slums.

Beginning in 1954, Mayor Richard Lee decided to do something about the city's decline. He planned to attract new investment, eliminate downtown slums, and stem the outflow of the white middle class. Urban renewal was a potentially divisive issue. However, according to research conducted at the time, key decisions were made in a highly democratic manner. The city government listened closely to all major groups. It adopted policies that reflected the diverse wishes and interests of city residents.

The social scientists who studied New Haven politics in the 1950s are known as **pluralists** (Polsby, 1959; Dahl, 1961). They argued that the city was highly democratic because power was widely dispersed. They showed that few of the most prestigious families in New Haven were economic leaders in the community. Moreover, neither economic leaders nor the social elite monopolized political decision making. Different groups of people decided various political issues. Some of these people had low status in the community. Moreover, power was more widely distributed than in earlier decades. The pluralists concluded that no single group exercised disproportionate power in New Haven.

The pluralists believed that politics worked much the same way in the United States as a whole and in other democracies such as Canada, too. Democracies, they said, are heterogeneous societies with many competing interests and centres of power. None of these power centres can dominate consistently. The owners of Stelco, for instance, may want tariffs on steel imports to protect the company's Canadian market. Meanwhile, the owners of General Motors Canada may oppose tariffs on steel because they want to keep their company's production costs down. The idea that "industry" speaks with one voice is thus a myth. Competing interests exist even within one industrial group, such as the automobile industry. For instance, a company like Vancouver's Ballard Power, a world leader in the production of electric fuel cells for automobiles, may favour tougher clean air laws now. A company specializing in the production of internal combustion engines may favour a go-slow approach to such laws. Because there is so much heterogeneity between and within groups, no single group can control political life. Sometimes one category of voters or one set of interest groups wins a political battle, sometimes another. Most often, however, politics involves negotiation and compromise between competing groups. Because no one group of people is always able to control the political agenda or the outcome of political conflicts, democracy is guaranteed, argued the pluralists.

## Elite Theory

**Elite theorists,** C. Wright Mills (1956) chief among them, sharply disagreed with the pluralist argument. According to Mills, **elites** are small groups that occupy the command posts of a society's most influential institutions. In the United States the country Mills analyzed, these institutions include the 200 to 300 biggest corporations, the executive branch of government, and the military. Mills wrote that the people (nearly all men) who control these institutions make important decisions that profoundly affect all members of society. Moreover, they do so without much regard for elections or public opinion.

Mills showed how the corporate, state, and military elites are connected. People move from one elite group to another during their careers. Their children intermarry. They maintain close social contacts. They tend to be recruited from upper-middle and upper classes. Yet Mills denied that these connections turn the three elites into what Marx called a **ruling class.** A ruling class is a self-conscious and cohesive group of people, led by corporate executives, who act to shore up capitalism. The three elites are relatively independent of one another, Mills insisted. They may see eye to eye on many issues, but each has its own sphere of influence. Conflict among elite groups is frequent (Alford and Friedland, 1985: 199; Mills, 1956: 277).

## The Elitist Critique of Pluralism

Most political sociologists today question the pluralist account of democratic politics. That is because research has established the existence of large, persistent, wealth-based inequalities in political influence and political participation.

John Porter's classic, *The Vertical Mosaic* (1965), was the first in a series of Canadian studies that demonstrate the weaknesses of pluralism and corroborate some aspects of elite theory (Brym, 1989; Clement, 1975; Olsen, 1980). These studies show that a disproportionately large number of people in Canada's political and other elites come from upper-class and upper-middle-class families. For example, about 40 percent of Canadian prime

Upper Canada College is an elite private school from which many Canadian politicians and business leaders have graduated since it was established in 1829. It is located on 17 hectares (43 acres) in the heart of Toronto. UCC also owns 181 hectares (450 acres) of rural property 80 km northwest of the Toronto campus. The downtown campus includes an indoor skating arena with artificial ice; tennis courts; a large indoor swimming pool; playing fields for soccer, lacrosse, football, cricket, rugby, and baseball; residences for out-of-town students; faculty residences; four gymnasia; outstanding computer and science facilities and library resources; and a fully equipped Creativity Centre for art, drama, music, and information technology. Ten percent of UCC students receive some financial aid to help with the hefty tuition. In 2001–02, annual tuition and incidental fees for a first-year student enrolled in the International Baccalaureate program, including room and board, was $32 315.

In a nationally televised address on January 17, 1961, U.S. President Eisenhower sounded much like C. Wright Mills and other elite theorists when he warned of the "undue influence" of the "military-industrial complex" in American society. Maintaining a large, permanent military establishment is "new in the American experience," he said. An "engaged society" offers the only effective defence against the "misplaced power" of the military-industrial lobby, according to Eisenhower.

ministers, premiers, and Cabinet ministers were born into the richest 10 percent of families in the country (Olsen, 1980: 129). In their youth, members of Canada's elites are likely to have attended expensive private schools. As adults, they tend to marry the offspring of other elite members and belong to exclusive private clubs. In the course of their careers, they often move from one elite group to another. Arguably, people with this sort of background cannot act dispassionately on behalf of all Canadians, rich and poor. Controversy persists over whether Canada's elites form a ruling class. Porter (1965), noting frequent conflict among elites, argued against the view that a ruling class controls Canada. His top students disagreed. They argued that the interests of large corporations dominate Canadian political life (Clement, 1975; Olsen, 1980). However, both Porter and his students did agree on one point: Contrary to pluralist claims, Canada's well-to-do consistently exercise disproportionate influence over political life in this country.

Studies of political participation in Canada add weight to the elitist view (Blais et al., 1997; Frank, 1992; Mishler, 1979: 88–97). Many surveys show that political involvement decreases with social class (see also Box 11.1). For example, the likelihood of voting falls with a person's class position. The likelihood of phoning or writing a member of Parliament, helping a candidate in an election campaign, contributing money to a political party, and running for office declines even more steeply as one moves down the class hierarchy. As intensity of political participation declines, so does political influence (e.g., Eagles, 1993). Consequently, although political apathy and cynicism are high among Canadians, the poorest Canadians are the most politically apathetic and cynical. They have less interest in politics than the well-to-do and they are more likely to think that government does not care what they think (see Figures 11.2 and 11.3). As one of the world's leading political sociologists writes: "The combination of a low vote and a relative lack of organization among the lower-status groups means that they will suffer from neglect by the politicians who will be receptive to the wishes of the more privileged, participating, and organized strata" (Lipset, 1981 [1960]: 226–7).

## The Marxist Critique of Elite Theory

Although compelling in some respects, elite theory has its critics, Marxists foremost among them. Some Marxists, known as "instrumentalists," deny that elites enjoy more or less equal power. Actually, they say, elites form a ruling class dominated by big business. From their point of view, the state, for example, is an arm (or "instrument") of the

BOX 11.1
IT'S YOUR CHOICE

### INCREASING THE PARTICIPATION OF WOMEN IN CANADIAN POLITICS

Just as political participation decreases with social class, so it varies by gender. On the whole, women are less politically active than men. The gender gap in political participation is due to sociological and historical factors. It has been reduced by political pressure and resulting public policy innovations. It can be further reduced by the same means.

By demonstrating, petitioning, and gaining the support of influential liberal-minded men, Canadian women won the right to vote federally in 1917, and in all provinces except Quebec by 1925. Quebec fell into line only in 1940. Some women have since been elected to Parliament and to provincial legislatures. As of 2000, about 21 percent of federal members of Parliament and provincial members of legislative assemblies were women. Many fewer women have been appointed to Cabinet positions both federally and provincially; and once, for four months (June to October 1993), Canada had a female prime minister (Kim Campbell). As these facts suggest, the more influential the form of political activity, the fewer women one finds (Bashevkin, 1993; "Women—Current Provincial and Territorial Party Standings," 2001; "Women—Party Standings in the House of Commons," 2000).

Active involvement in political life, especially running for office, requires such resources as time and money. Women are disadvantaged in this regard. As you saw in Chapter 9 (Sexuality and Gender), women have lower socio-economic status than men on average. As you will learn in Chapter 12 (Families), women are also saddled with more domestic responsibilities than men. These factors prevent many women from running for office. In addition, political parties influence the nomination of candidates for elected office and thus help determine where women run. Most parties tend to assign female candidates to ridings where chances of winning are low (Brodie, 1991).

Public policy analysts note that female political participation can increase if these barriers are removed (Boyd, 2001; Brodie, 1991). For example, laws could be passed that would allow candidates to take unpaid leave from their jobs to contest nominations and elections, set spending limits for nomination and election contests, make contributions for nomination contests tax deductible, treat child-care and housekeeping costs as reimbursable campaign expenses, and so forth. Additionally, laws could be enacted that make government subsidies to political party campaigns dependent on the proportion of their elected candidates that are women. In such a system, party subsidies would increase with the proportion of women elected, thus creating a powerful disincentive for parties to place most female candidates in ridings where they are likely to lose. Thus, the means to increase the participation of women in politics are available. Whether these means are implemented is your choice.

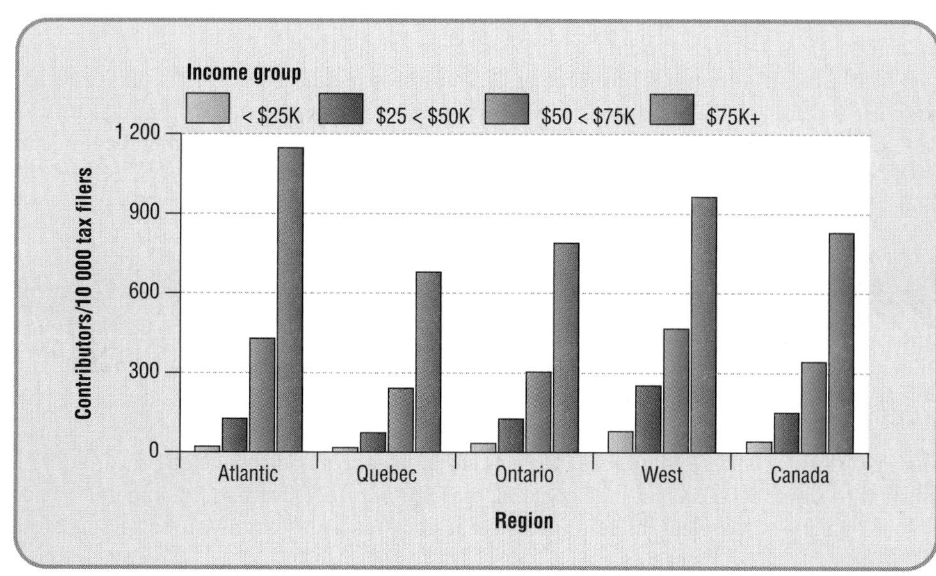


✦ **FIGURE 11.2** ✦
**Federal Political Contributors, by Income and Region, Canada, 1988**

Source: Frank (1992: 6).

✦ **FIGURE 11.3** ✦
**Political Apathy and Cynicism, by Annual Household Income, Canada, 1997**

Source: Blais et al. (1997).

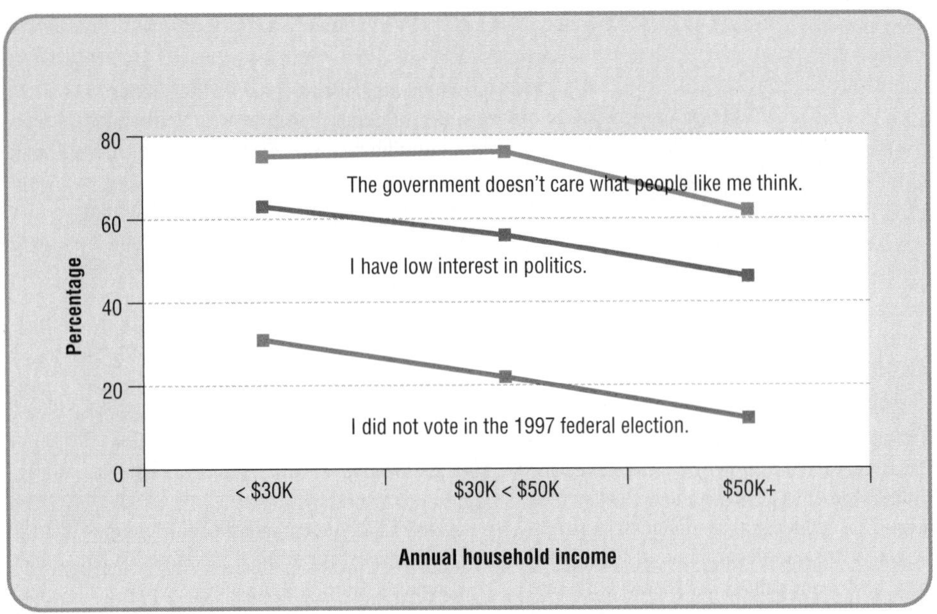


business elite. Big business gains control of the state in three main ways. First, members of wealthy families occupy important state positions in highly disproportionate numbers. Second, government officials rely mainly on the representatives of big business for advice. Third, political parties rely mainly on big business for financial support. According to some Marxists, members of different elites may disagree about specific issues. However, as a result of the three control mechanisms listed above, they always agree about one issue: the need to maintain the health of the capitalist system (Miliband, 1973 [1969]).

A second group of Marxists, known as "structuralists," offers a somewhat different interpretation of why the state in capitalist society is necessarily biased in favour of big business. For the structuralists, it is not so much the *social origins* of high government officials or the *social ties* linking them with big business that encourages the state to act with a pro-capitalist bias. Rather, they argue, the capitalist state acts as an arm of big business because it is constrained to do so by *the nature of the capitalist system itself.* For example, if Canadian government officials take actions that deeply damage capitalist interests, investment would be redirected to countries with regimes that are kinder to company profits. Such a move would cost Canada jobs and prosperity. It would be highly unpopular. The government could easily fall. Fearing this outcome, governments in capitalist societies find their field of action restricted to policies that ensure the well-being of big business. According to the structuralists, it is the very fact that the state is embedded in a capitalist system that forces it to act in this way (Poulantzas, 1975 [1968]).

It follows from both the instrumentalist and the structuralist positions that ordinary citizens, and especially members of the working class, rarely have much influence over state policy. According to Marxists, true democracy can emerge only if members of the working class and their supporters overthrow capitalism and establish a socialist system (see Chapter 10, Work and the Economy).

## Power Resource Theory

Both Marxist and elite theories leave some big political questions unanswered. For one thing, they pay little attention to how political parties lose office while other political parties get elected. Nor are they much concerned with the effect of one party or another on public policy. In fact, for Marxist and elite theorists, elections are little more than sideshows. They believe that elites or a ruling class always control society, regardless of election outcomes. Therefore, they contend, the victory of one party over another does not deserve much sociological attention because it does not substantially affect the lives of ordinary men and women.

In contrast, many political sociologists today think it matters a great deal which party is in office. After all, the lives of ordinary men and women are hugely affected by whether the governing party supports or opposes free trade, weaker environmental standards, less publicly funded medical care, bigger government subsidies for child care, abortion on demand, and so forth. Elite theorists are correct to claim that power is concentrated disproportionately in the hands of the well-to-do. But we still need a theory that accounts for the successes and failures of different parties and policies in different times and places.

That is where **power resource theory** is helpful. It focuses on how *variations* in the distribution of power affect the fortunes of parties and policies.

To understand power resource theory, first consider your own party preference. For many reasons, you may support one political party over another. For instance, your family may have a long tradition of voting for one party. You may have never really questioned this support. Maybe you support a party because you admire the energy, integrity, or track record of its leader. Or you might support a party because you agree with its policies on a range of issues. What factors lead *you* to prefer one party over another?

If a party's policies influence your vote, you are like many Canadians. In fact, Canadian voters cluster in two main policy groups. Voters on the *left* promote extensive government involvement in the economy. Among other things, this means they favour a strong "social safety net" of health and welfare benefits to help the less fortunate members of society. As a result, left-wing policies often lead to less economic inequality. In contrast, voters on the *right* favour a reduced role for government in the economy. They want to see a smaller welfare state and emphasize the importance of individual initiative in promoting economic growth. Economic issues aside, leftists and rightists also tend to differ on social or moral issues. Leftists tend to support equal rights for women and racial and sexual minorities. Rightists tend to support more traditional social and moral values.[3]

Figure 11.4 shows one indicator of how left and right sentiments were translated into support for Canada's five political parties in 1997. Using data from the 1997 Canadian Election Survey, we first found, for supporters of each political party, the percentage of people who favour tax increases for expanded social programs. This is one indicator of the percentage of people on the left. We then found the percentage of people who support tax cuts for reduced social programs. This is one indicator of the percentage of people on the right. Finally, we subtracted the percentage on the left from the percentage on the right. The absolute value of this difference is what we call the "Right Index." It shows how far to the right each party's supporters are. Clearly, there are big differences between parties. Reform Party supporters are furthest to the right, followed by the PCs.[4] Liberal supporters are in the middle. NDP supporters are furthest to the left, followed by Bloc Québécois supporters. Do you think of yourself as a supporter of one of these parties? Is your choice related to their policies?

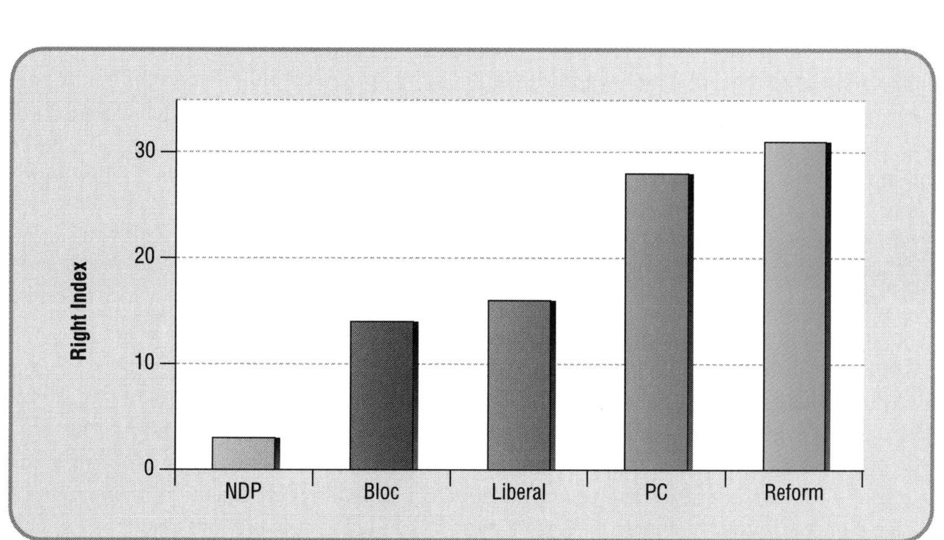


✦ **FIGURE 11.4** ✦

**How Right Are Canada's Political Parties?**

Source: Blais et al. (1997).

*Note*: The "Right Index" is the absolute value of (a) the percentage of party supporters favouring tax increases for expanded social programs minus (b) the percentage of party supporters favouring tax cuts for reduced social programs.

✦ **FIGURE 11.5** ✦
**Party Support by Household Income, Canada, 1997**

Source: Blais et al. (1997).

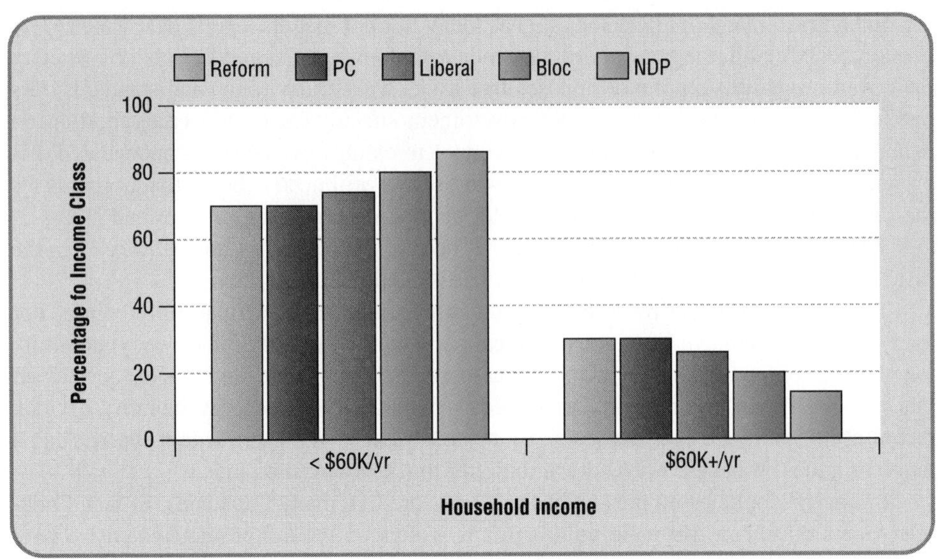


The policies favoured by different parties have different effects on different groups of people. Therefore, different parties tend to be supported by different classes, regions, religious groups, races, and other groups. Do you think the policies of your preferred party favour the class, region, religious group, or race to which you belong? If so, how? If not, why not?

In most Western democracies, the main factor that distinguishes political parties is differences in *class* support (Korpi, 1983: 35; Lipset and Rokkan, 1967; Manza, Hout, and Brooks, 1995). For example, as Figure 11.5 shows, low-income earners in Canada tend to support parties on the left. High-income earners tend to support parties on the right. This stands to reason since leftist parties favour policies that promote less inequality in society.

The tendency for people in different classes to vote for different parties varies from one country to the next. The strength of this tendency depends on many factors. One of the most important is how socially organized or cohesive classes are (Brym with Fox, 1989: 57–91; Brym, Gillespie, and Lenton, 1989). For example, an upper class that can create organizations such as the Business Council on National Issues and CATJO, which supported the PCs so effectively in the 1988 free trade election, is more powerful than an upper class that cannot take such action. If an upper class makes such efforts while a working class fails to organize itself, right-wing candidates have a better chance of winning office. Conservative policies are more likely to become law. Similarly, a working class that can unionize many workers is more powerful than one with few unionized workers. That is because unions often collect money for the party that is more sympathetic to union interests. They also lobby on behalf of their members and try to convince members to vote for the pro-union party. If workers become more unionized while an upper class fails to organize itself, then left-wing candidates have an improved chance of winning office. Policies that favour lower classes are more likely to become law. This is the main insight of power resource theory. *Organization is a source of power. Change in the distribution of power between major classes partly accounts for the fortunes of different political parties and different laws and policies* (Esping-Andersen, 1990; Korpi, 1983; O'Connor and Olsen, 1998; Shalev, 1983).

You can see how power resource theory works by looking at Table 11.1 on page 336. This table compares 18 industrialized democracies in the three decades after the Second World War. It divides the countries into three groups. In group one are countries such as Sweden, where socialist parties usually controlled governments. (Socialist parties are at least as left wing as the NDP in Canada.) In group two are countries such as Australia, where socialist parties *sometimes* controlled, or shared in the control of, governments. And in group three are countries such as Canada, where socialist parties rarely or never shared in the control of governments. The group averages in column two show that socialist par-

In the 2002 election for the French presidency, the right-wing candidate Maurice Le Pen placed second. Le Pen's anti-immigrant campaign highlighted the degree to which political cleavages in France are based not just on class but also on race.

ties are generally more successful where workers are more unionized. The group averages in columns four and five show there is more economic inequality in countries that are weakly unionized and have no socialist governments. In other words, by means of taxes and social policies, socialist governments ensure that the rich earn a smaller percentage of national income and the poor form a smaller percentage of the population. Studies of pensions, medical care, and other state benefits in the rich industrialized democracies reach similar conclusions. In general, where working classes are more organized and powerful, disadvantaged people are economically better off (Myles 1989 [1984]; O'Connor and Brym, 1988; Olsen and Brym, 1996).

Class is not the only factor that distinguishes political parties. Historically, *religion* has also been an important basis of party differences. For example, in West European countries with large Catholic populations, such as Switzerland and Belgium, parties are distinguished partly by the religious affiliation of their supporters. In recent decades, *ethnicity and race* have become cleavage factors of major and growing importance in some countries. For example, in the United States, African-Americans have overwhelmingly supported the Democratic Party since the 1960s (Brooks and Manza, 1997). Ethnicity has become an increasingly important division in French politics. This is due to heavy Arab immigration from Algeria, Morocco, and Tunisia since the 1950s and growing anti-immigration sentiment among a substantial minority of whites (Veugelers, 1997). *Regional* groups distinguish parties in other countries, such as Canada. In this country, some parties have been particularly attractive to Westerners, others to Québécois (see below). Power resource theory focuses mainly on how the shifting distribution of power between working and upper classes affects electoral success. However, one can also use the theory to analyze the electoral fortunes of parties that attract different religious groups, races, regional groups, and so on.

## State-Centred Theory

Democratic politics is a contest among various class, racial, ethnic, religious, and regional groups to control the state for their own advantage. When power is substantially redistributed

| | Percent of Nonagricultural Workforce Unionized | Socialist Share of Government | Percent of Total National Income to Top 10% Earners | Percent Poor |
|---|---|---|---|---|
| **Mainly Socialist Countries** | | | | |
| Sweden | 71 | High | 21.3 | 3.5 |
| Norway | 46 | High | 22.2 | 5.0 |
| **Average** | **68.5** | | **21.8** | **4.3** |
| **Partly Socialist Countries** | | | | |
| Austria | 55 | Medium | — | — |
| Australia | 50 | Medium | 23.7 | 8.0 |
| Denmark | 49 | Medium | — | — |
| Belgium | 47 | Medium | — | — |
| UK | 44 | Medium | 23.5 | 7.5 |
| New Zealand | 42 | Medium | — | — |
| Finland | 39 | Medium | — | — |
| **Average** | **46.6** | | **23.6** | **7.8** |
| **Mainly Nonsocialist Countries** | | | | |
| Ireland | 36 | Low | — | — |
| W. Germany | 35 | Low | 30.3 | 3.0 |
| Netherlands | 30 | Low | 27.7 | — |
| USA | 27 | Low | 26.6 | 13.0 |
| Japan | 27 | Low | 27.2 | — |
| Canada | 26 | Low | 25.1 | 11.0 |
| France | 25 | Low | 30.4 | 16.0 |
| Italy | 23 | Low | 30.9 | — |
| Switzerland | 23 | Low | — | — |
| **Average** | **28** | | **28.3** | **10.8** |

✦ **TABLE 11.1** ✦

**Some Consequences of Working Class Power in 18 Rich Industrialized Countries, 1946–1976**

Source: Korpi (1983: 40, 196).

*Note*: "Socialist share of government" is the proportion of seats in each Cabinet held by socialist parties weighted by the socialist share of seats in Parliament and the duration of the Cabinet. "Percent poor" is the average percentage of the population living in relative poverty according to OECD standards with the poverty line standardized according to household size.

because of such factors as change in the cohesiveness of these social groups, old ruling parties usually fall and new ones take office.

Note, however, that a winner-take-all strategy would be nothing short of foolish. If winning parties passed laws that benefit only their supporters, they might cause mass outrage and even violent opposition. Yet it would be bad politics to allow opponents to become angry, organized, and resolute. After all, winners want more than just a moment of glory. They want to be able to enjoy the spoils of office over the long haul. To achieve stability, they must give people who lose elections a voice in government. That way, even determined opponents are likely to recognize the government's **legitimacy.** Pluralists thus make a good point when they say that democratic politics is about accommodation and compromise. They only lose sight of how accommodation and compromise typically give more advantages to some rather than others, as both elite theorists and power resource theorists stress.

There is, however, more to the story of politics than conflict between classes, religious groups, regions, and so forth. Theda Skocpol and other **state-centred theorists** show how the state itself can structure political life (Block, 1979; Evans, Rueschemeyer, and Skocpol, 1985; Skocpol, 1979). They regard senior elected officials and state bureaucrats not as agents of economic elites but as major political players in their own right. Moreover, they hold that major political struggles become embodied in the very structure of states. That is, historically important political battles typically end with the passage of new laws and the creation of new political institutions. These laws and institutions go on to influence political life until political conflict becomes serious enough to alter them once again. Until then, the state influences political life *to some degree independently of day-to-day political conflict and the distribution of power at a given point in time*. This argument is a valuable supplement to power resource theory.

To illustrate state-centred theory, recall first that all societies are divided into different classes, religious groups, regions, and so forth. In principle, any one or a combination of these social divisions may be reflected in the policies of different political parties and the social characteristics of party supporters. For example, in some societies, politics is mostly about the attempts of different *classes* to control the state for their own advantage. In other societies, politics is more about the attempts of different *regions* to control the state for their own advantage; and so forth. What then determines which social division—class, region, or another factor—will predominate in political life? State-centred theory provides useful insights into this issue. For, according to state-centred theory, the state may be organized in such a way as to bias politics toward one social division or another.

Consider the Canadian case. We saw above that different Canadian political parties tend to attract people from different social classes. However, it may now be added that that tendency is relatively weak. That is, compared with most other democracies, class differences among parties are small in Canada. In contrast, regional differences are comparatively large (Butovsky, 2001; Gidengil, 1992). These large regional differences are evident, for example, in the results of the last federal election (see Figure 11.6). The results show that, in Quebec, the most popular federal political party is the Bloc Québécois. Most Bloc supporters want Quebec to form a sovereign country while retaining strong economic ties to Canada. By far the most popular political party in the West is the Canadian Alliance. Most members of the Alliance believe that the federal government has long ignored western interests. They want more regional say over taxation, public policy, and other areas of political life. The Liberals are the overwhelmingly dominant federal political party in Ontario. They claim to be the only truly national party in the country. However, few Westerners and Québécois see the Liberals that way; they think the Liberals strongly favour central-Canadian interests. Even the smaller political parties are regionally based. The Conservative Party is a significant presence only in Atlantic Canada. NDP support is substantial only in Atlantic Canada and the West. The results of the 2000 election mirror a long national tradition: politics in Canada is largely a regional phenomenon, a contest between people from different regions to attain state power for their own advantage.

Why? What is it that produces such a strong regional bias (and a correspondingly weak class bias) in Canadian political life? The answer must be sought in the history of Canadian politics and, in particular, in the way that history has structured the laws and policies of the Canadian state. In other words, the explanation for the regional bias of Canadian politics is state-centred.

Before Confederation in 1867, the British North American colonies enjoyed few unifying ties. Vast geographical barriers separated them. No railway or telegraph line linked them. Lower Canada (now Quebec) had become part of British North America by military conquest just a century earlier. It was still divided from the other colonies by religion (Catholic vs. Protestant), ethnicity (French vs. English), and lingering resentment.

Despite these deep divisions, British North American businessmen tried to forge a union among the colonies in the mid-1860s. They did so because they faced a huge problem that only unification could solve: the loss of their export markets. The British were dismantling the protected market known as the British Empire. The Americans had turned against free trade. To make matters worse, the British North American colonies had accumulated a crippling debt load (due mainly to borrowing money to help finance railroad construction), while certain elements in the United States were threatening to expand the border of their country northward. In this context, the business and political leaders of British North America regarded Confederation as a means of creating a new market and an expanded tax base by encouraging mass immigration and promoting economic growth.

To forge a union, however, the Fathers of Confederation had to be careful. For one thing, they had to avoid consulting ordinary citizens for fear of having their plan rejected. They knew the colonies had little in common and that most ordinary citizens had no interest in union. As Canada's first prime minister, John A. Macdonald, wrote to Leonard

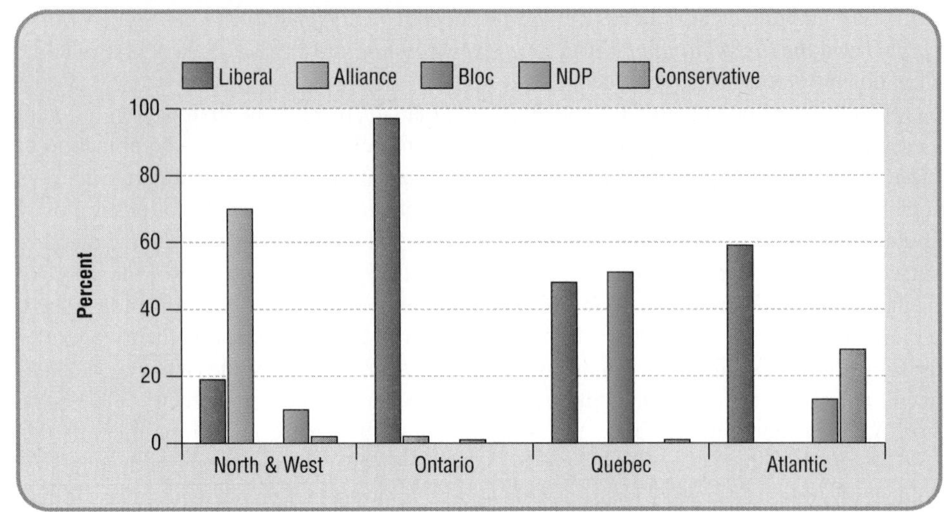


✦ **FIGURE 11.6** ✦
**Results of Canadian Federal Election, 2000, by Region (in percent)**

Source: "The Federal Election" (2000).

Tilley, New Brunswick's Father of Confederation, in October 1866: "The [passage of the British North America Act] must be carried out *per saltum* [in one leap], and no echo of it must reverberate through the British provinces till it becomes law.... The Act once passed and beyond remedy the people would soon learn to be reconciled to it" (quoted in Ryerson, 1973 [1968]: 355).

In addition, the Fathers of Confederation also found it necessary to draft a founding document, the British North America (BNA) Act, that played down the deep divisions between the British North American colonies. Most important, the BNA Act left ambiguous the question of how power would be distributed between federal and provincial governments. This vagueness enabled the Fathers of Confederation to forge their union, but it also left the door open to the bickering and bargaining that has characterized federal–provincial relations ever since 1867. Especially since the Second World War, the BNA Act (and later the Canadian Constitution) allowed the continuing drift of power from federal to provincial governments and thus entrenched regionalism in Canadian political life.

A landmark in the decentralization and regionalization of Canadian politics was reached in 1959. In that year, Quebec and the federal government agreed that a provincial government not wanting to participate in a federal program could receive federal funds to set up its own parallel program. Thereafter, the provincial right to "opt out" of federal programs was widely used not just by Quebec but also by the other provinces, which insisted on the same rights as Quebec (Bélanger, 2000). Thus, in the next four decades, power continued to decentralize and regionalize as the provinces gained more control over taxation, resource revenues, immigration policy, language use, and so on. Canada was a deeply regionally divided society from the start, and the state—the country's basic laws and policies—entrenched regional divisions. The result: a country in which politics is defined less as a struggle between classes than as a struggle between regions (Brym, 1992).[5] Said differently, from the perspective of state-centred theory, class conflict is given less voice than regional conflict in Canada because of the way the state structures politics.

In sum, political sociology has made good progress since the 1950s. Each of the field's major schools has made a useful contribution to our appreciation of political life (see Table 11.2). Pluralists teach us that democratic politics is about compromise and the accommodation of all group interests. Elite theorists teach us that, despite accommodation and compromise, power is concentrated in the hands of high-status groups, whose interests the political system serves best. Power resource theorists teach us that, despite the concentration of power in society, substantial shifts in the distribution of power do occur, and they have big effects on voting patterns and public policies. And state-centred theorists teach us that state structures also exert an important effect on politics.

✦ **TABLE 11.2** ✦
**Five Sociological Theories of Capitalist Democracy Compared**

| | Pluralist | Elite | Marxist | Power-resource | State-centred |
|---|---|---|---|---|---|
| How is power distributed? | Dispersed | Concentrated | Concentrated | Concentrated | Concentrated |
| Who are the main power holders? | Various groups | Elites | Ruling class | Upper class | State officials |
| On what is their power based? | Holding political office | Controlling major institutions | Owning substantial capital | Owning substantial capital | Holding political office |
| What is the main basis of public policy? | The will of all citizens | The interests of major elites | Capitalist interests | The balance of power among classes, etc. | The influence of state structures |
| Do lower classes have much influence on politics? | Yes | No | Rarely | Sometimes | Sometimes |

We now turn to an examination of the historical development of democracy, its sociological underpinnings, and its future.

## THE FUTURE OF DEMOCRACY

### Two Cheers for Russian Democracy

In 1989, the Institute of Sociology of the Russian Academy of Science invited Robert Brym, Neil Guppy, and eight other Canadian sociologists to attend a series of seminars in Moscow. The seminars were designed to acquaint some leading sociologists in the Soviet Union with Western sociology. The country was in the midst of a great thaw. Totalitarianism was melting, leaving democracy in its place. Soviet sociologists had never been free to read and research what they wanted, and they were eager to learn from North American and European scholars (Brym, 1990).

"Or at least so it seemed," says Robert. "One evening about a dozen of us were sitting around comparing the merits of Canadian whisky and Russian vodka. Soon, conversation turned from Crown Royal versus Moskovskaya to Russian politics. 'You must be so

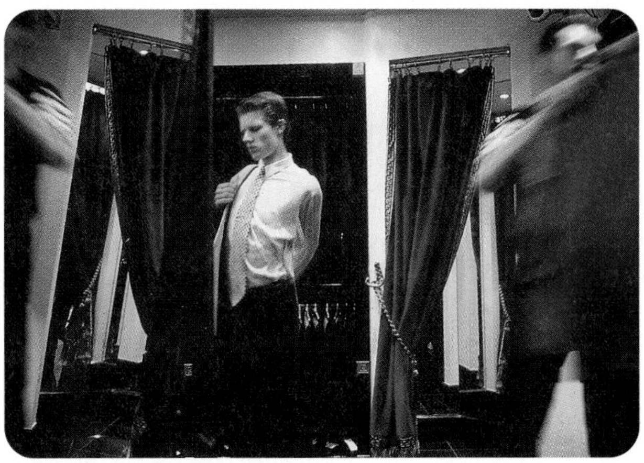

Although Versace does brisk business in Moscow, the streets are filled with homeless people. That is because the richest 10% of Russians earned 15 times more than the poorest 10%, making Russia one of the most inegalitarian countries in the world.

excited about what's happening here,' I said to my Russian hosts. 'How long do you think it will be before Russia will have multi-party elections? Do you think Russia will become a liberal democracy like Canada or a socialist democracy like Sweden?'

"One white-haired Russian sociologist slowly rose to his feet. His colleagues privately called him 'the dinosaur.' It soon became clear why. '*Nikogda*,' he said calmly and deliberately—'never.' '*Nikogda*,' he repeated, his voice rising sharply in pitch, volume, and emphasis. Then, for a full minute he explained that capitalism and democracy were never part of Russia's history, nor could they be expected to take root in Russian soil. 'The Russian people,' he proclaimed, 'do not want a free capitalist society. We know *freedom* means the powerful are free to compete unfairly against the powerless, exploit them, and create social inequality.'

"Everyone else in the room disagreed with the dinosaur's speech, in whole or in part. But not wanting to cause any more upset, we turned the conversation back to lighter topics. After 15 minutes, someone reminded the others that we had to rise early for the next day's seminars. The evening ended, its great questions unanswered."

Today, more than a decade later, the great questions of Russian politics remain unanswered. And it now seems there was some truth in the dinosaur's speech after all. Russia first held multi-party elections in 1991. Surveys found that most Russians favoured democracy over other types of rule. However, support for democracy soon fell because the economy collapsed (see Chapter 10, Work and the Economy, for details). According to official estimates, 39 percent of the population lived below the poverty line in 1999 (Brym, 1996a; 1996b; 1996c; Gerber and Hout, 1998; Handelman, 1995; Remnick, 1998).

Democratic sentiment weakened as economic conditions worsened (Whitefield and Evans, 1994). In elections held in 1995 and 1996, support for democratic parties plunged as support for communist and extreme right-wing nationalist parties surged (Brym, 1995; 1996d). Nationwide surveys conducted in 38 countries between 1995 and 1997 found that as many as 97 percent of the citizens of some countries viewed democracy as the ideal form of government. Russia ranked last, at a mere 51 percent (Klingemann, 1999). Democracy allowed a few people to enrich themselves at the expense of most Russians. Therefore, many citizens equated democracy not with freedom but with distress.

Russia's political institutions reflect the weakness of Russian democracy. Power is concentrated in the presidency to a much greater degree than in the United States. The parliament and the judiciary do not act as checks on executive power. Only a small number of Russians belong to political parties. Voting levels are low. And minority ethnic groups are sometimes treated arbitrarily and cruelly. Clearly, Russian democracy has a long way to go before it can be considered on par with democracy in the West.

The limited success of Russian democracy raises an important question. What social conditions must exist for a country to become fully democratic? This is the question to which we now turn. To gain some perspective, we first consider the three waves of democratization that have swept the world in the past 175 years (Huntington, 1991: 13–26; see Figure 11.7).

## The Three Waves of Democracy

The first wave of democratization began when more then half the white adult males in the United States became eligible to vote in the 1828 presidential election. By 1926, 33 countries enjoyed at least minimally democratic institutions. These countries included most of those in Western Europe, the British dominions (Australia, Canada, and New Zealand), Japan, and four Latin American countries (Argentina, Colombia, Chile, and Uruguay). However, just as an undertow begins when an ocean wave recedes, a democratic reversal occurred between 1922 and 1942. During that period, fascist, communist, and militaristic movements caused two-thirds of the world's democracies to fall under authoritarian or totalitarian rule.

The second wave of democratization took place between 1943 and 1962. Allied victory in the Second World War returned democracy to many of the defeated powers, including West Germany and Japan. The beginning of the end of colonial rule brought

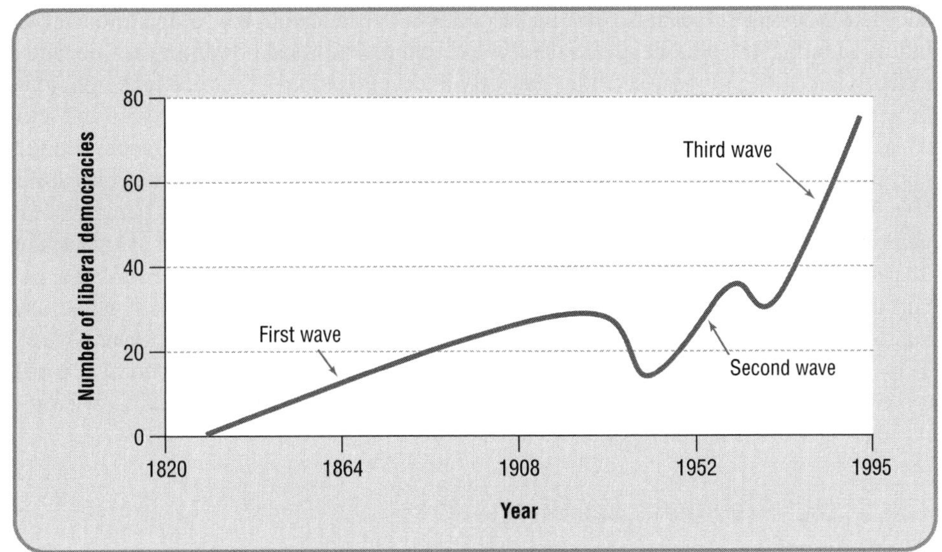


✦ **FIGURE 11.7** ✦
**The Three Waves of Democratization, 1828–1995**

Source: Diamond (1996: 28); Huntington (1991: 26).

democracy to some states in Africa and elsewhere. Some Latin American countries formed limited and unstable democracies. However, even by the late 1950s, the second wave was beginning to exhaust itself. Soon, the world was in the midst of a second democratic reversal. Military dictatorships replaced many democracies in Latin America, Asia, and Africa. One-third of the democracies that existed in 1958 were authoritarian regimes by the mid-1970s.

The third and biggest wave of democratization began in 1974 with the overthrow of military dictatorships in Portugal and Greece. It crested in the early 1990s. In Southern and Eastern Europe, Latin America, Asia, and Africa, a whole series of authoritarian regimes fell. In 1991, Soviet communism collapsed. By 1995, 117 of the world's 191 countries were democratic in the sense that their citizens could choose representatives in regular, competitive elections. That amounts to 61 percent of the world's countries containing nearly 55 percent of the world's population (Diamond, 1996: 26).

The third wave seems less dramatic, however, if we bear in mind that these figures refer to **formal democracies**—countries that hold regular, competitive elections. Many of these countries are not **liberal democracies.** That is, like Russia, they lack the freedoms

Nigeria celebrated independence from Britain in 1960 (left). In 1993, General Sani Abacha (right) annulled the presidential election, became head of state, and began a reign of brutal civil rights violations. The world's third wave of democratization was drawing to a close.

and constitutional protections that make political participation and competition meaningful. In formal but nonliberal democracies, substantial political power may reside with a military that is largely unaffected by the party in office. Certain cultural, ethnic, religious, or regional groups may not be allowed to take part in elections. The legislative and judicial branches of government may not constrain the power of the executive branch. Citizens may not enjoy freedom of expression, assembly, and organization. Instead, they may suffer from unjustified detention, exile, terror, and torture. At the end of 1995, 40 percent of the world's countries were liberal democracies, 21 percent were nonliberal democracies, and 39 percent were nondemocracies (calculated from Diamond, 1996: 28). The number of liberal democracies in the world fell nearly 2 percent between 1991 and 1995. Some new democracies, including large and regionally influential countries such as Russia, Nigeria, Turkey, Brazil, and Pakistan, experienced a decline in freedoms and protections. It is still too early to tell whether this marks the end of the third wave or the beginning of a third reversal (U.S. Information Agency, 1998–99).

## The Social Preconditions of Democracy

Liberal democracies emerge and endure when countries enjoy considerable economic growth, industrialization, urbanization, the spread of literacy, and a gradual decrease in economic inequality (Huntington, 1991: 39–108; Lipset, 1981 [1960]: 27–63, 469–76; 1994; Moore, 1967; Rueschemeyer, Stephens, and Stephens, 1992; Zakaria, 1997). Economic development creates middle and working classes that are large, well organized, literate, and well off. When these classes become sufficiently powerful, their demands for civil liberties and the right to vote and run for office have to be recognized. If powerful middle and working classes are not guaranteed political rights, they sweep away kings, queens, landed aristocracies, generals, and authoritarian politicians in revolutionary upsurges. In contrast, democracies do not emerge where middle and working classes are too weak to wrest big political concessions from pre-democratic authorities. In intermediate cases—where, say, a country's military is about as powerful a political force as its middle and working classes—democracy is precarious and often merely formal. The history of unstable democracies is largely a history of internal military takeovers (Germani and Silvert, 1961).

Apart from the socio-economic conditions noted above, favourable external political and military circumstances help liberal democracy endure. Liberal democracies, even strong ones such as France, collapse when fascist, communist, and military regimes and empires defeat them. They revive when democratic alliances win world wars and authoritarian empires break up. Less coercive forms of outside political intervention are sometimes effective, too. For example, in the 1970s and 1980s, the European Union helped liberal democracy in Spain, Portugal, and Greece by integrating these countries in the West European economy and giving them massive economic aid.

In sum, powerful, pro-democratic foreign states and strong, prosperous middle and working classes are liberal democracy's best guarantees. It follows that liberal democracy will spread in the less economically developed countries only if they prosper and enjoy support from the United States and the European Union, the world centres of liberal democracy.

Recognizing the importance of the United States and the European Union in promoting democracy in many parts of the world should not obscure two important facts, however. First, the United States is not always a friend of democracy. For example, between the end of the Second World War and the collapse of the Soviet Union in 1991, democratic regimes that were sympathetic to the Soviet Union were often destabilized by the United States and replaced by anti-democratic governments. American leaders were willing to export arms and offer other forms of support to anti-democratic forces in Iran, Indonesia, Chile, Nicaragua, Guatemala, and other countries because they believed it was in the United States' political and economic interest to do so (see Chapter 16, Population, Urbanization, and Development). For similar reasons, the United States supports nondemocratic regimes in Saudi Arabia, Kuwait, and elsewhere today. Desire for access to inexpensive oil, copper, and bananas (among other commodities), combined with fear of communist influence, have often outweighed democratic ideals in the United States. Meanwhile, anti-American attitudes in many parts of the world are based on American *opposition* to popular rule.

Second, just because the United States promotes democracy in many parts of the world, we should not assume that liberal democracy has reached its full potential in that country or, for that matter, in any of the other rich postindustrial countries that promote democracy internationally, including Canada. We saw otherwise in our discussion of the limited participation and influence of disadvantaged groups in Canadian politics. It seems fitting, therefore, to conclude this chapter by briefly assessing the future of liberal democracy in Canada.

Some analysts think the home computer will soon increase Canadians' political involvement. They think it will help solve the problem of unequal political participation by bringing more disadvantaged Canadians into the political process. Others think growing affluence means there are fewer disadvantaged Canadians to begin with. This makes economic or material issues less relevant than they used to be. In the concluding section, we dispute both contentions. We argue that political participation is likely to remain highly unequal in the future. Meanwhile, issues concerning economic inequality are likely to remain important for most people. Liberal democracy can realize its full potential only if both problems—political and economic inequality—are adequately addressed.

## Electronic Democracy

On October 20, 1935, the *Washington Post* ran a full-page story featuring the results of the world's first nationwide poll. The story also explained how the new method of measuring public opinion worked. George Gallup was the man behind the poll. In the article, he said that polls allow the people to reclaim their voice: "After one hundred and fifty years we return to the town meeting. This time the whole nation is within the doors" (quoted in London, 1994: 1). Gallup was referring to the lively New England assemblies that used to give citizens a direct say in political affairs. He viewed the poll as a technology that can bring the town hall to the entire adult population of the United States.

Gallup's idea seems naive today. Social scientists have shown that polls often allow politicians to mould public opinion, not just reflect it. For example, they can hire public opinion firms that word questions to increase the chance of eliciting preferred responses. Politicians can can then publicize the results to serve their own ends (Ginsberg, 1986). From this point of view, polls are little different from other media events that are orchestrated by politicians to sway public opinion (see Box 11.2).

Recently, however, some people have greeted a new technology with the same enthusiasm that Gallup lavished on polls. Computers linked to the Internet could allow citizens to debate issues and vote on them directly. This could give politicians a clear signal of how public policy should be conducted. Political participation is low and declining (see Figure 11.8). Some people think that computers can revive democracy. Public opinion would then become the law of the land (Westen, 1998).

It is a grand vision, but flawed. American social scientists have conducted more than a dozen experiments with electronic public meetings. They show that even if the technology needed for such meetings were available to everyone, interest is so limited that no more than a third of the population would participate (Arterton, 1987).

Subsequent experience supports this conclusion. The people most likely to take advantage of electronic democracy are those who have Internet access. They form a privileged and politically involved group. They are not representative of the adult population of Canada or any other country. That is apparent in Table 11.3. The table contains data from recent Canadian and international surveys of Internet access. Compared to the general population, Canadian Internet users are richer, better educated, more urban, and younger. Much the same holds true of international Internet users. We conclude that, if electronic democracy becomes widespread, it will probably reinforce the same inequalities

## BOX 11.2 SOCIOLOGY AT THE MOVIES

### *WAG THE DOG* (1997)

The American president is caught having an affair with his aide. What should be done? Tell the truth? Deny having sex with the woman? Get people to change their definition of "having sex"? Hire a media consultant? Start a war to distract the public?

*Wag the Dog* is a film about a sex scandal that embroils a fictional president. To cover up his sexual misconduct, the fictional president's advisers hire a Hollywood movie producer. The advisers and the producer create a fake crisis in a small, poor, remote country to divert attention from the president's misdeeds. The producer films a newsreel, complete with computer-generated special effects, of a young girl fleeing a military skirmish. Television news programs air it. Seeing a young girl in distress, the public registers strong support for U.S. intervention in the war.

Anne Heche, Dustin Hoffman, and Robert DeNiro conspire to cover up the president's sexual misdeeds by staging a phony war in *Wag the Dog.*

Rather than reality informing political decisions, political convenience creates reality in the world of *Wag the Dog*. Although some people may feel that the movie is too cynical and even paranoid in its caricature of modern politics, others would argue that it convincingly captures a key element of modern political life.

In fact, the movie seemed to predict a real-life event. Several months after its release, U.S. President Clinton's affair with White House intern Monica Lewinsky became a major scandal. For about a year, few people could fail to bring up the Lewinsky affair when talk turned to American politics. Politics in the United States seemed to focus on what "having sex" means. Moreover, in an eerie replication of the movie's plot, President Clinton ordered the bombing of Iraq soon after news of the affair broke. Regardless of the legitimacy of the military action, many concerned observers criticized Clinton's military tactic as a way of diverting the media's attention from his personal problems. Many viewers of the movie found it unsettling to see reality follow a movie script.

What does *Wag the Dog* tell us about politics? Does it merely caricature our media-obsessed, cynical view of politics? Or does it capture a slice of reality? Is it even useful to insist on the distinction between media and politics?

✦ **FIGURE 11.8** ✦

**Voter Turnout, Canadian Federal Elections, 1958–2000**

Source: "Canada: Parliamentary Elections" (2000); Naumetz (2000).

*Note:* If the trend in voter turnout continues to decline at the 1958–2000 rate, a minority of the voting-age population will vote in a federal election around 2051.

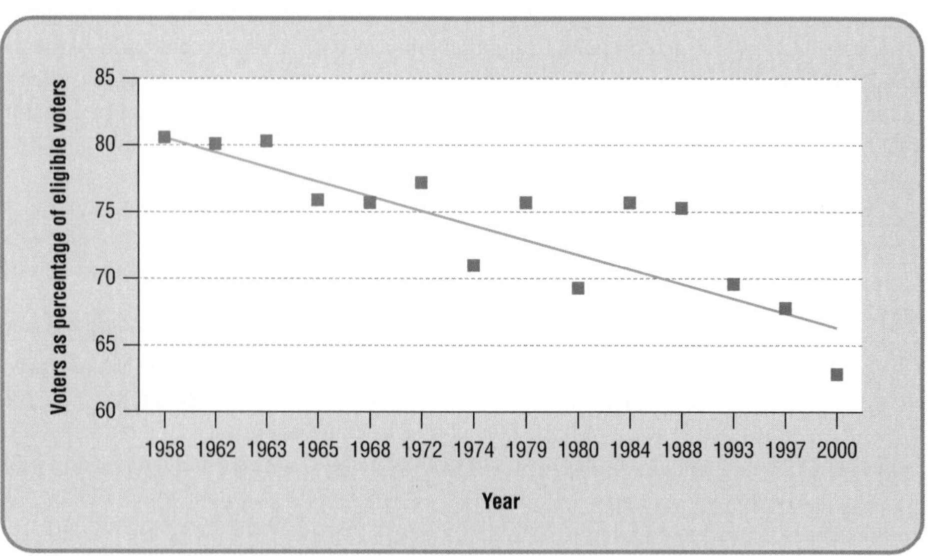

✦ **TABLE 11.3** ✦

**The Digital Divide: Social Characteristics of World Wide Web Users, Canada and International, 1998**

| **Canada (*n* = 38 030 households)** | |
|---|---|
| Percentage of households in top income quartile with Internet access at home | 45.1 |
| Percentage of households in bottom income quartile with Internet access at home | 7.1 |
| Percentage of households in top income quartile with Internet access at work | 50.4 |
| Percentage of households in bottom income quartile with Internet access at work | 4.1 |
| Percentage of households with Internet access at home, head of household with university degree | 46.7 |
| Percentage of households with Internet access at home, head of household without high-school diploma | 6.6 |
| Percentage of households in Canada's 15 largest Census Metropolitan Areas with Internet access at home | 40.4 |
| Percentage of households in Canada's outside 15 largest Census Metropolitan Areas with Internet access at home | 30.1 |
| Percentage of households with head of household age 35–54 regularly using Internet | 30.1 |
| Percentage of households with head of household age 65+ regularly using Internet | 5.3 |
| **International (*n* = 5022 individuals)** | |
| Under 41 years old | 59.6 |
| Completed college or higher | 70.2 |
| Annual household income CAD$75 000 or higher | 46.9 |

*Note*: The Canadian data come from a survey of a representative sample of households conducted by Statistics Canada (Dickinson and Ellison, 1999). The international data come from an online survey of Web users ("GVU's WWW User Surveys," 1999). In the latter, about 4% of respondents were from Canada, 7% from Europe, and 85% from the United States People learned about the survey on the Web and volunteered to participate in it. This produces sample bias. Respondents tend to be experienced and skilled Web users. However, comparing these results with survey results based on random samples suggests that the international figures reported here are accurate (Hoffman and Novak, 1998: 390–1).

in political participation that plague Canadian democracy today. It is unlikely to erase the political divide between classes. Instead, it is likely to help form a digital divide.

## Postmaterialism and the Dilemma of Canadian Politics

Believers in electronic democracy think the computer will solve the problem of unequal political participation. **Postmaterialists** believe that economic or material issues are becoming less important in Canadian politics. They argue as follows: Liberal democracies are less stratified than both nonliberal democracies and nondemocracies. That is, in liberal democracies, the gap between rich and poor is less extreme and society as a whole is more prosperous. In fact, say the postmaterialists, prosperity and the moderation of stratification have reached a point where they have fundamentally changed political life in Canada. They claim that, as recently as 50 years ago, most people were politically motivated mainly by their economic or material concerns. As a result, parties were distinguished from one another chiefly by the way they attracted voters from different classes. Now, however, many if not most Canadians have supposedly had their basic material wants satisfied. Particularly young people, who grew up in prosperous times, are less concerned with material issues, such as whether their next paycheque can feed and house their family. They are more concerned with postmaterialist issues, such as women's rights, civil rights, and the environment. The postmaterialists conclude that the old left–right political division, based on class differences and material issues, is being replaced. The new left–right political division, they say, is based on age differences and postmaterialist issues (Clark and Lipset, 1991; Clark, Lipset, and Rempel, 1993; Inglehart, 1997).

Although Canada is certainly more prosperous and less stratified than the less developed countries of the world, the postmaterialists are wrong to think that affluence is universal in this country, or that inequality is decreasing. These facts were documented at length in Chapter 7, Social Stratification: Canadian and Global Perspectives. Canada has one of the highest poverty rates of the rich industrialized countries and income equality has not increased in this country for three decades. Unemployment and poverty are particularly widespread among youth—the people who, in the postmaterialist view, are the most affluent and least concerned with material issues. About two-thirds of single Canadians under the age of 25 live below the poverty line. This suggests that, today, more new voters are poor than at any time since at least 1980, when data on youth poverty were first collected. Under these circumstances, we should not be surprised that bread-and-butter issues remain important to most voters. Canadian public opinion polls repeatedly show that the leading concerns of Canadians are unemployment and related material issues.

And so we arrive at the key dilemma of Canadian politics. Material issues—essentially problems of class inequality—continue to loom large in the minds of most Canadians. However, as we have seen, Canadian politics focuses on regional, not class issues. In other words, there is a disconnect between Canadian priorities and Canadian politics. This probably accounts in large measure for the declining rate of political participation and the high rates of political cynicism and apathy we have observed, particularly among lower classes (refer back to Figures 11.3 and 11.8). It probably also accounts in large measure for the fact that Canadians are increasingly turning to nonconventional means of influencing public policy. In 1980, 24 percent of Canadians said they had joined a boycott, attended an unlawful demonstration, joined an unofficial strike, or occupied a building or a factory at least once. Ten years later, that figure stood at 33 percent. Participation in such nonconventional political activities is most common among young, highly educated people (Nevitte, 1996: 75–109). This suggests that the future of Canadian politics may lie outside "normal" politics. We take up this fascinating theme again in Chapter 17, Collective Action and Social Movements.

## SUMMARY

1. The level of democracy in a society depends on how power is distributed. When power is concentrated in the hands of few people, society is less democratic.
2. Pluralists correctly note that democratic politics is about negotiation and compromise. However, they fail to appreciate that economically advantaged groups have more power than disadvantaged groups.
3. Elite theorists correctly note that power is concentrated in the hands of advantaged groups. However, they fail to appreciate how variations in the distribution of power influence political behaviour and public policy.
4. Power resource theorists usefully focus on changes in the distribution of power in society and their effects. However, they fail to appreciate what state-centred theorists emphasize—that state institutions and laws also affect political behaviour and public policy.
5. Many new democracies that emerged from the most recent wave of democratization are formal, not liberal, democracies. Their citizens enjoy regular, competitive elections but lack legal protection of rights and freedoms.
6. Citizens win legal protections of rights and freedoms when their middle and working classes become large, organized, and prosperous; and when powerful, friendly, pro-democratic foreign states support them.
7. Class inequality is a major barrier to increased political participation in Canada. That is likely to continue because the Canadian political system is biased toward regional rather than class politics. As a result, Canadians seem to be turning increasingly to nonconventional forms of political participation.

## GLOSSARY

**Authoritarian** states sharply restrict citizen control of the state.

**Authority** is legitimate, institutionalized power.

**Charismatic authority** is based on belief in the claims of extraordinary individuals to be inspired by a god or some higher principle.

**Civil society** is the private sphere of social life.

In a **democracy,** citizens exercise a high degree of control over the state. They do this mainly by choosing representatives in regular, competitive elections.

An **elite** is a group that controls the command posts of an institution.

**Elite theory** holds that small groups occupying the command posts of America's most influential institutions make the important decisions that profoundly affect all members of society. Moreover, they do so without much regard for elections or public opinion.

**Formal democracy** involves regular, competitive elections.

**Legal-rational authority** is typical of modern societies. It derives from respect for the law. Laws specify how one can achieve office. People generally believe these laws are rational. If someone achieves office by following these laws, people respect his or her authority.

The **legitimacy** of a government is its perceived right to rule.

A **liberal democracy** is a country whose citizens enjoy regular, competitive elections *and* the freedoms and constitutional protections that make political participation and competition meaningful.

**Lobbies** are organizations formed by special interest groups to advise and influence politicians.

The **mass media** in a democracy help keep the public informed about the quality of government.

**Pluralist theory** holds that power is widely dispersed. As a result, no group enjoys disproportionate influence and decisions are usually reached through negotiation and compromise.

**Political parties** are organizations that compete for control of government in regular elections. In the process, they give voice to policy alternatives and rally adult citizens to vote.

A **political revolution** is the overthrow of political institutions by an opposition movement and its replacement by new institutions.

**Postmaterialism** is a theory that claims that growing equality and prosperity in the rich industrialized countries have resulted in a shift from class-based politics to value-based politics.

**Power** is the ability to control others, even against their will.

**Power resource theory** holds that the distribution of power among major classes partly accounts for the successes and failures of different political parties.

**Public opinion** refers to the values and attitudes of the adult population as a whole. It is expressed mainly in polls and letters to lawmakers, and gives politicians a reading of citizen preferences.

A **ruling class** is a self-conscious, cohesive group of people in elite positions. They act to advance their common interests, and corporate executives lead them.

**Social movements** are collective attempts to change all or part of the political or social order.

The **state** consists of the institutions responsible for formulating and carrying out a country's laws and public policies.

**State-centred theory** holds that the state itself can structure political life, to some degree independently of the way power is distributed between classes and other groups at a given time.

In a **totalitarian** state, citizens lack almost any control of the state.

**Traditional authority,** the norm in tribal and feudal societies, involves rulers inheriting authority through family or clan ties. The right of a family or clan to monopolize leadership is widely believed to derive from the will of a god.

## QUESTIONS TO CONSIDER

1. Analyze any recent election. What issues distinguish the competing parties or candidates? What categories of the voting population does each party or candidate attract? Why?
2. Younger people are less likely to vote than older people. How would power resource theory explain this?
3. Do you think Canada will become a more democratic country in the next 25 years? Will a larger percentage of the population vote? Will class inequalities in political participation decline? Will public policy more accurately reflect the interests of the entire population? Why or why not?

## WEB RESOURCES

### Companion Web Site for This Book

http://www.brymsociologycompass.nelson.com

Begin by clicking on the Student Resources section of the Web site. Next, select the chapter you are currently studying from the pull-down menu. From the Student Resources page you will have easy access to InfoTrac College Edition®, MicroCase online exercises, and additional Web links. The Web site also has many useful tips to aid you in your study of sociology, including practice tests for each chapter.

## InfoTrac Search Terms

These search terms are provided to assist you in beginning to conduct research on this topic by visiting http://www.infotrac-college.com

**Civil society**
**Legitimacy**
**Political party**
**Ruling class**
**Voting**

## Recommended Web Sites

For data on Canadian elections, state revenues, and debt and expenditures, employment, visit the Statistics Canada Web site at http://www.statcan.ca/english/Pgdb/govern.htm.

The most important organization of international governance is the United Nations. For the UN Web site, go to http://www.un.org/.

For data on voter turnout in all democracies from 1945 to the present, go to the Web site of the International Institute for Democracy and Electoral Assistance at http://www.idea.int/.

# SUGGESTED READINGS

Doug Baer, ed. *Political Sociology: Canadian Perspectives* (Toronto: Oxford University Press, 2002). A compendium of Canadian writings in political sociology.

Samuel Huntington. *The Third Wave: Democratization in the Late Twentieth Century* (Norman, OK: University of Oklahoma Press, 1991). An account of the sweep and limits of democracy around the world.

Seymour Martin Lipset. *Political Man: The Social Bases of Politics*, 2nd ed. (Baltimore: Johns Hopkins University Press, 1981 [1960]). A classic introduction to the field.

Julia O'Connor and Gregg Olsen. *Power Resources Theory and the Welfare State: A Critical Approach* (Toronto: University of Toronto Press: 1998). A comprehensive and clear overview of power resource theory and its application to the contemporary analysis of the welfare state.

# NOTES

**1.** In early 2001, support for free trade had increased to 64 percent of Canadian adults, up from 46 percent in 1991 but down from 70 percent in 1999 (Tuck, 2001).

**2.** We say businessmen advisedly. Very few women are among Canada's richest people.

**3.** The clustering of voters on the left and the right does not mean that most Canadians know the difference between left and right in abstract terms or that they can identify specific parties as leftist or rightist. According to one recent poll, almost three-quarters of Canadians do not know, or are fuzzy on, the concept of a political right and left (Cobb, 2002).

**4.** In 2000, the Reform Party became the Canadian Alliance.

**5.** We emphasize political factors here, but the economic and cultural pull of the United States has also accentuated Canadian regionalism. North–south economic and cultural ties between Canada and the United States are arguably stronger than east–west ties between Canada's regions. For instance, the volume of trade between Canada and the United States is more than twice as large as the volume of trade among Canada's provinces ("Interprovincial Trade," 2001; "Imports and Exports of Goods on a Balance-of-Payments Basis," 2001). Similarly, a very large percentage of the most popular television programs, magazines, books, music, and movies in Canada are produced in the United States.

## IN THIS CHAPTER, YOU WILL LEARN THAT

- The traditional "nuclear" family is less common than it used to be. Several new family forms are becoming more popular. The frequency of one family form or another varies by class, ethnicity, sexual orientation, and region of the country.
- One of the most important forces underlying change from the traditional nuclear family is the entry of most women into the paid labour force. Doing paid work increases women's ability to leave unhappy marriages and control whether and when they will have children.
- Marital satisfaction increases as one moves up the class structure, where divorce laws are liberal, when teenage children leave the home, in families where housework is shared equally, and among spouses who enjoy a satisfying sex life.
- The worst effects of divorce on children can be eliminated if there is no parental conflict and the children's standard of living does not fall after divorce.
- The decline of the traditional nuclear family is sometimes associated with a host of social problems, such as poverty, welfare dependency, and crime. However, policies have been adopted in some countries that reduce these problems.

CHAPTER

# 12

# FAMILIES

## INTRODUCTION

One Saturday morning, Adie Nelson decided to enlist her children's help in reorganizing the contents of a large cabinet in their den. Inside the cabinet, along with an assortment of videos, CDs, video games, old report cards, and swimming badges, was a stack of old family photos. To Adie's surprise, both her children expressed great curiosity in the photos. "Who's that?" they asked repeatedly. "I wondered," says Adie, "whether their sudden interest in their relatives had anything to do with their lack of enthusiasm for cleaning out the cupboard. However, I thought it would be simple enough to explain who each person was. I was wrong.

"I got a hint that I might be in for a rough ride when my daughter asked, 'Oh, nasty! Who's the major geek kissing Auntie Reena?'

"'That's Auntie Reena's first husband, your cousin Adi's father,' I replied. 'And he's not really as big a geek as he looks.'

"'If he's Adi's dad, then why does she call Uncle Henry "Dad"?' my daughter asked, reasonably enough.

"'Well, Henry is actually Auntie Reena's second husband and Adi's stepdad,' I replied. 'But Adi calls him "Dad" because he acts like a dad to her.'

"My conviction that I could easily field my children's questions began to fade with my son's next query:

"'But Mom,' he interjected, 'if Auntie Reena and Uncle Henry aren't married any more and Lloyd's her husband, doesn't that make Uncle Henry Adi's ex-stepdad and our ex-uncle and Lloyd her new stepdad and our new uncle?'

"'No!' my daughter insisted. 'I like Uncle Henry and he's still my uncle even if he isn't married to Auntie Reena.'

"'Well, what about Lloyd?' my son asked. 'I thought you liked him, too.'

"'I do like him,' my daughter responded, 'but I can have more than one uncle, you know. There's no law says I can't. It's a free country.'

"My son stared at his sister in disbelief. 'Ronnie, you can't have a whole bunch of uncles with just one Auntie Reena. We're not talking about McNuggets.'

"At this point, we were still on the first photo. Feeling suddenly overwhelmed, I asked my children if, perhaps, they'd like to invite some friends over to play. They sprinted off, their great debate quickly forgotten.

"Now alone, I started sifting through the stack of photos. I began thinking about the myriad linkages among all the children, stepsiblings, spouses, ex-spouses, and same-sex partners of ex-in-laws that appeared in them. It seemed a huge and complicated task to get it right, and I soon gave up, exasperated as much by my inability to neatly map out our family ties for my kids as by the fact that the cabinet never did get organized.

"Later that day, I realized that my children and I had actually been engaged in one of the most difficult and controversial sociological tasks: defining 'family.' If I had been thinking sociologically rather than just feeling exasperated, I would have noted that even though some families are so complex they challenge our common-sense understanding of what a family should be like, their influence in our lives remains profound. For better or worse, our most intense emotional experiences are bound up with our families. We love, hate, protect, hurt, express generosity toward, and envy nobody as much as our parents, siblings, children, and mates. Little wonder, then, that most people are passionately concerned with the rights and wrongs, the dos and don'ts, of family life. Little wonder that family issues lie close to the centre of political debate in this country. Little wonder that attempts to define what is and is not a family often inspire intense emotion and impassionate debate."

Because families are emotional minefields, few subjects of sociological inquiry generate as much controversy. Much of the debate centres on a single question: Is the family in decline and, if so, what should be done about it? The question is hardly new. John Laing, a Protestant minister in Ontario, wrote in 1878, "We may expect to see further disintegration until the family shall disappear.... In all things civil and sacred the tendency of the age is towards individualism...its plausible aphorisms and popular usages silently undermining the divine institution of the family." In 1915, Canadian political economist and humorist Stephen Leacock remarked, "The home has passed, or at least is passing, out of existence. In place of it is the apartment—an incomplete thing, a mere part of something, where children are an intrusion, where hospitality is done through a caterer, and where Christmas is only the twenty-fifth of December" (as quoted in Sager, 2000: vii). Such statements, sounding the death knell of the family, seem more common whenever the family undergoes rapid change, and particularly when the divorce rate increases (see Box 12.1).

Today, when some people speak about "the decline of the family," they are referring to the **nuclear family.** The nuclear family is composed of a cohabiting man and woman who maintain a socially approved sexual relationship and have at least one child. Others are referring more narrowly to what might be called the **traditional nuclear family.** The traditional nuclear family is a nuclear family in which the wife works in the home without pay while the husband works outside the home for money. This makes him the "primary provider and ultimate authority" (Popenoe, 1988: 1).

## BOX 12.1 SOCIOLOGY AT THE MOVIES

Kevin Spacey and Mena Suvari in *American Beauty*

### *AMERICAN BEAUTY* (1999)

His wife wants to kill him. So does his daughter. His daughter's boyfriend, who has been supplying him with marijuana, is willing to kill him on his girlfriend's behalf. The boyfriend's father, a retired Marine, is convinced his son is having a homosexual affair with him. So he wants to kill him, too.

What does the character played by Kevin Spacey do to make so many people so angry in *American Beauty?* He gives up the pretenses of a middle-class, suburban husband. He returns in spirit (and in body, as well, by exercising furiously) to his teenage self. He quits his job as a magazine writer and gets a new one as a cook at a fast-food franchise. He trades in his "boring" late-model sedan for an old sports car. He is no longer willing to continue his loveless marriage or to suffer his daughter's taunts. He lusts after his teenage daughter's best friend. However, giving up such important family roles—dependable breadwinner, solid citizen, loving husband, sympathetic father—has big consequences. It enrages people enough that they want to kill him.

*American Beauty* offers a depressing portrait of suburban family life. The wife is a frustrated real estate broker. When she has an affair with a successful colleague, she appears more interested in advancing her career than in seeking pleasure or love. The pleasure and love she does experience seem to derive mainly from her lover's status. The retired Marine is an angry, violent, and obsessive-compulsive man. He has drained the life out of his wife. He is also homophobic, although it turns out that he harbours homosexual longings, as homophobes sometimes do (see Chapter 9, Sexuality and Gender). In fact, the only people who seem genuinely happy are the homosexual couple next door, who deviate from the suburban norm of heterosexual marriage.

Clearly, suburban family life is far from being a utopia. Well-manicured lawns and beautiful gardens sometimes mask deep frustrations and pathologies. What makes the Kevin Spacey character so subversive, however, is that he spurns the comforts of middle-class, suburban life and endangers the well-established norms of the nuclear family. But how should we understand the movie's challenge to conventional suburban family life? Does the movie merely illustrate a psychological problem—a midlife crisis—or does it illustrate a deeper, sociological problem—the collapse of conventional gender and family roles in a rapidly changing society?

In the 1940s and 1950s, many sociologists and much of the Canadian public considered the traditional nuclear family to be the most widespread and ideal family form. However, for reasons we will examine below, only 41 percent of Canadian families in 2001 took the form of the traditional nuclear family (married-couple families with children), compared with 69 percent in 1901 (see Figures 12.1 and 12.2). Between 1950 and 1998, the percentage of women over the age of 16 in the paid labour force increased from around 25 percent to 58 percent. In 1999, almost 80 percent of mothers with school-aged children were in the labour force. More than 6 in 10 mothers with children under the age of 3 were employed (Canadian Council on Social Development, 2001). As a result, only a minority of Canadian adults live in traditional nuclear families today. Many new family forms have become popular in recent decades.

✦ **FIGURE 12.1** ✦
**"Out of 100 Families" (Family Types, 2001)**

Source: Statistics Canada (2002e).

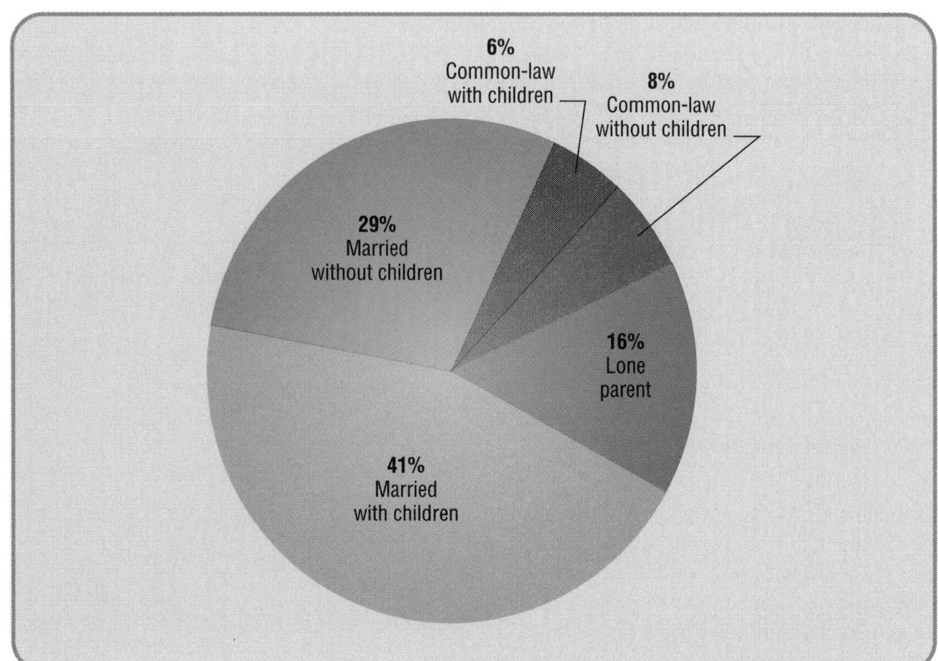


✦ **FIGURE 12.2** ✦
**Family Types, 1901**

Source: Canadian Families Project (1999).

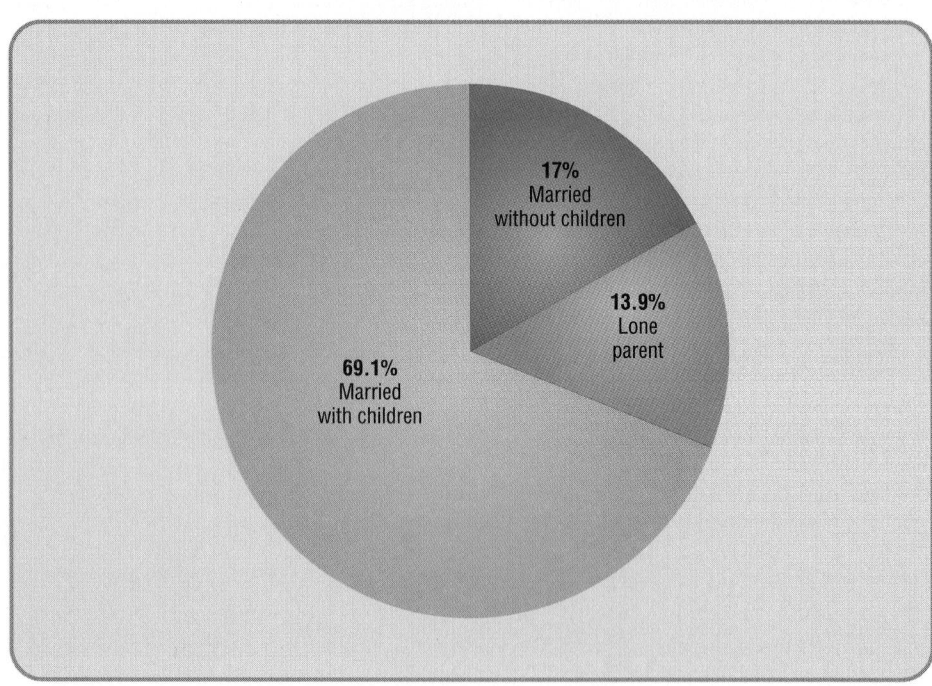

Some sociologists, many of them functionalists, view the decreasing prevalence of the married-couple family and the rise of the "working mother" as an unmitigated disaster (e.g., Gill, 1997; Popenoe, 1998, 1996). In their view, rising rates of crime, illegal drug use, poverty, and welfare dependency (among other social ills) can be traced to the fact that so many Canadian children are not living in two-parent households with stay-at-home mothers. They call for various legal and cultural reforms to shore up the traditional nuclear family. For instance, they want to make it harder to get a divorce and they want people to place less emphasis on individual happiness at the expense of family responsibility.

Other sociologists, influenced by conflict and feminist theories, disagree with the functionalist assessment (e.g., Coontz, 1992; Stacey, 1996). In the first place, they argue that it is inaccurate to talk about *the* family, as if this important social institution assumed or should assume only a single form. They emphasize that families have been structured in many ways and that the diversity of family forms is increasing as people accommodate the demands of new social pressures. Second, they argue that changing family forms do not necessarily represent deterioration in the quality of people's lives. In fact, such changes often represent *improvement* in the way people live. They believe that the decreasing prevalence of the traditional nuclear family and the proliferation of diverse family forms has benefited many men, women, and children and has not harmed other children as much as the functionalists think. They also believe that various economic and political reforms, such as the creation of an affordable nationwide daycare system, could eliminate most of the negative effects of single-parent households.

This chapter touches on divorce, reproductive choice, cohabitation, single-parent families, and other topics in the sociology of families. However, we have structured the chapter around the debate about the so-called decline of the Canadian family. We first outline the functional theory of the family because the issues raised by functionalism are still a focus of sociological controversy (Mann et al., 1997). Borrowing from the work of conflict theorists and feminists, we next present a critique of functionalism. In particular, we show that the nuclear family became the dominant and ideal family form only under specific social and historical conditions. Once these conditions changed, the nuclear family became less prevalent and a variety of new family forms proliferated. You will learn how these new family forms are structured and how their frequency varies by class, ethnicity, sexual orientation, and region. You will also learn that although postindustrial families solve some problems, they are hardly an unqualified blessing. The chapter's concluding section therefore considers the kinds of policies that might help alleviate some of the most serious concerns faced by families today. Let us, then, first review the functionalist theory of the family.

## FUNCTIONALISM AND THE NUCLEAR IDEAL

### Functional Theory

For any society to survive, its members must cooperate economically. They must have babies. And they must raise offspring in an emotionally supportive environment so the offspring can learn the ways of the group and eventually operate as productive adults. Since the 1940s, functionalists have argued that the nuclear family is ideally suited to meet these challenges. In their view, the nuclear family performs five main functions. It provides a basis for regulated sexual activity, economic cooperation, reproduction, socialization, and emotional support (Murdock, 1949: 1–22; Parsons, 1955).

Functionalists cite the pervasiveness of the nuclear family as evidence of its ability to perform the functions listed above. To be sure, other family forms exist. **Polygamy** expands the nuclear unit "horizontally" by adding one or more spouses (almost always wives) to the household. Polygamy is still legally permitted in many less industrialized countries of Africa and Asia. However, the overwhelming majority of families are monogamous because they cannot afford to support several wives and many children. The **extended family** expands the nuclear family "vertically" by adding another generation—

one or more of the spouse's parents—to the household. Extended families used to be common throughout the world. They still are in some places. However, according to the functionalists, the basic building block of the extended family (and of the polygamous family) is the nuclear unit.

George Murdock was a functionalist who conducted a famous study of 250 mainly preliterate societies in the 1940s. Murdock wrote: "Either as the sole prevailing form of the family or as the basic unit from which more complex familial forms are compounded, [the nuclear family] exists as a distinct and strongly functional group in every known society" (Murdock, 1949: 2). Moreover, the nuclear family, Murdock continued, is everywhere based on **marriage.** He defined marriage as a socially approved, presumably long-term, sexual and economic union between a man and a woman. It involves rights and obligations between spouses and between spouses and their children.

Let us consider the five main functions of marriage and the nuclear family in more detail:

1. *Sexual regulation.* Imagine a world without an institution that defines the boundaries within which legitimate sexual activity is permitted. Such a world would be disrupted by many people having sex wherever, whenever, and with whomever they pleased. An orderly social life would be difficult. Because marriage provides a legitimate forum for expressing the intense human need for sexual activity, says Murdock, it makes social order possible.

   Sex is not, however, the primary motive for marrying, he continues. After all, sex is readily available outside marriage. Only 54 of Murdock's 250 societies forbade or disapproved of premarital sex between nonrelatives. In most of those 250 societies, a married man could legitimately have an extramarital affair with one or more female relatives (Murdock, 1949: 5–6). It is hardly news that premarital and extramarital sex are common in contemporary Canada and other postindustrial societies. At present, Canadians living in Quebec evidence the most liberal sexual attitudes toward premarital, extramarital, and homosexual sex. However, based on current trends, it's been estimated that "by about the year 2010, close to 85 percent of Canadians will approve of nonmarital sex" (Bibby, 1995: 70).
2. *Economic cooperation.* Why then, apart from sex, do people marry? Murdock's answer is this: "By virtue of their primary sex difference, a man and a woman make an exceptionally efficient cooperating unit" (Murdock, 1949: 7). On average, women are physically weaker than men. Historically, pregnancy and nursing have restricted women in their activities. Therefore, writes Murdock, they can best perform lighter tasks close to home. These tasks include gathering and planting food, carrying water, cooking, making and repairing clothing, making pottery, and caring for children. Most men possess superior strength. They can therefore specialize in lumbering, mining, quarrying, land clearing, and house building. They can also range farther afield to hunt, fish, herd, and trade (Murdock, 1937). According to Murdock, this division of labour enables more goods and services to be produced than would otherwise be possible. People marry partly because of this economic fact. In Murdock's words: "Marriage exists only when the economic and the sexual are united into one relationship, and this combination occurs only in marriage" (Murdock, 1949: 8).
3. *Reproduction.* Before the invention of modern contraception, sex often resulted in the birth of a baby. According to Murdock, children are an investment in the future. By the age of six or seven, children in most societies do some chores. Their economic value to the family increases as they mature. When children become adults, they often help support their elderly parents. Thus, in most societies, there is a big economic incentive to having children.
4. *Socialization.* The investment in children can be realized only if adults rear the young to maturity. This involves not only caring for them physically but, as you saw in Chapter 4 (Socialization), teaching them language, values, beliefs, skills, religion,

and much else. Talcott Parsons (1955: 16) regarded socialization as the "basic and irreducible" function of the family.

5. *Emotional support.* Parsons also noted that the nuclear family universally gives its members love, affection, and companionship. He stressed that, in the nuclear family, it is mainly the mother who is responsible for ensuring the family's emotional well-being. She develops what Parsons calls the primary "expressive" role because she is the one who bears children and nurses them. It falls on the husband to take on the more "instrumental" role of earning a living outside the family (Parsons, 1955: 23). The fact that he is the "primary provider" makes him the ultimate authority.

## Foraging Societies

Does functionalism provide an accurate picture of family relations at any point in human history? To assess the adequacy of the theory, let us briefly consider family patterns in the two settings that were apparently foremost in the minds of the functionalists. We first discuss families in preliterate, foraging societies. In such societies, people subsist by hunting animals and gathering wild edible plants. Most of the cases in Murdock's sample are foraging societies. We then discuss families in urban and suburban middle-class Canada in the 1950s. The functionalists whose work we are reviewing lived in such families themselves.

Foraging societies are nomadic groups of 100 or fewer people. As we would expect from Murdock's and Parsons' analyses, a gender division of labour exists among foragers. Most men hunt and most women gather. Women also do most of the child care. However, research on foragers conducted since the 1950s, on which we base our analysis, shows that men often tend babies and children in such societies (Leacock, 1981; Lee, 1979; Turnbull, 1961). They often gather food after an unsuccessful hunt. In some foraging societies, women hunt. In short, the gender division of labour is less strict than Murdock and Parsons thought. What is more, the gender division of labour is not associated with large differences in power and authority. Overall, men have few if any privileges that women don't also enjoy. Relative gender equality is based on the fact that women produce up to 80 percent of the food.

Foragers travel in small camps or bands. The band decides by consensus when to send out groups of hunters. When they return from the hunt, they distribute game to all band members based on need. Each hunter does not decide to go hunting based on his or her own nuclear family's needs. Each hunter does not distribute game just to his or her own nuclear family. Contrary to what Murdock wrote, it is the band, not the nuclear family, that

There is rough gender equality among the !Kung-San, a foraging society in the Kalahari Desert in Botswana. That is partly because women play such a key economic role in providing food.

is the most efficient social organization for providing everyone with his or her most valuable source of protein.

In foraging societies, children are considered an investment in the future. However, it is not true that people always want more children for purposes of economic security. In fact, too many children are considered a liability. Subsistence is uncertain in foraging societies, and when band members deplete an area of game and edible plants, they move elsewhere. As a result, band members try to keep the ratio of children to productive adults low. In a few cases, such as the pre-twentieth-century Inuit, newborns were occasionally allowed to die if the tribe felt its viability was threatened by having too many mouths to feed.

Life in foraging societies is highly cooperative. For example, women and men care for—and women even breast-feed—each other's children. Despite Parsons' claim that socialization is the "basic and irreducible" function of the nuclear family, it is the band, not the nuclear family, that assumes responsibility for child socialization in foraging societies. Socialization is more a public than a private matter. As a seventeenth-century Innu man from northern Quebec said to a Jesuit priest who was trying to convince him to adopt European ways of raising children: "Thou hast no sense. You French people love only your own children; but we all love all the children of our tribe" (quoted in Leacock, 1981: 50).

In sum, recent research on foraging societies calls into question many of the functionalists' generalizations. In foraging societies, relations between the sexes are quite egalitarian. Children are not viewed just as an investment in the future. Each nuclear unit does not execute the important economic and socialization functions in isolation and in private. On the contrary, cooperative band members execute most economic and socialization functions in public.

Let us now assess the functionalist theory of the family in the light of evidence concerning Canadian middle-class families in the years just after the Second World War.

## The Canadian Middle Class in the 1950s

Functionalists recognized that the productive function of the family was less important after the Second World War than it had been in earlier times. In their view, the socialization and emotional functions of the family were now most important (Parsons, 1955). Thus, on the nineteenth-century family-owned farm, the wife played an indispensable productive role while the husband was out in the field or on the range. She took responsibility for the garden, the dairy, the poultry, and the management of the household. The children also did crucial chores with considerable economic value. But in the typical urban or suburban nuclear family of the late 1940s and 1950s, noted the functionalists, only one person played the role of breadwinner. That was usually the husband. Children enjoyed more time to engage in the play and leisure-time activities that were now considered necessary for healthy child development. For their part, most women got married, had babies, and stayed home to raise them. Strong normative pressures helped keep women at home. Thus, in the 1950s, sociologist David Riesman called a woman's failure to obey the strict gender division of labour a "quasi-perversion." *Esquire* magazine called women's employment in the paid labour force a "menace." *Life* magazine called it a "disease" (quoted in Coontz, 1992: 32).

As a description of family patterns in the 15 years after the Second World War, functionalism has its merits. During the Great Depression (1929–39) and after conscription began in 1942 (Oderkirk, 2000: 95), Canadians were forced to postpone marriage (if they married at all) because of widespread poverty, government-imposed austerity, and physical separation. After this long and dreadful ordeal, many Canadians just wanted to settle down, have children, and enjoy the peace, pleasure, and security that family life seemed to offer. Conditions could not have been better for doing just that. The immediate post-war era was one of unparalleled optimism and prosperity (Nelson and Robinson, 2002). Real per capita income rose, as did the percentage of Canadians who owned their own homes. By the mid-1950s, employment and personal income reached all-time highs. Various services and legislative amendments created during the Second World War to encourage wives and mothers to join the labour force were rescinded. The expectation was that a return to "normal" meant the resumption of the provider–housewife roles of men and women, respectively (Kingsbury and Scanzoni, 1993).

One result of these combined conditions was a "marriage boom" in Canada (see Figure 12.3). Increasingly, Canadians lived in married-couple families. The proportion of "never married" Canadians decreased and the average age at first marriage dropped from 24.4 years for brides and 27.6 for bridegrooms in 1941, to 23.4 and 26.1 years, respectively, by 1956 (McVey and Kalbach, 1995: 225; see Figure 12.4). A second result was a "baby boom." During this period in our history, Canadian families averaged four children—resulting in proportionally more boomers than in the United States, Australia, or New Zealand (Nikiforuk, 1999). And unlike the situation today, married men were much more likely than married women to be working for pay. For example, in 1951, 90.0 percent of married men but only 11.2 percent of married women were in the paid labour force.

Not all women, of course, could afford to stay out of the workforce. Poor women have often worked both inside and outside of the home. However, middle-class women engaged in what has been called an "orgy of domesticity" in the post-war years, devoting increasing attention to child rearing and housework. They also became increasingly concerned with

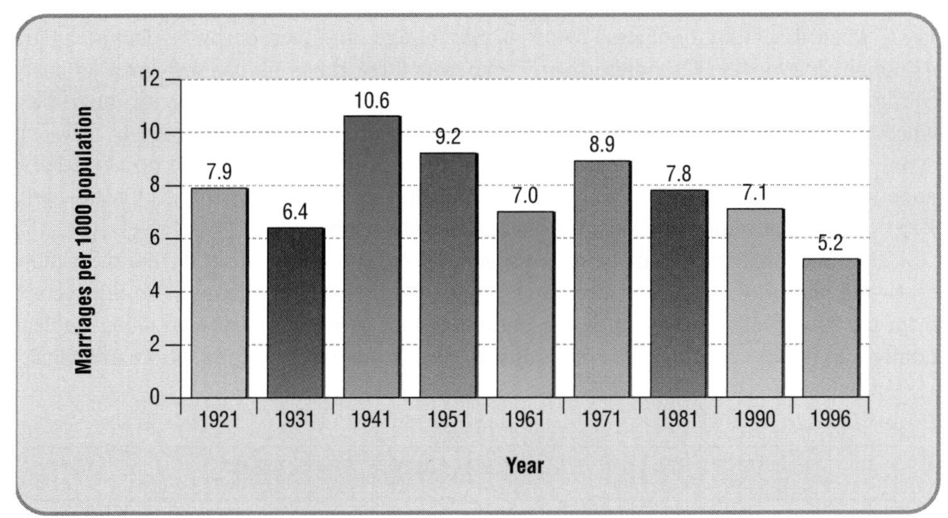


✦ **FIGURE 12.3** ✦
**Marriage Rates, 1921–1996**

Source: Statistics Canada, Selected Marriage Statistics 1921–1990. Cat. 82-552 and Statistics Canada, *The Daily*, 29 January 1998.

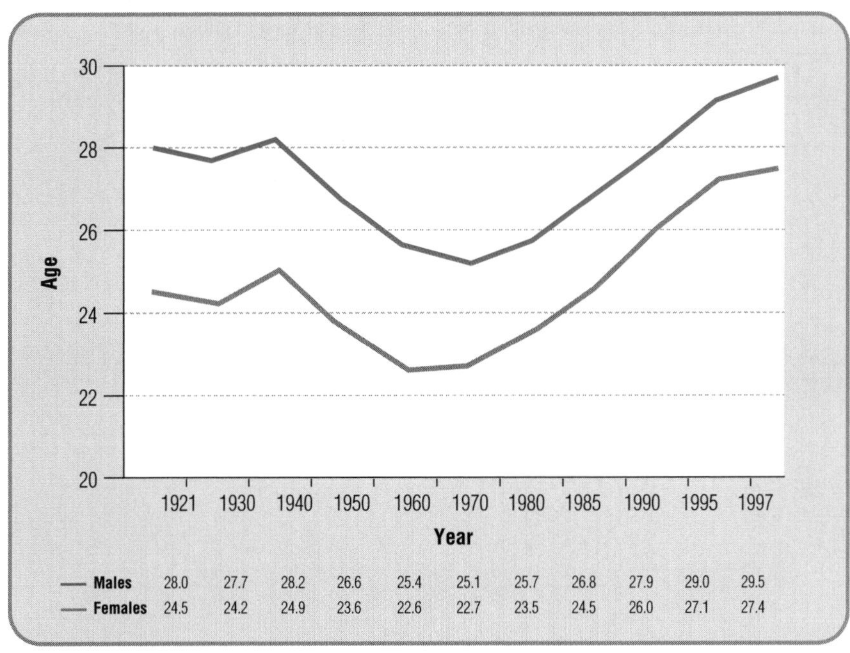


✦ **FIGURE 12.4** ✦
**Average Age at First Marriage**

Source: Statistics Canada (1992). *Current Demographic Analysis: Marriage and Conjugal Life in Canada*, Cat. 91-534, Statistics Canada, *The Daily*, 28 October 1999, 29 January 1998.

the emotional quality of family life as love and companionship became firmly established as the main motivation for marriage (Coontz, 1992: 23–41; Skolnick, 1991: 49–74).

Nevertheless, as sociologist Andrew J. Cherlin meticulously shows for the United States, the immediate post-war period was in many respects a historical aberration (Cherlin, 1992 [1981]: 6–30). Trends in divorce, marriage, and child-bearing show a gradual *weakening* of the nuclear family from the second half of the nineteenth century until the mid-1940s, and continued weakening after the 1950s. Specifically, throughout the nineteenth century, the **divorce rate** rose very slowly. The divorce rate is the number of divorces that occur in a year for every 1000 people in the population. Meanwhile, the **marriage rate** fell. The marriage rate is the number of marriages that occur in a year for every 1000 people in the population. The **total fertility rate** also fell. The total fertility rate is the average number of children that would be born to a woman during her lifetime, assuming she has the same number of children as the average for women in each age cohort. Only the peculiar historical circumstances of the post-war years, noted above, temporarily reversed these trends.

The pattern in Canada was much the same. Immediately following the Second World War, Canada's marriage and divorce rates both reached previously unprecedented highs. From a low of 6.4 marriages per 1000 population in 1931, the popularity of marriage peaked with 10.9 marriages per 1000 in both 1942 and 1946. It then gradually fell until 1971, when the "baby boomers" came of marital age, and then began to decline again. Although in 1946 the Canadian divorce rate was three times its pre-war level as hasty wartime marriages broke up, the divorce rate declined from that point until the 1960s, when the introduction of more liberal divorce legislation was accompanied by a rising divorce rate. In like fashion, although the fertility rate climbed during the post-war baby boom years, peaking in 1961, this pattern was also reversed (see Figure 12.5). By the early 1960s, the earlier trends in Canada had reasserted themselves.

The functionalists, we may conclude, generalized too hastily from the era they knew best—the period of their own adulthood. Contrary to what they thought, the big picture from the nineteenth century until the present is that of a gradually weakening nuclear family. Let us now consider the conditions that made other family forms more prevalent.

## CONFLICT AND FEMINIST THEORIES

I hadn't really wanted to marry at all. I wanted to make something of myself, not just give it away. But I knew if I didn't marry I would be sorry. Only freaks didn't. I knew I had to do it quickly, too, while there was still a decent selection of men to choose from . . . I was twenty . . .

✦ **FIGURE 12.5** ✦
**Total Fertility Rate, 1951–1996**

Source: For 1951 to 1992, *Canadian Families at the Approach of the Year 2000*; for 1993 to 1995, *The Daily*; for 1996, Annual Demographic Statistics 1998, Cat. #91-213.

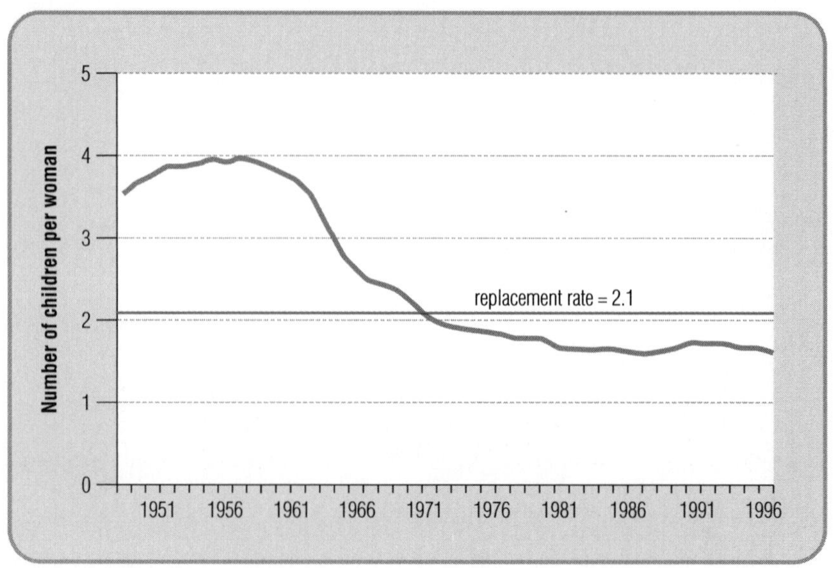

> Though I wanted to be a good wife, from the beginning I found it impossible to subdue my desires. I was in fierce competition with my husband, though Frank, completely absorbed in his own studies, was probably unaware of it. He believed he had married an impulsive girl, even a supergirl, but not a separate, feeling woman . . . Though we had agreed to study like fury till our money ran out and then take turns getting jobs, at bottom we knew it would be he who would get the degrees and I who would get the jobs. (Shulman, 1997 [1969]: 163, 173)

This quotation, from *Memoirs of an Ex-Prom Queen,* shows a side of family life entirely obscured by the functionalists. As the passage suggests, and as the novel establishes in biting and sometimes depressing detail, post-war families did not always operate like the smoothly functioning, happy, white, middle-class, mother-householder, father-breadwinner household portrayed every week in 1950s TV classics such as *Leave It to Beaver, Father Knows Best,* and *Ozzie and Harriet* (and revisited in the 1970s sitcom *Happy Days*).

Many men and women felt coerced into getting married, trapped in their families, unable to achieve the harmony, security, and emotional satisfaction they had been promised. As a result, the nuclear family was often a site of frustration and conflict. Surveys show that only about a third of working-class couples and two-thirds of middle-class couples were happily married (Bernard, 1972). Wives were less satisfied with marriage than husbands. They reported higher rates of depression, distress, and feelings of inadequacy. Dissatisfaction seems to have been especially high among those women who, during the Second World War, had operated cranes in steel mills, greased locomotives, riveted the hulls of ships, worked the assembly lines in munitions factories, planted and harvested crops, and felled Douglas firs. They were universally praised for their dedication and industry during the war. Many of them did not want to leave these well-paying jobs that gave them gratification and independence. Management fired most of them anyway and downgraded others to lower-paying "women's" jobs to make room for returning soldiers. The tedium of domestic labour must have been especially difficult for many of these women to accept (Coontz, 1992: 23–41; Skolnick, 1991: 49–74).

Also, many families were simply too poor to participate in the functionalists' celebration of the traditional nuclear unit. Others, because of divorce or widowhood, lacked a male "breadwinner" or "good provider" (Bernard, 1986 [1973]). For example, in 1951, 11.2 percent of married women and 19.3 percent of divorced and widowed women participated in the paid labour force. Then, as now, some of these women worked as "domestics," allowing their better-off counterparts to escape the drudgery of housework. Others

TV classics from the 1950s, such as *Father Knows Best,* portrayed smoothly functioning, happy, white, middle-class, mother-householder, father-breadwinner families.

provided child care as live-in or live-out nannies. Thus, to a degree not recognized by the functionalists, the role of the housewife sometimes meant the exploitation of lower-class and immigrant women.

Unlike the functionalists, Marxists had long seen the traditional nuclear family as a site of gender conflict and a basis for the perpetuation of social inequality. In the nineteenth century, Marx's close friend and co-author, Friedrich Engels, argued that the traditional nuclear family emerged along with inequalities of wealth. For once wealth was concentrated in the hands of a man, wrote Engels, he became concerned about how to transmit it to his children, particularly his sons. How could a man safely pass on an inheritance, asked Engels? Only by controlling his wife sexually and economically. Economic control ensured that the man's property would not be squandered and would remain his and his alone. Sexual control, in the form of enforced female monogamy, ensured that his property would be transmitted only to *his* offspring. It follows from Engels' analysis that only the elimination of private property and the creation of economic equality—in a word, communism—can bring an end to the traditional nuclear family and mark the arrival of gender equality (Engels, 1970 [1884]: 138–9).

Engels was right to note the long history of male economic and sexual domination in the traditional nuclear family. Early Canadian family law was informed by a vision of the family in which the role of the husband/father was pivotal and in which the labour and services of a wife belonged to her husband as a right. Although a series of legal reforms have altered the formerly harsh position of married women, as recently as a few decades ago a wife could not rent a car, take out a loan, or sign a contract without her husband's permission.

Despite the legally sanctioned domination of wives by husbands under capitalism, Engels was wrong to think that communism would eliminate gender inequality in the family. Gender inequality is as common in societies that call themselves communist as in those that call themselves capitalist. For example, the Soviet Union left "intact the fundamental family structures, authority relations, and socialization patterns crucial to personality formation and sex-role differentiation. Only a genuine sexual revolution [or, as we prefer to call it, a *gender revolution*] could have shattered these patterns and made possible the real emancipation of women" (Lapidus, 1978: 7).

Because gender inequality exists in noncapitalist (including precapitalist) societies, most feminists believe something other than, or in addition to, capitalism accounts for gender inequality. In their view, *patriarchy*—male dominance and norms justifying that dominance—is more deeply rooted in the economic, military, and cultural history of humankind than the classical Marxist account allows (see Chapter 9, Sexuality and Gender). For them, only a "genuine gender revolution" can alter this state of affairs.

Just such a revolution in family structures, authority relations, and socialization patterns picked up steam in Canada and other Western countries about 40 years ago, although its roots extend back to the eighteenth century. As you will see, the revolution is evident in the rise of romantic love and happiness as bases for marriage, women's increasing control over reproduction due to their use of contraceptives, and women's increasing participation in the system of higher education and the paid labour force. We next consider some consequences of the gender revolution for the selection of mates, marital satisfaction, divorce, reproductive choice, housework, and child care. We begin by considering the sociology of mate selection.

## POWER AND FAMILIES

### Love and Mate Selection

Most Canadians take for granted that marriage ought to be based on love (see Figure 12.6). Our assumption is evident, for example, in the way most popular songs celebrate love as the sole basis of long-term intimacy and marriage. In contrast, most of us view marriage devoid of love as tragic.

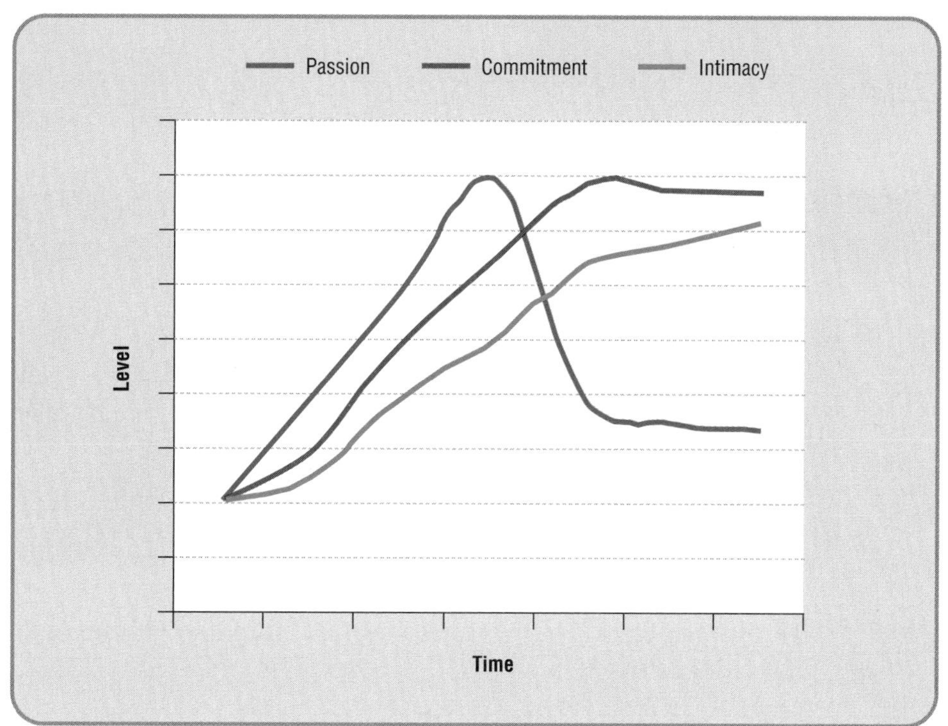


✦ **FIGURE 12.6** ✦

**The Components of Love**

According to psychologist Robert Sternberg, love can be built from three components: passion (erotic attraction), intimacy (confiding in others and shared feelings), and commitment (intention to remain in the relationship). In actual relationships, these components may be combined in various ways to produce different kinds of love. The fullest love requires all three components. Research shows that, in long-term relationships, passion peaks fairly quickly and then tapers off. Intimacy rises more gradually but remains at a higher plateau. Commitment develops most gradually but also plateaus at a high level.

Source: Sternberg (1986).

Yet in most societies throughout human history, love has had little to do with marriage. Some languages, such as the Chinese dialect spoken in Shanghai, even lack a word for love. Historically and across cultures, marriages were typically arranged by third parties, not by brides and grooms themselves. The selection of marriage partners was based mainly on calculations intended to maximize the prestige, economic benefits, and political advantages accruing to the families from which the bride and groom came. For a family of modest means, a small dowry might be the chief gain from allowing their son to marry a certain woman. For upper-class families, the benefits were typically bigger but no less strategic. In the early years of industrialization, for example, more than one old aristocratic family in economic decline scrambled to have its offspring marry into a family of the upstart bourgeoisie. This does not mean that such marriages were wholly devoid of loving feelings. However, "being in love" was not seen as an essential prerequisite for a successful marital union.

The idea that love should be important in the choice of a marriage partner first gained currency in eighteenth-century England with the rise of liberalism and individualism, philosophies that stressed freedom of the individual over community welfare (Stone, 1977). However, the intimate linkage between love and marriage that we know today emerged only in the early twentieth century, when Hollywood and the advertising industry began to promote self-gratification on a grand scale. For these new spinners of fantasy and desire, an important aspect of self-gratification was heterosexual romance leading to marriage (Rapp and Ross, 1986). Consider here, for example, the results of a recent study that asked 497 male and 673 female university undergraduates in 10 countries and Hong Kong the following question: "If a man (woman) had all the qualities you desired, would you marry this person if you were not in love with him (her)?" The results (presented in Figure 12.7) suggest that in free-choice cultures where the value of individualism is highly prized, love has come to be defined as *the* essential basis for marriage. In the United States, a country often considered to be the most individualistic society in the world, only 3.5 percent of the students said they would marry someone who they were not in love with—even if that person possessed all the qualities they were looking for in a partner (Levine et al., 1995).

Hollywood glamorized heterosexual, romantic love and solidified the intimate linkage between love and marriage that we know today. Clark Gable and Vivien Leigh *in Gone with the Wind* (1939).

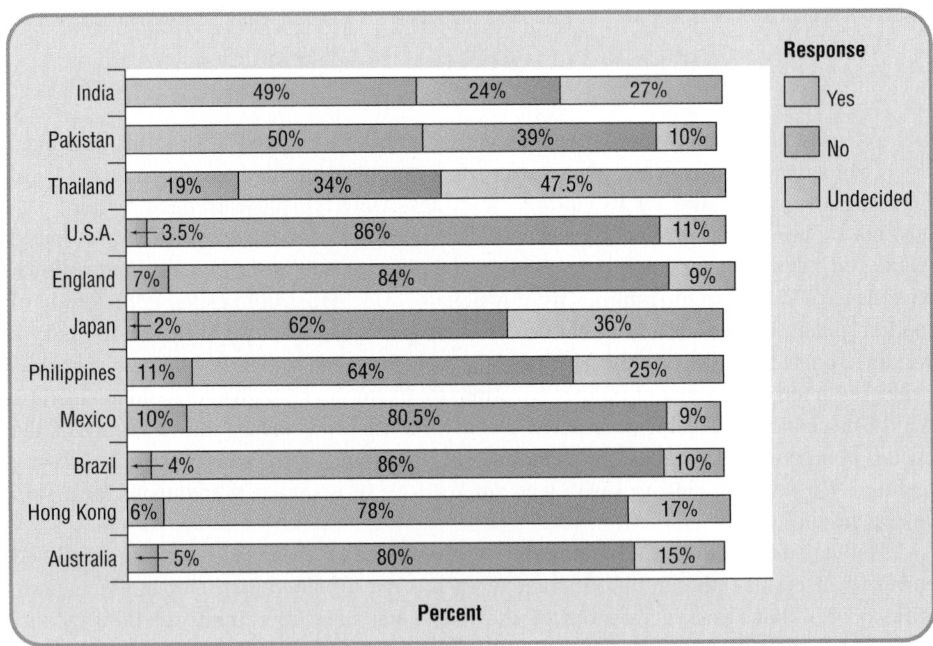


✦ **FIGURE 12.7** ✦

**Responses to Question: "If a man (woman) had all the other quantities you desired, would you marry this person if you were not in love with him (her)?"**

Note: Percentages may not add up to 100% because of rounding.

Source: Levine et al. (1995: 561).

Still, it would be a big mistake to think that love alone determines mate selection in our society—far from it. Three sets of social forces influence whom you are likely to fall in love with and marry (Kalmijn, 1998: 398–404):

1. *Marriage resources.* Potential spouses bring certain resources with them to the "marriage market." They use these resources to attract mates and compete against rivals. These resources include financial assets, status, values, tastes, and knowledge. Most people want to maximize the financial assets and status they gain from marriage and they want a mate who has similar values, tastes, and knowledge. As a result, whom you fall in love with and choose to marry is determined partly by the assets you bring to the marriage market.

2. *Third parties.* A marriage between people from two different groups may threaten the internal cohesion of one or both groups. Therefore, to varying degrees, families, neighbourhoods, communities, and religious institutions raise young people to identify with the groups they are members of and think of themselves as different from members of other groups. They may also apply sanctions to young people who threaten to marry outside the group. For example, although ethnic intermarriage has become increasingly common in Canada (Kalbach, 2000), parents often encourage their children to marry within their own ethnic group to preserve their unique culture (Kitano and Daniels, 1995). This is especially true among immigrants who come to Canada from more collectivist cultures in which arranged marriages have been the tradition (Dugger, 1996). As a result, whom you fall in love with and choose to marry is determined partly by the influence of third parties.
3. *Demographic and compositional factors.* The probability of marrying inside one's group increases with the group's size and geographical concentration. Conversely, if you are a member of a small group or a group that is dispersed geographically, you stand a greater chance of having to choose an appropriate mate from outside your group. There may simply be too few "prospects" in your group from which to choose (Brym, Gillespie, and Gillis, 1985). In addition, the ratio of men to women in a group influences the degree to which members of each sex marry inside or outside the group. For instance, war and incarceration may eliminate many male group members as potential marriage partners. This may encourage female group members to marry outside the group or forgo marriage altogether. Finally, since people usually meet potential spouses in "local marriage markets"—schools, universities and colleges, places of work, neighbourhoods, bars, and clubs—the degree to which these settings are socially segregated also influences mate selection. You are more likely to marry outside your group if local marriage markets are socially heterogeneous. As a result, whom you fall in love with and choose to marry is determined partly by the size, geographical dispersion, and sex ratio of the groups you belong to and the social composition of the local marriage markets you frequent.

As a result of the operation of these three sets of social forces, the process of falling in love and choosing a mate is far from random. Most of us will select a partner of similar ethnic background, age, and social class. Traditionally, the Protestant, Catholic, and Jewish religions, for example, as well as Muslim and Hindu religions, have encouraged **endogamy:** marrying within one's own social group. (The opposite of endogamy is **exogamy,** marrying outside one's group.)

In the past, social pressures to marry endogamously were more robust than they are today. Nevertheless, although interracial marriage has become more acceptable in Canada (Bibby, 2001: 216), the overwhelmingly majority of Canadian couples, whether married or living common law, with or without children, are racially homogeneous (Riedmann, Lamanna, and Nelson, 2003: 213)

## Marital Satisfaction

Just as mate selection came to depend more on romantic love over the years, so marital stability came to depend more on having a happy rather than merely a useful marriage. This change occurred because women in Canada and many other societies have become more autonomous, especially over the past 40 years or so. That is, one aspect of the gender revolution women are experiencing is that they are freer than ever to leave marriages in which they are unhappy.

One factor that contributed to women's autonomy was the legalization of birth control measures. Since 1969, birth control measures have been legal in Canada. The birth control pill made it easier for women to delay childbirth and have fewer children. A second factor that contributed to women's autonomy was their increased presence in the paid labour force. While in 1961 only about one in five husband-and wife families were dual-income families, by 1967 this had increased to just over one in three (Vanier Institute of the Family, 2000: 96). Once women enjoyed a source of income independent of their husbands, they gained the means to decide the course of their own lives to a greater extent than ever before. A married woman with a job outside the home is less tied to her marriage by economic necessity than a woman who works only at home. If she is deeply dissatisfied with her marriage, she can more easily leave. In addition, beginning in the late 1960s, laws governing divorce were changed to make divorce easier.

If marital stability now depends largely on marital satisfaction, what are the main factors underlying marital satisfaction? The sociological literature emphasizes five sets of forces (Collins and Coltrane, 1991 [1985]: 394–406, 454–64):

1. *Economic forces.* Money issues are the most frequent subjects of family quarrels, and money issues loom larger when there isn't enough money to satisfy a family's needs and desires. Accordingly, marital satisfaction tends to fall and the divorce rate tends to rise as you move down the socio-economic hierarchy. The lower the social class and the lower the educational level of the spouses, the more likely it is that financial pressures will make them unhappy and the marriage unstable. Marital dissatisfaction and divorce are also more common among groups with high poverty rates. In contrast, the marital satisfaction of wives and, even more, of husbands, generally *increases* when wives enter the paid labour force (Hughes, Galinsky, and Morris, 1992; Lupri and Frideres, 1988). This is mainly because of the beneficial financial effects. However, if *either* spouse spends so much time on the job that he or she neglects the family, marital satisfaction falls.
2. *Divorce laws.* Many surveys show that, on average, married people are happier than unmarried people. Moreover, when people are free to end unhappy marriages and remarry, the average level of happiness increases among married people. Thus, the level of marital happiness has increased in Canada over the past few decades, especially for wives, partly because it has become easier to get a divorce. For the same reason, in countries where getting a divorce is more difficult (e.g., Italy and Spain), husbands and wives tend to be less happy than in countries where getting a divorce is easier (e.g., Canada and the United States; Stack and Eshleman, 1998).
3. *The family life cycle.* Most divorces occur relatively early in marriage (Clarke, 1995). In Canada, the highest rate of divorce per 1000 population occurs at year 5 of marriage (with more than 3.5 divorces per 1000 population) and then falls each year thereafter (Ambert, 1998: 5). However, the proportion of divorces for couples married 20 years or more has increased in recent years (Wu and Penning, 1997). Marital satisfaction generally starts high, falls when children are born (especially for wives; Glenn, 1990: 825), reaches a low point when children are in their teenage years, and rises again when children reach adulthood (Rollins and Cannon, 1974).[1] Nonparents and parents whose children have left home (so-called "empty-nesters") enjoy the highest level of marital satisfaction. Parents who are just starting families or who have adult children living at home enjoy intermediate levels of marital satisfaction. Marital satisfaction is lowest during the "establishment" years, when children are attending school. Although most people get married at least partly to have children, it turns out that children, and especially teenagers, usually put big emotional and financial strains on families. This results in relatively low marital satisfaction.
4. *Housework and child care.* Marital happiness is higher among couples who perceive an equitable distribution of housework and child care (Rosenbluth, Steil, and Whitcomb, 1998). The farther couples are from an equitable sharing of domestic responsibilities, the more tension there is among all family members (Risman and Johnson-Sumerford, 1998). Some research finds that equitable sharing tends to increase with education (Berk, 1985).
5. *Sex.* Having a good sex life is associated with marital satisfaction. Contrary to popular belief, surveys show that sex generally improves during a marriage. Sexual intercourse is also more enjoyable and frequent among happier couples. From these

findings, some experts conclude that general marital happiness leads to sexual compatibility (Collins and Coltrane, 1991 [1985]: 344). However, the reverse may also be true. Good sex may lead to a good marriage. After all, sexual preferences are deeply rooted in our psyches and our earliest experiences. They cannot be altered easily to suit the wishes of our partners. If spouses are sexually incompatible, they may find it hard to change, even if they communicate well, argue little, and are generally happy on other grounds. On the other hand, if a husband and wife are sexually compatible, they may work harder to resolve other problems in the marriage for the sake of preserving their good sex life. Thus, the relationship between marital satisfaction and sexual compatibility is probably reciprocal. Each factor influences the other.

Religion, we note, has little effect on level of marital satisfaction. But religion does influence the divorce rate in a variety of ways. For example, a person may be influenced by biblical teaching that emphasizes the sanctity of marriage and prohibits adultery (Clark, 2000: 113). In addition, analysis of the 1995 General Social Survey data reveals that religious people are more likely than those who never attend religious services to report that they would remain married "for the sake of the children" and are less likely to view a partner's lack of love and respect or a partner's excessive drinking as grounds for divorce. However, religious people were just as likely as those who did not attend religious services to regard abusive behaviour and/or infidelity as valid reasons to divorce (Clark, 2000: 110).

Let us now see what happens when low marital satisfaction leads to divorce.

## Divorce

Before the turn of the twentieth century, divorce was a complex, drawn-out legal process in Canada. In some provinces, a "parliamentary" divorce was possible. However, this required that a private member's bill pass successfully through two readings in both the House of Commons and the Senate and then be approved by a special divorce committee (Boyd, 1998: 229). As a result, divorce was a rarity.

Prior to 1968, adultery was the only grounds for divorce in Canada, except in Nova Scotia, where cruelty was sufficient grounds even before Confederation (Morrison, 1987). The Divorce Act of 1968, the first federal divorce statute, expanded the "fault grounds" under which a divorce could be granted. In addition to adultery, proof that one's partner had engaged in prohibited activities such as mental or physical cruelty, rape, gross addiction to alcohol or other drugs, sodomy, bestiality, and homosexual acts, entitled the petitioner to an immediate divorce. This Act also took a first step toward "no-fault" divorce. The dissolution of a marriage was permitted on grounds of unspecified "marital breakdown," if couples had lived "separate and apart" for a three-year period before applying for a divorce and jointly consented to being divorced. In the event that one party did not wish to be divorced, the court required that five years pass from the time of the separation before applying for divorce.

With the amendment of Canada's Divorce Act in 1985, there is only one ground available for divorce—marital breakdown—but this is defined in three ways: (1) the spouses have lived apart for one year, (2) one of the spouses has committed an act of adultery, (3) one spouse has treated the other with mental or physical cruelty. Today, a spouse seeking divorce no longer has to prove grounds. Instead, a marriage is legally "dissolved" because the relationship is "irretrievably broken." Following these amendments, the divorce rate reached a historic high in 1987 and has since declined (Statistics Canada, 2000b). The 1998 crude divorce rate of 228 divorces for every 100 000 people is far below its peak in 1987 of 335 divorces per 100 000 people. Based on 1998 divorce rates, projections are that 36 percent of marriages will end in divorce within 30 years of marriage (Statistics Canada, 2000b).

### Economic Effects

After divorce, the most common pattern is a rise in the husband's income and a decline in the wife's (Vanier Institute of the Family, 2000). Indeed, "the longer the period of divorce (or widowhood) of a woman, the more she is likely to be poor" (Choi, 1992: 40). In

Canada, research indicates that in the first year following divorce, the income of Canadian women declines by about 50 percent while men's household income decreases by about 25 percent (Finnie, 1993). However, since the majority of children remain with their mothers following divorce,

> *when the figures are adjusted for family size, women's income drops by 40% while men's increases slightly*. Women's poverty rises from 16% before divorce to 43% after divorce. Even three years after divorce, women's income remains far below what they had during marriage and far below their ex-husbands' current income. (emphasis in original)

This pattern occurs because husbands tend to earn more, children typically live with their mothers, and support payments are often inadequate. Although child poverty in Canada is not restricted to single-parent families, a far higher proportion of children of single parents and, in particular, lone-parent mothers, live in low-income circumstances (see Figure 12.8). The younger the age of children at the time of divorce or dissolution of a common-law relationship, the more likely they are to be living in a low-income situation (Ambert, 1998: 9).

In the past, Canadian laws regarding the division of marital assets upon divorce and the awarding of alimony contributed to women's declining living standards post-divorce. For example, in the early 1970s, Irene Murdock, a farm wife, claimed that her labours over the course of 15 years had earned her a share in the family farm. However, the Supreme Court of Canada ruled that the labours were simply that of an "ordinary farm wife" and did *not* entitle Mrs. Murdock to share in the property that she and her husband had accumulated during their marriage (Steel, 1987: 159).

At present, there is no federal property law that applies throughout Canada. Although all Canadian provinces and territories have laws requiring spouses to share assets in the event of marital breakdown, the precise definition of what constitutes a "family asset" varies and creates inconsistencies across jurisdictions (Dranoff, 2001: 257). In addition, although the monetary value of tangible "family assets" (e.g., money in the bank, a house) can be calculated and shared, the valuable "new property" (Glendon, 1981) in today's society is the earning power of a professional degree, highly paid employment, work experience, a skilled trade, or other "human capital." Upon divorce, the wife *may* get an equal share of tangible property, but that does not usually result in her beginning post-divorce life on an equal footing with her former husband—especially if she retains physical custody of the couple's children.

**Child support** involves money paid by the noncustodial parent to the custodial parent for the purpose of supporting the children of a separated marital, cohabiting, or sexual rela-

✦ **FIGURE 12.8** ✦

**Poverty Rates among Canadian Families, 1980, 1989, and 1997**

Source: Based on Statistics Canada's low income cut-offs (1992 base).

*Note:* Elderly families are those with heads 65 years of age or older. Couples without children, two-parent, and lone-parent families are non-elderly. Two-parent and lone-parent families are restricted to those with at least one child under 18 living at home.

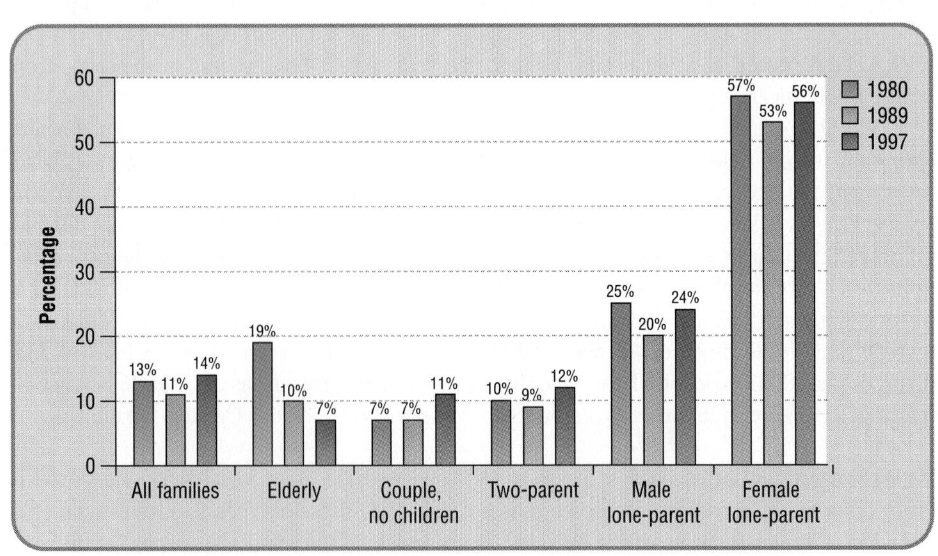

tionship. Under the Divorce Act, either parent may be ordered to pay child support. However, because mothers retain custody in the vast majority of cases—and because women are more likely to be economically disadvantaged in employment—the vast majority of those ordered to pay child support are fathers.

Every jurisdiction in Canada requires parents to support their children following separation or divorce. In 1997, the federal government introduced standardized formula guidelines, based on the income of the noncustodial parent only and the number of children involved, to establish the amount of mandatory payment for child-support orders granted from May 1, 1997, onwards under the Divorce Act. Although the intent of these guidelines is to provide more consistency across support orders, slight variations are permitted between provinces to reflect differences in cost of living. Judges may also increase support payments (e.g., to accommodate child care or medical costs) or decrease these payments (e.g., in joint custody cases where the noncustodial parent is responsible for a child at least 40 percent of the time).

Court orders in themselves, however, do not always guarantee that child support will be paid. In practice, orders for child and spousal support have often been difficult to enforce, and there have been very high default rates. All Canadian provinces now have their own programs to protect against nonpayment of child support. However, despite the increasing adoption of public enforcement strategies, the problem of "deadbeat parents" in Canada remains significant with more than $2 billion owed in child support (FAD, 2000).

Some analysts argue that the principal reason for nonpayment of child support is the unemployment or underemployment of the noncustodial parent (Meyer and Bartfield, 1996). If this is correct, "coercive child-support collection policies, such as automatic wage withholding, will have only limited success" and solving the problem "will be the old and unglamorous one, of solving un- and underemployment, both for the fathers and the mothers" (Braver, Fitzpatrick, and Bay, 1991: 184–5). Others recommend that Canada adopt the model of guaranteed child support used in France and Sweden. In these countries, the government gives the custodial parent the full amount of monies awarded in child support, even though this amount may not have been received from the noncustodial parent. The government would then assume responsibility for collecting the money owed from the parent who failed to provide it (Salt, 1991).

## Emotional Effects

Although divorce enables spouses to leave unhappy marriages, serious questions have been raised about the emotional consequences of divorce for children, particularly in the long term. Some scholars claim that divorcing parents are simply trading the well-being of their children for their own happiness. What does research say about this issue?

Research shows that children of divorced parents tend to develop behavioural problems and do less well in school than children in intact families. They are more likely to engage in delinquent acts and to abuse drugs and alcohol. They often experience an emotional crisis, particularly in the first two years after divorce. What is more, when children of divorced parents become adults, they are less likely than children of nondivorced parents to be happy. They are more likely to suffer health problems, depend on welfare, earn low incomes, and experience divorce themselves. In one study, almost half the children of divorced parents entered adulthood as worried, underachieving, self-deprecating, and sometimes angry young men and women (Wallerstein, Lewis, and Blakeslee, 2000). Clearly, divorce can have serious, long-term, negative consequences for children.

However, much of the research that seems to establish a link between divorce and long-term negative consequences for children is based on families who seek psychological counselling. Such families are a small and unrepresentative minority of the population. By definition, they have more serious emotional problems than the large majority, who do not need psychological counselling after divorce. One must be careful not to generalize from such studies. Another problem with much of this research is that some analysts fail to ask whether factors other than divorce might be responsible for the long-term distress experienced by many children of divorced parents.

A high level of parental conflict creates long-term distress among children. Divorce without parental conflict does children much less harm. Children in divorced families have a higher level of well-being on average than children in high-conflict, intact families.

Researchers who rely on representative samples and examine the separate effects of many factors on children's well-being provide the best evidence on the consequences of divorce for children. For example, a re-analysis of 92 relevant studies showed that, on average, the overall effect of divorce on children's well-being is not strong and is declining over time (Amato and Keith, 1991). This research also found that three factors account for much of the distress among children of divorce:

1. *A high level of parental conflict.* A high level of parental conflict creates long-term distress among children. Divorce without parental conflict does children much less harm. In fact, children in divorced families have a higher level of well-being on average than children in high-conflict, *intact* families. The effect of parental conflict on the long-term well-being of children is substantially greater than the effect of the next two factors discussed by Amato and Keith.
2. *A decline in living standards.* By itself, the economic disadvantage experienced by most children in divorced families exerts a small impact on their well-being. Nonetheless, it is clear that children of divorce who do not experience a decline in living standards suffer less harm.
3. *The absence of a parent.* Children of divorce usually lose a parent as a role model and a source of emotional support, practical help, and supervision. By itself, this factor also has a small effect on children's well-being, even if the child has continued contact with the noncustodial parent. According to the National Children's Survey, following parental separation, about one-third of children have very little contact with their noncustodial fathers (i.e., either irregular visits or no visits at all). Children born of common-law unions are even less likely to see their fathers than are children born to married parents. "Since fathers who have low levels of contact with their children are least likely to pay child support, these findings indicate that many, many Canadian children are at a high risk of losing both the personal and financial support of their fathers when their parents separate" (National Council on Welfare, 1999a: 5).

Subsequent studies confirm many of these generalizations and add an important observation. Many of the behavioural and adjustment problems experienced by children of divorce existed before the divorce took place. We cannot therefore attribute them to the divorce itself (Stewart et al., 1997).

In sum, claiming that divorcing parents selfishly trade the well-being of their children for their own happiness is an exaggeration. Although the heightened risk of poverty is real, high levels of parental conflict can also have serious negative consequences for children, even when they enter adulthood. In such high-conflict situations, divorce can benefit children. By itself, the absence of a parent has a small negative effect on children's well-being. But this effect is becoming smaller over time, perhaps in part because divorce is so common it is no longer a stigma.

## Reproductive Choice

We have seen that the power women gained from working in the paid labour force put them in a position to leave a marriage if it made them deeply unhappy. Another aspect of the gender revolution women are experiencing is that they are increasingly able to decide what happens in the marriage if they stay. For example, women now have more say over whether they will have children and, if so, when they will have them and how many they will have.

Children are increasingly expensive to raise. According to a 1998 estimate, "parents could expect to spend close to \$154,000 on rearing a child to age 18.... Boys cost \$154,367 while girls were a bargain at \$153,458" (Vanier Institute of the Family, 2000: 136). Children no longer give the family economic benefits, as they did, say, on the family farm. Most women want to work in the paid labour force, many of them to pursue a career. As a result, most women decide to have fewer children, to have them farther apart, and to have them at an older age. Some decide to have none at all (Dalphonse, 1997). In recent years, various organizations for childless couples have emerged, such as No Kidding, launched by a Canadian with chapters in several Canadian provinces and the United States, South Korea, and Côte d'Ivoire (http://www.nokidding.net).

Women's reproductive decisions are carried out by means of contraception and abortion. Throughout history, abortion has been a way of preventing birth. However, under section 179c of Canada's Revised Statutes of 1892, a woman who sought or succeeded in inducing her own abortion—as well as anyone who assisted her—committed a criminal offence. Until 1988, the Canadian Criminal Code defined any attempt to induce an abortion by any means as a crime for which the maximum penalty was life imprisonment or, if the woman herself was convicted, two years.

Laws prohibiting abortion established during the nineteenth century stood almost unchallenged until the 1960s, when an abortion reform movement, spearheaded by Canadian physician Dr. Henry Morgentaler, urged the repeal of abortion laws that, in his words, "compelled the unwilling to bear the unwanted" (in Dranoff, 2001: 16). The first such change occurred with the 1969 amendment that allowed for "therapeutic abortion" *if* performed by a physician in an accredited hospital and *if* a three-member committee certified that the continuation of the pregnancy would likely endanger the health of the mother. After this amendment, both the number and the rate of therapeutic abortions rose significantly. They then began to drop and stabilize beginning in 1983, and then rise substantially in 1988. In that year, the Supreme Court of Canada struck down the law on abortion on the grounds that it contravened a woman's right to control her own reproductive life and, as such, contravened her constitutionally protected guarantees to security of her person (under the equality rights provision of the Canadian Charter of Rights and Freedoms). The Supreme Court also unanimously determined that the civil law in Quebec, the Quebec Charter, and the common law do not protect fetal life or interests.

In 1989, in the case of *Tremblay v. Daigle*, the Supreme Court of Canada ruled that a fetus is not a person in law, and that a father of a fetus has no legal right of veto over a woman's decision with regards to the fetus she is carrying. In 1993, the Supreme Court of Canada struck down legislation that banned abortion clinics. By 1995, abortion clinics outside hospitals operated in all Canadian provinces except Prince Edward Island and Saskatchewan.

In 1998, one-third of all therapeutic abortions were performed in clinics and the remaining two-thirds were performed in hospitals. In that year, 110 331 women obtained therapeutic abortions in Canada. Women in their twenties accounted for half of all those who obtained abortions in 1998 (Health Canada, 1999; Statistics Canada, 2000g). However, on a global scale, abortion rates in Canada are low at 10.3 per 1000 women aged 15 to 44. In comparison, the rate in the United States is 21 per 1000 women, in Cuba 57, in Bulgaria 77, in Vietnam 84, in the Russian Federation 119, and in Romania 172 (Health Canada, 1999b).

Public opinion on the acceptability of abortion is mixed in Canada. According to Gallup polls agreement with the statement that abortion "should be legal under any circumstance" fell from 35 percent in 1995 to 28 percent in 1999. Agreement with the statement that "abortion should be illegal in all circumstances" rose from 13 percent in 1995 to 15 percent in 1999. In both years, the majority of Canadians were more likely to agree that abortion should be "legal only under certain [undefined] circumstances" (Tun, 2000).

Attitudes toward abortion vary by age, with Canadian teens more likely than Canadian adults to approve of the availability of legal abortion for any reason (55 versus 43 percent, respectively) (Bibby, 2001: 250–1). "Generation Xers" and adult baby boomer parents who participated in the sexual revolution of the 1960s show a slightly higher approval of abortion on demand (46 and 44 percent, respectively) than grandparents (36 percent). However, 90 percent of adults and 84 percent of teens support the availability of legal abortion when rape is involved.

Although Canadians are divided on the abortion issue, "right-to-life" versus "pro-choice" activists have been clashing since the 1970s. Right-to-life activists object to the decriminalization of abortion; pro-choice activists want the current situation preserved.

Both groups have tried to influence public opinion and lawmakers to achieve their aims. A few extreme right-to-life activists (almost all men) have resorted to violence (Gegax and Clemetson, 1998).

What are your views on abortion? Do you think your opinions are influenced by your social characteristics (income, education, occupation, religiousity, etc.)? In thinking about this issue, you will find it useful to know that right-to-life activists tend to be homemakers in religious, middle-income families. They argue that life begins at conception. Therefore, they say, abortion destroys human life and is morally indefensible. They advocate adoption instead of abortion. In their opinion, the pro-choice option is selfish, expressing greater concern for career advancement and sexual pleasure than moral responsibility (Erwin, 1988).

In contrast, pro-choice activists tend to be women pursuing their own careers. They are more highly educated, less religious, and better off financially than right-to-life activists. They argue that every woman has the right to choose what happens to her own body and that bearing an unwanted child can harm not only a woman's career but the child, too. For example, unwanted children are more likely to be neglected or abused. They are also more likely to get in trouble with the law because of inadequate adult supervision and discipline. Furthermore, according to pro-choice activists, religious doctrines claiming that life begins at conception are arbitrary. So, what is your view? And to what degree is it influenced by your social characteristics?

As sociologists Randall Collins and Scott Coltrane (1995) note, it seems likely that the criminalization of abortion would likely return us to the situation that existed in the 1960s. Specifically, they claim that, on a per capita basis, roughly as many abortions took place then as now. But because they were illegal, abortions were expensive, hard to obtain, and posed more dangers to women's health. Clearly, if abortion were criminalized, poor women and their unwanted children would suffer most.

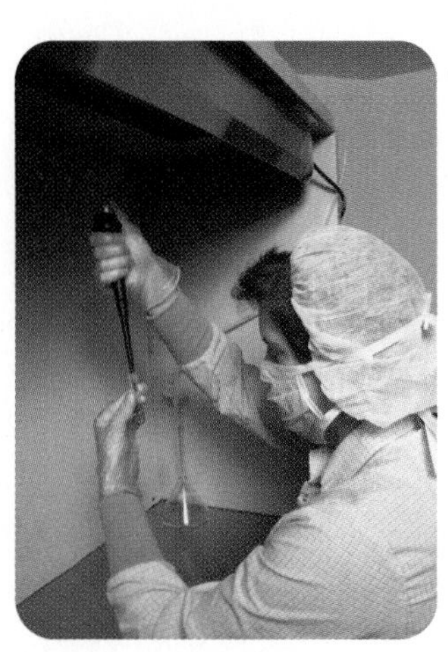

Fertilizing an egg in vitro.

## Reproductive Technologies

For most women, exercising reproductive choice means being able to prevent pregnancy and birth by means of contraception and abortion. For some women, however, it means *facilitating* pregnancy and birth by means of reproductive technologies. As many as 15 percent of couples are infertile. With a declining number of so-called "desirable" children (i.e., healthy, white newborns) available for adoption, and a persistent and strong desire by most people to have biologically related children, demand is strong for techniques to help infertile couples, some lesbian couples, and some single women have babies.

There are four main reproductive technologies. In *artificial insemination,* a donor's sperm is inserted in a woman's vaginal canal or uterus during ovulation. In *surrogate motherhood,* a donor's sperm is used to artificially inseminate a woman who has signed a contract to surrender the child at birth in exchange for a fee. In *in vitro fertilization,* eggs are surgically removed from a woman and joined with sperm in a culture dish, and an embryo is then transferred to the woman's uterus. Finally, various *screening techniques* are used on sperm and fetuses to increase the chance of giving birth to a baby of the desired sex and end pregnancies deemed medically problematic.

These procedures raise several sociological and ethical issues. We will mention two here (Achilles, 1993). The first problem is discrimination. Most reproductive technologies are expensive. Surrogate mothers charge $10 000 or more to carry a child. In vitro fertilization (IVF) fees are in the range of $25 000, and only Ontario's health insurance plan covers IVF (and then only in limited circumstances). Obviously, poor and middle-income earners who happen to be infertile cannot afford these procedures. In addition, according to the report of the Royal Commission on New Reproductive Technologies (1993), there is a strong tendency for members of the medical profession to deny single women and lesbian couples access to reproductive technologies. In other words, the medical community discriminates not just against those of modest means but against those wanting to rear children in nontraditional families.

A second problem introduced by reproductive technologies is that they render the terms *mother* and *father* obsolete, or at least vague. Is the mother the person who donates the egg, carries the child in her uterus, or raises the child? Is the father the person who donates the sperm or raises the child? As these questions suggest, a child conceived through a combination of reproductive technologies and raised by a heterosexual couple could have as many as three mothers and two fathers! This is not just a terminological problem. If it were, we could just introduce new distinctions such as *egg mother*, *uterine mother*, and *social mother* to reflect the new reality. The real problem is social and legal. The question of who has what rights and obligations to the child, and what rights and obligations the child has vis-à-vis each parent, is unclear. This lack of clarity has already caused anguished court battles over child custody (Franklin and Ragone, 1999).

Public debate on a wide scale is needed to decide who will control reproductive technologies and to what ends. On the one hand, reproductive technologies may bring the greatest joy to infertile people. They may also prevent the birth and suffering of children with chronic, progressive, and fatal diseases. On the other hand, reproductive technologies may continue to benefit mainly the well-to-do, reinforce traditional family forms that are no longer appropriate for many people, and cause endless legal wrangling and heartache.

## Housework and Child Care

As we have seen, women's increased participation in the paid labour force, their increased participation in the system of higher education, and their increased control over reproduction transformed several areas of family life. Despite this far-ranging gender revolution, however, one domain remains largely resistant to change: housework, child care, and senior care. This fact was first documented in detail by sociologist Arlie Hochschild. She showed that even women who work full time in the paid labour force usually begin a "second shift" when they return home. There, they prepare meals, help with homework, do laundry, and so forth (Hochschild with Machung, 1989).

To be sure, there has been *some* change as men take a more active role in the day-to-day running of the household. However, the change has been modest. For example, one study conducted in the late 1980s compared full-time female homemakers in first marriages with wives in first marriages who worked 30 hours or more per week outside the home. The wives working full time in the paid labour force did only 1 hour and 10 minutes less housework per day than the full-time homemakers. Husbands of women working full time in the paid labour force did a mere 37 minutes more housework per day than husbands of full-time homemakers (calculated from Demo and Acock, 1993). Studies estimate that, on average, men now do 20 to 35 percent of the housework and child care (Shelton and John, 1996: 299).

Figures 12.9 and 12.10 indicate that, whether or not they work in paid labour, "Canadian women bear a disportionate burden of unpaid labour in the home" (Health Canada, 1999b). Even these figures do not reveal the whole picture, however. Men tend to do low-stress chores that can often wait a day or a week. These jobs include mowing the lawn, repairing the car, and painting the fence. They also play with their children more than they used to. In contrast, women tend to do higher-stress chores that cannot wait. These jobs include getting kids dressed and out the door to school every day, preparing dinner and cleaning up after it is served, washing and ironing clothes, and the like. In short, the picture is hardly that of a revolution (Harvey, Marshall, and Frederick, 1991).

Two main factors shrink the gender gap in housework, child care, and senior care. First, the smaller the difference between the husband's and the wife's earnings, the more equal the division of household labour. Apparently, women are routinely able to translate earning power into domestic influence. Put bluntly, their increased financial status enables them to get their husbands to do more around the house. In addition, women who earn relatively high incomes are also able to use some of their money to pay outsiders to do domestic work.

Attitude is the second factor that shrinks the gender gap in domestic labour. The more that husband and wife agree there *should* be equality in the household division of labour, the more equality there is. Seeing eye to eye on this issue is often linked to both spouses

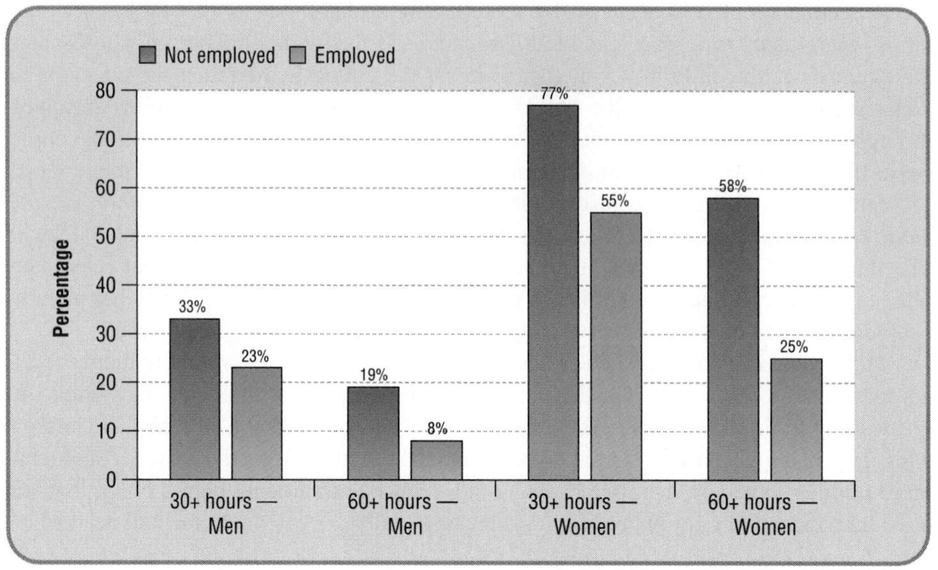


✦ **FIGURE 12.9** ✦
**Hours per Week Devoted to Child Care, Men and Women Living Together, with Children under Age 6, by Employment Status, 1995**

Source: Statistics Canada (1998e).

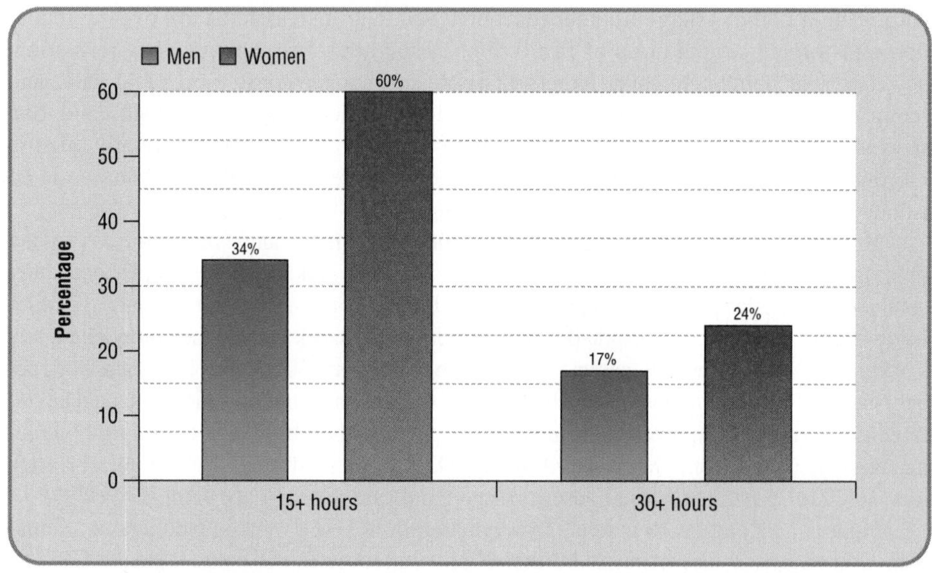


✦ **FIGURE 12.10** ✦
**Hours per Week Devoted to Unpaid Housework, Men and Women Living Together, with Children under Age 15, 1996**

Source: Statistics Canada (1998e).

having a post-secondary education (Greenstein, 1996). Thus, if there is going to be greater equality between men and women in doing household chores, two things have to happen. There must be greater equality between men and women in the paid labour force and broader cultural acceptance of the need for gender equality.

## Equality and Wife Abuse

Above we noted that more egalitarian couples are generally more happily married. Said differently, marital satisfaction increases as the statuses of husband and wife approach equality. Does it follow that higher levels of gender equality also result in lower rates of wife abuse? As we will now see, it does.

The 1999 General Social Survey (GSS), based on a large, representative nationwide sample, investigated the experiences of both women and men in relation to violence by current and/or previous spouses and common-law partners. A person was defined as having a current relationship if he or she was married, living common law, or had a same-sex partner.

The double day

Respondents were asked if, "in the past 5 years, your spouse/partner" has (1) threatened to hit you with his/her fist or anything else that could have hurt you, (2) thrown anything at you that could have hurt you, (3) pushed, grabbed, or shoved you in a way that could have hurt you, (4) slapped you, (5) kicked, bit, or hit you with his/her fist, (6) hit you with something that could have hurt you, (7) beaten you, (8) choked you, (9) used or threatened to use a gun or knife on you, or (10) forced you into any unwanted sexual activity by threatening you, holding you down, or hurting you in some way. Although this survey included questions about emotional abuse, the findings we present here do *not* include emotional abuse in the overall reported rates of spousal violence.

The results of this survey suggest that many Canadian women *and* men experience violence in their marriages or common-law relationships. Estimates derived from this survey suggest that 7 percent of Canadians who were in a marital or cohabiting relationship had experienced some form of violence at the hands of their partner over the past five years (Bunge, 2000a: 11). However, although the five-year rates of violence were similar for women (8 percent) and men (7 percent), women were more likely to experience severe forms of violence. Specifically, women were three times more likely to suffer an injury, five times more likely to receive medical attention, and five times more likely to report that the violence they had experienced caused them to fear for their lives (Bunge, 2000a: 11). Compared with men, women were more likely to report being beaten, choked, or threatened with a gun or knife, or having these weapons used against them. Women were also more likely than men to report multiple incidents of spousal violence. Compared with women, men were more likely to report being slapped, having something thrown at them, or being kicked, bit, or hit (Bunge, 2000a: 12).

The GSS survey data reveal that women and men from all income and educational levels experience spousal violence. In general, younger people face the greatest risk of experiencing spousal violence, with the highest rates reported by young women under the age of 25 (5 percent). Younger men aged 25 to 34 also reported higher rates of violence (4 percent) than those who were older (1 percent).

Consistent with earlier studies conducted in both Canada and the United States (Kong, 1997; U.S. Department of Justice, 1998), the risk of being a victim of spousal violence was higher for both women and men living in common-law unions (4 percent) than in legal marriages (1 percent). Individuals living in common-law relationships also experience a heightened level of lethal spousal violence (Hotton, 2001). This is particularly true for Aboriginal peoples. Aboriginal women in common-law relationships experience homicide rates that are almost eight times higher than those in legal marriages (111.0 per million and 13.9 per million, respectively). The rate of spousal homicide among Aboriginal men in common-law relationships is almost six times greater than that of Aboriginal men living with legal spouses (60.7 per million and 10.5 per million, respectively) (Johnson and Hotton, 2001: 31; see Figure 12.11).

Research suggests that men who abuse their partners may be attempting to compensate for general feelings of powerlessness or inadequacy in their jobs, marriages, or both. This form of family violence has been termed *patriarchal terrorism* (Johnson, 1995). As

✦ **FIGURE 12.11** ✦

**Aboriginal Women in Common-law Relationships Have Highest Rates of Spousal Homicide**

Source: Statistics Canada, Canadian Centre for Justice Statistics, Homicide Survey, 1991–1999.

*Note:* The 1991 Aboriginal Peoples Survey and the 1991 and 1996 Census were used to estimate the number of Aboriginal and non-Aboriginal women and men aged 15 and older who were married or in a common-law union. The denominators used for inter-censal years were estimated by averaging the difference from the known population figures in 1991 and 1996. Cases where the Aboriginal status of the victim was unknown were included in the non-Aboriginal rates.

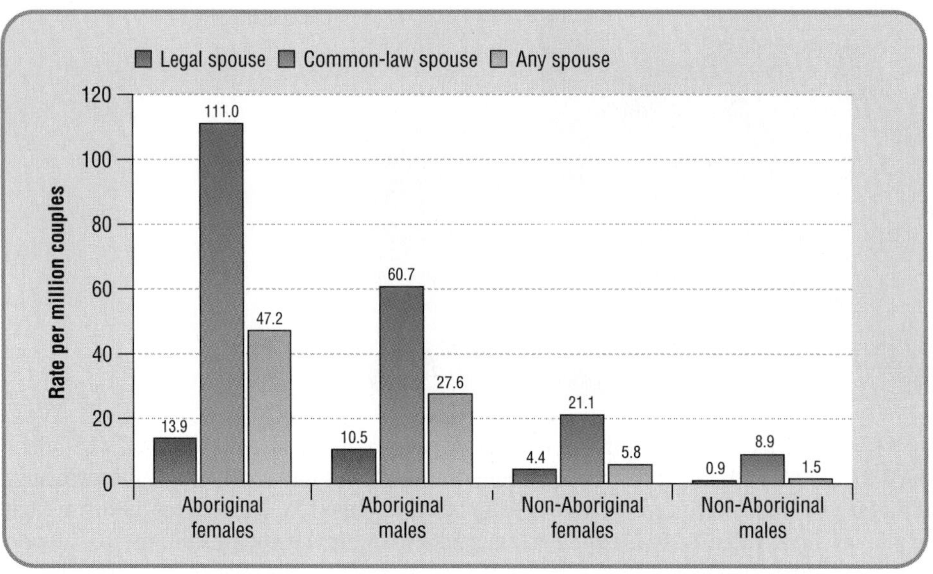


Chapter 9 (Sexuality and Gender) notes, cultural images of take-charge, aggressive masculinity may encourage some men to use physical expressions of power in an attempt to compensate for their perceived lack of occupational success, prestige, or satisfaction (Anderson, 1997). The men most likely to abuse women are between 18 and 30 years old, unemployed, users of illicit drugs or abusers of alcohol, and high-school dropouts. They are more likely than other men to have witnessed their mothers being abused, to have been abused themselves as children, and to believe that male domination is justified. Those who lack legitimate means of attaining personal or social power may resort to violence in an attempt to gain or regain feelings of personal power (Gelles, 1994, 1997; Pyke, 1997; Ronfeldt, Kimerling, and Arias, 1998; Smith, M., 1990).

Women also face a heightened risk of homicide following a marital separation (Johnson and Hotton, 2001: 33). Recognition that the most dangerous time for a victim of intimate violence is after leaving a violent relationship helped fuel the 1993 passage of Bill C-126, which made "criminal harassment" a criminal offence. This law is directed against "stalking." In 1999, 5382 incidents of criminal harassment were reported to 106 police forces in Canada (up 32 percent from 1996) (Greeno, 2000). Consistent with earlier research (Kong, 1997), women were the victims in 75 percent of reported cases. In most of these cases, the woman knew the stalker and, in many instances, had been involved with him in a previous relationship. Although women were most likely to be stalked by an ex-husband, boyfriend, or current husband, 44 percent of male victims were stalked by a casual acquaintance; few male victims of criminal harassment were stalked by an ex-wife or girlfriend. In addition, from 1997 to 1999 there were nine stalking-related homicides reported, each involving a woman being stalked by a former partner (Greeno, 2000).

We have seen that male domination in both childhood socialization and current family organization increases the likelihood of wife abuse. In addition, high levels of wife assault are associated with gender inequality in the larger society. For example, an American sociologist constructed a measure of wife assault for each U.S. state using data from a national survey (Straus, 1994). The measure shows the percentage of couples in each state in which the wife was physically assaulted by her partner during the 12 months preceding the survey. He then used government data to measure gender inequality in each state. His measure of gender inequality taps the economic, educational, political, and legal status of women. He found that wife assault and gender inequality vary proportionately. In other words, as gender equality increases—as women and men become more equal in the larger society—wife assault declines. The conclusion one must draw from this research is clear.

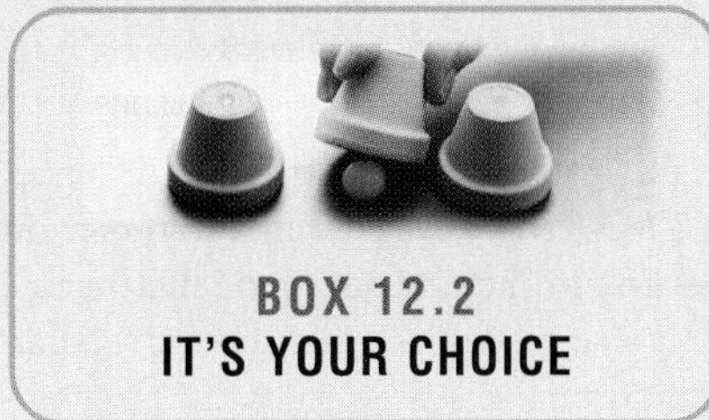

BOX 12.2
IT'S YOUR CHOICE

### IS SPANKING EVER APPROPRIATE?

On July 4, 2001, child welfare workers took 7 children, aged 6 to 14, from their home in southern Ontario amid concerns that they were being spanked with paddles by their fundamentalist Christian parents. The children's parents, members of the Church of God, admitted that they used paddles to discipline their children. However, they noted that doing so was consistent with the teachings of their religion. A media statement, released by the Church of God, noted the group's belief that "the Word of God advocates corporal punishment under certain circumstances" (Church of God, 2001). According to the group's spiritual adviser, Daniel Layne, "The whole issue is spanking and discipline, and how we see in modern times that when parents don't discipline their children it leads to all kinds of social problems.... Switching is used as a last resort, but the Scriptures clearly call for it and we won't give it up" (quoted in Clairborne, 2001).

The children were returned to their home on July 26, after their parents agreed to abstain from the use of corporal punishment while the case was before the courts. Children's Aid Society (CAS) workers were given unannounced access to the children in their homes and at school and allowed to discuss alternative methods of child discipline with the parents. However, more than 100 members of the Church of God fled Canada over fears that authorities would attempt to seize their children. In January 2002, the Ontario Court of Appeal found in favour of the children's parents and upheld the right of parents, teachers, and persons standing in place of parents to physically discipline their young charges (McCarten, 2002).

In stark contrast to such countries as Austria, Cyprus, Denmark, Finland, Italy, Norway, and Sweden, where the use of corporal punishment against children is prohibited by law, Canadian law has, since 1892, specifically allowed parents to use corporal punishment as a form of child discipline. However, not all Canadians would agree with the decision of the Ontario Court of Appeal in the Church of God case—or with the decisions rendered in other Canadian courtrooms. For example, one of the leading decisions used by our courts to interpret this section of the Criminal Code specifies that "the mere fact that the children disciplined suffered contusions and bruises is not in itself proof of exercise of undue force."

Is spanking ever appropriate? Experts themselves have conflicting opinions about this issue. Sociologist Murray Straus (1994) advises parents never to hit children of any age under any circumstances. There is considerable evidence to suggest that children who are spanked by their parents (including those who are otherwise loving) are more likely to cheat, lie, bully, be intentionally cruel to others, disobey in school, and misbehave in various ways (Stormshak et al., 2000; Straus, 1996; Straus and Mouradian, 1998; Straus and Stewart, 1999; Straus, Sugerman, and Giles-Sims, 1997). Research has also linked being spanked to depression and suicide in childhood, alcohol and/or drug abuse in adolescence, and, during adulthood, a heightened likelihood of abusing one's own children and/or engaging in spousal violence (Garvey, 1999; Turner and Finkelhor, 1996; Straus and Kantor, 1994). Spanking apparently teaches children that it is acceptable to hit someone and that those who love you may hit you with impunity. This message confuses love and violence—and sets the stage for subsequent abusive acts directed against intimate partners (Straus and Yodanis, 1996).

In contrast, other researchers contend that Straus and others may be overstating and oversimplifying the situation (Gilbert, 1997). One review of the literature on nonabusive and customary physical punishment by parents reports that the observed consequences of such punishment vary by method employed, the child's personality, subcultural factors, and so forth (Larzelere, 2000). Some studies find that nonabusive spanking as an occasional backup form of child discipline had such beneficial outcomes as reduced noncompliance and fighting among two- to six-year-olds.

What do you think? Do you agree with the decision of the Ontario Court of Appeal in the Church of God case? Is corporal punishment an appropriate form of child discipline? Is corporal punishment child abuse? Should parents spank their children? Should Canada repeal the law that allows corporal punishment? Is spanking a training ground for violence against intimate partners in later life? It's your choice.

The incidence of wife assault is highest where early socialization experiences predispose men to behave aggressively toward women, where norms justify the domination of women, and where a big power imbalance between men and women exists.

Summing up, we can say that conflict theorists and feminists have performed a valuable sociological service by emphasizing the importance of power relations in structuring family life. A substantial body of research shows that the gender revolution of the past 40 years has influenced the way we select mates, our reasons for being satisfied or dissatisfied with marriage, our propensity to divorce, the reproductive choices women make, the distribution of housework and child care, variations in the rate of wife abuse—in short, all aspects of family life. As you will now learn, the gender revolution has also created a much greater diversity of family forms.

# FAMILY DIVERSITY

## Sexual Orientation

Modifications in the Canadian census alert us to some of the changes that have occurred with respect to family structures. For example, the 1981 Census was the first to report on common-law marriages. The 2001 Census was the first to include questions that recognized same-sex partners in cohabiting relationships. It also recognized that some Canadian children are being raised in same-sex households.

Over the past decade, many rights and obligations that were once exclusively associated with heterosexual marriage (e.g., the right to spousal support) have been extended to couples living in both opposite-sex and same-sex marriage-like relationships. For example, the passage of the Modernization of Benefits and Obligations Act in 2000 resulted in changes to some 68 federal laws that made same-sex couples equal to opposite-sex couples. In June 2002, in a historic first, the adoption of Bill 84 in Quebec extended full parental rights to homosexual couples. It also gave same-sex couples who entered into a "civil union" the same status and obligations as heterosexual married couples (Seguin, 2002).

In 2001, the Netherlands became the first country in the world to legalize same-sex marriage. Prior to that time, *registered partnership* legislation (available in the Netherlands to both same-sex and opposite-sex couples) made partnership and marriage virtually identical in relation to rights and obligations. Currently, Cambodia and the Netherlands are the only countries that extend full and equal marriage rights to homosexuals. As of this writing, eight other countries allow homosexuals to register their partnerships under the law. They also recognize these partnerships as having some or all of the legal rights of marriage. These countries are Denmark (along with its dependency, Greenland), Hungary, Norway, Sweden, France, Iceland, Spain, and Germany. In the United States, there is considerable opposition to same-sex marriages. As of this writing, 32 states have passed laws *opposing* same-sex marriage and a nationwide Harris poll taken in February 2000 shows that about 56 percent of Americans oppose such unions. Nevertheless, the direction of change is clear. Amid sharp controversy, the legal and social definition of *family* is being broadened to include cohabiting, same-sex partners in long-term relationships (Ontario Consultants on Religious Tolerance, 2000b).

In 2002, in a precedent-setting move hailed by gay-right activists as the first of its kind in the world, full parental rights were extended to homosexual couples in Quebec. In addition, same-sex couples are granted the same status and obligations as heterosexual married couples when they enter into what is to be called a civil union. Here, lesbians react as the Quebec legislature passes the law.

Research shows that most homosexuals, like most heterosexuals, want a long-term, intimate relationship with one other adult (Kurdek, 1995). In fact, in Denmark, where homosexual couples can register partnerships under the law, the divorce rate for registered homosexual couples is lower than for heterosexual married couples (Ontario Consultants on Religious Tolerance, 2000b).

Many people believe that children brought up in homosexual families will develop a confused sexual identity, exhibit a tendency to become homosexuals themselves, and suffer discrimination from children and adults in the "straight" community. There is little research in this area and much of the research that exists is based on small, unrepresentative samples. Nevertheless, the findings are consistent. They suggest that children who grow up in homosexual families are much like children who grow up in heterosexual families. For example, a 14-year study assessed 25 young adults who were the offspring of lesbian families and 21 young adults who were the offspring of heterosexual families (Tasker and Golombok, 1997). The researchers reported that the two groups were equally well adjusted and displayed little difference in sexual orientation. Two respondents from the lesbian families considered themselves lesbians, while all of the respondents from the heterosexual families considered themselves heterosexual.

Homosexual and heterosexual families do differ in some respects. Lesbian couples with children record higher satisfaction with their partnerships than lesbian couples without children. In contrast, among heterosexual couples, it is the childless who record higher marital satisfaction (Koepke, Hare, and Moran, 1992). On average, the partners of lesbian mothers spend more time caring for children than the husbands of heterosexual mothers. Since children usually benefit from adult attention, this must be considered a plus. Finally, homosexual couples tend to be more egalitarian than heterosexual couples, sharing most decision making and household duties equally (Rosenbluth, 1997). That is because they tend to consciously reject traditional marriage patterns. The fact that they have the same gender socialization and earn about the same income also encourages equality (Kurdek, 1998; Reimann, 1997). In sum, available research suggests that raising children in lesbian families has no apparent negative consequences for the children. Indeed, there may be some benefits for all family members.

At the same time, however, it should be noted that homosexual families are not immune from abuse and violence. Although research on violence in gay and lesbian relationships is sparse, some studies suggest that violence between same-sex partners occurs at approximately the same rate as it does in heterosexual relationships (Chesley, MacAulay, and Ristock, 1991). Some of the dynamics involved are similar to those that mark violence in heterosexual relationships (Kurdek, 1998). For example, drug and/or alcohol abuse is often involved. In both cases, the abusive individual is typically jealous and possessive, and uses violence or its threat to control his/her partner (Renzetti, 1992). At the same time, there are some differences (Obejas, 1994). For example, one study found that while heterosexual men who abuse their partners often insist that it is their "right" to do so, lesbians who are abusive do not. As a result, lesbians who batter their partners are more likely to voluntarily seek treatment than their heterosexual male counterparts. Moreover, although it may be supposed that "butch/femme" roles and/or the woman's physical size influences the likelihood of being an abuser/victim, this is not the case.

## Cohabitation

Although both Canada and the United States have always been highly "married societies," with about 90 percent of each age cohort marrying at least once, some evidence suggests that the importance of marriage is waning for at least some Canadians. When asked the question, "In order for you to be happy in life, is it very important, important, not very important, or not at all important to be married?" just over 70 percent of Canadian women in 1984 and 67 percent of Canadian women in 1995 rated marriage as very important or important. Although the difference in slight, women in 1995 also placed less emphasis on the importance of marriage than Canadian men. Younger Canadians were less likely than older Canadians to place emphasis on marriage. Those living in Quebec were considerably less likely to rate marriage as very important or important. In that province, just over 53 percent of women and 59 percent of men did so (Wu, 2000: 65–6).

For some Canadians, living in a common-law relationship may simply be a prelude to marriage. For others, however, cohabitation has become an alternative to legal marriage.

Since the Canadian census first began to collect information on cohabitation in 1981, the number of cohabiting people 15 years of age and older has increased dramatically (see Figure 12.12). The 2001 census recorded 1 158 410 common-law families.

Although only about 8 percent of the population is currently cohabiting, cohabiting unions (also known as common-law unions) grew from 6 to 14 percent of all unions between 1981 and 2001. Although cohabitation is particularly popular in Quebec, residents of Quebec are clearly not alone in their changed attitude. Recent research finds that most Canadian women aged 18 to 49 approve of both premarital sex and nonmarital cohabitation when couples intend to marry at some point in the future. In addition, 55 percent of women outside Quebec and 73 percent of women in Quebec believe it is acceptable for couples to live together when they have no intention of making a long-term commitment and are simply sexually attracted to each other. In both cases, younger women and women in Quebec are particularly likely to voice such approval (Wu, 2000: 59).

Cohabitation is particularly common among the young and among those who are separated and divorced (Bumpass and Sweet, 1995). In Canada, the likelihood of cohabitation is higher among employed people, women with lower levels of education, nonstudents, people with no religious orientation, people born in Canada, Quebecers, women who are pregnant and men whose partners are pregnant, men who are just entering parenthood, people who had an unhappy childhood, people raised in a family in which there was a divorce, and people from a lower-class family background (Wu, 2000).

Research also reports a strong association between a couple's economic circumstances and the likelihood that their union will end in or be transformed into marriage (Pollard and Wu, 1998). The higher the woman's economic position, the less likely it is that she will marry her common-law partner and the more likely it is that she will leave the common-law union. For example, among semi-professional and skilled women, common-law unions are more likely to result in separation than marriage. In contrast, professional and semi-professional men are more likely to marry their common-law partners (Wu, 2000: 81).

Although some evidence suggests that previous cohabitation has a negative effect on marital happiness and stability (Wu, 2000: 131–2), not all researchers agree (White, 1992), and some predict that as common-law relationships become more institutionalized in our society, their stability will increase (Levine, 2001).

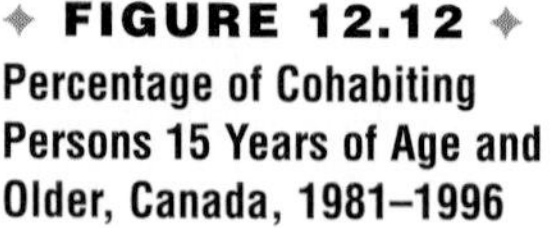

**✦ FIGURE 12.12 ✦**
**Percentage of Cohabiting Persons 15 Years of Age and Older, Canada, 1981–1996**

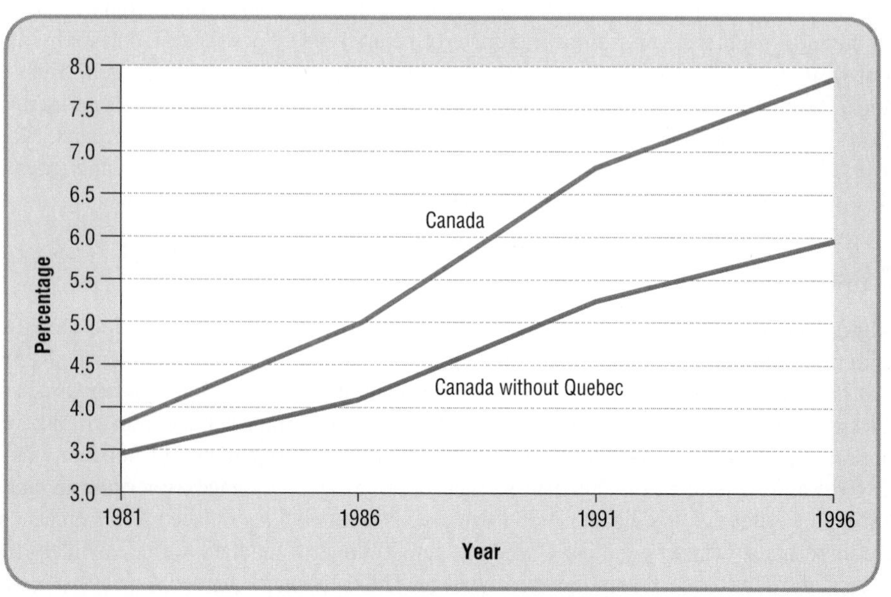

## Lone-Parent Families and Poverty

### Single-Mother Families

In 2001, 15.7 percent of all Canadian families were headed by a lone parent (Statistics Canada, 2002e). During the first half of the twentieth century, lone-parent families were generally the result of the death of one parent (Oderkirk and Lochhead, 1992). However, solo parenting today is most commonly the product of marital dissolution (either separation or divorce), after which child custody is typically granted to mothers. In 2001, the vast majority of lone-parent families were headed by women. Compared to lone-parent fathers, lone-parent mothers are more likely to be younger and less well educated, have lower earnings and less income, and be responsible for younger children (Oderkirk and Lochhead, 1992). In 1997, the average income for lone-parent families headed by women was $25 445. By comparison, the average income for two-parent families was $64 814 and for male-led, lone-parent families was $40 974 (Health Canada, 1999b).

Poverty is far more prevalent among female-headed single-parent households than among other types of family structures. Nearly two-thirds of families headed by single-parent mothers live below the poverty line. The poorest are families with young single-parent mothers (National Council on Welfare, 1999a). The situation is particularly bleak among women with disabilities. When compared with their counterparts without disabilities, both women and men with disabilities are more likely to be the sole providers of family income. For lone parents who work at jobs that pay minimum wage, poverty may be almost unavoidable: "In Winnipeg in 1999, a single parent with one child had to work 80 hours simply to get to the poverty line.... In Vancouver, where the minimum wage is the highest in the country, a single parent had to work 61 hours a week" (National Council on Welfare, 1999a: 18).

Poverty is not, of course, restricted to lone-parent families (refer back to Figure 12.8). Almost 1 in 5 Canadian children under the age of 18 lives in low-income families, while almost 1 in 7 Canadian children under the age of 18 was on welfare as of March 1997 (National Council on Welfare, 1999a). In 1996, 45 percent of children under the age of six in the visible minority population lived in low-income families (compared with 26 percent of all children). In the same year, Aboriginal children were especially likely to live in low-income families. In 1995, 3 out of 5 Aboriginal children under the age of 6 lived in low-income families. Among those aged 6 to 14, the incidence of low income was 48 percent, or more than twice the national rate of 22 percent (Statistics Canada, 1998f).

Divorce is responsible for the majority of lone-parent families in Canada today. Female-headed lone-parent families are a far more common form than male-headed lone-parent families.

It is still unclear "whether family structure is the cause or the victim of poverty. How many males disappear because they cannot support the children they have fathered? Are single-parent families poor because they are headed by a woman, or because the wage structure allows few mothers to earn their way out of poverty?" (Levitan, Mangum, and Mangum, 1998: 28). What is clear is that raising children in poverty involves doing without things that other Canadians may take for granted. Poor parents are often unable to provide their children with the opportunity to live in relatively safe neighbourhoods, undergo necessary dental work, or participate in such extracurricular activities as private music lessons (Canning and Strong, 1998). The capacity of parents to care for children and their children's developmental outcomes are better at each step up the income ladder. Low social support, family dysfunction, and parental depression, all of which have significant negative effects on children, are more common in low-income households (National Council on Welfare, 1999a). Child poverty is also related to school failure (Fields and Smith, 1998), negative involvement with parents (Harris and Marmer, 1996), stunted growth, reduced cognitive abilities, limited emotional development (Mayer, 1997), and a higher likelihood of dropping out of school (Duncan et al., 1998). In various ways, "economic insecurity, underemployment, and joblessness, on top of years of defeats and dashed hopes, have proven devastating to poor families" (Sugrue, 1999: 245).

## FAMILY POLICY

Having discussed several aspects of the decline of the traditional nuclear family and the proliferation of diverse family forms, we can now return to the big question posed at the beginning of this chapter: Is the decline of the nuclear family a bad thing for society? Said differently, do two-parent families—particularly those with stay-at-home moms—provide the kind of discipline, role models, help, and middle-class lifestyle that children need to stay out of trouble with the law and grow up to become well-adjusted, productive members of society? Conversely, are family forms other than the traditional nuclear family the main source of teenage crime, poverty, welfare dependency, and other social ills?

The answer suggested by research is clear: yes and no (Houseknecht and Sastry, 1996; Popenoe, 1996; Sandqvist and Andersson, 1992). Yes, the decline of the traditional nuclear family can be a source of many social problems. No, it doesn't have to be that way.

The United States is a good example of how social problems can emerge from the decline of the nuclear family. Sweden is a good example of how such problems can be averted. These two cases represent two models that Canadians should consider when thinking about our own family policies. The top panel of Table 12.1 shows that *on most indicators of nuclear family decline, Sweden leads the United States.* In Sweden, a smaller percentage of people get married. People usually get married at a later age than in the United States. The proportion of births outside of marriage is twice as high as in the United States. A much larger proportion of Swedish than American women with children under the age of three work in the paid labour force.

The bottom panel of Table 12.1 shows that *on most measures of children's well-being, Sweden also leads the United States.* Thus, in Sweden, children enjoy higher average reading test scores than in the United States. The poverty rate in two-parent families is only one-fifth the U.S. rate, while the poverty rate in single-parent families is only one-eleventh as high. The rate of infant abuse is one-eleventh the U.S. rate. The rate of juvenile drug offences is less than half as high. Sweden does have a higher rate of juvenile delinquency than the United States. However, the lead is slight and concerns only minor offences. Overall, then, the decline of the traditional nuclear family has gone farther in Sweden than in the United States, but children are much better off on average. How is this possible?

One explanation is that Sweden has something the United States lacks: a substantial family support policy. When a child is born in Sweden, a parent is entitled to 360 days of parental leave at 80 percent of his or her salary and an additional 90 days at a flat rate. Fathers can take an additional 10 days of leave with pay when the baby is born. Parents

| Indicators of Nuclear Family "Decline" | U.S.A. | Sweden | #1 "Decline" |
|---|---|---|---|
| Median age at first marriage | | | |
| Men | 26.5 | 29.4 | Sweden |
| Women | 24.4 | 27.1 | Sweden |
| Percentage of 45–49 population never married | | | |
| Men | 5.7 | 15.4 | Sweden |
| Women | 5.1 | 9.1 | Sweden |
| Nonmarital birth rate | 25.7 | 50.9 | Sweden |
| One-parent households with children < 15 as % of all households with children < 15 | 25.0 | 18.0 | U.S.A. |
| % of mothers in labour force with children < 3 | 51.0 | 84.0 | Sweden |
| Total fertility rate | 2.0 | 2.0 | Tie |
| Average household size | 2.7 | 2.2 | Sweden |
| **Indicators of Child Well-Being** | **U.S.A.** | **Sweden** | **#1 Well Being** |
| Mean reading performance score at 14 | 5.14 | 5.29 | Sweden |
| % of children in poverty | | | |
| Single-mother households | 59.5 | 5.2 | Sweden |
| Two-parent households | 11.1 | 2.2 | Sweden |
| Death rate of infants from abuse | 9.8 | 0.9 | Sweden |
| Suicide rate for children 15–19 (per 100 000) | 11.1 | 6.2 | Sweden |
| Juvenile delinquency rate (per 100 000) | 11.6 | 12.0 | U.S.A. |
| Juvenile drug offence rate (per 100 000) | 558.0 | 241.0 | Sweden |

**✦ TABLE 12.1 ✦**

**The "Decline" of the Nuclear Family and the Well-Being of Children: The United States and Sweden Compared**

Source: Adapted from Houseknecht and Sastry (1996).

are entitled to free consultations at "well baby clinics." Like all citizens of Sweden, they receive free health care from the state-run system. Temporary parental benefits are available for parents with a sick child under the age of 12. One parent can take up to 60 days off work per sick child per year at 80 percent of salary. All parents can send their children to heavily government-subsidized, high-quality daycare. Finally, Sweden offers its citizens generous direct cash payments based on the number of children in each family.[2]

Painting class in a state-subsidized daycare facility in Stockholm, Sweden.

Among industrialized countries, the United States stands at the other extreme. Since the Family and Medical Leave Act was passed in 1993, a parent is entitled to 12 weeks of *unpaid* parental leave. About 40 million citizens have no health care coverage. Health care is at a low standard for many millions more. There is no system of state daycare and no direct cash payments to families based on the number of children they have. The value of the dependant deduction on income tax has fallen by nearly 50 percent in current dollars since the 1940s. Thus, when an unwed Swedish woman has a baby, she knows she can rely on state institutions to maintain her standard of living and help give her child an enriching social and educational environment. When an unwed American woman has a baby, she is pretty much on her own. She is more likely than not to sink into poverty, with all the negative consequences that has for her and her child.

Canada rests midway between these two extremes. For example, a comparison of government-sponsored maternity, paternity, and parental leave programs in Canada, Belgium, the United Kingdom, Finland, Germany, Sweden, and the United States reveals that although Canada's maternity and parental leaves fall short of those offered in Finland, Germany, and Sweden, they are undeniably more generous than those in the United States or the United Kingdom (Marshall, 1999; see also Olsen and Brym, 1999).

In Canada, three criticisms are commonly raised against generous family support policies. First, some people say they encourage long-term dependence on welfare, illegitimate births, and the breakup of two-parent families. However, research shows that the divorce rate and the rate of births to unmarried mothers are not higher when welfare payments are more generous (Albelda and Tilley, 1997; Ruggles, 1997; Sweezy and Tiefenthaler, 1996).

It should also be evident that not all people who prefer to work are able to find full-time, secure employment, and part-time jobs offer little in the way of job security, decent wages, or benefits. "Part-time jobs are often the only real possibilities of employment, yet they cannot eliminate child and family poverty, no matter how hard a parent works. When lay-offs come, parents fall still further behind" (National Council on Welfare, 1999a: 16). Some provinces, such as Ontario, have incorporated "workfare" in their welfare systems. Workfare requires able-bodied people to do specific jobs as a condition of receiving welfare. However, most workfare jobs are menial dead-end jobs that are unlikely to lead to permanent employment. Finally, it is surely absurd to believe that living on welfare often represents a preferred lifestyle. For the overwhelming majority of welfare recipients, it indicates the loss of a job, spouse, or health—personal tragedies to which none of us is immune (National Council of Welfare, 1999a: 68).

A second criticism of generous family support policies focuses on child care. Some critics say that nonfamily child care is bad for children under the age of three. In their view, only parents can provide the love, interaction, and intellectual stimulation infants and toddlers need for proper social, cognitive, and moral development. However, when studies compare family care and daycare involving a strong curriculum, a stimulating environment, plenty of caregiver warmth, low turnover of well-trained staff, and a low ratio of caregivers to children, they find that daycare has no negative consequences for children over the age of one (Clarke-Stewart, Gruber, and Fitzgerald, 1994). A recent study of more than 6000 children found that a mother's employment outside the home does have a very small negative effect on the child's self-esteem, later academic achievement, language development, and compliance. However, this effect was apparent only if the mother returned to work within a few weeks or months of giving birth. Moreover, the negative effects usually disappeared by the time the child reached the age of five (Harvey, 1999). Research also shows that daycare has some benefits, notably enhancing a child's ability to make friends. The benefits of high-quality daycare are even more evident in low-income families, which often cannot provide the kind of stimulating environment offered by high-quality daycare.

The third criticism lodged against generous family support policies is that they are expensive and have to be paid for by high taxes. This is true. Swedes, for example, are more highly taxed than the citizens of any other country. They have made the political decision to pay high taxes, partly to avoid the social problems and associated costs that sometimes emerge when the traditional nuclear family is replaced with other family forms and no institutions are available to help family members in need. The Swedish experience teaches us, then, that there is a clear trade-off between expensive family support policies and low taxes. It is impossible to have both, and the degree to which any country favours one or the other is a political choice.

## SUMMARY

1. The traditional nuclear family consists of a father-provider, mother-homemaker, and at least one child.
2. Today, only a small minority of Canadians live in traditional nuclear families. Many different family forms have proliferated in recent decades, including same-sex and opposite-sex cohabiting relationships and lone-parent families.
3. In the 1950s, functionalist theory held that the traditional nuclear family is necessary because it performs essential functions in all societies. However, this theory is inaccurate.
4. Marxists stress how families operate to reproduce class inequality, while feminists stress how they operate to reproduce gender inequality.
5. The entry of women into the paid labour force increases their power to leave unhappy marriages and control whether and when they will have children. It does not, however, have a big effect on the gendered division of labour in families.
6. Marital satisfaction is lower at the bottom of the class structure, where divorce laws are strict, when children reach their teenage years, in families where housework is not shared equally, and among couples who do not have a good sexual relationship.
7. The effects of divorce on children are worst if there is a high level of parental conflict and the children's standard of living drops.
8. Although the family has been depicted as a "haven in a heartless world" (Lasch, 1977), family violence occurs in all types of families and can have lethal consequences.
9. People sometimes blame the decline of the traditional nuclear family for increasing poverty, welfare dependence, and crime. However, some countries have adopted policies that largely prevent these problems.

## GLOSSARY

**Child support** involves money paid by the noncustodial parent to the custodial parent for the purpose of supporting the children of a separated marital, cohabiting, or sexual relationship.

The **divorce rate** is the number of divorces that occur in a year for every 1000 people in the population.

**Endogamy** is marrying within one's own social group.

**Exogamy** is marrying outside one's own social group.

The **extended family** expands the nuclear family "vertically" by adding another generation—one or more of the spouses' parents—to the household.

**Marriage** is a socially approved, presumably long-term sexual and economic union between a man and a woman. It involves reciprocal rights and obligations between spouses and between parents and children.

The **marriage rate** is the number of marriages that occur in a year for every 1000 people in the population.

A **nuclear family** consists of a cohabiting man and woman who maintain a socially approved sexual relationship and have at least one child.

**Polygamy** expands the nuclear family "horizontally" by adding one or more spouses (usually women) to the household.

The **total fertility rate** is the average number of children born to women of the same age over their lifetime.

A **traditional nuclear family** is a nuclear family in which the husband works outside the home for money and the wife works without pay in the home.

## QUESTIONS TO CONSIDER

1. Do you agree with the functionalist view that the traditional nuclear family is the ideal family form for Canada today? Why or why not?
2. Ask your grandparents and parents how many people lived in their household when they were your age. Ask them to identify the role of each household member (mother, brother, sister, grandfather, boarder, etc.) and to describe the work done by each member inside and outside the household. Compare the size, composition, and division of labour of your household with that of your grandparents and parents. How have the size, composition, and division of labour of your household changed over three generations? Why have these changes occurred?

## WEB RESOURCES

### Companion Web Site for This Book

http://www.brymsociologycompass.nelson.com

Begin by clicking on the Student Resources section of the Web site. Next, select the chapter you are currently studying from the pull-down menu. From the Student Resources page you will have easy access to InfoTrac College Edition®, MicroCase online exercises, and additional Web links. The Web site also has many useful tips to aid you in your study of sociology, including practice tests for each chapter.

### InfoTrac Search Terms

These search terms are provided to assist you in beginning to conduct research on this topic by visiting http://www.infotrac-college.com

**Divorce**
**Extended family**
**Family values**
**Marriage**
**Nuclear family**

### Recommended Web Sites

"Marriage and Family Processes" at http://www.trinity.edu/~mkearl/family.html contains a wide range of valuable resources on family sociology.

You can find online tests and quizzes concerning love and relationships at http://dir.yahoo.com/society_and_culture/relationship/_quizzes_and_tests/.

"Kinship and Social Organization" at http://www.umanitoba.ca/anthropology/kintitle.html is an online interactive tutorial that teaches you about variations in patterns of descent, marriage, and residence using five case studies.

Visit these sites for statistics and information on families, http://www.vifamily.ca, lone-parent families, http://www.parentswithoutpartners.org, family violence, http://www.hc-sc.gc.ca/hppb/familyviolence/, sexual behaviour, http://purelove.org/statistics/index.html, and same-sex marriage, http://www.religioustolerance.org/hom_marr.htm.

## SUGGESTED READINGS

Katherine Arnup, ed. *Lesbian Parenting: Living with Pride & Prejudice* (Charlottetown: gynergy books, 1995). A rich collection of articles edited by a leading Canadian scholar working in the areas of lesbian parenting and reproductive rights for women.

Andrew J. Cherlin. *Marriage, Divorce, Remarriage,* revised and enlarged ed. (Cambridge, MA: Harvard University Press, 1992 [1981]). A concise and rock-solid presentation of some major issues in sociology of the family. Makes excellent use of demographic and survey data.

Martha McMahon. *Engendering Motherhood: Identity and Self-Transformation in Women's Lives* (New York: The Guilford Press, 1995). An important work that uses symbolic interaction as an analytical tool to suggest how class, marital status, and work shape the ways in which women create identities for themselves as mothers.

David Popenoe. *Life without Father: Compelling New Evidence that Fatherhood and Marriage Are Indispensable for the Good of Children and Society* (New York: Martin Kessler Books, 1996). The authoritative conservative view, this book relates today's major social problems to the breakdown of the traditional nuclear family.

Lillian B. Rubin. *The Transcendent Child: Tales of Triumph over the Past* (New York: HarperPerennial, 1997). Well-known sociologist Rubin talks about her own childhood, during which she was raised in poverty by an abusive mother, and addresses factors—using much empirical evidence besides her own—that affect children's ability to transcend difficult pasts (i.e., to be "resilient" children).

## NOTES

**1.** Research comparing marriages with and without children consistently finds marital happiness to be higher in child-free unions (Glenn and McLanahan, 1982; Houseknect, 1987; Somers, 1993). However, at least one analysis concludes that most of the difference in marital happiness between parents and nonparents is not due to a decline in marital happiness after the arrival of a child/children but to the fact that unhappy parents tend to stay married while unhappy nonparents are more likely to divorce. In consequence, when parents and nonparents are compared in cross-sample studies, still-married nonparents appear happier as a group (White, Booth, and Edwards, 1986).

**2.** We are grateful to Gregg Olsen, Department of Sociology, University of Manitoba, for this information.

## IN THIS CHAPTER, YOU WILL LEARN THAT

- The structure of society and one's place in it influence one's religious beliefs and practices.
- Under some circumstances, religion creates societal cohesion, while under other circumstances it promotes social conflict. When religion creates societal cohesion, it also reinforces social inequality.
- Religion governs fewer aspects of most people's lives than in the past. However, a religious revival has taken place in various parts of the world in recent decades and many people still adhere to religious beliefs and practices.
- Adults who were brought up in religious families attend religious services more frequently than adults who were brought up in nonreligious families. Attendance also increases with age and decreases with social status.
- Secular schools have substantially replaced the church and religious schools as educational institutions. Today, the educational system is second in importance only to the family as an agent of socialization.
- The educational system often creates social cohesion. In the process, it also reinforces existing inequalities in relation to class, race/ethnicity, and sexual orientation.

CHAPTER

# 13

# RELIGION AND EDUCATION

## INTRODUCTION

Robert Brym started writing the first draft of this chapter just after coming home from a funeral. "Roy was a fitness nut," says Robert, "and cycling was his sport. One perfect summer day, he was out training with his team. I wouldn't be surprised if the sunshine and vigorous exercise turned his thoughts to his good fortune. At 41, he was a senior executive in a medium-sized mutual funds firm. His boss, who treated him like a son, was grooming him for the presidency of the company. Roy had three vivacious children, ranging in age from 1 to 10, and a beautiful, generous, and highly intelligent wife. He was active in community volunteer work and everyone who knew him admired him. But on this particular summer day, he suddenly didn't feel well. He dropped back from the pack and then suffered a massive heart attack. Within minutes, he was dead.

"During shiva, the ritual week of mourning following the death of a Jew, hundreds of people gathered in the family's home and on their front lawn. I had never felt such anguish before. When we heard the steady, slow, clear voice of Roy's 10-year-old son solemnly intoning the mourner's prayer, we all wept. And we asked ourselves and each other the inevitable question: Why?"

In 1902, the great psychologist William James observed that this question lies at the root of all religious belief. Religion is the common human response to the fact that we all stand at the edge of an abyss. It helps us cope with the terrifying fact that we must die (James, 1976 [1902]: 116). It offers us immortality, the promise of better times to come, and the security of benevolent spirits who look over us. It provides meaning and purpose in a world that might otherwise seem cruel and senseless.

The motivation for religion may be psychological, as James argued. However, the content and intensity of our religious beliefs, and the form and frequency of our religious practices, are influenced by the structure of society and our place in it. In other words, the religious impulse takes literally thousands of forms. It is the task of the sociologist of religion to account for this variation. Why does one religion predominate here, another there? Why is religious belief more fervent at one time than another? Under what circumstances does religion act as a source of social stability and under what circumstances does it act as a force for social change? Are we becoming more or less religious? These are all questions that have occupied the sociologist of religion, and we will touch on all of them here. Note that we will not have anything to say about the truth of religion in general or the value of any religious belief or practice in particular. These are questions of faith, not science. They lie outside the province of sociology.

The cover of *Time* magazine once proclaimed, "God is dead." As a sociological observation, the assertion is preposterous. In a nationwide Canadian survey in 2000, 81 percent of adults and 71 percent of teenagers agreed with the statement "God or a higher power cares about you." Forty-six percent of adults and 36 percent of teens said they had felt the presence of God or a higher power (Bibby, 2001: 252). By these measures (and by other measures we will examine below), God is still very much alive in Canada. Nonetheless, as we will show, the scope of religious authority has declined in Canada and many other parts of the world. That is, religion governs fewer aspects of life than it used to. Some Canadians still look to religion to deal with all of life's problems. But more and more Canadians expect that religion can help them deal with only a restricted range of spiritual issues. Other institutions—medicine, psychiatry, criminal justice, education, and so forth—have grown in importance as the scope of religious authority has declined.

Foremost among these other institutions is the system of education. Organized religion used to be the main purveyor of formal knowledge and the most important agent of socialization apart from the family. Today, the education system is the main purveyor of formal knowledge and the most important agent of socialization apart from the family. It is this displacement of religion by the educational system that justifies our analyzing religion and education side by side in a single chapter.

Although Canadians hold a strong belief in the importance of education, we are increasingly likely to raise questions about its roles and central components. At present, it seems that we have only a moderate level of confidence in our public education system (Canadian Council on Social Development, 1999). A March 1999 Gallup poll reported that satisfaction with the educational system stood at 44 percent. In 1999, an Angus Reid survey asked Canadians to say whether they thought the education system was in better or worse shape now than it was 25 years earlier. More Canadians thought it was in worse shape. What are our chief educational concerns? Low academic performance, lack of discipline and respect, the future employability of students, and equality of opportunity (Bricker and Greenspon, 2001: 162–5). We will address these issues below, paying particular attention to the way they are related to the larger problem of social inequality.

By taking this approach, we follow tradition. Sociologists of education have long been interested in the relationship between education and inequality. Some say that education promotes upward mobility. Others argue that education faithfully reproduces inequality generation after generation. As you will see, the evidence offers stronger support for the second argument. Plenty of scope thus remains for educational reform. Through various parent–teacher initiatives, mentoring, and improved funding, individual citizens, politicians, and educational authorities can do much to improve academic standards and deal with the discipline problem, thus helping the school system perform more like a road to opportunity for all members of society. We will explore the educational issues at length below. First, however, we examine the influence of society on religion and the influence of religion on society.

## CLASSICAL APPROACHES IN THE SOCIOLOGY OF RELIGION

### Durkheim and the Problem of Order

Canadian economist Colin Jones said in a recent interview that hockey is Canada's "national religion" (*The Ring*, 2000). Do you agree with that opinion? Before making up your mind, consider the following facts. In February 2002, more than 3 million Canadians gathered in front of their TVs to watch the Canadian men's hockey team begin their pursuit of a gold medal at the Winter Olympic games. During the 1998 Winter Olympics, the Canada–Czech Republic game drew more than 2.5 million viewers—even though it was broadcast at 3:30 a.m. And, of course, when Canada's hockey team came from behind to defeat the Soviets in 1972, the nation "virtually came to a stop" (Kernaghan, 2002). It is also clear that few events attract the attention and enthusiasm of Canadians as much as the annual Stanley Cup finals (*Canadian Global Almanac 2002*, 2001: 627).

Apart from drawing a huge audience, the Stanley Cup playoffs generate a sense of what Durkheim would have called "collective effervescence." That is, the Stanley Cup excites us by making us feel part of something larger than us: the Montreal Canadiens, the Edmonton Oilers, the Toronto Maple Leafs, the Vancouver Canucks, the Calgary Flames, the Ottawa Senators, the institution of Canadian hockey, the spirit of Canada itself. As celebrated Canadian writer Roch Carrier (1979: 77) wrote in his famous short story "The Hockey Sweater": "[S]chool was...a quiet place where we could prepare for the next hockey game, lay out our next strategies. As for church...there we forgot school and dreamed about the next hockey game. Through our daydreams it might happen that we would recite a prayer: we would ask God to help us play as well as Maurice Richard." For many hours each year, hockey enthusiasts transcend their everyday lives and experience intense enjoyment by sharing the sentiments and values of a larger collective. In their fervour, they banish thoughts of their own mortality. They gain a glimpse of eternity as they immerse themselves in institutions that will outlast them and athletic feats that people will remember for generations to come.

So, do you think the Stanley Cup playoffs are a religious event? There is no god of the Stanley Cup (although the nickname of Canadian hockey legend Wayne Gretzky—The Great One—certainly suggests that he has transcended the status of a mere mortal). Nonetheless, the Stanley Cup playoffs meet Durkheim's definition of a religious experience.

From a Durkheimian point of view, Super Bowl Sunday can be considered a religious holiday.

Durkheim said that when people live together, they come to share common sentiments and values. These common sentiments and values form a **collective conscience** that is larger than any individual. On occasion, we experience the collective conscience directly. This causes us to distinguish the secular, everyday world of the **profane** from the religious, transcendent world of the **sacred.** We designate certain objects as symbolizing the sacred. Durkheim called these objects **totems.** We invent certain public practices to connect us with the sacred. Durkheim referred to these practices as **rituals.** The effect (or function) of rituals and of religion as a whole is to reinforce social solidarity, said Durkheim. He would have found support for his theory in research showing that the suicide rate dips during collective celebrations such as Thanksgiving—just as it does for the two days preceding Super Bowl Sunday and on Super Bowl Sunday itself, along with the final day of the World Series (Curtis, Loy, and Karnilowicz, 1986). Complementing these findings, research on suicides in Quebec from 1951–92 found that the early ousting of the Montreal Canadiens from the Stanley Cup playoffs was associated with an increased tendency for young men in Quebec to commit suicide during the hockey series (Trovato, 1998). These patterns are consistent with Durkheim's theory of suicide, which predicts a lower suicide rate when social solidarity increases (see Chapter 1, A Sociological Compass) and a higher suicide rate when social solidarity decreases.

Durkheim would consider the Stanley Cup and the team logos to be totems. The insignia represent groups we identify with. The trophy signifies the qualities that professional hockey stands for: competitiveness, sportsmanship, excellence, and the value of teamwork. The hockey game itself is a public ritual enacted according to strict rules and conventions. We suspend our everyday lives as we watch the ritual being enacted. The ritual heightens our experience of belonging to certain groups, increases our respect for certain institutions, and strengthens our belief in certain ideas. These groups, institutions, and ideas all transcend us. Thus, the game is a sacred event in Durkheim's terms. It cements society in the way Durkheim said all religions do (Durkheim, 1976 [1915]). Do you agree with this Durkheimian interpretation of the Stanley Cup playoffs? Why or why not? Do you see any parallels between the Durkheimian analysis of the Stanley Cup playoffs and sports in your community or university?

## Religion, Conflict, and Inequality

Durkheim's theory of religion is a functionalist account. It clearly offers some useful insights into the role of religion in society. However, critics lodge two main criticisms against it. First, it overemphasizes religion's role in maintaining social cohesion. In reality, religion often incites social conflict. Second, when religion does increase social cohesion, it often reinforces social inequality. Durkheim ignores this issue, too.

Consider first the role of religion in maintaining inequality. It was Marx who first stressed how religion often tranquilizes the underprivileged into accepting their lot in life. He called religion "the opium of the people" (Marx, 1970 [1843]: 131).

Evidence for Marx's interpretation may be drawn from many times and places. In medieval and early modern Europe, Christianity promoted the view that the Almighty ordains social inequality. In the words of an Anglican verse:

> The rich man at his castle,
> The poor man at his gate.
> God made them high or lowly
> And ordered their estate.

Nor were Western Christians alone in justifying social hierarchy on religious grounds. In Russian and other Slavic languages, the words for rich (*bogati*) and God (*bog*) have the same root. This suggests that wealth is God-given and perhaps even that it makes the wealthy godlike. The Hindu scriptures say that the highest caste sprang from the lips of the supreme creator, the next highest caste from his shoulders, the next highest from his thighs, and the lowest, "polluted" caste from his feet. And the Koran, the holy book of Islam, says that social inequality is due to the will of Allah (Ossowski, 1963: 19–20).

In Canada today, most people do not think of social hierarchy in such rigid terms—quite the opposite. Most people celebrate the alleged *absence* of social hierarchy. This is part of what sociologist Robert Bellah calls our **civil religion,** a set of quasi-religious beliefs and practices that binds the population together and justifies our way of life (Bellah, 1975).[1] When we think of Canada as a land of golden opportunity, a meritocracy in which everyone (regardless of race, creed, colour, or gender) can achieve success, we are giving voice to Canada's civil religion. The national anthem, the maple leaf, and great public events such as the Stanley Cup help make us feel at ease with our way of life, just as the Anglican verse cited above helped the British feel comfortable with their stratification system hundreds of years ago. Paradoxically, however, our civil religion may also help divert attention from the many inequalities that persist in Canadian society. Strong belief in the existence of equal opportunity, for instance, may lead people to overlook the lack of opportunity that remains in our society (see Chapter 7, Social Stratification: Canadian and Global Perspectives). In this manner, our civil religion functions much like the Anglican verse cited above, although its content is markedly different.

We can also find plenty of examples to illustrate religion's role in promoting conflict. One example is the role played by African-American churches during the 1950s and 1960s in spearheading the American civil rights movement. In the southern United States in the 1940s, whites sometimes allowed African Americans to sit at the back of their churches. More often, African-Americans had to worship in churches of their own. These separate churches were to form the breeding ground of the civil rights movement (Morris, 1984). Their impact was both organizational and inspirational. Organizationally, black churches supplied the ministers who formed the leadership of the civil rights movement. They also supplied the congregations within which marches, boycotts, sit-ins, and other forms of protest were coordinated. In addition, ideas from Christian doctrine inspired the protesters. Among the most powerful of these was the notion that African-Americans, like the Jews in Egypt, were slaves who would be freed. It was, after all, Michael—regarded by Christians as the patron saint of the Jews—who rowed the boat ashore. Some white segregationists reacted strongly against efforts at integration, often meeting the peaceful protesters with deadly violence. But the South was never the same again. Religion had helped promote the conflict needed to make the South a more egalitarian and racially integrated place.

Closer to home, it is worth remembering the important role played in the creation of our medicare system and our social welfare network by the "radical Christianity" of the early twentieth-century Social Gospel movement. The Social Gospel emphasized that

Christians should be as concerned with improving the here and now as with life in the hereafter. The efforts of Tommy Douglas, a Baptist minister, the leader of the Co-operative Commonwealth Federation (precursor of the New Democratic Party), and the "father of socialized medicine," exemplify the Social Gospel concern with social justice issues. More recently, a challenge to the status quo is evident in the policy pronouncements of the Social Affairs Commission of the Canadian Conference of Catholic Archbishops. This group has called on the Canadian government to base its economic and social policy "on the principle of a 'preferential option for the poor, the afflicted and the oppressed' as well as the notion that 'labour, not capital, must be given priority in the development of an economy based on justice'" (Dawson, 1993: 323). Similarly, the United Church of Canada has ignited conflict by declaring that "all persons, regardless of their sexual orientation, are welcome to become full members of the church and are eligible for ordination as ministers" (in Dawson, 1993: 323). These Canadian cases illustrate how religion can sometimes promote conflict and change.

In sum, religion can maintain social order under some circumstances, as Durkheim said. When it does so, however, it often reinforces social inequality. Moreover, under other circumstances religion can promote social conflict.

## Weber and the Problem of Social Change

If Durkheim highlighted the way religion contributes to social order, Max Weber stressed the way religion can contribute to social change. Weber captured the core of his argument in a memorable image: If history is like a train, pushed along its tracks by economic and political interests, then religious ideas are like railroad switches, determining exactly which tracks the train will follow (Weber, 1946: 280).

Weber's most famous illustration of his thesis is his short book, *The Protestant Ethic and Spirit of Capitalism*. Like Marx, Weber was interested in explaining the rise of modern capitalism. And, again like Marx, he was prepared to recognize the "fundamental importance of the economic factor" in his explanation (Weber, 1958 [1904–5]: 26). But Weber was also bent on proving the one-sidedness of any *exclusively* economic interpretation.

Weber made his case by first noting that the economic conditions Marx said were necessary for capitalist development existed in Catholic France during the reign of Louis XIV. Yet the wealth generated in France by international trade and commerce tended to be consumed by war and the luxurious lifestyle of the aristocracy rather than invested in the growth of capitalist enterprise. For Weber, what prompted vigorous capitalist development in non-Catholic Europe and North America was a combination of (a) favourable economic conditions such as those discussed by Marx, and (b) the spread of certain moral values by the Protestant reformers of the sixteenth century and their followers.

For specifically religious reasons, wrote Weber, followers of the Protestant theologian John Calvin stressed the need to engage in intense worldly activity and to display industry, punctuality, and frugality in their everyday life. In the view of men like John Wesley and Benjamin Franklin, people could reduce their religious doubts and assure a state of grace by working diligently and living simply. Many Protestants took up this idea. Weber called it the Protestant ethic (Weber, 1958 [1904–5]: 183).

According to Weber, the Protestant ethic had wholly unexpected economic consequences. Where it took root, and where economic conditions were favourable, early capitalist enterprise grew most robustly. Weber made his case even more persuasive by comparing Protestant Western Europe and North America with India and China. In Weber's view, Protestantism was constructed on the foundation of two relatively rational religions: Judaism and Catholicism. These religions were rational in two senses. First, their followers abstained from magic. Second, they engaged in legalistic interpretation of the holy writ. In contrast, said Weber, Buddhism in India and Confucianism in China had strong magical and otherworldly components. According to Weber, this hindered worldly success in competition and capital accumulation. As a result, capitalism developed slowly in Asia (Weber, 1963).

The port of Singapore. Some scholars argue that Confucianism in East Asia acted much like Protestantism in nineteenth-century Europe, invigorating rapid economic growth by virtue of its strong work ethic. This not only ignores the fact that Weber himself regarded Confucianism as a brake on economic growth in Asia, but it also plays down the economic and political forces that stimulated economic development in the region. This is the kind of one-sided explanation that Weber warned against.

In application, two problems have confronted Weber's argument. First, the correlation between the Protestant ethic and the strength of capitalist development is weaker than Weber thought. In some places, Catholicism has coexisted with vigorous capitalist growth and Protestantism with relative economic stagnation (Samuelsson, 1961 [1957]).

Second, Weber's followers have not always applied the Protestant ethic thesis as carefully as Weber did. For example, since the 1960s, the economies of Taiwan, South Korea, Hong Kong, and Singapore have grown quickly. Some scholars argue that Confucianism in East Asia acted much like Protestantism in nineteenth-century Europe, invigorating rapid economic growth by virtue of its strong work ethic (Lie, 1998). This ignores the fact that Weber himself regarded Confucianism as a brake on economic growth in Asia. In addition, it plays down the economic and political forces that stimulated economic development in the region. This is just the kind of one-sided explanation that Weber warned against (see Chapter 16, Population, Urbanization, and Development).

Despite these problems, Weber's treatment of the religious factor underlying social change is a useful corrective to Durkheim's emphasis of religion as a source of social stability. Along with Durkheim's work, Weber's contribution stands as one of the most potent insights into the influence of religion on society.

## THE RISE, DECLINE, AND PARTIAL REVIVAL OF RELIGION

### Secularization

In 1651, the British political philosopher Thomas Hobbes described life as "poore, nasty, brutish, and short" (Hobbes, 1968 [1651]: 150). His description fit the recent past. The standard of living in medieval and early modern Europe was abysmally low. On average, a person lived only about 35 years. The forces of nature and human affairs seemed entirely unpredictable. In this context, magic was popular. It offered easy answers to mysterious, painful, and capricious events.

As material conditions improved, popular belief in magic, astrology, and witchcraft gradually lost ground (Thomas, 1971). Christianity substantially replaced them. The better and more predictable times made Europeans more open to the teachings of organized religion. In addition, the Church campaigned vigorously to stamp out opposing belief systems and practices. The persecution of witches in this era was partly an effort to eliminate competition and establish a Christian monopoly over spiritual life.

The persecution of witches in the early modern era was partly an effort to eliminate competition and establish a Christian monopoly over spiritual life. Burning of Witches by Inquisition in a German Marketplace. After a drawing by H. Grobert.

The Church succeeded in its efforts. In medieval and early modern Europe, Christianity became a powerful presence in religious affairs, music, art, architecture, literature, and philosophy. Popes and saints were the rock musicians and movie stars of their day. The Church was the centre of life in both its spiritual and its worldly dimensions. Church authority was supreme in marriage, education, morality, economic affairs, politics, and so forth. European countries proclaimed official state religions. They persecuted members of religious minorities.

In contrast, a few hundred years later, Max Weber remarked on how the world had become thoroughly "disenchanted." By the turn of the twentieth century, he said, scientific and other forms of rationalism were replacing religious authority. His observations formed the basis of what came to be known as the **secularization thesis,** undoubtedly the most widely accepted argument in the sociology of religion until the 1990s. According to the secularization thesis, religious institutions, actions, and consciousness are unlikely to disappear, but they are certainly on the decline worldwide (Tschannen, 1991).

## Religious Revival

Despite the consensus about secularization that was still evident in the 1980s, many sociologists modified their judgments in the 1990s. There were two reasons for this. First, accumulated survey evidence showed that religion was not in an advanced state of decay. Actually, in many places, such as Canada, it was in fairly good health. Consider in this connection Table 13.1, which contains data from the *World Values Survey* (WVS), one of the most authoritative polls in the world. Table 13.1 allows us to compare Canada with 11 other postindustrial countries. In 1990, Canada ranked fifth in the percentage of respondents who said God is important to them. It fell to sixth place (tied with Belgium) in the percentage of people who attend religious services once a week or more. By these measures, Canada is not one of most religious postindustrial countries in the world. However, the evidence suggests that although Canadians are less likely to attend religious services than people in Ireland and the United States, religion continues to play an important role in the lives of many Canadians.

Both the history and the national identity of Canada are indelibly imprinted with the mark of religion. In the words of Reginald Bibby, Canada's leading sociologist of religion: "If one thinks of the past, it is impossible to imagine Quebec with no Roman Catholics, Ontario with no Anglicans or Presbyterians, the Prairies with no evangelical Protestants,

| | God Is Important in My Life | I Attend Religious Services Once a Week or More |
|---|---|---|
| United States | 70 | 44 |
| Ireland | 65 | 81 |
| Northern Ireland | 63 | 50 |
| Canada | 51 | 27 |
| Italy | 53 | 38 |
| Spain | 36 | 29 |
| Belgium | 30 | 27 |
| Britain | 28 | 14 |
| West Germany | 30 | 18 |
| Netherlands | 27 | 20 |
| France | 20 | 10 |
| Denmark | 13 | 3 |

✦ **TABLE 13.1** ✦

**The Importance of God and Church Attendance in 12 Postindustrial Societies, 1990 (in percent)**

Source: *The World Values Survey,* cited in Nevitte (1996: 210).

*Note:* All numbers are rounded. For column 1, the question read: "And how important is God in your life? (10 means very important and 1 means not at all important)." The figures indicate the percentage who indicated scores of 8, 9, or 10. For column 2, the question read: "Apart from weddings, funerals and christenings, about how often do you attend religious services these days?"

and British Columbia and the Atlantic region without the Church of England" (Bibby, 1993: 25). The 1982 Canadian Charter of Rights and Freedoms asserts that our country is founded on principles that recognize the supremacy of God. At the same time, it is evident that religion in Canada has been profoundly altered by social change after the Second World War. Since the 1970s, confidence in religious leaders has plummeted (Bibby, 1995: 123). In 1998, 36 percent of Canadians expressed a "lot of confidence" in religious organizations, 29 percent a "moderate amount," and 31 percent a "little" (Canadian Council on Social Development, 1999: 6). Participation levels have also fallen. In 1996 Canadians were far less likely than they were in the 1940s to attend religious services weekly (20 percent versus 67 percent). When compared to their parents or grandparents, Canadian teens are now far less likely to say that they were highly involved in religious groups as children (Bibby, 2001: 274). In addition, the number of Canadians reporting that they had "no religious affiliation" has been growing steadily since 1961, almost doubled between 1981 and 1991 (from 7.4 percent to 12.5 percent), and in 1996 reached 15 percent (see Figure 13.1). However, "demise is relative; organizationally, religion continues to be a significant force with a significant following in Canada" (Bibby, 2001: 114). Religion and spirituality remain of considerable interest to a sizable number of both young and old Canadians (see Table 13.2).

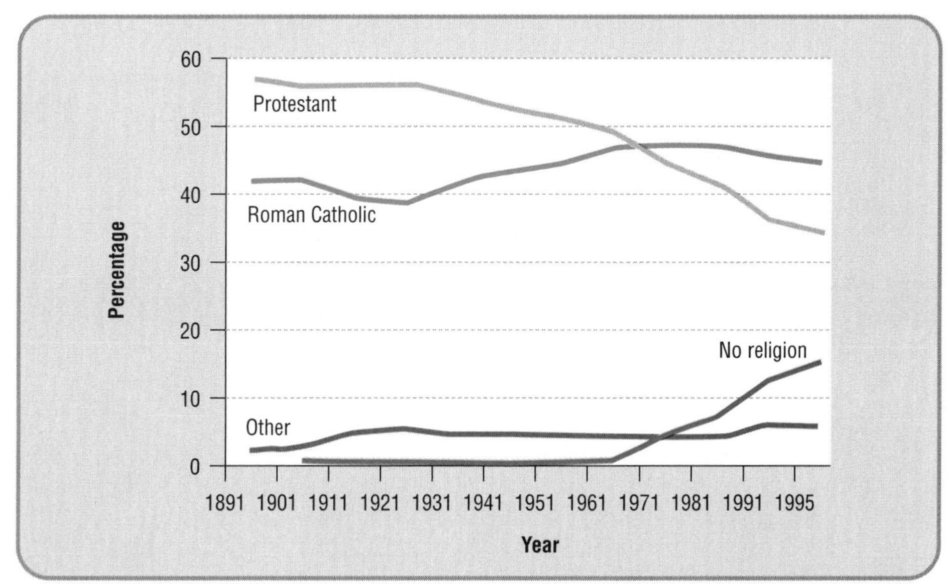


✦ **FIGURE 13.1** ✦

**Religious Affiliation of Canadians**

Source: Statistics Canada's Census, various years, 1995 data based on calculations from General Social Survey, 1995 Cycle 10.

✦ **TABLE 13.2** ✦
**Religious Involvement and Spirituality across Generations**

Source: Bibby (2001: 254).

| "I..." | ADULTS | TEENS |
|---|---|---|
| **Group Involvement** | | |
| Identify with a group | 86% | 76 |
| Am committed to Christianity or another faith | 55 | 48 |
| Attend weekly | 21 | 22 |
| Receive high level of enjoyment from group | 22 | 21 |
| Am open to possibility of greater involvement | 57 | 43 |
| **Spirituality** | | |
| Have spiritual needs | 73 | 48 |
| Have close friends interested in spirituality | 42 | 38 |
| Find spirituality very important | 34 | 30 |
| Pray privately weekly or more often | 47 | 33 |

The second circumstance that has caused many sociologists to revise their judgment about the secularization thesis is the revival of religious fundamentalism. Since the 1960s, fundamentalist religious organizations have rapidly increased their membership, especially among Protestants (Finke and Starke, 1992). **Fundamentalists** interpret their scriptures literally, seek to establish a direct, personal relationship with the higher being(s) they worship, and are relatively intolerant of nonfundamentalists (Hunter, 1991). Fundamentalists often support conservative social and political issues (Bruce, 1988; see Box 13.1).

During the same time period, religious movements became dominant forces in many less developed countries. Hindu nationalists formed the government in India. An Islamic revival swept Iran and other countries in the Middle East, Africa, and Asia. Religious fundamentalism became a worldwide phenomenon, sometimes leading to violence as a means of establishing fundamentalist ideas and institutions as the bases of nation-states (Juergensmeyer, 2000). Meanwhile, the Catholic Church played a critically important role in undermining communism in Poland, and Catholic "liberation theology" animated the successful fight against right-wing governments in Latin America (Kepel, 1994 [1991]; Segundo, 1976 [1975]; Smith, 1991). All these developments amount to a religious revival that was quite unexpected in, say, 1970.

Religious rituals are symbols that help unite people into a moral community.

BOX 13.1
SOCIOLOGY AT THE MOVIES

*Harry Potter and the Sorcerer's Stone* (2001)

### *HARRY POTTER AND THE SORCERER'S STONE* (2001)

*Harry Potter and the Sorcerer's Stone* introduces us to Harry Potter (played by Daniel Radcliffe) who, at the age of one, was orphaned when the most evil wizard of all, Lord Voldemort ("He-who-must-not-be-named"), murdered Harry's parents and tried to kill Harry. The infant Harry, who bears a thunderbolt-shaped scar on his forehead as the result of Lord Voldemort's attack, is deposited by the gentle giant Hagrid (played by Robbie Coltrane) on the doorstep of his unwelcoming relatives, the Dursleys. He lives a miserable, lonely existence, ignored by his aunt and uncle and bullied by their fat and pampered son. Shortly before his eleventh birthday, Harry's life is turned upside down. He is summoned by a blizzard of letters to Hogswarts School of Witchcraft and Wizardry. The school, housed in a 1000-year-old castle and headed by the renowned Professor Dumbledore (played by Richard Harris), provides select students with a seven-year program of instruction. Harry learns that although his relatives are muggles (non-witches), he is not.

At Hogwarts, Harry makes two great friends, Hermione Granger (played by Emma Watson) and Ron Weasley (played by Rupert Grint). He also acquires an enemy, Draco Malfoy (played by Tom Felton), and, for reasons that are unclear to him, evokes the displeasure of one of his instructors, the mysterious Professor Snape (played by Alan Rickman). At Hogwarts, Harry learns to concoct magical potions and perform spells. He participates in a sport called Quidditch that is played 15 or more metres in the air on flying brooms. He finds talking portraits on the walls, mirrors that reflect what Harry longs to see, and a cloak of invisibility that he can wear when he wishes to hide. All manner of magical creatures surround him. But danger lurks. For He-who-must-not-be-named stalks Harry, determined to accomplish what he earlier failed to do—kill the young wizard. Harry battles Lord Valdemort and destroys him. Or does he?

When *Harry Potter and the Sorcerer's Stone* opened in Canadian cinemas in November 2001, it enjoyed the largest debut in Canadian movie history (CBC News, 2001). Prominent in the lineups were children, many of whom were outfitted as if for Halloween in a variety of witch and wizard costumes. Some of the children were there on organized school field trips with their teachers and classmates after having studied the book. Although most people viewed *Harry Potter and the Sorcerer's Stone* as innocuous and interchangeable with numerous other films aimed at a youthful audience, others saw things differently. Various groups denounced both the film and the book on which it was based as "demonic." Many of these groups were conservative Protestants who claimed that the book glorifies witchcraft, makes "evil look innocent," and subtly draws "children into an unhealthy interest in a darker world that is occultic and dangerous to physical, psychological and spiritual well-being" (Shaw, 2001). According to Focus on the Family, a fundamentalist Christian ministry, "the effect of [the movie] is undoubtedly to raise curiosity about magic and wizardry. And any curiosity raised on this front presents a danger that the world will satisfy it with falsehood before the church or the family can satisfy it with truth" (Ontario Consultants on Religious Tolerance, 2002). Scenes from *Harry Potter and the Sorcerer's Stone* were scrutinized for possible demonic messages. A similarity was proclaimed between the lightning bolt that appears on Harry Potter's forehead and the symbol adopted by Hitler's SS. Similar claims in Durham, Ontario, led to a decision to ban the book on which the movie was based from any classes where at least one parent objected to its use. In the UK, the book was banished from a school in Kent after it was deemed at odds with the school's "church ethos." In the United States the American Library Association reported that the Harry Potter series was attacked in 13 states, making the books the most challenged novels of 1999. The most common complaint raised by critics? The book allegedly promoted "occult, Satanism and anti-family themes" (Ontario Consultants on Religious Tolerance, 2002).

Do you agree or disagree with the decision to ban to Harry Potter books and condemn the movie? Even if you disagree with the decision, do you think that individual schools should have the right to censor books and movies? For example, would it be acceptable if a predominantly white school were to ban the works of Toni Morrison and Maya Angelou on the grounds that they say derogatory things about whites? Would you agree with the right of a Jewish school to ban Shakespeare's *The Merchant of Venice* because it portrays Jews in a unflattering way? And what if students in an all-girls school decide they want to ban the works of Ernest Hemingway ("too sexist") while students in an all-boys school ban the writings of Margaret Atwood ("too anti-male")? In general, should schools have the freedom to censor or should censoring be banned?

## The Revised Secularization Thesis

The developments reviewed above led some sociologists to revise the secularization thesis in the 1990s. The revisionists acknowledge that religion has become increasingly influential in the lives of some individuals and groups over the past 30 years. They insist, however, that the scope of religious authority has continued to decline in most people's lives. That is, for most people, religion has less and less to say about education, family issues, politics, and economic affairs even though it may continue to be an important source of spiritual belief and practice. In this sense, secularization continues (Chaves, 1994; Yamane, 1997).

According to the **revised secularization thesis,** in most countries, worldly institutions have broken off (or "differentiated") from the institution of religion over time. One such worldly institution is the education system. Religious bodies used to run schools and institutions of higher learning that are now run almost exclusively by nonreligious authorities. Moreover, like other specialized institutions that separated from the institution of religion, the educational system is generally concerned with worldly affairs rather than spiritual matters. The overall effect of the differentiation of secular institutions has been to make religion applicable only to the spiritual part of most people's lives. Because the scope of religious authority has been restricted, people look to religion for moral guidance in everyday life less often than they used to. Moreover, most people have turned religion into a personal and private matter rather than one imposed by a powerful, authoritative institution. Said differently, people feel increasingly free to combine beliefs and practices from various sources and traditions to suit their own tastes. As supermodel Cindy Crawford said in a *Redbook* interview in 1992: "I'm religious but in my own personal way. I always say that I have a Cindy Crawford religion—It's my own" (quoted in Yamane, 1997: 116). No statement could more adequately capture the decline of religion as an authoritative institution suffusing all aspects of life.

# RELIGION IN CANADA

## Church, Sect, and Cult

Sociologists generally divide religious groups into just three types: churches, sects, and cults (Troeltsch, 1931 [1923]; Stark and Bainbridge, 1979; see Table 13.3).

In the sociological sense of the term, a **church** is any bureaucratic religious organization that has accommodated itself to mainstream society and culture. As a result, it may endure for many hundreds if not thousands of years. The bureaucratic nature of a church is evident in the formal training of its leaders, its strict hierarchy of roles, and its clearly drawn rules and regulations. Its integration into mainstream society is evident in its teachings, which are generally abstract and do not challenge worldly authority. In addition, churches integrate themselves into the mainstream by recruiting members from all classes of society.

Churches take two main forms. First are **ecclesia,** or state-supported churches. For example, Christianity became the state religion in the Roman Empire in 392 CE and Islam is the state religion in Pakistan, Afghanistan, and other countries today. State religions impose advantages on members and disadvantages on nonmembers. Tolerance of other religions is low in societies with ecclesia.

✦ **TABLE 13.3** ✦
**Church, Sect, and Cult Compared**

| | Church | Sect | Cult |
|---|---|---|---|
| Integration into society | High | Medium | Low |
| Bureaucratization | High | Low | Low |
| Longevity | High | Low | Low |
| Leaders | Formally trained | Charismatic | Charismatic |
| Class base | Mixed | Low | Various but segregated |

Alternatively, churches may be pluralistic, allowing diversity within the church and expressing tolerance of nonmembers. Pluralism allows churches to increase their appeal by allowing various streams of belief and practice to coexist under their overarching authority. These subgroups are called **denominations.** In 1991 (the latest year for which census data are available as of this writing), the major Protestant denominations in Canada were United Church, Anglican, Baptist, Lutheran, Presbyterian, and Pentecostal. The major Catholic denominations were Roman Catholic and Ukrainian Catholic. The major Jewish denominations were Orthodox, Conservative, Reform, and Reconstructionist. The major Muslim denominations were Shiite and Sunni. Many of these denominations are divided into even smaller groups. Table 13.4 shows the percentage of Canadians who belonged to the major religions and denominations in Canada in 1991.

**Sects** often form by breaking away from churches because of disagreement about church doctrine. Sometimes, sect members choose to separate themselves geographically, as the Hutterites do in their some 200 colonies, mostly within the Western provinces. However, even in urban settings, strictly enforced rules concerning dress, diet, prayer, and intimate contact with outsiders can separate sect members from the larger society. Hasidic Jews in Montreal and other large Canadian cities prove the viability of this isolation strategy. Sects are less integrated into society and less bureaucratized than churches. They are often led by **charismatic** leaders, men and women who claim to be inspired by supernatural powers and whose followers believe them to be so inspired. These leaders tend to be relatively intolerant of religious opinions other than their own. They tend to recruit like-minded members mainly from lower classes and marginal groups. Worship in sects tends

**✦ TABLE 13.4 ✦**
**Religious Adherence**

| | 1991 | |
|---|---|---|
| | **Number** | **Percentage** |
| **Total population[1]** | **26 994 045** | **100.0** |
| Catholic | 12 335 255 | 45.7 |
| Roman Catholic | 12 203 620 | 45.2 |
| Ukrainian Catholic | 128 390 | 0.5 |
| Other Catholic | 3 235 | — |
| Protestant | 9 780 715 | 36.2 |
| United Church | 3 093 120 | 11.5 |
| Anglican | 2 188 110 | 8.1 |
| Presbyterian | 636 295 | 2.4 |
| Lutheran | 636 205 | 2.4 |
| Baptist | 663 360 | 2.5 |
| Pentecostal | 436 435 | 1.6 |
| Other Protestant | 2 127 190 | 7.9 |
| Islam | 253 260 | 0.9 |
| Buddhist | 163 415 | 0.6 |
| Hindu | 157 010 | 0.6 |
| Sikh | 147 440 | 0.5 |
| Eastern Orthodox | 387 395 | 1.4 |
| Jewish | 318 065 | 1.2 |
| Para-religious groups | 28 155 | 0.1 |
| No religious affiliations | 3 386 365 | 12.5 |
| Other religions | 36 970 | 0.1 |

Source: Statistics Canada, Catalogue no. 93-319.

1 Based on sample data, which exclude institutional residents.

Even in urban settings, strictly enforced rules concerning dress, diet, prayer, and intimate contact with outsiders can separate sect members from the larger society.

to be highly emotional and based less on abstract principles than immediate personal experience (Stark, 1985: 314). Many sects are short-lived, but those that do persist tend to bureaucratize and turn into churches. If religious organizations are to enjoy a long life, they require rules, regulations, and a clearly defined hierarchy of roles.

**Cults** are small groups of people deeply committed to a religious vision that rejects mainstream culture and society. Cults are generally led by charismatic individuals. They tend to be class-segregated groups. That is, a cult tends to recruit members from only one segment of the stratification system, high, middle, or low. For example, many North American cults today recruit nearly all their members from among the university educated. Some of these cults seek converts almost exclusively on university and college campuses (Kosmin, 1991). Because they propose a radically new way of life, cults tend to recruit few members and soon disappear. There are, however, exceptions—and some extremely important ones at that. Jesus and Mohammed were both charismatic leaders of sects. They were so compelling that they and their teachings were able to inspire a large number of followers, including rulers of states. Their cults were thus transformed into churches.

In 1991, Roman Catholics remained the largest religious group in Canada with 12.2 million Canadians, or 45 percent of the population. Protestants were the second-largest group with 9.8 million Canadians, or 36 percent of the population. Nearly 13 percent of Canadians said they have no religious affiliation. Just over 1 percent of Canadians said they belong to "para-religious groups," that is, sects and cults.

All major religious groups in Canada draw from the nation's various racial, ethnic, and socio-economic groups. In spite of the common perception that the recent waves of immigrants have lessened the Christian domination of Canada, little, in fact, has changed. Most of the many recent immigrants from Asian and other Third World countries are Christians (Statistics Canada, 1998a). In 1991, one in three Asian immigrants identified with Protestantism or Roman Catholicism, while most Latin American immigrants were Roman Catholics (Bibby, 1993: 24). Only among African immigrants did the number of non-Christians exceed the number of Christians. Although each religious group draws on members from all social classes, sect-like groups tend to appeal to the less affluent and churchlike groups to the more affluent.

## Religiosity

We have reviewed the major classical theories of religion and society, the modern debate about secularization, and the major types of religious organizations. It is now time to consider some social factors that determine how important religion is to people, that is, their **religiosity.**

We can measure religiosity in various ways. Strength of belief, emotional attachment to a religion, knowledge about a religion, frequency of performing rituals, and frequency of applying religious principles in daily life all indicate how religious a person is (Glock,

1962). Ideally, one ought to examine many measures to get a fully rounded and reliable picture of the social distribution of religiosity. For simplicity's sake, however, we focus on just one measure here. In the 1995 and 2000 Project Canada Surveys, respondents were asked to indicate whether their level of involvement in religious activities at various points in their lives was "high," "moderate," "low," or "none." Figure 13.2 summarizes the results for 2000 (Bibby, 1995, 2000).

Some fascinating patterns emerge from the data. First, the people most heavily involved in religious activities are pre-teens and the elderly. As a result, involvement forms a U-shaped curve, falling among teenagers and young adults and then beginning to rise steadily after the age of 24.

How can we explain this pattern? Pre-teens have little say over whether they attend Sunday school, Hebrew school, confirmation classes, and the like. Their parents may even drop them off at special religious children's services. For many pre-teens, religious involvement is high because it is something that is required of them, even if their parents do not always follow suit. The elderly, for their part, have more time and more need for religion. Because they are not usually in school, employed in the paid labor force or busy raising a family, they have more opportunity than younger people to go to church, synagogue, mosque, or temple. Moreover, because elderly people are generally closer to illness and death than younger people, they are more likely to require the solace of religion. To a degree, then, involvement in religious activities is a life-cycle issue. That is, children are relatively actively involved in religious activities because they are required to be, and the elderly are relatively actively involved because they feel greater need for religious involvement and are in a position to act on that need. But there is another issue at stake here, too. Different age groups live through different times, and today's elderly reached maturity when religion was a more authoritative force in society. A person's current religious involvement depends partly on whether he or she grew up in more religious times. Thus, although young people are likely to become more religiously involved as they age, they are unlikely ever to become as involved as elderly people are today. This implies that "fewer young can be expected to...'return to church,' since fewer were ever active in the first place" (Bibby, 2001: 274–5).

Second, the region of the country in which you live is also correlated with the likelihood that you will attend religious services weekly. Canadians who live in the Atlantic provinces are more likely than other Canadians to attend church weekly (Bibby, 1995:

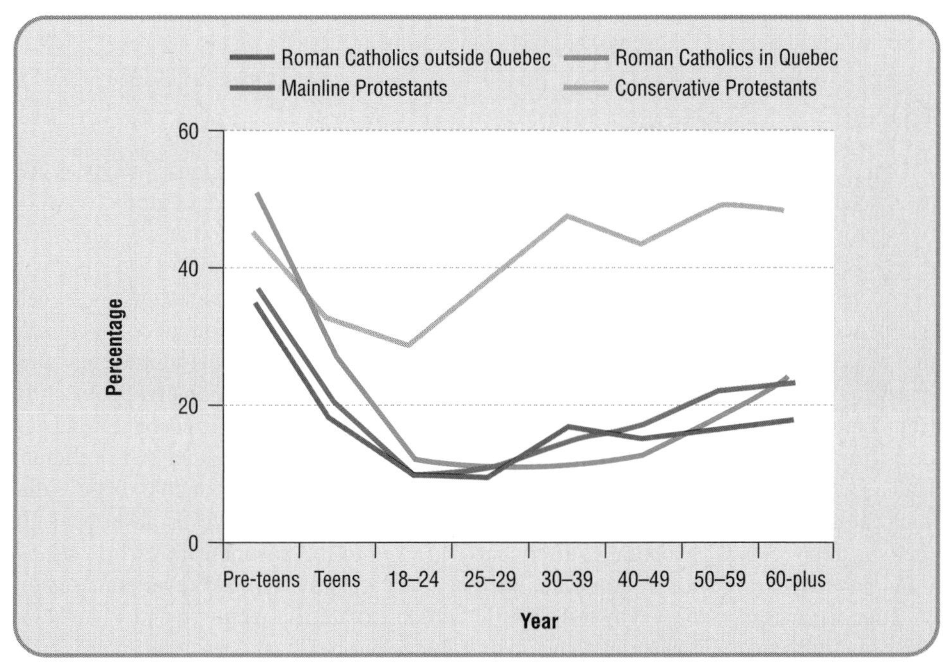


✦ **FIGURE 13.2** ✦
**Religious Involvement over Time by Group**

Source: Bibby (2001: 275).

Religiosity is partly a learned behaviour. Whether parents give a child a religious upbringing is likely to have a lasting impact on the child.

126). Quebec, in particular, has experienced a big decline in church attendance since the 1970s. Although in 1975, 35 percent of Quebecers attended at least one religious service a week, by 1995 only 19 percent did so.

Third, respondents whose parents attended religious services frequently are more likely to do so themselves (Jones, 2000). Religiosity is partly a *learned* behaviour. Whether parents give a child a religious upbringing is likely to have a lasting impact on the child. The New Testament recognizes this: "Whosoever shall not receive the kingdom of God as a little child, he shall not enter therein" (Mark 10:15).

This is by no means an exhaustive list of the factors that determine frequency of attending religious services. For example, research also indicates that social inequality may promote religiosity. If you re-examine Table 13.1, you will note that countries with the lowest level of social inequality, such as Denmark, tend to have the lowest level of church attendance. Countries with the highest level of social inequality, such as the United States, tend to have the highest level of church attendance. However, even this brief overview suggests that religiosity depends on obligation, opportunity, need, and learning. The people who attend religious services most frequently are those who must, those who were taught to be religious as children, those who need organized religion most because of their advanced age, and those who have the most time to go to services.

## The Future of Religion

A significant religious revival is taking place in Canada and other countries today. However, secularization seems to be the long-term trend, both in Canada and globally. In the twenty-first century, gradual secularization is likely to continue, although we can expect reversals at various times and in various places. A substantial minority of people will undoubtedly continue to want deep involvement with religious organizations, practices, and beliefs. Most others will probably want to maintain at least a minimal connection to organized religion. This will allow them to give added meaning to important events associated with celebration and mourning throughout the life cycle. Nationally, 9 out of 10 Canadian teenagers say they expect to have their marriages solemnized by a minister, priest, rabbi, or some other religious figure. Seven in 10 anticipate that such religious leaders will officiate at a birth-related event in their lives and nearly 9 out of 10 believe that such an official will officiate upon their death (Bibby, 2001: 118). However, as Weber said, the world is gradually becoming "disenchanted," even in the postindustrial world's most religious countries, as institutions such as the educational system take over some of the functions formerly performed by religion. In this context, it is important to understand how the rising influence of education came about. That is our next task.

# EDUCATION

## The Rise of Mass Schooling

By the time you finished high school you had spent nearly 13 000 hours in a classroom. This fact alone suggests that the educational system has displaced organized religion as the main purveyor of formal knowledge. It also suggests that the educational system is second only to the family as an important agent of socialization (see Chapter 4, Socialization).

Three hundred years ago only a small minority of people learned to read and write. A century ago most people in the world never attended school. As late as 1950 only about 10 percent of the world's countries boasted systems of compulsory mass education (Meyer, Ramirez, and Soysal, 1992). Even today, more than half of the people in developing nations are illiterate. In India alone, more than 400 million people cannot read or write and nearly 35 million children do not attend school (*Hindustan Times,* 1999). The situation in Canada is vastly different. In this country, there are almost 16 000 elementary and secondary schools employing a full-time teaching force of almost 300 000 and some 300 colleges and universities employing an additional 60 000 full-time educators (Statistics Canada, 1998a: 143). Canada currently ranks as one of the most highly educated societies in the world. The 1996 Census was the first Canadian census to record more university graduates than people with less than a grade nine education (see Figure 13.3). In that year, 69 percent of Canadians 20 years of age and older had completed at least high school (Health Canada, 1999a).

What accounts for the spread of mass schooling? Sociologists usually highlight three factors: the Protestant Reformation, the spread of democracy, and industrialization.

1. The Catholic Church relied on priests to convey dogma to believers. However, in the early sixteenth century, Martin Luther, a German monk, began to criticize the Catholic Church. Protestantism grew out of his criticisms. The Protestants believed that the Bible alone, and not Church doctrines, should guide Christians. They expected Christians to have more direct contact with the word of God than was allowed by the Catholic Church. Accordingly, Protestants needed to be able to read the scriptures for themselves. The rise of Protestantism was thus a spur to popular literacy.
2. The populations of France, Canada, the United States, and other new democracies demanded access to centres of learning, which had previously been restricted to the

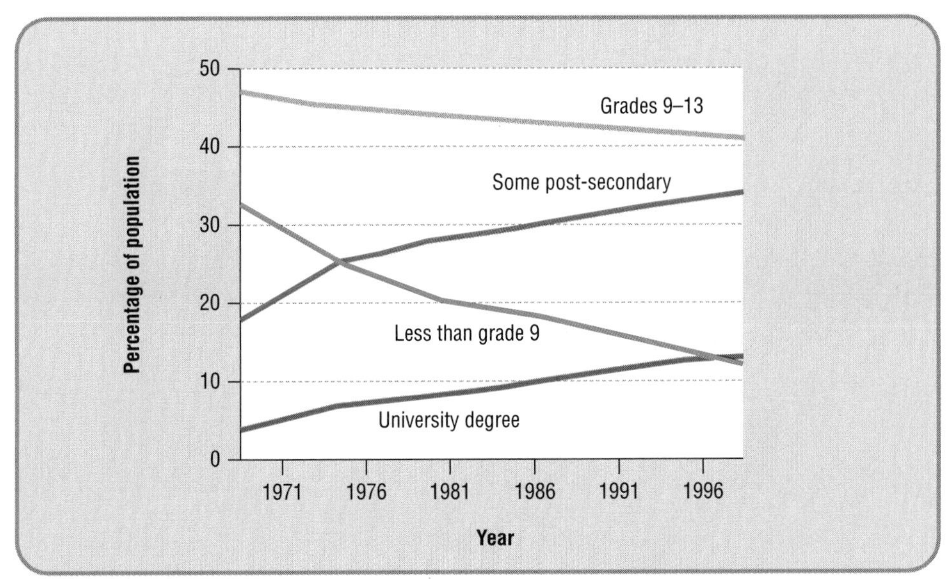


✦ **FIGURE 13.3** ✦
**Highest Level of Schooling, Age 15+, Canada, 1971 to 1996**

Source: Adapted from Statistics Canada, "Population 15 Years and Over by Age Groups (9), Sex (3) and School Attendance (4), Showing Highest Level of Schooling (15), for Canada, Provinces and Territories, 1991 and 1996 Censuses (20% Sample Data) (data products: The Nation: 1996 Census of Population)", Catalogue 93F0028, 1996.

wealthy. In Canada, educational opportunities expanded gradually in the nineteenth and twentieth centuries (Curtis, 1988). Women began to enter institutions of higher learning in the late nineteenth century and have surged into the higher education system in recent decades. By 1996, 12 percent of Canadian women 15 years of age and older had a university degree—double the figure in 1986 (6 percent) and four times that in 1971 (3 percent; see Figure 13.4). The gradual improvement in the **educational attainment** of Canadians is evident. (Educational attainment refers to the number of years of school completed and should not be confused with **educational achievement,** which refers to how much students actually learn.)

3. Before industrialization, people did not require formal education for many kinds of work (e.g., farming), while they could learn other occupations on the job (e.g., carpentry). In contrast, factories and offices called for literate and numerate workers. Furthermore, education became the key to a person's economic success. Each successive educational degree now boosts the likelihood of both employment and earning power. Among 1990 university graduates, about 8 in 10 who obtained a bachelor's degree or master's degree were working full time five years after graduation. Among those with a doctorate, about 9 in 10 had jobs. Although people with a bachelor's degree earned a median income of $38 000, people with a master's degree earned a median income of $50 000, and those with doctorates earned $54 000 (Statistics Canada, 1998a). In contrast, Canadians who did not complete high school reported income of $18 639 in 1995, a figure significantly below the Canadian average of $26 474 (Health Canada, 1999a). In 2001, Statistics Canada reported that although the average Canadian family headed by a high-school graduate had a net worth of about $65 000, a family headed by a university graduate enjoyed a net worth of almost $120 000. For families headed by a person with a degree in law, medicine, dentistry, or another profession, net worth soared to about $320 000 (Bricker and Greenspon, 2001: 158).

This last statistic points to an interesting exception. People who earn a doctorate (Ph.D.) typically earn less than professionals such as doctors and lawyers. Yet Ph.D.s usually have at least as many years of formal education as professionals. As you will learn in the next section, the reasons for this anomaly are connected to the phenomenon of "professionalization."

## Credential Inflation and Professionalization

Over the years, Canada and other countries have experienced what Randall Collins calls **credential inflation** (Collins, 1979). That is, it takes ever more certificates and diplomas

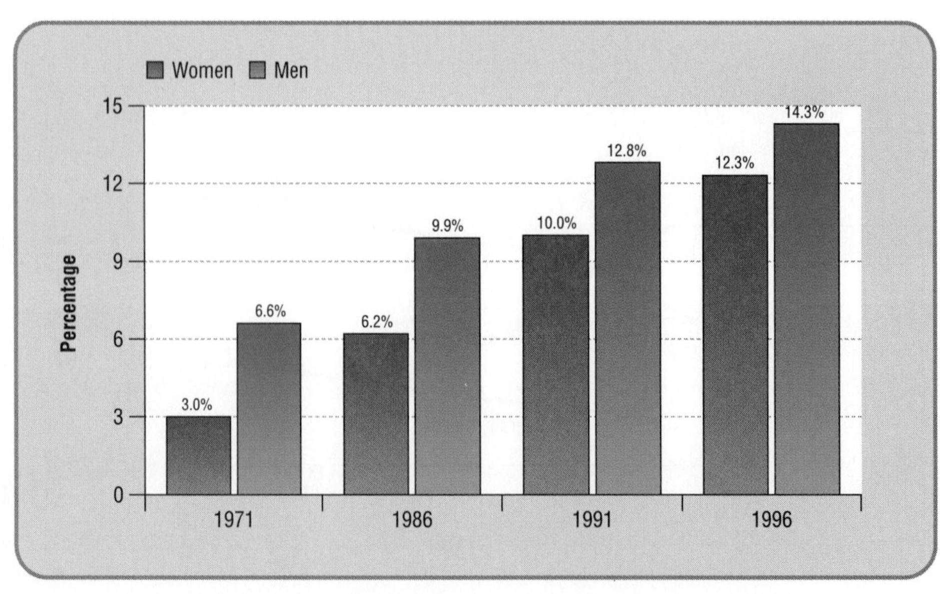


✦ **FIGURE 13.4** ✦
**Percentage of People Aged 15 and Over with a University Degree, 1971–1996**

Source: Adapted from Josee Normand (2000), "Education" in *Women in Canada* Ottawa: Statistics Canada, Catalogue no. 89-503, 2000, p. 85.

to qualify for a given job. A century ago, for example, many professors, even at the most prestigious universities, did not hold a doctoral degree. Today, most professors are Ph.D.s.

Part of the reason for credential inflation is the increasing technical requirements of many jobs. For example, because aircraft engines and avionics systems are more complex than they were, say, 75 years ago, working as an airplane mechanic today requires more technical expertise. Certification ensures that the airplane mechanic can meet the higher technical demands of the job. As Collins points out, however, in many jobs there is often a poor fit between one's credentials and one's specific responsibilities. On-the-job training, not a diploma or a degree, often gives people the skills they need to get the job done. Yet, according to Collins, credential inflation takes place partly because employers find it a convenient sorting mechanism. For example, an employer may assume that a university graduate has certain manners, attitudes, and tastes that will be useful in a high-profile managerial position. Just as family background used to serve as a way of restricting high-status occupations to certain people, credentials serve that purpose today.

Credential inflation is also fuelled by **professionalization,** which occurs when members of an occupation insist that people earn certain credentials in order to enter the occupation. Professionalization ensures that standards are maintained. It also keeps earnings high. After all, if "too many" people enter a given profession, the cost of services offered by that profession is bound to fall. This helps explain why, on average, physicians and lawyers earn more than university professors with a Ph.D. The Canadian Medical Association, for example, is a powerful organization that regulates and effectively limits entry into the medical professions. Canadian professors have never been in a position to form such powerful organizations (see Chapter 15, Health, Medicine, and Aging).

Since professionalization promotes high standards and high earnings, it has spread widely. Even some clowns now consider themselves professionals. Thus, there is a World Clown Association (WCA) that has turned rubber noses and big shoes into a serious business. At its eighteenth annual conference in 2000, the WCA held seminars on a wide variety of subjects including character development, on-target marketing, incredible bubbles, and simple but impressive balloons (Prittie, 2000). Sociologist David K. Brown tells the story of a friend who had been a successful plumber for more than 20 years but tired of the routine and decided to become a clown (Brown, 1995: xvii). His friend quickly found that becoming a clown is not just a matter of buying a costume and acting silly. First, he had to enter the Intensive Summer Clown Training Institute at a local college. The Institute awarded him a certificate signifying his competence as a clown. Based on his performance at the Institute, the prestigious Ringling Brothers Clown School in Florida invited him to enrol. Even a clown, it seems, needs credentials these days, and a really good clown can dream of going on to clown graduate school.

Since professionalization promotes high standards and high earnings, it has spread widely. Even some clowns now consider themselves professionals. Thus, there is a World Clown Association (WCA) that has turned rubber noses and big shoes into a serious business.

## The Functions of Education

Durkheim emphasized the role of schools in socializing the young and in promoting social integration. Human beings, he said, are torn between egoistic needs and moral impulses. Like religion in an earlier era, educational institutions must ensure that the moral side predominates. By instilling a sense of authority, discipline, and morality in children, schools make society cohesive (Durkheim, 1956, 1961 [1925]).

Contemporary sociologists have acknowledged Durkheim's point and broadened it. They point to a variety of manifest or intended functions performed by schools. Schools try to teach the young to view their nation with pride, respect the law of the land, think of democracy as the best form of government, and value capitalism (Callahan, 1962). Schools also transmit knowledge and culture from generation to generation, fostering a common cultural identity in the process. In recent decades, that common identity has been based on respect for the cultural diversity of Canadian society. In addition, it is often said that schools identify talent and skills, making sure that the brightest and most industrious students are selected and trained for the most challenging jobs. Schools have played a particularly important role in assimilating the disadvantaged, minorities, and successive waves of immigrants into Canadian society (Fass, 1989).

Schooling performs important latent or unintended functions, too. Schools encourage the development of a separate youth culture that often conflicts with parents' values (Coleman, 1961). At higher levels, educational institutions bring potential mates together, thus serving as a "marriage market." Schools perform a useful custodial service by keeping children under close surveillance for much of the day and freeing parents to work in the paid labour force. Universities and colleges, by keeping young people temporarily out of the full-time paid labour force, restrict job competition and support wage levels (Bowles and Gintis, 1976). Finally, because they can encourage critical, independent thinking, educational institutions sometimes become "schools of dissent" that challenge authoritarian regimes and promote social change (Brower, 1975; Freire, 1972).

## Reproducing Inequality

Many Canadians believe we enjoy equal access to basic schooling. They think schools identify and sort students based only on merit. They regard the educational system as an avenue of upward mobility. From this point of view, the best and the brightest are bound to succeed whatever their economic, ethnic, racial, linguistic, or religious background. The school system is the dream of a meritocracy—a system based solely on merit—in action.

Although some sociologists agree with this functionalist assessment, they are in a minority (Bell, 1973). Most sociologists find the conflict perspective on education more credible. In their view, the benefits of education are unequally distributed and tend to **reproduce the existing stratification system** (Jencks et al., 1972). We have already seen how schools help to reproduce the existing system of gender inequality (Chapter 9, Sexuality and Gender). Here we may add that they function similarly with respect to class. In

Schools encourage the development of a separate youth culture that often conflicts with parents' values.

other words, children from families at the bottom of the stratification system tend to get tracked into low- and middle-ability classes. When they finish school, they tend to wind up with jobs that keep them at the bottom of the stratification system. Meanwhile, children from families at the top of the stratification system tend to get tracked into middle- and high-ability classes. When they finish school, they tend to wind up with jobs that keep them at the top of the stratification system. Exceptions to this rule abound, but the basic pattern is clear.

Table 13.5 shows that young people from high-income families were 1.5 times more likely than those from low-income families to have been enrolled in a post-secondary institution in 1998 (71.0/48.8 = 1.5). Moreover, they were nearly 2.5 times more likely to have gone to university in 1998 (39.6/16.3 = 2.4). In other words, class determines whether one gets a post-secondary education in Canada, and it even more strongly determines whether one will get a university education.

Guppy and Davies (1998) analyzed 1994 Statistics Canada data on 25- to 34-year-old Canadians. Among those whose fathers were professionals or managers, about 60 percent attended university. The figure fell to 35 percent for those whose fathers were supervisory workers and to less than 30 percent for those whose fathers were skilled workers. Among those whose fathers were unskilled workers, fewer than 20 percent attended university. The figure was around 10 percent for those whose fathers were farmers. We conclude that class strongly influences whether one gets to study in university.

The sociological literature emphasizes three social mechanisms that operate within the school system to reproduce inequality:

- *The hidden curriculum.* In addition to academic and vocational subjects, students learn a **hidden curriculum** in school (Snyder, 1971; see also Chapter 4, Socialization). The hidden curriculum involves teaching obedience to authority and conformity to cultural norms. For example, from kindergarten to university, students are systematically taught to accept the curricula, routines, and grading systems imposed on them by teachers and professors. They are punished when they fail to do so (Gracey, 2001). Moreover, to the extent that a middle-class measuring rod is used to evaluate students, those from lower classes find themselves disadvantaged (Cohen, 1955). The middle-class measuring rod applies specific standards—fashionable attire, "proper" speech, deferred gratification, compliance—to judge competency in the student role. Those who do not meet this standard may be labelled "bad students."

  The hidden curriculum also influences the content of classroom lessons. For example, the development of the educational system in Ontario proceeded from the assumption that education would be an effective way to teach working-class children that their interests are identical to those of upper-class children. With memories of the failed Rebellion of 1837 in Upper Canada still fresh in his mind, the chief architect of the Ontario school system, Egerton Ryerson, set out to create a system in which young adults would be loyal to the Crown. As two sociologists note: "Ryerson's objective was social control, and he charged the schools with the responsibility of inculcating the beliefs and attitudes of mind that would accomplish it" (Curtis and Lambert, 1994: 12).

**✦ TABLE 13.5 ✦**
**Participation in Post-secondary Education and Family Income, 1998**

| Family Income | Bottom Quartile | Middle Half | Top Quartile |
|---|---|---|---|
| **Highest Level of Education in which Student Participated** | | | |
| College | 26.7 | 29.5 | 28.2 |
| University | 16.3 | 26.1 | 39.6 |
| All Post-secondary | 48.8 | 61.4 | 71.0 |

Source: Statistics Canada (2001a).

✦ *Testing and tracking.* Most schools in Canada are composed of children from various socio-economic, racial, and ethnic backgrounds. Testing and tracking maintain social inequality in these schools. IQ tests sort students, who are then channelled into high-ability ("enriched"), middle-ability, and low-ability ("special education") classrooms based on test scores. The result is often classrooms that are stratified by socio-economic status, race, and ethnicity, much like the larger society (Samueda et al., 1980).

For example, one study that examined the assessments made of the "academic potential" of 400 western Canadian students enrolled in an English-as-a-second-language program found that the tests used were frequently culturally biased. However, the psychologists who conducted the assessments were more likely to view the minority child as "deficient" rather than the tests that were used (Cummins, 1994). In addition, for more than a decade concern has been expressed over the streaming of black students in Ontario into low-level academic and vocational programs. According to research conducted by the Toronto Board of Education, while 1 in 5 black students was enrolled in a basic program, the comparable figures for white students was 1 in 10 and for Asians was 1 in 33 (Henry et al., 2000: 239).

Nobody denies that students vary in their abilities and that high-ability students require special challenges to reach their full potential. Nor does anyone deny that the underprivileged tend to score low on IQ tests. The controversial question is whether IQ is mainly genetic or social in origin. If IQ is genetic in origin, then it cannot be changed, so improving the quality of schooling for the underprivileged is arguably a waste of money (Herrnstein and Murray, 1994). If IQ is social in origin, IQ tests and tracking only reinforce social differences that could otherwise be reduced by changing the social circumstances of students.

Most sociologists think IQ is mainly a reflection of social standing, not genetic endowment (Fischer et al., 1996). They believe that members of underprivileged groups tend to score low on IQ tests because they do not have the training and the cultural background needed to score high. To support their argument, they point to cases where changing social circumstances resulted in changes in IQ scores. For instance, in the first decades of the twentieth century, most Jewish immigrants tested well below average on IQ tests. This was sometimes used as an argument against Jewish immigration (Gould, 1996 [1981]; Steinberg, 1989 [1981].) Today, most North American Jews test above average in IQ. Since the genetic makeup of Jews

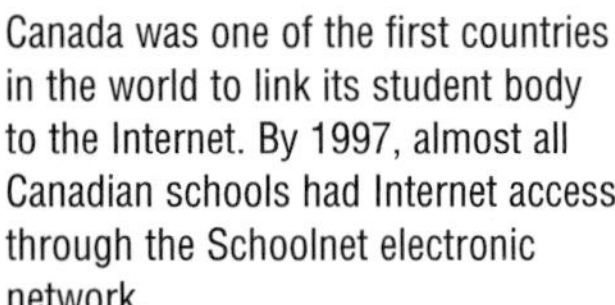
Canada was one of the first countries in the world to link its student body to the Internet. By 1997, almost all Canadian schools had Internet access through the Schoolnet electronic network.

has not changed in the past century, why the change in IQ scores? Sociologists point to upward mobility. During the twentieth century, most Jewish immigrants worked hard and moved up the stratification system. As their fortunes improved, they made sure their children had the skills and the cultural resources needed to do well in school. Average IQ scores rose as the social standing of Jews improved.

Here is an even more dramatic example of the effect of social circumstances on intelligence and school performance. In the United States, the 300 black and Latino students at the Hostos-Lincoln Academy of Science in the South Bronx were all written off as probable dropouts by their grade-eight counsellors. Yet most seniors in the school now take honours and university-level classes. Eighty percent of them go to university, well above the national U.S. average. The reason? The City of New York designated Hostos-Lincoln a special school in 1987. It is small, well equipped, attentive to individual students, and demanding. It stresses team teaching and a safe, family-like environment. Is Hostos-Lincoln an exception? No. A study of 820 high schools shows that where similar programs are introduced, students from grades 8 to 12 achieve 30 percent higher scores in math and 24 percent higher scores in reading compared to students in traditional schools (Hancock, 1994). Investing more in the education of the underprivileged can produce results (Schiff and Lewontin, 1986; see Box 13.2).

- *The self-fulfilling prophecy.* We noted in Chapter 4, Socialization, that a self-fulfilling prophecy is an expectation that helps cause what it predicts. In a classic study, Ray Rist (1970) revealed how a self-fulfilling prophecy influences one's educational chances. His participant observation research found that after merely eight days of observing students in a kindergarten classroom, the kindergarten teacher felt confident that she could assign the children to one of three tables. Students she designated "fast learners" were assigned to Table 1, closest to her own desk. Students she judged to be "slow learners" were assigned to Table 3, at the back of the class. Students she judged to be "average" were seated at Table 2, in the middle of the classroom. The students were not given any type of formal intelligence test, yet the teacher was confident she could distinguish bright, average, and slow students. On what basis did she make these distinctions? Probing the issue, Rist found that the key variable distinguishing the students was social class. Children at Table 1 were overwhelmingly middle class, while those assigned to Tables 2 and 3 were more likely to come from poorer homes. The assignment of these children was consequential because the children at Table 1 received more attention, were treated better, and, as the year progressed, came to see themselves as superior to the other children. In contrast, the other students, who tended to be ignored by the teacher and referred to by the Table 1 children as "dumb," did not fare well. The following year, the grade one teacher took notice of what the children had accomplished during kindergarten. Not surprisingly, the children who had been placed at Table 1 were assigned once again to places in the classroom that marked them as superior students.

  These findings suggest that, rather than valuing all students equally and treating them all as children with good prospects, teachers may suspect that disadvantaged and minority students are intellectually inferior. In turn, these students may come to feel rejected by teachers, other classmates, and the curriculum. Minority students may also be disadvantaged by overt racism and discrimination. In response, students presumed to be inferior and marginalized in the classroom often cluster together out of resentment and in defiance of authority. Some of them will eventually reject academic achievement as a goal. Discipline problems, ranging from apathy to disruptive and illegal behaviour, can result. Consistent with this argument, Aboriginal and black students in Canada have higher-than-average school dropout rates (Livingstone, 1999: 743; see also Toronto Board of Education, 1993). In contrast, research shows that challenging lower-class and minority students, giving them emotional support and encouragement, giving greater recognition in the curriculum to the accomplishments of the groups from which they originate, creating an environment

## BOX 13.2
## IT'S YOUR CHOICE

### IS SCHOOL ENOUGH?

Sociologists began to understand how little schools could do on their own to encourage upward mobility and end poverty in the 1960s, when sociologist James Coleman conducted a monumental study of academic performance and schools (Coleman et al., 1966). What he found was that differences in the quality of schools—measured by assessment of such factors as school facilities and curriculum—accounted at most for about a third of the variation in students' academic performance. At least two-thirds of the variation in academic performance was due to inequalities imposed on children by their homes, neighbourhoods, and peers. Three and a half decades later, little research contradicts Coleman's finding.

Various social commentators have argued that if we are to improve the success of disadvantaged students, we must develop policies that are aimed at improving the social environment of young, disadvantaged children *before* they enter the formal education system (Hertzman, 2000). Compensatory education programs for preschool children were largely developed in the United States and attempted to meet the needs of children who are socially and economically disadvantaged. In Canada, such programs have also been aimed at children with "special needs" and "at-risk" children—those who because of one or more factors in their background are believed to face a heightened risk of poor academic performance or social adjustment. Although the traditional focus of early childhood education has been on children's social and emotional development, at least some of these compensatory education programs focus on children's intellectual development.

Although noting that "[p]oor children are not always disadvantaged and disadvantaged children are not always poor" (Health Canada, 1999a: 73), the 1996–1997 National Longitudinal Survey of Children and Youth (NLSCY) found that household income was clearly associated with school; in fact, it was an important indicator of developmental maturity and future success at school (Doherty, 1997). In addition, as family income decreases, the likelihood that children will experience a host of other problems that will negatively influence their school performance increases. For example, poor health, hyperactivity, and delayed vocabulary development are all higher among children in low-income families than among children in middle- and higher-income families (Ross, 1998). Children who score low on school readiness are also more likely to have mothers with low levels of education and to be living in neighbourhoods that their mothers characterize as unsafe or as lacking in social cohesiveness (Health Canada, 1999a: 79).

It has been suggested that early developmental programs can decrease the chances of developmental problems in children and enhance their performance within schools. For example, Headstart programs are based on the belief that to assist children, the entire family must be helped. Evaluations of Headstart programs in Canada report such benefits as: "more students completing school and with better grades; fewer young people needing mental health services; fewer parents abusing alcohol with concurrent reductions of alcohol's impact on children; a reduction in family violence; [and] fewer students with preventable disabilities and reduced demand for medical services" (Government of Canada, 2001b). In Edmonton, for example, Headstart programs have existed for 25 years. These programs focus on preschool children ages three to five in low-income families, as well as the parents or other adults involved in raising these children. They are designed to respond to the needs of the community in which they are located. Among the forms of parental support provided are access to food banks, nutrition programs, literacy programs, parental support groups, and parenting courses. Promoting child readiness for school is also a key element of these programs.

Headstart programs have been identified as particularly important in increasing the educational success of Aboriginal students. Toward this end, the federal government announced in 1998 that it would provide permanent funding for the Aboriginal Headstart programs that already existed in Canada, as well as additional funds for the establishment of new Headstart programs on reserves. However, it is estimated that existing programs only reach about 5 percent of the Aboriginal children who could potentially benefit from their availability (George, 1998).

Admittedly, the costs of providing early childhood intervention programs are not insignificant. For example, in 1998 Health Canada spent approximately $22.5 million a year on Headstart programs that served approximately 4000 northern and urban Aboriginal children—merely 5 percent of those who required such programs. It was estimated that to reach its target audience would require spending 10 to 20 times that amount. However, the investments we make in the critical early years of a child's life not only benefit Canada's children but our economy as well. Indeed, one Canadian study reports that "every dollar spent in early intervention can save seven dollars in future expenditures in health and social spending" (Health Canada, 1999a: 88).

Do you believe that early childhood intervention programs would be useful in improving the educational success of children? If not, why not? If so, do you feel that attendance in these programs should be compulsory? Should parents who refuse to send their children to such programs be penalized for their decision? What background factors do you feel should be used to select children and their families for inclusion in such programs? It's your choice.

Although the composition of Canada's student population is becoming increasingly multicultural, this is less true of Canada's teachers. An ongoing debate in Canada is whether students, at all levels, would be better served by a faculty whose composition reflects the diversity of our population and who offer a more inclusive curriculum.

in which they can relax and achieve—all these strategies explode the self-fulfilling prophecy and improve academic performance (Steele, 1992).

In sum, schools reproduce the stratification system because of the hidden curriculum, IQ testing and tracking, and the self-fulfilling prophecy that disadvantaged and minority students are bound to do poorly. These social mechanisms increase the chance that those who are socially marginal and already disadvantaged will in fact earn low grades and wind up with jobs closer to the bottom than the top of the occupational structure.

## School Standards

When many students perform poorly in school, you can expect people to start complaining about low educational standards. And, in fact, many Canadians believe that the public school system has turned soft if not rotten. They argue that the youth of Japan and South Korea spend long hours concentrating on the basics of math, science, and language. Meanwhile, Canadian students spend fewer hours in school and study more nonbasic subjects that are of little practical value. From this point of view, art classes, drama programs, attention to athletics, and sensitivity to cultural diversity in the Canadian school curriculum are harmful distractions. If students do not spend more school time on subjects that "really" matter, the Canada can expect to suffer declining economic competitiveness in the twenty-first century.

Worrisome evidence apparently proving the inferiority of the Canadian school system appeared throughout the 1990s. One study of the math, science, and literacy scores of students in 30 countries showed that Canadian students hover near the middle, well behind students in such countries as the Netherlands and South Korea. In response, many Canadians began to clamour for the administration of provincewide standardized tests for both students and teachers. Such tests, it was argued, would allow school performance to be independently and objectively assessed. A May 2000 poll reported that more than 8 in 10 people support provincewide tests for students. A similar proportion believed that high-school students should be required to pass a compulsory literacy test and standardized provincewide knowledge test prior to graduation (Bricker and Greenspon, 2001: 165–6).

Some analysts emphasize that the results of international tests such as the one conducted in the 1990s are misleading (Barlow and Robertson, 1994; Bracey, 1998; Schrag, 1997). In the first place, most of the countries that participated in the study did not follow sampling guidelines. For political reasons, many of them excluded groups of students whom

Many Canadians believe that the public school system has turned soft if not rotten. They argue that the youth of Japan and South Korea spend long hours concentrating on the basics of math, science, and language. Meanwhile, Canadian students spend fewer hours in school and study more nonbasic subjects that are of little practical value. As the text shows, the reality is more complex than this simple characterization.

educational administrators thought would do poorly on the exam. These countries artificially inflated their scores. Second, different countries have different kinds of secondary school systems. For instance, some keep students in school for 14 years, while others, such as Canada, have 12-year systems (13 years in Ontario until 2001). Moreover, some countries have higher dropout rates than Canada has and siphon off poor academic performers to trades schools and job-training programs before they graduate high school. This leaves only the top academic performers in the last year of high school. In contrast, Canada tries to ensure that as many students as possible graduate high school since this enhances the quality of democracy, increases social cohesion in a culturally diverse society, and may improve economic performance. In short, international comparisons are often misleading.

Despite the limitations of international comparisons, many Canadians felt buoyed when the results of the most recent international tests in reading, math, and science were released in 2001. Among 32 countries, Canada ranked second overall in reading and fifth in math and science. When provincial results were analyzed separately, students in Alberta, Quebec, and British Columbia ranked among the best in the world. Indeed, Alberta students obtained the highest scores in the world in reading and placed third in both science and math. Quebec came second in math with scores that almost rivalled those obtained by students in Japan and placed fourth in reading and science. Other provinces, however, most notably those in the Atlantic region, did not fare as well (Sokolof, 2001).

Various social commentators claimed that Alberta's success stemmed from a provincial formula of frequent testing, standardized curriculum, financial support for disadvantaged schools and high expectations conveyed to students by teachers and parents. On a national scale, Canada's improved performance was seen to signify the narrowing of the achievement gap between poor and well-off students. Canada, it was noted, was one of six countries (the others being Finland, Iceland, Japan, Korea, and Sweden) singled out as providing good education to students from all socio-economic classes. At the same time, it would be premature to think that we can now rest on our laurels.

The 2001 international study also found that, throughout the world, students from wealthier backgrounds outperform students from poorer families. Family structure also contributes to student performance. Students from two-parent families fare better than those from single-parent families in half the countries surveyed. Although students at private schools outscored their public school counterparts in every province in Canada and every country examined, it is the socio-economic status of those who attend private schools rather than the type of school that seems responsible for the performance difference. Compared with students in the public system, students attending private schools in Canada are more likely to have parents with higher education and income. Predictably, students with such parents also perform well in the public system (Sokoloff, 2001).

## Dealing with the Public School Crisis

Despite the results of the international studies cited above, it would not be an exaggeration to claim that Canada's public schools are in crisis. Hundreds of millions of dollars have been removed from provincial education budgets since the early 1990s. As a result, schools are closing and "non-core" programs in art, music, drama, physical education, and special education are being cut. Parents are being asked to dig deeper into their pockets to pay for more books and supplies. Many teachers and staff members are required to work longer hours for salaries that do not keep pace with inflation. Demoralization results. More teachers and staff members are going on strike more often, while fewer young people are being attracted to the teaching profession. In 2001, Statistics Canada estimated that we suffered a shortfall of 20 000 teachers nationwide. To avoid these problems, an increasingly large number of parents who can afford it (now about 5 percent of Canadians with school-age children) are sending their children to private schools, where tuition fees can range as high as $32 000 a year (Schofield, 2001; see Chapter 11, Politics). Meanwhile, at the post-secondary level, tuition fees are increasing annually, making it more difficult for working-class and even middle-class families to send their adolescent children to college or university.

Although Canadians strongly believe that education is important, we are increasingly likely to raise questions about its role and central components. Recent surveys suggest that we have only a moderate level of confidence in the job being done by the public education sector.

Budget cuts are not the only change the Canadian school system has experienced since the early 1990s. In addition, provincial governments, particularly in Ontario, have centralized control of schools by imposing standardized testing and new curricula while reducing the power of school boards. Their stated aim is to do more with less, to improve school standards while removing resources from the educational system. In theory, this helps provincial governments balance their budgets and borrow less money while taxpayers can enjoy tax cuts. All of this presumably stimulates economic growth.

Nobody can reasonably object to the goals of stimulating economic growth and improving school standards. However, the way in which provincial governments have gone about the task of achieving these goals cuts two ways. For one thing, taking money out of the school system decreases the number of jobs available for principals, teachers, and support staff while keeping a lid on the purchasing power of the people who remain employed in the education sector. This decreases demand for goods and services and thus puts a damper on economic growth. In addition, taking money out of the school system increases educational inequality by robbing children from poor and modest economic backgrounds of growth opportunities. With fewer teachers, impoverished curricula, and increasing costs being shouldered by families rather than the state, the prospects of children from lower socio-economic strata have not looked so dim since the Second World War. As we have seen, the Canadian educational system has generally acted to reproduce the country's stratification system. Since the early 1990s, however, it has acted to help *increase* the degree of social stratification in Canadian society (Johnston, 2002).

Canadians can ponder two models of educational reform as they consider what to do with their public school system. One model is American. The other comes from the UK.

In the United States, two decades of cutbacks in public education have created a school system in which a third of the schools are merely "okay" and another third are in "terrible shape" (Bracey, 1998). The great majority of mediocre and bad schools are in the cores of big cities, which are disproportionately populated by racial minorities. In New York, 20 percent of schools are in need of immediate major repairs. Leaky ceilings, broken lights, and crumbling walls are common (Tornquist, 1998). On an average day in Chicago, teachers are unavailable for 57 000 downtown students. Many schools lack adequate furniture and books. Meanwhile, in an upper-middle-class Chicago suburb, spending per pupil is 78 percent higher than in downtown. Schools offer college-level courses and boast the latest audiovisual, computer, photographic, and sporting equipment (Kozol, 1991). A third of the schools in the United States are "world class," but only the well-to-do can attend most of them (Bracey, 1998). The American model, then, drains resources from the public school system, creating excellence for the few and mediocrity and demoralization for the majority.

The UK has taken a diametrically opposed approach since 1997. Education spending is on the increase, rising 8 percent in real terms in 2001 alone. Some 23 million new books have been purchased for the school system. Professional development is strongly emphasized. For example, nearly all of England's elementary teachers have been retrained so they can teach reading, writing, and math more effectively. A new National College for School Leadership has been created to develop top principals. Standardized testing has become more widespread so educators can pinpoint areas of weakness and improve them. Teachers' salaries are linked to performance. The results of these initiatives are already impressive. In 1997, 56 percent of 11-year-olds scored in the top two levels of the national

Concern with the quality of education has led to a boom in private tutoring schools. Leaders of supplemental education in Canada, Oxford Learning Centres®, were established 22 years ago in London, Ontario. There are now 65 centres in Canada and the United States.

literacy test. By 2001, the figure stood at 75 percent. Similar improvements have been registered in math. Areas of the country that in 1997 were below the national average in literacy and numeracy are now above the national average (Schofield, 2001).

Recent British educational reforms do not involve simply throwing more money at the school system. Rather, they involve establishing nationwide standards and then providing the resources necessary to meet those standards by creating "meaningful learning communities." The British reforms are based on the ideas of Michael Fullan, who is well known throughout much of the world, but not in Canada, as an educational reformer—which is ironic since Fullan is dean of the Ontario Institute for Studies in Education (OISE) at the University of Toronto (Fullan, 2001 [1982]; Hammonds, 2002).

In Fullan's use of the term, a *meaningful learning community* is a social setting in which all participants engage in education because it brings them substantial moral benefits. Students learn well when they feel they are actively engaged in achieving mastery of subjects that are relevant to their lives. Their opinions, needs, and backgrounds must therefore be taken into account in formulating curricula. Teachers teach well when they feel they are making a positive difference in the lives of their students. They require autonomy, resources, the support of their colleagues, and ongoing training or "professional development" to do so. Principals lead well when they feel they are creating a new school culture that facilitates beneficial social change. To achieve this they must forge consensus, encourage professional collaboration, ensure that top-quality instructional tools are readily available, and set expectations for students and teachers that are high, clear, and consistent. All of this is a recipe for excellence based on high standards gauged by nationwide testing. As Fullan notes, "student achievement increases substantially in schools with collaborative work cultures that foster a professional learning community among teachers and others, focus continuously on improving instructional practices in light of student performance data, and link to external standards and staff development support" (Fullan, 1998).

Admittedly, most Canadians are in no mood to pay higher taxes in the short term. But we need to consider the long term, too. In a world in which economic growth depends increasingly on the availability of a flexible, highly skilled, and well-educated labour force, do we want to provide most of our students with an inferior education? Do we want to live in a society whose educational system is a mechanism for increasing the distance between the affluent and the less well-to-do? In thinking about how we should deal with the public school crisis, these are surely questions worth pondering.

Some parents are choosing not to send their children to school at all but to teach them at home.

## SUMMARY

1. Durkheim argued that the main function of religion is to increase social cohesion by providing ritualized opportunities for people to experience the collective conscience.
2. Critics of Durkheim note that he ignored the ways in which religion can incite social conflict and reinforce social inequality.
3. Weber argued that religion acts like railroad switches, determining the tracks along which history will be pushed by the force of political and economic interest. Protestantism, for example, invigorated capitalist development.
4. Critics of Weber note that the correlation between economic development and the predominance of Protestantism is not as strong as Weber thought. They also note that some of Weber's followers offer one-sided explanations of the role of religion in economic development, which Weber warned against.
5. The secularization thesis holds that religious institutions, actions, and consciousness are on the decline worldwide.
6. Critics of the secularization thesis point out that there has been a worldwide religious revival over the past 30 years or so. They also note that survey evidence shows that religion in Canada is not in an advanced state of decay.
7. The revised secularization thesis recognizes the religious revival and the resilience of religion but still maintains that the scope of religious authority has declined over time. The revisionists say that religion is more and more restricted to the realm of the spiritual; it governs fewer aspects of people's lives and is more a matter of personal choice than it used to be.
8. Frequency of attending religious services is determined by opportunity (how much time people have available for attending), need (whether people are in a social position that increases their desire for spiritual answers to life's problems), and learning (whether people were brought up in a religious household).
9. Secular schools have substantially replaced the church and religious schools as educational institutions. Today, the educational system is second in importance only to the family as an agent of socialization.
10. The rise of mass schooling was stimulated by the Protestant Reformation (which demanded that people have more direct contact with the word of God), the spread of democracy (which involved people demanding access to previously restricted centres of learning), and industrialization (which required literate and numerate workers).
11. Credential inflation has taken place partly because of increased professionalization.
12. The educational system often creates social cohesion.
13. The educational system also reinforces existing class, racial, and ethnic inequalities. It reproduces the stratification system by means of the hidden curriculum, intelligence testing and tracking of students, and the operation of the self-fulfilling prophecy that poor and minority students will do poorly.
14. Although schools are supposed to provide all Canadian children with the academic and social foundations necessary to participate in society in a meaningful and productive way, some students do not enjoy the benefits as well as others.
15. Various suggestions have been made as to how we might improve our schools. These include a heightened emphasis on the human side of education and increasing the range of choices available to parents. A second type of solution involves substantially improving the social environment of young, disadvantaged children before and outside school.

## GLOSSARY

**Charismatic** leaders are men and women who claim to be inspired by supernatural powers and whose followers believe them to be so inspired.

A **church** is a bureaucratic religious organization that has accommodated itself to mainstream society and culture.

A **civil religion** is a set of quasi-religious beliefs and practices that bind a population together and justify its way of life.

The **collective conscience** is composed of the common sentiments and values that people share as a result of living together.

**Credential inflation** refers to the fact that it takes ever more certificates and diplomas to qualify for a given job.

**Cults** are small groups of people deeply committed to a religious vision that rejects mainstream culture and society.

**Denominations** are the various streams of belief and practice that some churches allow to coexist under their overarching authority.

**Ecclesia** are state-supported churches.

**Educational achievement** refers to how much students actually learn.

**Educational attainment** refers to the number of years of school students complete.

**Fundamentalists** interpret their scriptures literally, seek to establish a direct, personal relationship with the higher being(s) they worship, and are relatively intolerant of nonfundamentalists.

The **hidden curriculum** refers to the unwritten goals that education serves, such as teaching obedience to authority and conformity to cultural norms.

The **profane** refers to the secular, everyday world.

**Professionalization** takes place when members of an occupation insist that people earn certain credentials to enter the occupation. Professionalization ensures standards and keeps professional earnings high.

**Religiosity** refers to how important religion is to people.

The **reproduction of stratification by the school system** involves schools stratifying students so that they tend to wind up in roughly the same position in the class structure as their parents.

The **revised secularization thesis** holds that worldly institutions break off from the institution of religion over time. As a result, religion governs an ever-smaller part of most people's lives and has become largely a matter of personal choice.

**Rituals** are public practices designed to connect people to the sacred.

The **sacred** refers to the religious, transcendent world.

**Sects** usually form by breaking away from churches due to disagreement about church doctrine. Sects are less integrated into society and less bureaucratized than churches. They are often led by charismatic leaders, who tend to be relatively intolerant of religious opinions other than their own.

The **secularization thesis** says that religious institutions, actions, and consciousness are on the decline worldwide.

**Totems** are objects that symbolize the sacred.

# QUESTIONS TO CONSIDER

1. Does the sociological study of religion undermine one's religious faith, make one's religious faith stronger, or have no necessary implications for one's religious faith? On what do you base your opinion? What does your opinion imply about the connection between religion and science in general?
2. Students who drop out of school are often faulted for their lack of motivation. How might a student's decision to leave school be explained as a failure of the educational system rather than as a problem of motivation?
3. How would you try to solve the problem of unequal access to education? What do you think of the solutions to the education crisis discussed at the end of this chapter? Do you have some suggestions of your own?

# WEB RESOURCES

## Companion Web Site for This Book

http://www.brymsociologycompass.nelson.com

Begin by clicking on the Student Resources section of the Web site. Next, select the chapter you are currently studying from the pull-down menu. From the Student Resources page you will have easy access to InfoTrac College Edition®, MicroCase online exercises, and additional Web links. The Web site also has many useful tips to aid you in your study of sociology, including practice tests for each chapter.

## InfoTrac Search Terms

These search terms are provided to assist you in beginning to conduct research on this topic by visiting http://www.infotrac-college.com

**Cult**
**Educational achievement**
**Educational attainment**
**Fundamentalism**
**Secularization**

## Recommended Web Sites

The Canadian Education Association maintains a Web site at http://www.acea.ca.

The Canadian Federation of Students represents more than 450 000 students at colleges and universities across Canada through a cooperative alliance of more than 60 students' unions. This site is particularly helpful for those seeking information on issues that affect post-secondary students in Canada. Visit the Web site at http://www.cfs-fcee.ca.

Ontario Consultants on Religious Tolerance is an excellent Web site that provides basic, unbiased information on dozens of religions, religious tolerance and intolerance, religion and science, abortion and religion, and so forth. Visit the site at http://www.religioustolerance.org/.

Information on the SchoolNet eletronic network can be obtained at http://www.schoolnet.ca.

## SUGGESTED READINGS

Reginald W. Bibby. *Canada's Teens: Today, Yesterday and Tomorrow* (Toronto: Stoddart, 2001). One of Canada's most renowned sociologists of religion, Bibby has conducted nationwide surveys of Canadians from 1975 to 2000. Among the topics addressed are the religious and spiritual beliefs and practices of teenage and adult Canadians.

D. W. Livingstone. *The Education-Jobs Gap: Underemployment or Economic Democracy* (Toronto: Garamond Press, 1999). An important work that addresses the growing disjunction between education and pay in advanced industrial societies.

Neil Tudiver. *Universities for Sale: Resisting Corporate Control over Canadian Higher Education* (Toronto: James Lorimer and Company Ltd., 1999). Suggests that, if unchecked, corporations and economic expediency will erode scholarly independence and academic freedom.

Max Weber. *The Protestant Ethic and the Spirit of Capitalism* (New York: Scribner, 1958 [1904–5]). A classic—one of the most important works in the sociology of religion.

David Yamane. "Secularization on Trial: In Defense of a Neo-secularization Paradigm." *Journal for the Scientific Study of Religion* 36 (1997), pp. 109–22. A lively analysis of critiques of the secularization thesis and a convincing reformulation of the thesis.

## NOTE

1. Bellah's analysis is based in the United States, where civil religion is stronger than it is in Canada.

## IN THIS CHAPTER, YOU WILL LEARN THAT

- Movies, television, and other mass media sometimes blur the distinction between reality and fantasy.
- The mass media are products of the nineteenth and especially the twentieth centuries.
- Historically, the growth of the mass media is rooted in the rise of Protestantism, democracy, and capitalism.
- The mass media make society more cohesive.
- The mass media foster social inequality.
- Although the mass media are influential, audiences filter, interpret, resist, and even reject media messages if they are inconsistent with their beliefs and experiences.
- The interaction between producers and consumers of media messages is most evident on the new media frontier formed by the Internet, television, and other mass media.

CHAPTER

14

# THE MASS MEDIA

## THE SIGNIFICANCE OF THE MASS MEDIA

### Illusion Becomes Reality

The turn of the twenty-first century was thick with movies about the blurred line separating reality from fantasy. *The Truman Show* (1998) gave us Jim Carrey as an insurance sales agent who discovers that everyone in his life is an actor. He is the unwitting subject of a television program that airs 24 hours a day (see Box 14.1). In *The Matrix* (1999), Keanu Reeves finds that his identity and his life are illusions. Like everyone else in the world, Reeves is hard-wired to a giant computer that uses humans as an energy source. The computer supplies people with nutrients to keep them alive and simulated realities to keep them happy. Similar blurring between reality and media-generated illusion is evident in *Pleasantville* (1998), *EdTV* (1999), and *Nurse Betty* (2000).

The most disturbing movie in this genre is *American Psycho* (2000). Based on a novel that was banned in some parts of North America when it was first published in 1991, the movie is the story of Patrick Bateman, Wall Street yuppie by day, cold and meticulous serial killer by night. Unfortunately, the public outcry over the horrifying murder scenes virtually drowned out the book's important sociological point. *American Psycho* is really about how people become victims of the mass media and consumerism. Bateman, the

BOX 14.1
SOCIOLOGY AT THE MOVIES

#### *THE TRUMAN SHOW* (1998)

Whenever Truman tries to leave his hometown, something happens to prevent his departure. When he is about to board a boat, he becomes afraid of the water. When he drives down the freeway, the police turn him back on some pretext or another. Although he is a middle-aged, married man, he has never stepped outside of his hometown.

*The Truman Show* presents the life of Truman, played by Canadian actor Jim Carrey. Truman turns out to be the main character in a television show. He doesn't know it, but since birth his life has been televised in the world's longest-running soap opera. Unlike most soap operas, however, Truman's life is on television 24 hours a day, 365 days a year. He lives in a town created by the television producers. Actresses and actors play all the people in his life—including his wife. A young woman who once had a bit part in the show becomes an activist to free Truman. She even appears on the show to tell Truman the awful truth. Eventually, Truman manages to enter a new life by walking off the vast television set that had been his world until then.

*The Truman Show* suggests that the mass media are so powerful they have collapsed the distinction between illusion and reality. Until he escapes, Truman's reality is the creation of the television producers. His life is synonymous with his television show. Does *The Truman Show* overstate the power and influence of the mass media? Is it really the case that some people have trouble distinguishing fact from fiction, media representations from real-life events? In answering this question, you might research the 1999 Columbine high-school shootings on the World Wide Web to find out how well the teenagers who killed 13 of their fellow students were able to distinguish between reality and media-generated fantasy.

*The Truman Show,* starring Jim Carrey

To the degree the mass media shape our reality, is it possible to walk off the set, as Truman did? If so, how? Do people even want to walk off the set? In 2000, more than 11 000 cameras were connected to the World Wide Web—many of them in college dorms, apartments, and frat houses—and "reality TV," spearheaded by programs such as *Survivor* and *Big Brother,* was TV's hottest genre. Have the people who have connected cameras to their Web sites and starred on shows like *Survivor* and *Big Brother* become so many willing Trumans?

Many recent films—including *Nurse Betty,* starring Renée Zellweger and Morgan Freeman—suggest that the line between reality and media-generated illusion is becoming blurred.

serial murderer, says he is "used to imagining everything happening the way it occurs in movies." When he kisses his lover, he experiences "the 70 mm image of her lips parting and the subsequent murmur of 'I want you' in Dolby sound" (Ellis, 1991: 265). In Bateman's mind, his 14 murder victims are mere props in a movie in which he is the star. He feels no more empathy for them than an actor would for any other stage object. The mass media have so completely emptied him of genuine emotion he even has trouble remembering his victims' names. At the same time, however, the mass media have so successfully infused him with consumer values he can describe his victims' apparel in great detail—styles, brand names, stores where they bought their clothes, even prices. Thus, in *American Psycho,* killer and killed are both victims of consumerism and the mass media.

In different ways, these movies suggest that the fantasy worlds created by the mass media are increasingly the only realities we know, and they are every bit as pervasive and influential as religion was 500 or 600 years ago. Do you think this is an exaggeration dreamed up by filmmakers and novelists? If so, consider that the average Canadian spends more than three hours a day watching television, three hours listening to the radio, just under an hour reading magazines and books, and more than an hour reading newspapers (Moscovitch, 1998). Add to this the unknown number of hours Canadians spend going to the movies, using the Internet, listening to CDs, and playing video games, and it is clear that we spend close to 40 percent of our time interacting with the mass media: more than we do sleeping, working, or going to school. You might want to keep a tally of your activities for a couple of days to find out how you fit into this pattern of activity. Ask yourself, too, what you get out of your interactions with the mass media. Where do you get your ideas about how to dress, how to style your hair, and what music to listen to? Where do your hopes, aspirations, and dreams come from? If you're like most people, much of your reality is media generated. Canadian media guru Marshall McLuhan, who coined the term *global village* in the early 1960s, said the media are extensions of the human body and mind (McLuhan, 1964). Forty years later, it is perhaps equally valid to claim that the human body and mind are extensions of the mass media (Baudrillard, 1983, 1988; Bourdieu, 1998 [1996]).

The term **mass media** refers to print, radio, television, and other communication technologies. Often, *mass media* and *mass communication* are used interchangeably to refer to the transmission of information from one person or group to another. The word *mass* implies that the media reach many people. The word *media* signifies that communication does not take place directly through face-to-face interaction. Instead, technology intervenes or mediates in transmitting messages from senders to receivers. Furthermore, communication via the mass media is usually one-way, or at least one-sided. There are few senders (or producers) and many receivers (or audience members). Thus, most newspapers print a few readers' letters in each edition, but journalists and advertisers write virtually everything else. Ordinary people may appear on the Mike Bullard or Oprah Winfrey shows, enjoy play-along features on *Who Wants to Be a Millionaire?* and even delight in a slice of fame on *Survivor* or *Big Brother.* However, producers choose the guests and create the program content for these programs. Similarly, a handful of people may visit your personal Web site, but Yahoo.com boasts more than 200 million hits per day (Mosquera, 1999).

Usually, then, members of the audience cannot exert much influence on the mass media. They can only choose to tune in or tune out. And even tuning out is difficult because it excludes one from the styles, news, gossip, and entertainment most people depend on to grease the wheels of social interaction. Few people want to be cultural misfits. However, this does not mean that people are always passive consumers of the mass media. As noted below, we filter, interpret, and resist what we see and hear if it contradicts our experiences and beliefs. Even so, in the interaction between audiences and media sources, the media sources usually dominate.

To fully appreciate the impact of the mass media on life today, we need to trace their historical development. That is the first task we set ourselves below. We then critically review theories of the mass media's effects on social life. As you will see, each of these theories contributes to our appreciation of media effects. Finally, we assess developments on the media frontier formed by the Internet, television, and other mass media. We show that, to a degree, the new media frontier blurs the distinction between producer and consumer and has the potential to make the mass media somewhat more democratic for those who can afford access.

## The Rise of the Mass Media

John Lie once mentioned to his 11-year-old stepdaughter Jessie that when he grew up in Tokyo in the 1960s, not every household had a telephone. As someone who takes it for granted that she can pick up her brother's cellphone pretty much whenever she wants to call friends in California, Jessie was genuinely shocked. "How could you talk to your friends?" she asked.

"Well," John answered, "if a family was lucky enough to have a phone, it would be used not just by family members but by a whole network of relatives, friends, and neighbours. If you needed to call someone without a phone in his or her house, you had to call that person's closest neighbour who had a phone. The neighbour would then fetch the person you wanted to talk to. Some families even kept a little bowl next to their phone so nonfamily members could drop coins in to pay for their calls."

"Okay," said Jessie, "but that was in Japan. Here things were different, right?"

"They were different," replied John, "but in 1960 the United States was not all that far ahead of Japan in the use of telephones. One of my older colleagues told me that when he grew up in the United States in the 1940s, his parents had to make an appointment with the operator to phone long distance. Long-distance calls were so expensive, they used to time their calls to make sure they didn't exceed the standard three-minute rate."

Jessie shook her head, seeming to wonder whether people were still getting around by horse and buggy when John and his colleague were children.

"What seems quaint is largely a matter of perspective," concludes John. "I didn't find the scarcity of telephones strange when I was growing up. I did, however, find it shocking that television broadcast signals could not reach my grandparents in rural South Korea."

Similarly, it may be difficult for you to imagine a world without the mass media. Yet, as Table 14.1 shows, most of the mass media are recent inventions. The first developed systems of writing appeared only about 5500 years ago in Egypt and Mesopotamia (now southern Iraq). The print media became truly mass phenomena only in the nineteenth century. The inexpensive daily newspaper, costing a penny, first appeared in the United States in the 1830s. At that time, long-distance communication required physical transportation. To spread the news, you needed a horse, a railroad, or a ship. The slow speed of communication was costly. For instance, the last military engagement between Britain and the United States in the War of 1812–14 was the Battle of New Orleans. It took place 15 days

**✦ TABLE 14.1 ✦**
**The Development of the Mass Media**

| Year (CE) | Media Development |
|---|---|
| Circa 100 | Papermaking developed in China |
| Circa 1000 | Movable clay type used in China |
| Circa 1400 | Movable metal type developed in Korea |
| 1450 | Movable metal type used in Germany, leading to the Gutenberg Bible |
| 1702 | First daily newspaper, London's *Daily Courant* |
| 1833 | First mass-circulation newspaper, *New York Sun* |
| 1837 | Louis Daguerre invents a practical method of photography in France |
| 1844 | Samuel Morse sends the first telegraph message between Washington and Baltimore |
| 1875 | Alexander Graham Bell sends the first telephone message |
| 1877 | Thomas Edison develops the first phonograph |
| 1895 | Motion pictures are invented |
| 1901 | Italian inventor Guglielmo Marconi transmits the first transatlantic wireless message from England to Newfoundland |
| 1906 | First radio voice transmission |
| 1920 | First regularly scheduled radio broadcast, Pittsburgh |
| 1921 | First commercial TV broadcast |
| 1922 | Long-playing records (LPs) introduced |
| 1939 | Network TV begins in the United States |
| 1952 | VCR is invented |
| 1961 | First cable television, San Diego |
| 1969 | First four nodes of the United States Defense Department's ARPANET (precursor of the Internet) set up at Stanford University, UCLA, UC Santa Barbara, and the University of Utah |
| 1975 | First microcomputer marketed |
| 1983 | Cellphone invented |
| 1989 | World Wide Web conceived by Tim Berners-Lee at the European Laboratory for Particle Physics in Switzerland |

Sources: Berners-Lee (1999); Croteau and Hoynes (1997: 9–10); "The Silent Boom" (1998).

The newspaper was the dominant mass medium even as late as 1950.

One of the most famous photographs in Canadian history is the driving of the last spike of the Canadian Pacific Railway (CPR) on November 7, 1885, at Craigallachie, British Columbia. The man holding the hammer is Donald Smith, who financed much of the construction of the CPR. The taller man standing behind him to his right in the stovepipe hat is Sir Sandford Fleming, the mastermind behind standard time. The railroads spearheaded the introduction of standard time, which could be coordinated thanks to the introduction of the telegraph.

*after* a peace treaty was signed. The good news did not reach the troops near the mouth of the Mississippi until they had suffered 2100 casualties, including 320 dead.

The newspaper was the dominant mass medium even as late as 1950 (Smith, 1980; Schudson, 1991). However, change was in the air as early as 1844, when Samuel Morse sent the first telegraphic signal (Pred, 1973). From that time on, long-distance communication no longer required physical transportation. The transformative power of the new medium was soon evident. For example, until 1883, hundreds of local time zones existed in North America. The correct time was determined by local solar time and was typically maintained by a clock in a church steeple or a respected jeweller's shop window. Virtually instant communication by telegraph made it possible to coordinate time and establish just six time zones in Canada. Railroad companies spearheaded the move to standardize time. A Canadian civil and railway engineer, Sir Sandford Fleming, was the driving force behind the adoption of standard time in North America and worldwide (Blaise, 2001). The telegraph thus gave new meaning to the old expression "times change."

Most of the electronic media are creatures of the twentieth century. The first television signal was transmitted in 1928 and the first television broadcast in Canada took place in Montreal just three years later. The U.S. Department of Defense established ARPANET in 1969. It was designed as a system of communication between computers that would automatically find alternate transmission routes if one or more nodes in the network broke down because of, say, nuclear attack. ARPANET begat the Internet, which in turn begat the hyperlinked system of texts, images, and sounds known as the World Wide Web around 1991. By March 2002, an estimated 560 million people worldwide had access to the Web (Global Internet Statistics, 2002). It was a quick trip—a mere 140 years separate the Pony Express from the home video conference.

## Causes of Media Growth

The rise of the mass media can be explained by three main factors: one religious, one political, and one economic:

1. *The Protestant Reformation.* In the sixteenth century, Catholic people relied on priests to tell them what was in the Bible. In 1517, however, Martin Luther protested certain practices of the Church. Among other things, he wanted people to develop a more personal relationship with the Bible. Within 40 years, Luther's new form of Christianity, known as Protestantism, was established in half of Europe. Suddenly, millions of people were being encouraged to read. The Bible became the first mass media product in the West and by far the best-selling book.

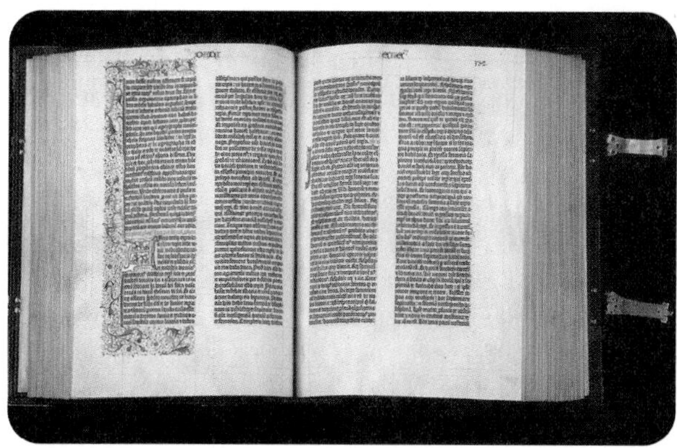
The Gutenberg Bible

Technological improvements in papermaking and printing made the diffusion of the Bible and other books possible (Febvre and Martin, 1976 [1958]). The most significant landmark was Johannes Gutenberg's invention of the printing press. In the 50 years after Gutenberg produced his monumental Bible in 1455, more books were produced than in the previous 1000 years. The printed book enabled the widespread diffusion and exchange of ideas. It contributed to the Renaissance (a scholarly and artistic revival that began in Italy around 1300 and spread to all of Europe by 1600) and to the rise of modern science (Johns, 1998).

A remarkable feature of the book is its durability. Many electronic storage media became obsolete just a few years after being introduced. For instance, eight-track tapes are icons of the 1970s and 5.25-inch floppy disks are icons of the early 1980s. They are barely remembered today. In contrast, books are still being published today, nearly 550 years after Gutenberg published his Bible. Approximately 10 000 books are published in Canada each year (Association of Canadian Publishers, 2002).

2. *Democratic movements.* A second force that promoted the growth of the mass media was political democracy. From the eighteenth century on, the citizens of France, the United States, and other countries demanded and achieved representation in government. At the same time, they wanted to become literate and gain access to previously restricted centres of learning. Democratic governments, in turn, depended on an informed citizenry and therefore encouraged popular literacy and the growth of a free press (Habermas, 1989).

Canadians now spend nearly 40 percent of their time interacting with the mass media.

Today, the mass media, and especially TV, mould our entire outlook on politics. TV's influence first became evident in the 1960 U.S. presidential election. That was the year of the first televised presidential debate—between John F. Kennedy and Richard Nixon. One of the four reporters who asked questions during the debate later recalled: "The people who watched the debate on their television sets apparently thought Kennedy came off better than Nixon. Those who heard the debate on radio thought Nixon was superior to Kennedy" (quoted in "The Candidates Debate," 1998). Kennedy smiled. Nixon perspired. Kennedy relaxed. Nixon fidgeted. The election was close, and most analysts believe that Kennedy got the edge simply because 70 million viewers thought he looked better on TV. Television was thus beginning to redefine the very nature of politics.

Soon, Canadian politicians were hiring "image consultants." Usually their advice led to the desired results. Sometimes, however, copying American media techniques could backfire. For instance, in recent decades Americans have often used "negative advertising" to trash political opponents, frequently on personal grounds. The Progressive Conservative Party of Canada briefly adopted this approach in the 1993 federal election campaign. They released two ads in English Canada that drew attention to Jean Chrétien's facial paralysis. The ads enraged many Canadians, who thought them grossly unfair. Support for the Conservative Party dropped sharply. Widely expected to win between 25 and 60 seats in the election, the PCs wound up with just 2 seats, partly because of the negative ads (Romanow et al., 1999).

The 1993 anti-Chrétien ads and the 1960 Kennedy–Nixon debate suggest that television has oversimplified politics. Some analysts say that politics has been reduced to a series of more or less well-managed images, catchy slogans, and ever-shorter uninterrupted comments or "sound bites." (In the United States, the average sound bite on nightly network news shrank from 42.3 seconds in 1968 to 8.4 seconds in 1992. The average sound bite on CBC News concerning the 1997 Canadian federal election was 8.2 seconds. On CTV News, the average was 7.1 seconds (Steward, 1999; Thelen, 1996). From this point of view, candidates are marketed for high office like Kellogg's sells breakfast cereal, and a politician's stage presence is more important than his or her policies in determining success at the polls.

3. *Capitalist industrialization.* The third major force that stimulated the growth of the mass media was capitalist industrialization. Modern industries required a literate and numerate workforce. They also needed rapid means of communication to do business efficiently. Moreover, the mass media turned out to be a major source of profit in their own right. In 1998, 67 percent of Canadian homes had a CD player, 99 percent had a colour television, and 73 percent had cable TV (Statistics Canada, 2000a). Film and video revenues reached $1.8 billion in 1997. Between 1986 and 1996, the consumer market for entertainment services grew by almost 50 percent, reaching almost $6 billion (Earl, 1999). Clearly, the mass media form a big business.

We conclude that the sources of the mass media lie deeply embedded in the religious, political, and economic needs of our society. Moreover, the mass media are among the most important institutions in our society today. How, then, do sociologists explain the effects of the mass media on society? To answer this question, we now summarize the relevant sociological theories.

## THEORIES OF MEDIA EFFECTS

### Functionalism

As societies develop, they become larger and more complex. The number of institutions and roles proliferate. Due to the sheer scale of a society, face-to-face interaction becomes less viable as a means of communication. As a result, the need increases for new means of coordinating the operation of the various parts of society. For example, people in New Brunswick must have at least a general sense of what is happening in Alberta and they need to share certain basic values with Albertans if they are going to feel they are citizens of the same country. The mass media do an important job in this regard. The nineteenth-century German philosopher Georg Hegel once said that the daily ritual of reading the newspaper unites the secular world, just as the ritual of daily prayer once united the Christian world. Stated more generally, his point is valid. The nationwide distribution of newspapers, magazines, movies, and television shows cements the large, socially diverse, and geographically far-flung population of Canada. In a fundamental sense, the nation is an imagined community, and the mass media make it possible for us to imagine it (Anderson, 1990).

Thus, the mass media perform an important function by *coordinating* the operation of industrial and postindustrial societies. But, according to functionalist theorists, their significance does not stop there (Wright, 1975). In addition, the mass media are also important agents of *socialization.* Families have relinquished their formerly nearly exclusive right to transmit norms, values, and culture. The mass media have stepped into the breech. They reinforce shared ideals of democracy, competition, justice, and so forth (see Chapter 4, Socialization).

A third function of the mass media involves *social control.* That is, the mass media help to ensure conformity. For example, news broadcasts, TV dramas, and "docutainment" programs such as *COPS* pay much attention to crime, and they regularly sing the praises of heroes who apprehend and convict criminals. By exposing deviants and showcasing law enforcement officials and model citizens, the mass media reinforce ideas about what kinds of people deserve punishment and what kinds of people deserve rewards. In this way, they reproduce the moral order. Some people think the Jenny Jones show and other similar programs are outlandish, and in a way they are. From a sociological point of view, however, they are also deeply conservative programs, for when television audiences become upset about marital infidelities and other outrages, they are reinforcing some of the most traditional norms of North American society and thus serving as agents of social control. As Nobel prize–winning author Saul Bellow wrote in *Herzog,* "a scandal [is] after all a sort of service to the community" (Bellow, 1964: 18).

The mass media's fourth and final function is to provide *entertainment.* Television, movies, magazines, and so forth give us pleasure, relaxation, and momentary escape from the tension and tedium of everyday life. How often have you come home after a long and frustrating day at university or work, picked up the remote control, channel surfed, concluded that there's nothing really worth watching, but settled for a soap opera or some other form of easily digestible entertainment? It is precisely because some products of the mass media require little effort on the part of the audience that they are important. They relieve stress. Moreover, they do so in a way that doesn't threaten the social order. Without such escapes, who knows how our daily tensions and frustrations might express themselves?

## Conflict Theory

Clearly, functionalism offers valuable insights into the operation of the mass media. However, conflict theorists have criticized the functional approach for paying insufficient attention to the social inequality fostered by the mass media. Specifically, conflict theorists say functionalism exaggerates the degree to which the mass media serve the interests of the entire society. They contend that some people benefit from the mass media more than others. In particular, the mass media favour the interests of dominant classes and political groups (Gitlin, 1983; Herman and Chomsky, 1988; Horkheimer and Adorno, 1986 [1944]; Iyengar, 1991).

Conflict theorists maintain that there are two ways in which dominant classes and political groups benefit disproportionately from the mass media. First, the mass media broadcast beliefs, values, and ideas that create widespread acceptance of the basic structure of society, including its injustices and inequalities. Second, ownership of the mass media is highly concentrated in the hands of a small number of people and is highly profitable for those people. Thus, the mass media are a source of economic inequality. Let us consider these issues in more detail.

## Media Ownership

For decades, most of the Canadian mass media have been owned by fewer than a dozen families: the Siftons, the Thomsons, the Bassetts, the Southams, the Irvings, the Honderichs, the Blacks, and, more recently, the Aspers, the Shaws, the Rogers, and the Péladeaus. As of this writing (August 2002), there are just six multimedia giants in the country, with combined revenue in 2001 of about $11.3 billion.[1] In order of size (as measured by annual revenue), they are as follows:

1. *CanWest Global Communications Corp.* Controlled by the Asper family of Winnipeg, CanWest Global owns the Global Television Network (composed of 11 stations across Canada), 3 independent television stations (CH TV Hamilton, CH TV Vancouver, and CH TV Montreal), *The National Post*, 14 major urban English-language daily newspapers (*St. John's Telegram, Charlottetown Guardian, Halifax Daily News,* Montreal *Gazette, Ottawa Citizen, St. Catharines Standard, Windsor Star, Regina Leader Post, Saskatoon Star Phoenix, Calgary Herald, Edmonton Journal, Vancouver Sun, Victoria Times-Colonist, Vancouver Province*), and so on. Revenue in 2001: $2.5 billion.
2. *Quebecor Inc.* Controlled by the Péladeau family of Montreal, Quebecor publishes eight major urban daily newspapers (*Le journal de Montréal, Le journal de Québec*, the *Ottawa Sun*, the *Toronto Sun*, the *London Free Press*, the *Winnipeg Sun*, the *Edmonton Sun*, the *Calgary Sun*). It also owns the largest cable TV provider in Quebec, Quebec's largest private TV network (TVA), Canoe.ca, and so on. Revenue in 2001: $2.4 billion.
3. *Rogers Communications Inc.* Controlled by Ted Rogers and based in Toronto, Rogers is one of the country's largest cable TV and broadband Internet service providers. It controls the Shopping Channel, CFMT (a multicultural television station in Toronto), Sportsnet, the Toronto Blue Jays, 29 radio stations, 62 consumer and business magazines (including *Maclean's*, *Flare*, and *Canadian Business*), and so on. Revenue in 2001: $2.2 billion.

The Asper family of Winnipeg owns CanWest Global Communications Corp., the biggest media conglomerate in Canada. In 2001 and 2002, the Aspers came under widespread criticism for controlling editorial content in their newspapers.

4. *Shaw Communications Inc.* Controlled by the Shaw family of Calgary, Shaw Communications is another of the country's largest cable TV and broadband Internet service providers. It also owns 49 radio stations and television specialty stations, including YTV, CMT, and Premium Pay TV Services. Revenue in 2001: $1.6 billion.
5. *CBC–Radio Canada.* The fifth-largest multimedia giant in Canada is the only one that is publicly owned. Its most important assets are an English-language television network, a French-language television network, and four commercial-free radio networks. Revenue in 2000: $1.4 billion, nearly two-thirds of which is a federal government grant and the balance of which comes from advertising, program sales, and so on.
6. *Bell Globemedia Inc.* Owned by Bell Canada Enterprises, based in Montreal, and the Thomson Corporation (which also owns Nelson, the publisher of the book you are holding in your hands), based in Toronto, Bell Globemedia controls the CTV television network, *The Globe and Mail*, CFCF (the biggest English-language television station in Montreal), CKY (Manitoba's biggest TV station), *Report on Business* TV, TSN (The Sports Network), etc. Revenue in 2001: $1.2 billion.

About 90 percent of the mass media in Canada are privately owned. Over time, concentration of the privately owned media has increased. That is, fewer and fewer people control Canada's mass media with every passing decade. Moreover, it is not just the *degree* of media concentration that has changed. The *form* of media concentration began to shift in the 1990s, too. Until the 1990s, media concentration involved mainly "horizontal integration." A small number of firms tried to control as much production as possible in their particular fields (newspapers, radio, television, etc.). In the 1990s, however, "vertical integration" became much more widespread. Media firms sought to control production and distribution in *many* fields. They became media "conglomerates." Today, a media conglomerate may own any combination of television networks, stations, and production facilities; magazines, newspapers, and book publishers; cable channels and cable systems; video store chains and sports teams; Web portals and software companies. A media conglomerate can create content and deliver it in a variety of forms. For instance, Rogers Communications Inc. owns the Toronto Blue Jays, creates sports entertainment, broadcasts it on its television stations, carries the signal to viewers' homes via its cable system, and spins off Blue Jays merchandise that it can sell at Rogers Video stores.

In the United States, the biggest media players include Disney, Viacom, and News Corporation. Other international giant media conglomerates include Bertelsmann (Germany), Sony (Japan), and Vivendi (France). By listing the countries in which the principal owners of these media conglomerates reside, we do not wish to suggest that they operate solely within their national boundaries. On the contrary, today's media conglomerates are increasingly global in their operations. For example, BMG records and Universal Studios are well known in North America but are owned by Bertelsmann and Vivendi, respectively. Moreover, citizenship is largely a matter of economic convenience for the owners of media conglomerates. Thus, Rupert Murdoch, principal shareholder of News Corporation (which owns the Fox network, 20th Century Fox, *The New York Post,* etc.), and Edgar Bronfman, a principal shareholder in Vivendi (which owns Universal Studios, Polygram records, etc.), are both American citizens. However, Murdoch is an expatriate Australian, Bronfman an expatriate Canadian.

The media conglomerates listed above are big, but the 600-pound gorilla among media conglomerates was born on January 10, 2000. On that day, the merger of two media behemoths into a single company, AOL/Time Warner, was announced. Its revenue in 2001 was US$36 billion. This makes AOL/Time Warner five times bigger than all six of Canada's media giants combined. The new company owns America Online, Warner Brothers, Time Warner Cable, CNN, HBO, *Time, People, Sports Illustrated, Life, Fortune,* DC Comics, Netscape, the Cartoon Network, the Atlanta Braves, the Atlanta Hawks, World Championship Wrestling, the Goodwill Games, Time-Life Books, and the Book-of-the-Month Club, to name only a few of its best-known companies ("That's AOL Folks . . . ," 2000). Ted Turner, who owned 100 million shares of Time-Warner, grew $3.5 billion richer in a single day when his stock soared upon news of the merger.

## Media Bias

Does the concentration of the mass media in fewer and fewer hands deprive the public of independent sources of information, limit the diversity of opinion, and encourage the public to accept their society as it is? Conflict theorists think so (see Box 14.2). They argue that when a few conglomerates dominate the production of news in particular, they squeeze out alternative points of view.

A recent example involves CanWest (Canada News Wire, 2002; International Federation of Journalists, 2002; Sallot, 2002; Siddiqui, 2002; Worthington, 2002). At the end of 2001, CanWest's owners, the Asper family, declared that editorials published in their newspapers should not contradict editorials written in their head office. The Aspers are strong supporters of the Liberal Party, staunchly pro-Israel, and in favour of increased military spending, increased protection of property rights, and an elected Senate. In 2002, two

### BOX 14.2 IT'S YOUR CHOICE

#### SHOULD CANADA'S BROADCASTERS BE SUBJECT TO MORE GOVERNMENT REGULATION?

*The use of the air...that lies over the...land of Canada is a natural resource over which we have complete jurisdiction.... I cannot think that any government would be warranted in leaving the air to private exploitation and not reserving it for...the use of the people. Without [complete government control of broadcasting from Canadian sources, radio] can never become the agency by which national consciousness may be fostered and national unity...strengthened.*

– Prime Minister R. B. Bennett, House of Commons, May 18, 1932 (quoted in Competition Bureau, 2002).

What was self-evident to Prime Minister Bennett more than 70 years ago is a matter of controversy today. Some Canadians, like Bennett, still argue for strict government control over the mass media. Like Bennett, they believe that the mass media should be used to strengthen Canadian culture. Others want a more or less free market in which the great bulk of programming is American in origin or, failing that, American in style. Here we review the state of government regulation of Canadian broadcasting and ask you to decide whether you approve of the status quo or think that more or less government regulation is needed.

The Canadian Radio-television and Telecommunications Commission (CRTC) was established by an Act of Parliament in 1968 as an independent agency responsible for regulating Canada's broadcasting and telecommunications systems. Its self-described mandate is to promote Canadian culture and economic competitiveness:

*Our mandate is to ensure that programming in the Canadian broadcasting system reflects Canadian creativity and talent, our linguistic duality, our multicultural diversity, the special place of aboriginal people within our society and our social values. At the same time, we must ensure that Canadians have access to reasonably priced, high-quality, varied and innovative communications services that are competitive nationally as well as internationally ("The CRTC's Mandate," 2002).*

In practice, promoting Canadian culture means ensuring that 35 percent of the popular music played on English-language commercial radio stations between 6 a.m. and 6 p.m., Monday through Friday, is Canadian. Regulations for "ethnic" and French-language stations are somewhat different. Privately owned television stations must achieve a yearly Canadian content level of 60 percent between 6 a.m. and midnight and 50 percent between 6 p.m. and midnight. Canadian content rules for the CBC are slightly more demanding. "Canadian" means that the producer of the program is Canadian, key creative personnel are Canadian, and 75 percent of service costs and post-production lab costs are paid to Canadians.

As a result of these regulations, about half of TV broadcasts in English Canada and 65 percent of popular music broadcasts are *American*. Moreover, many American TV and radio stations are widely available in Canada via cable, satellite, or the airwaves. (Roughly 75 percent of Canadian households subscribe to cable, and another 20 percent use satellite services; estimated from "Presentation by Canada's Cable Companies to the Standing Committee on Canadian Heritage, February 19, 2002," 2002; Statistics Canada, 2002a, 2002d). It seems reasonable to conclude that at least three-quarters of the TV and popular music to which Canadians have access is American.

Bearing the above facts in mind, do you think the Canadian government does enough or too much to ensure the preservation and enrichment of Canadian culture through the broadcast industry? Should the government be in the business of protecting Canadian culture at all? Should it allow free-market forces to shape the structure and content of Canadian broadcasting? Would a free-market approach to broadcasting enable Canadians to get what they really want, or would it allow powerful American broadcasters to completely dominate the marketplace and virtually eliminate Canadian content? These are policy questions that many Canadians debate on a regular basis. Their resolution is your choice.

reporters for the *Halifax Daily News* had their columns "killed" when they criticized the Asper policy. They were then asked if they wanted to continue to work for the paper. They said no. A reporter for the *Windsor Star* had his column killed for the same reason. An Aboriginal columnist for the *Regina Leader-Post* and *Saskatoon Star Phoenix* had a column killed when he expressed sympathy for stateless Palestinians. Yet another reporter was fired from the *Ottawa Citizen* after unearthing scandalous details about possible corruption involving Prime Minister Jean Chrétien. When reporters at the Montreal *Gazette* and the *Saskatoon Star Phoenix* protested the Aspers' attempts to control editorial policy, CanWest imposed a gag order on all reporters working for the organization, saying it would suspend journalists who publicly objected to its editorial policy. In March 2002, the gag order was extended to all Global TV employees. Then, in June 2002, Russell Mills, the long-time publisher of the *Ottawa Citizen*, was fired because of what the Aspers regarded as too much anti-Chrétien opinion on the editorial page. CanWest's actions are a form of corporate censorship, and they have been roundly criticized by the Newspaper Guild of Canada, the *Washington Post*, and the International Federation of Journalists, among other organizations.

CanWest is an extreme case. Such direct and open interference with editorial policy is not common in liberal democracies such as Canada. However, according to Edward Herman and Noam Chomsky (1988), several other, more subtle mechanisms help to bias the news in a way that supports powerful corporate interests and political groups. These biasing mechanisms include advertising, sourcing, and flak:

- *Advertising.* Most of the revenue earned by television stations, radio stations, newspapers, and magazines comes from advertising by large corporations. According to Herman and Chomsky, these corporations routinely seek to influence the news so it will reflect well on them. In one American survey, 93 percent of newspaper editors said advertisers have tried to influence their news reports. Thirty-seven percent of newspaper editors admitted to actually being influenced by advertisers (Bagdikian, 1997 [1983]). In addition, big advertisers may influence the news even without overtly trying to influence news carriers. For fear of losing business, news carriers may soften stories that big advertisers might find offensive.
- *Sourcing.* Studies of news gathering show that most news agencies rely heavily for information on press releases, news conferences, and interviews organized by large corporations and government agencies. These sources routinely slant information to reflect favourably on their policies and preferences. Unofficial news sources are consulted less often. Moreover, unofficial sources tend to be used only to provide reactions and minority viewpoints that are secondary to the official story.
- *Flak.* Governments and big corporations routinely attack journalists who depart from official and corporate points of view. For example, Brian Ross, the leading investigative reporter for *20/20,* prepared a segment about Disney World in 1998. Ross claimed that Disney was so lax in doing background checks on employees that it had hired pedophiles. ABC killed the story before airtime. ABC is owned by Disney (McChesney, 1999). Similarly, tobacco companies have systematically tried to discredit media reports that cigarettes cause cancer. In a notorious case, the respected public affairs show *60 Minutes* refused to broadcast a damaging interview with a former Philip Morris executive because CBS was threatened with legal action by the tobacco company. (This incident is the subject of the Oscar®-nominated 2000 movie *The Insider.*)

On the whole, the conflict theorists' arguments are compelling. We do not, however, find them completely convincing (Gans, 1979). After all, if 37 percent of newspaper editors have been influenced by advertisers, 63 percent have not. News agencies may rely heavily on government and corporate sources, but this does not stop them from routinely biting the hand that offers to feed them and evading flak shot their way. The daily newspaper is full of examples of mainstream journalistic opposition to government and corporate viewpoints. Even mainstream news sources, although owned by media conglomerates, do not always act like the lap dogs of the powerful (Hall, 1980).

Still, conflict theorists make a valid point if they restrict their argument to how the mass media support core societal values. In their defence of core values, the mass media *are* virtually unanimous. For example, the mass media enthusiastically support democracy and capitalism. We cannot think of a single instance of a major Canadian news outlet advocating a fascist government or a socialist economy in Canada.

Similarly, the mass media virtually unanimously endorse consumerism as a way of life. As discussed in Chapter 3, Culture, consumerism is the tendency to define oneself in terms of the goods and services one purchases. Endorsement of consumerism is evident in the fact that advertising fills the mass media and is its lifeblood. In 2000, advertising spending in Canada totalled \$5.3 billion, nearly half the amount spent on Canadian universities (Industry Canada, 2001; Statistics Canada, 2002b). We are exposed to a staggering number of ads each day; in fact, some estimates place the number in the thousands. Companies pay filmmakers to use their brand-name products conspicuously in their movies. In some magazines, ads figure so prominently one must search for the articles.

It is only when the mass media deal with news stories that touch on less central values that one may witness a diversity of media opinion. *Specific* government and corporate policies are often the subject of heated debate in the mass media.[2] Thus, despite the indisputable concentration of media ownership, the mass media are diverse and often contentious on specific issues that do not touch on core values (see Figure 14.1). To drive this point home, we must now say a few words about the sources of diversity and gender differences in the mass media.

## Diversity and Gender Differences in the Mass Media

Both functionalists and conflict theorists stress how the mass media bridge social differences and reinforce society's core values. The two schools of thought differ in that functionalists believe that core values serve everyone's interests while conflict theorists believe that they favour the interests of the rich and powerful. By focusing so closely on core values, however, both approaches understate the diversity of the mass media.

Like all societies, Canada is differentiated by generation, class, gender, race, and ethnicity. To a degree, the mass media reflect this social diversity. Many social differences are widening in Canadian society because of growing class inequality, increased immigration, the rise of a substantial middle class among racial minorities, and other social forces. The mass media must cater to this growing diversity or lose business. To entertain and sell products to a differentiated market, advertising and programming must appeal to specific market niches.

✦ **FIGURE 14.1** ✦
**The Relationship between Centrality of Values and Diversity of Media Opinion**

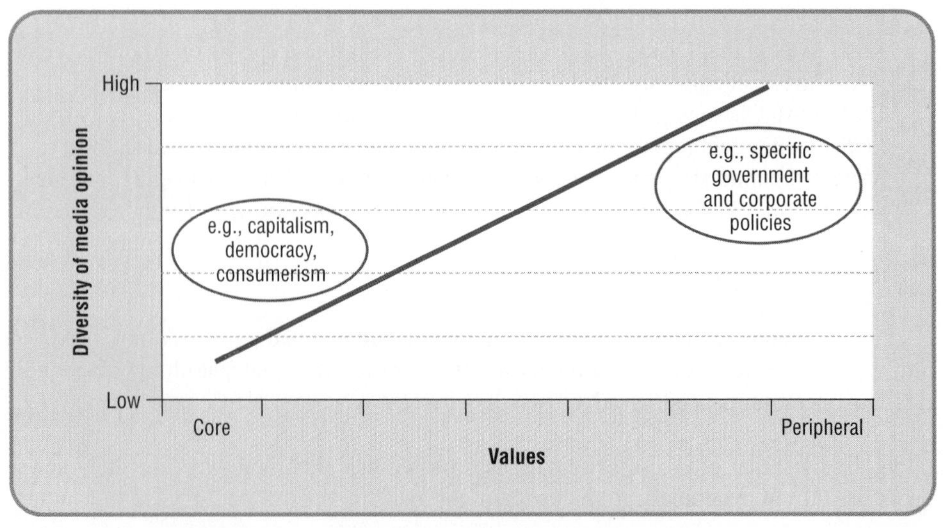

Technological advances, especially the computer, have made "niche marketing" possible. In the 1910s, when Henry Ford established the first assembly lines, his aim was to produce a standard automobile for a mass market. By standardizing production, Ford kept costs down and profits high. For about 60 years this was the aim of all big businesses. Some people knew that Ford's production and marketing model was not ideal. They understood that consumer tastes were diverse. However, limits existed on what they could do to satisfy that diversity, because it was less expensive to produce standardized commodities for large groups of people than a wide variety of products to suit the full range of consumer preferences. The computer changed all that. By allowing new forms of inventory control, short production runs, faster manufacturing, quick design changes, and so forth, computers allowed producers to cater to small market niches and increase profit margins. The mass media followed suit, diversifying their programming and advertising to reflect the needs of niche marketing.

Still, one must be careful not to exaggerate the degree to which the mass media reflect the diversity of Canadian society. Despite improvements in recent decades, critics who are sympathetic to feminism and the plight of racial minorities have charged the mass media with persistent *numerical underrepresentation* and *biased portrayal* of minority groups. Let us consider these charges.

MediaWatch describes itself as a "not-for-profit, feminist organization working to eliminate sexism in the media." In 1992–93 it sponsored an analysis of minority representation on Canadian television (MediaWatch, 1994). During the fall of 1992 its researchers classified actors by gender and race in eight popular dramatic series produced in Canada, some of which were also shown in the United States. In late 1993 and early 1994 the researchers classified newscasters by gender and race in four nationwide evening newscasts. Figure 14.2 summarizes the main results of their research. It compares (a) the representation of white men, white women, nonwhite men, and nonwhite women in dramatic and news programs with (b) the representation of these groups in the Canadian population as a whole. A score of 100 for any particular group means that there are proportionately as many members of that group on TV as there are in the general population. Scores above 100 indicate overrepresentation of the group on TV. Scores below 100 indicate underrepresentation. We see immediately that white men are overrepresented in both dramatic and news roles. Nonwhite men are substantially overrepresented in dramatic roles. All other groups are substantially underrepresented. The most underrepresented group is nonwhite women in news roles. They are underrepresented by 87 percent, which means there are 87 percent fewer nonwhite women reporting the news than there are nonwhite women in the Canadian population.

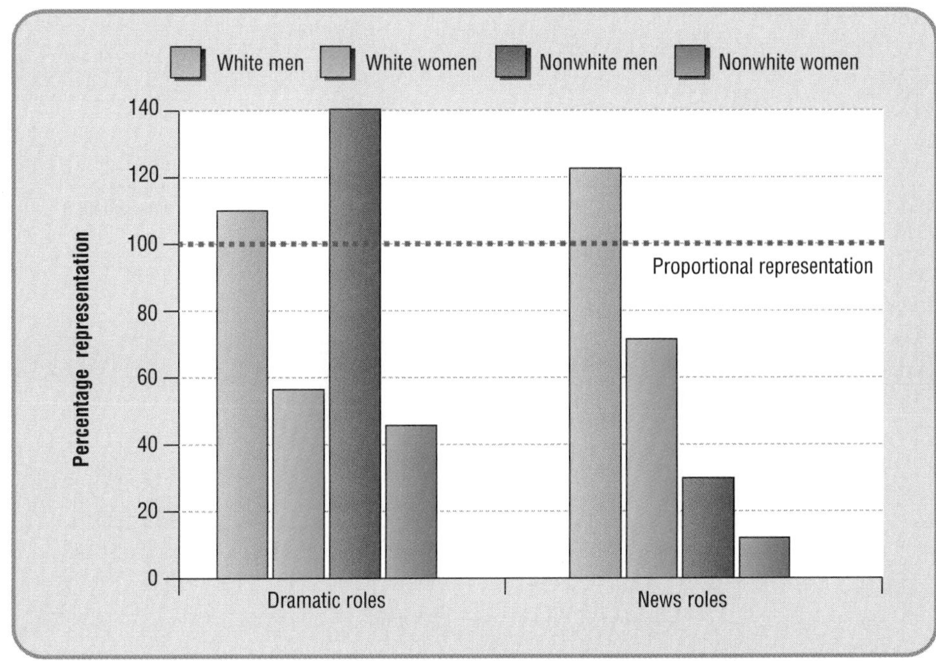


✦ **FIGURE 14.2** ✦

**Gender and Racial Distribution of Dramatic and News TV Roles, Canada, 1992–1993**

Sources: Brym (1999); MediaWatch (1994).

We can gain a more nuanced appreciation of the representation of minority groups on TV by examining research sponsored by the Screen Actors Guild (SAG), the professional organization of film and TV actors in the United States. This research concerns American television, but it is highly relevant to Canadian TV audiences because three-quarters or more of all TV programming available to Canadians comes from the United States. The SAG study focuses on fictional TV characters who appeared in prime-time and daytime series, films, and animated cartoons in the periods 1991–92 and 1994–97 (Gerbner, 1998). Figure 14.3 shows that in 1994–97 there were 29 percent more white men in fictional TV roles than white men in the U.S. population. At the same time, there were 28 percent fewer women in fictional TV roles than in the population, 46 percent fewer Native Americans, 61 percent fewer Asian-Pacific Americans, 66 percent fewer people 60 years of age or older, 76 percent fewer Hispanics, 88 percent fewer people with disabilities, and 89 percent fewer poor people. These figures demonstrate that TV falls short of reflecting the diversity of North American society in many crucial respects.

The SAG research demonstrates that the representation of minority groups improved during the 1990s. It also shows that the portrayal of women, racial minorities, the poor, and people with disabilities still tends to reinforce traditional, mainstream, negative stereotypes. For instance, fully 60 percent of fictional TV characters suffering from mental illness in the period 1994–97 were involved in crime or violence. Nonwhites tended to play comical or criminal characters rather than serious, heroic types. Characters of different races often interacted professionally, sometimes interacted socially, but were rarely romantically involved. Asian-Americans were typically portrayed as nerdy students, inscrutable martial arts masters, seductive Dragon Ladies, or clueless immigrants. Women were valued chiefly for their youth, sex appeal, and beauty, while older women were often associated with evil. Thus, in the 1990s, women playing fictional TV roles were on average younger than men and they became still younger relative to men in the course of the decade. Young women tended to play mainly romantic roles, but the proportion of villains among women increased with age. The tendency for villainy to increase among older men was much weaker (*Fall Colors II,* 2000; Gerbner, 1998). Canadian research shows that in TV drama, women outnumber men in family settings, child-care roles, and home management roles, while men outnumber women in paid employment settings and roles involving violence. In paid employment roles, men are more likely to be cast as managers, profes-

**✦ FIGURE 14.3 ✦**
**Representation of Minority Groups in Prime-Time and Daytime Television, United States, 1991–1992 and 1994–1997**

Source: Gerbner (1998)

*Note:* Data for white males, 1991–92 not reported.

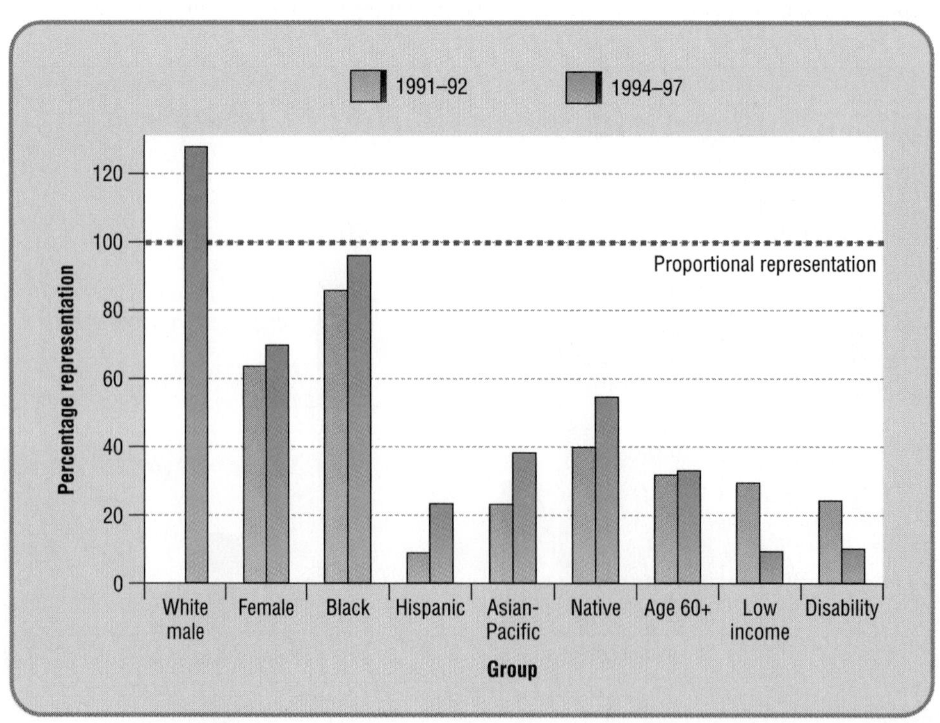

sionals, military personnel, and police officers, while women are more likely to be cast as sales and office workers. Thus, TV drama tends to reinforce gender stratification in the larger society (CRTC, 1990).

Much research points to positive change over time in the way the mass media treat various minority groups. We have come a long way since the 1950s, when the only blacks on TV played butlers and buffoons and the only Aboriginal peoples played brutal warriors or faithful sidekicks to the *real* heroes. At the same time, however, the research suggests that the mass media still have a long way to go before they cease reinforcing traditional class, race, and gender stereotypes in North American society (Dines and Humez, 1995). To a degree, the mass media influence the way audiences think about the world. Therefore, the perpetuation of stereotypes acts as a brake on social change.

That said, the *extent* to which TV and other mass media influence audiences is a subject of controversy in sociology. This will become clear as we consider the third major perspective on the sociological study of the mass media, the interpretive approach.

## The Interpretive Approach

The final episode of *Buffy the Vampire Slayer* in the 1999 season included a scene of a shooting spree at a high school. However, the Fox TV network cancelled the episode because it was scheduled to air shortly after 2 teenagers massacred 13 of their classmates at Columbine High School in Littleton, Colorado. In cancelling the show, network officials were reacting to members of the public who shared the widespread belief that airing it might incite more school violence.

The view that the mass media powerfully influence a passive public is common, not least among functionalists and conflict theorists. Many people believe that violence on TV causes violence in real life, pornography on the magazine stands leads to immoral sexual behaviour, and adolescents are more likely to start smoking cigarettes when they see popular movie stars lighting up. In a 1995 CBS/*New York Times* poll, for example, respondents said they thought television was the number-one cause of teenage violence (Kolbert, 1995).

Just how much influence do the mass media actually exert over their audiences? The question is mired in controversy. For example, recall our discussion of media violence in Chapter 2, Research Methods. There we found that most research on the subject is plagued by a big validity problem. Simply stated, experiments on media violence may not be measuring what they say they are. As a result, the degree to which TV violence encourages violent behaviour is unclear. The sociological consensus seems to be that TV violence has a weak effect on a small percentage of viewers (Felson, 1996: 123).

There are other reasons for questioning the strength of media effects. For instance, researchers have known for half a century that people do not change their attitudes and behaviours just because the media tell them to do so. That is because the link between persuasive media messages and actual behaviour is indirect. A **two-step flow of communication** takes place (Katz, 1957; Schiller, 1989; Schudson, 1995). In step 1, respected people of high status evaluate media messages. They are the opinion leaders of a neighbourhood or a community, people who are usually more highly educated, well-to-do, and/or politically powerful than others in their circle. Because of their high status, they exercise considerable independence of judgment. In step 2, opinion leaders *may* influence the attitudes and behaviours of others. In this way, opinion leaders filter media messages. The two-step flow of communication limits media effects. If people are influenced to vote for certain candidates, buy certain products, or smoke cigarettes, it is less because the media tell them to and more because opinion leaders suggest they should.

Yet another persuasive argument that leads one to question the effects of the mass media comes from interpretive sociologists such as symbolic interactionists and interdisciplinary **cultural studies** experts. They use in-depth interviewing and participant observation to study how people actually interpret media messages.

British sociologist Stuart Hall, one of the foremost proponents of this approach, emphasizes that people are not empty vessels into which the mass media pour a defined assortment of beliefs, values, and ideas. Rather, audience members take an active role in consuming the products of the mass media. They filter and interpret mass media messages in the context of their own interests, experiences, and values. Thus, in Hall's view, any adequate analysis of the mass media needs to take into account both the production and the consumption of media products. First, he says, we need to study the meanings intended by the producers. Then we need to study how audiences consume or evaluate media products. Intended and received meanings may diverge; audience members often interpret media messages in ways other than those intended by the producers (Hall, 1980; Seiter, 1999). Two sports examples from the summer of 2001 illustrate this. When Dale Earnhardt, Jr., won a NASCAR race at the track where his famous father had died in a crash a year earlier, some people cried "fix," just as they did when retiring baseball superstar Cal Ripken, Jr., hit a home run in the annual All-Star Game. This suggests that people are often skeptical if not downright cynical about what they see on TV (Brady, 2001). Here is a personal example of the way audiences may intepret media messages in unexpected ways: When John Lie's parents were preparing to emigrate to the United States in the late 1960s, his mother watched many American movies and television shows. One of her favourite TV programs was *My Three Sons,* a sitcom about three boys living with their father and grandfather. From the show she learned that boys wash dishes and vacuum the house in the United States. When the Lie family emigrated to Hawaii, John and his brother—but not his sister—had to wash dishes every night. When John complained, his mother reassured him that "in America, only boys wash dishes."

Even children's television viewing turns out to be complex when viewed through an interpretive lens. Research shows that young children clearly distinguish "make-believe" media violence from real-life violence (Hodge and Tripp, 1986). That is one reason why watching episode after episode of *South Park* has not produced a nation of *South Park* clones. Similarly, research shows differences in the way working-class and middle-class women relate to TV. Working-class women tend more than middle-class women to evaluate TV programs in terms of how realistic they are. This critical attitude reduces their ability to identify strongly with many characters, personalities, and story lines. For instance, working-class women know from their own experience that families often don't work the way they are shown on TV. They view the idealized, middle-class nuclear family depicted in many television shows with a mixture of nostalgia and skepticism (Press, 1991). Age also affects how one relates to television. Elderly viewers tend to be selective and focused in their television viewing. In contrast, people who grew up with cable TV and a remote control often engage in channel surfing, conversation, eating, and housework, zoning in and out of programs in anything but an absorbed fashion (Press, 1991). The idea that such viewers are sponges, passively soaking up the values embedded in TV programs and then mechanically acting on them, is inaccurate.

We conclude that each of the theoretical approaches reviewed above contributes to our understanding of how the mass media influence us:

- *Functionalism* usefully identifies the main social effects of the mass media: coordination, socialization, social control, and entertainment. By performing these functions, the mass media help make social order possible.
- *Conflict theory* offers an important qualification. As vast money-making machines controlled by a small group of increasingly wealthy people, the mass media contribute to economic inequality and to maintaining the core values of a stratified social order. However, dissent and diversity on non-core values is common.
- *Interpretive approaches* offer a second qualification. They remind us that audience members are people, not programmable robots. We filter, interpret, resist, and sometimes reject media messages according to our own interests and values. A full sociological appreciation of the mass media is obliged to recognize the interaction between producers and consumers of media messages.

In the final section of this chapter, we briefly explore the interaction between producers and consumers on the Internet. As you will see, the Internet provides fresh opportunities for media conglomerates to restrict access to paying customers and accumulate vast wealth. Simultaneously, however, it gives consumers new creative capabilities, partially blurring the distinction between producer and consumer. The Internet, we conclude, has the potential to make the mass media somewhat more democratic—at least for those who can afford access.

## THE INTERNET

The contradictory tendencies of the new media frontier are evident on the Internet. Let us first consider the forces that restrict Internet access and augment the power of media conglomerates. We then discuss countertrends.

### Access

The Internet requires an expensive infrastructure of personal computers, servers, and routers; an elaborate network of fibre optic, copper twist, and coaxial cables; and many other components. This infrastructure has to be paid for, primarily by individual users. As a result, access is not open to everyone. Far from it. In Canada, for example, households that are richer, better educated, urban, and younger are most likely to enjoy Internet access (see Chapter 11, Politics, Table 11.3).

Nor is Internet access evenly distributed globally. The United States is the overwhelming leader in terms of getting its population connected. Moreover, the *rate* of Internet connectivity (per 1000 people) in North America is more than double the rate in Western Europe, nearly 15 times higher than in Eastern Europe, and nearly 23 times higher than in South and Central America. It is more than 28 times higher than in the Asia-Pacific region and more than 68 times higher than in the Middle East and Africa. These figures show that international inequalities in Internet access mirror global inequalities (see Chapter 7, Social Stratification: Canadian and Global Perspectives).

### Content

U.S. domination is even more striking when it comes to Internet content. Roughly two-thirds of the servers that provide content on the Internet are in the United States (Internet Software Consortium, 2002). Some analysts say that American domination of the Web is an example of **media imperialism.** Media imperialism is the control of a mass medium by a single national culture and the undermining of other national cultures. Some media analysts in Canada, France, and other countries deeply resent the fact that the United States is the world's biggest exporter and smallest importer of mass media products, including Web content. They say that American media imperialism is a threat to their countries' national culture and identity. The problem of media imperialism is felt particularly acutely in Canadian television broadcasting because the country has a comparatively small population (smaller than California's), is close to the United States, and is about 75 percent English-speaking. Private broadcasters dominate the Canadian market and rely mainly on American entertainment programming. Moreover, the widespread use of cable and satellite dishes permits most Canadians to receive American programming directly from the source.

According to some media analysts, the Internet not only restricts access and promotes American content but also increases the power of media conglomerates. This is most evident in the realm of **media convergence.** Media convergence is the blending of the World Wide Web, television, and telephone into new, hybrid media forms. Many consumers find a PC too complex to operate and find TV limited in its functionality and entertainment value. Media convergence is intended to appeal mainly to such people (Dowling, Lechner, and Thielmann, 1998). The most visible form of media convergence today is interactive TV.

Media imperialism on Enaotai Island in West Papua New Guinea.

How will interactive TV operate in the near future? It will receive signals via cable, satellite dish, or fibre optic telephone line. It will be connected to the Web through a built-in computer with a hard drive big enough to record 12 to 30 hours of programming. If you have interactive TV in your household, you will be able to program and record the exact blend of programs you want to watch from a long menu of specialty channels. You will be able to order feature-length movies, use e-mail, make phone calls, and hold video conferences with people in remote locations. You will be able to call up Web sites that offer additional information on the programs or movies you are watching, shop for a wide variety of goods, do your banking, and pay your utility bills. And you will be able to do all this from the convenience of your couch. All the media giants are scrambling for market share. After all, the media conglomerates stand to earn many billions of dollars laying fibre optic cable, building new media appliances, writing software, creating TV programs, and selling goods and services online (Davis, 2000).

The control of interactive TV by huge media conglomerates may seem like an old story. In some respects it is. Ownership of every mass medium has become more concentrated over time. Interactive TV seems poised to repeat the pattern more quickly than any other mass medium. Because entry costs are so high, only media giants can become involved.

However, this is a media story with a twist, since consumers can *interact* with the new medium. The big media conglomerates may be able to carve out a new and lucrative niche for themselves by merging the Internet and television. However, they can never fully dominate the Internet. That is because it is the first mass medium that makes it relatively easy for consumers to become producers.

Millions of people are not just passive users of the Internet. Instead, they help create its content. For example, the Web boasts millions of personal Web sites. As of May 2002, it contained nearly 1800 role-playing communities (MUDs) with perhaps a million users ("The MUD Connector," 2001; see Chapter 4, Socialization). More than 26 000 cameras are connected to the Web. They open a window to the goings-on in people's offices, university dorms, apartments, and frat houses ("WebcamSearch.com," 2002). People have created more than 100 000 formal discussion groups on the Internet ("Liszt's Usenet NewsGroups Directory," 2000). Each group is composed of tens, hundreds, or thousands of individuals who discuss defined subjects by e-mail or in real time. Some discussion groups focus on particle physics. Others are devoted to banjos, lawyer jokes, Russian politics, sadomasochism, and just about every other human activity imaginable. The groups are self-governing bodies with their own rules and norms of "netiquette" (McLaughlin,

Osborne, and Smith, 1995; Sudweeks, McLaughlin, and Rafaeli, 1999). Chat groups such as ICQ and MSN Messenger involve more than 100 million users (ICQ.com, 2002). Entry costs are relatively low. All you need to contribute to a Web site, a MUD, a discussion group, or a chat group is your own PC, some free or inexpensive software, and an Internet connection. AOL/Time Warner and all the other media conglomerates have little control over the many thousands of communities that are proliferating online.

So we see that the image of the Internet as a medium that is subject to increasing domination by large conglomerates needs to be tempered by awareness of the contrary trend. Individual users are also making independent, creative contributions to Internet growth. Similarly, the view that the growth of the Web is an example of American media imperialism has not gone unchallenged. Where some media analysts see American media imperialism, others see globalization and postmodernization, social processes we introduced in Chapter 3, Culture. From the latter point of view, all cultures, including that of the United States, are becoming less homogeneous and more fragmented as they borrow elements from each other. Inexpensive international travel and telecommunications make this cultural blending possible. Thus, if you look carefully at the Web, you will see that even U.S. sites adopt content liberally from Latin America, Asia, and elsewhere. Just as international influences can be seen in today's hairstyles, clothing fashions, foods, and popular music, so can the Internet be seen as a site of globalization (Hall, 1992).

Shawn Fanning, creator of Napster. Napster allowed people to share recorded music on the World Wide Web, but media conglomerates took Napster to court, forcing it to stop the giveaway on the grounds that it was effectively stealing royalties from musicians and profits from music companies. Since then, alternative music sharing programs, such as Gnutella, Kazaa, and Morpheus, have become popular, suggesting that there is no end in sight to the tug of war between the forces for and against media conglomerates on the Web.

Of course, nobody knows exactly how the social forces outlined above will play themselves out. A phenomenon such as Napster emerges, enabling millions of people to freely share recorded music on the Web using a central server. Some analysts point to Napster as evidence of Internet democratization. Then the media conglomerates take Napster to court, forcing it to stop the giveaway on the grounds that it is effectively stealing royalties from musicians and profits from music companies. Some analysts see the shutdown of Napster as evidence of inevitable conglomeration on the Web. Then new Napster-like programs, such as Morpheus, Kazaa, and Gnutella emerge. (The name "Gnutella" comes from the popular nut-based paste, which spreads easily; see "Gnutella," 2000.) These programs allow people to share recorded music on the Web *without* a central server, making them virtually impossible to shut down. In mid-2002, the top five music-sharing Web sites had nearly 20 million unique users (White, 2002). And so the tug of war between conglomeration and democratization continues, with no end in sight. One thing is clear, however. The speed of technological innovation and the many possibilities for individual creativity on the new media frontier make this an exciting era to be involved in the mass media and to study it sociologically.

## SUMMARY

1. The mass media sometimes blur the line between reality and fantasy.
2. The mass media are means of transmitting information and entertainment from one person or group to another. The communication is typically from a few senders to many receivers.
3. The mass media became truly large-scale only when penny newspapers were published in the first half of the nineteenth century. The electronic media are products of the twentieth century.
4. Three main historical forces stimulated the growth of the mass media. The Protestant Reformation of the sixteenth century encouraged people to read the Bible themselves. The democratic movements that began in the late eighteenth century encouraged people to demand literacy. Beginning in the late nineteenth century, capitalist industrialization required rapid means of communication and fostered the mass media as important sources of profit.
5. Functionalism stresses that the mass media act to coordinate society, exercise social control, and socialize and entertain people.
6. Conflict theory stresses that the mass media reinforce social inequality. They do this both by acting as sources of profit for the few people who control media conglomerates and by promoting core values that help legitimize the existing social order.
7. Although the mass media promote social cohesion, they also differentiate groups by generation, gender, class, and ethnicity.
8. Interpretive approaches to studying the mass media stress that audiences actively filter, interpret, and sometimes even resist and reject media messages according to their interests and values.
9. The interaction between the producers and consumers of media messages is most evident on the new media frontier formed by the Internet, television, and other mass media.

## GLOSSARY

**Cultural studies** is an increasingly popular interdisciplinary area of media research. It focuses not just on the cultural meanings producers try to transmit but also on the way audiences filter and interpret mass media messages in the context of their own interests, experiences, and values.

The **mass media** are print, radio, television, and other communication technologies. The word *mass* implies that the media reach many people. The word *media* signifies that communication does not take place directly through face-to-face interaction. Instead, technology intervenes or mediates in transmitting messages from senders to receivers. Furthermore, communication via the mass media is usually one-way, or at least one-sided. There are few senders (or producers) and many receivers (or audience members).

**Media convergence** is the blending of the World Wide Web, television, and other communications media as new, hybrid media forms.

**Media imperialism** is the domination of a mass medium by a single national culture and the undermining of other national cultures.

The **two-step flow of communication** between mass media and audience members involves (a) respected people of high status and independent judgment evaluating media messages, and (b) other members of the community being influenced to varying degrees by these opinion leaders. Because of the two-step flow of communication, opinion leaders filter media messages.

## QUESTIONS TO CONSIDER

1. Locate Webcams in your region or community by searching on http://www.webcamsearch.com/. Who has set up these Webcams? For what purposes? How might they be used to strengthen ties among family members, friendship networks, special-interest groups, and so forth?
2. Phone TV and radio stations in your community to find out which are locally controlled and which are controlled by large media companies. If there are no locally controlled stations, does this have implications for the kind of news coverage and public affairs programming you may be watching? If there are locally controlled stations in your community, do they differ in terms of programming content, audience size, and audience type from stations owned by large media companies? If you can observe such differences, why do they exist?
3. The 1999 movie *Enemy of the State,* starring Will Smith, depicts one drawback of new media technologies: the possibility of intense government surveillance and violation of privacy rights. Do you think new media technologies are unqualified blessings or could they limit our freedom and privacy? If so, how? How could the capacity of new media technologies to limit freedom and privacy be limited?

## WEB RESOURCES

### Companion Web Site for This Book

http://www.brymsociologycompass.nelson.com

Begin by clicking on the Student Resources section of the Web site. Next, select the chapter you are currently studying from the pull-down menu. From the Student Resources page you will have easy access to InfoTrac College Edition®, MicroCase online exercises, and additional Web links. The Web site also has many useful tips to aid you in your study of sociology, including practice tests for each chapter.

### InfoTrac Search Terms

These search terms are provided to assist you in beginning to conduct research on this topic by visiting http://www.infotrac-college.com

**Cultural studies**
**Media bias**
**Media concentration**
**Media convergence**
**Media imperialism**

### Recommended Web Sites

NewsWatch Canada, from Simon Fraser University, "undertakes independent research on the diversity and thoroughness of news coverage in Canada's media, with a focus on identifying blindspots and double-standards." Go to http://newswatch.cprost.sfu.ca/intro.html.

Media Awareness Canada at http://www.media-awareness.ca/eng/ is a Canadian site dedicated to improving the mass media for children by focusing on media education in the home, school, and community.

*Media Magazine*, the journal of the Canadian Association of Journalists, is available online at http://www.caj.ca/mediamag/index.html

Excellent lists of Web links on the mass media, broadcasting, and communications compiled by the libraries at the University of British Columbia and at Simon Fraser University can be found at http://www.library.ubc.ca/poli/cpwebm.html and http://www.peak.sfu.ca/cmass/issue2/urls-media3.html.

The Media and Communications Studies Site at the University of Wales is one of the best sites on the Web devoted to the mass media. Among other interesting sections, it includes useful theoretical materials and resources on class, gender, and race in the mass media, mainly from a British perspective. Visit it at http://www.aber.ac.uk/media/Functions/mcs.html.

For useful resources on corporate ownership of the mass media and the social and political problems that result from increasingly concentrated media ownership, primarily with an American focus, go to http://www.fair.org/media-woes/corporate.html.

## SUGGESTED READINGS

Stuart Ewen. *PR! A Social History of Spin* (New York: Basic, 1997). Shows how various mass media organizations manipulate images and messages.

Douglas Kellner. *Media Culture: Cultural Studies, Identity and Politics Between the Modern and the Postmodern* (New York: Routledge, 1995). Assesses the production, meaning, and reception of contemporary American mass culture. A balanced and comprehensive interpretation.

Chris McCormick. *Constructing Danger: The Mis/respresentation of Crime in the News* (Halifax: Fernwood, 1995). A Canadian study of how the mass media shape our perceptions of crime.

David Taras. *Power and Betrayal in the Canadian Media*, updated ed. (Peterborough, ON: Broadview Press, 2001 [1999]). Another good Canadian study that analyzes how the power of media conglomerates and the weakness of government regulators have combined to create mass media that threaten democracy by minimizing our focus on politics and maximizing our focus on sensationalism.

## NOTES

1. The following synopsis is based on BCE (2002), CanWest Global Communications Corp. (2002), CBC Radio-Canada (2001), Chen and Graves (2001), Quebecor Inc. (2002), Rogers Communications Inc. (2002), Rogers Wireless Communications Inc. (2002), and Shaw Communications Inc. (2002). Revenue reported here for Quebecor does not include printing and related services. Revenue reported here for Rogers does not include wireless telephone services. Throughout, revenue is reported in Canadian dollars unless otherwise specified.
2. Conservatives often criticize the mass media for their allegedly liberal bias. We do not wish to enter into this highly charged political debate. It should be noted, however, that the conservative critique of the mass media focuses only on the media's analysis of specific government and corporate policies, not on their analysis of stories relating to core values.

## IN THIS CHAPTER, YOU WILL LEARN THAT

- Health risks are unevenly distributed in human populations. Men and women, upper and lower classes, rich and poor countries, and privileged and disadvantaged racial and ethnic groups are exposed to health risks to varying degrees.

- On several measures of health, Canada ranks among the top three countries in the world. Canada's health care system provides access to universal comprehensive coverage for medically necessary in-patient and out-patient physical services. However, income continues to affect the health of Canadians. As Canadians climb the income ladder, they experience less sickness, increased life expectancies, and better health. Many low-income and moderate-income Canadians have limited or no access to such health services as eye care, dentistry, mental health counselling, and prescription drugs.

- Medical successes created new problems. For instance, they allow people to live longer than they used to. This gives degenerative diseases such as cancer and heart disease more chance to develop. In turn, the increased incidence of such diseases raises new questions about when and how people should be allowed to die.

- The meaning people attach to aging and death varies historically and from one country to the next.

- The dominance of medical science is due to its successful treatments and the way in which doctors excluded competitors and established control over their profession and their clients.

- Patient activism, alternative medicine, and holistic medicine promise to improve the quality of health care in Canada and globally.

CHAPTER

# 15

# HEALTH, MEDICINE, AND AGING

## THE BLACK DEATH

In 1346, rumours reached Europe of a plague sweeping the East. Originating in Asia, the epidemic spread along trade routes to China and Russia. A year later, 12 galleys sailed from southern Russia to Italy. Diseased sailors were aboard. Their lymph nodes were terribly swollen and eventually burst, causing a painful death. Anyone who came in contact with the sailors was soon infected. As a result, their ships were driven out of several Italian and French ports in succession. Yet the disease spread relentlessly, again moving along trade routes to Spain, Portugal, and England. Within two years, the Black Death, as it came to be known, killed a third of Europe's population. Six hundred and fifty years later, the plague still ranks as the most devastating catastrophe in human history (Herlihy, 1998; McNeill, 1976; Zinsser, 1935).

Today we know that the cause of the plague was a bacillus that spread from lice to rats to people. It spread so efficiently because many people lived close together in unsanitary conditions. In the middle of the fourteenth century, however, nobody knew anything about germs. Therefore, Pope Clement VI sent a delegation to Europe's leading medical school in Paris to discover the cause of the plague. The learned professors studied the problem. They reported that a particularly unfortunate conjunction of Saturn, Jupiter, and Mars in the sign of Aquarius had occurred in 1345. The resulting hot, humid conditions caused the earth to emit poisonous vapours. To prevent the plague, they said, people should refrain from eating poultry, waterfowl, pork, beef, fish, and olive oil. They should not sleep during the daytime or engage in excessive exercise. Nothing should be cooked in rainwater. Bathing should be avoided at all costs.

We do not know whether the pope followed the professors' advice. We do know he made a practice of sitting between two large fires to breathe pure air. Since the plague bacillus is destroyed by heat, this may have saved his life. Other people were less fortunate. Some rang church bells and fired cannons to drive the plague away. Others burned incense, wore charms, and cast spells. But, other than the pope, the only people to have much luck in avoiding the plague were the well-to-do (who could afford to flee the densely populated cities for remote areas in the countryside) and the Jews (whose religion required that they wash their hands before meals, bathe once a week, and conduct burials soon after death).

Some of the main themes of the sociology of health, medicine, and aging are embedded in the story of the Black Death, or at least implied by it. First, recall that some groups were more likely to die of the plague than others. This is a common pattern. Health risks are always unevenly distributed. Women and men, upper and lower classes, rich and poor countries, and privileged and disadvantaged racial and ethnic groups are exposed to health risks to varying degrees. This suggests that health is not just a medical question but also a sociological issue. The first task we set ourselves below is to examine the sociological factors that account for the uneven distribution of health in society.

The story of the Black Death also suggests that health problems change over time. Epidemics of various types still break out, but there can be no Black Death where sanitation and hygiene prevent the spread of disease. Today we are also able to treat many infectious diseases, such as tuberculosis and pneumonia, with antibiotics. These wonder drugs and many other life-saving therapies were developed by twentieth-century medical science.

However, our medical successes have created new problems. For instance, because of the overuse of antibiotics, resistant microbes have developed through mutation. We are now faced with the spread of forms of tuberculosis and other infectious diseases once considered eliminated. Similarly, medical successes allow people to live longer than they used to. **Life expectancy** is the average age at death of the members of a population. Life expectancy in Canada in 1831 was approximately 40 years for men and 42 years for women (Lavoie and Oderkirk, 2000: 3). In contrast, a Canadian girl born in 2002 can hope to live to 83, a boy to 76 (Ash, 2001: 53). However, as a result of increased life expectancy, degenerative conditions such as cancer and heart disease have an opportunity to develop in a way that was not possible a century ago (see Table 15.1). The ability to prolong life by technical means also raises new questions about when people should be allowed to die and whether under some circumstances medical personnel should be allowed to assist them in bringing life to a close. The sociology of aging examines how society copes with such consequences of a growing elderly population. It is the second major issue we examine in this chapter.

The story of the Black Death raises a third issue, too. We cannot help being struck by the superstition and ignorance surrounding the treatment of the ill in medieval times. Remedies were often herbal but also included earthworms, urine, and animal excrement. People believed it was possible to maintain good health by keeping body fluids in balance. Therefore, cures that released body fluids were common. These included hot baths, laxatives, and diuretics, which increase the flow of urine. If these treatments didn't work, bloodletting was often prescribed. No special qualifications were required to administer medical treatment. Barbers doubled as doctors.

However, the backwardness of medieval medical practice, and the advantages of modern scientific medicine, can easily be exaggerated. For example, medieval doctors stressed the importance of prevention, exercise, a balanced diet, and a congenial environment in

**✦ TABLE 15.1 ✦**

**Leading Causes of Death, Canada, 1901 and 1997**

Source: 1901 data: Adapted from Table VI, "Principal Causes of Death," *Fourth Census of Canada, 1901, volume IV.* Ottawa: S. E. Dawson, 1906; 1997 data: Adapted from Statistics Canada, http://www.statcan.ca, Canadian Statistics, "Selected Leading Causes of Death by Sex, 1997."

| | Deaths per 100 000 Population | Percent of Deaths | Ratio Male: Female |
|---|---|---|---|
| **1901** | | | |
| 1. Tuberculosis | 180.8 | 12.0 | – |
| 2. Bronchitis and pneumonia | 150.9 | 10.0 | – |
| 3. Affections of the intestines | 136.9 | 9.1 | – |
| 4. Senile debility | 111.5 | 7.4 | – |
| 5. Congenital debility | 106.0 | 7.0 | – |
| 6. Diseases of the heart | 84.5 | 5.6 | – |
| 7. Apoplexy and paralysis | 67.2 | 4.4 | – |
| 8. Diphtheria and croup | 59.7 | 3.9 | – |
| 9. Accidents | 51.3 | 3.4 | – |
| 10. Cancers | 42.3 | 2.8 | – |
| 11. Influenza | 39.7 | 2.6 | – |
| **1997** | | | |
| 1. Cancers | 181.5 | 27.2 | 1.5 |
| 2. Heart disease | 173.0 | 26.6 | 1.8 |
| 3. Stroke (cerebrovascular) | 47.8 | 7.4 | 1.2 |
| 4. Lung disease | 29.0 | 4.5 | 2.2 |
| 5. Accidents | 27.6 | 4.0 | 2.1 |
| 6. Pneumonia/influenza | 23.7 | 3.7 | 1.6 |
| 7. Diabetes | 17.4 | 2.6 | 1.4 |
| 8. Diseases of central nervous system | 15.0 | 2.3 | 1.2 |
| 9. Diseases of arteries | 14.3 | 2.2 | 1.8 |
| 10. Psychoses | 13.6 | 2.2 | 1.0 |
| 11. Suicide | 12.0 | 1.7 | 4.0 |
| 12. Kidney diseases | 8.0 | 1.2 | 1.8 |
| 13. Liver diseases | 6.4 | 0.9 | 2.1 |
| 14. Neurotic and nonpsychotic illnesses | 3.5 | 0.5 | 1.9 |
| 15. HIV/AIDS | 2.0 | 0.3 | 7.2 |

maintaining good health. We now know this is sound advice. On the other hand, one of the great shortcomings of modern medicine is its emphasis on high-tech cures rather than preventive and environmental measures. Therefore, in the third section of this chapter, we investigate not just the many wonderful cures and treatments brought to us by modern scientific medicine but also its weaknesses. We also examine how the medical professions gained substantial control over health issues and promoted their own approach to well-being.

## HEALTH AND INEQUALITY

### Defining and Measuring Health

According to the World Health Organization (WHO), **health** is

> the ability of an individual to achieve his [or her] potential and to respond positively to the challenges of the environment . . . The basic resources for health are income, shelter and food. Improvement in health requires a secure foundation in these basics, but also information and life skills; a supportive environment, providing opportunities for making health choices among goods, services and facilities; and conditions in the economic, social and physical environments . . . that enhance health. (World Health Organization, 2000)

The WHO definition lists in broad terms the main factors that promote good health. However, when it comes to *measuring* the health of a population, sociologists typically examine the negative: rates of illness and death. They reason that healthy populations experience less illness and longer life than unhealthy populations. This is the approach we follow here.

Assuming ideal conditions, how long can a person live? In the twenty-first century, the **maximum human life span** may well increase because of medical advances. So far, however, the record is held by Jeanne Louise Calment, a French woman who died in 1997 at the age of 122. (Other people claim to be older, but they lack authenticated birth certificates.)

Calment was an extraordinary individual. She took up fencing at age 85, rode a bicycle until she was 100, gave up smoking at 120, and released a rap CD at 121 (Matalon, 1997). In contrast, only 1 in 100 people in the world's rich countries now lives to be 100. Medical scientists tell us that the **maximum average human life span**—the average age of death for an entire population under *ideal* conditions—is likely to increase in this century. Currently, the maximum average life span is roughly 87 years (Olshansky, Carnes, and Cassel, 1990).

In the twenty-first century, the maximum life span may increase because of medical advances. So far, the record is held by Jeanne Louise Calment, a French woman who died in 1997 at the age of 122.

Unfortunately, however, conditions are nowhere near ideal. Life expectancy throughout the world is less than 87 years. Figure 15.1 shows life expectancy in selected countries. Leading the list is Japan, where life expectancy was 81 years in 2000. Life expectancy was one to four years shorter in the other rich postindustrial countries, including Canada. But in India, life expectancy was only 61 years. The poor African country of Niger suffered the world's shortest life expectancy at 41 years (Population Reference Bureau, 2000). More than 50 million people today live in countries with a life expectancy shorter than 45 years, and about 300 million people live in 16 countries where life expectancy actually decreased between 1975 and 1995 (World Health Organization, 1998b).

Accounting for the difference between the maximum average human life span and life expectancy is one of the main tasks of the sociologist of health. For example, although the maximum average human life span is 87 years, life expectancy at birth in Canada in 2000 was 79 years. This implies that, on average, Canadians are being deprived of eight years of life due to avoidable *social* causes (87 – 79 = 8). Avoidable social causes deprive the average citizen of Niger of more than 46 years of life (87 – 41 = 46). Clearly, social causes have a big—and variable—impact on illness and death. We must therefore discuss them in detail.

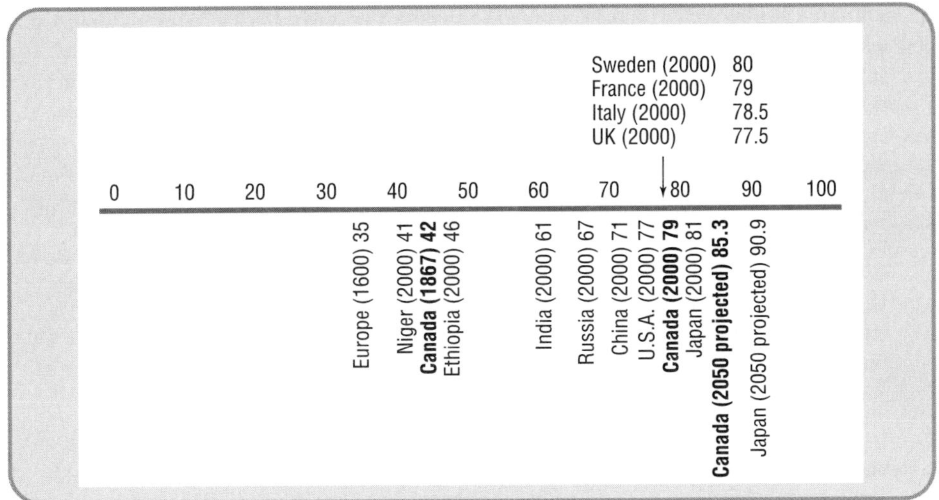


✦ **FIGURE 15.1** ✦
**Life Expectancy, Selected Countries (in years)**

Source: Population Reference Bureau (2000); Tuljapurkar, Li, and Boe (2000).

*Note:* We estimated some 2000 life expectancies by adding male and female life expectancies, dividing by 2, and adding 0.5 year to take account of the fact that the female:male population ratio is greater than 1.

## The Social Causes of Illness and Death

People get sick and die partly because of natural causes. One person may have a genetic predisposition to cancer. Another may come in contact with a deadly Ebola virus in the environment. However, over and above such natural causes of illness and death, we can single out three types of *social* causes:

1. *Human-environmental factors.* The environment constructed by humans poses major health risks. For example, the introduction of sour gas wells and logging operations around the reserves of the Lubicon First Nation in Alberta has resulted in a dramatic increase in illness. More than one in three members of the Lubicon population currently suffers from such health problems as tuberculosis, respiratory difficulties, and cancer at rates far above the national average (Barlow and May, 2000: 183). **Environmental racism,** or the tendency for hazardous waste sites and polluting industries to be located near First Nations communities or areas populated by the poor, the politically marginalized, or certain visible minorities, also contributes to lower levels of health. For example, in the 1980s, the mercury poisoning of the English-Wabigoon river system in western Ontario near the Manitoba border by the local pulp and paper industry led to the virtual destruction of the Grassy Narrows Indians' way of life and means of livelihood (Shkilnyk, 1985). More recently,

   > patterns of atmospheric cycling have made the North a dumping ground for industrial chemicals that ...[are] never used there. The chemicals bioaccumulate, delivering a higher level of toxic concentration to each level up the food chain. As a result, the breastmilk of Inuit mothers is ten times as contaminated as that of southern Canadian women. In both the North and the South, mother's milk is so laden with toxic substances such as PCBs, DDT (and its breakdown product DDE) and lindane, that if it were offered for sale, it would be too contaminated to be approved as human food. (Barlow and May, 2000: 184)

   This situation provides a striking illustration of how human-environmental conditions can cause illness and death (see also Chapter 18, Technology and the Global Environment).

2. *Lifestyle factors.* Smoking cigarettes, excessive use of alcohol and drugs, poor diet, lack of exercise, and social isolation are among the chief lifestyle factors associated with poor health and premature death. For example, smoking is associated with lung cancer, cardiovascular disease, strokes, emphysema, spontaneous abortion, premature birth, and neonatal death. In 1995, one in six deaths in Canada were caused by

smoking. In that year, there were 34 728 deaths and 500 345 years of potential life lost due to tobacco use (CCSA, 1999). It is estimated that smoking is responsible for at least one-quarter of all deaths in Canada of people between the ages of 35 and 84. As a cause of early death, smoking far outweighs the combined impact of suicide, vehicle crashes, and murder (Health Canada, 1999a, 2002b; Statistics Canada, 2001a). Social isolation, too, affects one's chance of becoming ill and dying prematurely. Thus, unmarried people have a greater chance of dying prematurely than do married people. At any age, the death of a spouse increases one's chance of dying, while remarrying decreases one's chance of dying (Helsing, Szklo, and Comstock, 1981). Social isolation is a particularly big problem among elderly people who retire, lose a spouse and friends, and cannot rely on family members or state institutions for social support. Such people are prone to fall into a state of depression that contributes to ill health.

3. *Factors related to the public health and health care systems.* The state of a nation's health depends partly on public and private efforts to improve people's well-being and treat their illnesses. The **public health system** is composed of government-run programs that ensure access to clean drinking water, basic sewage and sanitation services, and inoculation against infectious diseases. The absence of a public health system is associated with high rates of disease and low life expectancy. The **health care system** is composed of a nation's clinics, hospitals, and other facilities for ensuring health and treating illness. The absence of a system that ensures its citizens have access to a minimum standard of health care is also associated with high rates of disease and low life expectancy.

Exposure to all three sets of social causes of illness and death listed above is strongly related to country of residence, class, race, and gender. We now consider the impact of these factors, beginning with country of residence.

## Country of Residence

AIDS is the leading cause of death in urban Haiti. Extreme poverty has forced many Haitians to become prostitutes. They cater mainly to tourists from North America and Europe. Some of those tourists carried HIV, the virus that leads to AIDS, and they introduced it into Haiti. The absence of adequate health care and medical facilities in Haiti makes the epidemic's impact all the more devastating (Farmer, 1992).

AIDS is also the leading cause of death in the poverty-stricken part of Africa south of the Sahara desert. Table 15.2 shows that in December 1999, more than 8.5 percent of sub-Saharan Africans—24.5 million people—were living with AIDS/HIV (see also Figure 15.2). In contrast, 0.58 percent of North Americans and 0.23 percent of Western Europeans were living with AIDS/HIV. This means that AIDS/HIV is nearly 15 times more common in sub-Saharan Africa than in North America and almost 40 times more common than in Western Europe. As of June 30, 1998, 15 995 HIV/AIDS cases have been reported in

A health worker at Nazareth House in Cape Town, South Africa, lavishes care and attention on some of the 41 infected children in her care. Nearly one-fifth of South Africa's adult population is infected with AIDS/HIV.

✦ **TABLE 15.2** ✦

**A Global View of AIDS/HIV, December 1999**

Source: United Nations (2000b).

*Note:* The cumulative number of deaths due to AIDS on December 31, 1999, was about 14.5 million. More than 80% of these deaths had occurred in sub-Saharan Africa.

| | People Living with AIDS/HIV | Adult Rate (in percent) | AIDS Deaths, 1999 |
|---|---|---|---|
| **Began Late 1970s–Early 1980s** | | | |
| Sub-Saharan Africa | 24 500 000 | 8.57 | 2 200 000 |
| Latin America | 1 300 000 | 0.49 | 48 000 |
| Caribbean | 360 000 | 2.11 | 30 000 |
| Western Europe | 520 000 | 0.23 | 6 800 |
| North America | 900 000 | 0.58 | 20 000 |
| Australia & New Zealand | 15 000 | 0.13 | 120 |
| **Began Late 1980s** | | | |
| North Africa & Middle East | 220 000 | 0.12 | 13 000 |
| South & Southeast Asia | 5 600 000 | 0.54 | 460 000 |
| East Asia & Pacific | 530 000 | 0.06 | 18 000 |
| **Began Early 1990s** | | | |
| Eastern Europe & Central Asia | 420 000 | 0.21 | 8 500 |
| Total | 34 365 000 | 1.07 | 2 804 000 |

Canada, all but 158 of them among adults. Since the disease was first diagnosed in Canada in 1982, 11 046 Canadians have died because of HIV/AIDS infection (Statistics Canada, 1998c). Despite the much greater prevalence of AIDS/HIV in sub-Saharan Africa, however, spending on research and treatment is concentrated overwhelmingly in the rich countries of North America and Western Europe. As the case of AIDS/HIV illustrates, global inequality influences the exposure of people to different health risks.

You might think that prosperity increases health through biomedical advances, such as new medicines and diagnostic tools. If so, you are only partly correct. Biomedical advances do increase life expectancy. In particular, vaccines against infectious diseases have done much to improve health and ensure long life. However, the creation of a sound public health system was even more important in this regard. If a country can provide its citizens with clean water and a sewage system, epidemics decline in frequency and severity while life expectancy soars.

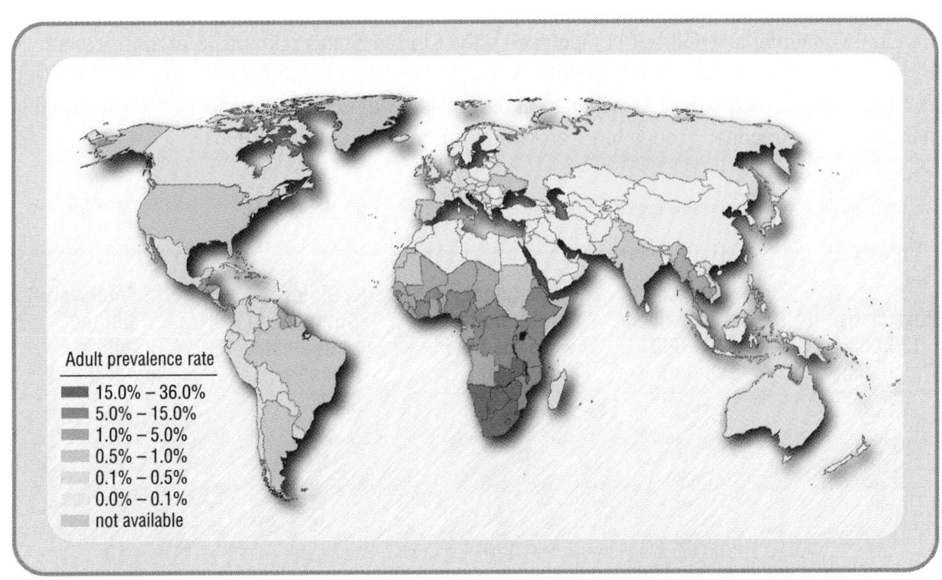


✦ **FIGURE 15.2** ✦

**Adult Prevalence Rate of AIDS/HIV Infection**

Source: UNAIDS/World Health Organization

The industrialized countries started to develop their public health systems in the mid-nineteenth century. Social reformers, concerned citizens, scientists, and doctors joined industrialists and politicians in urging governments to develop health policies that would help create a healthier labour force and citizenry (Bricker and Greenspon, 2001: 178–83; Goubert, 1989 [1986]; McNeill, 1976). But what was possible in North America and Western Europe 150 years ago is not possible in many developing countries today. Most of us take clean water for granted, but more than 1 billion of the world's 6 billion people do not have access to a sanitary water supply (de Villiers, 1999).

Other indicators of health inequality for selected countries are given in Table 15.3. We see immediately that there is a positive association between national wealth and good health. Canada, the United States, and Japan are rich countries. They spend a substantial part of their wealth on health care. Many physicians and nurses service their populations. As a result, **infant mortality** (the annual number of deaths before the age of 1 for every 1000 live births) is low. So is the rate of stunted growth due to malnutrition among children under the age of five. As noted above, rich countries also enjoy high life expectancy. Mexico, which is poorer than Canada, the United States, and Japan, spends a smaller proportion of its wealth on health care. Accordingly, its population is less healthy in a number of respects. The sub-Saharan country of Niger is one of the poorest countries in the world. It spends little on health care, has few medical personnel, and suffers from high rates of malnutrition stunting and infant mortality.

Closer inspection of Table 15.3 reveals an anomaly, however. The United States spends nearly twice as much per person on health care as Japan and more than 50 percent more than Canada. However, on average, Americans work nearly two months a year just to pay their medical bills. The United States has 11 percent more doctors per 100 000 people than Canada and 38 percent more than Japan. Yet the United States immunizes a smaller percentage of its children against measles, contains a higher percentage of malnourished children, and has a higher rate of infant mortality than Canada and Japan. On one measure—immunization of children against measles—the United States is substantially behind Mexico. The American case shows that spending more money on health care does not always improve the health of a nation.

## Class, Race, and Gender

What accounts for the American anomaly? Why do Americans spend far more on health care than any other country in the world yet wind up with a population that, on average, is less healthy than the population of other rich countries? Part of the answer is that the gap between rich and poor is greater in the United States than in Canada, Japan, Sweden, France, and other rich countries. In general, the higher the level of inequality in a country, the more unhealthy its population is (Wilkinson, 1996). Since, as we saw in Chapter 7 (Social Stratification: Canadian and Global Perspectives), the United States contains a higher percentage of poor people than other rich countries, its average level of health is lower. Moreover, because income inequality has widened in the United States since the early 1970s, health disparities among income groups have grown (Williams and Collins, 1995).

✦ **TABLE 15.3** ✦

**Health Indicators, Selected Countires, Mid-1990s**

Source: Adapted from World Health Organization (1999b).

*= estimate

| | Health Expenditures as % of GDP | Physicians/ 100 000 Population | Nurses and Midwives/ 100 000 Population | Infant Mortality/ 1000 Live Births | Children Immunized against Measles (%) | Malnutrition Stunting, Children under 5 (%) |
|---|---|---|---|---|---|---|
| USA | 14.0 | 245 | 878 | 7 | 82 | 2 |
| Canada | 9.0 | 221 | 958 | 6 | 98* | 1* |
| Japan | 7.2 | 177 | 641 | 4 | n.a. | 0* |
| Mexico | 4.2 | 107 | 40 | 31 | 97 | 23 |
| Niger | 2.0 | 3 | 17 | 115 | 42 | 40 |

In Canada, despite our system of universal health care, socio-economic status is related to numerous aspects of health and illness. On average, people with low income die at a younger age than do people with high income. Adults with low income are four to seven times more likely (depending on race, ethnicity, and gender) than those with high income to report fair or poor health. Poor Canadians are also more likely to report an unmet need for health care. In 1996–97, the highest rate of unmet health care needs was reported by Canadians in the lowest income bracket. They had an approximately 1 in 10 chance of reporting unmet needs, compared with a 1 in 20 chance among people at the highest income level (Health Canada, 1999a, 1999b; Statistics Canada, 1998a). Research finds that residents of the poorest neighbourhoods have death rates from circulatory disease, lung cancer, injuries, and suicide that are significantly higher than rates for residents of the richest neighbourhoods. Being poor is also associated with high rates of tobacco and alcohol consumption, being overweight, physical inactivity, and engaging in violence (Health Canada, 1999b). A broad range of psychiatric conditions is also associated with low socio-economic status (Williams and Collins, 1999).

Why does health deteriorate as we move down the class hierarchy? Sociologists have proposed several explanations:

1. *Unequal access to health resources.* A disproportionately large number of poor Canadians live in areas with inferior medical services. For example, there are fewer hospitals, physicians, and nurses per capita in rural areas than in urban areas. As well, the quality of preventive, diagnostic, and treatment facilities is generally superior in urban areas. Moreover, although access to health care remains largely unrelated to income due to Canada's medicare system, many low-income and moderate-income Canadians have limited or no access to eye care, dentistry, mental health counselling, and prescription drugs (Health Canada, 1999a; Boychuk, 2002). According to the National Population Health Survey, only 25 percent of Canadians in the low-income and middle-income groups had dental insurance, and only 34 percent visited a dentist in 1996–97. In contrast, 73 percent of high-income Canadians had dental insurance, and 81 percent visited a dentist in that same period (Health Canada, 1999b). According to the 1997–98 National Population Health Survey, just 47 percent of Canadians had insurance to cover at least part of the cost of eyeglasses or contact lenses. Few of them were members of lower classes (Health Canada, 1999a).
2. *Lack of knowledge.* If poor people have less access than others to doctors and hospitals, they also tend to have less knowledge about healthy lifestyles. For example, they are less likely to know what constitutes a nutritious diet. This, too, contributes to their propensity to illness. Illness, in turn, makes it more difficult for poor people to escape poverty (Abraham, 1993).
3. *High stress and the inability to cope with it.* People in lower classes experience relatively high stress levels because of their deprived and difficult living conditions (Kessler et al., 1994). Stress has been linked to a variety of physical and mental health problems, including high blood pressure, cancer, chronic fatigue, violence, and substance abuse. Moreover, people higher up in the class structure are often able to turn stress off. They can, for instance, more easily take a few days off work or go on vacation. People in lower classes have fewer resources that allow them to cope with stress by turning it off (Cockerham, 1998; Epstein, 1998; Evans, 1999). Finally, because they lack other resources for coping with stress, people in lower classes are more likely to turn to dangerous coping mechanisms, such as tobacco, alcohol, and illegal drugs. Of course, this results in a further deterioration of health.
4. *Environmental exposure.* As we saw above, poor people are more likely to be exposed to environmental risks that have a negative impact on health. There is a striking lack of pulp and paper mills, oil refineries, dump sites, factories, and mines in Westmount (Montreal), Tuxedo (Winnipeg), and other wealthy Canadian neighbourhoods. Racial disparities in health status are large. For example, the life expectancy of Status Indians is seven to eight years less than that of non-Aboriginal

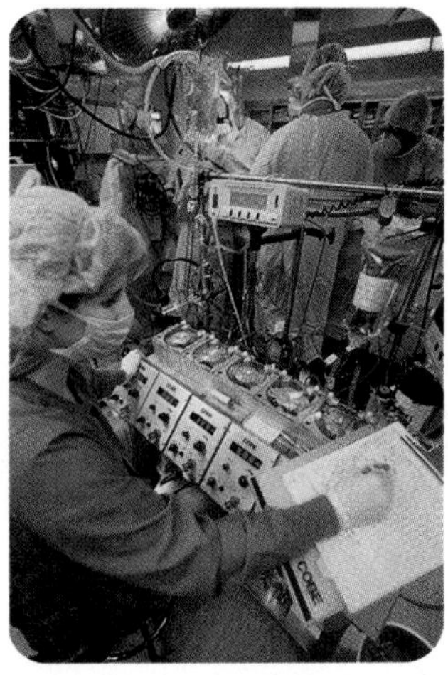

Biomedical advances increase life expectancy, but the creation of a sound public health system has even more dramatic effects.

Canadians (Status Indians are people whose names appear on the Indian Register maintained by the Department of Indian and Northern Affairs), and illegal drug use is high among Aboriginal peoples (Canadian Aboriginal News, 2001; Scott, 1997). Despite the health risks posed to both mother and the developing fetus, a national survey found that 76 percent of Inuit women and 54 percent of Indian women smoke during pregnancy, more than two to three times the national average (CCSA, 1999).

Such health disparities are partly, though not entirely, due to economic differences among racial groups. However, although Canadian research on this subject is sparse, American research shows that the health status of members of disadvantaged racial groups is lower than the health status of members of advantaged racial groups, *even within the same income group*. That is, if you compare an African-American and a white American who enjoy the same annual income, the African-American is likely to have poorer health. This suggests that racism affects health. It does so in three ways. First, income and other rewards do not have the same value across racial groups. For instance, due to discrimination, each year of education completed by an African-American results in smaller income gains than it does for white Americans. Since, as we have seen, income is associated with good health, blacks tend to be worse off than whites at the same income level. Second, racism affects access to health services. This is because African-Americans at all income levels tend to live in racially segregated neighbourhoods with fewer health-related facilities. Third, the experience of racism induces psychological distress that has a negative effect on health status. For example, racism increases the likelihood of drug addiction and participation in violence (Williams and Collins, 1995). Racism is also involved when some health care workers fail to provide services that are "racially sensitive, culturally appropriate and linguistically accessible" (Henry et al., 2000: 210). For example, with regards to victims of family violence, the assumption that certain races are "less credible" than others simply "adds another painful dimension to the experience and to the problem of finding help" (Henry et al., 2000: 214). Although one must be careful not to generalize too hastily from the United States to Canada, we think it is highly likely that Aboriginal peoples and some Afro-Canadians are affected by similar processes.

Finally, we must mention the health inequalities based on gender that some feminist scholars emphasize. In a review of the relevant literature in the *New England Journal of Medicine,* one researcher concluded that such gender inequalities are substantial (Haas, 1998).

- Gender bias exists in medical research. Worldwide, public health systems have been slower to address and more likely to neglect women's health issues than men's health issues. Thus, more research has focused on "men's diseases," such as cardiac arrest, than on "women's diseases," such as breast cancer. Similarly, women have been excluded from participating in major health research studies that have examined the relationship between aspirin use and heart disease and how cholesterol levels, blood pressure, and smoking affect heart disease (Johnson and Fee, 1997). Medical research is only beginning to explore the fact that women may react differently than men to some illnesses and may require different treatment regimes.
- Gender bias also exists in medical treatment. For example, women undergo fewer kidney transplants, various cardiac procedures, and other treatments than men.
- Because on average women live longer than men, they experience greater lifetime risk of functional disability and chronic illness, and greater need for long-term care. The low status of women in many less developed countries results in their being nutritionally deprived and having less access to medical care than do men. As a result, women in developing countries suffer high rates of mortality and **morbidity** (acute and chronic illness) because of the high rates of complications associated with pregnancy and childbirth. About one-quarter to one-half of deaths among women in developing countries are attributed to pregnancy-related complications ("Maternal Mortality," 1998). In rich developed countries such as Canada, the ratio of women to men is about 1.05. In poor less developed countries the ratio of women

to men is about 0.95. This means that more than 100 million women are "missing" in the poor less developed countries, largely because of gender inequality in health care (Sen, 1999: 104–7).

- Canadian women face a higher risk than men of poverty after marital disruption by divorce or widowhood. Since, as we have seen, poverty contributes to ill health, we could expect improvements in women's economic standing to be reflected in improved health status for women.

In sum, although on average women live longer than men, gender inequalities have a negative impact on women's health. Women's health is negatively affected by differences between women and men in access to gender-appropriate medical research and treatment as well as the economic resources needed to secure adequate health care.

## Health and Politics

Canada has a national health insurance system that is sometimes loosely described as **socialized medicine.** Despite differences in how socialized medicine works in such countries as Great Britain, Sweden, Germany, and Italy, common to all such systems is the fact that the government (1) directly controls the financing and organization of health services, (2) directly pays providers, (3) guarantees equal access to health care, and (4) allows some private care for individuals who are willing to pay for their medical expenses (Cockerham, 1998). However, Canada does not truly have a system of socialized medicine in that the government does not employ Canadian physicians. Rather, most of Canada's physicians are independent practitioners who are generally paid on a fee-for-service basis and submit claims directly to the provincial or territorial health insurance plan for payment.

Even though Canada's health care system is often lauded as among the best in the world, problems exist. For example, although our health care system is based on the premise that "all citizens will have access to the care they need within a reasonable time period" (Health Canada, 1999a), there are no precise definitions of what constitutes "needed care" or a "reasonable time period." For example, "support programs and services available to persons with disabilities, which are so essential to viability within the wider community, vary enormously from one part of the country to another" (Graham, 1999). In Lloydminster, which straddles the Saskatchewan–Alberta border, a person with a visual disability can obtain certain high-tech equipment on the Alberta side but not on the Saskatchewan side; "in other words, if you live in Saskatchewan you can get a white cane—but sorry, nothing high tech" (Graham, 1999: 48).

Despite a total health care bill that surpassed $100 billion in 2001 (Kennedy, 2001), Canadians still confront closings of emergency room departments; continuing shortages of nurses, physicians, specialists, and costly diagnostic equipment; persistent geographic differences in access to services; a decrease in the number of available hospital beds; and growing waiting lists for surgeries (Bricker and Greenspon, 2001; Health Canada, 2002a). Consider as well that, in the 12 months prior to their participation in the 1996–97 National Population Health Survey, approximately 5 percent of the Canadian population 12 years of age and older (1.2 million Canadians) required some health care or advice on at least one occasion and did not receive it. More than three-quarters of these needs were for physical health conditions (78 percent), and emotional health conditions and injuries were each reported by 9 percent of respondents.

A national survey conducted by the Canadian Medical Association (1998) suggests that Canadians perceived a decline in access to health care services between 1996 and 1998 (see Figure 15.3). Another national survey conducted by the Canadian Medical Association (2001) found that, "[w]hen asked to assign a letter grade to the current health care system, Canadians gave it, on average, a B for overall quality" (see Table 15.4). Although Canadians assigned a grade of A to access to family physicians, they awarded a grade of B to access to clinics and services for youth and seniors and a grade of C to access to modern diagnostic equipment, emergency room services, mental health services, and medical specialists.

✦ **FIGURE 15.3** ✦

**Canadians' Perceived Access to Health Care Services, 1998: Percentage Reporting Deteriorating Access in the Past Few Years**

Source: Canadian Medical Association (1998).

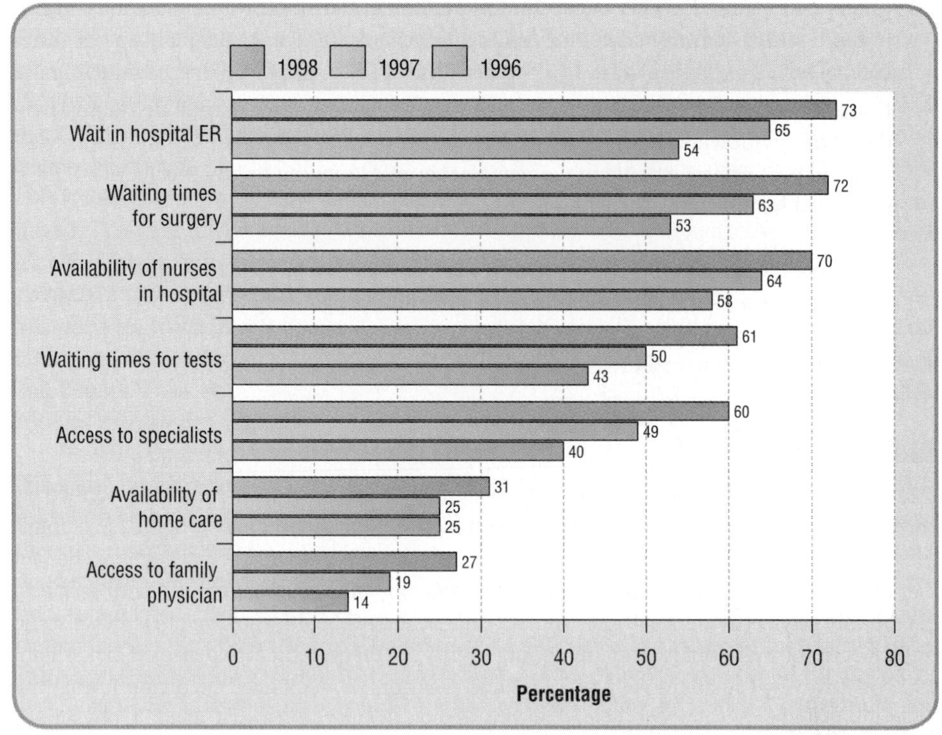


In general, Canadians were far more critical of the government's performance in the delivery of health care. Although health care providers, particularly physicians, were given a grade of B, the federal government was given a grade of C. Canadians gave a failing grade (F) to their provincial government's performance on health care issues. When asked how our current system could be improved, more than 8 in 10 Canadians identified the provision of long-term, sustainable funding. A second option, advanced by almost 6 in 10 Canadians, stressed more efficient management and the proper allocation of existing funds.

Patients are not the only Canadians complaining of inadequate services. At the 1999 annual meeting of the Canadian Medical Association, physicians asserted that Canada was heading toward a critical shortage of doctors that will threaten patient safety and emphasized that there already exists a serious shortage of physicians in rural areas and in certain specialties such as anaesthesia, radiology, and obstetrics. It was noted that even in major Canadian cities such as Toronto, patients are being forced to wait for needed surgery

✦ **TABLE 15.4** ✦

**Grading Our Health Care System**

Source: Canadian Medical Association (2001).

| GRADE | |
|---|---|
| Overall Quality of Health Care | B |
| **Access to Services** | |
| Family physicians | A |
| Clinics, services for youth and seniors | B |
| Emergency room services, diagnostic equipment and specialists | C |
| **Performance** | |
| Provincial governments | F |
| Federal government | C |
| Health care providers | B |

because of the shortage (Bricker and Greenspon, 2001: 217). Projecting into the future, the physicians estimated that the situation will worsen as a large wave of aging baby boomers become increasingly reliant on the health care system. They warned that by 2021 there will be only 1 doctor for every 718 patients, compared to the 1 doctor for every 548 patients in 1998 (Kennedy, 1999).

The news, however, is not altogether grim. Evidence suggests that Canada's health care system is, in fact, accomplishing what it originally set out to do: eliminate inequality among Canadians in relation to health care services. For example, poor women in Toronto have a survival rate for breast cancer that is 30 percent higher that of poor women in Detroit. For ovarian cancer the survival rate is 38 percent higher, and for cervical cancer it is 48 percent higher (Armstrong, Armstrong, and Fegan, 1998).

Nevertheless, the question of how to sustain—if not improve—public health care in Canada continues to be the subject of intense controversy and debate. For example, the premiers of Ontario and Alberta have both issued challenges to the federal government over health care. In Alberta, the provincial government seems poised to introduce changes that would allow for greater privatization. In Ontario, the provincial government has threatened that, if Ottawa does not increase transfer payments, it will withdraw pharmacare and home care services currently provided to senior citizens. Some critics have argued for privatization, that is, allowing private clinics to play an expanded role in the public system. They believe that privatization will facilitate timely access to quality care and allow provinces to cope with rising health costs (Boychuck, 2002). Others, however, suggest that privatization might result in the development of a two-tier system of health care: one tier for those who can pay for quality care and a second tier for those who cannot.

A two-tier system exists in the United States. The United States lacks a system of health insurance that covers the entire population. About 40 million Americans are not covered by health insurance at all. Another 40 million are inadequately covered. Only the elderly, the poor, and veterans receive medical benefits from the government under the Medicare and Medicaid programs (Starr, 1994 [1992]).

The vast majority of Americans are covered by private insurance programs run by employers and unions, although some people buy their own private coverage. Today, about 85 percent of employees buy their health coverage from health maintenance organizations (HMOs; Gorman, 1998). HMOs are private corporations that collect regular payments from employers and employees. When an employee needs medical treatment, it is administered by the HMO.

Like all corporations, HMOs pursue profit. They employ four main strategies to keep their shareholders happy. Unfortunately, all four strategies lower the average quality of health care in the United States (Kuttner, 1998a; 1998b):

1. Some HMOs avoid covering sick people and people who are likely to get sick. This keeps their costs down. For example, if an HMO can show that you had a medical condition before you came under its care, it won't cover you for that condition.
2. HMOs try to minimize the cost of treating sick people they can't avoid covering. Thus, HMOs use doctor-compensation formulas that reward doctors for withholding unprofitable treatments.
3. There have been allegations that some HMOs routinely inflate diagnoses to maximize reimbursements. For instance, at this writing, Columbia/HCA, the largest for-profit hospital chain in the United States, is under federal investigation for just that practice.
4. HMOs keep overhead charges high. In 1992, for example, administrative overhead accounted for 14 percent of total medical expenditures for private insurance companies. In contrast, administrative overhead amounts to 4 percent for Medicaid and 2 percent for Medicare. In Canada, administrative overhead amounts to 1 percent of expenditures (Folbre, 1995).

What is your opinion on Canadian health care? Do you favour the existing system, or would you like to see Canada move to the American model of a largely private system? Would you personally benefit more from one type of system than the other? If so, why? Does the type of system from which you would personally benefit influence the type of system you think is best for the country as a whole? Do you think it is possible to create a universal health care system that encourages cutting-edge research and development, attracts the best medical personnel, *and* maintains the level of health care that Canadians have come to expect? If so, how would you structure such a health care system? If not, what compromises do you think Canadians would have to make to achieve this ideal?

## AGING AS A SOCIAL PROBLEM

If health care is an attempt to prolong life and improve its quality, aging is health care's relentless foe. Many people think of aging simply as a natural, biological process that inevitably thwarts our best attempts to delay death. Sociologists, however, view aging in a more complex light. For them, aging is also a deeply social phenomenon. Specifically, as we saw in Chapter 4, Socialization, aging is a process of socialization, or learning new roles appropriate to different stages of life. The sociological nature of aging is also evident in the fact that its significance varies from one society to the next. That is, different societies attach different *meanings* to the progression of life through its various stages. Menopause, for example, occurs in all mature women. In Canada and the United States, it is often seen as a major life event. The old euphemism for menopause was the rather dramatic expression "change of life." In contrast, menopause is a relatively minor matter in Japan. Moreover, although menopausal women in Canada frequently suffer "hot flashes," menopausal Japanese women tend to complain mainly about "stiff shoulders" (Lock, 1993). In many Western countries, complaining about stiff shoulders is a classic symptom of having just given birth. As this example shows, the stages of life are not simply natural processes but events deeply rooted in society and culture. As we will see, the same holds for death.

### Aging and the Life Course

All individuals pass through distinct stages of life, which, taken together, sociologists call the **life course.** These stages are often marked by **rites of passage,** or rituals signifying the transition from one life stage to another (Fried and Fried, 1980). Circumcision, baptism, confirmation, the bar and bat mitzvah, university convocation, the wedding ceremony, and the funeral are among the best-known rites of passage in Canada.

As we saw in Chapter 4, Socialization, the duration of each stage of life differs from one society and historical period to the next. For example, there are no universal rules about when one becomes an adult. In preindustrial societies, adulthood arrived soon after puberty. In Japan, one becomes an adult at age 20. In Russia, you're not considered a fully developed adult until age 30, even though you can legally vote and drink alcohol at 18.

Even the *number* of life stages varies historically and across societies. For instance, childhood was a brief and insignificant stage of development in medieval Europe (Ariès, 1962 [1960]). In contrast, childhood is a prolonged stage of development in rich societies today, and adolescence is a new phase of development that was virtually unknown just a few hundred years ago (Kett, 1977). Increased life expectancy and the need for a highly educated labour force made childhood and adolescence both possible and necessary.

Finally, although some life-course events are universal—birth, puberty, marriage, and death—not all cultures attach the same significance to them. Thus, ritual practices to mark these events vary. For example, formal puberty rituals in many preindustrial societies are extremely important because they mark the transition to adult responsibilities. However, adult responsibilities do not immediately follow puberty in industrial and postindustrial societies because of the introduction of a prolonged period of childhood and adolescence. Therefore, formal puberty rituals do not exist in such societies.

## Sociological Aspects of Aging

As you pass through the life course, you new learn new patterns of behaviour that are common to people your age. Sociologically speaking, a category of people born in the same range of years is called an **age cohort.** For example, all Canadians born between 1980 and 1989 form an age cohort. **Age roles** are patterns of behaviour that are expected of people in different age cohorts. Age roles form an important part of our sense of self and others (Riley, Foner, and Waring, 1988). As we pass through the stages of the life course, we assume different age roles. To put it simply, a child is supposed to act like a child, an elderly person like an elderly person. We may find a 5-year-old dressed in a suit cute but look askance at a lone 50-year-old on a merry-go-round. The admonishment "act your age" can be applied to people of all ages who do not conform to their age roles. Many age roles are informally known by character types, such as "rebellious teenager" or "wise old woman." We formalize some age roles by law. For instance, establishing minimum ages for drinking, driving, and voting formalizes certain aspects of the adolescent and adult age roles.

We find it natural that children in the same age cohort, such as preschoolers in a park, should play together, or that people of similar age cluster at parties. Differences across age cohorts are sufficiently large in our society that some sociologists regard youth culture as a distinct subculture. Adolescents and teenagers—divided though they may be by gender, class, race, and ethnicity—frequently share common interests in music, movies, and so forth (Bibby, 2001).

A **generation** is a special type of age cohort. Many people think of a generation as people born within a 15- to 30-year span. Sociologists, however, usually define a generation more narrowly. From a sociological point of view, a generation is composed of members of an age cohort who have unique and formative experiences during their youth. Age cohorts are statistically convenient categories, but most members of a generation are conscious of belonging to a distinct age group. For example, "baby boomers" are North Americans who were born in the prosperous years of 1946 to 1964. Most of them came of age between the mid-1960s and the early 1970s. Common experiences that bind them together include major historical events (e.g., the war in Vietnam, Trudeaumania, Canada's centenary, the Watergate break-in, and the subsequent resignation of U.S. President Nixon) and popular music (e.g., the songs of Bob Dylan, the Beatles, and the Rolling Stones).

A generation is composed of members of an age cohort who have unique and formative experiences during their youth.

"Generation X" followed the baby boomers. Members of Generation X were born between 1965 and the early 1980s, and faced a period of slower economic growth and a job market glutted by the baby boomers. As a result, many of them resented having to take so-called McJobs when they entered the labour force. Douglas Coupland, the Vancouver writer credited with inventing the term *Generation X*, cuttingly defined a McJob as a "low-pay, low-prestige, low-dignity, low-benefit, no-future job in the service sector. Frequently considered a satisfying career choice by people who have never held one" (Coupland, 1991: 5).

Certain generationally defined moments sometimes help crystallize the feeling of being a member of a particular generation. For instance, when you are elderly you may still remember where you were when you first heard about the September 11, 2001, terrorist attacks on the United States or Princess Diana's fatal auto crash. Such memories may someday help you distinguish yourself from those who are too young to remember these tragic events. Finally, it should be noted that generations sometimes play a large role in history. Revolutionary movements, whether in politics or the arts, are sometimes led by members of a younger generation who aggressively displace members of an older generation (Eisenstadt, 1956; Mannheim, 1952; Spitzer, 1973).

**Age stratification** refers to social inequality between age cohorts. It exists in all societies and may be observed in everyday social interaction. For example, there is a clear status hierarchy in most schools. On average, students in higher grades enjoy higher status than students in lower grades. However, the strength of age stratification differs across social contexts. In Japan, for example, it is customary that elders are considered the head of the family; they sit at the head of the table, enter a room first, bathe first, and are honoured in a Respect for Elders Day. In contrast, the elderly in our own society are often viewed as "culturally irrelevant" (Kolland, 1994). Consider media representations of the young and the old in North America. While the young are featured in active, vital roles, the elderly are typically underrepresented or, when shown, presented as difficult, complaining, and burdensome. As a study of the elderly in popular films concluded, "older individuals of both genders were portrayed as less friendly, having less romantic activity, and enjoying fewer positive outcomes than younger characters at a movie's conclusion" (Brazzini et al., 1997: 541). Media depictions also may present the elderly as childlike in terms of their temperament, clothes, facial expressions, and activities—a phenomenon known as "infantalizing elders" (Arluke and Levin, 1990).

Some people think that ancient China and other societies were **gerontocracies,** that is, societies in which elderly men ruled, earned the highest incomes, and enjoyed the most prestige. Although some societies did approximate this model, its extent has been exaggerated. Powerful, wealthy, and prestigious "elders" are often mature, but not necessarily the oldest, men. Canada today is typical of most societies, past and present, in this regard. For example, median earned income for men gradually rises with age, reaching its peak at age 45, and then declines through later life (Guppy, Curtis, and Grabb, 1999: 249). Prestige and power follow the same course. This pattern reflects the fact that old age is usually not regarded as an unambiguous good. It denotes physical and mental decline and the nearness of death. Ambivalence about aging—especially as people reach the oldest age cohorts—is a cultural universal (Minois, 1989 [1987]). This ambivalence is accentuated by the common knowledge that the elderly face a host of social problems, the most serious of which we now examine.

## Social Problems of the Elderly

Canada's population, along with that of many other rich countries around the world, is "greying," that is, getting older. In 1901, only 5 percent of Canada's population was 65 or older, and almost 45 percent of the population was 19 or under. In that year, the median age of the Canadian population was 22.7 years (Novak, 1997). In contrast, Figure 15.4 shows a map of the projected median age in various parts of Canada for 2005.

Another way of considering the greying of Canada is to examine Figures 15.5 and 15.6, which provide **population pyramids,** graphs that show the percentage of the popu-

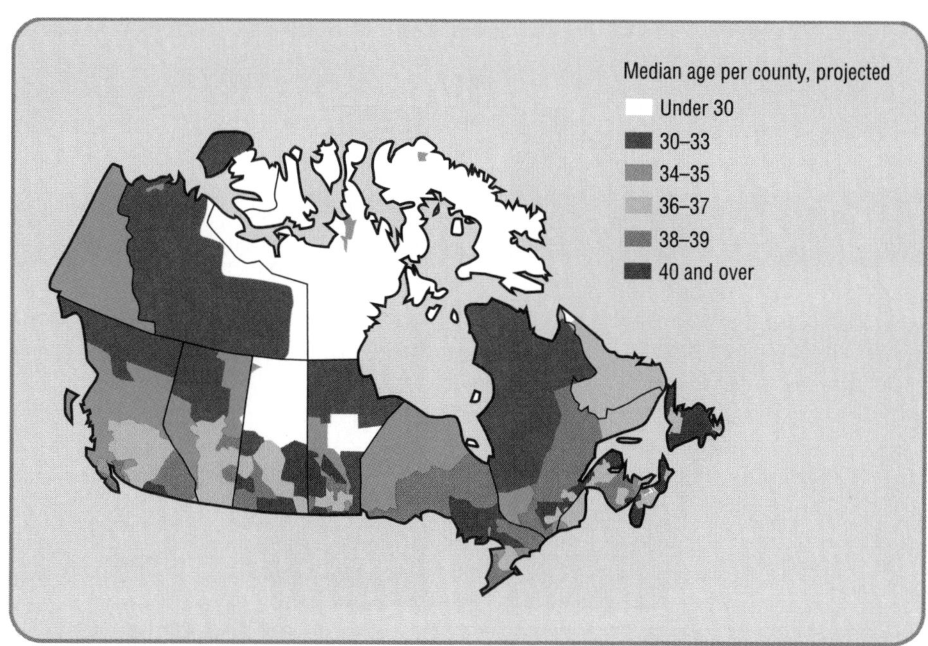


✦ **FIGURE 15.4** ✦
**Median Age, 2005**

Source: *Time* (1999).

lation in various age and sex cohorts, for 1901 and 2041 (projected). In 1901, Canada's population pyramid looked very much like a true pyramid: The base of the pyramid was wide, indicating that most people were younger, and the top was small, suggesting a small elderly population. However, by 2041, Canada's population "pyramid" will look more like a muffin, suggesting a small percentage of young people and a large percentage of old

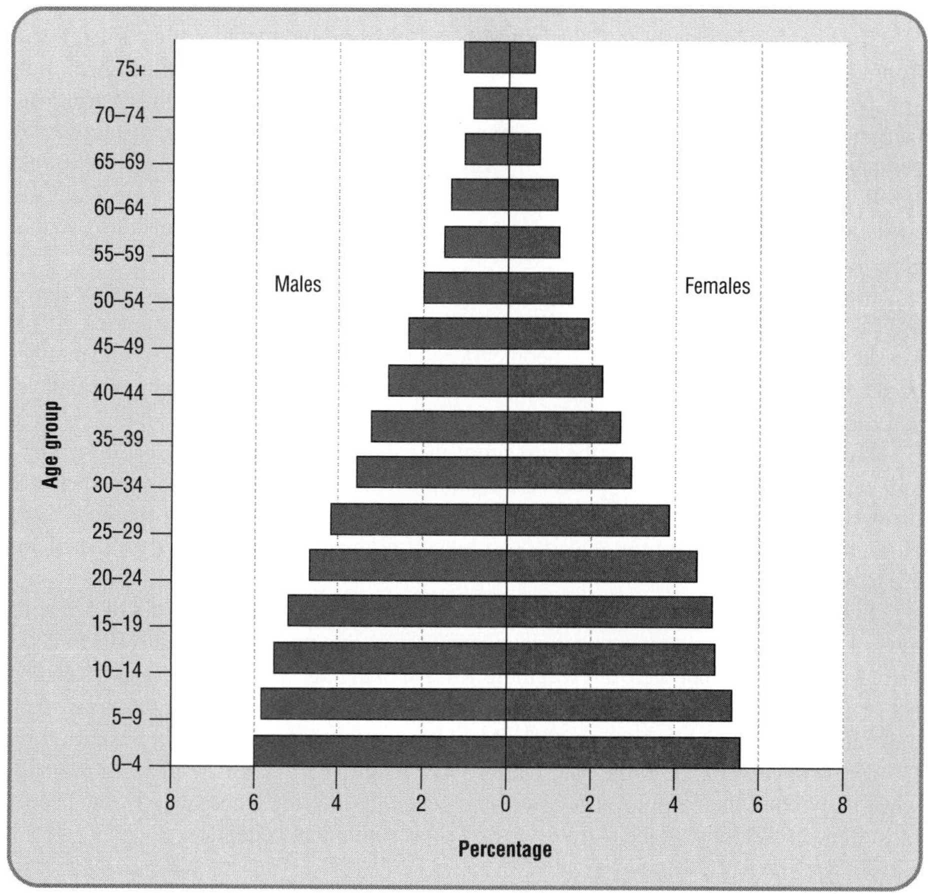


✦ **FIGURE 15.5** ✦
**Canadian Population Pyramids, 1901**

Source: McVey and Kalbach (1995).

✦ **FIGURE 15.6** ✦
**Canadian Population Pyramids, 2041[a]**

Source: George et al. (1994).

[a]low-population growth projection based on 1991 Census data

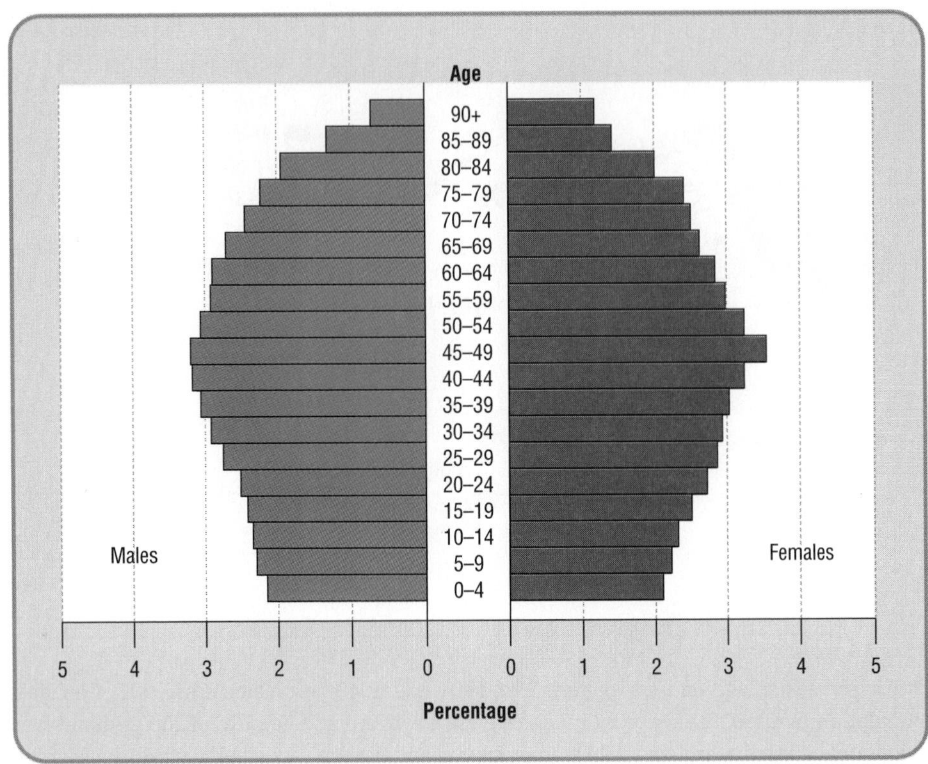


people. This change in the population composition of our society has wide-ranging implications for our social security system, as well as for housing, education, employment, and health care.

The number of elderly in Canada has increased for three main reasons. First, recall from Chapter 12, Families, that about a third of Canada's citizens (approximately 10 million people) were born during the 20-year "baby boom" after the Second World War. During this period, Canadian families averaged four children, resulting in more baby boomers per capita than in the United States, Australia, and New Zealand (Nikiforuk, 1999). Second, life expectancy has increased as a result of improvements in medical care, sanitation, nutrition, and housing. Third, Canada's low birth rate contributes to a higher percentage of elderly people.

Many sociologists of aging refer to elderly people who enjoy relatively good health—usually people between the ages of 65 and 74—as the "young old" (Neugarten, 1974; Laslett, 1991 [1989]). They refer to people 85 and over as the "old old." The rising number of old old concerns many people because the old old are most likely to suffer general physical decline, life-threatening diseases, social isolation, and poverty.

Significantly, the sex ratio (the number of men compared with the number of women) falls with age. In other words, because women live longer than men on average, there are many more women than men among the elderly. This imbalance is most marked in the oldest age cohorts. Therefore, poverty and related problems among the oldest Canadians are in part a gender issue.

Economic inequality between elderly women and men is largely the result of women's lower earning power when they are younger. Women are entering the paid workforce in increasing numbers, but there are still more women than men who are homemakers and do not work for a wage. Therefore, fewer women than men receive employer pensions when they retire (Nelson and Robinson, 2002). Moreover, as we saw in Chapter 9, Sexuality and Gender, women who are in the paid labour force tend to earn less than men. As a result, when they retire, their employer pensions are generally inferior. Consequently, the people most in need—elderly women—receive the fewest retirement benefits.

In addition to the old old and elderly women, the categories of elderly people most likely to be poor include those living alone, the disabled, and those living in rural areas (Siegel, 1996). However, declining income and poverty are not the only social problems faced by the elderly.

Because of the high value our society places on participation in the paid labour force, the end of full-time work signifies the end of meaningful life for at least some people. Especially in a society that puts a premium on vitality and youth, being elderly is a social stigma. **Ageism** is prejudice about, and discrimination against, elderly people. Ageism is evident, for example, when elderly men are stereotyped as "grumpy." Ageism affects women more than men. Thus, the same person who considers some elderly men "distinguished looking" may disparage elderly women as looking "haggard" (Banner, 1992).

Often, however, elderly people do not conform to the negative stereotypes applied to them. In Canada, 65 is sometimes considered the age at which people become elderly. (Sixty-five is the age at which Canadians become eligible to receive Old Age Security benefits, although some exemptions exist.) However, just because a person is 65 or over does not mean he or she is decrepit and dependent. On the contrary, most people who retire from active working life are far from being a tangle of health problems and a burden on society, due to the medical advances of recent decades, the healthier lifestyles followed by many elderly people, and the improved financial status of the elderly.

Contrary to stereotypes, the housing arrangements of elderly people are not usually desolate and depressing (Hochschild, 1973; Myerhoff, 1978). Although the likelihood that an individual will live in some type of special-care home for the elderly increases with age, only 1.4 percent of Canadian men and 1.7 percent of Canadian women between the ages of 65 and 74 live in such institutions. Among those age 85 and older, about one-quarter of men and slightly more than one-third of women lived in special-care homes (Novak, 1997; Statistics Canada, 1998a). In 1996, half of Canadian seniors over the age of 75 lived in private dwellings. Most of them lived with their spouses (Vanier Institute of the Family, 2000: 2).[1] In addition, if stereotypes often depict the elderly as a burden on their families, evidence shows that Canada's seniors contribute much to the lives of their children, grandchildren, friends, neighbours, and communities (Vanier Institute of the Family, 2000: 172; see Figure 15.7).

Only a small minority of elderly Canadians live in nursing homes.

✦ **FIGURE 15.7** ✦

**Percentage of Seniors Providing Assistance with Personal or Household Chores, 1996**

Source: Adapted from the Statistics Canada publication "A Portrait of Seniors in Canada, Third Edition," Catalogue 89-519, October 1999, page 45.

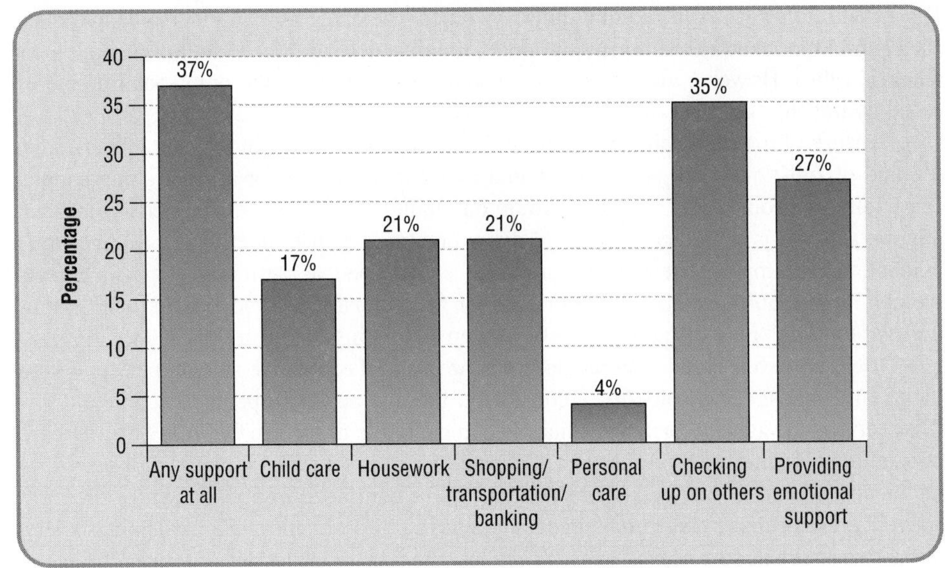


In the past four decades, seniors in Canada have benefited from rising incomes. Although in 1951 the average senior earned slightly more than half the income of Canadians of working age, in 1995 the average senior earned $20 300 or almost $84 for every $100 earned by Canadians of working age (Statistics Canada, 1998e). Because of income security programs such as the Guaranteed Income Supplement, the Old Age Security pension, and the Spouse's Allowance, Canadian seniors do not have to rely on welfare any more frequently than people in the general population (National Council on Welfare, 1998a). Moreover, between 1980 and 1996, the number of older Canadians who fell below Statistics Canada's low-income cutoff dropped substantially (on the low-income cutoff, see Chapter 7, Social Stratification: Canadian and Global Perspectives). Of the 20 percent of seniors living below the low-income cutoff in 1996, most were unattached women.

One reason for the relative economic security of the elderly is that they are well organized politically. Their voter participation rate is above average, and they are overrepresented among those who hold positions of political, economic, and religious power. Many groups seek to improve the status of the elderly. One of the earliest and most radical groups in North America was the Gray Panthers, founded in 1970 by Margaret Kuhn. With approximately 50 000 to 70 000 members, the Gray Panthers is a relatively small organization when compared with the Canadian Association of Retired Persons (CARP), an organization with about 370 000 members. CARP, Canada's largest 50-plus lobby group, is a nonprofit association that does not accept funding from any government body. It speaks out on a wide range of issues important to those over 50, and its mandate is "to protect what we have and improve our lifestyle" (www.fifty-plus.net/join/index-cfm). There are more than 1000 organizations working toward achieving greater political power, economic security, and better living conditions for the elderly. Indeed, global attention to the elderly led to 1999 being declared the International Year of Older Persons (DHHS, 1998). One economist, observing the elderly's considerable economic power, has referred to this group as a "revolutionary class" (Thurow, 1996). However, the elderly's activism may have led to a redistribution of resources away from young people. For example, educational funding has declined, while funding has increased for medical research related to diseases that disproportionately affect the elderly.

Conflict theorists would suggest that ongoing debates about funding for schools, daycare, social security, and medicare represent the conflicting interests of the young versus the old in our society. In this case, different age strata represent different interest groups that compete with one another for scare societal resources.

Reflecting this tension, the term **new ageism** is used with reference to the belief that the elderly are a burden on the economy and, especially, on a nation's youth. For example, it has been suggested that Canada's aging baby boomers will place an enormous strain on the social security system. As evidence of this, a 1996 government report predicted the emergence of a new "generation gap" between aging baby boomers, concerned with their pensions and personal security, and younger cohorts, who will be forced to bear some of the burden for the baby boomers' support (Peritz, 1999). According to a study conducted by the Organisation for Economic Co-operation and Development (OECD), there is already "growing evidence of disaffection among the young in communities with larger proportions of wealthy retired people" (in Peritz, 1999). In anticipation of government shortfalls, South Korea requires workers to save 35 percent of their income for retirement. In Japan, government benefits can be cancelled if redistribution of tax money is needed to ensure "equity between the generations" (Peterson, 1997). Whether Canadians are prepared to tolerate such a tax burden is questionable (see Box 15.1).

## Death and Dying

It may seem odd to say so, but the ultimate social problem the elderly must face is their own demise. Why are death and dying *social* problems and not just religious, philosophical, and medical issues?

In most traditional societies and in Europe until early modern times, most people accepted death (Ariès, 1982), partly because the dying were not isolated from other people. Instead, they continued to interact with household members and neighbours, who offered them continuous emotional support. Moreover, because the dying had previous experience of giving emotional support to other dying people, they could more easily accept death as part of everyday life.

In contrast, in Canada today, dying and death are usually separated from everyday life. Most terminally ill patients want to die peacefully and with dignity at home, surrounded by their loved ones. Yet the vast majority of Canadians die in hospitals. Often, hospital deaths are hygienic, noiseless, and lonely (Nuland, 1994: 242–62). Dying used to be

**BOX 15.1**
**IT'S YOUR CHOICE**

### THE SOCIAL SECURITY CRISIS

One of the greatest triumphs of public policy has been the development of the public health system, which has led to a substantial increase in life expectancy. Another major public policy achievement is social welfare, especially as it applies to the elderly. The combination of social security, medicare, and other government programs goes a long way toward ensuring that the elderly are not doomed to poverty and illness.

A longer and more secure life span is a wonderful thing. However, some scholars and policymakers worry that a major crisis is looming. Canada may not be able to afford government programs for the elderly in the future, due to the expected retirement of baby boomers, those born in the 20-year period after the Second World War. Many Canadians born in that period contribute to social security and other measures to support the aged. As the baby boomers begin to retire from the active labour force, however, fewer Canadians will be contributing to government coffers.

Some scholars argue that economic growth and higher immigration could offset the expected decline in the active labour force. However, others argue that we need more concrete measures to deal with the expected crisis in government support for the elderly. Some of the possible policy proposals include the following:

- Increase national savings.
- Lower health care costs, especially the disproportionately higher burden of medical cost for the elderly.
- Provide government support only to the truly needy, thereby eliminating or lowering social security and other federal benefits for the well-off.

What do you think? Should Canadians worry about the expected crisis in social security and other government programs that support the elderly? If you expect the potential crisis to erupt in your lifetime, what should you be doing now to avert the crisis? What are the advantages and disadvantages of each of the policy proposals listed above? What kind of lifestyle do you expect to lead when you are in your sixties, seventies, and eighties? Do you think you will be working full time, or will you be fully or partly retired? The policy proposals listed above are your choice.

public. It is now private. The lack of social support makes dying a more frightening experience for many people (Elias, 1985 [1982]). In addition, our culture celebrates youth and denies death (Becker, 1973). We use diet, fashion, exercise, makeup, and surgery to prolong youth, or at least the appearance of youth. This makes us less prepared for death than our ancestors were.

Adie Nelson was recently struck by our society's desire to keep death at a distance when she visited a colleague at home. "He lives in a house that was built in the 1850s," Adie explains. "In the front room, there is a large and beautiful bay window. When I complimented my colleague on the room, he asked if I knew the original reason for bay windows in homes. I said I did not. He then informed me that, historically, bay windows were the designated spot for the coffin of a deceased family member. The contours of the space would harbour the casket while people came to pay their last respects.

"My colleague's remarks surprised me. But they also started me thinking about all the ways in which we symbolically remove ourselves from death. Even though morticians earn more than pilots, we're typically uneasy around them and define 'death work' as somehow unseemly. I also began to think about the many euphemisms that we use to refer to the dying or the 'dearly departed'—again, a means of distancing ourselves from death. They are described as having 'passed on,' having 'entered the Pearly Gates,' or having gone 'to live with God,' 'to a better place,' to their 'final resting place,' or to 'meet their maker.' Individuals may be described as 'singing with the angels' or having joined 'God's heavenly choir.' Or, somewhat more bluntly, they may be described as having 'crapped out,' 'croaked,' 'bit the big one,' or 'curled up their toes.' Their 'number came up,' or their 'final curtain came down.' They have 'thrown in the towel,' 'gone belly up,' 'bit the dust,' 'given up the ghost,' 'kicked the bucket,' 'called it a day,' 'checked out,' 'struck out,' or 'cashed in their chips.' On occasion, we may express the optimistic view that those 'who are no longer with us' or 'who are no more' have 'found peace,' are 'deep in eternal slumber,' or are 'freed from their suffering.' Sometimes we may describe them in a more prosaic fashion—as 'feeding the worms,' being 'six feet under,' or 'pushing up daisies.' But, however we choose to describe them, they're rarely just 'dead.'"

The reluctance of many Canadians to accept death is clearly evident in the debate over euthanasia, also known as mercy killing or assisted suicide (Rothman, 1991). Various medical technologies, including machines that are able to replace the functions of the heart and lungs, can prolong life beyond the point that was possible in the past. This raises the question of how to deal with people who are near death. In brief, is it humane or immoral to hasten the death of terminally ill patients?

The term **euthanasia** can be broadly defined as any "deliberate act undertaken by one person with the intention of ending the life of another person to relieve that person's suffering, where that act is the cause of death" (McTeer, 1999: 117). A more narrow definition of euthanasia involves a doctor prescribing or administering medication or treatment that is *intended* to end a terminally ill patient's life. This form of euthanasia is sometimes referred to as *active euthanasia* inasmuch as it involves the commission of an act. A second form, sometimes referred to as *passive euthanasia*, involves intentionally withholding a life-saving medical procedure.

In Canada, assisting suicide or intentional killing, even in an attempt to end suffering, is criminal. In addition, doctors are legally prevented from withholding or withdrawing life-sustaining procedures. They are also legally obliged to ensure that patients whom they believe to be suicidal are prevented from harming themselves. Nevertheless,

> the reality of modern medicine is that doctors do practice passive euthanasia; not all of them, but rare is the doctor that has not, at the request of the patient, the patient's family, or on his or her own accord, decided to discontinue life-support. Studies also show that many doctors have acquiesced to life-ending drug dosages in cases of advanced terminal illness. (Duhaime, 1997)

A 2001 survey conducted by the Environics Research Group asked 2035 Canadians about their views on euthanasia. The results indicate that many Canadians support a ter-

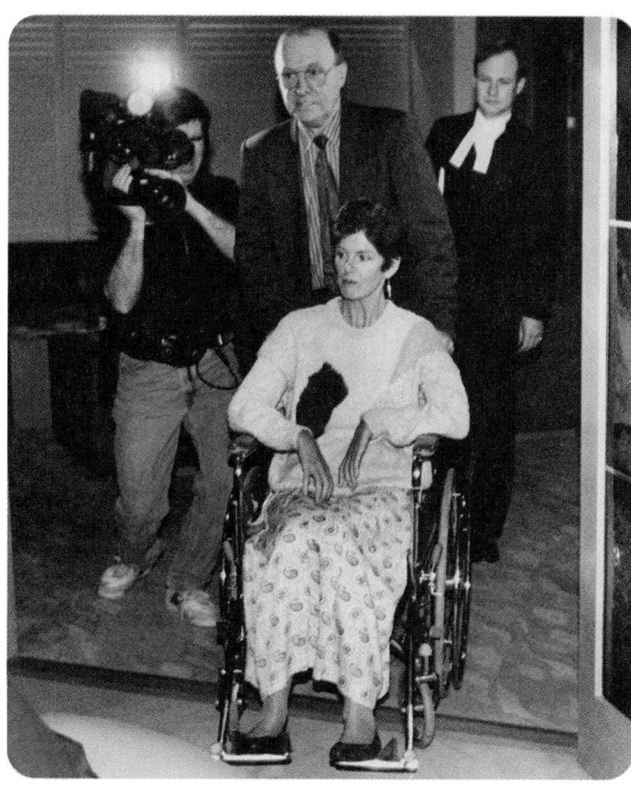

Sue Rodriguez, who suffered from amyotrophic lateral sclerosis (also known as Lou Gehrig's disease), launched a legal battle for the right to have a doctor help her die. She argued that the section of the Criminal Code that makes assisted suicide a criminal offence violates three rights guaranteed to all Canadians under the Charter of Rights and Freedoms: the right to life, liberty, and security of the person; the right not to be discriminated against on the basis of disability; and the right not to be subjected to cruel and unusual punishment. The Supreme Court of British Columbia dismissed her application. In 1993, the Supreme Court of Canada, in a 5–4 decision, dismissed her appeal.

minally ill person's right to die and believe that doctor-assisted suicide for terminally ill people should be legal in Canada. Just over three in four Canadians believe that an individual who helps end the life of a loved one suffering from an incurable and extremely painful illness should not be prosecuted. However, almost 6 in 10 Canadians oppose "mercy killing" of a severely disabled child by a parent. Although 42 percent believe that access to euthanasia is necessary for those who are critically ill or disabled because current nursing-home and end-of-life care is inadequate, almost three-quarters agree that "if people with disabilities, or those with chronic or terminal disease had access to adequate pain management and social services, there would be less demand for euthanasia" (Canada NewsWire, 2001).

Montreal physician Balfour Mount, who has been called Canada's father of palliative care,[2] has expressed a similar viewpoint. In the *Journal of the Royal College of Physicians and Surgeons of Canada*, Mount noted that "our courts voted against euthanasia by the narrowest of margins, while...our governments have failed to give adequate support to palliative care" ("Poor Palliative Care Encourages Euthanasia," 2001). Mount warns that unless more palliative care is provided, the "appeal of [euthanasia and assisted suicide] as a 'compassionate' alternative to overcrowded clinical services, inadequate fiscal resources, and increasing family caregiver burden is unlikely to lessen."

Euthanasia is bound to become a major political issue in coming decades as medical technologies for prolonging life improve, the number of elderly people increases, and the cost of medical care skyrockets. Some people will uphold extending the lives of terminally ill patients by all means possible as an ethical imperative. Others will regard it as immoral because it increases suffering and siphons scarce resources from other pressing medical needs.

To sum up our discussion, we may say that the apparently *natural* processes of death and dying are in fact highly *social* phenomena. For example, social circumstances account for variations in the definition and duration of life stages and the rituals associated with the transition from one life stage to the next. Similarly, the condition of the elderly depends in part on how numerous and powerful that group is as a political force. Finally, our attitudes toward death and dying reflect both our cultural values and our social conventions.

In the last section of this chapter, we make a similar argument about medicine. **Medicine** is a social institution devoted to prolonging life by fighting disease and promoting health. It may seem to lie squarely in the realm of pure science. However, as you will now learn, society shapes medical practice every bit as much as it influences the processes of aging and dying. We can see this clearly by examining how the medical and psychiatric professions have increased their control over people in the past 150 years or so. We begin this task by showing how forms of deviance that used to be considered the province of morality and the law have come increasingly under the sway of psychiatry. This change, we argue, is only partly because of the scientifically proven benefits of psychiatric care. We then examine how medicine drove other competing professions out of the health care market. Again, this demonstrates that the type of health care we receive is a product not just of scientific considerations but also of social forces.

# MEDICINE, POWER, AND CULTURE

## The Medicalization of Deviance

You may recall from our discussion of deviance that one of the preoccupations of symbolic interactionism is the labelling process (see Chapter 6, Deviance and Crime). According to symbolic interactionists, deviance results not just from the actions of the deviant but also from the responses of others, who define some actions as deviant and other actions as normal.

Here we may add that the *type* of label applied to a deviant act may vary widely over time and from one society to another, depending on how that act is interpreted. Consider, for instance, the **medicalization of deviance,** which refers to the fact that, over time, "medical definitions of deviant behaviour are becoming more prevalent in . . . societies like our own" (Conrad and Schneider, 1992 [1980]: 28–9). In an earlier era, much deviant behaviour was labelled "evil." Deviants tended to be chastised, punished, and otherwise socially controlled by members of the clergy, neighbours, family members, and the criminal justice system. Today, however, a person prone to drinking sprees is more likely to be declared an alcoholic and treated in a detoxification centre. A person predisposed to violent rages is more likely to be medicated. A person inclined to overeating is more likely to seek therapy and, in extreme cases, surgery. A heroin addict is more likely to seek the help of a methadone program. As these examples illustrate, what used to be regarded as wilful deviance is now often regarded as involuntary deviance. More and more, what used to be defined as "badness" is defined as "sickness." As our definitions of deviance change, deviance is increasingly coming under the sway of the medical and psychiatric establishments (see Figure 15.8).

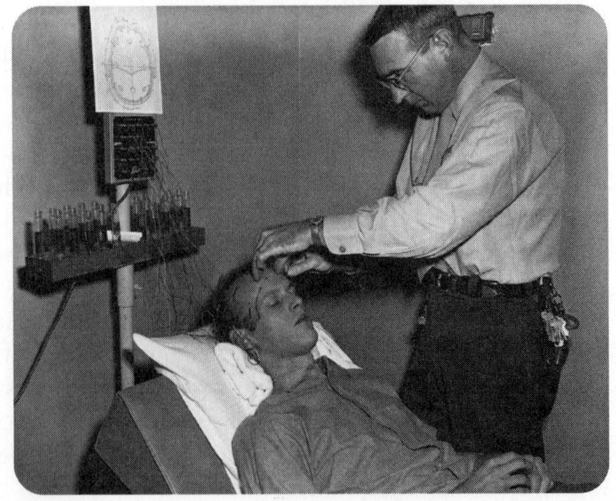

An example of the medicalization of deviance. A lobotomy is performed in a prison in the 1960s to "cure" the inmate of criminality.

> *"Now here's a young woman in her twenties, let's call her Betty Smith . . . she has never had a job, and she doesn't seem to want to go out and look for one. She is a very quiet girl, she doesn't talk much to anyone—even her own family, and she acts like she is afraid of people, especially young men her own age. She won't go out with anyone, and whenever someone comes to visit her family, she stays in her own room until they leave. She just stays by herself and daydreams all the time and shows no interest in anything or anybody."*

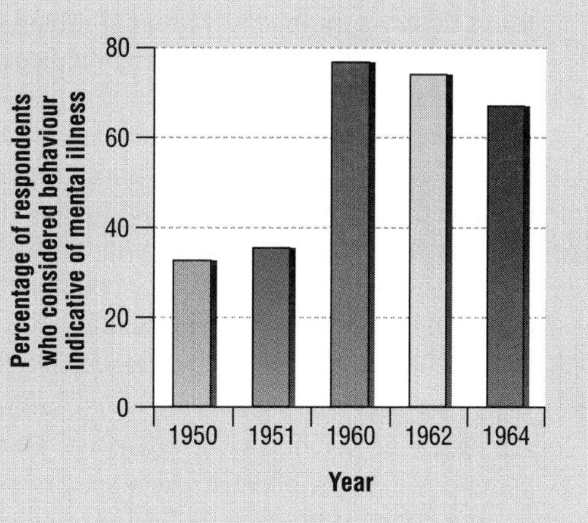


✦ **FIGURE 15.8** ✦

**An Example of the Medicalization of Deviance**

Five North American surveys conducted in the 1950s and 1960s presented respondents with the anecdote to the left. The graph shows the percentage of respondents who considered the behaviour described in the anecdote evidence of mental illness. Notice the difference between the 1950s and the 1960s. (Nearly 100% of the psychiatrists who evaluated the anecdote thought it illustrated "simple schizophrenia.")

How did the medicalization of deviance come about? What social forces are responsible for the growing capacity of medical and psychiatric establishments to control our lives? To answer this question, we first examine the fascinating case of mental illness. As you will see, our changing definitions of mental illness show perhaps more clearly than any other aspect of medicine how thin a line separates science from politics in the field of health care.

## The Political Sociology of Mental Illness

In 1974, a condition that had been considered a psychiatric disorder for more than a century ceased to be labelled as such by the American Psychiatric Association (APA). Did the condition disappear because it had become rare to the point of extinction? No. Did the discovery of a new wonder drug eradicate the condition virtually overnight? Again, no. In fact, in 1974 the condition was perhaps more widespread and certainly more public than ever before. However, paradoxically, just as the extent of the condition was becoming more widely appreciated, the APA's "bible," the *Diagnostic and Statistical Manual of Mental Disorders* (DSM), ceased to define it as a psychiatric disorder.

The "condition" we are referring to is homosexuality. In preparing the third edition of the DSM for publication, a squabble broke out among psychiatrists over whether homosexuality is in fact a psychiatric disorder. Gay and lesbian activists, who sought to destigmatize homosexuality, were partly responsible for a shift in the views of many psychiatrists on this subject. In the end, the APA decided that homosexuality is not a psychiatric disorder and deleted the entry in the DSM. The APA's membership confirmed the decision in 1974.

The controversy over homosexuality was only one of several *political* debates that erupted among psychiatrists in the 1970s and 1980s (Shorter, 1997: 288–327). Among others:

- ✦ The DSM task force initially decided to eliminate the term *neurosis* on the grounds that its role as a cause of mental disorder had never been proven experimentally. The decision outraged the psychoanalytic community, as *neurosis* is a keystone of its Freudian theories. As a result, psychoanalysts threatened to block publication of the third edition of DSM unless they were appeased. In 1979, the APA's board backed down, placing *neurosis* in parentheses after *disorder*. This compromise had nothing to do with science.
- ✦ When veterans of the Vietnam War began returning to the United States after 1971, they faced great difficulty re-entering American society. The war was unpopular, so veterans were not universally greeted as heroes. The U.S. economy went into a

tailspin in 1973, making jobs difficult to find. And the veterans had suffered high levels of stress during the war itself. Many of them believed their troubles were psychiatric in nature, and soon a nationwide campaign was underway, urging the APA to recognize post-traumatic stress disorder (PTSD) in its manual. Many psychiatrists were reluctant to do so. Nonetheless, PTSD was listed in the third edition of the DSM. To be sure, the campaign succeeded partly on the strength of evidence that extreme trauma has psychological (and at times physiological) effects. However, in addition, as one activist later explained, the PTSD campaign succeeded because "[we] were better organized, more politically active, and enjoyed more lucky breaks than [our] opposition" (Chaim Shatan, quoted in Scott, 1990: 308). Again, politics and not just science helped shape the definition of a mental disorder.

- Feminists were unhappy that the 1987 edition of DSM contained listings such as self-defeating personality disorder. The DSM claimed that this disorder is twice as common among women as it is among men. Feminists countered that the definition is an example of blaming the victim. Under pressure from feminists, the 1994 edition of DSM dropped the concept.

Some mental disorders have obvious organic causes, such as chemical imbalances in the brain. These organic causes can often be precisely identified. Often they can be treated with drugs or other therapies. Moreover, experiments can be conducted to verify their existence and establish the effectiveness of one treatment or another. However, the examples listed above show that the definition of a host of other mental disorders depends not just on scientific evidence but also on social values and political compromise. As psychologist John Goodman has stated, "no clear line divides the mentally healthy from the mentally unhealthy; and in addition, the definition of mental health is relative and is dependent on cultural context" (Goodman, 1999: 1469).

At the beginning of the twentieth century, just one mental disorder was recognized by the federal government: imbecility/insanity. By 1975, the DSM recognized 106 mental disorders. The 1994 edition of the DSM lists 297 mental disorders, a remarkable increase of 9.5 percent *per year* over 19 years. As the number of mental disorders has grown, so has the proportion of individuals presumably affected by them. In the mid-nineteenth century, few people were defined as suffering from mental disorders. However, the Canadian Mental Health Association (2001) estimates that one in five Canadians will be affected by a mental illness at some time in their lives. The most common mental disorder, depression, is supposed to affect 1 in 4 Canadian women and 1 in 10 Canadian men at some point in their lives (Canadian Psychiatric Association, 2002).

The University of Toronto's Edward Shorter, one of the world's leading historians of psychiatry, notes that in psychiatric practice, definitions of mental disorders are often expanded to include ailments with dubious or unknown biological foundations (e.g., "minor depression" and "borderline schizophrenia"; Shorter, 1997: 228). In addition, as we have seen, the sheer number of conditions labelled as mental disorders has increased rapidly during the twentieth century. We suggest four main reasons why the number and scope of such labels has expanded:

1. As we saw in Chapter 10, Work and the Economy, Canadians are now experiencing more stress and depression than ever before, due mainly to the increased demands of work and the growing time crunch. Mental health problems are thus more widespread than they used to be. At the same time, traditional institutions for dealing with mental health problems are less able to cope with them. The weakening authority of the church and the weakening grip of the family over the individual leave the treatment of mental health problems more open to the medical and psychiatric establishments.
2. The number of mental disorders has inflated because powerful organizations demand it. Because public and private organizations find the classification of mental disorders useful, they have proliferated. On occasion, the profit motive may be starkly

apparent as pharmaceutical companies rush to patent products they think will cure these conditions. Consider the repackaging of Prozac, the world's most widely prescribed anti-depressant, as Serafem, a treatment for women suffering from the newly named premenstrual dysphoric disorder. There can be no doubt that Prozac represented a pharmaceutical goldmine for Eli Lilly, its manufacturer, accounting for a third of the company's $6.5 billion in annual revenues. However, in 2001, Eli Lilly's patent on Prozac ended, allowing other manufacturers to sell generic versions of this drug at a fraction of the cost. In response, Prozac was quickly renamed and repatented as a treatment for another group of consumers (Bell, 2002: 34).

3. The cultural context stimulates inflation in the number and scope of mental disorders. Assailed by the latest best-sellers in the self-help section of our bookstores and lectured at by radio "therapists," we may be encouraged to turn our problems into medical and psychological conditions, sometimes without inquiring deeply into the disadvantages of doing so. For example, in 1980 the term *attention deficit disorder* (ADD) was coined to label hyperactive and inattentive schoolchildren, mainly boys. By the mid-1990s, North American doctors were writing more than 6 million prescriptions a year for Ritalin, an amphetamine-like compound that controls ADD. The organization Children and Adults with Attention Deficit Disorder (CHADD) now includes 600 chapters and 35 000 members worldwide, and has received almost US$1 million from Ritalin manufacturer Ciba Geigy (Bell, 2002: 34).

   Evidence shows that some children diagnosed with ADD have problems absorbing glucose in the brain or suffer from imbalances in chemicals that help the brain regulate behaviour (Optometrists Network, 2000). Yet the diagnosis of ADD is typically conducted *clinically*, that is, by interviewing and observing children to see if they exhibit signs of serious "inattention," "hyperactivity," and "impulsivity." This means that many children diagnosed with ADD may have no organic disorder at all. Some cases of ADD may be due to the school system failing to capture children's imagination. Some may involve children acting out because they are deprived of attention at home. Some may involve plain, old-fashioned high-spiritedness. A plausible case could be made that Winnie the Pooh suffers from ADD. In fact, this case *has* been made by psychiatrists at the Dalhousie University Medical School in Halifax (Shea et al., 2000). However, once hyperactivity and inattentiveness in school are defined as a medical and psychiatric condition, officials routinely prescribe drugs to control the problem and tend to ignore possible social causes.

4. The fourth main reason for inflation in the number and scope of mental disorders is that various professional organizations have promoted it. Consider post-traumatic stress disorder. There is no doubt that PTSD is a real condition, and that many veterans suffer from it. However, once the disorder was officially recognized in the 1970s, some therapists trivialized the term, for example, talking about PTSD "in children exposed to movies like *Batman*" (Shorter, 1997: 290). Some psychiatric social workers, psychologists, and psychiatrists may magnify the incidence of such mental disorders because doing so increases their stature and their patient load. Others may do so simply because the condition becomes "trendy." Whatever the motive, overdiagnosis is the result.

## The Professionalization of Medicine

The preceding discussion shows that the diagnosis and treatment of some mental disorders is not a completely scientific enterprise. Social and political processes are at least as important as scientific principles in determining how we treat some mental disorders. Various mental health professions compete for patients, as do different schools of thought within professions. Practitioners offer a wide and sometimes confusing array of treatments and therapies. In some cases their effectiveness is debatable, and there is at least some reason to remain skeptical of their ultimate worth.

In the early nineteenth century, the practice of medicine was in an even more chaotic state. Herbalists, faith healers, midwives, druggists, and medical doctors vied to meet the health needs of the public. A century later, the dust had settled. Medical science was victorious. Its first series of breakthroughs involved identifying the bacteria and viruses responsible for various diseases and then developing effective procedures and vaccines to combat them. These and subsequent triumphs in diagnosis and treatment convinced most people of the superiority of medical science over other approaches to health. Medical science worked, or at least it seemed to work more effectively and more often than other therapies.

It would be wrong, however, to think that scientific medicine came to dominate health care only because it produced results. A second, sociological reason for the rise and dominance of scientific medicine is that doctors were able to professionalize. As noted in Chapter 10, Work and the Economy, a profession is an occupation that requires extensive formal education. Professionals regulate their own training and practice. They restrict competition within the profession, mainly by limiting the recruitment of practitioners. They minimize competition with other professions, partly by laying exclusive claim to a field of expertise. Professionals are usually self-employed. They exercise considerable authority over their clients. And they profess to be motivated mainly by the desire to serve their community even though they earn a lot of money in the process. Professionalization, then, is the process by which people gain control and authority over their occupation and their clients. It results in professionals enjoying high occupational prestige and income, and considerable social and political power (Freidson, 1986; Johnson, 1972; Starr, 1982).

The professional organization of Canadian doctors is the Canadian Medical Association (CMA), founded in 1867 by 167 doctors in Quebec City. It quickly set about broadcasting the successes of medical science and criticizing alternative approaches to health as quackery and charlatanism. The CMA was able to have laws passed to restrict medical licences to graduates of approved schools and to ensure that only graduates of those schools could train the next generation of doctors. By restricting entry into the profession, and by specifying what "para-medical" practitioners could and could not do, members of the medical establishment ensured their own status, prestige, and high incomes. For example, midwifery was originally included in the work of the Victorian Order of Nurses, founded in 1897 by the National Council of Women to assist rural women who otherwise lacked access to health care. However, "the opposition of the medical establishment in Canada was so great to what it saw as an infringement of its prerogatives that the idea was allowed to die" (Mitchinson, 1993: 396). In short, when medicine became a profession, it also became a monopoly.

The modern hospital is the institutional manifestation of the medical doctor's professional dominance. Until the twentieth century, most doctors operated small clinics and visited patients in their homes. However, the rise of the modern hospital was guaranteed by medicine's scientific turn in the mid-nineteenth century. Expensive equipment for diagnosis and treatment had to be shared by many physicians. This required the centralization of medical facilities in large, bureaucratically run institutions that strongly resist deviations from professional conduct (see Box 15.2).

## Recent Challenges to Traditional Medical Science

### Patient Activism

By the mid-twentieth century, the dominance of medical science in Canada was virtually complete. Any departure from the dictates of scientific medicine was considered deviant. Thus, when sociologist Talcott Parsons defined the **sick role** in 1951, he first pointed out that illness suspends routine responsibilities and is not deliberate. Then he stressed that people playing the sick role must want to be well and must seek competent help, cooperating with health care practitioners at all times (Parsons, 1951: 428 ff.). Must they? According to Parsons' definition, a competent person suffering from a terminal illness cannot reasonably demand that doctors refrain from using heroic measures to prolong his

BOX 15.2
## SOCIOLOGY AT THE MOVIES

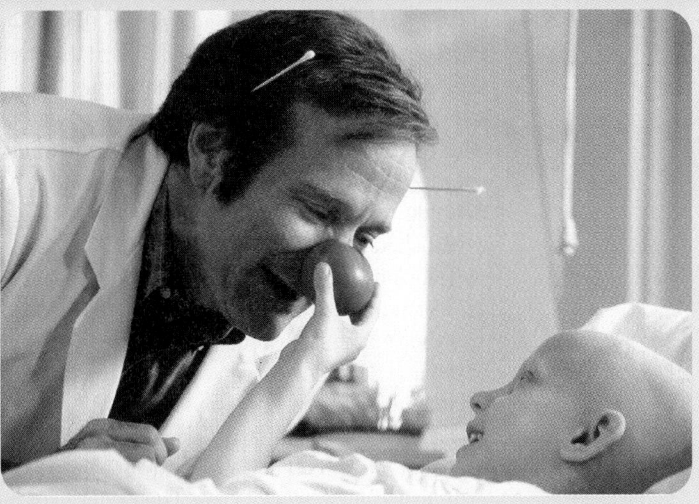

*Patch Adams,* starring Robin Williams

### *PATCH ADAMS* (1998)

Patch Adams, played by Robin Williams, is suicidal. Upon checking into a mental hospital, he finds that the doctors who are supposed to be helping him are indifferent to his plight. In contrast, other patients help him overcome his suicidal urges. Once better, he resolves to become a doctor to help other patients.

Patch Adams, based on a real person of the same name, breathes humour and life into the dreary world of the modern hospital. As an intern, Adams discovers that patients are identified by their ID number and disease. Doctors and nurses seem more concerned with medical charts than with their patients. Finally, Adams startles a nurse by asking her about a patient: "What's her name?" The very idea that a patient may be something more than his or her medical records reveals the impersonal and bureaucratic nature of the modern doctor–patient relationship.

Patch Adams becomes intent on infusing personal care, merriment, and humanity into the doctor–patient relationship. In dealing with children whose hair has fallen out because of chemotherapy, Patch plays a clown to bring smiles to their faces. He believes that laughter can be a great cure.

Not surprisingly, Adams faces resistance from medical school administrators. After all, he deviates significantly from the norm of impersonal professionalism. The administrators attempt to expel him from the medical school. With support from his friends and patients, however, Adams manages to win a court battle to remain in school. In real life, Patch Adams became a medical doctor who not only maintains a sense of humour but also continues to live up to his ideals, including by helping poor patients around the world.

*Patch Adams* is a sentimental movie that pits a humorous individual against a grim organization. However, critic Roger Ebert (1998) wrote: "To himself . . . [Patch Adams is] an irrepressible bundle of joy, a zany live wire who brings laughter into the lives of the sick and dying. To me, he's a pain in the wazoo. If this guy broke into my hospital room and started tap-dancing with bedpans on his feet, I'd call the cops." Here, Ebert is saying that the norm of professionalism—grim and impersonal though it may be—may be preferable to the antics of Patch Adams. Do you agree with Ebert? Would you prefer your doctor to be a "human being," or simply to play his or her professional role efficiently and effectively? What are the health advantages and disadvantages of each approach to doctoring?

or her life. And by his definition, a patient cannot reasonably question doctors' orders, no matter how well educated the patient and how debatable the effect of the prescribed treatment. Although Parsons' definition of the sick role may sound plausible to many people born before the Second World War, it probably sounds authoritarian and utterly foreign to most younger people.

That is because things have changed. The public is more highly educated now than it was 50 years ago. Many people now possess the knowledge, vocabulary, self-confidence, and political organization to participate in their own health care rather than passively accept whatever experts tell them. Research shows that this trend is evident even among older Canadians and lower-income earners. Canadian baby boomers and younger generations are even less likely to follow a doctor's advice uncritically; in fact, only one-third does so (Bricker and Greenspon, 2001: 221). Increasingly, patients are taught to perform simple, routine medical procedures themselves. Many people now use the Internet to seek information about various illnesses and treatments.[3] Increasingly, they are uncomfortable with doctors acting as authoritarian parents and patients acting as dutiful children. Indeed, surveys conducted in Canada reveal that 90 percent of Canadians now prefer that their doctor offer many treatment options rather than a single course of action, 86 percent say they usually ask their doctor many questions about procedures, 76 percent say they are more likely to question their doctor now than they were in the past, while about 70 percent claim to always ask their doctor about medicines that are prescribed (Bricker and Greenspon, 2001: 119–220). Doctors now routinely seek patients' informed consent for some procedures rather than deciding what to do on their own. Similarly, most hospitals have established ethics committees, which were unheard of only two decades ago (Rothman, 1991). These are responses to patients wanting a more active role in their own care.

Some recent challenges to the authority of medical science are organized and political. For example, when AIDS activists challenged the stereotype of AIDS as a "gay disease" and demanded more research funding to help find a cure, they changed research and treatment priorities in a way that could never have happened in, say, the 1950s or 1960s (Epstein, 1996). Similarly, when feminists supported the reintroduction of midwifery and argued against medical intervention in routine childbirths, they challenged the wisdom of established medical practice. The previously male-dominated profession of medicine considered the male body the norm and paid relatively little attention to "women's diseases," such as breast cancer, and "women's issues," such as reproduction. This, too, is now changing thanks to feminist intervention (Boston Women's Health Book Collective, 1998; Rothman, 1982, 1989; Schiebinger, 1993). And although doctors and the larger society traditionally treated people with disabilities as incompetent children, various movements now seek to empower them (Charlton, 1998; Zola, 1982). As a result, attitudes toward people with disabilities are changing.

## Alternative Medicine

Other challenges to the authority of medical science are less organized and less political than those just mentioned. Consider, for example, alternative medicine. According to the *1996–1997 National Population Health Survey*, 7 percent of Canadians 12 years of age and over report using the services of a narrowly defined list of alternative health care providers (see Figure 15.9). When the term *alternative care* is expanded to include such complementary and allied treatments as chiropractic and the herbal remedies used by

**✦ FIGURE 15.9 ✦**

**Percentage Who Use Alternative Health Care Services by Type of Practitioner Consulted, Canada, 1996–1997**

Source: Statistics Canada. *National Population Health Survey, 1996–1997.*

* Total exceeds 100% due to multiple responses.

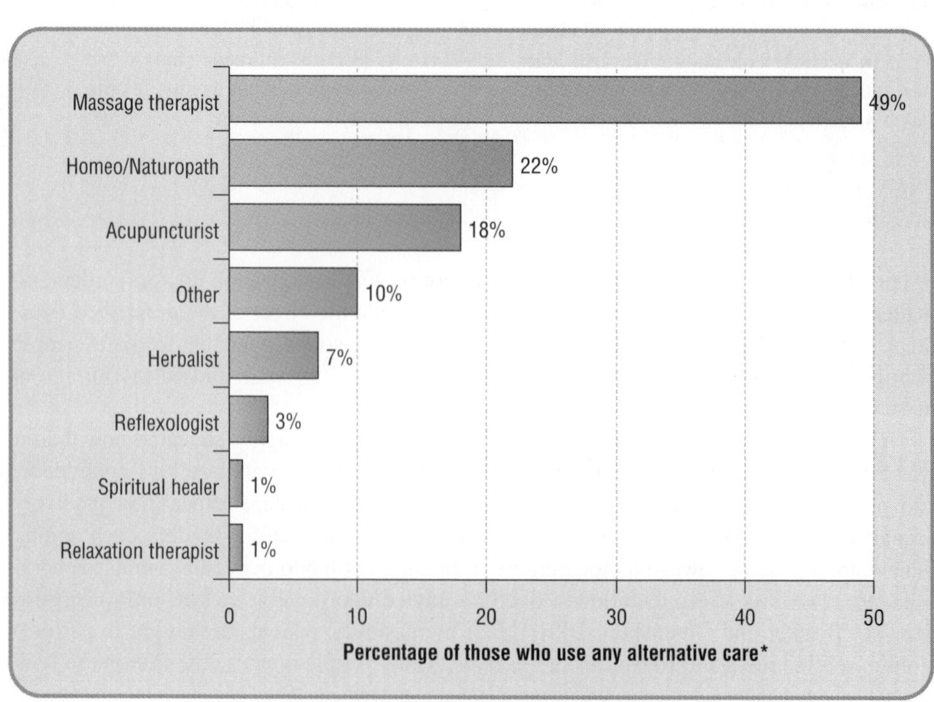

immigrants, the proportion of adult Canadians using such products and services increases to about 42 percent (Angus Reid Group, 1997). For example, 10 percent of men and 11 percent of women report at least one visit to a chiropractor in 1996–97 (Health Canada 1999b: 149). Alternative medicine is used mostly to treat back problems, chronic headache, arthritis, chronic pain, insomnia, depression, and anxiety.

In 1996–97, Canadian women were about 50 percent more likely than Canadian men to have consulted an alternative health care provider, defined narrowly as in Figure 15.9. The highest rate of use of such services is reported by women between the ages of 25 and 44 (11 percent), followed by women between the ages of 45 and 64 (10 percent). Use of alternative health care services (narrowly defined) is also higher among Canadians who have a university education, have high income, and live on the west coast and in the North. Thus, the *1996–1997 National Population Health Survey* reports that 9 percent of Canadians with a university degree, compared with 3 percent of those without a high-school diploma, had used an alternative health care provider in the previous year. Some 12 percent of high-income respondents reported a recent trip to a chiropractor, but only 6 percent of low-income respondents did so. Although individuals in British Columbia were the most likely to make use of alternative health care services, the use of alternative health care services was also relatively widespread in Yukon, the Northwest Territories, and Nunavut (Health Canada, 1999b: 149–53).

Despite its growing popularity, many medical doctors were hostile to alternative medicine until recently. They lumped all alternative therapies together and dismissed them as unscientific (Campion, 1993). By the late 1990s, however, a more tolerant attitude was evident in many quarters. For some kinds of ailments, physicians began to recognize the benefits of at least the most popular forms of alternative medicine. For example, a 1998 editorial in the respected *New England Journal of Medicine* admitted that the beneficial effect of chiropractic on low back pain is "no longer in dispute" (Shekelle, 1998). This change in attitude was due in part to new scientific evidence from Canadian research showing that spinal manipulation is a relatively effective and inexpensive treatment for low back pain (Manga, Angus, and Swan, 1993). At the same time, however, alternative forms of medicine should not be assumed to be entirely "risk-free." For example, to date, the majority of Canadian lawsuits against chiropractors have involved claims of muscular skeletal dysfunction, strains and sprains, and rib fractures. In other cases, however, more serious injury has occurred, including ruptured vertebral arteries and death (Cohen, 1999: 50).

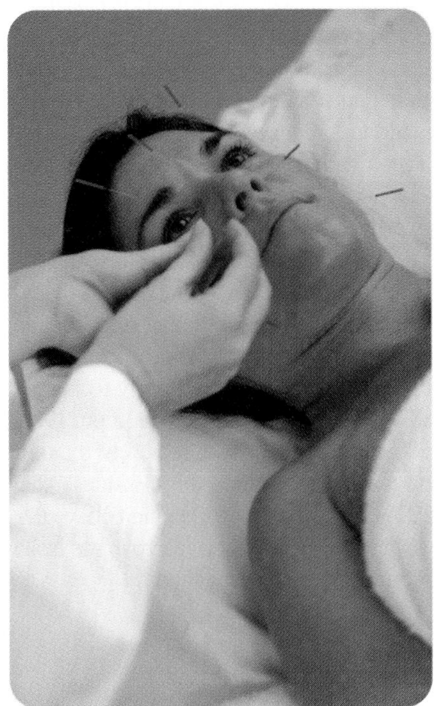

Acupuncture is one of the most widely accepted forms of alternative medicine.

Nevertheless, the medical profession's grudging acceptance of chiropractic in the treatment of low back pain indicates what we can expect in the uneasy relationship between scientific and alternative medicine in coming decades. Although many, if not most, alternative therapies (such as aromatherapy and foot reflexology) are noninvasive and relatively harmless, doctors will for the most part remain skeptical of alternative therapies unless properly conducted experiments demonstrate their beneficial effects. Part of their reluctance may be attributable to the fact that physicians who refer patients to alternative therapists become vulnerable to malpractice suits if the unconventional treatment goes wrong or if the referral falls below the reasonable standard of medical care. For example, the courts may rule that physicians are negligent if they refer patients to particular alternative therapies that have been proven to have no practical benefit or, on the basis of a misdiagnosis, send the patient for a form of therapy that aggravates the condition (Cohen, 1999: 50).

## Holistic Medicine

Medical doctors understand that a positive frame of mind often helps in the treatment of disease. For example, research shows that strong belief in the effectiveness of a cure can by itself improve the condition of about one-third of people suffering from chronic pain or fatigue (Campion, 1993). This is known as the **placebo effect.** Doctors also understand that conditions in the human environment affect people's health. However, despite their appreciation of the effect of mind and environment on the human body, traditional scientific medicine tends to respond to illness by treating disease symptoms as a largely physical and individual problem. Moreover, scientific medicine continues to subdivide into more specialized areas of practice that rely more and more heavily on drugs and high-tech machinery. Most doctors are less concerned with maintaining and improving health by understanding the larger mental and social context within which people become ill.

Traditional Indian and Chinese medicine takes a different approach. India's Ayurvedic medical tradition views individuals in terms of the flow of vital fluids or "humours" and their health in the context of their environment. In this view, maintaining good health requires not only balancing fluids in individuals but also balancing the relationship between individuals and the world around them (Zimmermann, 1987 [1982]). In spite of significant differences, the fundamental outlook is similar in traditional Chinese medicine. Chinese medicine and its remedies, ranging from acupuncture to herbs, seek to restore individuals' internal balance, as well as their relationship to the outside world (Unschuld, 1985). Contemporary **holistic medicine,** the third and final challenge to traditional scientific medicine we will consider, takes an approach similar to these "ethnomedical" traditions. Practitioners of holistic medicine argue that good health requires maintaining a balance between mind and body, and between the individual and the environment.

Most holistic practitioners do not reject scientific medicine. However, they emphasize disease *prevention*. When they treat patients, they take into account the relationship between mind and body and between the individual and his or her social and physical environment. Holistic practitioners thus seek to establish close ties with their patients and treat them in their homes or other relaxed settings. Rather than expecting patients to react to illness by passively allowing a doctor to treat them, they expect patients to take an active role in maintaining their good health. And, recognizing that industrial pollution, work-related stress, poverty, racial and gender inequality, and other social factors contribute heavily to disease, holistic practitioners often become political activists (Hastings, Fadiman, and Gordon, 1980).

In sum, patient activism, alternative medicine, and holistic medicine represent the three biggest challenges to traditional scientific medicine today. Few people think of these challenges as potential replacements for scientific medicine. However, many people believe that, together with traditional scientific approaches, these challenges will help improve the health status of people in Canada and throughout the world in the twenty-first century.

## SUMMARY


1. The social causes of illness and death include human-environmental factors, lifestyle factors, and factors related to the public health and health care systems. All three factors are related to country of residence, class, race, and gender.
2. Health risks are lower among the upper classes, rich countries, and privileged groups than among the lower classes, poor countries, and disadvantaged minority groups. In some respects related to health, men are in a more advantageous position than women.
3. Although Canada ranks high on most indicators of population health and there is much to be proud of in relation to our health care system, room for improvement remains. There are disparities in health status associated with socio-economic status, gender, and age. Minorities remain especially vulnerable to threats in the physical environment, including the dangers of damaging toxins and environmental pollutants.
4. Paradoxically, medical successes create new problems. For instance, they allow people to live longer than they used to. This gives degenerative diseases such as cancer and heart disease a chance to increase. Medical successes also raise new questions about when and how people should be allowed to die.
5. People attach different meanings to aging and death in different societies and historical periods. Thus, the stages of life vary in number and significance across societies. So does anxiety about death.
6. Canada's population is aging, and by 2031 more than a fifth of Canadians will be 65 or older. The ratio of men to women falls as age increases.
7. Between 1980 and 1996, the number of older Canadians whose income fell below Statistics Canada's low-income cutoff dropped significantly. However, one in five seniors, primarily unattached women, is still likely to be living in a low-income situation.
8. Over time, medical definitions of deviance have become more common. The recent history of psychiatry shows that social values and political compromise are at least as important as science in determining the classification of mental disorders.
9. Medical science came to dominate the health care system partly because it proved to be so successful in treating the ill. In addition, dominance was assured by doctors excluding competitors and establishing control over their profession and their clients.
10. Several challenges to traditional scientific medicine promise to improve the quality of health care in Canada and globally. These include patient activism, alternative medicine, and holistic medicine.


## GLOSSARY

An **age cohort** is a category of people born in the same range of years.

**Age roles** are norms and expectations about the behaviour of people in different age cohorts.

**Age stratification** refers to social inequality between age cohorts.

**Ageism** is prejudice about and discrimination against old people.

**Environmental racism** is the tendency for hazardous waste sites and polluting industries to be located near First Nations communities or areas populated by the poor, the politically marginalized, or certain visible minorities.

**Euthanasia** (also known as mercy killing and assisted suicide) involves a doctor prescribing or administering medication or treatment that is intended to end a terminally ill patient's life.

A **generation** is an age group that has unique and formative historical experiences.

A **gerontocracy** is a society ruled by elderly people.

**Health,** according to the World Health Organization, is "the ability of an individual to achieve his [or her] potential and to respond positively to the challenges of the environment."

The **health care system** is composed of a nation's clinics, hospitals, and other facilities for ensuring health and treating illness.

**Holistic medicine** emphasizes disease prevention. Holistic practitioners treat disease by taking into account the relationship between mind and body and between the individual and his or her social and physical environment.

**Infant mortality** is the number of deaths before the age of 1 for every 1000 live births in a population in 1 year.

The **life course** refers to the distinct phases of life through which people pass. These stages vary from one society and historical period to another.

**Life expectancy** is the average age at death of the members of a population.

The **maximum average human life span** is the average age of death for a population under *ideal* conditions. It is currently about 87 years.

The **maximum human life span** is the longest an *individual* can live under current conditions. It is currently about 122 years.

The **medicalization of deviance** is the tendency for medical definitions of deviant behaviour to become more prevalent over time.

**Medicine** is an institution devoted to fighting disease and promoting health.

**Morbidity** refers to acute and chronic illness.

The term **new ageism** is used with specific reference to the belief that the elderly are a burden on the economy and, especially, on a nation's youth.

The **placebo effect** is the positive influence on healing of a strong belief in the effectiveness of a cure.

**Population pyramids** are graphs that show the percentage of the population in various age and sex cohorts.

The **public health system** is composed of government-run programs that ensure access to clean drinking water, basic sewage and sanitation services, and inoculation against infectious diseases.

A **rite of passage** is a ritual that marks the transition from one stage of life to another.

Playing the **sick role,** according to Talcott Parsons, involves the nondeliberate suspension of routine responsibilities, wanting to be well, seeking competent help, and cooperating with health care practitioners at all times.

In a country with **socialized medicine,** the government (1) directly controls the financing and organization of health services, (2) directly pays providers, (3) guarantees equal access to health care, and (4) allows some private care for individuals who are willing to pay for their medical expenses.

## QUESTIONS TO CONSIDER

1. Since health resources are scarce, tough decisions have to be made about how they are allocated. For example, drug companies, physicians, hospitals, government research agencies, and other components of the health care system must decide how much to invest in trying to prolong the life of the elderly versus how much to invest in improving the health of the poor. What do you think are the main factors that help different components of the health care system decide how to allocate resources between these two goals? Specifically, how important is the profit motive? political pressure? Which components of the health system are most influenced by the profit motive? which by political pressure? If you were in charge of a major hospital or government funding for health research, how would you divide your scarce resources between these two goals? Why? What pressures might be placed on you to act differently than you would like to?
2. What generation do you belong to? What is the age range of people in your generation? What are some of the defining historical events that have taken place in your generation? How strongly do you identify with your generation? Ask the same questions of someone of a different race, gender, or class. How do these variables seem to influence the experience of a generation?
3. Do you believe that patient activism and alternative medicine improve health care or detract from the efforts of scientifically trained physicians and researchers to do the best possible research and administer the best possible treatments? Since patient activists may not be scientifically trained, and since alternative therapies may not be experimentally proven, are there inherent dangers in these challenges to traditional medicine? On the other hand, do biases in traditional medicine detract from health care by ignoring the needs of patient activists and the possible benefits of alternative therapies?

## WEB RESOURCES

### Companion Web Site for This Book

http://www.brymsociologycompass.nelson.com

Begin by clicking on the Student Resources section of the Web site. Next, select the chapter you are currently studying from the pull-down menu. From the Student Resources page you will have easy access to InfoTrac College Edition®, MicroCase online exercises, and additional Web links. The Web site also has many useful tips to aid you in your study of sociology, including practice tests for each chapter.

### InfoTrac Search Terms

These search terms are provided to assist you in beginning to conduct research on this topic by visiting http://www.infotrac-college.com

**Age discrimination**
**Euthanasia**
**Health maintenance organizations**
**Life expectancy**
**Public health**

### Recommended Web Sites

How long should you expect to live? Find out by answering questions on your health risks at http://www.msnbc.com/modules/quizzes/lifex.asp.

Health Canada has set up the Canadian Health Network Web site http://www.canadian-health-network.ca, which provides access to more than 400 Canadian health organizations. These range from the Aboriginal Nurses Association to the Canadian Cancer Society and the Heart and Stroke Foundation of Canada. Although based in Toronto, the network has operating partners in eastern and western Canada to ensure that regional interests are represented.

Visit the Web site of the Canadian Association for Retired People (CARP) at http://www.fifty-plus.net to learn about the many issues faced by retirees and the individual and collective actions they are taking to deal with these issues. CARP's services include discounted mail-order drugs, investment opportunities, travel information, volunteer opportunities, a *Spamhunter's Resource Guide* that offers practical advice for dealing with unwanted advertising offers, and news updates on issues of concern to those 50 and older.

## SUGGESTED READINGS

Pat Armstrong, Hugh Armstrong, and Claudia Fegan. *Universal Health Care: What the United States Can Learn from the Canadian Experience* (New York: The New Press, 1998). An insightful analysis that should sound a cautionary note in those who would advocate for the privatization of health care in Canada.

Maude Barlow and Elizabeth May. *Frederick Street: Life and Death on Canada's Love Canal* (Toronto: HarperCollins, 2000). A powerful book with an urgent message for Canadians about the dangers we face from toxic waste and environmental destruction within our communities.

Peter Conrad and Joseph W. Schneider. *Deviance and Medicalization: From Badness to Sickness,* expanded ed. (Philadelphia: Temple University Press, 1992 [1980]). This classic won the 1981 Charles Horton Cooley Award from the Society for the Study of Social Interaction. In a series of case studies on mental illness, alcoholism, opiate addiction, and other forms of deviance, it shows how the growth of the medical and psychiatric professions led to the medicalization of deviance in the twentieth century.

Peter Laslett. *A Fresh Map of Life: The Emergence of the Third Age* (Cambridge, MA: Harvard University Press, 1991 [1989]). A leading historical demographer reconsiders the role of the elderly.

Wendy Mitchinson. *The Nature of Their Bodies: Women and Their Doctors in Victorian Canada* (Toronto: University of Toronto Press, 1991). Historian Wendy Mitchinson provides a fascinating analysis of the evolution of Canadian medicine in this richly detailed book.

## NOTES

1. However, less than one half of seniors who are women lived with their spouse (42%), as compared with seven out of ten men (Vanier Institute of the Family, 2000: 3).
2. *Palliative care* refers to treatment that does not offer a "cure" for a specific illness or disease but, instead, serves primarily to lessen or manage the pain associated with the condition.
3. There are at least two health-related dangers to using the Internet, however. First, some people may misinterpret information or assume that unreliable sources are reliable. Second, sexual courtship on the Internet may lead to real-world meetings and therefore contribute to the spread of HIV/AIDS and other sexually transmitted diseases. Epidemiologists at the U.S. Centers for Disease Control and Prevention are now conducting a study on this subject (Roberts, 2000; SexQuiz.org, 2000).

PART

# V

# SOCIAL CHANGE

**CHAPTER 16**
POPULATION, URBANIZATION, AND DEVELOPMENT

**CHAPTER 17**
COLLECTIVE ACTION AND SOCIAL MOVEMENTS

**CHAPTER 18**
TECHNOLOGY AND THE GLOBAL ENVIRONMENT

## IN THIS CHAPTER, YOU WILL LEARN THAT

- Many people think that only natural conditions influence human population growth. However, social forces are important influences, too.
- In particular, sociologists have focused on two major social determinants of population growth: industrialization and social inequality.
- Industrialization also plays a major role in causing the movement of people from rural areas to cities.
- Cities are not as anonymous and alienating as many sociologists once believed them to be.
- The spatial and cultural forms of cities depend on the level of development of the societies in which they are found.
- Global inequality results less from deficiencies in poor societies than from relations between rich and poor countries.
- Under certain circumstances, poor societies can move along the path toward prosperity.

CHAPTER

# 16

# POPULATION, URBANIZATION, AND DEVELOPMENT

## INTRODUCTION

John Lie decided to study sociology because he was concerned about the poverty, pestilence, dictatorships, and natural disasters he had read about in books and observed during his travels in Asia and Latin America. "Initially," says John, "I thought I would major in economics because it seemed to me that much of the misery of the poor countries was a result of economic factors. In my economics classes, I learned about the importance of birth control programs to cap population growth, efforts to prevent the runaway growth of cities, and measures to spread Western knowledge, technology, and markets to people in less economically developed countries. My textbooks and professors assumed that if only the less developed countries would become more like the West, their populations, cities, economies, and societies would experience stable growth. Otherwise, the developing countries were doomed to suffer the triple catastrophe of overpopulation, too rapid urbanization, and economic underdevelopment.

"Equipped with this knowledge, I spent a summer in the Philippines working for an organization that offered farmers advice on how to promote economic growth. I assumed that, as in North America, farmers who owned large plots of land and used high technology would be more efficient and better off. However, I found the most productive villages were those in which most farmers owned *small* plots of land. In such villages, there was little economic inequality. The women in these villages enjoyed low birth rates, and the inhabitants were usually happier than the inhabitants of villages in which there was more inequality.

"What was going on? As I talked with the villagers, I came to realize that farmers who owned at least some of their own land had ample incentive to work hard. The harder they worked, the more they earned. With a higher standard of living, they didn't need to have as many children to help them on the farm. In contrast, in villages with greater inequality, many farmers owned no land. Some of them leased land, but many worked as farm labourers for wealthy landlords. They didn't earn more for working harder, so their productivity and their standard of living were low. As a result, they wanted to have more children to help bring income into their households.

"Few Filipino farms could match the productivity of high-tech North American farms, because even large plots were small by Canadian or American standards. Much high-tech agricultural equipment would have been useless there. Imagine trying to use a harvesting machine in a plot not much larger than some suburban backyards.

"Thus, my Western assumptions—that Filipino farmers needed big plots and high technology—turned out to be wrong. The Filipino farmers I met were knowledgeable and thoughtful about their needs and desires. When I started listening to them (and paying less attention to my economics textbooks and professors) I started to understand the real world of economic development. It was one of the most important sociological lessons I ever learned."

This chapter tackles the closely connected problems of population growth, urbanization, and economic development. It starts where John Lie did in the Philippines, with the realization that all is not as it seems. Specifically, we first show that population growth is a process governed less by natural laws than by social forces. We argue that these social forces are not related exclusively to industrialization, as social scientists commonly believed just a few decades ago. Instead, social inequality also plays a major role in shaping population growth. We next turn to the problem of urbanization. Today, population growth is typically accompanied by the increasing concentration of the world's people in urban centres. As recently as 40 years ago, sociologists believed that cities were typically alienating and anomic (or "normless"). We argue that this view is an oversimplification. We also outline the social roots of the city's physical and cultural evolution from preindustrial to postindustrial times. Finally, we turn to the distressing problem of global inequality among nations. We present and assess the major theoretical approaches to this problem in the light of available evidence and find some glimmers of hope in an otherwise troubling story.

# POPULATION

## The Population "Explosion"

Ten thousand years before the birth of Christ there were only about 6 million people in the world. By the time Christ was born, world population had risen to 250 million, and it increased to some 760 million by 1750. After that, world population skyrocketed. The number of humans reached 1 billion in 1804 and 5 billion in 1987 (see Figure 16.1). On July 1, 2001, there were an estimated 6.16 billion people in the world (U.S. Bureau of the Census, 1998d). Where 1 person stood 12 000 years ago, there are now 1025 people. Statistical projections suggest that, by 2100, there will be nearly 1700 people. Of those 1700, fewer than 250 will be standing in the rich countries of the world. More than 1450 of them will be in the developing countries of South America, Asia, and Africa.

Many analysts project that, after passing the 10 billion mark around 2100, world population will level off. But given the numbers cited above, is it any wonder that some population analysts say we're now in the midst of a population "explosion"? Explosions are horrifying events. They cause widespread and severe damage. They are fast and unstoppable. And that is exactly the imagery some population analysts, or **demographers,** wish to convey (e.g., Ehrlich, 1968; Ehrlich and Ehrlich, 1990; see Figure 16.2). They have written many books, articles, and television programs that deal with the population explosion. Images of an overflowing multitude in, say, Bangladesh, Nigeria, or Brazil remain fixed in our minds. Some people are frightened enough to refer to overpopulation as catastrophic. They link it to recurrent famine, brutal ethnic warfare, and other massive and seemingly intractable problems.

If this imagery makes you feel that the world's rich countries must do something about overpopulation, you're not alone. In fact, concern about the population "bomb" is as old as the social sciences. In 1798, Thomas Robert Malthus, a British clergyman of the Anglican faith, proposed a highly influential theory of human population (Malthus, 1966 [1798]). As you will soon see, contemporary sociologists have criticized, qualified, and in part rejected his theory. But because much of the sociological study of population is, in effect, a debate with Malthus' ghost, we must confront the man's ideas squarely.

## The Malthusian Trap

Malthus's theory rests on two undeniable facts and a questionable assumption. The facts: People must eat, and they are driven by a strong sexual urge. The assumption: Although

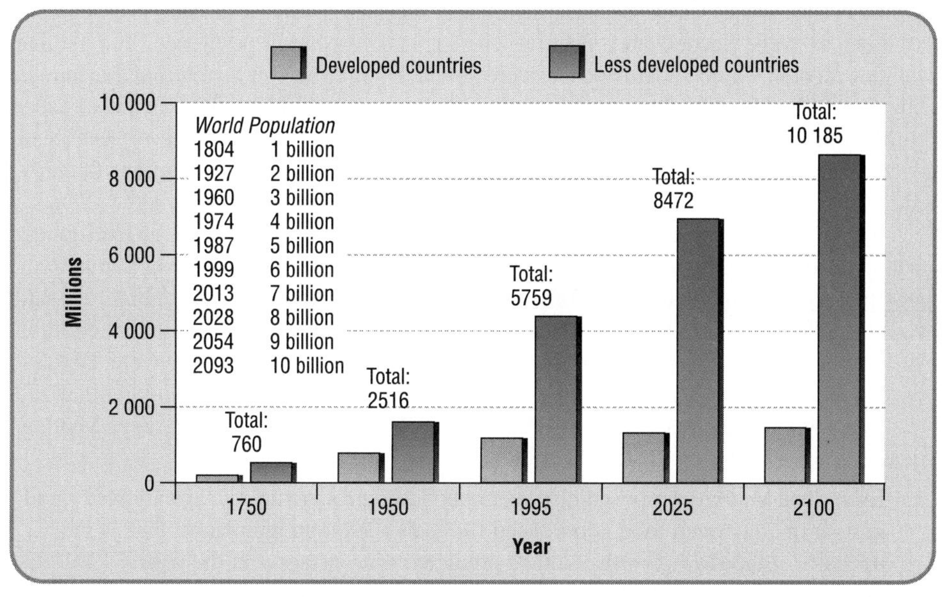


✦ **FIGURE 16.1** ✦
**World Population, 1750–2100 (in millions, projected)**

Sources: Livi-Bacci (1992: 31); Merrick et al. (1986: 12); United Nations (1993; 1998b).

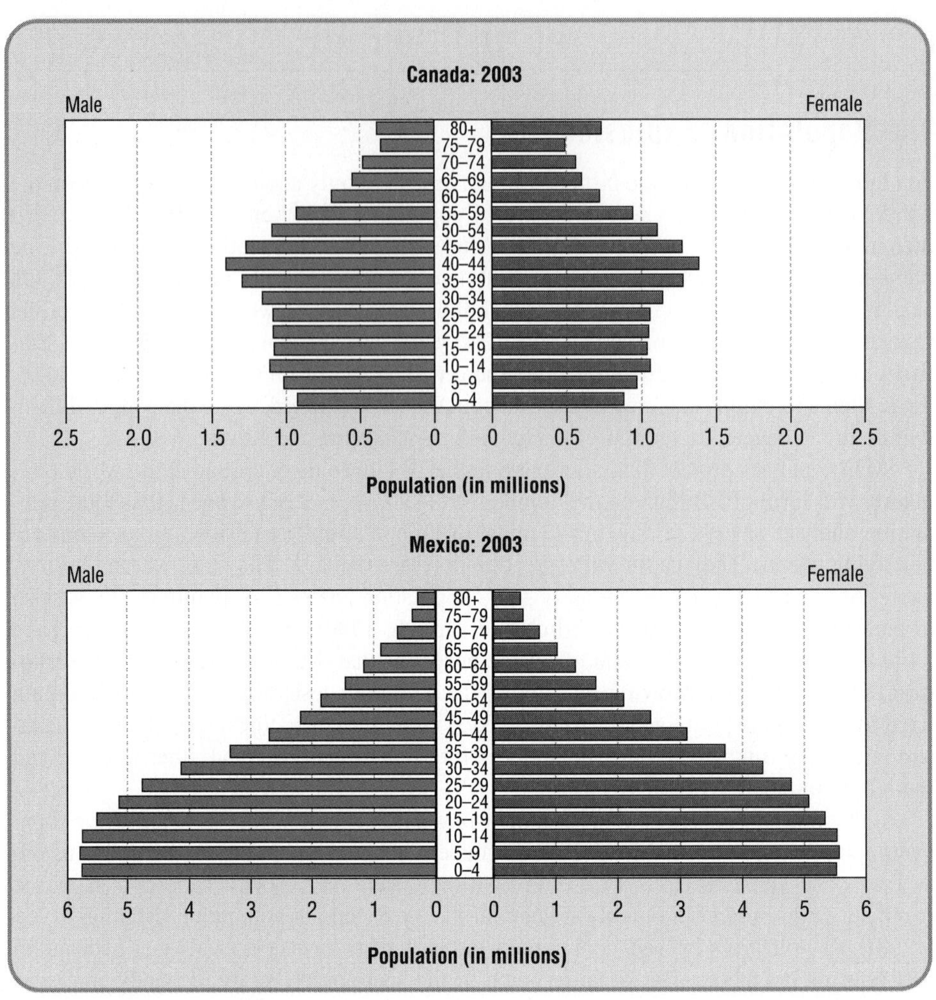


✦ **FIGURE 16.2** ✦

**How Demographers Analyze Population Changes and Composition**

The main purpose of demography is to figure out why the size, geographical distribution, and social composition of human populations change over time. The basic equation of population change is $P2 = P1 + B - D + I - E$, where $P2$ is population size at a given time, $P1$ is population size at an earlier time, $B$ is the number of births in the interval, $D$ is the number of deaths in the interval, $I$ is the number of immigrants arriving in the interval, and $E$ is the number of emigrants leaving in the interval. One basic tool for analyzing the composition of a population is the "age–sex pyramid" which shows the number of males and females in each age cohort of the population at a given point in time. Age–sex pyramids for Canada and Mexico are shown here, projected by the United States Census Bureau for 2003. Why do you think they look so different? Compare you answer to that of the theory of the demographic transition, discussed in this section.

Source: U.S Bureau of the Census (2002).

the food supply increases slowly and arithmetically (1, 2, 3, 4, etc.), population size grows quickly and geometrically (1, 2, 4, 8, etc.). Based on these ideas, Malthus concluded that "the superior power of population cannot be checked without producing misery or vice" (Malthus, 1966 [1798]: 217–8). Specifically, only two forces can hold population growth in check. First are "preventive" measures, such as abortion, infanticide, and prostitution. Malthus called these "vices" because he morally opposed them and thought everyone else ought to as well. Second are "positive checks," such as war, pestilence, and famine. Malthus recognized that positive checks create much suffering, yet he felt that they are the only forces that can be allowed to control population growth. Here, then, is the so-called **Malthusian trap:** a cycle of population growth followed by an outbreak of war, pestilence, or famine that keeps population growth in check. Population size might fluctuate, said Malthus, but it has a natural upper limit that Western Europe has reached.

Although many people supported Malthus's theory, others reviled him as a misguided prophet of doom and gloom (Winch, 1987). For example, people who wished to help the poor disagreed with Malthus. He felt such aid was counterproductive. Welfare, he said, would enable the poor to buy more food. With more food, they would have more children. And having more children would only make them poorer than they already were. Better to leave them alone, said Malthus. That will reduce the sum of human suffering in the world.

Although in some respects compelling, events have cast doubt on several of Malthus' ideas:

✦ Ever since Malthus proposed his theory, technological advances have allowed rapid growth in how much food is produced for each person on the planet. This is the opposite of the slow growth Malthus predicted. For instance, in the period 1991–93,

A "population explosion"? Hong Kong is one of the most densely populated places on earth.

India produced 23 percent more food per person than it did in 1979–81, and China produced 39 percent more. Moreover, except for Africa south of the Sahara, the largest increases in the food supply are taking place in the developing countries (Sen, 1994).

✦ If, as Malthus claimed, there is a natural upper limit to population growth, it is unclear what that limit is. Malthus thought the population could not grow much larger in early nineteenth-century Western Europe without "positive checks" coming into play. Yet the Western European population increased from 187 million people in 1801 to 321 million in 1900. It has now stabilized at about half a billion (McNeill, 1990). The Western European case suggests that population growth has an upper limit far higher than that envisaged by Malthus.

- Population growth does not always produce misery. For example, despite its rapid population increase over the past 200 years, Western Europe is one of the most prosperous regions in the world.
- Helping the poor does not generally result in the poor having more children. For example, in Western Europe, social welfare policies (unemployment insurance, state-funded medical care, paid maternity leave, pensions, etc.) are the most generous on the planet. Yet the size of the population is quite stable. In fact, as you will learn below, some forms of social welfare produce rapid and large *decreases* in population growth, especially in the poor, developing countries.
- Although the human sexual urge is as strong as Malthus thought, people have developed contraceptive devices and techniques to control the consequences of their sexual activity (Szreter, 1996). There is no necessary connection between sexual activity and childbirth.

The developments listed above all point to one conclusion. Malthus's pessimism was overstated. Human ingenuity seems to have enabled us to wriggle free of the Malthusian trap, at least for the time being.

We are not, however, home free. Today there are renewed fears that industrialization and population growth are putting severe strains on the planet's resources. As Chapter 18 (Technology and the Global Environment) establishes, we must take these fears seriously. It is encouraging to learn that the limits to growth are as much social as natural, and therefore avoidable rather than inevitable. However, we will see that our ability to avoid the Malthusian trap in the twenty-first century will require all the ingenuity and self-sacrifice we can muster. For the time being, however, let us consider the second main theory of population growth, the theory of the demographic transition.

## Demographic Transition Theory

According to **demographic transition theory,** the main factors underlying population dynamics are industrialization and the growth of modern cultural values (Notestein, 1945; Coale, 1974; Chesnais, 1992 [1986]; see Figure 16.3). The theory is based on the observation that the European population developed in four distinct stages:

1. In the first, *preindustrial stage* of growth, a large proportion of the population died every year because of inadequate nutrition, poor hygiene, and uncontrollable disease. In other words, the **crude death rate** was high. The crude death rate is the annual number of deaths (or "mortality") per 1000 people in a population. During this period, the **crude birth rate** was high, too. The crude birth rate is the annual number of live births per 1000 people in a population. In the preindustrial era, most people wanted to have as many children as possible. That was partly because relatively few children survived until adulthood. In addition, children were considered a valuable source of agricultural labour and a form of old age security in a society that consisted largely of peasants and lacked anything resembling a modern welfare state.
2. The second stage of European population growth was the *early industrial or transition period*. At this stage, the crude death rate dropped. People's life expectancy, or average life span, increased because economic growth led to improved nutrition and hygiene. However, the crude birth rate remained high. With people living longer and women having nearly as many babies as in the preindustrial era, the population grew rapidly. Malthus lived during this period of rapid population growth, and that accounts in part for his alarm.

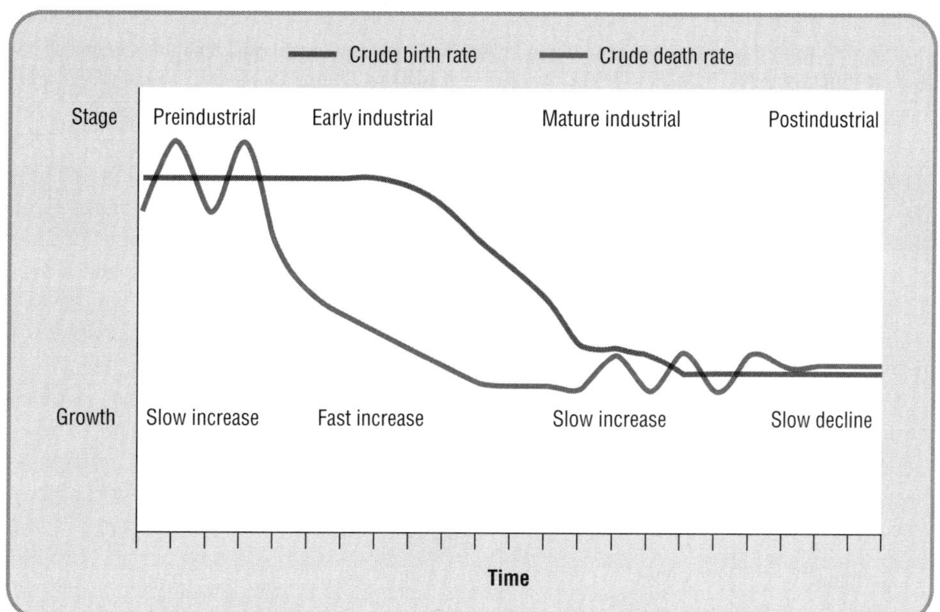


✦ **FIGURE 16.3** ✦
**Demographic Transition Theory**

3. The third stage of European population growth was the *mature industrial period*. At this stage, the crude death rate continued to fall. The crude birth rate fell even more dramatically, because economic growth eventually changed people's traditional beliefs about the value of having many children. Having a lot of children made sense in an agricultural society, where, as we have seen, children were a valuable economic resource. In contrast, children were more of an economic burden in an industrial society because breadwinners worked outside the home for a wage or a salary and children contributed little if anything to the economic welfare of the family. Note, however, that the crude birth rate took longer to decline than the crude death rate did. That is because people's values often change more slowly than their technologies. People can put in a sewer system or a water purification plant to lower the crude death rate faster than they can change their minds about something as fundamental as how many children to have. Eventually, however, the technologies and outlooks that accompany modernity led people to postpone getting married and to use contraceptives and other birth control methods. As a result, population stabilized during the mature industrial period. This demonstrates the validity of one of the demographer's favourite sayings: "Economic development is the best contraceptive."
4. In the last decades of the twentieth century (*the postindustrial period*), the total fertility rate continued to fall. The **total fertility rate** is the average number of children that would be born to a woman during her lifetime, assuming that she has the same number of children as the average for women in each age cohort. In fact, the total fertility rate fell below the **replacement level** in some countries. The replacement level is the number of children each woman must have on average for a population size to remain stable. Ignoring any inflow of settlers from other countries (**immigration** or **in-migration**) and any outflow to other countries (**emigration** or **out-migration**), the replacement level is 2.1. This means that, on average, each woman must give birth to slightly more than the two children needed to replace her and her mate. Slightly more than two children are required because some children die before they mature and reach reproductive age.

By the 1990s, some Europeans were worrying about declining fertility and its possible effects on population size. As you can see in Table 16.1, 21 countries, 18 of them in Europe, now have fertility rates below 1.5. In the period 1995–2000, 61 countries or areas of the world representing 44 percent of the world's population had a fertility rate below the

✦ **TABLE 16.1** ✦

**Countries with the Lowest and Highest Total Fertility Rates**

| Total Fertility Rate Less Than 1.5 (1995–2000) | | Total Fertility Rate More Than 6.0 (1995–2000) | |
|---|---|---|---|
| **Country** | **Fertility Rate** | **Country** | **Fertility Rate** |
| Bulgaria | 1.1 | Djibouti | 6.1 |
| Latvia | 1.1 | Madagascar | 6.1 |
| Spain | 1.2 | Zambia | 6.1 |
| Czech Republic | 1.2 | Benin | 6.1 |
| Italy | 1.2 | Rwanda | 6.2 |
| Russian Federation | 1.2 | Saudi Arabia | 6.2 |
| Slovenia | 1.2 | Guinea | 6.3 |
| Estonia | 1.2 | Congo | 6.3 |
| Hong Kong/China | 1.2 | Mozambique | 6.3 |
| Romania | 1.3 | Sierra Leone | 6.5 |
| Greece | 1.3 | Chad | 6.7 |
| Germany | 1.3 | Congo, Dem. Rep. of | 6.7 |
| Belarus | 1.3 | Malawi | 6.8 |
| Ukraine | 1.3 | Burundi | 6.8 |
| Armenia | 1.4 | Ethiopia | 6.8 |
| Hungary | 1.4 | Burkina Faso | 6.9 |
| Slovakia | 1.4 | Mali | 7.0 |
| Macau | 1.4 | Uganda | 7.1 |
| Austria | 1.4 | Angola | 7.2 |
| Lithuania | 1.4 | Yemen | 7.6 |
| Japan | 1.4 | Niger | 8.0 |

**Canada, 1995–2000: 1.6**

Source: Based on United Nations (2001: 154–7).

*Note:* Data refer to estimates for the period specified. Strict comparison between the two columns should be avoided because data collection is more sporadic in poor than in rich countries. As a result, the data in the right-hand column are on average seven years older than the data in the left-hand column. Over that period, fertility rates in Africa declined somewhat.

replacement level. That is 10 more countries than in the period 1990–95. Canada was a member of this group with a fertility rate of 1.6 in the period 1995–2000 (United Nations, 2001). Due to the proliferation of low-fertility societies, some scholars suggest that we have now entered a fourth, *postmodern stage* of population development. In this fourth stage of the demographic transition, the number of deaths per year exceeds the number of births (Van de Kaa, 1987).

As outlined above, the demographic transition theory provides a rough picture of how industrialization affects population growth. However, research has revealed a number of inconsistencies in the theory. Most of them are due to the theory placing too much emphasis on industrialization as the main force underlying population growth (Coale and Watkins, 1986). For example, demographers have found that reductions in fertility sometimes occur when standards of living stagnate or decline, not just when they improve because of industrialization. Thus, in Russia and some developing countries today, declining living standards have led to a deterioration in general health and a subsequent decline in fertility. Because of such findings, many scholars have concluded that an adequate theory of population growth must pay more attention to social factors other than industrialization and in particular to the role of social inequality.

## Population and Social Inequality

One of Malthus' staunchest intellectual opponents was Karl Marx. Marx argued that the problem of overpopulation is specific to capitalism (Meek, 1971). In his view, overpopulation is not a problem of too many people. Instead, it is a problem of too much poverty. Do away with the exploitation of workers by their employers, said Marx, and poverty will disappear. If a society is rich enough to eliminate poverty, then by definition its population is not too large. By eliminating poverty, one also solves the problem of overpopulation in Marx's view.

Marx's analysis makes it seem that capitalism can never generate enough prosperity to solve the overpopulation problem. He was evidently wrong. Overpopulation is not a serious problem in Canada, the United States, Japan, or Germany today.[1] It *is* a problem in most of Africa, where capitalism is weakly developed and the level of social inequality is much higher than in the postindustrial societies. Still, a core idea in Marx's analysis of the overpopulation problem rings true. As some contemporary demographers argue, social inequality is a main cause of overpopulation. Below, we illustrate this argument by first considering how gender inequality influences population growth. Then, we discuss the effects of class inequality on population growth.

## Gender Inequality and Overpopulation

The effect of gender inequality on population growth is well illustrated by the case of Kerala, a state in southern India with more than 30 million people. Kerala had a total fertility rate of just under 1.7 in 1998, half of India's national rate and well below the replacement level of 2.1. How did Kerala achieve this remarkable feat? Is it a highly industrialized oasis in the midst of a semi-industrialized country, as one might expect given the arguments of demographic transition theory? To the contrary, Kerala is not highly industrialized. In fact, it is among the poorer Indian states, with a per capita income estimated to be between $480 and $560 a year—below the national average of India, Cambodia, or the Sudan (Suzuki and Dressel, 2002: 326). Has the government of Kerala strictly enforced a state childbirth policy similar to China's? The Chinese government strongly penalizes families that have more than one child and it allows abortion at 8.5 months. As a result, China had a fertility rate of just 1.2 in 1995–2000 (United Nations, 2001: 154). In Kerala, however, the government stays out of its citizens' bedrooms. The decision to have children remains a strictly private affair.

The women of Kerala achieved a low total fertility rate because their government purposely and systematically raised their status over a period of decades (Franke and Chasin, 1992; Sen, 1994; Suzuki and Dressel, 2002: 326–8). The government helped create a realistic alternative to a life of continuous childbearing and child rearing. It helped women understand they could achieve that alternative if they wanted to. In particular, the government organized successful campaigns and programs to educate women, increase their participation in the paid labour force, and make family planning widely available. These government campaigns and programs resulted in Keralan women enjoying the highest literacy rate, the highest labour force participation rate, and the highest rate of political participation in India. Given their desire for education, work, and political involvement, most Keralan women want small families, so they use contraception to prevent unwanted births. Thus, by lowering the level of gender inequality, the government of Kerala solved its overpopulation problem. In general, where

> women tend to have more power [the society has] low rather than high mortality and fertility. Education and employment, for example, often accord women wider power and influence, which enhance their status. But attending school and working often compete with childbearing and childrearing. Women may choose to have fewer children in order to hold a job or increase their education. (Riley, 1997)

## Class Inequality and Overpopulation

Unravelling the Keralan mystery is an instructive exercise. It establishes that population growth depends not just on a society's level of industrialization but also on its level of gender inequality. *Class* inequality influences population growth, too. We turn to the South Korean case to illustrate this point.

In 1960, South Korea had a total fertility rate of 6.0. This prompted one North American official to remark that "if these Koreans don't stop overbreeding, we may have the choice of supporting them forever, watching them starve to death, or washing our hands of the problem" (quoted in Lie, 1998: 21). Yet by 1989, South Korea's total fertility rate had dropped to a mere 1.6; its estimated total fertility rate in 2000 remained low at 1.72 (*Canadian Global Almanac 2002*, 2001: 437). Why? The first chapter in this story involves land reform, not industrialization. The government took land from big landowners and gave it to small farmers. Consequently, the standard of living of small farmers improved. This eliminated a major reason for high fertility. Once economic uncertainty decreased, so did the need for child labour and support of elderly parents by adult offspring. Soon, the total fertility rate began to fall. Subsequent declines in the South Korean total fertility rate were due to industrialization, urbanization, and the higher educational attainment of the population. But a decline in class inequality in the countryside first set the process in motion.

The reverse is also true. Increasing social inequality can lead to overpopulation, war, and famine. For example, in the 1960s the governments of El Salvador and Honduras encouraged the expansion of commercial agriculture and the acquisition of large farms by wealthy landowners. The landowners drove peasants off the land. The peasants migrated to the cities. There they hoped to find employment and a better life. Instead, they often found squalor, unemployment, and disease. Suddenly, two countries with a combined population of fewer than 5 million people had a big "overpopulation" problem. Competition for land increased and contributed to rising tensions. This eventually led to the outbreak of war between El Salvador and Honduras in 1969 (Durham, 1979).

Similarly, economic inequality helps create famines. As Nobel prize winner Amartya Sen notes, "[f]amine is the characteristic of some people not *having* enough food to eat. It is not the characteristic of there not *being* enough food to eat" (Sen, 1981: 1; our emphasis). Sen's distinction is crucial, as his analysis of several famines shows. Sen found that, in some cases, while food supplies did decline, enough food was available to keep the stricken population fed. However, suppliers and speculators took advantage of the short supply. They hoarded grain and increased prices beyond the means of most people. In other cases, there was no decline in food supply at all. Food was simply withheld for political reasons, that is, to bring a population to its knees, or because many people were not considered entitled to receive it by the authorities. The source of famine, Sen concludes, is not underproduction or overpopulation but inequality of access to food (Drèze and Sen, 1989). In fact, even when starving people gain access to food, other forms of inequality may kill them. For instance, when food relief agencies delivered 3 million sacks of grain to prevent famine in Western Sudan in the mid-1980s, tens of thousands of people died anyway because they lacked clean water, decent sanitation, and vaccinations against various diseases (de Waal, 1989). Western aid workers failed to listen carefully to the Sudanese people about their basic medical and sanitary needs, with disastrous results.

## Summing Up

A new generation of demographers has begun to explore how class inequality and gender inequality affect population growth (Levine, 1987; Seccombe, 1992; Szreter, 1996). Their studies drive home the point that population growth and its negative consequences do not stem from natural causes (as Malthus held). Nor are they only responses to industrialization and modernization (as demographic transition theory suggests). Instead, population growth is influenced by a variety of social causes, social inequality chief among them.

Some undoubtedly well-intentioned Western analysts continue to insist that people in the developing countries should be forced to stop multiplying at all costs. Some observers even suggest diverting scarce resources from education, health, and industrialization into various forms of birth control, including, if necessary, forced sterilization (Riedmann, 1993). They regard the presumed alternatives—poverty, famine, war, ethnic violence, and the growth of huge, filthy cities—as too horrible to contemplate. However, they fail to see how measures that lower social inequality help control overpopulation and its consequences. Along with industrialization, lower levels of social inequality cause total fertility rates to fall.

## URBANIZATION

We have seen that overpopulation remains a troubling problem due to lack of industrialization and too much gender and class inequality in much of the world. We may now add that overpopulation is in substantial measure an *urban* problem. Driven by lack of economic opportunity in rural areas, political unrest, and other factors, many millions of people flock to big cities in the world's poor countries every year. Thus, most of the fastest-growing cities in the world today are in semi-industrialized countries where the factory system is not highly developed. As Table 16.2 shows, in 1900, 9 of the 10 biggest cities in the world were in industrialized Europe and the United States. By 2015, in contrast, 6 of the world's 10 biggest cities will be in Asia, 1 will be in Africa, and 2 will be in Latin America. Only 2 of the 10 biggest cities—Tokyo and New York—will be in highly industrialized countries. Urbanization is, of course, taking place in the world's rich countries, too. According to the 2001 Census, 8 in 10 Canadians now reside in cities, with approximately 48 percent living in Canada's 8 largest metropolitan areas: Toronto, Montreal, Vancouver, Ottawa-Hull, Calgary, Edmonton, Quebec City, and Winnipeg (Janigan, 2002: 22). In North America, the urban population is expected to increase from 76 to 84 percent of the total population between 1996 and 2030. In Africa and Asia, however, the urban population is expected to increase much faster—from about 35 to 55 percent of the total population in the same time period (United Nations, 1997b).

### From the Preindustrial to the Industrial City

To a degree, urbanization results from industrialization. As you will learn below, many great cities of the world grew up along with the modern factory, which drew hundreds of millions of people out of rural areas and transformed them into urban, industrial workers. Industrialization is not, however, the whole story behind the growth of cities. As we have just seen, the connection between industrialization and urbanization is weak in the world's less developed countries today. Moreover, cities first emerged in Syria, Mesopotamia, and Egypt 5000 or 6000 years ago, long before the growth of the modern factory. These early cities served as centres of religious worship and political administration. Similarly, it was not industry but international trade in spices, gold, cloth, and other precious goods that stimulated the growth of cities in preindustrial Europe and the Middle East. Thus, the correlation between urbanization and industrialization is far from perfect (Bairoch, 1988 [1985]; Jacobs, 1969; Mumford, 1961; Sjöberg, 1960).

Preindustrial cities differed from those that developed in the industrial era in several ways. Preindustrial cities were typically smaller, less densely populated, built within protective walls, and organized around a central square and places of worship. The industrial cities that began to emerge at the end of the eighteenth century were more dynamic and

✦ **TABLE 16.2** ✦

**World's 10 Largest Cities, 1900 and 2015, Projected (in millions)**

Source: Department of Geography, Slippery Rock University (1997, 1998); United Nations (1999c).

| 1900 | | 2015 | |
|---|---|---|---|
| London | 6.5 | Tokyo | 26.4 |
| New York | 4.2 | Bombay | 26.1 |
| Paris | 3.3 | Lagos | 23.2 |
| Berlin | 2.4 | Dhaka | 21.1 |
| Chicago | 1.7 | São Paulo | 20.4 |
| Vienna | 1.6 | Karachi | 19.2 |
| Tokyo | 1.5 | Mexico City | 19.2 |
| Saint Petersburg | 1.4 | New York | 17.4 |
| Philadelphia | 1.4 | Calcutta | 17.3 |
| Manchester | 1.3 | Jakarta | 17.1 |

Mexico City during one of its frequent smog alerts. Of the world's 10 biggest cities in 2015, only two—Tokyo and New York—will be in highly industrialized countries. All the others, including Mexico City, will be in developing countries.

complex social systems. A host of social problems, including poverty, pollution, and crime, accompanied their growth. The complexity, dynamism, and social problems of the industrial city were all evident in Chicago at the turn of the twentieth century. Not surprisingly, therefore, it was at the University of Chicago that North American urban sociology was born.

## The Chicago School and the Industrial City

From the 1910s to the 1930s, the members of the **Chicago school** of sociology distinguished themselves by their vividly detailed descriptions and analyses of urban life, backed up by careful, in-depth interviews, surveys, and maps showing the distribution of various features of the social landscape, all expressed in plain yet evocative language (Lindner, 1996 [1990]). Three of its leading members—Robert Park, Ernest Burgess, and Roderick McKenzie—proposed a theory of **human ecology** to illuminate the process of urbanization (Park, Burgess, and McKenzie, 1967 [1925]). Borrowing from biology and ecology, the theory highlights the links between the physical and social dimensions of cities and identifies the dynamics and patterns of urban growth.

The theory of human ecology, as applied to urban settings, holds that cities grow in ever-expanding concentric circles. It is sometimes called the "concentric zone model" of the city. Three social processes animate this growth (Hawley, 1950). **Differentiation** refers to the process by which urban populations and their activities become more complex and

Carcassone, France, a medieval walled city.

heterogeneous over time. For instance, a small town may have a diner, a pizza parlour, and a Chinese restaurant. But if that small town grows into a city, it will likely boast a variety of ethnic restaurants that reflect its more heterogeneous population. Moreover, in a city, members of different ethnic and racial groups and socio-economic classes may vie with one another for dominance in particular areas. Businesses may also try to push residents out of certain areas to establish commercial zones. When this happens, people are engaging in **competition,** an ongoing struggle by different groups to inhabit optimal locations. Finally, **ecological succession** takes place when a distinct group of people moves from one area to another, and another group moves into the old area to replace the first group. For example, a recurrent pattern of ecological succession involves members of the middle class moving to the suburbs, with working-class and poor immigrants moving into the inner city. The socio-economic scene of North America during the latter part of the nineteenth and early twentieth centuries, a time of large-scale immigration from Europe, provided the conceptual basis of this model. In Chicago in the 1920s, differentiation, competition, and ecological succession resulted in the zonal pattern illustrated in Figure 16.4.

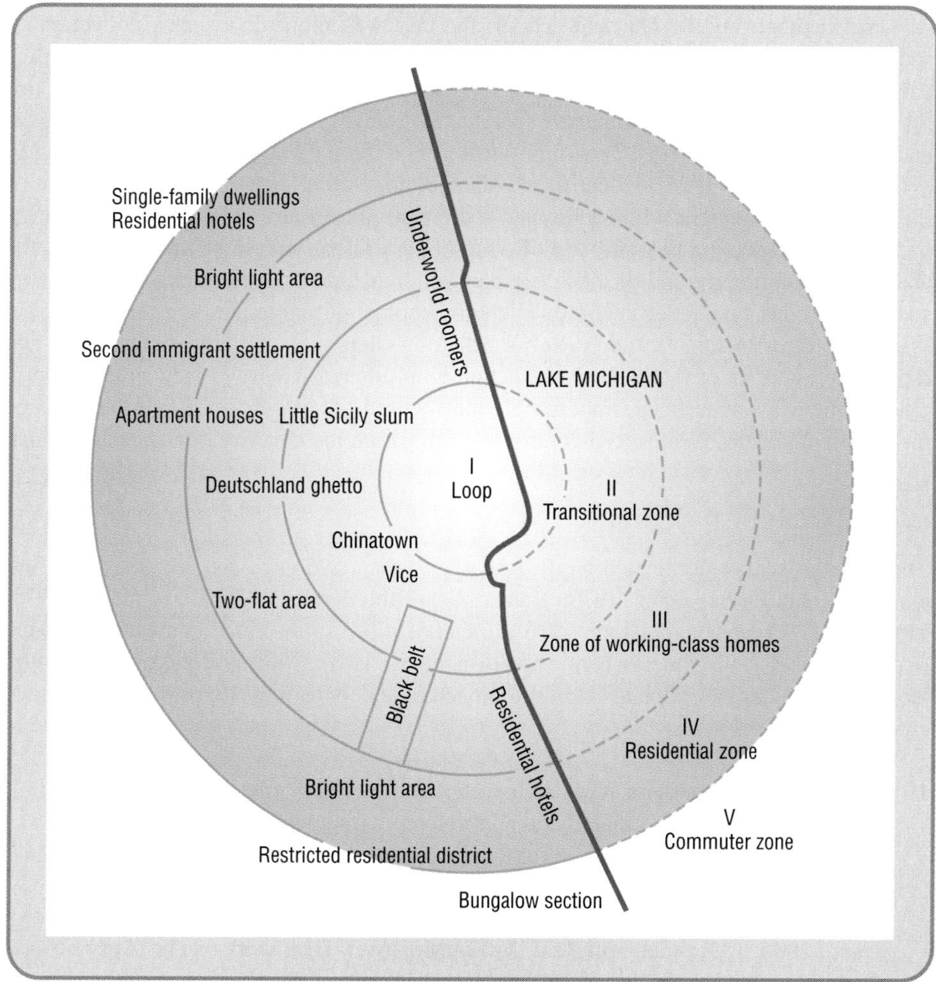


**✦ FIGURE 16.4 ✦**
**The Concentric Zone Model of Chicago, about 1920**

Source: Burgess (1967 [1925]).

1. Zone 1 was the central business district (known in Chicago as "the Loop"). It contained retail shopping areas, office buildings, and entertainment centres. The land in this zone was the most valuable in the city.
2. Zone 2, the "zone of transition," was the area of most intense competition between residential and commercial interests. The businesses usually succeeded in driving out middle-class residents by bidding up the price of land and having city governments rezone the area for commercial use. Homes then declined in value, and cheap

rental housing came to predominate. Eventually, the housing deteriorated into slums because speculators spent little on maintenance. They merely held on to the buildings until they could sell them for the commercial value of the land on which they stood. Where commercial development failed to materialize, the slums endured, attracting new immigrants, the poor, people with physical and mental disabilities, the unemployed, and criminals. The Chicago sociologists viewed this zone as "socially disorganized" because of its high level of deviance and crime.

3. When members of ethnic groups in Zone 2 could afford better housing, they moved to Zone 3, the "zone of working-class homes." These were mostly inexpensive, semi-detached buildings.
4. The upwardly mobile offspring of families in Zone 3 usually moved to Zone 4, the "residential zone," which contained small, middle-class, detached homes.
5. Zone 5, the "commuter zone," was where middle-class, upper-middle-class, and upper-class families lived in more expensive detached homes. These people also owned cars and commuted to work in the city.

For members of the Chicago school, the city was more than just a collection of socially segregated buildings, places, and people. It also involved a way of life that they called **urbanism.** They defined urbanism as "a state of mind, a body of customs[,] . . . traditions, . . . attitudes and sentiments" specifically linked to city dwelling (Park, Burgess, and McKenzie, 1967 [1925]: 1). Louis Wirth (1938) developed this theme. According to Wirth, rural life involves frequent face-to-face interaction among a few people. Most of these people are familiar with each other, share common values and a collective identity, and strongly respect traditional ways of doing things. Urban life, in contrast, involves the absence of community and of close personal relationships. Extensive exposure to many socially different people leads city dwellers to become more tolerant than rural folk, said Wirth (see also Wilson, 1991). However, urban dwellers also withdraw emotionally and reduce the intensity of their social interaction with others. In Wirth's view, interaction in cities is therefore superficial, impersonal, and focused on specific goals. People become more individualistic. Weak social control leads to a high incidence of deviance and crime.

## After Chicago: A Critique

The Chicago school dominated North American urban sociology for decades (e.g., Balakrishnan and Jarvis, 1976, 1979; Balakrishnan and Kralt, 1987; Berry, 1965, 1971; Murdie, 1969; Yeates and Garner, 1976). In fact, it still inspires much interesting research (e.g., Anderson, 1990; Balakrishnan and Selvanathan, 1990; Hou and Balakrishnan, 1996). However, three major criticisms of this approach to understanding city growth have gained credibility over the years:

1. One criticism focuses on Wirth's characterization of the "urban way of life." Research shows that social isolation, emotional withdrawal, stress, and other problems may be just as common in rural areas as in urban areas (Webb and Collette, 1977, 1979; Crothers, 1979). After all, in a small community a person may not be able to find anyone to share a particular interest or passion (Lamanna and Riedmann, 2000: 159; Small and Reid, 2002). Moreover, farm work can be every bit as stressful as work on an assembly line. Research also shows that urban life is less impersonal, anomic, and devoid of community than the Chicago sociologists made it appear. True, newcomers (of whom there were admittedly many in Chicago in the 1920s) may find city life bewildering if not frightening. Neighbourliness and friendliness to strangers are less common in cities than in small communities (Fischer, 1981). However, even in the largest cities, most residents create social networks and subcultures that serve functions similar to those performed by the small community (Carroll, 2002). Friendship, kinship, ethnic, and racial ties, as well as work and leisure relations, form the bases of these urban networks and subcultures (Fischer,

1984 [1976]; Hampton and Wellman, 1999; Jacobs, 1961; Wellman, 1979). Consider, in this context, that the United Nations has identified Toronto as the most multicultural city in the world. In 2001, for the first time, more Toronto residents were born outside than within Canada, making Toronto "earth's first global city not merely in the sense of being connected to the world, but of actually containing the world" (Bricker and Greenspon, 2001: 297). With more than 60 ethnic communities and 100 languages spoken, "[t]he 'vertical mosaic' of Toronto's multicultural population is a source of community support for people in everyday life" (Geddes, 1997: 91). Cities, it turns out, are clusters of many different communities. Herbert Gans found such a rich assortment of close social ties in his research he was prompted to call the people who live in cities "urban villagers" (Gans, 1962).

2. A second problem with the Chicago school's approach concerns the applicability of the concentric zone model to other times and places. In general, Canada, for example, has managed to avoid the U.S. ghetto syndrome. That is, in Canada we do not find the deep and enduring poverty that characterizes so many central neighbourhoods in the United States (Janigan, 2002: 26). True, we have not managed to evade the problem entirely. Thus, while the total metropolitan-area population of Canada grew by 6.9 percent between 1990 and 1995, the poor population in those areas grew by 33.8 percent. This population contains a large number of unemployed immigrants who know little English or French, Aboriginal peoples lacking much formal education, and single parents on social assistance (Janigan, 2002: 26). Research also shows that in the last few decades, socio-economic and ethnic residential segregation has increased in the large cities of Canada (and the United States). This led one urban sociologist to conclude that "Burgess was generally accurate" in observing that "[t]he socioeconomic status of urbanites increases directly with the distance of their residence from the city centre" (Gillis, 1995: 13.17; see also Kazemipur and Halli, 2000). Nonetheless, the core areas of most Canadian cities remain economically vibrant and socially viable, and they boast desirable and expensive housing. We conclude that the concentric zone theory has limited applicability to Canada.

   Evidence from preindustrial cities supports the view that the concentric zone model is most applicable to American industrial cities in the first quarter of the twentieth century. In preindustrial cities, slums are more likely to be found on the outskirts. Wealthy districts are more likely to be found in the city core. Commercial and residential buildings are often not segregated (Sjöberg, 1960).

   Finally, we note that after the automobile became a major means of transportation, some cities expanded not in concentric circles but in wedge-shaped sectors along natural boundaries and transportation routes (Hoyt, 1939). Others grew up around not one but many nuclei, each attracting similar kinds of activities and groups (Harris and Ullman, 1945; see Figure 16.5). All of this serves to case doubt on the universality of the concentric zone theory.

3. The third main criticism of the human ecology approach is that it presents urban growth as an almost natural process, slighting its historical, political, and economic foundations in capitalist industrialization. The Chicago sociologists' analysis of competition in the transitional zone came closest to avoiding this problem. However, their discussions of differentiation and ecological succession made the growth of cities seem almost like a force of nature rather than a process rooted in power relations and the urge to profit.

The so-called **new urban sociology,** heavily influenced by conflict theory, sought to correct this problem (Gottdiener and Hutchison, 2000 [1994]; Zukin, 1980). For new urban sociologists, urban space is not just an arena for the unfolding of social processes such as differentiation, competition, and ecological succession. Instead, they see urban space as a set of *commodified* social relations. That is, urban space, like all commodities, can be bought and sold for profit. As a result, political interests and conflicts shape the growth

✦ **FIGURE 16.5** ✦
**The Multiple-Nuclei Model of a City**

Source: Harris and Ullman (1945).

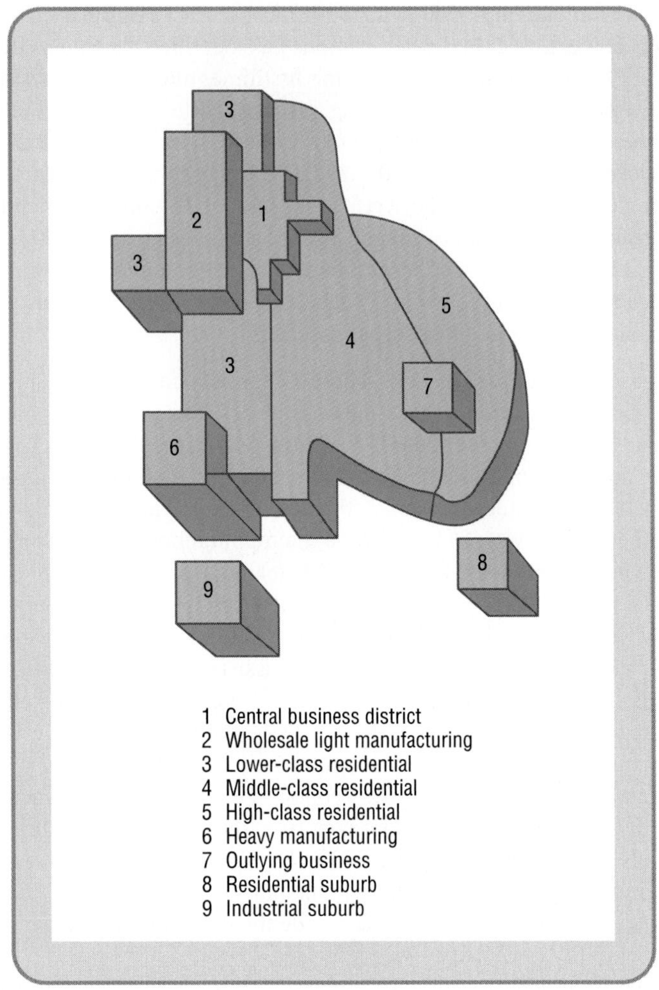


pattern of cities. John Logan and Harvey Molotch (1987), for example, portray cities as machines fuelled by a "growth coalition." This growth coalition is composed of investors, politicians, businesses, property owners, real estate developers, urban planners, the mass media, professional sports teams, cultural institutions, labour unions, and universities. All these partners try to get government subsidies and tax breaks to attract investment dollars. Reversing the pattern identified by the Chicago sociologists, this investment has been used to redevelop decaying downtown areas in many North American cities since the 1950s. In Canada, this approach is evident in the development of Harbourfront, a 28.3-hectare waterfront property along Toronto's Lake Ontario that has evolved "with mixed success into a recreational, cultural, residential, and commerical urban park" (Church, Greenberg, and McPhedran, 1997: 100). It is also notable in the reinvigoration of Gastown and the former Expo '86 lands in Vancouver, Quebec City's thriving Lower Town, and the restoration and revitalization of Calgary's downtown area (Janigan, 2002: 25).

According to Logan and Molotch, members of the growth coalition present redevelopment as a public good that benefits everyone. This tends to silence critics, prevent discussions of alternative ideas and plans, and veil the question of who benefits and who does not. In reality, the benefits of redevelopment are often unevenly distributed. Some maintain that most redevelopments are "pockets of revitalization surrounded by areas of extreme poverty" (Hannigan, 1998a: 53). It has additionally been claimed that local residents often enjoy few if any direct benefits from redevelopment. Indirectly, they also may suffer when budgets for public schooling, public transportation, and other amenities are cut to help pay for development subsidies and tax breaks.

For many, Africville serves as a cultural symbol of how urban development favours the interests of the haves at the expense of the have-nots. This photo shows former Africville resident Ruth Johnson, left, and Heritage Minister Sheila Copps, right, at a July 2002 ceremony to declare the former Halifax neighbourhood a national historic site.

For some Canadians, the case of the Africville relocation project in Halifax provides a powerful example of how urban redevelopment, renewal, and relocation may serve to disadvantage the marginal and powerless. Africville, a black community within the city of Halifax, was settled around 1850 by black refugees who had come to Nova Scotia, fleeing slavery in the United States. Like most black settlements in nineteenth-century Nova Scotia, Africville existed as a segregated community. Throughout its 125-year history, its inhabitants were poor and its population was small.

Even so, following the First World War, there was a drastic socio-economic decline in the community, with rampant unemployment and underemployment. Over time, Africville became viewed, at best, as an embarrassment and, at worst, as casting a blight on the city of Halifax. By the 1960s, years of civic mismanagement and discrimination by neglect had combined to make Africville one of the worst city slums in Canada's history. In 1963–64, Africville began to be phased out of existence by the City of Halifax and its inhabitants relocated.

However, despite their depressed living conditions, Africville's residents were often reluctant to move. As inducement, the city promised residents dramatically improved living conditions, including generous financial compensation for their homes, superior housing elsewhere, and monetary assistance following relocation. However, many of these promises were later broken or only partially kept. Residents who could not be cajoled into moving were threatened with the expropriation of their property by the city.

Eventually the residents of Africville were forced to move, and the community was bulldozed. The land that Africville had occupied remained vacant for many years. Although the land was designated at various times for industrial, warehouse, and highway use, none of these plans materialized. Seaview Memorial Park, the Fairview Cove Terminal, and A. Murray Mackay Bridge now mark the inland boundary of what was once Africville.

The question of why, precisely, the Africville relocation occurred continues to generate controversy and debate. One explanation is that during the 1940s and 1960s, urban renewal policies and relocation were seen as progressive and humanitarian social measures. It was felt that redevelopment and relocation would lead to better living conditions among the socially marginal and promote racial integration. A second explanation emphasizes Africville's identification by city officials and developers as potentially valuable land. In short, it suggests that events surrounding Africville are best viewed as attesting to how powerless people can be displaced from their community and their homes when it serves the interests of those who are more powerful.

Despite the events that occurred in Africville, the growth coalition is not all-powerful. Community activism often targets local governments and corporations that seek unrestricted growth. Sometimes activists meet with success (Castells, 1983). Yet for the past 50 years, the growth coalition has managed to reshape the face of North American cities, more or less in its own image.

## The Corporate City

The North American industrial city gave way after the Second World War to the **corporate city.** John Hannigan defines the corporate city as "a vehicle for capital accumulation—that is, . . . a money-making machine" (Hannigan, 1998b [1995]: 345).

In the suburbs, urbanized areas outside the political boundaries of cities, developers built thousands of single-family detached homes for the corporate middle class. These homes boasted large backyards and a car or two in every garage. A new way of life developed, which sociologists, appropriately enough, dubbed **suburbanism.** Every bit as distinctive as urbanism, suburbanism organizes life mainly around the needs of children. It also involves higher levels of conformity and sociability than life in the central city (Fava, 1956). Suburbanism became fully entrenched as developers built shopping malls to serve the needs of the suburbanites. This reduced the need to travel to the central city for consumer goods.

The suburbs were at first restricted to the well-to-do. However, following the Second World War, brisk economic growth, accompanied by higher wages and government assistance to veterans, put the suburban lifestyle within the reach of middle-class Canadians. Extensive road-building programs, the falling price of automobiles, and the "baby boom" that began in 1946 also stimulated mushroom-like suburban growth.

Due to the expansion of the suburbs and satellite communities, urban sociologists today often focus their attention not on cities but on "metropolitan areas" (a designation used by local governments) or "census metropolitan areas" (CMAs), a term coined by Statistics Canada. The latter refers to a large urban area (known as the urban core) along with adjacent urban and rural areas (urban and rural "fringes") that are highly integrated with the urban core. The formal definition of a CMA also specifies that it has an urban core population of at least 100 000 at the time of the most recent census. (However, once an area acquires the status of a CMA it retains its status even if the population of its urban core falls below 100 000.)

Metropolitan areas include downtown city cores and the surrounding suburbs (see Table 16.3). They also include two recent developments that indicate the continued change of the Canadian cityscape: the growth of rural residential areas within commuting distance of a city and the emergence of "edge cities," where clusters of malls, offices, and entertainment complexes arise, often beside major highways (Garrau, 1991). These are the "sprawling outer suburbs" (Janigan, 2002: 25) of major metropolitan areas. The growth of edge cities in Canada, though less pronounced than in the United States, has been stimulated by many factors. Among the most important are the mounting costs of operating businesses in city cores and the growth of new telecommunication technologies that are changing the location of work in the new millennium. Home offices, mobile employees, and decentralized business locations are all made possible by these technologies.

Although four decades ago Toronto-based urban critic Jane Jacobs (1961) warned of the dangers of sprawling suburbs and decaying downtowns in *The Death and Life of Great American Cities*, her premonitions would seem, in general, to be less valid in Canada. Jacobs' forecast has been avoided to some degree as the result of deliberate efforts undertaken by cities such as Vancouver, Quebec City, and Calgary to reinvigorate their downtowns. In addition, evidence of deteriorating conditions in our country's central cities has

**✦ TABLE 16.3 ✦**
**The 10 Largest Cities in Canada,* 2000 and 1901**

| City | Estimated Population on July 1, 2000 | City | Population in 1901 |
|---|---|---|---|
| 1. Toronto | 4 751 400 | Montreal | 266 826 |
| 2. Montreal | 3 480 300 | Toronto | 207 971 |
| 3. Vancouver | 2 048 800 | Quebec City | 68 834 |
| 4. Ottawa-Hull | 1 081 000 | Ottawa | 59 902 |
| 5. Calgary | 953 000 | Hamilton | 52 550 |
| 6. Edmonton | 944 200 | Winnipeg | 42 336 |
| 7. Quebec City | 689 700 | Halifax | 40 787 |
| 8. Winnipeg | 681 100 | Saint John | 40 711 |
| 9. Hamilton | 671 700 | London | 37 983 |
| 10. London | 421 300 | Vancouver | 26 196 |

Source: Adapted from Ash (2001: 89); Kearney and Ray (1999: 147).

* Based on census metropolitan areas (CMAs), which is defined as a large urban area, or urban core, along with the adjacent urban and rural areas that are highly integrated both socially and economically with that urban area.

sometimes been reduced by **gentrification**—a process whereby portions of the inner city are taken over by middle-class and/or higher-income groups and renovated and upgraded to desirable residential areas (Ley, 1996). Nevertheless, it remains true to at least some degree that in various Canadian cities, such as Winnipeg, the downtown core underwent a process of decline as the middle class fled, pulled by the promise of suburban lifestyle and pushed by such factors as racial animosity and fear of crime.

Some analysts suggest that many of the problems confronting cities are best resolved through the process of amalgamation. They view the creation of "megacities" such as Toronto, now the fifth-largest city in North America, with considerable optimism. They argue that bigger is, indeed, better in responding to such problems as inadequate road and public transit systems or environmental concerns, providing efficient and cost-effective services, and negotiating with provincial and federal governments. However, although Winnipeg, Halifax, Hamilton, and Fort McMurray number among those Canadian cities that have opted for amalgamation, others counter this trend, maintaining that "smaller is smarter."

Critics of amalgamation argue that it often *increases* costs (istar, 2001). Those opposed to amalgamation also argue that, when compared to larger governmental units, smaller units are more democratic, more accountable and responsive to their citizens, more sensitive to local, community, and neighbourhood issues, and more capable of responding to local opinion on the types and levels of services desired. Large governments, they claim, are difficult to control, show greater resistance to innovation and government reform, and are more likely to be influenced by special interests and professional advocates, such as lobbyists (Cox, 1997).

## The Postmodern City

Many of the conditions that plagued the industrial city—poverty, inadequate housing, structural employment—are evident in Canadian cities today. However, since about 1970, a new urban phenomenon has emerged alongside the legacy of old urban forms. This is the **postmodern city** (Hannigan, 1995b). The postmodern city has three main features.

**1.** The postmodern city is more *privatized* than the corporate city because access to formerly public spaces is increasingly limited to those who can afford to pay. Privatization is evident in the advertising claims of closed-off "gated communities" that boast of controlled-access front gates and foot patrols on the lookout for intruders. Privatization is also apparent in the construction of gleaming office towers and shopping areas that sometimes replace public urban green spaces. It is evident in pay-for-use public toilets and "patrons-only" washrooms. In the United States, this tendency is even more notable. For example, the private areas of downtown Los Angeles are increasingly intended for exclusive use by middle-class visitors and professionals who work in the information sector, including financial services, the computer industry, telecommunications, entertainment, and so forth.

2. The postmodern city is also more *fragmented* than the corporate city. That is, it lacks a single way of life, such as urbanism or suburbanism. Instead, a variety of lifestyles and subcultures proliferate in the postmodern city. They are based on race, ethnicity, immigrant status, class, sexual orientation, and so forth.
3. The postmodern city is more *globalized* than the corporate city. New York, London, and Tokyo epitomize the global city (Sassen, 1991). They are centres of economic and financial decision making. They are also sites of innovation, where new products and fashions originate. They have become the command posts of the globalized economy and its culture.

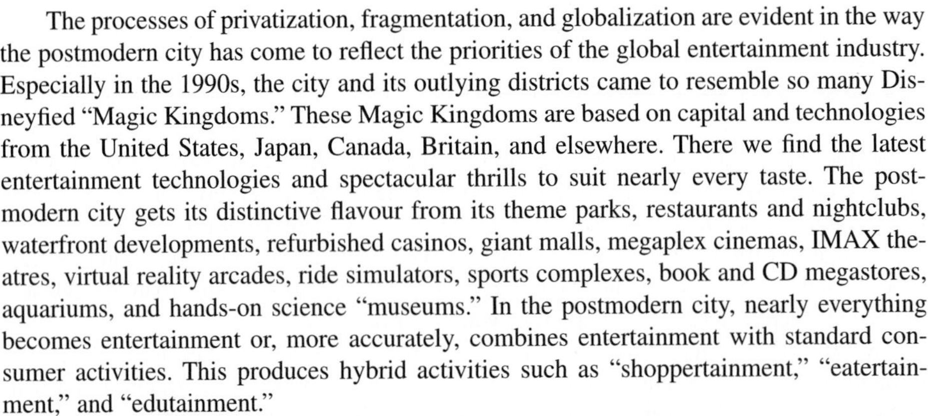
The processes of privatization, fragmentation, and globalization are evident in the way the postmodern city has come to reflect the priorities of the global entertainment industry. Especially in the 1990s, the city and its outlying districts came to resemble so many Disneyfied "Magic Kingdoms." These Magic Kingdoms are based on capital and technologies from the United States, Japan, Canada, Britain, and elsewhere. There we find the latest entertainment technologies and spectacular thrills to suit nearly every taste. The postmodern city gets its distinctive flavour from its theme parks, restaurants and nightclubs, waterfront developments, refurbished casinos, giant malls, megaplex cinemas, IMAX theatres, virtual reality arcades, ride simulators, sports complexes, book and CD megastores, aquariums, and hands-on science "museums." In the postmodern city, nearly everything becomes entertainment or, more accurately, combines entertainment with standard consumer activities. This produces hybrid activities such as "shoppertainment," "eatertainment," and "edutainment."

John Hannigan has shown how the new venues of high-tech urban entertainment manage to provide excitement—but all within a thoroughly clean, controlled, predictable, and safe environment (Hannigan, 1998a). The new Magic Kingdoms are kept spotless, in excellent repair, and fully temperature- and humidity-controlled. They also provide a sense of security by touting familiar name brands and rigorously excluding anything and anybody that might disrupt the fun. For example, entertainment developments often enforce dress codes, teenager curfews, and rules that ban striking workers and groups espousing social or political causes from their premises. The most effective barriers to potentially disruptive elements, however, are affordability and access. User surveys show that the new forms of urban entertainment tend to attract middle-class and upper-middle-class patrons, especially whites. That is because they are pricey and many are inaccessible by public transit and too expensive for most people to reach by taxi.

Referring to the major role played by the Disney Corporation in developing the new urban entertainment complexes, an architect once said that North American downtowns would be "saved by a mouse" (quoted in Hannigan, 1998a: 193). But do the new forms of entertainment that dot the urban landscape increase the economic well-being of the communities in which they are established? Not much, beyond creating some low-level, dead-end jobs (e.g., security guard, waiter, janitor). Do they provide ways of meeting new people, seeing old friends and neighbours, and in general improving urban sociability? Not really. You visit a theme park with family or friends, but you generally stick close to your group and rarely have chance encounters with other patrons or bump into acquaintances. Does the high-tech world of globalized urban entertainment enable cities and neighbourhoods to retain and enhance their distinct traditions, architectural styles, and ambience? It would be hard to destroy the distinctiveness of a city such as New York, Montreal, or Vancouver, but many large North American cities are becoming homogenized as they provide the same entertainment services—and the same global brands—as Tokyo, Paris, and Sydney. If the mouse is saving our cities, perhaps he is also gnawing away at something valuable in the process.

# DEVELOPMENT

## Global Inequality

The foregoing analysis shows that the *forms* assumed by urban social inequality in Canada and the United States have changed radically since the beginning of the twentieth century. Nevertheless, cities remain highly stratified places. If we now shift our attention from the national to the global level, we find an even more dramatic gap between rich and poor. In a Manhattan restaurant, pet owners can treat their cats to $100-a-plate birthday parties. In Cairo (Egypt) and Manila (the Philippines), garbage dumps are home to entire families who sustain themselves by picking through the foul refuse. The startling difference between these two worlds forms the subject of this chapter's last section. How did it come about that "[a] fifth of the developing world's population goes hungry every night, a quarter lack access to even a basic necessity like safe drinking water, and a third live in a state of abject poverty—at such a margin of human existence that words simply fail to describe it" (United Nations, 1994: 2)? How did it transpire that most of the citizens of the 20 or so rich, industrialized countries spend more on cosmetics or alcohol or ice cream or pet food than it would take to provide basic education, or water and sanitation, or basic health and nutrition for everyone in the world (see Table 16.4)? Let us examine how sociologists explain this gaping inequality.

## Theories of Development and Underdevelopment

Two sociological theories claim to explain global inequality. According to **modernization theory,** global inequality results from various inadequacies of poor societies themselves. Specifically, modernization theorists say that the citizens of poor societies lack sufficient *capital* to invest in Western-style agriculture and industry. They lack rational, Western-style *business techniques* of marketing, accounting, sales, and finance. As a result, their productivity and profitability remain low. They lack stable, Western-style *governments* that could provide a secure framework for investment. And, finally, they lack a Western *mentality*—that is, values that stress the need for savings, investment, innovation, education, high achievement, and self-control in having children (Berger, 1963; Huntington, 1968; Inkeles and Smith, 1976; Rostow, 1960). It follows that people living in rich countries can

✦ **TABLE 16.4** ✦

**Global Priorities: Annual Cost of Various Goods and Services, 1998 (in $US billion)**

| Good or Service | Annual Cost (in $US billion) |
|---|---|
| *Basic education for everyone in the world* | 6 |
| Cosmetics in the United States | 8 |
| *Water and sanitation for everyone in the world* | 9 |
| Ice cream in Europe | 11 |
| *Reproductive health for all women in the world* | 12 |
| Perfumes in Europe and the United States | 12 |
| *Basic health and nutrition for everyone in the world* | 13 |
| Pet foods in Europe and the United States | 17 |
| Business entertainment in Japan | 35 |
| Cigarettes in Europe | 50 |
| Alcoholic drinks in Europe | 105 |
| Narcotic drugs in the world | 400 |
| Military spending in the world | 780 |

Source: United Nations (1998a: 37).

*Note:* Items in italics represent estimates of what they would cost to achieve. Other items represent estimated actual cost.

A half-hour's drive from the centre of Manila, the capital of the Philippines, an estimated 70 000 Filipinos live on a 22.3-hectare mountain of rotting garbage, 50 metres high. It is infested with flies, rats, dogs, and disease. On a lucky day, residents can earn up to $5 retrieving scraps of metal and other valuables. On a rainy day, the mountain of garbage is especially treacherous: In July 2000, an avalanche buried 300 people alive. People who live on the mountain call it "the Promised Land."

best help their poor cousins by transferring Western culture and capital to them. Only then will the poor countries be able to cap population growth, stimulate democracy, and invigorate agricultural and industrial production. Government-to-government foreign aid can accomplish some of this. However, much also needs to be done to encourage Western businesses to invest directly in poor countries and to increase trade between rich and poor countries.

Critics have been quick to point out the chief flaw in modernization theory: For more than 200 years, the most powerful countries in the world deliberately impoverished the less powerful countries. It follows that an adequate theory of global inequality ought to focus on the relationship between rich and poor countries and not on the internal characteristics of poor countries themselves. Focusing on internal characteristics blames the victim rather than the perpetrator of the crime. This is the central argument of **dependency theory** (Baran, 1957; Frank, 1967; Wallerstein, 1974–89; Wolf, 1982).

According to dependency theorists, there was much less global inequality in 1750 than there is today. However, the Industrial Revolution enabled Western European countries, Russia, Japan, and the United States to amass enormous wealth. They used their wealth to establish powerful armies and navies. Their armed forces subdued and then annexed or colonized most of the rest of the world between the mid-eighteenth and the mid-twentieth centuries. The colonies were forced to become a source of raw materials, cheap labour, investment opportunities, and markets for the conquering nations. The colonizers thereby prevented industrialization and locked the colonies into poverty.

In the decades following the Second World War, nearly all of the colonies in the world became politically independent. However, say the dependency theorists, exploitation by direct political control was soon replaced by new means of achieving the same end: substantial foreign investment, support for authoritarian governments, and mounting debt. Let us consider each of these strategies in turn.

## Substantial Foreign Investment

Multinational corporations invested heavily in the poor countries to siphon off wealth in the form of raw materials and profits. True, they created some low-paying jobs in the process. However, they created many more high-paying jobs in the rich countries where the raw materials were used to produce manufactured goods. What is more, they sold part of the manufactured goods back to the poor, unindustrialized countries for additional profit.

## Support for Authoritarian Governments

According to dependency theorists, multinational corporations and rich countries continued their exploitation of the poor countries in the postcolonial period by giving economic and military support to local authoritarian governments (see Box 16.1). These governments managed to keep their populations subdued most of the time. When this was not possible, Western governments sent in their own troops and military advisers, engaging in what became known as "gunboat diplomacy." The term itself was coined in colonial times. In 1839, the Chinese rebelled against the British importation of opium into China and the British responded by sending a gunboat up the Yangtze River, starting the Opium War. The war resulted in Britain winning control of Hong Kong and access to five Chinese ports; what began as gunboat diplomacy ended as a rich feast for British traders. In the postcolonial period, the United States has been particularly active in using gunboat diplomacy in Central America. A classic case occurred in Guatemala in the 1950s. In 1952, the democratic government of Guatemala began to redistribute land to impoverished peasants. Some of the land was owned by the United Fruit Company, a huge U.S. multinational corporation and the biggest landowner in Guatemala. Two years later, the CIA backed a right-wing coup in Guatemala, preventing land reform and allowing the United Fruit Company to continue its highly profitable business as usual.

## Mounting Debt

The governments of the poor countries struggled to create transportation infrastructures (airports, roads, harbours, etc.), build up their education systems, and deliver safe water and at least the most basic health care to their people. To accomplish these tasks, they had to borrow money from Western banks and governments. So it came about that debt—and the interest payments that inevitably accompany debt—grew every year. By 1999, the poor countries owed the rich countries more than $2.5 trillion. That is 54 percent more than in 1992. At an average 7 percent rate of interest, it would cost $129 billion a year to service that debt. These crushing interest payments leave governments of poor countries with far too little money for development tasks. Foreign aid helps, but since it amounted to about $49 billion in 1999, it doesn't help much. At the end of the twentieth century, the poor countries were paying 2.6 times more interest to Western banks and governments than they were receiving as foreign aid (see Chapter 1, Figure 1.4). Recognizing the crippling impact of these repayments, former Canadian Minister of Finance Paul Martin is a prominent champion of the view that Western governments should cancel the debt obligation of poor countries.

Although Canada spent $2.1 billion in 2001 on foreign assistance, "Canada's international generosity reached an all time low of 0.24 percent of our Gross National Product in 2001/02, (CCIC, 2002). In comparison, Scandinavian countries maintain high levels of aid, consistently reaching or exceeding the UN target of 0.7 percent: Sweden, 0.7 percent; Norway, 0.9 percent; Denmark, 1 percent; the Netherlands, 0.8 percent. The Organisation

In 1893, leaders of the British mission pose before taking over what became Rhodesia and is now Zimbabwe. To raise a volunteer army, every British trooper was offered about 9 square miles (15 square kilometres) of native land and 20 gold claims. The Matabele and Mashona peoples were subdued in a three-month war. Nine hundred farms and 10 000 cattle were looted, leaving the native survivors without a livelihood. The British subsequently introduced forced labour so that the natives could pay a £2 per year tax.

BOX 16.1
## SOCIOLOGY AT THE MOVIES

*Three Kings* (1999), starring George Clooney, Mark Wahlberg, and Ice Cube

### *THREE KINGS* (1999)

It is 1991. A few months earlier, the army of Iraq invaded Kuwait, a small country in the enviable position of possessing 10 percent of the world's oil reserves. Now, the United States and its allies have declared victory over Iraq and its brutal leader, Saddam Hussein. They have pushed Iraqi forces out of Kuwait. American soldiers celebrate the restoration of the Kuwaiti people's freedom and the destruction of the Iraqi dictator's military might. The United States glories in its familiar role as the friend of democracy and the scourge of oppressors everywhere.

Then the picture becomes complicated. Some Americans discover a map on a captured Iraqi soldier. It leads to a bunker containing gold bars that Saddam Hussein looted from Kuwait. The Americans decide to do something for their families. As Major Archie Gates (played by George Clooney) says: "Saddam stole it from the [Kuwaiti] sheiks. I have no problem stealing it from Saddam." He assembles three trusted comrades, a Humvee, and some arms and other supplies. They head to the secret bunker, located in a small village.

What awaits the American soldiers is wholly unexpected. Remnants of Saddam's elite Revolutionary Guard protect the bunker. They are of no great danger to the Americans because a ceasefire has been declared. However, the villagers despise the Revolutionary Guard and Saddam. They have organized an armed resistance against the Iraqi leader and his troops. They cheer the arrival of the American soldiers. In response, the Revolutionary Guard shoots, imprisons, and tortures the rebels.

At first, the Americans ignore the plight of the freedom fighters because U.S. forces are under strict orders not to get involved. Their job as defined by the American government—securing the region's oil—is done. Suddenly, the "friend of democracy and the scourge of oppressors everywhere" is seen to be more self-interested than idealistic. The U.S. has ended the Iraqi military threat to the West's oil supply. (Saudi Arabia, with more than a quarter of the world's oil reserves, was next on Saddam's hit list.) Democracy, we learn, is a nice ideal when it suits American interests, but when it does not the United States is prepared to scatter that ideal to the winds.

In the movie, Archie Gates and his comrades develop sympathy for the village rebels. They help them overcome the Revolutionary Guard and lead them to sanctuary in neighbouring Iran. In a tense standoff with an American general and his troops at the Iraq–Iran border, Gates trades his knowledge of where the gold bars are stored for the safe passage of the villagers across the border. The movie leaves us with the feeling that while the U.S. government plays the game of oil politics, some American citizens really are idealistic and sympathetic to democracy and the oppressed everywhere.

In the real word, however, the United States abandoned Iraq's freedom fighters. The United States protected democracy in the region, such as it is. According to the CIA's *World Factbook 2001*, Kuwait allows just 10 percent of its population—adult men whose families lived in the country before 1920 or who have been Kuwaiti citizens for more than 30 years—to vote in elections. That is at least 10 percent better than democracy in Saudi Arabia, where there are no elections (Central Intelligence Agency, 2001). The West's oil supply is secure, although oil wealth in the region remains concentrated in the hands of the sheiks, their families, and their close supporters. Most of the Arab world remains impoverished as resentment builds against regimes like that of Kuwait and Saudi Arabia, fuelling Islamic militancy. Meanwhile, the United States prepares its next struggle on behalf of democracy and the oppressed.

for Economic Co-operation and Development (OECD)—composed of representatives of 29 industrialized nations who gather to discuss ways in which to promote economic growth, higher living standards, expanding trade, and free movement of investment—now ranks Canada seventeenth among 22 donor nations (Greenpeace, 2002). In 1995, Canada was ranked sixth (which was also our historical average for several decades). The 2001 federal budget included the largest increase in Canada's foreign aid spending in more than a decade and the creation of a new $500 million Africa Fund earmarked for the promotion of sustainable development (McIntosh, 2001). Yet these measures still fell well short of the 0.7 percent UN target (CCIC, 2002). At the same time, Canada's commitment has long contained the proviso that furnishing a specific level of support depends on a favourable assessment of our own fiscal situation.

Following the terrorist attacks of September 11, 2001, the Canadian public supported increased spending on security and the military (Gregg, 2002: 25). As a result, subsequent budgets are unlikely to include more spending on foreign aid. Even prior to the events of September 11, 2001, foreign aid has ranked fairly low on the list of what Canadians believe we should be spending money on: "When informed about the actual level of aid spending, 83% of Canadians think that this amount is either just right (50%) or not enough (33%)" (CCIC, 2002; see Box 16.2).

However, the consequences for the world's poor may be devastating. According to the World Bank, the economic downturn that occurred in the aftermath of the events of September 11, 2001, "will hit the world's poor the hardest. Some 10 million more men, women and children are likely to see their incomes drop below $1 a day, to say nothing of added insecurity, and feelings of powerless" (November 2001 Action Sheet, 2001).

## Assessment

Few sociologists would deny that the dependency theorists are correct on one score. In both the colonial and the postcolonial periods, Spain, Portugal, Holland, Britain, France, Italy, the United States, Japan, and Russia treated the world's poor with brutality to enrich themselves. Colonialism did have a devastating economic and human impact on the poor countries of the world. In the postcolonial era, the debt burden has crippled the development efforts of many poor countries.

That said, research has not yet answered one big question. Does foreign investment today have positive or negative effects on the developing countries? Much hinges on the answer to this question. Modernization theorists want more foreign investment in poor countries because they think it will promote economic growth and general well-being. They want trade and investment barriers to be dropped so free markets can bring prosperity to everyone. Dependency theorists diametrically oppose this strategy. They think foreign investment drains wealth out of poor countries. Therefore, they want the poor countries to revolt against the rich countries, throw up barriers to free trade and investment, and find their own paths to economic well-being.

Unfortunately, research conducted to date on the effects of foreign investment lends strong support to neither side in this debate. Some analysts find that foreign investment depresses economic growth in the poor countries in the medium to long term. This finding supports dependency theory (Bornschier and Chase-Dunn, 1985). Other analysts find that foreign investment increases growth and the well-being of even the most impoverished citizens of the poor countries. This finding supports modernization theory (Firebaugh and Beck, 1994). Whether analysts reach one conclusion or the other depends largely on which variables they include in their analyses and which statistical techniques they use.

There is, however, more to the story than that. Much research on the effects of foreign direct investment lumps together all poor countries. But there is good reason to believe that not all poor countries are alike. They have different histories and different social structures, and this may result in foreign investment having different effects in different times and places.

Immanuel Wallerstein proposes a variation on this theme. He argues that capitalist development has resulted in the creation of an integrated "world system" composed of three tiers. First are the **core** capitalist countries (the United States, Japan, Germany, etc.),

## BOX 16.2 IT'S YOUR CHOICE

### ATTITUDES TOWARD FOREIGN AID SPENDING

Do you think Canada is spending too much, too little, or about the right amount on foreign aid? A Southam News/CNC-ISS poll conducted in April 1998 attempted to answer this question. It subsequently reported that Canadians were divided about whether to increase or decrease foreign aid budgets, with those favouring an increase only slightly outnumbering those recommending cuts. Although respondents typically overestimated the share of the budget spent on foreign aid (estimating its share to be, on average, 11 percent versus its actual 2 percent), receiving accurate information about budget share did not result in a sizable change in their policy preferences.

According to this survey, Canadians' attitudes toward foreign aid are influenced "by a subtle form of self-interest involving an interplay of altruism and benefit" (Compas, 1998). Some, but not many, viewed foreign aid as promoting Canada's reputation in the world. Fifteen percent "strongly agreed" with the statement "Foreign aid is a matter of national power—Canada needs to give foreign aid in order to be taken seriously." Thirty-eight percent strongly agreed (and another 44 percent "agreed somewhat") with the statement "Canada gains when poor countries have economic hope because there's more trade, more stability and fewer refugees." Approximately the same percentage strongly agreed or somewhat agreed with the idea that "Giving foreign aid reflects pride in the values we stand for."

The most common reason given for cutting foreign aid was the belief that poor Canadians should be helped before the country spends on poor people abroad. This position has surfaced repeatedly in recent years. Consider, for example, that when increases in foreign aid spending were announced in the 2001 budget, MP Garry Breitkreuz rose in the House of Commons to hotly retort that the Canadian government should be direct money toward farmer's aid, not foreign aid: "The Prime Minister should look in his own backyard first.... Come to my home province of Saskatchewan and see the suffering going on in rural communities.... When will he realize that if he does not take any action on the prairies, he will have a third world country to bail out, but this time it will be his own?" (News Release, 1999). A second, but less strongly endorsed reason for decreasing the amount Canada gives in foreign aid was the belief that it serves primarily to enrich corrupt Third World leaders.

What do you think? Should Canada increase or decrease the amount it spends on foreign aid? Should the poor in Canada take precedence over the poor elsewhere? Why or why not? As a Canadian citizen, it's your choice.

which are major sources of capital and technology. Second are the **peripheral** countries (the former colonies), which are major sources of raw materials and cheap labour. Third are the **semiperipheral** countries (such as South Korea, Taiwan, and Israel), former colonies that are making considerable headway in their attempts to become prosperous (Wallerstein, 1974–89). To give just one dramatic illustration of this progress, South Korea and the African country of Ghana were among the poorest nations in the world in 1960. Ghana still is. But South Korea, the recipient of enormous foreign investment and aid, was nine times wealthier than Ghana in 1997 (as measured by per capita GNP; calculated from World Bank, 1999c: 193). Comparing the unsuccessful peripheral countries with the more successful semiperipheral countries presents us with a useful natural experiment. The comparison suggests circumstances that help some poor countries overcome the worst effects of colonialism.

The semiperipheral countries differ from the peripheral countries in four main ways (Hein, 1992; Kennedy, 1993: 193–227; Lie, 1998; Sanderson, 1995: 232–4): type of colonialism, geopolitical position, state policy, and social structure.

## Type of Colonialism

Around the turn of the twentieth century, Taiwan and Korea became colonies of Japan. They remained so until 1945. However, in contrast to the European colonizers of Africa, Latin America, and other parts of Asia, the Japanese built up their colonies' economies. They established transportation networks and communication systems. They built steel, chemical, and hydroelectric power plants. After Japanese colonialism ended, Taiwan and South Korea thus had a big advantage compared to, say, Ghana at the time Britain gave up control of that country or Brazil when Portuguese rule ended there. South Korea and Taiwan could use the Japanese-built infrastructure as a springboard to development.

A sixteenth-century engraving by Theodore de Bry of Amerindians crocodile hunting. Nearly a century after Europeans began subduing and conquering the Americas, de Bry provided the first high-quality European pictorial record of the New World.

## Geopolitical Position

By the end of the Second World War, the United States was the leading economic and military power in the world. However, it began to feel its supremacy threatened from the late 1940s on by the Soviet Union and China. Fearing that South Korea and Taiwan might fall to the communists, the United States poured unprecedented aid into both countries in the 1960s. It also gave them large low-interest loans and opened its domestic market to Taiwanese and South Korean products. Because the United States viewed Israel as a crucially important ally in the Middle East, it, too, received special economic assistance. Other countries with less strategic importance to the United States received less help in their drives to industrialize.

## State Policy

A third factor that accounts for the relative success of some countries in their efforts to industrialize and become prosperous concerns state policies. As a legacy of colonialism, the Taiwanese and South Korean states were developed on the Japanese model. They kept workers' wages low, restricted trade union growth, and maintained quasi-military discipline in the factories. Moreover, by placing high taxes on consumer goods, limiting the import of foreign goods, and preventing their citizens from investing abroad, they encouraged their citizens to put much of their money in the bank. This created a large pool of capital that the state made available for industrial expansion. Finally, from the 1960s on, the South Korean and Taiwanese states provided subsidies, training grants, and tariff protection to export-based industries. These policies did much to stimulate industrial growth.

## Social Structure

Taiwan and South Korea are socially cohesive countries. This makes it easy for them to generate consensus around development policies. It also allows them to get their citizens to work hard, save a lot, and devote their energies to scientific education.

Social solidarity in Taiwan and South Korea is based partly on the sweeping land reform they conducted in the late 1940s and early 1950s. By redistributing land to small farmers, both countries eliminated the class of large landowners, who usually oppose industrialization. A major source of social conflict was thus eliminated. In contrast, many countries in Latin America and Africa have not undergone land reform. The United States often intervened militarily to prevent land reform in Latin America. That is because U.S. commercial interests profited handsomely from the existence of large plantations (LaFeber, 1993).

Seoul, capital of South Korea. South Korea is one of the semiperipheral countries that are making headway in their attempts to become prosperous.

Another factor underlying social solidarity in Taiwan and South Korea is that both countries are more ethnically homogeneous than, say, countries in sub-Saharan Africa. British, French, and other West European colonizers often drew the borders of African countries to keep antagonistic tribes living side by side in the same jurisdiction. Maintaining tribal tensions made it easier for imperial powers to rule, as they could play one tribe off against another. However, this policy also caused much social and political conflict in postcolonial Africa. Today, the region suffers from frequent wars, coups, and uprisings. This high level of internal conflict acts as a barrier to economic development in Africa south of the Sahara Desert.

On balance, then, it seems that certain conditions do permit foreign investment to have positive economic effects. Postcolonial countries that enjoy an industrial infrastructure, strategic geopolitical importance, strong states with strong development policies, and socially cohesive populations are in the best position to join the ranks of the rich countries in the coming decades. Countries that have *some* of these characteristics may also be expected to experience some economic growth and increase in the well-being of their populations in the near future. Such countries include Chile, Thailand, Indonesia, perhaps Mexico and Brazil, and a few others in Latin America and Asia. In contrast, African countries south of the Sahara are in the worst position of all. They have inherited the most damaging consequences of colonialism and enjoy few of the conditions that could help them escape the history that has been imposed on them.

## Canada as a Semiperipheral Country

Many analysts regard Canada as a semiperipheral country that has managed to achieve prosperity despite its colonial past (Brym with Fox, 1989: 34–56; Laxer, 1989). In particular,

- The *type of colonialism* that Canada experienced is sometimes called "white settler colonialism." Like Australia, New Zealand, and the United States, Canada was settled by large numbers of Europeans who soon overwhelmed the Aboriginal population. They were determined to reproduce or improve the standard of living they enjoyed in the old country. Much of the wealth they produced was therefore reinvested locally. In contrast, when the European powers colonized Africa, they set up only small enclaves of white settlers. Their main aim was to exploit local resources and populations, sending nearly all of the wealth back to Europe.[2]
- Canada's *geopolitical position* has always been highly favourable to economic development. That is because it has served as a major supplier of raw materials and other goods to France, Great Britain, and the United States, and has fallen under the protective wing of each of these countries, all of which have viewed Canada as a staunch ally. For example, Canada played a disproportionately large role in the Second World War as a training ground, source of raw materials, and supplier of arms and soldiers to the Allies.
- Canada's *state policy* has sometimes acted to protect and stimulate the growth of Canadian industry, although admittedly not as consistently as the state policy of, say, South Korea. For example, the 1879 National Policy established a duty on imported manufactured goods. This sheltered the growth of Canadian industry, then in its infancy, by making foreign-made manufactured goods more expensive. Similarly, the 1965 Auto Pact required that foreign automobile companies wanting to sell cars in Canada duty-free manufacture cars in Canada and use a certain proportion of Canadian-made components. This stimulated the growth of an industry that, directly or indirectly, is now responsible for the employment of one-sixth of Ontario's labour force.

Canada's *social structure* has arguably had fewer positive effects on economic development than is the case in countries such as South Korean and Taiwan. In Canada, the French–English conflict has drawn attention away from development policy. And while strong farmers' and workers' movements have pushed governments in other countries to attend closely to development issues, these movements have been relatively weak in Canada (Brym, 1992; Laxer, 1989). Canada is not a world centre of capital. Our manufacturing sector is proportionately smaller than those of Germany, the United States, and Japan. An unusually large percentage of our industry is foreign owned. Still, Canada is one of the wealthiest countries in the world. Our semiperipheral status is clear.

## SUMMARY

1. Robert Malthus argued that although food supplies increase slowly, populations grow quickly. Because of these presumed natural laws, only war, pestilence, and famine can keep human population growth in check.
2. Rapid increases in food production, the existence of higher-than-expected upper limits to population size, the growth of large yet prosperous populations, the ability to provide generous social welfare and still maintain low population growth rates, and the widespread use of contraception have all cast doubt on Malthus's theory.
3. Demographic transition theory holds that the main factors underlying population dynamics are industrialization and the growth of modern cultural values. In the preindustrial era, both crude birth rates and crude death rates were high and population growth was therefore slow. In the first stages of industrialization, crude death rates fell, so population growth was rapid. As industrialization progressed and people's values about having children changed, the crude birth rate fell, resulting in slow growth again. Finally, in the postindustrial era, the crude death rate has risen above the crude birth rate in many societies. As a result, their populations slowly shrink unless in-migration augments their numbers.
4. Partially independent of the level of industrialization, the level of social inequality between women and men, and

between classes, affects population dynamics, with lower levels of social inequality typically resulting in lower crude birth rates and therefore lower population growth rates.

5. Much urbanization is associated with the growth of factories. However, religious, political, and commercial need gave rise to cities in the preindustrial era. Moreover, the fastest-growing cities in the world today are in semi-industrialized countries.
6. The members of the Chicago school famously described and explained the spatial and social dimensions of the industrial city. They developed a theory of human ecology that explained urban growth as the outcome of differentiation, competition, and ecological succession. They described the spatial arrangement of the industrial city as a series of expanding concentric circles. The main business, entertainment, and shopping area stands in the centre, with the class position of residents increasing as one moves from inner to outer rings.
7. Subsequent research showed that the city was not as anomic as the Chicago sociologists made it appear, and that the concentric zone pattern applies best to the industrial city in the first quarter of the twentieth century.
8. The new urban sociology criticized the Chicago school for making city growth seem like an almost natural process, playing down the power conflicts and profit motives that prompted the evolution of cities.
9. The corporate city that emerged after the Second World War was a vehicle for capital accumulation that stimulated the growth of the suburbs and resulted in the decline of inner cities.
10. The postmodern city that took shape in the last decades of the twentieth century is characterized by increased globalization of culture, fragmentation of lifestyles, and privatization of space.
11. Modernization theory argues that global inequality is due to some countries lacking sufficient capital, Western values, rational business practices, and stable governments.
12. Dependency theory counters modernization theory with the claim that global inequality results from the exploitative relationship between rich and poor countries.
13. An important test of the modernization and dependency theories concerns the effect of foreign investment on economic growth, but research on this subject is equivocal.
14. The poor countries best able to emerge from poverty have a colonial past that left them with industrial infrastructures, enjoy a favourable geopolitical position, implement strong growth-oriented economic policies, and have socially cohesive populations.

## GLOSSARY

The **Chicago school** founded urban sociology in the United States in the first decades of the twentieth century. Its members distinguished themselves by their vivid and detailed descriptions and analyses of urban life and their development of the theory of human ecology.

In the theory of human ecology, **competition** refers to the struggle by different groups for optimal locations in which to reside and set up businesses.

The **core** capitalist countries are rich countries such as the United States, Japan, and Germany that are the major sources of capital and technology in the world.

The **corporate city** refers to the growing post–Second World War perception and organization of the North American city as a vehicle for capital accumulation.

The **crude birth rate** is the annual number of live births per 1000 women in a population.

The **crude death rate** is the annual number of deaths per 1000 people in a population.

**Demographers** are social-scientific analysts of human population.

**Demographic transition theory** explains how changes in fertility and mortality have affected population growth from preindustrial to postindustrial times.

**Dependency theory** views economic underdevelopment as the result of exploitative relations between rich and poor countries.

In the theory of human ecology, **differentiation** refers to the process by which urban populations and their activities become more complex and heterogeneous over time.

In the theory of human ecology, **ecological succession** refers to the process by which a distinct urban group moves from one area to another and a second group comes in to replace the group that has moved out.

**Emigration,** or out-migration, is the outflow of people from one country and their settlement in one or more other countries.

**Gentrification** is the process by which certain deteriorated portions of the inner city are taken over by higher-income groups and upgraded through renovation to desirable residential areas.

**Human ecology** is a theoretical approach to urban sociology that borrows ideas from biology and ecology to highlight the links between the physical and social dimensions of cities and identify the dynamics and patterns of urban growth.

**Immigration,** or in-migration, is the inflow of people into one country from one or more other countries and their settlement in the destination country.

**In-migration,** see *immigration.*

The **Malthusian trap** refers to a cycle of population growth followed by an outbreak of war, pestilence, or famine that keeps population growth in check.

**Modernization theory** holds that economic underdevelopment results from poor countries lacking Western attributes. These attributes include Western values, business practices, levels of investment capital, and stable governments.

The **new urban sociology** emerged in the 1970s and stressed that city growth is a process rooted in power relations and the urge to profit.

**Out-migration,** see *emigration*.

The **peripheral** countries are former colonies that are poor and are major sources of raw materials and cheap labour.

The **postmodern city** is a new urban form that is more privatized and more socially and culturally fragmented and globalized than the corporate city.

The **replacement level** is the number of children that each woman must have on average for population size to remain stable. Ignoring any inflow of population from other countries and any outflow to other countries, the replacement level is 2.1.

The **semiperipheral** countries, such as South Korea, Taiwan, and Israel, consist of former colonies that are making considerable headway in their attempts to become prosperous.

**Suburbanism** is a way of life organized mainly around the needs of children and involving higher levels of conformity and sociability than life in the central city.

The **total fertility rate** is the annual number of live births per 1000 women in a population.

**Urbanism** is a way of life that, according to Louis Wirth, involves increased tolerance but also emotional withdrawal and specialized, impersonal, and self-interested interaction.

## QUESTIONS TO CONSIDER

1. Do you think that rapid global population growth is cause for alarm? If not, why not? If so, what aspects of global population growth are especially worrisome? What should be done about them?
2. Do you think of cities mainly as places of innovation and tolerance or mainly as sites of crime, prejudice, and anomie? Where does your image of the city come from? From your own experience? From the mass media? From your sociological reading?
3. Should Canadians do anything to help end global poverty? If so, why? If not, why not? If you think Canadians should be doing something to help end global poverty, what is it you think we should do?

## WEB RESOURCES

### Companion Web Site for This Book

http://www.brymsociologycompass.nelson.com

Begin by clicking on the Student Resources section of the Web site. Next, select the chapter you are currently studying from the pull-down menu. From the Student Resources page you will have easy access to InfoTrac College Edition®, MicroCase online exercises, and additional Web links. The Web site also has many useful tips to aid you in your study of sociology, including practice tests for each chapter.

### InfoTrac Search Terms

These search terms are provided to assist you in beginning to conduct research on this topic by visiting http://www.infotrac-college.com

**Dependency theory**
**Immigration**
**Migration**
**Modernization theory**
**Urbanization**

### Recommended Web Sites

Statistics Canada is perhaps the richest source of demographic data about Canada on the World Wide Web. It contains mainly Canadian, but also some international data, all easily accessible. Visit the Statistics Canada site at http://www.statscan.ca.

The World Wide Web Virtual Library: Demography & Population Studies at http://demography.anu.edu.au/VirtualLibrary/ offers a comprehensive list of international Web sites devoted to the social scientific study of population.

United Nations statisticians have created indicators of human development for every country in the period 1990–2002. The indicators are available at http://hdr.undp.org.

The Institute of Urban Studies is a policy research unit and resource centre associated with the University of Winnipeg. It features an extensive list of publications on urban issues in Canada. Visit its Web site at http://www.uwinnipeg.ca/~ius.

The International Development Research Centre (IDRC), a Canadian government agency that works on solutions to development problems through research, is a good resource for citizen-activists: http://www.idrc.ca.

## SUGGESTED READINGS

Donald H. Clairmont and Dennis W. Magill. *Africville: The Life and Death of a Canadian Black Community* (Toronto: Canadian Scholars' Press, 1999 [1974]). Originally published in 1974, it provides a social history Africville, a black community that fell victim to urban renewal and relocation policies of the 1960s. The third edition contains additional material that updates the original account and chronicles the ongoing efforts of Africville's residents to obtain compensation.

John Hannigan. *Fantasy City: Pleasure and Profit in the Postmodern Metropolis* (New York: Routledge, 1998). An entertaining and perceptive analysis of the postindustrial city as an entertainment hub.

John Lie. *Han Unbound: The Political Economy of South Korea* (Stanford, CA: Stanford University Press, 1998). A case study of the successes and limitations of development in one of the world's leading semi-peripheral countries.

Massimo Livi-Bacci. *A Concise History of World Population* (Cambridge, MA: Blackwell, 1992). A definitive introduction to world population by one of the world's leading demographers.

Eric R. Wolf. *Europe and the People without History* (Berkeley, CA: University of California Press, 1982). A broad and rich analysis of colonization and development from a dependency theory perspective.

## NOTES

1. However, since North Americans in particular consume so much energy and other resources, we have a substantial negative impact on the global environment. See Chapter 18, Technology and the Global Environment.
2. From this point of view, South Africa and, to a lesser degree, Rhodesia (now Zimbabwe) represent intermediate cases between the rest of Africa, on the one hand, and Canada, the United States, Australia, and New Zealand, on the other.

## IN THIS CHAPTER, YOU WILL LEARN THAT

- People sometimes riot, lynch, and engage in other forms of nonroutine group action to correct perceived injustices. Such events are rare, short-lived, spontaneous, and often violent. They subvert established institutions and practices. Nevertheless, most nonroutine collective action requires social organization, and people who take part in collective action often act in a calculated way.
- Collective action can result in the creation of one or more formal organizations or bureaucracies to direct and further the aims of its members. The institutionalization of protest signifies the establishment of a social movement.
- People are more inclined to rebel against existing conditions when strong social ties bind them to many other people who feel similarly wronged; when they have the time, money, and other resources needed to protest; and when political structures and processes give them opportunities to express discontent.
- For social movements to grow, members must make the activities, goals, and ideology of the movement consistent with the interests, beliefs, and values of potential recruits.
- The history of social movements is a struggle for the acquisition of constantly broadening citizenship rights—and opposition to those struggles.

CHAPTER

# 17

# Collective Action and Social Movements

## INTRODUCTION

Robert Brym almost sparked a small riot once. "It happened in grade 11," says Robert, "shortly after I learned that water combined with sulphur dioxide produces sulphurous acid. The news shocked me. To understand why, you have to know that I lived 100 kilometres east of the state of Maine and about 100 metres downwind of one of the largest pulp and paper mills in Canada. Waves of sulphur dioxide billowed from the mill's smokestacks day and night. The town's pervasive rotten-egg smell was a long-standing complaint in the area. But, for me, disgust turned to upset when I realized the fumes were toxic. Suddenly it was clear why many people I knew—especially people living near the mill—woke up in the morning with a kind of 'smoker's cough.' Through the simple act of breathing we were causing the gas to mix with the moisture in our bodies and form an acid that our lungs tried to expunge, with only partial success.

"Twenty years later, I read the results of a medical research report showing that area residents suffered from rates of lung disease, including emphysema and lung cancer, significantly above the North American average. But even in 1968 it was evident my hometown had a serious problem. I therefore hatched a plan. Our high school was about to hold its annual model parliament. The event was notoriously boring, partly because, year in, year out, virtually everyone voted for the same party, the Conservatives. But here was an issue, I thought, that could turn things around. A local man, K. C. Irving, owned the pulp and paper mill. *Forbes* magazine ranked him as one of the richest men in the world. I figured that when I told my fellow students what I had discovered, they would quickly demand the closure of the mill until Irving guaranteed a clean operation.

"Was *I* naive. As head of the tiny Liberal Party, I had to address the entire student body during assembly on election day to outline the party platform and rally votes. When I got to the part of my speech that explained why Irving was our enemy, the murmuring in the audience, which had been growing like the sound of a hungry animal about to pounce on its prey, erupted into loud "boos." A couple of students rushed the stage. The principal suddenly appeared from the wings and commanded the student body to settle down. He then took me by the arm and informed me that, for my own safety, my speech was finished. So, I discovered on election day, was our high school's Liberal Party. And so, it emerged, was my high-school political career.

"This incident troubled me for many years, partly because of the embarrassment it caused, partly because of the puzzles it presented. Why did I almost spark a small riot? Why didn't my fellow students rebel in the way I thought they would? Why did they continue to support an arrangement that was enriching one man at the cost of a community's health? Couldn't they see the injustice? Other people did. Nineteen sixty-eight was not just the year of my political failure in high school. It was also the year that student riots in France nearly toppled that country's government. In Mexico, the suppression of student strikes by the government left dozens of students dead. In the United States, students at Berkeley, Michigan, and other colleges demonstrated and staged sit-ins with unprecedented vigour. They supported free speech on their campuses, an end to American involvement in the war in Vietnam, increased civil rights for African-Americans, and an expanded role for women in public affairs. It was, after all, the 1960s."

Robert didn't know it at the time, but by asking why students in Paris, Mexico City, and Berkeley rebelled while his fellow high-school students did not, he was raising the main question that animates the study of collective action and social movements. Under what social conditions do people act in unison to change, or resist change to, society? That is the main issue we address in this chapter.

We have divided the chapter into three sections:

1. We first discuss the social conditions leading to the formation of lynch mobs, riots, and other types of nonroutine **collective action.** When people engage in collective action, they act in unison to bring about or resist social, political, and economic

change (Schweingruber and McPhail, 1999: 453). Some collective actions are "routine" and others are "nonroutine" (Useem, 1998: 219). Routine collective actions tend to be nonviolent and follow established patterns of behaviour in bureaucratic social structures. For instance, when Mothers Against Drunk Driving (MADD) lobbies for tougher laws against driving under the influence of alcohol, when members of a community organize a campaign against abortion or for freedom of reproductive choice, and when workers form a union, they are typically engaging in routine collective action. Sometimes, however, "usual conventions cease to guide social action and people transcend, bypass, or subvert established institutional patterns and structures" (Turner and Killian, 1987 [1957]: 3). On such occasions, people engage in nonroutine collective action, which tends to be short-lived and sometimes violent. They may, for example, form mobs and engage in riots. Until the early 1970s, it was widely believed that people who engage in nonroutine collective action lose their individuality and capacity for reason. Mobs and riots were often seen as wild and uncoordinated affairs, more like stampedes of frightened cattle than structured social processes. As you will see, however, sociologists later showed that this portrayal is an exaggeration. It deflects attention from the social organization and inner logic of extraordinary sociological events.[1]

2. We next outline the conditions underlying the formation of **social movements.** To varying degrees, social movements are enduring and bureaucratically organized collective attempts to change (or resist change to) part or all of the social order by petitioning, striking, demonstrating, and establishing lobbies, unions, and political parties. We will see that an adequate explanation of institutionalized protest also requires the introduction of a set of distinctively sociological issues. These concern the distribution of power in society and the framing of political issues in ways that appeal to many people.
3. Finally, we make some observations about the changing character of social movements. We argue that the history of social movements is the history of attempts by underprivileged groups to broaden their members' citizenship rights and increase the scope of protest from the local to the national to the global level.

We begin by considering the riot, a well-studied form of nonroutine collective action.

## NONROUTINE COLLECTIVE ACTION

### The Vancouver Riot of 1907

Just after 9 p.m. on September 7, 1907, following a rousing chorus of "Rule Britannia," A. E. Fowler rose to address a crowd of several thousand people outside Vancouver City Hall. Fowler was secretary of the Seattle branch of the Asiatic Exclusion League, an organization of white trade unionists who were trying to convince the American and Canadian governments to keep Chinese, Japanese, Hindus, and Sikhs out of North America. Fowler was a fanatic. He was discharged from the U.S. Army for "unfitness by character and temperament" (quoted in Wynne, 1996). According to rumour, he spent time in the Washington State Asylum at Steilacoom. He certainly knew how to whip up a crowd's emotions. Just two days earlier, he had participated in an anti-Asian riot in Bellingham, Washington, 80 kilometres southeast of Vancouver. He described how 500 white men had invaded the lodgings of more than 1000 Sikh and Hindu mill workers under cover of night, dragged them half-naked from their beds, and beat them. Six of the victims were in hospital. Four hundred were in jail, guarded by police. Seven hundred and fifty had been driven across the U.S.–Canada border.

The Vancouver crowd liked what it heard. They loudly cheered Fowler's impassioned description of the Bellingham violence as they waved little flags inscribed "A white

Canada for us." According to one source, Fowler "whipped the crowd into a frenzy" by calling for a "straight-from-the-shoulder blow" against Asian immigration ("Chinese Community," 2001). Suddenly, someone threw a stone. It shattered a window in a nearby Chinese-owned shop. The crowd, its prejudices having been reinforced and inflamed by Fowler, took this as a cue. Its members surged uncontrollably into Vancouver's Chinatown, hurling insults, throwing rocks through windows, and beating and occasionally stabbing any Chinese who were unable to flee or hide. With Chinatown reduced to a mass of broken glass, the crowd then moved on to the Japanese quarter, a few blocks away. The rioting continued for about three hours.

The next morning's papers in Toronto, Manchester, and London agreed on the main reason for the riot. The Toronto *Globe* said the riot was caused by "a gang of men from Bellingham." The *Manchester Guardian* said it had "proof of the correctness of the theory…that the anti-Japanese rioting in Vancouver was due to American agitators" (quoted in Wynne, 1996). In short, according to the papers, the riot resulted less from local social conditions than from the incitement of foreign hoodlums, the half-crazed Fowler foremost among them. Surely, the newspapers suggested, good white Canadian citizens could not be responsible for such an outrage.

## Breakdown Theory

Until about 1970, most sociologists believed at least one of three conditions must be met for nonroutine collective action, such as the 1907 Vancouver riot, to emerge. First, a group of people—leaders, led, or both—must be socially marginal or poorly integrated in society. Second, their norms must be strained or disrupted. Third, they must lose their capacity to act rationally by getting caught up in the supposedly inherent madness of crowds. Following Charles Tilly and his associates, we may group these three factors together as the **breakdown theory** of collective action. That is because all three factors assume collective action results from the disruption or breakdown of traditional norms, expectations, and patterns of behaviour (Tilly, Tilly, and Tilly, 1975: 4–6). At a more abstract level, breakdown theory may be seen as a variant of functionalism, for it regards collective action as a form of social imbalance that results from various institutions functioning improperly (see Chapter 1, A Sociological Compass). Specifically, most pre-1970 sociologists would have said that the Vancouver riot was caused by one or more of the following factors:

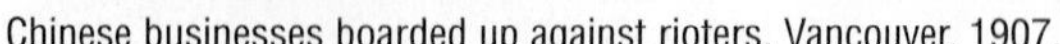
Chinese businesses boarded up against rioters, Vancouver, 1907.

Aftermath of the Vancouver riot, 1907.

1. *The discontent of socially marginal people.* This was the factor Ontario and British newspapers emphasized when they singled out "foreign agitators" as the main cause of the disturbance. According to the papers, the Vancouver rioters were galvanized by people from outside the community, people who had little in common with the solid citizens of Vancouver, people who, nonetheless, were skilled in whipping crowds into a frenzy and getting them to act in extraordinary and violent ways. Breakdown theorists often single out such socially marginal, outside agitators as a principal cause of riots and other forms of collective action.

   Sometimes, however, breakdown theorists focus on the social marginality of the led. Often, they say, a large number of the ordinary people who participate in riots, mobs, lynchings, and the like are poorly integrated in society. For example, they may be recent migrants to the area, that is, people who are unsettled and unfamiliar with the peaceable norms and conventions of the community. Pre-1970 sociologists could have made a case for the presence of many such people in Vancouver. After all, the completion of the Canadian Pacific Railway more than two decades earlier and the ongoing construction of other railways had stimulated rapid economic growth and urbanization in British Columbia. Construction, mining, and lumbering were all boom industries. It is at least possible (although it has never been demonstrated) that a large proportion of the rioters in 1907 were poorly integrated newcomers.

2. *The violation of norms* (sometimes called **strain**) is the second factor that pre-1970 sociologists would have stressed in trying to account for the 1907 Vancouver riot (Smelser, 1963: 47–8, 75). Arguably, two norms were violated in Vancouver in 1907, one cultural, the other economic. With rapid economic growth stimulating demand for labour, the number of Asian immigrants in British Columbia grew quickly in the early part of the twentieth century. By 1907, one-quarter of male workers in the province was of Asian origin. Their languages, styles of dress, religions, foods—in short, their entire way of life—offended many residents, who were of British origin. They regarded the Asian immigrants as "a threat to their cultural integrity" (Citizenship and Immigration Canada, 2000). From their point of view, Asian-Canadian cultural practices were violations of fundamental Anglo-Canadian norms.

   A second source of strain may have been the result of rapid economic growth causing British Columbians' material expectations to grow out of line with reality. According to proponents of breakdown theory, it is not grinding poverty, or **absolute deprivation,** that generates riots and other forms of collective action so much as **relative deprivation.** Relative deprivation refers to the growth of an intolerable gap between the social rewards people expect to receive and those they actually receive. Social rewards are widely valued goods such as money, education, security, prestige, and so forth. Accordingly, people are most likely to engage in collective action when rising expectations (brought on by, say, rapid economic growth and migration) exceed social rewards (sometimes brought on by economic recession or war) (Davies, 1969; Gurr, 1970). Neither recession nor war affected Vancouver in 1907. However, in that era of heady economic expansion, economic expectations may have risen beyond what society was able to provide. Hence the mounting frustration of Vancouver's workers that left them open to the influence of men like Fowler.

3. *The inherent irrationality of crowd behaviour* is the third factor likely to be stressed in any pre-1970 explanation of the Vancouver riot. Gustave Le Bon, an early French interpreter of crowd behaviour, wrote that an isolated person might be a cultivated individual. In a crowd, however, the individual is transformed into a "barbarian," a "creature acting by instinct" possessing the "spontaneity, violence," and "ferocity" of "primitive beings" (Le Bon, 1969 [1895]): 28). Le Bon argued that this transformation occurs because people lose their individuality and willpower when they join a crowd. Simultaneously, they gain a sense of invincible group power that derives from the crowd's sheer size. Their feeling of invincibility allows them to yield to

instincts they would normally hold in check. Moreover, if people remain in a crowd long enough, they enter something like a hypnotic state. This leaves them open to the suggestions of manipulative leaders and ensures that extreme passions spread through the crowd like a contagious disease. (Sociologists call Le Bon's argument the **contagion** theory of crowd behaviour.) For all these reasons, Le Bon held, people in crowds are often able to perform extraordinary and sometimes outrageous acts. *Extraordinary* and *outrageous* are certainly appropriate terms to describe the actions of the citizens of Vancouver in 1907.

## Assessing Breakdown Theory

Can social marginality, contagion, and strain fully explain what happened in Vancouver in 1907? Can breakdown theory adequately account for collective action in general? The short answer is no. Increasingly since 1970, sociologists have uncovered flaws in all three elements of breakdown theory and have proposed alternative frameworks for understanding collective action. To help you appreciate the need for these alternative frameworks, let us reconsider the three elements of breakdown theory in the context of the Vancouver riot.

*Social marginality*. Although it is true that Fowler and some of his associates were "outside agitators," the plain fact is that "if there had not been many local people who were deeply concerned about Oriental immigration, no amount of propaganda from the outside would have aroused the crowds" (Wynne, 1996). Moreover, the parade of 7000 to 9000 people that marched to city hall to hear Fowler's incendiary speech was organized locally by Vancouver trade unionists, ex-servicemen, and clergymen: all long-standing pillars of the community. This fits a general pattern: In most cases of collective action, leaders and early joiners tend to be well-integrated members of their communities, not socially marginal outsiders (Brym, 1980; Brym and Economakis, 1994; Economakis and Brym, 1995; Lipset, 1971 [1951]).

*Contagion*. No evidence suggests that the violence of September 7, 1907, was premeditated. However, the day's events were not spontaneous and unorganized acts of "contagion." A Vancouver branch of the Asiatic Exclusion League had been formed more than a month earlier and held three meetings before September 7. Two hundred people attended its third meeting on August 23. They carefully mapped out the route of the parade ending at city hall. They decided to hire a brass band. They arranged for the manufacture of flags emblazoned with racist slogans. They arranged to mobilize various local organizations to participate in the parade. They decided who would be invited to speak at city hall and what demands would be made of the government. Thus, sophisticated planning went into organizing the day's events.

As the Vancouver example shows, and as much research on riots, crowds, and demonstrations has confirmed, nonroutine collective action may be wild and violent but it is usually socially structured. In the first place, nonroutine collective action is socially structured by the predispositions that unite crowd members and predate their collective action. Thus, if the Vancouver rioters had not shared racist attitudes, they never would have organized and assembled for the parade and engaged in the riot in the first place (Berk, 1974; Couch, 1968; McPhail, 1991). Second, nonroutine collective action is socially structured by ideas and norms that emerge in the crowd itself, such as the idea to throw rocks through the windows of Chinese- and Japanese-owned shops in Vancouver (Turner and Killian, 1987 [1957]). Third, nonroutine collective action is structured by the degree to which different types of participants adhere to emergent and pre-existing norms. Leaders, rank-and-file participants, and bystanders adhere to such norms to varying degrees (Zurcher and Snow, 1981). Fourth, pre-existing social relationships among participants structure nonroutine collective action. For instance, relatives, friends, and acquaintances are more likely than strangers to cluster together and interact in riots, crowds, demonstrations, and lynchings (McPhail, 1991; McPhail and Wohlstein, 1983; Weller and Quarantelli, 1973). Thus, nonroutine collective action is socially organized in a number of ways, none of which is highlighted by focusing on "contagion."

*Strain.* Contrary to the argument of many breakdown theorists, a large body of post-1970 research shows that, in general, levels of deprivation, whether absolute or relative, are not commonly associated with the frequency or intensity of outbursts of collective action, either in Canada or elsewhere (McPhail, 1994; Torrance, 1986: 115–45). In other words, while feelings of deprivation are undoubtedly common among people who engage in collective action, they are also common among people who do not engage in collective action. Deprivation may therefore be viewed as a necessary, but not a sufficient, condition for collective action. For example, although Asian immigration upset many Anglo-Canadians in Vancouver, the roots of the 1907 riot ran deeper than the violation of their cultural norms. The roots of the riot were embedded in the way the local labour market was organized. Typically, where low-wage workers of one race and high-wage workers of another race compete for the same jobs, racist attitudes develop or are reinforced as high-wage workers resent the presence of low-wage competitors. Conflict almost inevitably results. This happened when African-Americans first migrated from the South to northern and western American cities in the early twentieth century. In Chicago, New York, and Los Angeles, the split labour market fuelled deep resentment, animosity, and even anti-black riots on the part of working-class whites (Bonacich, 1972). Similarly, in Vancouver the riot was ultimately the result of the way social life and, in particular, the labour market were organized in the city.

We conclude that nonroutine collective action is a two-sided phenomenon. Breakdown theory alerts us to one side. Collective action is partly a reaction to the violation of norms that threatened to *disorganize* traditional social life. But breakdown theory deflects attention from the other side of the phenomenon. Collective action is also a response to the *organization* of social life. And so we arrive at the starting point of post-1970 theories of collective action and social movements. For the past 30 years, most students of the subject have recognized that collective action is often not a short-term reaction to disorganization and deprivation. Instead, it is a long-term attempt to correct perceived injustice that requires a sound social-organizational basis.

## SOCIAL MOVEMENTS

### Solidarity Theory[2]

According to breakdown theory, people typically engage in nonroutine collective action soon after social breakdown occurs. In this view, rapid urbanization, industrialization, mass migration, unemployment, and war often lead to a buildup of deprivations or the violation of important norms. Under these conditions, people soon take to the streets.

In reality, however, people often find it difficult to turn their discontent into an enduring social movement. Social movements emerge from collective action only when the discontented succeed in building up a more or less stable membership and organizational base. Once this is accomplished, they typically move from an exclusive focus on short-lived actions such as demonstrations and riots to more enduring and routine activities. Such activities include establishing a publicity bureau, founding a newspaper, and running for public office. These and similar endeavours require hiring personnel to work full-time on various movement activities. Thus, the creation of a movement bureaucracy takes time, energy, and money. On these grounds alone, one should not expect social breakdown to result quickly in the formation of a social movement.

Research conducted since 1970 shows that, in fact, social breakdown often does not have the expected short-term effect. That is because several social-structural factors modify the effects of social breakdown on collective action. For example, Charles Tilly and his associates studied collective action in France, Italy, and Germany in the nineteenth and twentieth centuries (Lodhi and Tilly, 1973; Snyder and Tilly, 1972; Tilly, 1979a; Tilly, Tilly, and Tilly, 1975). They systematically read newspapers, government reports, and other sources so they could analyze a representative sample of strikes, demonstrations, and acts of collective violence. (They defined acts of collective violence as events in which groups of people seized or damaged persons or property.) They measured social breakdown by collecting data on rates of urban growth, suicide, major crime, prices, wages, and the value of industrial production. Breakdown theory would be supported if they found that levels of social breakdown rose and fell with rates of collective action. They did not.

As the top half of Table 17.1 shows for France, nearly all the correlations between collective violence and indicators of breakdown are close to zero. This means that acts of collective violence did not increase in the wake of mounting social breakdown, nor did they decrease in periods marked by less breakdown.

Significantly, however, Tilly and his associates found stronger correlations between collective violence and some other variables. You will find them in the bottom half of Table 17.1. These correlations hint at the three fundamental lessons of the **solidarity theory** of social movements, a variant of conflict theory (see Chapter 1, A Sociological Compass) and the most influential approach to the subject since the 1970s:

1. Inspecting Table 17.1, we first observe that collective violence in France increased when the number of union members rose. It decreased when the number of union members fell. Why? Because union organization gave workers more power, and that power increased their capacity to pursue their aims—if necessary, by demonstrating, striking, and engaging in collective violence. We can generalize from the French case as follows: Most collective action is part of a power struggle. The struggle usually intensifies as groups whose members feel disadvantaged become more powerful relative to other groups. How do disadvantaged groups become more powerful? By gaining new members, becoming better organized, and increasing their access to

**✦ TABLE 17.1 ✦**

**Correlates of Collective Violence, France, 1830–1960**

Source: Adapted from Tilly, Tilly, and Tilly (1975: 81–2).

*Notes:* (a) Correlations can range from −1.0 (indicating a perfect, inversely proportional relationship) to 1.0 (indicating a perfect, directly proportional relationship). A correlation of .00 indicates no relationship. (b) The correlation between the major crime and the rate of collective violence is negative, but it should be positive according to breakdown theory. (c) The exact years covered by each correlation vary.

| Variable | Correlation with Frequency of Collective Violence |
|---|---|
| **Breakdown variables** | |
| Number of suicides | .00 |
| Number of major crimes | −.16 |
| **Deprivation variables** | |
| Manufactured goods prices | .05 |
| Food prices | .08 |
| Value of industrial production | .10 |
| Real wages | .03 |
| **Organizational variable** | |
| Number of union members | .40 |
| **Political process variable** | |
| National elections | .17 |
| **State repression variable** | |
| Days in jail | −.22 |

scarce resources, such as money, jobs, and means of communication (Bierstedt, 1974). French unionization is thus only one example of **resource mobilization,** a process by which groups engage in more collective action as their power increases because of their growing size and increasing organizational, material, and other resources (Gamson, 1975; Jenkins, 1983; McCarthy and Zald, 1977; Oberschall, 1973; Tilly, 1978; Zald and McCarthy, 1979).

2. Table 17.1 also shows that there was somewhat more collective violence in France when national elections were held. Again, why? Because elections gave people new political opportunities to protest. In fact, by providing a focus for discontent and a chance to put new representatives with new policies in positions of authority, election campaigns often serve as invitations to engage in collective action. When else do new political opportunities open up for the discontented? Chances for protest also emerge when influential allies offer support, when ruling political alignments become unstable, and when elite groups are divided and come into conflict with one another (Tarrow, 1994: 86–9; Useem, 1998). Said differently, collective action takes place and social movements crystallize not just when disadvantaged groups become more powerful but when privileged groups and the institutions they control are divided and therefore become weaker. As economist John Kenneth Galbraith once said about the weakness of the Russian ruling class at the time of the 1917 revolution, if someone manages to kick in a rotting door, some credit has to be given to the door. In short, this second important insight of solidarity theory links the timing of collective action and social movement formation to the emergence of new **political opportunities** (McAdam, 1982; Piven and Cloward, 1977; Tarrow, 1994).
3. The third main lesson of solidarity theory is that government reactions to protest influence subsequent protest (see Box 17.1). Specifically, governments can try to lower the frequency and intensity of protest by taking various **social control** measures (Oberschall, 1973: 242–83). These measures include making concessions to protesters, co-opting the most troublesome leaders (for example, by appointing them advisers), and violently repressing collective action. The last point explains the modest correlation in Table 17.1 between frequency of collective violence and governments throwing more people into jail for longer periods of time. In France, more violent protest often resulted in more state repression. However, the correlation is modest because social control measures do not always have the desired effect. For instance, if grievances are very deeply felt, and yielding to protesters' demands greatly increases their hopes, resources, and political opportunities, government concessions may encourage protesters to press their claims further. And although the firm and decisive use of force usually stops protest, using force moderately or inconsistently often backfires. That is because unrest typically intensifies when protesters are led to believe that the government is weak or indecisive (Piven and Cloward, 1977: 27–36; Tilly, Tilly, and Tilly, 1975: 244).

Discussions of strain, deprivation, and contagion dominated analyses of collective action and social movements before 1970. Afterwards, analyses of resource mobilization, political opportunities, and social control dominated the field. Let us now make the new ideas more concrete. We do so by analyzing the ups and downs of one of the most important social movements in twentieth-century Canada, the union movement, and its major weapon, the strike.

## Strikes and the Union Movement in Canada

You can appreciate the significance of solidarity theory by considering patterns of strike activity in Canada. When blue-collar and white-collar workers go out on strike, they are withholding their labour to extract concessions from employers or governments in the form of higher wages and improved social welfare benefits. How do resource mobilization, political opportunity, and social control influence the willingness of workers to challenge the authority of employers and governments in this way?

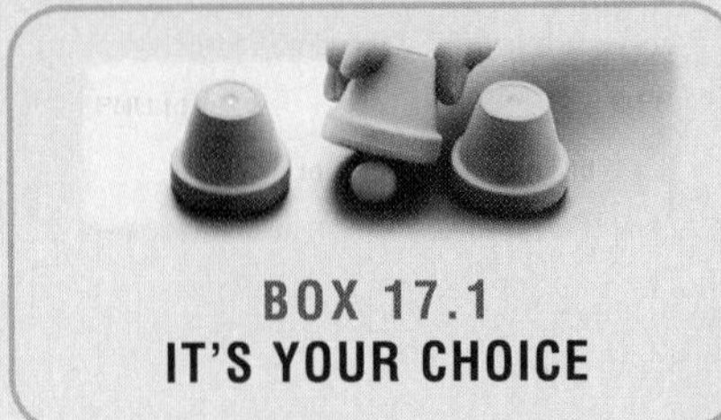

BOX 17.1
IT'S YOUR CHOICE

OCAP versus Premier Mike Harris, Toronto, June 15, 2000

### STATE SURVEILLANCE OF DEMONSTRATIONS

On June 15, 2000, members of the Ontario Coalition Against Poverty (OCAP) organized a demonstration of about 1000 people in front of the provincial legislature at Queen's Park to protest the policies of Mike Harris's Progressive Conservative government toward the poor and homeless. It didn't take long before a violent confrontation developed between protesters and the police. Gary Morton, one of the demonstrators, described the events as follows:

> An angry crowd of protesters, most of them wearing clothing to protect them from chemical attack by police, marches across the city to the legislature at Queen's Park. They make noise, bang drums and chant. When they arrive, huge numbers of riot police meet them... [T]he protesters send a delegation to the barricades at the front. Their demand—that they be allowed to address the legislature on homeless issues. The response is that no such thing will be allowed and no representative of the Harris Government will be speaking to them. The delegation informs the crowd of this and they surge forward to barricades... The people at the front grab the barricades and walk backward with them, opening a hole for the crowd to get through. Then all hell breaks loose. Gas smoke rolls and police charge out swinging batons. Some protesters struggle with them and others throw a few things like small water bottles. Horseback cops follow up, riding in from the north to force the crowd back and then swinging back in from the south. Between the horse sweeps the riot cops charge out and then get pushed back in. The police slowly gain ground. People are being picked off and beaten and cops begin to charge viciously into the larger body of peaceful protesters. At this point many people, myself included, begin to throw anything they can at the police. Bottles of water, mud and stones from the garden, picket signs. Brutality increases; anarchists tear apart a sidewalk and throw the chunks of stone at police. Horse charges swing in through the grassy area of the park and as the fight continues for some time we get forced out on the road, which we block... The police are now saying that they are going to review their videos frame by frame. (Morton, 2000)

The videos to which Morton refers came from seven cameras police set up to record the demonstration. In addition, police had a still photographer and several plainclothes officers with disposable cameras on duty. Two cameras belonging to Queen's Park security officers were also rolling during the melee. Finally, after the demonstration, the police seized film and videotape of the demonstration from television networks and newspapers (The CBC, CTV, ONtv, Global Television, *The Globe and Mail*, the *Toronto Star*, and *Sing Tao*).

What effect might police surveillance of demonstrations have on collective action? In the first place, if journalists fear their film and videos might be seized, they may be less likely to produce objective news reports. For example, a journalist might be disinclined to film a demonstrator being beaten by the police knowing that the film could be edited and used to identify and prosecute the demonstrator (Canadian Journalists for Free Expression, 2000). Moreover, according to sociologist Gary Marx, surveillance systems can be "used against those with the 'wrong' political beliefs; against racial, ethnic, or religious minorities; and against those with lifestyles that offend the majority" (quoted in Boal, 1998). One journalist comments: "Social psychologists say that taping political events can affect a participant's self-image, since being surveilled is unconsciously associated with criminality. Ordinary citizens shy away from politics when they see activists subjected to scrutiny. As this footage is splayed across the nightly news, everyone gets the meta-message: hang with dissenters and you'll end up in a police video" (Boal, 1998). In short, police surveillance of demonstrations may limit dissent and the free expression of political opinion.

What do you think? In the interest of maintaining law and order, should the police be entirely free to record demonstrations using cameras? Should they be allowed to seize film and videos from journalists? Or do such actions infringe the fundamental democratic rights of both the media and the citizenry? As a citizen, it's your choice.

1. Consider first the effect of *resource mobilization* on the frequency of strikes. Research shows that in Canada since the Second World War, strike activity has been high when (a) unemployment is low, (b) union membership is high, and (c) governments have shown themselves to be generous in their provision of social welfare benefits. Low unemployment indicates a strong economy. Workers are inclined to strike when business activity is robust because they know employers and governments can afford to make concessions. (Employers make bigger profits and governments collect more taxes during economic booms.) A high level of unionization is also conducive to more strike activity because unions provide workers with leadership, strike funds, and coordination. Thus, as resource mobilization principles suggest, strong social ties among workers (as indicated by a high level of unionization) and access to jobs and money (as indicated by a booming economy) increase challenges to authority (as indicated by strikes).[3]

   Figure 17.1 shows the pattern of strike activity in Canada between the end of the Second World War and 2000. It adds substance to the resource mobilization approach. Until 1974, the trend in strike activity was upward. In fact, in the 1970s, Canada was the most strike-prone country in the world. This was a period of growing prosperity, low unemployment, expanding state benefits, and increasing unionization. With access to increasing organizational and material resources, workers challenged authority increasingly more often in the three decades after the Second World War. In 1973, however, economic crisis struck. As a result of turmoil in the Middle East, oil prices tripled, and then tripled again at the end of the decade. Inflation increased and unemployment rose. Soon, the government was strapped for funds and had to borrow heavily to maintain social welfare programs. Eventually, the debt burden was so heavy the government felt obliged to cut various social welfare programs. At the same time, federal and provincial governments introduced laws and regulations limiting the right of some workers to strike and putting a cap on the wage gains that workers could demand. Unionization reached a peak in 1978, stabilized, and then began to decline (see Figure 17.2). Strike action was made even more difficult when Canada signed the free trade deal with the United States and Mexico. It was now possible for some employers to threaten to relocate to the United States or Mexico in the face of protracted strikes. Thus, in the post-1973 climate, the organizational and material resources of workers fell. As a result, strike activity plummeted. In 1974, nearly 16 strikes took place for every 100 000 Canadian nonagricultural workers. By 2000, that figure had fallen to 3 (Brym, 2003).

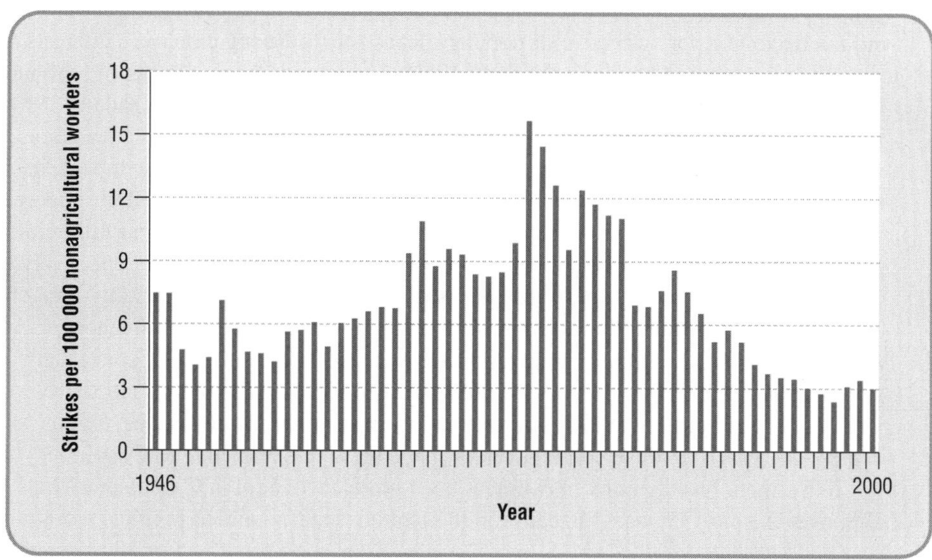


**✦ FIGURE 17.1 ✦**
**Weighted Frequency of Strikes, Canada, 1946–2000**

Sources: *Strikes and Lockouts in Canada 1968* (1970: 12–3); *Strikes and Lockouts in Canada 1985* (1985: 9); *Workplace Information Directorate* (1996); *Labour Organizations in Canada 1972* (1973: xxii–xxiii); *1994–1995 Directory of Labour Organizations in Canada* (1995: xiii); *1998 Directory of Labour Organizations in Canada* (1998: 15); "Chronological Perspective on Work Stoppage in Canada" (1999; 2001); "Chronological Perspective on Work Stoppages in Canada (Work Stoppages Involving One or More Workers), 1976–2000" (2001).

✦ **FIGURE 17.2** ✦
**Percentage of Nonagricultural Workers Unionized, Canada and United States, 1925–2000**

Sources: *Labour Organizations in Canada 1972* (1973: xxii–xxiii); *1994–1995 Directory of Labour Organizations in Canada* (1995: xiii); *1998 Directory of Labour Organizations in Canada* (1998: 15); "Union Membership in Canada—2000" (2000); U.S. Bureau of Labor Statistics (1998; 1999; 2001).

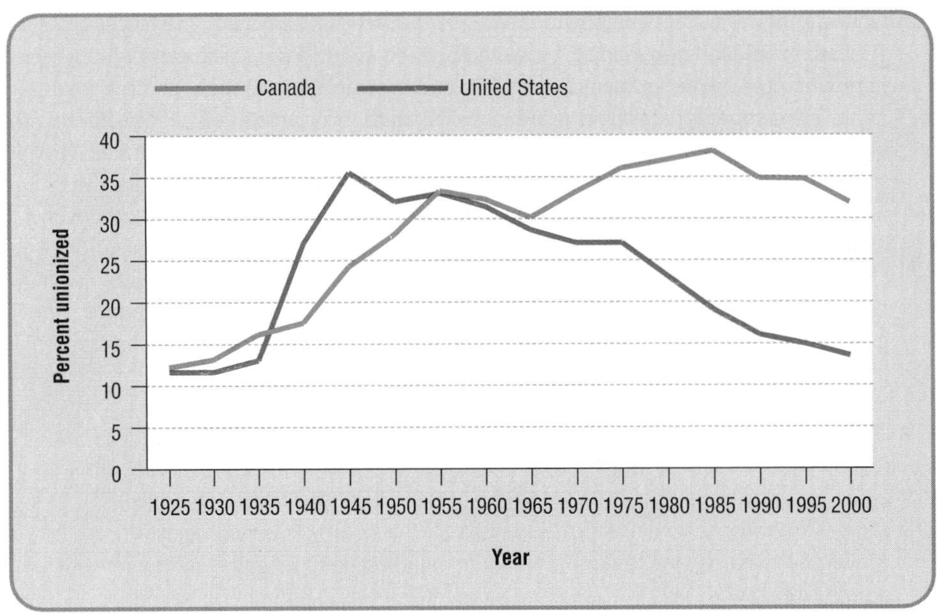


2. Comparing Canada and the United States allows us to highlight the effect of *political opportunities* on the health of the union movement. These two cases illustrate that opportunities for union growth are greater when privileged groups and the institutions they control are divided and therefore become weaker. Opportunities for union growth are fewer when privileged groups are socially cohesive and are backed by strong institutions.

The United Stastes and Canada have similar industrial and occupational structures. As the world's two largest trading partners, linked by a free trade agreement, they are subject to most of the same economic forces. Yet, as Figure 17.2 shows, trends in **union density** (the percentage of the nonagricultural labour force that is unionized) started to diverge in the mid-1960s. Today, fewer than one in eight nonagricultural employees in the United States is member of a union. The proportion of nonagricultural employees who belong to unions in Canada is about one in three. Why?

John F. Kennedy won the closely contested American presidential election of 1960 partly because of the union movement's support. As a result of his victory, government employees were awarded the right to unionize in 1961. However, their rights were sharply restricted. Striking, bargaining collectively over wages and benefits, and compulsory membership were not allowed. Therefore, public sector unions did not become a very effective or popular means for furthering employee interests.

The situation in Canada in the early 1960s was very different. A new pro-labour political party, the New Democratic Party (NDP), was established in Canada in 1961 with the support of the union movement. The NDP gained enough popularity among voters to be able to exert considerable influence over government policy. In fact, in the mid-1960s, the ruling Liberal Party would have lost office without NDP support. The NDP used its political leverage to convince the government to extend full union rights to public sector workers, including the right to strike and bargain collectively. Government employees soon joined unions in droves—and to a considerably greater extent than in the United States. Moreover, partly as a result of NDP influence, restrictions on private sector unionization were eased. Thus, in Canada, union density increased after the mid-1960s because political forces made unions attractive vehicles for furthering workers' interests. In contrast, in the United States, union density decreased because political forces made them less attractive to workers.

Why, then, has the union movement been more successful in Canada than the U.S. over the past 35 years? Because in the United States a unified political establishment was able to prevent the union movement from gaining rights that would make it attractive to more workers. Meanwhile, in Canada, a more divided political establishment could not prevent the creation of a legal environment that was favourable to union growth. In both cases, we see how political opportunities affect the growth or decline of social movements.

3. Finally, we turn to the most disruptive and violent strike in Canadian history—the Winnipeg General Strike of 1919—because it illustrates well three features of the use of *social control* on social movements:

   (a) *If authorities show indecision or weakness, movement partisans often become bolder.* In April 1918, three unions of Winnipeg city employees walked off the job, demanding higher wages. A month later, the strikers and their employers had nearly hammered out a settlement. However, just before signing off on the deal, the Winnipeg city council added a clause demanding that city workers pledge never to go out on strike again. In angry reaction, nearly *all* city employees walked off the job. That very same day, the city council capitulated. The striking workers got almost everything they demanded. After many bitter defeats, this victory convinced Winnipeg's workers they could get what they wanted by participating in a general strike, that is, a strike in which all employees walk off the job. Clearly, the city council's capitulation emboldened the workers (Bercuson, 1974: 7).

   (b) The second thing the Winnipeg strike teaches us about the use of social control on social movements is that *violence, especially the most extreme forms of violence, is most often initiated by authorities, not movement partisans.* On May 15, 1919, negotiations broke down over building and metal workers' demands for union recognition and higher wages. They called a general strike. The next morning, the city was paralyzed. Nearly all workers walked off the job. The strike leaders made every effort to keep the streets peaceful. The police, who supported the strike, even agreed to continue working to help maintain law and order. The city council, however, was opposed to having pro-strike police officers on duty. So they fired the entire police force, replacing them with a large

The Winnipeg General Strike of 1919 was the most disruptive and violent strike in Canadian history.

group of untrained "special police" who were hostile to the strike. The special police celebrated their first day of service by riding their horses and swinging their batons into a crowd listening to a speech downtown. This was the first act of violence during the Winnipeg General Strike but it was by no means the last. In addition to the special police, a mobile military force of 800 men armed with rifles and machine guns was recruited and trained to deal with the strikers. And on the afternoon of Saturday, June 21, that is just what they did. Striking workers had been gathering downtown to hold a parade in defiance of a ban issued by the mayor. They spotted a streetcar driven by a "scab" (replacement worker), cut the electricity powering it, smashed its windows, slashed its seats, and set the interior on fire. Fifty-four Royal Northwest Mounted Police on horses and 36 in trucks were dispatched to break up the crowd. They charged twice. The crowd responded with flying rocks and bottles. The Mounties then opened fire on the crowd and continued firing for several minutes. One worker was killed and many more were wounded. There is no evidence that workers fired any shots (Bercuson, 1974: 27). As is usually the case when one compares the violence exercised by authorities with the violence exercised by movement partisans, the authorities came out on top (Tilly, Tilly, and Tilly, 1975).

(c) Finally, the Winnipeg strike teaches us that *violent repression can still discontent, at least for a time*. This was certainly the case in Winnipeg. Four days after "Bloody Saturday," as June 21 came to be known, the Strike Committee called off the walkout, the strikers having failed to achieve any of their objectives. It took another quarter-century of strikes, many of them bitterly fought, before a larger and more powerful Canadian working class achieved the main demand of the Winnipeg General Strike and won the legal right to form unions.

## Framing Discontent

As we have seen, solidarity theory helps explain the emergence of many social movements. Still, the rise of a social movement sometimes takes strict solidarity theorists by surprise. So does the failure of an aggrieved group to press its claims by means of collective action. It seems, therefore, that something lies between (a) the capacity of disadvantaged people to mobilize resources for collective action, and (b) the recruitment of a substantial number of movement members. That "something" is **frame alignment** (Benford, 1997; Carroll and Ratner, 1996a; 1996b; Goffman, 1974; Snow, Rochford Jr., Worden, and Benford, 1986; Valocchi, 1996). Frame alignment is the process by which social movement leaders make their activities, ideas, and goals congruent with the interests, beliefs, and values of potential new recruits to their movement—or fail to do so. Thanks to the efforts of scholars operating mainly in the symbolic interactionist tradition (see Chapter 1, A Sociological Compass), frame alignment has recently become the subject of sustained sociological investigation (see Box 17.2).

Frame alignment can be encouraged in several ways. For example:

1. Social movement leaders can reach out to other organizations that, they believe, contain people who may be sympathetic to their movement's cause. Thus, leaders of an anti-nuclear movement may use the mass media, telephone campaigns, and direct mail to appeal to feminist, anti-racist, and environmental organizations. In doing so, they assume these organizations are likely to have members who would agree at least in general terms with the anti-nuclear platform.

2. Movement activists can stress popular values that have so far not featured prominently in the thinking of potential recruits. They can also elevate the importance of positive beliefs about the movement and what it stands for. For instance, in trying to win new recruits, movement members might emphasize the seriousness of the social movement's purpose. They might analyze the causes of the problem the movement is trying to solve in a clear and convincing way. Or they might stress the likelihood

## BOX 17.2 SOCIOLOGY AT THE MOVIES

Arabs led by Colonel T. E. Lawrence attack a Turkish supply train in *Lawrence of Arabia.*

### *LAWRENCE OF ARABIA* (1962)

One of the greatest movies of all time is a story about frame alignment. It is the Oscar®-winning account of how British Colonel T. E. Lawrence, brilliantly played by Peter O'Toole, helps turn fractious Arab tribes into a united movement for national independence from Turkey.

The Arabs had fallen under Turkish rule early in the 1500s. They subsequently endured a deep political and cultural decline. However, in the First World War (1914–18), Turkey fought against Britain, and Britain recognized in the Arabs a potential ally against the Turks. In the movie, the British deftly use Lawrence to unite the Arabs against their Turkish overlords.

At first, the British military dismiss the squabbling Arab tribes as "a nation of sheep stealers." Enter Lawrence. He sees in them a real people and a potentially valuable ally against the Turks. As a result, he sets out to align the beliefs of the Arabs with his own thinking. He accomplishes this task by word and example. By force of personality he convinces Bedouin tribal leaders that disunity will only ensure Arab status as a petty people, unable to gain its freedom and recapture the scientific, architectural, and literary glories it had achieved in medieval times. Conversely, he argues, unity will ensure political freedom and cultural flowering.

Words, however, are not enough to galvanize any more than a few tribes. Lawrence understands he can effectively align the beliefs of the Arabs with his own ambitions only by showing *in practice* how unity creates power. And so, in the movie, he proposes a land attack on the Turkish-controlled port of Aqaba. It is an outlandish idea because a land attack requires the nearly impossible crossing of a long stretch of barren desert known as "The Sun's Anvil." It is, however, an idea that is strategically dazzling, for the Turkish guns at Aqaba are stationary and they point out to the Red Sea, not inland. Fighting thirst, hunger, and fatigue, Lawrence leads his Bedouin supporters across the Sun's Anvil. In Aqaba, the Turks, defenceless against the land attack, lose hundreds in battle and quickly capitulate. It is a turning point. The British military, now convinced that Lawrence can unite the Arabs, gives him guns and artillery to continue his campaign against the Turks. Arabs throughout the Middle East take pride in their military accomplishments. They emerge at the end of the war by no means a fully united national independence movement, but one that is at least able to see the possibility of Arab unity.

*Lawrence of Arabia* is a great movie, but it is flawed because it gives too much credence to Lawrence's own self-promoting account of events and not enough to other credible historical sources that emphasize the native origins of Arab nationalism. Thus, the roots of the Arab national movement lay deeper than the movie allows. The movement first began to stir more than 60 years before Lawrence arrived in the Middle East, having sprung up among semi-Westernized Arab intellectuals in urban centres such as Beirut and Damascus in the late 1840s (Antonius, 1939: 35–60). Similarly, Arabs alone conceived and executed the all-important raid on Aqaba. Lawrence participated merely as "a trusted friend and companion-in-arms" of Faisal, the Bedouin leader and later king of Iraq (Antonius, 1939: 323). Lawrence's exercise in frame alignment certainly helped stimulate the Arab national movement, but, as these examples illustrate, by overstating and romanticizing Lawrence's role, *Lawrence of Arabia* underplays the Arabs' part in fashioning their own destiny.

The movie does, however, accurately portray the duplicity of the British, and it shows how they helped arouse a more militant Arab nationalism. The British promised the Arabs independence after the First World War in exchange for their support against the Turks. In 1916, however, they made a secret deal with France to divide up much of the region. After the war, Britain ruled part of the Middle East, France another. Increasingly, the United States, too, exercised substantial influence over parts of the region. This fuelled anti-Western resentment on the part of the Arabs. Western support for the creation of the State of Israel in 1948 further inflamed Arab nationalism and anti-Westernism. So did subsequent Western political and military intervention to ensure access to the region's enormous oil reserves. Thus, what began as an exercise in frame alignment turned out to be the world's most intractable political problem in the early twenty-first century.

The "Human Rights Now" tour, Los Angeles, 1988. Left to right: Peter Gabriel, Tracy Chapman, Youssou N'Dour, Sting, Joan Baez, and Bruce Springsteen. When bands play at protest rallies or festivals, it is not just for entertainment and not just because the music is relevant to a social movement's goals. The bands also attract nonmembers to the movement. This is one way of framing a social movement's goals to make them appealing to nonmembers.

of the movement's success. By doing so, they can increase the movement's appeal to potential recruits and perhaps win them over to the cause.

3. Social movements can stretch their objectives and activities to win recruits who are not initially sympathetic to the movement's original aims. This may involve a "watering down" of the movement's ideals. Alternatively, movement leaders may decide to take action calculated to appeal to nonsympathizers on grounds that have little or nothing to do with the movement's purpose. When rock, punk, or reggae bands play at nuclear disarmament rallies or gay liberation festivals, it is not necessarily because the music is relevant to the movement's goals. Nor do bands play just because movement members want to be entertained. The purpose is also to attract nonmembers. Once attracted by the music, however, nonmembers may make friends and acquaintances in the movement and then be encouraged to attend a more serious-minded meeting.

As we see, then, there are many ways in which social movements can make their ideas more appealing to a larger number of people. However, movements must also confront the fact that their opponents routinely seek to do just the opposite. That is, while movements seek to align their goals, ideas, and activities with the way potential recruits frame issues, their adversaries seek to *disalign* the way issues are framed by movements and potential recruits. The B.C. Forest Alliance provides a good illustration of this process (Doyle, Elliott, and Tindall, 1997 [1992]). Launched in British Columbia in 1991, the B.C. Forest Alliance was created and bankrolled by a group of senior forest industry executives and guided by the world's largest public relations firm. Its goal was to counter the province's environmental movement. It did so in two main ways. First, in its TV and print ads, the alliance claimed it represented the "middle ground" in the debate between forest companies and environmentalists. (In practice, the alliance rarely criticized forest companies while it routinely characterized environmentalists as dope-smoking hippies with untenable ideas such as shutting down the entire forest industry. Actually, very few environmentalists hold such extreme opinions, and research shows that that the middle class in B.C. broadly supports environmental groups.) The second way the alliance sought to counter the environmental movement was by arguing that more environmentalism means fewer jobs. (This was a huge oversimplification. Job losses in the forest industry were also caused by the introduction of new technologies in some areas, aging equipment in others, First Nations land claims, and resource depletion due to overharvesting and inadequate reforestation.) Muddying the waters in this way is typical of social movement opponents. Frame alignment should therefore be viewed as a conflict-ridden process in which social movement partisans and their opponents use all the resources at their disposal to compete for the way in which potential recruits and sympathizers view movement issues.

## Refrain: Back to 1968

Frame alignment theory stresses the strategies employed by movement members to recruit nonmembers who are like-minded, apathetic, or even initially opposed to the movement's goals. Resource mobilization theory focuses on the broad social-structural conditions that facilitate the emergence of social movements. One theory usefully supplements the other.

The two theories certainly help clarify the 1968 high-school incident described at the beginning of this chapter. In light of our discussion, it seems evident that two main factors prevented Robert Brym from influencing his classmates when he spoke to them about the dangers of industrial pollution from the local pulp and paper mill.

First, he lived in a poor and relatively unindustrialized region of Canada where people had few resources they could mobilize on their own behalf. Per capita income and the level of unionization were among the lowest of any state or province in North America. The unemployment rate was among the highest. In contrast, K. C. Irving, who owned the pulp and paper mill, was so powerful that most people in the region could not even conceive of the need to rebel against the conditions of life he created for them. He owned most of the industrial establishments in the province. Every daily newspaper, most of the weeklies, all of the TV stations, and most of the radio stations were his, too. Little wonder one rarely heard a critical word about his operations. Many people believed that Irving could make or break local governments single-handedly. Should one therefore be surprised that mere high-school students refused to take him on? In their reluctance, Robert's fellow students were only mimicking their parents, who, on the whole, were as powerless as Irving was mighty (Brym, 1979).

Second, many of Robert's classmates did not share his sense of injustice. Most of them regarded Irving as the great provider. They thought his pulp and paper mill, as well as his myriad other industrial establishments, gave many people jobs. They regarded that fact as more important for their lives and the lives of their families than the pollution problem Robert raised. Frame alignment theory suggests Robert needed to figure out ways to build bridges between their understanding and his. He did not. Therefore, he received an unsympathetic hearing.

Try applying solidarity and frame alignment theories to times when *you* felt a deep sense of injustice against an institution such as a school, an organization, a company, or a government. Did you do anything about your upset? If not, why not? If so, what did you do? Why were you able to act in the way you did? Did you try to get other people to join you in your action? If not, why not? If so, how did you manage to recruit them? Did you reach the goal you set out to achieve? If not, why not? If so, what enabled you to succeed? If you've never been involved in a collective action to correct a perceived injustice, try analyzing a movie about collective action using insights gleaned from solidarity and frame alignment theories. Classics movies on this subject include *Norma Rae* (1979), starring Sally Field. Field won the Best Actress Oscar® for her performance in this film as a Southern textile worker who joins with a labour organizer to unionize her mill. Another is *Matewan* (1987), a movie about the way employers prevented workers from organizing in the 1920s by fomenting racial and ethnic conflicts among them. See also Box 17.2.

## THE HISTORY AND FUTURE OF SOCIAL MOVEMENTS

Attempts to synthesize theories of collective action and social movement formation are in their infancy (Diani, 1996; Tarrow, 1994). Still, we can briefly summarize what we have learned about the causes of collective action and social movement formation with the aid of Figure 17.3. Breakdown theory partly answers the question of *why* discontent is sometimes expressed collectively and in nonroutine ways. Industrialization, urbanization, mass migration, economic slowdown, and other social changes often cause dislocations that engender feelings of strain, deprivation, and injustice. Solidarity theory focuses on *how* these social changes may eventually facilitate the emergence of social movements. They cause a reorganization of social relations, shifting the balance of power between disadvantaged and privileged groups. Solidarity theory also speaks to the question of *when* collective action erupts and social movements emerge. The opening and closing of political opportunities, as well as the exercise of social control by authorities, helps to shape the timing of collective action. Finally, by analyzing the day-to-day strategies employed to recruit nonmembers, frame alignment theory directs our attention to the question of *who* is recruited to social movements. Altogether, then, the theories we have considered provide a comprehensive picture of the why, how, when, and who of collective action and social movements.

Bearing this summary in mind, we can now turn to this chapter's final goal: sketching the historical development and future prospects of social movements in broad, rapid strokes. We begin three centuries ago.

In 1700, social movements were typically small, localized, and violent. In Europe, poor residents of a city might riot against public officials in reaction to a rise in bread prices or taxes. Peasants on an estate might burn their landowner's barns (or their landowner) in response to his demand for a larger share of the crop. However, as the state grew, the form of protest changed The state started taxing nearly all its citizens at higher and higher rates as government services expanded. It imposed a uniform language and often a common curriculum in a compulsory education system. It drafted most young men for army service. It instilled in its citizens all the ideological trappings of modern nationalism, from anthems to flags to historical myths.

✦ **FIGURE 17.3** ✦
**Determinants of Collective Action and Social Movement Formation**

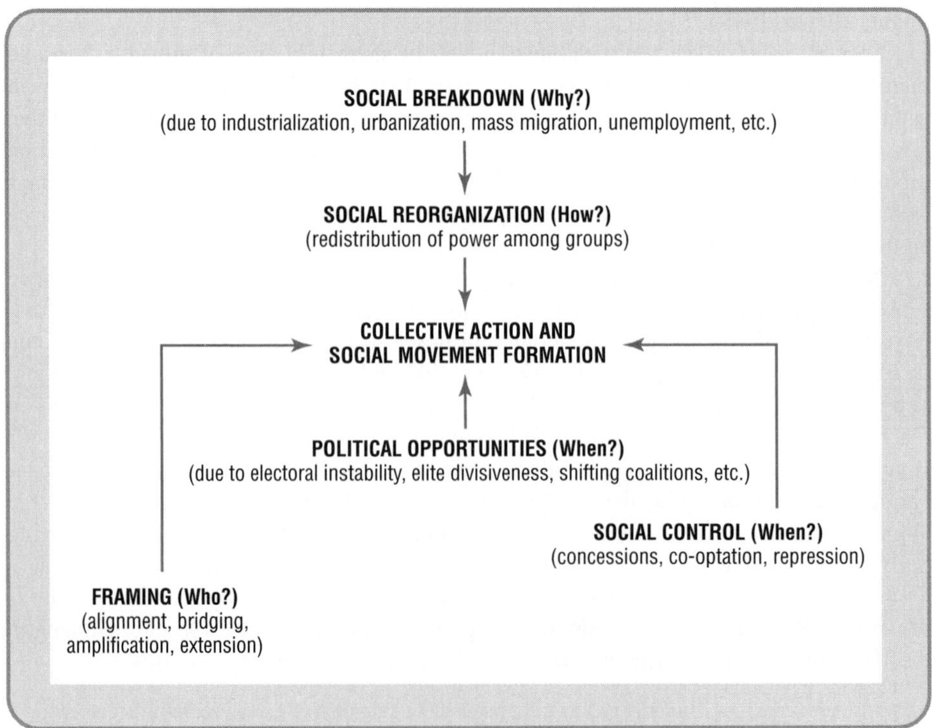

As the state came to encompass most aspects of life, social movements changed in three ways. First, they became national in scope. That is, they typically directed themselves against central governments rather than local targets. Second, their membership grew. This was partly because potential recruits were now literate and could communicate using the printed word. In addition, big new social settings—factories, offices, densely populated urban neighbourhoods—could serve as recruitment bases. Third, social movements became less violent. That is, their size and organization often allowed them to bureaucratize, stabilize, and become sufficiently powerful to get their way without frequent resort to extreme measures (Tilly, 1978; 1979a; 1979b; Tilly, Tilly, and Tilly, 1975).

Social movements often used their power to expand the rights of citizens. We may identify four stages in this process, focusing on Britain and the United States. In Britain, rich property owners fought against the king in the eighteenth century for **civil citizenship.** Civil citizenship is the right to free speech, freedom of religion, and justice before the law. The male middle class and the more prosperous strata of the working class fought against rich property owners in the nineteenth century for **political citizenship.** Political citizenship is the right to vote and run for office. In early-twentieth-century Britain, women and poorer workers succeeded in achieving these same rights despite the opposition of well-to-do men in particular. During the remainder of the century, blue-collar and white-collar workers fought against the well-to-do for **social citizenship.** Social citizenship is the right to a certain level of economic security and full participation in social life with the help of the modern welfare state (Marshall, 1965).

In medieval Europe, social movements were small, localized, and violent. For example, a medieval French historian reported that in 1358, "there were very strange and terrible happenings in several parts of the kingdom. . . . They began when some of the men from the country towns came together in the Beauvais region. They had no leaders and at first they numbered scarcely a hundred. One of them got up and said that the nobility of France . . . were disgracing and betraying the realm, and that it would be a good thing if they were all destroyed. At this they all shouted: 'He's right! He's right! Shame on any man who saves the gentry from being wiped out!' They banded together and went off, without further deliberation and unarmed except for pikes and knives, to the house of a knight who lived near by. They broke in and killed the knight, with his lady and children, big and small, and set fire to the house" (Froissart, 1968 [c. 1365]: 151).

The timing of the struggle for citizenship rights was different in the United States In particular, universal suffrage for white males was won earlier in the nineteenth century than in Europe. This accounts in part for the greater radicalism of the European working class. It had to engage in a long and bitter struggle for the right to vote while its U.S. counterpart was already incorporated into the political system (Lipset, 1977). Another important distinguishing feature of the United States concerns African-Americans. The 15th Amendment to the Constitution gave them the right to vote in 1870. However, most of them were unable to exercise that right, at least in the South, from the late nineteenth century until the 1960s. That was because of various restrictions on voter registration, including poll taxes and literacy tests. The civil rights movement of the 1960s was in part a struggle over this issue. It helped to create a community that is more politically radical than its white counterpart.

So-called **new social movements** emerged in the 1970s (Melucci, 1980; 1995). What is new about new social movements is the breadth of their goals, the kinds of people they attract, and their potential for globalization. Let us consider each of these issues in turn.

*Goals.* Some new social movements promote the rights not of specific groups but of humanity as a whole to peace, security, and a clean environment. Such movements include the peace movement, the environmental movement, and the human rights movement. Other new social movements, such as the women's movement and the gay rights movement, promote the rights of particular groups that have been excluded from full social participation. Accordingly, gay rights groups have fought for laws that eliminate all forms of discrimination based on sexual orientation. They have also fought for the repeal of laws that discriminate on the basis of sexual orientation, such as anti-sodomy laws and laws that negatively affect parental custody of children (Adam, Duyvendak, and Krouwel, 1999). Since the 1960s, the women's movement has succeeded in getting admission practices altered in professional schools, winning more freedom of reproductive choice for women, and opening up opportunities for women in the political, religious, military, educational, medical, and business systems (Adamson, Briskin, and McPhail, 1988; see Box 17.3). The emergence of the peace, environmental, human rights, gay rights, and women's movements marked the beginning of a fourth stage in the history of social movements. This fourth stage involves the promotion of **universal citizenship,** or the extension of citizenship rights to all adult members of society and to society as a whole (Roche, 1995; Turner, 1986: 85–105).

*Membership.* New social movements are also novel in that they attract a disproportionately large number of highly educated, relatively well-to-do people from the social, educational, and cultural fields. Such people include teachers, professors, journalists, social workers, artists, actors, writers, and student apprentices to these occupations. For several reasons, people in these occupations are more likely to participate in new social movements than are people in other occupations. Their higher education exposes them to radical ideas and makes those ideas appealing. They tend to hold jobs outside the business community, which often opposes their values. And they often become personally involved in the problems of their clients and audiences, sometimes even becoming their advocates (Brint, 1984; Rootes, 1995).

*Globalization potential.* Finally, new social movements are new in that they have more potential for globalization than did old social movements.

Up until the 1960s, social movements were typically *national* in scope. That is why, for example, the intensity and frequency of urban race riots in the United States in the 1960s did not depend on such local conditions as the degree of black–white inequality in a given city (Spilerman, 1970; 1976). Instead, African-Americans came to believe that racial problems are nationwide and capable of solution only by the federal government. Congressional and presidential action (and inaction) on civil rights issues, national TV coverage of race issues, and growing black consciousness and solidarity helped create this belief (Myers, 1997; Olzak and Shanahan, 1996; Olzak, Shanahan, and McEneaney, 1996).

Many new social movements that gained force in the 1970s increased the scope of protest beyond the national level. For example, members of the peace movement viewed federal laws banning nuclear weapons as necessary. Environmentalists felt the same way about federal laws protecting the environment. However, environmentalists also recognized that the

BOX 17.3

## THE WOMEN'S MOVEMENT IN CANADA

The women's movement was the first new social movement. It originated in the late nineteenth century. A century ago, women began to play a smaller role in domestic and farm work and started to enter the paid labour force in significant numbers. Owning more of their own economic resources, they became more independently minded. They began to realize they might free themselves of oppressive authority in the home. They also started to understand there was nothing inevitable about their receiving less pay and working in worse conditions than men with comparable jobs (Strong-Boag, 1986: 179).

Formulating a program for social change requires such resources as time, money, and education. Not surprisingly, therefore, the "first wave" of the women's movement was composed of highly educated professionals. A group of women with just that social profile established the Canadian Woman Suffrage Association in Toronto in 1883. By means of demonstrating, petitioning, and gaining the support of influential liberal-minded men, women won the right to vote federally in 1918, in all provinces but Quebec by 1925, and in Quebec in 1940.

Along with the right to vote, women won the right to run for public office. They immediately exercised that right, running mainly on the CCF and Liberal Party tickets. A woman was first elected to provincial office in Alberta in 1917 and to the federal Parliament in 1921.

In provincial legislatures and the federal Parliament women sought institutional reform through government action. Specifically, they pursued more equitable pay for women, easier access to higher education, protection from domestic violence, and a fair share of family assets and child support in case of divorce or desertion. But progress was slow on all these fronts. That was partly because women's representation in the country's legislatures remained meagre. Even as late as the 2000 federal election, women composed only 20.6 percent of federal MPs, placing Canada 25th among the world's countries. Moreover, some female MPs were hardly advocates of women's rights (Bashevkin, 1986; "Women in National Parliaments," 2001).

Because of this slow progress, feminists developed a strategy in the 1960s and 1970s that was less oriented toward established political institutions and more oriented toward grassroots action. The new strategy sought to achieve change not just "from above," by means of party politics, but also "from below," by creating a whole network of new organizations such as study groups, consciousness-raising circles, women's bookstores, rape crisis centres, abortion clinics, and shelters for battered women, and by creating opportunities to publicize the importance of feminist aims such as International Women's Day marches (Adamson, Briskin, and McPhail, 1988).

It was not only slow progress on the established political front that led women to create this network of new organizations. Many "second-wave" feminists were deeply involved in the student movement of the 1960s and 1970s. They were appalled to discover that, despite much rhetoric about liberation and equality, men controlled the student movement and men often refused to allow feminist issues to become part of their agenda. To pursue their aims they felt it was necessary to create new organizations run by women.

Today, then, the women's movement operates at both the grassroots level and within established political organizations to achieve its aims. It contains internal divisions. *Liberal feminists* believe that women can participate fully in society if they achieve equality of opportunity with men. They therefore advocate policies aimed at pay equity and the elimination of gender discrimination in the workplace. *Radical feminists* hold that male domination is rooted in the family. They champion free and safe contraception and abortion, an equitable division of domestic labour and the like. *Socialist feminists* maintain that legal equality is not enough to ensure that women can participate fully in society. In addition, they argue, the state should provide affordable and accessible daycare facilities and other services. These services, they say, could alleviate the economic burdens that prevent most women, especially those from the working class, from taking full advantage of available opportunities for education and employment. Thus, despite their different emphases, all three feminisms share a strong desire to see members of a previously marginal group expand their citizenship rights and become full participants in society.

condition of the Brazilian rain forest affects climactic conditions worldwide. Similarly, peace activists understood that the spread of weapons of mass destruction could destroy all of humanity. Therefore, members of the peace and environmental movements pressed for *international* agreements binding all countries to protect the environment and stop the spread of nuclear weapons. Social movements went global (see photos on the next page).

Inexpensive international travel and communication facilitated the globalization of social movements. New technologies made it easier for people in various national movements to work with like-minded activists in other countries. In the age of CNN, cheap jet transportation, fax machines, Web sites, and e-mail, it was possible not only to see the connection between apparently local problems and their global sources. It was also possible and, increasingly, desirable to act both locally and globally.

Consider the case of Greenpeace. Greenpeace is a highly successful environmental movement that originated in Vancouver in the mid-1970s. It now has offices in 41

The World Trade Organization (WTO) was set up by the governments of 134 countries in 1994 to encourage and referee global commerce. When the WTO met in Seattle in December 1999, 40 000 opponents of multinational corporations staged protests. Since then, protests have been staged wherever major international trade talks have been held. For example, when the Summit of the Americas took place in Quebec City in April 2001, more than 20 000 protesters took to the streets. They catapulted teddy bears, smoke bombs, and rocks at riot police and at one point breached the chain-link security fence surrounding the summit. Police responded with tear gas, water cannon, rubber bullets, and arrests. The accompanying photos were taken during the Quebec summit.

countries, with its international office in Amsterdam (Greenpeace, 2000). Among many other initiatives, it has mounted a campaign to eliminate the international transportation and dumping of toxic wastes. Its representatives visited local environmental groups in African and other developing countries. They supplied the Africans with organizing kits to help them tie their local concerns to global political efforts. They also published a newsletter to keep activists up to date on legal issues. Thus, Greenpeace coordinated a global campaign that enabled weak environmental organizations in developing countries to act more effectively. Their campaign also raised the costs of continuing the international trade in toxic waste.

Greenpeace is a highly successful global environmental movement that originated in Vancouver in the mid-1970s and now has offices in 41 countries.

Greenpeace is hardly alone in its efforts to go global. In 1953, 110 international social movement organizations spanned the globe. By 1993, there were 631. About a quarter were human rights organizations and about a seventh were environmental organizations. The latter are by far the fastest-growing organizational type (Smith, 1998: 97).

Even old social movements have gone global because of changes in the technology of mobilizing supporters. The anti-Western Muslim fundamentalist al-Qaeda terrorist movement can trace its political and intellectual roots to the formation of the Muslim Brotherhood in Egypt in 1928 ("Muslim Brotherhood Movement Homepage," 2002). By 2000, Osama bin Laden, the head of al-Qaeda, often used a satellite telephone to communicate with his operatives in as many as 60 countries—until U.S. law enforcement authorities inexplicably revealed they were tapping calls from his base in Afghanistan. Once he learned of these taps, bin Laden increased his use of another, more effective means of global communication: sending messages that are easily encrypted but difficult to decode via the Internet (Kelley, 2001; McCullagh, 2000). Some analysts think such messages were used to help plan and coordinate the complex, virtually simultaneous jet hijackings that resulted in the crash of an airliner in Pennsylvania and the destruction of the World Trade Center and part of the Pentagon on September 11, 2001, killing more than 3000 people.

Another example of an old social movement using modern technology to go global involves the peasants of Chiapas, a southern Mexican province. They participated in the 1910 Mexican Revolution and in a more globalized uprising against the Mexican government in 1994. Oppressed by Europeans and their descendants for nearly 500 years, the poor, indigenous people of southern Mexico were now facing a government edict preventing them from gaining access to farmland. They wanted the land for subsistence agriculture. But the government wanted to make sure the land stayed in the hands of large, Hispanic ranchers and farmers, who could earn foreign revenue by exporting goods to the United States and Canada under the terms of the new North American Free Trade Agreement. The peasants seized a large number of ranches and farms. A mysterious masked man known simply as Subcomandante Marcos was their leader (see photo). Effectively using the Internet and the international mass media as his secret weapon against the Mexican government, Marcos led what the *New York Times* called "the first postmodern revolution," combining a peasant uprising with the World Wide Web, short-wave radio, and photo spreads in *Marie Claire*. By ingeniously keeping the movement in the international public eye using modern technologies of communication, Marcos mobilized support abroad and limited the retaliatory actions of the Mexican government (*A Place Called Chiapas*, 1998; Jones, 1999).

Subcomandante Marcos, leader of the Zapatista National Liberation Army in southern Mexico. Effectively using the Internet and the international mass media as his secret weapon against the Mexican government, Marcos led what the *New York Times* called "the first postmodern revolution," combining a peasant uprising with the World Wide Web, short-wave radio, and photo spreads in *Marie Claire*. By keeping the movement in the international public eye using modern technologies of communication, Marcos mobilized support abroad and limited the retaliatory actions of the Mexican government.

The globalization of social movements can be further illustrated by coming full circle and returning to the anecdote with which we began this chapter. In 1991, Robert Brym visited his hometown. He hadn't been back in years. As he entered the city he vaguely sensed that something was different. "I wasn't able to identify the change until I reached the pulp and paper mill," says Robert. "Suddenly, it was obvious. The rotten-egg smell was virtually gone. I discovered that in the 1970s a local woman whose son developed a serious case of asthma took legal action against the mill and eventually won. The mill owner was forced by law to install a 'scrubber' in the main smokestack to remove most of the sulphur dioxide emissions. Soon, the federal government was putting pressure on the mill owner to purify the polluted water that poured out of the plant and into the local river system." Apparently, local citizens and the environmental movement had caused a deep change in the climate of opinion. This influenced the government to force the mill owner to spend millions of dollars to clean up his operation. It took decades, but what was political heresy in 1968 became established practice by 1991. That is because environmental concerns had been amplified by the voice of a movement that had grown to global proportions. In general, as this case illustrates, globalization helps ensure that many new social movements transcend local and national boundaries and promote universalistic goals.

## SUMMARY

1. In the short term, deprivation and strain due to rapid social change are generally *not* associated with increased collective action and social movement formation.
2. Mobs, riots, and other forms of crowd behaviour may be wild and violent. However, social organization and rationality underlie much crowd behaviour.
3. People are more inclined to rebel against the status quo when social ties bind them to many other people who feel similarly wronged and when they have the time, money, organization, and other resources needed to protest.
4. Collective action and social movement formation are more likely to occur when political opportunities allow them. Political opportunities emerge because of elections, increased support by influential allies, the instability of ruling political alignments, and divisions among elite groups.

5. Authorities' attempts to control unrest also influence the timing of collective action. They may offer concessions to insurgents, co-opt leaders, and employ coercion.
6. For social movements to grow, members must make the activities, goals, and ideology of the movement congruent with the interests, beliefs, and values of potential new recruits.
7. The history of social movements is a struggle for the acquisition of constantly broadening citizenship rights. These rights include (a) the right to free speech, religion, and justice before the law, (b) the right to vote and run for office, (c) the right to a certain level of economic security and full participation in the life of society, and (d) the right of marginal groups to full citizenship and the right of humanity as a whole to peace and security.

## GLOSSARY

**Absolute deprivation** is a condition of extreme poverty.

**Breakdown theory** suggests that social movements emerge when traditional norms and patterns of social organization are disrupted.

**Civil citizenship** recognizes the right to free speech, freedom of religion, and justice before the law.

**Collective action** occurs when people act in unison to bring about or resist social, political, and economic change. Some collective actions are routine; others are nonroutine. Routine collective actions are typically nonviolent and follow established patterns of behaviour in existing types of social structures. Nonroutine collective actions take place when usual conventions cease to guide social action and people transcend, bypass, or subvert established institutional patterns and structures.

**Contagion** is the process by which extreme passions supposedly spread rapidly through a crowd like a contagious disease.

**Frame alignment** is the process by which individual interests, beliefs, and values become congruent and complementary with the activities, goals, and ideology of a social movement.

**New social movements** became prominent in the 1970s. They attract a disproportionately large number of highly educated people in the social, educational, and cultural fields, and universalize the struggle for citizenship.

**Political citizenship** recognizes the right to run for office and vote.

**Political opportunities** for collective action and social movement growth occur during election campaigns, when influential allies offer insurgents support, when ruling political alignments become unstable, and when elite groups become divided and conflict with one another.

**Relative deprivation** is an intolerable gap between the social rewards people feel they deserve and the social rewards they expect to receive.

**Resource mobilization** refers to the process by which social movements crystallize because of increasing organizational, material, and other resources of movement members.

**Social citizenship** recognizes the right to a certain level of economic welfare security and full participation in the social life of the country.

**Social control** refers to the means by which authorities seek to contain collective action, including co-optation, concessions, and coercion.

**Social movements** are enduring collective attempts to change part or all of the social order by means of rioting, petitioning, striking, demonstrating, and establishing pressure groups, unions, and political parties.

**Solidarity theory** suggests that social movements are social organizations that emerge when potential members can mobilize resources, take advantage of new political opportunities, and avoid high levels of social control by authorities.

**Strain** refers to breakdowns in traditional norms that precede collective action.

**Union density** is the number of union members in a given location as a percentage of nonagricultural workers. It measures the organizational power of unions.

**Universal citizenship** recognizes the right of marginal groups to full citizenship and the rights of humanity as a whole.

## QUESTIONS TO CONSIDER

1. How would you achieve a political goal? Map out a detailed strategy for reaching a clearly defined aim, such as a reduction in income tax or an increase in government funding of universities. Who would you try to recruit to help you achieve your goal? Why? What collective actions do you think would be most successful? Why? To whose attention would these actions be directed? Why? Write a manifesto that frames your argument in a way that is culturally appealing to potential recruits.
2. Do you think that social movements will be more or less widespread in the twenty-first century than they were in the twentieth century? Why or why not? What kinds of social movements are likely to predominate?

## WEB RESOURCES

### Companion Web Site for This Book

http://www.brymsociologycompass.nelson.com

Begin by clicking on the Student Resources section of the Web site. Next, select the chapter you are currently studying from the pull-down menu. From the Student Resources page you will have easy access to InfoTrac College Edition®, MicroCase online exercises, and additional Web links. The Web site also has many useful tips to aid you in your study of sociology, including practice tests for each chapter.

### InfoTrac Search Terms

These search terms are provided to assist you in beginning to conduct research on this topic by visiting http://www.infotrac-college.com

**Collective action**
**Frame alignment**
**Relative deprivation**
**Resource mobilation**
**Unions**

### Recommended Web Sites

The environmental movement Greenpeace is one of the most successful cases of globalized protest. Greenpeace now has offices in 41 countries. Its Web site is at http://www.greenpeace.org/.

The use of the Internet to mobilize social movement support worldwide is well demonstrated by Mexico's Zapatista National Liberation Army in the southern province of Chiapas. Visit its Web site (mostly in Spanish, but with sections in French and Portuguese) at http://www.ezln.org/ and read about their information warfare in *Wired* magazine at http://www.wired.com/news/print/0,1294,17633,00.html.

Since 1910, March 8 has been celebrated as International Women's Day. For information about the demonstrations and other activities that took place around the world (including in Canada) on March 8, 2002, go to http://www.isis.aust.com/iwd/global.htm.

The Canadian Labour Congress (CLC) is the country's biggest umbrella labour organization, with more than 2.3 million members. To learn about the CLC's current projects, campaigns, and boycotts, visit the CLC Web site at http://www.clc-ctc.ca/eng-index.html.

## SUGGESTED READINGS

Benjamin R. Barber. "Jihad vs. McWorld," *The Atlantic Monthly* (March 1992), pp. 53–63. A compelling analysis of the fragmenting and globalizing forces affecting social movements today.

William K. Carroll, ed. *Organizing Dissent: Contemporary Social Movements in Theory and Practice*, 2nd ed. (Toronto: Garamond Press, 1997 [1992]). A useful survey of the theoretical and Canadian literature, plus case studies of contemporary Canadian social movements.

Hanspeter Kriesi, Hanspeter Kriese, and Jan Willem Duyvendak. *New Social Movements in Western Europe* (Minneapolis, MN: University of Minnesota Press, 1995). One of the best empirical analyses of new social movements.

Sidney Tarrow. *Power in Movement: Social Movements, Collective Action and Politics* (Cambridge, UK: Cambridge University Press, 1994). An excellent synthesis of resource mobilization and framing theories. Also underlines the importance of political structures in shaping discontent.

## NOTES

**1.** By the same token, bureaucracies may sometimes use nonroutine tactics. The distinction between routine and nonroutine collective action is thus a matter of degree, not of kind. Note in this connection that mobs, riots, and so on, used to be viewed as instances of "collective behaviour." Since the 1990s, however, that term has fallen into disfavour. That is because behaviour suggests a relatively low level of consciousness of self and therefore irrationality. Following Weber (1947), "action" denotes greater consciousness of self and therefore more rationality. Crowd action is not as nonroutine as was once believed.

**2.** The broad distinction between breakdown and solidarity theories is due to Tilly, Tilly, and Tilly (1975).

**3.** Some of these generalizations do not apply to countries with a long tradition of labour government. For example, since the Second World War, Sweden has experienced high levels of unionization and low strike rates. That is because Swedish workers and their representatives are involved in government policy making. Decisions about wages and benefits tend to be made in negotiations between unions, employer associations, and governments rather than on the picket line.

## IN THIS CHAPTER, YOU WILL LEARN THAT

- Some people think of technology as a useful magic that drives history forward.
- Others think of technology as a monster that has escaped human control and causes more harm than good.
- In reality, technology does transform society and history, but it is under human control since human need shapes technological growth.
- Increasingly, technological development has come under the sway of large multinational corporations and the military establishments of the major world powers.
- Widespread environmental degradation is the main negative consequence of technological development.
- Policy-oriented scientists, the environmental movement, the mass media, and respected organizations have to discover and promote environmental issues if they are to be turned into social problems. In addition, the public must connect the information learned from these groups to real-life events.
- Economically disadvantaged groups experience more environmental risks than economically advantaged groups.
- Most people are not prepared to pay the price to create a safe environment, but repeated environmental catastrophes could change our minds.
- By helping to make the public aware of the environmental and other choices we face in the twenty-first century, sociology can play an important role in the evolution of human affairs.

# CHAPTER 18

# TECHNOLOGY AND THE GLOBAL ENVIRONMENT

## TECHNOLOGY: SAVIOUR OR FRANKENSTEIN?

J. Robert Oppenheimer, the "father" of the atomic bomb.

On August 6, 1945, the United States Air Force dropped an atomic bomb on Hiroshima. The bomb killed about 200 000 Japanese, almost all of them civilians. It hastened the end of the Second World War, thus making it unnecessary for American troops to suffer heavy losses in a land invasion of Japan.

Scholars interested in the relationship between technology and society also recognize that Hiroshima divided the twentieth century into two distinct periods. We may call the period before Hiroshima the era of naive optimism. During that time, technology could do no wrong, or so it seemed to nearly all observers. **Technology** was widely defined as the application of scientific principles to the *improvement* of human life. It seemed to be driving humanity down a one-way street named progress, picking up speed with every passing year thanks to successively more powerful engines: steam, turbine, internal combustion, electric, jet, rocket, and nuclear. Technology produced tangible benefits. Its detailed workings rested on scientific principles that were mysterious to all but those with advanced science degrees. Therefore, most people regarded technologists with reverence and awe. They were viewed as a sort of priesthood whose objectivity allowed them to stand outside the everyday world and perform near-magical acts.

With Hiroshima, the blush was off the rose. Growing pessimism was in fact evident three weeks earlier, when the world's first nuclear bomb exploded at the Alamagordo Bombing Range in New Mexico. The bomb was the child of J. Robert Oppenheimer, who had been appointed head of the top-secret Manhattan Project just 28 months earlier. After recruiting what General Leslie Groves called "the greatest collection of eggheads ever," including three past and seven future Nobel prize winners, Oppenheimer organized the largest and most sophisticated technological project in human history up to that time. As an undergraduate at Harvard, Oppenheimer had studied Indian philosophy, among other subjects. On the morning of July 16, 1945, as the flash of intense white light faded and the purplish fireball rose, sucking desert sand and debris into a mushroom cloud more than 12 kilometres high, Oppenheimer quoted from Hindu scripture: "I am become Death, the shatterer of worlds" (quoted in Parshall, 1998).

Oppenheimer's misgivings continued after the war. Having witnessed the destructive power he helped unleash, he wanted the United States to set an example to the only other nuclear power at the time, the Soviet Union. He wanted both countries to halt thermonuclear research and refuse to develop the hydrogen bomb. But the governments of the United States and the Soviet Union had other plans. When Secretary of State Dean Acheson brought Oppenheimer to meet President Truman in 1946, Oppenheimer said, "Mr. President, I have blood on my hands." Truman later told Acheson, "Don't bring that fellow around again" (quoted in Parshall, 1998).

Overall, North Americans value science and technology highly. Thus, although Canada is a relatively small player in world scientific production (see Figure 18.1), Canadians are among the most optimistic about the benefits of science. Only Americans are more upbeat. Nevertheless, in the postwar years, a growing number of citizens have come to share Oppenheimer's doubts about the bomb. Indeed, they have extended those doubts not just to the peaceful use of nuclear energy but also to technology in general. Increasingly, people are beginning to think of technology as a monster run amok, a Frankenstein rather than a saviour (see Box 18.1).

It was only in the 1970s that a series of horrific disasters alerted many people (including some sociologists) to the fact that technological advance is not always beneficial, not even always benign. The most infamous technological disasters of the 1970s and 1980s include the following:

- An outbreak of Legionnaires' disease in a Philadelphia hotel in 1976 killed 34 people. It alerted the public to the possibility that the very buildings they live and work in can harbour toxic chemicals, lethal moulds, and dangerous germs.

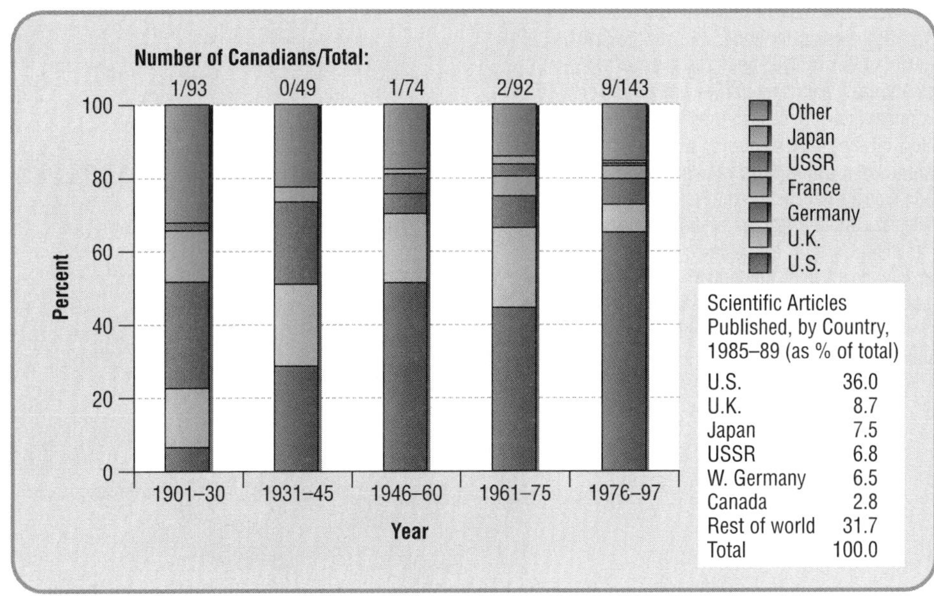


✦ **FIGURE 18.1** ✦

**Nobel Prizes in Natural Science by Country, 1901–1997 (in percent)**

Source: Council for Canadian Unity (1999); Kidron and Segal (1995: 92–3); U.S. Department of Commerce (1999: 628).

## BOX 18.1 SOCIOLOGY AT THE MOVIES

### *THE MATRIX* (1999)

*The Matrix*, starring Keanu Reeves

"Have you ever felt that there's something not right in the world?" With these words, *The Matrix* introduces Thomas Anderson, played by Keanu Reeves. Respectable software programmer by day, notorious hacker by night, Anderson, who goes by the handle Neo, has been plagued by the thought that there is something wrong with the world. "You don't know what it is, but it's there, like a splinter in your mind."

Neo knows somehow that something is wrong, but he cannot point to anything in particular. His moment of awareness comes when he encounters two legendary hackers, Morpheus and Trinity. They introduce him to the secret of his day world and the reality of the Matrix. It turns out that the "reality" lived by Neo and others is a form of collective imagination made possible by a gigantic computer, the Matrix. In fact, Neo and other people are nothing more than power supplies housed in liquid-filled containers. They supply energy for the Matrix. The Matrix, in turn, supplies these human "batteries" with images—making them feel they are living, not merely dreaming.

*The Matrix* is an exciting action-adventure film with extraordinary special effects. Beyond the glitz, however, the movie offers much to ponder, for it depicts a world in which information technology and the *representation* of reality have taken over the seemingly stable reality of the physical world. Is this what *our* world is becoming? *The Matrix* also poses a classic sociological question about technology. Is technology always a means of improving human life? Or is it sometimes antagonistic to human values?

The world's first major nuclear reactor accident occurred in December 1952 at the Chalk River nuclear facility about 125 km northwest of Ottawa. A partial meltdown of the reactor's uranium fuel core caused the 4-tonne lid to blow off the reactor, spurting radioactive water and creating lethal radiation levels. Some analysts consider the Chalk River Nuclear Laboratories one of the most contaminated pieces of real estate in Canada, with toxic radioactive pollution seeping from several nuclear waste dumps into aquifers, bogs, streams, and lakes, and ultimately into the Ottawa River.

- In 1977, dangerously high levels of toxic chemicals were discovered leaking into the basements and drinking water of the residents of Love Canal, near Niagara Falls, New York. This led to the immediate shutdown of an elementary school and the evacuation of residents from their homes.
- The partial meltdown of the reactor core at the Three Mile Island nuclear facility in Pennsylvania in 1979 caused lethal radioactive water and gas to pour into the environment. (A 1974 report by the Atomic Energy Commission said such an accident would likely occur only once in 17 000 years.)
- A gas leak at a poorly maintained Union Carbide pesticide plant in Bhopal, India, killed about 4000 people in 1984 and injured 30 000, a third of whom died excruciating deaths in the following years.
- In 1986, the No. 4 reactor at Chernobyl, Ukraine, exploded, releasing 30 to 40 times the radioactivity of the blast at Hiroshima. It resulted in mass evacuations, more than 10 000 deaths, countless human and animal mutations, and hundreds of square kilometres of unusable crop land.
- In 1989, the *Exxon Valdez* ran aground in Prince William Sound, Alaska, spilling 42 million litres of crude oil, producing a dangerous slick more than 1600 kilometres long, causing billions of dollars of damage, and killing hundreds of thousands of animals.

By the mid-1980s, sociologist Charles Perrow was referring to events such as those listed above as normal accidents. The term **normal accident** recognizes that the very complexity of modern technologies ensures they will *inevitably* fail, though in unpredictable ways (Perrow, 1984). For example, a large computer program contains many thousands of conditional statements. They take the form if $x = y$, do $z$; if $a = b$, do $c$. When in use, the program activates many billions of *combinations* of conditional statements. As a result, complex programs cannot be tested for all possible eventualities. Therefore, when rare combinations of conditions occur, they have unforeseen consequences that are usually minor, occasionally amusing, sometimes expensive, and too often dangerous. You experience normal accidents when your home computer "crashes" or "hangs." A few years ago, the avionics software for the F-16 jet fighter caused the jet to flip upside down whenever

A sea otter covered in oil spilled by the *Exxon Valdez* in 1989.

it crossed the equator. In January 1990, AT&T's entire long-distance network was crippled for nine hours due to a bug in the software for its routing switches. In Perrow's sense of the term, these are all normal accidents, although not as dangerous as the chemical and nuclear mishaps mentioned above.

German sociologist Ulrich Beck also coined a term that stuck when he said we live in a risk society. A **risk society** is a society in which technology distributes danger among all categories of the population. Some categories, however, are more exposed to technological danger than others. Moreover, in a risk society, danger does not result from technological accidents alone. In addition, increased risk is due to mounting *environmental* threats. Environmental threats are more widespread, chronic, and ambiguous than technological accidents. They are therefore more stressful (Beck, 1992 [1986]; Freudenburg, 1997). New and frightening terms—greenhouse effect, global warming, acid rain, ozone depletion, endangered species—have entered our vocabulary. To many people, technology seems to be spinning out of control. From their point of view, it enables the production of ever more goods and services, but at the cost of breathable air, drinkable water, safe sunlight, plant and animal diversity, and normal weather patterns. In the same vein, Neil Postman (1992) refers to the United States as a **technopoly**. He argues that the United States is the first country in which technology has taken control of culture. Technology, he says, compels people to try to solve all problems using technical rather than moral criteria, although technology is often the source of the problems.

The latest concern of technological skeptics is biotechnology. Molecular biologists have mapped the entire human gene structure and are also mapping the gene structures of selected animals and plants. They can splice genes together, creating plants and animals with entirely new characteristics. As we will see, the ability to create new forms of life holds incredible potential for advances in medicine, food production, and other fields. That is why the many advocates of this technology speak breathlessly of a "second genesis" and "the perfection of the human species." Detractors claim that, without moral and political decisions based on a firm sociological understanding of who benefits and suffers from these new techniques, the application of biotechnology may be a greater threat to our well-being than any other technology ever developed.

These considerations suggest five tough questions. We tackle each of them below. First, is technology *the* great driving force of historical and social change? This is the opinion of both cheerleaders and naysayers, those who view technology as our saviour and those who fear it as a Frankenstein. In contrast, we argue that technology is able to transform society only when it is coupled with a powerful social need. People control technology as much as technology transforms people. Second, if some people do control technology, then exactly who are they? We argue against the view that scientific and engineering wizards are in control. The military and big corporations now decide the direction of most technological research and its application. Third, what are the most dangerous spinoffs of technology and how is risk distributed among various social groups? We focus on global warming, industrial pollution, the decline of biodiversity, and genetic pollution. We show that although these dangers put all of humanity at risk, the degree of danger varies by class, race, and country. In brief, the socially and economically disadvantaged are most at risk. Fourth, how can we overcome the dangers of environmental degradation? We argue that market and technological solutions are insufficient by themselves. In addition, much self-sacrifice and cooperation will be required. The fifth and final question underlies all the others. It is the question with which we began this book: Why sociology?

## Technology *and* People Make History

Russian economist Nikolai Kondratiev was the first social scientist to notice that technologies are invented in clusters. As Table 18.1 shows, a new group of major inventions has cropped up every 40 to 60 years since the Industrial Revolution. Kondratiev argued that these flurries of creativity cause major economic growth spurts beginning 10 to 20 years later and lasting 25 to 35 years each. Thus, Kondratiev subscribed to a form of **technological determinism**, the belief that technology is the major force shaping human society and history (Ellul, 1964 [1954]).

Is it true that technology helps shape society and history? Of course it is. James Watt invented the steam engine in Britain in 1766. It was the main driving force in the mines, mills, factories, and railways of the Industrial Revolution. Gottlieb Daimler invented the internal combustion engine in Germany in 1883. It was the foundation stone of two of the world's biggest industries, automobiles and petroleum. John Atanasoff was among the first people to invent the computer in 1939 at Iowa State College (now University). It utterly transformed the way we work, study, and entertain ourselves. It also put the spurs to one of the most sustained economic booms ever. We could easily cite many more examples of how technology shapes history and transforms society.

However, if we probe a little deeper into the development of any of the technologies mentioned above, we notice a pattern: They did not become engines of economic growth until *social* conditions allowed them to do so. The original steam engine, for instance, was invented by Hero of Alexandria in the first century CE. He used it as an amusing way of opening a door. People then promptly forgot the steam engine. Some 1700 years later, when the Industrial Revolution began, factories were first set up near rivers and streams, where water power was available. That was several years before Watt patented his steam engine. Watt's invention was all the rage once its potential became evident. But it did not cause the Industrial Revolution and it was adopted on a wide scale only after the social need for it emerged (Pool, 1997: 126–7).

✦ **TABLE 18.1** ✦

**"Kondratiev Waves" of Modern Technological Innovation and Economic Growth**

Source: Adapted from Pacey (1983: 32).

| Wave | Invention Dates | New Technologies | Base | Economic Growth Spurt |
|---|---|---|---|---|
| 1 | 1760s–70s | Steam engine, textile manufacturing, chemistry, civil engineering | Britain | 1780–1815 |
| 2 | 1820s | Railways, mechanical engineering | Britain, Continental Western Europe | 1840–70 |
| 3 | 1870s–80s | Chemistry, electricity, internal combustion engine | Germany, United States | 1890–1914 |
| 4 | 1930s–40s | Electronics, aerospace, chemistry | United States | 1945–70 |
| 5 | 1970s | Microelectronics, biotechnology | United States, Japan | 1985–? |

Similarly, Daimler's internal combustion engine became the basis of the automobile and petroleum industries thanks to changes in the social organization of work wrought by Henry Ford, the self-defeating business practice of Ford's main competitors, the Stanley brothers, and, oddly enough, an epidemic of hoof-and-mouth disease. When Ford incorporated his company in 1903, a steam-driven automobile, the Stanley Steamer, was his main competition. Many engineers then believed the Stanley Steamer was the superior vehicle on purely technical grounds. Many engineers still think so today. (For one thing, the Stanley Steamer didn't require a transmission system.) But while the Stanley brothers built a finely tooled automobile for the well-to-do, Ford tried to figure out a way to produce a cheap car for the masses. His inspiration was the meatpacking plants of Cincinnati and Chicago. In 1913, he modelled the first car assembly line after those plants. Only then did he open a decisive lead in sales over the Stanleys. The Stanleys were finally done in a few years later. An outbreak of hoof-and-mouth disease led officials to close down the public watering troughs for horses that were widely used in American cities. Owners of the Stanley Steamer used the troughs to replenish its water supply. So we see it would be wrong to say, along with strict technological determinists, that Daimler's internal combustion engine *caused* the growth of the car industry and then the petroleum industry. The car and petroleum industries grew out of the internal combustion engine only because an ingenious entrepreneur efficiently organized work in a new way and because a chance event undermined access to a key element required by his competitor's product (Pool, 1997: 153–5).

And the computer? Atanasoff stopped work on it soon after the outbreak of the Second World War. However, once the military potential of the computer became evident, its development resumed. The British computer, Colossus, helped decipher secret German codes in the last two years of the war and played an important role in the Allied victory. The University of Illinois delivered one of the earliest computers, the ORDVAC, to the Ballistic Research Laboratory at the Aberdeen Proving Ground of the U.S. Army. Again we see how a new technology becomes a major force in society and history only after it is coupled with an urgent social need. We conclude that technology and society influence each other. Scientific discoveries, once adopted on a wide scale, often transform societies. But scientific discoveries are turned into useful technologies only when social need demands it.

## How High Tech Became Big Tech

Enjoying a technological advantage usually translates into big profits for businesses and military superiority for countries. In the nineteenth century, gaining technological advantage was still inexpensive. It took only modest capital investment, a little knowledge about the best way to organize work, and a handful of highly trained workers to build a shop to manufacture stirrups or even steam engines. In contrast, mass-producing cars, sending a

ORDVAC, an early computer developed at the University of Illinois, was delivered to the Ballistic Research Laboratory at the Aberdeen Proving Ground of the United States Army. Technology typically advances when it is coupled with an urgent social need.

man to the moon, and other feats of twentieth-century technology require enormous capital investment, detailed attention to the way work is organized, and legions of technical experts. Add to this the intensely competitive business and geopolitical environment of the twentieth century, and one can readily understand why ever-larger sums have been invested in research and development over the past hundred years.

It was in fact already clear in the last quarter of the nineteenth century that turning scientific principles into technological innovations was going to require not just genius but substantial resources, especially money and organization. Thus, Thomas Edison established the first "invention factory" at Menlo Park, New Jersey, in the late 1870s. Historian of science Robert Pool notes:

> [T]he most important factor in Edison's success—outside of his genius for invention—was the organization he had set up to assist him. By 1878, Edison had assembled at Menlo Park a staff of thirty scientists, metalworkers, glassblowers, draftsmen, and others working under his close direction and supervision. With such support, Edison boasted that he could turn out "a minor invention every ten days and a big thing every six months or so." (Pool, 1997: 22)

The phonograph and the electric light bulb were two such "big things." Edison inspired both. Both, however, were also expensive team efforts, motivated by vast commercial possibilities. (Edison founded General Electric, the most profitable company in the world in 1999 and the second most valuable based on market capitalization; see "Global 1000," 1999.)

At the beginning of the twentieth century, the scientific or engineering genius operating in isolation was only rarely able to contribute much to technological innovation. By mid-century, most technological innovation was organized along industrial lines. Entire armies of experts and vast sums of capital were required to run the new invention factories. The prototype of today's invention factory was the Manhattan Project, which built the nuclear bomb in the last years of the Second World War. By the time of Hiroshima, the manufacturing complex of the U.S. nuclear industry was about the same size as that of the U.S. automobile industry. The era of big science and big technology had arrived. Only governments and, increasingly, giant multinational corporations could afford to sustain the research effort of the second half of the twentieth century.

As the twentieth century ended, there seemed to be no upper limit to the amount that could be spent on research and development. In the course of the twentieth century, the number of research scientists in North America increased a hundredfold. In the last 40 years of the century, research and development spending tripled, taking inflation into account. In that same period, industry's share of spending rose from one-third to two-thirds of the total while government's share dropped proportionately (Hobsbawm, 1994: 523; U.S. Department of Commerce, 1998: 609; Woodrow Federal Reserve Bank of Minneapolis, 2000).

Because large multinational corporations now routinely invest astronomical sums in research and development to increase their chance of being the first to bring innovations to market, the time lag between new scientific discoveries and their technological application is continually shrinking. For instance, it was fully 38 years after the VCR was invented in 1952 before the device achieved 25 percent market penetration in North America. It took 18 years before the personal computer, invented in 1975, was owned by 25 percent of North Americans. The World Wide Web, invented in 1991, took only seven years to reach that level of market penetration ("The Silent Boom," 1998).

Because of these developments, it should come as no surprise that military and profit-making considerations now govern the direction of most research and development. A reporter once asked a bank robber why he robs banks. The robber answered: "Because that's where the money is." This is hardly the only motivation prompting scientists and engineers to research particular topics. Personal interests, individual creativity, and the state of a field's intellectual development still influence the direction of inquiry. This is especially true for theoretical work done in universities, as opposed to applied research funded by governments and private industry. It would, however, be naive to think that practicality doesn't also enter the scientist's calculation of what he or she ought to study. Even

Research in biotechnology is big business. Even in the late 1980s, nearly 40 percent of the biotechnology scientists who belonged to the prestigious National Academy of Sciences had industry affiliations.

in a more innocent era, Sir Isaac Newton studied astronomy partly because the explorers and mariners of his day needed better navigational cues. Similarly, Michael Faraday was partly motivated to discover the relationship between electricity and magnetism by his society's search for new forms of power (Bronowski, 1965 [1956]: 7–8). The connection between practicality and research is even more evident today. Many researchers—even many of those who do theoretically driven research in universities—are pulled in particular directions by large research grants, well-paying jobs, access to expensive state-of-the-art equipment, and the possibility of winning patents and achieving commercial success. For example, many leading molecular biologists in North America have established genetic engineering companies, serve on their boards of directors, or receive research funding from them. In not a few cases, major pharmaceutical and agrochemical corporations have bought out these companies because they see their vast profit potential (Rural Advancement Foundation International, 1999). Close to a majority of leading biotechnology scientists have industry affiliations (Rifkin, 1998: 56).

Economic lures, increasingly provided by the military and big corporations, have generated moral and political qualms among some researchers. Some scientists and engineers wonder whether work on particular topics achieves optimum benefits for humanity. Certain researchers are troubled by the possibility that some scientific inquiries may be harmful to humankind. However, a growing number of scientists and engineers recognize that to do cutting-edge research, they must still any residual misgivings, hop on the bandwagon, and adhere to military and industrial requirements and priorities. That, after all, is where the money is.

Because of global warming, glaciers are melting, the sea level is rising, and extreme weather events are becoming more frequent.

## Environmental Degradation

The side effect of technology that has given people the most serious cause for concern is environmental degradation. It has four main aspects: global warming, industrial pollution, the decline in biodiversity, and genetic pollution. Let us briefly consider each of these problems, beginning with global warming.

### Global Warming

Ever since the Industrial Revolution, humans have been burning increasing quantities of fossil fuels (coal, oil, gasoline, natural gas, etc.) to drive their cars, furnaces, and factories. Burning these fuels releases carbon dioxide into the atmosphere. The accumulation of carbon dioxide allows more solar radiation to enter the atmosphere and less heat to escape. This is the so-called **greenhouse effect**. Most scientists believe that the greenhouse effect contributes to **global warming**, a gradual increase in the world's average surface temperature. Using data from NASA's Goddard Institute for Space Studies, Figure 18.2 graphs the world's annual average surface air temperature and the concentration of carbon dioxide in the atmosphere from 1866 to 2000. The graph shows a warming trend that mirrors the increased concentration of carbon dioxide in the atmosphere. It also shows that the

✦ **FIGURE 18.2** ✦
**Annual Mean Global Surface Air Temperature and Carbon Dioxide Concentration, 1866–2000**

Source: Goddard Institute for Space Studies (2001); Karl and Trenberth (1999: 102).

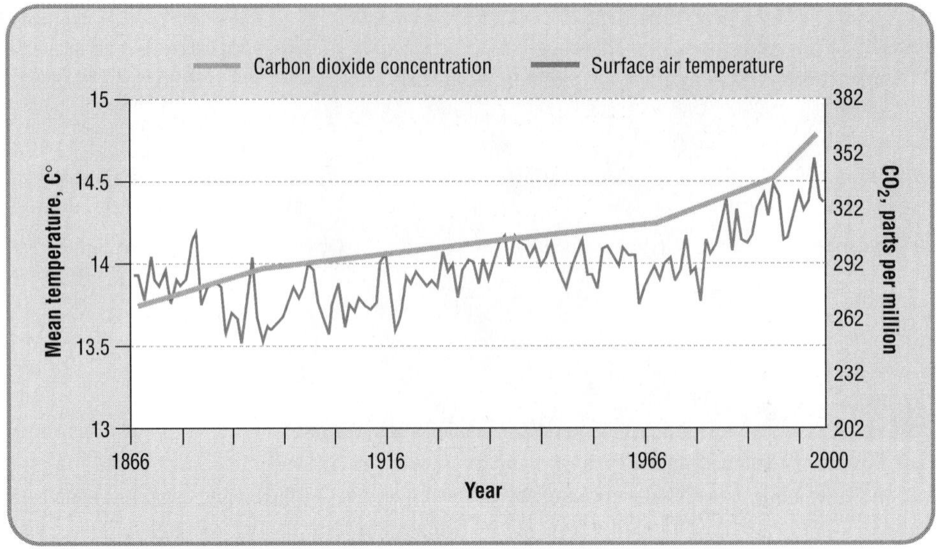


warming trend intensified sharply in the last third of the twentieth century. Between 1866 and 1965, average surface air temperature rose at a rate of 0.25 degrees Celsius per century. From 1966 to 2000, average surface air temperature rose at a rate of 1.69 degrees Celsius per century.

Many scientists believe global warming is already producing serious climactic change. For as temperatures rise, more water evaporates. This causes more rainfall and bigger storms, which leads to more flooding and soil erosion, which in turn leads to less cultivable land. People suffer and die all along the causal chain. This was tragically evident in 1998, when Hurricane Mitch caused entire mountainsides to collapse on poor villages in Guatemala and Honduras, killing thousands of inhabitants and ruining the fertile banana plantations of those countries.

Figure 18.3 graphs the worldwide dollar cost of damage due to "natural" disasters from 1980 to 1998. ("Natural" is in quotation marks because, as we have just seen, an increasingly large number of meteorological events are rendered extreme by human action.) Clearly, the damage caused by extreme meteorological events was on the upswing throughout the 1990s. This, however, may be only the beginning. It seems that global warming is causing the oceans to rise. That is partly because warmer water expands and partly because the partial melting of the polar ice caps puts more water in the oceans. In the twenty-first century, this may result in the flooding of some heavily populated coastal regions throughout the world. For instance, just a one-metre rise in the sea level would flood about 12 percent of the surface area of Egypt and Bangladesh (Kennedy, 1993: 110).

## Industrial Pollution

Industrial pollution is the emission of various impurities into the air, water, and soil due to industrial processes. It is a second major form of environmental degradation. Every day, we release a witch's brew into the environment. The more common ingredients include household trash, scrap automobiles, residue from processed ores, agricultural runoff containing dangerous chemicals, lead, carbon monoxide, carbon dioxide, sulphur dioxide, ozone, nitrogen oxide, various volatile organic compounds, chloroflourocarbons (CFCs), and various solids or "particulates" mixed with liquid droplets floating in the air. In Canada, most pollutants are especially highly concentrated in southern Ontario and southern Quebec. Old, heavy, dirty industries are centred in these densely populated areas. However, many other pollution "hot spots" dot the Canadian landscape. The petrochemical, mining, and pulp and paper industries are responsible for high levels of industrial pollution in Alberta, Saskatchewan, Manitoba, Yukon, Northwest Territories, and Nunavut.

Canada's biggest toxic dump is in Sydney, Nova Scotia, where waste from 100 years of nearly unregulated steel production has created the infamous Sydney "tar ponds." Containing 700 000 tonnes of toxic sludge in close proximity to residential neighbourhoods, the Syndey tar ponds hold 35 times more toxic waste than Love Canal in the United States The tar ponds are widely regarded as the second-worst toxic site in North America (Barlow and May, 2000).

Pollutants may affect us directly. For example, they seep into our drinking water and the air we breathe, causing a variety of ailments ranging from asthma to cancer, particularly among the young and the elderly. They also may affect us indirectly. For instance, sulphur dioxide and other gases are emitted by coal-burning power plants, pulp and paper mills, and motor-vehicle exhaust. They form **acid rain**. This is a form of precipitation whose acidity eats away at, and eventually destroys, forests and the ecosystems of lakes. Another example: CFCs are widely used in industry and by consumers, notably in refrigeration equipment. They contain chlorine, which is responsible for the depletion of the **ozone layer** 8 to 40 kilometres above the earth's surface. Ozone is a form of oxygen that blocks ultraviolet radiation from the sun. Let more ultraviolet radiation reach ground level and, as we are now witnessing, rates of skin cancer and crop damage increase.

Radioactive waste deserves special attention. There are five active commercial nuclear reactors in Canada today (Point Leprau in New Brunswick, Gentilly in Quebec, and Bruce, Darlington, and Pickering in Ontario). One hundred and three nuclear reactors are now generating commercial electricity in the United States. These facilities run on enriched uranium or plutonium fuel rods. Once these fuel rods decay beyond the point where they are useful in the reactor, they become waste material. This waste is highly radioactive. It must decay for about 10 000 years before humans can be safely exposed to it without protective equipment. The spent fuel rods need to be placed in sturdy, watertight copper canisters and buried deep in granite bedrock where the chance of seismic disturbance and water seepage is small. The trouble is, most North Americans are petrified at the prospect of having a nuclear waste facility anywhere near their families. As a result, spent fuel rods have been accumulating since the 1950s in "temporary" facilities. These are mainly pools of water near nuclear reactors. These facilities are a safety threat to the North American public. In 2002, the United States government announced plans to bury its 77 000 tonnes of nuclear waste deep in the Yucca Mountains of Nevada, 145 kilometres northwest of Las Vegas. The Canadian government has not come up with a plan for the burial of nuclear waste in this country (Canadian Coalition for Nuclear Responsibility, 2000; Pool, 1997).

## The Decline in Biodiversity

The third main form of environmental degradation is the decline in **biodiversity**, the enormous variety of plant and animal species inhabiting the earth. Biodiversity changes as new species emerge and old species die off because they cannot adapt to their environment.

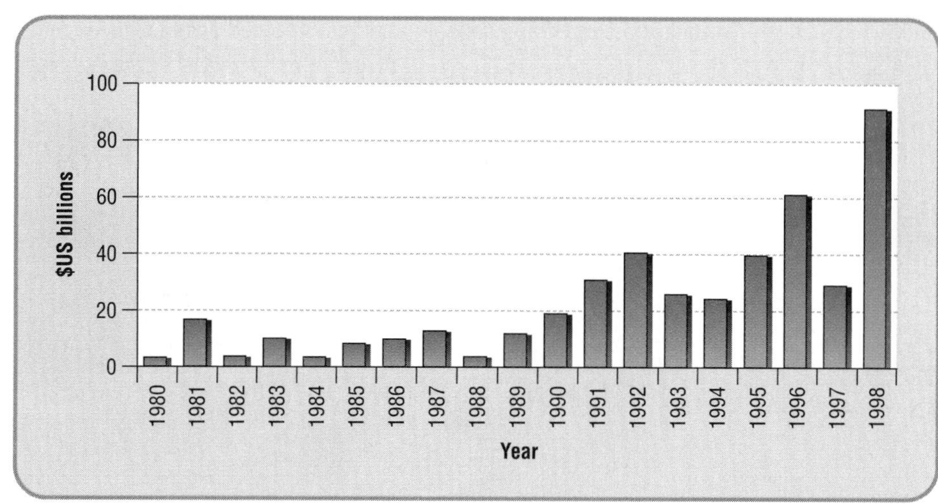


**✦ FIGURE 18.3 ✦**
**Worldwide Damage Due to "Natural" Disasters, 1980–1998 (in 1998 U.S. Dollars)**

Source: Abu-Nasr (1998); Vidal (1999).

This is all part of the normal evolutionary process. However, in recent decades the environment has become so inhospitable to so many species that the rate of extinction has accelerated greatly. Examination of fossil records suggests that, for millions of years, an average of one to three species became extinct annually. Today, about 1000 species are becoming extinct annually (Tuxill and Bright, 1998: 41). In 11 countries, 10 percent or more of bird species are threatened with extinction. In 29 countries, 10 percent or more of mammal species are similarly threatened (Kidron and Segal, 1995: 14–15).

The extinction of species is impoverishing in itself, but it also has practical consequences for humans. For example, each species of animal and plant has unique properties. When scientists discover that a certain property has a medically useful effect, they get busy trying to synthesize the property in the laboratory. Treatments for everything from headaches to cancer have been found in this way. Indeed, about a quarter of all drugs prescribed in North America today (including 9 of the top 10 in sales) include compounds first found in wild organisms. The single richest source of genetic material with pharmaceutical value is found in the world's rain forests, particularly in Brazil, where more than 30 million species of life exist. However, the rain forests are being rapidly destroyed by strip mining, the construction of huge pulp and paper mills and hydroelectric projects, and the deforestation of land by farmers and cattle grazers.

Similarly, fleets of trawlers belonging to the highly industrialized countries are now equipped with sonar to help them find large concentrations of fish. Some of these ships use fine mesh nets to increase their catch. They have been enormously "successful." Trawlers have depleted fish stocks in some areas of the world. In North America, for example, the depletion of cod, salmon, blue-fin tuna, and shark stocks has devastated fishing communities in Newfoundland and elsewhere, endangering one of the world's most important sources of protein. All told, 11 of the world's 15 main fishing grounds and 69 percent of the world's main fish species are in decline (McGinn, 1998: 60).

## Genetic Pollution

**Genetic pollution** is the fourth main form of environmental degradation. It refers to the health and ecological dangers that may result from artificially splicing genes together (Rifkin, 1998).

The genetic information of all living things is coded in a chemical called DNA. When members of a species reproduce, the characteristics of the mates are naturally transmitted to their offspring through DNA. **Recombinant DNA**, in contrast, is a technique developed by molecular biologists in the last few decades. It involves artificially joining bits of DNA from a donor to the DNA of a host. Donor and host may be of the same or different species. The donor DNA grows along with the host DNA, in effect creating a new form of life. For example, scientists inserted the gene that makes fireflies sparkle at night into a tobacco plant. The offspring of the plant had leaves that glowed in the dark. Researchers inserted human growth hormone into a mouse embryo. This created mice that grew twice as big and twice as fast as ordinary mice. Biologists combined embryo cells from a sheep and a

Artificially splicing genes together may yield benefits as well as dangers. Woody Allen in *Sleeper* (1973).

goat and placed them in the womb of a surrogate animal. The surrogate animal then gave birth to an entirely new species, half sheep, half goat.

These wonders of molecular biology were performed in the mid-1980s and helped to dramatize and publicize the potential of recombinant DNA. Since 1990, governments and corporations have been engaged in a multibillion-dollar international effort to create a complete genetic map of humans and various plants, micro-organisms, and animal species. With human and other genetic maps in hand, and using recombinant DNA and related techniques, it is possible to design what some people regard as more useful animals and plants and superior humans. By 2000, scientists had identified the location and chemical structure of every one of the approximately 40 000 human genes. This will presumably enable them to understand the function of each gene. They can then detect and eliminate hereditary propensities to a wide range of diseases. Recombinant DNA will also enable farmers to grow disease- and frost-resistant crops with higher yields. It will allow miners to pour ore-eating microbes into mines, pump the microbes aboveground after they have had their fill, and then separate out the ore. This will greatly reduce the cost and danger of mining. Recombinant DNA will allow companies to grow plants that produce cheap biodegradable plastic and micro-organisms that consume oil spills and absorb radioactivity. The potential health and economic benefits to humankind of these and many other applications of recombinant DNA are truly startling.

But so are the dangers genetic pollution poses to human health and the stability of ecosystems (Rifkin, 1998: 67–115). Consider, for example, the work of scientists at the National Institute of Allergy and Infectious Diseases. In the late 1980s, they introduced the genetic instructions for the human AIDS virus into mouse embryos. Subsequent generations of mice were born with AIDS and were used for research to find a cure for the disease. But what would happen if some of these mice got loose and bred with ordinary mice? In 1990, Dr Robert Gallo, co-discoverer of the AIDS virus, and a team of other scientists reported in the respected journal *Science* that the AIDS virus carried by the mice could combine with other mouse viruses. This could result in a new form of AIDS capable of reproducing more rapidly and being transmitted to humans through the air. Recognizing this danger, scientists housed the AIDS mice in stainless steel glove boxes surrounded by a moat of bleach. They enclosed the entire apparatus in the highest-level biosafety facility that exists. No mice have escaped so far, but the risk is still there.

Meanwhile, humans are already the recipients of transplanted bone marrow and hearts from baboons and pigs. Although the animals are screened for known problems, critics point out that such transplants could enable dangerous unknown viruses and retroviruses to jump between species and cause an epidemic among humans. If this seems farfetched, remember that the AIDS virus is widely believed to have jumped from a chimpanzee to a human in the late 1970s. By the end of 1999, the AIDS virus had killed about 14.5 million people worldwide and infected more than 34 million others (United Nations, 2000b). Ominously, in 1997 scientists discovered a previously unknown pig virus that can infect humans. And in 2000, scientists reported that at least three known pig retroviruses can infect human cells (Van der Laan et al., 2000).

Genetic pollution may also affect the stability of ecosystems. When a non-native organism enters a new environment, it usually adapts without a problem. Sometimes, however, it unexpectedly wreaks havoc. Kudzu vine, Dutch elm disease, the gypsy moth, chestnut blight, starlings, Mediterranean fruit flies, zebra mussels, rabbits, and mongooses have all done just that. Now, however, the potential for ecological catastrophe has multiplied, because scientists are regularly testing genetically altered plants (effectively, non-native organisms) in the field. Some have gone commercial, and many more will soon be grown on a wide scale. These plants are resistant to insects, disease, and frost. However, once their pollen and seeds escape into the environment, weeds, insects, and micro-organisms will eventually build up resistance to the genes that resist herbicides, pests, and viruses. Thus, superbugs, superweeds, and superviruses will be born. We cannot predict the exact environmental consequences of these developments. That is why the insurance industry refuses to insure genetically engineered crops against the possibility of their causing catastrophic ecological damage.

Global warming, industrial pollution, the decline in biodiversity, and genetic pollution threaten everyone. However, as you will now see, the degree to which they are perceived as threatening depends on certain social conditions being met. Moreover, the threats are not evenly distributed in society.

## THE SOCIAL CONSTRUCTION OF ENVIRONMENTAL PROBLEMS

Environmental problems do not become social issues spontaneously. Before they can enter the public consciousness, policy-oriented scientists, the environmental movement, the mass media, and respected organizations must discover and promote them. People have to connect real-life events to the information learned from these groups. Since some scientists, industrial interests, and politicians dispute the existence of environmental threats, the public can begin to question whether environmental issues are in fact social problems that require human intervention. We must not, then, think that environmental issues will inevitably be perceived as problematic. Rather, they are contested phenomena. They can be socially constructed by proponents, and they can be socially demolished by opponents. This is the key insight of the school of thought known as **social constructionism** (Hannigan, 1995a).

The controversy over global warming is a good example of how people create and contest definitions of environmental problems (Gelbspan, 1997; 1999; Hart and Victor, 1993; Mazur, 1998; Ungar, 1992; 1995; 1998; 1999). The theory of global warming was first proposed about a century ago. However, an elite group of scientists began serious research on the subject only in the late 1950s. They attracted no public attention until the 1970s. That is when the environmental movement emerged and gave new legitimacy and momentum to the scientific research and helped secure public funds for it. Respected and influential scientists now began to promote the issue of global warming. The mass media, always thirsting for sensational stories, were highly receptive to these efforts. Newspaper and television reports about the problem began to appear in the late 1970s. They proliferated in the mid- to late 1980s. Between 1988 and 1991, the public's interest in global warming reached an all-time high. That was because frightening events helped make the media reports more believable. For example, the summer of 1988 brought the worst drought in half a century. As crops failed, New York sweltered, and huge fires burned in Yellowstone National Park, *Time* magazine ran a cover story entitled "The Big Dry." It drew the connection between global warming and extreme weather. Many people became worried. Soon, respected organizations outside the scientific community, the mass media, and the environmental movement—such as the insurance industry and the United Nations—expressed concern about the effects of global warming. By 1994, 59 percent of Americans with an opinion on the subject thought that using coal, oil, and gas contributes to the greenhouse effect (calculated from National Opinion Research Center, 1999).

By 1994, however, public concern with global warming had already passed its peak. The eruption of Mount Pinatubo in the Philippines pumped so much volcanic ash into the atmosphere, clouding the sun, that global surface air temperatures fell in 1992–93. Media reports about global warming declined sharply. The media, always thirsting for new scares to capture larger audiences, thought the story had grown stale. Some scientists, industrialists, and politicians began to question whether global warming was in fact taking place. They cited satellite data showing the Earth's lower atmosphere had cooled in recent decades, published articles, and took out ads to express their opinion, thus increasing public skepticism.

With surface temperatures showing warming and lower atmospheric temperatures showing cooling, different groups lined up on different sides of the global warming debate. Those who had most to lose from the consequences of global warming or the least to lose from carbon emission cuts emphasized the surface data. Those who had most to lose from carbon emission cuts emphasized the lower atmospheric data. This latter group included

Western coal and oil companies, the member states of the Organization of Petroleum Exporting Countries (OPEC), and other coal- and oil-exporting nations, aided by right-wing think-tanks such as Canada's Fraser Institute in Vancouver, which is subsidized in part by major oil companies operating in Canada. "[B]ad scientific reporting, bad economics and bad judgement" is how the Fraser Institute summarized the analyses of those who wanted to solve the problem of global warming (Jones, 1997).

In August 1998 the global warming skeptics were dealt a serious blow when their satellite data were shown to be misleading. Until then, no one had taken into account that the satellites were gradually slipping from their orbits due to atmospheric friction, thus causing imprecise temperature readings. Allowing for the slippage, scientists from NASA and private industry now calculate that temperatures in the lower atmosphere are rising, just like temperatures on the Earth's surface (Wentz and Schabel, 1998; Hansen et al., 1998). These new findings may finally help lay to rest the claims of the global warming skeptics. However, one thing is certain. As the social constructionists suggest, the power of competing interests to get their definition of reality accepted as the truth will continue to influence public perceptions of the seriousness of global warming.

In addition to being socially defined, environmental problems are socially distributed. That is, environmental risks are greater for some groups than others. Let us now examine this issue.

## The Social Distribution of Risk

You may have noticed that after a minor twister touches down on some unlucky community, TV reporters often rush to interview the surviving residents of trailer parks. The survivors stand amid the rubble that was their lives. They heroically remark on the generosity of their neighbours, their good fortune in still having their family intact, and our inability to fight nature's destructive forces. Why trailer parks? Small twisters aren't particularly attracted to them, but reporters are. That is because trailers are pretty flimsy in the face of a small tornado. They often suffer a lot of damage from twisters, and therefore make a more sensational story than the minor damage typically inflicted on upper-middle-class homes with firmly shingled roofs and solid foundations. This is a general pattern. Whenever disaster strikes—from the sinking of the *Titanic* to the fury of Hurricane Mitch—economically and politically disadvantaged people almost always suffer most. That is because their circumstances render them most vulnerable.

In fact, the advantaged often consciously put the disadvantaged in harm's way to avoid risk themselves. For example, in the United States, oil refineries, chemical plants, toxic dumps, garbage incinerators, and other environmentally dangerous installations are more likely to be built in poor communities with a high percentage of African-Americans or Hispanic-Americans than in more affluent, mainly white communities. That is because disadvantaged people are often too politically weak to oppose such facilities and some may even value the jobs they create (Pool, 1997: 247–8; Szasz and Meuser, 1997: 100; Stretesky and Hogan, 1998). For instance, the 120-kilometre strip along the lower Mississippi River between New Orleans and Baton Rouge has been nicknamed "cancer alley" because the largely black population of that region suffers from unusually high rates of lung, stomach, pancreatic, and other cancers. The main reason? This small area is the source of fully one-quarter of the petrochemicals produced in the country, containing more than 100 oil refineries and chemical plants (Bullard, 1994 [1990]). This is just one example of **environmental racism,** the tendency to heap environmental dangers on the disadvantaged, and especially on disadvantaged racial minorities.

### The Canadian Case

Environmental racism is also evident in Canada. For example, the uranium used to construct the atom bombs that were dropped on Hiroshima and Nagasaki came from Port Radium in the Northwest Territories, the world's first uranium mine. More than 30 Dene hunters and trappers were recruited from the nearby village of Deline to haul and barge 45-kilogram burlap sacks of the raw ore along a 2100 kilometre route to Fort McMurray,

Alberta, for $3 a day. The American and Canadian governments had known about the dangers of exposure to uranium at least since 1931 (McClelland, 1931). However, they withheld this information from the workers, who were completely unprotected from the ore's deadly radiation. In the surrounding community, the Dene ate fish from contaminated dredging ponds and hunted and camped in contaminated areas. Dene children played with ore dust at docks and landings. Dene women sewed tents from used uranium sacks. Until recent decades, cancer was unknown in the community. Elders often lived into their nineties. By 1998, however, nearly half the uranium workers had died of cancer while still in their sixties and seventies. Cancer and lung disease are alarmingly widespread in the community. Deline is known locally as "The Village of the Widows." Neither the workers nor their families have received any compensation from the government, not even an apology (Nikiforuk, 1998).

Broadly similar stories of environmental racism are legion. In the late 1960s, the river running through the Ojibwa village of Grassy Narrows, near Kenora, Ontario, was poisoned for half a century by mercury contamination from a large pulp and paper mill. Mercury has devastating effects on the brain and central nervous system. The residents of Grassy Narrows were eventually relocated—but only after years of fishing in, bathing in, and drinking water from the river (Shkilnyk, 1985). In the early 1980s, more than 400 sour gas wells were drilled around the Lubicon First Nation village of Little Buffalo in Alberta. Residents experienced dramatic increases in the incidence of various illnesses immediately thereafter (Barlow and May, 2000: 183). In 2000, Toronto planned to ship its garbage—the equivalent of 250 truckloads a day—to the abandoned Adams mine pit near Kirkland Lake, Ontario. Local residents, many of whom are members of First Nations, fear widespread contamination. Nobody has suggested that the refuse be dumped in the ravine near the tony Toronto neighbourhood of Rosedale ("Adams Mine," 2000). As these examples suggest, there is a disturbing association in Canada between level of contamination and the concentration of Aboriginal populations. Figure 18.4 illustrates this association. Using a broad measure of airborne pollution, it shows that where Aboriginal Canadians form a larger proportion of the population, the per capita weight of particulates in the air is heaviest.

Class also structures exposure to environmental risk in Canada. Thus, Nova Scotia, one of Canada's poorest provinces, has the highest provincial cancer rate in the country. That is partly because the rate of cigarette smoking varies inversely with class, and Nova Scotians smoke more than any other Canadians (Bryden, Fife, and Hamilton, 2000). Cape Breton, Nova Scotia's poorest region, has the highest regional cancer rate in Nova Scotia. That is partly because Sydney, home to a large steel mill for a century, has the highest community cancer rate in Cape Breton. The people who live around Frederick Street, the poorest part of Sydney, have the highest neighbourhood cancer rate in town. Skin ailments,

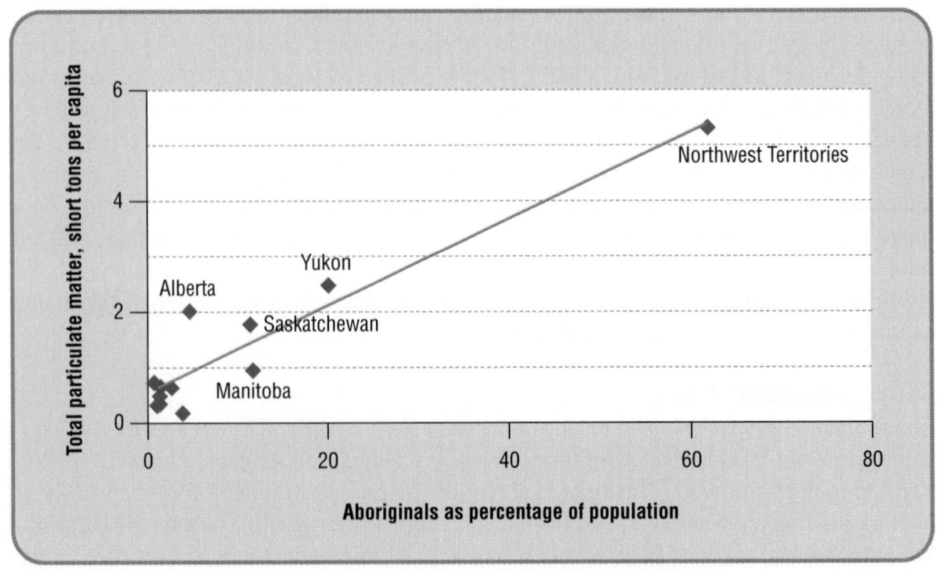


✦ **FIGURE 18.4** ✦
**Environmental Racism in Canada, 1995**

Source: Statistics Canada (2000e; 2000f); U.S. Environmental Protection Agency, Office of Air Quality Planning and Standards (2000).

birth defects, respiratory problems, diseases of the nervous system, and other medical conditions are also unusually common around Frederick Street. The main reason? The homes of Frederick Street border on the Sydney tar ponds, a 50-hectare site polluted to a depth of 24 metres with cancer-causing polycyclic aromatic hydrocarbons, toxic heavy metals, and arsenic. Sludge from the tar ponds oozes into people's basements, pervades their vegetable gardens, and runs in open streams where children play. Billions of federal and provincial tax dollars have been spent subsidizing the steel mill that is the source of the problem. Yet neither government nor private industry has ever done anything to clean up the scandalous mess (Barlow and May, 2000: 144 and *passim*).

## The Less Developed Countries

What is true for disadvantaged classes and racial groups in North America also holds for the world's less developed countries. The underprivileged face more environmental dangers than the privileged (Kennedy, 1993: 95–121). In North America, Western Europe, and Japan, population growth is low and falling. Industry and government are eliminating some of the worst excesses of industrialization. In contrast, world population will grow from about six to seven billion between 2000 and 2010, and nearly all of that growth will be in the less developed countries of the Southern Hemisphere. Moreover, Mexico, Brazil, China, India, and many other southern countries are industrializing rapidly. This is putting tremendous strain on their natural resources. Rising demand for water, electricity, fossil fuels, and consumer products is creating more polluted rivers, dead lakes, and industrial waste sites. At a quickening pace, rain forests, grazing land, cropland, and wetlands are giving way to factories, roads, airports, and housing complexes. Smog-blanketed megacities continue to sprawl. Eighteen of the world's 21 biggest cities are in less developed countries.

Given the picture sketched above, it should come as no surprise that, on average, people in less developed countries are more concerned about the environment than people in rich countries (Brechin and Kempton, 1994). However, the developing countries cannot afford much in the way of pollution control, so anti-pollution regulations are lax by North American, Western European, and Japanese standards. This is an incentive for some multinational corporations to situate some of their foulest operations in the Southern Hemisphere (Clapp, 1998). It is also the reason why the industrialization of the less developed countries is proving so punishing to the environment. When car ownership grows from, say, 5 percent to 20 percent of the population in China, and when 50 or 75 million Indians with motor scooters upgrade to cars, the result will be a choking mess. That is because the Chinese and the Indians simply cannot afford catalytic converters and electric cars. They have no regulations phasing in the use of these and other devices that save energy and pollute less.

For the time being, however, the rich countries do most of the world's environmental damage. That is because their inhabitants earn and consume more than the inhabitants of

Canada's biggest toxic dump is in Sydney, Nova Scotia, where waste from 100 years of nearly unregulated steel production has created the infamous Sydney tar ponds. Containing 700 000 tonnes of toxic sludge in close proximity to residential neighbourhoods, the Sydney tar ponds hold 35 times more toxic waste than Love Canal in the United States. The tar ponds are widely regarded as the second-worst toxic site in North America.

less developed countries. How much more? The richest fifth of humanity earns about 80 times more than the poorest fifth (up from 30 times more in 1950). In the past half-century, the richest fifth doubled its per capita consumption of energy, meat, timber, steel, and copper, and quadrupled its car ownership. In that same period, the per capita consumption of the poorest fifth hardly changed. The United States has only 4.5 percent of the world's population, but it uses about 25 percent of the Earth's resources. And it produces more than 20 percent of global emissions of carbon dioxide, the pollutant responsible for about half of global warming (Ehrlich et al., 1997). Thus, the inhabitants of the Northern Hemisphere cause a disproportionately large share of the world's environmental problems, enjoy a disproportionate share of the benefits of technology, and live with fewer environmental risks than people in the Southern Hemisphere.

### Inequality and Biotechnology

Social inequalities are also apparent in the field of biotechnology. For instance, the large multinational companies that dominate the pharmaceutical, seed, and agrochemical industries now routinely send anthropologists, biologists, and agronomists to all corners of the world. There they take samples of wild plants, the crops people grow, and human blood. They hope to find genetic material with commercial value in agriculture and medicine. If they discover genes with commercial value, the company they work for patents the discovery. This gives them the exclusive legal right to manufacture and sell the genetic material without compensating the donors. Thus, Indian farmers and then scientists worked for a hundred generations discovering, skilfully selecting, cultivating, and developing techniques for processing the neem tree, which has powerful antibacterial and pesticidal properties. However, a giant corporation based in a rich country is now the sole commercial beneficiary of their labour. Monsanto (U.S.), Novartis (Switzerland), Glaxo Wellcome (UK), and other prominent companies in the life sciences call this "protection of intellectual property." Indigenous people and their advocates throughout the world call it "biopiracy" (Rifkin, 1998: 37–66).

Finally, consider the possible consequences of people having their babies genetically engineered. This should be possible on a wide scale in 10 or 20 years. Free of inherited diseases and physical abnormalities, and perhaps genetically programmed to enjoy superior intellectual and athletic potential, these children would, in effect, speed up and improve the slow and imperfect process of natural evolution. That, at least, is the rosy picture sketched by proponents of the technology. In practice, since only the well-to-do are likely to be able to afford fully genetically engineered babies, the new technology could introduce an era of increased social inequality and low social mobility. Only the economically underprivileged would bear a substantial risk of genetic inferiority. This future was foreseen in the 1997 movie *Gattica*. The plot revolves around the tension between a society that genetically engineers all space pilots to perfection and a young man played by Ethan Hawke, who was born without the benefit of genetic engineering yet aspires to become a space pilot. Hawke's character manages to overcome his genetic handicap. It is clear from the movie, however, that his success is both illegal and extremely rare. The norm is rigid genetic stratification and it is strongly sanctioned by state and society. (For other examples of how new technologies can contribute to social inequality, see the discussion of job polarization in Chapter 10, Work and the Economy; the discussion of electronic democracy in Chapter 11, Politics; and Box 18.2).

## What Is to Be Done?

### The Market and High-Tech Solutions

Some people believe the environmental crisis will resolve itself. More precisely, they think we already have two weapons that will work together to end the crisis: the market and high technology. The case of oil illustrates how these weapons can combine forces. If oil reserves drop or oil is withheld from the market for political reasons, the price of oil goes up. This makes it worthwhile for oil exploration companies to develop new technologies to recover more oil. When they discover more oil and bring it to market, prices fall back

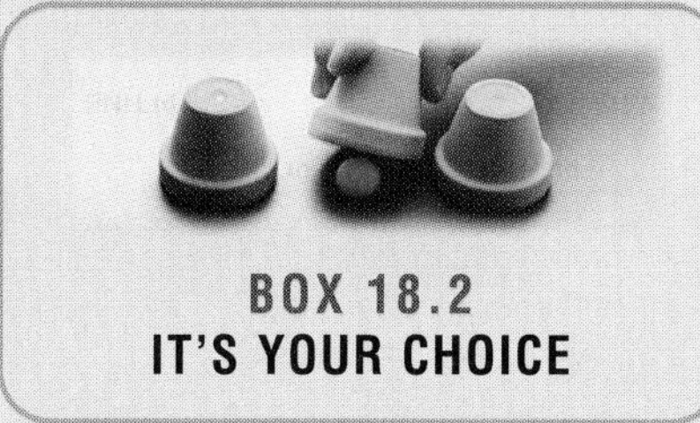

BOX 18.2
IT'S YOUR CHOICE

**WEB-BASED LEARNING AND HIGHER EDUCATION**

"I love it," says Carol Thibeault, a student at Central Connecticut State University. "With online classes, there's no set time that I have to show up. Sometimes I lug a heavy laptop onto the commuter bus and work on course files I've downloaded while I ride along. I even take my computer to the beach" (quoted in Maloney, 1999: 19). Carol is not alone in expressing her enthusiasm for the new information technology in higher education. E-mail and the World Wide Web are now about as exotic as the telephone in Canada and other rich countries. Some scholars see "online education" as the future of higher education.

The advantages of Web-based education are many. Parents with children—or students with jobs—can learn at their own speed, on their own schedule, and in their own style. This will make learning easier and more enjoyable. Potentially, many students can be taught efficiently and effectively, which will lower the cost of higher education.

Although few would argue for its elimination, many people think too much dependence on the "virtual classroom" has drawbacks. Some professors argue it is difficult to control the quality of online educational materials and instruction. That is why dropout rates for distance education courses tend to be significantly higher than rates for conventional classrooms (Merisotis, 1999). Others suggest that distance education will spread primarily among low-cost, low-status institutions. At elite institutions, they say, classroom contact and discussion will become even more important. So while one group of students will enjoy a great deal of personal attention from faculty members, another group will receive only cursory and impersonal attention.

What do you think the role of Web-based learning should be in higher education? Do you think distance learning is superior or inferior to traditional classroom learning? Is it better to learn from a professor and other students in a "real" classroom as opposed to a "virtual" classroom? Do you think online education will lead to an increase in social inequality?

to where they were. This is what happened following the oil crises of 1973 (when prices tripled) and 1978–79 (when prices tripled again). Reserves are higher now than they were in the 1970s and 1980s, and oil is less expensive. Similarly, if too little rice and wheat are grown to meet world demand, the price of these grains goes up. This prompts agrochemical companies to invent higher-yield grains. Farmers use the new grain seed to grow more wheat and rice, and prices eventually fall. This is what happened during the so-called "green revolution" of the 1960s. Projecting these experiences into the future, optimists believe that global warming, industrial pollution, and other forms of environmental degradation will be dealt with similarly. In their view, human inventiveness and the profit motive will combine to create the new technologies we need to survive and prosper in the twenty-first century.

Some evidence supports this optimistic scenario. In recent years, we have adopted new technologies to combat some of the worst excesses of environmental degradation. For example, we have replaced brain-damaging leaded gas with unleaded gas. We have developed environmentally friendly refrigerants, allowing the production of ozone-destroying CFCs to plummet. In a model of international cooperation, rich countries have even subsidized the cost of replacing CFCs in the developing countries. Efficient windmills and solar panels are now common. More factories are equipped with high-tech pollution control devices, preventing dangerous chemicals from seeping into the air and water. We have introduced cost-effective ways to recycle metal, plastic, paper, and glass. New methods are being developed for eliminating carbon dioxide emissions from the burning of fossil fuels (Parson and Keith, 1998). In November 1999, Ford and General Motors took the wraps off their diesel-electric hybrid cars, five-passenger sedans that get 35 kilometres to the litre (see photo on the next page). The widespread use of electric cars is only a decade away, thanks in part to the innovative work on fuel cells by Ballard Power Systems of Vancouver in conjunction with DaimlerChrysler and Ford.

Clearly, market forces are helping to bring environmentally friendly technologies on line. However, three factors suggest that market forces cannot solve environmental problems on their own. First, price signals often operate imperfectly. Second, political pressure is often required to stimulate policy innovation. Third, markets and new technologies are

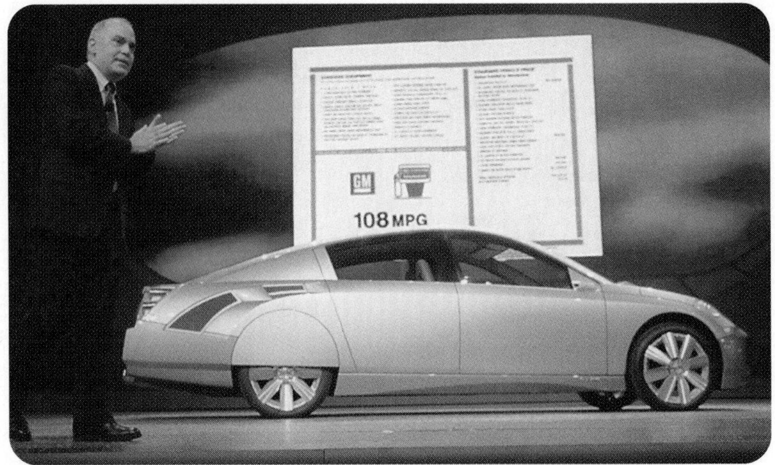


General Motors Vice-Chairman Harry Pearce presents the Precept, a fuel-cell powered vehicle that gets 46 km/L and has a 800-km range. High-tech inventions are one important part of the solution to the environmental crisis, but they are by no means sufficient.

not working quickly enough to deal adequately with the environmental crisis. Let us consider each of these issues in turn.

- *Imperfect price signals.* The price of many commodities does not reflect their actual cost to society. Gasoline in Canada sold for about 70 cents per litre at the time of this writing. But the *social* cost, which includes the cost of repairing the environmental damage caused by burning the gas, is at least $1.70 per litre. To avoid popular unrest, the government of Mexico City charges consumers only about 10 cents per cubic metre for water. The actual cost to society is about 10 times that amount (Ehrlich et al., 1997). Because of these and many other price distortions, the market often fails to send signals that might result in the speedy adoption of technological and policy fixes.
- *The importance of political pressure.* Political pressure exerted by environmental social movement activists, community groups, and public opinion is often necessary to motivate corporate and government action on environmental issues. For instance, organizations such as Greenpeace have successfully challenged the practices of logging companies, whalers, the nuclear industry, and other groups engaged in environmentally dangerous practices. Many less famous community associations have also played an important role in this regard (Brown, 1997; Mehta, 1997). The anti-nuclear movement is an outstanding example of a movement that forced a substantial turnaround in government and corporate policy. For instance, in Germany, which obtains a third of its electricity from nuclear power, the anti-nuclear movement has had a major effect on public opinion and in June 2000 the government decided to phase out all of the country's nuclear power plants within about 20 years. In Canada and the United States no more nuclear power plants are planned. Again, the anti-nuclear movement must be credited with helping to change the public mood and bring about the halt in construction of new nuclear facilities. Without the political efforts of pro-environment individuals, organizations, and social movements, it is doubtful that corporations and governments would define many environmental issues as social problems.
- *The slow pace of change.* We saw above how price signals and new technologies have created pockets of environmental improvement, especially in rich countries. However, it is unclear whether they can deal with the moral and political issues raised by biotechnology. Moreover, our efforts so far to clean up the planet are just not good enough. For example, carbon dioxide emissions from burning fossil fuels represent one of the biggest environmental hazards because they are the major source of global warming and climate change. Despite two international agreements on modest emission cutbacks, however, emissions continue to rise in Canada and most other countries (Environment Canada, 1997). This is partly because the per capita use of public transportation has been falling since 1990 (The Public Purpose,

1999). As a result, global warming continues to accelerate (refer back to Figure 18.2). After improving somewhat in the 1990s, air pollution in the world's biggest polluter, the United States is not expected to get any better between 1999 and 2010 (U.S. Environmental Protection Agency, Office of Air Quality Planning and Standards, 2000). Examining Figure 18.5, we see we can expect a substantial decrease in all of the world's renewable resources over the next decade. In 1993, 1680 of the world's leading scientists, including 104 Nobel prize winners, signed the "World Scientists' Warning to Humanity." It stated: "A great change in our stewardship of the earth and the life on it is required, if vast human misery is to be avoided and our global home on this planet is not to be irretrievably mutilated . . . Human beings and the natural world are on a collision course" (Union of Concerned Scientists, 1993). Evidence suggests we still are.

## The Cooperative Alternative

The alternative to the market and high-tech approach involves people cooperating to reduce greatly their overconsumption of just about everything. This strategy includes investing heavily in energy-saving technologies, environmental cleanup, and subsidized, environmentally friendly industrialization in the developing countries. It would require renewed commitment to voluntary efforts, new laws and enforcement bodies to ensure compliance, increased environmentally related research and development by industry and government, more environmentally directed foreign aid, and hefty new taxes to pay for everything (Livernash and Rodenburg, 1998). In addition, a cooperative strategy entails careful assessment of all the risks associated with biotechnology projects and consultation with the public before such projects are allowed to go forward. Profits from genetic engineering would also have to be shared equitably with donors of genetic material.

Is the solution realistic? Not in the short term. It would probably be political suicide for anyone in the rich countries to propose the drastic measures listed above. Not too many Canadian drivers would be happy paying $1.70 a litre for gas, for example. For the solution to be politically acceptable, the broad public in North America, Western Europe, and Japan must be aware of the gravity of the environmental problem and be willing to make substantial economic sacrifices to get the job done.

Survey data suggest that nearly all Canadians are aware of the environmental problem and are doing something about it. For instance, more than 81 percent of Canadians sort glass, cans, plastic, and paper for recycling. However, it seems that we are in general prepared to act only when it doesn't inconvenience us. Thus, when asked to indicate their main ways of getting to work, nearly 79 percent of Canadians said they usually drive and

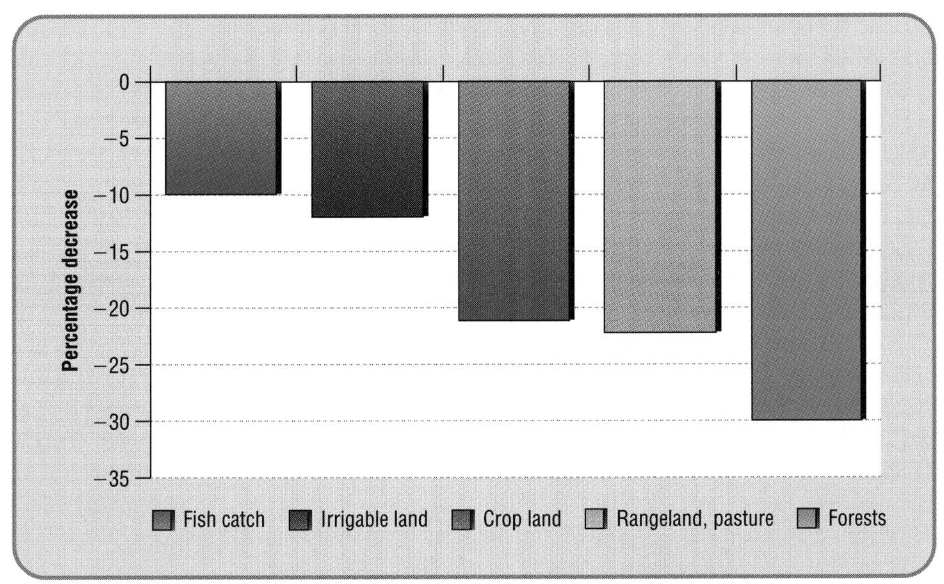


✦ **FIGURE 18.5** ✦
**Renewable Resources, World, Percent Change, 1990–2010 (projected)**

Source: Postel (1994: 11).

nearly 11 percent said they are usually passengers in a car. Fewer than 24 percent take public transit, cycle, or walk (Statistics Canada, 2000c).[1]

Other surveys conducted in the United States and elsewhere reveal much the same pattern. Most people know about the environmental crisis, say they want it dealt with, but are unwilling to be inconvenienced or pay much of the cost themselves. Most people regard environmental problems as remote and abstract, and people in general are not usually prepared to make big personal sacrifices for seemingly remote and abstract issues.

Sheldon Ungar shows in his analysis of the global warming issue that only when a social scare occurs are more people prepared to make bigger sacrifices to deal with the perceived problem. That is, people have to be able to connect real-life events, such as long droughts, catastrophic storms, scorching summers, and mild winters, with what they hear in the mass media about the environmental crisis before taking the problem more seriously and making the necessary commitment to help save the planet (Ungar, 1992; 1995; 1998; 1999). It follows that more and bigger environmental catastrophes may have to occur before more people are willing to take remedial action. The good news is that there is still time to change our culture of mass consumption.

## Evolution and Sociology

For many thousands of years, humans have thrived on this planet. That is because we have created cultural practices, including technologies, that allowed us to adapt to, and thrive in, our environment. Nonetheless, there have been some failures along the way. Many tribes and civilizations are extinct. And our success to date as a species is no warrant for the future. If we persist in using technologies that create an inhospitable environment, Nature will deal with us in the same way it always deals with species that cannot adapt.

Broadly speaking, we have two survival strategies to cope with the challenges that lie ahead: competition and cooperation. Charles Darwin wrote famously about competition in *On the Origin of Species by Means of Natural Selection* (1859). He observed that members of each species struggle against each other and against other species in their struggle to survive. Most of the quickest, the strongest, the best camouflaged, and the smartest live long enough to bear offspring. Most of the rest are killed off. Thus, the traits passed on to offspring are those most valuable for survival. Ruthless competition, it turns out, is a key survival strategy of all species, including humans.

In *The Descent of Man*, Darwin mentioned our second important survival strategy: cooperation. In some species mutual assistance is common. The species members who flourish are those who best learn to help each other (Darwin, 1871: 163). The Russian geographer and naturalist Petr Kropotkin (1908 [1902]) elaborated on this idea. After spending five years studying animal life in Siberia, he concluded that "mutual aid" is at least as important a survival strategy as competition. Competition takes place when members of the same species compete for limited resources, said Kropotkin. Cooperation occurs when species members struggle against adverse environmental circumstances. According to Kropotkin, survival in the face of environmental threat is best assured if species members help each other. Kropotkin also showed that the most advanced species in any group—ants among insects, mammals among vertebrates, humans among mammals—are the most cooperative. Many evolutionary biologists now accept Kropotkin's ideas (Gould, 1988). Recently, based on computer simulations involving competitive and cooperative strategies, mathematicians concluded that "cooperation [is] as essential for evolution as . . . competition" (Nowak, May, and Sigmund, 1995: 81).

As we have seen, a strictly competitive approach to dealing with the environmental crisis—relying on the market alone to solve our problems—now seems inadequate. Instead, it appears we require more cooperation and self-sacrifice. This involves substantially reducing consumption, paying higher taxes for environmental cleanup and energy-efficient industrial processes, subsidizing the developing countries to industrialize in an environmentally friendly way, and so forth. Above, we outlined some grave consequences of relying too little on a cooperative survival strategy at this historical juncture. But which strategy you emphasize in your own life is, of course, your choice.

Similarly, throughout this book—when we discussed families, gender inequality, crime, race, population, and many other topics—we raised social issues lying at the intersection point of history and biography—yours and ours. We set out alternative courses of action and outlined their consequences. We thus followed our disciplinary mandate: helping people make informed choices based on sound sociological knowledge (Wilensky, 1997; see Figure 18.6). In the context of the present chapter, however, we can make an even bolder claim for the discipline. Conceived at its broadest, sociology promises to help in the rational and equitable evolution of humankind.

**Calvin and Hobbes** by Bill Watterson

✦ **FIGURE 18.6** ✦
**The Advantage of Sociological Knowledge**

## SUMMARY

1. Technology is not beyond human control. For although technologies routinely transform societies, they are adopted only when there is a social need for them.
2. Since the last third of the nineteenth century, technological development has increasingly come under the control of multinational corporations and the military establishments of the major world powers.
3. Research scientists and engineers who work for these organizations normally must adhere to their research priorities.
4. A substantial and growing minority of North Americans is skeptical about the benefits of technology.
5. Four important negative consequences of technology are global warming, industrial pollution, the decline in biodiversity, and genetic pollution.
6. Disadvantaged classes, racial minorities, and countries are exposed to a disproportionately large share of the risks associated with environmental degradation.
7. Most North Americans are unwilling to undergo the personal sacrifices required to deal with environmental degradation. That could easily change in the face of repeated environmental catastrophes.
8. Sociology can play an important role in sensitizing the public to the social issues and choices humanity faces in the twenty-first century.

## GLOSSARY

**Acid rain** is precipitation whose acidity destroys forests and the ecosystems of lakes. It is formed by sulphur dioxide and other gases emitted by coal-burning power plants, pulp and paper mills, and motor-vehicle exhaust.

**Biodiversity** refers to the enormous variety of plant and animal species inhabiting the earth.

**Environmental racism** is the tendency to heap environmental dangers on the disadvantaged, and especially on disadvantaged racial minorities.

**Genetic pollution** refers to the potential dangers of mixing the genes of one species with those of another.

**Global warming** is the gradual worldwide increase in average surface temperature.

The **greenhouse effect** is the accumulation of carbon dioxide in the atmosphere that allows more solar radiation to enter the atmosphere and less solar radiation to escape.

**Normal accidents** are accidents that occur inevitably though unpredictably because of the very complexity of modern technologies.

The **ozone layer** is 8 to 40 kilometres above the earth's surface. It is depleted by CFCs. The depletion of the ozone layer allows more ultraviolet light to enter the earth's atmosphere, which increases the rate of skin cancer and crop damage.

**Recombinant DNA** involves taking a piece of DNA from one living species and inserting it into the DNA of another living species, where it grows along with the host DNA.

A **risk society** is a postmodern society defined by the way in which risk is distributed as a side effect of technology.

**Social constructionism** is a sociological approach to studying social problems such as environmental degradation. It emphasizes that social problems do not emerge spontaneously. Instead, they are contested phenomena whose prominence depends on the ability of supporters and detractors to make the public aware of them.

**Technological determinism** is the belief that technology is the main factor shaping human history.

**Technology** is the practical application of scientific principles.

**Technopoly** is a form of social organization in which technology compels people to try to solve all problems using technical rather than moral criteria, even though technology is often the source of the problems.

## QUESTIONS TO CONSIDER

1. What are the main environmental problems in your community? How are they connected to global environmental issues? (See "Web Resources," below, for useful leads.)
2. Take an inventory of your environmentally friendly and environmentally dangerous habits. In what ways can you act in a more environmentally friendly manner?

## WEB RESOURCES

### Companion Web Site for This Book

http://www.brymsociologycompass.nelson.com

Begin by clicking on the Student Resources section of the Web site. Next, select the chapter you are currently studying from the pull-down menu. From the Student Resources page you will have easy access to InfoTrac College Edition®, MicroCase online exercises, and additional Web links. The Web site also has many useful tips to aid you in your study of sociology, including practice tests for each chapter.

### InfoTrac Search Terms

These search terms are provided to assist you in beginning to conduct research on this topic by visiting http://www.infotrac-college.com

**Environmental problems**
**Environmental racism**
**Global warming**
**Human Genome Project**
**Technology**

### Recommended Web Sites

For the federal government's view of environmental issues in Canada, visit the Environment Canada Web site at http://www.ec.gc.ca/envhome.html.

Greenpeace is perhaps the most successful environmental organization in the world. Founded in Vancouver in the mid-1970s, it now has offices in 41 countries. Its Web site is at http://www.greenpeace.org.

Another important organization that works toward environmental awareness and public policy reform is the Sierra Club of Canada, founded in 1969. Its Web site is at http://www.sierraclub.ca/national/index.html.

Against All Reason is a provocative electronic journal devoted to "the radical nature of science as a route to knowledge and the radical critique of the social, political and economic roles of science and technology." Go to http://www.human-nature.com/reason/index.html.

## SUGGESTED READINGS

Maude Barlow and Eizabeth May. *Frederick Street: Life and Death on Canada's Love Canal* (Toronto: HarperCollins, 2000). An infuriating study of Canada's worst toxic nightmare, the tar ponds of Sydney, Nova Scotia.

Lester R. Brown, Christopher Flavin, Hilary French et al. *State of the World 2000* (New York: Norton, 2000). This popular annual contains a rich compendium of facts and interpretations about the environmental condition of the planet. It also proposes workable solutions.

Robert Pool. *Beyond Engineering: How Society Shapes Technology* (New York: Oxford University Press, 1997). A lucid analysis of how social factors influence technological development, with particular emphasis on nuclear power.

Jeremy Rifkin. *The Biotech Century: Harnessing the Gene and Remaking the World* (New York: Jeremy P. Tarcher/Putnam, 1998). An alarming account of the potential and problems of the technology that promises to change humanity more than any other.

## NOTE

1. The figures add up to more than 100 percent because more than one response was allowed.

# REFERENCES


Abraham, Laurie Kaye. 1993. *Mama Might Be Better Off Dead: The Failure of Health Care in Urban America.* Chicago: University of Chicago Press.

Abu-Nasr, Donna. 1998. "Natural Disaster Costs Soar to World Record." *Globe and Mail* 28 November: A25.

Achilles, Rhona. 1993. "Desperately Seeking Babies: New Technologies of Hope and Despair." Pp. 214–29 in Bonnie J. Fox, ed. *Family Patterns, Gender Relations*. Toronto: Oxford University Press.

Ad Critic.com. 2000. "Ad Critic: All Ads, All the Time." On the World Wide Web at http://www.adcritic.com (16 May 2000).

Adam, Barry, Jan Willem Duyvendak, and Andre Krouwel. 1999. *The Global Emergence of Gay and Lesbian Politics*. Philadelphia: Temple University Press.

Adams, Henry E., Lester W. Wright, Jr., and Bethany A. Lohr. 1998. "Is Homophobia Associated with Homosexual Arousal?" *Journal of Abnormal Psychology* 105: 440–45.

"Adams Mine." 2000. On the World Wide Web at http://server1.nt.net/customers/13/tpc/www/togarbag.htm#Anchor-First-14210 (8 October 2000).

Adams, R. J., G. Betcherman, and B. Bilson. 1995. *Good Job, Bad Jobs, No Jobs: Tough Choices for Canadian Labor Law*. Toronto: C.D. Howe Institute.

Adamson, Nancy, Linda Briskin, and Margaret McPhail. 1988. *Feminist Organizing for Change: The Contemporary Women's Movement in Canada*. Toronto: Oxford University Press.

Adler, Patricia A. and Peter Adler. 1998. *Peer Power: Preadolescent Culture and Identity*. New Brunswick, NJ: Rutgers University Press.

Akyeampong, E. B. 1999. "Unionization—An Update." *Perspectives on Labour and Income* 11, 3 (Autumn): 45–65.

Albas, Daniel and Cheryl Albas. 1989. "Modern Magic: The Case of Examinations." *The Sociological Quarterly* 30: 603–13.

Albelda, Randy and Chris Tilly. 1997. *Glass Ceilings and Bottomless Pits: Women's Work, Women's Poverty*. Boston, MA: South End Press.

Aldrich, Howard E. 1979. *Organizations and Environments*. Englewood Cliffs, NJ: Prentice-Hall.

Alford, Robert R. and Roger Friedland. 1985. *Powers of Theory: Capitalism, the State, and Democracy*. Cambridge, UK: Cambridge University Press.

Allen, Robert C. 1999. *Education and Technological Revolutions: The Role of the Social Sciences and the Humanities in the Knowledge Based Economy*. Ottawa: Social Sciences and Humanities Research Council of Canada. On the World Wide Web at http://www.sshrc.ca/english/resnews/researchresults/allen99.pdf (8 May 2001).

Amato, Paul R. and Bruce Keith. 1991. "Parental Divorce and the Well-Being of Children: A Meta-Analysis." *Psychological Bulletin* 110: 26–46.

Ambert, Anne-Marie. 1998. "Divorce: Facts, Figures and Consequences." Vanier Institute of the Family. On the World Wide Web at http://www.vifamily.ca/cft/divorce/divorcer.htm.

American Psychological Association. 1998. "Answers to Your Questions About Sexual Orientation and Homosexuality." On the World Wide Web at http://www.apa.org/pubinfo/orient.html (14 June 2000).

Amnesty International. 1998. "Female Genital Mutilation: A Human Rights Information Pack." On the World Wide Web at http://www.amnesty.org/ailib/intcam/femgen/fgm6.htm.

Anderson, Benedict O. 1990. *The Imagined Community*, rev. ed. London: Verso.

Anderson, Elijah. 1990. *Streetwise: Race, Class, and Change in an Urban Community*. Chicago: University of Chicago Press.

Anderson, Kristin L. 1997. "Gender, Status, and Domestic Violence: An Integration of Feminist and Family Violence Approaches." *Journal of Marriage and the Family* 59: 655–9.

Angus Reid Group. 1997. "Canadians and Alternative Medicines and Practices." *The Angus Reid Report* 12, 5 (September/October).

Antonius, George. 1939. *The Arab Awakening: The Story of the Arab National Movement*. Philadelphia: J. B. Lipincott.

Arace, Michael. 2000. "Oft-injured Forward Feels OK." *Columbus Dispatch* 17 September. On the World Wide Web at http://www.dispatch.com/news/sports00/sept00/424238.html (22 July 2002).

Arendt, Hannah. 1977 [1963]. *Eichmann in Jerusalem: A Report on the Banality of Evil*, rev. ed. Harmondsworth, UK: Penguin.

Ariès, Phillipe. 1962 [1960]. *Centuries of Childhood: A Social History of Family Life*, Robert Baldick, trans. New York: Knopf.

———. 1982. *The Hour of Our Death*. New York: Knopf.

Arluke, Arnold and Jack Levin. 1990. "'Second Childhood': Old Age in Popular Culture." Pp. 261–5 in W. Feigelman, ed. *Readings on Social Problems*. Fort Worth: Holt, Rinehart and Winston.

Armstrong, Pat, Hugh Armstrong, and Claudia Fegan. 1998. *Universal Health Care: What the United States Can Learn from the Canadian Experience*. New York: The New Press.

Arnett, Jeffrey Jensen. 1995. "Adolescents' Uses of Media for Self-Socialization." *Journal of Youth and Adolescence* 24: 519–33.

Arnup, Katherine, ed. 1995. *Lesbian Parenting: Living with Pride and Prejudice*. Charlottetown: gynergy books.

Arterton, F. Christopher. 1987. *Teledemocracy: Can Technology Protect Democracy?* Newbury Park, CA: Sage Publications.

Ash, Russell. 2001. *The Top 10 of Everything 2002*. Toronto: Dorling Kindersley Limited.

Associated Press. 2001. "Vancouver Gay Man Beaten to Death: Police Suspect Hate Crime." On the World Wide Web at http://www.planetqnews.com/0812/11.shtml.

Association of Canadian Publishers. 2002. "How to Get Published." On the World Wide Web at http://www.publishers.ca/published.html (15 May 2002).

Averett, Susan and Sanders Korenman. 1996. "The Economic Reality of The Beauty Myth." *Journal of Human Resources* 31: 304–30.

Babbie, Earl. 2000 [1973]. *The Practice of Social Research*, rev.ed. of 9th ed. Belmont, CA: Wadsworth.

Baer, Doug. 1999. "Educational Credentials and the Changing Occupational Structure." Pp. 92–106 in J. Curtis, E. Grabb, and N. Guppy, eds. *Social Inequality in Canada: Patterns, Problems, Policies*, 3rd ed. Scarborough, ON: Prentice Hall Allyn and Bacon Canada.

———, ed. 2002. *Political Sociology: Canadian Perspectives*. Toronto: Oxford University Press.

Bagdikian, Ben H. 1997 [1983]. *The Media Monopoly*, 5th ed. Boston: Beacon.

Bairoch, Paul. 1988 [1985]. *Cities and Economic Development: From the Dawn of History to the Present*, Christopher Braider, trans. Chicago: University of Chicago Press.

Baker, M. and D. Lero. 1996. "Division of Labour: Paid Work and Family Structure." Pp. 78–103 in Maureen Baker, ed. *Families: Changing Trends in Canada*, 3rd ed. Toronto: McGraw-Hill Ryerson.

Balakrishnan, T. R. 1979. "Changing Patterns of Spatial Differentiation in Urban Canada, 1961–1971." *Canadian Review of Sociology and Anthropology* 16, 2: 218–27.

Balakrishnan, T. R. and John Kralt. 1987. "Segregation of Visible Minorities in Montreal, Toronto, and Vancouver." In Leo Driedger, ed. *Ethnic Canada: Identities and Inequalities*. Toronto: Copp Clark Pitman.

Balakrishnan, T. R. and K. Jarvis. 1976. "Socioeconomic Differentiation in Urban Canada." *Canadian Review of Sociology and Anthropology* 13, 2: 204–16.

Balakrishnan, T. R. and K. Selvanathan. 1990. "Residential Segregation in Metropolitan Canada." In S. Halli, F. Travato, and L. Driedger, eds. *Ethnic Demography*. Ottawa: Carleton University Press.

Bales, Kevin. 1999. *Disposable People: New Slavery in the Global Economy*. Berkeley, CA: University of California Press.

Bank of Hawaii. 1999. *Commonwealth of the Northern Mariana Islands: Economic Report October*. On the World Wide Web at http://www.boh.com/econ/pacific/cnmi/1999/cnmi1999.pdf (23 June 2000).

Banner, Lois W. 1992. *In Full Flower: Aging Women, Power, and Sexuality*. New York: Knopf.

Bannon, Lisa. 2000. "Why Girls and Boys Get Different Toys." *The Wall Street Journal* 14 February: B1, B4.

Baran, Paul A. 1957. *The Political Economy of Growth*. New York: Monthly Review Press.

Barash, David. 1981. *The Whispering Within*. New York: Penguin.

Barber, Bernard. 1992. "Jihad vs. McWorld," *The Atlantic Monthly* March: 53–63. On the World Wide Web at http://www.theatlantic.com/politics/foreign/barberf.htm (28 April 2000).

———. 1996. *Jihad vs. McWorld: How Globalism and Tribalism Are Reshaping the World*. New York: Ballantine Books.

Baril, Alain and George A. Mori. 1994. "Leaving the Fold: Declining Church Attendance." Pp. 253–4 in *Canadian Social Trends* 2. Toronto: Thompson Educational Publishing.

Barlow, Maude and Elizabeth May. 2000. *Frederick Street: Life and Death on Canada's Love Canal*. Toronto: HarperCollins.

Barlow, Maude and Heather-Jane Robertson. 1994. *Class Warfare: The Assault on Canada's Schools*. Toronto: Key Porter Books.

Barnard, Chester I. 1938. *The Functions of the Executive*. Cambridge, MA: Harvard University Press.

Bar-On, D. 1999. *The Indescribable and the Undiscussable: Reconstructing Human Discourse after Trauma*. Ithaca, NY: Cornell University Press.

Bashevkin, Sylvia, 1986. "Independence versus Partisanship: Dilemmas in the Political History of Women in English Canada." Pp. 246–75 in V. Strong-Boag and A. Fellman, eds. *Rethinking Canada: The Promise of Women's History*. Toronto: Copp Clark Pitman.

——— 1993. *Toeing the Lines: Women and Party Politics in English Canada*, 2nd ed. Toronto: Oxford University Press.

Baudrillard, Jean. 1983. *Simulations*. New York: Semiotext(e).

———. 1988 [1986]. *America*. Chris Turner, trans. London: Verso.

———. 1988. *Selected Writings*, Mark Poster, ed. Stanford, CA: Stanford University Press.

Bauman, Zygmunt. 1991 [1989]. *Modernity and the Holocaust*. Ithaca, NY: Cornell University Press.

BCE. 2002. *2001 Annual Report*. On the World Wide Web at http://www.bce.ca/en/investors/reports/annual/bce/2001annua/BCEAREng.pdf (17 May 2002).

Beaudry, P. and D. Green. 1998. *Individual Responses to Changes in the Canadian Labour Market*, Paper Number 9. Ottawa: Industry Canada.

Beck, Ulrich. 1992 [1986]. *Risk Society: Towards a New Modernity*, Mark Ritter, trans. London, UK: Sage.

Becker, Ernest. 1973. *The Denial of Death*. New York: Free Press.

Becker, G. 1976. *The Economic Approach to Human Behavior*. Chicago: University of Chicago Press.

———. 1991. *A Treatise on the Family*. Cambridge, MA: Harvard University Press.

Bélanger, Claude. 2000. "Readings in Quebec History: Opting Out." On the World Wide Web at http://members.nbci.com/history_1/his951/readings/opting.htm (18 February 2001).

Bell, Daniel. 1973. *The Coming of Post-Industrial Society: A Venture in Social Forecasting*. New York: Basic Books.

———. 1976. *The Coming of Post-Industrial Society: A Venture in Social Forecasting*. New York: Basic Books.

Bell, Gregory Boyd. 2002. "No Strait Jacket Required." *This* January/February: 29.

Bellah, Robert A. 1975. *The Broken Covenant: American Civil Religion in a Time of Trial*. New York: Seabury Press.

Bellow, Saul. 1964. *Herzog*. New York: Fawcett World Library.

Benford, Robert D. 1997. "An Insider's Critique of the Social Movement Framing Perspective." *Sociological Inquiry* 67: 409–39.

Bercuson, David. 1974. "The Winnipeg General Strike" Pp. 1–32 in Irving Abella, ed. *On Strike: Six Key Labour Struggles in Canada, 1919–1949*. Toronto: James Lewis & Samuel.

Berger, Peter L. 1963. *Invitation to Sociology: A Humanistic Approach*. New York: Doubleday.

Berger, Peter L. and Thomas Luckmann. 1966. *The Social Construction of Reality: A Treatise in the Sociology of Knowledge*. Garden City, NY: Doubleday.

Berger, S., and R. Dore, eds. 1996. *National Diversity and Capitalism*. Ithaca, NY: Cornell University Press._

Berk, Richard A. 1974. *Collective Behavior*. Dubuque, IO: Wm. C. Brown.

Berk, Sarah Fenstermaker. 1985. *The Gender Factory: The Apportionment of Work in American Households*. New York: Plenum.

Bernard, Jessie. 1972. *The Future of Marriage*. New York: World.

———. 1986 [1973]. "The Good-Provider Role: Its Rise and Fall." Pp. 125–44 in Arlene S. Skolnick and Jerome H. Skolnick, eds. *Family in Transition: Rethinking Marriage, Sexuality, Child Rearing, and Family Organization*, 5th ed. Boston: Little, Brown.

Berners-Lee, Tim. 1999. "Tim Berners-Lee." On the World Wide Web at http://www.w3.org/People/Berners-Lee/Overview.html (2 May 2000).

Berry, B. J. L. 1965. "Internal Structure of the City." *Law and Contemporary Problems* 30: 111–9.

———. 1971. "Introduction: The Logic and Limitations of Comparative Factorial Ecology." *Economic Geography* (supplement) 47: 209–19.

Besserer, Sandra. 2002. "Criminal Victimization: An International Perspective: Results of the 2000 International Crime Victimization Survey." *Juristat* 22, 4 (May). Catalogue no. 85-002-XPE.

Betcherman, G. and G. Lowe. 1997. *The Future of Work in Canada: A Synthesis Report.* Ottawa: Canadian Policy Research Networks Inc.

Bianchi, Suzanne M. and Daphne Spain. 1996. "Women, Work, and Family in America." *Population Bulletin* 51, 3: 2–48.

Bibby, Reginald W. 1987. *Fragmented Gods: The Poverty and Potential of Religion in Canada*. Toronto: Irwin.

———. 1993. "Secularization and Social Change." Pp. 65–82 in W. E. Hewitt, ed. *The Sociology of Religion: A Canadian Focus*. Toronto: Butterworths.

———. 1995. *The Bibby Report: Social Trends Canadian Style.* Toronto: Stoddart.

———. 2001. *Canada's Teens: Today, Yesterday, and Tomorrow.* Toronto: Stoddart.

Biegler, Rebecca S. 1999. "Psychological Interventions Designed to Counter Sexism in Children: Empirical Limitations and Theoretical Foundations." Pp. 129–52 in W. B. Swann, Jr., J. H. Langlois, and L. A. Gilbert, eds. *Sexism and Stereotypes in Modern Society: The Gender Science of Janet Taylor Spence*. Washington, DC: American Psychological Association.

Bierstedt, Robert. 1963. *The Social Order*. New York: McGraw-Hill.

———. 1974. "An Analysis of Social Power." Pp. 220–41 in *Power and Progress: Essays in Sociological Theory*. New York: McGraw-Hill.

Birdwhistell, Ray L. 1970. *Kinesics and Context*. Philadelphia: Pennsylvania State University.

Bjorhus, J. 2000. "Gap Between Execs, Rank and File Grows Wider." *San Jose Mercury News* 18 June. On the World Wide Web at http://www.mercurycenter.com/premium/business/docs/ disparity18.htm (20 June 2000).

Black, Donald. 1989. *Sociological Justice*. New York: Oxford University Press.

Blais, André, Elisabeth Gidengil, Richard Nadeau, and Neil Nevitte. 1997. *1997 Canadian Election Survey*. Computer file on the World Wide Web at http://prod.library.utoronto.ca/datalib/codebooks/utm/elections/1997/ (1 December 1998).

Blaise, Clark. 2001. *Time Lord: The Remarkable Canadian Who Missed His Train and Changed the World*. Toronto: Knopf Canada.

Blau, Peter M. 1963 [1955]. *The Dynamics of Bureaucracy: A Study of Interpersonal Relationships in Two Government Agencies*, rev. ed. Chicago: University of Chicago Press.

———. 1964. *Exchange and Power in Social Life*. New York: Wiley.

Blauner, R. 1972. *Racial Oppression in America*. New York: Harper & Row.

Bliss, Jeff. 2000. "Getting a Life Offline." *Financial Post* 29 June: C3.

Block, Fred. 1979. "The Ruling Class Does Not Rule." Pp. 128–40 in R. Quinney, ed. *Capitalist Society*. Homewood, IL: Dorsey Press.

Blossfeld, H. and Y. Shavit, eds. 1993. *Persistant Inequality: Changing Educational Attainment in Thirteen Countries.* Boulder, CO: Westview Press.

Bluestone, B. and B. Harrison. 1982. *The Deindustrialization of America*. New York: Basic Books.

Blum, Deborah. 1997. *Sex on the Brain: The Biological Differences Between Men and Women*. New York: Penguin.

Blumberg, Paul. 1989. *The Predatory Society: Deception in the American Marketplace.* New York: Oxford University Press.

Blumer, Herbert. 1969. *Symbolic Interactionism: Perspective and Method*. Englewood Cliffs, NJ: Prentice-Hall.

Boal, Mark. 1998. "Spycam City." *The Village Voice* (30 September–6 October). On the World Wide Web at http://www.villagevoice.com/issues/9840/boal.shtml (26 March 2001).

Bonacich, Edna. 1972. "A Theory of Ethnic Antagonism: The Split Labor Market." *American Sociological Review* 37: 547–59.

——— 1973. "A Theory of Middleman Minorities." *American Sociological Review* 38: 583–94.

Bornholt, Laurel. 2001. "Self-Concepts, Usefulness and Behavioural Intentions on the Social Context of Schooling." *Educational Psychology* 21, 1 (March): 67–78.

Bornschier, Volker and Christopher Chase-Dunn. 1985. *Transnational Corporations and Underdevelopment*. New York: Praeger.

Boston Women's Health Book Collective, ed. 1998. *Our Bodies, Our Selves for the New Century: A Book by and for Women.* New York: Simon & Schuster.

Boswell, A. Ayres and Joan Z. Spade. 1996. "Fraternities and Collegiate Rape Culture: Why Are Some Fraternities More Dangerous Places for Women?" *Gender and Society* 10: 133–47.

Bouchard, Thomas J., Jr., David T. Lykken, Matthew McGue, Nancy L. Segal, and Auke Tellegen. 1990. "Sources of Human Psychological Differences: The Minnesota Study of Twins Reared Apart." *Science* 250, 4978: 223–6.

Bourdieu, Pierre. 1977 [1972]. *Outline of a Theory of Practice*, Richard Nice, trans. Cambridge, UK: Cambridge University Press.

———. 1984 [1979]. *Distinction: A Social Critique of the Judgment of Taste*, R. Nice, trans. Cambridge, MA: Harvard University Press.

———. 1998 [1996]. *On Television*. New York: New Press.

——— and J. Passeron. 1990. *Reproduction in Education, Society and Culture*, 2nd ed. R. Nice, trans. London: Sage.

Bowles, Samuel, and Herbert Gintis. 1976. *Schooling in Capitalist America: Educational Reform and the Contradictions of Economic Life*. New York: Basic Books.

Boychuk, Gerard W. 2002. "Federal Spending in Health: Why Here? Why Now?" Pp. 121–36 in G. Bruce Doern, ed. *How Ottawa Spends 2002–2003: The Security Aftermath and National Priorities*. Toronto: Oxford University Press.

Boyd, Monica. 1997. "Feminizing Paid Work." *Current Sociology* 45, 2 (April): 49–73.

———. 1999. "Canadian, eh? Ethnic Origin Shifts in the Canadian Census." *Canadian Ethnic Studies* 31, 3: 1–19

———. 2001. "Gender Inequality." Pp. 178–207 in Robert J. Brym, ed. *New Society: Sociology for the 21st Century*, 3rd ed. Toronto: Harcourt Canada.

Boyd, Monica and Doug Norris. 2001. "Who Are the 'Canadians'? Changing Census Responses, 1986–1996." *Canadian Ethnic Studies* 33, 1: 1–25.

Boyd, Monica, et al. 1985. *Ascription and Achievement: Studies on Mobility and Status Attainment in Canada*. Ottawa: Carleton University Press.

Boyd, Neil. 1998. *Canadian Law: An Introduction*. Toronto: Harcourt Brace Canada.

Bracey, Gerald W. 1998. "Are U.S. Students Behind?" *The American Prospect* 37, March–April: 54–70. On the World Wide Web at http://www.prospect.org/archives/37/37bracfs.html (1 May 2000).

Brady, Erik. 2001. "Too Good to Be True?" *USA Today* 12 July. On the Internet at wysiwyg://14/http://www.usatoday.com/sports/stories/2001-07-12-cover.htm (21 July 2001).

Braithwaite, John. 1981. "The Myth of Social Class and Criminality Revisited." *American Sociological Review* 46: 36–57.

———. 1989. *Crime, Shame and Reintegration*. New York: Cambridge University Press.

Brannigan, Augustine. 1984. *Crime, Courts and Corrections*. Toronto: Holt, Rinehart and Winston.

Brannock, K. C. and B. E. Champman. 1990. "Negative Sexual Experiences with Men among Heterosexual Women and Lesbians." *Journal of Homosexuality* 19: 105–10.

Braver, Sanford L., Pamela J. Fitzpatrick, and R. Curtis Bay. 1991. "Noncustodial Parent's Report of Child Support Payments." *Family Relations* 40, 2 (April): 180–5.

Braverman, H. 1974. *Labour and Monopoly Capital: The Degradation of Work in the Twentieth Century*. New York: Monthly Review Press.

Brazzini, D. G., W. D. McIntosh, S. M. Smith, S. Cook, and C. Harris. 1997. "The Aging Woman in Popular Film: Underrepresented, Unattractive, Unfriendly, and Unintelligent." *Sex Roles* 36: 531–43.

Brechin, Steven R. and Willett Kempton. 1994. "Global Environmentalism: A Challenge to the Postmaterialism Thesis." *Social Science Quarterly* 75: 245–69.

Bricker, Darrell and Edward Greenspon. 2001. *Searching for Certainty: Inside the New Canadian Mindset*. Toronto: Doubleday Canada.

Brieger, P., C. Cattaneo, M. Evans, P. Haavardsrud, D. Hasselback, K. Kalawsky, G. Marr, H. Shaw, B. Shecter, S. Silcoff, and R. Thompson. 2002. "Wealth Report." *National Post Online* 25 May. On the World Wide Web at http://www.nationalpost.com (26 May 2002).

Brint, Stephen. 1984. "New Class and Cumulative Trend Explanations of the Liberal Political Attitudes of Professionals." *American Journal of Sociology* 90: 30–71.

Brint, Stephen and Jerome Karabel. 1989. *The Diverted Dream: Community Colleges and the Promise of Educational References Opportunity in America, 1900–1985*. New York: Oxford University Press.

Brodie, Janine. 1991. "Women and the Electoral Process in Canada." Pp. 3–59 in Kathy Megyery, ed. *Women in Canadian Politics: Toward Equity in Representation*. Toronto: Dundurn Press.

Bromley, Julian V. 1982 [1977]. *Present-Day Ethnic Processes in the USSR*. Moscow: Progress Publishers.

Bronowski, J. 1965 [1956]. *Science and Human Values*, revised ed. New York: Harper & Row.

Brooks, Clem and Jeff Manza. 1997. "Social Cleavages and Political Alignments: U.S. Presidential Elections, 1960 to 1992." *American Sociological Review* 62: 937–46.

Brower, David. 1975. *Training the Nihilists: Education and Radicalism in Tsarist Russia*. Ithaca, NY: Cornell University Press.

Brown, David K. 1995. *Degrees of Control: A Sociology of Educational Expansion and Occupational Credentialism*. New York: Teachers College Press.

Brown, Laura S. 2000. "Dangerousness, Impotence, Silence, and Invisiblity: Heterosexism in the Construction of Women's Sexuality." Pp. 273–97 in Cheryl Brown Travis and Jacquelyn W. White, eds. *Sexuality, Society, and Feminism: Psychology of Women*. Washington, DC: American Psychological Association.

Brown, Lester R., Christopher Flavin, Hilary French et al. 2000. *State of the World 2000*. New York: Norton.

Brown, Lyn Mikel and Carol Gilligan. 1992. *Meeting at the Crossroads: Women's Psychology and Girls' Development*. Cambridge, MA: Harvard University Press.

Brown, P. and R. Rans. 1984. "Material Girl" (recorded by Madonna). On *Like a Virgin* (CD). New York: Sire Records/Warner.

Brown, Phil. 1997. "Popular Epidemiology Revisited." *Current Sociology* 45, 3: 137–56.

Browne, Malcolm W. 1998. "From Science Fiction to Science: The Whole Body Transplant." *New York Times* 5 May: B16.

Bruce, Steve. 1988. *The Rise and Fall of the New Christian Right: Conservative Protestant Politics in America 1978–1988*. Oxford, UK: Clarendon Press.

Brumberg, Joan Jacobs. 1997. *The Body Project: An Intimate History of American Girls*. New York: Random House.

Bryden, Joan, Robert Fife, and Graeme Hamilton. 2000. " Maritime Premiers Issue Health Ultimatum." *National Post* 8 September: A1, A7.

Brym, Robert J. 1979. "Political Conservatism in Atlantic Canada." Pp. 59–79 in Robert J. Brym and R. James

Sacouman, eds. *Underdevelopment and Social Movements in Atlantic Canada*. Toronto: New Hogtown Press.

———. 1980. *Intellectuals and Politics*. London, UK: George Allen and Unwin.

———. 1989. "Canada." Pp. 177–206 in Tom Bottomore and Robert J. Brym, eds. *The Capitalist Class: An International Study*. New York: New York University Press.

———. 1990. "Sociology, Perestroika, and Soviet Society." *Canadian Journal of Sociology* 15: 207–15.

———. 1992. "Some Advantages of Canadian Disunity: How Quebec Sovereignty Might Aid Economic Development in English-speaking Canada." *Canadian Review of Sociology and Anthropology* 29: 210–26.

———. 1995. "Voters Quietly Reveal Greater Communist Leanings." *Transition: Events and Issues in the Former Soviet Union and East-Central and Southeastern Europe* 1, 16: 32–5.

———. 1996a. "The Ethic of Self-reliance and the Spirit of Capitalism in Russia." *International Sociology* 11: 409–26.

———. 1996b. "Reevaluating Mass Support for Political and Economic Change in Russia." *Europe-Asia Studies* 48: 751–66.

———. 1996c. "'The Third Rome' and 'The End of History': Notes on Russia's Second Communist Revolution." *Canadian Review of Sociology and Anthropology* 33: 391–406.

———. 1996d. "The Turning Point in the Presidential Campaign." Pp. 44–9 in *The 1996 Presidential Election and Public Opinion*. Moscow: VTsIOM. [In Russian.]

———. 1999. *Canadian Society and the 1996 Census*. Toronto: Harcourt Brace Canada.

———. 2001a. "Hip-Hop from Dissent to Commodity: A Note on Consumer Culture." Pp. 78–81 in Robert J. Brym, ed. *New Society: Sociology for the 21st Century*, 3rd ed. Toronto: Harcourt Brace Canada.

———. 2001b. "Jewish Immigrants from the Former Soviet Union in Canada, 1996." *East European Jewish Affairs* 31: 36–43.

———. 2002. "Canadian Sociology: An Introduction to the upper thirteen." *The American Sociologist* 33, 1: 5–11.

———. 2003. "Affluence, Strikes, and Power in Canada, 1973–2000." J. Curtis, E. Grabb, and N. Guppy, eds. *Social Inequality in Canada: Patterns, Problems, Policies,* 4th ed. Scarborough, ON: Prentice-Hall.

Brym, Robert J. and Evel Economakis. 1994. "Peasant or Proletarian? Blacklisted Pskov Workers in St. Petersburg, 1913." *Slavic Review* 53: 120–39.

Brym, Robert J. with Bonnie J. Fox. 1989. *From Culture to Power: The Sociology of English Canada*. Toronto: Oxford University Press.

Brym, Robert J., Michael Gillespie, and A. Ron Gillis. 1985. "Anomie, Opportunity, and the Density of Ethnic Ties: Another View of Jewish Outmarriage in Canada." *Canadian Review of Sociology and Anthropology* 22: 102–12.

Brym, Robert J., Michael Gillespie, and Rhonda L. Lenton. 1989. "Class Power, Class Mobilization, and Class Voting: The Canadian Case." *Canadian Journal of Sociology* 14: 25–44.

Brym, Robert J. and Rhonda Lenton. 2001. *Love Online: A Report on Digital Dating in Canada*. Toronto: MSN.CA. On the World Wide Web at http://www.nelson.com/nelson/harcourt/sociology/newsociety3e/loveonline.pdf (20 December 2001).

Brym, Robert J. with the assistance of Rozalina Ryvkina. 1994. *The Jews of Moscow, Kiev and Minsk: Identity, Antisemitism, Emigration*. New York: New York University Press.

Brym, Robert J. and Céline Saint-Pierre. 1997. "Canadian Sociology." *Contemporary Sociology* 26: 543–6.

Brym, Robert J. William Shaffir, and Morton Weinfeld, eds. 1993. *The Jews in Canada*. Toronto: Oxford University Press.

Bukowski, W., C. Gauze, B. Hoza, and A. Newcomb. 1993. "Differences and Consistency in Relations with Same-sex and Other-sex Peers During Early Adolescence." *Developmental Psychology* 29: 255–63.

Bullard, Robert D. 1994 [1990]. *Dumping in Dixie: Race, Class and Environmental Quality*, 2nd ed. Boulder, CO: Westview Press.

Bullough, Vern L. 2000. "Transgenderism and the Concept of Gender." *International Journal of Transgenderism*, Special Issue 4, 3 (July–Sept).

Bumpass, Larry L. and James A. Sweet. 1995. "Cohabitation, Marriage, Nonmarital Childbearing, and Union Stability: Preliminary Findings from NSFH2." Population Association of America annual meeting, San Francisco, April.

Bunge, Valerie Pottie. 2000a. "Spousal Violence." Pp. 11–21 in Statistics Canada. *Family Violence in Canada: A Statistical Profile 2000*. Catalogue no. 85-224-XIE. Ottawa: Minister of Industry.

Burawoy, M. 1979. *Manufacturing Consent: Changes in the Labor Process Under Monopoly Capitalism*. Chicago: University of Chicago Press.

Burgess, Ernest. W. 1967 [1925]. "The Growth of the City: An Introduction to a Research Project." Pp. 47–62 in Robert E. Park, Ernest W. Burgess, and Roderick D. McKenzie. *The City*. Chicago: University of Chicago Press.

Burns, Tom and G. M. Stalker. 1961. *The Management of Innovation*. London, UK: Tavistock.

Bush, Irene R. and Anthony Sainz. 2001. "Competencies at the Intersection of Difference, Tolerance, and Prevention of Hate Crimes." Pp. 205–24 in Mary E. Swigonski and Robin S. Mama, eds. *From Hate Crimes to Human Rights: A Tribute to Matthew Shepard*. New York: Haworth Press.

Buss, David M. 2000. *Dangerous Passion: Why Jealousy is as Necessary as Love and Sex*. New York: Free Press.

Butovsky, Jonah. 2000. *The Decline of the New Democrats: The Politics of Postmaterialism or Neoliberalism?* Ph.D. dissertation, Department of Sociology, University of Toronto.

Buxton, L. H. D. 1963. "Races of Mankind." Pp. 864–6 in *Encyclopedia Britannica*, vol. 18. Chicago: Encyclopedia Britannica, Inc.

Cairns, Alan C. 2000. *Citizens Plus: Aboriginal Peoples and the Canadian State*. Vancouver: UBC Press.

Callahan, Raymond E. 1962. *Education and the Cult of Efficiency: A Study of the Social Forces That Have Shaped the Administration of the Public Schools*. Chicago: University of Chicago Press.

Campbell, D. and J. Stanley. 1963. *Experimental and Quasi-experimental Designs for Research*. Chicago: Rand McNally.

Campbell, F. A. and C. T. Ramey. 1994. "Effects of Early Intervention on Intellectual and Academic Achievement: A Follow-up Study of Children from Low-income Families." *Child Development* 65: 684–99.

Campion, Edward W. 1993. "Why Unconventional Medicine?" *New England Journal of Medicine* 328: 282.

Canada NewsWire. 2001. "Euthanasia Prevention Coalition Responds to Leger Marketing Poll." On the World Wide Web at http://www.newswire.ca/releases/July2001/03/c9446.html.

———. 2002. "CanWest Gag Order Now Extends to Global Television Reporters as Company Refuses to Lift Discipline against Regina 10." 13 March. On the World Wide Web at http://www.newswire.ca/releases/March2002/13/c0319.html (17 May 2002).

"Canada: Parliamentary Elections." 2000. On the World Wide Web at http://www.idea.int/Voter_turnout/northamerica/canada.html (29 November 2001).

Canadian Aboriginal News. 2001. "Innu, Health Officials Settle Differences over Treatment for Gas Sniffers." On the World Wide Web at http://www.candianaboriginal.com/health/health26b.htm.

Canadian Coalition for Nuclear Responsibility. 2000. On the World Wide Web at http://www.ccnr.org/#topics (8 October 2000).

Canadian Council on Social Development. 1999. *Thinking Ahead: Trends Affecting Public Education in the Future*. Ottawa: Canadian Council on Social Development.

———. 2001. *The Progress of Canada's Children 2001—Highlights*. On the World Wide Web at http://www.ccsd.ca/pubs/2—1/pcc2001.hl.htm.

Canadian Families Project. 1999. *Profiling Canada's Families in 1901*. Victoria: University of Victoria.

*Canadian Global Almanac 2000*. 1999. Toronto: Macmillan Canada.

*Canadian Global Almanac 2002*. 2001. Toronto: Macmillan Canada.

Canadian Journalists for Free Expression. 2000. "CJFE Disappointed at Ontario Superior Court Ruling Against Media Freedom." On the World Wide Web at http://www.cjfe.org/releases/2000/seizures.html (22 March 2001).

Canadian Medical Association. 1998. ©Canadian Medical Association. Canadians' Access to Quality Health Care: A System in Crisis. Brief submitted to the House of Commons Standing Committee on Finance; August 31, 1998; Ottawa, Canada. Reprinted from, by permission of the publisher. Available at: http://www.cma.ca/cma/common/displayPage.do?pageId=/staticContent/HTML/N0/12/advocacy/political/1998/08-31.htm.

———. 2001. Canadians give a B grade to the health care system. [news release]. Ottawa: ©Canadian Medical Association; August 13, 2001. Reprinted by permission of the publisher. Available at http://www.cma.ca/cma/common/displayPage.do?pageId=/staticContent/HTML/N0/12/ advocacy/news/2001/08-13.htm.

Canadian Mental Health Association. 2001. "Depression and Manic Depression." On the World Wide Web at http://www.cmha.ca/english/store/mh_pamphlets/mh.

Canadian Psychiatric Association. 2002. "Anxiety, Depression and Manic Depression." On the World Wide Web at http://www.cpa-apc.org/MIAW/pamphlets/Anxiety.arp.

Cancio, A. S., T. D. Evans, and D. J. Maume. 1996. "Reconsidering the Declining Significance of Race: Racial Differences in Early Career Wages." *American Sociological Review* 61: 541–56.

"The Candidates Debate." 1998. MSNBC News. On the World Wide Web at http://msnbc.com/onair/ msnbc/TimeAndAgain/archive/ken-nix/Default.asp?cp1=1 (2 May 2000).

Canning, Patricia M. and Charlotte Strong. 1998. *Families Adapting to the Cod Moratorium*. International Sociological Association (ISA).

CanWest Global Communications Corp. 2002. Annual Report 2001. On the World Wide Web at http://www.canwestglobal.com/annual/annual2001/3346_CWG_AR2001.pdf (17 May 2002).

Cardinal, H. 1977. *The Rebirth of Canada's Indians*. Edmonton: Hurtig Publishers.

Caron, Roger. 1979. *Go-Boy! The True Story of a Life Behind Bars*. London, UK: Arrow Books Limited.

Carrier, Roch. 1979. *The Hockey Sweater and Other Stories*, Sheila Fischman, trans. Toronto: Anansi.

Carroll, Barbara Wake. 2002. "Housing Policy in the New Millennium: The Uncompassionate Landscape." Pp. 69–89 in Edmund P. Fowler and David Siegel, eds. *Urban Policy Issues: Canadian Perspectives*, 2nd ed. Don Mills, ON: Oxford University Press.

Carroll, William. 1986. *Corporate Power and Canadian Capitalism*. Vancouver: University of British Columbia Press.

———, ed. 1997 [1992]. *Organizing Dissent: Contemporary Social Movements in Theory and Practice*, 2nd ed. Toronto: Garamond Press.

Carroll, William and Robert S. Ratner. 1996a. "Master Frames and Counter-Hegemony: Political Sensibilities in Contemporary Social Movements." *Canadian Review of Sociology and Anthropology* 33: 407–35.

———. 1996b. "Master Framing and Cross-Movement Networking in Contemporary Social Movements." *The Sociological Quarterly* 37, 4: 601–25.

Cassidy, B., R. Lord, and N. Mandell. 1998. "Silenced and Forgotten Women: Race, Poverty and Disability." Pp. 26–54 in Nancy Mandell, ed. *Race, Class and Sexuality*, 2nd ed. Scarborough: Prentice-Hall Allyn and Bacon.

Castells, Manuel. 1983. *The City and the Grassroots: A Cross-Cultural Theory of Urban Social Movements*. Berkeley, CA: University of California Press.

Cavalli-Sforza, L. L., P. Menozzi, and A. Piazza. 1994. *The History and Geography of Human Genes*. Princeton, NJ: Princeton University Press.

CBC. 2001. "Beauty by Design: Cosmetic Surgery in Canada." On the World Wide Web at http://www.cbc.ca/programs/sites/features/hm_cosmeticsurgery/overview.html (July 20, 2002).

CBC News. 2001. "Potter Craze Sweeps Theatres Across Canada." 16 November. On the World Wide Web at http://www.cbc.ca/cgi-bin/templates/view.cgi?/news2001/11/16/potter_0011116.

CBC-Radio Canada. 2001. Annual Report. On the World Wide Web at http://cbc.radio-canada/htmen/6_2_3_4_00.htm (17 May 2002).

CCIC (Canadian Council for International Cooperation). 2002. "Canadian Foreign Aid and the Upcoming 2002/03 Federal Budget: A CCIC Policy Briefing Note." On the World Wide Web at http://www.ccic.ca/devpol/canada_aid/ca40_briefing_note_budget_2002_2003.htm.

CCSA (Canadian Centre on Substance Abuse). 1999. *Canadian Profile 1999: Alcohol, Tobacco and Other Drugs*. Ottawa: Centre on Substance Abuse and Centre for Addiction and Mental Health.

Central Intelligence Agency. 2001. *The World Factbook 2001*. On the World Wide Web at http://www.cia.gov/cia/publications/factbook/ (25 June 2002).

CFS (Canadian Federation of Students). 2001. "Date Rape: No Means No." On the World Wide Web at http://www.cfs-fcee.ca/action/nmn.shtml.

Chambliss, Daniel F. 1996. *Beyond Caring: Hospitals, Nurses, and the Social Organization of Ethics*. Chicago: University of Chicago Press.

Chambliss, William J. 1989. "State-Organized Crime." *Criminology* 27: 183–208.

Chard, Jennifer. 2000. "Women in a Visible Minority." Pp. 219–44 in *Women in Canada, 2000: A Gender-Based Statistical Report*. Ottawa: Statistics Canada.

Charlton, James I. 1998. *Nothing about Us without Us: Disability Oppression and Empowerment*. Berkeley, CA: University of California Press.

Chaves, Mark. 1994. "Secularization as Declining Religious Authority." *Social Forces* 72: 749–74.

Chen, J., E. Ng, and R. Wilkins. 1994. "The Health of Canada's Immigrants in 1994–95." *Health Report* 7, 4 (Spring): 33–45. Statistics Canada Catalogue No. 82-003-XPB.

Chen, Jennifer and Gary Graves. 2001. "Media Ownership in Canada." CBC.CA May/August. On the World Wide Web at http://cbc.ca/news/indepth/background/mediaownership.html (17 May 2002).

Cherlin, Andrew J. 1992 [1981]. *Marriage, Divorce, Remarriage*, revised and enlarged ed. Cambridge, MA: Harvard University Press.

Chesley, L., D. MacAulay, and J. L. Ristock. 1991. *Abuse in Lesbian Relationships: A Handbook of Information and Resources*. Toronto: Counselling Centre for Lesbians and Gays.

Chesnais, Jean-Claude. 1992 [1986]. *The Demographic Transition: Stages, Patterns, and Economic Implications*, Elizabeth Kreager and Philip Kreager, trans. Oxford, UK: Clarendon Press.

"Chinese Canadian Historical Photo Exhibit." On the World Wide Web at http://www.ccnc.ca/toronto/history/pgallery.html (15 March 2001). [Original from Vancouver Public Archive, #939].

"Chinese Community." 2001. On the World Wide Web at http://www.direct.ca/news/cchi/chin02.shtml (15 March 2001).

Chisholm, Patricia. 1996. "The Body Builders: Canadians—Women and Men—Pay the High Price of Beauty." Originally published in *Maclean's* 8 July. On the World Wide Web at http://www.geocities.com/SunsetStrip/stage/2943/surgery.html (July 20, 2002).

Choi, Namkee G. 1992. "Correlates of the Economic Status of Widowed and Divorced Elderly Women." *Journal of Family Issues* 13, 1 (March): 38–54.

"Chronological Perspective on Work Stoppages in Canada." 1999. On the World Wide Web at http://labour.hrdc-drhc.gc.ca/doc/wid-dimt/eng/ws-at/table.cfm (30 June 2001).

"Chronological Perspective on Work Stoppages in Canada." 2001. On the World Wide Web at http://labour.hrdc-drhc.gc.ca/doc/wid-dimt/eng/ws-at/table.cfm (22 March 2001).

"Chronological Perspective on Work Stoppages in Canada (Work Stoppages Involving One or More Workers), 1976–2000." 2001. On the World Wide Web at http://labour-travail.hrdc-drhc.gc.ca/doc/wid-dimt/eng/ws-at/table.cfm (27 March 2001).

Church, Gardner, Kenneth Greenberg, and Marilou McPhedran. 1997. "Toronto: An Urban Alternative." Pp. 93–112 in Robert Geddes, ed. *Cities in Our Future: Growth and Form, Environmental Health and Social Equity*. Washington, DC: Island Press.

Church of God. 2001. On the World Wide Web at http://www.childrentaken.com/mediastatement.html.

Cicourel, Aaron. 1968. *The Social Organization of Juvenile Justice*. New York: Wiley.

Citizenship and Immigration Canada. 1997. *Facts and Figures 1996: Immigration Overview*. Ottawa. On the World Wide Web at http://www.cic.gc.ca/english/pub/facts96/index_e.html (18 April 2001).

———. 2000. "The Vancouver Riot of 1907." On the World Wide Web at http://www.cic.gc.ca/english/about/legacy/chap-3a.html (16 March 2001).

Clairborne, William. 2001. "Canadians from Sect Flee to U.S. over Right to Spank." On the World Wide Web at http://www.nospank.net/n-i27.htm.

Clairmont, Donald H. and Dennis W. Magill. 1999 [1974]. *Africville: The Life and Death of a Canadian Black Community*. Toronto: Canadian Scholars' Press.

Clapp, Jennifer. 1998. "Foreign Direct Investment in Hazardous Industries in Developing Countries: Rethinking the Debate." *Environmental Politics* 7, 4: 92–113.

Clark, S. D. 1968 [1962]. *The Developing Canadian Community*, 2nd ed. Toronto: University of Toronto Press.

Clark, Terry Nichols and Seymour Martin Lipset. 1991. "Are Social Classes Dying?" *International Sociology* 6: 397–410.

Clark, Terry Nichols, Seymour Martin Lipset, and Michael Rempel. 1993. "The Declining Political Significance of Class." *International Sociology* 8: 293–316.

Clark, Warren. 1998. "Religious Observance: Marriage and Family." *Canadian Social Trends* Autumn: 2–7.

———. 2000. "Religious Observance, Marriage and Family." Pp. 109–14 in *Canadian Social Trends: Volume 3*. Toronto: Thompson Educational Publishing, Inc.

Clarke, Harold D., Jane Jenson, Lawrence LeDuc, and Jon H. Pammett. 1996. *Absolute Mandate: Canadian Electoral Politics in an Era of Restructuring*, 3rd ed. Toronto: Gage.

Clarke, Sally. 1995. "Advance Report of Final Divorce Statistics, 1989 and 1990." *Monthly Vital Statistics Report* 43, 9 (Supp., March 22).

Clarke-Stewart, K. Alison, Christian P. Gruber, and Linda May Fitzgerald. 1994. *Children at Home and in Day Care*. Hillsdale, NJ: Lawrence Erlbaum.

Clawson, D. 1980. *Bureaucracy and the Labor Process: The Transformation of U.S. Industry, 1860–1920*. New York: Monthly Review Press.

Clement, W. 1975. *The Canadian Corporate Elite: An Analysis of Economic Power*. Toronto: McClelland & Stewart.

———, ed. 1997. *Understanding Canada: Building on the New Canadian Political Economy*. Montreal: McGill-Queen's University Press.

Clement, W. and J. Myles. 1994. *Relations of Ruling: Class and Gender in Postindustrial Societies*. Montreal and Kingston: McGill-Queen's University Press.

Clement, W. H. P. 1897. *The History of the Dominion of Canada*. Toronto: William Briggs.

Cleveland, Gordon and Michael Krashinsky. 1998. *The Benefits and Costs of Good Child Care: The Economic Rationale for*

*Public Investment in Young Children*. Toronto: University of Toronto.
Clinard, Marshall B. and Peter C. Yeager. 1980. *Corporate Crime*. New York: Free Press.
Cloward, Richard A. and Lloyd E. Ohlin. 1960. *Delinquency and Opportunity: A Theory of Delinquent Gangs*. New York: Free Press.
Coale, Ansley J. 1974. "The History of Human Population." *Scientific American* 23, 3: 41–51.
Coale, Ansley J. and Susan C. Watkins, eds. 1986. *The Decline of Fertility in Europe*. Princeton, NJ: Princeton University Press.
Cobb, Chris. 2002. "Canadian Confused by Left and Right." *National Post Online* 29 April. On the World Wide Web at http://www.nationalpost.com/search/story.html?f=/stories/20020429/63885.html&qs=left%20right (30 April 2002).
Cockerham, William C. 1998. *Medical Sociology*, 7th ed. Upper Saddle River, NJ: Prentice-Hall.
Cohen, Albert. 1955. *Delinquent Boys: The Subculture of a Gang*. New York: Free Press.
Cohen, Lynne. 1999. "Suing the Alternative Health-Care Provider." *Canadian Lawyer* November/December: 47–51.
Cohen, Stanley. 1972. *Folk Devils and Moral Panics: The Creation of the Mods and Rockers*. London: MacGibbon and Kee.
Colapinto, John. 2001. *As Nature Made Him: The Boy Who Was Raised as a Girl*. Toronto: HarperCollins.
Cole, Michael. 1995. *Cultural Psychology*. Cambridge, MA: Harvard University Press.
Cole, S., D. Denny, A. E. Eyler, and S. L. Samons. 2000. "Issues of Transgender." Pp. 149–95 in L. T. Szuchman and F. Mascarella, eds. *Psychological Perspectives on Human Sexuality*. New York: John Wiley & Sons.
Coleman, J. 1988. "Social Capital in the Creation of Human Capital." *American Journal of Sociology* 94: 95–120.
Coleman, James S. 1961. *The Adolescent Society*. New York: Free Press.
———. 1990. *Foundations of Social Theory*. Cambridge, MA: Harvard University Press.
Coleman, James, et al. 1966. *Equality of Educational Opportunity*. Washington, DC: United States Department of Health, Education, and Welfare, Office of Education.
Collins, Randall. 1975. *Conflict Sociology: Toward an Explanatory Science*. New York: Academic Press.
———. 1979. *The Credential Society: An Historical Sociology of Education*. New York: Academic Press.
———. 1982. *Sociological Insight: An Introduction to Nonobvious Sociology*. New York: Oxford University Press.
Collins, Randall and Scott Coltrane. 1991 [1985]. *Sociology of Marriage and the Family: Gender, Love, and Property*, 3rd ed. Chicago: Nelson-Hall.
———. 1995. *Sociology of Marriage and the Family*. Chicago: Nelson-Hall.
Commins, Patricia. 1997. "Foreign Sales Prop Up McDonald's." *Globe and Mail* 26 August: B8.
Compas. 1998. "Foreign Aid-Division over Money, Unity Over Principle." On the World Wide Web at http://www.compas.ca/html/archives/foreignaid>surv.htm.
Competition Bureau. 2002. Comments of the Commissioner of Competition to the Standing Committee on Canadian Heritage on the Study of the State of the Canadian Broadcasting System. Ottawa: Government of Canada. On the World Wide Web at http://strategis.ic.gc.ca/pics/ct/writtensubmission.pdf (19 May 2002).
Comte, Auguste. 1975. *Auguste Comte: The Foundation of Sociology*, Kenneth Thompson, ed. New York: Wiley.
Condry, J. and S. Condry. 1976. "Sex Differences: The Eye of the Beholder." *Child Development* 47: 812–19.
Conrad, Peter and Joseph W. Schneider. 1992 [1980]. *Deviance and Medicalization: From Badness to Sickness*, expanded ed. Philadelphia: Temple University Press.
Converse, J. M. and S. Presser. 1986. *Survey Questions: Handcrafting the Standardized Questionnaire*. Newbury Park, CA: Sage.
Conwell, Chic. 1937. *The Professional Thief: By A Professional Thief*, annotated and interpreted by Edwin H. Sutherland. Chicago: University of Chicago Press.
Cooley, Charles Horton. 1902. *Human Nature and the Social Order*. New York: Scribner's.
Coontz, Stephanie. 1992. *The Way We Never Were: American Families and the Nostalgia Trap*. New York: Basic Books.
Coontz, Stephanie and Peta Henderson. 1986. *Women's Work, Men's Property: The Origins of Gender and Class*. London, UK: Verso.
Couch, Carl J. 1968. "Collective Behavior: An Examination of Some Stereotypes." *Social Problems* 15: 310–22.
Council for Canadian Unity. 1999. "Canada's Nobel Prize Winners." On the World Wide Web at http://www.ccu-cuc.ca/en/library/nobel.html (7 October 2000).
Coupland, Douglas. 1991. *Generation X: Tales for an Accelerated Culture*. New York: St. Martin's Press.
Cox, Wendell. 1997. "Local and Regional Governance in the Greater Toronto Area: A Review of Alternatives." On the World Wide Web at http://www.publicpurpose.com/tor-demo.htm.
Creedon, Jeremiah. 1998. "God with a Million Faces." *Utne Reader* July–August: 42–8.
Creese, G. 1999. *Contracting Masculinity: Gender, Class, and Race in a White-Collar Union, 1944–1994*. Don Mills, ON: Oxford University Press Canada.
Creese, G. and B. Began. 1999. "Gender at Work: Seeking Solutions for Women's Equality." Pp.199–211 in J. Curtis, E. Grabb, and N. Guppy, eds. *Social Inequality in Canada*, 3rd ed. Toronto: Prentice-Hall.
Creighton, Sarah and Catherine Mihto. 2001. "Managing Intersex." *BMJ: British Medical Journal* 323, 7324 (December): 1264–5.
Crick, N. 1997. "Engagement in Gender Normative versus Nonnormative Forms of Aggression: Links to Social-psychological Adjustment." *Developmental Psychology* 33: 610–7.
Crompton, Susan, Jonathan Ellison, and Kathryn Stevenson. 2002. "Better Things to Do or Dealt out of the Game? Internet Dropouts and Infrequent Users." *Canadian Social Trends* Summer: 2–5.
Crompton, Susan and Michael Vickers. 2000. "One Hundred Years of Labour Force." *Canadian Social Trends* Summer: 2–6.
Croteau, David and William Hoynes. 1997. *Media/Society: Industries, Images, and Audiences*. Thousand Oaks, CA: Pine Forge Press.

Crothers, Charles. 1979. "On the Myth of Rural Tranquility: Comment on Webb and Collette." *American Journal of Sociology* 84: 429–37.

Crozier, Michel. 1964 [1963]. *The Bureaucratic Phenomenon*. Chicago: University of Chicago Press.

CRTC. 1990. *The Portrayal of Gender in Canadian Broadcasting: Summary Report*. Ottawa: Supply and Services Canada.

"The CRTC's Mandate." 2002. On the World Wide Web at http://www.crtc.gc.ca/eng/BACKGRND/Brochures/B29903.htm.

Cruikshank, J. 1997. "Negotiating with Narrative: Establishing Cultural Identity at the Yukon International Storytelling Festival." *American Anthropologist* 99: 55–69.

Cummins, Jim. 1994. "Lies We Live By: National Identity and Social Justice." *International Journal of the Sociology of Language* 110: 145–54.

Curran, John. 2000. "Thinner Miss Americas: Study: Some Contestants Undernourished." ABCNEWS.com. On the Internet at wysiwyg://7/http://abcnews.go.com/sections/living/DailyNews/missamerica000322.htmk.

Curtis, Bruce. 1988. *Building the Educational State: Canada West, 1836–1871*. London, ON: Althouse Press.

———. 2001. *The Politics of Population: State Formation, Statistics, and the Census of Canada, 1840-1875*. Toronto: University of Toronto Press.

Curtis, James, Edward Grabb, and Neil Guppy, eds. 1999. *Social Inequality in Canada: Patterns, Problems and Policies*. Scarborough, ON: Prentice Hall Allyn and Bacon Canada Inc.

Curtis, James, John Loy, and Wally Karnilowicz. 1986. "A Comparison of Suicide-Dip Effects of Major Sport Events and Civil Holidays." *Sociology of Sport Journal* 3: 1–14.

Curtis, James E. and Ronald D. Lambert. 1994. "Ideology and Social Change." Pp. 710–58 in Lorne Tepperman, James E. Curtis, and R. Jack Richardson, eds. *The Social World*, 3rd ed. Toronto: McGraw-Hill.

CyberPress. 2001. "The Recidivist Roger Caron Stopped Once Again" (translated from the French), 14 October. On the World Wide Web at http://216.239.37.120/transl.

Dahl, Robert A. 1961. *Who Governs?* New Haven, CT: Yale University Press.

Dalphonse, Sherri. 1997. "Childfree by Choice." *The Washingtonian* 32, 5: 48–57.

Darwin, Charles. 1859. *On the Origin of Species by Means of Natural Selection*. London: John Murray.

———. 1871. *The Descent of Man*. London: John Murray.

Davies, J. B. 1999. "Distribution of Wealth and Economic Inequality." Pp. 138–50 in J. Curtis, E. Grabb, and N. Guppy, eds. *Social Inequality in Canada: Patterns, Problems, Policies*, 3rd ed. Scarborough, ON: Prentice Hall Allyn and Bacon Canada.

Davies, James C. 1969. "Toward a Theory of Revolution." Pp. 85–108 in Barry McLaughlin, ed. *Studies in Social Movements: A Social Psychological Perspective*. New York: Free Press.

Davies, Mark, and Denise B. Kandel. 1981. "Parental and Peer Influences on Adolescents' Educational Plans: Some Further Evidence." *American Journal of Sociology* 87: 363–87.

Davies, S. 2003. "Stubborn Disparities: Explaining Class Inequalities in Schooling." In J. Curtis, E. Grabb, and N. Guppy, eds. *Social Inequality in Canada: Patterns, Problems, Policies*, 4th ed. Scarborough, ON: Prentice Hall Allyn and Bacon Canada.

Davis, Jim. 2000. "AOL Previews TV Plans." *CNET News* 6 January. On the World Wide Web at http://news.cnet.com/category/0-1006-200-1516271.html (2 May 2000).

Davis, K. and W. E. Moore. 1945. "Some Principles of Stratification." *American Sociological Review* 10: 242–9.

Dawidowicz, Lucy S. 1975. *The War Against the Jews, 1933–1945*. New York: Holt, Rinehart and Winston.

Dawson, Lorne. 1993. "Religion and Legitimacy." Pp. 311–27 in Peter S. Li and B. Singh Bolaria, eds. *Contemporary Sociology: Critical Perspectives*. Toronto: Copp Clark Pitman.

Deaux, Kay. 1999. "An Overview of Research on Gender: Four Themes from 3 Decades." Pp. 11–34 in William B. Swann, Jr., Judith H. Langlis, and Lucia Albino Gilbert, eds. *Sexism and Stereotypes in Modern Society: The Gender Science of Janet Taylor Spence*. Washington, DC: American Psychological Association.

"Defining a Common Language." n.d. Ramapo College, New Jersey, NYU Safe Zone Program Workshop. On the World Wide Web at http://www.content/student.resources/gayPeer/terminology.htm (25 July 2002).

DeKeseredy, Walter S. and Katherine Kelly. 1993. "The Incidence and Prevalence of Woman Abuse in Canadian University and College Dating Relationships." *Canadian Journal of Sociology* 18: 137–59.

Demo, David H. and Alan C. Acock. 1993. "Family Diversity and the Division of Domestic Labor: How Much Have Things Really Changed?" *Family Relations* 42: 323–31.

Denzin, Norman K. 1992. *Symbolic Interactionism and Cultural Studies: The Politics of Interpretation*. Oxford, UK: Blackwell.

Department of Geography, Slippery Rock University. 1997. "World's Largest Cities, 1900." On the World Wide Web at http://www.sru.edu/depts/artsci/ges/discover/d-6-8.htm (2 May 2000).

———. 1998. "World's Largest Urban Agglomerations, 2015." On the World Wide Web at http://www.sru.edu/depts/artsci/ges/discover/d-6-9b.htm (2 May 2000).

Department of Justice, Canada. 1995. "A Review of Firearm Statistics and Regulations in Selected Countries." On the World Wide Web at http://www.cfc-ccaf.gc.ca/research/publications/reports/1990%2D95/reports/siter_rpt_en.html (29 April 2000).

Derber, Charles. 1979. *The Pursuit of Attention: Power and Individualism in Everyday Life*. New York: Oxford University Press.

deSouza, Paul. 2002. "Youth Court Statistics, 2000/01." *Juristat* 22, 3 (March). Catalogue no. 85-002-XPE.

DeSteno, David and Peter Salovey. 2001. "Evolutionary Origins of Sex Differences in Jealousy: Questioning the 'Fitness' of the Model." Pp. 150–6 in W. Gerrod Parrott, ed. *Emotions in Social Psychology: Essential Readings*. Philadelphia: Psychology Press.

de Villiers, Marq. 1999. *Water*. Toronto: Stoddart Publishing.

de Waal, Alexander. 1989. *Famine That Kills: Darfur, Sudan, 1984–1985*. Oxford, UK: Clarendon Press.

DHHS (Department of Health and Human Services). 1998. "Statement of Jeanette Takamura." U.S. Department of Health and Human Services, Administration on Aging. 8 June. On the

World Wide Web at
http://www.aoa.dhhs.gov/pr/graying.html.

Diamond, Larry. 1996. "Is the Third Wave Over?" *Journal of Democracy* 7, 3: 20–37. On the World Wide Web at http://muse.jhu.edu/demo/jod/7.3diamond.html (1 May 2000).

Diamond, Milton. 1982. "Sexual Identity: Monozygotic Twins Reared in Discordant Sex Roles and a BBC Follow-up." *Archives of Sexual Behavior* 11: 181–6.

Diamond, Milton and H. Keith Sigmundson. 1999. "Sex Reassignment at Birth." Pp. 55–75 in Stephen J. Ceci and Wendy W. Williams, eds. *The Nature–Nurture Debate: The Essential Readings*. Maldan, MA: Blackwell.

Diani, Mario. 1996. "Linking Mobilization Frames and Political Opportunities: Insights from Regional Populism in Italy." *American Sociological Review* 61: 1053–69.

Dibbell, Julian. 1993. "A Rape in Cyberspace." *The Village Voice* 21 December: 36–42. On the World Wide Web at http://www.levity.com/julian/bungle.html (29 April 2000).

Dickens, Charles. *A Tale of Two Cities*. 2002 [1859]. On the World Wide Web at http://www.literature.org/authors/dickens-charles/two-cities/ (4 July).

Dickinson, Paul and Jonathan Ellison. 1999. *Getting Connected or Staying Unplugged: The Growing Use of Computer Communications Services*. Ottawa: Minister of Industry.

Dietz, Tracy L. 1998. "An Examination of Violence and Gender Role Portrayals in Video Games: Implications for Gender Socialization and Aggressive Behavior." *Sex Roles* 38: 425–42.

Dines, Gail and Jean McMahon Humez. 1995. *Gender, Race, and Class in Media: A Text-Reader*. Thousand Oaks, CA: Sage.

Doberman, J. 1997. *Darwin's Athletes: How Sport Has Damaged Black America and Preserved the Myth of Race*. Boston: Houghton Mifflin.

Doell, R. G. 1995. "Sexuality in the Brain." *Journal of Homosexuality* 29:345–56.

Doherty, G. 1997. *Zero to Six: The Basis for School Readiness*. Ottawa: Applied Research Branch, Human Resources Development Canada (#R-97-8E).

Donahue III, John J. and Steven D. Levitt. 2001. "The Impact of Legalized Abortion on Crime." *Quarterly Journal of Economics* 116: 379–420.

Doremus, P. N., W. W. Keller, L. W. Pauly, and S. Reich. 1998. *The Myth of the Global Corporation*. Princeton, NJ: Princeton University Press.

Douglas, Jack D. 1967. *The Social Meanings of Suicide*. Princeton, NJ: Princeton University Press.

Douglas, Susan J. 1994. *Where the Girls Are: Growing Up Female with the Mass Media*. New York: Random House.

Dowling, Michael, Christian Lechner, and Bodo Thielmann. 1998. "Convergence—Innovation and Change of Market Structures Between Television and Online Services." *Electronic Marketing* 8, 4. On the World Wide Web at http://www.electronicmarkets.com/netacademy/publications.nsf/all_pk/1124 (2 May 2000).

Doyle, Aaron, Brian Elliott, and David Tindall. 1997 [1992]. "Framing the Forests: Corporations, the B.C. Forest Alliance, and the Media." Pp. 240–68 in William Carroll, ed. *Organizing Dissent: Contemporary Social Movements in Theory and Practice*, 2nd ed. Toronto: Garamond Press.

Dranoff, Linda Silver. 2001. *Everyone's Guide to the Law*. Toronto: HarperCollins.

Drèze, Jean and Amartya Sen. 1989. *Hunger and Public Action*. Oxford, UK: Clarendon Press.

Drucker, P. 1993. *Post Capitalist Society*. New York: HarperBusiness.

Duffy, A., D. Glenday, and N. Pupo, eds. 1997. *Good Jobs, Bad Jobs, No Jobs: The Transformation of Work in the 21st Century*. Toronto: Harcourt Brace.

Duffy, Jim, Georg Gunther, and Lloyd Walters. 1997. "Gender and Mathematical Problem Solving." *Sex Roles* 37: 477–94.

Dugger, Karen. 1996. "Social Location and Gender-Role Attitudes: A Comparison of Black and White Women." Pp. 32–51 in Esther Ngan-Ling Chow, Doris Wilkinson, and Maxine Baca Zinn, eds. *Race, Class, and Gender*. Newbury Park, CA: Sage.

Duhaime, Lloyd. 1997. "Euthanasia in Canada." On the Internet at wysiwyg://17/http://www.duhaime.org/ca~euth.htm.

Duncan, Greg, W. Jean Yeung, Jeanne Brooks-Gunn, and Judith Smith. 1998. "How Much Does Childhood Poverty Affect the Life Chance of Children?" *American Sociological Review* 63: 402–23.

Dunk, T. 1991. *It's a Working Man's Town: Male Working Class Culture in Northwestern Ontario*. Montreal: McGill-Queens University Press.

Durham, William H. 1979. *Scarcity and Survival in Central America: Ecological Origins of the Soccer War*. Stanford, CA: Stanford University Press.

Durkheim, Émile. 1951 [1897]. *Suicide: A Study in Sociology*, G. Simpson, ed., J. Spaulding and G. Simpson, trans. New York: Free Press.

———. 1956. *Education and Sociology*, Sherwood D. Fox, trans. New York: Free Press.

———. 1961 [1925]. *Moral Education: A Study in the Theory and Application of the Sociology of Education,* Everett K. Wilson and Herman Schnurer, trans. New York: Free Press.

———. 1973 [1899–1900]. "Two Laws of Penal Evolution." *Economy and Society* 2: 285–308.

———. 1976 [1915]. *The Elementary Forms of the Religious Life*, Joseph Ward Swain, trans. New York: Free Press.

Dutton, Judy. 2000. "Detect His Lies Every Time." *Cosmopolitan* April: 126.

Eagles, Munroe. 1993. "Money and Votes in Canada: Campaign Spending and Parliamentary Election Outcomes, 1984 and 1988." *Canadian Public Policy* 19: 432–49.

Eagley, Alice H. and Wendy Wood. 1999. "The Origins of Sex Differences in Human Behaviour: Evolved Dispositions versus Social Roles." *American Psychologist* 54: 408–23.

Earl, Louise. 1999. *Entertainment Services: A Growing Consumer Market*. Ottawa: Statistics Canada. Catalogue no. 63-016-XPB.

Ebert, Roger. 1998. "Patch Adams." *Chicago Sun-Times*. On the World Wide Web at http://www.suntimes.com/ebert/ebert_reviews/1998/12/122504.html (2 May 2000).

Eccles, J. S., J. E. Jacobs, and R. D. Harold. 1990. "Gender Role Stereotypes, Expectancy Effects and Parents' Socialization of Gender Differences." *Journal of Social Issues* 46: 183–201.

Eccles, Jacquelynne S., Robert Roeser, Allan Wigfield, and Carol Freedman-Doen. 1999. "Academic and Motivational Pathways Through Middle Childhood." Pp. 287–377 in Lawrence Balter, ed. *Child Psychology*. Philadelphia: Psychology Press.

Economakis, Evel and Robert J. Brym. 1995. "Marriage and Militance in a Working Class District of St. Petersburg, 1896–1913." *Journal of Family History* 20: 23–43.

Edel, Abraham. 1965. "Social Science and Value: A Study in Interrelations." Pp. 218–38 in Irving Louis Horowitz, ed. *The*

*New Sociology: Essays in Social Science and Social Theory in Honor of C. Wright Mills*. New York: Oxford University Press.

EGALE. 2001. "Svend Robinson Introduces Bill, EGALE Renews Call for Hate Crimes Protection in Wake of Murder of Gay Man in Vancouver." Press release, 22 November. On the World Wide Web at http://www.egale.ca/pressrel/011122.htm.

e.Harlequin.com. 2000. "About eHarlequin.com." On the World Wide Web at http://eharlequin.women.com/harl/globals/about/00bkrd11.htm (17 May 2000).

Ehrlich, Paul R. 1968. *The Population Bomb*. New York: Ballantine.

Ehrlich, Paul R. and Anne H. Ehrlich. 1990. *The Population Explosion*. New York: Simon & Schuster.

Ehrlich, Paul R., Gretchen C. Daily, Scott C. Daily, Norman Myers, and James Salzman. 1997. "No Middle Way on the Environment." *Atlantic Monthly* 280, 6: 98–104. On the World Wide Web at http://www.theatlantic.com/issues/97dec/enviro.htm (8 October 2000).

Eichler, Margrit. 1987. *Nonsexist Research Methods*. Boston: Allen & Unwin.

———. 1988. *Nonsexist Research Methods: A Practical Guide*. Boston: Unwin Hyman.

——— .1988 [1983]. *Families in Canada Today*, 2nd ed. Toronto: Gage.

Eisenstadt, S. N. 1956. *From Generation to Generation*. New York: Free Press.

Eisler, Riane. 1995 [1987]. *The Chalice and the Blade: Our History, Our Future*. New York: HarperCollins.

Ekman, Paul. 1978. *Facial Action Coding System*. New York: Consulting Psychologists Press.

Elias, Norbert. 1985 [1982]. *The Loneliness of the Dying*, Edmund Jephcott, trans. Oxford, UK: Blackwell.

——— . 1994 [1939]. *The Civilizing Process*, Edmund Jephcott, trans. Cambridge, MA: Blackwell.

Elliott, H. L. 1995. "Living Vicariously Through Barbie." On the World Wide Web at http://ziris.syr.edu/path/public_html/barbie/main.html (19 November 1998).

Ellis, Brett Easton. 1991. *American Psycho*. New York: Vintage.

Ellis, Erin Brockovich. 2002. "The Power of One." On the World Wide Web at http://www.cincinnati.com/uniquelives/brockovich.html (30 June 2002).

Ellul, Jacques. 1964 [1954]. *The Technological Society*, John Wilkinson, trans. New York: Vintage.

Engels, Frederick. 1970 [1884]. *The Origins of the Family, Private Property and the State*, Eleanor Burke Leacock, ed., Alec West, trans. New York: International Publishers.

England, Paula. 1992. *Comparable Worth: Theories and Evidence*. Hawthorne, NY: Aldine de Gruyter.

Entine, J. 2000. *Taboo: Why Black Athletes Dominate Sports and Why We Are Afraid to Talk about It*. New York: Public Affairs.

Environics Research Group. 1999. *The Focus Canada Report* (March). Toronto.

Environment Canada. 1997. "Climate Change." On the World Wide Web at http://www.ec.gc.ca/science/eframe_b.htm (8 October 2000).

Epstein, Helen. 1998. "Life and Death on the Social Ladder." *New York Review of Books* 45, 12 (16 July): 26–30.

Epstein, Steven. 1996. *Impure Science: AIDS, Activism, and the Politics of Knowledge*. Berkeley, CA: University of California Press.

Erwin, J. 1988. "R.E.A.L. Women, Anti-Feminism, and the Welfare State." *Resources for Feminist Research* 17, 3 (September): 147–9.

Esping-Andersen, Gøsta. 1990. *The Three Worlds of Welfare Capitalism*. Princeton, NJ: Princeton University Press.

Estrich, Susan. 1987. *Real Rape*. Cambridge, MA: Harvard University Press.

Etcoff, Nancy. 1999. *Survival of the Prettiest: The Science of Beauty*. New York: Anchor Books.

Etzioni, Amitai. 1975. *A Comparative Analysis of Complex Organizations*, 2nd ed. New York: Free Press.

Evans, Peter B., Dietrich Rueschemeyer, and Theda Skocpol. 1985. *Bringing the State Back In*. Cambridge, UK: Cambridge University Press.

Evans, Robert G. 1999. "Social Inequalities in Health." *Horizons* (Policy Research Secretariat, Government of Canada) 2, 3: 6–7.

Everitt, J. 1998. "Public Opinion and Social Movements: The Women's Movement and the Gender Gap in Canada." *Canadian Journal of Political Science* 31: 743–65.

Ewen, Stuart. 1997. *PR! A Social History of Spin*. New York: Basic.

"Face of the Web Study Pegs Global Internet Population at More than 300 Million." 2000. On the World Wide Web at http://www.angusreid.com/media/content/displaypr.cfm?id_to_view=1001 (2 October 2000).

FAD (Families Against Deadbeats). 2000. On the World Wide Web at http://www.wantedposters.com.

Fagot, Berly I., Caire S. Rodgers, and Mary D. Leinbach. 2000. "Theories of Gender Socialization." Pp. 65–89 in Thomas Eckes, ed. *The Developmental Social Psychology of Gender*. Mahwah, NJ: Lawrence Erlbaum Associates.

*Fall Colors II: Exploring the Quality of Diverse Portrayals on Prime Time Television*. 2000. Oakland, CA: Children Now. On the World Wide Web at http://www.childrennow.org/media/fall-colors-2k/fc2-2k.pdf (5 August 2000).

Farmer, Paul. 1992. *AIDS and Accusation: Haiti and the Geography of Blame*. Berkeley, CA: University of California Press.

Farrell, Colin. n.d. "The Canadian Prison Strap." On the World Wide Web at http://www.corpun.com/canada2.html.

Fass, Paula S. 1989. *Outside In: Minorities and the Transformation of American Education*. New York: Oxford University Press.

Fattah, Ezzat A. 1991. *Understanding Criminal Victimization: An Introduction to Theoretical Victimology*. Scarborough, ON: Prentice Hall.

Faulkner, Anne H. and Kevin Cranston. 1998. "Correlates of Same-Sex Sexual Behavior in a Random Sample of Massachusetts High School Students." *Journal of Public Health* 88, February: 262–6.

Fava, Sylvia Fleis. 1956. "Suburbanism as a Way of Life." *American Sociological Review* 21: 34–7.

Fawcett, Diane. 1999. "Disability in the Labour Market: Barriers and Solutions." *Perception* 23, 3 (December). On the World Wide Web at http://www.ccsd.ca/perception/233/disab.htm.

Fearon, E. R. 1997. "Human Cancer Syndrome: Clues to the Origin and Nature of Cancer." *Science* 278: 1043–50.

Febvre, Lucien and Henri-Jean Martin. 1976 [1958]. *The Coming of the Book: The Impact of Printing 1450–1800*, David Gerard, trans. London: NLB.

"The Federal Election." 2000. On the World Wide Web at http://www.cbc.ca/ (28 November 2001).

Fedorowycz, Orest. 1999. "Homicide in Canada, 1998." *Juristat* 19, 10 (October). Canadian Centre for Justice Statistics. Cat. 85-002-XIE.

Feeley, Malcolm M. and Jonathan Simon. 1992. "The New Penology: Notes on the Emerging Strategy of Corrections and its Implications." *Criminology* 30: 449–74.

Fein, Helen. 1979. *Accounting for Genocide: National Responses and Jewish Victimization During the Holocaust*. New York: Free Press.

Fekete, John. 1994. *Moral Panics: Biopolitics Rising*. Toronto: Robert Davies.

Fellegi, I. 2000. "On Poverty and Low Income." In Statistics Canada. *Income in Canada 1998*. Ottawa: Ministry of Industry.

Felson, Richard B. 1996. "Mass Media Effects on Violent Behavior." *Annual Review of Sociology* 22: 103–28.

Fernandez-Dols, Jose-Miguel, Flor Sanchez, Pilar Carrera, and Maria-Angeles Ruiz-Belda. 1997. "Are Spontaneous Expressions and Emotions Linked? An Experimental Test of Coherence." *Journal of Nonverbal Behavior* 21: 163–77.

Fields, Jason and Kristin Smith. 1998. "Poverty, Family Structure, and Child Well-Being." Population Division. Washington, DC: U.S. Bureau of Census.

Figart, Deborah M. and June Lapidus. 1996. "The Impact of Comparable Worth on Earnings Inequality." *Work and Occupations* 23: 297–318.

Fineran, Susan. 2002. "Sexual Harassment Between Same-Sex Peers: Intersection of Mental Health, Homophobia, and Sexual Violence in Schools." *Social Work* 47, 1 (January): 65–74.

Finke, Roger, and Rodney Starke. 1992. *The Churching of America, 1776–1990: Winners and Losers in Our Religious Economy*. New Brunswick, NJ: Rutgers University Press.

Finnie, Ross. 1993. "Women, Men and the Economic Consequences of Divorce: Evidence from Canadian Longitudinal Data." *Canadian Review of Sociology and Anthropology* 30, 2: 205–41.

Firebaugh, Glenn and Frank D. Beck. 1994. "Does Economic Growth Benefit the Masses? Growth, Dependence and Welfare in the Third World." *American Journal of Sociology* 59: 631–53.

Fischer, Claude S. 1981. "The Public and Private Worlds of City Life." *American Sociological Review* 46: 306–16.

———. 1984 [1976]. *The Urban Experience*, 2nd ed. New York: Harcourt Brace Jovanovich.

Fischer, Claude S., Michael Hout, Martín Sánchez Jankowski, Samuel R. Lucas, Ann Swidler, and Kim Voss. 1996. *Inequality by Design: Cracking the Bell Curve Myth*. Princeton, NJ: Princeton University Press.

Fisher, John. 1999. *A Report on Lesbian, Gay and Bisexual Youth*. Ottawa: EGALE.

Flowers, Paul and Katie Buston. 2001. "'I Was Terrified of Being Different': Exploring Gay Men's Accounts of Growing-Up in a Heterosexist Society." *Journal of Adolescence, Special Issue: Gay, Lesbian, and Bisexual Youth* 24, 1 (February): 51–65.

Fludd, Robert. 1617–19. *Utriusque Cosmi Maioris Scilicet et Minoris Metaphysica, Physica Atqve Technica Historia*. Oppenheim, Germany: Johan-Theodori de Bry.

Folbre, Nancy. 1995. *The New Field Guide to the U.S. Economy: A Compact and Irreverent Guide to Economic Life in America*. New York: New Press.

Fong, E. and E. Ooka. (forthcoming). "The Social Consequences of Participating in Ethnic Economy." *International Migration Review*.

Förster, M., and M. Pellizzari. 2000. *Trends and Driving Factors in Income Distribution and Poverty in the OECD Area*. Labour Market and Social Policy Occasional Papers No. 42. Paris: OECD.

Foucault, Michel. 1977 [1975]. *Discipline and Punish: The Birth of the Prison*, Alan Sheridan, trans. New York: Pantheon.

Francis, D. 1992. *The Imaginary Indian: The Image of the Indian in Canadian Culture*. Vancouver, BC: Arsenal Pulp Press.

Frank, André Gundar. 1967. *Capitalism and Underdevelopment in Latin America: Historical Studies of Chile and Brazil*. New York: Monthly Review Press.

Frank, Jeffrey. 1992. "Voting and Contributing: Political Participation in Canada." *Canadian Social Trends* 27: 2–6.

Frank, Robert H. 1988. *Passions within Reason: The Strategic Role of the Emotions*. New York: Norton.

Frank, Thomas and Matt Weiland, eds. 1997. *Commodify Your Dissent: Salvos from the Baffler*. New York: W. W. Norton.

Frank Porter Graham Child Development Center. 1999. "Early Learning, Later Success: The Abecedarian Study." On the World Wide Web at http://www.fpg.unc.edu/~abc/abcedarianWeb/index.htm (10 August 2000).

Franke, Richard H. and James D. Kaul. 1978. "The Hawthorne Experiments: First Statistical Interpretation." *American Sociological Review* 43: 623–43.

Franke, Richard W. and Barbara H. Chasin. 1992. *Kerala: Development Through Radical Reform*. San Francisco: Institute for Food and Development Policy.

Franklin, Karen. 1998. "Psychosocial Motivations of Hate Crime Perpetrators." Paper presented at the annual meetings of the American Psychological Association (San Francisco: 16 August).

Franklin, Sara and Helen Ragone, eds. 1999. *Reproducing Reproduction*. Philadelphia: University of Pennsylvania Press.

Freidson, Eliot. 1986. *Professional Powers: A Study of the Institutionalization of Formal Knowledge*. Chicago: University of Chicago Press.

Freire, Paolo. 1972. *The Pedagogy of the Oppressed*. New York: Herder and Herder.

French, Marilyn. 1992. The War Against Women. New York: Ballantine Books.

Freud, Sigmund. 1962 [1930]. *Civilization and Its Discontents*, James Strachey, trans. New York: W. W. Norton.

———. 1973 [1915–17]. *Introductory Lectures on Psychoanalysis*, James Strachey, trans., James Strachey and Angela Richards, eds. Harmondsworth, UK: Penguin.

———. 1977 [1905]. *On Sexuality*, James Strachey, trans., Angela Richards, comp. and ed. Harmondsworth, UK: Penguin.

Freudenburg, William R. 1997. "Contamination, Corrosion and the Social Order: An Overview." *Current Sociology* 45, 3: 19–39.

Fried, Martha Nemes and Morton H. Fried. 1980. *Transitions: Four Rituals in Eight Cultures*. New York: W. W. Norton.

Friedenberg, Edgar Z. 1959. *The Vanishing Adolescent*. Boston: Beacon Press.

Froissart, Jean. 1968 [c. 1365]. *Chronicles*, selected and translated by Geoffrey Brereton. Harmondsworth, UK: Penguin.

Fullan, Michael. 1998. "Leadership for the 21st Century: Breaking the Bonds of Dependency." *Educational Leadership* 55, 7. On the World Wide Web at http://ascd.org/readingroom/edlead/9804/full.html.

———. 2001 (1982). *The New Meaning of Educational Change*, 3rd ed. New York: Teachers College Press.

Gabor, Thomas. 1994. *Everybody Does It: Crime by the Public*. Toronto: University of Toronto Press.

Gaines, Donna. 1990. *Teenage Wasteland: Suburbia's Dead End Kids*. New York: Pantheon.

Gallup Organization. 2000. "Gallup Poll Topics: A-Z." On the World Wide Web at http://www.gallup.com/poll/indicators/indhomosexual.asp (25 July 2002).

Galper, Joseph. 1998. "Schooling for Society." *American Demographics* 20, 3: 33–4.

Galt, Virginia. 1999. "Jack Falling behind Jill in School, Especially in Reading." *Globe and Mail* 30 October: A10.

Gambetta, Diego, ed. 1988. *Trust: Making and Breaking Cooperative Relations*. Oxford, UK: Blackwell.

Gamson, William A. 1975. *The Strategy of Social Protest*. Homewood, IL: Dorsey Press.

——— Bruce Fireman, and Steven Rytina. 1982. *Encounters with Unjust Authority*. Homewood, IL: Dorsey Press.

Gannon, Maire. 2001. "Crime Comparisons Between Canada and the United States." *Juristat* 21, 11 (December). Catalogue no. 85-002-XPE.

Gans, Herbert. 1962. *The Urban Villagers: Group and Class in the Life of Italian-Americans*. New York: Free Press.

———. 1979. *Deciding What's News: A Study of CBS Evening News, NBC Nightly News, Newsweek and Time*. New York: Pantheon.

———. 1991. "Symbolic Ethnicity: The Future of Ethnic Groups and Cultures in America." Pp. 430–43 in Norman R. Yetman, ed. *Majority and Minority: The Dynamics of Race and Ethnicity in American Life*, 5th ed. Boston, MA: Allyn and Bacon.

Gap.com. "Gap." 1999. On the World Wide Web at http://www.gap.com/onlinestore/gap/advertising/khakitv.asp (28 April 2000).

"Garciaparra Explains His Superstitions." 2000. On the World Wide Web at http://www.geocities.com/ Colosseum/Track4242/nomar3.wav (28 April 2000).

Garfinkel, Harold. 1967. *Studies in Ethnomethodology*. Englewood Cliffs, NJ: Prentice-Hall.

Garfinkel, Simson. 2000. *Database Nation: The Death of Privacy in the 21st Century*. Cambridge, MA: O'Reilly and Associates.

Garkawe, Sam. 1995. "The Impact of the Doctrine of Cultural Relativism on the Australian Legal System." *E Law* 2, 1. On the World Wide Web at http://www.murdoch.edu.au/elaw/issues/v2n1/garkawe.txt (10 May 2000).

Garland, David. 1990. *Punishment and Modern Society: A Study in Social Theory*. Chicago: University of Chicago Press.

Garner, David M. 1997. "The 1997 Body Image Survey Results." *Psychology Today* 30, 1: 30–44.

Garrau, Joel. 1991. *Edge City: Life on the New Frontier*. New York: Doubleday.

Garvey, Christine Ann. 1999. "The Intergenerational Transmission of Discipline." *Dissertation Abstracts International, Section A: The Sciences and Engineering* 60, 3-B (September): 1027.

Gaskell, Jane, Arlene McLaren, and Myra Novogrodsky. 1995. "What's Worth Knowing? Defining the Feminist Curriculum." Pp. 100–18 in E. D. Nelson and B. W. Robinson, eds. *Gender in the 1990s: Images, Realities, and Issues*. Scarborough: Nelson Canada.

Gates, W. with N. Myhrvold and P. Rinearson. 1996. *The Road Ahead*. New York: Penguin.

Gauvain, Mary, Beverly I. Fagot, Craig Leve, and Kate Kavanagh. 2002. "Instruction by Mothers and Fathers During Problem Solving with Their Young Children." *Journal of Family Psychology* 6, 1 (March): 81–90.

Geddes, Robert, ed. 1997. *Cities in Our Future: Growth and Form, Environmental Health and Social Equity*. Washington, DC: Island Press.

Gegax, T. Trent and Lynette Clemetson. 1998. "The Abortion Wars Come Home." *Newsweek* 9 November: 34–35.

Gelbspan, Ross. 1997. *The Heat Is On: The High Stakes Battle over Earth's Threatened Climate*. Reading, MA: Addison-Wesley.

———. 1999. "Trading Away Our Chances to End Global Warming." *Boston Globe* 16 May: E2.

Gelles, Richard J. 1994. "Ten Risk Factors." *Newsweek* 4 July: 29.

———. 1997. *Intimate Violence in Families*, 3rd ed. Thousand Oaks, CA: Sage.

Gellner, E. 1988. *Plough, Sword and Book: The Structure of Human History*. Chicago: University of Chicago Press.

George, Jane. 1998. "Kuujjuaq Daycare Thrives on Federal Head Start Program." Nunatsiaq News 29 October. On the World Wide Web at http://www.nunatsiaq.com/archives/nunavut981031/nvt81030_13.html.

George, M. V., M. J. Norris, F. Nault, S. Loh, and S. Y.Dai. 1994. *Population Projections for Canada, Provinces, and Territories 1993–2016*. Ottawa: Minister of Industry, Science and Technology.

Gerber, Theodore P. and Michael Hout. 1998. "More Shock than Therapy: Market Transition, Employment, and Income in Russia, 1991–1995." *American Journal of Sociology* 104: 1–50.

Gerbner, George. 1998. "Casting the American Scene: A Look at the Characters on Prime Time and Daytime Television from 1994–1997." *The 1998 Screen Actors Guild Report*. On the World Wide Web at http://www.media-awareness.ca/ eng/issues/minrep/resource/reports/gerbner.htm (5 August 2000).

Germani, Gino and Kalman Silvert. 1961. "Politics, Social Structure and Military Intervention in Latin America." *European Journal of Sociology* 11: 62–81.

Ghalam, Nancy Z. 1997. "Attitudes Towards Women, Work and Family." *Canadian Social Trends* 46: 13–7.

Giddens, Anthony. 1982. *Sociology: A Brief But Critical Introduction*. New York: Harcourt Brace Jovanovich.

Gidengil, Elizabeth. 1992. "Canada Votes: A Quarter Century of Canadian National Election Studies." *Canadian Journal of Political Science* 25: 219–48.

Gilbert, Susan. 1997. "2 Spanking Studies Indicate Parents Should Be Cautious." *New York Times* 20 August.

Gill, Richard T. 1997. *Posterity Lost: Progress, Ideology, and the Decline of the American Family*. London, UK: Rowman & Littlefield Publishers.

Gilligan, Carol. 1982. *In a Different Voice: Psychological Theory and Women's Development*. Cambridge, MA: Harvard University Press.

Gilligan, Carol, Nona P. Lyons, and Trudy J. Hanmer, eds. 1990. *Making Connections: The Relational Worlds of Adolescent Girls at Emma Willard School*. Cambridge, MA: Harvard University Press.

Gillis, A. R. 1995. "Urbanization." Pp. 13.1–13.35 in Robert J. Brym, ed. *New Society Brief Edition: Sociology for the 21st Century*. Toronto: Harcourt Brace.

Gilman, S. L. 1991. *The Jew's Body*. New York: Routledge.

Gimbutas, Marija. 1982. *Goddesses and Gods of Old Europe*. Berkeley and Los Angeles: University of California Press.

Ginsberg, Benjamin. 1986. *The Captive Public: How Mass Opinion Promotes States Power*. New York: Basic Books.

Gitlin, Todd. 1983. *Inside Prime Time*. New York: Pantheon.

Glaser, Barney and Anselm Straus. 1967. *The Discovery of Grounded Theory*. Chicago: Aldine.

Glazer, Nathan. 1997. *We Are All Multiculturalists Now*. Cambridge, MA: Harvard University Press.

Glendon, Mary Ann. 1981. *The New Family and the New Property*. Toronto: Butterworths.

Glenn, Norval D. 1990. "Quantitative Research on Marital Quality in the 1980s: A Critical Review." *Journal of Marriage and the Family* 52 (November): 818–31.

Glenn, Norval D. and Sara McLanahan. 1982. "Children and Marital Happiness: A Further Specifiction of the Relationship." *Journal of Marriage and the Family* 44: 63–72.

"Global Internet Statistics." 2002. On the World Wide Web at http://www.glreach.com/globstats/ (14 May 2002).

"Global Internet Statistics (by Language)." 2002. On the World Wide Web at http://www.glreach.com/globstats/index.php3 (22 July 2002).

"Global 1000." 1999. Business Week Online. On the World Wide Web at http://www.businessweek.com/ (8 October 2000).

Global Reach. 2001. "Global Internet Statistics (by Language)." On the World Wide Web at http://www.glreach.com/globstats/index.php3 (23 September 2001).

Glock, Charles Y. 1962. "On the Study of Religious Commitment." *Religious Education* 62, 4: 98–110.

"Gnutella." 2000. On the World Wide Web at http://gnutella.wego.com (7 August 2000).

Goddard Institute for Space Studies. 2001. "Annual Mean Temperature Anomalies in .01 C: Selected Zonal Means." On the World Wide Web at http://www.giss.nasa.gov/data/update/gistemp/ZonAnn.Ts.txt (10 May 2001).

Goffman, Erving. 1959 [1956]. *The Presentation of Self in Everyday Life*. Garden City, NY: Anchor.

———. 1961. *Asylums: Essays on the Social Situation of Mental Patients and Other Inmates*. Garden City, NY: Anchor Books.

———. 1963. *Stigma: Notes on the Management of Spoiled Identity*. Englewood Cliffs, NJ: Prentice-Hall.

———. 1974. *Frame Analysis*. Cambridge, MA: Harvard University Press.

Goldberg, M., and D. Green. 1999. *Raising the Floor: The Social and Economic Benefits of Minimum Wages in Canada*. Vancouver: Canadian Center for Policy Alternatives.

Goldhagen, Daniel Jonah. 1996. *Hitler's Willing Executioners: Ordinary Germans and the Holocaust*. New York: Knopf.

Goldie, Terry. 2001. *in a queer country: Gay & Lesbian Studies in the Canadian Context*. Vancouver: Arsenal Pulp Press.

Goldstein, Jay E. 1978. "The Prestige of Canadian Ethnic Groups: Some New Evidence." *Canadian Ethnic Studies* 10: 84–95

Goode, Erich and Nachman Ben-Yehuda. 1994. *Moral Panics: The Social Construction of Deviance*. Cambridge, MA: Blackwell.

Goodman, John T. 1999. "Mental Health." Pp. 1468–9 in James H. Marsh, ed. *The Canadian Encyclopedia: Year 2000 Edition*. Toronto: McClelland & Stewart.

Gordon, D. M., R. Edwards and M. Reich. 1982. *Segmented Work, Divided Workers: The Historical Transformation of Labor in the United States*. New York: Cambridge University Press.

Gorman, Christine. 1997. "A Boy without a Penis." *Time* 24 March: 83.

———. 1998. "Playing the HMO Game." *Time* 152, 2 (13 July). On the World Wide Web at http://www.time.com/time/magazine/1998/dom/980713/cover1.html (2 May 2000).

Gottdiener, Mark and Ray Hutchison. 2000 [1994]. *The New Urban Sociology*, 2nd ed. Boston: McGraw-Hill.

Gottfredson, Michael and Travis Hirschi. 1990. *A General Theory of Crime*. Stanford, CA: Stanford University Press.

Goubert, Jean-Pierre. 1989 [1986]. *The Conquest of Water*, Andrew Wilson, trans. Princeton, NJ: Princeton University Press.

Gould, Stephen Jay. 1996 [1981]. *The Mismeasure of Man*, rev. ed. New York: W. W. Norton.

———. 1988. "Kropotkin Was No Crackpot." *Natural History* 97, 7: 12–18.

Government of Canada. 2001a. "Early Intervention Programs." On the World Wide Web at http://www.crime-prevention.org/english/publications/youth/mobilize/early_e.html.

———. 2001b. *Job Futures*. On the World Wide Web at http://www.11hrdc-drhc.gc.ca/doc/jf/index.shtml (2 March 2001).

Goyder, J. 1997. *Technology and Society: A Canadian Perspective*. Peterborough, ON: Broadview Press.

Grabb, E. G. 1999. "Conceptual Issues in the Study of Social Inequality." Pp. vii–xxii in J. Curtis, E. Grabb, and N. Guppy, eds. *Social Inequality in Canada: Patterns, Problems, Policies*, 3rd ed. Scarborough, ON: Prentice Hall Allyn and Bacon Canada.

Gracey, Harry L. 2001. "Learning the Student Role: Kindergarten as Academic Boot Camp." Pp. 364–76 In James M. Henslin, ed. *Down to Earth Sociology: Introductory Readings*, 11th ed. New York: Free Press.

Graham, Mel. 1999. "Budget 2000 and People with Disabilities." *Abilities: Canadian Lifestyle Magazine for People with Disabilities* 41, Winter: 48.

Grange, Michael. 2000. "Recreational Hockey Not All Fun and Games." *Globe and Mail* 26 February: S1, S5.

Granovetter, Mark. 1973. "The Strength of Weak Ties." *American Sociological Review* 78: 1360–80.

———. 1995. *Getting a Job: A Study of Contacts and Careers*. Chicago: University of Chicago Press.

Grayson, P. 1985. *Corporate Strategies and Plant Closures: The SKF Experience*. Toronto: Our Times.

Greeley, Andrew. 1989. *Religious Change in America*. Cambridge, MA: Harvard University Press.

Greenhill, Pauline. 2001. "Can You See the Difference: Queerying the Nation, Ethnicity, Festival, and Culture in Winnipeg." Pp. 103–21 in Terry Goldie, ed. *in a queer country: Gay & Lesbian Studies in the Canadian Context*. Vancouver: Arsenal Pulp Press.

Greeno, Cherri. 2000. "Stalking Rate." *KW Record* 1 December: A1, A2.

Greenpeace. 2000. "Greenpeace Contacts Worldwide." On the World Wide Web at http://adam.greenpeace.org/information.shtml (2 May 2001).
———. 2002. "Rio + 10." On the World Wide Web at http://www.greenpeace.ca/Rio+10/ehtml/record.html.
Greenstein, Theodore N. 1996. "Husbands' Participation in Domestic Labor: Interactive Effects of Wives' and Husbands' Gender Ideologies." *Journal of Marriage and the Family* 58: 585–95.
Gregg, Allan R. 2002. "Scary New World." *Maclean's* 7 January: 22–5.
Grescoe, P. 1996. *The Merchants of Venus: Inside Harlequin and the Empire of Romance*. Vancouver: Raincoast.
Griffiths, C. T. and J. C. Yerbury. 1995. "Understanding Aboriginal Crime and Criminality: A Case Study." Pp. 383–98 in M. A. Jackson and C. T. Griffiths, eds. *Canadian Criminology: Perspectives on Crime and Criminality*, 2nd ed. Toronto: Harcourt, Brace Canada.
Grindstaff, Laura. 1997. "Producing Trash, Class, and the Money Shot: A Behind-the-Scenes Account of Daytime TV Talk Shows." Pp. 164–202 in James Lull and Stephen Hinerman, eds. *Media Scandals: Morality and Desire in the Popular Culture Marketplace*. Cambridge, UK: Polity Press.
Griswold, Wendy. 1992. "The Sociology of Culture: Four Good Arguments (and One Bad One)." *Acta Sociologica* 35: 322–8.
Grusky, David B., ed. 1994. *Social Stratification: Class, Race, and Gender in Sociological Perspective*. Boulder, CO: Westview.
Gunderson, Edna, Bill Keveney, and Ann Oldenburg. 2002. "The Osbournes' Find a Home in America's Living Rooms." *USA Today* 19 April:1A–2A.
Guppy, N. and S. Davies. 1998. *Education in Canada: Recent Trends and Future Challenges*. Ottawa: Ministry of Industry.
Guppy, Neil, James Curtis, and Edward Grabb. 1999. "Age-Based Inequalities in Canadian Society." Pp. 246–57 in James Curtis, Edward Grabb, and Neil Guppy, eds. *Social Inequality in Canada: Patterns, Problems, Policies*, 3rd ed. Scarborough, ON: Prentice Hall Allyn and Bacon.
Guppy, Neil and R. Alan Hedley. 1993. *Opportunities in Sociology*. Montreal: Canadian Sociology and Anthropology Association.
Gurr, Ted Robert. 1970. *Why Men Rebel*. Princeton, NJ: Princeton University Press.
"GVU's WWW User Surveys." 1999. On the World Wide Web at http://www.cc.gatech.edu/gvu/user_surveys/survey-1998-10/graphs/graphs.html#general (11 February 2001).
Haas, Jack and William Shaffir. 1987. *Becoming Doctors: The Adoption of a Cloak of Competence*. Greenwich, CT: JAI Press.
Haas, Jennifer. 1998. "The Cost of Being a Woman." *New England Journal of Medicine* 338: 1694–5.
Habermas, Jürgen. 1989. *The Structural Transformation of the Public Sphere*, Thomas Burger, trans. Cambridge, MA: MIT Press.
Hagan, John. 1989. *Structuralist Criminology*. New Brunswick, NJ: Rutgers University Press.
———. 1994. *Crime and Disrepute*. Thousand Oaks, CA: Pine Forge Press.
———. 2000. "White-Collar and Corporate Crime." Pp. 459–82 in Rick Linden, ed. *Criminology: A Canadian Perspective*, 4th ed. Toronto: Harcourt Canada.
Hagan, John, John Simpson, and A. R. Gillis. 1987. "Class in the Household: A Power-Control Theory of Gender and Delinquency." *American Journal of Sociology* 92: 788–816.
Haines, Herbert H. 1996. *Against Capital Punishment: The Anti-Death Penalty Movement in America, 1972–1994*. New York: Oxford University Press.
Hall, Edward, 1959. *The Silent Language*. New York: Doubleday.
———. 1966. *The Hidden Dimension*. New York: Doubleday.
Hall, Stuart. 1980. "Encoding/Decoding." Pp. 128–38 in Stuart Hall, Dorothy Hobson, Andrew Lowe, and Paul Willis, eds. *Culture, Media, Language: Working Papers in Cultural Studies, 1972–79*. London: Hutchinson.
———. 1992. "The Question of Cultural Identity." Pp. 274–313 in Stuart Hall, David Held, and Tim McGrew, eds. *Modernity and its Futures*. Cambridge, UK: Polity and Open University Press.
Hamer, D., P. F. Copeland, S. Hu, V. I. Magnuson, N. Hu, and A. M. I. Pattatucci. 1993. "A Linkage Between DNA Markers on the X Chromosome and Male Sexual Orientation." *Science* 261: 321–7.
Hamilton, Roberta. 1996. *Gendering the Vertical Mosaic: Feminist Perspectives on Canadian Society*. Toronto: Copp-Clark.
Hammer, Michael. 1999. "Is Work Bad for You?" *The Atlantic Monthly* August: 87–93.
Hammonds, Bruce. 2002. "The Latest Ideas on School Reform by Michael Fullan." *Leading and Learning for the 21st C* 1, 3. On the World Wide Web at http://www.leading-learning.co.nz/newsletters/vol101-no03-2002.html (29 June 2002).
Hampton, J., ed. 1998. *Internally Displaced People: A Global Survey*. London: Earthscan.
Hampton, Keith N. and Barry Wellman. 1999. "Netville On-Line and Off-Line: Observing and Surveying a Wired Suburb." *American Behavioral Scientist* 43: 475–92.
Hancock, Lynnell. 1994. "In Defiance of Darwin: How a Public School in the Bronx Turns Dropouts into Scholars." *Newsweek* 24 October: 61.
Handelman, Stephen. 1995. *Comrade Criminal: Russia's New Mafiya*. New Haven, CT: Yale University Press.
Haney, Craig, W. Curtis Banks, and Philip G. Zimbardo. 1973. "Interpersonal Dynamics in a Simulated Prison." *International Journal of Criminology and Penology* 1: 69–97.
Hanke, Robert. 1998. "'Yo Quiero Mi MTV!' Making Music Television for Latin America." Pp. 219–45 in Thomas Swiss, Andrew Herman, and John M. Sloop, eds. *Mapping the Beat: Popular Music and Contemporary Theory*. Oxford, UK: Blackwell.
Hannigan, John. 1995a. *Environmental Sociology: A Social Constructionist Perspective*. London: Routledge.
———. 1995b. "The Postmodern City: A New Urbanization?" *Current Sociology* 43, 1: 151–217.
———. 1998a. *Fantasy City: Pleasure and Profit in the Postmodern Metropolis*. New York: Routledge.
———. 1998b [1995]. "Urbanization." Pp. 337–59 in Robert J. Brym, ed. *New Society: Sociology for the 21st Century*, 2nd ed. Toronto: Harcourt Brace Canada.
Hannon, Roseann, David S. Hall, Todd Kuntz, Van Laar, and Jennifer Williams. 1995. "Dating Characteristics Leading to Unwanted vs. Wanted Sexual Behavior." *Sex Roles* 33: 767–83.
Hansen, James E., Makiko Sato, Reto Ruedy, Andrew Lacis, and Jay Glascoe. 1998. "Global Climate Data and Models: A Reconciliation." *Science* 281: 930–2.

Hao, Xiaoming. 1994. "Television Viewing among American Adults in the 1990s." *Journal of Broadcasting and Electronic Media* 38: 353–60.

Hare-Mustin, R. T. and J. Maracek. 1990. "Gender and the Meaning of Difference." Pp. 22–64 in R. T. Hare-Mustin and J. Maracek, eds. *Making a Difference: Psychology and the Construction of Gender*. New Haven, CT: Yale University Press.

Harrigan, Jinni A. and Kristy T. Taing. 1997. "Fooled by a Smile: Detecting Anxiety in Others." *Journal of Nonverbal Behavior* 21: 203–21.

Harris, Chauncy D. and Edward L. Ullman. 1945. "The Nature of Citite." *Annals of the American Academy of Political and Social Science* 242: 7–17.

Harris, Kathleen and Jeremy Marmer. 1996. "Poverty, Parental Involvement and Adolescent Well-Being." *Journal of Family Issues* 17, 5: 614–40.

Harris, Marvin. 1974. *Cows, Pigs, Wars and Witches: The Riddles of Culture*. New York, Random House.

Harrison, Bennett. 1994. *Lean and Mean: The Changing Landscape of Corporate Power in the Age of Flexibility*. New York: Basic Books.

Hart, David M. and David G. Victor. 1993. "Scientific Elites and the Making of U.S. Policy for Climate Change Research, 1957–74." *Social Studies of Science* 23: 643–80.

Hartnagel, Timothy F. 2000. "Correlates of Criminal Behaviour." Pp. 94–136 in Rick Linden, ed. *Criminology: A Canadian Perspective*, 4th ed. Toronto: Harcourt Canada.

Harvey, Andrew S., Katherine Marshall, and Judith A. Frederick. 1991. *Where Does the Time Go?* Ottawa: Statistics Canada.

Harvey, Elizabeth. 1999. "Sort-term and Long-term Effects of Early Parental Employment on Children of the National Longitudinal Survey of Youth." *Developmental Psychology* 35: 445–9.

Hastings, Arthur C., James Fadiman, and James C. Gordon, eds. 1980. *Health for the Whole Person: The Complete Guide to Holistic Medicine*. Boulder, CO: Westview Press.

Hawley, Amos. 1950. *Human Ecology: A Theory of Community Structure*. New York: Ronald Press.

Health Canada. 1994. *Suicide in Canada: Update of the Report of the Task Force on Suicide in Canada*. Ottawa: Mental Health Division, Health Services Directorate, Health Programs and Services Branch.

———. 1999a. *Statistical Report on the Health of Canadians*. Available on the World Wide Web at www.hc-sc.gc.ca/hppb/phdd/report/state/englover.html (December 25, 1999).

———. 1999b. *Toward a Healthy Future: Second Report on the Health of Canadians*. Prepared by the Federal, Provincial, and Territorial Advisory Committee on Population Health for the Meeting of Ministers of Health, Charlottetown, PEI. September. On the World Wide Web at http://www.hc-sc.gc.ca.

———. 2002a. Health Access Services Survey, 2001: Key Findings. On the World Wide Web at http://www.statcan.ca:80/english/freepub/82-575-XIE/findings.htm.

———. 2002b. "The Scoop on Smoking." On the World Wide Web at http://www.hc-sc.gc.ca/hecs-sesc/tobacco/youth/scoop.html.

Hechter, M. 1974. *Internal Colonialism: The Celtic Fringe in British National Development, 1536–1966*. Berkeley, CA: University of California Press.

Hechter, Michael. 1987. *Principles of Group Solidarity*. Berkeley, CA: University of California Press.

Hein, Simeon. 1992. "Trade Strategy and the Dependency Hypothesis: A Comparison of Policy, Foreign Investment, and Economic Growth in Latin America and East Asia." *Economic Development and Cultural Change* 40: 495–521.

Held, David. 1987. *Models of Democracy*. Stanford, CA: Stanford University Press.

Helsing, Knud J., Moyses Szklo, and George W. Comstock. 1981. "Factors Associated with Mortality after Widowhood." *American Journal of Public Health* 71: 802–9.

Henry, Frances, Carol Tator, Winston Mattis, and Tim Rees. 2000. *The Colour of Democracy: Racism in Canadian Society*, 2nd ed. Toronto: Harcourt Brace Canada.

Henry, Frances, et al. 2001. "The Victimization of Racial Minorities in Canada." Pp. 145–60 in Robert J. Brym, ed. *Society in Question: Sociological Readings for the 21st Century*. Toronto: Harcourt Canada.

Herdt, Gilbert. 2001. "Social Change, Sexual Diversity, and Tolerance for Bisexuality in the United States." Pp. 267–83 in Anthony R. D'Augelli and Charlotte J. Patterson, eds. *Lesbian, Gay, and Bisexual Identities and Youth: Psychological Perspectives*. New York: Oxford University Press.

Herlihy, David. 1998. *The Black Death and the Transformation of the West*. Cambridge, MA: Harvard University Press.

Herman, Edward S. and Noam Chomsky. 1988. *Manufacturing Consent: The Political Economy of the Mass Media*. New York: Pantheon.

Herman, Edward S. and Gerry O'Sullivan. 1989. *The "Terrorism" Industry: The Experts and Institutions That Shape Our View of Terror*. New York: Pantheon.

Herrnstein, Richard J., and Charles Murray. 1994. *The Bell Curve: Intelligence and Class Structure in American Life*. New York: Free Press.

Hersch, Patricia. 1998. *A Tribe Apart: A Journey into the Heart of American Adolescence*. New York: Ballantine Books.

Hertzman, Clyde, 2000. "The Case for Early Childhood Development Strategy." *Isuma: Canadian Journal of Policy Research* 1, 2: 11–18.

Hesse-Biber, Sharlene and Gregg Lee Carter. 2000. *Working Women in America: Split Dreams*. New York: Oxford University Press.

Hilberg, Raoul. 1961. *The Destruction of the European Jews*. Chicago: Quadrangle Books.

Hiller, Harry, ed. 2001. "Legacy for a New Millennium." Special issue of *The Canadian Journal of Sociology* 26, 3.

*Hindustan Times*. 1999. "40% Men and 60% Women Illiterate in India." 19 September. On the World Wide Web at http://www.hindutimes.com.

Hirschi, Travis. 1969. *Causes of Delinquency*. Berkeley, CA: University of California Press.

Hirschi, Travis and Hanan C. Selvin. 1972. "Principles of Causal Analysis." Pp. 126–47 in Paul F. Lazarsfeld, Ann K. Pasanella, and Morris Rosenberg, eds. *Continuities in the Language of Social Research*. New York: Free Press.

Hobart, Charles C. 1996. "Intimacy and Family Life: Sexuality, Cohabitation and Marriage." Pp. 143–73 in Maureen Baker, ed. *Families: Changing Trends in Canada*, 3rd ed. Toronto: McGraw-Hill Ryerson.

Hobbes, Thomas. 1968 [1651]). *Leviathan*. Middlesex, UK: Penguin.

Hobsbawm, Eric. 1994. *Age of Extremes: The Short Twentieth Century, 1914–1991*. London: Abacus.

Hochschild, Arlie Russell. 1973. *The Unexpected Community: Portrait of an Old Age Subculture*. Berkeley, CA: University of California Press.

Hochschild, Arlie Russell with Anne Machung. 1989. *The Second Shift: Working Parents and the Revolution at Home*. New York: Viking.

Hodge, Robert and David Tripp. 1986. *Children and Television: A Semiotic Approach*. Cambridge, UK: Polity.

Hodson, R., and T. Sullivan. 1995. *The Social Organization of Work*, 2nd ed. Belmont CA: Wadsworth.

Hoffman, Donna L. and Thomas P. Novak. 1998. "Bridging the Racial Divide on the Internet." *Science* 280: 390–1.

Hoggart, Richard. 1958. *The Uses of Literacy*. Harmondsworth, UK: Penguin.

Homans, George Caspar. 1950. *The Human Group*. New York: Harcourt, Brace.

———. 1961. *Social Behavior: Its Elementary Forms*. New York: Harcourt, Brace and World.

"Homosexuality and Bisexuality." 2000. *Report #5 to the Toronto Sun on the Third Annual Sun/COMPAS Sex Survey*. On the World Wide Web at http://www.compas.ca/html/archivesdocument.asp?compasSection=Sun+Media+Sex+Poll&GO=GO&compasID=61 (August 9, 2002).

hooks, bell. 1984. *Feminist Theory: From Margin to Center*. Boston: South End Press.

Hoover, Robert N. 2000. "Cancer—Nature, Nurture, or Both." *New England Journal of Medicine* 343, 2. On the World Wide Web at http://www.nejm.org/content/2000/0343/0002/0135.asp (16 July 2000).

Horkheimer, Max and Theodor W. Adorno. 1986 [1944]. *Dialectic of Enlightenment*, John Cumming, trans. London: Verso.

Hotton, Tina. 2001. "Spousal Violence After Marital Separation." *Juristat* 21, 7. Catalogue no. 85-002. Ottawa: Canadian Centre for Justice Statistics.

Hou, Feng and T. R. Balakrishnan. 1996. "Immigration and the Changing Ethnic Mosaic of Canadian Cities." Paper presented for the National Symposium on Immigration and Integration: New Challenges. Winnipeg. 25–27 October.

Houseknect, Sharon K. 1987. "Voluntary Childlessness." Pp. 369–418 in Marvin B. Sussman and Suzanne K. Steinmetz, eds. *Handbook of Marriage and the Family*. New York: Putnam.

Houseknect, Sharon K. and Jaya Sastry. 1996. "Family 'Decline' and Child Well-Being: A Comparative Assessment." *Journal of Marriage and the Family* 58: 726–39.

"How to Tell Your Friends from the Japs." 1941. *Time* 22 December: 33.

Howell, S. E. and C. L. Day. 2000. "Complexities of the Gender Gap." *Journal of Politics* 62: 858–75.

Hoyt, Homer. 1939. *The Structure and Growth of Residential Neighborhoods in American Cities*. Washington, DC: Federal Housing Authority.

Hughes, Diane, Ellen Galinsky, and Anne Morris. 1992. "The Effects of Job Characteristics on Marital Quality: Specifying Linking Mechanisms." *Journal of Marriage and the Family* 54, 1 (February): 31–42.

Hughes, Fergus P. 1995 [1991]. *Children, Play and Development*, 2nd ed. Boston: Allyn and Bacon.

Hughes, H. Stuart. 1967. *Consciousness and Society: The Reorientation of European Social Thought, 1890–1930*. London: Macgibbon and Kee.

Hughes, K., and G. Lowe. 2000. "Surveying the 'Post-Industrial' Landscape: Information Technologies and Labour Market Polarization in Canada." *Canadian Review of Sociology and Anthropology* 37, 1: 29–53.

Human Resources Development Canada. 2000. *Job Futures 2000*. On the World Wide Web at http://jobfutures.ca/doc/jf/emerging/emerging.shtml#sample (June 2001).

Human Rights Watch. 1995. *The Human Rights Watch Global Report on Women's Human Rights*. New York: Human Rights Watch.

Humphreys, L. 1975. *Tearoom Trade: Impersonal Sex in Public Places*. Chicago: Aldine de Gruyter.

Hunt, A. 1999. *Governing Morals: A Social History of Moral Regulation*. New York: Cambridge University Press.

Hunter, James Davison. 1991. *Culture Wars: The Struggle to Define America*. New York: Basic Books.

Huntington, Samuel. 1968. *Political Order in Changing Societies*. New Haven, CT: Yale University Press.

———. 1991. *The Third Wave: Democratization in the Late Twentieth Century*. Norman, OK: University of Oklahoma Press.

Hussein, Lula J. 1995. *Report on the Ottawa Consultations on Female Genital Mutilation*. On the World Wide Web at http://www.129.128.19.162.docs/fgmdoj.html.

ICQ.com. 2002. "What Is ICQ? About the Web's Largest Community." On the World Wide Web at http://www.icq.com/products/whatisicq.html (19 May 2002).

Ignatiev, N. 1995. *How the Irish Became White*. New York: Routledge.

*ILGA Annual Report 1996/1997*. On the World Wide Web at http://www.pangea.org/org/cgl/ilga/repilga97e.html (14 February 2002).

"Imports and Exports of Goods on a Balance-of-Payments Basis." 2001. On the World Wide Web at http://www.statcan.ca/english/Pgdb/Economy/International/gblec02a.htm (17 February 2001).

Industry Canada. 2001. "Advertising Services Industry." On the World Wide Web at http://strategis.ic.gc.ca/pics/dm/advertise-eng.pdf (17 May 2002).

Inglehart, Ronald. 1997. *Modernization and Postmodernization: Cultural, Economic, and Political Change in 43 Societies*. Princeton, NJ: Princeton University Press.

Ingram, Gordon Brent. 2001. "Redesigning Wreck: Beach Meets Forest as Location of Male Homoerotic Culture in Placemaking in Pacific Canada." Pp. 188–208 in Terry Goldie, ed. *in a queer country: Gay & Lesbian Studies in the Canadian Context*. Vancouver: Arsenal Pulp Press.

Inkeles, Alex and David H. Smith. 1976. *Becoming Modern: Individual Change in Six Developing Countries*. Cambridge, MA: Harvard University Press.

Integration Analysis Program. 1999. "Sex Offenders." Pp. 267–81 in Canadian Centre for Justice Statistics. *The Juristat Reader: A Statistical Overview of the Canadian Criminal Justice System*. Toronto: Thompson Educational Publishing.

International Federation of Journalists. 2002. "IFJ Condemns Attack on Canadian Journalists: 'Ugly and Intolerant' Vision of Modern Media." 14 March. On the World Wide Web at http://www.ifj.org/publications/press/pr/315.html (17 May 2002).

International Institute for Management Development. 2002. "The World Competitiveness Scoreboard" On the World Wide Web at http://www02.imd.ch/documents/wcy/content/ranking.pdf (11 June 2002).

Internet Software Consortium. 2002. "Distribution of Top-Level Domain Names by Host Count Jan 2002." On the World Wide Web at http://www.isc.org/ds/WWW-200201/dist-bynum.html (18 May 2002).

"Interprovincial Trade." 2001. On the World Wide Web at http://www.tc.gc.ca/pol/en/report/Truck_Corridors/Ch6E_HTM.htm (17 February).

Isajiw, W. W. 1978. "Olga in Wonderland: Ethnicity in a Technological Society." Pp. 29–39 in L. Driedger, ed. *The Canadian Ethnic Mosaic: A Quest for Identity*. Toronto: McClelland & Stewart.

istar. 2001. "Why Small Is Smarter." On the World Wide Web at http://home.istar.ca/~gskarzn/go/SMALL.HTM.

Iyengar, Shanto. 1991. *Is Anyone Responsible? How Television Frames Political Issues*. Chicago: University of Chicago Press.

Jackson, Carolyn and Ian David Smith. 2000. "Poles Apart? An Exploration of Single-Sex and Mixed-Sex Educational Environments in Australia and England." *Educational Studies* 26, 4 (December): 409–22.

Jacobs, J. A. 1993. "Careers in the U.S. service economy." Pp. 195–224 in G. Esping-Anderson, ed. *Changing Classes: Stratification and Mobility in Postindustrial Societies*. London, UK: Sage.

Jacobs, Jane. 1961. *The Death and Life of Great American Cities*. New York: Random House.

———. 1969. *The Economy of Cities*. New York: Random House.

Jagpal, Sarjeet Singh. 1994. "Becoming Canadian: Pioneer Sikhs in Their Own Words." On the World Wide Web at http://collections.ic.gc.ca/sikh/s1b.html (15 March 2001).

James, William. 1976 [1902]. *The Varieties of Religious Experience: A Study in Human Nature*. New York: Collier Books.

Janigan, Mary. 2002. "Saving Our Cities." *Maclean's* 3 June: 22–7.

Jencks, Christopher, Marshall Smith, Henry Acland, Mary Jo Bane, David Cohen, Herbert Gintis, Barbara Heyns, and Stephan Michelson. 1972. *Inequality: A Reassessment of the Effect of Family and Schooling in America*. New York: Basic Books.

Jenkins, J. Craig. 1983. "Resource Mobilization Theory and the Study of Social Movements." *Annual Review of Sociology* 9: 527–53.

Jensen, Margaret Ann. 1984. *Love's Sweet Return. The Harlequin Story*. Toronto: Women's Press.

John Howard Society. 1999a. *Check & Balance: The Facts about Facts*. Toronto: The John Howard Society of Ontario.

———. 1999b. *Fact Sheet: Population Trends and Crime*. Toronto: John Howard Society of Ontario.

Johns, Adrian. 1998. *The Nature of the Book: Print and Knowledge in the Making*. Chicago: University of Chicago Press.

Johnson, Holly and Tina Hotton. 2001. "Spousal Violence." Pp. 26–41 in Statistics Canada. *Family Violence in Canada: A Statistical Profile 2001*. Ottawa: Minister of Industry. Catalogue no. 85-224-XIE.

Johnson, Michael P. 1995. "Patriarchal Terrorism and Common Couple Violence: Two Forms of Violence Against Women." *Journal of Marriage and the Family* 57, 2 (May): 283–94.

Johnson, Terence J. 1972. *Professions and Power*. London: Macmillan.

Johnson, Tracy L. and Elizabeth Fee. 1997. "Women's Health Research: An Introduction." Pp. 3–26 in Florence P. Haseltine and Beverly Greenberg Jacobson, eds. *Women's Health Research: A Medical and Policy Primer*. Washington, DC: Health Press International.

Johnston, William A. 2002. "Class and Politics in the Era of the Global Economy." Pp. 288–306 in Douglas Baer, ed. *Political Sociology: Canadian Perspectives*. Toronto: Oxford University Press.

Jones, Christopher. 1999. "Chiapas' Well-Connected Rebels." Wired News 1 February. On the World Wide Web at http://www.wired.com/news/print/0,1294,17633,00.html (30 July 2000).

Jones, Frank. 2000. "Are Children Going to Religious Services?" Pp. 202–5 in *Canadian Social Trends* 3. Toronto: Thompson Educational Publishing.

Jones, Laura. 1997. "Global Warming Is All the Rage These Days...Which Enrages Many Doubting Scientists." *The Fraser Institute*. On the World Wide Web at http://oldfraser.lexi.net/media/media_releases/1997/19971201a.html (5 May 2002).

Jordan, Penny. 1999. *A Treacherous Seduction*. Toronto: Harlequin.

Joy, Bill. 2000. "Why the Future Doesn't Need Us." Wired 8, 4. On the World Wide Web at http://wired.com/wired/archive/8.04/joy_pr.html (4 November).

Juergensmeyer, Mark. 2000. *Terror in the Mind of God: The Global Rise of Religious Violence*. Berkeley, CA: University of California Press.

Kalbach, M. A. and W. E. Kalbach. 1998. "Becoming Canadian: Problems of an Emerging Identity." *Canadian Ethnic Studies* 31, 2: 1–17.

Kalbach, Madeline A. 2000. "Ethnicity and the Altar." Pp. 111–21 in Madeline A. Kalbach and Warren E. Kalbach, eds. *Perspectives on Ethnicity in Canada: A Reader*. Toronto: Harcourt Canada.

Kalmijn, Matthijs. 1998. "Intermarriage and Homogamy: Causes, Patterns, Trends." *Annual Review of Sociology* 24: 395–421.

Kanter, Rosabeth Moss. 1977. *Men and Women of the Corporation*. New York: Basic Books.

———. 1983. *The Change Masters: Innovation and Entrepreneurship in the American Corporation*. New York: Simon and Schuster.

———. 1989. *When Giants Learn to Dance: Mastering the Challenges of Strategy, Management, and Careers in the 1990s*. New York: Simon and Schuster.

Karklins, Rasma. 1986. *Ethnic Relations in the USSR: The Perspective from Below*. London: Unwin Hyman.

Karl, Thomas R. and Kevin E. Trenberth. 1999. "The Human Impact on Climate." *Scientific American* 281, 6 (September): 100–5.

Karraker, Katherine Hildebrandt, Dena Ann Vogel, and Margaret Ann Lake. 1995. "Parents' Gender-Stereotyped Perceptions of Newborns: The Eye of the Beholder Revisited." *Sex Roles* 33, 9–10 (November): 687–701.

Katz, Elihu. 1957. "The Two-Step Flow of Communication: An Up-to-Date Report on an Hypothesis." *Public Opinion Quarterly* 21: 61–78.

Katznelson, Ira, and Margaret Weir. 1985. *Schooling for All: Class, Race, and the Decline of the Democratic Ideal*. New York: Basic Books.

Kay, Fiona and John Hagan. 1998. "Raising the Bar: The Gender Stratification of Law Firm Capitalization." *American Sociological Review* 63: 728–43.

Kazemipur, Abdolmohammad and Shiva S. Halli. 2000. *The New Poverty: Ethnic Groups and Ghetto Neighbourhoods*. Toronto: Thompson Educational Publishing, Inc.

Kearney, Mark and Randy Ray. 1999. *The Great Canadian Book of Lists*. Toronto: The Dundurn Group.

Kelley, Jack. 2001. "Terror Groups Hide behind Web Encryption." *USA Today* 19 June. On the World Wide Web at http://www.usatoday.com/life/cyber/tech/2001-02-05-binladen.htm (13 September 2001).

Kellner, Douglas. 1995. *Media Culture: Cultural Studies, Identity and Politics Between the Modern and the Postmodern*. New York: Routledge.

Kennedy, Mark. 1999. "Doctors Warn Ottawa to Heed Physician Shortages Right Away." *National Post* 3 August: A6.

———. 2001. "Health Costs Rocket Past $100B." *National Post* 19 December: A1, A6.

Kennedy, Paul. 1993. *Preparing for the Twenty-First Century*. New York: HarperCollins.

Kepel, Gilles. 1994 [1991]. *The Revenge of God: The Resurgence of Islam, Christianity and Judaism in the Modern World*, Alan Braley, trans. University Park, PA: Pennsylvania State University Press.

Kerig, Patricia K., Philip A. Cowan, and Carolyn Pape Cowan. 1993. "Marital Quality and Gender Differences in Parent–Child Interaction." *Developmental Psychology* 29: 931–39.

Kernaghan, John. 2002. "A Hockey-Obsessed Nation Holds Its Breath." *Hamilton Spectator* 16 February. On the World Wide Web at http://www.hamiltonspectator.com/reports/534665.html.

Kessler, Ronald C., Katherine A. McGonagle, Shanyang Zhao, Christopher B. Nelson, Michael Hughes, Suzann Eshleman, Hans Ulrich Wittchen, and Kenneth S. Kendler. 1994. "Life-time and 12-Month Prevalence of DSM-III-R Psychiatric Disorders in the United States." *Archives of General Psychiatry* 51: 8–19.

Kett, Joseph F. 1977. *Rites of Passage: Adolescence in America, 1790 to the Present*. New York: Basic Books.

Kevles, Daniel J. 1999. "Cancer: What Do They Know?" *New York Review of Books* 46, 14: 14–21.

Kidron, Michael and Ronald Segal. 1995. *The State of the World Atlas*, 5th ed. London: Penguin.

King, Martin Luther. 1967. *Conscience for Change*. Toronto: CBC Learning Systems.

Kingsbury, Nancy and John Scanzoni. 1993. "Structural-Functionalism." Pp. 195–217 in Pauline G. Boss, William J. Doherty, Ralph LaRossa, Walter R. Schumm, and Suzanne K. Steinmetz, eds. *Sourcebook of Family Theories and Methods: A Contextual Approach*. New York: Plenum.

Kinsey, Alfred C., Wardell B. Pomeroy, and Clyde E. Martin. 1948. *Sexual Behavior in the Human Male*. Philadelphia: W. B. Saunders.

———. 1953. *Sexual Behaviour in the Human Female*. Philadelphia: W. B. Saunders.

Kitano, Harry and Roger Daniels. 1995. *Asian Americans: Emerging Minorities*, 2nd ed. Englewood Cliffs, NJ: Prentice-Hall.

Kling, Kristen C., Janet Shibley Hyde, Carolin J. Showers, and Brenda N. Buswell. 1999. "Gender Differences in Self-Esteem: A Meta-Analysis." *Psychological Bulletin* 125, 4: 470–500.

Klingemann, Hans-Dieter. 1999. "Mapping Political Support in the 1990s: A Global Analysis." In Pippa Norris, ed. *Critical Citizens: Global Support for Democratic Governance*. Oxford, UK: Oxford University Press. On the World Wide Web at http://ksgwww.harvard.edu/people/pnorris/Chapter_2.htm (20 October 2001).

Klockars, Carl B. 1974. *The Professional Fence*. New York: Free Press.

Koepke, Leslie, Jan Hare, and Patricia B. Moran. 1992. "Relationship Quality in a Sample of Lesbian Couples with Children and Child-Free Lesbian Couples." *Family Relations* 41: 224–9.

Kohlberg, Lawrence. 1981. *The Psychology of Moral Development: The Nature and Validity of Moral Stages*. New York: Harper and Row.

Kolbert, E. 1995. "Americans Despair of Popular Culture." *New York Times* 20 August: Section 2: 1, 23.

Kolland, Franz. 1994. "Contrasting Cultural Profiles Between Generations: Interests and Common Activities in Three Intrafamilial Generations." *Aging and Society* 14: 319–40.

Kong, Rebecca. 1997. "Criminal Harassment in Canada." *Canadian Social Trends* 45 (Autumn): 29–33.

Kornblum, William. 1997 [1988]. *Sociology in a Changing World*, 4th ed. Fort Worth: Harcourt Brace College Publishers.

Korpi, Walter. 1983. *The Democratic Class Struggle*. London: Routledge and Kegan Paul.

Kosmin, Barry A. 1991. *Research Report of the National Survey of Religious Identification*. New York: CUNY Graduate Center.

Kozol, Jonathan. 1991. *Savage Inequalities: Children in America's Schools*. New York: Crown.

Krahn, Harvey, and Graham S. Lowe, eds. 1998. *Work, Industry, and Canadian Society*, 3rd ed. Scarborough: Nelson.

Kriesi, Hanspeter, Hanspeter Kriese, and Jan Willem Duyvendak. 1995. *New Social Movements in Western Europe*. Minneapolis MN: University of Minnesota Press.

Kristof, Nicholas D. 1997. "With Stateside Lingo, Valley Girl Goes Japanese," *New York Times* 19 October: Section 1, 3.

Kropotkin, Petr. 1908 [1902]. *Mutual Aid: A Factor of Evolution*, revised ed. London: W. Heinemann.

Kuhn, Thomas. 1970 [1962]. *The Structure of Scientific Revolutions*, 2nd ed. Chicago: University of Chicago Press.

Kurdek, Lawrence A. 1995. "Assessing Multiple Determinants of Relationship Commitment in Cohabiting Gay, Cohabiting Lesbian, Cohabiting Heterosexual, and Married Heterosexual Couples." *Family Relations* 44: 261–6.

———. 1998. "Relationship Outcomes and Their Predictors: Longitudinal Evidence from Heterosexual Married, Gay Cohabiting and Lesbian Cohabiting Couples." *Journal of Marriage and the Family* 60, 3: 553–68.

Kurtz, Howard. 1997. "U.S. Television News Distorts Reality of Homicide Rates." *Edmonton Journal* 13 August: A5.

Kurzweil, Ray. 1999. *The Age of Spiritual Machines: When Computers Exceed Human Intelligence*. New York: Viking Penguin.

Kuttner, R. 1997. "The Limits of Markets." *The American Prospect* 31: 28–34. On the World Wide Web at http://www.prospect.org/archives/31/31kuttfs.html (30 April 2000).

Kuttner, Robert. 1998a. "In this For-Profit Age, Preventive Medicine Means Avoiding Audits." *Boston Globe* 22 March: E7.

———. 1998b. "Toward Universal Coverage." *The Washington Post* 14 July: A15.

*Labour Organizations in Canada 1972*. 1973. Ottawa: Economics and Research Branch, Canada Department of Labour. Cat. No. L2-2-1972.

LaFeber, Walter. 1993. *Inevitable Revolutions: The United States in Central America*, 2nd ed. New York: W. W. Norton.

Lamanna, Mary Ann and Agnes Riedmann. 2000. *Marriages and Families: Making Choices in a Diverse Society*, 7th ed. Belmont, CA: Wadsworth.

Lapidus, Gail Warshofsky. 1978. *Women in Soviet Society: Equality, Development, and Social Change*. Berkeley, CA: University of California Press.

La Prairie, Carol. 1996. *Examining Aboriginal Corrections in Canada*. Ottawa: Supply and Services Canada.

Larzelere, Robert E. 2000. "Child Outcomes of Nonabusive and Customary Physical Punishment by Parents: An Updated Literature Review." *Clinical Child & Family Psychology Review* 3, 4 (December): 199–221.

Lasch, Christopher. 1977. *Haven in a Heartless World: The Family Besieged*. New York: Basic Books.

Laslett, Peter. 1991 [1989]. *A Fresh Map of Life: The Emergence of the Third Age*. Cambridge, MA: Harvard University Press.

Lasswell, Harold. 1936. *Politics: Who Gets What, When and How*. New York: McGraw-Hill.

Laumann, Edward O., John H. Gagnon, Robert T. Michael, and Stuart Michaels. 1994. *The Social Organization of Sexuality: Sexual Practices in the United States*. Chicago: University of Chicago Press.

Lavoie, Yolande and Jillian Oderkirk. 2000. "Social Consequences of Demographic Change." Pp. 2–5 in *Canadian Social Trends: Volume 3*. Toronto: Thompson Educational Publishing, Inc.

Law, M. T. 1999. "The Economics of Minimum Wage Laws." *Public Policy Sources* 14. On the World Wide Web at http://www.fraserinstitute.ca/publications/pps/14/ (29 May 2000).

Laxer, Gordon. 1989. *Open for Business: The Roots of Foreign Ownership in Canada*. Toronto: Oxford University Press.

Lazare, Daniel. 1999. "Your Constitution Is Killing You: A Reconsideration of the Right to Bear Arms." *Harper's* 299, 1793 (October): 57–65.

Leacock, Eleanor Burke. 1981. *Myths of Male Dominance: Collected Articles on Women Cross-Culturally*. New York: Monthly Review Press.

Le Bon, Gustave. 1969 [1895]. *The Crowd: A Study of the Popular Mind*. New York: Ballantine Books.

Lee, K. 2000. *Urban Poverty in Canada: A Statistical Profile*. Ottawa: Canadian Council on Social Development.

Lee, Richard B. 1979. *The !Kung San: Men, Women and Work in a Foraging Society*. Cambridge, UK: Cambridge University Press.

Leidner, Robin. 1993. *Fast Food, Fast Talk: Service Work and the Routinization of Everyday Life*. Berkeley, CA: University of California Press.

Lenski, G. 1966. *Power and Privilege: A Theory of Social Stratification*. New York: McGraw Hill.

Lenski, G., P. Nolan, and J. Lenski. 1995. *Human Societies: An Introduction to Macrosociology*, 7th ed. New York: McGraw-Hill.

Lenton, Rhonda. 2001. "Sex, Gender, and Sexuality." Pp. 68–88 in Robert J. Brym, ed. *New Society: Sociology for the 21st Century*, 3rd ed. Toronto: Harcourt Canada.

Lerner, Gerda. 1986. *The Creation of Patriarchy*. New York: Oxford University Press.

Lever, J. 1994. "The 1994 Advocate Survey of Sexuality and Relationships: The Men." *Advocate* 23 August: 16–24.

Levine, David. 1987. *Reproducing Families: The Political Economy of English Population History*. Cambridge, UK: Cambridge University Press.

Levine, Elizabeth. 2001. "Living Together Can Double Separation Risk: Statscan Finding Applies to Couples Who Have Children." *National Post* 23 June. On the World Wide Web at wysiwyg://13/http://www.canada.com/cgi-bi...nationalpost/stories/200106 12/599934.html?.

Levine, Robert, Suguru Sato, Tsukasa Hashimoto, and Jyoti Verma. 1995. "Love and Marriage in Eleven Cultures." *Journal of Cross-Cultural Psychology* 26, 5: 554–71.

Levitan, S. A., Garth L. Mangum, and Stephen L. Mangum. 1998. *Programs in Aid of the Poor*, 7th ed. Baltimore: Johns Hopkins University Press.

Lewontin, R. C. 1991. *Biology as Ideology: The Doctrine of DNA*. New York: HarperCollins.

Ley, David. 1996. *The New Middle Class and the Remaking of the Central City*. Oxford, UK: Oxford University Press.

Li, P. 1995. "Racial Supremacism under Social Democracy." *Canadian Ethnic Studies* 27, 1: 1–17.

Li, Peter. 1998. *The Chinese in Canada*, 2nd ed. Toronto: Oxford University Press.

Lian, J. Z. and D. R. Matthews. 1998. "Does the Vertical Mosaic Still Exist? Ethnicity and Income in Canada, 1991." *Canadian Review of Sociology and Anthropology* 35: 461–81.

Lichtenstein, Paul, Niels V. Holm, Pia K. Verkasalo, Anastasia Iliadou, Jaakko Kaprio, Markku Koskenvuo, Eero Pukkala, Axel Skytthe, and Kari Hemminki. 2000. "Environment and Heritable Factors in the Causation of Cancer—Analyses of Cohorts of Twins from Sweden, Denmark, and Finland." *New England Journal of Medicine* 343, 2: On the World Wide Web at http://content.nejm.org/cgi/content/short/343/2/78 (12 July 2001).

Lie, John. 1998. *Han Unbound: The Political Economy of South Korea*. Stanford, CA: Stanford University Press.

———. 1992. "The Concept of Mode of Exchange." *American Sociological Review* 57: 508–23.

———. 2001. *Multiethnic Japan*. Cambridge, MA: Harvard University Press.

Liebow, Elliot. 1967. *Tally's Corner: A Study of Negro Street-Corner Men*. Boston: Little, Brown.

Light, I. 1991. "Immigrant and Ethnic Enterprise in North America." Pp. 307–18 in N. R. Yetman, ed. *Majority and Minority: The Dynamics of Race and Ethnicity in American Life*, 5th ed. Boston: Allyn and Bacon.

Lightfoot-Klein, Hanny, Cheryl Chase, Tim Hammond, and Ronald Goldman. 2000. "Genital Surgery on Children Below the Age of Consent." Pp. 440–79 in Lenore T. Szuchman and Frank Muscarella, eds. *Psychological Perspectives on Human Sexuality*. New York: John Wiley & Sons.

Linden, Rick, ed. 2000. *Criminology: A Canadian Perspective*, 4th ed. Toronto: Harcourt Canada.

Lindner, Rolf. 1996 [1990]. *The Reportage of Urban Culture: Robert Park and the Chicago School*, Adrian Morris, trans. Cambridge, UK: Cambridge University Press.

Linton, Ralph. 1936. *The Study of Man*. New York: Appleton-Century-Crofts.

Lips, Hilary M. 1999. *A New Psychology of Women: Gender, Culture and Ethnicity*. Mountain View, CA: Mayfield Publishing Company.

Lipset, Seymour Martin. 1971 [1951]. *Agrarian Socialism: The Cooperative Commonwealth Federation in Saskatchewan*, revised ed. Berkeley, CA: University of California Press.

———. 1977. "Why No Socialism in the United States?" Pp. 31–363 in Seweryn Bialer and Sophia Sluzar, eds. *Sources of Contemporary Radicalism*. Boulder, CO: Westview Press.

———. 1981 [1960]. *Political Man: The Social Bases of Politics*, 2nd ed. Baltimore: Johns Hopkins University Press.

———. 1994. "The Social Requisites of Democracy Revisited." *American Sociological Review* 59: 1–22.

Lipset, Seymour Martin and Stein Rokkan. 1967. "Cleavage Structures, Party Systems, and Voter Alignments: An Introduction." Pp. 1–64 in Seymour Martin Lipset and Stein Rokkan, eds. *Party Systems and Voter Alignments: Cross-National Perspectives*. New York: Free Press.

Lisak, David. 1992. "Sexual Aggression, Masculinity, and Fathers." *Signs* 16: 238–62.

"Liszt's Usenet NewsGroups Directory." 2000. On the World Wide Web at http://www.liszt.com/news (2 May 2000).

Livernash, Robert and Eric Rodenburg. 1998. "Population Change, Resources, and the Environment." *Population Bulletin* 53, 1. On the World Wide Web at http://www.prb.org/pubs/population_bulletin/bu53-1.htm (8 October 2000).

Livi-Bacci, Massimo. 1992. *A Concise History of World Population*. Cambridge, MA: Blackwell.

Livingstone, D. W. 1999. *The Education-Jobs Gap: Underemployment or Economic Democracy*. Toronto: Garamond Press.

Lock, Margaret. 1993. *Encounters with Aging: Mythologies of Menopause in Japan and North America*. Berkeley, CA: University of California Press.

Lodhi, Abdul Qaiyum and Charles Tilly. 1973. "Urbanization, Crime, and Collective Violence in 19th Century France." *American Journal of Sociology* 79: 296–318.

Lofland, John and Lyn H. Lofland. 1995 [1971]. *Analyzing Social Settings: A Guide to Qualitative Observation and Analysis*, 3rd ed. Belmont, CA: Wadsworth.

Logan, John R. and Harvey L. Molotch. 1987. *Urban Fortunes: The Political Economy of Place*. Berkeley, CA: University of California Press.

Logan, Ron. 2001. "Crime Statistics in Canada, 2000." *Juristat* 21, 8 (July). Catalogue no. 85-002-XPE.

London, Scott. 1994. "Electronic Democracy—A Literature Survey." On the World Wide Web at http:///www.west.net/~insight/london/ed.htm (15 August 1998).

Long, Elizabeth. 1997. *From Sociology to Cultural Studies*. Malden, MA: Blackwell.

Lonmo, Charlene. 2001. "Adult Correctional Services in Canada, 1999–00." *Juristat* 21, 5 (July). Catalogue no. 85-002-XPE.

Lorimer, J. 1981. "Canada's Oil Monopoly: The Story of the $12 Billion Rip-off of Canadian Consumers." In R. Bertrand, ed. *The State of Competition in the Canadian Petroleum Industry*. Toronto: James Lorimer & Company.

Lowe, G. S. 1987. *Women in the Administrative Revolution: The Feminization of Clerical Work*. Toronto: University of Toronto Press.

———. 2000. *The Quality of Work: A People-Centred Agenda*. Don Mills, ON: Oxford University Press.

———. 2001. "Quality of Work—Quality of Life." Keynote talk at the Work/Life Balance and Employee Wellness Strategies Conference, Edmonton. 14 May. On the World Wide Web at http://www.cprn.com/work/files/pzqwq_e.pdf (25 August 2002).

Lowman, John, Robert T. Menzies, and Ted S. Palys. 1987. *Transcarceration: Essays in the Sociology of Social Control*. Aldershot, ON: Gower.

Lupri, Eugen and James Frideres. 1988. "Marital Satisfaction over the Life Cycle." Pp 436–48 in Lorne Tepperman and James Curtis, eds. *Readings in Sociology: An Introduction*. Toronto: McGraw-Hill Ryerson.

Lurie, A. 1981. *The Language of Clothes*. New York: Random House.

Luxembourg Income Study. 1999a. "LIS Inequality Indices." On the World Wide Web at http://lissy.ceps.lu/ineq.htm (29 April 2000).

———. 1999b. "LIS Low Income Measures." On the World Wide Web at http://lissy.ceps.lu/lim.htm (29 April 2000).

Lynch, Michael, and David Bogen. 1997. "Sociology's Asociological 'Core': An Examination of Textbook Sociology in Light of the Sociology of Scientific Knowledge." *American Sociological Review* 62: 481-93.

Lyon, David and Elia Zureik, eds. 1996. *Computers, Surveillance, and Privacy*. Minneapolis: University of Minnesota Press.

Mackie, Marlene. 1991. *Gender Relations in Canada: Further Explorations*. Toronto: Butterworths.

MacKinnon, Catharine A. 1979. *Sexual Harassment of Working Women*. New Haven, CT: Yale University Press.

*Maclean's*. 2000. "Echoes of the Columbine Massacre." 1 May: 20.

———. 2002. "Acceptable but Not Equal." 3 June: 12.

MacLennan, Hugh. 1945. *Two Solitudes*. Toronto: Collins.

"Mad about Hockey: Superstitions." 2002. On the World Wide Web at http://www.mcg.org/societe/hockey/pages/aasuperstitions_2.html (20 June 2002).

Magro, Albert M. 1997. "Why Barbie Is Perceived as Beautiful." *Perceptual & Motor Skills* 85, 1 (August): 363–74.

Maguire, Mike, Rod Morgan, and Robert Reiner, eds. 1994. *The Oxford Handbook of Criminology*. Oxford, UK: Clarendon Press.

Maki, Allan. 2000. "Bad Enough to Kill Someone." *Globe and Mail* 23 February: A1.

Maloney, Wendi A. 1999. "Brick and Mortar." *Academe* 85, 5: 19–24.

Malthus, Thomas Robert. 1966 [1798]. *An Essay on the Principle of Population*, J. R. Bodnar, ed. London: Macmillan.

Manga, Pran, Douglas E. Angus, and William R. Swan. 1993. "Effective Management of Low Back Pain: It's Time to Accept the Evidence." *Journal of the Canadian Chiropractic Association* 37: 221–9.

Mankiw, N. G. 1998. *Principles of Macroeconomics*. Fort Worth, TX: The Dryden Press.

Mann, Susan A., Michael D. Grimes, Alice Abel Kemp, and Pamela J. Jenkins. 1997. "Paradigm Shifts in Family Sociology? Evidence from Three Decades of Family Textbooks." *Journal of Family Issues* 18: 315–49.

Mannheim, Karl. 1952. "The Problem of Generations." Pp. 276–320 in *Essays on the Sociology of Knowledge*, Paul Kecskemeti, ed. New York: Oxford University Press.

Manza, Jeff, Michael Hout and Clem Brooks. 1995. "Class Voting in Capitalist Democracies since World War II: Dealignment,

Realignment, or Trendless Fluctuation?" *Annual Review of Sociology* 21: 137–62.

Marchak, M. P. 1991. *The Integrated Circus: The New Right and the Restructuring of Global Markets*. Montreal: McGill-Queen's University Press.

Markowitz, Fran. 1993. *A Community in Spite of Itself: Soviet Jewish Émigrés in New York*. Washington, DC: Smithsonian Institute Press.

———. 2000. *Coming of Age in Post-Soviet Russia*. Urbana-Champaign, IL: University of Illinois Press.

Marrus, Michael Robert. 1987. *The Holocaust in History*. Hanover, NH: University Press of New England for Brandeis University Press.

Marshall, Katherine. 1999. "Employment after Childbirth." *Perspectives on Labour and Income* Autumn: 16–25. Catalogue 75-001-XPE.

———. 2001a. "Part-time by Choice." *Perspectives on Labour and Income* 13, 1: 20–7. Available on the World Wide Web at http://dsp-psd.pwgsc.gc.ca/dsp-psd/Pilot/Statcan/75-001-XIE/75-001-XIE.html.

———. 2001b. "Working with Computers." *Perspectives on Labour and Income* 13, 2: 5–11. Available on the World Wide Web at http://dsp-psd.pwgsc.gc.ca/dsp-psd/Pilot/Statcan/75-001-XIE/75-001-XIE.html.

Marshall, T. H. 1965. "Citizenship and Social Class." Pp. 71–134 in T. H. Marshall, ed. *Class, Citizenship, and Social Development: Essays by T. H. Marshall*. Garden City, NY: Anchor.

Martin, Carol Lynn. 1999. "A Developmental Perspective on Gender Effects and Gender Concepts." Pp. 45–74 in William B. Swann, Jr., Judith H. Langlois, and Lucia Albino Gilbert, eds. *Sexism and Stereotypes in Modern Science: The Gender Science of Janet Taylor Spence*. Washington, DC: American Psychological Association.

Martin, Joanne. 1992. *Cultures in Organizations*. New York: Oxford University Press.

Martineau, Harriet. 1985. *Harriet Martineau on Women*, Gayle Graham Yates, ed. New Brunswick, NJ: Rutgers University Press.

Marx, Karl. 1904 [1859]. *A Contribution to the Critique of Political Economy*, N. Stone, trans. Chicago: Charles H. Kerr.

———. 1970 [1843]. *Critique of Hegel's "Philosophy of Right"*, Annette Jolin and Joseph O'Malley, trans. Cambridge, MA: Harvard University Press.

Marx, Karl and Friedrich Engels. 1972 [1848]. "Manifesto of the Communist Party." Pp. 331–62 in R. Tucker, ed. *The Marx-Engels Reader*. New York: Norton.

Masters, William, Virginia E. Johnson. and Robert C. Kolodny. 1992. *Human Sexuality*, 4th ed. New York: HarperCollins.

———. 1994. *On Sex and Human Loving*. New York: HarperCollins.

Matalon, Jean-Marc. 1997. "Jeanne Calment, World's Oldest Person, Dead at 122." *The Shawnee News-Star* 5 August. On the World Wide Web at http://www.news-star.com/stories/080597/life1.html (2 May 2000).

"Maternal Mortality: A Preventable Tragedy." 1998. *Popline* 20: 4.

Matsueda, Ross L. 1988. "The Current State of Differential Association Theory." *Crime and Delinquency* 34: 277–306.

———. 1992. "Reflected Appraisals, Parental Labeling, and Delinquency: Specifying a Symbolic Interactionist Theory." *American Journal of Sociology* 97: 1577–611.

Mayer, J. P. 1944. *Max Weber and German Politics*. London: Faber and Faber.

Mayer, Susan E. 1997. *What Money Can't Buy: Family Income and Children's Life Chances*. Cambridge, MA: Harvard University Press.

Mazur, Allan. 1998. "Global Environmental Change in the News: 1987–90 vs. 1992–96." *International Sociology* 13: 457–72.

McAdam, Doug. 1982. *Political Process and the Development of Black Insurgency, 1930–1970*. Chicago: University of Chicago Press.

McCarten, James. 2002. "Child Spanking Law Upheld by Ontario Court: Childs' Rights Group Ponders Taking Case to Supreme Court." On the World Wide Web at http://www.oacas.org/Whatsnew/newsstories/jan02news/spankinglawupheld.pdf.

McCarthy, John D. and Mayer N. Zald. 1977. "Resource Mobilization and Social Movements: A Partial Theory." *American Journal of Sociology* 82: 1212–41.

McCarthy, Shawn. 1999. "Entrepreneurs Find a Place in the Sun." *Globe and Mail* 31 July: B1, B5.

McChesney, Robert W. 1999. "Oligopoly: The Big Media Game Has Fewer and Fewer Players." *The Progressive* November: 20–4. On the World Wide Web at http://www.progressive.org/mcc1199.htm (7 August 2000).

McClelland, W. R. 1931. "Precautions for Workers in the Treating of Radium Ores." *Investigations in Ore Dressing and Metallurgy*. Ottawa: Bureau of Mines. On the World Wide Web at http://www.ccnr.org/radium_warning.html (8 October 2000).

McCormick, Chris. 1995. *Constructing Danger: The Mis/representation of Crime in the News*. Halifax: Fernwood.

———, ed. 1999. *The Westray Chronicles: A Case Study in Corporate Crime*. Halifax: Fernwood.

McCrum, Robert, William Cran, and Robert MacNeil. 1992. *The Story of English*, new and rev. ed. London: Faber and Faber.

McCullagh, Declan. 2000. "Bin Laden: Steganography Master?" *Wired* February 7. On the World Wide Web at http://www.wired.com/news/print/0,1294,41658,00.html (13 September 2001).

McDonald's Corporation. 1999. "McDonald's Nutrition Facts." On the World Wide Web at http://www.mcdonalds.com/food/nutrition/index.html (16 August 1999).

"McDonald's Testing E-Burgers." 1999. *Wall Street Journal Interactive Edition* 11 August. On the World Wide Web at http://www.zdnet.com/zdnn/stories/news/0,4586,2312611,00.html (29 April 2000).

McGinn, Anne Platt. 1998. "Promoting Sustainable Fisheries." Pp. 59–78 in Lester R. Brown, Christopher Flavin, Hilary French et al. *State of the World 1998*. New York: Norton.

McIntosh, Andrew. 2001. "Foreign Aid Spending Increases by $1 Billion." *National Post* 11 December. On the World Wide Web at wysiwyg://1-/http://www.canada.com/compon..p?ud=f00fbafb-4db0-4b2d-b08d-cbc1421d1d54.

McKelvey, Bill. 1982. *Organizational Systematics: Taxonomy, Evolution, Classification*. Berkeley, CA: University of California Press.

McLaren, A. 1990. *Our Own Master Race: Eugenics in Canada, 1885–1945*. Toronto: McClelland & Stewart.

McLaren, Leah. 2002. "Aging Punks Jump on the Jubilee Bandwagon." *Globe and Mail* 1 June: R8.

McLaughlin, Margaret L., Kerry K. Osborne, and Christine B. Smith. 1995. "Standards of Conduct on Usenet." Pp. 90–111 in Steven G. Jones, ed. *CyberSociety*. Thousand Oaks, CA: Sage.

McLuhan, Marshall. 1964. *Understanding Media: The Extensions of Man*. New York: McGraw-Hill.

McMahon, Maeve W. 1992. *The Persistent Prison? Rethinking Decarceration and Penal Reform*. Toronto: University of Toronto Press.

McMahon, Martha. 1995. *Engendering Motherhood: Identity and Self-Transformation in Women's Lives*. New York: The Guilford Press.

McNeill, William H. 1976. *Plagues and Peoples*. Garden City, NY: Anchor Press.

———. 1990. *Population and Politics since 1750*. Charlottesville, WV: University Press of Virginia.

McPhail, Clark. 1991. *The Myth of the Madding Crowd*. New York: Aldine de Gruyter.

———. 1994. "The Dark Side of Purpose: Individual and Collective Violence in Riots." *The Sociological Quarterly* 35: 1–32.

McPhail, Clark and Ronald T. Wohlstein. 1983. "Individual and Collective Behaviors within Gatherings, Demonstrations, and Riots." *Annual Review of Sociology* 9: 579–600.

McRoberts, Kenneth. 1988 [1976]. *Quebec: Social Change and Political Crisis*, 3rd ed. Toronto: McClelland & Stewart.

McTeer, Maureen A. 1999. *Tough Choices: Living and Dying in the 21st Century*. Toronto: Irwin Law.

McVey, Wayne W., Jr. and Warren E. Kalbach. 1995. *Canadian Population*. Scarborough, ON: Nelson.

Mead, G. H. 1934. *Mind, Self and Society*. Chicago: University of Chicago Press.

Medawar, Peter. 1996. *The Strange Case of the Spotted Mice and Other Classic Essays on Science*. New York: Oxford University Press.

MediaWatch. 1994. *Front and Center: Minority Representation on Television*. On the World Wide Web at http://www.media.awareness.ca/fre/minorite/ressources/recherche/anglais/study.htm (17 May 2002).

Meek, Ronald L., ed. 1971. *Marx and Engels on the Population Bomb: Selections from the Writings of Marx and Engels Dealing with the Theories of Thomas Robert Malthus*. Dorothea L. Meek and Ronald L. Meek, trans. Berkeley, CA: Ramparts Press.

Mehta, Michael. 1997. "Re-Licensing of Nuclear Facilities in Canada: The 'Risk Society' in Action." *Electronic Journal of Sociology* 3, 1. On the World Wide Web at http://www.sociology.org/content/vol003.001/mehta.html (8 October 2000).

Meisenheimer II, Joseph R. 1998. "The Service Industry in the 'Good' versus 'Bad' Jobs Debate." *Monthly Labor Review* 121, 2: 22–47.

Melton, J. Gordon. 1996 [1978]. *Encyclopedia of American Religions*, 5th ed. Detroit: Gale.

Melucci, Alberto. 1980. "The New Social Movements: A Theoretical Approach." *Social Science Information* 19: 199–226.

———. 1995. "The New Social Movements Revisited: Reflections on a Sociological Misunderstanding." Pp. 107–19 in Louis Maheu, ed. *Social Classes and Social Movements: The Future of Collective Action*. London, UK: Sage.

Menzies, C. R. 1999. "First Nations, Inequality and the Legacy of Colonialism." Pp. 236–44 in J. Curtis, E. Grabb, and N. Guppy, eds. *Social Inequality in Canada*, 3rd ed. Scarborough, ON: Prentice Hall Allyn and Bacon Canada Inc.

Merisotis, Jamie P. 1999. "The 'What's-The-Difference?' Debate." *Academe* 85, 5: 47–51.

Merrick, Thomas W. et al. 1986. "World Population in Transition." *Population Bulletin* 41, 2.

Merton, Robert K. 1938. "Social Structure and Anomie." *American Sociological Review* 3: 672–82.

———. 1968 [1949]. *Social Theory and Social Structure*. New York: Free Press.

Messerschmidt, J.W. 1993. *Masculinities and Crime: Critique and Reconceptualization of Theory*. Lanhm, MD: Roman and Littlefield.

Messner, Michael. 1995 [1989]. "Boyhood, Organized Sports, and the Construction of Masculinities." Pp. 102–14 in Michael S. Kimmel and Michael A. Messner. *Men's Lives*, 3rd ed. Boston: Allyn and Bacon.

Messner, Michael A. 2000. "Barbie Girls versus Sea Monsters: Children Constructing Gender." *Gender & Society, Special Issue* 14, 6 (December): 765–84.

Meyer, David R. and Judi Bartfield. 1996. "Compliance with Child Support Orders in Divorce Cases." *Journal of Marriage and the Family* 58, 1: 201–12.

Meyer, John W., Francisco O. Ramirez, and Yasemin Nuhoglu Soysal. 1992. "World Expansion of Mass Education, 1870–1980." *Sociology of Education* 65: 128–49.

Meyer, John W. and W. Richard Scott. 1983. *Organizational Environments: Ritual and Rationality*. Beverly Hills, CA: Sage.

Meyer, Thomas. 1984. "'Date Rape': A Serious Campus Problem that Few Talk About." *Chronicle of Higher Education* 5 December: 1, 12.

Michael, Robert T., John H. Gagnon, Edward O. Laumann, and Gina Kolata. 1994. *Sex in America: A Definitive Survey*. Boston: Little, Brown and Company.

Michels, Robert. 1949 [1911]. *Political Parties: A Sociological Study of the Oligarchical Tendencies of Modern Democracy*, E. and C. Paul, trans. New York: Free Press.

Mickleburgh, Rod. 2000a. "Judge's Warning Rejected by NHL." *Globe and Mail* 7 October: A1, A9.

———. 2000b. "Hockey Tough Guy Pleads Not Guilty." *Globe and Mail* 21 September: A1.

"Mild Labor: The World at Work and Play." 1999. *Wired* 7, 12: 144.

Milem, Jeffrey F. 1998. "Attitude Change in College Students: Examining the Effect of College Peer Groups and Faculty Normative Groups." *The Journal of Higher Education* 69: 117–140.

Miles, R. 1989. *Racism*. London: Routledge.

Milgram, Stanley. 1974. *Obedience to Authority: An Experimental View*. New York: Harper.

Miliband, Ralph. 1973 [1969]. *The State in Capitalist Society*. London: Fontana.

Milloy, John S. 1999. *A National Crime: The Canadian Government and the Residential School System, 1879 to 1986*. Winnipeg: University of Manitoba Press.

Mills, C. Wright. 1956. *The Power Elite*. New York: Oxford University Press.

———. 1959. *The Sociological Imagination*. New York: Oxford University Press.

Minois, George. 1989 [1987]. *History of Old Age: From Antiquity to the Renaissance, Sarah Hanbury Tenison*, trans. Chicago: University of Chicago Press.

Mishler, William. 1979. *Political Participation in Canada*. Toronto: Macmillan of Canada.

Mitchinson, Wendy. 1991. *The Nature of Their Bodies: Women and Their Doctors in Victorian Canada*. Toronto: University of Toronto Press.

Mitchinson, Wendy. 1993. "The Medical Treatment of Women." Pp. 391–421 in Sandra Burt, Lorraine Code, and Lindsay Dorney, eds. *Changing Patterns: Women in Canada*, 2nd ed. Toronto: McClelland & Stewart.

Mizruchi, M. S. 1982. *The American Corporate Network, 1904–1974*. Beverly Hills, CA: Sage.

———. 1992. *The Structure of Corporate Political Action: Interfirm Relations and Their Consequences*. Cambridge, MA: Harvard University Press.

Mohr, Johann W. and Keith Spencer. 1999. "Crime." Pp. 587–9 in James H. Marsh, editor in chief. *The Canadian Encyclopedia*, Year 2000 Edition. Toronto: McClelland & Stewart, Inc.

Molm, Linda D. 1997. *Coercive Power in Social Exchange*. Cambridge, UK: Cambridge University Press.

Money, John and Anke Ehrhardt. 1972. *Man and Woman, Boy and Girl*. Boston: Little Brown.

Montgomery, M. 1965. "The Six Nations and the Macdonald Franchise." *Ontario History* 57: 13.

Mooney, Linda A., David Knox, Caroline Schacht, and Adie Nelson. 2001. *Understanding Social Problems*, 1st Canadian ed. Toronto: Nelson Thomson Learning.

Moore, Barrington, Jr. 1967. *Social Origins of Dictatorship and Democracy: Lord and Peasant in the Making of the Modern World*. Boston: Beacon.

Moore, D. S. 1995. *The Basic Practice of Statistics*. New York: W. H. Freeman.

Morissette, R., X. Zhang, and M. Drolet. 2002. *The Evolution of Wealth Inequality in Canada, 1984–1999*. On the World Wide Web at http://www.statcan.ca (March 2002).

Morris, Aldon D. 1984. *The Origins of the Civil Rights Movement: Black Communities Organizing for Change*. New York: Free Press.

Morris, Norval and David J. Rothman, eds. 1995. *The Oxford History of the Prison: The Practice of Punishment in Western Society*. New York: Oxford University Press.

Morrison, Nancy. 1987. "Separation and Divorce." Pp. 125–43 in M. J. Dymond, ed. *The Canadian Woman's Legal Guide*. Toronto: Doubleday.

Mortimer, Jeylan T. and Roberta G. Simmons. 1978. "Adult Socialization." *Annual Review of Sociology* 4: 421–54.

Morton, Gary. 2000. "Showdown at Queen's Park." On the World Wide Web at http://www.tao.ca/earth/toronto/archive/1999/toronto01278.html (22 March 2001).

Moscovitch, Arlene. 1998. "Electronic Media and the Family." The Vanier Institute of the Family. On the World Wide Web at http://www.vifamily.ca/cft/media/media.htm (14 May 2002).

Mosquera, Mary. 1999. "Yahoo Beats Estimates." *TechWeb* 7 April. On the World Wide Web at http://www.techweb.com/wire/story/TWB19990407S0029 (2 May 2000).

"The MUD Connector." 2001. On the World Wide Web at http://www.mudconnect.com/ (19 May 2002).

Mumford, Lewis. 1961. *The City in History: Its Origins, Its Transformations, and Its Prospects*. New York: Harcourt, Brace, and World.

Murdie, R. A. 1969. "Factorial Ecology of Metropolitan Toronto, 1951–1961." Research Paper 116, Department of Geography. Chicago: University of Chicago Press.

Murdock, George Peter. 1937. "Comparative Data on the Division of Labor by Sex." *Social Forces* 15: 551–3.

———. 1949. *Social Structure*. New York: Macmillan.

Murnen, Sarah K., Annette Perot, and Don Byrne. 1989. "Coping with Unwanted Sexual Activity: Normative Responses, Situational Determinants and Individual Differences." *Journal of Sex Research* 26: 85–106.

"Muslim Brotherhood Movement Homepage." 2002. On the World Wide Web at http://www.ummah.org.uk/ikhwan/ (7 May 2001).

Myerhoff, Barbara. 1978. *Number Our Days*. New York: Dutton.

Myers, Daniel J. 1997. "Racial Rioting in the 1960s: An Event History Analysis of Local Conditions." *American Sociological Review* 62: 94–112.

Myles, John. 1989 [1984]. *Old Age in the Welfare State: The Political Economy of Public Pensions*, 2nd ed. Lawrence, KA: University Press of Kansas.

Myles, John, and Adnan Turegun. 1994. "Comparative Studies in Class Structure." *Annual Review of Sociology* 20: 103–24.

Nagle, Matt. 2001. "Gay Man Murdered in Vancouver's Stanley Park." *Seattle Gay News* 23 November. On the World Wide Web at http://www.sgn.org/2001/11/23.

Nakhaie, M. R. 1997. "Vertical Mosaic among the Elites: The New Imagery Revisited." *Canadian Review of Sociology and Anthropology* 34, 1: 1–24.

National Coalition of Anti-Violence Programs. 1998. *Anti-Lesbian, Gay, Bisexual and Transgendered Violence in 1997*. New York: The New City Gay & Lesbian Anti-Violence Project.

National Council of Welfare. 1998a. *Profiles of Welfare: Myths and Realities: A Report by the National Council of Welfare*. On the World Wide Web at http://www.ncwnbes.net/htmdocument/ reportprowelfare.repprowelfare.htm.

———. 1998b. *Banking and Poor People: Talk Is Cheap*. Ottawa: The Council.

———. 1998c. *Profiles of Welfare: Myths and Realities*. Ottawa: Ministry of Public Works.

———. 1999a. *Children First: A Pre-Budget Report by the National Council of Welfare*. On the World Wide Web at http://www.ncwcnbes.net.htmdocument/reportchildfirst.htm.

———. 1999b. "No Such Thing as a 'Typical' Welfare Case, Says National Council of Welfare Report." On the World Wide Web at http://www.ncwcnbes.net/htmdocument/reportprowelfare/PRESSPROWELFARE.htm.

———. 1999c. Preschool Children: Promises to Keep. On the World Wide Web at http://www.ncwcnbes/net/htmdocument/reportpromise/firstpag.html.

———. 1999. *A New Poverty Line: Yes, No or Maybe?* Ottawa: Ministry of Public Works.

———. 2000. *Poverty Profile 1998*. Ottawa: Ministry of Public Works.

National Opinion Research Center. 1999. *General Social Survey, 1972–98*. Chicago: University of Chicago. Machine-readable file.

Naumetz, Tim. 2000. "Snow, Easy Call Kept Voters Away, Chrétien Says." *National Post* 29 November: A8.

Neal, Mark Anthony. 1999. *What the Music Said: Black Popular Music and Black Public Culture*. New York: Routledge.

Nelson, Adie and Barrie W. Robinson. 2002. *Gender in Canada*, 2nd ed. Toronto: Prentice Hall.

Neugarten, Bernice. 1974. "Age Groups in American Society and the Rise of the Young Old." *Annals of the American Academy of Political and Social Science* 415: 187–98.

Nevitte, Neil. 1996. *The Decline of Deference*. Peterborough, ON: Broadview Press.

"New York Knicks History." 2000. On the World Wide Web at http://www.nba.com/knicks/news/00400499.html?nav=ArticleList#2 (9 May 2000).

Newman, K. 1999. *No Shame in My Game: The Working Poor in the Inner City*. New York: Knopf and the Russell Sage Foundation.

News Release. 1999. "Breitkreuz Tells PM Farm Aid—not Foreign Aid is Needed." On the World Wide Web at http://www.garrybreitkreuz.com/breitkreuzgpress/agri40.htm.

Nicolaiedis, Nicos. 1998. "Pierre Marty's 'Doll' and Today's Barbies." *Revue française de psychanalyse, Special Issue: Psychosomatique et pulsionnalité* 62, 5 (Nov–Dec): 1579–81.

Nie, Norman H., Sidney Verba, and John R. Petrocik. 1979 [1976]. *The Changing American Voter*, revised ed. Cambridge, MA: Harvard University Press.

"The Nike Campaign." 2000. On the World Wide Web at http://www.web.net/~msn/3nike.htm (23 June 2000).

Nikiforuk, Andrew. 1998. "Echoes of the Atomic Age: Cancer Kills Fourteen Aboriginal Uranium Workers." *Calgary Herald* 14 March: A1, A4. On the World Wide Web at http://www.ccnr.org/deline_deaths.html (8 October 2000).

———. 1999. "A Question of Style." *Time* 31 May: 58–9.

*1994–1995 Directory of Labour Organizations in Canada*. 1995. Ottawa: Minister of Supply and Services Canada. Cat. No. L2-2-1995.

*1998 Directory of Labour Organizations in Canada*. 1998. Ottawa: Workplace Information Directorate.

Nisbett, Richard E., Kaiping Peng, Incheol Choi, and Ara Norenzayan. 2001. "Culture and Systems of Thought: Holistic versus Analytic Cognition." *Psychological Review* 108: 291–310.

Nolen, Stephanie. 1999. "Gender: The Third Way." *Globe and Mail* 25 September: D1, D4.

Normand, Josee. 2000. "Education." Pp. 85–96 in *Women in Canada 2000: A Gender-Based Statistical Report*. Ottawa: Statistics Canada.

Norton, Kevin I., Timothy S. Olds, Scott Olive, and Stephen Dank. 1996. "Ken and Barbie at Life Size." *Sex Roles* 34, 3–4 (February): 287–94.

Notestein, F. W. 1945. "Population—The Long View." Pp. 36–57 in T. W. Schultz, ed. *Food for the World*. Chicago: University of Chicago Press.

Novak, Mark. 1997. *Aging and Society: A Canadian Perspective*, 3rd ed. Scarborough, ON: Nelson.

November 2001 Action Sheet. 2001. "The December Federal Budget: Will the World's Poor Pay for September 11?" On the World Wide Web at wysiwyg://7/http://www.results-resultats.ca/actions/2001-11-en.html?mode=print.

Nowak, Martin A., Robert M. May, and Karl Sigmund. 1995. "The Arithmetics of Mutual Help." *Scientific American* 272, 6: 76–81.

Nowell, Amy and Larry V. Hedges. 1998. "Trends in Gender Differences in Academic Achievement from 1960 to 1994: An Analysis of Differences in Mean, Variance, and Extreme Scores." *Sex Roles* 39: 21–43.

Nuland, Sherwin B. 1994. *How We Die: Reflections on Life's Final Chapter*. New York: Vintage.

Oates, Joyce Carol. 1999. "The Mystery of JonBenét Ramsey." *New York Review of Books* 24 (June): 31–7.

Obejas, Achy. 1994. "Women Who Batter Women." *Ms.* September/October: 53.

Oberschall, Anthony. 1973. *Social Conflict and Social Movements*. Englewood Cliffs, NJ: Prentice-Hall.

O'Connor, Julia S. and Robert J. Brym. 1988. "Public Welfare Expenditure in OECD Countries: Towards a Reconciliation of Inconsistent Findings." *British Journal of Sociology* 39: 47–68.

O'Connor, Julia S. and Gregg M. Olsen, eds. 1998. *Power Resources Theory and the Welfare State: A Critical Approach*. Toronto: University of Toronto Press.

Oderkirk, Jillian. 2000. "Marriage in Canada: Changing Beliefs and Behaviours, 1600–1990." *Canadian Social Trends* 3: 93–8. Toronto: Thompson Educational Publishing, Inc.

Oderkirk, Jillian and Clarence Lochhead. 1992. "Lone Parenthood: Gender Differences." *Canadian Social Trends* 27, Spring: 16–9.

OECD (Organization for Economic Co-operation and Development). 2001. *Knowledge and Skills for Life: First Results from PISA 2000.* On the World Wide Web at http://www.pisa.oecd.org/knowledge/summary/g.htm (5 December 2001).

Ogmundson, R., and J. McLaughlin. 1992. "Trends in the Ethnic Origins of Canadian Elites: The Decline of the BRITS?" *The Canadian Review of Sociology and Anthropology* 29: 227–42.

Olsen, Dennis. 1980. *The State Elite*. Toronto: McClelland & Stewart.

Olsen, Gregg M. 2002. *The Politics of the Welfare State: Canada, Sweden, and the United States*. Don Mills, ON: Oxford University Press Canada.

Olsen, Gregg and Robert J. Brym. 1996. "Between American Exceptionalism and Swedish Social Democracy: Public and Private Pensions in Canada." Pp. 261–79 in Michael Shalev, ed. *The Privatization of Social Policy? Occupational Welfare and the Welfare State in America, Scandinavia and Japan*. London: Macmillan.

Olshansky, S. Jay, Bruce A. Carnes, and Christine Cassel. 1990. "In Search of Methusaleh: Estimating the Upper Limits of Human Longevity." *Science* 250: 634–40.

Olzak, Susan, and Suzanne Shanahan. 1996. "Deprivation and Race Riots: An Extension of Spilerman's Analysis." *Social Forces* 74: 931–62.

Olzak, Susan, Suzanne Shanahan, and Elizabeth H. McEneaney. 1996. "Poverty, Segregation, and Race Riots: 1960 to 1993." *American Sociological Review* 61: 590–614.

O'Malley, Martin and Amina Ali. 2001. "Sticks, Stones and Bullies." CBC.CA. On the World Wide Web at http://cbc.ca/national/ news/bully/ (23 June 2002).

Omega Foundation. 1998. "An Appraisal of the Technologies of Political Control: Summary and Options Report for the European Parliament." On the World Wide Web at http://home.icdc.com/~paulwolf/eu_stoa_2.htm (29 April 2000).

Omi, M. and H. Winant. 1986. *Racial Formation in the United States*. New York: Routledge.

Ontario Coalition Against Poverty. 2000. "Harris Can Be Stopped March: Reports on June 15th, 2000." On the World Wide Web at http://www.interlog.com/~cjazz/june15.htm#su (22 March 2000).

"Ontario Coalition Against Poverty." 2001. On the World Wide Web at http://www.tao.ca/~ocap/ (22 March 2001).

Ontario Consultants on Religious Tolerance. 2000a. "Female Genital Mutilation (Female Circumcision)" On the World Wide Web at http://www.religioustolerance.org/femcirm.htm.

———. 2000b. "Homosexual (Same-Sex) Marriages." On the World Wide Web at http://www.religioustolerance.org/hom_marr.htm (20 August 2000).

———. 2002. "The Harry Potter Books: Efforts to Ban Books." On the World Wide Web at http://www.religioustolerance.org/potter3.htm.

Optometrists Network. 2000. "Attention Deficit Disorder." On the World Wide Web at http://www.add-adhd.org/ADHD_attention-deficit.html (14 August 2000).

Ornstein, Michael D. 1983. "The Development of Class in Canada." Pp. 224–66 in J. Paul Grayson, ed. *Introduction to Sociology: An Alternate Approach*. Toronto: Gage.

———.1998. "Survey Research." *Current Sociology* 46, 4: 1–87.

Ossowski, Stanislaw. 1963. *Class Structure in the Social Consciousness*, S. Patterson, trans. London: Routledge and Kegan Paul.

Owen, Michelle K. 2001. "'Family' as a Site of Contestation: Queering the Normal or Normalizing the Queer?" Pp. 86–102 in Terry Goldie, ed. *in a queer country: Gay and Lesbian Studies in the Canadian Context*. Vancouver: Arsenal Pulp Press.

Pacey, Arnold. 1983. *The Culture of Technology*. Cambridge, MA: MIT Press.

Pammett, Jon H. 1997. "Getting ahead Around the World." Pp. 67–86 in Alan Frizzell and Jon H. Pammett, eds. *Social Inequality in Canada*. Ottawa: Carleton University Press.

Park, Robert. E. 1950 [1914]. *Race and Culture*. New York: Free Press.

Park, Robert Ezra, Ernest W. Burgess, and Roderick D. McKenzie. 1967 [1925]. *The City*. Chicago: University of Chicago Press.

Parke, Ross D. 2001. "Paternal Involvement in Infancy: The Role of Maternal and Paternal Attitudes." *Journal of Family Psychology* 15, 4 (December): 555–8.

———. 2002. "Parenting in the New Millenium: Prospects, Promises and Pitfalls." Pp. 65–93 in James P. McHale and Wendy S. Grolnick, eds. *Retrospect and Prospect in the Psychological Study of Families*. Mahwah, NJ: Lawrence Erlbaum Associates, Inc.

Parshall, Gerald. 1998. "Brotherhood of the Bomb." *US News and World Report* 125, 7 (17–24 August): 64–8.

Parson, E. A. and D. W. Keith. 1998. "Fossil Fuels without $CO_2$ Emissions." *Science* 282: 1053–4.

Parsons, Talcott. 1951. *The Social System*. New York: Free Press.

———. 1955. "The American Family: Its Relation to Personality and to the Social Structure." Pp. 3–33 in Talcott Parsons and Robert F. Bales, eds. *Family, Socialization and Interaction Process*. New York: Free Press.

Pendakur, K. and R. Pendakur. 1998. "The Colour of Money: Earnings Differentials among Ethnic Groups in Canada." *Canadian Journal of Economics* 31: 518–48.

Pendakur, R. 2000. *Immigrants and the Labour Force: Policy, Regulation and Impact*. Montreal: McGill-Queens University Press.

Peritz, Ingrid. 1999. "Birth Rate in Quebec Lowest Since 1908." *Globe and Mail* 4 October: A1.

Perrow, Charles B. 1984. *Normal Accidents*. New York: Basic Books.

Perry-Castañeda Library Map Collection. 2000. "Comparative Soviet Nationalities by Republic." On the World Wide Web at http://www.lib.utexas.edu/Libs/PCL/Map_collection/commonwealth/USSR_NatRep_89.jpg (23 November 2000).

Peters, John F. 1994. "Gender Socialization of Adolescents in the Home: Research and Discussion." *Adolescence* 29: 913–34.

Peterson, Peter. 1997. "Will America Grow Up Before It Grows Old?" P. 70 in Harold A. Widdison, ed. *Social Problems: Annual Editions*. Guilford, CN: Dushkin.

Piaget, Jean and Bärbel Inhelder. 1969. *The Psychology of the Child*, Helen Weaver, trans. New York: Basic Books.

Pillard, Richard C. and J. Michael Bailey. 1998. "Human Sexuality Has a Heritable Component." *Human Biology* 70, April: 347–65.

Pineo, P. C. and J. Porter. 1985. "Ethnic Origin and Occupational Attainment." In M. Boyd, J. Goyder, F. E. Jones, H. A. McRoberts, P. C. Pineo, and J. Porter, eds. *Ascription and Achievement: Studies in Mobility and Status Attainment*. Ottawa: Carleton University Press.

Pinker, Steven. 1994. "Apes—Lost for Words." *New Statesman and Society* 15 April: 30–1.

Piven, Frances Fox and Richard A. Cloward. 1977. *Poor People's Movements: Why They Succeed, How They Fail*. New York: Vintage.

*A Place Called Chiapas*. 1998. *Vancouver: Canada Wild Productions*. (Movie).

Plummer, Kenneth. 1995. *Telling Sexual Stories: Power, Change and Social Worlds*. London, UK: Routledge.

Podolny, Joel M. and Karen L. Page. 1998. "Network Forms of Organization." *Annual Review of Sociology* 24: 57–76.

Polanyi, K. 1957 [1944]. *The Great Transformation: The Political and Economic Origins of Our Time*. Boston: Beacon.

Pold, H. 2001. "Trends in Part-Time Work." *Perspectives on Labour and Income* 13, 1: 13–5. Available on the World Wide Web at http://dsp-psd.pwgsc.gc.ca/dsp-psd/Pilot/Statcan/75-001-XIE/75-001-XIE.html.

Pollard, Michael and Zheng Wu. 1998. *Economic Circumstances and the Stability of Nonmarital Cohabitation*. Statistics Canada Income Research Paper Series. Catalogue no. 75F0002M1E98010.

Polsby, Nelson W. 1959. "Three Problems in the Analysis of Community Power." *American Sociological Review* 24: 796–803.

Pool, Robert. 1997. *Beyond Engineering: How Society Shapes Technology*. New York: Oxford University Press.

"Poor Palliative Care Encourages Euthanasia." 2001. 19 March. On the World Wide Web at http://www.savemedicare.com/n19ma01a.htm.

Pope, Harrison G., Jr., Roberto Olivardia, Amanda Gruber, and John Borowiecki. 1999. "Evolving Ideals of Male Body Image as Seen Through Action Toys." *International Journal of Eating Disorder* 26, 1 (July): 65–72.

Popenoe, David. 1988. *Disturbing the Nest: Family Change and Decline in Modern Societies*. New York: Aldine de Gruyter.

———. 1996. *Life without Father: Compelling New Evidence that Fatherhood and Marriage Are Indispensable for the Good of Children and Society*. New York: Martin Kessler Books.

———. 1998. "The Decline of Marriage and Fatherhood." Pp. 312–9 in John J. Macionis and Nijole V. Benokraitis, eds.

*Seeing Ourselves: Classic, Contemporary and Cross-Cultural Readings in Sociology*, 4th ed. Upper Saddle River, NJ: Prentice Hall.

Population Reference Bureau. 2000. "2000 World Population Data Sheet." On the World Wide Web at http://www.prb.org/pubs/wpds2000/wpds2000_Infant_Mortality-Life_Expectancy_At_Birth.html (16 August 2000).

Porter, John. 1965. *The Vertical Mosaic: An Analysis of Social Class and Power in Canada*. Toronto: University of Toronto Press.

———. 1979. *The Measure of Canadian Society: Education, Equality, and Opportunity*. Toronto: Gage.

Portes, A. and R. D. Manning. 1991. "The Immigrant Enclave: Theory and Empirical Examples." Pp. 319–32 in N. R. Yetman, ed. *Majority and Minority: The Dynamics of Race and Ethnicity in American Life*, 5th ed. Boston: Allyn and Bacon.

Portes, Alejandro. 1996. "Global Villagers: The Rise of Transnational Communities." *The American Prospect* 25: 74–77. On the World Wide Web at http://www.prospect. org/archives/25/25port.html (29 April 2000).

Postel, Sandra. 1994. "Carrying Capacity: Earth's Bottom Line." Pp. 3–21 in Linda Starke, ed. *State of the World 1994*. New York: Norton.

Postman, Neil. 1982. *The Disappearance of Childhood*. New York: Delacorte.

———. 1992. *Technopoly: The Surrender of Culture to Technology*. New York: Vintage.

Poulantzas, Nicos. 1975 [1968]. *Political Power and Social Classes*, T. O'Hagan, trans. London: New Left Books.

Pred, Allan R. 1973. *Urban Growth and the Circulation of Information*. Cambridge, MA: Harvard University Press.

"Presentation by Canada's Cable Companies to the Standing Committee on Canadian Heritage, February 19, 2002." 2002. On the World Wide Web at http://www.ccta.ca/english/publications/speeches-presentations/ 2002/ppt/e-02-19.ppt (20 May 2002).

Press, Andrea. 1991. *Women Watching Television: Gender, Class and Generation in the American Television Experience*. Philadelphia: University of Pennsylvania Press.

Prittie, Jennifer. 2000. "The Serious Business of Rubber Noses and Big Shoes." *National Post* 29 March: A1–A2.

The Public Purpose. 1999. "Annual Per Capita Public Transport Ridership, Canada and United States: 1960–1995." On the World Wide Web at http://www.publicpurpose.com/ut-canus.htm (8 October 1999).

Pyke, Karen D. 1997. "Class-Based Masculinities: The Interdependence of Gender, Class, and Interpersonal Power." *Gender and Society* 10: 527–49.

Quebecor Inc. 2002. *2001 Annual Report*. On the World Wide Web at http://www.quebecor.com/htmen/0_0/pdf/ Annual_Report 2001_EN.pdf (17 May 2002).

Raag, Tarja and Christine L. Rackliff. 1998. "Preschoolers' Awareness of Social Expectations of Gender: Relationships to Toy Choices." *Sex Roles* 38: 685–700.

Rapp, R. and E. Ross. 1986. "The 1920s: Feminism, Consumerism and Political Backlash in the U.S." Pp. 52–62 in J. Friedlander, B. Cook, A. Kessler-Harris, and C. Smith-Rosenberg, eds. *Women in Culture and Politics*. Bloomington, IN: Indiana University Press.

Reimann, Renate. 1997. "Does Biology Matter? Lesbian Couples' Transition to Parenthood and Their Division of Labor." *Qualitative Sociology* 20, 2: 153–85.

Reiter, Ester. 1991. *Making Fast Food: From the Frying Pan into the Fryer*. Montreal: McGill-Queen's University Press.

Reitz, J. G. (in press) "Immigrant Success in the Knowledge Economy: Institutional Change and the Immigrant Experience in Canada, 1970–1995." *Journal of Social Issues*.

Reitz, J. G. and R. Breton. 1994. *The Illusion of Difference: Realities of Ethnicity in Canada and the United States*. Toronto: C. D. Howe Institute.

Remennick, Larissa I. 1998. "The Cancer Problem in the Context of Modernity: Sociology, Demography, Politics." *Current Sociology* 46, 1: 1–150.

Remnick, David. 1998. "How Russia Is Ruled." *New York Review of Books* 45, 6: 10–15.

Renzetti, Claire M. 1992. *Violent Betrayal: Partner Abuse in Lesbian Relationships*. Newbury Park, CA: Sage.

Richardson, J. 1832. *Wacousta; Or the Prophecy: A Tale of the Canadas*. London, UK: Cadell.

Richardson, R. Jack. 1996. "Canada and Free Trade: Why Did It Happen?" Pp. 200–9 in Robert J. Brym, ed. *Society in Question*. Toronto: Harcourt Brace Canada.

Richler, Mordecai. 1959. *The Apprecenticeship of Duddy Kravitz*. Don Mills ON: A. Deutsch.

Ridgeway, Cecilia L. 1983. *The Dynamics of Small Groups*. New York: St. Martin's Press.

Riedmann, Agnes. 1993. *Science That Colonizes: A Critique of Fertility Studies in Africa*. Philadelphia: Temple University Press.

Riedmann, Agnes, Mary Ann Lamanna, and Adie Nelson. 2003. *Marriages and Families,* 1st Canadian ed. Toronto: Nelson.

Rifkin, Jeremy. 1998. *The Biotech Century: Harnessing the Gene and Remaking the World*. New York: Jeremy P. Tarcher/Putnam.

———. 1995. *The End of Work: The Decline of the Global Labor Force and the Dawn of the Post Market Era*. New York: G. P. Putnam's Sons.

Riley, Matilda White, Anne Foner, and Joan Waring. 1988. "Sociology of Age." Pp. 243–90 in Neil Smelser, ed. *Handbook of Sociology*. Newbury Park, CA: Sage.

Riley, Nancy. 1997. "Gender, Power, and Population Change." *Population Bulletin* 52, 1. On the World Wide Web at http://www.prb.org/pubs/population_bulletin/bu52-1.htm (25 August 2000).

Rinehart, J. W. 2001. *The Tyranny of Work: Alienation and the Labour Process*, 4th ed. Toronto: Harcourt Brace.

*The Ring* (University of Victoria's community newspaper). 2000. "Comment." 4 February. On the World Wide Web at http://www.communications.uvic.ca/Ring/00feb04/cover.html.

Risman, B.J. and D. Johnson-Sumerford. 1998. "Doing It Fairly: A Study of Postgender Marriages." *Journal of Marriage and the Family* 60: 23–40.

Rist, Ray. 1970. "Student Social Class and Teacher Expectations: The Self-Fulfilling Prophecy in Ghetto Education." *Harvard Educational Review* 40, 3 (August): 411–51.

Ritzer, George. 1993. *The McDonaldization of Society*. Thousand Oaks, CA: Pine Forge Press.

——— 1996. "The McDonalidzation Thesis: Is Expansion Inevitable?" *International Sociology* 11: 291–307.

Roberts, C. G. D. 1915. *A History of Canada for High Schools and Academics*. Toronto: Macmillan.

Roberts, Julian and Thomas Gabor. 1990. "Race and Crime: A Critique." *Canadian Journal of Criminology* 92, 2 (April): 291–313.

Roberts, Siobhan. 2000. "Web Could Be New STD Breeding Ground." *National Post* 17 June: A2.

Robertson, Ian. 1977. *Sociology*. New York: Worth Publishing.

Robinson, David, Frank J. Porporino and William A. Millson. 1999. "A One-Day Snapshot of Inmates in Canada's Adult Correctional Facilities." Pp. 53–68 in Canadian Centre for Justice Statistics. *The Juristat Reader: A Statistical Overview of the Canadian Justice System*. Toronto: Thompson Educational Publishing, Inc.

Robinson, John P. and Suzanne Bianchi. 1997. "The Children's Hours." *American Demographics* December: 20–4.

Roche, Maurice. 1995. "Rethinking Citizenship and Social Movements: Themes in Contemporary Sociology and Neoconservative Ideology." Pp. 186–219 in Louis Maheu, ed. *Social Classes and Social Movements: The Future of Collective Action*. London, UK: Sage.

Roediger, D. R. 1991. *The Wages of Whiteness: Race and the Making of the American Working Class*. London: Verso.

Roethlisberger, Fritz J. and William J. Dickson. 1939. *Management and the Worker*. Cambridge, MA: Harvard University Press.

Rogan, Mary. 2001. "An Epidemic of Gas Sniffing Decimates Arctic Indian Tribe." *New York Times on the Web*. On the World Wide Web at http://www.uwec.edu/Academic/Curric/majstos/p390/Articles/030301gas-sniffing-Indians.htm (4 March).

Rogers, Jackie Krasas and Kevin D. Henson. 1997. "'Hey, Why Don't You Wear a Shorter Skirt?' Structural Vulnerability and the Organization of Sexual Harassment in Temporary Clerical Employment." *Gender and Society* 11: 215–37.

Rogers Communications Inc. 2002. 2001 Annual Report. On the World Wide Web at http://media.corporate-ir.net/media_files/TOR/RCI.B.TO/reports/rci_ar01_eng.pdf (17 May).

Rogers Wireless Communications Inc. 2002. *2001 Annual Report*. On the World Wide Web at http://media.corporate-ir.net/media_files/TOR/RCI.B.TO/reports/ratt_ar01_eng.pdf (17 May).

Rollins, Boyd C. and Kenneth L. Cannon. 1974. "Marital Satisfaction over the Family Life Cycle." *Journal of Marriage and the Family* 36: 271–84.

Romaniuc, A. 1984. "Fertility in Canada: From Baby-boom to Baby-bust." *Current Demographic Analysis*. Ottawa: Statistics Canada.

Romanow, Walter I., Michel de Repentigny, Stanley B. Cunningham, Walter C. Soderlund, and Kai Hildebrandt, eds. 1999. *Television Advertising in Canadian Elections: The Attack Mode, 1993*. Waterloo, ON: Wilfrid Laurier Press.

Ronfeldt, Heidi M., Rachel Kimerling, and Ilena Arias. 1998. "Satisfaction with Relationship Power and the Perpetuation of Dating Violence." *Journal of Marriage and the Family* 60: 70–8.

Rootes, Chris. 1995. "A New Class? The Higher Educated and the New Politics." Pp. 220–35 in Louis Maheu, ed. *Social Classes and Social Movements: The Future of Collective Action*. London, UK: Sage.

Rosenberg, Janet, Harry Perlstadt, and William Phillips. 1997. "Now That We Are Here: Discrimination, Disparagement and Harassment at Work and the Experience of Women Lawyers." Pp. 247–59 in Dana Dunn, ed. *Workplace/Women's Place*. Los Angeles: Roxbury.

Rosenbluth, Susan C. 1997. "Is Sexual Orientation a Matter of Choice?" *Psychology of Women Quarterly* 21: 595–610.

Rosenbluth, Susan C., Janice M. Steil, and Juliet H. Whitcomb. 1998. "Marital Equality: What Does It Mean?" *Journal of Family Issues* 19, 3: 227–44.

Rosenthal, Robert and Lenore Jacobson. 1968. *Pygmalion in the Classroom: Teacher Expectation and Pupils' Intellectual Development*. New York: Holt, Rinehart, and Winston.

Rosin, Hanna and Richard Morin. 1999. "In One Area, Americans Still Draw a Line on Acceptability." *Washington Post, National Weekly Edition*, 16, 11 (11 January): 8.

Ross, D., P. Roberts, and K. Scott. 2000. "Family Income and Child Well-Being." *Isuma, Canadian Journal of Policy Research* 1, 2 (Autumn): 51–6.

Ross, David. 1998. "Rethinking Child Poverty." *Insight, Perception* 22, 1: 9–11.

Rostow, W. W. 1960. *The Stages of Economic Growth: A Non-Communist Manifesto*. New York: Cambridge University Press.

Rothman, Barbara Katz. 1982. *In Labor: Women and Power in the Birthplace*. New York: W. W. Norton.

———. 1989. *Recreating Motherhood: Ideology and Technology in a Patriarchal Society*. New York: W. W. Norton.

Rothman, D. J., E. Rose, T. Awaya, B. Cohen, A. Daar, S. L. Dzemeshkevich, C. J. Lee, R. Munro, H. Reyes, S. M. Rothman, K. F. Schoen, N. Scheper-Hughes, Z. Shapira, and H. Smit. 1997. *The Bellagio Task Force Report on Transplantation, Bodily Integrity, and the International Traffic in Organs*. On the World Wide Web at http://www.icrc.org/icrceng.nsf/5cacfdf48ca698b641256242003b3295/e1c0f992370a3032412565a2002f88ba?OpenDocument (8 December 2000).

Rothman, David J. 1991. *Strangers at the Bedside: A History of How Law and Bioethics Transformed Medical Decision Making*. New York: Basic Books.

———. 1998. "The International Organ Traffic." *New York Review of Books* 45, 5: 14–7.

Royal Commission on New Reproductive Technologies. 1993. *Proceed with Caution: Final Report of the Royal Commission on New Reproductive Technologies*. Ottawa: Canadian Communications Groups.

Rubin, J. Z., F. J. Provenzano, and Z. Lurra. 1974. "The Eye of the Beholder." *American Journal of Orthopsychiatry* 44: 512–9.

Rubin, Lillian B. 1997. *The Transcendent Child: Tales of Triumph over the Past*. New York: HarperPerennial.

Rueschemeyer, Dietrich, Evelyne Huber Stephens, and John Stephens. 1992. *Capitalist Development and Democracy*. Chicago: University of Chicago Press.

Ruggles, Steven. 1997. *Prolonged Connections: The Rise of the Extended Family in 19th-century England and America*. Madison, WI: University of Wisconsin Press.

Rural Advancement Foundation International. 1999. "The Gene Giants." On the World Wide Web at http://www.rafi.org/web/allpub-one.shtml?dfl=allpub.db&tfl= allpub-one-frag.ptml&operation=display&ro1= recNo&rf1=34&rt1=34&usebrs=true (2 May 2000).

Rushton, J. P. 1995. *Race, Evolution and Behaviour: A Life History Perspective*. New Brunswick, NJ: Transaction Publishers.

Russell, Bob. 1999. *More with Less: Work Reorganization in the Canadian Mining Industry*. Toronto: University of Toronto Press.

Russett, Cynthia Eagle. 1966. *The Concept of Equilibrium in American Social Thought*. New Haven, CT: Yale University Press.

Ryan, Kathryn M. and Jeanne Kanjorski. 1998. "The Enjoyment of Sexist Humor, Rape Attitudes, and Relationship Aggression in College Students." *Sex Roles* 38: 743–56.

Ryerson, Stanley. 1973 [1968]. *Unequal Union: Roots of Crisis in the Canadas, 1815–1873*, 2nd ed. Toronto: Progress.

Sager, Eric W. 2000. "Canada's Families—An Historian's Perspective." Pp.vii–xi in Vanier Institute of the Family. *Profiling Canada's Families II*. Nepean, ON: Vanier Institute of the Family.

Sallot, Jeff. 2002. "Mills Flouted Principle, CanWest Says." *Globe and Mail* 21 June: A4.

Salt, Robert. 1991. "Child Support in Context: Comments on Rettig, Christensen, and Dahl." *Family Relations* 40, 2 (April): 175–8.

Sampson, Robert. 1997. "The Embeddedness of Child and Adolescent Development: A Community-Level Perspective on Urban Violence." Pp. 31–77 in Joan McCord, ed. *Violence and Childhood in the Inner City*. Cambridge, UK: Cambridge University Press.

Sampson, Robert and John H. Laub. 1993. *Crime in the Making: Pathways and Turning Points through Life*. Cambridge, MA: Harvard University Press.

Samson, Colin, James Wilson, and Jonathan Mazower. 1999. *Canada's Tibet: The Killing of the Innu*. London UK: Survival. On the World Wide Web at http://www.survival.org.uk/pdf/Innu%20report.pdf (1 May 2001).

Samuda, R. J., D. Crawford, C. Philip, and W. Tinglen. 1980. *Testing, Assessment, and Counselling of Minority Students: Current Methods in Ontario*. Toronto: Ontario Ministry of Education.

Samuelsson, Kurt. 1961 [1957]. *Religion and Economic Action*, E. French, trans. Stockholm: Scandinavian University Books.

Sanderson, Stephen K. 1995. *Macrosociology: An Introduction to Human Societies*, 3rd ed. New York: Harper Collins.

Sandqvist, Karin and Bengt-Erik Andersson. 1992. "Thriving Families in the Swedish Welfare State." *Public Interest* 109: 114–16.

Sarlo, C. 2001. *Measuring Poverty in Canada*. Vancouver: The Fraser Institute.

Sartre, J. 1965 [1948]. *The Anti-Semite and Jew*, G. J. Becker, trans. New York: Schocken.

Sassen, Saskia. 1991. *The Global City: New York, London, Tokyo*. Princeton, NJ: Princeton University Press.

Sauve, Roger. 2002. "Job, Family and Stress among Husbands, Wives and Lone-Parents 15–64 from 1990 to 2000." On the World Wide Web at http://www.vifamily.ca/cft/connect.htm.

Saxton, Lloyd. 1990. *The Individual, Marriage, and the Family*, 9th ed. Belmont, CA: Wadsworth.

Scarr, Sandra and Richard A. Weinberg. 1978. "The Influence of 'Family Background' on Intellectual Attainment." *American Sociological Review* 43: 674–92.

Schiebinger, Londa L. 1993. *Nature's Body: Gender in the Making of Modern Science*. Boston: Beacon Press.

Schiff, Michel, and Richard Lewontin. 1986. *Education and Class: The Irrelevance of IQ Genetic Studies*. Oxford, UK: Clarendon Press.

Schiller, Herbert I. 1989. *Culture Inc.: The Corporate Takeover of Public Expression*. New York: Oxford University Press.

Schlesinger, Arthur. 1991. *The Disuniting of America: Reflections on a Multicultural Society*. New York: W. W. Norton.

Schmidtke, A., B. Weinacker, A. Apter, A. Batt, A. Berman, U. Bille-Brahe, A. Botsis, D. DeLeo, A. Doneux, R. Goldney, O. Grad, C. Haring, K. Hawton, H. Hjelmeland, M. Kelleher, A. Kerkhof, A. Leenaars, J. Lännqvist, K. Michel, A. Ostamo, E. Salander Renberg, L. Sayil, Y. Takahashi, C. van Heeringen, A. Värnik, and D. Wasserman. 1998. "Suicide Rates in the World (Update)." On the World Wide Web at http://www.uniwuerzburg.de/IASR/suicide-rates.htm (2 May 2001).

Schneider, Barbara and David Stevenson. 1999. *The Ambitious Generation: America's Teenagers: Motivated but Directionless*. New Haven, CT: Yale University Press.

Schneider, Margaret and Susan Phillips. 1997. "A Qualitative Study of Sexual Harassment of Female Doctors by Patients." *Social Science and Medicine* 45: 669–76.

Schofield, John. 2001. "Saving Our Schools." *Maclean's* 14 May. On the World Wide Web at http://www.macleans.ca/ (29 June 2002).

Schor, Juliet B. 1992. *The Overworked American: The Unexpected Decline of Leisure*. New York: Basic Books.

———. 1999. *The Overspent American: Why We Want What We Don't Need*. New York: Harper.

Schrag, Peter. 1997. "The Near-Myth of Our Failing Schools." *The Atlantic Monthly* October. On the World Wide Web at http://www.theatlantic.com/issues/97oct/fail.htm (2 May 2000).

Schroeder, K.A., L.L. Blood and D. Maluso. 1993. "Gender Differences and Similarities Between Male and Female Undergraduate Students regarding Expectations for Career and Family Roles." *College Student Journal* 27: 237–49.

Schudson, Michael. 1991. "National News Culture and the Rise of the Informational Citizen." Pp. 265–82 in Alan Wolfe, ed. *America at Century's End*. Berkeley, CA: University of California Press.

———. 1995. *The Power of News*. Cambridge, MA: Harvard University Press.

Schweingruber, David and Clark McPhail. 1999. "A Method for Systematically Observing and Recording Collective Action." *Sociological Methods and Research* 27: 451–98,

Scott, James C. 1998. *Seeing Like a State: How Certain Schemes to Improve the Human Condition Have Failed*. New Haven, CT: Yale University Press.

Scott, K. 1997. "Indigenous Canadians." Pp. 133–64 in D. McKenzie, R. Williams and E. Single, eds. *Canadian Profile: Alcohol, Tobacco and Other Drugs, 1997*. Ottawa: Canadian Centre on Substance Abuse.

Scott, Peter Dale and Jonathan Marshall. 1991. *Cocaine Politics: Drugs, Armies, and the CIA in Central America*. Berkeley, CA: University of California Press.

Scott, Sarah. 2000. "The Deepest Cut of All." On the World Wide Web at http://www.chatelaine.com/read/news+views/fgm.html.

Scott, Wilbur J. 1990. "PTSD in DSM-III: A Case in the Politics of Diagnosis and Disease." *Social Problems* 37: 294–310.

Scully, Diana. 1990. *Understanding Sexual Violence: A Study of Convicted Rapists*. Boston: Unwin Hyman.

Seccombe, Wally. 1992. *A Millennium of Family Change: Feudalism to Capitalism in Northwestern Europe*. London: Verso.

Seguin, Rheal. 2002. "Gay Couples in Quebec Get Full Parental Rights." *Globe and Mail* 8 June: A1, A7.

Segundo, Juan Luis, S. J. 1976 [1975]. *The Liberation of Theology*, John Drury, trans. Maryknoll, NY: Orbis.

Seiter, Ellen. 1999. *Television and New Media Audiences*. Oxford, UK: Clarendon Press.

Selznick, Philip. 1957. *Leadership in Administration: A Sociological Interpretation*. New York: Harper and Row.

Sen, Amartya. 1981. *Poverty and Famines: An Essay on Entitlement and Deprivation*. Oxford, UK: Clarendon Press.

———. 1994. "Population: Delusion and Reality." *New York Review of Books* 41, 15: 62–71.

———. 1999. *Development as Freedom*. New York: Anchor.

Senn, Charlene Y., Serge Desmarais, Norine Veryberg, and Eileen Wood. 2000. "Predicting Coercive Sexual Behavior Across the Lifespan in a Random Sample of Canadian Men." *Journal of Social and Personal Relationships* 17, 1 (February): 95–113.

Sentencing Project. 2001. "News & Updates." August. On the World Wide Web at http://www.sentencingproject.org/news/news.html#newpop (22 July 2002).

Sewell, William H. 1958. "Infant Training and the Personality of the Child." *American Journal of Sociology* 64: 150–9.

"SexQuiz.org." 2000. On the World Wide Web at http://www.sexquiz.org (12 August 2000).

Shain, A. 1995. "Employment of People with Disabilities." *Canadian Social Trends* 38: 8–13.

Shakur, Sanyika (a.k.a. Monster Kody Scott). 1993. *Monster: The Autobiography of an L.A. Gang Member*. New York: Penguin.

Shalev, Michael. 1983. "Class Politics and the Western Welfare State." Pp. 27–50 in S. E. Spiro and E. Yuchtman-Yaar, eds. *Evaluating the Welfare State: Social and Political Perspectives*. New York: Academic Press.

Shattuck, Roger. 1980. *The Forbidden Experiment: The Story of the Wild Boy of Aveyron*. New York: Farrar, Straus, and Giroux.

Shaw, Karen. 2001. "Harry Potter Books: My Concerns." On the World Wide Web at http://www.reachouttrust.org/regulars/articles/occult/hpotter2.htm.

Shaw Communications Inc. 2002. *Annual Report 2001*. On the World Wide Web at http://www.shaw.ca/investors/Annual_Report/01/ShawAR.pdf (17 May 2002).

Shea, Sarah E., Kevin Gordon, Ann Hawkins, Janet Kawchuk, and Donna Smith. 2000. "Pathology in the Hundred Acre Wood: A Neurodevelopmental Perspective on A. A. Milne." *Canadian Medical Association Journal* 163, 12: 1557–9. On the World Wide Web at http://www.cma.ca/cmaj/vol-163/issue-12/1557.htm (12 December 2000).

Shekelle, Paul G. 1998. "What Role for Chiropractic in Health Care?" *New England Journal of Medicine* 339: 1074–5.

Shelton, Beth Anne and Daphne John. 1996. "The Division of Household Labor." *Annual Review of Sociology* 22: 299–322.

Sherrill, Robert. 1997. "A Year in Corporate Crime." *The Nation* 7 April: 11–20.

Shields, M. 1999. "Long Working Hours and Health." *Health Reports* 11, 2: 33–48.

Shkilnyk, Anastasia. 1985. *A Poison Stronger than Love: The Destruction of an Ojibway Community*. New Haven, CT: Yale University Press.

Short, James F., Jr. and Fred L. Strodtbeck. 1965. *Group Process and Gang Delinquency*. Chicago: University of Chicago Press.

Shorter, Edward. 1997. *A History of Psychiatry: From the Era of the Asylum to the Age of Prozac*. New York: John Wiley and Sons.

Shulman, Alix Kates. 1997 [1969]. *Memoirs of an Ex-Prom Queen*. New York: Penguin.

Siddiqui, Haroon. 2002. "CanWest Censorship Is Shameful." *The Star.com* 10 March. On the World Wide Web at http://www.thestar.com/NASApp/cs/ContentServer?pagename=thestar/Layout/Article_Type1&c=Article&cid=1015585330473&call_page=TS_Opinion&call_pageid=96825 (17 May 2002).

Siegel, Jacob. 1996. "Aging into the 21st Century." Administration on Aging. On the World Wide Web at http://www.aoa.dhhs.gov/aoa/stats/aging21/default.htm (2 May 2000).

Signorielli, Nancy. 1998. "Reflections of Girls in the Media: A Content Analysis Across Six Media Overview." On the World Wide Web at http://childrennow.org/media/mc97/ReflectSummary.html.

Silberman, Steve. 2000. "Talking to Strangers." *Wired* 8, 5: 225–33, 288–96. On the World Wide Web at http://www.wired.com/wired/archive/8.05/translation.html (23 May 2002).

"The Silent Boom." 1998. *Fortune* 7 July: 170–1.

Simmel, George. 1950. *The Sociology of Georg Simmel*, Kurt H. Wolff, trans and ed. New York: Free Press.

Simon, Jonathan. 1993. *Poor Discipline: Parole and the Social Control of the Underclass, 1890–1990*. Chicago: University of Chicago Press.

Sissing, T. W. 1996. "The Black Community in the History of Québec and Canada." On the World Wide Web at http://www.qesnrecit.qc.ca/mpages/title.htm (14 June 2002).

Sjöberg, Gideon. 1960. *The Preindustrial City: Past and Present*. New York: Free Press.

Skinner, B. F. 1953. *Science and Human Behavior*. New York: Macmillan.

Skocpol, Theda. 1979. *States and Revolutions: A Comparative Analysis of France, Russia, and China*. Cambridge, UK: Cambridge University Press.

Skolnick, Arlene. 1991. *Embattled Paradise: The American Family in an Age of Uncertainty*. New York: Basic Books.

Small, Bryan J. A. and Donald G. Reid. 2002. "Public Policy on Recreation and Leisure in Urban Canada." Pp. 172–93 in Edmund P. Fowler and David Siegel, eds. *Urban Policy Issues: Canadian Perspectives*, 2nd ed. Don Mills, ON: Oxford University Press.

Smelser, Neil. 1963. *Theory of Collective Behavior*. New York: Free Press.

Smith, Adam. 1776/1981. *An Inquiry into the Nature and Causes of the Wealth of Nations*, vols. 1 and 2. Indianapolis, IN: Liberty Press.

Smith, Anthony. 1980. *Goodbye Gutenberg: The Newspaper Revolution of the 1980s*. New York: Oxford University Press.

Smith, Christian. 1991. *The Emergence of Liberation Theology: Radical Religion and Social Movement Theory*. Chicago: University of Chicago Press.

Smith, Donna. 1990. *Stepmothering*. New York: St. Martin's Press.

Smith, Jackie. 1998. "Global Civil Society? Transnational Social Movement Organizations and Social Capital." *American Behavioral Scientist* 42: 93–107.

Smith, Michael. 1990. "Patriarchal Ideology and Wife Beating: A Test of a Feminist Hypothesis." *Violence and Victims* 5: 257–73.

Smith, Tom W. 1992. "A Methodological Analysis of the Sexual Behavior Questions on the GSS." *Journal of Official Statistics* 8: 309–25.

Snider, Laureen. 1999. "White-Collar Crime." Pp. 2504 in James H. Marsh, editor in chief. *The Canadian Encyclopedia, Year 2000 Edition*. Toronto: McClelland & Stewart Inc.

Snow, David A., E. Burke Rochford Jr., Steven K. Worden, and Robert D. Benford. 1986. "Frame Alignment Processes, Micromobilization, and Movement Participation." *American Sociological Review* 51: 464–81.

Snyder, Benson R. 1971. The Hidden Curriculum. New York: Alfred A. Knopf.

Snyder, David and Charles Tilly. 1972. "Hardship and Collective Violence in France, 1830–1960." *American Sociological Review* 37: 520–32.

Sofsky, Wolfgang. 1997 [1993]. *The Order of Terror: The Concentration Camp*, William Templer, trans. Princeton, NJ: Princeton University Press.

Sokoloff, Heather. 2001. "Wealth Affects Test Scores." *National Post* 5 December: A17.

Solomon, Charlene Marmer. 1999. "Stressed to the Limit." *Workforce* 78, 9: 48–54.

Somers, Marsha D. 1993. "A Comparison of Voluntarily Childfree Adults and Parents." *Journal of Marriage and the Family* 55, 3 (August): 643–50.

Sorenson, Elaine. 1994. *Comparable Worth: Is It a Worthy Policy?* Princeton, NJ: Princeton University Press.

Spilerman, Seymour. 1970. "The Causes of Racial Disturbances: A Comparison of Alternative Explanations." *American Sociological Review* 35: 627–49.

———. 1976. "Structural Characteristics of Cities and the Severity of Racial Disorders." *American Sociological Review* 41: 771–93.

Spitz, René A. 1945. "Hospitalism: An Inquiry into the Genesis of Psychiatric Conditions in Early Childhood." Pp. 53–74 in *The Psychoanalytic Study of the Child*, vol. 1. New York: International Universities Press.

———. 1962. "Autoerotism Re-examined: The Role of Early Sexual Behavior Patterns in Personality Formation." Pp. 283–315 in *The Psychoanalytic Study of the Child*, vol. 17. New York: International Universities Press.

Spitzer, Allan. 1973. "The Historical Problem of Generations." *American Historical Review* 78: 1353–85.

Spitzer, Steven. 1980. "Toward a Marxian Theory of Deviance." Pp. 175–91 in Delos H. Kelly, ed. *Criminal Behavior: Readings in Criminology*. New York: St. Martin's Press.

Srinivas, M. N. 1952. *Religion and Society among the Coorgs of South India*. Oxford, UK: Oxford University Press.

Stacey, Judith. 1996. *Brave New Families: Stories of Domestic Upheaval in Late Twentieth Century America*. New York: Basic Books.

Stack, Carol. 1974. *All Our Kin: Strategies for Survival in a Black Community*. New York: Harper.

Stack, Stephen and J. Ross Eshleman. 1998. "Marital Status and Happiness: A 17-Nation Study." *Journal of Marriage and the Family* 60: 527–36.

Stark, Rodney. 1985. *Sociology*. Belmont, CA: Wadsworth.

Stark, Rodney and William Sims Bainbridge. 1979. "Of Churches, Sects, and Cults: Preliminary Concepts for a Theory of Religious Movements." *Journal for the Scientific Study of Religion* 18: 117–31.

Starr, Paul. 1982. *The Social Transformation of American Medicine*. New York: Basic Books.

———. 1994 [1992]. *The Logic of Health Care Reform: Why and How the President's Plan Will Work*, rev. ed. New York: Penguin.

Statistics Canada. 1997a. *Earnings of Men and Women*, Annual. Cat. No. 13-217-XPB.

———. 1997b. "1996 Census: Marital Status, Common-Law Unions and Families." *The Daily* 14 October. On the World Wide Web at http://www.statcan.ca/Daily/English/971014/d971014.htm.

———. 1998a. *Canada Yearbook 1999*. Ottawa: Minister of Industry.

———. 1998b. *Canada Yearbook 2000*. Ottawa: Minister of Industry.

———. 1998c. "HIV/AIDS." *The Daily* 29 October. On the World Wide Web at http://www.statcan.ca:80/Daily/English/981029/d981029.htm.

———. 1998d. "1996 Census: Census Families in Private Households by Age Groups of Never-married Sons and/or Daughters at Home (15), Showing Family Structure (7), for Canada, Provinces, Territories and Census Metropolitan Areas." 93F22009.ivt.

———. 1998e. "1996 Census: Labour Force Activity, Occupation and Industry, Place of Work, Mode of Transportation to Work, Unpaid Work." *The Daily* 17 March. On the World Wide Web at http://www.statcan.ca/Daily/English/980317/d980317.htm.

———. 1998f. "1996 Census: Sources of Income, Earnings and Total Income, and Family Income." *The Daily* 12 May. On the World Wide Web at http://www.statscan.ca:80/Daily/English/980512/d980512.htm.

———. 1999a. "The Gender Gap in Earnings." *The Daily* 20 December. On the World Wide Web at http://www.statcan.ca/Daily/English/991220.d991220.htm.

———. 1999b. *Health Indicators Data Base*, revised ed. Ottawa. Machine-readable file. Catalogue #82-221-XCB.

———. 2000a. *Canada at a Glance*. Ottawa. Catalogue 12-581-XPE.

———. 2000b. "Divorces, 1998." *The Daily* 28 September. On the World Wide Web at http://www.statcan.ca/Daily/English/000928/d000926.htm.

———. 2000c. "Household Environmental Practices." On the World Wide Web at http://www.statcan.ca/english/Pgdb/Land/Environment/envir01a.htm (7 October).

———. 2000d. *Income in Canada 1998*. Ottawa: Ministry of Industry.

———. 2000e. "Population." On the World Wide Web at http://www.statcan.ca/english/Pgdb/People/Population/demo02.htm (7 October 2000).

———. 2000f. "Population by Aboriginal Group, 1996 Census." On the World Wide Web at http://www.statcan.ca/english/Pgdb/People/Population/demo39a.htm (7 October 2000).

———. 2000g. "Therapeutic Abortions, 1998." *The Daily* 18 December. On the World Wide Web at http://www.statcan.ca/Daily/English/001218/d001218d.htm.

———. 2000h. *Women in Canada, 2000: A Gender-Based Statistical Report*. Ottawa: Statistics Canada.

———. (2000i). *1997 Economic Dynamics*. Catalogue Number 61F0020XCB Ottawa: Minister of Public Works and Government Services.

———. 2001a. "Impact of Smoking on Life Expectancy and Disability." *The Daily* 22 June. On the World Wide Web at http://www.statcam.ca/Daily/English/010622/d010622a.htm.

———. 2001b. "Participation in Postsecondary Education and Family Income, 1998." *The Daily* 7 December. On the World Wide Web at http://www.statcan.ca/Daily/English/011207/d011207c.htm (28 June 2002).

———. 2001c. "Television Viewing: Fall 1999." *The Daily* 25 January. On the World Wide Web at http://www.statcan.ca/Daily/English/010125/d010125a.htm (23 July 2002).

———. 2002a. "Cable Television Industry." On the World Wide Web at http://www.statcan.ca/english/Pgdb/People/Culture/arts11.htm (20 May 2002).

———. 2002b. "Expenditures on Education, by Education Level." On the World Wide Web at http://www.statcan.ca/english/Pgdb/People/Education/educ14a.htm (17 May 2002).

———. 2002c. "Immigrant Population by Place of Birth and Period of Immigration, 1996 Census, Canada." On the World Wide Web at http://www.statcan.ca/english/Pgdb/People/Population/demo25a.htm (14 June 2002).

———. 2002d. "Population, Occupied Private Dwellings, Private Households, Collective Dwellings, Population in Collective Dwellings, and Average Number of Persons per Private Household, 1961–1996 Censuses, Canada." On the World Wide Web at http://www.statcan.ca/english/Pgdb/People/Families/famil66.htm (20 May 2002).

———. 2002e. "2001 Census: Marital Status, Common-Law Status, Families, Dwellings and Households." *The Daily* (22 October 2002). On the World Wide Web at http://www.statcan.ca/Daily/English/021022/td021022.htm.

Steel, Freda M. 1987. "Alimony and Maintenance Orders." Pp. 155–67 in Sheilah L. Martin and Kathleen E. Mahoney, eds. *Equality and Judicial Neutrality*. Toronto: Carswell.

Steele, Claude M. 1992. "Race and the Schooling of Black Americans." *The Atlantic Monthly* April. On the World Wide Web at http://www.theatlantic.com/unbound/flashbks/blacked/steele.htm (2 May 2000).

Steinberg, Stephen. 1989 [1981]. *The Ethnic Myth: Race, Ethnicity, and Class in America*, updated ed. Boston: Beacon Press.

Steinem, Gloria. 1994. *Moving Beyond Words*. New York: Simon & Schuster.

Stephens, W. Richard, Jr. 1999. *Careers in Sociology*, 2nd ed. Boston: Allyn and Bacon. On the World Wide Web at http://www.abacon.com/socsite/careers.html (15 May 2001).

Sternberg, Robert J. 1986. "A Triangular Theory of Love." *Psychological Review* 93: 119–35.

Steward, Gillian. 1999. "Politicians and the Shrinking Soundbite." *Media Spring*. On the World Wide Web at http://www.caj.ca/mediamag/spring99/media99_11.html (19 May 2002).

Stewart, Abigail, Anne P. Copeland, Nia Lane Chester, Janet E. Malley, and Nicole B. Barenbaum. 1997. *Separating Together: How Divorce Transforms Families*. New York: The Guilford Press.

Stone, Lawrence. 1977. *The Family, Sex and Marriage in England, 1500–1800*. New York: Harper and Row.

Stormshak, Elizabeth A., Karen L. Bierman, Robert J. McMahon, and Liliana J. Lengua. 2000. "Parenting Practices and Child Disruptive Behavior Problems in Early Elementary School." *Journal of Clinical Child Psychology* 29, 1 (March): 17–29.

Stotsky, Sandra. 1999. *Losing Our Language: How Multicultural Classroom Instruction Is Undermining Our Children's Ability to Read, Write, and Reason*. New York: Free Press.

Straus, Murray A. 1994. *Beating the Devil Out of Them: Corporal Punishment in American Families*. New York: Lexington Books.

———. 1996. "Presentation: Spanking and the Making of a Violent Society." *Pediatrics* 98: 837–49.

Straus, Murray A. and Carrie L. Yodanis. 1996. "Corporal Punishment in Adolescence and Physical Assaults on Spouses Later in Life: What Accounts for the Link?" *Journal of Marriage and the Family* 58, 4: 825–924.

Straus, Murray A., David B. Sugerman, and Jean Giles-Sims. 1997. "Spanking by Parents and Subsequent Antisocial Behavior of Children." *Archives of Pediatrics & Adolescent Medicine* 151, 8: 761–73.

Straus, Murray A. and Glenda Kaufman Kantor. 1994. "Corporal Punishment of Adolescents by Parents: A Risk Factor in the Epidemiology of Depression, Suicide, Alcohol Abuse, Child Abuse, and Wife Beating." *Adolescence* 29, 115: 543–56.

Straus, Murray A. and Julie H. Stewart. 1999. "Corporal Punishment by American Parents: National Data on Prevalence, Chronicity, Severity, and Duration in Relation to Child and Family Characteristics." *Clinical Child & Family Psychology Review* 2, 2 (June): 55–70.

Straus, Murray A. and Vera E. Mouradian. 1998. "Impulsive Corporal Punishment by Mothers and Antisocial Behavior and Impulsiveness of Children." *Behavioral Science & the Law* 16, 3: 353–62.

Strauss, Anselm L. 1993. *Continual Permutations of Action*. New York: Aldine de Gruyter.

Stretesky, Paul and Michael J. Hogan. 1998. "Environmental Justice: An Analysis of Superfund Sites in Florida." *Social Problems* 45: 268–87.

*Strikes and Lockouts in Canada 1968*. 1970. Ottawa: Economic and Research Branch, Canada Department of Labour. Cat. No. L2-1/1968.

*Strikes and Lockouts in Canada 1985*. 1985. Ottawa: Minister of Supply and Services Canada. Cat. No. L160-2999/85B.

Strong-Boag, Veronica. 1986. "Ever a Crusader: Nellie McClung, First-Wave Feminist." Pp. 178–90 in V. Strong-Boag and A. Fellman, eds. *Rethinking Canada: The Promise of Women's History*. Toronto: Copp Clark Pitman.

Subrahmanyam, Kaveri and Patricia M. Greenfield. 1998. "Computer Games for Girls: What Makes Them Play?" Pp. 46–71 in Justine Cassell and Henry Jenkins, eds. *From Barbie to Mortal Kombat: Gender and Computer Games*. Cambridge, MA: MIT Press.

Sudweeks, Fay, Margaret McLaughlin, and Sheizaf Rafaeli, eds. 1999. *Network and Netplay: Virtual Groups on the Internet*. Menlo Park, CA: AAAI Press.

Sugrue, Thomas J. 1999. "Poor Families in an Era of Urban Transformation: The 'Underclass' Family in Myth and Reality." Pp. 243–57 in Stephanie Coontz, ed. *American Families: A Multicultural Reader*. New York: Routledge.

Sumner, William Graham. 1940 [1907]. *Folkways*. Boston: Ginn.

Sutherland, Edwin H. 1939. *Principles of Criminology*. Philadelphia: Lippincott.

———. 1949. *White Collar Crime*. New York: Dryden.
Suttles, G. D. 1968. *The Social Order of the Slum: Ethnicity and Territory in the Inner City*. Chicago: University of Chicago Press.
Suzuki, David and Holly Dressel. 2002. *Good News for a Change: Hope for a Troubled Planet*. Toronto: Stoddart.
Sweezy, Kate and Jill Tiefenthaler. 1996. "Do State-Level Variables Affect Divorce Rates?" *Review of Social Economy* 54: 47–65.
Sykes, Gresham and David Matza. 1957. "Techniques of Neutralization: A Theory of Delinquency." *American Sociological Review* 22: 664–70.
Szasz, Andrew and Michael Meuser. 1997. "Environmental Inequalities: Literature Review and Proposals for New Directions in Research and Theory." *Current Sociology* 45, 3: 99–120.
Szreter, Simon. 1996. *Fertility, Class and Gender in Britain, 1860–1940*. Cambridge, UK: Cambridge University Press.
Tannen, Deborah. 1990. *You Just Don't Understand Me: Women and Men in Conversation*. New York: William Morrow.
———. 1994a. *Talking from 9 to 5: How Women's and Men's Conversational Styles Affect Who Gets Heard, Who Gets Credit, and What Gets Done at Work*. New York: William Morrow.
———. 1994b. *Gender and Discourse*. New York: Oxford University Press.
Taras, David. 2001 [1999]. *Power and Betrayal in the Canadian Media*, updated ed. Peterborough, ON: Broadview Press.
Tarrow, Sidney. 1994. *Power in Movement: Social Movements, Collective Action and Politics*. Cambridge, UK: Cambridge University Press.
Tasker, Fiona L. and Susan Golombok. 1997. *Growing Up in a Lesbian Family: Effects on Child Development*. New York: The Guilford Press.
Tavris, C. 1992. *The Mismeasure of Woman*. New York: Simon & Schuster.
Taylor, Charles. 1994. *Multiculturalism: Examining the Politics of Recognition*. Princeton, NJ: Princeton University Press.
Tec, Nechama. 1986. *When Light Pierced the Darkness: Christian Rescue of Jews in Nazi-Occupied Poland*. New York: Oxford University Press.
"That's AOL Folks . . ." 2000. *CNNfn*. On the World Wide Web at http://cnnfn.com/2000/01/10/deals/aol_warner (2 May 2000).
Thelen, David. 1996. *Becoming Citizens in the Age of Television: How Americans Challenged the Media and Seized Political Initiative during the Iran-Contra Debate*. Chicago: University of Chicago Press.
Thomas, Keith. 1971. *Religion and the Decline of Magic*. London: Weidenfeld and Nicholson.
Thomas, Mikhail. 2002. "Adult Criminal Court Statistics, 2000/01." *Juristat* 22, 2 (March). Catalogue no. 85-002-XPE.
Thomas, W. I. and F. Znaniecki. 1958 [1918–20]. *The Polish Peasant in Europe and America: Monograph of an Immigrant Group*, 2nd ed. (2 vols.). New York: Dover Publications.
Thomas, William Isaac. 1966 [1931]. "The Relation of Research to the Social Process." Pp. 289–305 in Morris Janowitz, ed. *W.I. Thomas on Social Organization and Social Personality*. Chicago: University of Chicago Press.
Thompson, E. P. 1967. "Time, Work Discipline, and Industrial Capitalism." *Past and Present* 38: 59–67.
———. 1968. *The Making of the English Working Class*. Harmondsworth, UK: Penguin.
Thorne, Barrie. 1993. *Gender Play: Girls and Boys in School*. New Brunswick, NJ: Rutgers University Press.
Thurow, Lester C. 1996. "The Birth of a Revolutionary Class." *New York Times Magazine* 19 May: 46–7.
Tierney, John. 1997. "Our Oldest Computer, Upgraded." *New York Times Magazine* 28 (September): 46-9, 97, 100, 104-5.
Tigert, Leanne M. 2001. "The Power of Shame: Lesbian Battering as a Manifestation of Homophobia." *Women & Therapy, Special Issue: Intimate Betrayal: Domestic Violence in Lesbian Relationships* 23, 3: 73–85.
Tilly, C., L. Tilly and R. Tilly. 1975. *The Rebellious Century, 1830–1930*. Cambridge, MA: Harvard University Press.
Tilly, Charles. 1978. *From Mobilization to Revolution*. Reading, MA: Addison-Wesley.
———. 1979a. "Collective Violence in European Perspective." Pp. 83–118 in H. Graham and T. Gurr, eds. *Violence in America: Historical and Comparative Perspective*, 2nd ed. Beverly Hills: Sage.
———. 1979b. "Repertoires of Contention in America and Britain, 1750–1830." Pp. 126–55 in Mayer N. Zald and John D. McCarthy, eds. *The Dynamics of Social Movements: Resource Mobilization, Social Control, and Tactics*. Cambridge, MA: Winthrop Publishers.
Tilly, Charles, Louise Tilly, and Richard Tilly. 1975. *The Rebellious Century, 1830–1930*. Cambridge, MA: Harvard University Press.
*Time*. 1999. "A Changing People." Canadian Edition 31 May: 30–4.
Toffler, Alvin. 1990. *Powershift: Knowledge, Wealth, and Violence at the Edge of the 21st Century*. New York: Bantam.
Tong, Rosemarie. 1989. *Feminist Thought: A Comprehensive Introduction*. Boulder, CO: Westview.
Tönnies, Ferdinand. 1957 [1887]. *Community and Society*. Charles P. Loomis, ed. and trans. East Lansing, MI: Michigan State University Press.
Tonry, Michael. 1995. *Malign Neglect: Race, Crime, and Punishment in America*. New York: Oxford University Press.
Tornquist, Cynthia. 1998. "Students Head Back to Decaying Classrooms." *CNN.COM* 30 August. On the World Wide Web http://www.cnn.co.uk/US/9808/30/hazardous.schools (11 August 2000).
Toronto Board of Education. 1993. *The 1991 Every Secondary Student Survey. Part II: Detailed Profiles of Toronto's Secondary School Students*. Toronto: Toronto Board of Education Research Services.
Toronto Stock Exchange. 2000. *2000 Canadian Shareowners Study*. Toronto.
Torpey, J. 2001. "Making Whole What Has Been Smashed: Reflections on Reparations." *The Journal of Modern History* 73: 333–58.
Torrance, Judy M. 1986. *Public Violence in Canada*. Toronto: University of Toronto Press.
Tovee, M. J., S. M. Mason, J. L. Emery, S. E. McClusky, and E. M. Cohen-Tovee. 1997. "Supermodels: Stick Insects or Hourglasses?" *Lancet* 350: 1474–5.
Troeltsch, Ernst. 1931 [1923]. *The Social Teaching of the Christian Churches*, Olive Wyon, trans. 2 vols. London, UK: George Allen and Unwin.
Trovato, Frank. 1998. "The Stanley Cup of Hockey and Suicide in Quebec, 1951–1992." *Social Forces* 77, 1 (September): 105–27.

Tschannen, Olivier. 1991. "The Secularization Paradigm: A Systematization." *Journal for the Scientific Study of Religion* 30: 395–415.

Tsutsui, William M. 1998. *Manufacturing Ideology: Scientific Management in Twentieth-Century Japan*. Princeton, NJ: Princeton University Press.

Tuck, Simon. 2001. "Fewer Canadians Support Free Trade." *Globe and Mail* 5 February: A1.

Tudiver, Neil. 1999. *Universities for Sale: Resisting Corporate Control over Canadian Higher Education*. Toronto: James Lorimer and Company Ltd.

Tufts, Jennifer. 2000. "Public Attitudes Toward the Criminal Justice System." *Juristat* 20, 12 (December). Catalogue no. 85-002-XPE.

Tuljapurkar, Shripad, Nan Li, and Carl Boe. 2000. "A Universal Pattern of Mortality Decline in the G7 Countries." *Nature* 405: 789–92.

Tumin, M. 1953. "Some Principles of Stratification: A Critical Analysis." *American Sociological Review* 18: 387–94.

Tun, Paul. 2000. "Polls Show Canadians Not Settled on Abortion." *The Interim* August. On the World Wide Web at http://www.lifesite.net/interim/2000/aug/09pollsshow.html.

Turkel, Ann Ruth. 1998. "All About Barbie: Distortions of a Transitional Object." *Journal of the American Academy of Psychoanalysis* 26, 1 (Spring): 165–77.

Turkle, Sherry. 1995. *Life on the Screen: Identity in the Age of the Internet*. New York: Simon & Schuster.

Turnbull, Colin M. 1961. *The Forest People*. New York: Doubleday.

Turner, Bryan S. 1986. *Citizenship and Capitalism: The Debate over Reformism*. London, UK: Allen and Unwin.

Turner, Heather A. and David Finkelhor. 1996. "Corporal Punishment as a Stressor among Youth." *Journal of Marriage and the Family* 58, 1: 155–66.

Turner, Ralph H. and Lewis M. Killian. 1987 [1957]. *Collective Behavior*, 3rd ed. Englewood Cliffs, NJ: Prentice-Hall.

Tuxill, John and Chris Bright. 1998. "Losing Strands in the Web of Life." Pp. 41–58 in Lester R. Brown, Christopher Flavin, Hilary French et al. *State of the World 1998*. New York: Norton.

Twenge, Jean M. 1997. "Changes in Masculine and Feminine Traits over Time: A Meta-analysis." *Sex Roles* 36: 305–25.

Ungar, Sheldon. 1992. "The Rise and (Relative) Decline of Global Warming as a Social Problem." *Sociological Quarterly* 33: 483–501.

———. 1995. "Social Scares and Global Warming: Beyond the Rio Convention." *Society and Natural Resources* 8: 443–56.

———. 1998. "Bringing the Issue Back In: Comparing the Marketability of the Ozone Hole and Global Warming." *Social Problems* 45: 510–27.

———. 1999. "Is Strange Weather in the Air? A Study of U.S. National Network News Coverage of Extreme Weather Events." *Climatic Change* 41: 133–50.

"Union Membership in Canada—2000." 2000. *Workplace Gazette: An Industrial Relations Quarterly* 3, 3: 68–75.

Union of Concerned Scientists. 1993. "World Scientists' Warning to Humanity." On the World Wide Web at http://www.englib.cornell.edu/scitech/u95/warn.html (2 May 2000).

United Nations. 1993. *The Age and Sex Distribution of the World Population*. New York.

———. 1994. *Human Development Report 1994*. New York: Oxford University Press.

———. 1997b. "Percentage of Population Living in Urban Areas in 1996 and 2030." On the World Wide Web at http://www.undp.org/popin/wdtrends/ura/uracht1.htm (2 May 2000).

———. 1998a. *Human Development Report 1998*. New York: Oxford University Press.

———. 1998b. "World Population Growth from Year 0 to 2050." On the World Wide Web at http://www.popin.org/pop1998/4.htm (3 July 1999).

———. 1999a. "Gender Empowerment Measure." On the World Wide Web at http://www.undp.org/hdro/98gem.htm (28 April 2000).

———. 1999b. "Human Development Index." On the World Wide Web at http://www.undp.org/hdro/98hdi1.htm (28 April 2000).

———. 1999c. *World Urbanization Prospects: The 1999 Revision*. On the World Wide Web at http://www.un.org/esa/population/publications/wup1999/wup99.htm (27 August 2002).

———. 2000a. "Indicators on Income and Economic Activity." On the World Wide Web at http://www.un.org/Depts/unsd/social/inc-eco.htm (28 April 2000).

———. 2000b. Report on the Global HIV/AIDS Epidemic. On the World Wide Web at http://www.unaids.org/epidemic_update/report/Epi_report.htm (12 August 2000).

———. 2001. *Human Development Report 2001*. New York: Oxford University Press.

United Nations Development Programme. 2001. Table 22, "Gender Employment Measure." Pp 214–7 in *Human Development Indicators 2001*.

Unschuld, Paul. 1985. *Medicine in China*. Berkeley, CA: University of California Press.

Ursel, Jane. 2000. "Family Violence Courts." Pp. 45–8 in Statistics Canada. *Family Violence in Canada: A Statistical Profile 2000*. Catalogue 85-224-XIE. Ottawa: Minister of Industry.

U.S. Bureau of Labor Statistics. 1998. "Union Members Summary." On the World Wide Web at http://stats.bls.gov/news.release/union2.nws.htm (2 January 2001).

———. 1999. "Union Members Summary." On the World Wide Web at http://stats.bls.gov/news.release/union2.nws.htm (17 March 2001).

———. 2001. "Union Members Summary." On the World Wide Web at http://stats.bls.gov/news.release/union2.nws.htm (21 March 2001).

U.S. Bureau of the Census. 1998d. "Total Midyear Population for the World: 1950–2050." On the World Wide Web at http://www.census.gov/ipc/www/worldpop.html (2 May 2000).

———. 1999. Statistical Abstract of the United States: 1999. On the World Wide Web at http://www.census.gov/prod/99pubs/99statab/sec04.pdf (15 January 2001).

———. 2002. "IDB Population Pyramids." On the World Wide Web at http://www.census.gov./ipc/www/idbpyr.html (5 June 2002).

U.S. Department of Commerce. 1998. *Statistical Abstract of the United States: 1998*. On the World Wide Web at http://www.census.gov/prod/3/98pubs/98statab/sasec1.pdf (8 October 2000).

———. Statistical Abstract of the United States: 1999. On the World Wide Web at http://www.census.gov/prod/99pubs/99statab/sec20.pdf (19 November 2002).

U.S. Department of Health and Human Services. 1999. *Healthy People 2000: National Health Promotion and Disease Prevention Objectives*. Hyattsville, MD: Centers for Disease Control and Prevention, National Center for Health Statistics. On the World Wide Web at http://www.cdc.gov/nchswww/data/hp2k99.pdf (29 April 2000).

U.S. Department of Justice. 1998. *Stalking and Domestic Violence: The Third Annual Report to Congress under the Violence Against Women Act*. Washington, DC: Violence Against Women Grants Office.

U.S. Environmental Protection Agency, Office of Air Quality Planning and Standards. 2000. *National Air Pollutant Emission Trends, 1900–1998*. On the World Wide Web at http://www.epa.gov/ttn/chief/trends98/emtrnd.html (3 August 2000).

U.S. Information Agency. 1998–99. *The People Have Spoken: Global Views of Democracy*, 2 vols. Washington, D.C.: Office of Research and Media Reaction.

Useem, Bert. 1998. "Breakdown Theories of Collective Action." *Annual Review of Sociology* 24: 215–38.

Valocchi, Steve. 1996. "The Emergence of the Integrationist Ideology in the Civil Rights Movement." *Social Problems* 43: 116–30.

Valverde, M. 1991. *The Age of Light, Soap and Water: Moral Reform in English Canada, 1885–1925*. Toronto: McClelland & Stewart.

———, ed. 1994. "Moral Regulation." *Canadian Journal of Sociology* 19, 2: vi–xii.

Van de Kaa, Dirk. 1987. "Europe's Second Demographic Transition." *Population Bulletin* 42, 1: 1–58.

Van der Laan, Luc J. W., Christopher Lockey, Bradley C. Griffeth, Francine S. Frasier, Carolyn A. Wilson, David E. Onions, Bernhard J. Hering, Zhifeng Long, Edward Otto, Bruce E. Torbett, and Daniel R. Salomon. 2000. "Infection by Porcine Endogenous Retrovirus After Islet Xenotransplantation in SCID Mice." *Nature* 407: 501–4. On the World Wide Web at http://www.nature.com/cgi-taf/DynaPage.taf?file=/nature/journal/v407/n6800/full/407501a0_fs.html.

Vanier Institute of the Family. 2000. *Profiling Canada's Families II*. Nepean, ON: Vanier Institute of the Family.

———. 2001. *Profiling Canada's Families II*. Nepean, ON: Vanier Institute of the Family.

Veblen, T. 1899. *The Theory of the Leisure Class*. On the World Wide Web at http://socserv2.socsci.mcmaster.ca/~econ/ugcm/3ll3/veblen/leisure/index.html (29 April 2000).

Vernarec, E. 2000. "Depression in the Work Force: Seeing the Cost in a Fuller Light." *Business and Health* 18, 4: 48–55.

Veugelers, John. 1997. "Social Cleavage and the Revival of Far Right Parties: The Case of France's National Front." *Acta Sociologica* 40: 31–49.

Vidal, John. 1999. "World Burdened by Wars and Pollution." *The Guardian* 6 June: 7.

Vygotsky, Lev S. 1987. *The Collected Works of L. S. Vygotsky*, vol. 1, N. Minick, trans. New York: Plenum.

Waldfogel, Jane. 1997. "The Effect of Children on Women's Wages." *American Sociological Review* 62: 209–17.

Wallace, James and Jim Erickson. 1992. *Hard Drive: Bill Gates and the Making of the Microsoft Empire*. New York: John Wiley.

Wallerstein, Immanuel. 1974–89. *The Modern World-System*, 3 vols. New York: Academic Press.

———, ed. 1998. "The Heritage of Sociology and the Future of the Social Sciences in the 21st Century." *Current Sociology* 46, 2.

Wallerstein, Judith S., Julia Lewis, and Sandra Blakeslee. 2000. *The Unexpected Legacy of Divorce: A 25 Year Landmark Study*. New York: Hyperion.

Wallich, P., and M. Mukerjee. 1996. "Regulating the Body Business." *Scientific American* 274, 3 (March): 12–3.

Wanner, R. 1999. "Expansion and Ascription: Trends in Educational Opportunity in Canada, 1920–1994." *Canadian Review of Sociology and Anthropology* 36 (August): 409–42.

Webb, Eugene J., Donald T. Campbell, Richard D. Schwartz, and Lee Sechrest. 1966. *Unobtrusive Measures: Nonreactive Research in the Social Sciences*. Chicago: Rand McNally.

Webb, Stephen D. and John Collette. 1977. "Rural–Urban Differences in the Use of Stress-Alleviating Drugs." *American Journal of Sociology* 83: 700–7.

———. 1979. "Reply to Comment on Rural–Urban Differences in the Use of Stress-Alleviating Drugs." *American Journal of Sociology* 84: 1446–52.

"WebcamSearch.com." 2002. On the World Wide Web at http://www.webcamsearch.com/ (19 May 2002).

Weber, Max. 1946. *From Max Weber: Essays in Sociology*, rev. ed., H. Gerth and C. W. Mills, eds. and trans. New York: Oxford University Press.

———. 1947. *The Theory of Social and Economic Organization*, T. Parsons, ed., A. M. Henderson and T. Parsons, trans. New York: Free Press.

———. 1958 [1904–5]. *The Protestant Ethic and the Spirit of Capitalism*. New York: Scribner.

———. 1963. *The Sociology of Religion*, Ephraim Fischoff, trans. Boston: Beacon Press.

———. 1964 [1949]. "'Objectivity' in Social Science and Social Policy." Pp. 49–112 in Edward A. Shils and Henry A. Finch, trans. and eds. *The Methodology of the Social Sciences*. New York: Free Press of Glencoe.

———. 1978a [1968]. *Economy and Society*, Guenther Roth and Claus Wittich, eds. Berkeley, CA: University of California Press.

Weeks, Jeffrey. 2000. *Making Sexual History*. Cambridge, UK: Polity Press.

Weis, Joseph G. 1987. "Class and Crime." Pp. 71–90 in Michael Gottfredson and Travis Hirschi, eds. *Positive Criminology*. Beverly Hills, CA: Sage.

Weissman, M. 1992. "The Changing Rate of Major Depression: Cross-National Comparisons." *Journal of the American Medical Association* 268, 21: 3098–105.

Welch, Michael. 1997. "Violence Against Women by Professional Football Players: A Gender Analysis of Hypermasculinity, Positional Status, Narcissism, and Entitlement." *Journal of Sport and Social Issues* 21: 392–411.

Weller, Jack M. and E. L. Quarantelli. 1973. "Neglected Characteristics of Collective Behavior." *American Journal of Sociology* 79: 665–85.

Wellman, Barry. 1979. "The Community Question: The Intimate Networks of East Yorkers." *American Journal of Sociology* 84: 201–31.

Wellman, Barry, and Stephen Berkowitz, eds. 1997 [1988]. *Social Structures: A Network Approach*, updated ed. Greenwich, CT: JAI Press.

Wellman, Barry, et al. 1996. "Computer Networks as Social Networks: Collaborative Work, Telework, and Virtual Community." *Annual Review of Sociology* 22: 213–38.

Welsh, Sandy. 1999. "Gender and Sexual Harassment." *Annual Review of Sociology* 25: 169–90.

Wentz, Frank J. and Matthias Schabel. 1998. "Effects of Orbital Decay on Satellite-Derived Lower-Tropospheric Temperature Trends." *Nature* 394: 661–4.

West, Candace and Don Zimmerman. 1987. "Doing Gender." *Gender and Society* 1: 125–51.

Westen, Tracy. 1998. "Can Technology Save Democracy?" *National Civic Review* 87: 47–56.

Wetzel, Janice Wood. 2001. "Human Rights in the 20th Century: Weren't Gays and Lesbians Human?" Pp. 15–31 in Mary E. Swigonski and Robin S. Mama, eds. *From Hate Crimes to Human Rights: A Tribute to Matthew Shepard*. New York: Haworth Press.

Wheeler, Stanton. 1961. "Socialization in Correctional Communities." *American Sociological Review* 26: 697–712.

Whitaker, Reg. 1987. *Double Standard*. Toronto: Lester and Orpen Dennys.

White, James. 1992. "Marital Status and Well-Being in Canada: An Analysis of Age Group Variations." *Journal of Family Issues* 13: 390–409.

White, Lynn K., Alan Booth, and John N. Edwards. 1986. "Children and Marital Happiness." *Journal of Families Issues* 7, 2: 131–47.

White, Roy B. 2002. "Trading Places." *Time*, Canadian ed. 27 May: 66.

Whitefield, S. and G. Evans. 1994. "The Russian Election of 1993: Public Opinion and the Transition Experience." *Post-Soviet Affairs* 10: 38–60.

Whittington, L. 1999. *The Banks: The Ongoing Battle for Control of Canada's Richest Business*. Toronto: Stoddart.

Whyte, W. F. 1981 [1943]. *Street Corner Society: The Social Structure of an Italian Slum*, 3rd ed. Chicago: University of Chicago Press.

Wilensky, Harold L. 1967. *Organizational Intelligence: Knowledge and Policy in Government and Industry*. New York: Basic Books.

———. 1997. "Social Science and the Public Agenda: Reflections on the Relation of Knowledge to Policy in the United States and Abroad." *Journal of Health Politics, Policy and Law* 22: 1241–65.

Wiley, Norbert. 1994. *The Semiotic Self*. Chicago: University of Chicago Press.

Wilkinson, Richard G. 1996. *Unhealthy Societies: The Afflictions of Inequality*. London: Routledge.

Willardt, Kenneth. 2000. "The Gaze He'll Go Gaga For." *Cosmopolitan* April: 232–7.

Williams, David R. and Chiquita Collins. 1995. "U.S. Socioeconomic and Racial Differences in Health: Patterns and Explanations." *Annual Review of Sociology* 21: 349–86.

———. 1999. "U.S. Socioeconomic and Racial Differences in Health: Patterns, and Explanations." Pp. 349–76 in Kathy Charmaz and Debora A. Paterniti, eds. *Health, Illness, and Healing: Society, Social Context, and Self*. Los Angeles: Roxbury Publishing Co.

Willis, Paul. 1984 [1977]. *Learning to Labour: How Working-Class Kids Get Working-Class Jobs*. New York: Columbia University Press.

Wilson, Edward O. 1975. *Sociobiology: The New Synthesis*. Cambridge, MA: Belknap Press of the Harvard University Press.

Wilson, Elizabeth. 1991. *The Sphinx in the City: Urban Life, the Control of Disorder and Women*. Berkeley, CA: University of California Press.

Winch, Donald. 1987. *Malthus*. Oxford, UK: Oxford University Press.

*Wired*. 1999. December.

Wirth, Louis. 1938. "Urbanism as a Way of Life." *American Journal of Sociology* 44: 1–24.

Wolf, D. L. 1992. *Factory Daughters: Gender, Household Dynamics, and Rural Industrialization in Java*. Berkeley, CA: University of California Press.

Wolf, Eric R. 1982. *Europe and the People without History*. Berkeley, CA: University of California Press.

Wolf, Naomi. 1997. *Promiscuities: The Secret Struggle for Womanhood*. New York: Vintage.

Wolff, Janet. 1999. "Cultural Studies and the Sociology of Culture." *Invisible Culture* 1. On the World Wide Web at http://www.rochester.edu/in_visible_culture/issue1/wolff/wolff.html (10 May 2000).

"Women—Current Provincial and Territorial Party Standings." 2001. On the World Wide Web at http://www.parl.gc.ca/information/about/related/province/StandingsProvGlobal.asp?Language=E&Cat=F (20 February 2001).

"Women in National Parliaments." 2001. On the World Wide Web at http://www.ipu.org/wmn-e/classif.htm (27 March 2001).

"Women—Party Standings in the House of Commons." 2000. On the World Wide Web at http://www.parl.gc.ca/information/about/people/House/StandingsHofCwm.asp?Language=E (20 February 2001).

Wong, L. and M. Ng. 1998. "Chinese Immigrant Entrepreneurs in Vancouver: A Case Study of Ethnic Business Development." *Canadian Ethnic Studies* 30: 64–85.

Wood, Julia and Angela Henry. 2002. *Everyday Encounters: An Introduction to Interpersonal Communication*, 2nd Canadian ed. Toronto: Nelson.

Wood, W., F. Y. Wong, and J. G. Chachere. 1991. "Effects of Media Violence on Viewers' Aggression in Unconstrained Social Interaction." *Psychological Bulletin* 109: 371–83.

Woodrow Federal Reserve Bank of Minneapolis. 2000. "What's a Dollar Worth?" On the World Wide Web at http://woodrow.mpls.frb.fed.us/economy/calc/cpihome.html (8 October 2000).

Workplace Information Directorate. 1996. Special tabulation of strikes statistics for 1986–95. Ottawa: Human Resources Development Canada.

"Work-related Stress: A Condition Felt 'Round the World.'" 1995. *HR Focus* 72, 4 (April): 17.

World Bank. 1999a. "Aid Dependency." On the World Wide Web at http://www.worldbank.org/data/wdi/pdfs/tab6_10.pdf (27 April 2000).

———. 1999b. "Global Development Finance 1999." On the World Wide Web at http://www.worldbank.org/prospects/gdf99/tables.pdf (27 April 2000).

———. 1999c. "GNP Per Capita 1997, Atlas Method and PPP." On the World Wide Web at http://www.worldbank.org/data/databytopic/GNPPC97.pdf (10 July 1999).

World Health Organization. 1998a. Female Genital Mutilation, Table 1. On the World Wide Web at http://www.who.int/dsa/cat98/fgmbook.htm.

———. 1998b. "Fifty Facts from the World Health Report 1998." 8 August. On the World Wide Web at http://www.who.int/whr/1998/facse/htm.

———. 1999b. "World Health Report 1999: Basic Indicators for All Member States." On the World Wide Web at http://www.who.int/whr/1999/en/indicators.htm (2 May 2000).

———. 2000. "WHO Terminology Information System." On the World Wide Web at http://www.who.int/terminology/ter/wt001.html#health (2 May 2000).

*World Values Survey, 1990–1993*. 1994. Ann Arbor, MI: Inter-University Consortium for Political and Social Research.

Worthington, Peter. 2002. "Aspers Get Press in U.S.: Washington Post Weighs in on 'Free-Speech' Debate." *Toronto Sun* 28 January. On the World Wide Web at http://www.friendscb.org/articles/TorontoSun/torsun020128.htm (17 May 2002).

Wortley, Scot, David Brownfield and John Hagan. 1996. "The Usual Suspects: Race, Age and Gender Differences in Police Contact." Paper Presented at the 48th Annual Conference of the American Society of Criminology, Chicago: November.

Wright, Charles Robert. 1975. *Mass Communication: A Sociological Perspective*. New York: Random House.

Wright, Erik Olin, Janeen Baxter, with Gunn Elisabeth Birkelund. 1995. "The Gender-Gap in Workplace Authority: A Cross-National Study." *American Sociological Review* 60: 407–35.

Wu, Zheng. 2000. *Cohabitation: An Alternative Form of Family Living*. Don Mills, ON: Oxford University Press.

Wu, Zheng and Margaret J. Penning. 1997. "Marital Instability after Midlife." *Journal of Family Issues* 18, 5: 459–78.

Wynne, Robert E. 1996. "American Labor Leaders and the Vancouver Anti-Oriental Riot." *Pacific Northwest Quarterly* 86: 172–9. On the World Wide Web at http://www.vcn.bc.ca/acww/html/body_riot.html (15 March 2001).

X, Malcolm. 1965. *The Autobiography of Malcolm X*. New York: Grove.

Yamane, David. 1997. "Secularization on Trial: In Defense of a Neosecularization Paradigm." *Journal for the Scientific Study of Religion* 36: 109–22.

Yancey, W. L, E. P. Ericksen, and G. H. Leon. 1979. "Emergent Ethnicity: A Review and Reformulation." *American Sociological Review* 41: 391–403.

Yeates, Maurice H. and Barry Garner. 1976. *The North American City*, 2nd ed. New York: Harper & Row.

Zakaria, Fareed. 1997. "The Rise of Illiberal Democracy." *Foreign Affairs* 76, 6: 22–43.

Zald, Meyer N. and John D. McCarthy. 1979. *The Dynamics of Social Movements*. Cambridge, MA: Winthrop.

Zaslavsky, Victor, and Robert J. Brym. 1978. "The Functions of Elections in the USSR." *Soviet Studies* 30: 62–71.

———. 1983. *Soviet Jewish Emigration and Soviet Nationality Policy*. London: Macmillan.

Zimbardo, Philip G. 1972. "Pathology of Imprisonment." *Society* 9, 6: 4–8.

Zimmermann, Francis. 1987 [1982]. *The Jungle and the Aroma of Meats: An Ecological Theme in Hindu Medicine*, Janet Lloyd, trans. Berkeley, CA: University of California Press.

Zimring, Franklin E. and Gordon Hawkins. 1995. *Incapacitation: Penal Confinement and the Restraint of Crime*. New York: Oxford University Press.

Zinsser, Hans. 1935. *Rats, Lice and History*. Boston: Little, Brown.

Zola, Irving Kenneth. 1982. *Missing Pieces: A Chronicle of Living with a Disability*. Philadelphia: Temple University Press.

Zuboff, S. 1988. *In the Age of the Smart Machine: The Future of Work and Power*. New York: Basic Books.

Zukin, Sharon. 1980. "A Decade of the New Urban Sociology." *Theory and Society* 9: 539–74.

Zurcher, Louis A. and David A. Snow. 1981. "Collective Behavior and Social Movements." Pp. 447–82 in Morris Rosenberg and Ralph Turner, eds. *Social Psychology: Sociological Perspectives*. New York: Basic Books.

# INDEX

**I**

## J

# Credits and Acknowledgments

## Photo Credits

**Chapter 1** p. 7: Courtesy of A.C. Fine Art; p. 8: © Photodisc; p. 13: © Phillip Caruso/The Everett Collection; p. 14: © Paul Almasy/Corbis; p. 15: © Musee du Louvre, Paris/Giraudon, Paris/Superstock; p. 16: Diego Rivera. *Detroit Industry,* North Wall. 1932–33. Fresco (detail). Copyright 1997. Photograph Copyright © 2001 The Detroit Institute of the Arts; Courtesy of Ed Clark; p. 18: Carleton University Archives; p. 19: American Sociological Association; p. 20: Photo courtesy of Margrit Eichler; pp. 22–23: Copyright © 2001 Time Inc. Reprinted by permission. TIME graphic by Joe Lertola.

**Chapter 2** p. 36: Top: © Archivo Iconografico, S.A./Corbis/ Magma; Bottom: © Bettman/Corbis/Magma; p. 43: © Index Stock/ James Frank; p. 45: © Alan Oddie/Photo Edit; p. 47: The Everett Collection; p. 48: CP Picture Archive/Ken Frayer; p. 50: © Antonio Rosario/The Image Bank; p. 51: Bob Marshak/The Everett Collection; p. 52: Index Stock/Brad Bartholomew; p. 57: Courtesy of Tom Campbell.

**Chapter 3** p. 68: CP Picture Archive/Ron Frehm; p. 69: Index Stock/Frank Chmura; p. 74: Photofest; p. 75: © Dinodia/V.H. Mishra; p. 77: CP Picture Archive/Kevin Frayer; p. 80: Courtesy of Kellogg's; p. 83: © Owen Franklin/Corbis/Magma; p. 85: The Everett Collection; p. 87: © Superstock; p. 89: CP Picture Archive/Nick Ut.

**Chapter 4** p. 96: © Corbis/Magma; p. 98: Index Stock/Key Color; p. 99: The Everett Collection; p. 100: © Myrleen Cate/ PhotoEdit; p. 103: Top: Courtesy of Carol Gilligan; Bottom: ©Spencer Grant/PhotoEdit; p. 106: © Photodisc; p. 107: Paul Conklin/Photo Edit; p. 112: © Jonathan Blair/Corbis/Magma; p. 117: CP Picture Archive/Mike Ridewood.

**Chapter 5** p. 125: The Everett Collection; p. 127: © Photodisc; p. 129: CP Picture Archive/Peter Bregg; p. 133: Mills, Janet Lee. 1985 "Body Language Speaks Louder Than Words," *Horizons*, February, pp.6–12; p. 137: © Erich Lessing/Art Resource, N.Y.; p. 139: © Brandom Films/The Everett Collection, NY; p. 141: The Everett Collection.

**Chapter 6** p. 150: CP Picture Archive/Frank Gunn; p. 152: National Library of Medicine, Washington, DC; p. 153: WeeGEE/ICP/Getty Images; p. 157: David James/The Everett Collection; p. 163: The Everett Collection; p. 165: The Everett Collection; p. 169: New York Public Library; p. 171: CP Picture Archive/Fred Chartrand; p. 173: CP Picture Archive/Frank Gunn.

**Chapter 7** p. 183: © Christie's Images /Corbis/Magma; p. 186: CP Picture Archive/Tibor Kolley; p. 198: Left: From *Saturday Night,* June 3, 2000, "The War Next Store", p. 48 Story and photographs by Ami Vitale; Right: From *Saturday Night,* June 3, 2000, "The War Next Store", p. 49 Story and photographs by Ami Vitale; p. 200: © Art Resource, NY; p. 205: Left: Agriculture and Agri-Food Canada; Right: BSIP Agency/Index Stock Imagery; p. 207: CP Picture Archive/Alex Urosevic; p. 210: Left: CP Picture Archive/Stan Behal; Right: CP Picture Archive/Hans Deryk.

**Chapter 8** p. 221: From *Mismeasurement of Man* by Stephen Jay Gould (Norton); p. 223: CP Picture Archive/Andrew Vaughan; p. 227: Courtesy of The Everett Collection; p. 229: © Eyewire; p. 233: CP Picture Archives/AP Photo/Eddie Adams; p. 236: National Archives of Canada/C-030939; p. 238: The Phillips Collection, Washington DC; p. 242: Courtesy of the Pier 21 Society; p. 243: Canadian Pacific Airlines/National Archives of Canada/C-45080.

**Chapter 9** p. 253: © Bernard and Catherine Desjeux/Corbis/ Magma; p. 258: Photofest; p. 259: Bottom: Reuters News Media, Inc./Corbis; p. 261: Myrleen Cate/IndexStock; p. 263: Top: CP Picture Archive/Adam Butler; p. 267: © Michael Kooren/Archive Photos, NY; p. 269: CP Picture Archive/ David Lucas; p. 271: The Granger Collection, New York; p. 274: Steve Dunwell Photography Inc/IndexStock; p. 276: Courtesy of the Canadian Federation of Students; p. 281: © SuperStock; p. 282: CP Picture Archive/Jonathan Hayward.

**Chapter 10** p. 291: Cover of *Wired Magazine*, Dec. 1999. Photography by James Porto/Courtesy of Wired Magazine, Conde Nast Publications; p. 292: CP Picture Archive/Andrew Vaughan; p. 295: The Everett Collection, New York; p. 299: Copyright © 1999 SoundStage!; p. 300: © Spencer Grant/PhotoEdit; p. 306: The Everett Collection, New York; p. 307: Meri Simon, *San Jose Mercury News* (in Bliss, 2000). Copyright © San Jose Mercury News; 295. Found in Bliss, Jeff (2000), "Getting a Life Offline," *Financial Post*, 29 June: C3; p. 314: CP Picture Archive/Bill Becker; p. 316: CP Picture Archive/Jeff McIntosh.

**Chapter 11** p. 324: George Bush Presidential Library and Museum; p. 327: Top: © Archivo Iconografico, S.A./Corbis/Magma; Centre: © SuperStock; Bottom: CP Picture Archive/Fred Chartrand; p. 329: Dick Hemingway; p. 330: © Mark Richards/Photo Edit; p. 335: CP Picture Archive/Michel Euler; p. 339: Left: © 1995 Lise Sarfati/Magnum Photos, Inc; Right: © AFP/Corbis/Magma; p. 341: Left: © Marc Riboud/Magnum Photos, Inc; Right: ©Reuters/Jeremiah Kamau/Archive Photos; p. 344: The Everett Collection.

**Chapter 12** p. 353: The Everett Collection, New York; p. 357: © Peter Johnson/Corbis/Magma; p. 361: The Everett Collection, New York; p. 364: The Everett Collection, New York; p. 370: © SuperStock; p. 372: © Jacques M. Chenet/Corbis/Magma; p. 375: © Michael Newman/PhotoEdit; p. 378: CP PictureArchive/Clement Allard; p. 381: © Photodisc; p. 383: © Jonathan Blair/Corbis/Magma.

**Chapter 13** p. 392: © Michael Newman/PhotoEdit; p. 395: © 1994 Wendy Chan/The Image Bank; p. 396: © Bettmann/Corbis/Magma; p. 398: © A. Ramey/PhotoEdit; p. 399: Photofest; p. 402: © Bill Varie/Corbis/Magma; p. 404: © Omni Photo Communications Inc./Index Stock; p. 407: © Eyewire; p. 408: CP Picture Archive/Jacques Boissinot; p. 410: CP Picture Archive/Don Healy; p. 413: © Photodisc; p. 414: © The Purcell Team/Corbis/Magma;

p. 415: CP Picture Archive/Chuck Stoody; p. 416: Oxford Learning Centres; p. 417: CP Picture Archive/John Ulan.

**Chapter 14** p. 424: The Everett Collection, NY; p. 425: © Renee Zellweger/The Everett Collection; p. 427: CP Picture Archive/Wayne Hiebert; p. 428: CP Picture Archive/National Archives; p. 429: Top: © The Pierpont Morgan Library/Art Resource, New York; Bottom: © Reed Kaestner/Corbis/Magma; p. 432: CP Picture Archive/Kevin Frayer; p. 442: © Associated Press, Melbourne Age/AP/Wide World Photos; p. 443: © Reuters New-Media,Inc./Corbis/Magma.

**Chapter 15** p. 450: CP Picture Archive/Associated Press AP; p. 452: © Mike Hutchings/Reuters/Archive Photos; p. 455: © Mark Richards/PhotoEdit; p. 461: © Spencer Grant/PhotoEdit; p. 465: CP Picture Archive/Philip Walker; p. 469: CP Picture Archive/Chuck Stoody; p. 470: © Ted Streshinsky/ Corbis/Magma; p. 475: © Melinda Sue Gordon/The Everett Collection, NY; p. 477: © Francisco Cruz/SuperStock.

**Chapter 16** p. 489: © The Purcell Group/Corbis/Magma; p. 496: Top: © Murry Sill/Index Stock Imagery; Bottom: The Granger Collection, NY; p. 501: CP Picture Archive/Andrew Vaughan; p. 506: Photo by Miro Cernetig, Globe and Mail, Toronto. Reprinted with permission from The Globe and Mail; p. 507: Weidenfeld and Nicolson Archives; p. 508: © Sunset Boulevard/Corbis Sygma/Magma; p. 511: © Giraudon /Art Resource NY; p. 512: Craig Brown/Index Stock.

**Chapter 17** p. 522: Left: Vancouver Public Library, #939; Right: Rare Books and Special Collections, University of British Columbia Library, Photo XXXVI-17; p. 17: CP Picture Archive/Maclean's Photo/Phil Snel; p. 531: National Archives of Canada/PA-163001; p. 533: The Everett Collection, NY; p. 534: ©Hintz Diltz/Corbis/Magma; p. 537: Bibliotheque Nationale de France; p. 540: Top Left: CP Picture Archive/Ryan Remiorz; Top Right: CP Picture Archive/Fred Chartrand; Bottom: CP Picture Archive/Frank Gunn; p. 541: © Reuters News Media, Inc./ Corbis/Magma.

**Chapter 18** p. 546: © Bettman/Corbis/Magma; p. 547: © 1999 WB & Village Roadshow Film Limited/The Everett Collection, NY; p. 548: CP Picture Archive/Grant Collins; p. 549: © Gary Braasch/ Corbis/Magma; p. 551: U.S. Army Photos; p. 553: Top: Index Stock Imagery/Jacob Halaska; Bottom: © SuperStock; p. 556: The Everett Collection; p. 561: CP Picture Archive/Ray Fahey; p. 564: © Joe Polemi/Reuters/Archive Photos. NY; p. 567: Copyright © 1990 Bill Watterson. Reprinted with permission of Universal Press Syndicate. All rights reserved.

## Literary Acknowledgments

**Chapter 1** pp. 12–13: From *The Sociological Imagination* by C. Wright Mills, copyright © 2000 by Oxford University Press, Inc. Used by permission of Oxford University Press, Inc.

**Chapter 4** p. 105: Figure from *The Ambitious Generation* by Schneider and Stevenson. © by Yale University Press. Reprinted by permission.

**Chapter 5** p. 126: Bar graph based on information in Chapter 4, Closeness of the Victim from *Obedience to Authority: An Experimental View* by Stanley Milgram. © 1974 by Stanley Milgram. Reprinted by permission of HarperCollins Publishers, Inc.

**Chapter 6** p. 152: Figure from *Crime and Disrepute* by John Hagan. Copyright © 1994 Pine Forge Press. Reprinted by permission of Sage Publications; p. 172: www.sentencingproject.org/brief/usvsrus.pdf Reprinted by permission of The Sentencing Project.

**Chapter 7** p. 189: Bottom: Human Resources Development Canada, "Selected occupations, average annual incomes and average income ranges" http://jobfutures.ca/noc/browse-occupations-alphabet.shtml Retrieved March, 2, 2001. Reproduced with the permission of the Minister of Public Works and Government Services Canada, 2002. p. 193: Top: National Council of Welfare, 2000: http://www.ncwcnbes.net. Reproduced with the permission of the Minister of Public Works and Government Services Canada, 2002; Bottom: *Child Poverty Profile 1998* (Autumn 2001) National Council on Welfare. On the World Wide Web at http://www.ncwcnbes.net/htmdocument/reportchildpoverty98/reportchildpoverty98.html#_Toc522256760 7 June 2002. Reproduced with the permission of the Minister of Public Works and Government Services Canada, 2002; p. 198: United Nations. (1998). *Human Development Report 1998*. Copyright © 1998 by The United Nations Development Program. Used by permission of Oxford University Press, Inc.

**Chapter 8** p. 224: "How to Tell your Friends from the Japs," 1941, Time Magazine, Dec. 22, p. 33. Copyright © 1941 Time, Inc. Reprinted by permission. p. 244: Bottom: Figure from *Sociology in a Changing World*, Fourth Edition by William Kornblum, copyright © 1997. Reprinted by permission of Wadsworth, a division of Thomson Learning: www.thomsonrights.com. Fax 800-730-2215.

**Chapter 9** p. 264: Top: "The 1997 Body Image Results" by David M. Garner, *Psychology Today*, Vol. 30, No. 1, pp. 30–44. Reprinted with permission from Psychology Today Magazine. Copyright © 1997 Sussex Publishers, Inc.

**Chapter 10** p. 290: *From In the Age of the Smart Machine: The Future of Work and Power* by Shoshana Zuboff, © 1988 by Basic Books, Inc. Reprinted by permission of Basic Books, a member of Perseus Books, L.L.C.

**Chapter 12** p. 364: Robert Levine, Suguru Sato, Tsukasa Hashimoto and Jyoti Verma. Journal of Cross-Cultural Psychology 26(5): pp. 554–71. Copyright 1995 by Sage Publications. Reprinted with permission of Sage Publications, Inc.; p. 380: From *Cohabitation: An Alternative Form of Family Living* by Zheng Wu. Copyright © Oxford University Press Canada 2000. Reprinted with permission of the Oxford University Press Canada.

**Chapter 15** p. 463: Time. 1999. "A Changing People." Canadian Edition 31 May: 30–4. © 1999 TIME Inc. Reprinted by permission.

**Chapter 16** p. 497: From "The Growth of the City: An Introduction to a Research Project" Ernest W. Burgess, pp. 47–62 in *The City* by Robert E. Park et al. Copyright © 1967 University of Chicago Press. Used with permission.